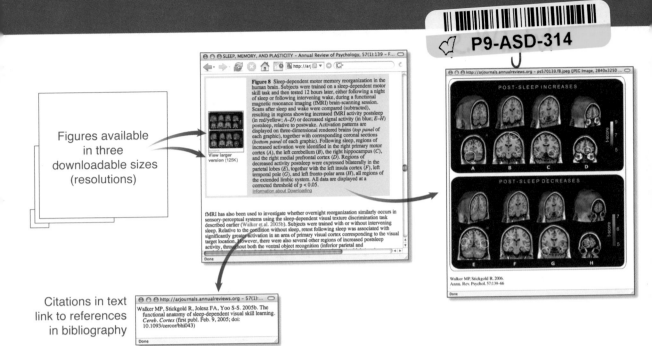

Figures available in three downloadable sizes (resolutions)

Citations in text link to references in bibliography

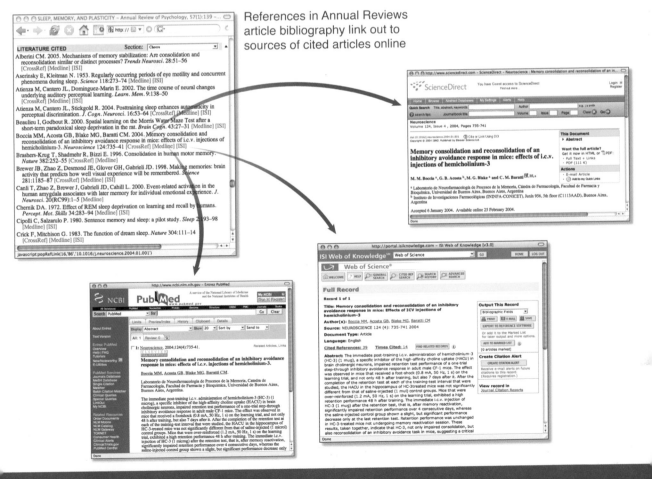

References in Annual Reviews article bibliography link out to sources of cited articles online

Annual Review of
Psychology

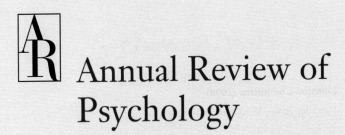

Annual Review of Psychology

Volume 59, 2008

Susan T. Fiske, *Editor*
Princeton University

Daniel L. Schacter, *Associate Editor*
Harvard University

Robert Sternberg, *Associate Editor*
Tufts University

www.annualreviews.org • science@annualreviews.org • 650-493-4400

Annual Reviews
4139 El Camino Way • P.O. Box 10139 • Palo Alto, California 94303-0139

Annual Reviews
Palo Alto, California, USA

International Standard Serial Number: 0066-4308
International Standard Book Number: 978-0-8243-0259-7
Library of Congress Catalog Card Number: 50-13143

TYPESET BY APTARA, INC.
PRINTED AND BOUND BY MALLOY INCORPORATED, ANN ARBOR, MICHIGAN

Contents

**Annual Review of
Psychology**

Volume 59, 2008

Errata

An online log of corrections to *Annual Review of Psychology* articles may be found at
http://psych.annualreviews.org/errata.shtml

Related Articles

The Evolution of a Cognitive Psychologist: A Journey from Simple Behaviors to Complex Mental Acts

Gordon H. Bower

Department of Psychology, Stanford University, Stanford, California 94305;
email: Gordon@psych.Stanford.edu

Annu. Rev. Psychol. 2008. 59:1–27

The *Annual Review of Psychology* is online at
http://psych.annualreviews.org

This article's doi:
10.1146/annurev.psych.59.103006.093722

Key Words

human memory, skilled reading, mental models, knowledge
representation, narrative focus, cognitive revolution, associative
networks, chunking, memory organization, story grammars

Abstract

The author summarizes his evolving interests from conditioning
studies within a behaviorist orientation, thence to human memory,
knowledge representation, and narrative understanding and memory. Arguing that the study of skilled reading provides a microcosm
for revealing cognitive processes, he illustrates this by reviewing his
research on the use of spatial priming to investigate readers' on-line
updating of their situational models of texts. Conceptual entities
close to the reader's focus of attention within the model are readily
retrieved. Retrieval speed from memory declines with the probed object's distance from the current focus and decays with time elapsed
in the narrative since the item was last in focus. The focus effect
varies with the character's perspective, his status in the story, his active goals, and other factors. The results are accommodated within
an associative network model distinguishing just-read sentences in
short-term memory from activated portions of long-term memory
structures to which they refer.

Contents

INTRODUCTION

Authors of prefatory chapters for earlier *Annual Review of Psychology* volumes wrote scholarly reviews setting forth their contributions to a single major line of research. I am opting instead for an autobiographic approach that touches on the major research topics that I have pursued over successive phases of my career. Each topic could be elaborated to chapter lengths, but page limits constrain that impulse and rescue undaunted readers. Accordingly, this narrative briefly tracks my progression from simple animal conditioning experiments within the behaviorist tradition to cognitive approaches to human learning and memory, and, then, to human knowledge representation and utilization. The arc reaches its culmination, and longest description, in the research on narrative comprehension and memory that I carried out with several collaborators. I view my path as a conceptual progression from the simple to the complex, and as reflecting the expanding horizons and theoretical ambitions of cognitive science.

Early College Years

Influenced by a high school teacher, I acquired an early interest in Freudian psychoanalysis, reading the psychoanalytic canon extensively—Freud, Adler, Jung, Horney, Fenichel, Sullivan, Rank, and Melanie Klein—during late high school and early college at Western (now Case Western) Reserve University in Cleveland, Ohio. As an aspiring psychiatrist, I waded through two years of premed courses. After my freshman year, I worked as a summer ward attendant at the Cleveland State mental hospital; later, during my sophomore year, I was a part-time research assistant to the psychology staff there. Those sobering experiences convinced me of the somewhat primitive state of psychiatric knowledge and discouraged me from a career in psychiatry. At the same time, I became engrossed in an experimental psychology class taught by a young ex-Yalie, Charles R. Porter, who introduced me to learning theory, especially touting the quantitative approach of Clark Hull (1952). That interest put me on a path that led to Yale graduate school and study with Neal Miller. At the time, Miller was a premier learning theorist whose sympathies for psychoanalytic theory were evident throughout the book *Personality and Psychotherapy* that he coauthored with John Dollard (Dollard & Miller 1950).

Yale Graduate School and Early Stanford Years

I arrived at Yale in September 1955, just as Miller was shifting his research focus to identifying the areas of the mammalian brain that control reward, punishment, and biological drives. My early work tested cats and rats to plumb the motivational effects of brain stimulation. My first publication with Miller reported a dual reward-punishment effect from stimulating spots in the rat's limbic system (Bower & Miller 1958). My rats would press a lever to turn on the brain stimulation at these spots, but it quickly became aversive so they would rotate a wheel in the cage to turn it off. The animals would repeat this on-off behavior until both rodents and their observers grew weary of it. Although I took courses in physiological psychology and learned techniques of precise electrode implantation, recording, preparation, and histological examination of brain tissue, I preferred the more "behavioral" side of learning theory. While continuing work with Miller, I concentrated my behavioral research increasingly with Yale's Frank Logan (1956, 1960). When I received my PhD in 1959, I was a committed Hullian theorist with a strong "animal learning" orientation.

I set up an animal-learning lab when I started my first job at Stanford University's Psychology Department in fall, 1959. The lab was located in a Quonset hut leftover from World War II. I built my rat runways, shuttle boxes, and operant conditioning chambers there, using electrical components cannibalized from junked pinball machines. With this hardware, I investigated such diverse conditioning topics as transfer of training between Pavlovian and instrumental conditioning, schedules for developing avoidance and escape learning, reward contrast effects among reinforcement conditions, frustration from reward-reductions, "observing responses" in rats and pigeons, and errorless discrimination learning. I was happily and productively occupied, doing the kinds of research I was trained to do. But seeds of doubt about my animal-learning approach germinated as the allure of mathematical psychology increasingly attracted my attention.

Mathematical Models and Human Learning

Although I had started with an interest in quantitative learning theory, this was not Yale's strength. Fortunately, I got a crash course in mathematical learning theory after my second year in graduate school by attending a 1957 summer institute on mathematical psychology sponsored by the Social Science

Research Council. There I met many leaders, or soon-to-be leaders, of the emerging mathematical psychology movement that was a prominent stream within learning theory in the 1955 to 1975 era. That summer I formed a close intellectual bond with the leader of that movement, Bill Estes, who became my mentor. By the early 1960s, Estes, Dick Atkinson, and I had been hired to join Patrick Suppes at Stanford to fill out the mathematical learning theory segment of its department. In those heady years, we attracted some of the brightest graduate students who would help lead the next generation, including (alphabetically) John Anderson, Bobby Klatzky, Steve Kosslyn, Douglas Hintzman, David Rumelhart, and Richard Shiffrin.

MOVING INTO COGNITIVE PSYCHOLOGY

We tested most of our mathematical models on data collected from college students learning such experimental tasks as paired associates, free recall, serial learning, or simple category (classification) learning. Since massive amounts of data are easier to harvest from college students than from rats, my animal research was gradually displaced by my studies of human learning.

So two years after I received my Yale degree, I was deeply engaged in studying human "verbal learning" (as it was then called) despite having had no graduate training in this field. To get up to speed, I read widely and prepared a lengthy review of human learning research in 1962, although the entire book was not published until five years later (Bower 1967). At Yale, we had regarded Hullian behavior theory and animal learning, specifically studies of motivation and reinforcement, as royal roads to enlightenment, and we viewed studies of human learning as dull dead-ends. The apparent dullness of this field seemed to be captured in its major text at that time, *The Psychology of Human Learning*, by McGeogh & Irion (1952). Yet, human memory was one of the first barricades of tradition stormed and

breached by the forays of the revolutionary cognitive psychologists. The sudden contrast and jolt of this intellectual shift taught me to stay nimble and be ready to move with the winds of change in academic psychology.

Major Influences Toward Cognitive Psychology

The information-processing viewpoint. The mid-1960s was a time of conceptual turmoil in experimental psychology. I was swept up in several of its waves. The most powerful of these was the "information-processing" approach, which viewed perception and memory as the taking in, transforming, storing, and retrieving of packets of information. Leading proponents of this approach were George Miller, Jerome Bruner, and Ulric Neisser. The movement's seminal works were *Plans and the Structure of Behavior* by George Miller et al. (1960) and *Cognition* by Neisser (1967). Both treatises upset the worldview of traditional behaviorists. Donald Broadbent (1957, 1958), the influential British leader of the information-processing approach, played a key role in directing the field into studies of selective attention and immediate memory. Broadbent and Arthur Melton (1963) spearheaded the popularity of research studies of short-term memory. Several of us at Stanford developed mathematical models using an information-processing metaphor for short-term memory and its transfer to long-term memory (Bower 1967). The dual-storage model of Atkinson & Shiffrin (1968) became the leading theory of that era.

Computer simulation modeling. Related revolutionary influences were computer simulation models of psychological processes as exemplified in the work of Allen Newell and Herbert Simon (1961, 1963). Their models of psychological processes were arguably even better specified than our mathematical models, and their simulations could be run under differing experimental circumstances to gauge whether the models predicted the behavior of real subjects. My first exposure to computer-simulation modeling was in a 1963 summer workshop at RAND Corporation with Simon, Newell, and several of their students, including Ed Feigenbaum. The first viable simulation project I was associated with was the "Stimulus and Association Learner" (SAL) model of my student, Douglas Hintzman (1968). Doug and I showed how many standard results in human verbal learning could be simulated by an elementary information-processing model. Specifically, SAL incrementally learned a discrimination net of features to distinguish among and respond to the stimuli of a paired associate list. These experiences instilled in me an abiding appreciation for the artificial-intelligence approach to knowledge acquisition and utilization.

Chomsky and psycholinguistics. Another major influence in cognitive psychology was the Chomskian revolution in linguistics (Chomsky 1957, 1965). I had met Noam Chomsky at that 1957 Social Science Research Council summer institute, when he was assisting George Miller with a workshop on the psychology of language. Yet, I did not grasp the significance of Chomsky's approach until I read his devastating critique (Chomsky 1959) of Fred Skinner's book, *Verbal Behavior* (1957). In his critique, Chomsky ripped the veil from our eyes, revealing that, regarding the complexities of linguistic performance, our behaviorist emperor had no clothes. Chomsky persuasively argued that the stimulus-response approach was too impoverished to explain the complexities of verbal behavior, suggesting that the behaviorist analysis would be useless for understanding the learning and use of language. This unmasking came as a shock to those of us raised on psychologists' "internal stimuli and response hierarchies," which was the behaviorists' main tool in attempting to understand what language could do (Dollard & Miller 1950, Osgood 1953, Staats 1968). Chomsky countered that psychologists should develop more complex information-processing models of language, a challenge that gave birth to psycholinguistics. Leading the first halting steps of this incipient field were George Miller and his colleagues at the Harvard Cognitive Sciences Center. Chomsky and Miller were largely responsible for promoting language learning and language use as hot topics in cognitive psychology.

Organizational Factors in Memory

Having worked on mathematical descriptions of transfers of information from short-term to long-term memory, I wanted to know more about what caused these transfers to succeed. So my students and I studied the cognitive maneuvers that people use to learn and remember things (Bobrow & Bower 1969, Bower & Winzenz 1970). Many of us found that sheer repetition and rote rehearsal of an item in short-term memory was woefully insufficient for recording a more long-lasting memory. So what would accomplish this?

Chunking in memory. I found clues in the literature describing the role that organization plays in memorizing. My studies of organizational aids to memory were greatly influenced by the ideas of George Katona (1940) on how subjects' "understanding" of materials promotes memory, of George Miller (1956) on chunking, and of Endel Tulving (1962) and George Mandler (1967) on participants' subjective organization in free recall. Tulving and Mandler studied how people learned to free-recall lists of "unrelated" words studied repeatedly. They found that adult subjects spontaneously look for meaningful relations among the items, grouping them into "chunks," and perhaps even organizing the chunks into larger memory chunks. That prompted my research into the processes that created or disrupted chunks in memory (Bower 1970a, 1972).

Perceptual chunking and memory. In this work, I was influenced by Solomon Asch's thesis that memory was an incidental by-product of the person organizing the materials into a perceptual or conceptual unity or whole (Asch 1969, Asch et al. 1960). By one or another means, people come to view disparate elements as inseparable parts of a single unit. This hypothesis guided my studies on the learning of "unrelated" pieces of information that we experimenters perceptually unitized (or not) for our subjects (Bower et al. 1969, Bower & Winzenz 1969). Asch's thesis also extended to the process of conceptual unitization and drew upon insights from mnemonic devices and mental imagery. As one consequence, I began studies of mnemonic devices (Bower & Clark 1969, Bower 1970b).

Mnemonics and Mental Imagery

Magicians and stage performers have long used mnemonic devices to enhance their memorization for disparate information, be it shopping lists, lecture topics, associating faces with names, their phone numbers, occupations, spouses, hometowns, and so on. I published studies on the mnemonic coding (translation) of "meaningless nonsense" into "meaningful sense" and on how people use language and imagery to form conceptual units. We found that in learning to associate pairs of unrelated words, memory was greatly improved by instructing subjects to search out and form meaningful relationships between the items, such as might be expressed in a sentence—no matter how bizarre. Similarly, asking subjects to construct a visual image of some interaction between the referents of a pair of nouns greatly facilitated their recall of the pair (Bower 1972b). At this time, Allan Paivio and his group at Western Ontario University were leading the research on mental imagery in learning (Paivio 1971). These studies of associative learning via conceptual or imagery combinations became a popular trend of the times, and were in sympathy with the contemporaneous "depth of processing"

metaphor of Gus Craik and Bob Lockhart (1972, Craik & Tulving 1975).

During this period, the style and content of experimentation were markedly different from our previous learning research. Earlier mathematical models had attempted to describe trial-by-trial performance of subjects who were studying a collection of items repeated over many trials. The newer memory experiments typically involved single exposures to the information to be remembered. Also, those later experiments often involved unintentional learning created by instructing subjects to carry out some specified "processing" of the material (e.g., categorizing or imaging it) with no mention of its being memorized. These topics and experimental methods were increasingly far removed from the former mathematical models of learning on which I had been working.

Human Associative Memory

While depth of processing is an arresting metaphor, it was not entirely satisfying for me (cf. Ross 1981). I wanted to understand what created "meaningful combinations" of materials that caused them to be learned so quickly. The easiest approach was to study the meaningfulness of conceptual combinations generated through language. This belief led my student, John Anderson, and me to propose a theory of how people use conceptual knowledge to encode and remember new combinations of concepts, especially descriptions of events and factual assertions. That theory was set forth in several articles and our book, *Human Associative Memory*, affectionately known as *HAM* (Anderson & Bower 1973).

Anderson and I began with the ideas about semantic memory and question answering that Ross Quillian (1968) and Allan Collins (1969) had popularized (Collins & Quillian 1969, 1972). That approach (Minsky 1968) represents knowledge as a huge associative network. Within this network, a concept was represented by a structured set of labeled associations among its related properties and among other concepts. The meaning of a concept is the collection of other concepts as well as referent sensory shapes and features to which it is related. Memory retrieval was conceived as the cues in the question sending activation into corresponding regions of the associative network, searching for a matching structure. Although mildly adequate for representing static knowledge, this approach did not address the learning of any new facts or concepts. Anderson and I wanted to encompass new learning using an augmented association theory. We believed that people learn such new information by interassociating instances of familiar concepts, thereby creating novel configurations that describe the information.

Tests of HAM. We tested our theory by providing college students with many interrelated facts about people in a small town. They would read, for example, that "The town mayor owns a local restaurant" and "The town sheriff drives a white Chevy." The HAM theory was written as a computer simulation model. Anderson programmed a language parser that would take such typed sentences into its short-term memory and set up simple associative structures. As each fact was read, we supposed that subjects (as did the computer program) performed three tasks: (*a*) established a new unit in memory for the configuration of underlying propositions describing the fact or episode; (*b*) composed these propositions by creating new instances, or tokens, of pre-existing concepts that already had been stored in the person's (and computer's) memory; and (*c*) linked them together in a pattern of subject-predicate structures. These labeled associations enabled the simulated system to answer questions about who was doing what to whom, when, and where. Because the system used familiar concepts (Chevy, sheriff), the new fact could be combined with pre-existing knowledge that enabled the simulation to draw simple inferences, such as inferring that the person who enforces the law in town drives a white car.

The Zeitgeist surrounding HAM. Our efforts were part of the contemporary Zeitgeist. Psychologists and artificial intelligence (AI) researchers were then building computer models of knowledge representation and language understanding (Kintsch 1974; Rumelhart et al. 1972; Schank 1975a,b; Winograd 1972). What set our work apart was that Anderson and I explicitly sought to relate our computer simulation model to the systematic laws and generalizations found in the human memory and learning tradition. Relying on simple assumptions, for example, that associations are strengthened by repetition and weakened by time decay and interference, our model explained findings from our experiments on fact learning and retrieval. Significantly, our model was extendable so it could encompass many traditional findings of the experimental literature on human learning.

Part of our goal was to recast the laboratory findings from memory research to relate them to novel ideas about knowledge representation coming out of AI. These AI topics included perceptual pattern recognition, propositional analysis of knowledge, semantic memory, labeled associative networks, retrieval by fitting a question to a content-addressable structure stored in memory, and answering questions by using a collection of specific strategies. Importantly, we demonstrated how to move laboratory research on memory away from its traditional lists of nonsense syllables and unrelated words toward more realistic materials, including coherent text.

Anderson later developed HAM into a far more powerful theory and simulation system. He introduced, for example, the important idea of "productions": the learned routines that move the cognitive system from one subtask to another as it works on a larger problem. Refinements of this production system, along with the labeled associative network and improvements in the perceptual front end of the system, enabled Anderson and his associates to develop cognitive psychology's most powerful and successful theoretical system (Anderson & Lebiere 1998). It is a major achievement. I am proud to have contributed to its origins in the early 1970s.

MOVING UP TO COHERENT TEXT

Anderson and I had addressed such prototypic "memory experiment" materials as single experiences (unrelated word lists) and single sentences (and their underlying propositions). Yet we understood that cognitive psychology had a long way to go before it could model the understanding of, and memory for, such coherent prose as a simple story or history lesson. Prose has properties that greatly transcend collections of unrelated or scrambled sentences. In meaningful prose, successive sentences are connected by a variety of coherence principles. For example, successive sentences should carry forward somewhat the same topic (concepts) and introduce new facts about it in a multilayered, interwoven way (Fletcher et al. 1996). Impressed by the pioneering theories of Walter Kintsch (1974), Roger Schank (1975b), and David Rumelhart (1975), my students and I began investigations of narrative comprehension and memory. Despite my primary interest in memory, I knew text comprehension had to be studied as well, because it is a major determinant of what people remember from a text.

Why Study Narrative Understanding and Memory?

Although there are many types of prose, psychologists began to focus on the study of narratives and story understanding in the 1980s. Several reasons led to this common interest. First, understanding of any text depends critically on the reader's expertise regarding the topic under discussion. Most adults already possess the requisite common knowledge of human affairs required to understand simple stories and folktales. For example, most adults understand basic human motives, goals,

causes of purposive actions, and simple rules of social reciprocity. This homogeneity of subjects' knowledge eliminates what would otherwise be a major source of variability in experimental data. Second, reading, remembering, and summarizing narratives are familiar cognitive tasks for most literate people. Moreover, researchers using simple narratives as experimental materials can carefully construct variations in texts to create controlled comparisons and to isolate specific components of the comprehension process. In short, narrative understanding offers an excellent experimental test tube within which to study general aspects of people's understanding and memory.

Story Grammars

Our early efforts, as with many research ventures, followed other work in the area. After a few minor studies of text memory (Bower 1974, 1978), my student, Perry Thorndyke, and I became attracted to the story-grammar approach to understanding (Bower 1976, Thorndyke 1977). Simple stories and folktales contain such recurring components as a setting, characters, a theme (main goal), a plot, episodes, and a resolution. Colby (1973) and Rumelhart (1975) even conjectured that there might be something like a context-free story grammar. That is, some rewrite rules would specify how large narrative components would be expressed in terms of smaller constituents or terminal elements. For example, a narrative consists of a setting, a theme, episodes, and an outcome. The setting in turn can be rewritten as a list of characters and places. The theme is one or more goals, and an episode is made up of characters' actions in a setting that yields outcomes. Those outcomes, in turn, may establish new narrative subgoals. Rumelhart proposed that readers use this framework to interpret, understand, and recall simple problem-solving stories.

Our early research showed that adults not only prefer stories that follow the canonical grammar but also recall them far better than they do randomly scrambled sentences (Bower 1976, Thorndyke 1977). A crucial element for recall is the overall goal of the protagonist. If no overall goal is expressed or strongly implied, comprehension and recall plummet. Comprehension also suffers if subgoals, actions, and outcomes are spread out and misaligned over different episodes of the story. Furthermore, when summarizing a story, people typically recite the "higher" units of the grammatical hierarchy by naming the main characters, main setting, main goal, and main outcome. In other words, as the grammar expected, people recall the essential gist of the story, while letting go of lesser details. Kintsch (1974) similarly found that people recall the main points (generalizations) rather than finer details of expository text. This and other research (e.g., Mandler & Johnson 1977, Stein 1988) established that people in our culture acquire and use a schema that allows them to identify the principal elements of a well-formed narrative and how these elements are structured. This schema also guides their later recall of the narrative.

But story grammars had their shortcomings. A first shortcoming is that story grammars only specified abstract components (e.g., settings, goals) but said nothing about what kinds of content would fill those components. Yet, it is the content that makes any story concrete and interesting. A second shortcoming, in violation of proposed context-free story grammar rules, is the many constraints and relations among the elements that fill the constituents of a typical narrative. For example, the main goal must be that of the main character. His or her actions must be plausible within the context of the story and relevant to those goals. And the final outcome must be related to the initial goal. A third shortcoming is that the early story grammars ignored the critical role that the readers' inferences play in understanding—the grammar applies only to the surface sentences of the text. Yet, many important elements of a text are implied rather than stated explicitly. The inferences that people draw from events in a story (or in real life)

reflect their pre-existent knowledge and beliefs. These shortcomings of the story grammar approach led researchers to the study of the conceptual meaning of narrative events, which provides a far richer lode to be mined.

Consensus View of Event Understanding

Dating from van Dijk & Kintsch (1983), researchers have developed the consensus that as people read or hear a story about events, a cascade of different cognitive processes go on in parallel, building multilevel representations of the information. First, readers take in the surface structure of the printed (or spoken) sentences and hold it in their working memory for several seconds. From this surface structure, they extract a propositional text base containing the logical relations between the concepts and the predicates stated in the text. Finally, a referential representation of what the text is about is constructed. This situation model or a mental model (Bower 1989, Johnson-Laird 1983, Zwaan & Radvansky 1998) is not the text itself but rather is what the text refers to. In some respects, the situation model is like a mental image of the story's settings and actions that the reader constructs and modifies based on clues in the text. In other respects, however, the model differs from an image. It contains, for example, hidden information that would not be visible in an image, such as characters' motives, thoughts, and hidden weapons.

The situational model includes mental tokens corresponding to the characters mentioned in the text, the approximate locations and arrays of objects in the scenes, the goal and actions taken by the characters, events, and so on. A situation model is constructed by connecting the concepts that are in the text to the real world or some imaginary world referents. Situation models draw upon the schematic knowledge the reader already has about the general situation that the text describes. This dependence acknowledges the role of expertise in understanding particular topics.

Theorists of situation models (as articulated by Zwaan et al. 1995) have hypothesized that the more significant attributes or dimensions of story situations include variations in story time, space, the current actor, his goals, emotions, and important causal relationships between events. What makes a text coherent is a high degree of overlap or constancy of these attributes from one clause to the next. Major changes in any of these attributes usually cause readers to update their current model. Research has shown that the greater the number of these attributes that are changed from one sentence to the next, the greater the updating that must occur, and the more time readers take to read and process those changes.

Causal Analyses of Motives, Actions, and Outcomes

A major clue about a situational change is a change in the characters' goals—their achievement, frustration, or failure. Therefore, I moved my research increasingly from full-blown stories to concentrate on how people recognize and understand characters' motives, plans, and actions (Black & Bower 1980; Bower 1978, 1983; Foss & Bower 1986). The causal linkages among these elements heavily influence a reader's representation of the meaning of the narrative. Tracking a reader's understanding of characters' plans and goals has been the focus of research on causal analysis of narratives (Black & Bower 1980, Schank & Abelson 1977, Trabasso & Sperry 1985).

Most simple stories introduce a main character who has a complicated problem to solve. The story describes the character's actions to overcome obstacles to achieve the solution. Readers assume that the character's actions can be explained by his goals as played out within the constraints of the situation. While frustration of a goal may prompt the character to abandon it, more often he responds by establishing subgoals that, once conquered, pave the way to achieving the principal goal. Readers use everyday psychology to try to explain the character's motives and actions. In this way, readers connect new narrative events to earlier goals or actions in the text. Readers build a network of causal connections among the events of the story—going from some initiating event (for example, the sheriff learns that rustlers have stolen cattle) through the various goals, subgoals, and actions of the main character (the sheriff chases them), overcoming obstacles (they hide and ambush him), and arriving at some final resolution (he captures the rustlers and retrieves the cattle).

Readers consider events along this main causal chain to be the most significant parts of a story (Schank 1975b, Schank & Abelson 1977). Tom Trabasso and his associates (Suh & Trabasso 1993, Trabasso & Sperry 1985, Trabasso & Suh 1993, Trabasso & van den Broek 1985) analyzed many simple narratives, asking whether each event (described in a story statement) was enabled or caused by earlier events or whether it enables or causes later events. In a coherent story, the enabling events and causes form a web of connections. The importance of a statement in a story turns out to be determined by its number of connections. This connectivity is what determines the likelihood that readers will recall a given statement (or the event that it describes) or will include it when summarizing the story. This causal analysis replaces the empty platitude that readers recall the gist of a story (Bartlett 1932)—a statement that is useless until we know what determines the gist. Causal connectivity, based simply on analysis of the text itself, is an excellent predictor of what readers consider the gist of a narrative.

Goal-Based Explanations

Because character goals are the most important causes of character actions, my associates and I investigated how readers search in memory for goals to explain actions. For example, plans and actions for achieving goals range from the well trod to the unexpected. We showed that when the number of subgoal inferences required to connect a character's action to his or her primary goal increases, it takes readers longer to comprehend the action in question (Foss & Bower 1986). Thus, we understand immediately why a hungry man eats a pizza. But it takes an extra step—and moment—to deduce why he might open the yellow pages of the phone book. We also know that in stories involving conflict, readers attribute competence and noble motives to characters with whom they identify, whereas they attribute negative traits to their adversaries. Moreover, their later recollections often contain distortions that justify these attributions (Bower 1978).

Readers establish a goal list in memory for each character and monitor how story events relate to those goals. Along the way, the character may add a goal, move closer to completing a goal, drop a completed goal, or abandon a frustrated (unachievable) goal. The more independent goals the character is juggling simultaneously, the longer it takes readers to understand the character's actions. We hypothesize that as each action occurs, the reader scans that actor's goal list, taking more time to find one that explains that action. The extra time readers take to sort through a character's multiple goals is shortened if the character's action satisfies several goals simultaneously (Sharkey & Bower 1984, 1987). Studies of goal monitoring and action explanation reveal much about how people comprehend actions in stories as well as in real life.

The Spatial Dimension

An important dimension of the situational model is the spatial location where significant story events take place. This spatial information may include a mental map of the story's places, landmarks, and objects as they are laid out in space, as well as the locations of the characters as they move about. Furthermore, to be coherent, the description of the spatial layout and of the characters' movements should be consistent. If a tower is said to be north of Bill's current location, then he can-

not see it by looking to the south. O'Brien & Albrecht (1992) have used detection of such inconsistencies to measure the accessibility of spatial information. A major narrative change in spatial location often flags the start of a new episode, signaling readers that the current model must be updated to incorporate the change. For example, the sentence "Meanwhile, back at the ranch, the outlaws..." signals a location change and a likely change in the current actor(s).

Not every story requires a detailed spatial situation. A sketchy default location often suffices. For example, stories beginning "There was once an old king who lived in a beautiful castle..." rarely provide details about the castle or where in the world it is located because such details may be irrelevant to the character's pursuit of his goals. Readers pay little attention to, and do not encode, detailed setting information unless or until it becomes relevant to the actions of the story. Black & Bower (1982) showed that setting information is best remembered when it causally relates to, or enables, later significant plot actions. For example, an earlier description of a telephone in an office becomes relevant and memorable if the character later has to telephone to report a crime.

Similarly, changes in spatial attributes of the scene do not routinely cause situational shifts unless they are both large and relevant to ongoing actions (Zwaan & van Oostendorp 1993). When spatial location is relevant to ongoing actions, readers carefully track the locations of the main character and critical objects. This point was demonstrated by Sundermeier et al. (2005). They found that objects and spatial locations were kept accessible in a reader's model and were reactivated if the current action or outcome hinged upon that information.

FOCUS AND UPDATING WITHIN SITUATION MODELS

As readers take in successive clauses of a story, they update their current model, making some elements more active in memory even as they drop other entities that had been active previously. This updating process is controlled by what readers deem significant to a story's plot. A convenient way to study this updating of situational models is by observing how readers track the changing locations of the main character. This especially holds true when the location is relevant to the main character's goal and likely actions. The remainder of this chapter summarizes what colleagues and I have found about updating caused by changes in the character's location.

Readers focus on that part of their situational model where a significant change occurs, which implies that they typically focus on the main character, his goal, and movements. This moment-by-moment tracking defines the "here and now" point in the progress of the narrative. Linguists, who call this focal point the deictic center, refer to items in the focus as being foregrounded in the reader's consciousness. Psychologists think of focus as a particularly active portion of the current model in the reader's working memory. Language provides many ways to shift this focus to a new person, place, time, or topic. This is often done explicitly, as in "Later, inside the bank vault, Jack worked furiously to crack the safe." Once mentioned, this new person and place moves to the foreground until another shift is introduced.

In research I started with postdoctoral students Dan Morrow and Steve Greenspan and further advanced with Mike Rinck, we explored the psychological consequences of such shifts of focus. We hypothesized that memory-representations of focused objects are highly activated. If so, they would be readily accessible for answering questions about them. This increased accessibility reflects nonconscious activation of memory-representations of objects near the focus. As one implication, Morrow (1985) found that items near the current focus (i.e., the current actor in a story) are likely to be selected as the referent for ambiguous pronouns. Consider, for example, the sentence "John walked past

the car and up to the house; its windows were dirty." Most people assume that the house, not the car, had dirty windows because the narrative locates John near the house now.

Paradigm for Studying Spatial Priming

To study the role of focus in updating, we familiarized our college student with a map or floor plan of the spatial layout of a building to which later experimental stories would refer (Morrow et al. 1987). The memorized map would serve as the long-term memory base for the later stories. Across different experiments, we varied the floor plan as well as the stories and test items to measure the influence of several variables on the accessibility of different objects in the situational model. **Figure 1** shows an example map used in some of our experiments.

Our standard experiments had college students memorize a map and then read 10 to 20 brief stories that were each about 20 lines long. Each story introduced a new character whose goal required him or her to move around the previously mapped building. These stories described the characters' thoughts, plans, and actions as they moved between rooms. For example, in one story a research lab manager, Wilbur, is assigned the goal of cleaning up lab rooms for an upcoming inspection by the Board of Directors. In another story, a security officer named Jack has to search throughout the building for a burglar who reportedly broke into the building. Participants read the stories at a computer terminal, presenting them line-by-line at their own pace, and their reading times per sentence were recorded.

The focus hypothesis directs interest to the movement sentences, such as "Wilbur walked from the Reception Room into the Library." Following linguists' conventions, the place the character just left is called the Source room and the place he just entered is called the Goal (or Current Location) room. As characters moved about, we measured how quickly

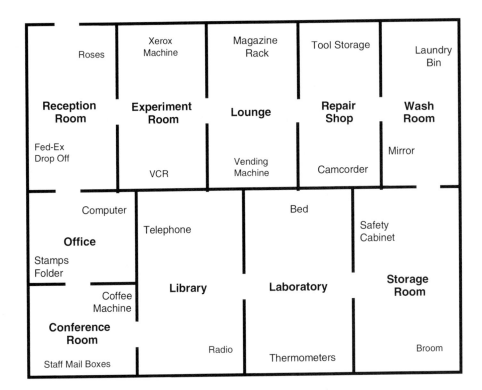

Figure 1

Example of a building layout studied by participants in our experiments. The number and location of objects as well as the room layouts were varied across different experiments.

subjects remembered from memory places and objects that were temporally or spatially near their focus of attention. To this end, after self-paced reading of a movement sentence, readers were occasionally interrupted and given a probe test. The probes required subjects to quickly answer either a yes/no question about the location of an object or whether or not two objects were located in the same room. The correct answer to a random half of the questions was "yes," while "no" was the correct answer to the rest. Our interest centered on the "yes" probes. To increase observation samples, each story contained three or four such interruptions. To ensure that readers consistently tracked the current location of the main character, occasional questions tested subjects' knowledge of his or her current location. After indicating their decision (with a yes or no key press), subjects continued reading the story until the next interruption or the end of the story. To encourage good comprehension, each story concluded with two or three yes/no questions about it.

We rewarded subjects for accuracy; those who were too inaccurate on the questions were replaced.

The following sections summarize what we have learned by considering spatial priming as a window on readers' updating of their situation model (for other reviews, see Bower & Morrow 1990, Bower & Rinck 1999, Rinck & Bower 2003).

The Basic Distance-Effect

We hypothesized that memory activation would be greatest for objects in the location currently in focus (where the protagonist is now) with activation diminishing the further the object was from the focus. We found this distance-effect in our first experiments, in which subjects learned the floor plans of two buildings: a lab and a storage barn (Morrow et al. 1987, 1989). Probe tests given after a movement sentence clocked the fastest retrieval speeds for the current Location room, followed by the Source room, and then by more distant Other rooms in the building the current story was about. The slowest retrieval speeds involved probe tests about objects from the other building not mentioned in the current story. The Other room was presumably faster than objects from the other building because it had been activated by mention of the current building and sometimes by the character having been there earlier during his tour of the building. Objects in the room farther along the path in the direction just ahead of the character's current location had a level of activation (retrieval speed) that fell between that of the Source room and the Other room.

Our initial experiments also ruled out two extraneous factors: (*a*) The same distance effect arose regardless of whether the movement sentence mentioned the Source room before or after the Location room; and (*b*) an incidental mention of a room that the character does not enter or think about results in negligible activation. An example might be, "Wilbur went into his office to review the messages that had been sent over earlier from the reception room." Such a sentence activates objects in the office but not in the reception room.

Major Versus Minor Characters

If the main character recruits a minor character to help achieve his goal, readers continue to focus more attention on the major character. In tests for this effect, the narratives included several critical sentences that described the movements of the two characters. A story might relate that Wilbur (major character) went into room A, while John (minor) went into room B, or it might reverse the order of the two clauses. A test probe followed such sentences, naming the major or minor character plus an object from the building. Subjects had to decide whether the probed character was in the same room as the object. We found that questions about the major character were answered more quickly than were those about the minor character. This suggested that read-

ers could split their attention between both characters, but the main character continued to command more of their attention.

Intermediate Locations

We found that intermediate landmarks along an implied path were activated somewhat by the character passing through their room. Critical motion sentences in this experiment took such forms as, "Wilbur walked from room A into room C." In this case, the memorized map made clear to the reader that Wilbur would have to pass through an intermediate room, B, when walking from room A to C. We found that retrieval speeds were fastest for items in the Goal room, C; next fastest for those in the intermediate (Path) room, B; next for objects in the Source room, A; and slowest for objects in some Other, more distant room that had not been activated by the sentence just read. We presume that this gradient arises because readers mentally simulate the character's imagined movement as he passed—and briefly activated—objects in the implied Path room. This Path room activation immediately begins to decay as soon as the character enters the Goal room. Significantly, the implied Path room caused greater activation than the explicitly mentioned Source room. I present a theory below that accounts for this intermediate-path effect.

Mental Location

We have also found that the most activated location is the place that the character is currently thinking about, which is not necessarily where he is currently located. After a movement sentence, the critical sentence described the character thinking about an activity in another room, e.g., remembering that he had to paint its walls or sand its floors. Test probes showed that readers accessed unmentioned objects in the thought-about room more quickly than those in the current location room. In fact, when the character's thoughts were elsewhere, subjects' access to objects in the Location room was only slightly faster than to objects from some distant Other room. Apparently, readers track the thoughts of the character more than his physical location.

This mental-location advantage would probably be reversed if readers know that the character's physical location at the moment is more important than his present thought-location, for example, if he is sitting on a ticking time bomb about to explode as he is thinking about another place. The underlying principle in such examples is that readers focus on places where they expect significant events to occur that will either advance or foil the protagonist's goals. Here again, fate of the character's goal is a major determinant of what readers identify as the crux of a story.

Objects Accompanying the Main Character

Consistent with these distance effects, Glenberg et al. (1987) showed that mentioned objects carried by the main character as he moves around are relatively accessible for as long as this character is in focus. Their vignettes introduced a character and mentioned an object that he either took with him on a walk or left behind. They found that after an intervening sentence or two, the object the character carried with him was more accessible for recognition memory and for pronoun resolution than was the object left behind.

Spatial Perspective Within the Situation

The situation model of readers mirrors the main character's perspective. Consequently, readers answer questions best from the character's vantage point. DeVega (1994) had subjects memorize locations of four buildings, such as around a town square. They then read vignettes about a main character walking through the square in a specific direc-

tion. The vignettes then introduce a second character who is walking in the same direction as the first character or in the opposite direction (that is, they are approaching one another). Probe questions then asked readers to quickly identify where a landmark was (ahead, behind, left, right) relative to one of the characters. Responses were slower for left-right rather than for ahead-behind judgments, slower for questions about the character not currently in focus, and much slower when the orientations of the two characters were opposite rather than congruent. This research indicated that readers construct and view their situation model from a particular perspective and orientation (see also Taylor & Tversky 1996).

Distance Effects in Anaphor Resolution

A criticism of the map-then-story procedure is that it overemphasizes spatial information (learning the map and then answering spatial questions), a process that might prompt subjects to read unnaturally. Perhaps readers do not normally pay so much attention to spatial information (Zwaan & van Oostendorp 1993). In response, Mike Rinck and I (Rinck & Bower 1995) conducted experiments that assessed focus effects without using any interrupting location probes. Instead, we simply measured the time subjects took to read a target sentence that contained an anaphor (such definite noun phrases as "the telephone") that referred to an object in one of the rooms of a building. Having just moved from a Source into a Goal room, the character thought about (or remembered, planned, envisioned, etc.) doing something with a critical object in another room, e.g., "Wilbur remembered that he should check the VCR in the experiment room." We found that the further the object (in this case, the VCR) was from the focus on the character's location, the longer it took subjects merely to read the anaphor sentence. Moreover, the reading time per syllable was quickened when the anaphor sentence specifically mentioned the room where the critical object was located (in the just-cited example, the target sentence reminds readers that the VCR is in the experiment room). The extra room cue presumably saves subjects the time that they otherwise would expend retrieving which room contains the object in question. This is a familiar result in memory retrieval: Two converging cues elicit a satisfactory answer more readily than either cue alone. The important result is that subjects reading "naturally" are showing the distance-from-focus effect even though they are not being interrupted to answer location questions.

Interference in Resolving Ambiguous Anaphors

If anaphor resolution involves memory retrieval, then it should be slowed by associative interference. If, for example, "the table" could refer to any one of several tables scattered throughout several rooms in the building, readers should read it faster if they are told the room-location of the mentioned table. Otherwise, readers are left in limbo, awaiting information that is more specific. In our experiment, subjects memorized a map that contained one, three, or five different example objects such as tables, chairs, and computers, distributed throughout different rooms in a building (Bower & Rinck 2001). Next, they read stories that moved the character into a specific room (e.g., the Reception room), and then they read critical sentences such as "Sally remembers having had her lecture notes while she was standing *at the table in the library.*" The alternate rendering reversed the final noun phrases, e.g., while she was standing "in the library at the table." Precise measurements of the time subjects took to read the critical anaphor (i.e., the table) were obtained by having subjects press the space bar to read each successive word on the computer screen. This method, known as "rapid serial visual presentation," is often used in reading research.

As predicted, subjects took more time to read the ambiguous anaphor (the table) when it preceded (rather than followed) the specific room name in the sentence. Subjects also took longer to read the anaphor when there were more examples of the mentioned category (e.g., tables) in different rooms. The time they took to read the room name reflected the usual distance-from-focus effect. In contrast, the increased reading time associated with increasing the number of instances of the object anaphor (from one to three to five tables) was considerably offset when the room name preceded the anaphor. In these cases, the room name clearly flags which table is being discussed, thereby reducing competing claims on memory retrieval. These results confirm the earlier finding that "natural" readers who are not interrupted by location questions nonetheless show the distance-from-focus effect. They also show how interference slows anaphor resolution. In addition, the results support the "immediacy" assumption (Just & Carpenter 1992), which posits that readers immediately attempt to identify the referent for each anaphor as they encounter it in a sentence.

What's the Distance Metric?

We wondered if the distance-from-focus effect should be measured by a Euclidean metric (in a straight line as the crow flies) or by route distance: the number of rooms or spatial segments separating the focus from the mentioned object. In experiments by Rinck et al. (1997), these two types of distance were varied independently. The memorized maps allowed the stories and test-probes to put either a long or a short metric distance between the current focus and the referent object. Additionally, this distance either was divided into two rooms or was left as an undivided room. Following a movement across this distance, the character thought about an object along the path. This object was either metrically near or far from the focus room, and that distance either was divided into two rooms or was not. The dependent variables were the time subjects took to read the movement sentence itself and the "think about" object-anaphor sentence.

The experiment produced several clear results. Overall, the primary determinant of reading time was the route (room) distance, and not the Euclidean metric distance. Subjects took longer to read the movement sentence when its path traversed two rooms rather than one, whereas room length had no effect on reading time. Also, the reading time for the anaphor in the thought-about object sentence increased dramatically when the path was divided into two rooms compared to one. Here again, the metric length of this room (or rooms) was immaterial. Readers' references to an object on the other side of a shared wall (a minimal metric distance), for example, required no more reading time than references to an object on the other side of the building (a long metric distance). Although room segments had a major impact on reading, metric distances had no measurable impact.

What is odd about this finding is that we know that subjects had recorded metric information in memory. When asked to draw maps from memory of the rooms and their objects, they do a reasonably good job of reproducing relative locations and distances. Yet, in our reading task, they skipped from one landmark to another without regard for metric distances. Why? A plausible answer is that they do not need to keep metric information active while reading since they are never asked questions about it, so it remains inactive. I presumed that if subjects were required to pay attention to metric distances in order to answer relevant questions (i.e., "Is object A or B metrically closer to the character now?"), then their reaction times would show metric distance effects, e.g., two objects close to the focus would lead to faster decisions than two objects far from the focus. This leaves open the question of whether such metric influences would then appear in readers' anaphor look-up times.

Learning a Spatial Layout from a Verbal Description

Spatial distance effects do not depend upon learning layouts from a map. Similar distance effects occur when subjects learn spatial arrangements of rooms and objects from detailed verbal descriptions. Relying exclusively on verbal descriptions, our subjects memorized a rectangular preschool with five rooms (Rinck et al. 1996). Each room had two doors leading to adjacent rooms and a third door opening into a common inner courtyard. The rooms contained common school objects and each room was named for the teacher (e.g., Ms. Hill's room). The verbal descriptions also located the rooms relative to the outer shell of the building. Subjects were not allowed to physically draw maps of the building (although most undoubtedly constructed mental images of its presumed layout).

Compared to our earlier physical map learners, those relying just on verbal descriptions took far longer to memorize the spatial layout. They also later read the stories slightly slower. Nonetheless, during the standard story reading following map learning, the distance gradient for the retrieval of probed objects remained orderly and significant across both groups. Regardless of whether subjects had learned from physical maps or verbal descriptions, their retrieval speeds were fastest for objects in the Goal room, followed by those in the Path room, then those in the Source room, and finally were slowest for objects found in some Other room.

Whether or not memory for the spatial array is identical for map learners and verbal-description learners, we note that the distance effects in both cases appear to reflect the connectivity structures among rooms that both types of subjects memorized. Similarly, Taylor & Tversky (1992) found that subjects who studied maps and those receiving verbal descriptions of maps performed comparably on tests of spatial knowledge.

Using Prelearned Spatial Arrays

To insure homogeneity of spatial knowledge, subjects in the foregoing experiments memorized a map of a unique space in which the story events take place. Some evidence suggests that a distance effect occurs when the stories refer to a spatial layout that is already familiar to subjects before they show up to participate in the experiment. In pilot work, my student, Saskia Trail, found a small but significant distance effect for subjects who read many stories about characters driving long distances between major United States cities, pursuing a goal such as delivering furniture or selling encyclopedias to libraries. The critical sentences had the character drive from one city to another (e.g., San Diego to Miami). In the destination city, he would think about some activity (e.g., spending his bonus pay) in the current Location city (Miami), the Source city (San Diego), or a city along the just-completed driving Path (e.g., New Orleans).

Trail measured how quickly subjects, who were never shown a map, read those critical "thinking" sentences depending on which city the character was thinking about. These anaphor reading times showed the usual distance gradient, with reading time for Path cities being intermediate between the times for the shorter Goal city and the longer Source city. In an unforeseen complication to her experiment, Trail found that her college subjects' pre-existent map knowledge often was fuzzy and imprecise. Morrow et al. (2004) did a more substantial follow-up study that found that senior citizens showed a more robust "city-distance" effect in anaphor reading times than did young people. The authors suggested that the weaker effect for younger subjects might have resulted from their poorer knowledge of geographic locations of the cities in the stories.

Clearly, more research is needed regarding distance effects with familiar arrays. One logistical challenge is identifying highly familiar spatial arrays (such as floor plans, towns, or campuses) for a large sample of subjects and then writing stories about characters moving around in those spaces. Trail and I tried using our own university campus as the known spatial array. But we abandoned this approach after discovering surprisingly large variation in students' knowledge of different campus spots (such as dorms, lecture halls, and eateries).

Elapsed Story Time

Once a character leaves one place and enters another, distinct space, we hypothesize that activation on the initial place decays as its relevance to the character recedes into the past. This decay process turns out to be determined by the lapse of time spelled out in the story, not the real time that passes as subjects read intervening sentences before they hit an anaphor referring back to the original location.

Rinck et al. (2000) investigated this question in experiments that built on the work of Rolf Zwann (1996). Our movement sentences moved the story character from a Source room through a Path room into a Goal room. Significantly, he carries out an activity in the Goal room that alternately is described as taking either a short time (e.g., two minutes) or a long time (e.g., two hours). In addition, we varied the number of intervening sentences separating the movement event from the elapsed story-time statement, following which we presented the probe test. The probe measured the accessibility of an object in the Path room. For example, Wilbur walks from room A (through room B) into room C, where he notices that room C needs to be cleaned up. This action was followed by zero or five sentences elaborating on the activity in room C before the critical time-lapse sentence stated that Wilbur took either two minutes or two hours to clean up room C. We probe-tested the subject, asking about an object in either Path room B or Goal room C. If elapsed story time is critical for deactivation of earlier entities, then objects in the Path room will have notably less activation after a stated two-hour cleanup than a cleanup said to take just two minutes.

The results in this experiment were striking: The elapsed story time caused a large and consistent slowing of object retrieval time, whereas actual elapsed reading time (determined by the zero versus five intervening sentences) had virtually no effect. Retrieval times for objects in the just-left room were markedly slower following elapsed hours than elapsed minutes. This occurred even though subjects took no longer to read the elapsed-hours statements than the elapsed-minutes statements. Apparently, readers of the longer (hours) verb-modifier deactivated Path-room objects significantly more than did readers of the shorter (minutes) verb modifier. This inhibition occurs very quickly given that the test probe immediately followed the subject's self-paced reading of the elapsed time sentence. Such rapid suppression of activation has been a premise of several language-processing theories (Gernsbacher 1990).

Although we found little effect resulting from our manipulation of the number of intervening sentences, the maximum number we tested was only five sentences. We would expect a larger effect if this cap was pumped up to hundreds of intervening sentences before the test probe. However, this would introduce logistical and conceptual problems. Namely, it is difficult to interject so many intervening sentences without introducing new topics, subgoals, and episodes. These changes would shift the situation away from the one that immediately follows the critical movement sentence. This shift, in and of itself, likely would deaden accessibility related to the prior Path room.

Priming by a Momentary Active Goal

Earlier we found that activation tracks the place that the character is thinking about as he plans to do something there. Readers can predict what is on a character's mind by knowing his active goal (wish, desire, plan). Thus, if they read that the character is hungry, then food items and their associated places in the building should be activated in the readers' mind.

In our goal-activation experiments (Rinck & Bower 1999, 2003), each story tested several goal-related probes by introducing a momentary, minor goal that temporarily interrupts the character's overarching main goal. For example, Wilbur's main goal in one story was to clean up all the rooms in the research building before tomorrow's inspection by the board of directors. During this lengthy chore, however, he has the apparently spontaneous thought that he also needs to make copies of a handout for his speech to the directors the next day. Once Wilbur addresses this momentary copying goal and we have probed the accessibility of some related object, the narrative returns Wilbur to his chief goal: cleaning up the building.

At each critical point in the text, we introduced either of two momentary goals (such as to make photocopies or to videotape his practice speech), followed by a probe referring to a goal-object probe that was either in the current Location room or in the prior Source room. We created four experimental conditions: The goal-object probe in the Location or Source room was either relevant to the temporary goal (for example, the Xerox machine is relevant to the copying goal) or it was irrelevant because the object probe did not relate to the temporary goal (for example, although Wilbur wanted to videotape, the probe tested the location of the Xerox machine).

This experiment revealed major effects of spatial distance and goal relevance on memory-retrieval times. As expected, Location-room probes always were answered more quickly than Source-room probes. Independently, probes of goal-relevant objects were always answered more quickly than probes of goal-irrelevant objects. Significantly, these two factors did not interact: The speed-up advantage of goal-relevant over goal-irrelevant probes was about the same for objects in the Location room as for those in the Source room.

Priming by Active, Completed, or Postponed Goals

The accessibility of goals and their relevant objects vary throughout a story, reflecting their evolving status with the protagonist. Earlier research has shown that a character's active, uncompleted goals remain more accessible than completed goals (Dopkins et al. 1993, Lutz & Radvansky 1997, Suh & Trabasso 1993). Presumably, a protagonist's uncompleted goals are kept active in the reader's working memory, as opposed to completed goals, which fall victim either to passive decay or by inhibition. Readers expect that completed goals will no longer motivate the character and, therefore, will no longer be needed to explain the character's later actions.

Our experiments compared active and completed goals to a third type of goal, namely, those that the character briefly considers, but then postpones or abandons. Our postponement-narratives had the character set aside the briefly considered goal due to his pressing need to finish the overarching goal. We tested whether a mentioned but then postponed goal retains any more activation than a completed goal. We modified the texts and test probes of previous "goal" experiments to include the postponed goal condition along with the active and completed goal conditions. After introducing a momentary interrupting goal, the narrative then described it as either active, completed, or postponed—that is, considered briefly but rejected. Immediately thereafter, the probe-object test was presented. All probe objects were goal relevant and located in either the current Location room or the preceding Source room.

The results showed strong main effects of goal status as well as spatial distance to the goal object. Specifically, subjects always retrieved objects relevant to the active goal fastest and always retrieved those related to the postponed goal the slowest. Retrieval time for the completed goal-object varied with its spatial location: Subjects retrieved a completed goal-object as quickly as an active goal-object when it was in the current Location room where the character had just used it. However, retrieval time for the completed goal-object slowed to that of an object related to a postponed goal when the completed goal was in the just-preceding Source room. To clarify this result, a second experiment varied the number of sentences (zero or three) between the goal-status sentence and presentation of the probe test. The intervening three sentences described the character's return to his overarching goal. In this experiment, we replicated the previous results for active and postponed goals; furthermore, we found that the completed-goal condition yielded fast retrieval when no sentences intervened before the test probe, but much slower retrieval after three intervening sentences.

The results suggest that readers may process postponed versus completed goals differently. The sudden drop in accessibility of postponed-goal objects suggests that readers actively inhibit postponed goals and related objects. In contrast, the decrease in accessibility of completed-goal objects probably reflects a gradual decay of activation (from zero to three intervening sentences).

A NETWORK EXPLANATION OF FINDINGS

Activating Associative Networks in Long-term Memory

I will invoke a familiar conceptual framework to summarize our findings. First, consider the long-term memory structure that our subjects might use to represent the maps of the experimental buildings. Following long-standing conventions in AI (Anderson 1978, Kosslyn 1980, Pylyshyn 1973), the memorized map may be represented as a hierarchical tree structure containing units or nodes (denoting objects, rooms, buildings) with labeled links or associations (containment of objects in rooms, paths between rooms, geometric relationships, etc.). The upper part of **Figure 2**, labeled "Long-Term Memory,"

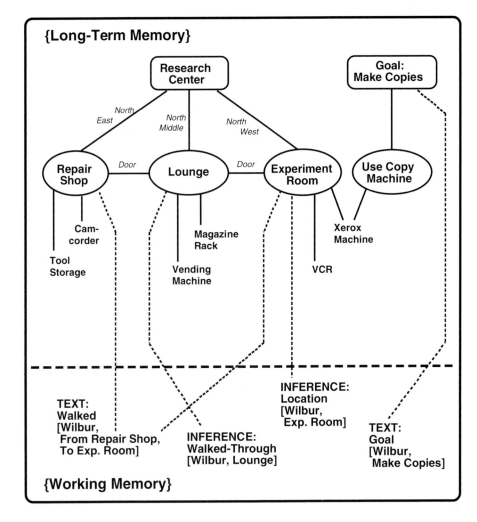

{Long-Term Memory}

Research Center

Goal: Make Copies

North East — North Middle — North West

Repair Shop — Door — Lounge — Door — Experiment Room

Use Copy Machine

Cam-corder

Magazine Rack

Xerox Machine

Tool Storage

Vending Machine

VCR

INFERENCE: Location [Wilbur, Exp. Room]

TEXT: Walked [Wilbur, From Repair Shop, To Exp. Room]

INFERENCE: Walked-Through [Wilbur, Lounge]

TEXT: Goal [Wilbur, Make Copies]

{Working Memory}

Figure 2

An associative network in long-term memory encoding knowledge of the building's spatial layout. Conceptual units (nodes) denote rooms and objects, and links denote spatial relationships and connections. Working memory (lower part) contains the "Here-Now" focus on the current location, the currently active sentence, and a spatial inference from it. The unit representing the goal of making photocopies is also shown in the right side of the figure. Reproduced with permission from Rinck & Bower 2003, Figure 8.

depicts part of such a hypothetical spatial encoding of several rooms, with each room containing several objects. The rooms also have various access relations and locations relative to one another (Bower & Rinck 1999). The bottom part of **Figure 2**, labeled "Working Memory," holds the most recent sentence the subject has read and parsed into basic propositions (such as "Wilbur walked from the Repair Shop into the Experiment Room"). The theory supposes that the concepts mentioned in this sentence are temporarily linked to their corresponding referents in long-term memory. This is depicted by dashed lines connecting the working-memory concepts to their corresponding units in the hierarchy. These linkages pass activation from working memory to the units in the long-term memory structure. An example would be to activate the proposition that the camcorder is in the repair shop. Below I discuss the goal-plan features on the right side of **Figure 2**.

In this scheme, the focus of attention (or foregrounded concepts) zeroes in on currently active concepts in working memory and their counterparts in long-term memory. It also is the narrative's here-and-now point. As the narrative flows, the concepts that are active evolve and change, as does the Here-and-Now pointer. In this network model, questions about object locations require the processor to activate and retrieve propositions from long-term memory, for example, "The Experiment Room contains the Xerox machine" (Collins & Loftus 1975). Because such concepts have received spreading activation from the preceding movement sentences, they have a head-start advantage relative to entities more distant in the network, so the network can more readily retrieve them and answer questions about them. The farther is the queried room from the focus in the network, the weaker the spread of activation and the slower the time to retrieve information to answer questions. This property yields the basic categorical ("room") distance gradient independently of the Euclidian metric distance.

These object-concepts now in the spotlight (speaking metaphorically) are more accessible for answering related questions than are objects lying outside the spotlight. The distance-from-focus gradient suggests two possible metaphors. One features a fuzzy spotlight that scatters light in a gradient around its center. The more peripheral an object is to the center, the dimmer is its lighting, so the more time required for checking and verifying an answer. An alternative metaphor invokes a sharply defined spotlight that must be swung from its current location to focus on a probed object. The time for the spotlight to traverse the path in the model would be presumed to reflect greater distances. Both metaphors correspond to plausible models of attention focus.

Explaining the Intermediate-Room Effect

To illustrate the workings of the spatial network model in **Figure 2**, consider how it explains two of our results. Consider first the intermediate-room result of an earlier experiment. We assume that the character's movement from room A (**Figure 2**, Repair Shop) to C (**Figure 2**, Experiment Room) invokes a conscious or unconscious inference (via the network linkages) that the character passed through room B (**Figure 2**, Lounge). This inference is reflected in the proposition "Wilbur

walked through the Lounge," which **Figure 2** shows as now active in working memory. This inference activates the Lounge room concept in memory, so that questions about its objects are answered more readily than objects in other, more distant rooms. Likewise, once the story moves on to other rooms and topics, the activations of previously visited rooms decay back to the baseline, losing their temporary accessibility boost. As they read, subjects create a dynamic wave of activation spreading across their network memory structure. This wave's surge creates peaks and valleys of activation (and accessibility) that sweeps across the concept units that track the character's current location, thoughts, and goals (see also van Den Broek et al. 1998).

Explaining the Goal-Relevance Effect

As a second example, the effects of goal relevance on accessibility can be explained by the associative network outlined in **Figure 2**. We begin with the plausible assumption that readers track the character's active goals, retaining them in working memory. Each familiar goal is associated with plan structures in long-term memory that guide inferences about instrumental objects typically used in those plans. For instance, educated readers know that copy machines make photocopies, camcorders make videotapes, and so on. Likely goal-related links between the "Make photocopies" plan units are depicted in the upper right side of **Figure 2**.

When a goal is active in working memory, it presumably activates its corresponding goal-plan structure in long-term memory, which, in turn, activates associated instruments—such as the copy machine in the preceding example. The activation of the goal-relevant object enhances the activation coming from the room location unit that has also just been activated by its concept in working memory. We therefore expect reaction time to be further reduced by the combined relevance of the goal and location of focus. Moreover, activation caused by these goal-based instrumental inferences should be kept aroused as long as the current goal is active. Yet, this elevated activation on this goal should decay once this goal is completed and the character moves on to another goal and, perhaps, another location. On the other hand, if the goal is abandoned or postponed, then the goal activation is quickly and actively inhibited, much as Gernsbacher (1990) suggested.

In conclusion, this network model—combined with some auxiliary assumptions about automatic inferences, goal activation, and decay—readily accounts for the bulk of our experimental findings about memory access during narrative comprehension. More specifically, it appears to help explain focus effects in spatial priming within situation models.

SUMMARY AND CONCLUDING COMMENT

To summarize, I have argued that one goal of reading research should be an understanding of how people process narratives and construct situation models from them. A major factor in updating a situation model is how the text guides the reader's momentary focus of attention. The last part of this chapter has reviewed many results on how narrative focus changes or "primes" the accessibility of entities in the situation model. This priming was examined using both subjects' times to read an anaphor referring to an object and to answer explicit questions about its location.

The primary findings indicate that narrative focus enhances accessibility of nearby objects in the model. The effect during reading appears determined not by Euclidean distance but by route distance from the focus. Readers'

focus follows the major character and tracks his location, goals, and thoughts. Readers' retrieval of an anaphoric reference to an object is slowed by their momentary uncertainty (e.g., which of several instances of a category is being referred to). The enhanced accessibility of the current place or goal fades as the character, and hence the focus, moves on to other places and topics. This fading is quickened when the text states that a long time has elapsed in the story.

Readers construct their situation models from a given perspective and orientation; questions about object locations are most readily answered from that perspective. The distance-from-focus effect arises when the spatial layout is learned from a verbal description as well as from a map. Some evidence suggests that distance effects also arise for narrative questions about familiar maps not studied in the experiment.

Explicit mention of a character's goal increases the accessibility of objects relevant to that goal. This accessibility is highest when a goal is being actively pursued, it fades soon after a goal is achieved, and is absent if a considered goal is abandoned. I proposed an associative network model with retrieval determined by spreading activation as a way of summarizing some of the major findings.

The research described in this review is a selected sample of topics my collaborators and I have investigated throughout my career. I have had a stellar collection of graduate and postgraduate students and colleagues who have contributed their ideas and experimental labors to this research. Many of them have gone on to illustrious research careers. I consider them my lasting legacy to cognitive psychology, outweighing by far the findings summarized here.

ACKNOWLEDGMENT

Parts of this chapter are adapted from the author's autobiographical chapter in *A History of Psychology in Autobiography*, Vol. 8, edited by G. Lindsey & W. Runyan, APA Books 2007, and from Bower & Morrow (1990).

LITERATURE CITED

Anderson JR. 1978. Arguments concerning representations for mental imagery. *Psychol. Rev.* 85:249–77

Anderson JR, Bower GH. 1973. *Human Associative Memory.* Washington, DC: Hemisphere

Asch SE. 1969. Reformulation of the problem of association. *Am. Psychol.* 24:92–102

Asch SE, Ceraso J, Heimer W. 1960. Perceptual conditions of association. *Psychol. Monogr.* 57:No. 3

Atkinson RC, Shiffrin R. 1968. Human memory: a proposed system and its control processes. In *Psychology of Learning and Motivation*, ed. KW Spence, JT Spence, Vol. 2, pp. 90–195. New York: Academic

Bartlett FC. 1932. *Remembering.* Cambridge, UK: Cambridge Univ. Press

Black J, Bower GH. 1980. Story understanding as problem-solving. *Poetics* 9:223–50

Bobrow S, Bower GH. 1969. Comprehension and recall of sentences. *J. Exp. Psychol.* 80:515–18

Bower GH, Miller NE. 1958. Rewarding and punishing effects from stimulating the same place in the rat's brain. *J. Comp. Physiol. Psychol.* 51:669–74

Bower GH. 1967. A descriptive theory of memory. In *The Organization of Recall*, ed. DP Kimble, pp. 112–85. New York: N.Y. Acad. Sci.

Bower GH. 1970a. Organizational factors in memory. *Cogn. Psychol.* 1:18–46

Bower GH. 1970b. Analysis of a mnemonic device. *Am. Sci.* 58:496–519

Bower GH. 1972a. A selective review of organizational factors in memory. See Tulving & Donaldson 1972, pp. 93–137

Bower GH. 1972b. Mental imagery and associative learning. In *Cognition in Learning and Memory*, ed. L Gregg, pp. 51–88. New York: Wiley

Bower GH. 1974. Selective facilitation and interference in retention of prose. *J. Educ. Psychol.* 66:1–8

Bower GH. 1976. Experiments on story understanding and recall. *Q. J. Exp. Psychol.* 28:511–34

Bower GH. 1978a. Interference paradigms for meaningful propositional memory. *Am. J. Psychol.* 91:575–85

Bower GH. 1978b. Experiments on story comprehension and recall. *Discourse Process.* 1:211–31

Bower GH. 1983. Plans and goals in understanding episodes. In *Discourse Processing*, ed. A Flammer, W Kintsch, pp. 2–15. Amsterdam: North Holland

Bower GH. 1989. Mental models in narrative understanding. In *Cognition in Individual and Social Contexts*, ed. AF Bennett, KM McConkey, pp. 129–44. Netherlands: Elsevier

Bower GH, Clark M. 1969. Narrative stories as mediators for serial learning. *Psychonom. Sci.* 14:181–82

Bower GH, Lesgold A, Tieman D. 1969. Grouping operations in free recall. *J. Verbal Learn. Verbal Behav.* 8:481–93

Bower GH, Morrow DG. 1990. Mental models in narrative comprehension. *Science* 247:44–48

Bower GH, Rinck M. 1999. Priming access to entities in spatial mental models. In *Proc. 41st Cong. German Psychol. Soc.*, ed. W Hacker, M Rinck. pp. 74–85. Berlin: Pabst Sci.

Bower GH, Rinck M. 2001. Selecting one among many referents in spatial situation models. *J. Exp. Psychol. Learn. Mem. Cogn.* 27(1):81–98

Bower GH, Winzenz D. 1969. Group structure coding and memory for digit series. *J. Exp. Psychol. Monogr.* 80:2(Pt. 2)

Bower GH, Winzenz D. 1970. Comparison of associative learning strategies. *Psychonom. Sci.* 20(2):119–20

Broadbent DE. 1958. *Perception and Communication.* London: Pergamon

Chomsky N. 1965. *Aspects of a Theory of Syntax.* Cambridge, MA: MIT Press

Chomsky N. 1959. Review of Skinner's *Verbal Behavior*. *Language* 35:26–58

Colby BN. 1973. A partial grammar of Eskimo folktales. *Am. Anthropol.* 75:645–62

Collins AM, Quillian MR. 1972. How to make a language user. See Tulving & Donaldson 1972, pp. 310–51

Collins AM, Loftus EF. 1975. A spreading-activation theory of semantic processing. *Psychol. Rev.* 82:407–28

Craik FIM, Lockhart RS. 1972. Levels of processing: a framework for memory research. *J. Verbal Learn. Verbal Behav.* 11:671–81

deVega M. 1994. Characters and their perspectives in narratives describing spatial environments. *Psychol. Res.* 56:116–26

Bobrow DG, Collins A, eds. 1975. *Representation and Understanding*. New York: Academic

Dollard J, Miller NE. 1950. *Personality and Psychotherapy*. New York: McGraw-Hill

Dopkins S, Klin C, Myers JL. 1993. Accessibility of information about goals during the processing of narrative text. *J. Exp. Psychol. Learn. Mem. Cogn.* 19:70–80

Fletcher CR, Van Den Broek P, Authur EJ. 1996. A model of narrative comprehension and recall. In *Models of Understanding Text*, ed. BK Britten, AE Graesser, pp. 141–63. Hillsdale, NJ: Erlbaum

Foss CL, Bower GH. 1986. Understanding actions in relation to goals. In *Advances in Cognitive Science*, ed. NE Sharkey. 1:94–124. Chichester, UK: Ellis Horwood

Gernsbacher MA. 1990. *Language Comprehension as Structure Building*. Hillsdale, NJ: Erlbaum

Glenberg AM, Meyer M, Lindem K. 1987. Mental models contribute to foregrounding during text comprehension. *J. Mem. Lang.* 26:69–83

Hintzman D. 1968. Explorations with a discrimination net model of paired-associate learning. *J. Math. Psychol.* 5:123–62

Hull CL. 1952. *A Behavior System*. New Haven, CT: Yale Univ. Press

Johnson-Laird PN. 1983. *Mental Models: Towards a Cognitive Psychology of Language, Inference, and Consciousness*. Cambridge, MA: Harvard Univ Press

Just MA, Carpenter PA. 1992. A capacity theory of comprehension: individual differences in working memory. *Psychol. Rev.* 99:122–49

Kintsch W. 1974. *The Representation of Meaning in Memory*. Hillsdale, NJ: Erlbaum

Kosslyn SM. 1980. *Image and Mind*. Cambridge, MA: Harvard Univ. Press

Logan FA. 1956. A micromolar approach to behavior theory. *Psychol. Rev.* 63:63–73

Logan FA. 1960. *Incentive*. New Haven, CT: Yale Univ. Press

Lutz MF, Radvansky GA. 1997. The fate of completed goal information in narrative comprehension. *J. Mem. Lang.* 36:293–310

Mandler JM, Johnson NJ. 1977. Remembrance of things parsed: story structure and recall. *Cogn. Psychol.* 9:111–51

Mandler G. 1967. Organization and memory. In *The Psychology of Learning and Motivation*, ed. KW Spence, JT Spence, Vol. 1, pp. 328–72. New York: Academic

McGeogh GA, Irion Al. 1952. *The Psychology of Human Learning*. New York: Longmans. Rev. ed.

Melton A. 1963. Implications of short-term memory for the general theory of memory. *J. Verbal Learn. Verbal Behav.* 3:1–21

Miller GA. 1956. The magical number seven plus or minus two: some limits on our capacity for processing information. *Psychol. Rev.* 3:81–97

Miller GE, Galanter E, Pribram K. 1960. *Plans and the Structure of Behavior*. New York: Holt, Rinehart & Winston

Morrow DG. 1985. Prominent characters and events organize narrative understanding. *J. Mem. Lang.* 24:390–404

Morrow DG, Bower GH, Greenspan SL. 1989. Updating situation models during narrative comprehension. *J. Mem. Lang.* 28:292–312

Morrow DG, Greenspan S, Bower GH. 1987. Accessibility and situation models in narrative comprehension. *J. Mem. Lang.* 26:165–87

Morrow DG, Stine-Morrow E, Sanborn A, Ridolfo H. 2004. *Older adults create situation models from geographical knowledge when reading narratives.* Poster presented at Conf. Cogn. Aging, Atlanta, GA

Neisser U. 1967. *Cognitive Psychology.* New York: Appleton-Century-Crofts

Newell A, Simon HA. 1961. Computer simulation of human thinking. *Science* 134:2011–17

O'Brien EJ, Albrecht JE. 1992. Comprehension strategies in the development of a mental model. *J. Exp. Psychol. Learn. Mem. Cogn.* 18:777–84

Osgood CE. 1953. *Method and Theory in Experimental Psychology.* New York: Oxford Univ. Press

Owens J, Bower GH, Black JB. 1979. The "Soap Opera" effect in story recall. *Mem. Cogn.* 7:185–91

Paivio A. 1971. *Imagery and Verbal Processes.* New York: Holt, Rinehart & Winston

Pylyshyn ZW. 1973. What the mind's eye tells the mind's brain: a critique of mental imagery. *Psychol. Bull.* 80:1–24

Rinck M, Bower GH. 1995. Anaphora resolution and the focus of attention in mental models. *J. Mem. Lang.* 34:110–31

Rinck M, Bower GH. 1999. Goals as generators of activation in narrative understanding. In *Narrative Comprehension, Causality, and Coherence: Essays in Honor of Tom Trabasso*, ed. S Goldman, A Graesser, P van den Broek, pp. 111–34. Saddle River, NJ: Erlbaum

Rinck M, Bower GH. 2003. Goal-based accessibility of entities within situation models. In *The Psychology of Learning and Motivation: Advances in Research and Theory*, ed. B Ross, 39:213–45. New York: Academic

Rinck M, Bower GH, Wolf K. 2000. Temporal and spatial distance in situation models. *Mem. Cogn.* 29:1310–20

Rinck M, Hahnal A, Bower GH, Glowalla M. 1997. The metrics of spatial situation models. *J. Exp. Psychol. Learn. Mem. Cogn.* 23:622–37

Rinck M, Williams P, Bower GH, Becker ES. 1996. Spatial situation models and narrative understanding: some generalizations and extensions. *Discourse Process.* 21:23–55

Ross BH. 1981. The more, the better? Number of decisions as a determinant of memorability. *Mem. Cogn.* 9:23–33

Rumelhart DE. 1975. Notes on a schema for stories. See Bobrow & Collins 1975, pp. 211–36

Rumelhart DE, Lindsay PH, Norman DA. 1972. A process model for long-term memory. See Tulving & Donaldson 1972, pp. 197–246

Schank RC. 1975a. *Conceptual Information Processing.* Amsterdam: North-Holland

Schank RC. 1975b. The structure of episodes. See Bobrow & Collins 1975, pp. 237–72

Schank RC, Abelson RP. 1977. *Scripts, Plans, Goals, and Understanding.* Hillsdale, NJ: Erlbaum

Sharkey N, Bower GH. 1984. The integration of goals and actions in text understanding. In *Proc. Sixth Annu. Conf. Cogn. Sci. Soc.*, pp. 315–17, Boulder, CO

Sharkey NE. Bower GH. 1987. A model of memory organization for interacting goals. In *Modeling Cognition*, ed. PE Morris, pp. 231–48. Chichester, UK: Wiley

Skinner BF. 1957. *Verbal Behavior.* Englewood Cliffs, NJ: Prentice-Hall

Stein NL. 1988. The development of storytelling skills. In *Child Language: A Book of Readings*, ed. MB Franklin, S Barten, pp. 282–97. New York: Cambridge Univ. Press

Suh SY, Trabasso T. 1993. Inferences during reading: converging evidence from discourse analysis, talk-aloud protocols, and recognition priming. *J. Mem. Lang.* 32:279–300

Sundermeier BA, Van Den Broek P, Zwaan RA. 2005. Causal coherence and the availability of locations and objects during narrative comprehension. *Mem. Cogn.* 33:462–70

Taylor HA, Tversky B. 1992. Descriptions and depictions of environments. *Mem. Cogn.* 20:483–96

Taylor HA, Tversky B. 1996. Perspective in spatial descriptions. *J. Mem. Lang.* 35:371–91

Thorndyke PW. 1977. Cognitive structures in comprehension and memory for narrative discourse. *Cogn. Psychol.* 89:77–110

Trabasso T, Sperry LL. 1985. Causal relatedness and importance of story events. *J. Mem. Lang.* 24:595–611

Trabasso T, Van Den Broek P. 1985. Causal thinking and representation of narrative events. *J. Mem. Lang.* 24:612–30

Trabasso T, Suh SY. 1993. Understanding text: achieving explanatory coherence through on-line inferences and mental operations in working memory. *Discourse Process.* 16:3–34

Tulving E. 1962. Subjective organization in the free recall of "unrelated" words. *Psychol. Rev.* 69:344–54

Tulving E, Donaldson W, eds. 1972. *Organization of Memory.* New York: Academic

Van Den Broek P, Young M, Tzeng Y, Linderholm T. 1998. The Landscape model of reading: inferences and the online construction of a memory representation. In *The Construction of Mental Representations During Reading*, ed. H van Oostendorp, SR Goldman, pp. 71–98. Mahwah, NJ: Erlbaum

van Dijk TA, Kintsch W. 1983. *Strategies of Discourse Comprehension.* New York: Academic

Winograd T. 1972. Understanding natural language. *Cogn. Psychol.* 3:1–191

Zwaan RA. 1996. Processing narrative time shifts. *J. Exp. Psychol. Learn. Mem. Cogn.* 22:1196–207

Zwaan RA, van Oostendorp H. 1993. Do readers construct spatial representations in naturalistic story comprehension? *Discourse Process.* 16:125–43

Zwaan RA, Radvansky GA. 1998. Situation models in language comprehension and memory. *Psychol. Bull.* 123:162–85

Zwaan RA, Magliano JP, Graesser AC. 1995. Dimensions of situation model construction in narrative comprehension. *J. Exp. Psychol. Learn. Mem. Cogn.* 21:386–97

Addiction and the Brain Antireward System

George F. Koob[1] and Michel Le Moal[2]

[1]Committee on the Neurobiology of Addictive Disorders, The Scripps Research Institute, La Jolla, California 92037; email: gkoob@scripps.edu

[2]Institut François Magendie, Institut National de la Santé et de la Recherche Médicale, Unité 862, Université Victor Segalen Bordeaux 2, Bordeaux 33076, France; email: lemoal@bordeaux.inserm.fr

Annu. Rev. Psychol. 2008. 59:29–53

The *Annual Review of Psychology* is online at
http://psych.annualreviews.org

This article's doi:
10.1146/annurev.psych.59.103006.093548

0066-4308/08/0203-0029$20.00

Key Words

extended amygdala, allostasis, opponent process, drug addiction, neuroadaptation

Abstract

A neurobiological model of the brain emotional systems has been proposed to explain the persistent changes in motivation that are associated with vulnerability to relapse in addiction, and this model may generalize to other psychopathology associated with dysregulated motivational systems. In this framework, addiction is conceptualized as a cycle of decreased function of brain reward systems and recruitment of antireward systems that progressively worsen, resulting in the compulsive use of drugs. Counteradaptive processes, such as opponent process, that are part of the normal homeostatic limitation of reward function fail to return within the normal homeostatic range and are hypothesized to repeatedly drive the allostatic state. Excessive drug taking thus results in not only the short-term amelioration of the reward deficit but also suppression of the antireward system. However, in the long term, there is worsening of the underlying neurochemical dysregulations that ultimately form an allostatic state (decreased dopamine and opioid peptide function, increased corticotropin-releasing factor activity). This allostatic state is hypothesized to be reflected in a chronic deviation of reward set point that is fueled not only by dysregulation of reward circuits per se but also by recruitment of brain and hormonal stress responses. Vulnerability to addiction may involve genetic comorbidity and developmental factors at the molecular, cellular, or neurocircuitry levels that sensitize the brain antireward systems.

Contents

Drug addiction: a chronically relapsing disorder characterized by: compulsion to seek and take the drug, loss of control in limiting intake, and emergence of a negative emotional state (e.g., dysphoria, anxiety, and irritability) when access to the drug is prevented

Neuroadaptation: change in neuronal function of a system with repeated challenge to that system

INTRODUCTION

What is Addiction? The Clinical Syndrome

Drug addiction, also known as substance dependence, is a chronically relapsing disorder characterized by (*a*) compulsion to seek and take the drug, (*b*) loss of control in limiting intake, and (*c*) emergence of a negative emotional state (e.g., dysphoria, anxiety, irritability) when access to the drug is prevented (defined here as dependence) (Koob & Le Moal 2005). The terms addiction and substance dependence (as currently defined by the *Diagnostic and Statistical Manual of Mental Disorders*, fourth edition; Am. Psychiatric Assoc. 1994) are used interchangeably throughout this review and refer to a final stage of a usage process that moves from drug use to addiction.

Clinically, the occasional but limited use of a drug with the potential for abuse or dependence is distinct from the emergence of a chronic drug-dependent state. An important goal of current neurobiological research is to understand the molecular and neuropharmacological neuroadaptations within specific neurocircuits that mediate the transition from occasional, controlled drug use and the loss of behavioral control over drug seeking and drug taking that defines chronic addiction. The thesis of this review is that a key element of the addiction process is the underactivation of natural motivational systems such that the reward system becomes compromised and that an antireward system becomes recruited to provide the powerful motivation for drug seeking associated with compulsive use (see Antireward sidebar).

A Motivational Perspective of Addiction

Motivation is a state that varies with arousal; it guides behavior in relationship to changes in the environment and shares key common characteristics with our concepts of addiction. The environment can be external (incentives) or internal (central motive states or drives), and such motivation or motivational states are not constant and vary over time. The concept of motivation was linked inextricably with hedonic, affective, or emotional states in addiction in the context of temporal dynamics by Solomon's opponent-process theory of motivation. Solomon & Corbit (1974) postulated that hedonic, affective, or emotional states, once initiated, are automatically modulated by the central nervous system with mechanisms that reduce the intensity of hedonic feelings. Solomon argued that there is affective or hedonic habituation (or tolerance) and affective or hedonic withdrawal (abstinence). He defined two processes: the a-process and the b-process. The a-process could consist of either positive or negative hedonic responses. It occurs shortly after presentation of a stimulus, correlates closely with the stimulus intensity, quality, and duration of the reinforcer, and shows tolerance. In contrast, the b-process appears after the a-process has terminated. It is sluggish in onset, slow to build up to an asymptote, slow to decay, and gets larger with repeated exposure. Thus, the affective dynamics of opponent process theory generate new motives and new opportunities for reinforcing and energizing behavior (Solomon 1980).

From a drug-taking perspective of brain motivational systems, it was hypothesized that the initial acute effect of a drug was opposed or counteracted by homeostatic changes in brain systems. Certain systems in the brain were hypothesized to suppress or reduce all departures from hedonic neutrality (Solomon & Corbit 1974). This affect control system was conceptualized as a single negative feedback, or opponent, loop that opposes the stimulus-aroused affective state (Poulos & Cappell

ANTIREWARD

The concept of an antireward system was developed to explain one component of time-dependent neuroadaptations in response to excessive utilization of the brain reward system. The brain reward system is defined as activation of circuits involved in positive reinforcement with an overlay of positive hedonic valence. The neuroadaptation simply could involve state-shifts on a single axis of the reward system (within-system change; dopamine function decreases). However, there is compelling evidence that brain stress/emotional systems are recruited as a result of excessive activation of the reward system and provide an additional source of negative hedonic valence that are defined here as the antireward system (between-system change; corticotropin-releasing factor function increases). The combination of both a deficit in the reward system (negative hedonic valence) and recruitment of the brain stress systems (negative hedonic valence) provides a powerful motivational state mediated in part by the antireward system (Koob & Le Moal 2005).

1991, Siegel 1975, Solomon & Corbit 1974). Affective states—pleasant or aversive—were hypothesized to be automatically opposed by centrally mediated mechanisms that reduce the intensity of these affective states; in this opponent-process theory, tolerance and dependence are inextricably linked (Solomon & Corbit 1974). In the context of drug dependence, Solomon argued that the first few self-administrations of an opiate drug produce a pattern of motivational changes similar to that of an a-process or euphoria, which is followed by a decline in intensity. Then, after the drug wears off, an opposing, aversive negative emotional state emerges, which is the b-process.

More recently, opponent-process theory has been expanded into the domains of the neurocircuitry and neurobiology of drug addiction from a physiological perspective. An allostatic model of the brain motivational systems has been proposed to explain the persistent changes in motivation that are associated with vulnerability to relapse in addiction, and this model may generalize to other psychopathology associated with dysregulated

Antireward: a concept based on the hypothesis that there are brain systems in place to limit reward that are triggered by excessive activity in the reward system

Opponent process: affective or hedonic habituation (tolerance) and affective or hedonic withdrawal (abstinence)

motivational systems (Koob & Le Moal 2001). In this framework, addiction is conceptualized as a cycle of spiraling dysregulation of brain reward/antireward mechanisms that progressively increases, resulting in the compulsive use of drugs. Counteradaptive processes such as opponent-process that are part of the normal homeostatic limitation of reward function fail to return within the normal homeostatic range and are hypothesized to form an allostatic state. These counteradaptive processes are hypothesized to be mediated by two processes: within-system neuroadaptations and between-system neuroadaptations (Koob & Bloom 1988). A within-system neuroadaptation is a molecular or cellular change within a given reward circuit to accommodate overactivity of hedonic processing associated with addiction, resulting in a decrease in reward function. A between-system neuroadaptation is a circuitry change where a different circuit (brain stress circuit) is activated by excessive engagement of the reward circuit and has opposing actions, again limiting reward function (see Antireward sidebar). The extension of such an allostatic state is further hypothesized to be reflected in a chronic deviation of reward set point that is fueled both by dysregulation of reward circuits per se and by recruitment of brain and hormonal stress responses. The purpose of this review is to explore what neuroadaptational changes occur in the brain emotional systems to account for the allostatic changes in motivation that produce the compulsivity of addiction.

DRUG USE, ABUSE, AND DEPENDENCE: DYNAMICS OF MOTIVATION

Drug Use: Drug Dependence

From a psychiatric-motivational perspective, drug addiction has aspects of both impulse control disorders and compulsive disorders. Impulse control disorders are characterized by an increasing sense of tension or arousal before committing an impulsive act; plea-sure, gratification, or relief at the time of committing the act; and there may or may not be regret, self-reproach, or guilt following the act (Am. Psychiatric Assoc. 1994). A classic impulse control disorder is kleptomania, where there is an increase in tension before stealing an object or objects that are not needed and relief after the act but little or no regret or self-reproach. In contrast, compulsive disorders are characterized by anxiety and stress before committing a compulsive repetitive behavior and relief from the stress by performing the compulsive behavior. A classic compulsive disorder is obsessive-compulsive disorder, where obsessions of contamination or harm drive anxiety, and performing repetitive compulsive acts reduces the anxiety. As an individual moves from an impulsive disorder to a compulsive disorder, there is a shift from positive reinforcement driving the motivated behavior to negative reinforcement driving the motivated behavior (Koob 2004). Drug addiction has been conceptualized as a disorder that progresses from impulsivity to impulsivity/compulsivity in a collapsed cycle of addiction composed of three stages: preoccupation/anticipation, binge/intoxication, and withdrawal/negative affect (**Figure 1**, see color insert). Different theoretical perspectives ranging from experimental psychology, social psychology, and neurobiology can be superimposed on these three stages, which are conceptualized as feeding into each other, becoming more intense, and ultimately leading to the pathological state known as addiction (Koob & Le Moal 1997).

Patterns of Drug Dependence

Different drugs produce different patterns of addiction with emphasis on different components of the addiction cycle. Opioids are a classic drug of addiction, in which an evolving pattern of use includes intravenous or smoked drug taking, an intense intoxication with opioids, the development of tolerance, and escalation in intake, as well as profound dysphoria, physical discomfort, and somatic withdrawal signs during abstinence. Intense preoccupation with obtaining opioids (craving) develops and often precedes the somatic signs of withdrawal. This preoccupation is linked not only to stimuli associated with obtaining the drug but also to stimuli associated with withdrawal and internal and external states of stress. A pattern develops wherein the drug must be obtained to avoid the severe dysphoria and discomfort of abstinence. Alcoholism follows a similar pattern, but the intoxication is less intense and the pattern of drug taking often is characterized by binges of alcohol intake that can be daily episodes or prolonged days of heavy drinking. A binge is now defined as consumption of five standard drinks for males and four standard drinks for females in a two-hour period, or obtaining a blood alcohol level of 0.08 gram percent (Natl. Inst. Alcohol Abuse Alcohol. 2004). Alcoholism is characterized by a severe emotional and somatic withdrawal syndrome and intense craving for the drug that is often driven by negative emotional states but also by positive emotional states. Many alcoholics continue with such a binge/withdrawal pattern for extended periods, but for others the pattern evolves into an opioid-like addiction in which they must have alcohol available at all times to avoid the consequences of abstinence. Nicotine addiction contrasts with the above patterns in that nicotine is associated with even less of a binge/intoxication stage. Cigarette smokers who meet the criteria for substance dependence are likely to smoke throughout the waking hours and to experience negative emotional states with dysphoria, irritability, and intense craving during abstinence. The binge/intoxication stage forms a minor component of nicotine dependence, with the pattern of intake one of highly titrated intake of the drug except during periods of sleep. Psychostimulants such as cocaine and amphetamines show a pattern with a greater emphasis on the binge/intoxication stage. The duration of such binges can be hours or days; binges are often followed by a crash that is characterized by extreme dysphoria and inactivity. Intense craving follows later and is driven by both environmental cues signifying availability of the drug and by internal states often linked to negative emotional states and stress. Marijuana dependence follows a pattern similar to that of opioids and tobacco in that there is a significant intoxication stage, but as chronic use continues, subjects begin to show a pattern of chronic intoxication during waking hours. Withdrawal is characterized by dysphoria, irritability, and sleep disturbances, and although marijuana craving has been less studied to date (Heishman et al. 2001), it is most likely linked both to environmental and internal states similar to those of other drugs of abuse.

Craving: memory of the rewarding aspects of drug use superimposed on a negative emotional state

NEUROBIOLOGICAL SUBSTRATES OF DRUG USE AND DEPENDENCE

Animal Models of Addiction

Much of the recent progress in understanding the neurobiology of addiction has derived from the study of animal models of addiction to specific drugs such as stimulants, opioids, alcohol, nicotine, and Δ^9-tetrahydrocannabinol. Although no animal model of addiction fully emulates the human condition, animal models do permit investigation of specific elements of the process of drug addiction. Such elements can be defined by models of different stages of the addiction cycle, models of psychological constructs such as positive and negative reinforcement, and models of actual symptoms of addiction.

Animal models for the binge/intoxication stage of the addiction cycle can be conceptualized as measuring acute drug reward; reward can be defined as a positive reinforcer with some additional emotional value such as pleasure. Animal models of reward are extensive and well validated. Animals and humans will readily self-administer drugs in the nondependent state. Drugs of abuse have powerful reinforcing properties in that animals will perform many different tasks and procedures to obtain the drugs, even in the nondependent state. Drugs that are self-administered by animals correspond well with those that have high abuse potential in humans, and intravenous drug self-administration is considered an animal model that is predictive of abuse potential (Collins et al. 1984). Using this procedure, the dose, cost of responding, and second-order schedules [working for a stimulus (cue) that then allows the reinforcer to be delivered] all can be manipulated to determine the value of the reward. Oral self-administration of alcohol has also been used as a reward in similar studies in which animals will work to obtain meaningful blood alcohol levels (Samson 1986). Two other animal models have been used extensively to measure indirectly drug reward: conditioned place preference and brain reward thresholds. Animals typically exhibit a conditioned place preference for an environment associated with drugs that are self-administered by humans, and they avoid environments that induce aversive states (conditioned place aversion) (Carboni & Vacca 2003). Lowering of brain-stimulation reward thresholds are also reliable measures of drug reward. Drugs of abuse decrease thresholds for brain stimulation reward, and there is good correspondence between the ability of drugs to decrease brain reward thresholds and their abuse potential (Kornetsky & Bain 1990).

Animal models of the negative reinforcing effects of dependence include the same models used for the rewarding effects of drugs of abuse (described above). However, changes in valence of the reward occur where spontaneous withdrawal from all drugs of abuse increases, instead of lowers, brain reward thresholds (Koob 2004). Animals also show a conditioned place aversion, instead of preference, to precipitated withdrawal from chronic administration of a drug.

More recently, animal models for the transition to addiction have been demonstrated that incorporate animal models of the rewarding effects of drugs as well as the induction of dependence. Rodents will increase the intravenous self-administration of drugs with extended access to the drugs and during withdrawal from the dependent state, as measured both by increased amount of drug administration and working harder to obtain the drug. Such increased self-administration in dependent animals has now been observed with cocaine, methamphetamine, nicotine, heroin, and alcohol (Ahmed & Koob 1998, Ahmed et al. 2000, Kitamura et al. 2006, O'Dell & Koob 2007, Roberts et al. 2000). Equally compelling are studies that show drug taking in the presence of aversive consequences in animals given extended access to the drug. Rats with extended access to cocaine did not suppress drug seeking in the presence of an aversive conditioned stimulus or punishment, which has face validity for the DSM-IV criteria of "continued substance use despite knowledge of having a persistent physical or psychological problem" (Deroche-Gamonet et al. 2004, Vanderschuren & Everitt 2004).

Animal models of craving (preoccupation/anticipation stage) involve the conditioned rewarding effects of drugs of abuse and measures of the conditioned aversive effects of dependence, as well as resistance to extinction and second-order schedules (Shippenberg & Koob 2002). Many of the measures of craving assess the motivational properties of the drugs themselves or of a cue paired with the drugs after extinction. Drug-induced reinstatement involves first extinction and then presentation of a priming injection of a drug. Latency to reinitiate responding, or the amount of responding on the previously extinguished lever, is hypothesized to reflect the motivation for drug-seeking behavior. Similarly, drug-paired or drug-associated stimuli can reinitiate drug-seeking behavior (cue-induced reinstatement). Stress-induced reinstatement occurs when acute stressors can also reinitiate drug-seeking behavior that previously has been extinguished in animals. Protracted abstinence has been linked to the increased brain reward thresholds, and increases in anxiety-like behavior have been shown to persist after acute withdrawal in animals with a history of dependence. Finally, conditioned opioid withdrawal—where previously neutral stimuli are paired with precipitated opioid withdrawal—has been shown not only to produce place aversions but also to have motivational properties in increasing self-administration of opioids (Kenny et al. 2006).

Neural Basis of Drug Reward— Positive Reinforcing Effects

A key element of drug addiction is neuroadaptation within the brain reward system during the development of addiction, and one must understand the neurobiological bases for acute drug reward to understand how the reward systems change with the development of addiction. A principal focus of research on the neurobiology of the positive reinforcing effects of drugs with dependence potential has been on the activation of the circuitry related to the origins and terminals of the mesocorticolimbic dopamine system. Compelling evidence exists for a critical role of this system in drug reward associated with psychostimulant drugs, and there is evidence that all major drugs of abuse activate this system as measured either by increased extracellular levels of dopamine in the terminal areas [such as medial (shell) point of the nucleus accumbens] or by activation of the firing of neurons in the ventral tegmental area (Di Chiara 2002, Koob 1992). However, although selective neurotoxin-induced lesions of the mesolimbic dopamine system do block cocaine, amphetamine, and nicotine self-administration, rats continue to self-administer heroin and alcohol in the absence of the mesocorticolimbic dopamine system (Pettit et al. 1984, Rassnick et al. 1993b), and place-preference studies show robust place preferences to morphine and nicotine in the presence of major dopamine receptor blockade (Bechara & van der Kooy 1992, Laviolette & van der Kooy 2003). Indeed, an impor-

tant role for opioid peptides in drug reward, independent of a direct action on dopamine neurons, has been proposed (Koob 1992). Together, these results suggest that multiple parallel pathways mediate drug reward.

Specific components of the basal forebrain associated with the amygdala also have been identified with drug reward, particularly alcohol (Koob 2003a). One hypothetical construct, the extended amygdala, includes not only the central nucleus of the amygdala (CeA), but also the bed nucleus of the stria terminalis (BNST) and a transition zone in the medial subregion of the nucleus accumbens (shell of the nucleus accumbens), and these regions share certain cytoarchitectural and circuitry similarities (Heimer & Alheid 1991). As the neural circuits for the reinforcing effects of drugs with dependence potential have evolved, the role of neurotransmitters/neuromodulators also has evolved, and those that have been identified to have a role in the acute reinforcing effects of drugs of abuse in these basal forebrain areas include mesolimbic dopamine, opioid peptide, γ-aminobutyric acid (GABA), glutamate, endocannabinoids, and serotonin (**Table 1**).

Neural Basis of Drug Dependence: Within-System Neuroadaptational Processes

The neural substrates and neuropharmacological mechanisms for the negative motivational effects of drug withdrawal may involve disruption of the same neurochemical systems and neurocircuits implicated in the positive reinforcing effects of drugs of abuse, termed a within-system neuroadaptation (**Table 2**). All drugs of abuse produce elevations in brain reward thresholds during acute withdrawal (Koob & Le Moal 2005), and in animal models of the transition to addiction, increases in brain reward threshold (decreased reward) occur that temporally precede and highly correlate with the increase in drug intake with extended access (Ahmed et al. 2002, Kenny et al. 2006).

Extended amygdala: regions of the basal forebrain that share certain cytoarchitectural and circuitry similarities. The regions are the central nucleus of the amygdala, the bed nucleus of the stria terminalis, and a transition zone in the medial subregion of the nucleus accumbens (shell of the nucleus accumbens)

CeA: central nucleus of the amygdala

BNST: bed nucleus of the stria terminalis

GABA: γ-aminobutyric acid

Table 1 Neurobiological substrates for the acute reinforcing effects of drugs of abuse

Drug of abuse	Neurotransmitter	Site
Cocaine and amphetamines	Dopamine	Nucleus accumbens
	γ-aminobutyric acid	Amygdala
Opiates	Opioid peptides	Nucleus accumbens
	Dopamine	Ventral tegmental area
	Endocannabinoids	
Nicotine	Nicotinic acetylcholine	Nucleus accumbens
	Dopamine	Ventral tegmental area
	γ-aminobutyric acid	Amygdala
	Opioid peptides	
Δ^9-Tetrahydrocanna-binol	Endocannabinoids	Nucleus accumbens
	Opioid peptides	Ventral tegmental area
	Dopamine	
Alcohol	Dopamine	Nucleus accumbens
	Opioid peptides	Ventral tegmental area
	γ-aminobutyric acid	Amygdala
	Endocannabinoids	

Table 2 Neurotransmitters implicated in the motivational effects of withdrawal from drugs of abuse

Neurotransmitter	Functional effect
↓ Dopamine	"Dysphoria"
↓ Serotonin	"Dysphoria"
↓ γ-Aminobutyric acid	Anxiety, panic attacks
↓ Neuropeptide Y	Antistress
↑ Dynorphin	"Dysphoria"
↑ Corticotropin-releasing factor	Stress
↑ Norepinephrine	Stress

HPA: hypothalamic-pituitary-adrenal axis

CRF: corticotropin-releasing factor

ACTH: adrenocorticotropic hormone

During such acute withdrawal, there is decreased activity of the mesocorticolimbic dopamine system as well as decreased activity in opioid peptide, GABA, and glutamate in the nucleus accumbens or the amygdala. Repeated administration of psychostimulants produces an initial facilitation of dopamine and glutamate neurotransmission in the nucleus accumbens (Ungless et al. 2001, Vorel et al. 2002). However, chronic administration leads to decreases in dopaminergic and glutamatergic neurotransmission in the nucleus accumbens during acute withdrawal (Kalivas et al. 2003, Weiss et al. 1992), opposite responses of opioid receptor transduction

mechanisms in the nucleus accumbens during opioid withdrawal (Shaw-Lutchman et al. 2002), changes in GABA-ergic neurotransmission during alcohol withdrawal (Grobin et al. 1998, Roberto et al. 2004), and differential regional changes in nicotinic acetylcholine receptor function during nicotine withdrawal.

Human imaging studies of addicts during withdrawal or protracted abstinence give results that are consistent with animal studies. There are decreases in dopamine D_2 receptors (hypothesized to reflect hypodopaminergic functioning) and hypoactivity of the orbitofrontal-infralimbic cortex system (Volkow et al. 2003). Decreases in reward neurotransmitter function have been hypothesized to contribute significantly to the negative motivational state associated with acute drug abstinence and may trigger long-term biochemical changes that contribute to the clinical syndrome of protracted abstinence and vulnerability to relapse.

Neural Basis of Drug Dependence: Between-System Neuroadaptational Processes

Different neurochemical systems involved in stress modulation also may be engaged within the neurocircuitry of the brain stress systems in an attempt to overcome the chronic presence of the perturbing drug and to restore normal function despite the presence of drug, termed a between-system neuroadaptation. The hypothalamic-pituitary-adrenal (HPA) axis and the brain stress system, both mediated by corticotropin-releasing factor (CRF), are dysregulated by chronic administration of drugs of abuse, with a common response of elevated adrenocorticotropic hormone (ACTH) and corticosterone and extended amygdala CRF during acute withdrawal from all major drugs of abuse (Koob & Le Moal 2005, Kreek & Koob 1998). Acute withdrawal from drugs of abuse also may increase the release of norepinephrine in the bed nucleus of the stria terminalis and decrease functional levels of neuropeptide Y (NPY) in the extended amygdala (Olive et al. 2002, Roy & Pandey 2002).

For example, with alcohol, CRF may have a key role in mediating the neuroendocrine, autonomic, and behavioral responses to stress and anxiety that drive excessive drinking in dependence (Koob & Heinrichs 1999). Regions of the extended amygdala (including the CeA) contain high amounts CRF terminals, cell bodies, and receptors and comprise part of the "extrahypothalamic" CRF-stress system. (Merchenthaler et al. 1982); numerous studies have demonstrated the involvement of the extended amygdala CRF system in mediating the behavioral responses associated with fear and anxiety (Koob & Heinrichs 1999). During ethanol withdrawal, extrahypothalamic CRF systems become hyperactive, with an increase in extracellular CRF within the CeA and BNST of dependent rats (Funk et al. 2006, Merlo-Pich et al. 1995, Olive et al. 2002, Zorrilla & Koob 2004), and this dysregulation of brain CRF systems is hypothesized to underlie both the enhanced anxiety-like behaviors and the enhanced ethanol self-administration associated with ethanol withdrawal. Supporting this hypothesis, the subtype nonselective CRF-receptor antagonists α-helical CRF_{9-41} and D-Phe CRF_{12-41} (intracerebroventricular administration) reduce both ethanol withdrawal-induced anxiety-like behavior and ethanol self-administration in dependent animals (Baldwin et al. 1991, Valdez et al. 2002). When administered directly into the CeA, CRF receptor antagonists also attenuate anxiety-like behavior (Rassnick et al. 1993a) as well as ethanol self-administration in ethanol-dependent rats (Funk et al. 2006). These data suggest an important role of CRF, primarily within the CeA, in mediating the increased self-administration associated with dependence. Similar results have been observed with the increased intravenous self-administration associated with extended access

to heroin (Greenwell et al. 2007), cocaine (Specio et al. 2007), and nicotine (George et al. 2007).

These results suggest not only a change in the function of neurotransmitters associated with the acute reinforcing effects of drugs of abuse during the development of dependence, such as decreases in dopamine, opioid peptides, serotonin, and GABA function, but also recruitment of the CRF system (**Figure 2**, see color insert). Additional between-system neuroadaptations associated with motivational withdrawal include activation of the dynorphin-κ opioid system, activation of the norepinephrine brain stress system, and dysregulation of the NPY brain antistress system (Koob & Le Moal 2005) (**Table 2**). Additionally, activation of the brain stress systems may contribute not only to the negative motivational state associated with acute abstinence, but also to the vulnerability to stressors observed during protracted abstinence in humans.

The neuroanatomical entity termed the extended amygdala thus may represent a neuroanatomical substrate for the negative effects on reward function produced by stress that help drive compulsive drug administration. As stated above, the extended amygdala is composed of the BNST, the CeA, and a transition zone in the medial subregion of the nucleus accumbens (shell of the nucleus accumbens). The extended amygdala receives numerous afferents from limbic structures such as the basolateral amygdala and hippocampus and sends efferents to the medial part of the ventral pallidum and to the lateral hypothalamus, thus further defining the specific brain areas that interface classical limbic (emotional) structures with the extrapyramidal motor system (Alheid et al. 1995) (**Figure 3**, see color insert).

However, perhaps even more compelling support of the integration of the extended amygdala and emotional states comes from the extensive data from the classical studies of Le Doux, which show a convergence of the

NPY: neuropeptide Y

expression of the conditioned fear response in the CeA (Phelps & Le Doux 2005) and data showing that the central nucleus of the amygdala is a key component of neurocircuitry involved in emotional pain processing (Price 2002) (**Figure 3**). Studies on the neurocircuitry of fear conditioning show that auditory stimuli from the auditory cortex and pain from the somatosensory cortex converge on the lateral amygdala, which then projects to the CeA to elicit the various autonomic and behavioral responses to conditioned fear (Phelps & Le Doux 2005). The spino (trigemino)-ponto-amygdaloid pathway that projects from the dorsal horn to the mesencephalic parabrachial area to the CeA has been hypothesized to be involved in emotional pain processing (Bester et al. 1995). Together, these neurochemical studies (from addiction neurobiology) and neuroanatomical studies (from behavioral neuroscience) point to a rich substrate for the integration of emotional stimuli related to the "dark side of addiction," defined as the development of the aversive emotional state that drives the negative reinforcement of addiction.

The dark side of addiction (Koob & Le Moal 2005) is hypothesized to involve a long-term, persistent plasticity in the activity of neural circuits mediating motivational systems that derives from recruitment of antireward systems that drive aversive states. The withdrawal/negative affect stage defined above consists of key motivational elements such as chronic irritability, emotional pain, malaise, dysphoria, alexithymia, and loss of motivation for natural rewards, and is characterized in animals by increases in reward thresholds during withdrawal from all major drugs of abuse. Antireward is a concept developed based on the hypothesis that there are brain systems in place to limit reward (Koob & Le Moal 1997). As dependence and withdrawal develop, brain antireward systems such as CRF, norepinephrine, and dynorphin are recruited (**Figures 2** and **3**), producing aversive or stress-like states (Aston-Jones et al. 1999, Koob 2003a, Nestler 2001). At the same time, within the motivational circuits of the ventral striatum-extended amygdala, there are decreases in reward function. The combination of decreases in reward neurotransmitter function and recruitment of antireward systems provides a powerful source of negative reinforcement that contributes to compulsive drug-seeking behavior and addiction.

Neural Bases of Protracted Abstinence and Relapse

The dark side may also contribute to the critical problem in drug addiction of chronic relapse, wherein addicts return to compulsive drug taking long after acute withdrawal. Neurotransmitter/neuromodulator systems implicated in stress-induced relapse include CRF, glucocorticoids, and norepinephrine in stress-induced relapse, suggesting reactivation of antireward systems during relapse (Piazza & Le Moal 1996, See et al. 2003, Shaham et al. 2000). Thus, the dysregulations that comprise the dark side of drug addiction persist during protracted abstinence to set the tone for vulnerability to craving by activation of the drug-, cue-, and stress-induced reinstatement neurocircuits now driven by a reorganized and hypofunctioning prefrontal system (Le Moal 1995).

The preoccupation/anticipation stage of the addiction cycle has long been hypothesized to be a key element of relapse in humans and defines addiction as a chronic relapsing disorder. Although often linked to the construct of craving, craving per se has been difficult to measure in human clinical studies (Tiffany et al. 2000) and often does not correlate with relapse. Craving can be defined as memory of the rewarding effects of a drug superimposed upon a negative emotional state. Nevertheless, the stage of the addiction cycle in which the individual reinstates drug-seeking behavior after abstinence remains a challenging focus for identifying neurobiological mechanisms and developing medications for treatment.

Table 3 Craving

Craving: a hypothetical construct that can be defined as the memory of the rewarding effects of a drug, superimposed upon a
  negative motivational state (Markou et al. 1998).
Craving Type 1: craving induced by drugs or stimuli, such as environmental cues, that have been paired with drug
  self-administration.
Animal models of Craving Type 1: drug or cue-induced reinstatement where administration of a drug previously
  self-administered or a cue previously paired with access to drug reinstates responding for a lever that has been extinguished.
Craving Type 2: a state change characterized by anxiety and dysphoria or a residual negative emotional state that combines with
  Craving Type 1 situations to produce relapse to drug seeking.
Animal models of Craving Type 2: stress-induced reinstatement of drug seeking after extinction, or increased drug taking in
  animals after a prolonged deprivation.

Animal models of craving can be divided into two domains: drug seeking induced by stimuli paired with drug taking, and drug seeking induced by an acute stressor or a state of stress (**Table 3**). Craving Type 1 animal models involve the use of drug-primed reinstatement and cue-induced reinstatement in animals that have acquired drug self-administration and then had been subjected to extinction of responding for the drug. Craving Type 2 animal models involve stress-induced reinstatement in animals that have acquired drug self-administration and then have been subjected to extinction of responding for the drug (Shippenberg & Koob 2002) (see sidebar Memory of Addiction: An Allostatic View).

Most evidence from animal studies suggests that drug-induced reinstatement is by the medial prefrontal cortex/nucleus accumbens/glutamatergic circuit modulated by dopamine in the frontal cortex (McFarland & Kalivas 2001). In contrast, neuropharmacological and neurobiological studies using animal models for cue-induced reinstatement involve a glutamatergic projection from the basolateral amygdala to the nucleus accumbens as a critical substrate with a possible feed-forward mechanism through the prefrontal cortex system involved in drug-induced reinstatement and dopamine modulation in the basolateral amygdala (Everitt & Wolf 2002, Weiss et al. 2001). In contrast, stress-induced reinstatement of drug-related responding in animal models appears to depend on the activation of both CRF and norepinephrine in elements of the ex-

MEMORY OF ADDICTION: AN ALLOSTATIC VIEW

Craving has been defined as the memory of the pleasant rewarding effects of drugs of abuse superimposed on a negative emotional state (Koob 2000). In the context of the present treatise, the memory linked to drug cues (Craving Type 1) and mediated by the reward system becomes even more powerful when superimposed on a residual negative emotional state hypothesized to exist in protracted abstinence. The Craving Type 2 state also can be potentiated by associations formed from the linking of previously neutral stimuli with the motivational effects of drug withdrawal (Kenny et al. 2006). Interestingly, these Craving Type 2 associations appear to be processed via the same structures as those linked to Craving Type 1 associations (i.e., basolateral amygdala) (Schulteis et al. 2002). Thus, memory mechanisms may contribute to the allostatic state by associative mechanisms linked to both the reward and antireward systems.

tended amygdala (CeA and BNST) (Shaham et al. 2003, Shalev et al. 2002). Protracted abstinence, largely described in alcohol-dependence models, appears to involve overactive glutamatergic and CRF systems (De Witte et al. 2005, Valdez et al. 2002).

VULNERABILITY TO ADDICTION

Individual Differences—Drug Seeking

Large individual differences and diverse sources of vulnerability account for the passage from controlled social or occasional use to dependence and the propensity to enter the addiction cycle. The number of individuals meeting the criteria for drug addiction for a given drug as a function of ever having used the drug varies significantly between drugs, ranging from approximately 9% for marijuana to 31% for tobacco (Anthony et al. 1994). These differences may relate to the rate of access of the drug to the brain, which may be as basic as drug pharmacology and pharmacokinetics or as complicated as the social environmental access. In contrast, individual variables such as genetic background and environmental history, and their addition, correlation, or interaction, may also play key roles and may interconnect with availability (Rutter et al. 2006) (**Figure 4**).

Other factors that can contribute to individual vulnerability for drug use initiation or relapse are (*a*) comorbidity with psychopathological conditions, (*b*) temperamental and personality traits and genetic factors, developmental factors, and socioeconomic status, and (*c*) stress and life events. Each of these factors presumably interacts with the neurobiological processes involved in the sensitivity to drugs and in self-regulation and executive capacities. Initiation of use and abuse is more associated with vulnerability factors, whereas the movement to addiction is more associated with neurobiological factors (Glantz & Pickens 1992).

Individual Differences—Sensitivity to Antireward Neuroadaptations

Preadolescent and adolescent exposure to alcohol, tobacco, or drugs of abuse significantly increases the propensity for dependence in adulthood. Adolescents first intoxicated with alcohol at age 16 or younger are two to three times more likely to develop dependence (Hingson et al. 2003). Similar results have been reported for tobacco, where there is a relation between the age of initiation and the intensity of smoking later in life. It has been argued that regular smoking during adolescence raises the risk for adult smoking by a factor of 16 compared to nonsmoking during young ages (Chassin et al. 1990). Thus, early onset of drug use is a predictor of subsequent drug problems, and it is a linear relationship with age from 13–21 (Grant & Dawson 1998).

In humans, rates of drug and alcohol abuse and dependence are higher in males than in females (SAMHSA 2004). The relatively lower rate in females has long reflected the fact that women experience more social and educational constraints, which may serve as protective factors; however, evidence from recent surveys indicates that identical percentages of girls and boys had used alcohol, tobacco, and illicit drugs for the period of observation. Indeed, recent clinical evidence suggests that in comparison with males, females meet criteria for drug dependence more quickly and the course to addiction is faster. In addition, females differ in their vulnerability to relapse to drug use during abstinence periods and are more likely to relapse owing to stress and depression (see review in Lynch 2006).

Clear evidence also shows that adverse early experiences contribute to adolescent and adult psychopathology. Early experiences, prenatal or postnatal stress, and deleterious life events have pervasive and profound effects on adaptive abilities, and these changes reflect permanently altered gene expression—epigenetic changes—and their downstream effects on the HPA axis (Meaney & Szyf 2005). In rats, prenatally stressed offspring will present as adults with increased vulnerability to drug abuse, and the increased sensitivity correlates with a dysregulated HPA axis (Deminière et al. 1992). Preadolescence and adolescence are particularly sensitive periods that are affected by social and familial environments as well as social status, but individual responses to experiences during these periods also reflect a genetic contribution (Gunnar & Quevedo 2006) and the development of coping strategies (Skinner & Zimmer-Gembeck 2006). The ways in which this early exposure changes the brain to make it more sensitive to reward and stress dysregulation is largely unknown at this time.

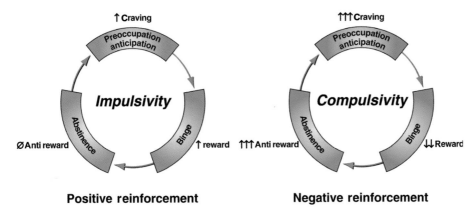

Positive reinforcement   **Negative reinforcement**

Figure 1

Diagram describing the addiction cycle that is conceptualized as having three major components: pre-occupation/anticipation ("craving"), binge/intoxication, and withdrawal/negative affect. Note that as the individual moves from the impulsivity stage to the compulsivity stage, there is a shift from positive reinforcement associated with the binge/intoxication component to negative reinforcement associated with the withdrawal/negative affect component. Craving is hypothesized to increase in the compulsivity stage because of an increase in the need state for the drug that is driven not only by loss of the positive reinforcing effects of the drugs (tolerance), but also by generation of an antireward state that supports negative reinforcement.

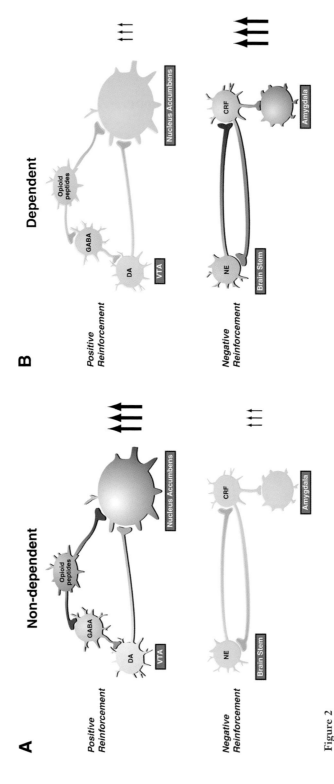

Figure 2

Neurocircuitry associated with the acute positive reinforcing effects of drugs of abuse and the negative reinforcement of dependence and how it changes in the transition from non-dependent drug taking to dependent drug taking. Key elements of the reward circuit are dopamine and opioid peptide neurons that intersect at both the ventral tegmental area and the nucleus accumbens and are activated during initial use and the early binge/intoxication stage. Key elements of the stress circuit are CRF and noradrenergic neurons that converge on GABA interneurons in the central nucleus of the amygdala that are activated during the development of dependence. CRF, corticotropin-releasing factor; DA, dopamine; GABA, gamma-aminobutyric acid; NE, norepinephrine; VTA, ventral tegmental area. Figure modified with permission from Nestler (2005).

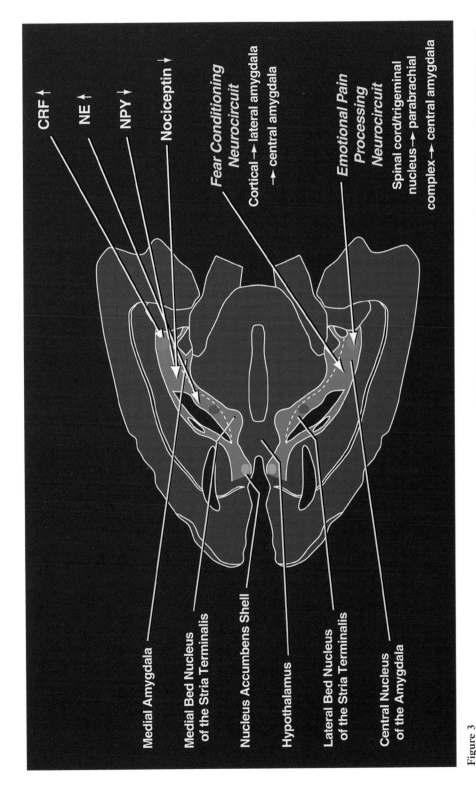

CRF ↑
NE ↑
NPY ↓
Nociceptin ↓

Fear Conditioning Neurocircuit
Cortical → lateral amygdala
→ central amygdala

Emotional Pain Processing Neurocircuit
Spinal cord/trigeminal nucleus → parabrachial complex → central amygdala

Medial Amygdala

Medial Bed Nucleus of the Stria Terminalis

Nucleus Accumbens Shell

Hypothalamus

Lateral Bed Nucleus of the Stria Terminalis

Central Nucleus of the Amygdala

Figure 3

Construct of the extended amygdala illustrated in a horizontal plane of a rodent brain. Key elements include the central nucleus of the amygdala, the bed nucleus of the stria terminalis, and a transition zone in the medial (shell) part of the nucleus accumbens. The extended amygdala receives significant projections from the prefrontal cortex and insular cortex and sends efferent projections to the lateral hypothalamus and ventral tegmental area. Neuropharmacological components that contribute to the constructs of the "dark side" include activation of CRF in the central nucleus of the amygdala, activation of norepinephrine in the bed nucleus of the stria terminalis, and decreases in function of neuropeptide Y and nociceptin in the central nucleus of the amygdala. The central nucleus of the amygdala is also a key structure integrating neurocircuitry of the expression fear and conditioned fear as well as emotional pain responses. CRF, corticotropin-releasing factor; NE, norepinephrine; NPY, neuropeptide Y. Brain schematic modified with permission from Heimer & Alheid (1991).

Vulnerability Targets in Addiction

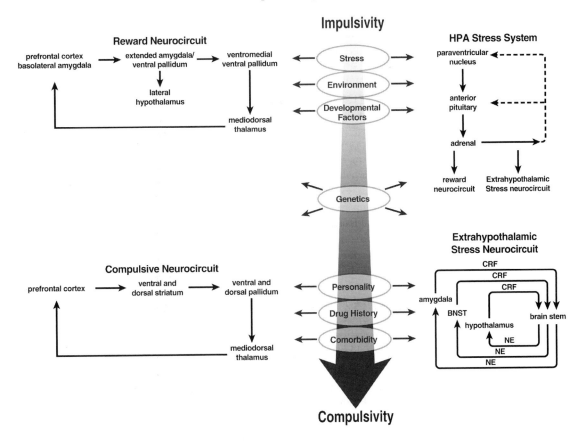

Figure 4

Brain circuits hypothesized to be recruited at different stages of the addiction cycle as addiction moves from positive reinforcement to negative reinforcement. The top left diagram illustrates an increase in the inactivity of a brain reward system circuit with a focus on the extended amygdala and an increase in the drug- and cue-induced reinstatement circuit with a focus on the prefrontal cortex and basolateral amygdala, which both drive positive reinforcement and impulsivity. The bottom left diagram illustrates a decrease in the brain reward circuit and an increase in the behavioral output or compulsivity circuit, both involved in driving negative reinforcement and compulsivity. The top right diagram refers to the hypothalamic-pituitary-adrenal axis, which (*a*) feeds back to regulate itself, (*b*) activates the brain reward neurocircuit, and (*c*) facilitates the extrahypothalamic stress neurocircuit. The bottom right diagram refers to the brain stress circuits in feed-forward loops. Superimposed on the transition from impulsivity to compulsivity are sources of vulnerability. Stress, development, and the environment are hypothesized to have an early influence in the process. Comorbidity, personality, and drug history are hypothesized to have a later influence. Genetics interacts at all levels with these factors both directly and through epigenetic mechanisms. BNST, bed nucleus of the stria terminalis; CRF, corticotropin-releasing factor; HPA, hypothalamic-pituitary-adrenal axis; NE, norepinephrine. Figure adapted from Koob & LeMoal (2004, 2006).

Psychopathological comorbidities are prominent factors in vulnerability for addiction and overlap significantly with the dark side perspective (**Figure 4**). A psychodynamic self-medication hypothesis deeply rooted in clinical research focuses on underlying developmental difficulties, emotional disturbances, structural factors, building of the self, and personality organization (Khantzian 1985, 1990). Two critical elements, disordered emotions and disordered self-care, and two contributory elements, disordered self-esteem and disordered relationships, are hypothesized to be the basis for drug self-medication. Individuals are hypothesized to take drugs as a means to cope with painful and threatening emotions, in an attempt to medicate dysregulated affective states, unbearable painful affect, or an inability to express personal feelings and/or use appropriate language to express feelings. The choice of drug is hypothesized to be appropriate to the emotional state being self-medicated (Khantzian 1997). An extension of the Khantzian hypothesis is that excessive drug taking can cause the dysregulated emotional state that leads to each class of drugs being self-administered as an antidote to dysphoric states and act temporarily as a replacement for a defect in the psychological structure of these individuals caused by the drug (Koob 2003b).

From the perspective of comorbid psychiatric disorders, some of the strongest associations are found with mood disorders, antisocial personality disorders, and conduct disorders (Glantz & Hartel 1999). Approximately 35% of the subjects with dependence met lifetime criteria for mood disorders, 45% for anxiety, and 50% for conduct or antisocial disorders (Merikangas et al. 1998). Recent data (Grant et al. 2004a–c) show similar results (21%–29% for mood disorders, 22%–25% for anxiety, and 32%–70% for personality disorders).

A key neurobiological element involved in all of the above-identified vulnerabilities to drug use initiation and dependence is stress axis dysregulation. Drugs of abuse acutely activate the HPA response to stress, and as dependence develops, ultimately engage brain stress systems. These basic observations have led to the hypothesis that the brain and brain pituitary stress systems have a role in the initial vulnerability to drugs, the development of dependence, and the vulnerability to

stress-induced relapse (Kreek & Koob 1998; Piazza & Le Moal 1996, 1998) (**Figure 4**). The enhanced propensity to self-administer drugs that is produced by stressors is linked to increased activation of the mesolimbic dopamine system mediated by stress hormone release. Glucocorticoids via glucocorticoid receptors facilitate dopamine-dependent behaviors by modulating dopamine transmission in the ventral striatum and the shell part of nucleus accumbens and thus may drive the extrahypothalamic CRF system (see above).

Genetic and Epigenetic Mechanisms

Genetic contributions to drug addiction face methodologically complex problems and interpretive issues as observed with other psychopathologies. Twin studies and analogous family studies with other sorts of biological relatives, coupled with epidemiological analyses, have provided evidence of genetic influences on addictions (Merikangas et al. 1998). However, there is no single gene for addiction. Genetic contributions to addiction result from complex genetic differences, ranging from alleles that control drug metabolism to hypothesized genetic control over drug sensitivity and environmental influences (Crabbe 2002, Rutter et al. 2006, Uhl & Grow 2004). Estimates from twin and adoption studies give ranges of 40% to 60% heritability. To date, molecular gene-finding methods and association and linkage studies are still inherently limited by relatively weak effects of specific genes and methodological problems.

In contrast, studies using genetic animal models have provided some insights into potential genetic targets from inbred strains, selected lines, quantitative trait loci mapping, and knockout methodology. Rats exposed to a mildly stressful situation display differential levels of reactivity, a measure of novelty seeking and disinhibition. High responders subsequently display higher responses to drugs of abuse than do low responders with a higher reactivity of the stress axis and a higher utilization of dopamine in the ventral striatum

(Piazza & Le Moal 1996, 1998). High-alcohol-preferring rats have been selectively bred to show high voluntary consumption of alcohol, increased anxiety-like responses, and numerous neuropharmacological phenotypes, such as decreased dopaminergic activity and decreased NPY activity. In an alcohol-preferring and alcohol-nonpreferring cross, a quantitative trait locus was identified on chromosome 4, a region to which the gene for NPY has been mapped. In the inbred preferring and nonpreferring quantitative trait loci analyses, loci on chromosomes 3, 4, and 8 have been identified that correspond to loci near the genes for the dopamine D_2 and serotonin $5HT_{1B}$ receptors (Carr et al. 1998).

Advances in molecular biology have led to the ability to systematically inactivate the genes that control the expression of proteins that make up receptors or neurotransmitter/neuromodulators in the central nervous system using the gene knockout and transgenic knock-in approaches. Although such an approach does not guarantee that these genes are the ones that convey vulnerability in the human population, they provide viable candidates for exploring the genetic basis of endophenotypes associated with addiction.

For opioids, the μ-opioid receptor has been identified as a key site for the acute reinforcing effects of opioids. Opiate (morphine) reinforcement as measured by conditioned place preference or self-administration is absent in μ-knockout mice, and there is no development of somatic signs of dependence to morphine in these mice. Knockout of the μ-opioid receptor also decreases nicotine reward, cannabinoid reward, and alcohol drinking in mice, which suggests a more global role of the μ-opioid receptor in drug reinforcement (Gaveriaux-Ruff & Kieffer 2002).

For ethanol, knockout studies have implicated numerous neurotransmitter systems in ethanol preference, again a measure of initial acute reinforcing effects of ethanol but not necessarily a measure of vulnerability to addiction. Known reward neurotransmitters (e.g., opioid, dopamine, GABA, and serotonin) and novel modulators (e.g., protein kinases and G-protein-activated inwardly rectifying K^+ channels) have been suggested by knockout studies to modulate ethanol preference (see Crabbe et al. 2006 for a review).

In studies involving psychostimulants, dopamine D_1 receptor knockout mice show no response to D_1 receptor agonists or antagonists and show a blunted response to the locomotor-activating effects of cocaine and amphetamine. D_1 knockout mice also are impaired in their acquisition of intravenous cocaine self-administration in comparison with wild-type mice. D_2 knockout mice have severe motor deficits and blunted responses to psychostimulants and opiates, but the effects on psychostimulant reward are less consistent. Dopamine-transporter knockout mice are dramatically hyperactive but also show a blunted response to psychostimulants. Thus, knockout studies suggest key roles for D_1 receptors and the dopamine transporter in the actions of psychomotor stimulants (Caine et al. 2002).

Finally, new vistas in vulnerability focus on the genetic-environment interface. These mechanisms, termed epigenetic, can maintain an acquired differentiated characteristic to strengthen synaptic connections and trace associations to long-term behavioral changes. A dramatic feature of addiction is the striking longevity of the behavioral abnormalities, which indicates that addiction processes produce long-term and probably permanent changes in specific circuitry in the brain. Such permanent changes in gene expression patterns may be obtained through permanent changes in chromatin remodeling without changes in DNA sequences. The concept of chromatin remodeling (an important determinant of gene expression) has provided one example of how stable changes in gene expression may be produced in neurons and glia to provoke long-lasting changes in physiology and behavior (Colvis et al. 2005, Levenson & Sweatt 2005). Thus, stress, trauma, prenatal stress, and early-life rearing experiences may alter addiction pathology later in life, via gene expression changes (Lemaire et al. 2006, Meaney 2001, Vallée et al. 1999, Weaver et al. 2004). Chronic use of drugs, presumably via regulation of intracellular signaling cascades, leads to the regulation of specific transcription factors, and regulation of these factors causes changes in histone acetylation and even DNA modification at particular target genes (Colvis et al. 2005). Such a schema expands the realm of factors that control individual susceptibility to addiction.

ALLOSTATIC VIEW OF ADDICTION

Homeostasis to Allostasis of the Reward System

An overall conceptual theme argued here is that drug addiction represents a break with homeostatic brain regulatory mechanisms that regulate the emotional state of the animal. However, the view that drug addiction represents a simple break with homeostasis is not sufficient to explain a number of key elements of addiction. Drug addiction, as with other chronic physiological disorders such as high blood pressure, worsens over time, is subject to significant environmental influences, and leaves a residual neuroadaptive trace that allows rapid "readdiction" even months and years after detoxification and abstinence. These characteristics of drug addiction have led us to reconsider drug addiction as not simply a homeostatic dysregulation of hedonic function and executive function, but rather as a dynamic break with homeostasis of these systems, termed allostasis.

Allostasis as a physiological concept was developed originally by neurobiologist Peter

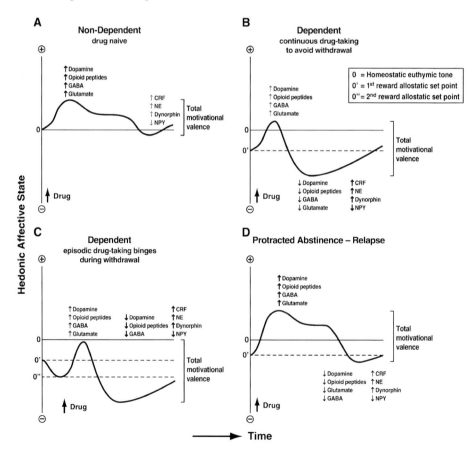

Sterling and epidemiologist James Eyer to explain the basis for the increase in patterns of human morbidity and mortality associated with the baby boom generation (individuals born after World War II), and has been argued to provide a more parsimonious explanation of the neuroadaptive changes that occur in the brain reward and stress systems to drive the pathological condition of addiction (Koob & Le Moal 2001).

Allostasis is defined as stability through change. Allostasis is far more complex than homeostasis and has several unique characteristics that differ from homeostasis (Sterling & Eyer 1988). Allostasis involves a feed-forward mechanism rather than the negative feedback mechanisms of homeostasis. A feed-forward mechanism has many advantages because when increased need produces a signal in homeostasis, negative feedback can correct the need, but the time required may be long and the resources may not be available. In allostasis, however, there is continuous re-evaluation of need and continuous readjustment of all parameters toward new set points. Thus, there is a fine matching of resources to needs.

Yet, it is precisely this ability to mobilize resources quickly and use feed-forward mechanisms that leads to an allostatic state and an ultimate cost to the individual that is known as allostatic load (McEwen 1998). An allostatic state can be defined as a state of chronic deviation of the regulatory system from its normal (homeostatic) operating level. An allostatic load can be defined as the "long-term cost of allostasis that accumulates over time and reflects the accumulation of damage that can

←

Figure 5

Conceptualization of the hedonic responses associated with drug intake at various stages of drug addiction correlated with changes in neurotransmitter systems within the extended amygdala circuitry hypothesized to mediate drug reward [arbitrarily defined as dopamine, opioid peptides, γ-aminobutyric acid (GABA), and glutamate] and antireward [arbitrarily defined as corticotropin-releasing factor (CRF), norepinephrine (NE), neuropeptide Y (NPY), and dynorphin]. (*A*) The hedonic response to an acute drug administration in a drug-naive individual with activity in neurotransmitter systems involved in reward predominating with a minor antireward opponent process-like response. (*B*) The hedonic response to an acute drug administration in a drug-Dependent (big "D"; see What is Addiction? section) individual while taking drug regularly. Initial activity in neurotransmitter systems involved in reward is followed by a decrease in function of neurotransmitter systems involved in reward and a major antireward opponent process-like response. $0'$ (zero prime) refers to the change in hedonic set point produced by chronic dysregulation of reward neurotransmitters and chronic recruitment of antireward neurotransmitters. This change in hedonic set point is the allostatic state of reward dysregulation conceptualized in Koob & Le Moal (2001). (*C*) The hedonic response to an acute drug administration in a drug-Dependent individual during withdrawal. A major antireward opponent process-like response at the beginning of the time course is followed by modest activity in neurotransmitter systems involved in reward triggered by a drug administration during withdrawal. $0'$ (zero prime) refers to the change in hedonic set point associated with the development of Dependence while still taking drug. $0''$ (zero double prime) refers to the hedonic set point during peak withdrawal after cessation of drug taking. (*D*) The hedonic response to an acute drug administration in a formerly drug-Dependent individual during protracted abstinence. Note that a previously drug-Dependent individual was hypothesized to remain at a residual $0'$ state, termed protracted abstinence. Robust activity in neurotransmitter systems involved in reward triggered by a drug administration is followed by an exaggerated antireward opponent process-like response (i.e., dysregulation of reward neurotransmitters and recruitment of antireward neurotransmitters) that drives the subject back to below $0'$. "Total motivational valence" refers to the combined motivation for compulsive drug use driven by both positive reinforcement (the most positive state above the 0 euthymic set point) and negative reinforcement (movement from the most negative state to 0 set point). The magnitude of a response is designated by the thickness of the arrows. The large upward arrow at the bottom of each panel refers to drug administration. The total time scale is estimated to be approximately eight hours. Figure modified with permission from Koob & Le Moal (2006).

lead to pathological states." Allostatic load is the consequence of repeated deviations from homeostasis that take on the form of changed set points that require increasing amounts of energy to defend, and ultimately reach, the level of pathology (McEwen 2000).

Temporal Dynamics of Allostasis

The failure of allostatic change to habituate or not to shut off is inherent in a feed-forward system that is in place for rapid, anticipated challenge to homeostasis. However, the same physiological mechanism that allows rapid response to environmental challenge becomes the engine of pathology if adequate time or resources are not available to shut off the response. Thus, for example, chronically elevated blood pressure is "appropriate" in an allostasis model to meet environmental demand of chronic arousal but is "certainly not healthy" (Sterling & Eyer 1988). Another example of such a feed-forward system is illustrated in the interaction between CRF and norepinephrine in the brainstem and basal forebrain that could lead to pathological anxiety (Koob 1999). Allostatic mechanisms also have been hypothesized to be involved in maintaining a functioning brain reward system that has relevance for the pathology of addiction (Koob & Le Moal 2001). Two components are hypothesized to adjust to challenges to the brain produced by drugs of abuse: overactivation of brain reward transmitters and circuits, and recruitment of the brain antireward or brain stress systems (**Figure 5**). Repeated challenges, as in the case of drugs of abuse, lead to attempts of the brain via molecular, cellular, and neuro-circuitry changes to maintain stability, but at a cost. For the drug addiction framework elaborated here, the residual deviation from normal brain-reward threshold regulation is described as an allostatic state. This state represents a combination of chronic elevation of reward set point fueled by decreased function of reward circuits, recruitment of antireward systems, loss of executive control, and facili-

tation of stimulus-response associations, all of which lead to the compulsivity of drug seeking and drug taking (see below).

Addiction as a Model of Psychopathology of Motivational Processes: "Nondrug Addictions"

Allostatic-like changes in reward function also may apply to any number of pathological states that are challenged by external and internal events, including depression and drug addiction. Other impulse control disorders, some listed by the DSM-IV, have characteristics similar to drug addiction in several domains. Such disorders include those with documented diagnostic criteria such as kleptomania, trichotillomania, pyromania, and compulsive gambling. Other disorders such as compulsive shopping, compulsive sexual behavior, compulsive eating, compulsive exercise, and compulsive computer use have fallen outside the realm of accepted diagnostic disorders. However, many of these disorders take on characteristics of impulsivity and compulsivity and have common face validity with the phenotype of addiction. For example, many of these disorders are associated with self-regulation failures from a social psychology perspective (Baumeister et al. 1994), and many have characteristic impulsivity problems associated with impulse control disorders and can move to compulsivity as the disorder progresses. A case can be made that there is strong face validity with the addiction cycle of preoccupation/anticipation (craving), binge/intoxication, and withdrawal/negative affect stages for compulsive gambling, compulsive shopping, compulsive eating, compulsive sexual behavior, and compulsive exercise.

Neurobiological studies are under way with these "nondrug addictions" and suggest some similarities with the neurobiological profiles associated with drug addiction. For example, there is a decrease in dopamine D_2 receptor activity in compulsive eating (Wang et al. 2002) and gambling (Comings et al. 1996, Zack & Poulos 2007) and some evidence of frontal cortex deficits in compulsive gambling (Tanabe et al. 2007). Stressors also have been shown to affect relapse in these disorders (Ledgerwood & Petry 2006). Refinement of the human neuropsychological and neu- robiological measures will further elucidate whether the same neurobiological circuits related to emotional function dysregulated in drug addiction are dysregulated in nondrug addiction.

SUMMARY POINTS

1. A key element of addiction is the development of a negative emotional state during drug abstinence.

2. The neurobiological basis of the negative emotional state derives from two sources: decreased reward circuitry function and increased antireward circuitry function.

3. The antireward circuitry function recruited during the addiction process can be localized to connections of the extended amygdala in the basal forebrain.

4. Neurochemical elements in the antireward system of the extended amygdala have as a focal point the extrahypothalamic corticotropin-releasing factor system.

5. Other neurotransmitter systems implicated in the antireward response include norepinephrine, dynorphin, neuropeptide Y, and nociceptin.

6. Vulnerability to addiction involves multiple targets in both the reward and antireward system, but a common element is sensitization of brain stress systems.

7. Dysregulation of the brain reward system and recruitment of the brain antireward system are hypothesized to produce an allostatic emotional change that can lead to pathology.

8. Nondrug addictions may be hypothesized to activate similar allostatic mechanisms.

LITERATURE CITED

Ahmed SH, Kenny PJ, Koob GF, Markou A. 2002. Neurobiological evidence for hedonic allostasis associated with escalating cocaine use. *Nat. Neurosci.* 5:625–26

Ahmed SH, Koob GF. 1998. Transition from moderate to excessive drug intake: change in hedonic set point. *Science* 282:298–300

Ahmed SH, Walker JR, Koob GF. 2000. Persistent increase in the motivation to take heroin in rats with a history of drug escalation. *Neuropsychopharmacology* 22:413–21

Alheid GF, De Olmos JS, Beltramino CA. 1995. Amygdala and extended amygdala. In *The Rat Nervous System*, ed. G Paxinos, pp. 495–578. San Diego, CA: Academic

Am. Psychiatric Assoc. (APA). 1994. *Diagnostic and Statistical Manual of Mental Disorders.* Washington, DC: Am. Psychiatric Press. 4th ed.

Anthony JC, Warner LA, Kessler RC. 1994. Comparative epidemiology of dependence on tobacco, alcohol, controlled substances, and inhalants: basic findings from the National Comorbidity Survey. *Ex. Clin. Psychopharmacol.* 2:244–68

Aston-Jones G, Delfs JM, Druhan J, Zhu Y. 1999. The bed nucleus of the stria terminalis: a target site for noradrenergic actions in opiate withdrawal. *Ann. NY Acad. Sci.* 877:486–98

Baldwin HA, Rassnick S, Rivier J, Koob GF, Britton KT. 1991. CRF antagonist reverses the "anxiogenic" response to ethanol withdrawal in the rat. *Psychopharmacology* 103:227–32

Baumeister RF, Heatherton TF, Tice DM, eds. 1994. *Losing Control: How and Why People Fail at Self-Regulation*. San Diego, CA: Academic

Bechara A, van der Kooy D. 1992. Lesions of the tegmental pedunculopontine nucleus: effects on the locomotor activity induced by morphine and amphetamine. *Pharmacol. Biochem. Behav.* 42:9–18

Bester H, Menendez L, Besson JM, Bernard JF. 1995. Spino (trigemino) parabrachiohypothalamic pathway: electrophysiological evidence for an involvement in pain processes. *J. Neurophysiol.* 73:568–85

Caine SB, Negus SS, Mello NK, Patel S, Bristow L, et al. 2002. Role of dopamine D2-like receptors in cocaine self-administration: studies with D2 receptor mutant mice and novel D2 receptor antagonists. *J. Neurosci.* 22:2977–88

Carboni E, Vacca C. 2003. Conditioned place preference: a simple method for investigating reinforcing properties in laboratory animals. *Methods Mol. Med.* 79:481–98

Carr LG, Foroud T, Bice P. 1998. A quantitative trait locus for alcohol consumption in selectively bred rat lines. *Alcohol Clin. Exp. Res.* 22:884–87

Chassin L, Presson CC, Sherman SJ, Edwards DA. 1990. The natural history of cigarette smoking: predicting young-adult smoking outcomes from adolescent smoking patterns. *Health Psychol.* 9:701–16

Collins RJ, Weeks JR, Cooper MM, Good PI, Russell RR. 1984. Prediction of abuse liability of drugs using IV self-administration by rats. *Psychopharmacology* 82:6–13

Colvis CM, Pollock JD, Goodman RH, Impey S, Dunn J, et al. 2005. Epigenetic mechanisms and gene networks in the nervous system. *J. Neurosci.* 25:10379–89

Comings DE, Rosenthal RJ, Lesieur HR, Rugle LJ, Muhleman D, et al. 1996. A study of the dopamine D2 receptor gene in pathological gambling. *Pharmacogenetics* 6:223–34

Crabbe JC. 2002. Genetic contributions to addiction. *Annu. Rev. Psychol.* 53:435–62

Crabbe JC, Phillips TJ, Harris RA, Arends MA, Koob GF. 2006. Alcohol-related genes: contributions from studies with genetically engineered mice. *Addict. Biol.* 11:195–269

Deminière JM, Piazza PV, Guegan G, Abrous DN, Maccari S, et al. 1992. Increased locomotor response to novelty and propensity to intravenous amphetamine self-administration in adult offspring of stressed mothers. *Brain Res.* 586:135–39

Deroche-Gamonet V, Belin D, Piazza PV. 2004. Evidence for addiction-like behavior in the rat. *Science* 305:1014–17

De Witte P, Littleton J, Parot P, Koob G. 2005. Neuroprotective and abstinence-promoting effects of acamprosate: elucidating the mechanism of action. *CNS Drugs* 19:517–37

Di Chiara G. 2002. Nucleus accumbens shell and core dopamine: differential role in behavior and addiction. *Behav. Brain Res.* 137:75–114

Everitt BJ, Wolf ME. 2002. Psychomotor stimulant addiction: a neural systems perspective. *J. Neurosci.* 22:3312–20. Erratum. 2002. *J. Neurosci.* 22(16):1a

Funk CK, O'Dell LE, Crawford EF, Koob GF. 2006. Corticotropin-releasing factor within the central nucleus of the amygdala mediates enhanced ethanol self-administration in withdrawn, ethanol-dependent rats. *J. Neurosci.* 26:11324–32

Gaveriaux-Ruff C, Kieffer BL. 2002. Opioid receptor genes inactivated in mice: the highlights. *Neuropeptides* 36:62–71

George O, Ghozland S, Azar MR, O'Dell LE, Zorrilla EP, et al. 2007. A neurobiological mechanism for the "hook" in nicotine dependence. *Proc. Natl. Acad. Sci. USA.* In press

Glantz MD, Hartel CR, eds. 1999. *Drug Abuse: Origins and Interventions*. Washington, DC: Am. Psychol. Assoc.

Glantz MD, Pickens RW, eds. 1992. *Vulnerability to Drug Abuse*. Washington, DC: Am. Psychol. Assoc.

Grant BF, Dawson DA. 1998. Age of onset of drug use and its association with DSM-IV drug abuse and dependence: results from the National Longitudinal Alcohol Epidemiologic Survey. *J. Subst. Abuse* 10:163–73

Grant BF, Hasin DS, Chou SP, Stinson FS, Dawson DA. 2004a. Nicotine dependence and psychiatric disorders in the United States: results from the national epidemiologic survey on alcohol and related conditions. *Arch. Gen. Psychiatry* 61:1107–15

Grant BF, Stinson FS, Dawson DA, Chou SP, Dufour MC, et al. 2004b. Prevalence and co-occurrence of substance use disorders and independent mood and anxiety disorders: results from the National Epidemiologic Survey on Alcohol and Related Conditions. *Arch. Gen. Psychiatry* 61:807–16

Grant BF, Stinson FS, Dawson DA, Chou SP, Ruan WJ, Pickering RP. 2004c. Co-occurrence of 12-month alcohol and drug use disorders and personality disorders in the United States: results from the National Epidemiologic Survey on Alcohol and Related Conditions. *Arch. Gen. Psychiatry* 61:361–68

Greenwell TN, Funk CK, Cottone P, Richardson HN, Chen SA, et al. 2007. Corticotropin-releasing factor-1 receptor antagonists decrease heroin self-administration in long-, but not short-access rats. Manuscr. submitted

Grobin AC, Matthews DB, Devaud LL, Morrow AL. 1998. The role of GABA(A) receptors in the acute and chronic effects of ethanol. *Psychopharmacology* 139:2–19

Gunnar M, Quevedo K. 2006. The neurobiology of stress and development. *Annu. Rev. Psychol.* 58:145–73

Heimer L, Alheid GF. 1991. Piecing together the puzzle of basal forebrain anatomy. *Adv. Exp. Med. Biol.* 295:1–42

Heishma SJ, Singleton EG, Liguori A. 2001. Marijuana Craving Questionnaire: development and initial validation of a self-report instrument. *Addiction* 96:1023–34

Hingson R, Heeren T, Zakocs R, Winter M, Wechsler H. 2003. Age of first intoxication, heavy drinking, driving after drinking and risk of unintentional injury among U.S. college students. *J. Stud. Alcohol* 64:23–31

Kalivas PW, McFarland K, Bowers S, Szumlinski K, Xi ZX, Baker D. 2003. Glutamate transmission and addiction to cocaine. *Ann. NY Acad. Sci.* 1003:169–75

Kenny PJ, Chen SA, Kitamura O, Markou A, Koob GF. 2006. Conditioned withdrawal drives heroin consumption and decreases reward sensitivity. *J. Neurosci.* 26:5894–900

Khantzian EJ. 1985. The self-medication hypothesis of addictive disorders: focus on heroin and cocaine dependence. *Am. J. Psychiatry* 142:1259–64

Khantzian EJ. 1990. Self-regulation and self-medication factors in alcoholism and the addictions. Similarities and differences. *Recent Dev. Alcohol* 8:255–71

Khantzian EJ. 1997. The self-medication hypothesis of substance use disorders: a reconsideration and recent applications. *Harv. Rev. Psychiatry* 4:231–44

Kitamura O, Wee S, Specio SE, Koob GF, Pulvirenti L. 2006. Escalation of methamphetamine self-administration in rats: a dose-effect function. *Psychopharmacology* 186:48–53

Koob GF. 1992. Drugs of abuse: anatomy, pharmacology, and function of reward pathways. *Trends Pharmacol. Sci.* 13:177–84

Koob GF. 1999. Corticotropin-releasing factor, norepinephrine and stress. *Biol. Psychiatry* 46:1167–80

Koob GF. 2000. Animal models of craving for ethanol. *Addiction* 95(Suppl. 2):s73–81

Koob GF. 2003a. Alcoholism: allostasis and beyond. *Alcohol Clin. Exp. Res.* 27:232–43

Koob GF. 2003b. The neurobiology of self-regulation failure in addiction: an allostatic view. *Neuro-Psychoanal.* 5:35–39

Koob GF. 2004. Allostatic view of motivation: implications for psychopathology. *Nebr. Symp. Motiv.* 50:1–18

Koob GF, Bloom FE. 1988. Cellular and molecular mechanisms of drug dependence. *Science* 242:715–23

Koob GF, Heinrichs SC. 1999. A role for corticotropin-releasing factor and urocortin in behavioral responses to stressors. *Brain Res.* 848:141–52

Koob GF, Le Moal M. 1997. Drug abuse: hedonic homeostatic dysregulation. *Science* 278:52–58

Koob GF, Le Moal M. 2001. Drug addiction, dysregulation of reward, and allostasis. *Neuropsychopharmacology* 24:97–129

Koob GF, Le Moal M. 2004. Drug addiction and allostasis. In *Allostasis, Homeostasis, and the Costs of Physiological Adaptation,* ed. J Schulkin, pp. 150–63. New York: Cambridge Univ. Press

Koob GF, Le Moal M. 2005. Plasticity of reward neurocircuitry and the "dark side" of drug addiction. *Nat. Neurosci.* 8:1442–44

Koob GF, Le Moal M. 2006. *Neurobiology of Addiction.* London: Academic

Kornetsky C, Bain G. 1990. Brain-stimulation reward: a model for drug induced euphoria. *Mod. Methods Pharmacol.* 6:211–31

Kreek MJ, Koob GF. 1998. Drug dependence: stress and dysregulation of brain reward pathways. *Drug Alcohol Depend.* 51:23–47

Laviolette SR, van der Kooy D. 2003. Blockade of mesolimbic dopamine transmission dramatically increases sensitivity to the rewarding effects of nicotine in the ventral tegmental area. *Mol. Psychiatry* 8:50–59

Ledgerwood DM, Petry NM. 2006. What do we know about relapse in pathological gambling? *Clin. Psychol. Rev.* 26:216–28

Le Doux JE, Iwata J, Cicchetti P, Reis DJ. 1988. Different projections of the central amygdaloid nucleus mediate autonomic and behavioral correlates of conditioned fear. *J. Neurosci.* 8:2517–29

Lemaire V, Lamarque S, Le Moal M, Piazza PV, Abrous DN. 2006. Postnatal stimulation of the pups counteracts prenatal stress-induced deficits in hippocampal neurogenesis. *Biol. Psychiatry* 59:786–92

Le Moal M. 1995. Mesocorticolimbic dopaminergic neurons: functional and regulatory roles. In *Psychopharmacology: The Fourth Generation of Progress*, ed. FE Bloom, DJ Kupfer, pp. 283–94. New York: Raven

Levenson JM, Sweatt JD. 2005. Epigenetic mechanisms in memory formation. *Nat. Rev. Neurosci.* 6:108–18

Lynch WJ. 2006. Sex differences in vulnerability to drug self-administration. *Exp. Clin. Psychopharmacol.* 14:34–41

Markou A, Kosten TR, Koob GF. 1998. Neurobiological similarities in depression and drug dependence: a self-medication hypothesis. *Neuropsychopharmacology* 18:135–74

Markou A, Weiss F, Gold LH, Caine SB, Schulteis G, Koob GF. 1993. Animal models of drug craving. *Psychopharmacology* 112:163–82

McEwen BS. 1998. Stress, adaptation, and disease: allostasis and allostatic load. *Ann. NY Acad. Sci.* 840:33–44

McEwen BS. 2000. Allostasis and allostatic load: implications for neuropsychopharmacology. *Neuropsychopharmacology* 22:108–24

McFarland K, Kalivas PW. 2001. The circuitry mediating cocaine-induced reinstatement of drug-seeking behavior. *J. Neurosci.* 21:8655–63

Meaney MJ. 2001. The development of individual differences in behavioral and endocrine responses to stress. *Annu. Rev. Neurosci.* 24:1161–92

Meaney MJ, Szyf M. 2005. Environmental programming of stress responses through DNA methylation: life at the interface between a dynamic environment and a fixed genome. *Dialogues Clin. Neurosci.* 7:103–23

Merchenthaler I, Vigh S, Petrusz P, Schally AV. 1982. Immunocytochemical localization of corticotropin-releasing factor (CRF) in the rat brain. *Am. J. Anat.* 165:385–96

Merikangas KR, Mehta RL, Molnar BE, Walters EE, Swendsen JD, et al. 1998. Comorbidity of substance use disorders with mood and anxiety disorders: results of the International Consortium in Psychiatric Epidemiology. *Addict. Behav.* 23:893–907

Merlo-Pich E, Lorang M, Yeganeh M, Rodriguez de Fonseca F, Raber J, et al. 1995. Increase of extracellular corticotropin-releasing factor-like immunoreactivity levels in the amygdala of awake rats during restraint stress and ethanol withdrawal as measured by microdialysis. *J. Neurosci.* 15:5439–47

Natl. Inst. Alcohol Abuse Alcohol. 2004. NIAAA council approves definition of binge drinking. *NIAAA Newsl.* No. 3

Nestler EJ. 2001. Molecular basis of long-term plasticity underlying addiction. *Nat. Rev. Neurosci.* 2:119–28

Nestler EJ. 2005. Is there a common molecular pathway for addiction? *Nat. Neurosci.* 8:1445–49

O'Dell LE, Koob GF. 2007. "Nicotine deprivation effect" in rats with intermittent 23-hour access to intravenous nicotine self-administration. *Pharmacol. Biochem. Behav.* 86:346–53

Olive MF, Koenig HN, Nannini MA, Hodge CW. 2002. Elevated extracellular CRF levels in the bed nucleus of the stria terminalis during ethanol withdrawal and reduction by subsequent ethanol intake. *Pharmacol. Biochem. Behav.* 72:213–20

Pettit HO, Ettenberg A, Bloom FE, Koob GF. 1984. Destruction of dopamine in the nucleus accumbens selectively attenuates cocaine but not heroin self-administration in rats. *Psychopharmacology* 84:167–73

Phelps EA, Le Doux JE. 2005. Contributions of the amygdala to emotion processing: from animal models to human behavior. *Neuron* 48:175–87

Piazza PV, Le Moal M. 1996. Pathophysiological basis of vulnerability to drug abuse: role of an interaction between stress, glucocorticoids, and dopaminergic neurons. *Annu. Rev. Pharmacol. Toxicol.* 36:359–78

Piazza PV, Le Moal M. 1998. The role of stress in drug self-administration. *Trends Pharmacol. Sci.* 19:67–74

Poulos CX, Cappell H. 1991. Homeostatic theory of drug tolerance: a general model of physiological adaptation. *Psychol. Rev.* 98:390–408

Price DD. 2002. Central neural mechanisms that interrelate sensory and affective dimensions of pain. *Mol. Interv.* 2:392–403

Rassnick S, Heinrichs SC, Britton KT, Koob GF. 1993a. Microinjection of a corticotropin-releasing factor antagonist into the central nucleus of the amygdala reverses anxiogenic-like effects of ethanol withdrawal. *Brain Res.* 605:25–32

Rassnick S, Stinus L, Koob GF. 1993b. The effects of 6-hydroxydopamine lesions of the nucleus accumbens and the mesolimbic dopamine system on oral self-administration of ethanol in the rat. *Brain Res.* 623:16–24

Roberto M, Madamba SG, Stouffer DG, Parsons LH, Siggins GR. 2004. Increased GABA release in the central amygdala of ethanol-dependent rats. *J. Neurosci.* 24:10159–66

Roberts AJ, Heyser CJ, Cole M, Griffin P, Koob GF. 2000. Excessive ethanol drinking following a history of dependence: animal model of allostasis. *Neuropsychopharmacology* 22:581–94

Roy A, Pandey SC. 2002. The decreased cellular expression of neuropeptide Y protein in rat brain structures during ethanol withdrawal after chronic ethanol exposure. *Alcohol Clin. Exp. Res.* 26:796–803

Rutter M, Moffitt TE, Caspi A. 2006. Gene-environment interplay and psychopathology: multiple varieties but real effects. *J. Child. Psychol. Psychiatry* 47:226–61

Samson HH. 1986. Initiation of ethanol reinforcement using a sucrose-substitution procedure in food- and water-sated rats. *Alcohol Clin. Exp. Res.* 10:436–42

Schulteis G, Ahmed SH, Morse AC, Koob GF, Everitt BJ. 2000. Conditioning and opiate withdrawal: the amygdala links neutral stimuli with the agony of overcoming drug addiction. *Nature* 405:1013–14

See RE, Fuchs RA, Ledford CC, McLaughlin J. 2003. Drug addiction, relapse, and the amygdala. *Ann. NY Acad. Sci.* 985:294–307

Shaham Y, Erb S, Stewart J. 2000. Stress-induced relapse to heroin and cocaine seeking in rats: a review. *Brain Res. Rev.* 33:13–33

Shaham Y, Shalev U, Lu L, De Wit H, Stewart J. 2003. The reinstatement model of drug relapse: history, methodology and major findings. *Psychopharmacology* 168:3–20

Shalev U, Grimm JW, Shaham Y. 2002. Neurobiology of relapse to heroin and cocaine seeking: a review. *Pharmacol. Rev.* 54:1–42

Shaw-Lutchman TZ, Barrot M, Wallace T, Gilden L, Zachariou V, et al. 2002. Regional and cellular mapping of cAMP response element-mediated transcription during naltrexone-precipitated morphine withdrawal. *J. Neurosci.* 22:3663–72

Shippenberg TS, Koob GF. 2002. Recent advances in animal models of drug addiction and alcoholism. In *Neuropsychopharmacology: The Fifth Generation of Progress*, ed. KL Davis, D Charney, JT Coyle, C Nemeroff, pp. 1381–97. Philadelphia, PA: Lippincott Williams & Wilkins

Siegel S. 1975. Evidence from rats that morphine tolerance is a learned response. *J. Comp. Physiol. Psychol.* 89:498–506

Skinner EA, Zimmer-Gembeck MJ. 2006. The development of coping. *Annu. Rev. Psychol.* 58:119–44

Solomon RL. 1980. The opponent-process theory of acquired motivation: the costs of pleasure and the benefits of pain. *Am. Psychol.* 35:691–712

Solomon RL, Corbit JD. 1974. An opponent-process theory of motivation: 1. Temporal dynamics of affect. *Psychol. Rev.* 81:119–45

Specio SE, Wee S, O'Dell LE, Boutrel B, Zorrilla EP, Koob GF. 2007. CRF1 receptor antagonists attenuate escalated cocaine self-administration in rats. Manuscr. submitted

Sterling P, Eyer J. 1988. Allostasis: a new paradigm to explain arousal pathology. In *Handbook of Life Stress, Cognition and Health*, ed. S Fisher, J Reason, pp. 629–49. Chichester, UK: Wiley

Substance Abuse Ment. Health Serv. Adm. (SAMHSA). 2004. *Overview of Findings from the 2003 National Survey on Drug Use and Health* (Off. Appl. Stud., NHSDA Ser. H-21, DHHS Publ. No. SMA 03–3774). Rockville, MD: SAMHSA

Tanabe J, Thompson L, Claus E, Dalwani M, Hutchison K, Banich MT. 2007. Prefrontal cortex activity is reduced in gambling and nongambling substance users during decision-making. *Hum. Brain Mapp.* In press

Tiffany ST, Carter BL, Singleton EG. 2000. Challenges in the manipulation, assessment and interpretation of craving relevant variables. *Addiction* 95(Suppl. 2):S177–87

Uhl GR, Grow RW. 2004. The burden of complex genetics in brain disorders. *Arch. Gen. Psychiatry* 61:223–29

Ungless MA, Whistler JL, Malenka RC, Bonci A. 2001. Single cocaine exposure in vivo induces long-term potentiation in dopamine neurons. *Nature* 411:583–87

Valdez GR, Koob GF. 2004. Allostasis and dysregulation of corticotropin-releasing factor and neuropeptide Y systems: implications for the development of alcoholism. *Pharmacol. Biochem. Behav.* 79:671–89

Valdez GR, Roberts AJ, Chan K, Davis H, Brennan M, et al. 2002. Increased ethanol self-administration and anxiety-like behavior during acute withdrawal and protracted abstinence: regulation by corticotropin-releasing factor. *Alcohol Clin. Exp. Res.* 26:1494–501

Vallée M, Maccari S, Dellu F, Simon H, Le Moal M, Mayo W. 1999. Long-term effects of prenatal stress and postnatal handling on age-related glucocorticoid secretion and cognitive performance: a longitudinal study in the rat. *Eur. J. Neurosci.* 11:2906–16

Vanderschuren LJ, Everitt BJ. 2004. Drug seeking becomes compulsive after prolonged cocaine self-administration. *Science* 305:1017–19

Volkow ND, Fowler JS, Wang GJ. 2003. The addicted human brain: insights from imaging studies. *J. Clin. Invest.* 111:1444–51

Vorel SR, Ashby CR Jr, Paul M, Liu X, Hayes R, et al. 2002. Dopamine D3 receptor antagonism inhibits cocaine-seeking and cocaine-enhanced brain reward in rats. *J. Neurosci.* 22:9595–603

Wang GJ, Volkow ND, Fowler JS. 2002. The role of dopamine in motivation for food in humans: implications for obesity. *Expert Opin. Ther. Targets* 6:601–9

Weaver IC, Cervoni N, Champagne FA, D'Alessio AC, Sharma S, et al. 2004. Epigenetic programming by maternal behavior. *Nat. Neurosci.* 7:847–54

Weiss F, Ciccocioppo R, Parsons LH, Katner S, Liu X, et al. 2001. Compulsive drug-seeking behavior and relapse: neuroadaptation, stress, and conditioning factors. *Ann. NY Acad. Sci.* 937:1–26

Weiss F, Markou A, Lorang MT, Koob GF. 1992. Basal extracellular dopamine levels in the nucleus accumbens are decreased during cocaine withdrawal after unlimited-access self-administration. *Brain Res.* 593:314–18

Zack M, Poulos CX. 2007. A D2 antagonist enhances the rewarding and priming effects of a gambling episode in pathological gamblers. *Neuropsychopharmacology* 32:1678–86

Zorrilla EP, Koob GF. 2004. The therapeutic potential of CRF1 antagonists for anxiety. *Expert Opin. Invest. Drugs* 13:799–828

The Brain, Appetite, and Obesity

Hans-Rudolf Berthoud and Christopher Morrison

Neurobiology of Nutrition Laboratory, Pennington Biomedical Research Center,
Louisiana State University System, Baton Rouge, Louisiana;
email: berthohr@pbrc.edu, morriscd@pbrc.edu

Annu. Rev. Psychol. 2008. 59:55–92

The *Annual Review of Psychology* is online at
http://psych.annualreviews.org

This article's doi:
10.1146/annurev.psych.59.103006.093551

Key Words

food intake, homeostatic regulation of body weight, food reward,
taste hedonics, gut-brain axis

Abstract

Food intake and energy expenditure are controlled by complex, redundant, and distributed neural systems that reflect the fundamental
biological importance of adequate nutrient supply and energy balance. Much progress has been made in identifying the various hormonal and neural mechanisms by which the brain informs itself about
availability of ingested and stored nutrients and, in turn, generates
behavioral, autonomic, and endocrine output. While hypothalamus
and caudal brainstem play crucial roles in this homeostatic function,
areas in the cortex and limbic system are important for processing
information regarding prior experience with food, reward, and emotion, as well as social and environmental context. Most vertebrates
can store a considerable amount of energy as fat for later use, and this
ability has now become one of the major health risks for many human
populations. The predisposition to develop obesity can theoretically
result from any pathological malfunction or lack of adaptation to
changing environments of this highly complex system.

Contents

INTRODUCTION

An appropriate supply of micro- and macronutrients is absolutely required for life. Therefore, strong biological mechanisms have evolved that rigorously defend food supply just as they do for other biological needs. However, unlike oxygen, most vertebrates can store a considerable amount of energy and some micronutrients for later use. Eating more food than necessary for daily energy expenditure when food was plenty served as a hedge against subsequent periods of famine. However, this ability to store surplus energy as fat has now become one of the biggest health risks for many human populations (Prentice et al. 2005, Weinsier et al. 1998, Wells 2006). The uninterrupted supply of cheap energy-dense foods together with an increasingly sedentary lifestyle has led to obesity in a large segment of the human population. Obesity is thus a state of excessive chronic fat storage that goes beyond natural fluctuations caused by changes in nutrient availability in the environment. The prevalence of obesity is particularly high in populations that rapidly changed from a restrictive environment to an environment of plenty. Although not experimentally proven, one view is that thrifty genes were selected to guarantee optimal survival of periods of famine in these populations, and that these same genes have now become a liability (Neel 1962, Prentice et al. 2005, Ravussin & Bogardus 2000).

OVERVIEW: FOOD INTAKE IS CONTROLLED BY A COMPLEX AND DISTRIBUTED NEURAL SYSTEM

Because of its biological importance, food intake is controlled by a highly complex system that is redundant but extremely reliable. Neural control mechanisms are typically regarded as "input-integration-output" systems (**Figure 1**). For the control of ingestive behavior, it seems obvious that smelling and tasting a delicious bowl of soup are examples of input systems at work, and that taking a spoonful to the mouth and swallowing it are examples of output systems in action. It is less obvious how relevant information is integrated and where this integration takes place. The combined sensory perceptions of the taste and smell leading to a neural representation and subjective experience of the flavor of the soup may serve as an example of integration at work. Before we discuss specific components of this regulatory system in detail, let us quickly introduce the major systems involved.

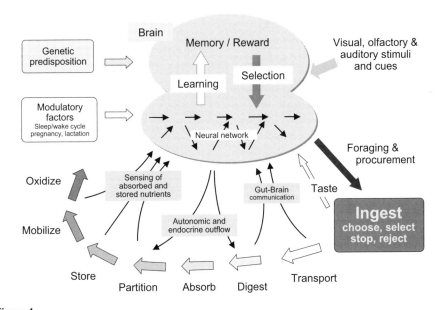

Figure 1

General flow diagram depicting the major factors and mechanisms determining the control of ingestive behavior and energy balance.

CCK:
cholecystokinin

Sensory Input to the Brain: Information About Nutrients Through Many Senses and Routes

Figure 1 provides an overview of the major categories of input signals and factors that allow the brain to decide whether it should engage in ingestive behavior or not. Relevant signals from the outside world come mainly through the classical senses of sight and smell. These visual and olfactory signals do not necessarily have to directly identify specific foods (e.g., seeing a banana). Cues previously associated with particular foods can acquire predictive value through learning, and as such do not only operate through visual and olfactory but also through auditory and somatosensory input channels.

Once put into the mouth, foods elicit taste and mechanical sensations, which are arguably the most important for ingestive behavior. Taste functions predominantly as a feed-forward stimulus, anecdotally known as the French saying "l'appétit vient en mangeant." Acceptable foods are then swallowed and further processed within the gastrointestinal tract. There, different components of foods interact with mechano- and chemosensors that send neural signals via mainly vagal afferents and/or hormonal signals through the bloodstream to the brain (**Figure 1**). Although most of these signals, such as cholecystokinin (CCK), have negative feedback functions, at least two signals with feed-forward characteristics have recently been described, namely ghrelin secreted from the stomach mucosa (Asakawa et al. 2001) and the reward-generating signals emanating from small intestinal nutrient infusions (Sclafani 2004). Gut-to-brain communication is increasingly recognized as playing an important role not just in the determination of meal size but also in overall food intake. Current hypotheses explaining the remarkable efficacy of various types of bariatric surgeries to reverse type-2 diabetes and obesity include changes in the release patterns of various gastrointestinal hormones (Cummings et al. 2004).

Once absorbed, macronutrients are partitioned into either storage or immediate metabolism in various tissues (**Figure 1**). The pancreas plays a special role in that circulating fuels and certain gastrointestinal hormones, the incretins, determine the release of the pancreatic hormones insulin, glucagon, amylin, and pancreatic polypeptide, all signaling to brain (Burcelin 2005, Drucker & Nauck 2006). Other nutrient sensors are located in the portal vein and liver (Matveyenko & Donovan 2006, Thorens & Larsen 2004). Adipose tissue is another major player in sending feeding-relevant signals to the brain. Adipose tissue secretes leptin, adiponectin, resistin, and certain cytokines, which all play important roles in the neural and peripheral regulation of food intake and energy balance (Trayhurn et al. 2006).

Information from recall of memorial representations can also be considered as inputs to the integrative neural circuits responsible for the control of ingestive behaviors. The neural mechanisms involved in learning about foods and the use of such mnemonic representations for guiding feeding behavior are discussed in more detail below.

Integrative Processes: Not Just the Hypothalamus

Clearly, the hypothalamus is a crucial player in the control of food intake and energy balance. Some of the key neuronal populations have been identified in the arcuate nucleus, and much of the molecular mechanisms of intracellular integration of various hormonal and nutrient signals are currently under intensive investigation. How this integrated metabolic information generated in arcuate nucleus neurons is passed on to other brain areas is already less clear, and details about how the brain as a whole integrates all the information from inside and outside the body into adaptive biological responses regarding ingestive behavior are still ill defined. It is recognized that the neural network responsible for the overall integration is not limited to the hypothalamus, but includes important areas in the limbic system, cortex, midbrain, and brainstem. All these aspects of neural integration are discussed in more detail below.

Output from the Brain: Behavioral, Autonomic, and Endocrine

The three arms of brain output, skeletal motor action (behavior), autonomic, and endocrine outflow, are shown in **Figure 1**. The autonomic and enteric nervous systems and the pituitary-endocrine axis should be considered as part of the overall effector or output system because they significantly modulate gastrointestinal handling and metabolic processing of food as well as partitioning and oxidation of metabolites, and thus codetermine the level of signals on the sensory side of the regulatory loop. Food intake and selection in the narrower sense are controlled by the skeletal motor system, including the final common pathways for locomotion important for foraging and the procurement phase of ingestive behavior. Perhaps the most interesting aspect of the organization of output is how motivation to eat is translated into action. This translation is really at the center of integration, dealing with the convergence of metabolic, cognitive, emotional, and volitional controls on the final common output path. This is discussed in detail below.

Modulatory Factors: Rhythms and Cycles

The function of the feeding control system is modulated or biased by a number of factors, notably circadian and circannual rhythms (see sidebar Circadian Rhythms), gender-related reproductive cycle, and relative stage of the lifespan. Feeding activity is intimately tied to the sleep-wake cycle and level of arousal throughout the circadian rhythm (Vanitallie 2006). In addition to the simple fact that decreased duration of sleep with the modern lifestyle provides more opportunities to eat, relative sleep deprivation may favor development of obesity through other mechanisms.

CIRCADIAN RHYTHMS

The relationship between feeding, metabolism, and circadian time was strikingly highlighted when the disruption of clock genes (Clock, Bmal1) produced mice with obesity, hyperphagia, and abnormal glucose homeostasis (Rudic et al. 2004, Turek et al. 2005). Components of the clock appear to directly regulate genes controlling behavior and metabolism, whereas metabolism conversely alters the expression of clock genes. This reciprocal molecular relationship is mirrored in physiology and behavior, as feeding behavior is clearly influenced by circadian time, yet nutrient ingestion is also sufficient to entrain certain circadian rhythms. These observations (a) highlight a research area that provides a physiological and molecular framework to explain the coordinated regulation of both behavior and metabolism, and (b) provide mechanistic support for evidence that the disruption of circadian patterns produces alterations in ingestive behavior and metabolism (Moynihan Ramsey et al. 2007).

Hibernators and animals with ultracircadian rhythms are extremely useful models for the study of ingestive behavior controls and energy balance regulation. Their remarkable reversible hyperphagia and obesity are discussed in the next main section.

During pregnancy and lactation, powerful hormones are at work profoundly shifting metabolism and energy requirements (Eckel 2004) (see sidebar Gender Differences). Similarly, during childhood, energy requirements and composition are higher, and toward the end of the lifespan, they tend to decrease (Hays & Roberts 2006).

Genetic Predisposition: "Thrifty Genes" versus "Random Drift"

In most humans, genes do not directly cause obesity, but they predispose to becoming obese in the changed environment of the modern world. Because it is clear that genes and their products ultimately control all bodily functions, including food intake, energy expenditure, and energy balance, it can be said that a fraction of the population is genetically prone to the environmental and lifestyle push

GENDER DIFFERENCES

Food intake and body weight are influenced by gender. A classic example of body weight modulation by gender is the tendency of males to deposit visceral fat (apple shape) and females to deposit subcutaneous fat (pear shape). Variations in sex steroids clearly contribute to this difference, as these hormones directly alter both food intake and body fat distribution. Sex steroids also interact with nutrient-sensing pathways, by modulating the signaling capacity of leptin and insulin. The cellular and molecular mechanisms underlying these gender differences are only beginning to be unraveled (Clegg et al. 2006, Woods et al. 2003).

toward obesity, while another fraction is resistant (Friedman 2003, Neel 1962, Speakman 2004). Thus, each of the many factors by which lifestyle and environment influence energy balance interacts with specific sets of susceptibility genes, the variations of which determine the physiological impact of the particular factor (Boutin & Froguel 2001). Consequently, some individuals respond strongly (prone) and others weakly or not at all (resistant) to a given factor. For example, resistant individuals may decrease meal size in response to increased caloric density, while prone individuals do not. In response to overeating a palatable meal, resistant individuals may increase physical activity while prone individuals may not. There are two fundamentally opposing theories regarding the evolution of such susceptibility genes. The "thrifty gene" hypothesis introduced above suggests that genes determining high efficiency in the acquisition and usage of energy were selected over millions of years in human and human ancestral populations that experienced frequent famines (Prentice et al. 2005). As much as this theory makes sense intuitively, there is little experimental data to support it. For one, few thrifty genes have been identified, and the frequency of famines is difficult to document. Therefore, an alternative or competing hypothesis that has recently gained momentum suggests gene drift through random

mutations allowed by a relaxation of the strict upper limits for body weight caused by the disappearance of predators (Speakman 2006).

This brief overview shows the multiplicity of input signals that ultimately determine body weight regulation and give a hint at the complexity of underlying integrative processes. In the following sections, we discuss some of these processes in more detail.

SENSING OF INGESTED NUTRIENTS AND THE INTERNAL MILIEU: POSITIVE AND NEGATIVE FEEDBACK FROM MULTIPLE LOCATIONS

The major sensors and pathways supplying the brain with information about ingested nutrients are depicted in **Figure 2**. Sensory information from the nutrient-handling periphery is signaled to the central nervous system either via circulating hormones and other factors or via sensory nerves, particularly vagal afferents.

Taste: The Gatekeeper of the Body

The most significant and exciting progress in taste perception has taken place in the periphery, with the discovery of the gene families and signaling mechanisms responsible for detecting sweet, sour, bitter, and savory (umami) foods by taste receptor cells in the oral cavity (Adler et al. 2000, Huang et al. 2006, Laugerette et al. 2005, Nelson et al. 2001, Zhang et al. 2003, Zhao et al. 2003). An in-depth discussion of the peripheral transduction mechanisms and central pathways of the gustatory system is beyond the scope of this review and can be found in other review articles (e.g., Chandrashekar et al. 2006).

Gastrointestinal Tract: Beyond Satiation?

Once food is recognized as safe and beneficial by the gustatory gatekeeper, it is processed and eventually absorbed into the blood circulation or lymph within the alimentary canal.

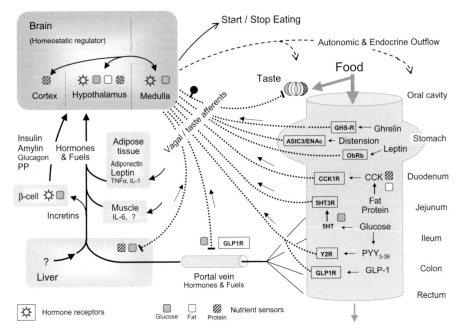

Figure 2

Schematic diagram showing signals and pathways used by the brain to sense nutrients after ingestion.

The gastrointestinal tract communicates intensely in a reciprocal fashion with the brain through the vagus nerve, the sympathetic nervous system, and hormones. Vagal afferents provide a particularly dense sensory innervation to the gastrointestinal tract, reaching as far down as the descending colon (Berthoud et al. 2004, Berthoud & Neuhuber 2000).

Stomach. Far from being a passive reservoir for ingested food, the stomach is a highly regulated organ with elaborate neural and hormonal control mechanisms. The presence of ingested food is detected by a variety of mechanosensory vagal afferent terminals (Berthoud et al. 2004, Berthoud & Neuhuber 2000, Phillips & Powley 2000, Zagorodnyuk et al. 2001) (**Figure 2**).

Vagal afferent fibers are also innervating the gastric mucosa, where they are likely to detect locally released hormones such as leptin and ghrelin. Leptin is produced in the mucosa of the stomach and rapidly mobilized by feeding and high doses of exogenous CCK (Bado et al. 1998), and it appears to activate vagal afferents (Wang et al. 1997), which have been shown to express the long form of leptin receptor (Burdyga et al. 2002, Buyse et al. 2001). Small doses of leptin infused into the celiac artery significantly decreased sucrose intake; this effect was not observed in rats with subdiaphragmatic vagotomy or perivagal capsaicin-treatment aimed to selectively ablate vagal afferent fibers (Peters et al. 2006).

The very recent discovery of ghrelin was particularly exciting because it is the first and only peripherally secreted hormone with a stimulatory effect on appetite. Ghrelin is mainly secreted from oxyntic gland cells in the mucosa of the empty stomach, and secretion is rapidly suppressed upon the ingestion of food (Cummings 2006, Cummings et al. 2001). There is evidence from one laboratory that ghrelin secreted from the gastric mucosa stimulates appetite by inhibiting activity of vagal afferents. Ghrelin's appetite-stimulating effect was abolished in rats with subdiaphragmatic vagotomy and in rats with

PYY: peptide YY

capsaicin-induced vagal deafferentation (Date et al. 2002). Ghrelin receptor is expressed by a subset of vagal afferent neurons in the nodose ganglia and appears to regulate expression of other peptide receptors in vagal afferents (Burdyga et al. 2006, Date et al. 2002). Furthermore, ghrelin does not stimulate food intake in patients with surgical procedures involving vagotomy (le Roux et al. 2005).

Upper small intestine. Vagal afferent nerve fibers also innervate all compartments of the small intestinal wall and are in a position to sense nutrients after they are absorbed from the lumen (for a review, see Berthoud & Neuhuber 2000). The demonstration that vagal afferents express CCK-1 receptors (Broberger et al. 1999, Moriarty et al. 1997, Patterson et al. 2002) and numerous functional studies strongly suggest that luminal nutrients, particularly lipids and proteins, activate vagal afferents via release of CCK from adjacent enteroendocrine cells (Geary 2004, Raybould et al. 2006, Smith et al. 1985).

Since glucose is a very poor stimulator of CCK release, it is not clear whether a similar mechanism exists for the sensing of glucose by vagal afferents. There is some limited evidence that 5-HT-secreting enteroendocrine cells and the 5-HT3 receptor might be involved (Freeman et al. 2006). The 5-HT3 receptor is expressed in vagal afferent neurons (Morales & Wang 2002), and stimulation of c-Fos in nodose ganglion neurons by luminal administration of 5-HT or maltose was blocked by prior vagotomy or 5-HT3 receptor antagonist treatment (Wu et al. 2005).

An emerging concept is the role of the gut in generating positive feelings and emotions or reward. This concept has been pioneered by Sclafani's (2004) electronic esophagus experiments, in which the animal learns to associate a particular taste that has no nutritive value with the infusion of various nutrients into the duodenum. In later two-bottle preference tests, rats and mice highly prefer the taste paired with duodenal infusion of nu-

trients such as corn oil or glucose over the taste paired with isotonic saline infusion, suggesting that a signal generated by nutrients in the gut is positively reinforcing (Sclafani 2004). Although the signal in these experiments does not seem to be mediated to the brain via vagal afferents, the concept of reward from the gut resonates well with the view that subconscious perception of viscerosensory information contributes to a sense of internal well-being (Craig 2003). Thus, the popular expression "gut feeling" may have a plausible neurological explanation after all.

Lower gut. Converging recent evidence suggests that peptide YY (PYY) and glucagon-like peptide 1 secreted from L-cells mainly in the ileum, colon, and rectum seem to be most relevant for the control of appetite. Once PYY is released into the circulation, the first two amino acids are rapidly cleaved by dipeptidyl peptidase IV, resulting in PYY_{3-36} (Eberlein et al. 1989). This truncated peptide has a high affinity for the Y2 receptor and has anorexigenic potency in both rats and humans (Batterham et al. 2002, 2006; Chelikani et al. 2005b, 2006; Larhammar 1996), whereas PYY_{1-36} has a higher affinity for the Y1 and Y5 receptors and is orexigenic if injected into the brain. A physiological role for PYY in satiation is supported by the observation that PYY-null mice are slightly hyperphagic and develop obesity, both effects being reversible with PYY3-36 administration (Batterham et al. 2006). PYY thereby appears to selectively affect the satiating effects of proteins but not fats and carbohydrates (Batterham et al. 2006).

Because PYY_{3-36} can easily cross the blood-brain barrier, and direct application of PYY_{3-36} to neurons in the arcuate nucleus inhibits their activity, it has been suggested that the anorectic effect of peripheral PYY_{3-36} is mediated by Y2 receptors in the arcuate nucleus (Batterham et al. 2002). However, vagal afferents may also be involved in the anorectic effects of PYY_{3-36}, as abdominal vagotomy abolished both the anorectic effect and c-Fos expression in the arcuate nucleus following peripherally administered PYY_{3-36} (Koda et al. 2005). The Y2 receptor is expressed in at least some vagal afferents (Ghilardi et al. 1994, Koda et al. 2005, Zhang et al. 1997), and PYY stimulates firing of gastric vagal afferents (Koda et al. 2005).

Glucagon-like peptide-1 (GLP-1), also secreted from L-cells, is the site-specific splice product of the proglucagon gene also expressed in pancreatic islet cells, where its major cleavage product is glucagon. Not unlike PYY, GLP-1 release also appears to be stimulated by all three macronutrients by both an indirect, partly neural reflex originating in the upper small intestine and by direct mucosal contact in the lower gut (Anini et al. 2002, Herrmann et al. 1995, Herrmann-Rinke et al. 1995). GLP-1 actions on pancreatic hormone secretion and gastric emptying make it a powerful regulator of glycemic homeostasis (D'Alessio et al. 1995, Ritzel et al. 1995, Schirra & Goke 2005).

Peripheral administration of GLP-1 or its stable analog exendin-4, the naturally occurring peptide from the Gila monster lizard, enhance satiation and reduce food intake in humans and rats (Chelikani et al. 2005a, Gutzwiller et al. 1999). Because of rapid breakdown by dipeptidyl peptidase-VI, endogenously secreted GLP-1 has a very short half-life in plasma. Thus, although endogenous GLP-1 may partly act as a true hormone through the circulation on feeding circuits in the brain, it could also act in a paracrine fashion on vagal afferent nerve fibers within the gut mucosa. This view is supported by observations that GLP-1 receptor is expressed in nodose ganglion and that GLP-1 increases cytosolic Ca^{2+} and evokes action potentials in vagal afferent neurons (Kakei et al. 2002, Nakagawa et al. 2004). In addition, GLP-1 released from the ileum can also act through GLP-1 receptors expressed in the area postrema (Merchenthaler et al. 1999, Yamamoto et al. 2003) to activate catecholaminergic neurons with projections to the nucleus tractus solitarii (NTS), ventrolateral

medulla, and parabrachial nucleus (Yamamoto et al. 2003). The study of the site of action for the anorectic action of GLP-1 is complicated by the fact that the peptide is also expressed in a small population of neurons in the NTS with projections to the hypothalamus (Tang-Christensen et al. 2001).

In summary, vagal afferent nerve fibers in the gastrointestinal tract are in an excellent position to pick up information regarding volume and composition of luminal contents. They can directly detect mechanical touch, distension, and stretch at any location. In addition, they can indirectly detect the presence and concentration of all three macronutrients through mediation by peptides and transmitters released from specialized endothelial cells. These peptides are also absorbed into the bloodstream and can interact with receptors in specialized brain areas. There are still many unsolved issues regarding nutrition-related gut-to-brain communication. The relative contributions of the hormonal versus the paracrine, vagally mediated mode of action, to the control of satiation and appetite, as well as reflex control of gastrointestinal, pancreatic, and hepatic functions are uncertain. The relationship between individual vagal primary afferent neurons and the various populations of peptide-secreting enteroendocrine cells is ill defined.

Postabsorptive Sites: Pancreas, Liver, and Muscle

Portal vein. Except for longer-chain fatty acids reaching the general circulation through lymph vessels, absorbed nutrients are collected in the hepatic portal vein and first reach the liver, the most important metabolic factory in the body. The wall of the portal vein is innervated by vagal afferent fibers (Berthoud et al. 1992) that act as glucosensors (Burcelin et al. 2000, 2001; Niijima 1982). They have been implicated in the hypoglycemia-induced sympathoadrenal (Hevener et al. 1997, 2000) and feeding responses (Friedman et al. 1986), and in the satiating properties of glucose in

GLP-1: glucagon-like peptide-1

TNF: tumor
necrosis factor

the presence of insulin (Friedman et al. 1986, Stricker et al. 1977). More recently, vagal afferent portal vein glucosensors have also been implicated in the food intake–suppressing effects of high-protein diets mediated by intestinal gluconeogenesis (Mithieux et al. 2005).

Liver. The liver itself provides some information about availability of fuels that is used by the brain for the control of food intake, but the role of primary afferent nerve fibers is controversial. There are studies showing that changes in fatty acid oxidation and adenosine triphosphate (ATP) production are reflected in hepatocyte membrane potential and electrical activity of vagal afferent neurons (Horn et al. 2001, Lutz et al. 1996) (for reviews, see Friedman 1997, Langhans 2003). However, in a number of studies, careful denervation of the liver did not result in significant changes of ingestive behavior (for review, see Bellinger 1999), and few vagal afferent fibers are found in the hepatic parenchyma (Berthoud et al. 1992). Only the portal vein and portions of the liver are exclusively exposed to the hormonal and nutrient output of the gut; all other organs, including the brain, pancreas, and adipose tissue, receive these signals only after passing through heart and lungs.

Pancreas. Pancreatic β-cells have glucose-sensing capabilities, and signaling to the brain by their secretory products insulin and amylin are thus encoding glucose availability. Insulin acts directly on the hypothalamus and other brain areas (see next section), and amylin acts to decrease food intake and gastric emptying via receptors in the area postrema and ascending pathways to the hypothalamus and limbic structures (Lutz et al. 2001, Young 2005). Thus, absorbed nutrients on their way to storage, transformation, or utilization have available a number of communication pathways to the brain.

Stored Nutrients: Leptin and More

With the discovery of leptin, the existence and importance of direct signals from white adipose tissue, the major site of stored energy, to the brain has become clear. How leptin affects the brain is discussed in detail in the next section. Besides leptin, adipose tissue releases additional messengers such as the cytokines TNF-α and IL-1, which have potent effects on vagal primary afferent neurons (Ek et al. 1998) and dorsal vagal complex neurons (Emch et al. 2000, 2002). Adipose tissue also may send sensory information to the brain via dorsal root spinal afferent neurons (Bartness & Bamshad 1998).

The other functional energy store is hepatic glycogen. Although it has long been hypothesized that hepatic glycogen generates a signal to the brain by affecting hepatocyte membrane potential and vagal sensory neurons (Russek 1981), this hypothesis has not yet received general acceptance. In light of the discovery of leptin, it is interesting to speculate that an analogous hormonal signal is generated by hepatic glycogen. It is interesting to note that the liver is the only major peripheral organ from which no circulating factor (except for glucose and other metabolites) informing the brain regarding metabolism relevant for energy status has been identified.

INTEGRATION OF METABOLIC INFORMATION: IMPORTANCE OF THE HYPOTHALAMUS

Just as the brain must sense and respond to a large variety of external cues related to food availability, the brain also processes an array of internal signals. These signals convey information about the presence and type of nutrients within the gut, the quantity of fuels circulating within the blood, and the level of energy stored as fat. Although multiple brain areas are clearly involved, the hypothalamus has received the most attention as a primary site involved in the initial sensing of circulating nutritional cues (**Figure 3**).

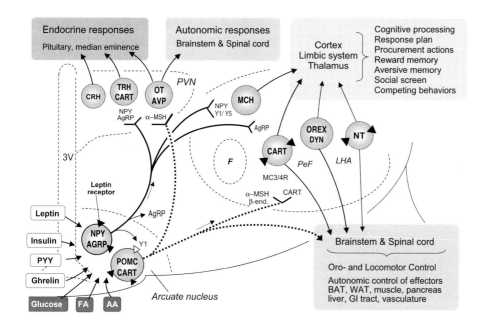

Figure 3

Hypothalamic peptidergic circuitry related to feeding and energy balance.

The Arcuate Nucleus: Critical Site for Regulation of Energy Balance

Much of our understanding of how the hypothalamus influences energy homeostasis stems from work on leptin action within the arcuate nucleus (ARC), although leptin is just one of many signals acting on ARC neurons and leptin also acts on sites outside the ARC. One population of leptin-sensitive neurons in the ARC expresses the potent orexigenic peptides neuropeptide Y (NPY) and Agouti-related protein (AgRP). These NPY/AgRP neurons are primary drivers of food intake, as central injection of either NPY or AgRP leads to a profound increase in food intake. Although constitutive genetic knockout of either NPY or AgRP exerts only subtle effects on body weight regulation or leptin sensitivity, acute ablation of the NPY/AgRP neurons in adult animals leads to significant hypophagia and weight loss (Gropp et al. 2005, Luquet et al. 2005). Thus, NPY/AgRP neurons play a significant role in the stimulation of feeding behavior, although other pathways can compensate for the loss of NPY and AgRP in early development.

Another population of ARC neurons expresses proopiomelanocortin (POMC) and cocaine- and amphetamine-regulated transcript (CART) (**Figure 3**). POMC is a large precursor protein that is processed into a variety of smaller products, notably alpha-melanocyte stimulating hormone (α-MSH). Central injection of α-MSH or its stable analog melanotan II (MTII) produces a marked suppression of food intake, whereas genetic deletion of POMC results in an obese phenotype (Krude et al. 1998, Yaswen et al. 1999). These observations suggest that POMC neurons exert a tonic inhibitory influence on food intake that is necessary for appropriate regulation of energy homeostasis. A model has emerged in which these two populations of neurons exert opposing effects on feeding behavior and energy metabolism, resulting in regulation of body weight and adiposity within normal levels (Morton et al. 2006). This scenario is not unlike the accelerator and brake of an automobile, and as such, these neurons are positioned to rapidly and robustly influence feeding behavior.

NPY/AgRP and POMC neurons interact on several levels. One is the local inhibition of POMC neurons via local axon collaterals from NPY neurons (Cowley et al. 2001, Roseberry et al. 2004). Since NPY neurons

NPY:
neuropeptide Y

AgRP:
Agouti-related peptide

POMC:
proopiomelanocortin

CART: cocaine-and amphetamine-regulated transcript

MTII: melanotan II

GABA: gamma-aminobutyric acid

Stat3: signal transducer and activator of transcription3

ERK: extracellular regulated kinase

cAMP: cyclic adenosine monophosphate

PDE3B: phosphodiesterase 3B

can also produce gamma-aminobutyric acid (GABA), if activated, they inhibit POMC neurons through both Y1 and GABA receptors. In the absence of reciprocal inhibition of NPY neurons by POMC neurons, this arrangement may be interpreted as a fail-safe system to protect eating as the default mode of action.

A second level of interaction occurs at downstream target neurons, as NPY/AgRP and POMC projections frequently converge on common downstream sites both within and outside the hypothalamus (see below).

Integration of Hormone and Nutrient Signals

The two neuron populations in the arcuate nucleus of the hypothalamus are sensitive to a number of signals conveying the overall availability of fuels that are either (*a*) circulating in the plasma, (*b*) ready to be absorbed from the gastrointestinal tract, or (*c*) stored as glycogen or fat.

As mentioned above, both NPY/AgRP and POMC neurons express leptin receptors and are directly regulated by leptin. Selective deletion of leptin receptors within POMC neurons results in an obese phenotype (Balthasar et al. 2005), although the effect is much less robust than loss of POMC or deletion of leptin receptors in all neurons. Leptin acts on NPY/AgRP and POMC neurons in an opposing fashion, inhibiting NPY/AgRP neurons while stimulating POMC neurons. Thus, while low leptin levels result in a profound stimulation of food intake and suppression of energy expenditure, high leptin levels result in suppression of food intake and stimulation of energy expenditure. The mechanism by which leptin regulates these neurons involves changes in both gene expression and acute membrane effects (Cowley et al. 2001; Schwartz et al. 1996, 1997; Spanswick et al. 1997). These observations suggest that leptin engages multiple signaling pathways to impact neuronal function, and recent data clearly support this observation (Munzberg & Myers 2005). The leptin receptor is a type 1 cytokine receptor traditionally proposed to signal through the Janus kinase-signal transducer and activator of transcription (Jak-Stat) pathway. Jak-Stat signaling is critical for leptin action on ARC neurons; leptin induces Stat3 activation in both POMC and NPY neurons (Elias et al. 1999, Hakansson & Meister 1998, Munzberg et al. 2003) and loss of leptin's ability to activate Stat3 leads to obesity (Bates et al. 2003, Xu et al. 2007). However, leptin also engages other intracellular pathways, including ERK, PI3K, and cAMP/PDE3B (Niswender et al. 2001, Zhao et al. 2002). Of these, PI3K signaling has received the most attention, as loss of PI3K signaling attenuates leptin-induced inhibition of food intake, regulation of neuropeptide expression, and stimulation of sympathetic nervous system activity (Morrison et al. 2005, Niswender et al. 2001, Rahmouni et al. 2003). Hypothalamic PI3K signaling also influences hepatic glucose production (Obici et al. 2002). Thus, even for this single hormone, the cellular and molecular mechanisms mediating its effects are complex. Yet leptin is not the only hormone to converge on hypothalamic neurons.

Fasting plasma insulin levels correlate positively with adiposity, and insulin acts in the brain to suppress activity of NPY neurons and stimulate POMC neurons, much like leptin does (Plum et al. 2006a, Woods & Seeley 2001). Furthermore, insulin injection into the third ventricle suppresses food intake and enhances peripheral glucose metabolism, whereas selective deletion of brain insulin receptor leads to obesity (Bruning et al. 2000, Obici et al. 2002, Woods et al. 1979). The overlapping actions of leptin and insulin are mediated in part by the overlapping signaling pathways activated by these hormones, as both leptin and insulin activate PI3K within hypothalamic neurons and require intact PI3K signaling to suppress food intake (Niswender et al. 2001, 2003). Whether leptin and insulin actually activate PI3K signaling within the same population of neurons is less clear. Recent data suggest that leptin and insulin commonly activate PI3K signaling within

POMC neurons but that these hormones may differentially regulate PI3K signaling within NPY/AgRP neurons (Plum et al. 2006b, Xu et al. 2005). Although the regulation and interaction is undoubtedly complex, the conclusion is that two seemingly disparate hormones converge on a common signaling molecule within a common neuronal population.

Availability of fuels in the near future is signaled from the gut by gastrointestinal hormones such as ghrelin, GLP-1, and PYY. Ghrelin stimulates NPY neurons through growth-hormone secretagogue receptors (GHS-R) (Kohno et al. 2003), whereas PYY(3-36) directly inhibits NPY neurons via Y2 autoreceptors (Riediger et al. 2004). In addition, gut signals can influence activity of neurons in the arcuate nucleus via ascending projections from the dorsal vagal complex.

Immediate availability of fuels is signaled by glucose, fatty acids, and amino acids, for which specific sensing mechanisms have been described in arcuate nucleus and other neurons of the hypothalamus. Some neurons are sensitive to physiological variations in glucose concentrations (Levin 2002), and these changes are mediated in part via signaling pathways similar to those mediating glucose-stimulated insulin secretion in pancreatic beta cells (van den Top & Spanswick 2006). The relevance of these pathways is evident from recent work demonstrating that deletion of hypothalamic glucose transporter 2 (GLUT2) (Marty et al. 2006) or glucokinase (Yang et al. 2007) induces significant increases in feeding behavior and hypothalamic gene expression, presumably by altering cellular energy status and/or AMP-kinase activity (Li et al. 2006). ARC neurons also utilize defined signaling mechanisms to respond to fatty acids and amino acids, which both suppress food intake and alter peripheral glucose metabolism when administered into the brain ventricles (Cota et al. 2006, Kahn et al. 2005, Obici & Rossetti 2003). The ability of these molecules to alter neuronal function appears to be mediated by evolutionarily conserved nutrient-sensing pathways such

as AMP-activated protein kinase and mammalian target of rapamycin. These signaling molecules are acutely responsive to variations in cellular energy status, and thus it is not surprising that they also function within nutrient sensing neurons.

Finally, it should be recognized that arcuate NPY and POMC neurons are not isolated from the rest of the brain, but rather receive neural inputs from various brain areas, notably from orexin/hypocretin neurons in the lateral hypothalamus (Horvath et al. 1999, Muroya et al. 2004) and several limbic forebrain sites (DeFalco et al. 2001). The role that these synaptic inputs play in modulating their response to circulating hormones and nutrients is unknown.

The New Frontier: Neural Integration Through Converging Intracellular Signaling Cascades

As progress has been made in defining the intracellular signaling pathways mediating the effects of these various hormonal, transmitter, and metabolite signals, it becomes apparent that the richness of these intracellular signaling pathways and their coupling to changes in neuronal excitability, peptide expression, and synaptic connectivity may provide the major substrate for integrative processes (**Figure 4**). The convergence of insulin and leptin signaling on PI3K, mentioned above, is one example. This opens new possibilities for the development of pharmacological and behavioral tools in the fight against obesity.

Two of the most exciting new players in intraneuronal integration are AMP-activated kinase (AMPK) and mammalian target of rapamycin (mTOR). AMPK is an evolutionarily conserved serine-threonine kinase that responds to changes in cellular energy levels (Xue & Kahn 2006). AMPK is sensitive to the AMP/ATP ratio, such that depletion of cellular energy stores activates AMPK signaling. Whereas in peripheral tissues, AMPK activation leads to rigorous defense of cellular energy availability through

GLUT2: glucose transporter 2

AMPK: adenosine monophosphate activated protein kinase

mTOR: mammalian target of rapamycin

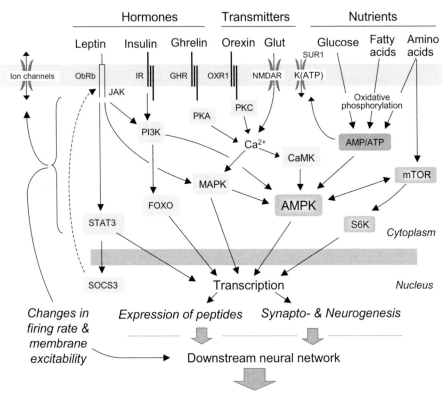

Hormones: Leptin, Insulin, Ghrelin

Transmitters: Orexin, Glut

Nutrients: Glucose, Fatty acids, Amino acids

Ion channels, ObRb, IR, GHR, OXR1, NMDAR, K(ATP), SUR1

JAK, PKA, PKC, PI3K, Ca²⁺, CaMK, MAPK, FOXO, STAT3, AMPK, AMP/ATP, mTOR, S6K, SOCS3

Oxidative phosphorylation

Cytoplasm

Transcription — Nucleus

Changes in firing rate & membrane excitability

Expression of peptides

Synapto- & Neurogenesis

Downstream neural network

Changes in food intake & autonomic/endocrine function

Figure 4

Molecular mechanisms of integration of various signals by hypothetical "nutrient-sensing neurons" in the mediobasal hypothalamus.

increased oxidation, in the arcuate nucleus, AMPK activation increases food intake and energy conservation (Minokoshi et al. 2004). Glucose, leptin, and insulin each inhibit (Lee et al. 2005, Minokoshi et al. 2004), and ghrelin increases, hypothalamic AMPK activity (Andersson et al. 2004). In addition, constitutive activation of AMPK is sufficient to block leptin-dependent decreases in food intake, suggesting that the inhibition of AMPK is necessary for leptin action (Minokoshi et al. 2004). Taken together, these observations provide strong support for AMPK signaling as a key component in the hypothalamic regulation of food intake and indicate that multiple hormone- and nutrient-signaling pathways converge on hypothalamic AMPK.

mTOR is another evolutionarily conserved energy sensor that has assumed a specific functional role in hypothalamic regula-

tion of energy balance (Cota et al. 2006). In many peripheral tissues, mTOR plays a key role in coupling cellular energy status and growth factor signaling to protein synthesis, growth, and division. Recent data indicate that mTOR is expressed within key populations of mediobasal hypothalamic neurons and is sensitive to metabolic state, and that the ability of amino acids to suppress food intake and regulate neuropeptide expression may depend on mTOR (Cota et al. 2006, Morrison et al. 2007). Evidence also suggests that hypothalamic mTOR contributes to leptin action, with leptin activating hypothalamic mTOR and inhibition of mTOR blocking leptin-dependent suppression of food intake (Cota et al. 2006). Considering that insulin is also a classic regulator of mTOR signaling, likely via activation of PI3K, this activation of mTOR by leptin may reflect a downstream effect of PI3K signaling. Although this work is very early, it suggests that mTOR, much like AMPK, represents a potential site of convergence for both hormonal and nutrient sensing. To add to this complexity, there is also strong evidence for an interaction between AMPK and mTOR (Marshall 2006).

One important unanswered question is how much of these converging signaling cascades are represented within single neurons of a particular phenotype such as NPY and POMC neurons, or whether they are represented in separate neurons. Another question that has not received much attention is how information from other brain areas mediated by neural afferents to the leptin receptor-bearing arcuate nucleus neurons (DeFalco et al. 2001, Horvath et al. 1999, Muroya et al. 2004) is integrated with the metabolic signals. Nevertheless, the consensus is that the hypothalamus, and particularly key neuronal populations within the ARC, are capable of responding to an array of nutritional signals, and that these signals are transmitted to downstream brain areas involved in satiation, autonomic outflow, neuroendocrine regulation, learning and memory, and reward.

Translating Metabolic Sensor Output into Adaptive Biological Responses

ARC neurons respond to a variety of circulating nutrient signals, but their ability to regulate food intake is dependent on downstream neuronal targets. These downstream neurons are thus second-order targets and exist in many areas both within and outside the hypothalamus (**Figure 3**). The major recipients of arcuate input are other hypothalamic areas, in particular the paraventricular nucleus (PVN) and lateral/perifornical hypothalamic areas (LHA). These two brain regions are classically associated with the regulation of food intake and autonomic output, and each brain area contains a variety of neuropeptides associated with energy balance control. The prevailing model suggests that input from NPY/AgRP neurons is opposed by input from POMC neurons, this "metabolic" informa-

tion is integrated with input from additional brain areas, and these downstream neurons in turn project widely to third- and higher-order neurons located in many areas of the brain and spinal cord (Berthoud 2002).

This downstream convergence is particularly true for AgRP and aMSH, as these two molecules act on the same population of melanocortin 3 and 4 receptors (MC3R and MC4R). AgRP antagonizes melanocortin receptors while POMC-derived aMSH stimulates these receptors, and the competition occurring at these receptors is significant for the regulation of food intake, energy expenditure, sympathetic outflow, neuroendocrine function, and glucose homeostasis (Cone 2005). MC4R is particularly significant, as MC4R deficiency induces profound obesity, hyperphagia, and hyperglycemia (Butler 2006), and is currently the most common monogenetic cause of human obesity (Farooqi & O'Rahilly 2006).

The lateral/perifornical hypothalamus provides a compelling example of this interconnection and integration. LHA neurons are classically associated with feeding behavior, and electrical stimulation of the LHA produces a rapid and profound induction of feeding that ends immediately upon cessation of the stimulation. Neurons within the LHA contain several food-regulatory neuropeptides (hypocretin/orexin, melanin-concentrating hormone, neurotensin, and histamine), and many of these neurons receive direct input from ARC NPY/AgRP and POMC neurons. In addition to this metabolic information, the LHA also receives information from brain areas associated with reward, motivation, learning, and memory (orbitofrontal cortex, nucleus accumbens, amygdala, and ventral tegmental area), from areas associated with sensory input (insular and olfactory cortex), and from brainstem areas associated with vagal and visceral sensory input, sensory motor coordination, and arousal (NTS, parabrachial nucleus, and locus coeruleus). Although the role that many of these specific connections play is unclear,

aMSH:
alpha-melanocyte stimulating hormone

MC3R:
melanocortin receptor 3

MC4R:
melanocortin receptor 4

the consensus is that the LHA is receiving input from a wide variety of areas, including ARC-derived metabolic information. In turn, the LHA projects widely through the entire brain (Berthoud 2002), from the cortex to the spinal cord. Consequently, information processed within the LHA has the capacity to affect nearly every neural activity.

Similarly, the PVN also represents a downstream target of ARC neurons, which also receives information from a variety of locations and equally projects to a variety of locations. In particular, the PVN is classically associated with neuroendocrine function via the hypothalamic pituitary axis, as well as a regulation of the autonomic nervous system. For example, thyrotropin-releasing hormone neurons receive direct input from ARC neurons, and their opposing regulation of the thyrotropin-releasing hormone neuron contributes to the metabolic regulation of the thyroid axis (Lechan & Fekete 2006). Thus, ARC-derived metabolic information has the capacity to influence a variety of behavioral endpoints via the LHA as well as neuroendocrine and autonomic endpoints via the PVN.

In addition, ARC neurons also project to a variety of additional areas besides the PVN and LHA. For example, leptin-sensitive POMC neurons project directly to brainstem areas associated with the response to satiety signals and autonomic outflow (Berthoud et al. 2006, Zheng et al. 2005). The reciprocal relationship between areas in the brainstem and hypothalamus is particularly important for understanding the coordination between food intake and autonomic nervous system activity. This issue has been addressed in several recent reviews (Berthoud 2004, Ellacott & Cone 2004, Grill & Kaplan 2002) and is not further discussed here.

Taken together, available evidence clearly indicates that this neural network is positioned to modulate an array of neuronal processes that play critical roles in the regulation of feeding behavior, autonomic outflow, neuroendocrine function, and more cognitive aspects such as reward, learning, and memory.

DEALING WITH FOOD IN THE ENVIRONMENT: FORAGING, PERCEPTION, AND PROCUREMENT

The metabolic controls of eating discussed above are embedded in a much larger neural system allowing animals and humans to interact with the food-providing environment. In the mostly restrictive environments of the past, evolutionary pressures forged development of neural systems that made it easy to locate, secure, store, preserve, prepare, and cook high-quality foods, and to pass valuable experience with these activities on to offspring. These activities require neural functions that are very different from the ones involved in managing the internal milieu, but they are at the same time powerfully influenced by the metabolic state. Although these neural systems and functions are used for most other behaviors, their evolution must have been shaped to a large extent by the need to procure and eat food.

The relationship between the internal regulatory system that is termed "metabolic" and these externally oriented systems termed "cognitive-hedonic" is shown in **Figure 5**. Major factors operating during the foraging and procurement phase are prior experience,

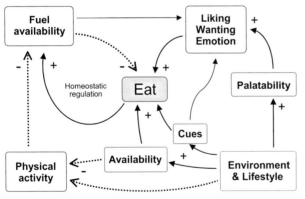

Figure 5

Interactions between metabolic-homeostatic and cognitive-hedonic processes in the control of food intake and energy balance.

availability, and cost. Factors operating during the consummatory phase are cephalic and postingestive feed-forward mechanisms such as the sight, smell, and taste (flavor, palatability) of already familiar foods. Other factors include social context as well as ethnic and religious habits and rules. The many changes in environment and modern lifestyle that put pressure on food intake and energy balance have been discussed elsewhere (Hill & Peters 1998, Hill et al. 2003, Levitsky 2005, Rolls 2003, Ulijaszek 2002).

We discuss below some of the basic neural mechanisms and systems thought to be involved in this interaction with the food environment. First, we draw attention to the elaborate sensory and cognitive mechanisms necessary for successful foraging and procurement of food. Then we discuss the concepts and potential neural substrates of reward, liking, and wanting, and their role in ingestive behavior.

Foraging and Procurement: Lots of Brain and Muscle Work

Procurement of food and water is one of the most important behaviors for any life form. Invertebrate animals that are even more primitive, such as insects, use elaborate navigation and communication strategies to secure food sources and guarantee survival. An example is the honeybee, which engages in a dance to communicate the location and abundance of a food source to other worker bees in the hive (von Frisch 1967). Recent studies capitalizing on advancements in radar technology demonstrated that recruits use the information embedded in the waggle dance to find the food location hundreds of meters away, even taking into consideration strong side winds, suggesting, "[T]he bee's experience of the terrain modulates the encoding of spatial information in the dance and that interactions between path integration and visual landmarks are computed in the context of dance communication" (Riley et al. 2005). Although the bee's brain is relatively small, it is able to generate such a complex memory, encode the salient information into dance movements, and, in the reverse, lay down a working memory from watching the dance and use it to find the food source—and all this not for immediate personal reward, but for the future benefit of the bee society. Ants use similarly elaborate communication skills to teach each other to find food on their long journeys through the forest floor (Franks & Richardson 2006).

These examples illustrate that, even early in evolution, large portions of the nervous system have been dedicated to survival mechanisms such as procuring food. It should not be surprising that the huge cortex of modern humans harbor an extraordinary ability to deal with the procurement of food. Memorial representations of foods and food cues are available to the foraging human long before food is actually seen, smelled, or tasted.

Multisensory Perception Leads to the Generation of Food Representations

A growing number of electrophysiological recording studies in monkeys and neuroimaging studies in humans suggest that representations of experience with foods are generated in areas of the prefrontal cortex, insular cortex, and perhaps the amygdala. These areas receive converging information through all sensory modalities (**Figure 6**), and thus representations contain any number of sensory attributes, including shape, color, taste, and flavor, as well as links to time, location, and social context (see bee example above). Furthermore, links to significant (positive or negative) consequences of ingestion of the food, its reward value, can also be bundled into the same representations (de Araujo et al. 2005).

Olfactory information is relayed through the olfactory bulb and primary olfactory cortex (consisting of mainly piriform cortex) to the orbitofrontal cortex (de Araujo et al. 2003c; Rolls et al. 1998, 2003a; Verhagen 2006). Odor molecules are detected by a large number of receptor cells in the olfactory epithelium that each project to glomeruli in the olfactory bulb. In the mouse, there are about 1000 and in primates about 350 genes encoding different receptor proteins (Buck & Axel 1991, Zhang & Firestein 2002). Odor stimuli produce specific spatial patterns of activity, so-called odor images or odor maps across the olfactory bulb glomeruli that are not unlike electrical activity maps produced by the visual system (Shepherd 2006). The mammalian olfactory system is characterized by two modes of perception. Orthonasal olfaction is mainly used to detect potentially beneficial or harmful signals in the environment, whereas retronasal olfaction is used in combination with the gustatory and somatosensory systems to generate the sense of flavor (Murphy et al. 1977, Rozin 1982) (**Figure 6**).

Visual and auditory information are also relayed via their respective thalamic relays to the orbitofrontal cortex (Verhagen 2007). Visual information plays a key role in the recognition of potential foods, particularly when it

is serving as a cue in the form of a picture or image in the absence of smell and taste, for example on the television screen.

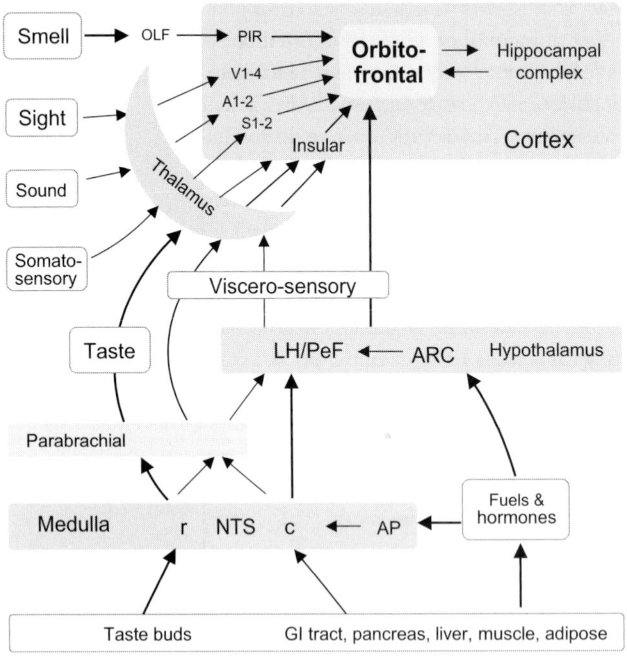

Gustatory and visceroceptive information reaches the orbitofrontal cortex via relays in the solitary nucleus, thalamus, and insular cortex (Craig 2003; de Araujo et al. 2003a,c; Verhagen 2006). In addition, metabolic information from circulating fuels and hormones can potentially reach the orbitofrontal cortex via sensors in the caudal medulla and hypothalamus as discussed in the previous section. Information from mediobasal hypothalamic nutrient sensors is relayed to the lateral hypothalamus, which has profuse projections to most of the cortex (Saper 2000).

Finally, somatosensory information, particularly from the oral cavity, also reaches the orbitofrontal cortex via thalamus and somatosensory cortex (for review, see Verhagen 2006). It includes the sensations of fine touch (creaminess) (de Araujo et al. 2003b, Rolls et al. 1999), deep pressure (crunchiness) (Rolls et al. 2003b), temperature and pain (burning sensation of hot chili pepper) (Kadohisa et al. 2004), and astringency (e.g., dry wine) (Kadohisa et al. 2005), which are major determinants for the palatability of everyday foods and criteria for the development of commercial foods.

The orbitofrontal cortex does not, of course, work in isolation, but is in intimate contact with other cortical areas, such as the prefrontal, anterior cingulate, insular, perirhinal, and entorhinal cortices, as well as with the hippocampal formation and the amygdala, collectively often referred to as paralimbic cortex (for review, see Verhagen 2006). It is within these areas that polymodal representations of experiences with foods are thought to be stored, updated, and retrieved for guiding future appetitive behavior. Interference or loss of memorial representations can have powerful effects on food intake. It has been long known that amnesic patients readily eat a second meal offered immediately after a full meal (Hebben et al. 1985, Higgs 2005). On the other hand, enhancing memory for a

Figure 6

Converging of sensory pathways to areas of the polymodal association cortex thought to result in the formation of food representations.

recent meal, by cuing study participants to re-call items eaten at lunch, suppresses intake in an afternoon snack (Higgs 2005). Studies in rats also suggest that the hippocampus may be critically involved with a specific type of memory-inhibition function that could nor-mally lead to the suppression of food intake (Davidson et al. 2005).

REWARD AND PUNISHMENT AS BASIC PRINCIPLES GUIDING BEHAVIOR

The first step in dealing with food in the envi-ronment is to know what is beneficial and what is harmful, and most, but not all, of this knowl-edge is acquired through learning processes. As discussed above, neural representations of experience with particular foods together with environmental and social context information are available from constantly updated memo-rial traces laid down in a network including the orbitofrontal, prefrontal, anterior cingu-late, and insular cortices and the hippocampal formation. Noninvasive imaging techniques have clearly demonstrated that simply think-ing about food can modulate neural activity in specific brain areas known to be involved in the cognitive controls of appetitive behav-iors (Arana et al. 2003) and can lead to physi-ological responses such as saliva, gastric acid, and insulin secretion. Also, in the absence of real food, food cues that have been previously linked to specific foods can serve as condi-tioned stimuli to recall their memorial rep-resentations (Davidson 2000, Davidson et al. 2000).

Conditioned Food Intake and Aversion

Conditioned taste aversion (CTA) is the best-characterized appetitive learning phe-nomenon, with extensive data regarding par-ticipating brain structures and neurotransmit-ters and their receptors, as well as intracellular signaling pathways (Berman & Dudai 2001, Desmedt et al. 2003; see also review by Welzl

et al. 2001). Many of the brain structures in-volved in CTA such as parabrachial nucleus, amygdala, insular cortex, and nucleus accum-bens are also involved in the sensory and re-warding aspects of taste processing.

Learning about the rewarding effects of palatable food is less well characterized. Le-sion experiments in rats suggest different but complementary roles for the orbitofrontal cortex and basomedial amygdala in learning about representations of specific experiences with food and using them to guide appeti-tive behavior. It had long been demonstrated that food intake can be conditioned over time by repeatedly pairing the presentation of food with a tone or light (conditioned stimulus, or CS+) in hungry rats. After learning this task, even sated rats will approach and consume food upon exposure to the CS+ (Weingarten 1983). When the reinforcer (food) in this Pavlovian conditioning task is later deval-ued by pairing it with LiCl, rats will ex-hibit reduced approach behavior to the food cup (conditioned response). Rats with ex-citotoxic lesions placed before learning the conditioning task in the orbitofrontal cortex (Gallagher et al. 1999) or basolateral amyg-dala (Hatfield et al. 1996), although still able to learn the conditioning task, no longer ex-hibited the reduced approach behavior af-ter LiCl devaluation. When placed after the food approach-conditioning phase, only le-sions in the orbitofrontal cortex, but not the basolateral amygdala, resulted in loss of the devaluation-induced reduction in approach behavior (Pickens et al. 2003). Thus, the baso-lateral amygdala seems to be critical to learn-ing representations that link cues to the in-centive properties of outcomes but not for maintaining such representations. In contrast, the orbitofrontal cortex seems to be criti-cal for maintaining memorial representations that link cues to the incentive properties of outcomes, for updating them with new infor-mation, and for using them to guide appetitive behavior (Pickens et al. 2003).

Imaging studies in human subjects point to the same cortical areas for encoding the predictive reward value of olfactory cues. In hungry subjects scanned during learning and anticipation of food-based olfactory rewards, neural responses associated with the acquisition of picture-odor contingencies were found in the insular and orbitofrontal cortices and in the amygdala (Gottfried et al. 2003). There are many more neuroimaging studies, all pointing to the prefrontal/orbitofrontal cortex and amygdala as playing crucial roles in dealing with the acquisition, storage, and recall of representations of experience with food. Representations of experience with food are not only important for the procurement process. Because they contain an emotional component, they are also important for the determination of the subjective value we assign to a particular food. This emotional component, the rewarding or pleasurable aspect of food, is discussed below.

These conditioning and learning mechanisms are exploited by the advertisement industry (Hoek & Gendall 2006, Linn 2004). It is well known to parents that when shopping, children who are television watchers are more likely to demand certain food items. The power of culturally based brand images to influence behavioral choices through measurable changes in neural activity has been recently demonstrated in a human imaging study (McClure et al. 2004).

Neural Correlates of Liking

Emotions may have evolved to make animals engage in behaviors with a beneficial outcome and to avoid engaging in behaviors that potentially diminish survival (Cardinal et al. 2002). Applied to nutrition, tasting physiologically beneficial foods elicits a feeling of pleasure, while tasting bitter, potentially toxic foods elicits negative emotions. Although the neural pathways necessary for taste perception are well described, the mechanisms by which pleasurable taste and flavor guide intake are less well understood.

Berridge & Robinson (2003) have outlined the potential psychological components that

constitute reward into learning, liking, and wanting, as well as the major brain structures most likely involved. The characteristic orofacial expressions displayed by decerebrate rats (Grill & Norgren 1978) and anencephalic infants (Steiner 1973) in response to sweet taste strongly suggest that the forebrain is not the only brain area involved in experiencing the hedonic impact or liking of pleasant stimuli. Berridge & Robinson (2003) refer to these expressions as objective affective reactions or implicit affect, and to the psychological process as "liking."

Besides neural circuits in the hindbrain, the nucleus accumbens and ventral pallidum in the limbic forebrain are other key components of the distributed neural network mediating liking of palatable foods (**Figure 7**). The mu-opioid receptor appears to play a crucial role. Local injection of the selective mu-opioid agonist DAMGO into the nucleus accumbens elicits voracious food intake, particularly of palatable sweet or high-fat foods (Kelley et al. 2002, Will et al. 2003, Zhang & Kelley 2000). This increased consumption of highly palatable foods appears to be due to increased liking, as morphine microinjections into this area increased the number of positive affective reactions (Pecina & Berridge 2000), and microinjection of a selective mu-opioid antagonist reduced sucrose drinking (Kelley et al. 1996). Based on the resulting c-Fos plumes, the most sensitive area for this effect was the caudal shell of the nucleus accumbens, near the border with the adjacent core (Pecina & Berridge 2000). Contrary to the long-held view, the mesolimbic dopamine system does not play any role in the affect or liking of pleasurable stimuli but is crucial for the mobilization of motor behavior to obtain pleasurable stimuli, and was termed "wanting" by Berridge and Robinson (Berridge 1996, Berridge & Robinson 2003) (see below).

To consciously experience and give subjective ratings of pleasure from palatable foods (liking), humans very likely use areas in the prefrontal and cingulate cortex (Kringelbach 2004). Thus, the neurological substrate

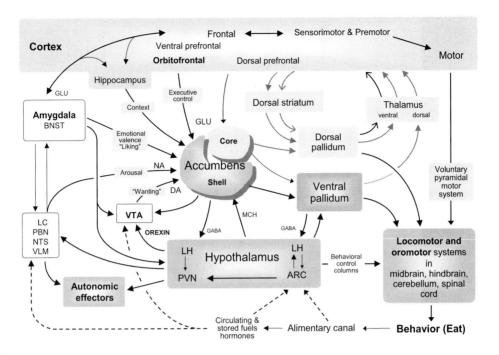

Figure 7

Translation of food motivation into action.

responsible for experiencing pleasure from food is complex and distributed throughout the neuraxis and cannot be conveniently eliminated by tissue lesions (**Figure 7**). One of the common denominators of the distributed network may be opioidergic transmission, particularly through the mu-opioid receptor. However, chronic treatment with the nonselective opioid receptor antagonist naloxone, although clearly curbing intake of palatable foods (Levine & Billington 2004, Levine et al. 1995), has not resulted in significant changes of energy balance (de Zwaan & Mitchell 1992). The mu-opioid receptor-deficient mouse showed some resistance to diet-induced obesity, but the effect was apparently not mediated by changes in food intake (Tabarin et al. 2005). Newer, more selective opioid antagonists currently tested in rats may be more promising (Statnick et al. 2003, Zhang et al. 2006). Another possible denominator of the distributed pleasure network may be signaling through the CB1 cannabinoid receptor, which is distributed throughout most

of the components of the network. Like opioids, endocannabinoids signaling through the CB1 receptor may also selectively suppress appetite for palatable foods (Cooper 2004).

Neural Correlates of Wanting

The other psychological process involved in reward is motivation, incentive salience, or "wanting," as termed by Berridge and Robinson (Berridge 1996, Berridge & Robinson 2003). Although liking a food is typically followed by wanting and eating it, wanting is a dissociable process that has a distinct underlying neural substrate. This distinction grew mainly out of research on drug addiction, where stimuli that are often no longer liked are still intensely wanted. Just as learning and liking do, motivation has a conscious or explicit and an unconscious or implicit aspect. As stated by Berridge & Robinson, "[W]anting or incentive salience is a motivational, rather than an affective, component of reward. Its attribution transforms mere sensory information about rewards and their cues (sights, sounds and smells) into attractive, desired, riveting incentives" (Berridge & Robinson 2003, p. 510). Dopaminergic projections from the ventral tegmental area to the nucleus accumbens (part of the mesolimbic dopamine system) are the most crucial component of the implicit or unconscious wanting system (Dayan & Balleine 2002, Kaczmarek & Kiefer 2000, Wyvell & Berridge 2000) (**Figure 7**). Manipulation of this dopamine system powerfully influences wanting (instrumental performance for and consumption of) drugs or food, but not liking (Berridge & Robinson 2003, Cannon & Palmiter 2003, Pecina et al. 2003, Wyvell & Berridge 2001). The lateral hypothalamus is also involved in wanting, as electrical stimulation of this area induces rats to vigorously self-stimulate and eat (want) food, even though it does not make them like the food more (Berridge & Valenstein 1991).

The mesolimbic wanting system is intimately connected with elements of the metabolic regulatory system. Leptin and insulin can act directly on mesolimbic dopamine neurons to modulate wanting for food (Figlewicz 2003, Fulton et al. 2006, Hommel et al. 2006). Leptin can also indirectly modulate mesolimbic dopamine neurons via action on lateral hypothalamic orexin and neurotensin neurons with projections to the ventral tegmental area (Harris et al. 2005).

TOP-DOWN EXECUTIVE CONTROL OF INGESTIVE BEHAVIOR

Corticolimbic mechanisms of reward appear to be under executive control of the prefrontal cortex. The prefrontal cortex receives sensory information from inside and outside the body as well as emotional and cognitive information from the limbic system, and it is intimately connected to cortical areas involved in motor planning and execution. It is thus in an ideal position to translate all available homeostatic and environmental information into adaptive behavioral responses—in brief, to make choices and decisions (Balleine 2007, Murray et al. 2007).

The right prefrontal cortex appears to play a critical role in behavioral restraint and moral self-control by keeping reward-generating mechanisms in check. Damage to the right frontal cortex can lead to a general disregard for the long-term adverse consequences of behavioral choices, such as increased risk taking and excessive food intake (Alonso-Alonso & Pascual-Leone 2007). A "gourmand syndrome," associated with passion for eating highly palatable foods, was reported in two case studies of humans with damage to the right frontal hemisphere (Regard & Landis 1997, Uher & Treasure 2005). It is interesting to speculate that part of this asymmetry is based on the asymmetries in the peripheral autonomic nervous system representing homeostatic activity in the dorsal posterior insula, known to be densely connected with the prefrontal cortex (Craig 2003, 2005).

Modern neuroimaging studies also support the importance of a balanced control by distinct areas of the prefrontal cortex in the control of food intake. Successful dieters who have significantly higher levels of dietary restraint in comparison with nondieters show increased neural activity in the right dorsolateral prefrontal cortex in response to food consumption (DelParigi et al. 2007). In contrast, obese subjects show less activation of the left dorsolateral prefrontal cortex in response to food (Le et al. 2006), and patients suffering from the Prader-Willi syndrome, who experience severe disturbances in appetite control resulting in hyperphagia and obesity, show increased activity in the ventromedial prefrontal cortex when viewing pictures of food after glucose consumption (Miller et al. 2007). This latter finding is consistent with a role of the ventromedial prefrontal cortex in the mediation of food intake driven by conditioned (learned) motivational cues in sated rats (Petrovich et al. 2007).

THE CAUSES OF OBESITY

Predisposition to develop obesity can theoretically result from any pathological malfunction or lack of adaptation to environmental influences of the highly complex control systems discussed above. Current research is mainly focusing on two major aspects of the control system: inadequate sensing of ingested nutrients and overstimulation of reward mechanisms.

Loss of Appropriate Nutrient Sensing

When signals that inform the brain about the availability of nutrients lose their capacity to modulate energy balance effectors, either starvation or obesity results. This is best illustrated by the extreme obesity resulting from defects in leptin signaling and its rapid reversal upon leptin treatment in leptin-deficient mice and humans. However, the overwhelming majority of obese humans do not lack leptin, but instead have paradoxically high circulating-leptin levels consistent with their obesity. Very few respond favorably to exogenous leptin (Heymsfield et al. 1999, Hukshorn et al. 2000), suggesting a state of leptin resistance. Obesity and leptin resistance also develop in mice and rats put on a high-fat diet, in cats and dogs fed today's palatable foods, and in bears and baboons eating from garbage cans (Banks et al. 2006, Wilsey & Scarpace 2004). In seasonal animals, leptin is effective when endogenous leptin levels are low during winter, but it is ineffective when leptin levels are high during summer (Rousseau et al. 2003). The modern human environment could thus be regarded as the equivalent of continuous "summer" with natural leptin resistance. Before the modern era, this "summer" used to be broken by periods of scarcer food supply that quickly restored leptin sensitivity. This seems to be confirmed by better success with leptin treatment when it is given as an adjunct to moderate food-intake restriction (Fogteloo et al. 2003, Rosenbaum et al. 2002) (see sidebar Current Obesity Treatment Options).

CURRENT OBESITY TREATMENT OPTIONS

Only a few drugs currently have approval by the Food and Drug Administration for the long-term treatment of obesity in the United States. Unfortunately, weight loss with these medications is usually not more than 10%, and substantial motivation and lifestyle modification remain essential. The most efficacious current treatment is bariatric surgery, which although highly invasive produces significant and sustained reductions in body weight in many patients. Considering that many major advances in the neurobiology of ingestive behavior have occurred only within the past 10–15 years, it is perhaps too early for much of this information to translate to drug development and clinical testing.

If leptin is the main negative feedback signal for the putative adipostat, why does this seemingly maladaptive response occur? Why does leptin stop signaling when it is most needed? Several explanations have been offered. One intriguing possibility is that high-fat diets and obesity damage or alter the blood-brain barrier, such that leptin is less capable of accessing brain areas regulating food intake. A putative mechanism for reduced leptin transport is the increase in triglycerides that occurs in response to high-fat feeding (Banks et al. 2004, 2006). Interestingly, triglycerides are also increased during periods of prolonged starvation, and in these times a mechanism to suppress the anorectic effects of leptin may have proved advantageous (Banks et al. 2004, 2006). An alternative explanation is that elevated triglycerides signal dependence on milk ingestion after birth, a time when food intake can hardly be too high and there is no use for satiety signaling by leptin. This would fit the observation that the blockade of leptin transport through the blood-brain barrier is specific to milk triglycerides (Banks et al. 2004). In any case, the thought that the obesity crisis might be caused by a case of "mistaken identity" is puzzling and requires careful further testing.

Others find the explanation in defective leptin receptor–mediated signaling within critical hypothalamic neurons. As discussed in detail above, leptin engages multiple intracellular-signaling pathways to regulate feeding relevant neurons. Like most signaling cascades, these pathways are both negatively and positively regulated, and suppression of positive or induction of negative regulators of leptin signaling has been suggested as a potential mechanism for leptin resistance. Neuron-specific deletion of two negative regulators, suppressor of cytokine signaling 3 (Mori et al. 2004) or protein tyrosine phosphatase-1B (Bence et al. 2006), protects mice from developing leptin resistance, hyperphagia, and dietary obesity. Therefore, leptin resistance is necessary for the development of obesity in response to high-fat diet in rodents, and interventions that improve leptin sensitivity would be expected to similarly protect humans against obesity. Data from polygenic models of obesity indicate that obesity-prone rats display a reduced sensitivity to at least central leptin and insulin even prior to exposure to high-fat diets (Clegg et al. 2005, Levin et al. 2004). These observations suggest that genetic variation in leptin sensitivity may underlie variations in susceptibility to obesity.

In many cases, this leptin resistance appears to be reversible. In hibernators, leptin resistance turns on and off during periods of weight gain or loss, suggesting that the ability to stimulate or suppress leptin signaling is a normal physiological property of these critical neurons (Krol et al. 2006). Leptin resistance also does not only result from high-fat feeding, but additional conditions such as age (Wilsey & Scarpace 2004) or pregnancy (Denis et al. 2003) are associated with leptin resistance, while prolonged receptor stimulation also leads to resistance (Pal & Sahu 2003). The fact that diet-induced leptin resistance is easily reversible by putting animals back on normal chow diet also supports this conclusion.

Finally, an alternative explanation for the obesity epidemic is that leptin has not evolved as a signal to prevent obesity. This model suggests that leptin's biological action happens only at low circulating levels, where its absence is a very strong survival signal to find and eat food, and normal levels merely stop this emergency mode but do little in preventing increases in adiposity. As an extension of this model, it is possible that mechanisms have evolved to actively dampen the anorectic effects of supranormal leptin levels, as this action of leptin may have conferred a disadvantage in a restrictive environment. Therefore, this model would propose that leptin resistance does not represent pathological damage to the regulatory system, but instead is an appropriate physiological reaction to positive energy balance. Leptin-resistance in hibernating animals in late summer, a time when they are already obese but need to continue eating for winter, supports this possibility.

Overstimulation of Reward Mechanisms

Most rodent strains are susceptible to diet-induced obesity, and the changes in food intake and body weight in rats given access to a variety of palatable foods are striking (Sclafani & Springer 1976). This diet is very similar to the cafeteria diet many modern humans are faced with every day. As discussed in detail above, the hedonic impact of heightened palatability appears to be one of the most important factors for stimulating appetite and consumption.

Given that at least parts of the reward system are subject to negative feedback control by the availability of endogenous nutrients such as leptin and insulin (Figlewicz 2003, Hommel et al. 2006), this strong and sustained response to palatable diets may be surprising. Surprising, that is, unless the same rapid resistance to these feedback signals develops in reward circuits, as it does in the hypothalamus, and/or the modulation of reward mechanisms by metabolic signals is mainly active in the starved state. Few studies have addressed this important question. In one study, diet-induced leptin resistance was limited to the arcuate nucleus, with other hypothalamic and extrahypothalamic leptin receptors retaining sensitivity (Munzberg et al. 2004). If leptin sensitivity in reward circuits would not be compromised by palatable diets, and increased consumption would continue even in the presence of elevated leptin levels commensurate with the developing obesity, one would have to conclude that the effectiveness of leptin to curb reward is low. Maybe the major function of leptin in these circuits is to heighten reward of even bland food when food is hard to find. In addition to increased palatability, availability—in terms of both access to prepared foods and portion sizes—is also important for increased consumption. The neural systems underlying changes in intake induced by availability and the ways in which neural systems interact with other systems are poorly understood issues and deserve attention.

Finally, imbalanced executive functions in the prefrontal cortex, such as weakened inhibitory control by the right dorsolateral or increased activity in the ventromedial prefrontal cortex, could result in a hyperactive reward mechanism.

CONCLUSIONS

We have made a great deal of progress in identifying the neural mechanisms involved in the controls of ingestive behavior and responsible for the maintenance of energy balance. The hypothalamus has been confirmed as a crucial node in the homeostatic regulatory system keeping body weight within normal limits. In addition, important roles for the reciprocal gut-brain communication pathways are emerging, and the neural organization of cross talk between hypothalamus and brainstem is beginning to be better defined. Within the hypothalamus, there is a new appreciation for the highly complex intracellular-signaling pathways that serve to integrate the numerous nutrient, hormonal, and neural signals informing the brain about the internal milieu.

However, despite this remarkable regulatory system, the prevalence of obesity is increasing at an alarming pace in genetically predisposed segments of the global population. Although it is clear that the cause of this obesity epidemic has to be found in the rapid changes in environment and lifestyle, it is far from clear what specific neural systems and mechanisms are affected by these changes and why the homeostatic regulation breaks down. Because food-related signals and cues from the external world interact primarily with the cognitive and emotional brain, it will be important to study the underlying neural mechanisms and pathways with the same vigor and sophisticated tools that have been applied to the hypothalamic homeostatic regulation. In fact, it is artificial to distinguish homeostatic from nonhomeostatic mechanisms, as recent findings show that the cognitive, emotional, and rewarding brain is intimately linked to the internal metabolic regulatory systems.

Unfortunately, current pharmacological treatment options for obese patients are limited to a few drugs with moderate effectiveness, and only invasive obesity surgery guarantees somewhat larger and sustained weight loss. If it is difficult to design highly efficacious drugs targeting more peripheral aspects of the regulatory system, it might be even more difficult to find drugs targeting the higher neural functions involved in appetite control, particularly when "feeling good" in our often stressful environment is intricately correlated with consuming palatable food. It is also hard to imagine children taking drugs their entire life to keep obesity in check. Therefore, adequate environmental changes and behavioral therapies should be rigorously explored in parallel with the development of new drugs.

ACKNOWLEDGMENT

Work on this review was supported by NIH grants DK47348 and DK52257.

LITERATURE CITED

Adler E, Hoon MA, Mueller KL, Chandrashekar J, Ryba NJ, Zuker CS. 2000. A novel family of mammalian taste receptors. *Cell* 100:693–702

Alonso-Alonso M, Pascual-Leone A. 2007. The right brain hypothesis for obesity. *JAMA* 297:1819–22

Andersson U, Filipsson K, Abbott CR, Woods A, Smith K, et al. 2004. AMP-activated protein kinase plays a role in the control of food intake. *J. Biol. Chem.* 279:12005–8

Anini Y, Hansotia T, Brubaker PL. 2002. Muscarinic receptors control postprandial release of glucagon-like peptide-1: in vivo and in vitro studies in rats. *Endocrinology* 143:2420–26

Arana FS, Parkinson JA, Hinton E, Holland AJ, Owen AM, Roberts AC. 2003. Dissociable contributions of the human amygdala and orbitofrontal cortex to incentive motivation and goal selection. *J. Neurosci.* 23:9632–38

Asakawa A, Inui A, Kaga T, Yuzuriha H, Nagata T, et al. 2001. Ghrelin is an appetite-stimulatory signal from stomach with structural resemblance to motilin. *Gastroenterology* 120:337–45

Bado A, Levasseur S, Attoub S, Kermorgant S, Laigneau JP, et al. 1998. The stomach is a source of leptin. *Nature* 394:790–93

Balleine BW. 2007. The neural basis of choice and decision making. *J. Neurosci.* 27:8159–60

Balthasar N, Dalgaard LT, Lee CE, Yu J, Funahashi H, et al. 2005. Divergence of melanocortin pathways in the control of food intake and energy expenditure. *Cell* 123:493–505

Banks WA, Coon AB, Robinson SM, Moinuddin A, Shultz JM, et al. 2004. Triglycerides induce leptin resistance at the blood-brain barrier. *Diabetes* 53:1253–60

Banks WA, Farr SA, Morley JE. 2006. The effects of high fat diets on the blood-brain barrier transport of leptin: failure or adaptation? *Physiol. Behav.* 88:244–48

Bartness TJ, Bamshad M. 1998. Innervation of mammalian white adipose tissue: implications for the regulation of total body fat. *Am. J. Physiol.* 275:R1399–411

Bates SH, Stearns WH, Dundon TA, Schubert M, Tso AW, et al. 2003. STAT3 signalling is required for leptin regulation of energy balance but not reproduction. *Nature* 421:856–59

Batterham RL, Cowley MA, Small CJ, Herzog H, Cohen MA, et al. 2002. Gut hormone PYY(3-36) physiologically inhibits food intake. *Nature* 418:650–54

Batterham RL, Heffron H, Kapoor S, Chivers JE, Chandarana K, et al. 2006. Critical role for peptide YY in protein-mediated satiation and body-weight regulation. *Cell Metab.* 4:223–33

Bellinger LL. 1999. A nonessential role of liver innervation in controlling feeding behavior. *Nutrition* 15:506

Bence KK, Delibegovic M, Xue B, Gorgun CZ, Hotamisligil GS, et al. 2006. Neuronal PTP1B regulates body weight, adiposity and leptin action. *Nat. Med.* 12:917–24

Berman DE, Dudai Y. 2001. Memory extinction, learning anew, and learning the new: dissociations in the molecular machinery of learning in cortex. *Science* 291:2417–19

Berridge KC. 1996. Food reward: brain substrates of wanting and liking. *Neurosci. Biobehav. Rev.* 20:1–25

Berridge KC, Robinson TE. 2003. Parsing reward. *Trends Neurosci.* 26:507–13

Berridge KC, Valenstein ES. 1991. What psychological process mediates feeding evoked by electrical stimulation of the lateral hypothalamus? *Behav. Neurosci.* 105:3–14

Berthoud H-R. 2002. Multiple neural systems controlling food intake and body weight. *Neurosci. Biobehav. Rev.* 26:393–428

Berthoud H-R. 2004. The caudal brainstem and the control of food intake and energy balance. In *Handbook of Behavioral Neurobiology*, ed. EM Stricker, SC Woods, pp. 195–240. New York: Plenum

Berthoud H-R, Blackshaw LA, Brookes SJ, Grundy D. 2004. Neuroanatomy of extrinsic afferents supplying the gastrointestinal tract. *Neurogastroenterol. Motil.* 16(Suppl. 1):28–33

Berthoud H-R, Kressel M, Neuhuber WL. 1992. An anterograde tracing study of the vagal innervation of rat liver, portal vein and biliary system. *Anat. Embryol. (Berl.)* 186:431–42

Berthoud H-R, Neuhuber WL. 2000. Functional and chemical anatomy of the afferent vagal system. *Auton. Neurosci.* 85:1–17

Berthoud H-R, Sutton GM, Townsend RL, Patterson LM, Zheng H. 2006. Brainstem mechanisms integrating gut-derived satiety signals and descending forebrain information in the control of meal size. *Physiol. Behav.* 89:517–24

Boutin P, Froguel P. 2001. Genetics of human obesity. *Best Pract. Res. Clin. Endocrinol. Metab.* 15:391–404

Broberger C, Holmberg K, Kuhar MJ, Hokfelt T. 1999. Cocaine- and amphetamine-regulated transcript in the rat vagus nerve: a putative mediator of cholecystokinin-induced satiety. *Proc. Natl. Acad. Sci. USA* 96:13506–11

Bruning JC, Gautam D, Burks DJ, Gillette J, Schubert M, et al. 2000. Role of brain insulin receptor in control of body weight and reproduction. *Science* 289:2122–25

Buck L, Axel R. 1991. A novel multigene family may encode odorant receptors: a molecular basis for odor recognition. *Cell* 65:175–87

Burcelin R. 2005. The incretins: a link between nutrients and well-being. *Br. J. Nutr.* 93(Suppl. 1):S147–56

Burcelin R, Da Costa A, Drucker D, Thorens B. 2001. Glucose competence of the hepatoportal vein sensor requires the presence of an activated glucagon-like peptide-1 receptor. *Diabetes* 50:1720–28

Burcelin R, Dolci W, Thorens B. 2000. Glucose sensing by the hepatoportal sensor is GLUT2-dependent: in vivo analysis in GLUT2-null mice. *Diabetes* 49:1643–48

Burdyga G, Spiller D, Morris R, Lal S, Thompson DG, et al. 2002. Expression of the leptin receptor in rat and human nodose ganglion neurones. *Neuroscience* 109:339–47

Burdyga G, Varro A, Dimaline R, Thompson DG, Dockray GJ. 2006. Ghrelin receptors in rat and human nodose ganglia: putative role in regulating CB-1 and MCH receptor abundance. *Am. J. Physiol. Gastrointest. Liver Physiol.* 290:G1289–97

Butler AA. 2006. The melanocortin system and energy balance. *Peptides* 27:281–90

Buyse M, Ovesjo ML, Goiot H, Guilmeau S, Peranzi G, et al. 2001. Expression and regulation of leptin receptor proteins in afferent and efferent neurons of the vagus nerve. *Eur. J. Neurosci.* 14:64–72

Cannon CM, Palmiter RD. 2003. Reward without dopamine. *J. Neurosci.* 23:10827–31

Cardinal RN, Parkinson JA, Hall J, Everitt BJ. 2002. Emotion and motivation: the role of the amygdala, ventral striatum, and prefrontal cortex. *Neurosci. Biobehav. Rev.* 26:321–52

Chandrashekar J, Hoon MA, Ryba NJ, Zuker CS. 2006. The receptors and cells for mammalian taste. *Nature* 444:288–94

Chelikani PK, Haver AC, Reeve JR Jr, Keire DA, Reidelberger RD. 2006. Daily, intermittent intravenous infusion of peptide YY(3–36) reduces daily food intake and adiposity in rats. *Am. J. Physiol. Regul. Integr. Comp. Physiol.* 290:R298–305

Chelikani PK, Haver AC, Reidelberger RD. 2005a. Intravenous infusion of glucagon-like peptide-1 potently inhibits food intake, sham feeding, and gastric emptying in rats. *Am. J. Physiol. Regul. Integr. Comp. Physiol.* 288:R1695–706

Chelikani PK, Haver AC, Reidelberger RD. 2005b. Intravenous infusion of peptide YY(3–36) potently inhibits food intake in rats. *Endocrinology* 146:879–88

Clegg DJ, Benoit SC, Reed JA, Woods SC, Dunn-Meynell A, Levin BE. 2005. Reduced anorexic effects of insulin in obesity-prone rats fed a moderate-fat diet. *Am. J. Physiol. Regul. Integr. Comp. Physiol.* 288:R981–86

Clegg DJ, Brown LM, Woods SC, Benoit SC. 2006. Gonadal hormones determine sensitivity to central leptin and insulin. *Diabetes* 55:978–87

Cone RD. 2005. Anatomy and regulation of the central melanocortin system. *Nat. Neurosci.* 8:571–78

Cooper SJ. 2004. Endocannabinoids and food consumption: comparisons with benzodiazepine and opioid palatability-dependent appetite. *Eur. J. Pharmacol.* 500:37–49

Cota D, Proulx K, Smith KA, Kozma SC, Thomas G, et al. 2006. Hypothalamic mTOR signaling regulates food intake. *Science* 312:927–30

Cowley MA, Smart JL, Rubinstein M, Cerdan MG, Diano S, et al. 2001. Leptin activates anorexigenic POMC neurons through a neural network in the arcuate nucleus. *Nature* 411:480–84

Craig AD. 2003. Interoception: the sense of the physiological condition of the body. *Curr. Opin. Neurobiol.* 13:500–5

Craig AD. 2005. Forebrain emotional asymmetry: a neuroanatomical basis? *Trends Cogn. Sci.* 9:566–71

Cummings DE. 2006. Ghrelin and the short- and long-term regulation of appetite and body weight. *Physiol. Behav.* 89:71–84

Cummings DE, Overduin J, Foster-Schubert KE. 2004. Gastric bypass for obesity: mechanisms of weight loss and diabetes resolution. *J. Clin. Endocrinol. Metab.* 89:2608–15

Cummings DE, Purnell JQ, Frayo RS, Schmidova K, Wisse BE, Weigle DS. 2001. A preprandial rise in plasma ghrelin levels suggests a role in meal initiation in humans. *Diabetes* 50:1714–19

D'Alessio DA, Prigeon RL, Ensinck JW. 1995. Enteral enhancement of glucose disposition by both insulin-dependent and insulin-independent processes. A physiological role of glucagon-like peptide I. *Diabetes* 44:1433–37

Date Y, Murakami N, Toshinai K, Matsukura S, Niijima A, et al. 2002. The role of the gastric afferent vagal nerve in ghrelin-induced feeding and growth hormone secretion in rats. *Gastroenterology* 123:1120–28

Davidson TL. 2000. Pavlovian occasion setting: a link between physiological change and appetitive behavior. *Appetite* 35:271–72

Davidson TL, Kanoski SE, Walls EK, Jarrard LE. 2005. Memory inhibition and energy regulation. *Physiol. Behav.* 86:731–46

Davidson TL, Morell JR, Benoit SC. 2000. Memory and macronutrient regulation. In *Neural and Metabolic Control of Macronutrient Intake*, ed. HR Berthoud, RJ Seeley, pp. 203–17. Boca Raton, FL: CRC Press

Dayan P, Balleine BW. 2002. Reward, motivation, and reinforcement learning. *Neuron* 36:285–98

de Araujo IE, Kringelbach ML, Rolls ET, Hobden P. 2003a. Representation of umami taste in the human brain. *J. Neurophysiol.* 90:313–19

de Araujo IE, Kringelbach ML, Rolls ET, McGlone F. 2003b. Human cortical responses to water in the mouth, and the effects of thirst. *J. Neurophysiol.* 90:1865–76

de Araujo IE, Rolls ET, Kringelbach ML, McGlone F, Phillips N. 2003c. Taste-olfactory convergence, and the representation of the pleasantness of flavour, in the human brain. *Eur. J. Neurosci.* 18:2059–68

de Araujo IE, Rolls ET, Velazco MI, Margot C, Cayeux I. 2005. Cognitive modulation of olfactory processing. *Neuron* 46:671–79

DeFalco J, Tomishima M, Liu H, Zhao C, Cai X, et al. 2001. Virus-assisted mapping of neural inputs to a feeding center in the hypothalamus. *Science* 291:2608–13

DelParigi A, Chen K, Salbe AD, Hill JO, Wing RR, et al. 2007. Successful dieters have increased neural activity in cortical areas involved in the control of behavior. *Int. J. Obes. (Lond.)* 31:440–48

Denis RG, Bing C, Naderali EK, Vernon RG, Williams G. 2003. Lactation modulates diurnal expression profiles of specific leptin receptor isoforms in the rat hypothalamus. *J. Endocrinol.* 178:225–32

Desmedt A, Hazvi S, Dudai Y. 2003. Differential pattern of cAMP response element-binding protein activation in the rat brain after conditioned aversion as a function of the associative process engaged: taste vs context association. *J. Neurosci.* 23:6102–10

de Zwaan M, Mitchell JE. 1992. Opiate antagonists and eating behavior in humans: a review. *J. Clin. Pharmacol.* 32:1060–72

Drucker DJ, Nauck MA. 2006. The incretin system: glucagon-like peptide-1 receptor agonists and dipeptidyl peptidase-4 inhibitors in type 2 diabetes. *Lancet* 368:1696–705

Eberlein GA, Eysselein VE, Schaeffer M, Layer P, Grandt D, et al. 1989. A new molecular form of PYY: structural characterization of human PYY(3-36) and PYY(1-36). *Peptides* 10:797–803

Eckel LA. 2004. Estradiol: a rhythmic, inhibitory, indirect control of meal size. *Physiol. Behav.* 82:35–41

Ek M, Kurosawa M, Lundeberg T, Ericsson A. 1998. Activation of vagal afferents after intravenous injection of interleukin-1beta: role of endogenous prostaglandins. *J. Neurosci.* 18:9471–79

Elias CF, Aschkenasi C, Lee C, Kelly J, Ahima RS, et al. 1999. Leptin differentially regulates NPY and POMC neurons projecting to the lateral hypothalamic area. *Neuron* 23:775–86

Ellacott KL, Cone RD. 2004. The central melanocortin system and the integration of short- and long-term regulators of energy homeostasis. *Recent Prog. Horm. Res.* 59:395–408

Emch GS, Hermann GE, Rogers RC. 2000. TNF-alpha activates solitary nucleus neurons responsive to gastric distension. *Am. J. Physiol. Gastrointest. Liver Physiol.* 279:G582–86

Emch GS, Hermann GE, Rogers RC. 2002. Tumor necrosis factor-alpha inhibits physiologically identified dorsal motor nucleus neurons in vivo. *Brain Res.* 951:311–15

Farooqi S, O'Rahilly S. 2006. Genetics of obesity in humans. *Endocr. Rev.* 27:710–18

Figlewicz DP. 2003. Adiposity signals and food reward: expanding the CNS roles of insulin and leptin. *Am. J. Physiol. Regul. Integr. Comp. Physiol.* 284:R882–92

Fogteloo AJ, Pijl H, Frolich M, McCamish M, Meinders AE. 2003. Effects of recombinant human leptin treatment as an adjunct of moderate energy restriction on body weight, resting energy expenditure and energy intake in obese humans. *Diabetes Nutr. Metab.* 16:109–14

Franks NR, Richardson T. 2006. Teaching in tandem-running ants. *Nature* 439:153

Freeman SL, Bohan D, Darcel N, Raybould HE. 2006. Luminal glucose sensing in the rat intestine has characteristics of a sodium-glucose cotransporter. *Am. J. Physiol. Gastrointest. Liver Physiol.* 291:G439–45

Friedman JM. 2003. A war on obesity, not the obese. *Science* 299:856–58

Friedman MI. 1997. An energy sensor for control of energy intake. *Proc. Nutr. Soc.* 56:41–50

Friedman MI, Tordoff MG, Ramirez I. 1986. Integrated metabolic control of food intake. *Brain Res. Bull.* 17:855–59

Fulton S, Pissios P, Manchon RP, Stiles L, Frank L, et al. 2006. Leptin regulation of the mesoaccumbens dopamine pathway. *Neuron* 51:811–22

Gallagher M, McMahan RW, Schoenbaum G. 1999. Orbitofrontal cortex and representation of incentive value in associative learning. *J. Neurosci.* 19:6610–14

Geary N. 2004. Endocrine controls of eating: CCK, leptin, and ghrelin. *Physiol. Behav.* 81:719–33

Ghilardi JR, Allen CJ, Vigna SR, McVey DC, Mantyh PW. 1994. Cholecystokinin and neuropeptide Y receptors on single rabbit vagal afferent ganglion neurons: site of prejunctional modulation of visceral sensory neurons. *Brain Res.* 633:33–40

Gottfried JA, O'Doherty J, Dolan RJ. 2003. Encoding predictive reward value in human amygdala and orbitofrontal cortex. *Science* 301:1104–7

Grill HJ, Kaplan JM. 2002. The neuroanatomical axis for control of energy balance. *Front. Neuroendocrinol.* 23:2–40

Grill HJ, Norgren R. 1978. The taste reactivity test. II. Mimetic responses to gustatory stimuli in chronic thalamic and chronic decerebrate rats. *Brain Res.* 143:281–97

Gropp E, Shanabrough M, Borok E, Xu AW, Janoschek R, et al. 2005. Agouti-related peptide-expressing neurons are mandatory for feeding. *Nat. Neurosci.* 8:1289–91

Gutzwiller JP, Goke B, Drewe J, Hildebrand P, Ketterer S, et al. 1999. Glucagon-like peptide-1: a potent regulator of food intake in humans. *Gut* 44:81–86

Hakansson ML, Meister B. 1998. Transcription factor STAT3 in leptin target neurons of the rat hypothalamus. *Neuroendocrinology* 68:420–27

Harris GC, Wimmer M, Aston-Jones G. 2005. A role for lateral hypothalamic orexin neurons in reward seeking. *Nature* 437:556–59

Hatfield T, Han JS, Conley M, Gallagher M, Holland P. 1996. Neurotoxic lesions of basolateral, but not central, amygdala interfere with Pavlovian second-order conditioning and reinforcer devaluation effects. *J. Neurosci.* 16:5256–65

Hays NP, Roberts SB. 2006. The anorexia of aging in humans. *Physiol. Behav.* 88:257–66

Hebben N, Corkin S, Eichenbaum H, Shedlack K. 1985. Diminished ability to interpret and report internal states after bilateral medial temporal resection: case H.M. *Behav. Neurosci.* 99:1031–39

Herrmann C, Goke R, Richter G, Fehmann HC, Arnold R, Goke B. 1995. Glucagon-like peptide-1 and glucose-dependent insulin-releasing polypeptide plasma levels in response to nutrients. *Digestion* 56:117–26

Herrmann-Rinke C, Voge A, Hess M, Goke B. 1995. Regulation of glucagon-like peptide-1 secretion from rat ileum by neurotransmitters and peptides. *J. Endocrinol.* 147:25–31

Hevener AL, Bergman RN, Donovan CM. 1997. Novel glucosensor for hypoglycemic detection localized to the portal vein. *Diabetes* 46:1521–25

Hevener AL, Bergman RN, Donovan CM. 2000. Portal vein afferents are critical for the sympathoadrenal response to hypoglycemia. *Diabetes* 49:8–12

Heymsfield SB, Greenberg AS, Fujioka K, Dixon RM, Kushner R, et al. 1999. Recombinant leptin for weight loss in obese and lean adults: a randomized, controlled, dose-escalation trial. *JAMA* 282:1568–75

Higgs S. 2005. Memory and its role in appetite regulation. *Physiol. Behav.* 85:67–72

Hill JO, Peters JC. 1998. Environmental contributions to the obesity epidemic. *Science* 280:1371–74

Hill JO, Wyatt HR, Reed GW, Peters JC. 2003. Obesity and the environment: Where do we go from here? *Science* 299:853–55

Hoek J, Gendall P. 2006. Advertising and obesity: a behavioral perspective. *J. Health Commun.* 11:409–23

Hommel JD, Trinko R, Sears RM, Georgescu D, Liu ZW, et al. 2006. Leptin receptor signaling in midbrain dopamine neurons regulates feeding. *Neuron* 51:801–10

Horn CC, Tordoff MG, Friedman MI. 2001. Role of vagal afferent innervation in feeding and brain Fos expression produced by metabolic inhibitors. *Brain Res.* 919:198–206

Horvath TL, Diano S, van den Pol AN. 1999. Synaptic interaction between hypocretin (orexin) and neuropeptide Y cells in the rodent and primate hypothalamus: a novel circuit implicated in metabolic and endocrine regulations. *J. Neurosci.* 19:1072–87

Huang AL, Chen X, Hoon MA, Chandrashekar J, Guo W, et al. 2006. The cells and logic for mammalian sour taste detection. *Nature* 442:934–38

Hukshorn CJ, Saris WH, Westerterp-Plantenga MS, Farid AR, Smith FJ, Campfield LA. 2000. Weekly subcutaneous pegylated recombinant native human leptin (PEG-OB) administration in obese men. *J. Clin. Endocrinol. Metab.* 85:4003–9

Kaczmarek HJ, Kiefer SW. 2000. Microinjections of dopaminergic agents in the nucleus accumbens affect ethanol consumption but not palatability. *Pharmacol. Biochem. Behav.* 66:307–12

Kadohisa M, Rolls ET, Verhagen JV. 2004. Orbitofrontal cortex: neuronal representation of oral temperature and capsaicin in addition to taste and texture. *Neuroscience* 127:207–21

Kadohisa M, Rolls ET, Verhagen JV. 2005. Neuronal representations of stimuli in the mouth: the primate insular taste cortex, orbitofrontal cortex and amygdala. *Chem. Senses* 30:401–19

Kahn BB, Alquier T, Carling D, Hardie DG. 2005. AMP-activated protein kinase: ancient energy gauge provides clues to modern understanding of metabolism. *Cell Metab.* 1:15–25

Kakei M, Yada T, Nakagawa A, Nakabayashi H. 2002. Glucagon-like peptide-1 evokes action potentials and increases cytosolic Ca2+ in rat nodose ganglion neurons. *Auton. Neurosci.* 102:39–44

Kelley AE, Bakshi VP, Haber SN, Steininger TL, Will MJ, Zhang M. 2002. Opioid modulation of taste hedonics within the ventral striatum. *Physiol. Behav.* 76:365–77

Kelley AE, Bless EP, Swanson CJ. 1996. Investigation of the effects of opiate antagonists infused into the nucleus accumbens on feeding and sucrose drinking in rats. *J. Pharmacol. Exp. Ther.* 278:1499–507

Koda S, Date Y, Murakami N, Shimbara T, Hanada T, et al. 2005. The role of the vagal nerve in peripheral PYY3-36-induced feeding reduction in rats. *Endocrinology* 146:2369–75

Kohno D, Gao HZ, Muroya S, Kikuyama S, Yada T. 2003. Ghrelin directly interacts with neuropeptide-Y-containing neurons in the rat arcuate nucleus: Ca2+ signaling via protein kinase A and N-type channel-dependent mechanisms and cross-talk with leptin and orexin. *Diabetes* 52:948–56

Kringelbach ML. 2004. Food for thought: hedonic experience beyond homeostasis in the human brain. *Neuroscience* 126:807–19

Krol E, Duncan JS, Redman P, Morgan PJ, Mercer JG, Speakman JR. 2006. Photoperiod regulates leptin sensitivity in field voles, *Microtus agrestis*. *J. Comp. Physiol. [B]* 176:153–63

Krude H, Biebermann H, Luck W, Horn R, Brabant G, Gruters A. 1998. Severe early-onset obesity, adrenal insufficiency and red hair pigmentation caused by POMC mutations in humans. *Nat. Genet.* 19:155–57

Langhans W. 2003. Role of the liver in the control of glucose-lipid utilization and body weight. *Curr. Opin. Clin. Nutr. Metab. Care* 6:449–55

Larhammar D. 1996. Structural diversity of receptors for neuropeptide Y, peptide YY and pancreatic polypeptide. *Regul. Pept.* 65:165–74

Laugerette F, Passilly-Degrace P, Patris B, Niot I, Febbraio M, et al. 2005. CD36 involvement in orosensory detection of dietary lipids, spontaneous fat preference, and digestive secretions. *J. Clin. Invest.* 115:3177–84

Le DS, Pannacciulli N, Chen K, Del Parigi A, Salbe AD, et al. 2006. Less activation of the left dorsolateral prefrontal cortex in response to a meal: a feature of obesity. *Am. J. Clin. Nutr.* 84:725–31

Lechan RM, Fekete C. 2006. The TRH neuron: a hypothalamic integrator of energy metabolism. *Prog. Brain Res.* 153:209–35

Lee K, Li B, Xi X, Suh Y, Martin RJ. 2005. Role of neuronal energy status in the regulation of adenosine 5'-monophosphate-activated protein kinase, orexigenic neuropeptides expression, and feeding behavior. *Endocrinology* 146:3–10

le Roux CW, Neary NM, Halsey TJ, Small CJ, Martinez-Isla AM, et al. 2005. Ghrelin does not stimulate food intake in patients with surgical procedures involving vagotomy. *J. Clin. Endocrinol. Metab.* 90:4521–24

Levin BE. 2002. Metabolic sensors: viewing glucosensing neurons from a broader perspective. *Physiol. Behav.* 76:397–401

Levin BE, Dunn-Meynell AA, Banks WA. 2004. Obesity-prone rats have normal blood-brain barrier transport but defective central leptin signaling before obesity onset. *Am. J. Physiol. Regul. Integr. Comp. Physiol.* 286:R143–50

Levine AS, Billington CJ. 2004. Opioids as agents of reward-related feeding: a consideration of the evidence. *Physiol. Behav.* 82:57–61

Levine AS, Weldon DT, Grace M, Cleary JP, Billington CJ. 1995. Naloxone blocks that portion of feeding driven by sweet taste in food-restricted rats. *Am. J. Physiol.* 268:R248–52

Levitsky DA. 2005. The nonregulation of food intake in humans: hope for reversing the epidemic of obesity. *Physiol. Behav.* 86:623–32

Li B, Lee K, Martin RJ. 2006. Overexpression of glucose transporter 2 in GT1–7 cells inhibits AMP-activated protein kinase and agouti-related peptide expression. *Brain Res.* 1118:1–5

Linn SE. 2004. Food marketing to children in the context of a marketing maelstrom. *J. Public Health Policy* 25:367–78

Luquet S, Perez FA, Hnasko TS, Palmiter RD. 2005. NPY/AgRP neurons are essential for feeding in adult mice but can be ablated in neonates. *Science* 310:683–85

Lutz TA, Mollet A, Rushing PA, Riediger T, Scharrer E. 2001. The anorectic effect of a chronic peripheral infusion of amylin is abolished in area postrema/nucleus of the solitary tract (AP/NTS) lesioned rats. *Int. J. Obes. Relat. Metab. Disord.* 25:1005–11

Lutz TA, Niijima A, Scharrer E. 1996. Intraportal infusion of 2,5-anhydro-D-mannitol increases afferent activity in the common hepatic vagus branch. *J. Auton. Nerv. Syst.* 61:204–8

Marshall S. 2006. Role of insulin, adipocyte hormones, and nutrient-sensing pathways in regulating fuel metabolism and energy homeostasis: a nutritional perspective of diabetes, obesity, and cancer. *Sci. STKE* 2006:re7

Marty N, Bady I, Thorens B. 2006. Distinct classes of central GLUT2-dependent sensors control counterregulation and feeding. *Diabetes* 55(Suppl. 2):S108–13

Matveyenko AV, Donovan CM. 2006. Metabolic sensors mediate hypoglycemic detection at the portal vein. *Diabetes* 55:1276–82

McClure SM, Li J, Tomlin D, Cypert KS, Montague LM, Montague PR. 2004. Neural correlates of behavioral preference for culturally familiar drinks. *Neuron* 44:379–87

Merchenthaler I, Lane M, Shughrue P. 1999. Distribution of prepro-glucagon and glucagon-like peptide-1 receptor messenger RNAs in the rat central nervous system. *J. Comp. Neurol.* 403:261–80

Miller JL, James GA, Goldstone AP, Couch JA, He G, et al. 2007. Enhanced activation of reward mediating prefrontal regions in response to food stimuli in Prader-Willi syndrome. *J. Neurol. Neurosurg. Psychiatry* 78:615–19

Minokoshi Y, Alquier T, Furukawa N, Kim YB, Lee A, et al. 2004. AMP-kinase regulates food intake by responding to hormonal and nutrient signals in the hypothalamus. *Nature* 428:569–74

Mithieux G, Misery P, Magnan C, Pillot B, Gautier-Stein A, et al. 2005. Portal sensing of intestinal gluconeogenesis is a mechanistic link in the diminution of food intake induced by diet protein. *Cell Metab.* 2:321–29

Morales M, Wang SD. 2002. Differential composition of 5-hydroxytryptamine3 receptors synthesized in the rat CNS and peripheral nervous system. *J. Neurosci.* 22:6732–41

Mori H, Hanada R, Hanada T, Aki D, Mashima R, et al. 2004. Socs3 deficiency in the brain elevates leptin sensitivity and confers resistance to diet-induced obesity. *Nat. Med.* 10:739–43

Moriarty P, Dimaline R, Thompson DG, Dockray GJ. 1997. Characterization of cholecystokininA and cholecystokininB receptors expressed by vagal afferent neurons. *Neuroscience* 79:905–13

Morrison CD, Morton GJ, Niswender KD, Gelling RW, Schwartz MW. 2005. Leptin inhibits hypothalamic Npy and AgRP gene expression via a mechanism that requires phosphatidylinositol 3-OH-kinase signaling. *Am. J. Physiol. Endocrinol. Metab.* 289:E1051–57

Morrison CD, Xi X, White CL, Ye J, Martin RJ. 2007. Amino acids inhibit AgRP gene expression via an mTOR-dependent mechanism. *Am. J. Physiol. Endocrinol. Metab.* 293:E165–71

Morton GJ, Cummings DE, Baskin DG, Barsh GS, Schwartz MW. 2006. Central nervous system control of food intake and body weight. *Nature* 443:289–95

Moynihan Ramsey K, Marcheva B, Kohsaka A, Bass J. 2007. The clockwork of metabolism. *Annu. Rev. Nutr.* 27:219–40

Munzberg H, Flier JS, Bjorbaek C. 2004. Region-specific leptin resistance within the hypothalamus of diet-induced obese mice. *Endocrinology* 145:4880–89

Munzberg H, Huo L, Nillni EA, Hollenberg AN, Bjorbaek C. 2003. Role of signal transducer and activator of transcription 3 in regulation of hypothalamic proopiomelanocortin gene expression by leptin. *Endocrinology* 144:2121–31

Munzberg H, Myers MG Jr. 2005. Molecular and anatomical determinants of central leptin resistance. *Nat. Neurosci.* 8:566–70

Muroya S, Funahashi H, Yamanaka A, Kohno D, Uramura K, et al. 2004. Orexins (hypocretins) directly interact with neuropeptide Y, POMC and glucose-responsive neurons to regulate Ca2+ signaling in a reciprocal manner to leptin: orexigenic neuronal pathways in the mediobasal hypothalamus. *Eur. J. Neurosci.* 19:1524–34

Murphy C, Cain WS, Bartoshuk LM. 1977. Mutual action of taste and olfaction. *Sens. Processes* 1:204–11

Murray EA, O'Doherty JP, Schoenbaum G. 2007. What we know and do not know about the functions of the orbitofrontal cortex after 20 years of cross-species studies. *J. Neurosci.* 27:8166–69

Nakagawa A, Satake H, Nakabayashi H, Nishizawa M, Furuya K, et al. 2004. Receptor gene expression of glucagon-like peptide-1, but not glucose-dependent insulinotropic polypeptide, in rat nodose ganglion cells. *Auton. Neurosci.* 110:36–43

Neel JV. 1962. Diabetes mellitus: a "thrifty" genotype rendered determined by progress? *Am. J. Hum. Genet.* 14:353–63

Nelson G, Hoon MA, Chandrashekar J, Zhang Y, Ryba NJ, Zuker CS. 2001. Mammalian sweet taste receptors. *Cell* 106:381–90

Niijima A. 1982. Glucose-sensitive afferent nerve fibres in the hepatic branch of the vagus nerve in the guinea-pig. *J. Physiol.* 332:315–23

Niswender KD, Morrison CD, Clegg DJ, Olson R, Baskin DG, et al. 2003. Insulin activation of phosphatidylinositol 3-kinase in the hypothalamic arcuate nucleus: a key mediator of insulin-induced anorexia. *Diabetes* 52:227–31

Niswender KD, Morton GJ, Stearns WH, Rhodes CJ, Myers MG Jr, Schwartz MW. 2001. Intracellular signalling. Key enzyme in leptin-induced anorexia. *Nature* 413:794–95

Obici S, Rossetti L. 2003. Nutrient sensing and the regulation of insulin action and energy balance. *Endocrinology* 144:5172–78

Obici S, Zhang BB, Karkanias G, Rossetti L. 2002. Hypothalamic insulin signaling is required for inhibition of glucose production. *Nat. Med.* 8:1376–82

Pal R, Sahu A. 2003. Leptin signaling in the hypothalamus during chronic central leptin infusion. *Endocrinology* 144:3789–98

Patterson LM, Zheng H, Berthoud HR. 2002. Vagal afferents innervating the gastrointestinal tract and CCKA-receptor immunoreactivity. *Anat. Rec.* 266:10–20

Pecina S, Berridge KC. 2000. Opioid site in nucleus accumbens shell mediates eating and hedonic "liking" for food: map based on microinjection Fos plumes. *Brain Res.* 863:71–86

Pecina S, Cagniard B, Berridge KC, Aldridge JW, Zhuang X. 2003. Hyperdopaminergic mutant mice have higher "wanting" but not "liking" for sweet rewards. *J. Neurosci.* 23:9395–402

Peters JH, Ritter RC, Simasko SM. 2006. Leptin and CCK selectively activate vagal afferent neurons innervating the stomach and duodenum. *Am. J. Physiol. Regul. Integr. Comp. Physiol.* 290:R1544–49

Petrovich GD, Ross CA, Holland PC, Gallagher M. 2007. Medial prefrontal cortex is necessary for an appetitive contextual conditioned stimulus to promote eating in sated rats. *J. Neurosci.* 27:6436–41

Phillips RJ, Powley TL. 2000. Tension and stretch receptors in gastrointestinal smooth muscle: re-evaluating vagal mechanoreceptor electrophysiology. *Brain Res. Brain Res. Rev.* 34:1–26

Pickens CL, Saddoris MP, Setlow B, Gallagher M, Holland PC, Schoenbaum G. 2003. Different roles for orbitofrontal cortex and basolateral amygdala in a reinforcer devaluation task. *J. Neurosci.* 23:11078–84

Plum L, Belgardt BF, Bruning JC. 2006a. Central insulin action in energy and glucose homeostasis. *J. Clin. Invest.* 116:1761–66

Plum L, Ma X, Hampel B, Balthasar N, Coppari R, et al. 2006b. Enhanced PIP3 signaling in POMC neurons causes KATP channel activation and leads to diet-sensitive obesity. *J. Clin. Invest.* 116:1886–901

Prentice AM, Rayco-Solon P, Moore SE. 2005. Insights from the developing world: thrifty genotypes and thrifty phenotypes. *Proc. Nutr. Soc.* 64:153–61

Rahmouni K, Haynes WG, Morgan DA, Mark AL. 2003. Intracellular mechanisms involved in leptin regulation of sympathetic outflow. *Hypertension* 41:763–67

Ravussin E, Bogardus C. 2000. Energy balance and weight regulation: genetics vs environment. *Br. J. Nutr.* 83(Suppl. 1):S17–20

Raybould HE, Glatzle J, Freeman SL, Whited K, Darcel N, et al. 2006. Detection of macronutrients in the intestinal wall. *Auton. Neurosci.* 125:28–33

Regard M, Landis T. 1997. "Gourmand syndrome": eating passion associated with right anterior lesions. *Neurology* 48:1185–90

Riediger T, Bothe C, Becskei C, Lutz TA. 2004. Peptide YY directly inhibits ghrelin-activated neurons of the arcuate nucleus and reverses fasting-induced c-Fos expression. *Neuroendocrinology* 79:317–26

Riley JR, Greggers U, Smith AD, Reynolds DR, Menzel R. 2005. The flight paths of honeybees recruited by the waggle dance. *Nature* 435:205–7

Ritzel R, Orskov C, Holst JJ, Nauck MA. 1995. Pharmacokinetic, insulinotropic, and glucagonostatic properties of GLP-1 [7-36 amide] after subcutaneous injection in healthy volunteers. Dose-response relationships. *Diabetologia* 38:720–25

Rolls BJ. 2003. The supersizing of America: portion size and the obesity epidemic. *Nutr. Today* 38:42–53

Rolls ET, Critchley HD, Browning A, Hernadi I. 1998. The neurophysiology of taste and olfaction in primates, and umami flavor. *Ann. N. Y. Acad. Sci.* 855:426–37

Rolls ET, Critchley HD, Browning AS, Hernadi I, Lenard L. 1999. Responses to the sensory properties of fat of neurons in the primate orbitofrontal cortex. *J. Neurosci.* 19:1532–40

Rolls ET, Kringelbach ML, de Araujo IE, 2003a. Different representations of pleasant and unpleasant odours in the human brain. *Eur. J. Neurosci.* 18:695–703

Rolls ET, Verhagen JV, Kadohisa M. 2003b. Representations of the texture of food in the primate orbitofrontal cortex: neurons responding to viscosity, grittiness, and capsaicin. *J. Neurophysiol.* 90:3711–24

Roseberry AG, Liu H, Jackson AC, Cai X, Friedman JM. 2004. Neuropeptide Y-mediated inhibition of proopiomelanocortin neurons in the arcuate nucleus shows enhanced desensitization in ob/ob mice. *Neuron* 41:711–22

Rosenbaum M, Murphy EM, Heymsfield SB, Matthews DE, Leibel RL. 2002. Low-dose leptin administration reverses effects of sustained weight-reduction on energy expenditure and circulating concentrations of thyroid hormones. *J. Clin. Endocrinol. Metab.* 87:2391–94

Rousseau K, Atcha Z, Loudon AS. 2003. Leptin and seasonal mammals. *J. Neuroendocrinol.* 15:409–14

Rozin P. 1982. "Taste-smell confusions" and the duality of the olfactory sense. *Percept. Psychophys.* 31:397–401

Rudic RD, McNamara P, Curtis AM, Boston RC, Panda S, et al. 2004. BMAL1 and CLOCK, two essential components of the circadian clock, are involved in glucose homeostasis. *PLoS Biol.* 2:e377

Russek M. 1981. Current status of the hepatostatic theory of food intake control. *Appetite* 2:137–43

Saper CB. 2000. Hypothalamic connections with the cerebral cortex. *Prog. Brain Res.* 126:39–48

Schirra J, Goke B. 2005. The physiological role of GLP-1 in human: incretin, ileal brake or more? *Regul. Pept.* 128:109–15

Schwartz MW, Seeley RJ, Campfield LA, Burn P, Baskin DG. 1996. Identification of targets of leptin action in rat hypothalamus. *J. Clin. Invest.* 98:1101–6

Schwartz MW, Seeley RJ, Woods SC, Weigle DS, Campfield LA, et al. 1997. Leptin increases hypothalamic pro-opiomelanocortin mRNA expression in the rostral arcuate nucleus. *Diabetes* 46:2119–23

Sclafani A. 2004. Oral and postoral determinants of food reward. *Physiol. Behav.* 81:773–79

Sclafani A, Springer D. 1976. Dietary obesity in adult rats: similarities to hypothalamic and human obesity syndromes. *Physiol. Behav.* 17:461–71

Shepherd GM. 2006. Smell images and the flavour system in the human brain. *Nature* 444:316–21

Smith GP, Jerome C, Norgren R. 1985. Afferent axons in abdominal vagus mediate satiety effect of cholecystokinin in rats. *Am. J. Physiol.* 249:R638–41

Spanswick D, Smith MA, Groppi VE, Logan SD, Ashford ML. 1997. Leptin inhibits hypothalamic neurons by activation of ATP-sensitive potassium channels. *Nature* 390:521–25

Speakman JR. 2004. Obesity: the integrated roles of environment and genetics. *J. Nutr.* 134:2090–105S

Speakman JR. 2006. Thrifty genes for obesity and the metabolic syndrome—time to call off the search? *Diab. Vasc. Dis. Res.* 3:7–11

Statnick MA, Tinsley FC, Eastwood BJ, Suter TM, Mitch CH, Heiman ML. 2003. Peptides that regulate food intake: antagonism of opioid receptors reduces body fat in obese rats by decreasing food intake and stimulating lipid utilization. *Am. J. Physiol. Regul. Integr. Comp. Physiol.* 284:R1399–408

Steiner JE. 1973. *The Gustofacial Response: Observations on Normal and Anancephalic Newborn Infants.* Bethesda, MD: U.S. Dept. Health, Educ., Welfare

Stricker EM, Rowland N, Saller CF, Friedman MI. 1977. Homeostasis during hypoglycemia: central control of adrenal secretion and peripheral control of feeding. *Science* 196:79–81

Tabarin A, Diz-Chaves Y, Carmona Mdel C, Catargi B, Zorrilla EP, et al. 2005. Resistance to diet-induced obesity in mu-opioid receptor-deficient mice: evidence for a "thrifty gene." *Diabetes* 54:3510–16

Tang-Christensen M, Vrang N, Larsen PJ. 2001. Glucagon-like peptide containing pathways in the regulation of feeding behaviour. *Int. J. Obes. Relat. Metab. Disord.* 25(Suppl. 5):S42–47

Thorens B, Larsen PJ. 2004. Gut-derived signaling molecules and vagal afferents in the control of glucose and energy homeostasis. *Curr. Opin. Clin. Nutr. Metab. Care* 7:471–78

Trayhurn P, Bing C, Wood IS. 2006. Adipose tissue and adipokines—energy regulation from the human perspective. *J. Nutr.* 136:1935–39S

Turek FW, Joshu C, Kohsaka A, Lin E, Ivanova G, et al. 2005. Obesity and metabolic syndrome in circadian Clock mutant mice. *Science* 308:1043–45

Uher R, Treasure J. 2005. Brain lesions and eating disorders. *J. Neurol. Neurosurg. Psychiatry* 76:852–57

Ulijaszek SJ. 2002. Human eating behaviour in an evolutionary ecological context. *Proc. Nutr. Soc.* 61:517–26

van den Top M, Spanswick D. 2006. Integration of metabolic stimuli in the hypothalamic arcuate nucleus. *Prog. Brain Res.* 153:141–54

Vanitallie TB. 2006. Sleep and energy balance: interactive homeostatic systems. *Metabolism* 55:S30–35

Verhagen JV. 2007. The neurocognitive bases of human multimodal food perception: consciousness. *Brain Res. Brain Res. Rev.* 53:271–86

von Frisch K. 1967. *Dance Language and Orientation of Bees.* Cambridge, MA: Harvard Univ. Press

Wang YH, Tache Y, Sheibel AB, Go VL, Wei JY. 1997. Two types of leptin-responsive gastric vagal afferent terminals: an in vitro single-unit study in rats. *Am. J. Physiol.* 273:R833–37

Weingarten HP. 1983. Conditioned cues elicit feeding in sated rats: a role for learning in meal initiation. *Science* 220:431–33

Weinsier RL, Hunter GR, Heini AF, Goran MI, Sell SM. 1998. The etiology of obesity: relative contribution of metabolic factors, diet, and physical activity. *Am. J. Med.* 105:145–50

Wells JC. 2006. The evolution of human fatness and susceptibility to obesity: an ethological approach. *Biol. Rev. Camb. Philos. Soc.* 81:183–205

Welzl H, D'Adamo P, Lipp HP. 2001. Conditioned taste aversion as a learning and memory paradigm. *Behav. Brain Res.* 125:205–13

Will MJ, Franzblau EB, Kelley AE. 2003. Nucleus accumbens mu-opioids regulate intake of a high-fat diet via activation of a distributed brain network. *J. Neurosci.* 23:2882–88

Wilsey J, Scarpace PJ. 2004. Caloric restriction reverses the deficits in leptin receptor protein and leptin signaling capacity associated with diet-induced obesity: role of leptin in the regulation of hypothalamic long-form leptin receptor expression. *J. Endocrinol.* 181:297–306

Woods SC, Gotoh K, Clegg DJ. 2003. Gender differences in the control of energy homeostasis. *Exp. Biol. Med. (Maywood)* 228:1175–80

Woods SC, Lotter EC, McKay LD, Porte D Jr. 1979. Chronic intracerebroventricular infusion of insulin reduces food intake and body weight of baboons. *Nature* 282:503–5

Woods SC, Seeley RJ. 2001. Insulin as an adiposity signal. *Int. J. Obes. Relat. Metab. Disord.* 25(Suppl. 5):S35–38

Wu XY, Zhu JX, Gao J, Owyang C, Li Y. 2005. Neurochemical phenotype of vagal afferent neurons activated to express C-Fos in response to luminal stimulation in the rat. *Neuroscience* 130:757–67

Wyvell CL, Berridge KC. 2000. Intra-accumbens amphetamine increases the conditioned incentive salience of sucrose reward: enhancement of reward "wanting" without enhanced "liking" or response reinforcement. *J. Neurosci.* 20:8122–30

Wyvell CL, Berridge KC. 2001. Incentive sensitization by previous amphetamine exposure: increased cue-triggered "wanting" for sucrose reward. *J. Neurosci.* 21:7831–40

Xu AW, Kaelin CB, Takeda K, Akira S, Schwartz MW, Barsh GS. 2005. PI3K integrates the action of insulin and leptin on hypothalamic neurons. *J. Clin. Invest.* 115:951–58

Xu AW, Ste-Marie L, Kaelin CB, Barsh GS. 2007. Inactivation of signal transducer and activator of transcription 3 in proopiomelanocortin (Pomc) neurons causes decreased Pomc expression, mild obesity, and defects in compensatory refeeding. *Endocrinology* 148:72–80

Xue B, Kahn BB. 2006. AMPK integrates nutrient and hormonal signals to regulate food intake and energy balance through effects in the hypothalamus and peripheral tissues. *J. Physiol.* 574:73–83

Yamamoto H, Kishi T, Lee CE, Choi BJ, Fang H, et al. 2003. Glucagon-like peptide-1-responsive catecholamine neurons in the area postrema link peripheral glucagon-like peptide-1 with central autonomic control sites. *J. Neurosci.* 23:2939–46

Yang XJ, Mastaitis J, Mizuno T, Mobbs C. 2007. Glucokinase regulates reproductive function, glucocorticoid secretion, food intake, and hypothalamic gene expression. *Endocrinology* 148:1928–32

Yaswen L, Diehl N, Brennan MB, Hochgeschwender U. 1999. Obesity in the mouse model of pro-opiomelanocortin deficiency responds to peripheral melanocortin. *Nat. Med.* 5:1066–70

Young A. 2005. Inhibition of gastric emptying. *Adv. Pharmacol.* 52:99–121

Zagorodnyuk VP, Chen BN, Brookes SJ. 2001. Intraganglionic laminar endings are mechano-transduction sites of vagal tension receptors in the guinea-pig stomach. *J. Physiol.* 534:255–68

Zhang J, Frassetto A, Huang RR, Lao JZ, Pasternak A, et al. 2006. The mu-opioid receptor subtype is required for the anorectic effect of an opioid receptor antagonist. *Eur. J. Pharmacol.* 545:147–52

Zhang M, Kelley AE. 2000. Enhanced intake of high-fat food following striatal mu-opioid stimulation: microinjection mapping and Fos expression. *Neuroscience* 99:267–77

Zhang X, Firestein S. 2002. The olfactory receptor gene superfamily of the mouse. *Nat. Neurosci.* 5:124–33

Zhang X, Shi T, Holmberg K, Landry M, Huang W, et al. 1997. Expression and regulation of the neuropeptide Y Y2 receptor in sensory and autonomic ganglia. *Proc. Natl. Acad. Sci. USA* 94:729–34

Zhang Y, Hoon MA, Chandrashekar J, Mueller KL, Cook B, et al. 2003. Coding of sweet, bitter, and umami tastes: different receptor cells sharing similar signaling pathways. *Cell* 112:293–301

Zhao AZ, Huan JN, Gupta S, Pal R, Sahu A. 2002. A phosphatidylinositol 3-kinase phosphodiesterase 3B-cyclic AMP pathway in hypothalamic action of leptin on feeding. *Nat. Neurosci.* 5:727–28

Zhao GQ, Zhang Y, Hoon MA, Chandrashekar J, Erlenbach I, et al. 2003. The receptors for mammalian sweet and umami taste. *Cell* 115:255–66

Zheng H, Patterson LM, Phifer CB, Berthoud HR. 2005. Brainstem melanocortinergic modulation of meal size and identification of hypothalamic POMC projections. *Am. J. Physiol. Regul. Integr. Comp. Physiol.* 289:247–58

Neuroendocrine Regulation of Feminine Sexual Behavior: Lessons from Rodent Models and Thoughts About Humans

Jeffrey D. Blaustein

Center for Neuroendocrine Studies, Neuroscience and Behavior Program and Psychology Department, University of Massachusetts, Amherst, Massachusetts 01003-9271; email: blaustein@cns.umass.edu

Annu. Rev. Psychol. 2008. 59:93–118

First published online as a Review in Advance on August 2, 2007

The *Annual Review of Psychology* is online at http://psych.annualreviews.org

This article's doi: 10.1146/annurev.psych.59.103006.093556

0066-4308/08/0203-0093$20.00

Key Words

estradiol, progesterone, estrogen receptors, progestin receptors, reproductive behavior, lordosis, sexuality, preclinical models

Abstract

Much has been learned concerning the neuroendocrine processes and cellular mechanisms by which steroid hormones influence reproductive behaviors in rodents and other animals. In this review, a short discussion of hormones and feminine sexual behavior in some rodent species is followed by an outline of the main principles that have been learned from these studies. Examples are given of the importance of considering the timing of hormone treatments, dosage of hormone, use of a specific hormone, particular class of hormones, or form of hormone, interactions between hormones, route of administration, peripheral factors that influence hormonal response, and the possible mechanisms of action by which hormones and other factors influence sexual behaviors. Although cellular studies in humans are presently impossible to perform, mechanistic studies in rodents may provide clues about the neuroendocrine mechanisms by which hormones act and interact in the brain to influence behavior in all species, including humans.

Contents

INTRODUCTION

Beach, one of the pioneers of behavioral endocrinology, ended his 1981 classic historical review of the field, "Historical origins of modern research on hormones and behavior," with the comment:

> Scientists with their doctorates in psychology study development of progesterone receptors in neurons of the rat hypothalamus while other investigators initially trained in pharmacology invent elegant behavioral measures of sexual motivation in the estrous female. These developments appear to represent more than a mere borrowing of techniques by one discipline from another. Instead they seem to reflect progress toward recognition of common goals and shared

theoretical interests. If such is indeed the case, behavioral endocrinology may well be a discipline *in statu nascendi*. (Beach 1981)

Beach's monograph was written when research on the hormonal regulation of sexual behavior was fairly well developed, but research on the cellular mechanisms of hormone action on the behavior was still in its infancy. In addition to more progress on the understanding of neuroendocrine regulation of sexual behavior, a great deal has been learned in the past 25 years about the important and multifaceted roles that steroid receptors play in the regulation of sexual behavior in rodents. In contrast to other recent reviews of subfields of hormones and feminine sexual behavior (Blaustein & Erskine 2002, Blaustein & Mani 2007, Pfaff et al. 1994, Pfaus 1999), this review is an attempt to articulate the main lessons that have come from the study of both—the neuroendocrine regulation of sexual behaviors and of neural mechanisms of action of steroid hormones—in rodents. It ends with thoughts on the potential relevance of this work to human sexual health.

BEHAVIOR CAN INFORM PHYSIOLOGY AND CELLULAR AND MOLECULAR BIOLOGY

In his historical paper, Beach relayed a story about an event that has a prominent role in the history of this field. In the mid-1930s, William Caldwell Young, another parent of this field, and his collaborators were working to understand the hormonal factors that contribute to the expression of feminine sexual behavior in female rats and guinea pigs. To their surprise, they learned that during the estrous cycle, the sexually receptive posture, lordosis, could first be elicited when the ovarian follicle was ripening, well before ovulation had occurred. And after many insightful studies, they learned that the optimal treatment for inducing feminine sexual behavior in guinea pigs and rats in which ovaries had been

Table 1 Effects of typical hormone treatments on sexual behavior in ovariectomized rats

0 hours	42 hours	Lordosis?[1]
Oil	Oil	No
Estradiol (low dose)	Oil	Usually low
Oil	Progesterone	No
Estradiol	Progesterone	High

[1]Copulatory behavior (lordosis) is typically tested four to six hours after second progesterone injection.

removed to eliminate the principal sources of estradiol and progesterone secretion, was injection of estradiol followed a day or two later with an injection of progesterone (see Young 1969 for a review) (**Table 1**). Although the data were incontrovertible, they presented a conundrum: the expression of feminine sexual behavior, which they had shown required exposure to progesterone, most definitely commenced prior to ovulation during the estrous cycle, yet progesterone was believed to be secreted only from the corpus luteum, a structure definitely formed at the time of ovulation.

Not surprisingly, since dogma in any field is difficult to refute (Blaustein 2004a), Young's heretical work was rejected by the leading endocrinologists of the day. It was not until three decades later (Feder et al. 1967, 1968) that the work of Young's group was vindicated when the first assays of progesterone across the rat and guinea pig estrous cycle revealed that progesterone was in fact secreted well before ovulation (**Figure 1**). Indeed, progesterone could not have been secreted solely from the corpus luteum, as early researchers had assumed. It was later learned that there was a previously unknown source of progesterone in the cells of the follicle and interstitium (Leavitt et al. 1971). Unfortunately, the false belief that the corpus luteum was the only source of progesterone (as well as the false belief that the endocrinologists of the day knew all that there was

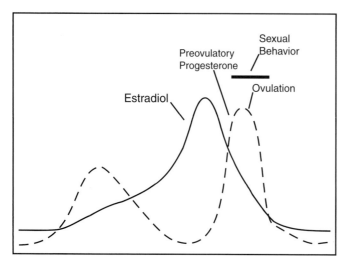

Metestrus   **Diestrus**   **Proestrus**   **Estrus**

Figure 1

Patterns of estradiol and progesterone over a typical four-day estrous cycle in rats and relationship to the period of sexual behavior and ovulation. The patterns of hormone levels have been plotted without regard to actual levels, as the peak level of progesterone is nearly 1000 times that of estradiol (levels adapted from Butcher et al. 1974). The approximate time of the period of sexual receptivity and ovulation are indicated.

to know about ovarian function) had led some researchers to abide by the dogma that no progesterone was secreted prior to ovulation. The study of feminine sexual behavior in rodents using a behavioral endocrinology approach suggested quite correctly that progesterone was secreted from another source prior to ovulation.

Subsequently, through the use of timed ovariectomies at different stages of the estrous cycle with exogenous hormone replacement, others (Joslyn et al. 1971, Powers 1970) demonstrated the necessity for preovulatory progesterone during the estrous cycle for the facilitation of sexual receptivity in rats and guinea pigs. Thus, given the opportunity, behavior can inform physiology. Since these studies then led to research on the cellular and molecular mechanisms of progesterone's influence on sexual behavior, it is fair to say that the study of behavior can inform cellular and molecular biology as well.

THERE IS MORE TO ANIMAL SEXUAL BEHAVIOR THAN JUST THE REFLEXIVE, SEXUALLY RECEPTIVE POSTURE, LORDOSIS

Although much of the early work in this field simplified the characteristics of feminine sexual behavior, tending primarily to the immobile lordosis posture to appropriate mating stimulation as an index of sexual receptivity, sexual behavior is far more complex than this. Beach (1976) described three elements of sexual behavior—receptivity, proceptivity, and attractivity. Blaustein & Erskine (2002) recently modified this terminology and described copulatory, paracopulatory, and progestative behaviors. Copulatory behaviors are behaviors that result in successful transfer of sperm from the male to the female and are analogous to Beach's term "receptivity," but the term emphasizes the active role of the female. Paracopulatory behaviors were defined as species-typical behaviors displayed by females that arouse the male and stimulate him to mount. This is comparable to Beach's term, proceptivity. Other terms that have been used for these behaviors are precopulatory (Hlinak & Madlafousek 1977) or solicitation (Erskine 1989) behaviors. This includes behaviors such as ear wiggling, darting, and hopping. Progestative behaviors include behaviors that the female uses to regulate contact with the male (pacing) that facilitate or initiate pregnancy.

There is no question that female rodents, particularly well-studied rats, express a host of behaviors in addition to the lordosis posture. Some of these serve to attract the male to the female; others increase the probability that copulation will result in offspring. However, before accepting the idea that study of additional aspects of sexual behavior beyond lordosis (receptive behavior) is essential, we can ask whether the most commonly measured response, lordosis, is itself useful as a behavioral readout, even when studied to the exclusion of other very important parameters.

The necessity and appropriateness of studying parameters beyond copulatory behavior, or lordosis, depends entirely on the questions being asked. If sexual behavior is used as a readout for the actions of hormones or drugs on a particular neural substrate, then lordosis is quite adequate. It is reliable, quantifiable, and replicable, and it lends itself to reductionistic, mechanistic study. If, however, the goal is to fully understand the complexities, idiosyncrasies, and/or evolution of hormonal regulation of feminine sexual behavior in a particular species, then the study of lordosis in a vacuum is no more appropriate than the study of jaw movements alone in an attempt to understand the complexities of appetite and body weight regulation. Finally, if the goal is to provide a reliable, preclinical model for human sexual behavior, then it is appropriate to address the many issues that are considered later in this review.

SPECIFICS OF HORMONE TREATMENTS AND INTERACTIONS BETWEEN HORMONES ARE CRITICAL TO RESPONSE: TIME COURSE, DOSE, ROUTE OF ADMINISTRATION, FORM OF HORMONE, AND PATTERN OF ADMINISTRATION

Whereas estradiol requires about a day to effectively prime ovariectomized guinea pigs and rats to respond to progesterone, progesterone facilitates the expression of sexual behaviors in estradiol-primed animals with a very short latency (Boling & Blandau 1939, Boling et al. 1938, Collins et al. 1938). In fact, some studies demonstrated extraordinarily rapid effects of progesterone on feminine rat sexual behavior, with some reports of onset of sexual behavior in less than ten minutes (Lisk 1960, Meyerson 1972) if the progesterone was administered intravenously rather than subcutaneously. However, in other studies, longer latencies of 30 minutes for lordosis (Glaser et al. 1983, McGinnis et al. 1981)

and two hours or more for onset of proceptive/paracopulatory behaviors (Glaser et al. 1983) have been reported. Interestingly, these rapid effects of intravenous progesterone have never been observed in guinea pigs (unpublished observations of R.W. Goy, D.A. Goldfoot, and W.D. Joslyn, cited in Terasawa et al. 1976), although after intrahypothalamic administration, many of the guinea pigs responded by the first test at one hour (Morin & Feder 1974). Although there are various inconsistencies in the precise time course of progesterone action, caused in part by the competing anesthetic effects of progesterone (Meyerson 1972), the effects of progesterone on feminine sexual behavior are considerably more rapid than those of estradiol, a feature that must be considered in all studies of the mechanisms of action of estradiol and progesterone. This also provides a dramatic illustration that the route of administration is critically important to the time course of response.

The particular effects of hormones on behavior and other physiological end points are also critically dependent on the dosage and timing of administration. For example, progesterone has very different effects on feminine sexual behavior depending on the timing of administration and dose relative to estradiol as follows:

A. Estradiol alone may induce the expression of feminine sexual behavior (known as estrogen heat or progesterone-independent sexual behavior), but treatment with progesterone facilitates the expression, allows a lower dose of estradiol to be used, induces expression with short latency, and is required during the estrous cycle. Furthermore, the nature of progesterone-facilitated sexual behavior more closely resembles behavior seen during estrous cycle. (For a review, see Blaustein & Erskine 2002.)

B. Progesterone treatment concurrent with or before estradiol treatment may inhibit the expression of sexual

ERs: estrogen
receptors

behavior (Blaustein & Wade 1977a, Wallen et al. 1975), a feature of progesterone's actions that is sometimes called concurrent inhibition (Blaustein & Wade 1977a); however, in some cases it may facilitate the expression of sexual behavior, depending on the dosage of each hormone (Blaustein & Wade 1977a).

C. Progesterone may desensitize subsequent response to itself, depending on the dosage and timing of each injection (Blaustein 1982, Blaustein & Wade 1977b), a feature of progesterone that has been called sequential inhibition or desensitization.

D. Progesterone administered in the absence of estradiol has no effect on sexual receptivity. To my knowledge, there has never been a report of progesterone influencing the expression of feminine sexual behavior in the absence of an estrogen. This is understandable, since animals are never exposed to progesterone in the absence of an estrogen during the reproductive cycle.

Dramatic differences among estrogens must be taken into account in the interpretation of experiments. First, although the dominant naturally occurring estrogen circulating in mammals is estradiol-17β (usually referred to as estradiol), it is typically injected subcutaneously in an esterified form, estradiol benzoate, that is slowly released. The benzoate group is hydrolyzed, releasing estradiol-17β into the circulation. The effectiveness of estradiol in contrast with estradiol benzoate differs dramatically, with considerably lower doses of estradiol benzoate required for the equivalent behavioral response as doses of free estradiol (Feder & Silver 1974). Likewise, estradiol, the predominant, circulating estrogen, is more potent than the other estrogens, estrone and estriol (Feder & Silver 1974). On the other hand, if the free estradiol is administered in the form of low-dose pulses separated by 3 to 36 hours (Clark & Roy 1987),

quite small quantities are sufficient to induce full behavioral response.

The influence of the form of hormone used and the pattern of administration is most dramatically illustrated in contrasts between males and females. Feminine sexual behavior is considered to be sexually differentiated because gonadectomized female rats, guinea pigs, and many other animals tend to express feminine sexual behavior in response to estradiol and progesterone in adulthood, but males do not (Wallen & Baum 2002). There is ample evidence that this is due to the actions of sex steroids acting during the neonatal period to alter the bias of brain areas involved in feminine sexual behavior to be responsive or not. Surprisingly, if the estradiol is given in the form of two small pulses of free estradiol separated by about a day, male rats and guinea pigs are quite behaviorally responsive (Olster & Blaustein 1988, 1990; Sodersten et al. 1983).

The fact that behavioral response and even the appearance of sex differences in response to hormones are so dependent on dosage and timing of administration of the hormones drives home the important message that results from single-dose/single-time-point experiments can be very misleading. In fact, this accounts for the early misconception that progesterone inhibited the expression of sexual behavior in guinea pigs but not in rats (Zucker 1967).

CELLULAR MECHANISMS OF HORMONAL REGULATION OF FEMININE SEXUAL BEHAVIOR

Steroid receptors are protein molecules that bind hormones and are believed to mediate the effects of hormones on particular responses in a variety of tissues. Although estrogen receptors (ERs), intracellular binding proteins that bind estrogens with high affinity and specificity, were first discovered and characterized in peripheral reproductive tissues (Gorski et al. 1968, Jensen et al. 1968), the work of many researchers (Eisenfeld 1969, Kahwanago et al. 1969, Michael 1962,

Pfaff 1968a, Stumpf 1968, Zigmond & McEwen 1969) collectively demonstrated that ERs were present in the brain, a tissue once considered a negative control for peripheral reproductive tissues.

After ERs were discovered in the brain, it followed that ERs might be involved in the cellular mechanisms by which estrogens act in the brain to influence sexual behavior. The first studies on the cellular underpinnings of the effects of estradiol on behavior implicated ERs in the mechanism of action. The receptors were found in the neuroanatomical sites at which estradiol implants induced sexual behaviors, and blocking the receptors so that they did not bind estradiol inhibited the effects of estradiol on sexual behavior (e.g., Luttge 1976, Roy & Wade 1977).

Because of the apparent discrepancy in the time that it takes for estradiol and progesterone to influence sexual behavior, it had been speculated that estrogens acted through what has been called a cell nuclear or direct genomic mechanism involving ERs, whereas progesterone influenced sexual behavior by an unspecified membrane mechanism (e.g., McEwen et al. 1978). However, the discovery of progestin receptors (PRs) in the brain with binding affinities and steroid specificity matching those in other reproductive tissues (Kato & Onouchi 1977; MacLusky & McEwen 1978, 1980), as well as cell nuclear progestin binding in the brain (Blaustein & Wade 1978, Sar & Stumpf 1973, Warembourg 1978), suggested that the PR might mediate the effects of progesterone on sexual behavior. Although this hypothesis was controversial at first (Etgen 1984), work by many labs supported the involvement of intracellular PRs in the brain in the mechanisms by which progesterone facilitates sexual behavior (Blaustein & Feder 1980; Blaustein et al. 1980; Moguilewsky & Raynaud 1979a,b; Parsons et al. 1980).

As discussed above, the sequential inhibition effect of progesterone refers to the finding that progesterone first facilitates sexual behavior, but once the period of sexual receptivity (heat) terminates, a second progesterone injection no longer facilitates the expression (Blaustein & Wade 1977a, Marrone et al. 1977, Morin 1977). The study of cellular mechanisms of progesterone action led to the hypothesis that although progesterone can inhibit the effects of estradiol on the induction of sexual receptivity, its role in progesterone-facilitated sexual behavior is to desensitize subsequent response to itself (Blaustein & Brown 1985) by the down-regulation of PRs. It has also been proposed that this down-regulation of PRs in relevant neurons is the basis for termination of the period of sexual receptivity (Blaustein & Brown 1985). Failure to respond to progesterone a short time after heat termination can be seen as a continuation of the process by which progesterone brings about heat termination. Recent work on the cellular process by which PRs are down-regulated, which demonstrates that blocking the degradation of PRs blocks the desensitization to a subsequent progesterone injection (Gonzalez-Flores et al. 2004), supports the hypothesis that down-regulation of PRs is responsible for this sequential inhibition or desensitization to progesterone.

STEROID HORMONE RECEPTORS ARE DEFINITELY INVOLVED, BUT THERE ARE MANY CANDIDATES

The cloning and sequencing of the ER (Greene et al. 1986) and PR genes (Jeltsch et al. 1986) made possible the study of the regulation and function of each of these genes. As has been the case with numerous receptors, early experiments and interpretations were complicated by discoveries of new forms of the receptors. A second ER coded by a separate gene was identified in peripheral reproductive tissues in 1996 (Kuiper et al. 1996), and then it was shown to be expressed in the brain (Li et al. 1997, Shughrue et al. 1996). Although this ER, termed ERβ, has a great deal of structural homology with the original ER, later named ERα, it is less homologous in the region that binds to DNA, suggesting

PRs: progestin receptors

that when ERβ is activated, it may influence different genes or influence genes in different ways than does ERα. In fact, studies using genetically modified strains of mice with a disrupted ERα or ERβ gene (gene knockout strains) have found that ERα is essential for the expression of sexual behavior in response to estradiol and progesterone (Rissman et al. 1997), whereas ERβ either is without obvious effect (Kudwa & Rissman 2003) or may have an opposing influence (Ogawa et al. 1999).

The early discovery of two forms of the PR (Schrader & O'Malley 1972) complicated an understanding of its role. However, in this case, the same PR gene is capable of synthesizing two different receptors, PRA and PRB (Conneely et al. 1987, Kastner et al. 1990). PRA has an amino acid sequence that is identical to PRB, except that it is truncated and missing a stretch of amino acids at its N terminus. This finding complicates study of the two receptors, since they bind the same hormones, and antibodies that bind to PRA also bind to PRB, making it difficult to distinguish the two using immunocytochemistry, a standard anatomical technique for visualizing the receptors in brain sections. The recent development of genetically engineered strains of mice with disrupted genes for either PRA or PRB (PRA and PRB knockout mice) has resulted in evidence that, while PRA is essential for progesterone-facilitated sexual behavior, the PRB isoform has an important role as well (Mani et al. 2006).

These intracellular receptors are referred to by many names—nuclear receptors, because they were believed to act in the cell nucleus; genomic receptors, because they influence gene activity; classic steroid hormone receptors, because they were the first class of receptors characterized; transcription factor receptors, because they are modifiers of gene transcription; and direct genomic receptors because, in contrast to membrane receptors (discussed below) that may influence gene activity indirectly, they influence gene expression directly (Blaustein & Mani 2007).

Membrane receptors that are coded for by completely independent genes have been described (Filardo & Thomas 2005, Zhu et al. 2003), as have membrane receptors that seem to be post-translational modifications of the same genes that code for the transcription factor receptors discussed here (Razandi et al. 1999, Wade et al. 2001). It has also been shown anatomically that steroid hormone receptors are present at sites outside of cell nuclei of brain cells. In fact, ERs have been reported at a variety of cytoplasmic sites, including presynaptic terminals and postsynaptic densities (Blaustein et al. 1992), each suggestive of direct effects of steroid hormones on neurotransmitter release or synaptic signaling (Blaustein 1994). Although it is unclear what roles these synaptic ERs play in sexual behavior, recent work in the hippocampus suggests that they may be involved in mobilization of vesicles in presynaptic boutons (Hart et al. 2007). Although there is good evidence that, in addition to the well-characterized role of the transcription factor receptors, membrane receptors have a role in feminine sexual behavior (Debold & Frye 1994, Kow & Pfaff 2004), it is still too early in the development of this field to provide a comprehensive summary of that role.

STEROID RECEPTORS ARE INVOLVED IN SEXUAL BEHAVIORS IN EVERY INFRAHUMAN VERTEBRATE SPECIES IN WHICH THEY HAVE BEEN STUDIED

The transcription factor steroid hormone receptors in the brain are not a curiosity of rats, or for that matter, of rodents. They are present in all vertebrate species studied (Pfaff et al. 1994), including species as diverse as lizards (Young & Crews 1995), rhesus monkeys (Michael et al. 2005), and humans (Donahue et al. 2000, Osterlund & Hurd 2001). Furthermore, in all species in which their role in feminine sexual behavior has been studied, the receptors have been shown to be involved, although as discussed above, this is not the only mechanism by which hormones influence sexual behaviors. Therefore, as we learn more about the roles and regulation of various steroid receptors in rodents, it is reasonable to consider analogies with other species, including humans.

THERE IS MORE TO STEROID HORMONE ACTION THAN JUST BINDING TO RECEPTORS

It is now known that the transcriptional regulation by steroid receptors is more complex than hormones merely binding to them and inducing a cellular response. Numerous coregulators that influence transcriptional activity of ERs or PRs have been discovered and characterized (McKenna et al. 1999, O'Malley 2007). Although it is clear from in vitro work that these coregulators influence the transcriptional activity of steroid receptors, scant work has been done on their involvement in the brain in the regulation of feminine sexual behavior. However, three coactivators, steroid receptor coactivator-1 (SRC-1), SRC-2, and cAMP binding protein, have been shown to have a modulatory role in the mechanism of action of both ERs (Molenda et al. 2002) and PRs (Apostolakis et al. 2002, Molenda-Figueira et al. 2006) in feminine sexual behavior. Similarly, consistent with their involvement in feminine sexual behavior, these coregulators are coexpressed with ERs and PRs in brain areas involved in the behavior (Tetel et al. 2007).

NEUROANATOMICAL SUBSTRATES ARE COMPLEX: IT IS NOT JUST THE VENTROMEDIAL NUCLEUS OF THE HYPOTHALAMUS

Although full treatment of the subject is beyond the scope of this review, a discussion of the neuroendocrine mechanisms involved in feminine sexual behavior would not be complete without at least a short account of neuroanatomical substrates where the

hormones may act in this process. Although the neuroanatomical substrates for feminine sexual behavior are often oversimplified to suggest that the ventromedial nucleus of the hypothalamus (VMN) is the critical site for hormonal regulation of feminine sexual behavior, it must be noted that the VMN per se should not be considered the critical center for this regulation. Although small lesions of the VMN suppress sexual behavior induced by estradiol alone, they have little effect on progesterone-facilitated sexual behavior (Mathews & Edwards 1977). In fact, when the VMN is lesioned in rats, sexual behavior (at least that induced by repeated injections of estradiol alone, i.e., progesterone-independent sexual behavior) does not fully diminish for 48 hours (Pfaff & Sakuma 1979). Consequently, caution must be used in the interpretation of the cellular or molecular microanalysis of the cells in the VMN per se with the intent of elucidating the cellular mechanisms specific to sexual behavior.

The misunderstanding about the role of the VMN may be in part the result of imprecise anatomical descriptions and the fact that neurochemical systems often do not segregate into clear Nissl-defined densities of cells. Although the distinction is not uniformly accepted, some researchers distinguish the VMN (the distinct density of cells identified by the presence of Nissl substance in stained sections) from the ventromedial hypothalamus (VMH) (which also includes many cells in the shell surrounding the dense core of cells). This is a useful distinction, because many of the cells with qualities that would be expected of neurons involved in mediating the effects of hormones on feminine sexual behavior lie in the neuropil outside the VMN, but within the broader VMH. For example, in the careful tract-tracing work of Flanagan-Cato and collaborators (Calizo & Flanagan-Cato 2003, Daniels & Flanagan-Cato 2000, Flanagan-Cato et al. 2001), many neurons that are of likely importance to sexual behavior, because of their projections to the lumbar epaxial muscles involved in the

VMN: ventromedial nucleus of the hypothalamus

VMH: ventromedial hypothalamus

vlVMN:
ventrolateral aspect
of the ventromedial
nucleus of the
hypothalamus

lordosis response, have been shown to lie in the shell of the VMN rather than the core. Likewise, early autoradiographic studies of ER-containing cells (Pfaff 1968b, Pfaff & Keiner 1973, Stumpf 1968) all found many ER-containing cells in this area, and the same has been seen for PRs (Auger & Blaustein 1997, Blaustein et al. 1988). In fact, the cells adjacent to the VMN have been suggested as part of the site critical for estradiol priming of sexual behavior in guinea pigs (Delville & Blaustein 1988). It is essential in evaluating studies of particular cells hypothetically involved in the regulation of sexual behaviors to determine precisely which cells were sampled, and it is critical that studies not focus solely on the core VMN or ventrolateral aspect of the ventromedial nucleus of the hypothalamus (vlVMN) (e.g., Mo et al. 2006, White et al. 2007) to the exclusion of potentially important cells in the neuropil shell.

The VMH is definitely an important site in the regulation of feminine sexual behaviors. Furthermore, many other neuroanatomical areas have also been implicated in the hormonal regulation of feminine sexual behavior. These have been discussed in other reviews of this field (Blaustein & Erskine 2002, Pfaff et al. 1994).

ALL TYPES OF MATING STIMULATION ARE NOT EQUAL

When a male rat attempts to copulate with a female rat, he exhibits three very specific stereotyped behaviors, each having distinct physiological/behavioral consequences. The male may mount without intromission. This results in stimulation to the flanks and perineal region and is all that is required for eliciting the lordosis response if the female is sexually receptive (Kow et al. 1979). If he is successful in achieving intromission, he provides much of the same stimulation, as well as additional stimulation to the vagina. Since the rat penis is covered with keratinous spines, the stimulation to the vaginal wall is likely to be quite intense as the spines rake across the

vaginal wall (Phoenix et al. 1976, Taylor et al. 1983). Finally, if and when the male ejaculates, he provides similar stimulation as with intromissions, although perhaps of longer duration and greater intensity. In addition, by depositing the sperm plug, the male provides stimulation to the female's cervix as well (Sachs et al. 1984). The question of whether cervical stimulation occurs during intromissions without ejaculation cannot be answered at present.

It should not be surprising that each of these types of stimulation has different effects on the behavior of the female. While all that is necessary for the expression of lordosis is the stimulation that accompanies a mount, cervical stimulation (Pfaus et al. 2000), apparently conveyed by the pelvic nerve (Lodder & Zeilmaker 1976), results in increased rejection of the male and termination of the period of sexual receptivity.

Furthermore, in a paced-mating testing situation in which the female, rather than the male, sets the pace of copulatory stimulation and in which progestative behaviors can be studied, females return to the male sooner after intromission than ejaculation, and sooner after a mount than after an intromission (Bermant 1961, Erskine 1985, Peirce & Nuttall 1961). Although it has been suggested that only paced-mating behavior is rewarding to the female (Paredes & Vazquez 1999), a recent report suggests that nonpaced mating is rewarding as well (Meerts & Clark 2007). However, allowing the female to pace the rate of sexual stimulation enhances her chance of entering a progestative state, a time of high levels of circulating progesterone, essential for either pregnancy or pseudopregnancy (Erskine 1995).

HORMONES AND BEHAVIOR WITHOUT THE HORMONES: STEROID HORMONE RECEPTORS DO NOT NEED HORMONES

Steroid receptors, mediators of many of the effects of steroid hormones on target cells, are each named for the class of hormones to which they bind. ERs bind estrogens, PRs bind progestins, androgen receptors bind androgens, etc., and for many years, it had been assumed that hormone binding was essential to activate the receptors. The steroid receptors are often referred to as ligand-activated proteins. As of the writing of this review, even the Nuclear Receptor Signaling Atlas (NURSA; **http://www.nursa.org/**) still refers to ERα as "an estrogen-activated member of the nuclear receptor superfamily of transcription factors." However, ERs and PRs can be activated by mechanisms that do not require binding to their cognate hormone ligand (Power et al. 1991). Various steroid receptors can be activated indirectly by dopamine acting via the cAMP/adenylate cyclase intracellular signaling pathway, as well as by a host of other membrane receptors and intracellular signaling pathways (Blaustein 2004b). It is essential to consider these alternate pathways of "hormone-independent activation" when considering the possible mechanisms by which steroid receptors might be activated to influence sexual behaviors.

Although the vast majority of work in the field of hormones and feminine sexual behavior has focused on the mechanisms by which the two hormones, estradiol and progesterone, act at the cellular level in the brain to influence behavior, more recent work has demonstrated that the ovarian hormones aren't always necessary. While a number of other examples have now been reported (Blaustein & Mani 2007), the first example of the involvement of this mechanism in the regulation of sexual behavior was the report that dopamine agonists can substitute for progesterone in facilitating sexual behavior in estradiol-primed rats and mice by a process that requires PRs (Mani et al. 1994a,c, 1996). Subsequently, a variety of neurotransmitters and signaling pathways, including gonadotropin-releasing hormone, delta opioid receptors, cAMP, and cGMP, have been shown to facilitate feminine sexual behavior by this mechanism (Acosta-Martinez et al.

2006; Beyer et al. 1997; Chu et al. 1999; Mani et al. 1994b, 2006).

This mechanism of facilitation of feminine sexual behavior by ligand-independent activation of PRs goes beyond pharmacology. Copulatory attempts by male rats, which were known to increase levels of sexual receptivity in nonreceptive, estradiol-primed rats (Foreman & Moss 1977), have been shown to do so by hormone-independent activation of PRs (Auger 2001, Auger et al. 1997). Since mating stimulation induces dopamine release into a variety of forebrain sites (Etgen & Morales 2002, Matuszewich et al. 2000, Meisel et al. 1993), and since mating stimulation induces a genomic response (expression of the immediate early gene product, Fos) in neurons containing both ERs (Tetel et al. 1994) and PRs (Auger et al. 1996), it is possible that mating stimulation activates PRs indirectly via dopamine release (Meredith et al. 1998) by the process of hormone-independent activation. Therefore, although steroid receptors can be activated by their cognate hormone ligands (e.g., estradiol, progesterone), they can also be activated by nonhormonal mechanisms after appropriate neuronal stimulation.

In the first studies on mating enhancement via activation of PRs, it was determined that the proximal stimulus for the enhancement of sexual behavior was stimulation of the vagina and cervix (Auger et al. 1997, Bennett et al. 2002). Recent work, however, suggests that nonintromissive stimuli are sufficient for the enhancement (S. Farrell, G. Ghavami, J. Laroche, G. Mohan, and J.D. Blaustein, unpublished observations). Intromissive stimuli, in fact, often have a negative influence on sexual behaviors (Bennett et al. 2002, Pfaus et al. 2000).

PERIPHERAL REPRODUCTIVE ORGANS INFLUENCE RESPONSE OF THE BRAIN TO HORMONES

Although we tend to think of hormones acting on the brain to influence sexual behavior, in addition to the endocrine glands that secrete the hormones, peripheral reproductive organs are involved in other ways. For example, removal of the uterus increases the effectiveness and/or response of a given dose of estradiol and/or progesterone (Siegel et al. 1978).

In other experiments, systemic administration of the neuropeptide oxytocin or the prostaglandin, PGE_2, facilitates the expression of feminine sexual behavior after estradiol treatment in rats. However, the effectiveness of oxytocin is blocked by a section of the pelvic nerve (Moody et al. 1994), one of the principal nerves innervating the uterus. In fact, the effectiveness of each hormone is diminished by removal of the uterus, and even more so, by removal of the cervix (Moody & Adler 1995). Therefore, the response to systemic oxytocin injection seems to be secondary at least in part to uterine and/or cervical contractions induced by oxytocin and PGE_2. Because stimulation of the cervix, for example, rapidly influences gene expression in neurons containing ERs and PRs in the same areas that are involved in mediating the effects of sex steroid hormones on feminine sexual behavior (Auger et al. 1996, Tetel et al. 1994), it is quite reasonable to suggest that response of those neurons is heightened by feedback relating to muscular contractions in those peripheral reproductive organs. Because neural stimulation can activate steroid hormone receptors in neurons involved in the regulation of sexual behavior (described above), it is also possible that this uterus/cervix-mediated enhancement of sexual responding involves activation of steroid receptors in these neurons. The potentially important role of interactions between peripheral reproductive organs and the brain cannot be ignored.

MICE ARE NOT LITTLE RATS; EACH RODENT SPECIES HAS ITS OWN IDIOSYNCRACIES

Many similarities exist in the neuroendocrine underpinnings of feminine sexual behavior among different species of rodents (e.g., rats,

guinea pigs, hamsters, and mice). Each species has a similar pattern of hormonal secretion preceding the onset of estrous behavior—secretion of estradiol for about a day followed by a preovulatory surge in progesterone. However, there are some extreme differences among rodent species in the hormonal regulation of sexual behaviors. For example, the expression of feminine sexual behavior in estradiol-primed prairie voles is induced by exposure to male prairie voles (Carter et al. 1987).

Likewise, although there are similarities in the hormonal regulation of sexual behavior among rats, guinea pigs, hamsters, and mice, there also are rather large differences. The paracopulatory behaviors expressed differ among species, and the duration that the lordosis posture is held differs dramatically as well. Furthermore, although the other common laboratory rodent species tend to respond to the first exposure to estradiol and progesterone after ovariectomy with the expression of feminine sexual behaviors, mice require multiple, sequential (often weekly) treatments with testing before they express optimal levels (Kudwa & Rissman 2003, Mani et al. 1997, Thompson & Edwards 1971). No explanation for this difference has been forthcoming, although the use of inappropriate doses of hormones has been eliminated as a likely cause (J. Laroche and J.D. Blaustein, unpublished observations). Nevertheless, this dramatic difference in response must be taken into account in design, interpretation, and generalizations of experiments using mice. Likewise, although there are similarities in the hormonal and even cellular mechanisms, there are also robust species differences in the sexual behaviors themselves.

CAN NEUROENDOCRINE PRINCIPLES LEARNED IN RATS AND OTHER RODENTS BE APPLIED TO HUMANS?

Sexual behaviors in rodents obviously differ in many ways from sexual behaviors in humans. First and foremost, there are elements of sexual behavior in rodents that are reflexive; sexual behavior in humans is not reflexive. Second, whereas sexual receptivity is expressed only at well-defined periods during the reproductive cycle of rats, this is not true in humans or in primates in general. While appreciating the dramatic differences between humans and rodents, we can ask if there are commonalities in hormonal influences on particular aspects of sexual behavior.

Evidence from a variety of studies supports the view that hormones influence sexual behaviors in primates (Wallen 2001, Wallen et al. 1984, Wilson et al. 1982, Zehr et al. 1998), including influencing sexual desire and/or motivation in humans (Adams et al. 1978, Bancroft 2005, Basaria & Dobs 2006, Bolour & Braunstein 2005, Bullivant et al. 2004, Sherwin & Gelfand 1987, Stanislaw & Rice 1988). Although the specific hormones involved in sexual motivation and behavior in rodents and primates, including humans, may differ (Agmo & Ellingsen 2003), hormones are involved in all species. Therefore, it is reasonable to consider applying the basic endocrine concepts gleaned from work in rodents to humans.

As has been discussed in this review, a great deal is known about the hormonal and cellular mechanisms involved in the regulation of sexual behaviors in rats and other mammals. The question is whether the treatment of female sexual disorders in humans can be informed by the work in rats and other sub-human species. Pfaus and colleagues (Pfaus et al. 2003) have suggested that although the copulatory behavior, lordosis, does not have a counterpart in human female sexual function, measures of solicitation (paracopulatory behavior) are analogous to sexual desire in women. In contrast, Agmo and coworkers (Agmo et al. 2004) have suggested that measures of solicitation are not isomorphic with elements of human sexual behavior. They suggest that the display of lordosis may be as useful as more sophisticated measures in studies aimed at a basic understanding of the neuro-

biological underpinnings of feminine sexual behavior.

Rat paracopulatory behavior is sometimes used as a model for sexual desire in humans (Pfaus et al. 2004). The premise is that while women have sexual desire, unlike rodents they do not have reflexive components to their sexual behavior (i.e., lordosis). Therefore, the finding that stimulation of melanocortin-3/4 receptors with PT-141 (bremelanotide) increased paracopulatory behaviors in female rats suggested to researchers that this class of receptor might enhance sexual desire in humans. Subsequent work confirmed this initial finding by showing that another melanocortin agonist, melanotan II, increased the paracopulatory behaviors, ear-wiggling and darting and hopping, but only in the presence of both estradiol and progesterone (Rossler et al. 2006). Although the authors of both of these studies suggested that the effects of the drug are selective for proceptive (paracopulatory) behaviors without effect on lordosis, caution must be exercised in this interpretation. The influence on receptivity (lordosis) may not have been adequately tested, because in most of these experiments the level of lordosis response was already at or close to ceiling levels. Even so, there was a strong trend for an increase in lordosis after treatment with the melanocortin agonist (Rossler et al. 2006), suggesting that although the drugs increase sexual behavior, they may not be specific for paracopulatory/soliciting behaviors.

Nevertheless, if the rat model has predictive validity, then a melanocortin receptor agonist should have positive effects on sexual arousal in women. This idea was tested in a recent study in which PT-141 was administered to premenopausal women with female sexual arousal disorder (Diamond et al. 2006). These investigators reported a positive effect on subjective sexual response after intranasal administration of the drug in contrast to women receiving a placebo. Although this suggests that tests of paracopulatory behavior may have predictive validity for humans, it does not shed light on whether the more common tests of copulatory behavior (i.e., lordosis) are without validity. Most treatments that induce the expression of high levels of paracopulatory behavior also induce high levels of receptive behaviors.

When considering the preclinical value of a particular rodent model for human sexual disorders, work in rodents informs us that the etiology of, and the endocrine context accompanying, the low level of sexual desire should be considered. In most rodent studies, response to a particular compound in ovariectomized animals is dependent on pretreatment with either estradiol alone or followed by progesterone. In light of this, we have to consider the possibility that, as in other species, a particular therapy in humans might only be effective on a particular endocrine background.

If hormones influence sexual desire in humans—and the evidence suggests that they do—then it is critical to consider the endocrine context accompanying the disorder. It should be noted that hormone levels change dramatically and sometimes rapidly during the menstrual cycle, not in the controlled fashion of preclinical rat models. Is the particular human disorder likely to be secondary to changes in ovarian hormones, as is the case after ovariectomy, or is it present during typical menstrual cycles? It is likely that the estradiol-only primed rat model would have the most homology to human sexual disorders in which the etiology may be hormone deficiency (e.g., after ovariectomy), while the rat model treated with estradiol plus progesterone would be more appropriate for disorders that occur in the presence of typical levels of hormones during particular stages of the menstrual cycle.

Unfortunately, there are very few examples of treatments facilitating the expression of sexual behaviors in rats in the absence of ovarian hormones. In fact, only two treatments have been reported to be effective in the absence of a baseline level of the critical hormones, estradiol and/or estradiol and progesterone. These treatments are short-latency in-

duction of lordosis after cervical probing with a glass rod (Rodriguez-Sierra et al. 1975) and treatment with prostaglandin E_2 (Rodriguez-Sierra & Komisaruk 1978). Therefore, it is not surprising that preclinical models generally include hormone priming, but it should be noted that they may not be an ideal model for human sexual disorders that occur in the absence of typical hormones.

Although it is now accepted that hormones influence sexual desire or motivation in humans, there is currently debate about whether sexual desire in women is more dependent on estrogens or androgens. Increases in androgens increase sexual desire or motivation (see, e.g., de Paula et al. 2007, Sherwin et al. 1985, Simon et al. 2005). However, it has been suggested that the mechanism for this effect could be via an increase in circulating estrogens secondary to a release of estrogens from their protein carrier in the blood, sex hormone–binding globulin (Wallen & Parsons 1998).

In contrast to the androgens and estrogens, the role of progesterone, which has a robust influence on the sexual behavior of rats, guinea pigs, hamsters, and mice, has been largely unexplored in women. Although progestins are considered to have inhibitory effects on sexual desire based on results of one study (Dennerstein et al. 1980), it must be noted that a synthetic progestin, not progesterone, was used in this study, and the progestin was administered chronically for months.

Although yet untested, results from experiments in a variety of rodent models predict two means by which progesterone and/or the progestin response system could be involved in a positive influence on female sexual desire. First, if progesterone levels were to increase prior to the onset of peak sexual desire, as they do prior to the onset of sexual behaviors in rats, then it might be reasonable to suggest that a causal relationship exists between the peak in progesterone at this stage of the reproductive cycle and the increase in sexual desire, an idea that has recently been suggested (Bullivant et al. 2004). In fact, a mid-cycle progesterone surge was reported in one study that sampled blood levels of progesterone repeatedly at short intervals (Hoff et al. 1983). This finding opens up the possibility that preovulatory progesterone secretion might be involved in some aspects of the periovulatory increase in sexual desire that has been reported (Bullivant et al. 2004). Also, the possibility cannot be ignored that like in rats (Micevych et al. 2003, Sinchak et al. 2003), progesterone might be synthesized in the hypothalamus in humans. Support for the possibility that progesterone has a facilitating role in primates comes from work in rhesus monkeys; progesterone, although not responsible for initiation of sexual behavior, may enhance ongoing behavior (Wallen et al. 1984, Wilson et al. 1982) prior to subsequently inhibiting it.

Even if it were found that progesterone does not influence sexual behaviors or desire during the preovulatory period in humans, it is reasonable to consider the possibility that PRs are involved in the increase in sexual desire often seen in women around this time. As discussed earlier, estradiol-primed rats do not require exposure to progesterone in order to activate PRs and to express high levels of PR-dependent sexual behaviors if they receive appropriate neuronal stimulation. Although in the case of sexual behavior, the stimulation involves mating by a male rat, it has also been shown that the surge of gonadotropin-releasing hormone in estrous-cycling rats requires hormone-independent activation of PRs by an endogenous neural stimulus (Chappell & Levine 2000). Thus, just as progesterone is not necessary in rats for PR-dependent influences on behavior and physiology, there is the unexplored possibility that a similar, PR-dependent process influences sexual desire in humans. Is it also reasonable to consider the possibility that some drugs that apparently influence sexual desire in humans (Bechara et al. 2004, Caruso et al. 2004, Diamond et al. 2006) do so by indirect activation of steroid hormone receptors, as occurs with similar drugs in rats (Mani et al. 1994a).

Some misunderstanding and misinterpretation of results of studies in humans relates to nomenclature. The term "estrogen" is sometimes used by researchers to refer to estradiol-17β, sometimes to any of the endogenous estrogens, sometimes to any compound of the class called estrogens, and sometimes to the entire class of hormones. The problems associated with use of this imprecise terminology are apparent in the hormone replacement therapy debate. The well-publicized studies by the Women's Health Initiative (Rossouw et al. 2002) and the Women's Health Initiative Memory Study (Rapp et al. 2003, Shumaker et al. 2003) investigated the effects of either Premarin[TM] or Prempro[TM] on a wide variety of health parameters. Despite the fact that Premarin[TM] is a collection of a variety of conjugated equine estrogens (CEEs) and not specifically estradiol-17β, and Prempro[TM] is a mixture of these CEEs and the synthetic progestin, medroxyprogesterone acetate, and not progesterone, these studies are often misinterpreted as having investigated the effects of "estradiol" or "estradiol and progesterone." It is not at all clear if these results have relevance to the effects of specific estrogens, such as estradiol-17β, or the naturally occurring progestin, progesterone. It is also critical to bear in mind, as discussed above, that a particular hormone can have very different effects depending on the endocrine context in which it is administered, yet in these studies, as is typically the case in work in humans, both classes of hormones were administered concurrently and daily for extended durations.

As has been pointed out recently (Gleason et al. 2005), the specific form of the estrogen used and route of administration can have dramatic influence on efficacy in humans, as is the case in rodents (discussed above). Failure to take into account dosage and time course of hormone action and interactions with other hormones may lead to misunderstanding of the effects of particular hormones in human studies in which these issues are often not considered for logistical reasons. In human studies, the route of administration (oral in the case of CEEs), context (treatment started premenopausally, perimenopausally, or postmenopausally, or decades later), specific chemical structure (e.g., progesterone versus synthetic progestin, estradiol versus CEEs), and pattern of exposure (both classes of steroids administered concurrently versus sequentially) must be considered in the interpretation of results. Does concurrent administration of an estrogen and a progestin inform us about their role during typical reproductive cycles in which hormones are dynamically secreted in particular patterns? Does treatment with a synthetic progestin inform us about the role of progesterone?

The Women's Health Initiative study (Hays et al. 2003) found no effect of Premarin™ on sexual satisfaction. Besides the problems already mentioned, this study asked only one question relating to sexual satisfaction, so for many reasons it is regrettably of no value in a discussion of the influences of hormones on sexual response in women. Unfortunately, the vast majority of research in humans has been on the effects of these nonphysiological treatments and often has not used the naturally secreted hormones estradiol and progesterone in their physiological patterns.

CONCLUSIONS AND FUTURE ISSUES

Studies of hormones and feminine sexual behavior primarily in rodents (but also in other nonhuman species) have taught us a great deal about the factors that are important in determining whether a particular treatment will influence a particular response as well as informed us about the possible cellular mechanisms that might be involved. Neuroendocrinological issues that should be kept in mind when designing and evaluating studies, in both humans and other animals, include the following:

- dose of hormone (less hormone can sometimes be more effective than more hormone)
- form of hormone administered and the specific estrogen (all estrogens are not the same as estradiol, and even estradiol benzoate is not the same as estradiol)
- timing of treatment (some responses of hormones are rapid, and some are slow)
- route of administration, which influences the response to hormone
- interactions with other hormones (the presence of one hormone can dramatically alter the efficacy and even the effects of another hormone)
- cellular mechanisms involved (sometimes a nonhormonal factor can use the same response system as a missing hormone, and regulation of relevant receptors should be considered)
- peripheral factors (e.g., stimulation of peripheral reproductive organs) and environmental factors (e.g., behavior of conspecifics), which can robustly influence behavior and response to hormones
- species differences that exist even among similar rodent models (e.g., mice are not little rats or little guinea pigs)
- specific neuroanatomical sites under investigation. Researchers must be aware that a precise understanding of the neuroanatomical structures involved is essential to molecular and cellular studies (i.e., studies that solely examine cells within the VMN or vlVMN may be too focused at this time).

The jury will be out for some time concerning the question of whether or not research on sexual behaviors in rodents has predictive validity for developing therapies for women with hypoactive sexual disorders. However, many of the basic principles and factors discussed here should be considered in the design and interpretation of studies of hormones and sexual desire in humans. In addition, although this review is focused specifically on sexual behavior, the research that has been carried out on neuroendocrine mechanisms of the regulation of sexual behavior is not idiosyncratic to that behavior. These studies have elucidated basic neuroendocrinological principles, which can inform work on other behaviors, cognitive function, regulation of ovulation, and any other brain-related end point that is influenced by steroid hormones. Regardless of whether rodent models have predictive validity for human sexual disorders, basic neuroendocrine principles gleaned from these studies should inform research on all of these behavioral and physiological end points.

ACKNOWLEDGMENTS

Research related to this review in the author's laboratory was funded by NS 19327 from the National Institutes of Health. I am grateful to all of my colleagues and trainees with whom I have spoken over the years regarding the issues raised in this review. I am especially grateful to Dr. Kim Wallen for providing thoughts on nonhuman primate models.

LITERATURE CITED

Acosta-Martinez M, Gonzalez-Flores O, Etgen AM. 2006. The role of progestin receptors and the mitogen-activated protein kinase pathway in delta opioid receptor facilitation of female reproductive behaviors. *Horm. Behav.* 49:458–62

Adams DB, Gold AR, Burt AD. 1978. Rise in female-initiated sexual activity at ovulation and its suppression by oral contraceptives. *N. Engl. J. Med.* 299:1145–50

Agmo A, Ellingsen E. 2003. Relevance of nonhuman animal studies to the understanding of human sexuality. *Scand. J. Psychol.* 44:293–301

Agmo A, Turi AL, Ellingsen E, Kaspersen H. 2004. Preclinical models of sexual desire: conceptual and behavioral analyses. *Pharmacol. Biochem. Behav.* 78:379–404

Apostolakis EM, Ramamurphy M, Zhou D, Onate S, O'Malley BW. 2002. Acute disruption of select steroid receptor coactivators prevents reproductive behavior in rats and unmasks genetic adaptation in knockout mice. *Mol. Endocrinol.* 16:1511–23

Auger AP. 2001. Ligand-independent activation of progestin receptors: relevance for female sexual behaviour. *Reproduction* 122:847–55

Auger AP, Blaustein JD. 1997. Progesterone treatment increases Fos-immunoreactivity within some progestin receptor-containing neurons in localized regions of female rat forebrain. *Brain Res.* 746:164–70

Auger AP, Moffatt CA, Blaustein JD. 1996. Reproductively-relevant stimuli induce Fos-immunoreactivity within progestin receptor-containing neurons in localized regions of female rat forebrain. *J. Neuroendocrinol.* 8:831–38

Auger AP, Moffatt CA, Blaustein JD. 1997. Progesterone-independent activation of rat brain progestin receptors by reproductive stimuli. *Endocrinology* 138:511–14

Bancroft J. 2005. The endocrinology of sexual arousal. *J. Endocrinol.* 186:411–27

Basaria S, Dobs AS. 2006. Clinical review: controversies regarding transdermal androgen therapy in postmenopausal women. *J. Clin. Endocrinol. Metab.* 91:4743–52

Beach FA. 1976. Sexual attractivity, proceptivity, and receptivity in female mammals. *Horm. Behav.* 7:105–38

Beach FA. 1981. Historical origins of modern research on hormones and behavior. *Horm. Behav.* 15:325–76

Bechara A, Bertolino MV, Casabe A, Fredotovich N. 2004. A double-blind randomized placebo control study comparing the objective and subjective changes in female sexual response using sublingual apomorphine. *J. Sex Med.* 1:209–14

Bennett AL, Blasberg ME, Blaustein JD. 2002. Mating stimulation required for mating-induced estrous abbreviation in female rats: effects of repeated testing. *Horm. Behav.* 42:206–11

Bermant G. 1961. Response latencies of female rats during sexual intercourse. *Science* 133:1771–73

Beyer C, Gonzalez-Flores O, Gonzalez-Mariscal G. 1997. Progesterone receptor participates in the stimulatory effect of LHRH, prostaglandin E_2, and cyclic AMP on lordosis and proceptive behaviours in rats. *J. Neuroendocrinol.* 9:609–14

Blaustein JD. 1982. Progesterone in high doses may overcome progesterone's desensitization effect on lordosis by translocation of hypothalamic progestin receptors. *Horm. Behav.* 16:175–90

Blaustein JD. 1994. Estrogen receptors in neurons: new subcellular locations and functional implications. *Endocrine J.* 2:249–58

Blaustein JD. 2004a. Can you teach an old dogma new tricks? *Endocrinology* 145:1055–56

Blaustein JD. 2004b. Minireview: neuronal steroid hormone receptors: they're not just for hormones anymore. *Endocrinology* 145:1075–81

Blaustein JD, Brown TJ. 1985. Neural progestin receptors: regulation of progesterone-facilitated sexual behaviour in female guinea pigs. In *Neurobiology: Current Comparative Approaches*, ed. R Gilles, J Balthazart, pp. 60–76. Berlin: Springer-Verlag

Blaustein JD, Erskine MS. 2002. Feminine sexual behavior: cellular integration of hormonal and afferent information in the rodent forebrain. In *Hormones, Brain and Behavior*, ed. DW Pfaff, AP Arnold, AM Etgen, SE Fahrbach, RT Rubin, pp. 139–214. New York: Academic

Blaustein JD, Feder HH. 1980. Nuclear progestin receptors in guinea pig brain measured by an in vitro exchange assay after hormonal treatments that affect lordosis. *Endocrinology* 106:1061–69

Blaustein JD, King JC, Toft DO, Turcotte J. 1988. Immunocytochemical localization of estrogen-induced progestin receptors in guinea pig brain. *Brain Res.* 474:1–15

Blaustein JD, Lehman MN, Turcotte JC, Greene G. 1992. Estrogen receptors in dendrites and axon terminals in the guinea pig hypothalamus. *Endocrinology* 131:281–90

Blaustein JD, Mani SK. 2007. Feminine sexual behavior from neuroendocrine and molecular neurobiological perspectives. In *Behavioral Neurochemistry, Neuroendocrinology and Molecular Neurobiology*, ed. JD Blaustein, pp. 95–150. Berlin: Springer-Verlag

Blaustein JD, Ryer HI, Feder HH. 1980. A sex difference in the progestin receptor system of guinea pig brain. *Neuroendocrinology* 31:403–9

Blaustein JD, Wade GN. 1977a. Concurrent inhibition of sexual behavior but not brain (^{3}H)estradiol uptake by progesterone in female rats. *J. Comp. Physiol. Psychol.* 91:742–51

Blaustein JD, Wade GN. 1977b. Sequential inhibition of sexual behavior by progesterone in female rats: comparison with a synthetic antiestrogen. *J. Comp. Physiol. Psychol.* 91:752–60

Blaustein JD, Wade GN. 1978. Progestin binding by brain and pituitary cell nuclei and female rat sexual behavior. *Brain Res.* 140:360–37

Boling J, Young WC, Dempsey EW. 1938. Miscellaneous experiments on the estrogen progesterone induction of heat in the spayed guinea pig. *Endocrinology* 23:182–87

Boling JL, Blandau RJ. 1939. The estrogen-progesterone induction of mating responses in the spayed female rat. *Endocrinology* 25:359–64

Bolour S, Braunstein G. 2005. Testosterone therapy in women: a review. *Int. J. Impot. Res.* 17:399–408

Bullivant SB, Sellergren SA, Stern K, Spencer NA, Jacob S, et al. 2004. Women's sexual experience during the menstrual cycle: identification of the sexual phase by noninvasive measurement of luteinizing hormone. *J. Sex Res.* 41:82–93

Butcher RL, Collins WE, Fugo NW. 1974. Plasma concentration of LH, FSH, prolactin, progesterone and estradiol-17β throughout the 4-day estrous cycle of the rat. *Endocrinology* 94:1704–8

Calizo LH, Flanagan-Cato LM. 2003. Hormonal-neural integration in the female rat ventromedial hypothalamus: triple labeling for estrogen receptor-alpha, retrograde tract tracing from the periaqueductal gray, and mating-induced Fos expression. *Endocrinology* 144:5430–40

Carter CS, Witt DM, Schneider J, Harris ZL, Volkening D. 1987. Male stimuli are necessary for female sexual behavior and uterine growth in prairie voles (*microtus ochrogaster*). *Horm. Behav.* 221:74–82

Caruso S, Agnello C, Intelisano G, Farina M, Di ML, Cianci A. 2004. Placebo-controlled study on efficacy and safety of daily apomorphine SL intake in premenopausal women affected by hypoactive sexual desire disorder and sexual arousal disorder. *Urology* 63:955–59

Chappell PE, Levine JE. 2000. Stimulation of gonadotropin-releasing hormone surges by estrogen. I. Role of hypothalamic progesterone receptors. *Endocrinology* 141:1477–85

Chu HP, Morales JC, Etgen AM. 1999. Cyclic GMP may potentiate lordosis behaviour by progesterone receptor activation. *J. Neuroendocrinol.* 11:107–13

Clark AS, Roy EJ. 1987. Effective intervals for the administration of estradiol pulses and the induction of sexual behavior in female rats. *Physiol. Behav.* 39:665–67

Collins VJ, Boling JI, Dempsey EW, Young WC. 1938. Quantitative studies of experimentally induced sexual receptivity in the spayed guinea pig. *Endocrinology* 23:188–96

Conneely OM, Maxwell BL, Toft DO, Schrader WT, O'Malley BW. 1987. The A and B forms of the chicken progesterone receptor arise by alternate initiation of translation of a unique mRNA. *Biochem. Biophys. Res. Comm.* 149:493–501

Daniels D, Flanagan-Cato LM. 2000. Functionally defined compartments of the lordosis neural circuit in the ventromedial hypothalamus in female rats. *J. Neurobiol.* 45:1–13

de Paula FJ, Soares JM Jr, Haidar MA, de Lima GR, Baracat EC. 2007. The benefits of androgens combined with hormone replacement therapy regarding to patients with postmenopausal sexual symptoms. *Maturitas* 56:69–77

Debold JF, Frye CA. 1994. Progesterone and the neural mechanisms of hamster sexual behavior. *Psychoneuroendocrinology* 19:563–79

Delville Y, Blaustein JD. 1988. Neural site of action of estradiol in the induction of sexual receptivity in female guinea pigs. *Abstr. Annu. Meet. Soc. Neurosci. Toronto #1748* (Abstr.)

Dennerstein L, Burrows GD, Wood C, Hyman G. 1980. Hormones and sexuality: effect of estrogen and progestogen. *Obstet. Gynecol.* 56:316–22

Diamond LE, Earle DC, Heiman JR, Rosen RC, Perelman MA, Harning R. 2006. An effect on the subjective sexual response in premenopausal women with sexual arousal disorder by bremelanotide (PT-141), a melanocortin receptor agonist. *J. Sex Med.* 3:628–38

Donahue JE, Stopa EG, Chorsky RL, King JC, Schipper HM, et al. 2000. Cells containing immunoreactive estrogen receptor-alpha in the human basal forebrain. *Brain Res.* 856:142–51

Eisenfeld AJ. 1969. Hypothalamic oestradiol-binding macromolecules. *Nature* 224:1202–3

Erskine MS. 1985. Effects of paced coital stimulation on estrous duration in intact cycling rats and ovariectomized and ovariectomized-adrenalectomized hormone-primed rats. *Behav. Neurosci.* 99:151–61

Erskine MS. 1989. Solicitation behavior in the estrous female rat: a review. *Horm. Behav.* 23:473–502

Erskine MS. 1995. Prolactin release after mating and genitosensory stimulation in females. *Endocr. Rev.* 16:508–28

Etgen AM. 1984. Progestin receptors and the activation of female reproductive behavior: a critical review. *Horm. Behav.* 18:411–30

Etgen AM, Morales JC. 2002. Somatosensory stimuli evoke norepinephrine release in the anterior ventromedial hypothalamus of sexually receptive female rats. *J. Neuroendocrinol.* 14:213–18

Feder HH, Resko JA, Goy RW. 1967. Progesterone levels in the arterial plasma of preovulatory and ovariectomized rats. *J. Endocrinol.* 41:563–69

Feder HH, Resko JA, Goy RW. 1968. Progesterone concentrations in the arterial plasma of guinea pigs during the oestrous cycle. *J. Endocrinol.* 40:505–13

Feder HH, Silver R. 1974. Activation of lordosis in ovariectomized guinea pigs by free and esterified forms of estrone, estradiol-17B and estriol. *Physiol. Behav.* 13:251–55

Filardo EJ, Thomas P. 2005. GPR30: a seven-transmembrane-spanning estrogen receptor that triggers EGF release. *Trends Endocrinol. Metab.* 16:362–67

Flanagan-Cato LM, Calizo LH, Daniels D. 2001. The synaptic organization of VMH neurons that mediate the effects of estrogen on sexual behavior. *Horm. Behav.* 40:178–82

Foreman MM, Moss RL. 1977. Effects of subcutaneous injection and intrahypothalamic infusion of releasing hormones upon lordotic response to repetitive coital stimulation. *Horm. Behav.* 8:219–34

Glaser JH, Rubin BS, Barfield RJ. 1983. Onset of the receptive and proceptive components of feminine sexual behavior in rats following the intravenous administration of progesterone. *Horm. Behav.* 17:18–27

Gleason CE, Carlsson CM, Johnson S, Atwood C, Asthana S. 2005. Clinical pharmacology and differential cognitive efficacy of estrogen preparations. *Ann. N. Y. Acad. Sci.* 1052:93–115

Gonzalez-Flores O, Guerra-Araiza C, Cerbon M, Camacho-Arroyo I, Etgen AM. 2004. The 26S proteasome participates in the sequential inhibition of estrous behavior induced by progesterone in rats. *Endocrinology* 145:2328–36

Gorski J, Toft D, Shyamala G, Smith D, Notides A. 1968. Hormone receptors: studies on the interaction of estrogen with the uterus. *Recent Prog. Horm. Res.* 24:45–80

Greene GL, Gilna P, Waterfield M, Baker A, Hort Y, Shine J. 1986. Sequence and expression of human estrogen receptor complementary DNA. *Science* 231:1150–54

Hart SA, Snyder MA, Smejkalova T, Woolley CS. 2007. Estrogen mobilizes a subset of estrogen receptor-alpha-immunoreactive vesicles in inhibitory presynaptic boutons in hippocampal CA1. *J. Neurosci.* 27:2102–11

Hays J, Ockene JK, Brunner RL, Kotchen JM, Manson JE, et al. 2003. Effects of estrogen plus progestin on health-related quality of life. *N. Engl. J. Med.* 348:1839–54

Hlinak Z, Madlafousek J. 1977. Female precopulatory behaviour as a determinant of sexual activity in male rats [proceedings]. *Act. Nerv. Super. (Praha)* 19:242–43

Hoff JD, Quigley ME, Yen SS. 1983. Hormonal dynamics at midcycle: a reevaluation. *J. Clin. Endocrinol. Metab.* 57:792–96

Jeltsch JM, Krozowski Z, Quirin-Stricker C, Gronemeyer H, Simpson RJ, et al. 1986. Cloning of the chicken progesterone receptor. *Proc. Natl. Acad. Sci. USA* 83:5424–28

Jensen EV, Suzuki T, Kawasima T, Stumpf WE, Jungblut PW, de Sombre ER. 1968. A two-step mechanism for the interaction of estradiol with rat uterus. *Proc. Natl. Acad. Sci. USA* 59:632–38

Joslyn WD, Feder HH, Goy RW. 1971. Estrogen conditioning and progesterone facilitation of lordosis in guinea pigs. *Physiol. Behav.* 7:477–82

Kahwanago I, Heinrichs WL, Herrmann WL. 1969. Isolation of oestradiol "receptors" from bovine hypothalamus and anterior pituitary gland. *Nature* 223:313–14

Kastner P, Krust A, Turcotte B, Stropp U, Tora L, et al. 1990. Two distinct estrogen-regulated promoters generate transcripts encoding the two functionally different human progesterone receptor forms A and B. *EMBO J.* 9:1603–14

Kato J, Onouchi T. 1977. Specific progesterone receptors in the hypothalamus and anterior hypophysis of the rat. *Endocrinology* 101:920–28

Kow LM, Montgomery MO, Pfaff DW. 1979. Triggering of lordosis reflex in female rats with somatosensory stimulation: quantitative determination of stimulus parameters. *J. Neurophysiol.* 42:195–202

Kow LM, Pfaff DW. 2004. The membrane actions of estrogens can potentiate their lordosis behavior-facilitating genomic actions. *Proc. Natl. Acad. Sci. USA* 101:12354–57

Kudwa AE, Rissman EF. 2003. Double oestrogen receptor alpha and beta knockout mice reveal differences in neural oestrogen-mediated progestin receptor induction and female sexual behaviour. *J. Neuroendocrinol.* 15:978–83

Kuiper GGJM, Enmark E, Peltohuikko M, Nilsson S, Gustafsson JA. 1996. Cloning of a novel estrogen receptor expressed in rat prostate and ovary. *Proc. Natl. Acad. Sci. USA* 93:5925–30

Leavitt WW, Bosley CG, Blaha GC. 1971. Source of ovarian preovulatory progesterone. *Nature* 234:283–84

Li X, Schwartz PE, Rissman EF. 1997. Distribution of estrogen receptor-beta-like immunoreactivity in rat forebrain. *Neuroendocrinology* 66:63–67

Lisk RD. 1960. A comparison of the effectiveness of intravenous, as opposed to subcutaneous, injection of progesterone for the induction of estrous behavior in the rat. *J. Biochem. Physiol.* 38:1381–83

Lodder J, Zeilmaker GH. 1976. Role of pelvic nerves in the postcopulatory abbreviation of behavioral estrus in female rats. *J. Comp. Physiol. Psychol.* 90:925–29

Luttge WG. 1976. Intracerebral implantation of the antiestrogen CN-69, 725-27: effects on female sexual behavior in rats. *Pharmacol. Biochem. Behav.* 4:685–88

MacLusky NJ, McEwen BS. 1978. Oestrogen modulates progestin receptor concentrations in some rat brain regions but not in others. *Nature* 274:276–78

MacLusky NJ, McEwen BS. 1980. Progestin receptors in rat brain: distribution and properties of cytoplasmic progestin-binding sites. *Endocrinology* 106:192–202

Mani SK, Allen JMC, Clark JH, Blaustein JD, O'Malley BW. 1994a. Convergent pathways for steroid hormone- and neurotransmitter-induced rat sexual behavior. *Science* 265:1246–49

Mani SK, Allen JMC, Lydon JP, Mulac-Jericevic B, Blaustein JD, et al. 1996. Dopamine requires the unoccupied progesterone receptor to induce sexual behavior in mice. *Mol. Endocrinol.* 10:1728–37

Mani SK, Allen JMC, Rettori V, McCann SM, O'Malley BW, Clark JH. 1994b. Nitric oxide mediates sexual behavior in female rats. *Proc. Natl. Acad. Sci. USA* 91:6468–72

Mani SK, Blaustein JD, Allen JM, Law SW, O'Malley BW, Clark JH. 1994c. Inhibition of rat sexual behavior by antisense oligonucleotides to the progesterone receptor. *Endocrinology* 135:1409–14

Mani SK, Blaustein JD, O'Malley BW. 1997. Progesterone receptor function from a behavioral perspective. *Horm. Behav.* 31:244–55

Mani SK, Reyna AM, Chen JZ, Mulac-Jericevic B, Conneely OM. 2006. Differential response of progesterone receptor isoforms in hormone-dependent and -independent facilitation of female sexual receptivity. *Mol. Endocrinol.* 20:1322–32

Marrone BL, Rodriguez-Sierra JF, Feder HH. 1977. Lordosis: inhibiting effects of progesterone in the female rat. *Horm. Behav.* 8:391–402

Mathews D, Edwards DA. 1977. The ventromedial nucleus of the hypothalamus and the hormonal arousal of sexual behaviors in the female rat. *Horm. Behav.* 8:40–51

Matuszewich L, Lorrain DS, Hull EM. 2000. Dopamine release in the medial preoptic area of female rats in response to hormonal manipulation and sexual activity. *Behav. Neurosci.* 114:772–82

McEwen BS, Krey LC, Luine VN. 1978. Steroid hormone action in the neuroendocrine system: When is the genome involved? In *The Hypothalamus*, ed. S Reichlin, RJ Baldessarini, JB Martin, pp. 255–68. New York: Raven

McGinnis MY, Parsons B, Rainbow TC, Krey LC, McEwen BS. 1981. Temporal relationship between cell nuclear progestin receptor levels and sexual receptivity following intravenous progesterone administration. *Brain Res.* 218:365–71

McKenna NJ, Lanz RB, O'Malley BW. 1999. Nuclear receptor coregulators: cellular and molecular biology. *Endocr. Rev.* 20:321–44

Meerts SH, Clark AS. 2007. Female rats exhibit a conditioned place preference for nonpaced mating. *Horm. Behav.* 51:89–94

Meisel RL, Camp DM, Robinson TE. 1993. A microdialysis study of ventral striatal dopamine during sexual behavior in female Syrian hamsters. *Behav. Brain Res.* 55:151–57

Meredith JM, Moffatt CA, Auger AP, Snyder GL, Greengard P, Blaustein JD. 1998. Mating-related stimulation induces phosphorylation of dopamine- and cyclic AMP–regulated phosphoprotein-32 in progestin receptor-containing areas in the female rat brain. *J. Neurosci.* 18:10189–95

Meyerson B. 1972. Latency between intravenous injection of progestins and the appearance of estrous behavior in estrogen-treated ovariectomized rats. *Horm. Behav.* 3:1–9

Micevych P, Sinchak K, Mills RH, Tao L, LaPolt P, Lu JKH. 2003. The luteinizing hormone surge is preceded by an estrogen-induced increase of hypothalamic progesterone in ovariectomized and adrenalectomized rats. *Neuroendocrinology* 78:29–35

Michael RP. 1962. Estrogen-sensitive neurons and sexual behavior in female cats. *Science* 136:322–23

Michael RP, Clancy AN, Zumpe D. 2005. Mating activates estrogen receptor-containing neurons in the female monkey brain. *Physiol. Behav.* 85:404–13

Mo B, Callegari E, Telefont M, Renner KJ. 2006. Proteomic analysis of the ventromedial nucleus of the hypothalamus (*pars lateralis*) in the female rat. *Proteomics* 6:6066–74

Moguilewsky M, Raynaud JP. 1979a. Estrogen-sensitive progestin-binding sites in the female rat brain and pituitary. *Brain Res.* 164:165–75

Moguilewsky M, Raynaud JP. 1979b. The relevance of hypothalamic and hypophyseal progestin receptor regulation in the induction and inhibition of sexual behavior in the female rat. *Endocrinology* 105:516–22

Molenda HA, Griffin AL, Auger AP, McCarthy MM, Tetel MJ. 2002. Nuclear receptor coactivators modulate hormone-dependent gene expression in brain and female reproductive behavior in rats. *Endocrinology* 143:436–44

Molenda-Figueira HA, Williams CA, Griffin AL, Rutledge EM, Blaustein JD, Tetel MJ. 2006. Nuclear receptor coactivators function in estrogen receptor– and progestin receptor–dependent aspects of sexual behavior in female rats. *Horm. Behav.* 50:383–92

Moody KM, Adler NT. 1995. The role of the uterus and cervix in systemic oxytocin-PGE$_2$ facilitated lordosis behavior. *Horm. Behav.* 29(4):571–80

Moody KM, Steinman JL, Komisaruk BR, Adler NT. 1994. Pelvic neurectomy blocks oxytocin-facilitated sexual receptivity in rats. *Physiol. Behav.* 56:1057–60

Morin LP. 1977. Progesterone: inhibition of rodent sexual behavior. *Physiol. Behav.* 18:701–15

Morin LP, Feder HH. 1974. Hypothalamic progesterone implants and facilitation of lordosis behavior in estrogen-primed ovariectomized guinea pigs. *Brain Res.* 70:81–93

O'Malley BW. 2007. Coregulators: from whence came these "master genes." *Mol. Endocrinol.* 21(5):1009–13

Ogawa S, Chan J, Chester AE, Gustafsson JA, Korach KS, Pfaff DW. 1999. Survival of reproductive behaviors in estrogen receptor β gene-deficient (β ERKO) male and female mice. *Proc. Natl. Acad. Sci. USA* 96:12887–92

Olster DH, Blaustein JD. 1988. Progesterone facilitation of lordosis in male and female Sprague-Dawley rats following priming with estradiol pulses. *Horm. Behav.* 22:294–304

Olster DH, Blaustein JD. 1990. Biochemical and immunocytochemical assessment of neural progestin receptors following estradiol treatments that eliminate the sex difference in progesterone-facilitated lordosis in guinea- pigs. *J. Neuroendocrinol.* 2:79–86

Osterlund MK, Hurd YL. 2001. Estrogen receptors in the human forebrain and the relation to neuropsychiatric disorders. *Prog. Neurobiol.* 64:251–67

Paredes RG, Vazquez B. 1999. What do female rats like about sex? Paced mating. *Behav. Brain Res.* 105:117–27

Parsons B, MacLusky NJ, Krey L, Pfaff DW, McEwen BS. 1980. The temporal relationship between estrogen-inducible progestin receptors in the female rat brain and the time course of estrogen activation of mating behavior. *Endocrinology* 107:774–79

Peirce JT, Nuttall RL. 1961. Self-paced sexual behavior in the female rat. *J. Comp. Physiol. Psychol.* 54:310–13

Pfaff D, Keiner M. 1973. Atlas of estradiol-concentrating cells in the central nervous system of the female rat. *J. Comp. Neurol.* 151:121–58

Pfaff DW. 1968a. Autoradiographic localization of radioactivity in rat brain after injection of tritiated sex hormones. *Science* 161:1355–56

Pfaff DW. 1968b. Uptake of ^{3}H-estradiol by the female rat brain. An autoradiographic study. *Endocrinology* 83:1149–55

Pfaff DW, Sakuma Y. 1979. Deficit in the lordosis reflex of female rats caused by lesions in the ventromedial nucleus of the hypothalamus. *J. Physiol.* 288:203–10

Pfaff DW, Schwartz-Giblin S, McCarthy MM, Kow L-M. 1994. Cellular and molecular mechanisms of female reproductive behaviors. In *The Physiology of Reproduction*, ed. E Knobil, JD Neill, pp. 107–220. New York: Raven. 2nd ed.

Pfaus JG. 1999. Neurobiology of sexual behavior. *Curr. Opin. Neurobiol.* 9:751–58

Pfaus JG, Kippin TE, Coria-Avila G. 2003. What can animal models tell us about human sexual response? *Annu. Rev. Sex Res.* 14:1–63

Pfaus JG, Shadiack A, Van Soest T, Tse M, Molinoff P. 2004. Selective facilitation of sexual solicitation in the female rat by a melanocortin receptor agonist. *PNAS* 101:10201–4

Pfaus JG, Smith WJ, Byrne N, Stephens G. 2000. Appetitive and consummatory sexual behaviors of female rats in bilevel chambers. II. Patterns of estrus termination following vaginocervical stimulation. *Horm. Behav.* 37:96–107

Phoenix CH, Copenhaver KH, Brenner RM. 1976. Scanning electron microscopy of penile papillae in intact and castrated rats. *Horm. Behav.* 7:217–27

Power RF, Mani SK, Codina J, Conneely OM, O'Malley BW. 1991. Dopaminergic and ligand-independent activation of steroid hormone receptors. *Science* 254:1636–39

Powers JB. 1970. Hormonal control of sexual receptivity during the estrous cycle of the rat. *Physiol. Behav.* 5:831–35

Rapp SR, Espeland MA, Shumaker SA, Henderson VW, Brunner RL, et al. 2003. Effect of estrogen plus progestin on global cognitive function in postmenopausal women. The Women's Health Initiative Memory Study: a randomized controlled trial. *JAMA* 289:2663–72

Razandi M, Pedram A, Greene GL, Levin ER. 1999. Cell membrane and nuclear estrogen receptors (ERs) originate from a single transcript: studies of ERα and ERβ expressed in Chinese hamster ovary cells. *Mol. Endocrinol.* 13:307–19

Rissman EF, Early AH, Taylor JA, Korach KS, Lubahn DB. 1997. Estrogen receptors are essential for female sexual receptivity. *Endocrinology* 138:507–10

Rodriguez-Sierra JF, Crowley WR, Komisaruk BR. 1975. Vaginal stimulation in rats induces prolonged lordosis responsiveness and sexual receptivity. *J. Comp. Physiol. Psychol.* 89:79–85

Rodriguez-Sierra JF, Komisaruk BR. 1978. Lordosis induction in the rat by prostaglandin E_2 systemically or intracranially in the absence of ovarian hormones. *Prostaglandins* 15:513–24

Rossler AS, Pfaus JG, Kia HK, Bernabe J, Alexandre L, Giuliano F. 2006. The melanocortin agonist, melanotan II, enhances proceptive sexual behaviors in the female rat. *Pharmacol. Biochem. Behav.* 85:514–21

Rossouw JE, Anderson GL, Prentice RL, LaCroix AZ, Kooperberg C, et al. 2002. Risks and benefits of estrogen plus progestin in healthy postmenopausal women: principal results from the Women's Health Initiative randomized controlled trial. *JAMA* 288:321–33

Roy EJ, Wade GN. 1977. Binding of [^{3}H]estradiol by brain cell nuclei and female rat sexual behavior: inhibition by antiestrogens. *Brain Res.* 126:73–87

Sachs BD, Glater GB, O'Hanlon JK. 1984. Morphology of the erect glans penis in rats under various gonadal hormone conditions. *Anat. Rec.* 210:45–52

Sar M, Stumpf WE. 1973. Neurons of the hypothalamus concentrate [^{3}H]progesterone or its metabolites. *Science* 183:1266–68

Schrader WT, O'Malley BW. 1972. Progesterone-binding components of chick oviduct. IV. Characterization of purified subunits. *J. Biol. Chem.* 247:51–59

Sherwin BB, Gelfand MM. 1987. The role of androgen in the maintenance of sexual functioning in oophorectomized women. *Psychosom. Med.* 49:397–409

Sherwin BB, Gelfand MM, Brender W. 1985. Androgen enhances sexual motivation in females: a prospective, crossover study of sex steroid administration in the surgical menopause. *Psychosom. Med.* 47:339–51

Shughrue PJ, Komm B, Merchenthaler I. 1996. The distribution of estrogen receptor-β mRNA in the rat hypothalamus. *Steroids* 61:678–81

Shumaker SA, Legault C, Rapp SR, Thal L, Wallace RB, et al. 2003. Estrogen plus progestin and the incidence of dementia and mild cognitive impairment in postmenopausal women. The Women's Health Initiative Memory Study: a randomized controlled trial. *JAMA* 289:2651–62

Siegel HI, Ahdieh HB, Rosenblatt JS. 1978. Hysterectomy-induced facilitation of lordosis behavior in the rat. *Horm. Behav.* 11:273–78

Simon J, Braunstein G, Nachtigall L, Utian W, Katz M, et al. 2005. Testosterone patch increases sexual activity and desire in surgically menopausal women with hypoactive sexual desire disorder. *J. Clin. Endocrinol. Metab.* 90:5226–33

Sinchak K, Mills RH, Tao L, LaPolt P, Lu JK, Micevych P. 2003. Estrogen induces de novo progesterone synthesis in astrocytes. *Dev. Neurosci.* 25:343–48

Sodersten P, Pettersson A, Eneroth P. 1983. Pulse administration of estradiol-17β cancels sex difference in behavioral estrogen sensitivity. *Endocrinology* 112:1883–85

Stanislaw H, Rice FJ. 1988. Correlation between sexual desire and menstrual cycle characteristics. *Arch. Sex Behav.* 17:499–508

Stumpf WE. 1968. Estradiol-concentrating neurons: topography in the hypothalamus by dry-mount autoradiography. *Science* 162:1001–3

Taylor GT, Komitowski D, Weiss J. 1983. Light and scanning electron microscopic study of testosterone-restored penile papillae in castrated rats. *Anat. Rec.* 205:277–86

Terasawa E, Goldfoot DA, Davis GA. 1976. Pentobarbital inhibition of progesterone-induced behavioral estrus in ovariectomized guinea pigs. *Brain Res.* 107:375–83

Tetel MJ, Celentano DC, Blaustein JD. 1994. Intraneuronal convergence of tactile and hormonal stimuli associated with female reproduction in rats. *J. Neuroendocrinol.* 6:211–16

Tetel MJ, Siegal NK, Murphy SD. 2007. Cells in behaviourally relevant brain regions coexpress nuclear receptor coactivators and ovarian steroid receptors. *J. Neuroendocrinol.* 19(4):262–71

Thompson ML, Edwards DA. 1971. Experiential and strain determinants of the estrogen-progesterone induction of sexual receptivity in spayed female mice. *Horm. Behav.* 2:299–305

Wade CB, Robinson S, Shapiro RA, Dorsa DM. 2001. Estrogen receptor (ER)α and ERβ exhibit unique pharmacologic properties when coupled to activation of the mitogen-activated protein kinase pathway. *Endocrinology* 142:2336–42

Wallen K. 2001. Sex and context: hormones and primate sexual motivation. *Horm. Behav.* 40:339–57

Wallen K, Baum MJ. 2002. Masculinization and defeminization in altricial and precocial mammals: comparative aspects of steroid hormone action. In *Hormones, Brain and Behavior*, ed. DW Pfaff, AP Arnold, AM Etgen, SE Fahrbach, RT Rubin, pp. 385–423. Amsterdam: Academic

Wallen K, Goy RW, Phoenix CH. 1975. Inhibitory actions of progesterone on hormonal induction of estrus in female guinea pigs. *Horm. Behav.* 6:127–38

Wallen K, Parsons WA. 1998. Androgen may increase sexual motivation in estrogen-treated ovariectomized rhesus monkeys by increasing estrogen availability. *Serono Int. Symp. Biol. Menopause*, Newport Beach, Calif.

Wallen K, Winston LA, Gaventa S, vis-DaSilva M, Collins DC. 1984. Periovulatory changes in female sexual behavior and patterns of ovarian steroid secretion in group-living rhesus monkeys. *Horm. Behav.* 18:431–50

Warembourg M. 1978. Radioautographic study of the brain and pituitary after [³H]progesterone injection into estrogen-primed ovariectomized guinea pigs. *Neurosci. Lett.* 7:1–5

White MM, Sheffer I, Teeter J, Apostolakis EM. 2007. Hypothalamic progesterone receptor-A mediates gonadotropin surges, self priming and receptivity in estrogen-primed female mice. *J. Mol. Endocrinol.* 38:35–50

Wilson ME, Gordon TP, Collins DC. 1982. Variation in ovarian steroids associated with the annual mating period in female rhesus monkeys (*Macaca mulatta*). *Biol. Reprod.* 27:530–39

Young LJ, Crews D. 1995. Comparative neuroendocrinology of steroid receptor gene expression and regulation: relationship to physiology and behavior. *Trends Endocrinol. Metab.* 6:317–23

Young WC. 1969. Psychobiology of sexual behavior in the guinea pig. In *Advances in the Study of Behavior*, ed. DS Lehrman, RA Hinde, E Shaw, pp. 1–110. New York: Academic

Zehr JL, Maestripieri D, Wallen K. 1998. Estradiol increases female sexual initiation independent of male responsiveness in rhesus monkeys. *Horm. Behav.* 33:95–103

Zhu Y, Rice CD, Pang YF, Pace M, Thomas P. 2003. Cloning, expression, and characterization of a membrane progestin receptor and evidence it is an intermediary in meiotic maturation of fish oocytes. *Proc. Natl. Acad. Sci. USA* 100:2231–36

Zigmond RE, McEwen BS. 1969. Selective retention of oestradiol by cell nuclei in specific brain regions of the ovariectomized rat. *J. Neurobiol.* 17:889–99

Zucker I. 1967. Actions of progesterone in the control of sexual receptivity of the spayed female rat. *J. Comp. Physiol. Psychol.* 63:313–16

The Biological Basis of Audition

Gregg H. Recanzone and Mitchell L. Sutter

Center for Neuroscience and Section of Neurobiology, Physiology & Behavior, University of California at Davis, California 95618; email: ghrecanzone@ucdavis.edu, mlsutter@ucdavis.edu

Annu. Rev. Psychol. 2008. 59:119–42

First published online as a Review in Advance on August 3, 2007

The *Annual Review of Psychology* is online at http://psych.annualreviews.org

This article's doi: 10.1146/annurev.psych.59.103006.093544

Key Words

temporal processing, spatial processing, macaque monkey, human imaging, audition, perception

Abstract

Interest has recently surged in the neural mechanisms of audition, particularly with regard to functional imaging studies in human subjects. This review emphasizes recent work on two aspects of auditory processing. The first explores auditory spatial processing and the role of the auditory cortex in both nonhuman primates and human subjects. The interactions with visual stimuli, the ventriloquism effect, and the ventriloquism aftereffect are also reviewed. The second aspect is temporal processing. Studies investigating temporal integration, forward masking, and gap detection are reviewed, as well as examples from the birdsong system and echolocating bats.

Contents

INTRODUCTION

Humans and animals use many different senses to explore and experience the world around them. Of all of the mammalian sensory systems, we currently have the best understanding of the visual system, largely due to the consistent interest in this topic and the tremendous effort that has been made to explore and attempt to understand the neural mechanisms of visual perception. Our understanding of the neural basis of auditory perception is far behind that of vision, but interest in this area has surged over the past decade. Two major strategies that are used to elucidate the neural correlates of auditory perception are functional imaging techniques in humans and single-neuron responses in macaque monkeys. This review highlights some of these studies and places them in a broader context of the neurological basis of auditory perception.

The auditory system must process many different features of an acoustic stimulus to give rise to the salient features that we perceive; one must determine where a sound came from, what different spectral and temporal properties it has, and what exactly the sound represents. This complexity is much too great to be dealt with in a single review, so we have elected to focus on spatial and temporal processing. Further, this review focuses on the cortical mechanisms most closely related to auditory perception, i.e., what the listener actually perceives. In the auditory system, the acoustic signal is extensively processed by nuclei in the brainstem, midbrain, and thalamus (**Figure 1**). Clearly, the role of these subcortical structures is paramount in providing the necessary input to the cerebral cortex for auditory perception. For instance, bilateral cochlear lesions result in deafness regardless of cortical function. Similarly, lesions of the superior olivary complex in the brainstem result in sound localization deficits despite an intact auditory cortex (see Masterton et al. 1967). However, the cerebral cortex is necessary for the perception of auditory signals (see Heffner 1997, Heffner & Heffner 1990). The focus of this review is on recent studies using both single-neuron recordings in animal preparations and functional imaging in humans that have shed new light on how neural processing gives rise to auditory perception.

THE ORGANIZATION OF THE PRIMATE AUDITORY CORTEX

The use of the macaque monkey as an animal model in studies of the neural basis of audition has increased dramatically in the past few years. Monkeys and humans share similarities in the anatomical, electrophysiological, and functional role that these cortical areas play in audition. Recent studies have investigated the role of the primate cerebral cortex in auditory spatial processing, which is one

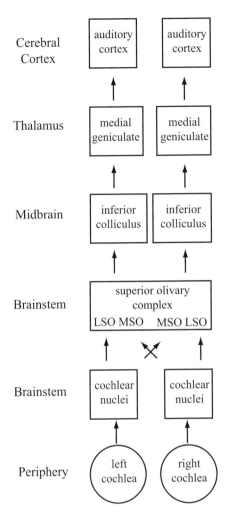

| Cerebral Cortex | auditory cortex | auditory cortex |

Thalamus — medial geniculate / medial geniculate

Midbrain — inferior colliculus / inferior colliculus

Brainstem — superior olivary complex / LSO MSO MSO LSO

Brainstem — cochlear nuclei / cochlear nuclei

Periphery — left cochlea / right cochlea

Figure 1

Schematic diagram of the ascending auditory system. Shown are the major subcortical nuclei that process acoustic information. Each cochlea projects to the ipsilateral cochlear nucleus in the brainstem. Not shown are the three different subdivisions of this nucleus, the dorsal cochlear nucleus, the anterior ventral cochlear nucleus, and the posterior ventral cochlear nucleus. These neurons project to the superior olivary complex (SOC) in the brainstem, which contains the lateral superior olive (LSO) and medial superior olive (MSO). Each cochlear nucleus projects to the SOC bilaterally; thus, neurons in these regions have binaural response properties that are projected upward to each ascending nucleus. The nucleus of the trapezoid body is not shown. SOC neurons project to the inferior colliculus (IC), which itself is composed of several subnuclei. The IC is the obligatory relay nucleus to the thalamus. Not shown is the nucleus of the lateral lemniscus. The IC neurons project to the medial geniculate body of the dorsal thalamus, which in turn projects to the auditory cortex.

emphasis of this review, so this section provides an overview of the basic organization of these areas.

The auditory cortex of the primate can be divided into three main regions, each composed of several cortical areas (**Figure 2**; see Jones 2003, Kaas & Hackett 2000, Pandya 1995, Rauschecker & Tian 2000). The organization can be described as a core-belt-parabelt arrangement, with the cortical hierarchy advancing at each stage. Each of these fields can be distinguished based on histological appearance, corticocortical and thalamocortical connections, and functional response properties (Hackett et al. 2001, Jones et al. 1995, Kosaki et al. 1997, Merzenich &

Brugge 1973, Molinari et al. 1995, Morel et al. 1993, Rauschecker & Tian 2004, Rauschecker et al. 1995, Recanzone et al. 2000a, Tian & Rauschecker 2004, Woods et al. 2006). The core region is composed of three cortical areas. The primary auditory cortex, A1, has koniocortical cytoarchitecture and is believed to be homologous with A1 in other mammals (Hackett et al. 2001). Rostral to A1 are two other core cortical fields, the rostral field (R) and rostrotemporal field (RT). Physiologically, A1 and R are organized tonotopically (Merzenich & Brugge 1973, Morel et al. 1993, Recanzone et al. 2000b), with a reversal at the low-frequency border between the two fields. Area RT is also suspected of having a tonotopic organization, but this has yet to be explicitly demonstrated. Surrounding the core field are several belt fields. In the lateral belt (caudolateral, mediolateral, and anterolateral, or CL, ML, and AL, respectively), neurons respond better to broad spectral stimuli, such as broadband and narrowband noise, than to tones (Merzenich & Brugge 1973, Rauschecker & Tian 2004,

A1: primary auditory cortex

Koniocortical cytoarchitecture: cortical areas characterized by a well-developed inner granular layer (layer 4) corresponding to primary sensory areas

Tonotopic organization: the regular and progressive spatial arrangement of tone frequency representations

IC: inferior colliculus

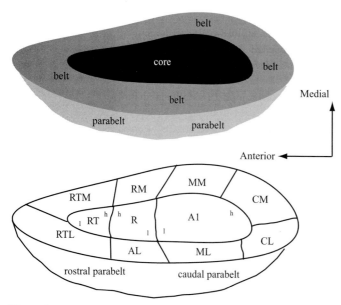

Medial

Anterior

Figure 2

Schematic diagram of the primate auditory cortex. Top schematic shows the general organization of core (*black*), belt (*gray*), and parabelt (*light gray*). Bottom schematic shows the approximate locations of the different cortical areas. The core is made up of the primary auditory cortex (AI), the rostral field (R), and the rostrotemporal (RT) area. These three fields have a tonotopic organization as shown by the lower-case letters h (high frequency) and l (low frequency). The medial belt includes the caudomedial (CM) area, middle medial (MM) area, rostromedial (RM) area, and medial rostrotemporal (RTM) area. The lateral belt includes the caudolateral (CL) area, middle lateral (ML) area, anterolateral (AL) area, and the lateral rostrotemporal (RTL) area. The parabelt is divided into rostral and caudal areas. Drawing is not to scale as the medial belt is significantly narrower than the lateral belt. Adapted from (Kaas & Hackett 2000).

Rauschecker et al. 1995, Recanzone et al. 2000a, Tian & Rauschecker 2004). However, if narrowband noise is used, the corresponding center frequency of the stimulus that elicits the best response does show tonotopy, with reversals at the borders between these lateral belt fields (Rauschecker & Tian 2004). The medial belt fields have been less well defined physiologically, although they generally also show broad spatial tuning (Kosaki et al. 1997, Woods et al. 2006).

Lateral to the belt fields is the parabelt, which is subdivided into rostral and caudal regions. The thalamocortical and corticocortical connections have been described (Hackett et al. 1998a,b; see Jones 2003), but there have

been relatively few published electrophysiology studies of neurons in these areas. Two imaging studies in the macaque monkey have been able to define the parabelt cortex (as well as the other fields shown in **Figure 2**) by the change in the blood oxygenation level–dependent response to acoustic stimulation (Kayser et al. 2007, Petkov et al. 2006). The results from these anatomical and functional imaging studies in monkeys and functional imaging studies in humans (referenced below) indicate that the parabelt is likely processing complex acoustic features.

In humans, multiple studies over the past decade have explored the functional organization of the auditory cortex. These experiments have been hampered by the wide individual variability of the gross anatomical landmarks of the upper bank of the superior temporal gyrus (e.g., Leonard et al. 1998) that does not consistently identify the locations of the different cortical fields (see also Morosan et al. 2001, Petkov et al. 2004). The human auditory cortex is also composed of three core fields defined histologically as in the macaque (Morosan et al. 2001, Rademacher et al. 2001). Functional imaging studies note that there are several tonotopic fields in the human auditory cortex (e.g., Bilecen et al. 1998, Talavage et al. 2000). Other features of auditory responses in different cortical areas are consistent with the results seen in macaques (e.g., Ahveninen et al. 2006, Altmann et al. 2007, Brunetti et al. 2005, Krumbholz et al. 2005, Petkov et al. 2004, Viceic et al. 2006, Wessinger et al. 2001, Zimmer & Macaluso 2005).

One central theme in investigating auditory cortical processing is the working hypothesis that spatial and nonspatial features of acoustic stimuli are processed in two parallel streams (Rauschecker 1998) similar to that proposed for the dorsal "where" and ventral "what" streams in visual cortex (Ungerleider & Haxby 1994, Ungerleider & Mishkin 1982). Work in both nonhuman primates (Recanzone et al. 2000b, Romanski et al. 1999, Tian et al. 2001, Woods et al. 2006; see Kaas & Hackett 2000, Rauschecker

& Tian 2000) and humans (Ahveninen et al. 2006, Altmann et al. 2007, Arnott et al. 2004, Sestieri et al. 2006) tends to support this model in that spatial features are preferentially processed in caudal cortical areas, and nonspatial features are processed in more ventral cortical areas. Thus, it appears that the macaque monkey is an excellent animal model for human auditory cortical processing.

AUDITORY SPATIAL PROCESSING

Auditory spatial processing has been a topic of interest ever since the auditory system has been experimentally investigated. One key feature of spatial processing in the auditory system is that, unlike the visual and somatosensory systems, space is not directly represented in the sensory epithelium. The central nervous system must compute the spatial location of a stimulus by integrating the information provided by many individual inner hair cells and their corresponding spiral ganglion cells. These computations are initiated very early, at the level of the second synapses in the central nervous system in the superior olivary complex (**Figure 1**). These early processing stations have been the topic of much interest and research, and the contribution of these stations to spatial processing is too extensive to review here. Instead, we focus on the cortical mechanisms of spatial localization and how these responses can potentially account for the sound localization ability of humans and nonhuman primates. In this section, we describe psychophysical studies and the potential spatial cues that can be used to compute the spatial location of stimuli. The electrophysiological and functional imaging evidence in support of a caudal processing stream of acoustic space is then summarized.

Sound Localization Psychophysics

The ability of humans and animals to detect either changes in or the absolute location of an acoustic stimulus has been studied extensively for several decades (see Blauert 1997, Carlile et al. 1997, Heffner 2004, Populin & Yin 1998, Recanzone & Beckerman 2004, Recanzone et al. 1998, Su & Recanzone 2001). These studies have noted that two basic parameters influence sound localization ability (see Blauert 1997). The first is spectral bandwidth. The greater the bandwidth, the better subjects are able to localize the stimuli, particularly in elevation. For example, broadband noise is better localized than band-passed noise, which is better localized than tones (see Recanzone et al. 2000b for examples in monkeys). This is likely due to the ability to recruit more neurons to provide information about stimulus location as more neurons are activated by the greater spectral energy of the stimulus. The second basic stimulus parameter is the intensity of the stimulus, with low-intensity stimuli being most difficult to localize and louder stimuli more easily localized (e.g., Altshuler & Comalli 1975, Comalli & Altshuler 1976, Recanzone & Beckerman 2004, Sabin et al. 2005, Su & Recanzone 2001). Again, as the louder sounds will engage a greater population of neurons, it is possible that the size of the neuronal pool is important in processing acoustic space information. This is reasonable to assume, as the individual binaural cues can be ambiguous when only a single frequency is present, and the monaural cues depend on both a broad spectral bandwidth and reasonable intensity levels to be effective, as described below.

Binaural Cues

Two binaural cues can be used to calculate the location of an acoustic source. The first is interaural intensity differences. If a sound source is not in the plane of the midline, primarily the head but also the body will absorb some of the energy and shadow the far ear from the acoustic source, thereby making the intensity of the stimulus at that ear less than the intensity of the closer ear (**Figure 3A**). The second binaural cue results from the fact

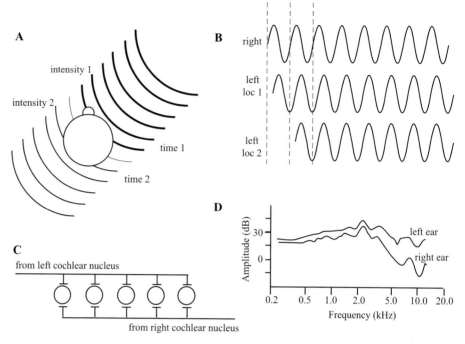

A intensity 1 intensity 2 time 1 time 2

B right left loc 1 left loc 2

C from left cochlear nucleus from right cochlear nucleus

D Amplitude (dB) 30 0 left ear right ear 0.2 0.5 1.0 2.0 5.0 10.0 20.0 Frequency (kHz)

Figure 3

Sound localization cues. (*A*) Interaural intensity and timing cues. The head and body will absorb some of the sound energy, resulting in a lower-intensity stimulus at the far ear (intensity 2) in comparison with the near ear (intensity 1), represented here by the lines becoming thinner. The wave fronts will also arrive at the near ear (time 1) before the far ear (time 2), giving rise to interaural timing cues. (*B*) Interaural time and phase cues. The waveform will reach the far ear at a later time than the near ear. Ambiguities exist when only considering the phase and not the onset, as two locations can have the same phase disparity if they differ by multiples of a single cycle. (*C*) Jeffress's model of computing interaural timing differences. The lengths of the axons will result in coincident activation of only one neuron, depending on the location of the stimulus. (*D*) Head-related transfer functions. The acoustic energy measured at the eardrum varies between the two ears as a function of the stimulus location. (*D*) is adapted from (Wightman & Kistler 1989a).

that any sound deviating from the midline will arrive at the near ear before it arrives at the far ear. This interaural timing difference can occur at the onset of the stimulus, but can also continue as a phase difference of the signal between the two ears. One advantage of encoding phase differences is that there are multiple samples (each phase of the stimulus) that can be compared. The disadvantage is that ambiguities can exist for higher frequencies as the same phase difference will occur when the location corresponds to multiples of a full cycle of the stimulus (**Figure 3***B*).

The superior olivary complex (SOC) of the brainstem is the first processing stage

of these binaural interactions, and lesions of these structures can cause sound localization deficits (see Casseday & Neff 1975, Kavanagh & Kelly 1992, Masterton et al. 1967). Binaural processing seems to be selectively disrupted, as the animals can still hear the sounds but make random responses with respect to the perceived location of the stimulus. Jeffress (1948) presented one initial hypothesis, based on a place code in the SOC (**Figure 3***C*), that could account for the ability to make microsecond discriminations. In this model, the length of the axons determines a place code where the action potentials from the two cochlear nuclei arrive at the postsynaptic cell

Place code:
encoding a specific stimulus parameter by the activity of neurons located at a particular place within the structure

simultaneously. This is an attractively simple model that has been shown to exist in the avian brain, but it has yet to be demonstrated in the mammalian brain (see Carr & Koppl 2004, McAlpine 2005), which may use a different mechanism.

Monaural Cues

The binaural cues are quite effective in providing the necessary information to the brain to localize acoustic stimuli in azimuth, as evidenced by deficits in sound localization perception in the unilaterally deaf or after one ear is plugged or occluded (see Blauert 1997, Middlebrooks & Green 1991). However, binaural cues cannot provide information with respect to the elevation of the stimulus, as mammalian ears are symmetrically placed on the head in elevation. There is a class of monaural cues that provide both azimuth, and especially elevation, cues (see Wightman & Kistler 1989a,b). As the sound travels to the listener, the reflections of the sounds off the head, body, and particularly the pinna cause the energy at certain frequencies to be cancelled out and therefore reduced. This leaves a characteristic sound spectrum, called the head-related transfer function (HRTF; **Figure 3D**), that is different from that of the sound in the air. Transforming sounds using the HRTF to recreate spatial location and presenting them via earphones permits the sound to be perceived from outside the listener's head (Wightman & Kistler 1989b), allowing spatial hearing to be studied in small environments such as in functional magnetic resonance imaging (fMRI) scanners (Altmann et al. 2007, Fujiki et al. 2002, Hunter et al. 2003, Pavani et al. 2002, Warren et al. 2002).

For these spectral cues to be effective, the stimulus must have a broad spectral bandwidth. These cues also require that the stimulus be loud enough to permit detection of all of the decreases in energy, or notches. Thus, pure tone stimuli are extremely difficult to localize in elevation (e.g., Recanzone et al. 2000b), as are very-low-intensity stimuli

(e.g., Recanzone & Beckerman 2004, Sabin et al. 2005, Su & Recanzone 2001). Because the spectral bandwidth of neurons in the primary auditory cortex can be quite narrow (Recanzone et al. 2000a), a population-coding scheme is necessary to encode acoustic space at the cortical level. Several varieties of such models have been proposed (Fitzpatrick et al. 1997, Furukawa et al. 2000, Harper & McAlpine 2004, Recanzone et al. 2000b, Skottun 1998, Stecker et al. 2005a).

Lesion Experiments

Lesions in normal animals have shown that the auditory cortex is necessary for the perception of acoustic space. Early studies in cats suggested that the primary auditory cortex (A1) is both necessary and sufficient to account for sound localization ability (Jenkins & Merzenich 1984; see King et al. 2007 for review). More recent studies have suggested that although AI is certainly necessary, it may not be sufficient for sound localization (Malhotra & Lomber 2007). Experiments in primates have concurred with the necessity argument but have not addressed whether A1 is sufficient for sound location perception (Heffner & Heffner 1990, Sanchez-Longo & Forster 1958, Thompson & Cortez 1983, Zatorre & Penhune 2001; see also Beitel & Kaas 1993). The sound localization deficits are rarely complete, and lesioned animals are able to detect the same acoustic stimuli; thus, it seems the best explanation is that the animals are unable to perceive the location of the sound (see Heffner 1997).

Physiology Experiments

The spatial response properties of cortical neurons have been studied extensively over the years and have primarily used the cat as an animal model (e.g., Brugge et al. 1996, Imig et al. 1990, Middlebrooks et al. 1994, Middlebrooks & Pettigrew 1981, Rajan et al. 1990). A handful of studies have investigated spatial response properties in the macaque

HRTF: head-related transfer function

fMRI: functional magnetic resonance imaging

monkey, in both anesthetized (Rauschecker & Tian 2000, 2004; Tian et al. 2001) and alert preparations (Ahissar et al. 1992, Benson et al. 1981, Recanzone et al. 2000b, Woods et al. 2006). Tian et al. (2001) tested whether neurons were better tuned to the spatial location or to the type of stimulus (monkey vocalization) in three different areas of the lateral belt (CL, ML, and AL). They found that neurons in the caudal fields are much more sharply spatially tuned than neurons in the more rostral fields, which were more selective for the type of vocalization. In a similar study in alert monkeys, Recanzone et al. (2000b) showed that neurons in the caudal belt field CM had sharper spatial tuning functions than those in A1 in both azimuth and elevation. Furthermore, the population response indicated that CM neurons could account for the localization performance of these animals as a function of the frequency and spectral bandwidth of the stimulus. Most recently, Woods et al. (2006) measured the spatial receptive fields of neurons in two core (A1 and R) and four belt (MM, CL, CM, and ML) cortical areas. As predicted by Rauschecker (1998), neurons in the caudal fields had sharper spatial tuning to broadband noise stimuli presented at different stimulus intensities.

Imaging Experiments

There has been a surge of functional imaging experiments investigating auditory spatial processing in humans. Initial studies in humans primarily used magnetoencephalography or positron emission tomography imaging techniques because it is difficult to create external sound sources in the confines of an fMRI magnet (e.g., Weeks et al. 1999). More recently, fMRI studies have taken advantage of HRTFs to externalize the stimuli (Altmann et al. 2007, Fujiki et al. 2002, Hunter et al. 2003, Pavani et al. 2002, Warren et al. 2002). These studies, as well as those using traditional headphone stimuli, have indicated that the posterior regions of auditory cortex, both Heschl's gyrus and the planum temporale,

are preferentially activated by the spatial aspects of the stimulus location (Ahveninen et al. 2006, Altmann et al. 2007, Brunetti et al. 2005, Krumbholz et al. 2005, Viceic et al. 2006, Zimmer & Macaluso 2005; see Arnott et al. 2004 for a review of earlier work) whereas nonspatial aspects of the stimuli are preferentially processed by more rostral regions. This is consistent with single-neuron experiments in nonhuman primates, as discussed above.

Visual Influences on Auditory Spatial Processing

The spatial resolution of the auditory system is quite remarkable given that acoustic space must be calculated by the nervous system. However, it is clearly inferior to the spatial resolution of the visual or somatosensory system, where the spatial features of the stimulus are encoded by the location of the sensory receptor. In some cases, both spatially disparate auditory and visual stimuli can be perceived to originate from the location of the visual stimulus. This type of intersensory bias is known as the ventriloquism effect (Howard & Templeton 1966), but similar interactions occur between the auditory, visual, and proprioceptive senses in both space and time (see Bertelson 1999, Recanzone 2003, Welch 1999, Welch & Warren 1980). Both cognitive and noncognitive factors influence the incidence and magnitude of the ventriloquism effect (see Welch 1999). The cognitive factors include the "unity assumption," which is that the subject has the a priori assumption that the two stimuli are part of the same real-world object or event.

Three main noncognitive factors affect the strength of the ventriloquism effect. The first is timing, as there has to be close temporal synchrony between the auditory and visual stimuli for the illusion to occur (Slutsky & Recanzone 2001). Subjects also are more likely to report the two stimuli as different if the visual stimulus leads the auditory stimulus compared to the reverse. The second parameter is compellingness (Warren et al. 1981), which is how well the sound matches what the listener expects of the visual object, i.e., deep pitches for large objects and high pitches for small objects. Finally, there is a spatial influence (Jack & Thurlow 1973). If the auditory and visual stimuli are too far apart spatially, the illusion breaks down. Of course, all three of these parameters interact. For example, the distance between a tone and flash of light where the illusion breaks down is much smaller than when voices are presented with images of people talking.

Early studies interpreted the sensory bias on the idea that one sensory modality would capture the other based on the relative acuities between the two, with little sensory bias of the dominant sensory modality by the nondominant sensory modality. For the ventriloquism effect, therefore, the high-acuity visual system will capture the location of the auditory stimulus, with little or no bias of the visual location by the auditory stimulus (see Warren et al. 1981). More recently, Alais & Burr (2004) have hypothesized that a model of optimal combination can explain this phenomenon. In this case, the variance in the prediction for the location of the stimulus in each modality is taken into account to determine where the bisensory stimulus originated. By increasing the difficulty in localizing the visual stimuli, they showed that subjects would increase the variance of the localization estimates, and for conditions where the visual acuity was very low, the auditory stimulus tended to dominate the percept of where both stimuli were located.

The results from a second set of experiments are consistent with the idea that the sensory system with the highest acuity dominates the percept (Phan et al. 2000). Those experiments tested a subject with bilateral parietal lobe lesions. This subject could detect visual stimuli across the entire visual field, but had extreme difficulty discriminating whether two visual stimuli came from the same location or different locations, particularly in the right visual field. His auditory localization was relatively normal. When he was discrim-

inating the location of visual stimuli while unattended auditory stimuli were simultaneously presented from the same location, his visual acuity was greatly improved. Again, the sensory modality that has the greater acuity, regardless of which it is, tends to dominate the percept of where both stimuli are located.

Ventriloquism Aftereffect

An intriguing aspect of the ventriloquism effect is that it can be long lasting (Lewald 2002, Radeau & Bertelson 1974, Recanzone 1998, Woods & Recanzone 2004). If a subject is presented with auditory and visual stimuli with a consistent spatial disparity for a period of tens of minutes, the subject's percept of acoustic space will be shifted in the direction of the visual stimulus when tested in complete darkness. This indicates that the representation of acoustic space has somehow been altered by the disparate visual experience. This can occur when the auditory and visual stimuli are displaced by a small amount and are consistently perceived to be from the same location (Recanzone 1998) or when the spatial disparity is quite large (Lewald 2002). Under either condition, the effect does not transfer across frequencies, i.e., training at one frequency does not influence the spatial representation at other frequencies. The frequency range over which this integration occurs remains to be explored. Recanzone (1998) used 750 Hz and 3000 Hz stimuli, and Lewald (2002) used 1000 Hz and 4000 Hz, so potentially a frequency difference of less than two octaves could show a transference effect. The duration of the effect also remains untested. It is possible that the effect will remain until the subject is put back into the "normal" environment and the auditory and visual stimuli are again spatially coincident.

It is important to note that this aftereffect is quite different from other aftereffects that are the result of adaptation of neurons in the visual motion processing areas, such as the waterfall illusion (Hautzel et al. 2001, Tootell et al. 1995, van Wezel & Britten 2002). The ventriloquism aftereffect lasts tens of minutes, does not transfer across frequencies, and more importantly, is in the same direction as the adapting stimulus.

Potential Neural Mechanisms of the Ventriloquism Effect

The underlying neuronal mechanisms of the ventriloquism effect and aftereffect remain unclear. It remains difficult to test where in the brain neurons shift their spatial receptive fields to account for this change in perception. Functional imaging studies in humans do not currently have the spatial resolution to detect such subtle differences in spatial processing, and the broad spatial receptive fields increase the difficulty of determining changes in spatial processing at the single-neuron level. Although the ventriloquism aftereffect has been shown in macaque monkeys (Woods & Recanzone 2004), it is always difficult to have an animal perform a task in which an illusion may (or may not) occur. Does the experimenter reward the animal for responding as though it experienced the illusion and run the risk that the animal learns to make the experimenter-desired response even though it did not perceive the illusion? The alternative is to not reward the animal on illusion trials, and run the risk that the animal does experience the illusion and will not be able to form a relationship between the stimulus, the response, and the reward. One way around this is to use "probe" trials that are very infrequent and either are never or are randomly rewarded. The inherent disadvantage of probe trials is that very few of the interesting trials are presented, which either vastly increases the time to perform the experiment or greatly decreases the amount of data collected.

Regardless, several candidate structures could be involved in this multisensory processing. First, there is a direct projection from the auditory cortex to the visual cortex representing the periphery in primates (Falchier et al. 2002, Rockland & Ojima 2003), and visual cortex projects to auditory cortical fields

in ferrets (Bizley et al. 2006). Indeed, visual influences at early auditory cortical levels have been demonstrated. Ghazanfar et al. (2005) showed that the majority of locations tested had either an enhanced and/or a suppressed response when video images of monkeys making vocalizations were paired with the vocalization as opposed to just the video or audio component alone. This effect was greater in the lateral belt areas than in A1 and was consistent with earlier reports of audio-visual interactions in speech processing in humans (Calvert et al. 1999). In addition, other nonauditory factors such as eye position and task demands can also influence the responses of auditory cortical neurons (Brosch et al. 2005, Fu et al. 2004, Werner-Reiss et al. 2003, Woods et al. 2006), indicating that there is processing beyond simple acoustic feature representations even in core auditory cortex in the primate.

Previous studies have documented several regions of the nonhuman primate brain that have multisensory responses, including the superior temporal sulcus (e.g., Benevento et al. 1977, Bruce et al. 1981, Cusick 1997), the parietal lobe (e.g., Cohen et al. 2005, Mazzoni et al. 1996, Stricanne et al. 1996), and the frontal lobe (Benevento et al. 1977, Russo & Bruce 1994). Each of these areas could potentially be involved in multisensory processing leading to the ventriloquism effect, but to date studies that directly investigate how these illusions are represented at the level of the single neuron have not been reported.

Human imaging studies have used a wide variety of different auditory and visual stimuli with a variety of different tasks that the subjects have to perform. The results from these studies have been quite varied in detail. The variances are likely due to the differences in experimental paradigms and the difficulty in comparing cross-modal matching, intramodal matching, spatial attention, and cross-modal learning paradigms (see Calvert 2001). Nonetheless, these studies are consistent in implicating a number of different cortical areas, including the superior temporal sulcus, inferior parietal lobe, prefrontal cortex, and the insula (e.g., Bushara et al. 2001, 2003; Lehmann et al. 2006; Sestieri et al. 2006). A few studies have directly assessed audio-visual interactions that are relevant to the ventriloquism effect (Bischoff et al. 2007, Busse et al. 2005, Stekelenburg & Vroomen 2005, Stekelenburg et al. 2004). Findings from these studies are consistent in showing differential activation of the multisensory processing areas noted above, namely, the superior temporal sulcus, intraparietal areas, insula, and frontal cortex, when sensory binding occurs in contrast to when it does not. How these different brain pathways integrate or parse these different sensory modalities into the percept of a single or two different sensory objects or events remains unknown.

TEMPORAL PROCESSING

The ability of the auditory system to process the temporal features of sounds also has a long history. Only recently have the neural mechanisms of this processing been explored in nonhuman primate models (e.g., Bartlett & Wang 2005, Phan & Recanzone 2007, Werner-Reiss et al. 2006), although there is a rich literature on human auditory temporal processing using event-related recording and magnetoencephalography techniques. For the purposes of this review, we concentrate on five basic temporal processing features and draw from a number of different species to illustrate potential neural correlates.

With respect to the auditory system, the term "temporal processing" can be ambiguous. Temporal processing can either refer to the ability of the auditory system to process temporal components of the acoustic stimulus, or it can refer to the ability of the neurons to encode acoustic parameters in the temporal pattern of neural activity. For this review, unless otherwise noted, we use the term to refer to the former. An additional point of confusion can come about from the auditory usage of the term "temporal processing" when it is contrasted with spectral processing. Spectral processing refers to the ability of the nervous system to analyze the frequencies of a sound; technically, sound frequency is a temporal property. In general, spectral processing is used to refer to analysis of sound where frequency can be resolved by place on the cochlea. Spectral processing has recently been reviewed elsewhere (Sutter 2005) and is not the topic of this article. Finally, investigators often discuss two types of temporal processing: temporal integration and temporal resolution (for a review, see Eddins & Green 1995). In this article, we focus on forms of temporal integration and resolution that have been studied both psychophysically and electrophysiologically.

Temporal Integration

Temporal integration refers to the ability to integrate acoustic features over time. This integration is ecologically important because it takes time to transmit large quantities of high-quality information and because integrating over time in realistic noisy environments allows random noise to be averaged out, thereby making the signal easier to detect. However, many realistic biological problems, like hunting prey or avoiding predation, require a rapid response for which integrating over long times would be counterproductive. Therefore, a compromise or tradeoff must be established.

One basic way to assess this tradeoff is by measuring the ability of subjects to detect a sound as a function of its duration. Increasing the duration of a sound decreases the detection threshold up to a point, after which longer durations do not lead to further improvements (Dallos & Olsen 1964, Garner & Miller 1947, Hughes 1946). This type of relationship has been modeled primarily in two ways. One is to reciprocally relate threshold and duration (Bloch's law). Another is through the leaky integrator model, which models temporal integration as the charging of a capacitor in parallel with a resistor (Munson 1947, Plomp & Bouman 1959,

Bloch's law: the perceived loudness and sound duration are reciprocally related so that their product is constant (loudness × sound duration = constant)

Zwislocki 1960). With this model, a time constant (in milliseconds) can be calculated that reflects how long it takes integration to reach 63% of asymptotic value.

Integration time constants of 50–200 msec have been found in most investigations of human subjects (Eddins & Green 1995; Eddins et al. 1992; Garner & Miller 1947; Gerken et al. 1983, 1990; Green & Birshall 1957; Plomp & Bouman 1959; Watson & Gengel 1969) and other animal subjects (Clack 1966, Costalupes 1983, Fay & Coombs 1983, O'Connor et al. 1999, Solecki & Gerken 1990), although there has been significant variation of estimates both within and across species. A more recent reanalysis (with nonlinear curve fitting) of the data available in the literature suggests mean integration time constants of ~30 msec in humans and medians of ~45 msec in other animals, but there still was a large degree of variation, with time constants from 25–150 msec in humans and 25–350 msec in other animals (O'Connor & Sutter 2003, O'Connor et al. 1999). Several sources of experimental differences can account for the large range of values. These include the use of arbitrary subjective criteria for curve fitting (O'Connor & Sutter 2003) and the possibility that neither the power law nor the leaky integrator models completely captures temporal integration because performance for very short stimuli deviates substantially from the model predictions, resulting in a strong relationship between reported time constants and the minimum duration stimulus used in the experiments. In addition, the frequencies used can influence the estimate of integration times. The general results of these behavioral and psychophysical studies, therefore, are mixed, which makes it difficult to interpret comparisons across studies.

There have only been a few single-unit studies of temporal integration. One has found very similar time constants for cochlear nucleus neurons and behavior in chinchillas (Clack et al. 1993). The results using the exponential (leaky integrator) function fit the behavioral data very well. However, when the same analysis was applied to auditory nerve data, the neurons of the auditory nerve had time constants much longer than neurons in the cochlear nucleus. One possible explanation for this is that the longest stimulus used was one second. By counting spikes (a form of integration) for the entire second, the integration time of neurons could have been exceeded and therefore the calculations of adding spikes would continue to show improvement (even if the animal could not use this). Because this technique integrates the neural data, it is quite possible that the slower cochlear nucleus integration times (relative to the auditory nerve) reflect adaptation of the cochlear nucleus neurons. Further analysis would need to be performed to determine whether the cochlear nucleus neurons themselves appear to integrate or receive an already integrated signal.

In the dorsal zone of the cat auditory cortex (Middlebrooks & Zook 1983, Sutter & Schreiner 1991), neurons have been found with integrative properties on the timescale observed in temporal integration (He 1998, He et al. 1997). These neurons have long latencies and are tuned to respond to longer sounds. These responses appear to have an already integrated output, except that the response is transient. A caveat that needs to be brought up is that this result is based on the subset of dorsal zone neurons with latencies greater than 30 msec, yet approximately one third of dorsal zone neurons have shorter latencies (Middlebrooks & Zook 1983, Stecker et al. 2005b, Sutter & Schreiner 1991). A little more than half (78/150) of the neurons with latencies greater than 30 msec had responses that increased with greater duration and at some point reached an asymptotic value. However, in 36% (54/150) of the neurons the activity decreased as duration was increased. This does not pose a major problem for a population code because the joint activity of a neuron that increases rate with increasing duration and one that decreases rate provides more information than either one individually. Although curves were not fit to the data, inspection suggests that the time constants of the duration firing rate curves were 100–200 msec, consistent with the psychophysical literature. One important limitation of this study, with respect to this review, is that most of these recordings were made at highly suprathreshold intensities. Neurons in the dorsal zone are known to have relatively high thresholds (Middlebrooks & Zook 1983, Sutter & Schreiner 1991). Thus, how dorsal zone neurons could contribute to detection thresholds remains unclear. However, it should be noted that temporal integration of loudness shares many properties with that of detection (Zwislocki 1960).

Forward Masking

Temporal integration has also been studied using a forward masking paradigm. Two sounds are presented sequentially and subjects' ability to detect the second sound (thresholds in dB) is measured as a function of the duration of the first. Masking occurs when the ability to detect the second sound decreases. There is a rich psychophysical literature on this topic and, in general, as the masker (first sound) duration is increased, the ability to detect the target (second sound) decreases (**Figure 4**; e.g., Weber & Green 1978). The idea with respect to integration is that the masker causes adaptation or habituation to energy at the frequencies present in the sound, and therefore the target is less perceivable. The difficulty in comparing perceptual masking to physiology is that results are influenced by many stimulus variables in addition to masker duration (shown by arrows in **Figure 4**). Therefore, in almost all of the reported studies, the differences in results can be accounted for by differences in the employed stimulus set. Nevertheless, based on physiological data, several neural mechanisms have been proposed for forward masking, including adaptation of auditory nerve fibers (Harris & Dallos 1979). Although peripheral adaptation almost certainly contributes to forward masking, a signal detection analysis indicates that limitations introduced more

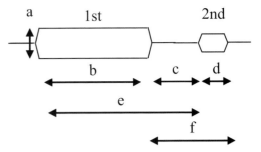

Figure 4

Stimulus parameters in forward masking experiments. The first stimulus is the masker and the subject is asked to detect the second stimulus. Parameters that influence the strength of masking include the intensity of the masker (*a*), the duration of the masker (*b*), the interstimulus interval (*c*), the duration of the target (*d*), the onset interval between the masker and target (*e*), and the combined interstimulus interval and target duration (*f*).

central to the auditory nerve are also necessary (Relkin & Turner 1988). Findings indicate roles for central adaptation and inhibition in areas including the cochlear nucleus (Boettcher et al. 1990, Kaltenbach et al. 1993) and cortex (Brosch & Schreiner 1997, Calford & Semple 1995). Most single-unit studies of forward masking have focused on how the response to the target sound recovers with a longer delay between the first and second sound. In the few studies that have investigated the effect of masker duration (Harris & Dallos 1979), the general trend is for more masking as the duration is increased, a trend consistent with the psychophysical results.

Neuroethological Studies

Other interesting properties of the biological basis of temporal integration can be gleaned from neuroethological studies. In songbirds, the ability to discriminate a song improves by increasing the sample time of the song (Ratcliffe & Weisman 1986). Neurons in a part of the forebrain called high vocal center (also known as hyperventrale pars caudalis) selectively respond to the bird's own song (Margoliash 1983, 1986; Margoliash & Konishi 1985; Theunissen & Doupe 1998). The pronounced selectivity of these neurons was investigated by dissecting the song into individual syllables. The results showed that these neurons integrate across several syllables, sometimes up to the order of a second (Margoliash & Fortune 1992, Margoliash et al. 1994). For these neurons, if the song's structure was degraded in any manner prior to the integration time, responsiveness dropped dramatically. Such neuronal response selectivity achieved by combining elements over such a long time is a very rare finding. Furthermore, it was found that within the high vocal center (or hyperventrale pars caudalis) most neurons responded similarly to song. However, by changing the width of the analysis window, selectivity to different syllables in the song could be revealed (Sutter & Margoliash 1994). In other words, the bird's forebrain could pull different features out of a sound by applying different integration times. The combination of results in the bird suggests that neurons in the forebrain can analyze a sound by simultaneously applying multiple integration times in parallel.

Echolocating bats provide another neuroethological example of neural integration. In these bats, neurons in one cortical area are highly selective for delays between echolocation emission and the returning echo (O'Neill & Suga 1979, Suga & O'Neill 1979). These neurons will only respond to a very narrow range of delays. To achieve this, these neurons integrate the emission and returning echo over a timescale of approximately 10–20 msec. In both of the provided examples (birds and bats) we can see cases where neurons that are highly selective for biologically relevant sounds can be found at higher levels in the brain, and that such selectivity comes about by integrating different sequentially occurring components of the auditory signal over time.

Gap Detection

Contrasting temporal integration is temporal resolution: the ability to resolve time. One way to study temporal resolution is to measure the ability to detect a gap or silent period in a sound. Gap detection can be studied with broadband noise or narrowband sounds such as tones. Because gap detection in narrowband sounds contains strong spectral cues that subjects can use, we first focus on the ability to detect a gap in noise. Humans' ability to detect a gap in a broadband noise is on the scale of a few milliseconds (Eddins et al. 1992, Forrest & Green 1987, Snell et al. 1994). Remarkably similar results across many animal studies report gap detection that is similar to humans in the 2–6 msec range for broadband noise (e.g., Ison et al. 1991, Leitner et al. 1997, Syka et al. 2002, Wagner et al. 2003), including macaques (personal observation). Although gap detection appears to be fairly simple, there is strong support for a role of the auditory cortex (Bowen et al. 2003, Ison et al. 1991, Kelly et al. 1996, Syka et al. 2002). Thresholds usually increase with auditory cortical lesions, inactivation, or interference. There have been surprisingly few studies of the neural correlate of gap detection. One difficulty in finding a single-unit response correlated with gap detection is that it is difficult to detect a dip in the response of neurons with sustained firing rates. In the auditory nerve, fibers reduce activity during a gap in broadband noise, and then give a slightly elevated onset response followed by sustained activity. For short gaps down to 1–2 msec, this can be seen in the average activity (Salvi & Arehole 1985). The average value for all single units sampled was significantly different at gap widths ≥ 2 msec compared with the response when no gap was present. This suggests that the population of auditory nerve fibers sampled have the information to detect a gap that is consistent with psychophysical performance.

As the auditory system ascends to the IC, the representation becomes much more dependent on phasic responses to the re-onset of the tone (Walton et al. 1997, 1998). Here the most sensitive neurons are those with an onset response to noise. The trend toward onset response encoding strengthens even more at the cortical level (Eggermont 1999). The IC and auditory cortex studies indicate sensitivity comparable to behavioral thresholds; however, since they are based on observations from averaged activity and don't employ signal detection metrics, it is not possible to make definitive statements. Nevertheless, the finding that such activity is obvious in the averaged responses suggests that these higher-level areas can encode gaps by pooling across neurons.

There is a wide variety of results with respect to the ability to detect gaps in narrowband sounds. This is partially because rapid transitions in narrowband sounds (like tones) generate additional frequencies, making a click-like artifact that can be used by the subjects to determine that there is a gap, and different methods are more or less effective at eliminating this cue. However, an interesting illusion can be created by introducing a gap into a "foreground" sound and then filling the gap with broadband noise (Bashford et al. 1988; Warren 1970; Warren et al. 1972, 1988). Under these conditions, not only is gap detection impaired but subjects also report the foreground as being continuous. This effect has several names (auditory induction, continuity illusion, perceptual or phonemic restoration,

amodal completion, and auditory fill-in) and can be thought of as resulting from the auditory system reallocating the energy present in the noise to the foreground (Bregman 1990). Induction occurs for the spectral content of sounds, but recently it has also been demonstrated for the temporal properties of amplitude-modulated sounds (Lyzenga et al. 2005). Induction has also been found in cats (Sugita 1997), cotton-top tamarin monkeys (Miller et al. 2001), and macaque monkeys (Petkov et al. 2003). Recent studies in macaques compared the single-neuron responses in A1 to stimuli that produce induction in these animals (Petkov et al. 2007). As was the case with gap detection, teasing apart the contribution of onset, offset, and sustained responses was useful. Onset, offset, and sustained responders contribute such that the noise removes the ability to observe the foreground sound's transitions by obliterating an onset of responses, and it induces a continuous foreground sound perception with the sustained response. An inability to hear transitions of foreground sounds has been shown psychophysically to be a requirement for induction (Bregman & Dannenbring 1977).

SUMMARY POINTS

1. The functional and anatomical organization of the primate auditory cortex is organized in a core-belt-parabelt manner and is similar between macaque monkeys and humans.

2. Spatial processing is equivalent between humans and macaques, and both appear to selectively process acoustic spatial information in caudal regions of the auditory cortex.

3. Visual stimuli can strongly influence auditory spatial representations and could do so by influencing early cortical areas, including A1, as well as multisensory areas.

4. Temporal integration time constants are similar between humans and other animals.

5. Gap detection is mainly processed by onset responses, and there is a cortical correlate to auditory fill-in in the auditory cortex of macaque monkeys.

ACKNOWLEDGMENTS

The authors thank C. Broaddus, K. Campi, J. Engle, M. Fletcher, J. Johnson, M. Niwa, S. Nyon, and K. O'Connor for their contributions to the manuscript. The authors are supported by NIH grants EY013458 and AG024372 (GHR) and DC02514 (MLS), and the McDonnel Foundation (MLS).

LITERATURE CITED

Ahissar M, Ahissar E, Bergman H, Vaadia E. 1992. Encoding of sound-source location and movement: activity of single neurons and interactions between adjacent neurons in the monkey auditory cortex. *J. Neurophysiol.* 67:203–15

Ahveninen J, Jääskeläinen IP, Raij T, Bonmassar G, Devore S, et al. 2006. Task-modulated "what" and "where" pathways in human auditory cortex. *Proc. Natl. Acad. Sci. USA* 103:14608–13

Alais D, Burr D. 2004. The ventriloquist effect results from near-optimal bimodal integration. *Curr. Biol.* 14:257–62

Altmann CF, Bledowski C, Wibral M, Kaiser J. 2007. Processing of location and pattern changes of natural sounds in the human auditory cortex. *NeuroImage* 35:1192–200

Altshuler MW, Comalli PE. 1975. Effect of stimulus intensity and frequency on median horizontal plane sound localization. *J. Aud. Res.* 15:262–65

Arnott SR, Binns MA, Grady CL, Alain C. 2004. Assessing the auditory dual-pathway model in humans. *NeuroImage* 22:401–8

Bartlett EL, Wang X. 2005. Long-lasting modulation by stimulus context in primate auditory cortex. *J. Neurophysiol.* 94:83–104

Bashford JA Jr, Meyers MD, Brubaker BS, Warren RM. 1988. Illusory continuity of interrupted speech: speech rate determines durational limits. *J. Acoust. Soc. Am.* 84:1635–38

Beitel RE, Kaas JH. 1993. Effects of bilateral and unilateral ablation of auditory cortex in cats on the unconditioned head orienting response to acoustic stimuli. *J. Neurophysiol.* 70:351–69

Benevento LA, Fallon J, Davis BJ, Rezak M. 1977. Auditory-visual interaction in single cells in the cortex of the superior temporal sulcus and the orbital frontal cortex of the macaque monkey. *Exp. Neurol.* 57:849–72

Benson DA, Hienz RD, Goldstein MH Jr. 1981. Single-unit activity in the auditory cortex of monkeys actively localizing sound sources: spatial tuning and behavioral dependency. *Brain Res.* 219:249–67

Bertelson P. 1999. Ventriloquism: a case of crossmodal perceptual grouping. In *Cognitive Contributions to the Perception of Spatial and Temporal Events*, ed. G Aschersleben, T Bachmann, J Musseler, pp. 346–62. New York: Elsevier

Bilecen D, Scheffler K, Schmid N, Tschopp K, Seelig J. 1998. Tonotopic organization of the human auditory cortex as detected by BOLD-fMRI. *Hear. Res.* 126:19–27

Bischoff M, Walter B, Blecker CR, Morgen K, Vaitl D, Sammer G. 2007. Utilizing the ventriloquism-effect to investigate audio-visual binding. *Neuropsychologia* 45:578–86

Bizley JK, Nodal RF, Bajo VM, Nelken I, King AJ. 2006. Physiological and anatomical evidence for multisensory interactions in auditory cortex. *Cereb. Cortex* Nov. 29 (Epub ahead of print)

Blauert J. 1997. *Spatial Hearing: The Psychophysics of Human Sound Localization.* Cambridge, MA: MIT Press

Boettcher FA, Salvi RJ, Saunders SS. 1990. Recovery from short-term adaptation in single neurons in the cochlear nucleus. *Hear. Res.* 48:125–44

Bowen GP, Lin D, Taylor MK, Ison JR. 2003. Auditory cortex lesions in the rat impair both temporal acuity and noise increment thresholds, revealing a common neural substrate. *Cereb. Cortex* 13:815–22

Bregman AS. 1990. *Auditory Scene Analysis*. Cambridge, MA: MIT Press

Bregman AS, Dannenbring GL. 1977. Auditory continuity and amplitude edges. *Can. J. Psychol.* 31:151–59

Brosch M, Schreiner CE. 1997. Time course of forward masking tuning curves in cat primary auditory cortex. *J. Neurophysiol.* 77:923–43

Brosch M, Selezneva E, Scheich H. 2005. Nonauditory events of a behavioral procedure activate auditory cortex of highly trained monkeys. *J. Neurosci.* 25:6797–806

Bruce C, Desimone R, Gross CG. 1981. Visual properties of neurons in a polysensory area in superior temporal sulcus of the macaque. *J. Neurophysiol.* 46:369–84

Brugge JF, Reale RA, Hind JE. 1996. The structure of spatial receptive fields of neurons in primary auditory cortex of the cat. *J. Neurosci.* 16:4420–37

Brunetti M, Belardinelli P, Caulo M, Del Gratta C, Della Penna S, et al. 2005. Human brain activation during passive listening to sounds from different locations: an fMRI and MEG study. *Hum. Brain Mapp.* 26:251–61

Bushara KO, Grafman J, Hallett M. 2001. Neural correlates of auditory-visual stimulus onset asynchrony detection. *J. Neurosci.* 21:300–4

Bushara KO, Hanakawa T, Immisch I, Toma K, Kansaku K, Hallett M. 2003. Neural correlates of cross-modal binding. *Nat. Neurosci.* 6:190–95

Busse L, Roberts KC, Crist RE, Weissman DH, Woldorff MG. 2005. The spread of attention across modalities and space in a multisensory object. *Proc. Natl. Acad. Sci. USA* 102:18751–56

Calford MB, Semple MN. 1995. Monaural inhibition in cat auditory cortex. *J. Neurophysiol.* 73:1876–91

Calvert GA. 2001. Crossmodal processing in the human brain: insights from functional neuroimaging studies. *Cereb. Cortex* 11:1110–23

Calvert GA, Brammer MJ, Bullmore ET, Campbell R, Iversen SD, David AS. 1999. Response amplification in sensory-specific cortices during crossmodal binding. *NeuroReport* 10:2619–23

Carlile S, Leong P, Hyams S. 1997. The nature and distribution of errors in sound localization by human listeners. *Hear. Res.* 114:179–96

Carr CE, Koppl C. 2004. Coding interaural time differences at low best frequencies in the barn owl. *J. Physiol. Paris* 98:99–112

Casseday JH, Neff WD. 1975. Auditory localization: role of auditory pathways in brain stem of the cat. *J. Neurophysiol.* 38:842–58

Clack TD. 1966. Effect of signal duration on the auditory sensitivity of humans and monkeys (*Macaca mulatta*). *J. Acoust. Soc. Am.* 40:1140–46

Clock AE, Salvi RJ, Saunders SS, Powers NL. 1993. Neural correlates of temporal integration in the cochlear nucleus of the chinchilla. *Hear. Res.* 71:37–50

Cohen YE, Russ BE, Gifford GW III. 2005. Auditory processing in the posterior parietal cortex. *Behav. Cogn. Neurosci. Rev.* 4:218–31

Comalli PE, Altshuler MW. 1976. Effect of stimulus intensity, frequency, and unilateral hearing loss on sound localization. *J. Aud. Res.* 16:275–79

Costalupes JA. 1983. Temporal integration of pure tones in the cat. *Hear. Res.* 9:43–54

Cusick CG. 1997. The superior temporal polysensory region in monkeys. *Cereb. Cortex* 12:435–68

Dallos PJ, Olsen WO. 1964. Integration of energy at threshold with gradual rise-fall tone pips. *J. Acoust. Soc. Am.* 36:743–51

Eddins DA, Green DM. 1995. Temporal integration and temporal resolution. In *Hearing (Handbook of Perception and Cognition)*, ed. BCJ Moore, pp. 207–42. San Diego, CA: Academic. 2nd ed.

Eddins DA, Hall JW 3rd, Grose JH. 1992. The detection of temporal gaps as a function of frequency region and absolute noise bandwidth. *J. Acoust. Soc. Am.* 91:1069–77

Eggermont JJ. 1999. Neural correlates of gap detection in three auditory cortical fields in the cat. *J. Neurophysiol.* 81:2570–81

Falchier A, Clavagnier S, Barone P, Kennedy H. 2002. Anatomical evidence of multimodal integration in primate striate cortex. *J. Neurosci.* 22:5749–59

Fay RR, Coombs S. 1983. Neural mechanisms in sound detection and temporal summation. *Hear. Res.* 10:69–92

Fitzpatrick DC, Batra R, Stanford TR, Kuwada S. 1997. A neuronal population code for sound localization. *Nature* 388:871–74

Forrest TG, Green DM. 1987. Detection of partially filled gaps in noise and the temporal modulation transfer function. *J. Acoust. Soc. Am.* 82:1933–43

Fu KM, Shah AS, O'Connell MN, McGinnis T, Eckholdt H, et al. 2004. Timing and laminar profile of eye-position effects on auditory responses in primate auditory cortex. *J. Neurophysiol.* 92:3522–31

Fujiki N, Riederer KAJ, Jousmaki V, Makela JP, Hari R. 2002. Human cortical representation of virtual auditory space: differences between sound azimuth and elevation. *Eur. J. Neurosci.* 16:2207–13

Furukawa S, Xu L, Middlebrooks JC. 2000. Coding of sound-source location by ensembles of cortical neurons. *J. Neurosci.* 20:1216–28

Garner WR, Miller GA. 1947. The masked threshold of pure tones as a function of duration. *J. Exp. Psychol.* 37:293–303

Gerken GM, Bhat VK, Hutchison-Clutter M. 1990. Auditory temporal integration and the power function model. *J. Acoust. Soc. Am.* 88:767–78

Gerken GM, Gunnarson AD, Allen CM. 1983. Three models of temporal summation evaluated using normal-hearing and hearing-impaired subjects. *J. Speech Hear. Res.* 26:256–62

Ghazanfar AA, Maier JX, Hoffman KL, Logothetis NK. 2005. Multisensory integration of dynamic faces and voices in rhesus monkey auditory cortex. *J. Neurosci.* 25:5004–12

Green DM, Birshall TG. 1957. Signal detection as a function of signal intensity and duration. *J. Acoust. Soc. Am.* 29:523–31

Hackett TA, Preuss TM, Kaas JH. 2001. Architectonic identification of the core region in auditory cortex of macaques, chimpanzees, and humans. *J. Comp. Neurol.* 441:197–222

Hackett TA, Stepniewska I, Kaas JH. 1998a. Subdivisions of auditory cortex and ipsilateral cortical connections of the parabelt auditory cortex in macaque monkeys. *J. Comp. Neurol.* 394:475–95

Hackett TA, Stepniewska I, Kaas JH. 1998b. Thalamocortical connections of the parabelt auditory cortex in macaque monkeys. *J. Comp. Neurol.* 400:271–86

Harper NS, McAlpine D. 2004. Optimal neural population coding of an auditory spatial cue. *Nature* 430:682–86

Harris DM, Dallos P. 1979. Forward masking of auditory nerve fiber responses. *J. Neurophysiol.* 42:1083–107

Hautzel H, Taylor JG, Krause BJ, Schmitz N, Tellmann L, et al. 2001. The motion aftereffect: more than area V5/MT? Evidence from 15O-butanol PET studies. *Brain Res.* 892:281–92

He J. 1998. Long-latency neurons in auditory cortex involved in temporal integration: theoretical analysis of experimental data. *Hear. Res.* 121:147–60

He J, Hashikawa T, Ojima H, Kinouchi Y. 1997. Temporal integration and duration tuning in the dorsal zone of cat auditory cortex. *J. Neurosci.* 17:2615–25

Heffner HE. 1997. The role of macaque auditory cortex in sound localization. *Acta Otolaryngol. Stockh. Suppl.* 532:22–27

Heffner HE, Heffner RS. 1990. Effect of bilateral auditory cortex lesions on sound localization in Japanese macaques. *J. Neurophysiol.* 64:915–31

Heffner RS. 2004. Primate hearing from a mammalian perspective. *Anat. Rec. A Discov. Mol. Cell Evol. Biol.* 281A:1111–22

Howard IP, Templeton WB. 1966. *Human Spatial Orientation*. New York: Wiley

Hughes JW. 1946. The threshold of audition for short periods of stimulation. *Proc. R. Soc. Lond. B Biol. Sci.* 133:486–90

Hunter MD, Griffiths TD, Farrow TFD, Zheng Y, Wilkinson ID, et al. 2003. A neural basis for the perception of voices in external auditory space. *Brain* 126:161–69

Imig TJ, Irons WA, Samson FR. 1990. Single-unit selectivity to azimuthal direction and sound pressure level of noise bursts in cat high-frequency primary auditory cortex. *J. Neurophysiol.* 63:1448–66

Ison JR, O'Connor K, Bowen GP, Bocirnea A. 1991. Temporal resolution of gaps in noise by the rat is lost with functional decortication. *Behav. Neurosci.* 105:33–40

Jack CE, Thurlow WR. 1973. Effects of degree of visual association and angle of displacement on the "ventriloquism" effect. *Percept. Mot. Skills* 37:967–79

Jeffress LA. 1948. A place theory of sound localization. *J. Comp. Psychol.* 41:35–39

Jenkins WM, Merzenich MM. 1984. Role of cat primary auditory cortex for sound-localization behavior. *J. Neurophysiol.* 52:819–47

Jones EG. 2003. Chemically defined parallel pathways in the monkey auditory system. *Ann. N.Y. Acad. Sci.* 999:218–33

Jones EG, Dell'Anna ME, Molinari M, Rausell E, Hashikawa T. 1995. Subdivisions of macaque monkey auditory cortex revealed by calcium-binding protein immunoreactivity. *J. Comp. Neurol.* 362:153–70

Kaas JH, Hackett TA. 2000. Subdivisions of auditory cortex and processing streams in primates. *Proc. Natl. Acad. Sci. USA* 97:11793–99

Kaltenbach JA, Meleca RJ, Falzarano PR, Myers SF, Simpson TH. 1993. Forward masking properties of neurons in the dorsal cochlear nucleus: possible role in the process of echo suppression. *Hear. Res.* 67:35–44

Kavanagh GL, Kelly JB. 1992. Midline and lateral field sound localization in the ferret (*Mustela putorius*): contribution of the superior olivary complex. *J. Neurophysiol.* 67:987–1016

Kayser C, Petkov CI, Augath M, Logothetis NK. 2007. Functional imaging reveals visual modulation of specific fields in auditory cortex. *J. Neurosci.* 27:1824–35

Kelly JB, Rooney BJ, Phillips DP. 1996. Effects of bilateral auditory cortical lesions on gap-detection thresholds in the ferret (*Mustela putorius*). *Behav. Neurosci.* 110:542–50

King AJ, Bajo VM, Bizley JK, Campbell RAA, Nodal FR, et al. 2007. Physiological and behavioral studies of spatial coding in the auditory cortex. *Hear. Res.* Jan. 19 (Epub ahead of print)

Kosaki H, Hashikawa T, He J, Jones EG. 1997. Tonotopic organization of auditory cortical fields delineated by parvalbumin immunoreactivity in macaque monkeys. *J. Comp. Neurol.* 386:304–16

Krumbholz K, Schonwiesner M, Rubsamen R, Zilles K, Fink GR, Yves von Cramon D. 2005. Hierarchical processing of sound location and motion in the human brainstem and planum temporale. *Eur. J. Neurosci.* 21:230–38

Lehmann C, Herdener M, Esposito F, Hubl D, di Salle F, et al. 2006. Differential patterns of multisensory interactions in core and belt areas of human auditory cortex. *NeuroImage* 31:294–300

Leitner DS, Carmody DP, Girten EM. 1997. A signal detection theory analysis of gap detection in the rat. *Percept. Psychophys.* 59:774–82

Leonard CM, Puranik C, Kuldau JM, Lombardino LJ. 1998. Normal variation in the frequency and location of human auditory cortex landmarks. Heschl's gyrus: Where is it? *Cereb. Cortex* 8:397–406

Lewald J. 2002. Rapid adaptation to auditory-visual spatial disparity. *Learn. Mem.* 9:268–78

Lyzenga J, Carlyon RP, Moore BC. 2005. Dynamic aspects of the continuity illusion: perception of level and of the depth, rate, and phase of modulation. *Hear. Res.* 210:30–41

Malhotra S, Lomber SG. 2007. Sound localization during homotopic and heterotopic bilateral cooling deactivation of primary and nonprimary auditory cortical areas in the cat. *J. Neurophysiol.* 97:26–43

Margoliash D. 1983. Acoustic parameters underlying the responses of song-specific neurons in the white-crowned sparrow. *J. Neurosci.* 3:1039–57

Margoliash D. 1986. Preference for autogenous song by auditory neurons in a song system nucleus of the white-crowned sparrow. *J. Neurosci.* 6:1643–61

Margoliash D, Fortune ES. 1992. Temporal and harmonic combination-sensitive neurons in the zebra finch's HVc. *J. Neurosci.* 12:4309–26

Margoliash D, Fortune ES, Sutter ML, Yu AC, Wren-Hardin BD, Dave A. 1994. Distributed representation in the song system of oscines: evolutionary implications and functional consequences. *Brain Behav. Evol.* 44:247–64

Margoliash D, Konishi M. 1985. Auditory representation of autogenous song in the song system of white-crowned sparrows. *Proc. Natl. Acad. Sci. USA* 82:5997–6000

Masterton B, Jane JA, Diamond IT. 1967. Role of brainstem auditory structures in sound localization. I. Trapezoid body, superior olive, and lateral lemniscus. *J. Neurophysiol.* 30:341–59

Mazzoni P, Bracewell RM, Barash S, Andersen RA. 1996. Spatially tuned auditory responses in area LIP of macaques performing delayed memory saccades to acoustic targets. *J. Neurophysiol.* 75:1233–41

McAlpine D. 2005. Creating a sense of auditory space. *J. Physiol.* 566:21–28

Merzenich MM, Brugge JF. 1973. Representation of the cochlear partition on the superior temporal plane of the macaque monkey. *Brain Res.* 50:275–96

Middlebrooks JC, Clock AE, Xu L, Green DM. 1994. A panoramic code for sound location by cortical neurons. *Science* 264:842–44

Middlebrooks JC, Green DM. 1991. Sound localization by human listeners. *Annu. Rev. Psychol.* 42:135–59

Middlebrooks JC, Pettigrew JD. 1981. Functional classes of neurons in primary auditory cortex of cat distinguished by sensitivity to sound location. *J. Neurosci.* 1:107–20

Middlebrooks JC, Zook JM. 1983. Intrinsic organization of the cat's medial geniculate body identified by projections to binaural response-specific bands in the primary auditory cortex. *J. Neurosci.* 3:203–24

Miller CT, Dibble E, Hauser MD. 2001. Amodal completion of acoustic signals by a nonhuman primate. *Nat. Neurosci.* 4:783–84

Molinari M, Dell'Anna ME, Rausell E, Leggio MG, Hashikawa T, Jones EG. 1995. Auditory thalamocortical pathways defined in monkeys by calcium-binding protein immunoreactivity. *J. Comp. Neurol.* 362:171–94

Morel A, Garraghty PE, Kaas JH. 1993. Tonotopic organization, architectonic fields, and connections of auditory cortex in macaque monkeys. *J. Comp. Neurol.* 335:437–59

Morosan P, Rademacher J, Schleicher A, Amunts K, Schormann T, Zilles K. 2001. Human primary auditory cortex: cytoarchitectonic subdivisions and mapping into a spatial reference system. *NeuroImage* 13:684–701

Munson WA. 1947. The growth of auditory sensation. *J. Acoust. Soc. Am.* 19:584–91

O'Connor K, Sutter ML. 2003. Auditory temporal integration in primates: a comparative analysis. In *Primate Audition: Ethology and Neurobiology*, ed. A Ghazanfar, pp. 27–43. Boca Raton, FL: CRC Press

O'Connor KN, Barruel P, Hajalilou R, Sutter ML. 1999. Auditory temporal integration in the rhesus macaque (*Macaca mulatta*). *J. Acoust. Soc. Am.* 106:954–65

O'Neill WE, Suga N. 1979. Target range-sensitive neurons in the auditory cortex of the mustache bat. *Science* 203:69–73

Pandya DN. 1995. Anatomy of the auditory cortex. *Rev. Neurol. (Paris)* 151:486–94

Pavani F, Macaluso E, Warren JD, Driver J, Griffiths TD. 2002. A common cortical substrate activated by horizontal and vertical sound movement in the human brain. *Curr. Biol.* 12:1584–90

Petkov CI, Kang X, Alho K, Bertrand O, Yund EW, Woods DL. 2004. Attentional modulation of human auditory cortex. *Nat. Neurosci.* 7:658–63

Petkov CI, Kayser C, Augath M, Logothetis NK. 2006. Functional imaging reveals numerous fields in the monkey auditory cortex. *PLoS Biol.* 4:e215

Petkov CI, O'Connor KN, Sutter ML. 2003. Illusory sound perception in macaque monkeys. *J. Neurosci.* 23:9155–61

Petkov CI, O'Connor KN, Sutter ML. 2007. Encoding of illusory continuity in primary auditory cortex. *Neuron* 54:153–65

Phan ML, Recanzone GH. 2007. Single-neuron responses to rapidly presented temporal sequences in the primary auditory cortex of the awake macaque monkey. *J. Neurophysiol.* 97:1726–37

Phan ML, Schendel KL, Recanzone GH, Robertson LC. 2000. Auditory and visual spatial localization deficits following bilateral parietal lobe lesions in a patient with Balint's syndrome. *J. Cogn. Neurosci.* 12:583–600

Plomp R, Bouman MS. 1959. Relation between hearing threshold and duration for tone pulses. *J. Acoust. Soc. Am.* 31:749–58

Populin LC, Yin TCT. 1998. Behavioral studies of sound localization in the cat. *J. Neurosci.* 18:2147–60

Radeau M, Bertelson P. 1974. The after-effects of ventriloquism. *Q. J. Exp. Psychol.* 26:63–71

Rademacher J, Morosan P, Schleicher A, Freund HJ, Zilles K. 2001. Human primary auditory cortex in women and men. *NeuroReport* 12:1561–65

Rajan R, Aitkin LM, Irvine DR, McKay J. 1990. Azimuthal sensitivity of neurons in primary auditory cortex of cats. I. Types of sensitivity and the effects of variations in stimulus parameters. *J. Neurophysiol.* 64:872–87

Ratcliffe L, Weisman RG. 1986. Song sequence discrimination in the black-capped chickadee (*Parus atricapillus*). *J. Comp. Psychol.* 100:361–67

Rauschecker JP. 1998. Parallel processing in the auditory cortex of primates. *Audiol. Neurootol.* 3:86–103

Rauschecker JP, Tian B. 2000. Mechanisms and streams for processing of "what" and "where" in auditory cortex. *Proc. Natl. Acad. Sci. USA* 97:11800–6

Rauschecker JP, Tian B. 2004. Processing of band-passed noise in the lateral auditory belt cortex of the rhesus monkey. *J. Neurophysiol.* 91:2578–89

Rauschecker JP, Tian B, Hauser M. 1995. Processing of complex sounds in the macaque nonprimary auditory cortex. *Science* 268:111–14

Recanzone GH. 1998. Rapidly induced auditory plasticity: the ventriloquism aftereffect. *Proc. Natl. Acad. Sci. USA* 95:869–75

Recanzone GH. 2003. Auditory influences on visual temporal rate perception. *J. Neurophysiol.* 89:1078–93

Recanzone GH, Beckerman NS. 2004. Effects of intensity and location on sound location discrimination in macaque monkeys. *Hear. Res.* 198:116–24

Recanzone GH, Guard DC, Phan ML. 2000a. Frequency and intensity response properties of single neurons in the auditory cortex of the behaving macaque monkey. *J. Neurophysiol.* 83:2315–31

Recanzone GH, Guard DC, Phan ML, Su TK. 2000b. Correlation between the activity of single auditory cortical neurons and sound localization behavior in the macaque monkey. *J. Neurophysiol.* 83:2723–39

Recanzone GH, Makhamra SDDR, Guard DC. 1998. Comparison of relative and absolute sound localization ability in humans. *J. Acoust. Soc. Am.* 103:1085–97

Relkin EM, Turner CW. 1988. A reexamination of forward masking in the auditory nerve. *J. Acoust. Soc. Am.* 84:584–91

Rockland KS, Ojima H. 2003. Multisensory convergence in calcarine visual areas in macaque monkey. *Int. J. Psychophysiol.* 50:19–26

Romanski LM, Tian B, Fritz J, Mishkin M, Goldman-Rakic PS, Rauschecker JP. 1999. Dual streams of auditory afferents target multiple domains in the primate prefrontal cortex. *Nat. Neurosci.* 2:1131–36

Russo GS, Bruce CJ. 1994. Frontal eye field activity preceding aurally guided saccades. *J. Neurophysiol.* 71:1250–53

Sabin AT, Macpherson EA, Middlebrooks JC. 2005. Human sound localization at near-threshold levels. *Hear. Res.* 199:124–34

Salvi RJ, Arehole S. 1985. Gap detection in chinchillas with temporary high-frequency hearing loss. *J. Acoust. Soc. Am.* 77:1173–77

Sanchez-Longo LP, Forster FM. 1958. Clinical significance of impairment of sound localization. *Neurology* 8:119–25

Sestieri C, Di Matteo R, Ferretti A, Del Gratta C, Caulo M, et al. 2006. "What" versus "where" in the audiovisual domain: an fMRI study. *NeuroImage* 33:672–80

Skottun BC. 1998. Sound localization and neurons. *Nature* 393:531

Slutsky DA, Recanzone GH. 2001. Temporal and spatial dependency of the ventriloquism effect. *NeuroReport* 12:7–10

Snell KB, Ison JR, Frisina DR. 1994. The effects of signal frequency and absolute bandwidth on gap detection in noise. *J. Acoust. Soc. Am.* 96:1458–64

Solecki JM, Gerken GM. 1990. Auditory temporal integration in the normal-hearing and hearing-impaired cat. *J. Acoust. Soc. Am.* 88:779–85

Stecker GC, Harrington IA, Macpherson EA, Middlebrooks JC. 2005b. Spatial sensitivity in the dorsal zone (area DZ) of cat auditory cortex. *J. Neurophysiol.* 94:1267–80

Stecker GC, Harrington IA, Middlebrooks JC. 2005a. Location coding by opponent neural populations in the auditory cortex. *PLoS Biol.* 3:e78

Stekelenburg JJ, Vroomen J. 2005. An event-related potential investigation of the time-course of temporal ventriloquism. *NeuroReport* 6:641–44

Stekelenburg JJ, Vroomen J, de Gelder B. 2004. Illusory sound shifts induced by the ventriloquist illusion evoke the mismatch negativity. *Neurosci. Lett.* 357:163–66

Stricanne B, Andersen RA, Mazzoni P. 1996. Eye-centered, head-centered and intermediate coding of remembered sound locations in area LIP. *J. Neurophysiol.* 76:2071–76

Su K, Recanzone GH. 2001. Differential effect of near-threshold stimulus intensities on sound localization performance in azimuth and elevation in normal human subjects. *J. Assoc. Res. Otolaryngol.* 2:246–56

Suga N, O'Neill WE. 1979. Neural axis representing target range in the auditory cortex of the mustache bat. *Science* 206:351–53

Sugita Y. 1997. Neuronal correlates of auditory induction in the cat cortex. *NeuroReport* 8:1155–59

Sutter ML. 2005. Spectral processing in the auditory cortex. *Int. Rev. Neurobiol.* 70:253–98

Sutter ML, Margoliash D. 1994. Global synchronous response to autogenous song in zebra finch HVc. *J. Neurophysiol.* 72:2105–23

Sutter ML, Schreiner CE. 1991. Physiology and topography of neurons with multipeaked tuning curves in cat primary auditory cortex. *J. Neurophysiol.* 65:1207–26

Syka J, Rybalko N, Mazelova J, Druga R. 2002. Gap detection threshold in the rat before and after auditory cortex ablation. *Hear. Res.* 172:151–59

Talavage TM, Ledden PJ, Benson RR, Rosen BR, Melcher JR. 2000. Frequency-dependent responses exhibited by multiple regions in human auditory cortex. *Hear. Res.* 150:225–44

Theunissen FE, Doupe AJ. 1998. Temporal and spectral sensitivity of complex auditory neurons in the nucleus HVc of male zebra finches. *J. Neurosci.* 18:3786–802

Thompson GC, Cortez AM. 1983. The inability of squirrel monkeys to localize sound after unilateral ablation of auditory cortex. *Behav. Brain Res.* 8:211–16

Tian B, Rauschecker JP. 2004. Processing of frequency-modulated sounds in the lateral auditory belt cortex of the rhesus monkey. *J. Neurophysiol.* 92:2993–3013

Tian B, Reser D, Durham A, Kustov A, Rauschecker JP. 2001. Functional specialization in rhesus monkey auditory cortex. *Science* 292:290–93

Tootell RB, Reppas JB, Dale AM, Look RB, Sereno MI, et al. 1995. Visual motion aftereffect in human cortical area MT revealed by functional magnetic resonance imaging. *Nature* 375:139–41

Ungerleider LG, Haxby JV. 1994. "What" and "where" in the human brain. *Curr. Opin. Neurobiol.* 4:157–65

Ungerleider LG, Mishkin M. 1982. Two cortical visual systems. In *Analysis of Visual Behavior*, ed. DJ Ingle, MA Goodale, RJW Mansfield, pp. 549–86. Cambridge, MA: MIT Press

Van Wezel RJ, Britten KH. 2002. Motion adaptation in area MT. *J. Neurophysiol.* 88:3469–76

Viceic D, Fornari E, Thiran JP, Maeder PP, Meuli R, et al. 2006. Human auditory belt areas specialized in sound recognition: a functional magnetic resonance imaging study. *NeuroReport* 17:1659–62

Wagner E, Klump GM, Hamann I. 2003. Gap detection in Mongolian gerbils (*Meriones unguiculatus*). *Hear. Res.* 176:11–16

Walton JP, Frisina RD, Ison JR, O'Neill WE. 1997. Neural correlates of behavioral gap detection in the inferior colliculus of the young CBA mouse. *J. Comp. Physiol. A Neuroethol. Sens. Neural Behav. Physiol.* 181:161–76

Walton JP, Frisina RD, O'Neill WE. 1998. Age-related alteration in processing of temporal sound features in the auditory midbrain of the CBA mouse. *J. Neurosci.* 18:2764–76

Warren DH, Welch RB, McCarthy TJ. 1981. The role of visual-auditory "compellingness" in the ventriloquism effect: implications for transitivity among the spatial senses. *Percept. Psychophys.* 30:557–64

Warren JD, Zielinski BA, Green GGR, Rauschecker JP, Griffiths TD. 2002. Perception of sound-source motion by the human brain. *Neuron* 34:139–48

Warren RM. 1970. Perceptual restoration of missing speech sounds. *Science* 167:392–93

Warren RM, Obusek CJ, Ackroff JM. 1972. Auditory induction: perceptual synthesis of absent sounds. *Science* 176:1149–51

Warren RM, Wrightson JM, Puretz J. 1988. Illusory continuity of tonal and infratonal periodic sounds. *J. Acoust. Soc. Am.* 84:1338–42

Watson CS, Gengel RW. 1969. Signal duration and signal frequency in relation to auditory sensitivity. *J. Acoust. Soc. Am.* 46:989–97

Weber DL, Green DM. 1978. Temporal factors and suppression effects in backward and forward masking. *J. Acoust. Soc. Am.* 64:1392–99

Weeks RA, Aziz-Sultan A, Bushara KO, Tian B, Wessinger CM, et al. 1999. A PET study of human auditory spatial processing. *Neurosci. Lett.* 262:155–58

Welch RB. 1999. Meaning, attention, and the "unity assumption" in the intersensory bias of spatial and temporal perceptions. In *Cognitive Contributions to the Perception of Spatial and Temporal Events*, ed. G Aschersleben, T Bachmann, J Musseler, pp. 371–87. New York: Elsevier

Welch RB, Warren DH. 1980. Immediate perceptual response to intersensory discrepancy. *Psychol. Bull.* 88:638–67

Werner-Reiss U, Kelly KA, Trause AS, Underhill AM, Groh JM. 2003. Eye position affects activity in primary auditory cortex of primates. *Curr. Biol.* 13:554–62

Werner-Reiss U, Porter KK, Underhill AM, Groh JM. 2006. Long lasting attenuation by prior sounds in auditory cortex of awake primates. *Exp. Brain Res.* 168:272–76

Wessinger CM, VanMeter J, Tian B, Van Lare J, Pekar J, Rauschecker JP. 2001. Hierarchical organization of the human auditory cortex revealed by functional magnetic resonance imaging. *J. Cogn. Neurosci.* 13:1–7

Wightman FL, Kistler DJ. 1989a. Headphone simulation of free-field listening I: stimulus synthesis. *J. Acoust. Soc. Am.* 85:858–67

Wightman FL, Kistler DJ. 1989b. Headphone simulation of free-field listening II: psychophysical validation. *J. Acoust. Soc. Am.* 85:868–78

Woods TM, Lopez SE, Long JH, Rahman JE, Recanzone GH. 2006. Effects of stimulus azimuth and intensity on the single-neuron activity in the auditory cortex of the alert macaque monkey. *J. Neurophysiol.* 96:3323–37

Woods TM, Recanzone GH. 2004. Visually induced plasticity of auditory spatial perception in macaques. *Curr. Biol.* 14:1559–64

Zatorre RJ, Penhune VB. 2001. Spatial localization after excision of human auditory cortex. *J. Neurosci.* 21:6321–28

Zimmer U, Macaluso E. 2005. High binaural coherence determines successful sound localization and increased activity in posterior auditory areas. *Neuron* 47:893–905

Zwislocki J. 1960. Theory of temporal auditory summation. *J. Acoust. Soc. Am.* 32:1046–60

Color in Complex Scenes

Steven K. Shevell[1] and Frederick A. A. Kingdom[2]

[1] Departments of Psychology and Ophthalmology & Visual Science, University of Chicago, Chicago, Illinois 60637; [2] McGill Vision Research, McGill University, Montreal H3A 1A1, Canada; email: shevell@uchicago.edu, fred.kingdom@mcgill.ca

Annu. Rev. Psychol. 2008. 59:143–66

The *Annual Review of Psychology* is online at http://psych.annualreviews.org

This article's doi: 10.1146/annurev.psych.59.103006.093619

Key Words

chromatic adaptation, equivalent-uniform-background hypothesis, color constancy, color and form, color and motion

Abstract

The appearance of an object or surface depends strongly on the light from other objects and surfaces in view. This review focuses on color in complex scenes, which have regions of different colors in view simultaneously and/or successively, as in natural viewing. Two fundamental properties distinguish the chromatic representation evoked by a complex scene from the representation for an isolated patch of light. First, in complex scenes, the color of an object is not fully determined by the light from that object reaching the eye. Second, the chromatic representation of a complex scene contributes not only to hue, saturation, and brightness, but also to other percepts such as shape, texture, and object segmentation. These two properties are cornerstones of this review, which examines color perception with context that varies over space or time, including color constancy, and chromatic contributions to such percepts as orientation, contour, depth, and motion.

Contents

INTRODUCTION

Seeing in color has many advantages. Apart from the enrichment of our visual experience, more information is in a colored than in a black-and-white world. Flowers on a shrub escape notice in a black-and-white image but are seen immediately with color (**Figure 1a**; see color insert). Objects in colored scenes are more easily detected (Domini & Lucas 2001, Mollon 2000, Sumner & Mollon 2000), more easily identified (Mollon 1989; **Figure 1b**), more easily grouped (**Figure 1c**), and more easily remembered (Gegenfurtner & Rieger 2000) than objects in black-and-white scenes.

In natural viewing, colored objects are seen within a complex surrounding context. Within the eye and brain, the neural representations of color in complex scenes can be influenced by complicated, and sometimes subtle, aspects of the natural viewing environment. These representations allow the chromatic property of an object to be extracted from the light entering the eye, even though this light depends in part on the source of illumination and on shading. These representations also carry information about the spatial and temporal structure of the scene. In this review, we examine how context affects color perception and also how chromatic representations serve other visual percepts such as form, depth, motion, and object segmentation.

Color is Not in Light

The practice of describing light by its hue, for example a "yellow light," confuses a perceptual phenomenon (the hue yellow) with the physical world (light). True, a particular physical wavelength near 580 nm appears yellow, 540 nm lime green, 600 nm orange, and 660 nm red. But a yellow indistinguishable from 580 nm is seen also with a mixture of only 540 nm and 600 nm; or only 540 nm and 660 nm; or an infinite number of other light mixtures. The identical color percept from all these physically distinct lights is mediated by identical neural responses evoked by the lights. The determination of color by neural responses to light—not apprehension of color within the light rays themselves—is a foundational and functional property of color vision.

The Significance of Context in Color Perception

The world we see would be chaotic if an object's color were directly determined by the wavelengths from it that enter the eye. An egg that appears white and an eggplant that is seen as purplish at an outdoor market would be, respectively, yellow and a shade of orange in a kitchen illuminated by a common screw-in light bulb. Of course, this does not happen, and the reason is that neural representations for the color of the egg and the eggplant compensate for the change in wavelengths reflected from objects when moving from outdoor to indoor illumination. More generally, neural processes that mediate perception exploit the spectral and spatial distribution of light so we experience objects with a nearly stable color, despite changes in the wavelengths from the objects that reach the eye.

These neural processes cannot operate when the light from an object is seen without context. Consider an isolated piece of paper that normally appears white and another paper printed with an ink that reflects only long wavelengths. In daylight, one paper appears white and the other red, but if the first paper is illuminated by only long wavelengths and the second paper by daylight, then the wavelengths of light that reach the eye are the same from both papers. There is no information to distinguish their appearance, so they must look identical. In natural viewing, light reflected from other objects in view—that is, context—provides the critical information required to perceive the papers as different in color under various typical spectral distributions of illumination.

Classical theories of color vision focus on isolated patches of light unaffected by context (Wright 1946). They reveal fundamental properties of photoreceptors, which transduce physical light into neural responses at the first stage of vision. Context, however, alters responses within the retina, lateral geniculate nucleus, and visual cortex, so it is hardly surprising that light that is nearby or was viewed previously can change the color appearance of a particular fixed physical stimulus. An example of color-appearance changes induced by context is shown in **Figure 2** (see color insert), where the words ANNUAL and REVIEW are printed in the same ink but within different contexts (similarly OF and PSYCHOLOGY share a common ink). In natural viewing, variegation in the retinal image is abundant over space and time. Such complex visual stimuli excite neural mechanisms that underlie color perception of natural scenes but that are not revealed by an isolated patch of light.

The Principle of Trichromacy and Why it Fails to Explain Color in Natural Viewing

Most human observers can match any spectral distribution of light by a mixture of three primary lights. This is the principle of trichromacy, which follows from neural coding: any uniform, isolated patch of light is encoded by exactly three distinct neural responses. Two physically different distributions of light will be indistinguishable if they result in the same three responses. Trichromacy, however, is silent about the colors one perceives; that is, it explains which lights look alike but not what lights look like.

The distinction between the neural responses that determine trichromacy versus neural representations of hue, while critical, is sometimes lost. The three types of photoreceptor that mediate color vision were called at one time the red, green, and blue cones. Just as "yellow light" inappropriately confuses perception with physical light, the term "blue cone" wrongly confuses perception with a type of neuron. The response of this type of cone is neither restricted to those wavelengths that appear bluish (it responds

Spectral distribution of light: a function giving the amount of energy at each wavelength of light

also to wavelengths well beyond 500 nm, which in isolation appear yellowish green) nor is essential for the sensation of the hue blue, which can be experienced with a small, sharply focused retinal stimulus that does not fall on any so-called blue cones (Hofer et al. 2005). Modern terminology includes no color percepts in the names of receptors; the cones are labeled L, M, and S (for long-, middle-, and short-wavelength sensitive, respectively) instead of red, green, and blue. Trichromacy follows from responses of the L, M, and S cones irrespective of the hue they evoke.

Trichromacy implies that any isolated patch of light can be matched by a mixture of three primary lights, but the range of colors we see with all possible mixtures of primaries is much smaller than the gamut of colors we commonly experience. The reason is context, which not only alters color perception (**Figure 2**) but also vastly expands the domain of colors we see. A mixture alone never appears brown, maroon, or gray, which are commonly experienced but evoked only when a light is viewed with other light nearby (that is, with context). Trichromacy also implies that two physically different patches of light that look alike in the dark will look alike in any shared context. The two patches evoke the same neural responses at the first stage of vision, so they are substitutable for one another (Grassmann 1853). Context can affect the patches' color appearance but it does so equally; thus, trichromacy cannot reveal what lights look like in a complex scene.

To distinguish light from the percept it evokes, light is described here by its wavelength or spectral distribution. A nonselective spectral distribution, such as equal energy at all wavelengths, is called "broadband." Color names (e.g., brown, red, green, pink, and white) are reserved exclusively for percepts, as is the term "achromatic," which refers to a percept of white, gray, or black. Luminance or radiance is a magnitude of physical light, whereas brightness refers to the perceived level of emitted light.

CONTEXT IN COMPLEX SCENES

Complex Context Cannot be Reduced to Simple Context

The simplest context is a uniform background field, which has been studied extensively for over a century (e.g., Chichilnisky & Wandell 1995, Jameson & Hurvich 1972, Shevell 1982, von Kries 1905, Walraven 1976; for review, see Shevell 2003). The influence of the context in a complex scene might be understood with theories that explain color changes from a uniform background, a possibility called the equivalent-uniform-background hypothesis.

The hypothesis has alternative forms. The strongest form holds that complex context is equivalent to a uniform field at the space-average chromaticity and luminance of the context. In this form, averaging is at the level of physical light and the context is reduced to a trichromatic description of the space-average stimulus. A different form holds that the effect of each region within a complex background can be represented by its effect as a uniform background; the effects from multiple regions are combined to explain the influence of complex context. This implies aggregation at a neural level. A third form posits that some (unspecified) uniform background is equivalent to (that is, completely substitutable for) any complex context.

The equivalent-uniform-background hypothesis provides a first-order account of some studies of color (Bauml 1995, Brainard & Wandell 1992, Valberg & Lange-Malecki 1990), but none of its variants is consistent with color perception in complex scenes. The space-average form is tested explicitly by substituting different inhomogeneous backgrounds that have the same space-average chromaticity and luminance. Such substitutions alter color appearance, even with a locally uniform field surrounding the region judged in color so that edge contrast is fixed (Barnes et al. 1999, Mausfeld & Andres 2002). Also, adding retinal disparity and thus stereoscopic depth to a complex scene changes the influence of context without altering the space average of light in each eye (Yang & Shevell 2002).

Aggregation of neural influences from each distinct region fails a test of independence. Consider three lights: 540 nm, which appears yellowish green; 660 nm, which appears red; and a broadband light that appears white. Initial measurements can establish the color change caused by a uniform background of only 540 nm, 660 nm, or broadband light; as expected, the broadband background has little effect on color. Next, consider (*a*) a new background with two separate regions, one composed of 540 nm and one composed of the broadband light; and (*b*) a second new background with 660 nm in place of 540 nm in one region and the same broadband region as in (*a*). Identical broadband regions should have the same influence, whether paired with 540 or 660 nm; moreover, that influence should be weak because of the minimal influence of the broadband background alone.

Measurements, however, show a substantial change in color perception when the broadband region is introduced within either a 540 nm or 660 nm background. Furthermore, the direction of color change evoked by adding the broadband region to 540 nm [background (*a*)] is opposite in direction to the change due to adding the broadband region to 660 nm [background (*b*)]. This implies that even minimally complex backgrounds composed of only two chromaticities fail the independence condition implicit in this form of the equivalent-uniform-background hypothesis (Wesner & Shevell 1992). Independence is inconsistent also with the color induced by chromatic patterns, each one at a single spatial frequency, in comparison with a compound pattern with both frequencies. The compound pattern reveals nonlinear spatial interactions (Zaidi et al. 1992).

The form that posits the existence of some uniform background equivalent to any complex context fails to account for color-appearance shifts caused specifically by chromatic variegation within a scene (Brenner &

Cornelissen 2002, Ekroll et al. 2004, Shevell & Wei 2000, Singer & D'Zmura 1994). For example, different chromatic lights perceived as green, red, blue, or yellow (rectangles, *upper panel* of **Figure 3**; see color insert) lose most of their color when viewed against a background pattern containing strong chromatic contrast (*lower panel* of **Figure 3**; from Brown & MacLeod 1997). This gamut compression with high-contrast context occurs even with thin gray "grout" between the elements of the background mosaic, a result that excludes local contrast at the edge of the rectangles as the cause of the color differences in the two panels of **Figure 3**. Gamut compression is separable for color and brightness (Brown & MacLeod 1997).

Color Perception with Context that Varies Over Space or Time

Background context that varies in space or time may influence separate processes at distinct levels of the visual system. Background light at spatial frequencies above 4 cycles per degree alters the number of photons absorbed by receptors in nearby regions due to imperfections in the eye's optics, which cause spread light (Smith et al. 2001). Spread light varies with the specific wavelengths in the stimulus and increases with spatial frequency (Marimont & Wandell 1994).

With complex context, separate neural processes can be influenced by the mean and the variability within a background over time and/or space. For example, a spatially uniform background that oscillates slowly in time (1 Hz) between two chromaticities causes a light at their physical average to have an appearance approaching achromatic; at the same time, the hues of other lights are compressed along the axis of chromatic oscillation (Webster & Mollon 1994, 1995). Consider a range of lights that all appear bluish but are somewhat dissimilar in hue because of modestly different L-, M-, and S-cone stimulation. After viewing a steady uniform background at their mean chromaticity, these

Gamut compression: the phenomenon in which colors or brightnesses that normally cover a given range appear to cover a smaller range

Spatial-frequency tuning: a function giving relative sensitivity at each spatial frequency of a visual stimulus. Spatial frequency is the number of cycles of a repeating pattern within a given visual angle (for example, the number of cycles within one degree of visual angle)

Equiluminant: constant in luminance (i.e., may vary in only chromaticity)

same lights appear to have a range of different hues around white. These percepts are described fairly well by adaptation-induced rescaling of L-, M-, and S-cone responses. If, however, a temporally oscillating field with the same time-average chromaticity replaces the steady background, then further color shifts occur. The variability of the background light over time causes compression of a separate postreceptoral chromatic neural representation. Furthermore, this compression of the range of perceived color occurs selectively along virtually any direction of chromatic oscillation, which implicates a neural representation of dimensionality exceeding the three of trichromacy, presumably at a cortical locus.

Steady backgrounds with spatial variation (as in **Figure 3**, *lower panel*) rather than temporal variation cause similar compression when chromaticities in a background mosaic are selected randomly from a line in color space. Color-selective compression in any chromatic direction again suggests a non-trichromatic cortical process (Webster et al. 2002).

A central neural mechanism is revealed also by chromatically varying spatial context in one eye, which evokes the same shift in the color of a light presented to either the same eye or fellow eye (Shevell & Wei 2000). A cortical neural process may be inferred also for the perceived color differences in **Figure 2**. The spatial-frequency tuning and chromatic selectively of the color shifts implicate an S-cone antagonistic center-surround (+S/−S) receptive-field (Shevell & Monnier 2005). No such neuron is found in the retina (Calkins 2001; Dacey 1996, 2000), but physiological studies reveal cortical neurons with S-cone center-surround organization (Conway 2001, Solomon et al. 2004).

Chromatic variation within background context alters perceived chromatic contrast as well as hue. A region with a fixed magnitude of L-cone/M-cone chromatic contrast appears to have less contrast when surrounded by a background of high rather than low L-cone/M-cone variation. Chromatic selectivity

of perceived contrast reduction is substantial though not complete: perceived L-cone/M-cone contrast is more strongly compressed by an equiluminant background that varies stimulation of the L and M cones, compared with a background with only S-cone contrast (**Figure 4**; see color insert); similarly, perceived S-cone contrast is more strongly reduced by an equiluminant background with S-cone than L-cone/M-cone contrast (Singer & D'Zmura 1994). Compression of perceived chromatic contrast shows interocular transfer (chromatic-contrast background in one eye, test presented to the other eye), which implicates a central neural mechanism.

Context that contains chromatic variation typical of natural scenes points to the functional significance of these neural mechanisms. Chromatically selective compression along any direction of chromatic variation, as discussed above, allows adaptation to the specific color gamut within individual scenes and natural environments. Chromatic compression varies according to (*a*) the colors found in different natural scenes (Webster & Mollon 1997, Webster et al. 2002) and (*b*) the chromatic variation within a single scene, which shifts under different spectral illuminations (Webster & Mollon 1995).

Chromatically selective neural responses within the retina, lateral geniculate, and visual cortex have been studied extensively [reviewed by Gegenfurtner (2003) and Solomon & Lennie (2007)]. A general conclusion is that cortical responses show a greater diversity of chromatic selectivity than responses from subcortical neurons. The multiple levels of chromatic representation imply that a full understanding of color perception in complex scenes requires knowledge of the influence of context at each level.

COLOR CONSTANCY

Most objects we see are visible only when they reflect illumination from a light source, such as a lamp or the sun. The objects cannot be seen when the lights go off or the sun goes down, which reveals a basic confound: The light from an object depends on both the selective spectral reflectance of the object and the spectral composition of the illumination. In normal viewing, however, the color of an object remains quite stable under different illuminants even though only the object's spectral reflectance (irrespective of the illumination) defines the object's chromatic characteristic. Color constancy is the stable perceived color of an object under different light sources, despite the different spectral distributions of light from object to eye. Recall the example of the egg and the eggplant mentioned above.

Perceptual constancy would be a minor issue if changes of illumination caused small differences in the spectral distribution of light entering the eye, but exactly the opposite is true. If the color of an object depended on only the light reflected from it, the shifts would be dramatic. A mosaic of colored objects known as the Macbeth ColorChecker (Munsell Color Laboratory, New Windsor, New York) gives a full range of colors under sunlight (**Figure 5**, *top*; see color insert). The same mosaic illuminated by an indoor (tungsten) light bulb reflects much less short-wavelength light to the eye; this change of illumination would cause substantial shifts if just the light from each region within the mosaic mediated its perceived color (as simulated in **Figure 5**, *bottom*). In general, the changes in receptoral stimulation from a single object due to changes in everyday illumination are comparable to the differences in receptoral excitation when one light illuminates separate objects of categorically different hue (Shevell 2003).

Context provides the biologically available information necessary (though not sufficient) to achieve color constancy. Theories of constancy differ in terms of how context contributes to the color appearance of objects.

Color Constancy is Imperfect

Color perception is closer to constancy than to the color percept expected from the wave-

lengths reflected by an object, but constancy is not complete. Estimates of the degree of color constancy vary widely with the viewing context and the task asked of the observer which, in different studies (reviewed by Smithson 2005), requires full color matching of an object under different illuminants, a judgment of the chromaticity that appears colorless ("gray" or "white"), assignment of color names to objects, categorization of the color of a surface as one of a small number of possible hues, or identification of identical surfaces under different illuminants. Color constancy indexes range from zero (no constancy) to 1.0 (perfect constancy). Constancy is found to be nearly perfect when categorizing the hue of a pulsed stimulus seen on a larger field reflecting the illuminant, but it falls by about half if the same stimulus is viewed steadily and the illuminant is in only a remote, spatially separated region (Hansen et al. 2007). Constancy can be high (index >0.8) for the judgment of a colorless percept in a room with real illuminated objects and surfaces but drops substantially if the change of illuminant fails to alter local edge contrast, the spatial average of light in view, or the most intense stimulus (Kraft & Brainard 1999). Constancy index values below 0.7 are common in studies employing various experimental approaches (e.g., Arend et al. 1991, Smithson & Zaidi 2004, Yang & Maloney 2001).

Receptoral Responses are Always Ambiguous

The light from an object absorbed by each type of cone L, M, or S, Q_L, Q_M, or Q_S, is

$$Q_L = \int_\lambda \{E(\lambda)R(\lambda)\}q_L(\lambda)d\lambda,$$

$$Q_M = \int_\lambda \{E(\lambda)R(\lambda)\}q_M(\lambda)d\lambda \quad \text{and}$$

$$Q_S = \int_\lambda \{E(\lambda)R(\lambda)\}q_S(\lambda)d\lambda.$$

The integration is over the wavelengths λ of visible light from 400 to 700 nm; $E(\lambda)$ is a function with the (unknown) energy level of

Spectral reflectance: a function giving the fraction of energy reflected from an object or surface at each wavelength of light

Color constancy index: a summary measure of the degree to which perception follows color constancy in a given situation

the illuminating light at each wavelength; $R(\lambda)$ is a function with the (unknown) proportion of incident light reflected from the object at each wavelength; and $q_L(\lambda)$, $q_M(\lambda)$, and $q_S(\lambda)$ are functions with the physiological spectral sensitivity of each type of cone L, M, and S. Only the spectral reflectance at each wavelength, $R(\lambda)$, carries the intrinsic chromatic characteristic of an object; as shown by the equations, however, the biologically available information (Q_L, Q_M, and Q_S) depends on the product $E(\lambda)R(\lambda)$ at each wavelength.

In natural environments, the integrals that give Q_L, Q_M, and Q_S are approximated very closely by summing values at 10 nm intervals (that is, at 400, 410, 420, . . . , 700 nm). In this case, $E(\lambda)$, $R(\lambda)$, $q_L(\lambda)$, $q_M(\lambda)$, and $q_S(\lambda)$ are each vectors with 31 values, and the light absorbed by each cone type is

$$Q_L = \sum_\lambda \{E(\lambda)R(\lambda)\}q_L(\lambda),$$
$$Q_M = \sum_\lambda \{E(\lambda)R(\lambda)\}q_M(\lambda) \quad \text{and}$$
$$Q_S = \sum_\lambda \{E(\lambda)R(\lambda)\}q_S(\lambda).$$

This summation form makes clear that adding more objects (i.e., context), each with its own spectral reflectance $R(\lambda)$, does not deterministically solve the constancy problem because each new object adds three biologically available quantities (Q_L, Q_M, and Q_S) as well as an additional unknown spectral reflectance vector $R(\lambda)$ with 31 values [$R(400)$, $R(410)$, . . . , $R(700)$]. The neural responses of receptors, therefore, carry insufficient information to specify the chromatic characteristic of the object. Theories of color constancy must resolve this implicit ambiguity by applying assumptions about the visual system and/or the physical world.

Modeling Illumination and Reflectance

With N objects, each with its own reflectance $R(\lambda)$ and all under a single illuminant with energy distribution $E(\lambda)$, summation at 10 nm intervals requires 31 unknown values for each object's reflectance plus 31 additional

unknowns for the illuminant [thus $31(N+1)$ unknown values in all]. Each object results in three separate receptoral quantal absorptions, Q_L, Q_M, and Q_S, so there are $3*N$ neural responses available to determine $31(N+1)$ unknowns, which, of course, is too little biological information to solve for so many unknown reflectance values. Models of illuminant spectra and reflectance spectra reduce the number of unknowns so the biological information is sufficient to determine the reflectance vectors $R(\lambda)$. For example, the illumination $E(\lambda)$ can be posited to be some weighted sum of three known, fixed spectral energy distributions $e_1(\lambda)$, $e_2(\lambda)$, and $e_3(\lambda)$. Then the 31 unknowns for $E(\lambda)$ are reduced to just three unknowns: the weights a_1, a_2, and a_3 that give the illuminant $E(\lambda) = a_1 e_1(\lambda) + a_2 e_2(\lambda) + a_3 e_3(\lambda)$. Similarly, all reflectances can be posited to be a weighted sum of three known, fixed reflectance distributions $r_1(\lambda)$, $r_2(\lambda)$, and $r_3(\lambda)$, so the reflectance of any object depends on just three weights, b_1, b_2, and b_3; then, an object's reflectance $R(\lambda)$ is given by $b_1 r_1(\lambda) + b_2 r_2(\lambda) + b_3 r_3(\lambda)$. Under these assumptions, and with a reference patch of known (or assumed) reflectance $R_{STANDARD}(\lambda)$, the 3N quantal catches are sufficient to determine the values b_1, b_2, and b_3 and thus establish color constancy (Buchsbaum 1980, Sallstrom 1973).

The assumptions that all illuminants and reflectances can be expressed as a weighted sum of just three spectral distributions are reasonable approximations of the variations of natural illumination that occur with weather and over the course of a day (Judd et al. 1964) and of the spectral reflectances found in natural scenes (Cohen 1964, Dannemiller 1992). Neither assumption is perfect but neither is color constancy. If reflectance is assumed to be a weighted sum of only two distributions, so $R(\lambda) = b_1 r_1(\lambda) + b_2 r_2(\lambda)$, then the 3N quantal catches ($N \geq 3$) give constancy without requiring a reflectance standard in view (Maloney & Wandell 1986). Other models of illumination and reflectance invoke alternative assumptions (reviewed by Shevell 2003).

Estimating Illumination

Since Helmholtz (1866/1962), the stable color percept of an object has been attributed to our ability to "eliminate" (volume II, p. 287) differences in spectral illumination. This can be wrongly interpreted to mean that the intrinsic chromatic property of an object [that is, its reflectance $R(\lambda)$] can be determined by directly viewing the illuminant (or inferring an equivalent neural representation) so that the illuminant can be eliminated. The idea may be that receptoral stimulations from an object, which depend on the product $E(\lambda)R(\lambda)$, can reveal the reflectance $R(\lambda)$ if there is a neural representation of the illuminant alone. Viewing the illuminant, however, provides only a trichromatic neural representation: the amount of illuminating light absorbed by each type of cone, Q_L, Q_M, and Q_S. This biologically available information is insufficient to determine either the spectral energy distribution of illumination $E(\lambda)$ or the intrinsic chromatic property of an object $R(\lambda)$ (Maloney 1999).

Nonetheless, estimating the illuminant can be an integral component of a theory of color constancy that includes other assumptions, such as a model of illumination and reflectance (discussed above). Simple estimates of illumination can be based on the receptoral responses to the average light over the entire scene ("gray world assumption"; Buchsbaum 1980) or to the brightest patch in view (Land & McCann 1971), though these fail to capture many available physical cues to illumination. These cues include specular reflections from surfaces, shadows, mutual inter-reflections among objects, and luminance-chromaticity correlation within a scene (Golz & MacLeod 2002, MacLeod & Golz 2003, Maloney 2002; reviewed by Smithson 2005); some cues require a three-dimensional scene (Maloney 1999). A further complication is multiple sources of light (Yang & Shevell 2003), which are common in natural viewing. Given the availability of multiple cues, which may not be equally informative about illumination or even be available in some environments, two basic questions are how each cue is selected (or ignored) and how the selected cues are aggregated. This is the cue combination problem (Maloney 2002), which optimally should consider each cue's reliability as well as its relative value for estimating the illuminant.

Another approach to illuminant estimation exploits features of the natural environment. The spectral characteristics of lights in natural scenes are not random. This property can be used to determine the most likely combination of illumination and object reflectance consistent with the ambiguous receptoral responses. For example, the two papers described in the Introduction section that reflect identical long-wavelength light to the eye and thus cannot be distinguished by photoreceptor signals would, on this account, be seen as reddish because an object reflecting only long wavelengths under daylight illumination is more likely in the natural environment than is an object that reflects all wavelengths equally under only long-wavelength illumination. Object color so determined goes beyond the biologically available information from the scene by using prior knowledge about illuminated objects in the natural world. Such estimates of illumination and the consequent color percepts are called Bayesian, after the eighteenth-century mathematician Thomas Bayes, who formulated an approach that incorporates prior knowledge with new information to assess the likelihood of events. A Bayesian illuminant-estimation model can account well for a surface perceived to be colorless (gray or white) when part of a complex (simulated) scene under various different spectral illuminants (Brainard et al. 2006; see Knill & Richards 1996 for other applications of the Bayesian approach to visual perception).

Relational Color Constancy

Color constancy is the stable perceived color of objects under different spectral light sources. This definition, based on color appearance, is akin to a similar problem called relational color constancy (Foster & Nascimento 1994): Is a change in light from a scene perceived as a change in object color or, instead, only spectral illumination? Relational color constancy would provide the functional ability to discriminate a change in a physical object (ripening of fruit) from a change in ambient lighting (long-wavelength light at sunset). Although the color appearance of the object could change with illumination, its inferred chromatic properties would not when the difference in the visual stimulus is attributed entirely to an illumination change.

There is a close relationship between standard and relational color constancy for an ideal visual system viewing surfaces under a single illuminant, though in practice, the two types of constancy are empirically dissociable (Foster et al. 1997). Relational color constancy is tested by asking an observer to judge whether the difference between two separate visual stimuli is due to a change in illumination or a change in object reflectance. Humans make this discrimination accurately and reliably. This ability can be modeled by the relative receptor stimulation across space for each type of cone (L, M, or S), which changes very little with changes in spectral illumination (Foster & Nascimento 1994). In fact, a scene undergoing a (simulated) change in only natural spectral illumination but that causes a modest change in a cone-type's relative excitation across space is often misperceived as a change in object reflectance; furthermore, nearly the same change but with artificial manipulation that preserves relative receptor excitation is judged wrongly as a change in only illumination (Nascimento & Foster 1997).

CHROMATIC REPRESENTATIONS IN SERVICE OF VISUAL PERCEPTS OTHER THAN COLOR

The primary function of color vision is the percepts of hue and saturation. In fact, color vision is defined as the ability to distinguish two lights regardless of their luminance levels. Chromatic neural representations, however, contribute also to other visual percepts such as shape, texture, and object segmentation. For example, color vision can reveal objects that are camouflaged in a black-and-white image (**Figure 1a**); in this case, a chromatic representation serves object segmentation. As with the perception of hue, context is critical for understanding the role of color vision in the perception of form and motion, which by definition refer to relations within a stimulus across space and/or time. A poignant indicator that hue and form are separate functions of color vision comes from cerebral achromatopsic patients, who through brain injury have lost all sensation of hue yet often perceive the form of purely chromatic patterns as well as normal persons do (Heywood et al. 1998).

A number of interrelated questions concern the contributions of chromatic neural responses to form, motion, and other percepts. First, is there evidence that purely chromatic stimuli drive percepts of form or motion? Second, if such evidence indeed exists, is a chromatic neural representation better or worse than a spectrally unselective representation based only on luminance? Third, how do chromatic and spectrally unselective representations combine, if at all, to determine perceived form or motion? Fourth, are there circumstances in which a particular combination of chromatic and spectrally unselective information alters the percept of form or motion? Although the first two of these questions have received considerable attention over the past 20 years (reviewed by Regan 2000 and Gegenfurtner & Kiper 2003), the question of how chromatic and spectrally unselective representations interact for form and motion perception has only recently begun to be addressed. To approach these questions, first consider the relations among chromaticity, luminance, and form in the physical world, and the manner in which these physical features are initially encoded by the visual system.

(a)

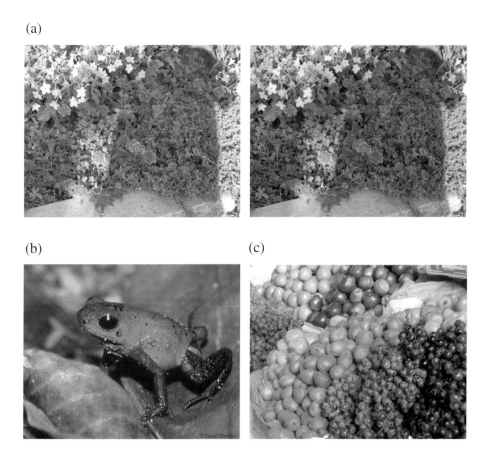

(b)

(c)

Figure 1

Some of the many functions of color vision. (*a*) Color reveals otherwise camouflaged objects. (*b*) The aptly named Blue Jeans frog (*Dendrobates pumilio*) is easily identified from its coloration (photo courtesy of D. Montero). (*c*) Color is useful for grouping and identifying fruit (photo courtesy of D.I. Thompson).

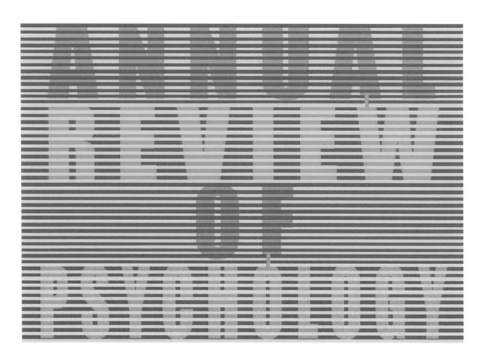

Figure 2

The words ANNUAL and REVIEW are printed in identical ink (check the connector bar above W). They appear different in color because of the patterned context in which they are seen. Similarly, OF and PSYCHOLOGY are in the same ink (check the connector bar below F).

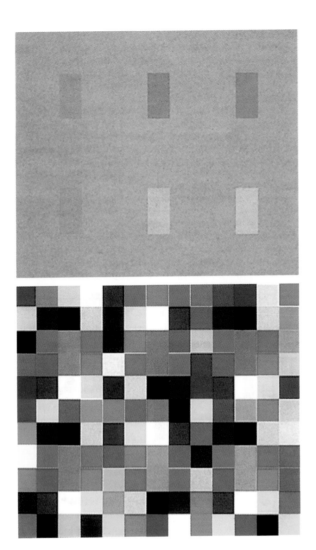

Figure 3

(*Upper panel*) Six rectangles within a uniform surround. (*Lower panel*) The same six rectangles are within a surround that has chromatic and luminance contrast. Both surrounds have the same space-average chromaticity and luminance. From Brown & MacLeod 1997 (copyright 1997, reprinted with permission from Elsevier).

Figure 4

A small circular equiluminant grating with only L-cone/M-cone contrast (*left*) has a greater reduction in perceived contrast when within a surrounding equiluminant grating at the same chromaticities (*center*) compared with an equiluminant grating with only S-cone contrast (*right*). (Limitations of color reproduction and individual observer differences do not allow exact cone isolation.) After D'Zmura & Singer 1999 (images courtesy of M. D'Zmura).

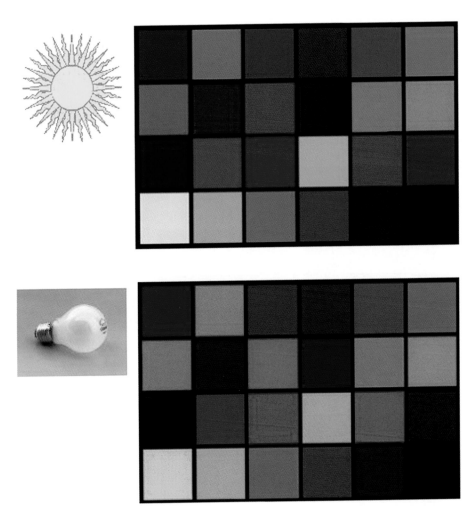

Figure 5

The chromatic surfaces of the Macbeth ColorChecker (Munsell Color Laboratory, New Windsor, New York) as it appears under sunlight (*top*) and as it would appear under tungsten illumination (*bottom*) if color perception followed directly from the wavelengths from each region reaching the eye.

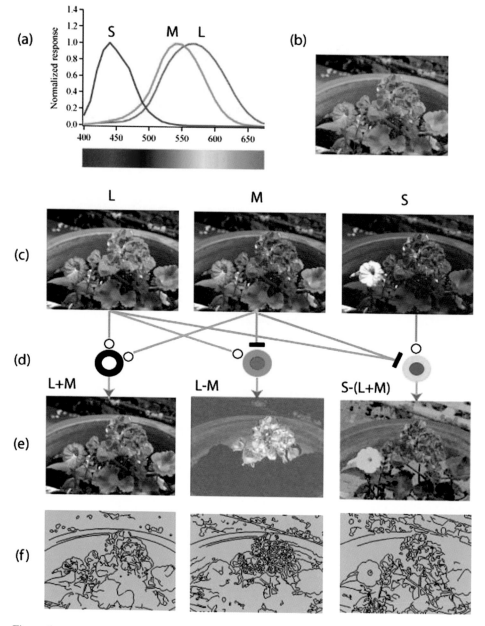

Figure 6

Stages of chromatic neural responses. (*a*) Spectral sensitivities of the L, M, and S cones. (*b*) Original image. (*c*) Responses of the three types of cones to the image. (*d*) Cone signals combine to give postreceptoral responses. (*e*) Postreceptoral responses to the image. (*f*) Edge maps from postreceptoral responses. (Original image from the McGill Calibrated Color Image database: **http://tabby. vision.mcgill.ca**.)

Figure 7

Simulated appearance of flowers as seen by (*a*) normal trichromats, (*b*) protanopes, (*c*) deuteranopes, or (*d*) tritanopes. After Viénot et al. (1995) (images courtesy of F. Viénot).

Figure 8

Shadow cast across a grass-pavement border. At the grass-pavement border, there is a large change in both color and luminance (and texture); at the shadow border, the change is primarily in luminance with little change in color (no change in texture).

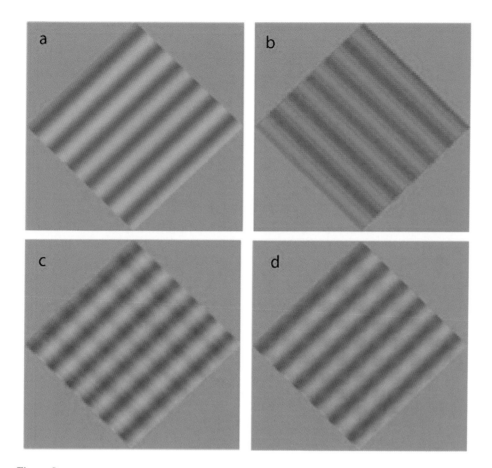

Figure 9

Color can promote or inhibit shape-from-shading. (*a*) Right oblique luminance grating. (*b*) Left oblique chromatic grating. (*c*) Combining (*a*) and (*b*) gives the impression of a depth-corrugated surface. (*d*) Adding a second chromatic grating aligned with the luminance grating in (*a*) inhibits the impression of depth.

Figure 10

The tall building in sunset illumination appears to many observers as if painted two-thirds orange (photo courtesy of B. Micklethwait).

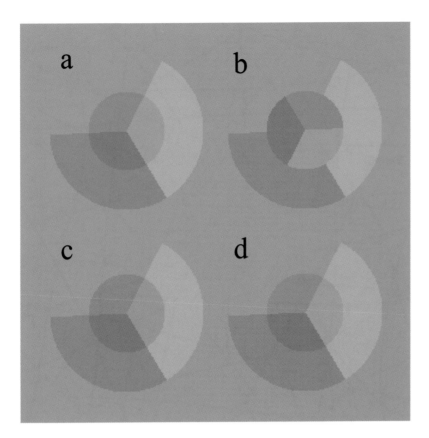

Figure 11

Color and transparency. (*a*) Simulated spectrally unselective transparency on a chromatically variegated background. (*b*) Rotating the central region destroys the impression of transparency. (*c*) Introducing random chromatic changes across the surround's border reduces the impression of transparency. (*d*) Consistent chromatic changes across the surround's border create the impression of a colored transparency.

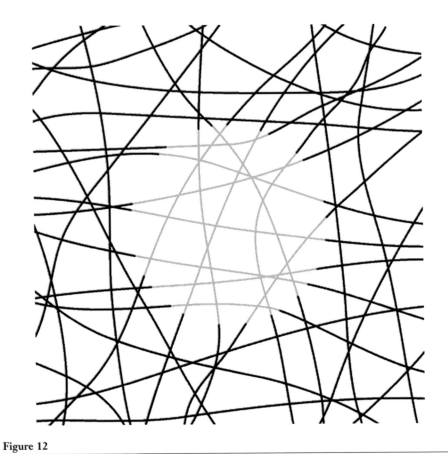

Figure 12

Neon-color spreading. (Image courtesy of Hans Knuchel, **www.blelb.ch**.)

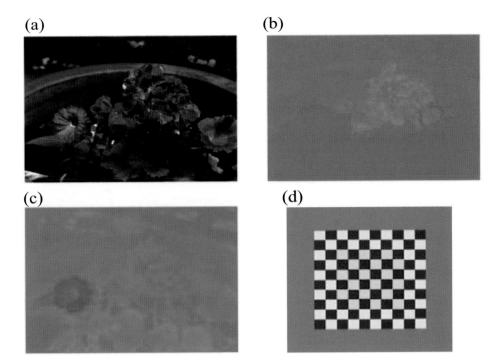

Figure 13

Color and resolution. The three postreceptoral representations of the image in **Figure 6b**: (*a*) L+M, (b) L-M, and (c) S-(L+M). [The images in (*b*) and (*c*) are not exactly equiluminant due to limitations of color reproduction and individual observer differences.] (*d*) A demonstration of poor chromatic resolution. As one walks away from the image, the blue and yellow checks become increasingly desaturated and eventually appear black and white (after Moulden et al. 1993).

(a) (b)

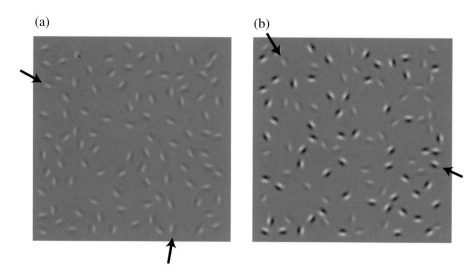

Figure 14

Color and contour linking. (*a*) The pattern is constructed from red-green equiluminant gabor micropatterns. The arrows show the beginning and end of the target path—a string of orientationally aligned gabor micropatterns that the observer must detect. (*b*) When the path alternates between equiluminant red-green and isochromatic white-black gabors, it is more difficult to detect. After McIlhagga & Mullen (1996) (images courtesy of K. Mullen).

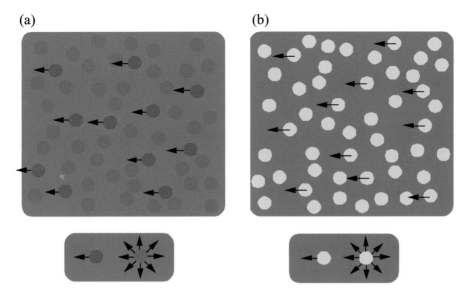

Figure 15

Color and global motion. In (*a*), the target elements (moving in one direction) and distractor elements (moving in random directions) have different colors, but in (*b*) they have the same color. Fewer target elements are needed in (*a*) than in (*b*) to identify the target's direction of motion. After Croner & Albright (1997).

Correlations Among Cone and Cone-Opponent Responses

Visual information about form and motion is provided by the spatiotemporal pattern of luminance and chromaticity in the image. The advantage provided by color vision depends on at least two neural representations that are not confounded, for if every spatiotemporal change in brightness were accompanied by a comparable change in color, there would be no biologically useful information in the representation of color. In daylight vision, the retinal image captured by the L, M, and S cones (**Figure 6a**; see color insert) is transformed into three postreceptoral responses (Derrington et al. 1984, DeValois 1965, Krauskopf et al. 1982): a luminance response, which sums the signals from the L and M cones, and two chromatically selective pathways, one of which compares the responses of the L and M cones (the L-M response) and one of which compares the response of the S cones with the summed responses from the L and M cones [the S-(L+M) response]. [These postreceptoral chromatic responses are sometimes—and again inappropriately—labeled "red-green" and "yellow-blue," respectively. This is a carryover from the misnomers for cones, discussed above. Although each response encodes chromatic information, neither one is mapped to only one pair of hues (Knoblauch & Shevell 2001, Mollon & Cavonius 1987, Wuerger et al. 2005)].

The three postreceptoral responses decorrelate the cone signals; that is, they remove information that is redundant in the signals by virtue of the close overlap in the cones' spectral sensitivities (Buchsbaum & Gottschalk 1983, Fine et al. 2003, Johnson et al. 2005, Ruderman et al. 1998, Zaidi 1997; but see also Lee et al. 2002). The responses of each cone-type to the image in **Figure 6b** are shown in **Figure 6c**, where cone-response magnitudes are represented by gray level. The Pearson correlation coefficient R between the image pixel values of each pair of cone responses is 0.96 for L and M, 0.78 for M and S, and 0.73

for L and S. These values are typical for natural scenes (Ruderman et al. 1998) and Munsell papers (McIlhagga & Mullen 1997). They show that the L-, M-, and S-cone responses are in most instances highly correlated. The postreceptoral responses formed by combining cone signals are shown in **Figure 6e**. The figure is drawn in black and white to reinforce the point that each response alone cannot signal hue. Hue is only made explicit at a later stage, where the postreceptoral responses (or subsequent recodings of them) are compared to each other (DeValois & DeValois 1993, Wuerger et al. 2005). The correlations among the postreceptoral responses in **Figure 6e** are much smaller than the correlations among the cone signals: 0.17 for L+M with L-M, 0.14 for L+M with S-(L+M), and –0.16 for L-M with S-(L+M). Decorrelation is a fundamental property of sensory systems (Barlow & Foldiak 1989, Field 1994, Simoncelli & Olshausen 2001) and means that the L-M, S-(L+M), and L+M signals are largely independent. There are, however, some consistent correlations among the postreceptoral responses in natural scenes, and these can be important for perception. Correlations between "redness" and "luminance" (L-M with L+M) are exploited for color constancy (Golz & Macleod 2002). The negative correlation between L-M and S-(L+M) in **Figure 6e** is found across scenes (Johnson et al. 2005, Webster & Mollon 1997) and is especially pronounced in scenes with arid landscapes and blue skies (Webster & Mollon 1997), revealing a tendency for colors to fall along a continuum between the hues blue and yellow.

The relative independence of the L-M and S-(L+M) responses highlights that color-defective individuals lack certain types of form information normally provided by chromatic coding. About 8% of the male population is born without normal L- or M-cone photopigment (Smith & Pokorny 2003). A quarter of these, known as dichromats, are missing altogether either functional L or M cones and experience only those color percepts carried by the S-cone pathway. Loss of functional

S cones, resulting in tritanopia, is extremely rare. The information loss experienced by dichromats can be modeled by transforming a natural image into a two-cone, as opposed to the normal three-cone, representation. As dichromats can have no appreciation of the hues experienced by trichromats (and vice versa), any model of dichromatic hues inevitably requires some assumptions (Viénot et al. 1995). Nevertheless, **Figure 7*b*,*c*** (see color insert) suggests the reduction of color differences for protanopes and deuteranopes compared with normals: The red flowers are no longer conspicuous against the green foliage. Tritanopes, on the other hand, might be expected to miss violet flowers. The figure emphasizes that what is missing from the visual world of the dichromat is not just the ability to experience and discriminate certain hues, but also the ability to detect certain types of objects.

Correlations Among Higher-Order Representations

The strongest correlations among the three postreceptoral neural representations are found not among pixel intensities but rather among pixel-intensity relations. The relations among points in an image define higher-order structures such as edges, contours, shapes, and textures. In the three postreceptoral representations, the higher-order structures have similar mathematical properties (Parraga et al. 2002, Wachtler et al. 2001) and for a given scene are positively correlated. For example, in **Figure 6*e***, the shape of the violet flower is visible in both the S-(L+M) and L+M postreceptoral representations, and the upper edge of the terracotta pot can be seen in all three responses. The edge maps (**Figure 6*f***) reinforce the point that the three postreceptoral responses are closely related when image structure is considered (Fine et al. 2003, Johnson et al. 2005).

The reason for higher-order correlations among the postreceptoral responses to everyday scenes is that a change in chromaticity is accompanied by a change in luminance at most object borders; thus, a change in one postreceptoral response is typically accompanied by a change in another. Given the importance of object boundaries to visual object recognition, neurons in the visual cortex might be expected to be tuned simultaneously to both chromatic and luminance contrasts, and many such neurons are reported (Horwitz et al. 2005, Johnson et al. 2001; reviewed by Solomon & Lennie 2007).

Does it follow, then, that color is made redundant by considering change relations rather than point intensities? The answer is no for illuminated objects, as in natural viewing. Object boundaries typically cause luminance changes together with chromatic changes, but shadows and shading tend to cause luminance changes free of chromatic change (Kingdom et al. 2004, Rubin & Richards 1982). These relations are illustrated in **Figure 8** (see color insert). Chromatic variations, therefore, are more reliable indicators of material boundaries than are luminance variations (e.g., see also Switkes et al. 1988), particularly in scenes where shadows and shading are prevalent.

Experimental evidence shows that the visual system uses these chromatic-luminance relations in a way that directly influences perception. The luminance grating in **Figure 9*a*** (see color insert) appears almost flat, yet when combined with the orthogonally oriented chromatic grating in **Figure 9*b***, produces a "plaid" (**Figure 9*c***) that appears markedly corrugated in depth (an example of shape-from-shading). The changes in luminance are not tied to the changes in chromaticity; this promotes the perceptual interpretation that the plaid in **Figure 9*c*** is a material surface with differences in shading (just as the luminance but not chromatic change in **Figure 8** is interpreted as shading). This shading is characteristic of a corrugated material illuminated obliquely, which is what is perceived. If, on the other hand, the luminance changes are accompanied by corresponding chromaticity changes, then the percept of shading and thus depth should be lost. This is exactly what happens. Adding a second chromatic grating in alignment with the luminance grating, as in **Figure 9d**, strongly reduces the impression of corrugated depth. Now, the changes in luminance are perceived to belong to the material rather than to shading of the illuminant. These percepts from chromatic-luminance patterns (Kingdom 2003) reveal that color vision helps segment a retinal image into perceived material and illumination components, which is critical for object perception. The color-as-material assumption can sometimes lead to striking perceptual errors. The building in **Figure 10** (see color insert) appears to be painted two-thirds orange, yet the orange part is in fact sunset illumination shining on a spectrally unselective reflecting surface.

Not only does color affect perceived shape, but perceived shape also affects color perception. Consider a card that is painted magenta on its left half and white on its right half. When folded vertically along the central color boundary, with the fold more distant than the card's edges (like so >, viewed from the left), the concave shape causes some light to be reflected from the magenta half onto the white half, resulting in a perceived pinkish glow on the white side. The perceived shape of the card can be inverted with an optical device (a pseudoscope) that reverses binocular disparities so the fold appears to be nearer than the edges (perceived shape like so <, viewed from the left), even though the card itself and the physical reflection of light from the magenta half is unchanged. Now the white half of the card appears a deep magenta color (Bloj et al. 1999). The substantial color shift caused by a change in perceived shape implies the visual system uses information about shape to counteract the physical interreflection of light between surfaces. Specifically, the reflected light from the magenta half that falls on the white half tends to be discounted when the geometry is consistent with interreflection between surfaces. On the other hand, when the card is perceived with the center fold forward (like looking at a peaked roof from a helicopter), the geometry does not support interreflection;

in this case, the light reflected from the magenta half is attributed to the surface of the white half, which appears magenta.

The spatial relations between color and luminance are important also for the percept of transparency that we experience when viewing materials we can see through. Spectrally unselective transparencies, such as dark glasses or the simulated transparency in the center of **Figure 11a** (see color insert), reduce the level of light without altering its chromatic content, akin to how a cast shadow is primarily a change in luminance, not chromaticity (**Figure 8**). In chromatically variegated scenes, a sharp change in luminance unaccompanied by a change in chromaticity is therefore consistent not only with a shadow but also with a spectrally unselective transparency (Kingdom et al. 2004), though a compelling impression of transparency often requires additional cues, such as sharp borders and X-junctions (Kanizsa 1979). Introducing random chromatic changes across the borders of an otherwise compelling spectrally unselective transparency (**Figure 11c**) reduces or eliminates the impression of transparency (Kingdom et al. 2004, Ripamonti & Westland 2003). But this does not mean that continuity of color across the transparency border per se is the prerequisite for the impression of transparency. Provided that the changes in chromaticity across the transparency border are consistent along the length of the border (that is, always toward a particular color—blue in the example in **Figure 11d**), a strong impression of transparency results, but now of a colored transparency such as color-tinted acetate (D'Zmura et al. 1997, Fulvio et al. 2006, Khang & Zaidi 2002, Ripamonti & Westland 2003). It would appear that the critical chromatic requirement for transparency perception is consistency, rather than absence, of chromatic change across the transparency border. Cross-border chromatic consistency is an important factor also in the related phenomenon known as neon-color spreading (**Figure 12**, see color insert; Anderson 1997, van Tuijl 1975).

X-junction: a feature of a stimulus where four distinct regions meet such that the boundaries between them form an X (for example, when an edge created by a shadow falls perpendicular to an edge of an object)

Equiluminance

Despite the importance of the interaction between representations of chromaticity and luminance for perceived form, as discussed above, most studies use equiluminant stimuli to assess the chromatic contribution to form or motion perception. Equiluminant (that is, constant-luminance) stimuli are designed to evoke only chromatic neural representations in order to probe their isolated contributions. They are often employed to answer the question: Are the neural responses that are driven by only chromaticity "better or worse" than the responses to luminance? A difficulty, however, arises in comparing chromaticity and luminance for a given form/motion task because performance usually improves with stimulus contrast, and there is no common metric to equate chromatic contrast and luminance contrast. One approach to this problem is to use a behavioral measure that is independent of how contrast is measured physically. One such measure defines contrast in multiples of the amount of contrast required to detect the stimulus. With contrast defined in this way, form and motion tasks at equiluminance (that is, purely chromatic stimuli) tend to require higher contrast to achieve a given level of performance than do their isochromatic counterparts with luminance contrast (Morgan & Aiba 1985, Mullen & Boulton 1992, Simmons & Kingdom 1994, Webster et al. 1990). The precise reason for this is not clear, but two possible reasons are that chromatic form/motion mechanisms (*a*) have higher internal noise levels and/or (*b*) employ fewer neurons in comparison with the mechanisms involved in chromatic detection (Kingdom & Simmons 2000, Solomon & Lennie 2007).

Recall that equiluminant stimuli have an inherent limitation in that they cannot reveal how chromaticity and luminance jointly contribute to percepts of form or motion. In a given natural scene, for example, chromatic contrast might contribute very little to some types of form or motion because sufficient luminance contrast is present to produce asymptotic performance. On the other hand, certain benefits of color vision might be revealed only when chromatic and luminance variations are both present, as discussed above.

Color and Spatial Resolution

When the L-M and S-(L+M) component images of **Figure 6** are rendered in colors that isolate their respective postreceptoral representations, as shown in **Figure 13*b,c*** (see color insert), there is a striking lack of fine detail compared with both the original (**Figure 6*b***) and the L+M image (**Figure 13*a***). This is due to two possibly related reasons. First, the chromatic content in natural scenes tends to be less densely variegated (that is, more patch-like) than the luminance content. This is due mainly to shading and shadows, which often proliferate in the luminance representation but tend to be free of chromatic differences (as discussed above). Second, color vision is a "low spatial-resolution" system (Granger & Heurtley 1973, Mullen 1985), as can be seen in **Figure 13*d*** from the desaturation of the regions that appear yellow and blue when viewed from a distance of a few meters. One consequence of color vision's poor spatial resolution is that pure colored edges are blurred in the neural representation, yet we are unaware of this fact in our everyday visual experience (e.g., **Figure 6*b*** and plate 7 of Wandell 1995) in spite of our good judgment of blur at equiluminance (Webster et al. 2006, Wuerger et al. 2001). This may be because color tends to spread into areas defined by borders with sharp luminance contrast (Boynton 1978, Mollon 1995, Pinna et al. 2001), a phenomenon exploited by watercolor artists.

Color and Position, Orientation, Contour, and Texture

Contours often delineate the shapes of objects and therefore are important for object recognition (Marr 1982). The orientations and positions of local parts of contours are first detected in the early stages of vision. After these contour parts are linked to form whole contours, the contour shapes are encoded at higher levels of the visual system. Studies using equiluminant test patterns reveal that color can mediate positional judgments (Krauskopf & Forte 2002, Morgan & Aiba 1985), orientation judgments (Beaudot & Mullen 2005, Clifford et al. 2003, Webster et al. 1990), judgments of blur (Webster et al. 2006, Wuerger et al. 2001), contour linking (McIlhagga & Mullen 1996, Mullen et al. 2000), and contour shape processing (Gheorghiu & Kingdom 2007, Mullen & Beaudot 2002). Contour linking by color has been studied using an innovative stimulus that was originally designed by Field et al. (1993) and is shown in **Figure 14a** (see color insert). The task is to find the string of elements that are collinearly arranged in the form of a path. Paths constructed from equiluminant elements that appear red and green (**Figure 14a**) are detected as easily as paths constructed from isochromatic elements that vary only in luminance (not shown; McIlhagga & Mullen 1996). When the path elements, however, alternate between equiluminant and isochromatic (**Figure 14b**) or between L-M and S-(L+M), performance declines considerably (McIlhagga & Mullen 1996, Mullen et al. 2000). This shows that contour linking is selective along chromatic and luminance dimensions.

Dense arrays of local orientations produce textures, and the detection of spatial variation in texture is important to vision for segmenting a scene into surfaces and determining their three-dimensional shapes. Equiluminant texture variations are detectable (Cardinal & Kiper 2003, McIlhagga et al. 1990, Pearson & Kingdom 2002) by visual mechanisms broadly tuned for color (Cardinal & Kiper 2003), though, unlike contour linking, not independently from isochromatic texture variations (Pearson & Kingdom 2002). Equiluminant textures can elicit an impression of three-dimensional shape (Troscianko et al. 1991,

Zaidi & Li 2006), which suggests that chromatic signals contribute to neural processes mediating shape-from-texture.

Luminance-defined texture boundaries are camouflaged by random chromatic variations that appear red and green. This can give a rare advantage to individuals with a dichromatic red-green color defect: Such observers can break the camouflage because they do not perceive the chromatic variation (Morgan et al. 1992).

Color and Stereopsis

Small differences in the two eyes' views of a scene provide the basis for stereoscopic depth perception (Howard & Rogers 2002, Julesz 1971). A compelling observation is that a random-dot stereogram that contains a depth-target, which is visible only when viewed stereoscopically, disappears when the display is made equiluminant (de Weert 1979, Gregory 1977, Livingstone 1996, Livingstone & Hubel 1987). This has led some to conclude that color vision is stereoblind (Livingstone 1996, Livingstone & Hubel 1987). Yet stereoscopic depth is perceived at equiluminance with relatively simple stimuli such as bars or grating patches (de Weert & Sazda 1983, Kingdom & Simmons 2000, Scharff & Geisler 1992), so for these stimuli there is evidence for stereo mechanisms sensitive to chromaticity (Simmons & Kingdom 1997, Ts'o et al. 2001). The poor depth quality in equiluminant random-dot stereograms probably results from a specific deficit in integrating many local chromatic depth signals in order to generate a depth-defined surface (Kingdom et al. 1999).

A prerequisite for successful stereopsis is correct matching of the corresponding parts of the scene in each eye's view. Spurious matches tend to occur in scenes containing dense arrays of similar elements lying in multiple depth planes. However, even if the elements have similar luminance contrasts, orientations, and sizes, chromatic differences could reduce the number of false matches

Stereoscopic depth perception: the ability to perceive the relative depth of objects from the slight difference between the two eyes' views of the world

Random-dot stereogram: two stimuli, one to each eye, consisting of an identical array of dense dots, except for a subset of the dots in one eye that is slightly offset horizontally relative to this subset in the other eye. When viewed stereoscopically, the subset of dots appears to be in a different depth plane than the other dots if the visual system matches corresponding chromatic responses. A number of studies demonstrate that the introduction of chromatic differences to complex stereo displays indeed reduces the number of false matches, to the benefit of stereopsis (den Ouden et al. 2005, Jordan et al. 1990, Julesz 1971).

Color and Motion

Equiluminant objects appear to move more slowly than their luminance counterparts (Cavanagh et al. 1984, Lu et al. 1999, Mullen & Boulton 1992, Troscianko & Fahle 1988), and the target shapes in random-dot kinematograms, which are only visible when the dots are moving (analogous to the random-dot stereograms mentioned above), are difficult or impossible to discern at equiluminance (Livingstone & Hubel 1987, Ramachandran & Gregory 1978). Furthermore, motion of simple stimuli such as equiluminant chromatic L-M grating patches can be masked by the addition of randomly moving luminance "noise" (Yoshizawa et al. 2000). This last result, if taken alone, might be explained by chromatic signals that feed into a common chromatic-luminance motion mechanism; however, the finding that moving chromatic L-M noise fails to mask luminance motion (except at very high contrasts) makes this possibility unlikely (Yoshizawa et al. 2000).

An alternative proposal is that perceived motion of simple L-M chromatic stimuli is mediated by a luminance artifact generated within the visual system, possibly due to a temporal difference in the L- and M-cone signals (Mullen et al. 2003). Although this suggestion runs counter to other evidence for chromatic contributions to simple-stimulus motion, albeit ones that can interact with luminance signals (Cropper & Derrington 1996, Dobkins & Albright 1993, Gegenfurtner & Hawken 1996, Morgan & Ingle 1994; reviewed by Cropper & Wuerger 2005), the chromatic

contribution to motion for simple stimuli is at best very weak.

The consensus is more favorable for a chromatic contribution to motion for more complex objects, such as those defined by variations in chromatic contrast rather than color (Cropper & Derrington 1995, Yoshizawa et al. 2000). Some have argued, however, that for both simple and complex objects, perceived motion at equiluminance is mediated by only a general-purpose, attention-based, high-level mechanism that responds to the movement of any figure-ground relation, whether defined by color, luminance, or texture (Lu et al. 1999). Such a mechanism is implicated by the ability to attentionally track an equiluminant moving object even where the motion percept itself is severely degraded (Cavanagh 1992).

The question of whether there exists a chromatic contribution to motion, as opposed to a general-purpose, attention-based, figure-ground mechanism, emerges also from studies of color in "global motion" (**Figure 15**; see color insert). In this type of display, most of the elements—the "distractors"—move in random directions, but a subset—the "targets"—moves coherently in one direction or another. Studies disagree as to whether coherent motion in these displays is perceptible at equiluminance (e.g., against, Bilodeau & Faubert 1999; in favor, Ruppertsberg et al. 2006). In studies using nonequiluminant global motion displays, in which all elements have luminance contrast, the introduction of a color difference between the target and distractor elements reduces the number of target dots needed to identify the direction of motion (Croner & Albright 1997; **Figure 15**), and this could be taken to imply a chromatic contribution to global motion. If, however, subjects are prevented from selectively attending to the target dots in these displays (Snowden & Edmunds 1999), or if the displays are designed in such a way as to render selective attention useless (Li & Kingdom 2001a), the chromatic-difference advantage disappears. Thus, while

Random-dot kinematogram: a stimulus consisting of a dense array of dots in which a subset of dots is visually segmented from the other dots only when the subset is in motion

Global motion: the overall perceived direction of motion from an array of objects with different individual motion directions

global-motion experiments using nonequiluminant displays implicate color as a useful cue for picking out moving objects that would otherwise be camouflaged, the experiments provide no evidence that the chromatic difference actually contributes to motion. A failure to find evidence for a chromatic contribution to global motion in nonequiluminant displays emerges also from studies in which local motion signals are used to generate an impression of global three-dimensional structure (Li & Kingdom 2001b).

There is a caveat, however, to these conclusions. It was pointed out above that in mixed color-luminance stimuli there are likely to be cases in which color contributes little or nothing to the task because the luminance contrast alone drives asymptotic performance. Thus, it is possible that besides the role of color in attentional cuing, there is a weak chromatic contribution to global motion, but in nonequiluminant displays, it does not manifest itself because it is swamped by the luminance signal. Some support for this idea comes from physiological studies of the chromatic sensitivity of neurons in monkey middle temporal (MT) area, which forms part of the dorsal pathway and is believed to be specialized for global motion processing (reviewed by Gegenfurtner & Kiper 2003). Most studies reveal that MT neurons are sensitive to both L-M (Gegenfurtner et al. 1994; Thiele et al. 1999, 2001) and S-(L+M) chromatic contrast (Barberini et al. 2005), though in general sensitivity to L-M chromatic contrast is low (e.g., Gegenfurtner et al. 1994). Importantly, however, when sufficiently high luminance contrast is present in the stimulus, the chromatic contribution from L-M contrast to MT responses becomes negligible (Thiele et al. 1999). This last finding might be a physiological correlate of the apparently contradictory psychophysical findings described above, namely perceptible global motion at equiluminance (Ruppertsberg et al. 2006) and absence of chromatic contributions to global motion with nonequiluminant stimuli (Li & Kingdom 2001a,b; Snowden & Edmunds 1999).

CONCLUSION

Complex scenes reveal the rich contribution to perception from light varying in spectral composition. Chromatic variation within a scene over space or time alters the hue of a given light; moreover, it allows the intrinsic color of an object to be separated from the light illuminating it despite the ambiguity of receptoral responses that vary with the spectral distribution of illumination. Furthermore, chromatic features of a complex scene influence percepts other than color, including orientation, shape, texture, and object segmentation.

The ambiguity implicit in the early encoding of light is resolved by neural processes that often exploit properties of the natural world. This suggests a fundamental limitation of research conducted with equiluminant chromatic patterns, which lack the complexity of natural scenes required to investigate two implicit aspects of normal viewing: (a) congruent (or incongruent) changes in chromaticity and luminance and (b) the relative importance of chromaticity when both chromatically selective and spectrally unselective neural responses contribute to the same percept. The many levels of chromatic neural representation reinforce the importance of using complex visual stimuli, including ones that vary in both chromaticity and luminance, to advance our understanding of chromatic contributions to vision.

ACKNOWLEDGMENTS

We thank D. MacLeod, L. Maloney, M. Michna, K. Mullen, J. Pokorny, M. Webster, and A. Yoonessi for comments on an earlier draft. Supported by National Institutes of

Health grant EY-04802 (S.S.) and Canadian Institute of Health Research grant #MOP-11554 (F.K.).

LITERATURE CITED

Anderson BL. 1997. A theory of illusory lightness and transparency in monocular and binocular images: the role of contour junctions. *Perception* 26:419–53

Arend L, Reeves A, Schirillo J, Goldstein R. 1991. Simultaneous color constancy: papers with divers Munsell values. *J. Opt. Soc. Am. A* 8:661–72

Barberini CL, Cohen MR, Wandell BA, Newsome WT. 2005. Cone signal interactions in direction-selective neurons in the middle temporal visual area (MT). *J. Vision* 5:603–21

Barlow HB, Foldiak P. 1989. Adaptation and decorrelation in the cortex. In *The Computing Neuron*, ed. C Miall, RM Durbin, GJ Mitchison, pp. 54–72. Wokingham, UK: Addison-Wesley

Barnes CS, Wei J, Shevell SK. 1999. Chromatic induction with remote chromatic contrast varied in magnitude, spatial frequency, and chromaticity. *Vision Res.* 39:3561–74

Bauml KH. 1995. Illuminant changes under different surface collections: examining some principles of color appearance. *J. Opt. Soc. Am. A* 12:261–71

Beaudot WH, Mullen KT. 2005. Orientation selectivity in luminance and color vision assessed using 2-d band-pass filtered spatial noise. *Vision Res.* 45:687–96

Bilodeau L, Faubert J. 1999. Global motion cues and the chromatic motion system. *J. Opt. Soc. Am. A* 16:1–5

Bloj MG, Kersten D, Hurlbert AC. 1999. Perception of three-dimensional shape influences colour perception through mutual illumination. *Nature* 402:877–79

Boynton RM. 1978. Ten years of research with the minimally distinct border. In *Visual Psychophysics and Physiology*, ed. JC Armington, J Krauskopf, BR Wooten, pp. 193–207. New York: Academic

Brainard DH, Longere P, Delahunt PB, Freeman WT, Kraft JM, Xiao B. 2006. Bayesian model of human color constancy. *J. Vision* 6:1267–81

Brainard DH, Wandell BA. 1992. Asymmetric color matching: how color appearance depends on the illuminant. *J. Opt. Soc. Am. A* 9:1433–48

Brenner E, Cornelissen FW. 2002. The influence of chromatic and achromatic variability on chromatic induction and perceived colour. *Perception* 31:225–32

Brown RO, MacLeod DIA. 1997. Color appearance depends on the variance of surround colors. *Curr. Biol.* 7:844–49

Buchsbaum G. 1980. A spatial processor model for object colour perception. *J. Franklin Inst.* 310:1–26

Buchsbaum G, Gottschalk A. 1983. Trichromacy, opponent colour coding and optimum colour information transmission in the retina. *Proc. R. Soc. Lond. B Biol. Sci.* 220:89–113

Calkins DJ. 2001. Seeing with S cones. *Prog. Retin. Eye Res.* 20:255–87

Cardinal KS, Kiper DC. 2003. The detection of colored Glass patterns. *J. Vision* 3:199–208

Cavanagh P. 1992. Attention-based motion perception. *Science* 257:1563–65

Cavanagh P, Tyler CW, Favreau OE. 1984. Perceived velocity of moving chromatic gratings. *J. Opt. Soc. Am. A* 1:893–99

Chichilnisky EJ, Wandell BA. 1995. Photoreceptor sensitivity changes explain color appearance shifts induced by large uniform backgrounds in dichoptic matching. *Vision Res.* 35:239–54

Clifford CW, Spehar B, Solomon SG, Martin PR, Zaidi Q. 2003. Interactions between color and luminance in the perception of orientation. *J. Vision* 3:106–15

Cohen J. 1964. Dependency of the spectral reflectance curves of the Munsell color chips. *Psychonom. Sci.* 1:369–70

Conway BR. 2001. Spatial structure of cone inputs to color cells in alert macaque primary visual cortex (V-1). *J. Neurosci.* 21:2768–83

Croner LJ, Albright TD. 1997. Image segmentation enhances discrimination of motion in visual distractors. *Vision Res.* 37:1415–27

Cropper SJ, Derrington AM. 1995. Detection and motion-detection in chromatic and luminance beats. *J. Opt. Soc. Am. A* 13:401–7

Cropper SJ, Derrington AM. 1996. Rapid colour-specific detection of motion in human vision. *Nature* 379:72–74

Cropper SJ, Wuerger SM. 2005. The perception of motion in chromatic stimuli. *Behav. Cogn. Neurosci. Rev.* 4:192–217

Dacey DM. 1996. Circuitry for color coding in the primate retina. *Proc. Natl. Acad. Sci. USA* 93:582–88

Dacey DM. 2000. Parallel pathways for spectral coding in primate retina. *Annu. Rev. Neurosci.* 23:743–75

Dannemiller JL. 1992. Spectral reflectance of natural objects: How many basis functions are necessary? *J. Opt. Soc. Am. A* 9:507–15

den Ouden HEM, van Ee R, de Haan EHF. 2005. Colour helps to solve the binocular matching problem. *J. Physiol.* 567:665–71

Derrington AM, Krauskopf J, Lennie P. 1984. Chromatic mechanisms in lateral geniculate nucleus of macaque. *J. Physiol.* 357:241–65

DeValois RL. 1965. Analysis and coding of color vision in the primate visual system. *Cold Spring Harb. Symp. Quant. Biol.* 30:567–79

DeValois RL, DeValois KK. 1993. A multi-stage color model. *Vision Res.* 33:1053–65

de Weert CMM. 1979. Colour contours and stereopsis. *Vision Res.* 19:555–64

de Weert CMM, Sadza KJ. 1983. New data concerning the contribution of colour differences to stereopsis. In *Colour Vision: Physiology and Psychophysics*, ed. JD Mollon, LT Sharpe, pp. 553–62. London: Academic

Dobkins KR, Albright TD. 1993. What happens if it changes color when it moves? Psychophysical experiments on the nature of chromatic input to motion detectors. *Vision Res.* 33:1019–36

Domini NJ, Lucas PW. 2001. Ecological importance of trichromatic vision to primates. *Nature* 410:363–65

D'Zmura M, Colantoni P, Knoblauch K, Laget B. 1997. Color transparency. *Perception* 26:471–92

D'Zmura M, Singer B. 1999. Contrast gain control. In *Color Vision: From Genes to Perception*, ed. KR Gegenfurtner, LT Sharpe, pp. 369–85. London: Cambridge Univ. Press

Ekroll V, Faul F, Niederee R. 2004. The peculiar nature of simultaneous colour contrast in uniform surrounds. *Vision Res.* 44:1765–86

Field DJ. 1994. What is the goal of sensory coding? *Neural Comput.* 6:559–601

Field DJ, Hayes A, Hess RF. 1993. Contour integration by the human visual system: evidence for a local association field. *Vision Res.* 33:173–93

Fine I, MacLeod DIA, Boynton GM. 2003. Surface segmentation based on the luminance and color statistics of natural scenes. *J. Opt. Soc. Am. A* 20:1283–91

Foster DH, Nascimento SM. 1994. Relational colour constancy from invariant cone-excitation ratios. *Proc. R. Soc. Lond. B Biol. Sci.* 257:115–21

Foster DH, Nascimento SM, Craven BJ, Linnell KJ, Cornelissen FW, Brenner E. 1997. Four issues concerning colour constancy and relational colour constancy. *Vision Res.* 37:1341–45

Fulvio JM, Singh M, Maloney LT. 2006. Combining achromatic and chromatic cues to transparency. *J. Vision* 6:760–76

Gegenfurtner KR. 2003. Cortical mechanisms of colour vision. *Nat. Rev. Neurosci.* 4:563–72

Gegenfurtner KR, Hawken MJ. 1996. Interaction of motion and color in the visual pathways. *Trends Neurosci.* 19:394–401

Gegenfurtner KR, Kiper DC. 2003. Color vision. *Annu. Rev. Neurosci.* 26:181–206

Gegenfurtner KR, Kiper DC, Beusmans J, Carandini M, Zaidi Q. 1994. Chromatic properties of neurons in macaque MT. *Visual Neurosci.* 11:455–56

Gegenfurtner KR, Rieger J. 2000. Sensory and cognitive contributions of color to the recognition of natural scenes. *Curr. Biol.* 10:805–8

Gheorghiu E, Kingdom FAA. 2007. Chromatic tuning of contour shape mechanisms revealed through the shape-frequency and shape-amplitude after-effects. *Vision Res.* 47:1935–49

Golz J, MacLeod DIA. 2002. Influence of scene statistics on colour constancy. *Nature* 415:637–40

Granger EM, Heurtley JC. 1973. Visual chromaticity-modulation transfer function. *J. Opt. Soc. Am. A* 63:1173–74

Grassmann HG. 1853. Theory of compound colors. *Annalen der Physik und Chemie* (Poggendorf) 89:69–84. Transl. (anon.). 1854. *Philosophic Mag.* 4:254–64

Gregory RL. 1977. Vision with isoluminant colour contrast: 1. A projection technique and observations. *Perception* 6:113–19

Hansen T, Walter S, Gegenfurtner KR. 2007. Effects of spatial and temporal context on color categories and color constancy. *J. Vision* 7:1–15

Helmholtz H. 1866/1962. *Helmholtz's Treatise on Physiological Optics.* 3rd ed. Transl. JPC Southall. 1962. New York: Dover

Heywood CA, Kentridge RW, Cowey A. 1998. From and motion from colour in cerebral achromatopsia. *Exp. Brain Res.* 123:145–53

Hofer H, Singer B, Williams DR. 2005. Different sensations from cones with the same photopigment. *J. Vision* 5:444–54

Horwitz GD, Chichilnisky EJ, Albright TD. 2005. Blue-yellow signals are enhanced by spatiotemporal luminance contrast in macaque V1. *J. Neurosci.* 93:2263–78

Howard IP, Rogers BJ. 2002. *Seeing in Depth.* Vol. I and II. Ontario, Canada: Porteus

Jameson D, Hurvich LM. 1972. Color adaptation: sensitivity, contrast, after-images. In *Handbook of Sensory Physiology, Vol. VII/4, Visual Psychophysics*, ed. D Jameson, LM Hurvich, pp. 568–81. Berlin: Springer-Verlag

Johnson AP, Kingdom FAA, Baker CL Jr. 2005. Spatiochromatic statistics of natural scenes: first- and second-order information and their correlational structure. *J. Opt. Soc. Am. A* 22:2050–59

Johnson EN, Hawken MJ, Shapley R. 2001. The spatial transformation of color in the primary visual cortex of the macaque monkey. *Nat. Neurosci.* 4:409–16

Jordan JR, Geisler WS, Bovik AC. 1990. Color as a source of information in the stereo correspondence process. *Vision Res.* 30:1955–70

Judd DB, MacAdam DL, Wyszecki G. 1964. Spectral distribution of typical daylight as a function of correlated color temperature. *J. Opt. Soc. Am.* 54:1031–40

Julesz B. 1971. *Foundations of Cyclopean Perception.* Chicago: Univ. Chicago Press

Kanizsa G. 1979. *Organization in Vision.* New York: Praeger

Khang B-G, Zaidi Q. 2002. Accuracy of color scission for spectral transparencies. *J. Vision* 2:451–66

Kingdom FAA. 2003. Colour brings relief to human vision. *Nat. Neurosci.* 6:641–44

Kingdom FAA, Beauce C, Hunter L. 2004. Colour vision brings clarity to shadows. *Perception* 33:907–14

Kingdom FAA, Simmons DR. 2000. The relationship between colour vision and stereoscopic depth perception. *J. Soc. 3D Broadcasting and Imaging* 1:10–19

Kingdom FAA, Simmons DR, Rainville SJM. 1999. On the apparent collapse of stereopsis in random-dot-stereograms at isoluminance. *Vision Res.* 39:2127–41

Knill DC, Richards W, eds. 1996. *Perception as Bayesian Inference*. London: Cambridge Univ. Press

Knoblauch K, Shevell SK. 2001. Relating cone signals to color appearance: failure of monotonicity in yellow/blue. *Visual Neurosci.* 18:901–6

Kraft JM, Brainard DH. 1999. Mechanisms of color constancy under nearly natural viewing. *Proc. Natl. Acad. Sci. USA* 96:307–12

Krauskopf J, Forte JD. 2002. Influence of chromaticity on vernier and stereo acuity. *J. Vision* 2:645–52

Krauskopf J, Williams DR, Heeley DW. 1982. Cardinal directions of colour space. *Vision Res.* 22:1123–31

Land EH, McCann JJ. 1971. Lightness and Retinex theory. *J. Opt. Soc. Am.* 61:1–11

Lee T-W, Wachtler T, Sejnowski TJ. 2002. Color opponency is an efficient representation of spectral properties in natural scenes. *Vision Res.* 42:2095–103

Li H-CO, Kingdom FAA. 2001a. Segregation by colour/luminance does not necessarily facilitate motion discrimination in noise. *Percept. Psychophys.* 63:660–75

Li H-CO, Kingdom FAA. 2001b. Motion-surface labeling by orientation, spatial frequency and luminance polarity in 3-D structure-from-motion. *Vision Res.* 41:3873–82

Livingstone M. 1996. Differences between stereopsis, interocular correlation and binocularity. *Vision Res.* 36:1127–40

Livingstone MS, Hubel DH. 1987. Psychophysical evidence for separate channels for the perception of form, color, movement, and depth. *J. Neurosci.* 7:3416–68

Lu Z-L, Lesmes LA, Sperling G. 1999. Perceptual motion standstill in rapidly moving chromatic displays. *Proc. Natl. Acad. Sci. USA* 96:15374–79

MacLeod DIA, Golz J. 2003. A computational analysis of colour constancy. In *Colour Perception: Mind and the Physical World*, ed. R Mausfeld, D Heyer, pp. 205–46. London: Oxford Univ. Press

Maloney LT. 1999. Physics-based approaches to modeling surface color perception. In *Color Vision: From Genes to Perception*, ed. KR Gegenfurtner, LT Sharpe, pp. 387–416. London: Cambridge Univ. Press

Maloney LT. 2002. Illuminant estimation as cue combination. *J. Vision* 2:493–504

Maloney LT, Wandell BA. 1986. Color constancy: a method for recovering surface spectral reflectances. *J. Opt. Soc. Am. A* 3:29–33

Marimont DH, Wandell BA. 1994. Matching color images: the effects of axial chromatic aberration. *J. Opt. Soc. Am. A* 11:3113–22

Marr D. 1982. *Vision*. New York: Freeman

Mausfeld R, Andres J. 2002. Second-order statistics of colour codes modulate transformations that effectuate varying degrees of scene invariance and illumination invariance. *Perception* 31:209–24

McIlhagga W, Hine T, Cole GR, Snyder AW. 1990. Texture segregation with luminance and chromatic contrast. *Vision Res.* 30:489–95

McIlhagga WH, Mullen KT. 1996. Contour integration with color and luminance contrast. *Vision Res.* 36:1265–79

McIlhagga WH, Mullen KT. 1997. The contribution of colour to contour detection. In *John Dalton's Colour Vision Legacy. Selected Proceedings of the International Conference*, ed. CD Dickinson, I Murray, D Carden, pp. 187–96. London: Taylor & Francis

Mollon JD. 1989. "Tho' she kneel'd in that place where they grew…" The uses and origins of primate colour vision. *J. Exp. Biol.* 146:21–38

Mollon JD. 1995. Seeing color. In *Colour, Art and Science*, ed. T Lamb, J Bourriau, Ch. 5, pp. 127–50. London: Cambridge Univ. Press

Mollon JD. 2000. Cherries among the leaves: the evolutionary origins of color vision. In *Color Perception: Philosophical, Psychological, Artistic and Computational Perspectives*, ed. S David, pp. 10–30. New York: Oxford Univ. Press

Mollon JD, Cavonius CR. 1987. The chromatic antagonisms of opponent process theory are not the same as those revealed in studies of detection and discrimination. In *Colour Vision Deficiencies VIII*, ed. G Verriest, pp. 473–83. Dordrecht, The Netherlands: Junk

Morgan MJ, Adam A, Mollon JD. 1992. Dichromats detect colour-camouflaged objects that are not detected by trichromats. *Proc. R. Soc. Lond. B Biol. Sci.* 248:291–95

Morgan MJ, Aiba TS. 1985. Positional acuity with chromatic stimuli. *Vision Res.* 25:689–95

Morgan MJ, Ingle G. 1994. What direction of motion do we see if luminance but not colour contrast is reversed during displacement? Psychophysical evidence for a signed-colour input to motion detection. *Vision Res.* 34:2527–35

Moulden B, Kingdom F, Wink B. 1993. Colour pools, brightness pools, assimilation, and the spatial resolving power of the human colour-vision system. *Perception* 22:343–51

Mullen KT. 1985. The contrast sensitivity of human colour vision to red-green and blue-yellow gratings. *J. Physiol.* 359:381–409

Mullen KT, Beaudot WH. 2002. Comparison of color and luminance vision on a global shape discrimination task. *Vision Res.* 42:565–75

Mullen KT, Beaudot WH, McIlhagga WH. 2000. Contour integration in color vision: a common process for the blue-yellow, red-green and luminance mechanisms? *Vision Res.* 40:639–55

Mullen KT, Boulton JC. 1992. Absence of smooth motion perception in color vision. *Vision Res.* 32:483–88

Mullen KT, Yoshizawa T, Baker CL. 2003. Luminance mechanisms mediate the motion of red-green isoluminant gratings: the role of "temporal chromatic aberration." *Vision Res.* 43:1235–47

Nascimento SM, Foster DH. 1997. Detecting natural changes of cone-excitation ratios in simple and complex coloured images. *Proc. R. Soc. Lond. B Biol. Sci.* 264:1395–402

Parraga CA, Troscianko T, Tolhurst DJ. 2002. Spatio-chromatic properties of natural images and human vision. *Curr. Biol.* 12:483–87

Pearson PM, Kingdom FAA. 2002. Texture-orientation mechanisms pool colour and luminance. *Vision Res.* 42:1547–58

Pinna B, Brelstaff G, Spillmann L. 2001. Surface color from boundaries: a new "watercolor" illusion. *Vision Res.* 41:2669–76

Ramachandran VS, Gregory RL. 1978. Does colour provide an input to human motion perception? *Nature* 275:55–56

Regan D. 2000. *Human Perception of Objects*. Sunderland, MA: Sinauer

Ripamonti C, Westland S. 2003. Prediction of transparency perception based on cone-excitation ratios. *J. Opt. Soc. Am. A* 20:1673–80

Rubin JM, Richards WA. 1982. Color vision and image intensities: When are changes material? *Biol. Cybern.* 45:215–26

Ruderman DL, Cronin TW, Chiao C-C. 1998. Statistics of cone responses to natural images: implications for visual coding. *J. Opt. Soc. Am. A* 15:2036–45

Ruppertsberg AI, Wuerger SM, Bertami M. 2006. When S-cones contribute to chromatic global motion. *Visual Neurosci.* 23:1–8

Sallstrom P. 1973. *Color and Physics: Some Remarks Concerning the Physical Aspects of Human Color Vision*. Univ. Stockholm: Inst. Physics

Scharff LV, Geisler WS. 1992. Stereopsis at isoluminance in the absence of chromatic aberrations. *J. Opt. Soc. Am. A* 9:868–76

Shevell SK. 1982. Color perception under chromatic adaptation: equilibrium yellow and long-wavelength adaptation. *Vision Res.* 22:279–92

Shevell SK. 2003. Color appearance. In *The Science of Color*, ed. SK Shevell, pp. 149–90. Oxford, UK: Elsevier. 2nd ed.

Shevell SK, Monnier P. 2005. Color shifts from S-cone patterned backgrounds: contrast sensitivity and spatial frequency selectivity. *Vision Res.* 45:1147–54

Shevell SK, Wei J. 2000. A central mechanism of chromatic contrast. *Vision Res.* 40:3173–80

Simmons DR, Kingdom FAA. 1994. Contrast thresholds for stereoscopic depth identification with isoluminant and isochromatic stimuli. *Vision Res.* 34:2971–82

Simmons DT, Kingdom FAA. 1997. On the independence of chromatic and achromatic stereopsis mechanisms. *Vision Res.* 37:1271–80

Simoncelli EP, Olshausen BA. 2001. Natural image statistics and neural representation. *Annu. Rev. Neurosci.* 24:1193–216

Singer B, D'Zmura M. 1994. Color contrast induction. *Vision Res.* 34:3111–26

Smith VC, Jin PQ, Pokorny J. 2001. The role of spatial frequency in color induction. *Vision Res.* 41:1007–21

Smith VC, Pokorny J. 2003. Color matching and discrimination. In *The Science of Color*, ed. SK Shevell, pp. 103–48. Oxford, UK: Elsevier. 2nd ed.

Smithson HE. 2005. Sensory, computational and cognitive components of human colour constancy. *Philos. Trans. R. Soc. Lond. B Biol. Sci.* 360:1329–46

Smithson HE, Zaidi Q. 2004. Colour constancy in context: roles for local adaptation and levels of reference. *J. Vision* 4:693–710

Snowden RJ, Edmunds R. 1999. Colour and polarity contributions to global motion perception. *Vision Res.* 39:1813–22

Solomon SG, Lennie P. 2007. The machinery of colour vision. *Nat. Rev. Neurosci.* 8:276–86

Solomon SG, Peirce JW, Lennie P. 2004. The impact of suppressive surrounds on chromatic properties of cortical neurons. *J. Neurosci.* 24:148–60

Sumner P, Mollon JD. 2000. Catarrhine photopigments are optimised for detecting targets against a foliage background. *J. Exp. Biol.* 23:1963–86

Switkes E, Bradley A, DeValois KK. 1988. Contrast dependence and mechanisms of masking interactions among chromatic and luminance gratings. *J. Opt. Soc. Am. A* 5:1149–62

Thiele A, Dobkins KR, Albright TD. 1999. The contribution of color to motion processing in macaque middle temporal area. *J. Neurosci.* 19:6571–87

Thiele A, Dobkins KR, Albright TD. 2001. Neural correlates of chromatic motion perception. *Neuron* 32:351–58

Troscianko T, Fahle M. 1988. Why do isoluminant stimuli appear slower. *J. Opt. Soc. Am. A* 5:871–80

Troscianko T, Montagnon R, Le Clerc J, Malbert E, Chanteau PL. 1991. The role of colour as a monocular depth cue. *Vision Res.* 31:1923–29

Ts'o DY, Roe AW, Gilbert CD. 2001. A hierarchy of the functional architecture for color, form and disparity in primate visual area V2. *Vision Res.* 41:1333–49

Valberg A, Lange-Malecki B. 1990. "Colour constancy" in Mondrian patterns: a partial cancellation of physical chromaticity shifts by simultaneous contrast. *Vision Res.* 30:371–80

van Tuijl HFJM. 1975. A new visual illusion: neonlike color spreading and complementary color induction between subjective contours. *Acta Psychol.* 39:441–45

Viénot F, Brettel H, Ott L, Ben M'Barek A, Mollon JD. 1995. What do colour-blind people see? *Nature* 376:127–28

von Kries J. 1905. Influence of adaptation on the effects produced by luminous stimuli. In *Sources of Color Science 1970*, ed. DL MacAdam, pp. 120–26. Cambridge, MA: MIT Press

Wachtler T, Lee T-W, Sejnowski TJ. 2001. Chromatic structure of natural scenes. *J. Opt. Soc. Am. A* 18:65–77

Walraven J. 1976. Discounting the background—the missing link in the explanation of chromatic induction. *Vision Res.* 16:289–95

Wandell BA. 1995. *Foundations of Vision*. Sunderland, MA: Sinauer

Webster MA, DeValois KK, Switkes E. 1990. Orientation and spatial frequency discrimination for luminance and chromatic gratings. *J. Opt. Soc. Am. A* 7:1034–49

Webster MA, Malkoc G, Bilson AC, Webster SM. 2002. Color contrast and contextual influences on color appearance. *J. Vision* 2:505–19

Webster MA, Mizokami Y, Svec LA, Elliott SL. 2006. Neural adjustments to chromatic blur. *Spatial Vision* 19:111–32

Webster MA, Mollon JD. 1994. The influence of contrast adaptation on color appearance. *Vision Res.* 34:1993–2020

Webster MA, Mollon JD. 1995. Colour constancy influenced by contrast adaptation. *Nature* 373:694–98

Webster MA, Mollon JD. 1997. Adaptation and the color statistics of natural images. *Vision Res.* 37:3283–98

Wesner MF, Shevell SK. 1992. Color perception within a chromatic context: changes in red/green equilibria caused by noncontiguous light. *Vision Res.* 32:1623–34

Wright WD. 1946. *Researches on Normal and Defective Colour Vision*. London: Kimpton

Wuerger SM, Atkinson P, Cropper SJ. 2005. The cone inputs to the unique-hue mechanisms. *Vision Res.* 45:3210–23

Wuerger SM, Owens H, Westland S. 2001. Blur tolerance for luminance and chromatic stimuli. *J. Opt. Soc. Am. A* 18:1231–39

Yang JN, Maloney LT. 2001. Illuminant cues in surface color perception: tests of three candidate cues. *Vision Res.* 41:2581–600

Yang JN, Shevell SK. 2002. Stereo disparity improves color constancy. *Vision Res.* 42:1979–89

Yang JN, Shevell SK. 2003. Surface color perception under two illuminants: the second illuminant reduces color constancy. *J. Vision* 3:369–79

Yoshizawa T, Mullen KT, Baker CL. 2000. Absence of a chromatic linear motion mechanism in human vision. *Vision Res.* 40:1993–2010

Zaidi Q. 1997. Decorrelation of L- and M-cone signals. *J. Opt. Soc. Am. A* 14:3420–31

Zaidi Q, Li A. 2006. Three-dimensional shape from chromatic orientation flows. *Visual Neurosci.* 3–4:323–30

Zaidi Q, Yoshimi B, Flanigan N, Canova A. 1992. Lateral interactions within color mechanisms in simultaneous induced contrast. *Vision Res.* 32:1695–707

Visual Perception and the Statistical Properties of Natural Scenes

Wilson S. Geisler

Center for Perceptual Systems and Department of Psychology, University of Texas at Austin, Austin, Texas 78712-1062; email: geisler@psy.utexas.edu

Annu. Rev. Psychol. 2008. 59:167–92

First published online as a Review in Advance on August 15, 2007

The *Annual Review of Psychology* is online at http://psych.annualreviews.org

This article's doi:
10.1146/annurev.psych.58.110405.085632

Key Words

natural scene statistics, spatial vision, motion perception, color vision, ideal observer theory

Abstract

The environments in which we live and the tasks we must perform to survive and reproduce have shaped the design of our perceptual systems through evolution and experience. Therefore, direct measurement of the statistical regularities in natural environments (scenes) has great potential value for advancing our understanding of visual perception. This review begins with a general discussion of the natural scene statistics approach, of the different kinds of statistics that can be measured, and of some existing measurement techniques. This is followed by a summary of the natural scene statistics measured over the past 20 years. Finally, there is a summary of the hypotheses, models, and experiments that have emerged from the analysis of natural scene statistics.

Contents

RATIONALE FOR MEASURING NATURAL SCENE STATISTICS

The process of natural selection guarantees a strong connection between the design of an organism's perceptual systems and the properties of the physical environment in which the organism lives. In humans, this connection is implemented through a mixture of fixed (hardwired) adaptations that are present at birth and facultative (plastic) adaptations that alter or adjust the perceptual systems during the lifespan.

The link between perceptual systems and environment is most obvious in the design of sensory organs. The physical properties of electromagnetic waves, acoustic waves, and airborne molecules and their relation to the properties of objects and materials are clearly a driving force behind the evolution of eyes, ears, and noses. Not surprisingly, central perceptual mechanisms that process the outputs of sensory organs also tend to be closely related to specific physical properties of the environment.

The design of a perceptual system is also constrained by the particular tasks the organism evolved to perform in order to survive and reproduce. For example, mammals that suffer high rates of predation have a strong need to detect predators and hence tend to have laterally placed eyes that maximize field of view, whereas mammals that are predators have a strong need to capture moving prey and hence tend to have frontally placed eyes that maximize binocular overlap (Walls 1942). Furthermore, there are purely biological constraints on the design of perceptual systems, including the biological materials available to construct the sensory organs and competition for space with other organs and systems within the body.

Our often-veridical perceptions of the world give the impression of a deterministic connection between perception and environment; however, this is largely an illusion. Most perceptual capabilities depend upon combining many very different sources of stimulus information, each of which is only probabilistically predictive in the task the organism is trying to perform. For example, our estimates of physical object size and shape are often based upon a combination of information sources, including lighting/shading, texture, occlusion, motion, and binocular disparity. Each of these sources is only probabilistically related to object shape and size, but together they provide us with very robust perceptions and perceptual performance. Furthermore, all visual measurements are noisy due to the inherent randomness of light absorption and chemical events within the photoreceptors. Consequently, the appropriate way to characterize natural stimuli is in statistical terms.

The primary aim of this review is to demonstrate the great potential value of analyzing the statistical properties of natural scenes,[1] especially within the context of developing statistical models of perception. Another aim is to demonstrate that the Bayesian framework for statistical inference is particularly appropriate for characterizing natural scene statistics and evaluating their connection to performance in specific tasks. In principle, measuring natural scene statistics allows one to identify sources of stimulus information available for performing different perceptual tasks and to determine the typical ranges and reliabilities of those sources of information. Analyzing natural scene statistics within the Bayesian framework allows one to determine how a rational visual system should exploit those sources of information. This approach can be valuable for generating hypotheses about visual mechanisms, for designing appropriate experiments to test those hypotheses, and for gaining insight into why specific design features of the visual system have evolved or have been learned.

Roots of the Natural Scene Statistics Approach

The natural scene statistics approach originates in physics. Historically, physics has been concerned with topics of direct relevance to understanding the design of visual systems including the properties of light, the laws of image formation, the reflectance, scattering, and transmittance properties of natural materials, and the laws of motion and gravity. Against this backdrop, biologists began asking how visual systems are adapted to the physical environment and to the tasks that the organism performs. Most early work on the ecology and evolutionary biology of vision was concerned with the optics and the photoreceptors of eyes (e.g., Cronly-Dillon & Gregory 1991, Lythgoe 1979, Walls 1942). This early work emphasized the relationship between design,

function, and the properties of the environment, but because of the issues being investigated, gave little consideration to the statistical properties of natural stimuli.

Interest in the statistical properties of natural visual stimuli began with the discovery in physics of the inherent Poisson randomness of light (quantal fluctuations). Human and animal studies by early sensory scientists subsequently showed that under some circumstances behavioral and neural performance is limited by a combination of quantal fluctuations and internal sources of noise (e.g., Barlow 1957, Barlow & Levick 1969, Hecht et al. 1942). This work, along with parallel work in audition, led to the development of signal detection theory and Bayesian ideal observer theory (e.g., see Green & Swets 1966), which provides an appropriate formal framework for proposing and testing hypotheses about the relationship between perceptual performance and the statistical properties of stimuli and neural responses. However, early work on the statistical properties of visual stimuli and neural responses focused on simple detection and discrimination tasks, paying little attention to sources of stimulus variation other than quantal fluctuations and pixel noise.

Some early perception scientists (e.g., Gibson 1966, 1979) did appreciate the importance of the complex properties of natural stimuli for solving perceptual tasks, but they paid little attention to statistical variations of those properties in natural scenes. An exception was Brunswik (1956), who realized that the relationship between distal and proximal stimuli is inherently statistical; in fact, he demonstrated, by analyzing natural images, that perceptual biases such as the Gestalt rule of proximity have a statistical basis in natural scenes (Brunswik & Kamiya 1953).

Recent years have seen rapid growth in the statistical analyses of natural images (for a review, see Simoncelli & Olshausen 2001) as well as in the analysis and modeling of complex perceptual tasks within the framework of Bayesian ideal observer theory (for reviews,

---

[1]Natural scenes refer to real environments, as opposed to laboratory stimuli, and may include human-made objects. Most of the studies described here concern measurements of outdoor environments without human-made objects.

see Geisler & Diehl 2003, Kersten et al. 2004, Knill & Richards 1996). A central tenet of this review is that combining measurements of natural scene statistics with Bayesian ideal observer analysis provides an important new approach in the study of sensory and perceptual systems.

Within-Domain Statistics

Natural scene statistics have been measured at various stages (domains) along the path from physical environment to behavioral response. The simpler and more common kinds of measurements are what I call within-domain statistics (first column in **Figure 1A**, see color insert). The purpose of within-domain statistics is to characterize the probability distribution of properties within a specific domain such as the (distal) environment or (proximal) retinal image. The more complex and less common kinds of measurements are what I call across-domain statistics (other columns in **Figure 1A**). Their purpose is to characterize the joint probability distribution of properties across specific domains. Across-domain statistics are essential for analyzing natural scene statistics within the Bayesian ideal observer framework.

In the case of within-domain statistics for the environment, a vector of physical scene properties ω is selected and then those properties are measured in a representative set of scenes in order to estimate the probability distribution of the properties $p(\omega)$. For example, ω might be the reflectance function at a point on a surface in a natural scene; that is, a vector giving the fraction of light reflected from the surface for a number of different wavelengths, $\omega = [\rho(\lambda_1), L, \rho(\lambda_n)]$. Making these physical measurements for a large number of surface points in natural scenes would make it possible to estimate the probability distribution of natural surface reflectance. Similarly, in the case of within-domain statistics for images, a vector of retinal image properties s is selected and their distribution measured. For example, s might be a vector rep-

resenting the wavelength spectrum at a retinal image location, $s = [I(\lambda_1), \ldots, I(\lambda_n)]$ (see plots in **Figure 1B**). For the domain of neural response, a set of response properties for a population of neurons is selected and their distribution measured for a representative set of natural stimuli. In this case, z might be a vector of the spike counts of each neuron, $z = [count_1, \ldots, count_n]$. Finally, for the domain of behavior, a vector of properties for some class of behavior is selected and their distribution measured for a representative set of natural stimuli. For example, r might be the eye fixation locations in a natural image during free viewing, $r = [fixation_1, \ldots, fixation_n]$.

Measurements of within-domain statistics are highly relevant for understanding neural coding and representation. A plausible hypothesis is that the retina and other stages of the early visual pathway have evolved (or learned) to efficiently code and transmit as much information about retinal images as possible, given the statistics of natural images and biological constraints such as the total number of neurons and the dynamic range of neural responses. Variants of this efficient coding hypothesis have been widely proposed and evaluated (Atick & Redlich 1992; Attneave 1954; Barlow 1961, 2001; Field 1994; Laughlin 1981; van Hateren 1992). For example, the efficient coding hypothesis predicts many of the response characteristics of neurons in the retina directly from the joint probability distributions of the intensities at two pixel locations in natural images, $p(s) = p(I_1, I_2)$, measured for various separations of the pixels in space and time. The measurement of within-domain statistics is central to the enterprise of testing the efficient coding hypothesis: To determine what would be an efficient code, it is essential to know the probability distribution of the image properties to be encoded.

Across-Domain Statistics

Within-domain statistics say nothing about the relationship between the domains listed in **Figure 1A**, such as the relationship between properties of the environment and the images formed on the retina. Natural visual tasks generally involve making inferences about specific physical properties of the environment from the images captured by the eyes. These tasks include classifying materials, discriminating object boundary contours from shadow contours, estimating object shape, identifying objects, estimating the distance or motion of an object, or estimating one's own motion direction and speed. The relevant statistics for understanding how the visual system performs such tasks are the joint distributions of physical scene properties and image properties, $p(\omega, \mathbf{s})$, or equivalently, $p(\omega)$ and the conditional distribution $p(\mathbf{s}|\omega)$ for each value of ω. [Note that $p(\omega, \mathbf{s}) = p(\mathbf{s}|\omega)p(\omega)$.] Using Bayes' rule, these across-domain statistics specify the posterior probabilities of different states of the world (physical environment properties) given particular observed retinal image properties $p(\omega|\mathbf{s})$. It is the characteristics of the posterior probability distributions that visual systems evolve or learn to exploit in performing specific natural visual tasks.

Suppose an organism's task is to identify (for a given species of tree) whether a randomly selected location (small patch) in the retinal image corresponds to the surface of a fruit or the surface of a leaf, based solely on the information available in the wavelength spectrum at that randomly selected location (see **Figure 1B**). In this case, there are just two relevant states of the environment (distal stimuli): $\omega = fruit$ and $\omega = leaf$, and due to variations in lighting and reflectance, a large number of possible wavelength spectra (proximal stimuli) for each distal stimulus. In principle, $p(\omega)$ could be measured by randomly selecting lines of sight from a large number of example scenes and counting the proportion of times a fruit surface is the first surface encountered along that line of sight. Similarly, $p(\mathbf{s}|\omega)$ could be measured by recording the wavelength spectra for each of the randomly sampled lines of sight, sorting them according to whether they are from fruit or leaf, and then analyzing them separately to estimate the two conditional probability distributions. The statistical regularities represented by $p(\mathbf{s}|\omega)$ and $p(\omega)$ could be exploited by the visual system for identifying fruits and leaves from the wavelength spectra that reach the eye. On the other hand, knowing only the within-domain statistics, $p(\mathbf{s})$ and $p(\omega)$, is not useful for identifying fruits and leaves because the statistics do not specify the relationship between the image properties (wavelength spectra) and the physical objects (fruits and leaves) of relevance in the task. This example illustrates the use of across-domain statistics for characterizing the connection between environmental properties and image properties; comparable examples can be generated for the other kinds of across-domain statistics (see table in **Figure 1A**).

Bayesian ideal observer theory provides an appropriate formal framework for understanding how across-domain statistics might be exploited by the visual system to perform specific tasks (Geisler & Diehl 2003). The Bayesian approach in perception research has been discussed at length elsewhere and is only briefly summarized here, as a prelude to some of the studies described below. An "ideal observer" is a theoretical device that performs a task in an optimal fashion given the available information (and possibly other constraints). Deriving an ideal observer can be very useful because (a) the derivation usually leads to a thorough understanding of the computational requirements of the perceptual task, (b) the ideal observer provides the appropriate benchmark for comparison with behavioral performance, and (c) ideal observers often reduce to, or can be approximated by, relatively simple decision rules or procedures that can serve as initial hypotheses for the actual processing carried out in a perceptual system.

The logic behind deriving an ideal observer is straightforward. Consider an ideal observer that wishes to perform a specific task in its current environment and has access to some vector of properties in the retinal image. Upon receiving a particular stimulus vector

S, an ideal observer should make the response that maximizes the utility (gain/loss) averaged over all possible states of the environment,

$$\mathbf{r}_{opt}(\mathbf{S}) = \arg\max_{\mathbf{r}} \left(\sum_{\omega} \gamma(\mathbf{r}, \omega) p(\mathbf{S}|\omega) p(\omega) \right)$$

(1)

where $\gamma(\mathbf{r}, \omega)$ is the utility of making response **r** when the true state of the environment is ω, and the function arg max returns the response that maximizes the sum in the brackets. In other words, once the relevant across-domain statistics have been estimated and the utility function for the task has been specified, then Equation (1) can be used to determine (via simulation or calculation) the optimal performance in the task.

Think back to the hypothetical task described above: identifying whether a small patch of retinal image corresponds to a fruit or a leaf. There are two possible responses, $\mathbf{r} = fruit$ and $\mathbf{r} = leaf$. To maximize accuracy, an appropriate utility function is $\gamma(\mathbf{r}, \omega) = 1$, if $\mathbf{r} = \omega$, and $\gamma(\mathbf{r}, \omega) = -1$, if $\mathbf{r} \neq \omega$ (i.e., equal but opposite weights for corrects and errors). Substituting this utility function and the measured probability distributions into Equation (1) gives the (parameter-free) optimum decision rule. The performance accuracy of this decision rule can be determined by applying the rule to random samples $(\Omega, \mathbf{S})$ from the across-domain probability distribution, $p(\omega, \mathbf{s})$, or alternatively, by directly calculating the probability that $\mathbf{r}_{opt}(\mathbf{S}) = \Omega$. The optimal decision rule (or an approximation to it) could serve as a principled hypothesis about the perceptual mechanisms in the organism that discriminate fruits from leaves.

MEASURING NATURAL SCENE STATISTICS

A variety of devices and techniques has been used to measure natural scene properties. Spectrophotometric devices measure the wavelength distribution (radiance as a function of wavelength) of the light that reaches their sensors. They can be used to measure reflectance spectra of materials, irradiance spectra of light sources (illuminants), as well as radiance spectra that reach the eye. Spectrophotometers collect light over only one small patch at a time, making them impractical for collecting data from a large number of locations in a scene. Hyperspectral cameras can measure radiance spectra at each camera pixel location, but require relatively long exposure time, and thus are practical only for conditions where effects of object and shadow motion are minimized (e.g., long distances or indoor environments). The most common method of measuring natural scene properties has been to analyze images captured by digital still cameras and digital movie cameras. Digital cameras usually provide either 8-bit grayscale or 24-bit color (8 bits per color) images, although some high-end cameras provide 36-bit color (12 bits per color) images, which is desirable for some kinds of measurements. A weakness of standard digital cameras is that they cannot provide detailed spectral (chromatic) information, although with proper calibration it is possible to obtain images that give, for each pixel location, the approximate luminance and/or the approximate amount of radiant power absorbed in each of the three classes of cone photoreceptor, the long (L), middle (M), and short (S) wavelength cones. Many studies have analyzed uncalibrated camera images, which is justifiable if the scene statistics of interest (e.g., contour geometry) are little affected by monotonic transformations of the camera's color responses.

Another useful class of device is the range finder, which measures distance to each point in a scene by measuring return time for an emitted pulse of infrared laser light. These devices are accurate for large distances (a few meters to a kilometer or more). A related class of device is the three-dimensional scanner, which uses triangulation rather than time-of-flight, and is useful for making precise range measurements at near distances (e.g., measuring the shape of a face). A weakness of both devices is that the scans take substantial time (typically seconds), and thus motion in the scene can produce significant distortions.

The above devices are the most common for measuring natural scene statistics, and they can be used in a fairly straightforward manner to measure within-domain statistics for the image or environment. Measuring across-domain statistics is more difficult because both image and environment properties must be measured for the same scene. One approach is to combine environment measurements from one instrument with image measurements from another instrument. For example, monocular across-domain statistics for depth can be measured by combining a calibrated camera image with a distance map obtained with a range finder.

An expedient approach for measuring across-domain statistics involves hand segmentation. The central assumption of this approach is that under some circumstances humans are able to make veridical assignments of image pixels to physical sources in the environment. When this assumption holds, the pixel assignments are useful measurements of environmental properties.

For example, consider the close-up image of foliage in **Figure 2A** (see color insert). When observers are asked to segment individual leaves and branches that are within or touching the orange dashed circle, the result in **Figure 2B** is obtained. The colored leaves and branches show the segmented objects, the red/brown shaded leaf shows one individual segmented object. These segmentations are performed with high confidence and repeatability, and hence generally provide an accurate measurement of the physical source (the specific leaf or branch) that gave rise to a given pixel. Many across-domain statistics can be measured with a large set of such segmentation data. To take one simple example, it is straightforward to measure the posterior probability of the same or different object [ω = same or ω = different], given the distance between a pair of image pixels and their luminance values [$\mathbf{s} = (d_{12}, l_1, l_2)$].

Hand segmentation methods are useful for measuring across-domain statistics only to the extent that the segmentations are veridical (i.e., represent physical "ground truth"), and there are cases (e.g., distant images of foliage) where some image regions are ambiguous and difficult to segment.[2] In cases where hand segmentation methods fail, accurate ground truth measurements require more direct physical measurement. Another strategy for measuring across-domain statistics combines computer-graphics simulation with direct measurements of scene statistics.

NATURAL SCENE STATISICS

It is difficult to know ahead of time which specific statistics will prove most informative for understanding vision. At this time, progress is being made by selecting statistics based on intuition, historical precedence, and mathematical tractability. It is important to note that the number of samples required for estimating a probability distribution grows exponentially with the number of properties/dimensions ("the curse of dimensionality"), and hence most studies measure natural scene statistics for only one or a few properties at a time. This is a significant limitation because perceptual mechanisms exploit complex regularities in natural scenes that may only be fully characterized by measuring joint distributions over a substantial number of dimensions. Nonetheless, the published work has demonstrated that much can be learned from low-dimensional measurements and that there are useful methods for learning about the structure of probability distributions in high-dimensional spaces. This section presents a somewhat eclectic summary of some of the natural scene statistics that have been measured.

---

[2]Hand segmentation has also been used to measure how humans segment scenes into regions without specific instructions to be exhaustive or identify physical sources; in this case, the aim is not to precisely measure physical ground truth but rather to obtain a useful data set for training image-processing algorithms (e.g., Martin et al. 2004).

Luminance and Contrast

PCA: principal components analysis

Luminance and contrast, fundamental stimulus dimensions encoded by visual systems, vary both within a given scene and across scenes. Most studies have involved measuring the statistics of luminance and contrast within images of natural scenes (e.g., Brady & Field 2000, Frazor & Geisler 2006, Laughlin 1981, Ruderman 1994, Tadmor & Tolhurst 2000). The distribution of local luminance within a given image is typically obtained by first dividing the luminance at each pixel by the average for the whole image.[3] Combining these distributions across images and then scaling to the average luminance of the images gives the distribution of luminance in the typical natural image. As shown in **Figure 3A** (see color insert), this distribution is approximately symmetric on a logarithmic axis and hence positively skewed on a linear scale (Brady & Field 2000, Laughlin 1981, Ruderman et al. 1998). In other words, relative to the mean luminance, there are many more dark pixels than light pixels.

The distribution of local contrast within images has been measured using various definitions of contrast. **Figure 3B** shows the distribution of local root-mean-squared contrast (the standard deviation of luminance divided by the mean luminance in a small neighborhood) in the typical natural image. Another more specialized measure is an equivalent Michelson contrast—the Michelson contrast of a sine wave grating (sine wave amplitude divided by mean) that would produce the same contrast response as the local image patch, where the contrast response is from a filter designed to mimic a typical receptive field at some level of the visual system (Brady & Field 2000, Tadmor & Tolhurst 2000). These latter distributions tend to be similar in shape to the one in **Figure 3B**, but (as expected given

the selectivity of the filter) are shifted toward lower contrasts.

There are large variations of local luminance and local contrast in natural images, and these variations tend to be statistically independent. The average joint distribution of luminance and contrast has a slight negative correlation ($r = -0.2$) primarily due to the fact that sky regions tend to be both bright and low in contrast (**Figure 3C**). Low correlations between luminance and contrast are also observed within the constituents of natural images. For example, the joint distribution of luminance and contrast in purely foliage regions (**Figure 3D**) has a slight positive correlation ($r = 0.15$). As discussed below, the large variations in local luminance and contrast and their low correlation have important implications for neural coding.

Color

Interest in natural scene statistics was stimulated by the discoveries that the chromatic power spectra of natural light sources (Dixon 1978, Judd et al. 1964) and the reflectance spectra of natural materials (Maloney 1986, Maloney & Wandell 1986) are highly constrained and can be characterized with just a few numbers. These studies used the standard statistical technique of principal components analysis (PCA) to describe the structure of the probability distributions. For example, each reflectance spectrum can be represented by a single vector in a high-dimensional space, where each dimension of the space is the reflectance at a particular wavelength. A large set of reflectance spectra create a cloud of vectors in this space. Under the assumption of normality, PCA finds the principal axes of this cloud. The first principal axis is the one that accounts for the most variance in the distribution (i.e., it is the direction in the space along which the cloud is most spread out); the second principal axis is the one perpendicular to the first that accounts for most of the remaining variance, and so on. Principal components are unit vectors along the principal axes; in

---

[3]One could regard the ratio of pixel luminance to global luminance as a form of Weber contrast, but here the term "contrast" is reserved for measurements of luminance variation relative to the average luminance in a small neighborhood.

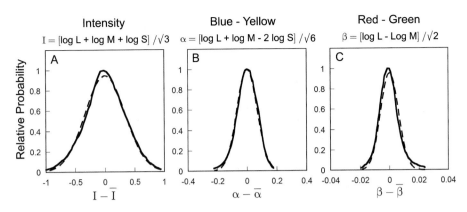

Figure 4

Probability distributions for color in natural foliage scenes. (*A*) Distribution along the first principal axis in log cone response space, minus the average in the image. (*B*) Distribution along the second principal axis. (*C*) Distribution along the third principal axis. The dashed curves are best-fitting Gaussian distributions. The joint probability distribution is approximately the product of these three marginal distributions (adapted from Ruderman et al. 1998).

other words, they describe the directions of the principal axes.

The important discovery of these studies is that most of the variance is accounted for by the first few principal axes. The implications are that the probability distribution of natural irradiance spectra and of natural reflectance spectra can each be described in a rather small dimensional (tractable) space and that natural images can be coded relatively accurately with just a few classes of cone receptor, although three classes (the number in humans) is somewhat short of optimal (Brainard & Freeman 1997, D'Zmura & Iverson 1993, Maloney & Wandell 1986).

The chromatic properties of natural images captured with digital cameras are often described in terms of the number of photons absorbed in the three types of cones, at each image location. Thus, analogous to measuring the distribution of local luminance in natural images (**Figure 3*A***), one can measure the distribution of cone responses in natural images. As it turns out, the joint distribution of the logarithm of the cone responses in natural images is approximately Gaussian. A convenient way to describe Gaussian distributions is to determine the marginal distributions along the principal axes with PCA. This

is convenient because the joint distribution is then the product of the marginal distributions (note that the aim of using PCA is different here than in the case of analyzing natural irradiance and reflectance spectra). **Figure 4** shows the three principal axes (specified by the equations above each panel) and marginal distributions for foliage-dominated natural images obtained with a hyperspectral camera (Ruderman et al. 1998). Exactly the same principal components for close-up foliage images (e.g., **Figure 2**) were obtained with a calibrated digital camera (Ing & Geisler 2006).

Spatial Structure

Much of the information in retinal images is contained in the spatial pattern of luminance and color. One overall spatial statistic of natural images, which is relatively consistent across scenes, is the Fourier amplitude spectrum (or equivalently the spatial autocorrelation function). **Figure 5*A*** (see color insert) shows the amplitude spectra of six different natural images plotted on logarithmic axes (each was obtained from the two-dimensional Fourier power spectrum by summing across orientation and then taking the square root). The solid line represents a slope of −1.0;

thus the amplitude spectra fall approximately as $1/f^n$, where f is spatial frequency and the exponent n is approximately 1.0 (Burton & Moorehead 1987, Field 1987, Ruderman & Bialek 1994). One consequence is that the amplitude spectra of natural images are relatively scale invariant, in the sense that scaling all frequencies by a factor (e.g., moving forward or backward in a scene) has little effect on the shape of the amplitude spectrum. For more discussion of scale invariance, see Ruderman (1997, 2002), Lee et al. (2001), and Balboa et al. (2001).

Based on **Figure 5A**, the simplest model of the spatial structure of natural images would be that produced by a $1/f$ amplitude spectrum and a random phase spectrum. An image created in this fashion is a sample of filtered Gaussian noise, often called $1/f$ noise. Such a sample of filtered noise does not contain recognizable objects or regions, but does contain complex random features. Thus, it is reasonable to ask if $1/f$ noise can serve as a statistical model of the local properties of images. One way to address this question is to compare how local sensors like those in visual cortex respond to $1/f$ noise versus actual natural images. A local sensor with an oriented receptive field (similar to an orientation-selective cortical neuron) computes a weighted sum across a small patch of image. Because $1/f$ noise is Gaussian distributed, any given weighted sum will also be Gaussian distributed (dashed curve in **Figure 5B**). However, in natural images the probability distribution of local sensor responses is generally not Gaussian, but rather is sharply peaked at zero response with heavy tails (solid curve in **Figure 5B**). In other words, for real images a given local sensor tends to respond relatively infrequently, but when it does respond it tends to produce a relatively large response (Field 1987, Olshausen & Field 1997).

One way that $1/f$ noise differs from natural images is that the local luminance distribution of natural images is not Gaussian on a luminance axis, but rather is approximately Gaussian on a log luminance axis (**Figures 3A**

and **4**). Thus, a more realistic model of the spatial structure of natural images would be that of noise having a $1/f$ amplitude spectrum and a local luminance distribution that matches natural scenes. Frazor & Geisler (2006) call this first-order $1/f$ noise because the local luminance distribution is the first-order statistic of an image and the amplitude spectrum corresponds to the second-order statistic. Sensor responses to first-order $1/f$ noise peak more strongly at zero and have heavier tails than those for $1/f$ noise; however, the peaks and the tails of the distributions are not as pronounced as they are for natural images.

A more complete description of the spatial structure of natural images can be obtained by examining the joint statistics of responses from pairs of local sensors. As one would expect, there are significant correlations between pairs of nonoverlapping sensors. For example, if there is a large response from an oriented edge sensor, then it is likely that a neighboring colinear (or cocircular) edge sensor also has a large response (Geisler et al. 2001, Sigman et al. 2001). This occurs because natural scenes contain many contours that tend to be relatively smooth and to have significant spatial extent (e.g., see **Figure 2**). Similarly, if there is a large response from an oriented edge sensor, then it is likely that a neighboring parallel (but not colinear) edge sensor will have a large response (Geisler et al. 2001). This occurs because there is much parallel structure in natural images (e.g., see branches and leaf markings in **Figure 2**). Importantly, however, even when there is no correlation between the responses of a pair of sensors, the responses are often statistically dependent. For example, **Figure 5C** shows the distribution of responses of an orientation-selective sensor conditional on the response of another nonoverlapping orientation selective sensor at a nearby location (Schwartz & Simoncelli 2001). The responses are uncorrelated, but the variance of the response of one sensor (RF2) increases as function of the magnitude of the response of the

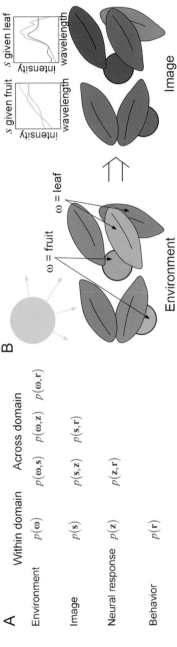

A

	Within domain	Across domain	
Environment	$p(\omega)$	$p(\omega,s)$ $p(\omega,z)$ $p(\omega,r)$
Image	$p(s)$	$p(s,z)$ $p(s,r)$
Neural response	$p(z)$	$p(z,r)$
Behavior	$p(r)$	

B

$\omega = $ fruit

$\omega = $ leaf

Environment

s given fruit

intensity / wavelength

s given leaf

intensity / wavelength

Image

Figure 1

Kinds of natural scene statistics. (*A*) There are two general kinds of natural scene statistics that can be measured at various stages (domains) from environment to behavior. Within-domain statistics describe the probability distribution of a vector of properties within a given domain. Across-domain statistics describe the joint probability distribution of properties across domains. (*B*) Hypothetical example. Suppose an organism's task is to identify whether a randomly selected location in the retinal image corresponds to the surface of a fruit or the surface of a leaf. The relevant property of the environment takes on just one of two possible values ($\omega = fruit$ or $\omega = leaf$). The relevant property of the image is a wavelength spectrum **s** (the plots show a few examples of spectra for fruits and leaves). Measuring the probability of fruit or leaf is an example of measuring $p(\omega)$. Measuring the probability distribution of wavelength spectra without regard to the source (leaf or fruit) is an example of measuring $p(s)$. Measuring the probability distribution of wavelength spectra separately for fruit and leaves and then combining with the probability of fruit or leaf is an example of measuring an across-domain statistic $p(\omega, s)$. See text for more details.

Figure 2

Using hand segmentation to measure across-domain statistics. (*A*) Close-up image of foliage obtained with a 36-bit calibrated camera. The orange circle indicates the region to be hand segmented. (*B*) The colored leaves and branches show the result of the hand segmentation. The orange shaded leaf is an individual segmented object.

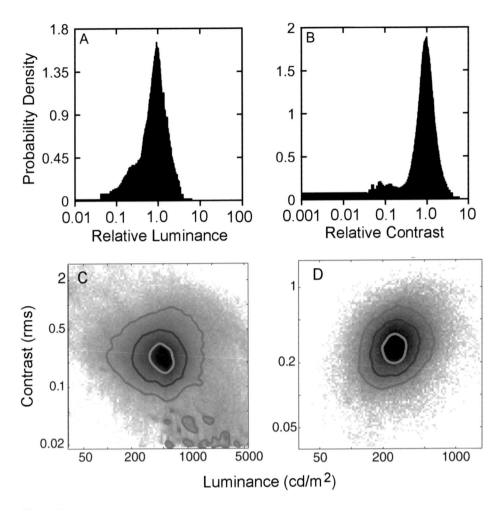

Figure 3

Luminance and contrast in natural images. (*A*) Average distribution of local luminance levels within a natural image, relative to the mean luminance of the image. (*B*) Average distribution of local contrast in natural images, relative to the mean contrast of the image. (*C*) Average joint distribution of local luminance and local contrast in natural images, scaled to the average luminance and average contrast in natural images. (Contours enclose 90%, 65%, and 40% of the observations.) (*D*) Average joint distribution of local luminance and local contrast within foliage regions of natural images.

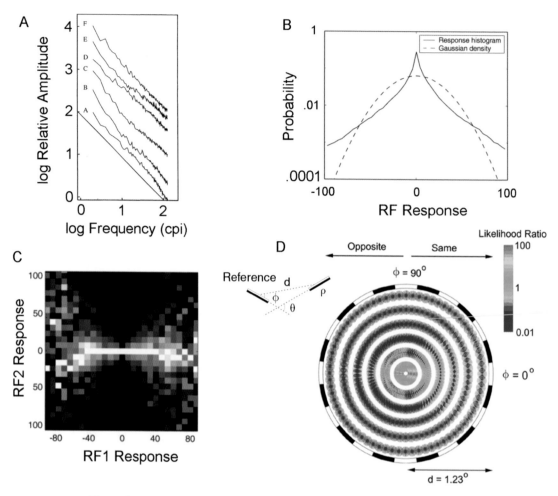

Figure 5

Spatial properties of natural images. (*A*) Amplitude spectra of six natural images (adapted from Field 1987). The spectrum for each image has been displaced vertically for display purposes. The diagonal line has a slope of -1.0. (*B*) Histogram of responses to natural images of a sensor having a receptive field profile representative of those in primary visual cortex. The dashed line shows the best-fitting Gaussian distribution. (*C*) Histograms of responses to natural images of a sensor (RF2) conditional on the response of a nearby but nonoverlapping sensor (RF1). The histograms are represented by the vertical columns of pixels (the brighter the pixel the greater the frequency). For display purposes, each column of pixels has been scaled to use the full grayscale range. (*D*) Histogram showing the ratio of the likelihood that a particular pair of edge elements belongs to the same physical contour to the likelihood that the pair belong to different physical contours. In this plot, the central horizontal line segment represents one of the pair of edge elements (the reference); each ring represents a distance bin d; each location around the diagram represents a direction bin ϕ; each line element plotted at a given distance and direction represents an orientation difference bin θ. The right side of the plot shows the likelihood ratios when the contrast polarity is the same, the left side when the contrast polarity is opposite.

other sensor (RF1). In other words, strong features tend to cluster in natural images; thus, when a strong response occurs in a local sensor, the responses tend to be strong in other nearby sensors, although the sign of the response may be random (as in **Figure 5C**).

Another strategy for characterizing spatial structure in natural images is to measure general properties of the joint probability distribution of pixels within a spatial neighborhood of a given size. Two popular approaches have been to apply either PCA or independent components analysis (ICA) to a collection of patches sampled from natural images (for another approach, see Lee et al. 2003). If the patch size is, say, 12×12 pixels, then (ignoring color) each patch can be represented as a point in a 144-dimensional space where each dimension is the luminance at one of the 144 pixel locations. Applying PCA to natural image patches shows that a large number of principal axes are required to capture a substantial fraction of the variance in the distribution of image patches, and hence PCA does not lead to a compact summary of the spatial structure of natural images in the same way it does for natural irradiance and reflectance spectra.

ICA is a conceptually different approach. Rather than assuming, like PCA, that the whole space is described by a single multidimensional Gaussian distribution, ICA assumes that the space is described by a sum of statistically independent distributions, each representing a different unknown "source." The aim of ICA is to estimate, from a large collection of samples, the vector corresponding to each source (the direction of the primary axis of each source). This is an interesting approach because images probably are the result of independent physical sources (e.g., contours produced by different surface boundaries, surface markings, and shadows). ICA may discover some of those sources. Furthermore, the filters obtained from ICA, which recover (measure) the sources in an image, might be plausible candidates for neural receptive fields. Applying ICA to natural image patches yields filters similar in appearance to receptive fields of simple cells found in the visual cortex of mammals (Bell & Sejnowski 1997, Hyvarinen & Hoyer 2000, van Hateren & van der Schaaf 1998). (For ICA of natural auditory stimuli, see Lewicki 2002.) A conceptually related analysis producing similar results involves estimating independent sources, with the additional constraint that the sources are "sparse," in the sense that when a given source has a large value, other potential sources are constrained to have small values (Olshausen & Field 1997).

The studies of spatial structure described so far concern within-domain statistics, which are particularly relevant to issues of image coding (see below). There have also been attempts to measure across-domain statistics, which are more relevant to the performance of specific tasks. For example, Elder & Goldberg (1998, 2002) and Geisler et al. (2001, Geisler & Perry 2006) measured the pair-wise statistics of image contours that were hand segmented from natural images. Geisler et al. (2001, Geisler & Perry 2006) used an automatic algorithm to detect small edge elements from natural images and then had observers assign edge elements to physical contours in the image. Thus, with respect to the notation in **Figure 1A**, the state of the environment ω could take on one of two values ($\omega = c$ if two edge elements came from the same physical contour and $\omega = \sim c$ if two elements came from different physical contours). For each pair of edge elements, they determined the distance d between the elements, the direction θ of one of the elements with respect to the other element, the difference in orientation θ between the elements, and the difference in contrast polarity (same or opposite) ρ between the elements (**Figure 5D**). Thus, with respect to the notation in **Figure 1A**, the retinal image properties were defined by the vector $\mathbf{s} = (d, \phi, \theta, \rho)$. **Figure 5D** plots the ratio of the measured likelihood distributions for the cases where edge element pairs belong to the same contour and different contours:

ICA: independent components analysis

$l(d, \phi, \theta, \rho) = p(\mathbf{s}|\omega = c)/p(\mathbf{s}|\omega = {\sim}c)$. As can be seen, edge elements in natural images that are cocircular (which includes colinear) and of the same contrast polarity are more likely to come from the same physical contour; edge elements that deviate substantially from cocircularity or are of opposite polarity are likely to come from different physical contours. (Note, however, that even when the polarity is opposite, nearby edge elements are more likely to come from the same contour if they are approximately colinear; this presumably occurs because physical contours often cross backgrounds that modulate substantially in intensity.) These results have direct relevance for understanding the perceptual mechanisms underlying tasks such as contour grouping and contour completion.

Range

An important task for visual systems is estimating distance and three-dimensional shape from the two-dimensional images formed on each retina. A relevant statistic is the distribution of distances (ranges) in natural environments. **Figure 6A** shows a range image (over an extent of 259° horizontal and 80° vertical) measured in a forest environment with a laser range finder. In this image, lighter pixels denote greater distances. The solid curve in **Figure 6B** shows the probability of each

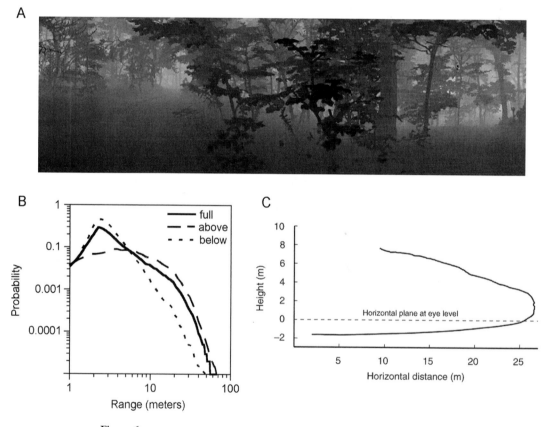

Figure 6

Range properties of forest environments. (*A*) Range image—the lighter the color, the greater the distance. (*B*) Histogram of range based upon 54 forest range images (adapted from Huang et al. 2000). (*C*) Average range as a function of elevation based upon a combination of 23 forest and 51 outdoor (Duke campus) range images (adapted from Yang & Purves 2003).

distance based upon 54 such forest range images (Huang et al. 2000). The distribution of distances is different above (dashed curve) and below (dotted curve) the line of sight. **Figure 6C** shows that average distance decreases rapidly below the line of sight due to the effect of the ground plane and decreases more gradually above the line of sight presumably due to the foliage canopy (Yang & Purves 2003). Huang et al. (2000) showed that their observed distributions of range in forest scenes can be approximated by a model consisting of a flat ground plane populated by a spatial Poisson distribution of cylinders (trees).

When coupled with other measurements, range statistics are of relevance for understanding depth and motion coding. For example, **Figure 7** shows the distribution of binocular disparity implied by the statistics of Yang & Purves (2003) when combined with the distribution of human fixation points measured as observers walk through forest environments (Cormack et al. 2005). Most binocular disparities fall within a modest range of ±1.5 degrees. Potetz & Lee (2003) measured range images along with coregistered grayscale images and discovered several modest correlations (e.g., range and luminance are negatively correlated).

Spatiotemporal Structure

The spatial structure of a retinal image changes over time due to self motion and to motion in the environment. The dynamical properties of natural retinal images are important to characterize because they contain useful information for many perceptual tasks, including heading estimation, image segmentation, distance estimation, and shape estimation. However, measuring and characterizing the spatiotemporal statistics of natural images are difficult because there is almost always some component of image motion that results from self-motion (i.e., the receptor array is almost always translating and/or rotating because of eye, head, and body movements).

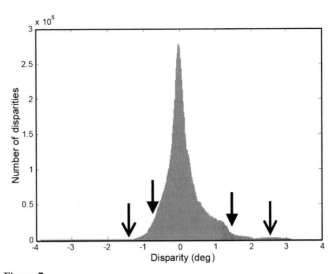

Figure 7

Distribution of binocular disparity for human observers when walking in forest environments. The solid arrows mark the upper and lower 2.5% quantiles; the open arrows mark the upper and lower 0.5% quantiles.

Thus, normal retinal image dynamics cannot be fully measured by a fixed camera or a camera attached to the head or body. Rather, one would like to move the image plane of the camera along the same trajectories typically undergone by the receptor array. This has been done for a flying insect by recording flight path and body orientation and then moving a camera along the same path with a robotic gantry (Boeddeker et al. 2005), but it has not been done for humans or for other mammals.

Nonetheless, systematic results have been obtained by analyzing video clips from movies and handheld cameras. For example, the symbols in **Figure 8** show the average spatiotemporal power spectra for natural image video reported by Dong & Atick (1995a). Contrast power decreases smoothly with increases in either spatial frequency or temporal frequency. The authors find the pattern of results can be fitted approximately (solid curves) by modeling the world as a collection of patches of spatial $1/f$ noise that are each undergoing translation at some random velocity. This is a plausible model for this image statistic because even nontranslational motion flow

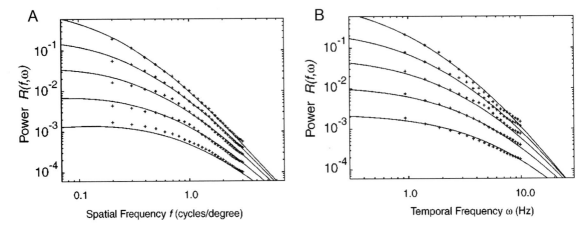

Figure 8

Spatiotemporal power spectra of natural images. (*A*) Spatial power spectra measured at different temporal frequencies (1.4, 2.3, 3.8, 6, and 10 Hz, from top to bottom). (*B*) Temporal spectra measured at different spatial frequencies (0.3, 0.5, 0.8, 1.3, and 2.1 cpd, from top to bottom). The solid curves show the expected spectra if the world is modeled as collection of patches of spatial $1/f$ noise that are each undergoing translation locally at some random velocity. (Adapted from Dong & Atick 1995a.)

patterns, such as those produced by moving through the three-dimensional environment, will most often produce approximately translational motion in a small neighborhood over a small time period.

These within-domain statistics are relevant for understanding motion coding. To measure across-domain statistics relevant for tasks such as heading estimation, it would also be necessary to measure the range at each pixel, as the image plane moves through space (Roth & Black 2005, Tversky & Geisler 2007).

Eye Movements and Foveation

The spatial resolution of the primate retina is high in the center of the fovea and falls off smoothly, but rapidly, as a function of retinal eccentricity. Information is collected from the environment by coupling this variable-resolution retina with a motor system that can rapidly direct the eyes in arbitrary directions, and indeed, most natural visual tasks involve selecting a series of locations to fixate. This implies that the relevant across-domain statistics for such tasks must take into account the foveated spatial resolution of the retina.

In other words, we need to measure the statistical relationship between environmental properties and properties of the retinal output and/or between properties of the retinal image and retinal output. In the terminology of **Figure 1*A*** this means measuring $p(\omega, \mathbf{z})$ and/or $p(\mathbf{s}, \mathbf{z})$, where $\mathbf{z}$ represents the specific properties of the retinal output that are of interest.

To make such measurements, Raj et al. (2005) modeled the spatial resolution (transfer function) of the human retina with a human contrast sensitivity function, which is also consistent with primate ganglion cell density and receptive field size as a function of eccentricity (Geisler & Perry 1998). They then considered the task of selecting fixations to maximally reduce total uncertainty about local contrast in natural images. The relevant across-domain statistics for this task are conditional probability distributions describing the probability of each possible local image contrast given a particular local contrast observed in the retinal output. **Figure 9** shows four of these conditional distributions. Note that the mode and variance of the distributions increase as function of both the retinal

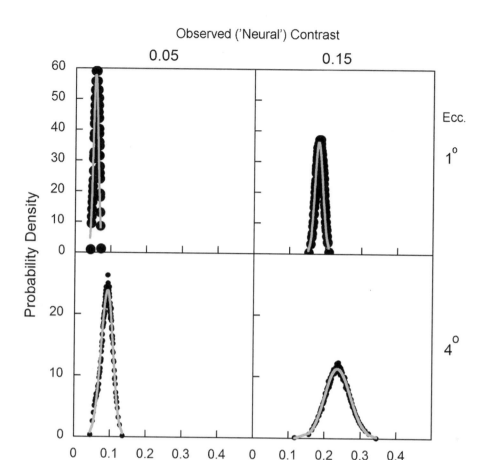

Figure 9

Example conditional probability distributions of local retinal image contrast given an eccentricity and an observed contrast at the output of a foveated retina, which was modeled after the primate retina. Such statistics are relevant for understanding how a rational visual system with a foveated retina should select fixation locations in order to accurately encode the image.

eccentricity and contrast observed in the retinal output. The increase in variance with eccentricity is intuitive because spatial resolution is decreasing with eccentricity. More surprising is that variance increases with observed contrast in the retinal output: the greater the response in the retinal output, the greater the uncertainty about the contrast in the retinal image. This finding may be related to the finding of Schwartz & Simoncelli (2001) that strong features tend to cluster in natural images (**Figure 5C**).

EXPLOITING NATURAL SCENE STATISTICS

The previous section summarized some of the measured natural scene statistics relevant for visual perception. This section considers how some of those statistical properties might be exploited by the human (or nonhuman primate) visual system. One aim is to convince the reader that measuring natural scene statistics can be useful for generating quantitative, testable hypotheses about perceptual mechanisms, can be useful for designing

LGN: lateral
geniculate nucleus

V1: primary visual
cortex

experiments and stimuli, and can provide useful insight into design features of the visual system. This section focuses on a few examples from the topics of coding and representation, grouping and segregation, identification, and estimation.

Coding and Representation of the Visual Image

Within-domain statistics are the easiest to measure and are of particular relevance to coding and representation of the retinal image (the proximal stimulus). Hence more studies of natural scene statistics have been devoted to this topic than to any other. A central hypothesis about coding and representation is that neural resources are limited (in number of neurons, spikes per neuron, synaptic contacts per neuron, etc.), thus pushing visual systems to efficiently use those resources (Attneave 1954, Barlow 1961; for reviews, see Barlow 2001, Simoncelli 2003, Simoncelli & Olshausen 2001).

One important resource limitation is that neurons have a limited dynamic range, presumably for fundamental metabolic and biophysical reasons. A plausible hypothesis is that sensory neurons match their limited ranges to the dynamic range of the natural signals that they encode. This ensures that the full response range is used while minimizing the likelihood of overdriving or underdriving the neuron. One way to match the dynamic range of responses with that of the input signals is via histogram equalization: Adjust the shape of the neuron's response function so that all response levels occur equally often under natural stimulus conditions. Laughlin (1981) compared the probability distribution of local luminance (Weber contrast) in natural images with the luminance response functions of the large monopolar neurons in the eye of the blowfly and found that the response functions are consistent with the histogram equalization hypothesis. Subsequently, the hypothesis has been tested for the contrast responses of neurons in lateral geniculate nucleus (LGN) and

primary visual cortex (V1) of cats and primates (e.g., Brady & Field 2000, Clatworthy et al. 2003, Tadmor & Tolhurst 2000). Although the results depend somewhat on the specific definition of contrast used (Frazor & Geisler 2006), there is evidence for a rough match between the contrast response functions of neurons in the early visual system and the distribution of contrasts encountered by the eye in natural environments.

For natural images, there is a low correlation between luminance and contrast at the same retinal location (see **Figure 3C,D**); furthermore, it can be shown that for normal saccadic inspection of natural images there is little correlation in luminance at the same retinal location across fixations (Frazor & Geisler 2006) or in contrast at the same retinal location across fixations (Frazor & Geisler 2006, Reinagel & Zador 1999). The implication is that neurons whose receptive fields are spatially localized will typically receive random samples of luminance and contrast from distributions like those in **Figure 3**, several times per second. This fact raises questions about the coding of luminance and contrast in the visual system. The most obvious is how neurons in the visual system respond to simultaneous, frequent, and statistically independent variations in local luminance and contrast over their natural ranges. Geisler et al. (2007) measured response functions of individual neurons in V1 and found them to be separable in luminance and contrast; i.e., response as a function of luminance and contrast is the product of a single function for luminance and a single function for contrast: $r(C, L) = r_C(C) r_L(L)$. Similarly, Mante et al. (2005) measure responses of individual neurons in the LGN and found responses to be consistent with separable luminance and contrast gain control mechanisms. Separable responses are expected under the efficient coding hypothesis, if local luminance and contrast are statistically independent.

The results of Geisler et al. (2007) point to a new hypothesis about how local luminance is coded in the cortex. The classic hypothesis is that most neurons in V1 respond poorly to luminance, and that luminance is coded by a specialized set of luminance-responding cells (for a review, see Peng & Van Essen 2005). Although most cortical neurons do not respond to uniform luminance stimulation, by parametrically varying luminance and contrast, Geisler et al. (2007) found that local luminance strongly modulates contrast response in the same separable fashion as other stimulus dimensions such as orientation, spatial frequency, and direction of motion. Thus, local luminance appears to be coded in the cortex in the same fashion as other well-known stimulus dimensions. Specialized luminance-responding cells may code uniform areas such as patches of sky. The studies of Mante et al. (2005) and Geisler et al. (2007) were motivated by measured natural scene statistics, and hence they demonstrate the potential value of natural scene statistics in guiding neurophysiology.

Another form of histogram equalization is to match the tuning characteristics across a population of neurons to the distribution of natural signals. For example, Cormack et al. (2005) found that the probability distribution of binocular disparities that occur during navigation through forest environments by humans (see **Figure 7**) corresponds reasonably well with the distribution of preferred disparities of single neurons in area MT of the macaque monkey (DeAngelis & Uka 2003). The results of Cormack et al. (2005) suggest that disparity tuning of neurons in monkey visual cortex conforms (in at least some ways) to an efficient coding of natural binocular images.

Another way to use neural resources efficiently is to remove redundant information across a population of neurons. A classic example concerns the coding of chromatic information with opponent color mechanisms. The spectral sensitivities of the L, M, and S cones overlap substantially (especially the L and M cones), creating highly correlated responses. Thus, if one observes a large response from, say, an L cone, it is very likely that a large re-

sponse will be observed from a spatially adjacent M cone. Rather than represent these two large responses with two high spike rates, it is more efficient (in terms of utilizing neural dynamic range) to transform the cone responses so that they are statistically independent. Interestingly, applying such a transformation predicts chromatic receptive fields that are similar to the color opponent mechanisms that have been estimated from psychophysical studies (Buchsbaum & Gottschalk 1983, Ruderman et al. 1998; see **Figure 4**). Similarly, spatial and temporal decorrelation (whitening) of the receptor responses to natural images predicts spatial (Atick & Redlich 1992, Srinivasan et al. 1982) and spatio-temporal receptive field shapes (Dong & Atick 1995b) similar to those found in the retina and LGN. Thus, in a number of ways, the design of the retina seems to be consistent with the efficient coding hypothesis.

The evidence is less clear with respect to coding and representation in V1. V1, like the retina and LGN, is laid out in a topographic map; however, for each ganglion cell or LGN relay neuron there are hundreds of V1 neurons, and thus V1 could potentially contain a large number of lossless (and efficient) representations of the retinal output, each tailored to a different task. Another hypothesis is that V1 provides a sparse, statistically independent representation of the retinal output. Field (1987) noted that (linear) receptive fields similar to those measured in V1 respond very infrequently to natural images and produce relatively large responses when they do respond. In other words, the probability distribution of responses to natural images is highly peaked at zero and has heavy tails (see **Figure 5B**). The implication is that a natural image will produce a pattern of strong responses in a rather sparse subset of cortical neurons. Olshausen & Field (1997) showed that simultaneously optimizing sparseness and statistical independence in the responses to natural images yields receptive fields similar to those of V1 neurons, suggesting that a sparse, statistical independent representation may be the goal of

V1 coding. However, this begs the question of the functional advantages of a sparse code. Possibly a sparse code provides a more meaningful (immediately interpretable) representation of the image than would highly compact codes, or possibly a sparse code facilitates subsequent processing (Olshausen 2003). Other possibilities are that a sparse code, which concentrates strong activity in a few neurons, might be less susceptible to neural noise arising in later cortical areas or might consume less metabolic energy than more distributed codes.

Interestingly, Schwartz & Simoncelli (2001) show that contrast normalization, an important nonlinear response property of V1 neurons (Albrecht & Geisler 1991, Carandini et al. 1997, Heeger 1991), should increase statistical independence by largely eliminating variance dependences such as the one illustrated in **Figure 5C**. However, contrast normalization has other potentially functional advantages that are not obviously related to efficient coding or natural image statistics, advantages such as contrast-invariant feature tuning (Albrecht & Geisler 1991, Heeger 1991) and enhanced feature identification performance (Geisler & Albrecht 1995). Perhaps all of these advantages have contributed to the evolution of contrast normalization mechanisms.

Other nonlinear response properties of retinal and cortical neurons have been inferred from measurements of their responses to natural images. In general, receptive fields estimated with linear systems analysis techniques (e.g., spike-triggered averaging) do not make accurate predictions of responses to natural images. There is not space here to review the literature directed at measuring and characterizing responses of neurons to natural stimuli; however, for recent reviews, see Reinagel (2001) and Wu et al. (2006), and for discussion, see Felson & Dan (2005) and Rust & Movshon (2005).

In addition to removing redundant information from the image, the retina removes nonredundant information by having a highly foveated retina with many fewer receptors than needed to fully code the image, and even fewer ganglion cells than receptors. The visual system compensates for the reduction in number of receptors and ganglion cells by having an eye movement system that can rapidly point the eye in desired directions. Thus, fully encoding the retinal image requires making a series of fixations. One hypothesis is that when the task is specifically to encode and remember an image, humans make eye movements that acquire as much image information as possible with the fewest number of fixations. Across-level statistics, such as those in **Figure 9**, can be combined with a Bayesian ideal observer analysis to determine the optimal procedure for selecting fixations in natural scenes. Raj et al. (2005) determined how to select successive fixations that maximally reduce the total uncertainty (entropy) about the contrast at every location in the image (see also Renninger et al. 2005). They then showed that the fixations selected by this algorithm are also near optimal for reducing total uncertainty about the detailed structure of the image. It remains to be seen how well human eye movements match the optimal eye movements, but it is likely that humans display (qualitatively) some of the optimal behaviors, which include moderate length saccades, avoidance of very-low-contrast regions of the image, a moderate percentage of fixations near high-contrast features, and avoidance of fixations near the boundaries of the image.

Grouping and Segregation

Efficiently encoding and representing the images falling on the retina may be the primary goal of initial visual processing, especially in the human retina, because the optic nerves create a severe information-transmission bottleneck and because the information transmitted up the optic nerve must support a very wide range of perceptual tasks. On the other hand, central processing is more likely to reflect specific tasks. The mechanisms of perceptual grouping and segregation fall into this category. Their purpose is undoubtedly to group together image features that arise from the same physical source in the environment (e.g., the same surface or object) and segregate features that arise from different physical sources. In other words, grouping and segregation mechanisms are designed to make inferences about the environment from image information collected by the eyes, and hence across-domain statistics are particularly relevant.

Geisler et al. (2001) used the across-domain statistics in **Figure 5D** (averaged over contrast polarity) as the basis for a one-parameter model of contour grouping in random contour-element displays. In the model, contour elements are grouped together when the likelihood ratio given by **Figure 5D** exceeds a criterion. This model, based directly on natural scene statistics, was able to predict human contour grouping performance under a wide range of stimulus conditions. More recently, Geisler & Perry (2006) used the statistics in **Figure 5D** to derive a parameter-free Bayesian ideal observer for a contour completion task where the observer reports whether or not contour segments passing under an occluding surface belong to the same physical contour (source). The results showed that humans parallel optimal performance in all conditions and perform only slightly below optimal. These two studies strongly suggest that the human visual system incorporates and properly exploits the across-domain statistics represented in **Figure 5D**.

Fine et al. (2003) took an interesting approach to measuring across-domain color statistics relevant for region grouping/segregation. They assumed that the probability distribution of color differences ($s = \Delta I, \Delta \alpha, \Delta \beta$) between adjacent pixels approximates the distribution of color differences between pixels from the same physical surface ($\omega = same$), and that the probability distribution of color differences between pixels taken from different natural images approximates the distribution of color differences for pixels from different physical surfaces ($\omega = different$). (See **Figure 4** for the definition of I, α, β.) Starting from these distributions, they derived a Bayesian decision rule for segmenting pixels into regions. They compared segmentations using this decision rule with those of human observers and found a fairly high correlation. Although it is likely that nearby pixels usually belong to the same physical surface, their implicit assumption that the distribution of color differences within a surface does not vary with distance between pixels probably doesn't hold. Analyzing many hand-segmented images like the one in **Figure 2**, Wilson et al. (2006) found that the color difference distributions within surfaces vary substantially with distance. Nonetheless, the two studies show there is much useful information for region grouping and segregation in the across-domain statistics of color differences.

Identification

Although the retina may have evolved primarily to efficiently encode the retinal images, as mentioned above, there can be no doubt (even for general-purpose organisms like humans, who perform a wide range of tasks) that the design of the eye is constrained by the family of tasks the organism performs. Further, there may be specific aspects of retinal processing that are tailored to specific sources in the environment. For example, measurements of across-domain statistics suggest that the positioning of the cone spectral sensitivities along the wavelength axis may be optimal for identifying sources of food. Lythgoe & Partridge (1989) showed that in mammals, the S and M cones (most mammals have only these two cone types) are generally well positioned to discriminate between different kinds of foliage. Similarly, Osorio & Vorobyev (1996), Regan et al. (2001), and Parraga et al. (2002) show that the L and M cones in trichromatic primates are often well positioned for identifying fruit in foliage.

Identification of behaviorally relevant sources in the environment, such as specific materials, surfaces, and objects, strongly depends on grouping and segregation mechanisms. Conversely, grouping and segregation undoubtedly depend on certain top-down and bottom-up identification mechanisms. Thus, grouping, segregation, and identification are best thought of as part of an integrated system for interpreting retinal images. A key goal of this integrated system is identifying the source of an image contour. In natural images, a contour could be the result of a surface boundary, a surface marking (i.e., a surface reflectance change), a cast shadow, or a shading boundary due to a change in surface orientation relative to the illumination. These are very different sources and their proper identification is crucial for arriving at the correct physical interpretation of the image. Measurements of across-level statistics could give us principled hypotheses for the brain mechanisms that identify contour sources given a retinal image.

To make a start at these measurements, Ing & Geisler (2006) analyzed a large set of hand-segmented, close-up foliage images like the one in **Figure 2**. They chose this class of images because they are relatively easy to segment and because foliage environments are the natural environment of the macaque monkey (the primary animal model for human vision). In addition to hand-segmenting leaves and branches, they also segmented shadow boundaries and surface markings. Using this segmentation data as the ground truth measurements of the sources, they measured the joint probability distribution of intensity and contrast differences (in I, α, β space; see **Figure 4**) across contours, given that the source contour was a surface boundary, a shadow boundary, or a surface-marking boundary. Finally, by combining these measured probability distributions with an ideal classifier, they demonstrated that for moderate length contours it is possible to discriminate between any two sources with 85% to 90% accuracy. This is a promising initial result because it shows that simple local image properties alone provide useful information

for contour source identification. Further, the simple decision rules derived from the measured distributions provide concrete hypotheses for source identification mechanisms in the visual system, although global and top-down factors are also likely to contribute.

Estimation

Many natural perceptual tasks involve estimation of continuous environmental properties such as the reflectance spectrum, illumination spectrum, surface orientation, distance, or velocity, at one or more locations in the visual field. Across-level statistics are providing new hypotheses and valuable insights into such estimation tasks.

Under the assumption that retinal images can be approximated as the combination of a randomly selected natural illuminant and a collection of surfaces, each with a randomly selected natural reflectance spectrum, Maloney & Wandell (1986) showed it is possible to estimate the illuminant and reflectance spectra of surfaces with remarkably few classes of receptor (approximately four). (Note that estimating the reflectance function is equivalent to solving the color constancy problem.) This result may help explain why most organisms have relatively few classes of receptor. Subsequently, Brainard & Freeman (1997) described how to optimally estimate reflectance and illumination within the Bayesian ideal observer framework. Although these and similar studies provide valuable insight into the problem of color constancy, they assume uniform illumination and matt surface patches, neither of which occur very frequently in natural scenes (e.g., see Boyaci et al. 2006, Dror et al. 2004, Fleming et al. 2003, Khang et al. 2006). Thus, reflectance estimation given real illumination patterns and surface properties requires more complex perceptual mechanisms than the ones suggested by earlier work. However, real illumination and surface complexity may also provide additional information the visual system can use. For example, Sharan et al. (2005) and Motoyoshi et al. (2007) show that humans can judge (with reasonable accuracy) the reflectance of natural materials from grayscale images that have been equated for mean luminance. Statistical analysis of the images shows that the shape of the pixel luminance distribution varies systematically with the reflectance of the material and that humans are able to exploit these statistics (and possibly other image statistics) when judging reflectance.

When retinal image information is poor, a rational visual system will put greater reliance on the prior probability distributions of different possible environmental states and bias its estimates accordingly (e.g., see Knill & Richards 1996, Torralba 2003). Weiss et al. (2002) show this principle could explain various motion illusions, under the assumption that the prior probability for local speed decreases monotonically with speed. This general assumption is likely to be true, but the specific predictions depend upon the shape of the prior probability distribution, which they did not measure (however, see Stocker & Simoncelli 2006). Yang & Purves (2003) applied a similar analysis in an attempt to predict apparent distance illusions. Using statistical measurements obtained with a range finder, they were able to qualitatively account for several distance-estimation biases that have been reported in the literature.

To circumvent some of the difficulties associated with measuring across-domain motion statistics, Tversky & Geisler (2007) combined graphics simulations with measured natural scene statistics. Specifically, they created model environments based on the measured range statistics of Huang et al. (2000; see **Figure 6B**) and the local $1/f$ statistics of natural image patches (**Figure 5A**). They then simulated various kinds of self motion through these environments and measured the scene statistics produced by these motions. These statistics were used to determine optimal integration area (receptive field size) of local motion sensors for heading estimation. The primary finding is that integration area should increase with the speed being estimated. This

hypothesis should be testable in physiological and psychophysical studies. Similar statistical measurements could potentially be used to estimate the approximate prior probability distribution of ground truth velocities needed for analyses like that of Weiss et al. (2002).

CONCLUSION

In the traditional approach to perception research, the scientist (*a*) thinks informally or casually about natural tasks and environments, (*b*) generates or modifies hypotheses about perceptual or neural mechanisms, (*c*) conducts controlled behavioral or physiological experiments to test those hypotheses and then cycles back to (*b*). Although there is nothing wrong with this approach (which has produced a vast amount of knowledge), a potential weakness is that hypotheses and experimental paradigms tend to be formulated from informal thinking about natural environments and stimuli rather than from principled physical measurements. By directly measuring statistical regularities of natural environments and stimuli it may be possible to derive novel and plausible hypotheses for perceptual mechanisms and to design experimental paradigms that better reflect the important characteristics of natural stimuli. Indeed, the studies described here demonstrate the value of measuring and characterizing natural scene statistics. Measurements of within-domain statistics have revealed much about the structure and variability of natural images. This has made it possible to test various forms of the efficient coding hypothesis and has led to novel models and experiments that would not have been conceived otherwise. Measurements of across-domain statistics, especially when combined with Bayesian ideal observer theory, are proving to be particularly useful in generating new insights and testable (parameter-free or nearly parameter-free) models for performance in tasks such as fixation selection, contour grouping, contour classification, motion estimation, and reflectance estimation.

Measuring and characterizing the statistical properties of natural environments and stimuli are difficult tasks, but the potential for payoff appears to be great.

ACKNOWLEDGMENTS

The author's work is supported by NIH grants EY11747 and EY02688. E. Adelson, R. Blake, R. Diehl, B. Olshausen, and E. Simoncelli provided useful comments and discussion.

LITERATURE CITED

Albrecht DG, Geisler WS. 1991. Motion selectivity and the contrast-response function of simple cells in the visual cortex. *Vis. Neurosci.* 7:531–46

Atick JJ, Redlich AN. 1992. What does the retina know about natural scenes? *Neural Comput.* 4:196–210

Attneave F. 1954. Some informational aspects of visual perception. *Psychol. Rev.* 61:183–93

Balboa RM, Tyler CW, Grzywacz NM. 2001. Occlusions contribute to scaling in natural images. *Vision Res.* 41:955–64

Barlow HB. 1957. Increment thresholds at low intensities considered as signal/noise discriminations. *J. Physiol. Lond.* 136:469–88

Barlow HB. 1961. Possible principles underlying the transformations of sensory messages. In *Sensory Communication*, ed. WA Rosenblith, pp. 217–34. Cambridge, MA: MIT Press

Barlow HB. 2001. Redundancy reduction revisited. *Network* 12:241–53

Barlow HB, Levick WR. 1969. Three factors limiting the reliable detection of light by retinal ganglion cells of the cat. *J. Physiol.* 200:1–24

Bell AJ, Sejnowski TJ. 1997. The "independent components" of natural scenes are edge filters. *Vision Res.* 37:3327–38

Boeddeker N, Lindemann JP, Egelhaaf M, Zeil J. 2005. Responses of blowfly motion-sensitive neurons to reconstructed optic flow along outdoor flight paths. *J. Comp. Physiol. A* 191:1143–55

Boyaci H, Doerchner K, Snyder JL, Maloney LT. 2006. Surface color perception in three-dimensional scenes. *Vis. Neurosci.* 23:311–21

Brady N, Field DJ. 2000. Local contrast in natural images: normalization and coding efficiency. *Perception* 29:1041–55

Brainard DH, Freeman WT. 1997. Bayesian color constancy. *J. Opt. Soc. Am. A* 14:1393–411

Brunswik E. 1956. *Perception and the Representative Design of Psychological Experiments.* Berkeley: Univ. Calif. Press

Brunswik E, Kamiya J. 1953. Ecological cue-validity of "proximity" and other Gestalt factors. *Am. J. Psychol.* 66:20–32

Buchsbaum G, Gottschalk A. 1983. Trichromacy, opponent colours coding and optimum colour information transmission in the retina. *Proc. R. Soc. Lond. B Biol. Sci.* 220:89–113

Burton GJ, Moorehead IR. 1987. Color and spatial structure in natural scenes. *Appl. Opt.* 26:157–70

Carandini M, Heeger DJ, Movshon JA. 1997. Linearity and normalization in simple cells of the macaque primary visual cortex. *J. Neurosci.* 17:8621–44

Clatworthy PL, Chirimuuta M, Lauritzen JS, Tolhurst DJ. 2003. Coding of the contrasts in natural images by populations of neurons in primary visual cortex (V1). *Vis. Res.* 43:1983–2001

Cormack LK, Liu Y, Bovik AC. 2005. Disparity statistics in the natural environment. *J. Vis.* 5(8):604 (Abstr.)

Cronly-Dillon JR, Gregory RL, eds. 1991. *Evolution of the Eye and Visual System, Vol. 2.* Boca Raton, FL: CRC Press

DeAngelis GC, Uka T. 2003. Coding of horizontal disparity and velocity by MT neurons in the alert macaque. *J. Neurophysiol.* 89:1094–111

Dixon RE. 1978. Spectral distribution of Australian daylight. *J. Opt. Soc. Am.* 68:437–50

Dong DW, Atick JJ. 1995a. Statistics of natural time-varying images. *Netw. Comput. Neural Syst.* 6:345–58

Dong DW, Atick JJ. 1995b. Temporal decorrelation: a theory of lagged and nonlagged responses in the lateral geniculate nucleus. *Netw. Comput. Neural Syst.* 6:159–78

Dror RO, Willsky AS, Adelson EH. 2004. Statistical characterization of real-world illumination. *J. Vis.* 4:821–37

D'Zmura M, Iverson G. 1993. Color constancy. I. Basic theory of two-stage linear recovery of spectral descriptions for lights and surfaces. *J. Opt. Soc. Am. A* 10:2148–65

Elder JH, Goldberg RM. 1998. *The statistics of natural image contours.* Presented at 1998 IEEE Comput. Soc. Workshop Percept. Org. Comput. Vis., Santa Barbara, Calif.

Elder JH, Goldberg RM. 2002. Ecological statistics for the Gestalt laws of perceptual organization of contours. *J. Vis.* 2:324–53

Felson G, Dan Y. 2005. A natural approach to studying vision. *Nat. Neurosci.* 8:1643–46

Field DJ. 1987. Relations between the statistics of natural images and the response properties of cortical cells. *J. Opt. Soc. Am. A* 4:2379–94

Field DJ. 1994. What is the goal of sensory coding? *Neural Comput.* 6:559–601

Fine I, MacLeod DIA, Boynton GM. 2003. Surface segmentation based on the luminance and color statistics of natural scenes. *J. Opt. Soc. Am. A* 20:1283–91

Fleming RW, Dror RO, Adelson EH. 2003. Real-world illumination and the perception of surface reflectance properties. *J. Vis.* 3:347–68

Frazor RA, Geisler WS. 2006. Local luminance and contrast in natural images. *Vis. Res.* 46:1585–98

Geisler WS, Albrecht DG. 1995. Bayesian analysis of identification performance in monkey visual cortex: nonlinear mechanisms and stimulus certainty. *Vis. Res.* 35:2723–30

Geisler WS, Albrecht DG, Crane AM. 2007. Responses of neurons in primary visual cortex to transient changes in local contrast and luminance. *J. Neurosci.* 27:5063–67

Geisler WS, Diehl RL. 2003. A Bayesian approach to the evolution of perceptual and cognitive systems. *Cogn. Sci.* 27:379–402

Geisler WS, Perry JS. 1998. A real-time foveated multi-resolution system for low-bandwidth video communication. In *Human Vision and Electronic Imaging, SPIE Proceedings*, ed. B Rogowitz, T Pappas, 3299:294–305. Bellingham, WA: SPIE

Geisler WS, Perry JS. 2006. Efficiency of contour grouping across occlusions in natural images. *J. Vis.* 6:336 (Abstr.)

Geisler WS, Perry JS, Super BJ, Gallogly DP. 2001. Edge co-occurrence in natural images predicts contour grouping performance. *Vis. Res.* 41:711–24

Gibson JJ. 1966. *The Senses Considered as Perceptual Systems.* Boston, MA: Houghton-Mifflin

Gibson JJ. 1979. *The Ecological Approach to Visual Perception.* Boston, MA: Houghton-Mifflin

Green DM, Swets JA. 1966. *Signal Detection Theory and Psychophysics.* New York: Wiley

Hecht S, Shlaer S, Pirenne MH. 1942. Energy, quanta, and vision. *J. Gen. Physiol.* 25:819–40

Heeger DJ. 1991. Computational model of cat striate physiology. In *Computational Models of Visual Perception*, ed. MS Landy, AJ Movshon, pp. 119–33. Cambridge, MA: MIT Press

Huang J, Lee AB, Mumford D. 2000. Statistics of range images. *Proc. IEEE Conf. Comput. Vis. Pattern Recognit.*, 1: 324–31. Piscataway, NJ: IEEE

Hyvarinen A, Hoyer P. 2000. Emergence of topography and complex cell properties from natural images using extensions of ICA. In *Advances in Neural Information Processing Systems*, ed. SA Solla, TK Leen, K-R Muller, pp. 827–33. Cambridge, MA: MIT Press

Ing AD, Geisler WS. 2006. Ribbon analysis of contours in natural images. *J. Vis.* 6:103 (Abstr.)

Judd DB, MacAdam DL, Wyszecki GW. 1964. Spectral distribution of typical daylight as a function of correlated color temperature. *J. Opt. Soc. Am.* 54:1031–40

Kersten D, Mamassian P, Yuille AL. 2004. Object perception as Bayesian inference. *Annu. Rev. Psychol.* 55:271–304

Khang BG, Koenderink JJ, Kappers AML. 2006. Perception of illumination direction in images of 3-D convex objects: influence of surface materials and light fields. *Perception* 35:625–45

Knill DC, Richards W, eds. 1996. *Perception as Bayesian Inference*. Cambridge, MA: Cambridge Univ. Press

Laughlin SB. 1981. A simple coding procedure enhances a neuron's information capacity. *Z. Naturforsch. C* 36:910–12

Lee AB, Mumford D, Huang J. 2001. Occlusion models for natural images: a statistical study of a scale-invariant dead leaves model. *Int. J. Comput. Vis.* 41:35–59

Lee AB, Pedersen KS, Mumford D. 2003. Nonlinear statistics of high-contrast patches in natural images. *Int. J. Comput. Vis.* 54:83–103

Lewicki MS. 2002. Efficient coding of natural sounds. *Nat. Neurosci.* 5:356–63

Lythgoe JN. 1979. *The Ecology of Vision*. New York: Oxford Univ. Press

Lythgoe JN, Partridge JC. 1989. Visual pigments and the acquisition of visual information. *J. Exp. Biol.* 146:1–20

Maloney LT. 1986. Evaluation of linear models of surface spectral reflectance with small numbers of parameters. *J. Opt. Soc. Am. A* 3:1673–83

Maloney LT, Wandell BA. 1986. Color constancy: a method for recovering surface spectral reflectance. *J. Opt. Soc. Am. A* 3:29–33

Mante V, Bronin V, Frazor RA, Geisler WS, Carandini M. 2005. Independence of gain control mechanisms in early visual system matches the statistics of natural images. *Nat. Neurosci.* 8:1690–97

Martin DR, Fowlkes CC, Malik J. 2004. Learning to detect natural image boundaries using local brightness, color and texture cues. *IEEE Trans. Pattern Anal. Mach. Intell.* 26:530–49

Motoyoshi I, Nishida1 S, Sharan L, Adelson EH. 2007. Image statistics and the perception of surface qualities. *Nature* 447:206–9

Olshausen BA. 2003. Principles of image representation in visual cortex. In *The Visual Neurosciences*, ed. LM Chalupa, JS Werner, pp. 1603–15. Cambridge, MA: MIT Press

Olshausen BA, Field DJ. 1997. Sparse coding with an overcomplete basis set: a strategy by V1? *Vis. Res.* 37:3311–25

Osorio D, Vorobyev M. 1996. Colour vision as an adaptation to frugivory in primates. *Proc. R. Soc. Lond. B Biol. Sci.* 263:593–99

Parraga CA, Troscianko T, Tolhurst DJ. 2002. Spatiochromatic properties of natural images and human vision. *Curr. Biol.* 12:483–87

Peng X, Van Essen DC. 2005. Peaked encoding of relative luminance in macaque areas V1 and V2. *J. Neurophysiol.* 93:1620–32

Potetz B, Lee TS. 2003. Statistical correlations between two-dimensional images and three-dimensional structures in natural scenes. *J. Opt. Soc. Am. A* 20:1292–303

Raj R, Geisler WS, Frazor RA, Bovik AC. 2005. Contrast statistics for foveated visual systems: fixation selection by minimizing contrast entropy. *J. Opt. Soc. Am. A* 22:2039–49

Regan BC, Julliot C, Simmen B, Vienot F, Charles-Dominique P, Mollon JD. 2001. Fruits, foliage and the evolution of primate colour vision. *Philos. Tran. R. Soc. Lond. B* 356:229–83

Reinagel P. 2001. How do visual neurons respond in the real world? *Curr. Opin. Neurobiol.* 11:437–42

Reinagel P, Zador AM. 1999. Natural scene statistics at the centre of gaze. *Comput. Neural Syst.* 10:1–10

Renninger LW, Coughlan J, Verghese P, Malik J. 2005. An information maximization model of eye movements. In *Advances in Neural Information Processing Systems 17*, ed. LK Saul, Y Weiss, L Bottou, pp. 1121–28. Boston, MA: MIT Press

Roth S, Black MJ. 2005. On the spatial statistics of optical flow. *Proc. 10th IEEE Int. Conf. Comput. Vis.* 1:42–49. Boston, MA: IEEE

Ruderman DL. 1994. The statistics of natural images. *Comput. Neural Syst.* 5:517–48

Ruderman DL. 1997. Origins of scaling in natural images. *Vis. Res.* 37:3385–98

Ruderman DL. 2002. Letter to the editor. *Vis. Res.* 42:2799–801

Ruderman DL, Bialek W. 1994. Statistics of natural images: scaling in the woods. *Phys. Rev. Lett.* 73:814–17

Ruderman DL, Cronin TW, Chiao C. 1998. Statistics of cone responses to natural images: implications for visual coding. *J. Opt. Soc. Am. A* 15:2036–45

Rust NC, Movshon AJ. 2005. In praise of artifice. *Nature Neurosci.* 8:1647–50

Schwartz O, Simoncelli EP. 2001. Natural signal statistics and sensory gain control. *Nat. Neurosci.* 4:8 19–25

Sharan L, Li Y, Adelson EH. 2005. Image statistics and reflectance estimation. *J. Vis.* 5(8):375 (Abstr.)

Sigman M, Cecchi GA, Gilbert CD, Magnasco MO. 2001. On a common circle: natural scenes and Gestalt rules. *Proc. Natl. Acad. Sci. USA* 98:1935–40

Simoncelli EP. 2003. Vision and the statistics of the visual environment. *Curr. Opin. Neurobiol.* 13:144–49

Simoncelli EP, Olshausen BA. 2001. Natural image statistics and neural representation. *Annu. Rev. Neurosci.* 24:1193–216

Srinivasan MV, Laughlin SB, Dubs A. 1982. Predictive coding: a fresh view of inhibition in the retina. *J. R. Soc. London Ser. B* 216:427–59

Stocker A, Simoncelli EP. 2006. Noise characteristics and prior expectations in human visual speed perception. *Nat. Neurosci.* 9:578–85

Tadmor Y, Tolhurst DJ. 2000. Calculating the contrasts that retinal ganglion cells and LGN neurones encounter in natural scenes. *Vis. Res.* 40:3145–57

Torralba A. 2003. Modeling global scene factors in attention. *J. Opt. Soc. Am. A* 20:1407–18

Tversky T, Geisler WS. 2007. Optimal sensor design for estimating local velocity in natural environments. In *Human Vision and Electronic Imaging, SPIE Proceedings*, ed. B Rogowitz, T Pappas, S Daly, Vol. 6492. Bellingham, WA: SPIE. In press

van Hateren JH. 1992. A theory of maximizing sensory information. *Biol. Cybern.* 68:23–29

van Hateren JH, van der Schaaf A. 1998. Independent component filters of natural images compared with simple cells in primary visual cortex. *Proc. R. Soc. London B Biol. Sci.* 265:359–66

Walls GL. 1942. *The Vertebrate Eye and Its Adaptive Radiation*. Bloomfield Hills, Mich.: Cranbrook Inst. Sci.

Weiss Y, Simoncelli E, Adelson EH. 2002. Motion illusions as optimal percepts. *Nat. Neurosci.* 5:598–604

Wilson JA, Ing AD, Geisler WS. 2006. Chromatic differences within surfaces and across surface boundaries. *J. Vis.* 6(6):559 (Abstr.)

Wu MC-K, David SV, Gallant JL. 2006. Complete functional characterization of sensory neurons by system identification. *Annu. Rev. Neurosci.* 29:477–505

Yang Z, Purves D. 2003. A statistical explanation of visual space. *Nat. Neurosci.* 6:632–40

The Mind and Brain of Short-Term Memory

John Jonides, Richard L. Lewis, Derek Evan Nee,
Cindy A. Lustig, Marc G. Berman,
and Katherine Sledge Moore

Department of Psychology, University of Michigan, Ann Arbor, Michigan 48109;
email: jjonides@umich.edu

Annu. Rev. Psychol. 2008. 59:193–224

First published online as a Review in Advance on
September 12, 2007

The *Annual Review of Psychology* is online at
http://psych.annualreviews.org

This article's doi:
10.1146/annurev.psych.59.103006.093615

Key Words

working memory, attention, encoding, storage, retrieval

Abstract

The past 10 years have brought near-revolutionary changes in psychological theories about short-term memory, with similarly great advances in the neurosciences. Here, we critically examine the major psychological theories (the "mind") of short-term memory and how they relate to evidence about underlying brain mechanisms. We focus on three features that must be addressed by any satisfactory theory of short-term memory. First, we examine the evidence for the architecture of short-term memory, with special attention to questions of capacity and how—or whether—short-term memory can be separated from long-term memory. Second, we ask how the components of that architecture enact processes of encoding, maintenance, and retrieval. Third, we describe the debate over the reason about forgetting from short-term memory, whether interference or decay is the cause. We close with a conceptual model tracing the representation of a single item through a short-term memory task, describing the biological mechanisms that might support psychological processes on a moment-by-moment basis as an item is encoded, maintained over a delay with some forgetting, and ultimately retrieved.

Contents

INTRODUCTION

Mentally add 324 and 468.

Follow the instructions to complete any form for your federal income taxes.

Read and comprehend this sentence.

What are the features of the memory system that allows us to complete these and other complex tasks? Consider the opening example. First, you must create a temporary representation in memory for the two numbers. This representation needs to survive for several seconds to complete the task. You must then allocate your attention to different portions of the representation so that you can apply the rules of arithmetic required by the task. By one strategy, you need to focus attention on the "tens" digits ("2" and "6") and mitigate interference from the other digits (e.g., "3" and "4") and from partial results of previous operations (e.g., the "12" that results from

adding "4" and "8"). While attending to local portions of the problem, you must also keep accessible the parts of the problem that are not in the current focus of attention (e.g., that you now have the units digit "2" as a portion of the final answer). These tasks implicate a short-term memory (STM). In fact, there is hardly a task that can be completed without the involvement of STM, making it a critical component of cognition.

Our review relates the psychological phenomena of STM to their underlying neural mechanisms. The review is motivated by three questions that any adequate account of STM must address:

1. What is its structure?

A proper theory must describe an architecture for short-term storage. Candidate components of this architecture include storage buffers, a moving and varying focus of attention, or traces with differing levels of activation. In all cases, it is essential to provide a mechanism that allows a representation to exist beyond the sensory stimulation that caused it or the process that retrieved the representation from long-term memory (LTM). This architecture should be clear about its psychological constructs. Furthermore, being clear about the neural mechanisms that implement those constructs will aid in development of psychological theory, as we illustrate below.

2. What processes operate on the stored information?

A proper theory must articulate the processes that create and operate on representations. Candidate processes include encoding and maintenance operations, rehearsal, shifts of attention from one part of the representation to another, and retrieval mechanisms. Some of these processes are often classified as executive functions.

3. What causes forgetting?

A complete theory of STM must account for the facts of forgetting. Traditionally, the two leading contending accounts of forgetting have relied on the concepts of decay and interference. We review the behavioral and neurophysiological evidence that has traditionally been brought to the table to distinguish decay and interference accounts, and we suggest a possible mechanism for short-term forgetting.

Most models of STM fall between two extremes: Multistore models view STM and LTM as architecturally separate systems that rely on distinct representations. By contrast, according to unitary-store models, STM and LTM rely largely on the same representations, but differ by (a) the level of activation of these representations and (b) some of the processes that normally act upon them. We focus on the distinctions drawn by these theories as we examine the evidence concerning the three questions that motivate our review. In this discussion, we assume that a representation in memory consists of a bundle of features that define a memorandum, including the context in which that memorandum was encountered.

WHAT IS THE STRUCTURE OF SHORT-TERM MEMORY?

Multistore Models that Differentiate Short- and Long-Term Memory

In his *Principles of Psychology*, William James (1890) articulated the view that short-term ("primary") memory is qualitatively different from long-term ("secondary") memory (see also Hebb 1949). The most influential successor to this view is the model of STM developed by Baddeley and colleagues (e.g., Baddeley 1986, 1992; Baddeley & Hitch 1974; Repov & Baddeley 2006). For the years 1980 to 2006, of the 16,154 papers that cited "working memory" in their titles or abstracts, fully 7339 included citations to Alan Baddeley.

According to Baddeley's model, there are separate buffers for different forms of information. These buffers, in turn, are separate from LTM. A verbal buffer, the phonological loop, is assumed to hold information that can be rehearsed verbally (e.g., letters, digits). A visuospatial sketchpad is assumed to maintain visual information and can be further fractionated into visual/object and spatial stores (Repov & Baddeley 2006, Smith et al. 1995). An episodic buffer that draws on the other buffers and LTM has been added to account for the retention of multimodal information (Baddeley 2000). In addition to the storage buffers described above, a central executive is proposed to organize the interplay between the various buffers and LTM and is implicated in controlled processing.

In short, the multistore model includes several distinctions: (a) STM is distinct from LTM, (b) STM can be stratified into different informational buffers based on information type, and (c) storage and executive processes are distinguishable. Evidence in support of these claims has relied on behavioral interference studies, neuropsychological studies, and neuroimaging data.

Evidence for the distinction between short- and long-term memory. Studies of brain-injured patients who show a deficit in STM but not LTM or vice versa lead to the implication that STM and LTM are separate systems.[1] Patients with parietal and temporal lobe damage show impaired short-term phonological capabilities but intact LTM (Shallice & Warrington 1970, Vallar & Papagno 2002). Conversely, it is often claimed that patients with medial temporal lobe (MTL) damage demonstrate impaired LTM but preserved STM (e.g., Baddeley & Warrington 1970, Scoville & Milner 1957; we reinterpret these effects below).

Neuroimaging data from healthy subjects have yielded mixed results, however. A meta-analysis comparing regions activated during verbal LTM and STM tasks indicated a great deal of overlap in neural activation for the tasks in the frontal and parietal lobes (Cabeza et al. 2002, Cabeza & Nyberg 2000). Three studies that directly compared LTM and STM in the same subjects did reveal some regions selective for each memory system (Braver et al. 2001, Cabeza et al. 2002, Talmi et al. 2005). Yet, of these studies, only one found that the MTL was uniquely activated for LTM (Talmi et al. 2005). What might account for the discrepancy between the neuropsychological and neuroimaging data?

One possibility is that neuroimaging tasks of STM often use longer retention intervals than those employed for neuropsychological tasks, making the STM tasks more similar to LTM tasks. In fact, several studies have shown that the MTL is important when retention intervals are longer than a few seconds (Buffalo et al. 1998, Cabeza et al. 2002, Holdstock et al. 1995, Owen et al. 1995). Of the studies that compared STM and LTM in the same subjects, only Talmi et al. (2005) used an STM retention interval shorter than five seconds. This study did find, in fact, that the MTL was uniquely recruited at longer retention intervals, providing support for the earlier neuropsychological work dissociating long- and short-term memory. As we elaborate below, however, there are other possible interpretations, especially with regard to the MTL's role in memory.

Evidence for separate buffers in short-term memory. The idea that STM can be parceled into information-specific buffers first received support from a series of studies of selective interference (e.g., Brooks 1968, den Heyer & Barrett 1971). These studies relied on the logic that if two tasks use the same processing mechanisms, they should show interfering effects on one another if performed concurrently. This work showed a double dissociation: Verbal tasks interfered with verbal STM but not visual STM, and visual tasks interfered with visual STM but not verbal STM, lending support to the idea of separable memory systems (for reviews, see Baddeley 1986 and Baddeley & Hitch 1974).

The advent of neuroimaging has allowed researchers to investigate the neural correlates of the reputed separability of STM buffers. Verbal STM has been shown to rely primarily on left inferior frontal and left parietal cortices, spatial STM on right posterior dorsal frontal and right parietal cortices, and object/visual STM on left inferior frontal, left parietal, and left inferior temporal cortices (e.g., Awh et al. 1996, Jonides et al. 1993, Smith & Jonides 1997; see review by Wager & Smith 2003). Verbal STM shows a marked left hemisphere preference, whereas spatial and object STM can be distinguished mainly by a dorsal versus ventral separation in posterior cortices (consistent with Ungerleider & Haxby 1994; see Baddeley 2003 for an account of the function of these regions in the service of STM).

The more recently postulated episodic buffer arose from the need to account for interactions between STM buffers and LTM. For example, the number of words recalled in an STM experiment can be greatly increased if the words form a sentence (Baddeley et al.

---

[1]Another line of neural evidence about the separability of short- and long-term memory comes from electrophysiological studies of animals engaged in short-term memory tasks. We review this evidence and its interpretation in The Architecture of Unitary-Store Models section.

1987). This "chunking" together of words to increase short-term capacity relies on additional information from LTM that can be used to integrate the words (Baddeley 2000). Thus, there must be some representational space that allows for the integration of information stored in the phonological loop and LTM. This ability to integrate information from STM and LTM is relatively preserved even when one of these memory systems is damaged (Baddeley & Wilson 2002, Baddeley et al. 1987). These data provide support for an episodic buffer that is separable from other short-term buffers and from LTM (Baddeley 2000, Baddeley & Wilson 2002). Although neural evidence about the possible localization of this buffer is thin, there is some suggestion that dorsolateral prefrontal cortex plays a role (Prabhakaran et al. 2000, Zhang et al. 2004).

Evidence for separate storage and executive processes. Baddeley's multistore model assumes that a collection of processes act upon the information stored in the various buffers. Jointly termed the "central executive," these processes are assumed to be separate from the storage buffers and have been associated with the frontal lobes.

Both lesion and neuroimaging data support the distinction between storage and executive processes. For example, patients with frontal damage have intact STM under conditions of low distraction (D'Esposito & Postle 1999, 2000; Malmo 1942). However, when distraction is inserted during a delay interval, thereby requiring the need for executive processes to overcome interference, patients with frontal damage show significant memory deficits (D'Esposito & Postle 1999, 2000). By contrast, patients with left temporo-parietal damage show deficits in phonological storage, regardless of the effects of interference (Vallar & Baddeley 1984, Vallar & Papagno 2002). Consistent with these patterns, a meta-analysis of 60 functional neuroimaging studies indicated that increased demand for executive processing recruits dorsolateral frontal cortex and posterior parietal cortex (Wager & Smith 2003). By contrast, storage processes recruit predominately posterior areas in primary and secondary association cortex. These results corroborate the evidence from lesion studies and support the distinction between storage and executive processing.

Unitary-Store Models that Combine Short-Term and Long-Term Memory

The multistore models reviewed above combine assumptions about the distinction between short-term and long-term systems, the decomposition of short-term memory into information-specific buffers, and the separation of systems of storage from executive functions. We now consider unitary models that reject the first assumption concerning distinct systems.

Contesting the idea of separate long-term and short-term systems. The key data supporting separable short-term and long-term systems come from neuropsychology. To review, the critical contrast is between patients who show severely impaired LTM with apparently normal STM (e.g., Cave & Squire 1992, Scoville & Milner 1957) and those who show impaired STM with apparently normal LTM (e.g., Shallice & Warrington 1970). However, questions have been raised about whether these neuropsychological studies do, in fact, support the claim that STM and LTM are separable. A central question is the role of the medial temporal lobe. It is well established that the MTL is critical for long-term declarative memory formation and retrieval (Gabrieli et al. 1997, Squire 1992). However, is the MTL also engaged by STM tasks? Much research with amnesic patients showing preserved STM would suggest not, but Ranganath & Blumenfeld (2005) have summarized evidence showing that MTL is engaged in short-term tasks (see also Ranganath & D'Esposito 2005 and Nichols et al. 2006).

In particular, there is growing evidence that a critical function of the MTL is to establish representations that involve novel relations. These relations may be among features or items, or between items and their context. By this view, episodic memory is a special case of such relations (e.g., relating a list of words to the experimental context in which the list was recently presented), and the special role of the MTL concerns its binding capabilities, not the timescale on which it operates. STM that is apparently preserved in amnesic patients may thus reflect a preserved ability to maintain and retrieve information that does not require novel relations or binding, in keeping with their preserved retrieval of remote memories consolidated before the amnesia-inducing lesion.

If this view is correct, then amnesic patients should show deficits in situations that require STM for novel relations, which they do (Hannula et al. 2005, Olson et al. 2006b). They also show STM deficits for novel materials (e.g., Buffalo et al. 1998, Holdstock et al. 1995, Olson et al. 1995, 2006a). As mentioned above, electrophysiological and neuroimaging studies support the claim that the MTL is active in support of short-term memories (e.g., Miyashita & Chang 1968, Ranganath & D'Esposito 2001). Taken together, the MTL appears to operate in both STM and LTM to create novel representations, including novel bindings of items to context.

Additional evidence for the STM-LTM distinction comes from patients with perisylvian cortical lesions who are often claimed to have selective deficits in STM (e.g., Hanley et al. 1991, Warrington & Shallice 1969). However, these deficits may be substantially perceptual. For example, patients with left perisylvian damage that results in STM deficits also have deficits in phonological processing in general, which suggests a deficit that extends beyond STM per se (e.g., Martin 1993).

The architecture of unitary-store models. Our review leads to the conclusion that short- and long-term memory are not architecturally separable systems—at least not in the strong sense of distinct underlying neural systems. Instead, the evidence points to a model in which short-term memories consist of temporary activations of long-term representations. Such unitary models of memory have a long history in cognitive psychology, with early theoretical unification achieved via interference theory (Postman 1961, Underwood & Schultz 1960). Empirical support came from demonstrations that memories in both the short and long term suffered from proactive interference (e.g., Keppel & Underwood 1962).

Perhaps the first formal proposal that short-term memory consists of activated long-term representations was by Atkinson & Shiffrin (1971, but also see Hebb 1949). The idea fell somewhat out of favor during the hegemony of the Baddeley multistore model, although it was given its first detailed computational treatment by Anderson (1983). It has recently been revived and greatly developed by Cowan (1988, 1995, 2000), McElree (2001), Oberauer (2002), Verhaeghen et al. (2004), Anderson et al. (2004), and others. The key assumption is the construct of a very limited focus of attention, although as we elaborate below, there are disagreements regarding the scope of the focus.

One shared assumption of these models is that STM consists of temporary activations of LTM representations or of representations of items that were recently perceived. The models differ from one to another regarding specifics, but Cowan's model (e.g., Cowan 2000) is representative. According to this model, there is only one set of representations of familiar material—the representations in LTM. These representations can vary in strength of activation, where that strength varies as a function of such variables as recency and frequency of occurrence. Representations that have increased strength of activation are more available for retrieval in STM experiments, but they must be retrieved nonetheless to participate in cognitive action. In addition, these representations are subject to forgetting over time. A special but limited set of these representations, however, can be within the focus of attention, where being within the focus makes these representations immediately available for cognitive processing. According to this and similar models, then, STM is functionally seen as consisting of LTM representations that are either in the focus of attention or at a heightened level of activation.

These unitary-store models suggest a different interpretation of frontal cortical involvement in STM from multistore models. Early work showing the importance of frontal cortex for STM, particularly that of Fuster and Goldman-Rakic and colleagues, was first seen as support for multistore models (e.g., Funahashi et al. 1989, Fuster 1973, Jacobsen 1936, Wilson et al. 1993). For example, single-unit activity in dorsolateral prefrontal cortex regions (principal sulcus, inferior convexity) that was selectively responsive to memoranda during the delay interval was interpreted as evidence that these regions were the storage sites for STM. However, the sustained activation of frontal cortex during the delay period does not necessarily mean that this region is a site of STM storage. Many other regions of neocortex also show activation that outlasts the physical presence of a stimulus and provides a possible neural basis for STM representations (see Postle 2006). Furthermore, increasing evidence suggests that frontal activations reflect the operation of executive processes [including those needed to keep the representations in the focus of attention; see reviews by Postle (2006), Ranganath & D'Esposito (2005), Reuter-Lorenz & Jonides (2007), and Ruchkin et al. (2003)]. Modeling work and lesion data provide further support for the idea that the representations used in both STM and LTM are stored in those regions of cortex that are involved in initial perception and encoding, and that frontal activations reflect processes involved in selecting this information for the focus of attention and keeping it there (Damasio 1989, McClelland et al. 1995).

The principle of posterior storage also allows some degree of reconciliation between multi- and unitary-store models. Posterior regions are clearly differentiated by information type (e.g., auditory, visual, spatial), which could support the information-specific buffers postulated by multistore models. Unitary-store models focus on central capacity limits, irrespective of modality, but they do allow for separate resources (Cowan 2000) or feature components (Lange & Oberauer 2005, Oberauer & Kliegl 2006) that occur at lower levels of perception and representation. Multi- and unitary-store models thus both converge on the idea of modality-specific representations (or components of those representations) supported by distinct posterior neural systems.

Controversies over Capacity

Regardless of whether one subscribes to multi- or unitary-store models, the issue of how much information is stored in STM has long been a prominent one (Miller 1956). Multistore models explain capacity estimates largely as interplay between the speed with which information can be rehearsed and the speed with which information is forgotten (Baddeley 1986, 1992; Repov & Baddeley 2006). Several studies have measured this limit by demonstrating that approximately two seconds worth of verbal information can be recirculated successfully (e.g., Baddeley et al. 1975).

Unitary-store models describe capacity as limited by the number of items that can be activated in LTM, which can be thought of as the bandwidth of attention. However, these models differ on what that number or bandwidth might be. Cowan (2000) suggested a limit of approximately four items, based on performance discontinuities such as errorless performance in immediate recall when the number of items is less than four, and sharp increases in errors for larger numbers. (By this view, the classic "seven plus or minus two" is an overestimate because it is based on studies that allowed participants to engage in processes of rehearsal and chunking, and reflected contributions of both the focus and LTM; see also Waugh & Norman 1965.) At the other extreme are experimental paradigms suggesting that the focus of attention consists of a single item (Garavan 1998, McElree 2001, Verhaeghen & Basak 2007). We briefly consider some of the central issues behind current controversies concerning capacity estimates.

Behavioral and neural evidence for the magic number 4. Cowan (2000) has reviewed an impressive array of studies leading to his conclusion that the capacity limit is four items, plus or minus one (see his Table 1). Early behavioral evidence came from studies showing sharp drop-offs in performance at three or four items on short-term retrieval tasks (e.g., Sperling 1960). These experiments were vulnerable to the criticism that this limit might reflect output interference occurring during retrieval rather than an actual limit on capacity. However, additional evidence comes from change-detection and other tasks that do not require the serial recall of individual items. For example, Luck & Vogel (1997) presented subjects with 1 to 12 colored squares in an array. After a blank interval of nearly a second, another array of squares was presented, in which one square may have changed color. Subjects were to respond whether the arrays were identical. These experiments and others that avoid the confound of output-interference (e.g., Pashler 1988) likewise have yielded capacity estimates of approximately four items.

Electrophysiological and neuroimaging studies also support the idea of a four-item capacity limit. The first such report was by Vogel & Machizawa (2004), who recorded event-related potentials (ERPs) from subjects as they performed a visual change-detection task. ERP recording shortly after the onset of the retention interval in this task indicated a negative-going wave over parietal and occipital sites that persisted for the duration of the retention interval and was sensitive to the number of items held in memory. Importantly, this signal plateaued when array size reached between three and four items. The amplitude

of this activity was strongly correlated with estimates of each subject's memory capacity and was less pronounced on incorrect than correct trials, indicating that it was causally related to performance. Subsequent functional magnetic resonance imaging (fMRI) studies have observed similar load- and accuracy-dependent activations, especially in intraparietal and intraoccipital sulci (Todd & Marois 2004, 2005). These regions have been implicated by others (e.g., Yantis & Serences 2003) in the control of attentional allocation, so it seems plausible that one rate-limiting step in STM capacity has to do with the allocation of attention (Cowan 2000; McElree 1998, 2001; Oberauer 2002).

Evidence for more severe limits on focus capacity. Another set of researchers agree there is a fixed capacity, but by measuring a combination of response time and accuracy, they contend that the focus of attention is limited to just one item (e.g., Garavan 1998, McElree 2001, Verhaeghen & Basak 2007). For example, Garavan (1998) required subjects to keep two running counts in STM, one for triangles and one for squares—as shape stimuli appeared one after another in random order. Subjects controlled their own presentation rate, which allowed Garavan to measure the time spent processing each figure before moving on. He found that responses to a figure of one category (e.g., a triangle) that followed a figure from the other category (e.g., a square) were fully 500 milliseconds longer than responses to the second of two figures from the same category (e.g., a triangle followed by another triangle). These findings suggested that attention can be focused on only one internal counter in STM at a time. Switching attention from one counter to another incurred a substantial cost in time. Using a speed-accuracy tradeoff procedure, McElree (1998) came to the same conclusion that the focus of attention contained just one item. He found that the retrieval speed for the last item in a list was substantially faster than for any other item in the list, and that other

COGNITIVE EVENTS

NEURAL EVENTS

TASK EVENTS

encoding | maintenance in focus | highly available representation out of the focus, degraded by interference and decay | retrieval and maintenance in focus

Prefrontal control systems
Parietal attentional systems

Posterior high-level perceptual systems
Posterior low-level perception systems
Medial-temporal binding systems

Representation by active neuronal firing
Representation by synaptic changes

(5) Iconic memory at stimulus offset

(3) Speed-accuracy trade-off in perceptual encoding

(6) Active maintenance mediated by frontal-parietal systems; decay caused by stochastic drift

(9) Focus shifts to second stimulus; first stimulus pattern ceases active firing

(7) Reuse of perceptual systems for STM and imagery, mediated by frontal-parietal systems

(2) Active MTL role in binding in STM

(10) Retroactive interference caused by disruption of short-term synaptic enhancement by active neural patterns of second and third stimuli

(11) Decay of representation outside of focus caused by decay of short-term synaptic enhancement

(12) Cue-based parallel retrieval, subject to proactive interference

(13) Frontal-parietal mediated active maintenance of retrieved pattern

Extent and basis of neural representation

Time (ms)

stimulus | delay | second stimulus and delay | third stimulus and delay | probe

Figure 1

The processing and neural representation of one item in memory over the course of a few seconds in a hypothetical short-term memory task, assuming a simple single-item focus architecture. The cognitive events are demarcated at the top; the task events, at the bottom. The colored layers depict the extent to which different brain areas contribute to the representation of the item over time, at distinct functional stages of short-term memory processing. The colored layers also distinguish two basic types of neural representation: Solid layers depict memory supported by a coherent pattern of active neural firing, and hashed layers depict memory supported by changes in synaptic patterns. The example task requires processing and remembering three visual items; the figure traces the representation of the first item only. In this task, the three items are sequentially presented, and each is followed by a delay period. After the delay following the third item, a probe appears that requires retrieval of the first item. See the text for details corresponding to the numbered steps in the figure.

items were retrieved at comparable rates to each other even though the accuracy of retrieval for these other items varied.

Oberauer (2002) suggested a compromise solution to the "one versus four" debate. In his model, up to four items can be directly accessible, but only one of these items can be in the focus of attention. This model is similar to that of Cowan (2000), but adds the assumption that an important method of accessing short-term memories is to focus attention on one item, depending on task demands. Thus, in tasks that serially demand attention on several items (such as those of Garavan 1998 or McElree 2001), the mechanism that accomplishes this involves changes in the focus of attention among temporarily activated representations in LTM.

Alternatives to capacity limits based on number of items. Attempting to answer the question of how many items may be held in the focus implicitly assumes that items are the appropriate unit for expressing capacity limits. Some reject this basic assumption. For example, Wilken & Ma (2004) demonstrated that a signal-detection account of STM, in which STM capacity is primarily constrained by noise, better fit behavioral data than an item-based fixed-capacity model. Recent data from change-detection tasks suggest that object complexity (Eng et al. 2005) and similarity (Awh et al. 2007) play an important role in determining capacity. Xu & Chun (2006) offer neuroimaging evidence that may reconcile the item-based and complexity accounts: In a change-detection task, they found that activation of inferior intra-parietal sulcus tracked a capacity limit of four, but nearby regions were sensitive to the complexity of the memoranda, as were the behavioral results.

Other researchers disagree with fixed item-based limits because they have demonstrated that the limit is mutable. Practice may improve subjects' ability to use processes such as chunking to allow greater functional capacities (McElree 1998, Verhaeghen et al. 2004; but see Oberauer 2006). However, this type of flexibility appears to alter the amount of information that can be compacted into a single representation rather than the total number of representations that can be held in STM (Miller 1956). The data of Verhaegen et al. (2004; see Figure 5 of that paper) suggest that the latter number still approximates four, consistent with Cowan's claims.

Building on these findings, we suggest a new view of capacity. The fundamental idea that attention can be allocated to one piece of information in memory is correct, but the definition of what that one piece is needs to be clarified. It cannot be that just one item is in the focus of attention because if that were so, hardly any computation would be possible. How could one add 3+4, for example, if at any one time, attention could be allocated only to the "3" or the "4" or the "+" operation? We propose that attention focuses on what is bound together into a single "functional context," whether that context is defined by time, space, some other stimulus characteristic such as semantic or visual similarity or momentary task relevance. By this account, attention can be placed on the whole problem "3+4," allowing relevant computations to be made. Complexity comes into play by limiting the number of subcomponents that can be bound into one functional context.

Summary

What are we to conclude from the data concerning the structure of STM? We favor the implication that the representational bases for perception, STM, and LTM are identical. That is, the same neural representations initially activated during the encoding of a piece of information show sustained activation during STM (or retrieval from LTM into STM; Wheeler et al. 2000) and are the repository of long-term representations. Because regions of neocortex represent different sorts of information (e.g., verbal, spatial), it is reasonable to expect that STM will have an organization by type of material as well. Functionally, memory in the short term seems to consist of items in the focus of attention along with recently attended representations in LTM. These items in the focus of attention number no more than four, and they may be limited to just a single representation (consisting of items bound within a functional context).

We turn below to processes that operate on these representations.

WHAT PROCESSES OPERATE ON THE STORED INFORMATION?

Theoretical debate about the nature of STM has been dominated by discussion of structure and capacity, but the issue of process is also important. Verbal rehearsal is perhaps most intuitively associated with STM and plays a key role in the classic model (Baddeley 1986). However, as we discuss below, rehearsal most likely reflects a complex strategy rather than a primitive STM process. Modern approaches offer a large set of candidate processes, including encoding and maintenance (Ranganath et al. 2004), attention shifts (Cowan 2000), spatial rehearsal (Awh & Jonides 2001), updating (Oberauer 2005), overwriting (Neath & Nairne 1995), cue-based parallel retrieval (McElree 2001), and interference-resolution (Jonides & Nee 2006).

Rather than navigating this complex and growing list, we take as our cornerstone the concept of a limited focus of attention. The central point of agreement for the unitary-store models discussed above is that there is a distinguishable focus of attention in which representations are directly accessible and available for cognitive action. Therefore, it is critical that all models must identify the processes that govern the transition of memory representations into and out of this focused state.

The Three Core Processes of Short-Term Memory: Encoding, Maintenance, and Retrieval

If one adopts the view that a limited focus of attention is a key feature of short-term stor-age, then understanding processing related to this limited focus amounts to understanding three basic types of cognitive events[2]: (a) encoding processes that govern the transformation from perceptual representations into the cognitive/attentional focus, (b) maintenance processes that keep information in the focus (and protect it from interference or decay), and (c) retrieval processes that bring information from the past back into the cognitive focus (possibly reactivating perceptual representations).

Encoding of items into the focus. Encoding processes are the traditional domain of theories of perception and are not treated explicitly in any of the current major accounts of STM. Here we outline three implicit assumptions about encoding processes made in most accounts of STM, and we assess their empirical and theoretical support.

First, the cognitive focus is assumed to have immediate access to perceptual processing—that is, the focus may include contents from the immediate present as well as contents retrieved from the immediate past. In Cowan's (2000) review of evidence in favor of the number four in capacity estimates, several of the experimental paradigms involve focused representations of objects in the immediate perceptual present or objects presented less than a second ago. These include visual tracking experiments (Pylyshyn et al. 1994), enumeration (Trick & Pylyshyn 1993), and whole report of spatial arrays and spatiotemporal arrays (Darwin et al. 1972, Sperling 1960). Similarly, in McElree's (2006) and Garavan's (1998) experiments, each incoming item in the stream of material (words or letters or objects) is assumed to be represented momentarily in the focus.

---

[2]This carving up of STM processes is also consistent with recent approaches to individual differences in working memory, which characterize individual variation not in terms of variation in buffer capacity, but rather in variation in maintenance and retrieval processes (Unsworth & Engle 2007).

Second, all of the current theories assume that perceptual encoding into the focus of attention results in a displacement of other items from the focus. For example, in McElree's single-item focus model, each incoming item not only has its turn in the focus, but it also replaces the previous item. On the one hand, the work reviewed above regarding performance discontinuities after the putative limit of STM capacity has been reached appears to support the idea of whole-item displacement. On the other hand, as also described above, this limit may be susceptible to factors such as practice and stimulus complexity. An alternative to whole-item displacement as the basis for interference is a graded similarity-based interference, in which new items entering the focus may partially overwrite features of the old items or compete with old items to include those featural components in their representations as a function of their similarity. At some level, graded interference is clearly at work in STM, as Nairne (2002) and others have demonstrated (we review this evidence in more detail below). But the issue at hand is whether the focus is subject to such graded interference, and if such interference is the process by which encoding (or retrieving) items into the focus displaces prior items. Although there does not appear to be evidence that bears directly on this issue (the required experiments would involve manipulations of similarity in just the kinds of paradigms that Cowan, McElree, Oberauer, and others have used to provide evidence for the limited focus), the performance discontinuities strongly suggest that something like displacement is at work.

Third, all of the accounts assume that perceptual encoding does not have obligatory access to the focus. Instead, encoding into the focus is modulated by attention. This follows rather directly from the assumptions about the severe limits on focus capacity: There must be some controlled way of directing which aspects of the perceptual present, as well as the cognitive past, enter into the focused state. Stated negatively, there must be some way of preventing aspects of the perceptual present from automatically entering into the focused state. Postle (2006) recently found that increased activity in dorsolateral prefrontal cortex during the presentation of distraction during a retention interval was accompanied by a selective decrease in inferior temporal cortical activity. This pattern suggests that prefrontal regions selectively modulated posterior perceptual areas to prevent incoming sensory input from disrupting the trace of the task-relevant memorandum.

In summary, current approaches to STM have an obligation to account for how controlled processes bring relevant aspects of perception into cognitive focus and leave others out. It is by no means certain that existing STM models and existing models of perceptual attention are entirely compatible on this issue, and this is a matter of continued lively debate (Milner 2001, Schubert & Frensch 2001, Woodman et al. 2001).

Maintenance of items in the focus. Once an item is in the focus of attention, what keeps it there? If the item is in the perceptual present, the answer is clear: attention-modulated, perceptual encoding. The more pressing question is: What keeps something in the cognitive focus when it is not currently perceived? For many neuroscientists, this is the central question of STM—how information is held in mind for the purpose of future action after the perceptual input is gone. There is now considerable evidence from primate models and from imaging studies on humans for a process of active maintenance that keeps representations alive and protects them from irrelevant incoming stimuli or intruding thoughts (e.g., Postle 2006).

We argue that this process of maintenance is not the same as rehearsal. Indeed, the number of items that can be maintained without rehearsal forms the basis of Cowan's (2000) model. Under this view, rehearsal is not a basic process but rather is a strategy for accomplishing the functional demands for sustaining memories in the short term—a strategy composed of a series of retrievals and re-encodings. We consider rehearsal in more detail below, but we consider here the behavioral and neuroimaging evidence for maintenance processes.

There is now considerable evidence from both primate models and human electroencephalography and fMRI studies for a set of prefrontal-posterior circuits underlying active maintenance. Perhaps the most striking is the classic evidence from single-cell recordings showing that some neurons in prefrontal cortex fire selectively during the delay period in delayed-match-to-sample tasks (e.g., Funahashi et al. 1989, Fuster 1973). As mentioned above, early interpretations of these frontal activations linked them directly to STM representations (Goldman-Rakic 1987), but more recent theories suggest they are part of a frontal-posterior STM circuit that maintains representations in posterior areas (Pasternak & Greenlee 2005, Ranganath 2006, Ruchkin et al. 2003). Furthermore, as described above, maintenance operations may modulate perceptual encoding to prevent incoming perceptual stimuli from disrupting the focused representation in posterior cortex (Postle 2006). Several computational neural-network models of circuits for maintenance hypothesize that prefrontal cortical circuits support attractors, self-sustaining patterns observed in certain classes of recurrent networks (Hopfield 1982, Rougier et al. 2005, Polk et al. 2002). A major challenge is to develop computational models that are able to engage in active maintenance of representations in posterior cortex while simultaneously processing, to some degree, incoming perceptual material (see Renart et al. 1999 for a related attempt).

Retrieval of items into the focus. Many of the major existing STM architectures are silent on the issue of retrieval. However, all models that assume a limited focus also assume that there is some means by which items outside that focus (either in a dormant long-term store or in some highly activated portion of LTM) are brought into the focus by switching the attentional focus onto those items. Following Sternberg (1966), McElree (2006), and others, we label this process "retrieval." Despite this label, it is important to keep in mind that the associated spatial metaphor of an item moving from one location to another is misleading given our assumption about the common neural representations underlying STM and LTM.

There is now considerable evidence, mostly from mathematical models of behavioral data, that STM retrieval of item information is a rapid, parallel, content-addressable process. The current emphasis on parallel search processes is quite different from the earliest models of STM retrieval, which postulated a serial scanning process (i.e., Sternberg 1966; see McElree 2006 for a recent review and critique). Serial-scanning models fell out of favor because of empirical and modeling work showing that parallel processes provide a better account of the reaction time distributions in STM tasks (e.g., Hockley 1984). For example, McElree has created a variation on the Sternberg recognition probe task that provides direct support for parallel, rather than serial, retrieval. In the standard version of the task, participants are presented with a memory set consisting of a rapid sequence of verbal items (e.g., letters or digits), followed by a probe item. The task is to identify whether the probe was a member of the memory set. McElree & Dosher's (1989) innovation was to manipulate the deadline for responding. The time course of retrieval (accuracy as a function of response deadline) can be separately plotted for each position within the presentation sequence, allowing independent assessments of accessibility (how fast an item can be retrieved) and availability (asymptotic accuracy) as a function of set size and serial position. Many experiments yield a uniform rate of access for all items except for the most recent item, which is accessed more quickly. The uniformity of access rate is evidence for parallel access, and the distinction between the most recent item and the other items is evidence for a distinguished focus of attention.

Neural Mechanisms of Short- and Long-Term Memory Retrieval

The cue-based retrieval processes described above for STM are very similar to those posited for LTM (e.g., Anderson et al. 2004, Gillund & Shiffrin 1984, Murdock 1982). As a result, retrieval failures resulting from similarity-based interference and cue overlap are ubiquitous in both STM and LTM. Both classic studies of recall from STM (e.g., Keppel & Underwood 1962) and more recent studies of interference in probe-recognition tasks (e.g., Jonides & Nee 2006, McElree & Dosher 1989, Monsell 1978) support the idea that interference plays a major role in forgetting over short retention intervals as well as long ones (see below). These common effects would not be expected if STM retrieval were a different process restricted to operate over a limited buffer, but they are consistent with the notion that short-term and long-term retrieval are mediated by the same cue-based mechanisms.

The heavy overlap in the neural substrates for short-term and long-term retrieval provides additional support for the idea that retrieval processes are largely the same over different retention intervals. A network of medial temporal regions, lateral prefrontal regions, and anterior prefrontal regions has been extensively studied and shown to be active in long-term retrieval tasks (e.g., Buckner et al. 1998, Cabeza & Nyberg 2000, Fletcher & Henson 2001). We reviewed above the evidence for MTL involvement in both short- and long-term memory tasks that require novel representations (see section titled "Contesting the Idea of Separate Long-Term and Short-Term Systems"). Here, we examine whether the role of frontal cortex is the same for both short- and long-term retrieval.

The conclusion derived from neuroimaging studies of various different STM procedures is that this frontal role is the same in short-term and long-term retrieval. For example, several event-related fMRI studies of the retrieval stage of the probe-recognition task found increased activation in lateral prefrontal cortex similar to the activations seen in studies of LTM retrieval (e.g., D'Esposito et al. 1999, D'Esposito & Postle 2000, Manoach et al. 2003). Badre & Wagner (2005) also found anterior prefrontal activations that overlapped with regions implicated in episodic recollection. The relatively long retention intervals often used in event-related fMRI studies leaves them open to the criticism that by the time of the probe, the focus of attention has shifted elsewhere, causing the need to retrieve information from LTM (more on this discussion below). However, a meta-analysis of studies that involved bringing very recently presented items to the focus of attention likewise found specific involvement of lateral and anterior prefrontal cortex (Johnson et al. 2005). These regions appear to be involved in retrieval, regardless of timescale.

The same conclusion may be drawn from recent imaging studies that have directly compared long- and short-term retrieval tasks using within-subjects designs (Cabeza et al. 2002, Ranganath et al. 2003, Talmi et al. 2005). Ranganath et al. (2003) found the same bilateral ventrolateral and dorsolateral prefrontal regions engaged in both short- and long-term tasks. In some cases, STM and LTM tasks involve the same regions but differ in the relative amount of activation shown within those regions. For example, Cabeza et al. (2002) reported similar engagement of medial temporal regions in both types of task, but greater anterior and ventrolateral activation in the long-term episodic tasks. Talmi et al. (2005) reported greater activation in both medial temporal and lateral frontal cortices for recognition probes of items presented early in a 12-item list (presumably necessitating retrieval from LTM) versus items presented later in the list (presumably necessitating retrieval from STM). One possible reason for this discrepancy is that recognition for late-list items did not require retrieval because these items were still in the focus of attention. This account is plausible since late-list items were drawn either from the last-presented or second-to-last presented item and preceded the probe by less than two seconds.

In summary, the bulk of the neuroimaging evidence points to the conclusion that the activation of frontal and medial temporal regions depends on whether the information is currently in or out of focus, not whether the task nominally tests STM or LTM. Similar reactivation processes occur during retrieval from LTM and from STM when the active maintenance has been interrupted (see Sakai 2003 for a more extensive review).

The Relationship of Short-Term Memory Processes to Rehearsal

Notably, our account of core STM processes excludes rehearsal. How does rehearsal fit in? We argue that rehearsal is simply a controlled sequence of retrievals and re-encodings of items into the focus of attention (Baddeley 1986, Cowan 1995). The theoretical force of this assumption can be appreciated by examining the predictions it makes when coupled with our other assumptions about the structures and processes of the underlying STM architecture. Below we outline these predictions and the behavioral, developmental, neuroimaging, and computational work that support this view.

Rehearsal as retrieval into the focus. When coupled with the idea of a single-item focus, the assumption that rehearsal is a sequence of retrievals into the focus of attention makes a very clear prediction: A just-rehearsed item should display the same retrieval dynamics as a just-perceived item. McElree (2006) directly tested this prediction using a version of his response-deadline recognition task, in which subjects were given a retention interval between presentation of the list and the probe rather than presented with the probe immediately after the list. Subjects were ex-plicitly instructed to rehearse the list during this interval and were trained to do so at a particular rate. By controlling the rate, it was possible to know when each item was rehearsed and hence re-established in the focus. The results were compelling: When an item was predicted to be in focus because it had just been rehearsed, it showed the same fast retrieval dynamics as an item that had just been perceived. In short, the speed-accuracy tradeoff functions showed the familiar in-focus/out-of-focus dichotomy of the standard paradigm, but the dichotomy was established for internally controlled rehearsal as well as externally controlled perception.

Rehearsal as strategic retrieval. Rehearsal is often implicitly assumed as a component of active maintenance, but formal theoretical considerations of STM typically take the opposite view. For example, Cowan (2000) provides evidence that although first-grade children do not use verbal rehearsal strategies, they nevertheless have measurable focus capacities. In fact, Cowan (2000) uses this evidence to argue that the performance of very young children is revealing of the fundamental capacity limits of the focus of attention because it is not confounded with rehearsal.

If rehearsal is the controlled composition of more primitive STM processes, then rehearsal should activate the same brain circuits as the primitive processes, possibly along with additional (frontal) circuits associated with their control. In other words, there should be overlap of rehearsal with brain areas subserving retrieval and initial perceptual encoding. Likewise, there should be control areas distinct from those of the primitive processes.

Both predictions receive support from neuroimaging studies. The first prediction is broadly confirmed: There is now considerable evidence for the reactivation of areas associated with initial perceptual encoding in tasks that require rehearsal (see Jonides et al. 2005 for a recent review; note also that evidence exists for reactivation in LTM retrieval: Wheeler 2000, 2006).

The second prediction—that rehearsal engages additional control areas beyond those participating in maintenance, encoding, and retrieval—receives support from two effects. One is that verbal rehearsal engages a set of frontal structures associated with articulation and its planning: supplementary motor, premotor, inferior frontal, and posterior parietal areas (e.g., Chein & Fiez 2001, Jonides et al. 1998, Smith & Jonides 1999). The other is that spatial rehearsal engages attentionally mediated occipital regions, suggesting rehearsal processes that include retrieval of spatial information (Awh et al. 1998, 1999, 2001).

Computational modeling relevant to strategic retrieval. Finally, prominent symbolic and connectionist computational models of verbal STM tasks are based on architectures that do not include rehearsal as a primitive process, but rather assume it as a strategic composition of other processes operating over a limited focus. The Burgess & Hitch (2005, 2006) connectionist model, the Executive-Process/Interactive Control (EPIC) symbolic model (Meyer and Kieras 1997), and the Atomic Components of Thought (ACT-R) hybrid model (Anderson & Matessa 1997) all assume that rehearsal in verbal STM consists of a controlled sequence of retrievals of items into a focused state. They all assume different underlying mechanisms for the focus (the Burgess & Hitch model has a winner-take-all network; ACT-R has an architectural buffer with a capacity of one chunk; EPIC has a special auditory store), but all assume strategic use of this focus to accomplish rehearsal. These models jointly represent the most successful attempts to account for a range of detailed empirical phenomena traditionally associated with rehearsal, especially in verbal serial recall tasks. Their success therefore provides further support for the plausibility of a compositional view of rehearsal.

WHY DO WE FORGET?

Forgetting in STM is a vexing problem: What accounts for failures to retrieve something encoded just seconds ago? There are two major explanations for forgetting, often placed in opposition: time-based decay and similarity-based interference. Below, we describe some of the major findings in the literature related to each of these explanations, and we suggest that they may ultimately result from the same underlying principles.

Decay Theories: Intuitive but Problematic

The central claim of decay theory is that as time passes, information in memory erodes, and so it is less available for later retrieval. This explanation has strong intuitive appeal. However, over the years there have been sharp critiques of decay, questioning whether it plays any role at all (for recent examples, see Lewandowsky et al. 2004 and the review in this journal by Nairne 2002).

Decay explanations are controversial for two reasons: First, experiments attempting to demonstrate decay can seldom eliminate alternative explanations. For example, Keppel & Underwood (1962) demonstrated that forgetting in the classic Brown-Peterson paradigm (designed to measure time-based decay) was due largely, if not exclusively, to proactive interference from prior trials. Second, without an explanation of how decay occurs, it is difficult to see decay theories as more than a restatement of the problem. Some functional arguments have been made for the usefulness of the notion of memory decay—that decaying activations adaptively mirror the likelihood that items will need to be retrieved (Anderson & Schooler 1991), or that decay is functionally necessary to reduce interference (Altmann & Gray 2002). Nevertheless, McGeoch's famous (1932) criticism of decay theories still holds merit: Rust does not occur because of time itself, but rather from oxidation processes that occur with time. Decay theories must explain the processes by which decay could occur, i.e., they must identify the oxidation process in STM.

Retention-interval confounds: controlling for rehearsal and retroactive interference.

The main problem in testing decay theories is controlling for what occurs during the retention interval. Many experiments include an attention-demanding task to prevent participants from using rehearsal that would presumably circumvent decay. However, a careful analysis of these studies by Roediger et al. (1977) makes one wonder whether the use of a secondary task is appropriate to prevent rehearsal at all. They compared conditions in which a retention interval was filled by nothing, by a relatively easy task, or by a relatively difficult one. Both conditions with a filled interval led to worse memory performance, but the difficulty of the intervening task had no effect. Roediger et al. (1977) concluded that the primary memory task and the interpolated task, although demanding, used different processing pools of resources, and hence the interpolated tasks may not have been effective in preventing rehearsal. So, they argued, this sort of secondary-task technique may not prevent rehearsal and may not allow for a convincing test of a decay hypothesis.

Another problem with tasks that fill the retention interval is that they require subjects to use STM (consider counting backward, as in the Brown-Peterson paradigm). This could lead to active displacement of items from the focus according to views (e.g., McElree 2001) that posit such displacement as a mechanism of STM forgetting, or increase the noise according to interference-based explanations (see discussion below in What Happens Neurally During the Delay?). By either account, the problem with retention-interval tasks is that they are questionable ways to prevent rehearsal of the to-be-remembered information, and they introduce new, distracting information that may engage STM. This double-edged sword makes it difficult to tie retention-interval manipulations directly to decay.

Attempts to address the confounding factors.

A potential way out of the rehearsal conundrum is to use stimuli that are not easily converted to verbal codes and that therefore may be difficult to rehearse. For example, Harris (1952) used tones that differed so subtly in pitch that they would be difficult to name by subjects without perfect pitch. On each trial, participants were first presented with a to-be-remembered tone, followed by a retention interval of 0.1 to 25 seconds, and finally a probe tone. The accuracy of deciding whether the initial and probe tones were the same declined with longer retention intervals, consistent with the predictions of decay theory.

Using another technique, McKone (1995, 1998) reduced the probability of rehearsal or other explicit-memory strategies by using an implicit task. Words and nonwords were repeated in a lexical-decision task, with the measure of memory being faster performance on repeated trials than on novel ones (priming). To disentangle the effects of decay and interference, McKone varied the time between repetitions (the decay-related variable) while holding the number of items between repetitions (the interference-related variable) constant, and vice versa. She found that greater time between repetitions reduced priming even after accounting for the effects of intervening items, consistent with decay theory. However, interference and decay effects seemed to interact and to be especially important for nonwords.

Procedures such as those used by Harris (1952) and McKone (1995, 1998) do not have the problems associated with retention-interval tasks. They are, however, potentially vulnerable to the criticism of Keppel & Underwood (1962) regarding interference from prior trials within the task, although McKone's experiments address this issue to some degree. Another potential problem is that these participants' brains and minds are not inactive during the retention interval (Raichle et al. 2001). There is increasing evidence that the processes ongoing during nominal "resting states" are related to memory, including STM (Hampson et al. 2006). Spontaneous retrieval by participants during the retention interval could interfere with memory for the experimental items. So, although experiments that reduce the influence of rehearsal provide some of the best evidence of decay, they are not definitive.

What happens neurally during the delay? Neural findings of delay-period activity have also been used to support the idea of decay. For example, at the single-cell level, Fuster (1995) found that in monkeys performing a delayed-response task, delay-period activity in inferotemporal cortex steadily declined over 18 seconds (see also Pasternak & Greenlee 2005). At a molar level, human neuroimaging studies often show delay-period activity in prefrontal and posterior regions, and this activity is often thought to support maintenance or storage (see review by Smith & Jonides 1999). As reviewed above, it is likely that the posterior regions support storage and that frontal regions support processes related to interference-resolution, control, attention, response preparation, motivation, and reward.

Consistent with the suggestive primate data, Jha & McCarthy (2000) found a general decline in activation in posterior regions over a delay period, which suggests some neural evidence for decay. However, this decline in activation was not obviously related to performance, which suggests two (not mutually exclusive) possibilities: (*a*) the decline in activation was not representative of decay, so it did not correlate with performance, or (*b*) these regions might not have been storage regions (but see Todd & Marois 2004 and Xu & Chun 2006 for evidence more supportive of load sensitivity in posterior regions).

The idea that neural activity decays also faces a serious challenge in the classic results of Malmo (1942), who found that a monkey

with frontal lesions was able to perform a delayed response task extremely well (97% correct) if visual stimulation and motor movement (and therefore associated interference) were restricted during a 10-second delay. By contrast, in unrestricted conditions, performance was as low as 25% correct (see also Postle & D'Esposito 1999). In summary, evidence for time-based declines in neural activity that would naturally be thought to be part of a decay process is at best mixed.

Is there a mechanism for decay? Although there are data supporting the existence of decay, much of these data are subject to alternative, interference-based explanations. However, as Crowder (1976) noted, "Good ideas die hard." At least a few key empirical results (Harris 1952; McKone 1995, 1998) do seem to implicate some kind of time-dependent decay. If one assumes that decay happens, how might it occur?

One possibility—perhaps most compatible with results like those of Malmo (1942)—is that what changes over time is not the integrity of the representation itself, but the likelihood that attention will be attracted away from it. As more time passes, the likelihood increases that attention will be attracted away from the target and toward external stimuli or other memories, and it will be more difficult to return to the target representation. This explanation seems compatible with the focus-of-attention views of STM that we have reviewed. By this explanation, capacity limits are a function of attention limits rather than a special property of STM per se.

Another explanation, perhaps complementary to the first, relies on stochastic variability in the neuronal firing patterns that make up the target representation. The temporal synchronization of neuronal activity is an important part of the representation (e.g., Deiber et al. 2007, Jensen 2006, Lisman & Idiart 1995). As time passes, variability in the firing rates of individual neurons may cause them to fall increasingly out of synchrony unless they are reset (e.g., by rehearsal). As the neurons fall out of synchrony, by this hypothesis, the firing pattern that makes up the representation becomes increasingly difficult to discriminate from surrounding noise [see Lustig et al. (2005) for an example that integrates neural findings with computational (Frank et al. 2001) and behaviorally based (Brown et al. 2000) models of STM].

Interference Theories: Comprehensive but Complex

Interference effects play several roles in memory theory: First, they are the dominant explanation of forgetting. Second, some have suggested that STM capacity and its variation among individuals are largely determined by the ability to overcome interference (e.g., Hasher & Zacks 1988, Unsworth & Engle 2007). Finally, differential interference effects in STM and LTM have been used to justify the idea that they are separate systems, and common interference effects have been used to justify the idea that they are a unitary system.

Interference theory has the opposite problem of decay: It is comprehensive but complex (Crowder 1976). The basic principles are straightforward. Items in memory compete, with the amount of interference determined by the similarity, number, and strength of the competitors. The complexity stems from the fact that interference may occur at multiple stages (encoding, retrieval, and possibly storage) and at multiple levels (the representation itself or its association with a cue or a response). Interference from the past (proactive interference; PI) may affect both the encoding and the retrieval of new items, and it often increases over time. By contrast, interference from new items onto older memories (retroactive interference; RI) frequently decreases over time and may not be as reliant on similarity (see discussion by Wixted 2004).

Below, we review some of the major findings with regard to interference in STM, including a discussion of its weaknesses in

explaining short-term forgetting. We then present a conceptual model of STM that attempts to address these weaknesses and the questions regarding structure, process, and forgetting raised throughout this review.

Interference Effects in Short-Term Memory

Selection-based interference effects. The Brown-Peterson task, originally conceived to test decay theory, became a workhorse for testing similarity-based interference as well. In the "release-from-PI" version (Wickens 1970), short lists of categorized words are used as memoranda. Participants learn one three-item list on each trial, perform some other task during the retention interval, and then attempt to recall the list. For the first three trials, all lists consist of words from the same category (e.g., flowers). The typical PI effects occur: Recall declines over subsequent trials. The critical manipulation occurs at the final list. If it is from a different category (e.g., sports), recall is much higher than if it is from the same category as preceding trials. In some cases, performance on this set-shift or release-from-PI trial is nearly as high as on the very first trial.

The release-from-PI effect was originally interpreted as an encoding effect. Even very subtle shifts (e.g., from "flowers" to "wild-flowers") produce the effect if participants are warned about the shift before the words are presented (see Wickens 1970 for an explanation). However, Gardiner et al. (1972) showed that release also occurs if the shift-cue is presented only at the time of the retrieval test—i.e., after the list has been encoded. They suggested that cues at retrieval could reduce PI by differentiating items from the most recent list, thus aiding their selection.

Selection processes remain an important topic in interference research. Functional neuroimaging studies consistently identify a region in left inferior frontal gyrus (LIFG) as active during interference resolution, at least for verbal materials (see a review by Jonides & Nee 2006). This region appears to be generally important for selection among competing alternatives, e.g., in semantic memory as well as in STM (Thompson-Schill et al. 1997). In STM, LIFG is most prominent during the test phase of interference trials, and its activation during this phase often correlates with behavioral measures of interference resolution (D'Esposito et al. 1999, Jonides et al. 1998, Reuter-Lorenz et al. 2000, Thompson-Schill et al. 2002). These findings attest to the importance of processes for resolving retrieval interference. The commonality of the neural substrate for interference resolution across short-term and long-term tasks provides yet further support for the hypothesis of shared retrieval processes for the two types of memory.

Interference effects occur at multiple levels, and it is important to distinguish between interference at the level of representations and interference at the level of responses. The LIFG effects described above appear to be familiarity based and to occur at the level of representations. Items on a current trial must be distinguished and selected from among items on previous trials that are familiar because of prior exposure but are currently incorrect. A separate contribution occurs at the level of responses: An item associated with a positive response on a prior trial may now be associated with a negative response, or vice versa. This response-based conflict can be separated from the familiarity-based conflict, and its resolution appears to rely more on the anterior cingulate (Nelson et al. 2003).

Other mechanisms for interference effects? Despite the early work of Keppel & Underwood (1962), most studies examining encoding in STM have focused on RI: how new information disrupts previous memories. Early theorists described this disruption in terms of displacement of entire items from STM, perhaps by disrupting consolidation (e.g., Waugh & Norman 1965). However, rapid serial visual presentation studies sug-

gest that this type of consolidation is complete within a very short time—approximately 500 milliseconds, and in some situations as short as 50 milliseconds (Vogel et al. 2006).

What about interference effects beyond this time window? As reviewed above, most current focus-based models implicitly assume something like whole-item displacement is at work, but these models may need to be elaborated to account for retroactive similarity-based interference, such as the phonological interference effects reviewed by Nairne (2002). The models of Nairne (2002) and Oberauer (2006) suggest a direction for such an elaboration. Rather than a competition at the item level for a single-focus resource, these models posit a lower-level similarity-based competition for "feature units." By this idea, items in STM are represented as bundles of features (e.g., color, shape, spatial location, temporal location). Representations of these features in turn are distributed over multiple units. The more two items overlap, the more they compete for these feature units, resulting in greater interference. This proposed mechanism fits well with the idea that working memory reflects the heightened activation of representations that are distributed throughout sensory, semantic, and motor cortex (Postle 2006), and that similarity-based interference constrains the capacity due to focusing (see above; Awh et al. 2007). Hence, rather than whole-item displacement, specific feature competition may underlie the majority of encoding-stage RI.

Interference-based decay? Above, we proposed a mechanism for decay based on the idea that stochastic variability causes the neurons making up a representation to fall out of synchrony (become less coherent in their firing patterns). Using the terminology of Nairne (2002) and Oberauer (2006), the feature units become less tightly bound. Importantly, feature units that are not part of a representation also show some random activity due to their own stochastic variability, creating a noise distribution. Over time, there is an increasing likelihood that the feature units making up the to-be-remembered item's representation will overlap with those of the noise distribution, making them increasingly difficult to distinguish. This increasing overlap with the noise distribution and loss of feature binding could lead to the smooth forgetting functions often interpreted as evidence for decay.

Such a mechanism for decay has interesting implications. It may explain why PI effects interact with retention interval. Prior trials with similar items would structure the noise distribution so that it is no longer random but rather is biased to share components with the representation of the to-be-remembered item (target). Representations of prior, now-irrelevant items might compete with the current target's representation for control of shared feature units, increasing the likelihood (rate) at which these units fall out of synchrony.

Prior similar items may also dampen the fidelity of the target representation to begin with, weakening their initial binding and thus causing these items to fall out of synchrony more quickly. In addition, poorly learned items might have fewer differentiating feature units, and these units may be less tightly bound and therefore more vulnerable to falling out of synchrony. This could explain why Keppel & Underwood (1962) found that poorly learned items resulted in retention-interval effects even on the first trial. It may also underlie the greater decay effects that McKone (1995, 1998) found for nonwords than for words, if one assumes that nonwords have fewer meaning-based units and connections.

A SUMMARY OF PRINCIPLES AND AN ILLUSTRATION OF SHORT-TERM MEMORY AT WORK

Here we summarize the principles of STM that seem best supported by the behavioral and neural evidence. Building on these principles, we offer a hypothetical sketch of the processes and neural structures that are engaged by a canonical STM task, the probe recognition task with distracting material.

Principles of Short-Term Memory

We have motivated our review by questions of structure, process, and forgetting. Rather than organize our summary this way, we wish to return here to the title of our review and consider what psychological and neural mechanisms seem best defended by empirical work. In that we have provided details about each of these issues in our main discussion, we summarize them here as bullet points. Taken together, they provide answers to our questions about structure, process, and forgetting.

The mind of short-term memory. Representations in memory are composed of bundles of features for stored information, including features representing the context in which that information was encountered.

- Representations in memory vary in activation, with a dormant state characterizing long-term memories, and varying states of activation due to recent perceptions or retrievals of those representations.
- There is a focus of attention in which a bound collection of information may be held in a state that makes it immediately available for cognitive action. Attention may be focused on only a single chunk of information at a time, where a chunk is defined as a set of items that are bound by a common functional context.
- Items may enter the focus of attention via perceptual encoding or via cue-based retrieval from LTM.
- Items are maintained in the focus via a controlled process of maintenance, with rehearsal being a case of controlled sequential allocation of attentional focus.
- Forgetting occurs when items leave the focus of attention and must compete

with other items to regain the focus (interference), or when the fidelity of the representation declines over time due to stochastic processes (decay).

The brain of short-term memory. Items in the focus of attention are represented by patterns of heightened, synchronized firing of neurons in primary and secondary association cortex.

- The sensorimotor features of items in the focus of attention or those in a heightened state of activation are the same as those activated by perception or action. Information within a representation is associated with the cortical region that houses it (e.g., verbal, spatial, motor). In short, item representations are stored where they are processed.

- Medial temporal structures are important for binding items to their context for both the short- and long-term and for retrieving items whose context is no longer in the focus of attention or not yet fully consolidated in the neocortex.

- The capacity to focus attention is constrained by parietal and frontal mechanisms that modulate processing as well as by increased noise in the neural patterns arising from similarity-based interference or from stochastic variability in firing.

- Frontal structures support controlled processes of retrieval and interference resolution.

- Placing an item into the focus of attention from LTM involves reactivating the representation that is encoded in patterns of neural connection weights.

- Decay arises from the inherent variability of the neural firing of feature bundles that build a representation: The likelihood that the firing of multiple features will fall out of synchrony increases with time due to stochastic variability.

A Sketch of Short-Term Memory at Work

The theoretical principles outlined above summarize our knowledge of the psychological and neural bases of STM, but further insight can be gained by attempting to see how these mechanisms might work together, moment-by-moment, to accomplish the demands of simple tasks. We believe that working through an illustration will not only help to clarify the nature of the proposed mechanisms, but it may also lead to a picture of STM that is more detailed in its bridging of neural process and psychological function.

Toward these ends, we present here a specific implementation of the principles that allows us to give a description of the mechanisms that might be engaged at each point in a simple visual STM task. This exercise leads us to a view of STM that is heavily grounded in concepts of neural activation and plasticity. More specifically, we complement the assumptions about cognitive and brain function above with simple hypotheses about the relative supporting roles of neuronal firing and plasticity (described below). Although somewhat speculative in nature, this description is consistent with the summary principles, and it grounds the approach more completely in a plausible neural model. In particular, it has the virtue of providing an unbroken chain of biological mechanisms that supports the encoding of short-term memories over time.

Figure 1 (see color insert) traces the representation of one item in memory over the course of a few seconds in our hypothetical task. The cognitive events are demarcated at the top of the figure, and the task events at the bottom. In the hypothetical task, the subject must keep track of three visual items (such as novel shapes). The first item is presented for 700 milliseconds, followed by a delay of 2 seconds. The second stimulus then appears, followed by a delay of a few seconds, then the third stimulus, and another delay. Finally, the probe appears, and contact must be made with the memory for the first item. The assumption is that subjects will engage in a strategy of actively maintaining each item during the delay periods.

Before walking through the timeline in **Figure 1**, let us take a high-level view. At any given time point, a vertical slice through the figure is intended to convey two key aspects of the neural basis of the memory. The first is the extent to which multiple cortical areas contribute to the representation of the item, as indicated by the colored layers corresponding to different cortical areas. The dynamic nature of the relative sizes of the layers captures several of our theoretical assumptions concerning the evolving contribution of those different areas at different functional stages of STM. The second key aspect is the distinction between memory supported by a coherent pattern of active neural firing (captured in solid layers) and memory supported by synaptic plasticity (captured in the hashed layers) (Fuster 2003, Grossberg 2003, Rolls 2000). The simple hypothesis represented here is that perceptual encoding and active-focus maintenance are supported by neuronal firing, and memory of items outside the focus is supported by short-term synaptic plasticity (Zucker & Regehr 2002).[3]

We now follow the time course of the neural representation of the first item (in the order indicated by the numbers in the figure). (*1*) The stimulus is presented and rapidly triggers a coherent pattern of activity in posterior perceptual regions, representing both low-level visual features of the item content and its abstract identification in higher-level regions. (*2*) There is also a rapid onset of the representation of item-context binding (temporal context in our example) supported by the medial-temporal lobes (see section titled "Contesting the Idea of Separate Long-Term and Short-Term Systems") (Ranganath & Blumenfeld 2005). (*3*) Over the first few hundred milliseconds, this pattern increases in quality, yielding speed-accuracy tradeoffs in perceptual identification. (*4*) Concurrent with the active firing driven by the stimulus, very short-term synaptic plasticity across cortical areas begins to encode the item's features and its binding to context. Zucker & Regehr (2002) identify at least three distinct plasticity mechanisms that begin to operate on this time scale (tens of milliseconds) and that together are sufficient to produce memories lasting several seconds. (For the use of this mechanism in a prominent neural network model of STM, see Burgess & Hitch 1999, 2005, 2006.) (*5*) At the offset of the stimulus, the active firing pattern decays very rapidly (consistent with identified mechanisms of rapid decay in short-term potentiation; Zucker & Regehr 2002), but (*6*) active maintenance, mediated by increased activity in frontal and parietal systems, maintains the firing pattern during the delay period (see sections titled "The Architecture of Unitary-Store Models" and "Maintenance of Items in the Focus") (Pasternak & Greenlee 2005, Ranganath 2006, Ruchkin et al. 2003). This active delay firing includes sustained contribution of MTL to item-context binding (see section titled "Contesting the Idea of Separate Long-Term and Short-Term Systems"). Significant reduction in coherence of the firing pattern may occur as a result of stochastic drift as outlined above (in sections titled "What Happens Neurally During the Delay?" and "Interference-Based Decay?"), possibly leading to a kind of short-term decay during maintenance (see section titled "What Happens Neurally During the Delay?") (Fuster 1995, Pasternak & Greenlee 2005). (*7*) The active maintenance involves the reuse of posterior perceptual regions in the service of the task demands on STM. This reuse includes even early perceptual areas, but we show

---

[3]The alternative to this strong claim is that memory items outside the focus might also be supported by residual active firing. The empirical results reviewed above indicating load-dependent posterior activation might lend support to this alternative if one assumes that the memory load in those experiments was not entirely held in the focus, and that these activations exclusively index firing associated with the memory load itself.

here a drop in the contribution of primary perceptual regions to maintenance in order to indicate a relatively greater effect of top-down control on the later high-level regions (Postle 2006, Ranganath 2006). (*8*) During this delay period of active maintenance, short-term potentiation continues to lay down a trace of the item and its binding to context via connection weights both within and across cortical regions. The overall efficacy of this memory encoding is the result of the interaction of the possibly decaying active firing pattern with the multiple plasticity mechanisms and their individual facilitation and depression profiles (Zucker & Regehr 2002).

(*9*) At the end of the delay period and the onset of the second stimulus, the focus rapidly shifts to the new stimulus, and the active firing of the neural pattern of the target stimulus ceases. (*10*) The memory of the item is now carried completely by the changed synaptic weights, but this change is partially disrupted by the incoming item and its engagement of a similar set of neural activity patterns. Cognitively, this disruption yields similarity-based retroactive interference (see "Other Mechanisms for Interference Effects?") (Nairne 2002). (*11*) Even in the absence of interference, a variety of biochemical processes give rise to the decay of short-term neural change and therefore the gradual loss of the memory trace over time. This pattern of interference and decay continues during processing of both the second and third stimulus. The probe triggers a rapid memory retrieval of the target item (*12*), mediated in part by strategic frontal control (see "Neural Mechanisms of Short- and Long-Term Memory Retrieval") (Cabeza et al. 2002, Ranganath et al. 2004). This rapid retrieval corresponds to the reinstantiation of the target item's firing pattern in both posterior perceptual areas (*13*) and medial-temporal regions, the latter supporting the contextual binding. A plausible neural mechanism for the recovery of this activity pattern at retrieval is the emergent pattern-completion property of attractor networks

(Hopfield 1982). Attractor networks depend on memories encoded in a pattern of connection weights, whose formation and dynamics we have sketched above in terms of short-term synaptic plasticity. Such networks also naturally give rise to the kind of similarity-based proactive interference clearly evident in STM retrieval (see "Selection-Based Interference Effects") (Jonides & Nee 2006, Keppel & Underwood 1962).

We have intentionally left underspecified a precise quantitative interpretation of the *y*-axis in **Figure 1**. Psychologically, it perhaps corresponds to a combination of availability (largely driven by the dichotomous nature of the focus state) and accessibility (driven by a combination of both firing and plasticity). Neurally, it perhaps corresponds to some measure of both firing amplitude and coherence and potential firing amplitude and coherence.

We are clearly a long way from generating something like the plot in **Figure 1** from neuroimaging data on actual tasks—though plots of event-related potentials in STM tasks give us an idea of what these data may look like (Ruchkin et al. 2003). There no doubt is more missing from **Figure 1** than is included (e.g., the role of subcortical structures such as the basal ganglia in the frontal/parietal mediated control, or the reciprocal cortical-thalamic circuits that shape the nature of the neocortical patterns). We nevertheless believe that the time course sketched in **Figure 1** is useful for making clear many of the central properties that characterize the psychological and neural theory of human STM outlined above: (*a*) STM engages essentially all cortical areas—including medial temporal lobes—and does so from the earliest moments, though it engages these areas differentially at different functional stages. (*b*) STM reuses the same posterior cortical areas and representations that subserve perception, and active maintenance of these representations depends on these posterior areas receiving input from frontal-parietal circuits. (*c*) Focused items are distinguished both functionally and neurally by active firing patterns, and nonfocused memories depend on synaptic potentiation and thereby suffer from decay and retroactive interference. (*d*) Nonfocused memories are reinstantiated into active firing states via an associative retrieval process subject to proactive interference from similarly encoded patterns.

Postscript: Revisiting Complex Cognition

A major goal of this review has been to bring together psychological theorizing (the mind) and neuroscientific evidence (the brain) of STM. However, any celebration of this union is premature until we address this question: Can our account explain how the mind and brain accomplish the everyday tasks (e.g., completing a tax form) that opened this review? The recognition probe task used in our example and the other procedures discussed throughout the main text are considerably simpler than those everyday tasks. Is it plausible to believe that the system outlined here, particularly in light of its severely limited capacity, could support human cognition in the wild?

It is sobering to note that Broadbent (1993) and Newell (1973, 1990) asked this question nearly two decades ago, and at that time they were considering models of STM with even larger capacities than the one advocated here. Even so, both observed that none of the extant computational models of complex cognitive tasks (e.g., the Newell & Simon 1972 models of problem solving) used contemporary psychological theories of STM. Instead, the complex-cognition models assumed much larger (in some cases, effectively unlimited) working memories. The functional viability of the STM theories of that time was thus never clearly demonstrated. Since then, estimates of STM capacity have only grown smaller, so the question, it would seem, has grown correspondingly more pressing.

Fortunately, cognitive modeling and cognitive theory have also developed over that time, and in ways that would have pleased both Broadbent and Newell. Importantly, many computational cognitive architectures now make assumptions about STM capacity that are congruent with the STM models discussed in this review. The most prominent example is ACT-R, a descendent of the early Newell production-system models. ACT-R continues to serve as the basis of computational models of problem solving (e.g., Anderson & Douglass 2001), sentence processing (Lewis & Vasishth 2005, Lewis et al. 2006), and complex interactive tasks (Anderson et al. 2004). However, the current version of ACT-R has a focus-based structure with an effective capacity limit of four or fewer items (Anderson et al. 2004).

Another important theoretical development is the long-term working memory approach of Ericsson & Kintsch (1995). This approach describes how LTM, using the kind of fast-encoding and cue-based associative retrieval processes assumed here, can support a variety of complex cognitive tasks ranging from discourse comprehension to specialized expert performance. In both the modern approaches to computational architecture and long-term working memory, the power of cognition resides not in capacious short-term buffers but rather in the effective use of an associative LTM. A sharply limited focus of attention does not, after all, seem to pose insurmountable functional problems.

In summary, this review describes the still-developing convergence of computational models of complex cognition, neural network models of simple memory tasks, modern psychological studies of STM, and neural studies of memory in both humans and primates. The points of contact among these different methods of studying STM have multiplied over the past several years. As we have pointed out, significant and exciting challenges in furthering this integration lie ahead.

LITERATURE CITED

Altmann EM, Gray WD. 2002. Forgetting to remember: the functional relationship of decay and interference. *Psychol. Sci.* 13(1):27–33

Anderson JR. 1983. Retrieval of information from long-term memory. *Science* 220(4592):25–30

Anderson JR, Bothell D, Byrne MD, Douglass S, Lebiere C, Qin Y. 2004. An integrated theory of mind. *Psychol. Rev.* 111:1036–60

Anderson JR, Douglass S. 2001. Tower of Hanoi: evidence for the cost of goal retrieval. *J. Exp. Psychol.: Learn. Mem. Cogn.* 27:1331–46

Anderson JR, Matessa M. 1997. A production system theory of serial memory. *Psychol. Rev.* 104(4):728–48

Anderson JR, Schooler LJ. 1991. Reflections of the environment in memory. *Psychol. Sci.* 2(6):396–408

Atkinson RC, Shiffrin RM. 1971. The control of short-term memory. *Sci. Am.* 224:82–90

Awh E, Barton B, Vogel EK. 2007. Visual working memory represents a fixed number of items regardless of complexity. *Psychol. Sci.* 18(7):622–28

Awh E, Jonides J. 2001. Overlapping mechanisms of attention and spatial working memory. *Trends Cogn. Sci.* 5(3):119–26

Awh E, Jonides J, Reuter-Lorenz PA. 1998. Rehearsal in spatial working memory. *J. Exp. Psychol.: Hum. Percept. Perform.* 24:780–90

Awh E, Jonides J, Smith EE, Buxton RB, Frank LR, et al. 1999. Rehearsal in spatial working memory: evidence from neuroimaging. *Psychol. Sci.* 10(5):433–37

Awh E, Jonides J, Smith EE, Schumacher EH, Koeppe RA, Katz S. 1996. Dissociation of storage and rehearsal in verbal working memory: evidence from PET. *Psychol. Sci.* 7:25–31

Baddeley AD. 1986. *Working Memory*. Oxford: Clarendon

Baddeley AD. 1992. Working memory. *Science* 225:556–59

Baddeley AD. 2000. The episodic buffer: a new component of working memory? *Trends Cogn. Sci.* 4(11):417–23

Baddeley AD. 2003. Working memory: looking back and looking forward. *Nat. Rev. Neurosci.* 4(10):829–39

Baddeley AD, Hitch G. 1974. Working memory. In *Recent Advances in Learning and Motivation*, Vol. 8, ed. GA Bower, pp. 47–90. New York: Academic

Baddeley AD, Thomson N, Buchanan M. 1975. Word length and structure of short-term memory. *J. Verbal Learn. Verbal Behav.* 14(6):575–89

Baddeley AD, Vallar G, Wilson BA. 1987. Sentence comprehension and phonological working memory: some neuropsychological evidence. In *Attention and Performance XII: The Psychology of Reading*, ed. M Coltheart, pp. 509–29. London: Erlbaum

Baddeley AD, Warrington EK. 1970. Amnesia and the distinction between long- and short-term memory. *J. Verbal Learn. Verbal Behav.* 9:176–89

Baddeley AD, Wilson BA. 2002. Prose recall and amnesia: implications for the structure of working memory. *Neuropsychologia* 40:1737–43

Badre D, Wagner AD. 2005. Frontal lobe mechanisms that resolve proactive interference. *Cereb. Cortex* 15:2003–12

Braver TS, Barch DM, Kelley WM, Buckner RL, Cohen NJ, et al. 2001. Direct comparison of prefrontal cortex regions engaged by working and long-term memory tasks. *Neuroimage* 14:48–59

Broadbent D. 1993. Comparison with human experiments. In *The Simulation of Human Intelligence*, ed. D Broadbent, pp. 198–217. Oxford: Blackwell Sci.

Brooks LR. 1968. Spatial and verbal components of the act of recall. *Can. J. Psychol.* 22:349–68

Brown GDA, Preece T, Hulme C. 2000. Oscillator-based memory for serial order. *Psychol. Rev.* 107(1):127–81

Buckner RL, Koutstaal W, Schacter DL, Wagner AD, Rosen BR. 1998. Functional-anatomic study of episodic retrieval using fMRI: I. Retrieval effort versus retrieval success. *NeuroImage* 7(3):151–62

Buffalo EA, Reber PJ, Squire LR. 1998. The human perirhinal cortex and recognition memory. *Hippocampus* 8:330–39

Burgess N, Hitch GJ. 1999. Memory for serial order: a network model of the phonological loop and its timing. *Psychol. Rev.* 106(3):551–81

Burgess N, Hitch GJ. 2005. Computational models of working memory: putting long-term memory into context. *Trends Cogn. Sci.* 9:535–41

Burgess N, Hitch GJ. 2006. A revised model of short-term memory and long-term learning of verbal sequences. *J. Mem. Lang.* 55:627–52

Cabeza R, Dolcos F, Graham R, Nyberg L. 2002. Similarities and differences in the neural correlates of episodic memory retrieval and working memory. *Neuroimage* 16:317–30

Cabeza R, Nyberg L. 2000. Imaging cognition II: an empirical review of 275 PET and fMRI studies. *J. Cogn. Neurosci.* 9:254–65

Cave CB, Squire LR. 1992. Intact verbal and nonverbal short-term memory following damage to the human hippocampus. *Hippocampus* 2:151–63

Cowan N. 1988. Evolving conceptions of memory storage, selective attention, and their mutual constraints within the human information processing system. *Psychol. Bull.* 104:163–91

Cowan N. 1995. *Attention and Memory: An Integrated Framework*. New York: Oxford Univ. Press

Cowan N. 2000. The magical number 4 in short-term memory: a reconsideration of mental storage capacity. *Behav. Brain Sci.* 24:87–185

Crowder R. 1976. *Principles of Learning and Memory*. Hillsdale, NJ: Erlbaum

Damasio AR. 1989. Time-locked multiregional retroactivation: a system-level proposal for the neuronal substrates of recall and recognition. *Cognition* 33:25–62

Darwin CJ, Turvey MT, Crowder RG. 1972. Auditory analogue of Sperling partial report procedure—evidence for brief auditory storage. *Cogn. Psychol.* 3(2):255–67

Deiber MP, Missonnier P, Bertrand O, Gold G, Fazio-Costa L, et al. 2007. Distinction between perceptual and attentional processing in working memory tasks: a study of phase-locked and induced oscillatory brain dynamics. *J. Cogn. Neurosci.* 19(1):158–72

den Heyer K, Barrett B. 1971. Selective loss of visual and verbal information in STM by means of visual and verbal interpolated tasks. *Psychon. Sci.* 25:100–2

D'Esposito M, Postle BR. 1999. The dependence of span and delayed-response performance on prefrontal cortex. *Neuropsychologia* 37(11):1303–15

D'Esposito M, Postle BR. 2000. Neural correlates of processes contributing to working memory function: evidence from neuropsychological and pharmacological studies. In *Control of Cognitive Processes*, ed. S Monsell, J Driver, pp. 580–602. Cambridge, MA: MIT Press

D'Esposito M, Postle BR, Jonides J, Smith EE, Lease J. 1999. The neural substrate and temporal dynamics of interference effects in working memory as revealed by event-related fMRI. *Proc. Natl. Acad. Sci. USA* 96:7514–19

Eng HY, Chen DY, Jiang YH. 2005. Visual working memory for simple and complex visual stimuli. *Psychon. Bull. Rev.* 12:1127–33

Ericsson KA, Kintsch W. 1995. Long-term working memory. *Psychol. Rev.* 102:211–45

Fletcher PC, Henson RNA. 2001. Frontal lobes and human memory—insights from functional neuroimaging. *Brain* 124:849–81

Frank MJ, Loughry B, O'Reilly RC. 2001. Interactions between the frontal cortex and basal ganglia in working memory: a computational model. *Cogn. Affect. Behav. Neurosci.* 1:137–60

Funahashi S, Bruce CJ, Goldman-Rakic PS. 1989. Mnemonic coding of visual space in the monkey's dorsolateral prefrontal cortex. *J. Neurophysiol.* 61:331–49

Fuster JK. 2003. Thoughts from the long-term memory chair. *Behav. Brain Sci.* 26:734–35

Fuster JM. 1973. Unit activity in prefrontal cortex during delayed response performance: neuronal correlates of transient memory. *J. Neurophysiol.* 36:61–78

Fuster JM. 1995. *Memory in the Cerebral Cortex.* Cambridge, MA: MIT Press

Gabrieli JDE, Brewer JB, Desmond JE, Glover GH. 1997. Separate neural bases of two fundamental memory processes in the human medial temporal lobe. *Science* 276:264–66

Garavan H. 1998. Serial attention within working memory. *Mem. Cogn.* 26:263–76

Gardiner JM, Craik FIM, Birtwist J. 1972. Retrieval cues and release from proactive inhibition. *J. Verbal Learn. Verbal Behav.* 11(6):778–83

Gillund G, Shiffrin RM. 1984. A retrieval model for both recognition and recall. *Psychol. Rev.* 91(1):1–67

Goldman-Rakic PS. 1987. Circuitry of primate pre-frontal cortex and regulation of behavior by representational memory. In *Handbook of Physiology: The Nervous System*, Vol. 5, ed. F. Plum, pp. 373–417. Bethesda, MD: Am. Physiol. Soc.

Grossberg S. 2003. From working memory to long-term memory and back: linked but distinct. *Behav. Brain Sci.* 26:737–38

Hampson M, Driesen NR, Skudlarski P, Gore JC, Constable RT. 2006. Brain connectivity related to working memory performance. *J. Neurosci.* 26(51):13338–43

Hanley JR, Young AW, Pearson NA. 1991. Impairment of the visuo-spatial sketch pad. *Q. J. Exp. Psychol. Hum. Exp. Psychol.* 43:101–25

Hannula DE, Tranel D, Cohen NJ. 2006. The long and the short of it: relational memory impairments in amnesia, even at short lags. *J. Neurosci.* 26(32):8352–59

Harris JD. 1952. The decline of pitch discrimination with time. *J. Exp. Psychol.* 43(2):96–99

Hasher L, Zacks RT. 1988. Working memory, comprehension, and aging: a review and a new view. In *The Psychology of Learning and Motivation*, Vol. 22, ed. GH Bower, pp. 193–225. New York: Academic

Hebb DO. 1949. *The Organization of Behavior.* New York: Wiley

Hockley WE. 1984. Analysis of response-time distributions in the study of cognitive-processes. *J. Exp. Psychol.: Learn. Mem. Cogn.* 10(4):598–615

Holdstock JS, Shaw C, Aggleton JP. 1995. The performance of amnesic subjects on tests of delayed matching-to-sample and delayed matching-to-position. *Neuropsychologia* 33:1583–96

Hopfield JJ. 1982. Neural networks and physical systems with emergent collective computational abilities. *Proc. Natl. Acad. Sci. USA* 79(8):2554–58

Jacobsen CF. 1936. The functions of the frontal association areas in monkeys. *Comp. Psychol. Monogr.* 13:1–60

James W. 1890. *Principles of Psychology.* New York: Henry Holt

Jensen O. 2006. Maintenance of multiple working memory items by temporal segmentation. *Neuroscience* 139:237–49

Jha AP, McCarthy G. 2000. The influence of memory load upon delay-interval activity in a working-memory task: an event-related functional MRI study. *J. Cogn. Neurosci.* 12:90–105

Johnson MK, Raye CL, Mitchell KJ, Greene EJ, Cunningham WA, Sanislow CA. 2005. Using fMRI to investigate a component process of reflection: prefrontal correlates of refreshing a just-activated representation. *Cogn. Affect. Behav. Neurosci.* 5:339–61

Jonides J, Lacey SC, Nee DE. 2005. Processes of working memory in mind and brain. *Curr. Dir. Psychol. Sci.* 14:2–5

Jonides J, Nee DE. 2006. Brain mechanisms of proactive interference in working memory. *Neuroscience* 139:181–93

Jonides J, Smith EE, Koeppe RA, Awh E, Minoshima S, Mintun MA. 1993. Spatial working memory in humans as revealed by PET. *Nature* 363:623–25

Jonides J, Smith EE, Marshuetz C, Koeppe RA, Reuter-Lorenz PA. 1998. Inhibition in verbal working memory revealed by brain activation. *Proc. Natl. Acad. Sci. USA* 95:8410–13

Keppel G, Underwood BJ. 1962. Proactive-inhibition in short-term retention of single items. *J. Verbal Learn. Verbal Behav.* 1:153–61

Lange EB, Oberauer K. 2005. Overwriting of phonemic features in serial recall. *Memory* 13:333–39

Lewandowsky S, Duncan M, Brown GDA. 2004. Time does not cause forgetting in short-term serial recall. *Psychon. Bull. Rev.* 11:771–90

Lewis RL, Vasishth S. 2005. An activation-based theory of sentence processing as skilled memory retrieval. *Cogn. Sci.* 29:375–419

Lewis RL, Vasishth S, Van Dyke J. 2006. Computational principles of working memory in sentence comprehension. *Trends Cogn. Sci.* 10:447–54

Lisman JE, Idiart MAP. 1995. Storage of 7+/–2 short-term memories in oscillatory subcycles. *Science* 267:1512–15

Luck SJ, Vogel EK. 1997. The capacity of visual working memory for features and conjunctions. *Nature* 390:279–81

Lustig C, Matell MS, Meck WH. 2005. Not "just" a coincidence: frontal-striatal interactions in working memory and interval timing. *Memory* 13:441–48

Malmo RB. 1942. Interference factors in delayed response in monkeys after removal of frontal lobes. *J. Neurophysiol.* 5:295–308

Manoach DS, Greve DN, Lindgren KA, Dale AM. 2003. Identifying regional activity associated with temporally separated components of working memory using event-related functional MRI. *NeuroImage* 20(3):1670–84

Martin RC. 1993. Short-term memory and sentence processing: evidence from neuropsychology. *Mem. Cogn.* 21:176–83

McClelland JL, McNaughton BL, O'Reilly RC. 1995. Why there are complementary learning systems in the hippocampus and neocortex: insights from the successes and failures of connectionist models of learning and memory. *Psychol. Rev.* 102:419–57

McElree B. 1998. Attended and nonattended states in working memory: accessing categorized structures. *J. Mem. Lang.* 38:225–52

McElree B. 2001. Working memory and focal attention. *J. Exp. Psychol.: Learn. Mem. Cogn.* 27:817–35

McElree B. 2006. Accessing recent events. *Psychol. Learn. Motiv.* 46:155–200

McElree B, Dosher BA. 1989. Serial position and set size in short-term memory: time course of recognition. *J. Exp. Psychol.: Gen.* 118:346–73

McGeoch J. 1932. Forgetting and the law of disuse. *Psychol. Rev.* 39:352–70

McKone E. 1995. Short-term implicit memory for words and non-words. *J. Exp. Psychol.: Learn. Mem. Cogn.* 21(5):1108–26

McKone E. 1998. The decay of short-term implicit memory: unpacking lag. *Mem. Cogn.* 26(6):1173–86

Meyer DE, Kieras DE. 1997. A computational theory of executive cognitive processes and multiple-task performance: 1. Basic mechanisms. *Psychol. Rev.* 104(1):3–65

Miller GA. 1956. The magical number seven, plus or minus two: some limits on our capacity for processing information. *Psychol. Rev.* 63:81–97

Milner PM. 2001. Magical attention. *Behav. Brain Sci.* 24(1):131

Miyashita Y, Chang HS. 1968. Neuronal correlate of pictorial short-term memory in the primate temporal cortex. *Nature* 331:68–70

Monsell S. 1978. Recency, immediate recognition memory, and reaction-time. *Cogn. Psychol.* 10(4):465–501

Murdock BB. 1982. A theory for the storage and retrieval of item and associative information. *Psychol. Rev.* 89(6):609–26

Nairne JS. 2002. Remembering over the short-term: the case against the standard model. *Annu. Rev. Psychol.* 53:53–81

Neath I, Nairne JS. 1995. Word-length effects in immediate memory: overwriting trace decay theory. *Psychon. Bull. Rev.* 2:429–41

Nelson JK, Reuter-Lorenz PA, Sylvester CYC, Jonides J, Smith EE. 2003. Dissociable neural mechanisms underlying response-based and familiarity-based conflict in working memory. *Proc. Natl. Acad. Sci. USA* 100:11171–75

Newell A. 1973. You can't play 20 questions with nature and win: projective comments on the papers of this symposium. In *Visual Information Processing*, ed. WG Chase, pp. 283–310. New York: Academic

Newell A. 1990. *Unified Theories of Cognition*. Cambridge, MA: Harvard Univ. Press

Newell A, Simon H. 1972. *Human Problem Solving*. Englewood Cliffs, NJ: Prentice-Hall

Nichols EA, Kao Y-C, Verfaellie M, Gabrieli JDE. 2006. Working memory and long-term memory for faces: evidence from fMRI and global amnesia for involvement of the medial temporal lobes. *Hippocampus* 16:604–16

Oberauer K. 2002. Access to information in working memory: exploring the focus of attention. *J. Exp. Psychol.: Learn. Mem. Cogn.* 28:411–21

Oberauer K. 2006. Is the focus of attention in working memory expanded through practice? *J. Exp. Psychol.: Learn. Mem. Cogn.* 32:197–214

Oberauer K, Kliegl R. 2006. A formal model of capacity limits in working memory. *J. Mem. Lang.* 55:601–26

Olson IR, Moore KS, Stark M, Chatterjee A. 2006a. Visual working memory is impaired when the medial temporal lobe is damaged. *J. Cogn. Neurosci.* 18:1087–97

Olson IR, Page K, Moore KS, Chatterjee A, Verfaellie M. 2006b. Working memory for conjunctions relies on the medial temporal lobe. *J. Neurosci.* 26:4596–601

Owen AM, Sahakian BJ, Semple J, Polkey CE, Robbins TW. 1995. Visuo-spatial short-term recognition memory and learning after temporal lobe excisions, frontal lobe excisions or amygdala-hippocampectomy in man. *Neuropsychologia* 33:1–24

Pashler H. 1988. Familiarity and visual change detection. *Percept. Psychophys.* 44:369–78

Pasternak T, Greenlee MW. 2005. Working memory in primate sensory systems. *Nat. Rev. Neurosci.* 6:97–107

Polk TA, Simen P, Lewis RL, Freedman E. 2002. A computational approach to control in complex cognition. *Cogn. Brain Res.* 15(1):71–83

Postle BR. 2006. Working memory as an emergent property of the mind and brain. *Neuroscience* 139:23–38

Postle BR, D'Esposito M. 1999. "What"—then—"where" in visual working memory: an event-related, fMRI study. *J. Cogn. Neurosci.* 11(6):585–97

Postman L. 1961. Extra-experimental interference and retention of words. *J. Exp. Psychol.* 61(2):97–110

Prabhakaran V, Narayanan ZZ, Gabrieli JDE. 2000. Integration of diverse information in working memory within the frontal lobe. *Nat. Neurosci.* 3:85–90

Pylyshyn ZW. 1994. Some primitive mechanisms of spatial attention. *Cognition* 50:363–84

Pylyshyn ZW, Burkell J, Fisher B, Sears C, Schmidt W, Trick L. 1994. Multiple parallel access in visual-attention. *Can. J. Exp. Psychol. Rev. Can. Psychol. Exp.* 48(2):260–83

Raichle ME, MacLeod AM, Snyder AZ, Powers WJ, Gusnard DA, Shulman GL. 2001. A default mode of brain function. *Proc. Natl. Acad. Sci. USA* 98:676–82

Ranganath C. 2006. Working memory for visual objects: complementary roles of inferior temporal, medial temporal, and prefrontal cortex. *Neuroscience* 139:277–89

Ranganath C, Blumenfeld RS. 2005. Doubts about double dissociations between short- and long-term memory. *Trends Cogn. Sci.* 9:374–80

Ranganath C, DeGutis J, D'Esposito M. 2004. Category-specific modulation of inferior temporal activity during working memory encoding and maintenance. *Cogn. Brain Res.* 20:37–45

Ranganath C, D'Esposito M. 2001. Medial temporal lobe activity associated with active maintenance of novel information. *Neuron* 31:865–73

Ranganath C, D'Esposito M. 2005. Directing the mind's eye: prefrontal, inferior and medial temporal mechanisms for visual working memory. *Curr. Opin. Neurobiol.* 15:175–82

Ranganath C, Johnson MK, D'Esposito M. 2003. Prefrontal activity associated with working memory and episodic long-term memory. *Neuropsychologia* 41(3):378–89

Renart A, Parga N, Rolls ET. 1999. Backward projections in the cerebral cortex: implications for memory storage. *Neural Comput.* 11(6):1349–88

Repov G, Baddeley AD. 2006. The multi-component model of working memory: explorations in experimental cognitive psychology. *Neuroscience* 139:5–21

Reuter-Lorenz PA, Jonides J. 2007. The executive is central to working memory: insights from age, performance and task variations. In *Variations in Working Memory*, ed. AR Conway, C Jarrold, MJ Kane, A Miyake, JN Towse, pp. 250–70. London/New York: Oxford Univ. Press

Reuter-Lorenz PA, Jonides J, Smith EE, Hartley A, Miller A, et al. 2000. Age differences in the frontal lateralization of verbal and spatial working memory revealed by PET. *J. Cogn. Neurosci.* 12:174–87

Roediger HL, Knight JL, Kantowitz BH. 1977. Inferring decay in short-term-memory—the issue of capacity. *Mem. Cogn.* 5(2):167–76

Rolls ET. 2000. Memory systems in the brain. *Annu. Rev. Psychol.* 51:599–630

Rougier NP, Noelle DC, Braver TS, Cohen JD, O'Reilly RC. 2005. Prefrontal cortex and flexible cognitive control: rules without symbols. *Proc. Natl. Acad. Sci. USA* 102(20):7338–43

Ruchkin DS, Grafman J, Cameron K, Berndt RS. 2003. Working memory retention systems: a state of activated long-term memory. *Behav. Brain Sci.* 26:709–77

Sakai K. 2003. Reactivation of memory: role of medial temporal lobe and prefrontal cortex. *Rev. Neurosci.* 14(3):241–52

Schubert T, Frensch PA. 2001. How unitary is the capacity-limited attentional focus? *Behav. Brain Sci.* 24(1):146

Scoville WB, Milner B. 1957. Loss of recent memory after bilateral hippocampal lesions. *J. Neurol. Neurosurg. Psychiatry* 20:11–21

Shallice T, Warrington EK. 1970. Independent functioning of verbal memory stores: a neuropsychological study. *Q. J. Exp. Psychol.* 22:261–73

Smith EE, Jonides J. 1997. Working memory: a view from neuroimaging. *Cogn. Psychol.* 33:5–42

Smith EE, Jonides J. 1999. Neuroscience—storage and executive processes in the frontal lobes. *Science* 283:1657–61

Smith EE, Jonides J, Koeppe RA, Awh E, Schumacher EH, Minoshima S. 1995. Spatial vs object working-memory: PET investigations. *J. Cogn. Neurosci.* 7:337–56

Sperling G. 1960. The information available in brief visual presentations. *Psychol. Monogr.* 74:Whole No. 498

Squire L. 1992. Memory and the hippocampus: a synthesis from findings with rats, monkeys, and humans. *Psychol. Rev.* 99:195–231

Sternberg S. 1966. High-speed scanning in human memory. *Science* 153:652–54

Talmi D, Grady CL, Goshen-Gottstein Y, Moscovitch M. 2005. Neuroimaging the serial position curve. *Psychol. Sci.* 16:716–23

Thompson-Schill SL, D'Esposito M, Aguirre GK, Farah MJ. 1997. Role of left inferior prefrontal cortex in retrieval of semantic knowledge: a reevaluation. *Proc. Natl. Acad. Sci. USA* 94:14792–97

Thompson-Schill SL, Jonides J, Marshuetz C, Smith EE, D'Esposito M, et al. 2002. Effects of frontal lobe damage on interference effects in working memory. *J. Cogn. Affect. Behav. Neurosci.* 2:109–20

Todd JJ, Marois R. 2004. Capacity limit of visual short-term memory in human posterior parietal cortex. *Nature* 428(6984):751–54

Todd JJ, Marois R. 2005. Posterior parietal cortex activity predicts individual differences in visual short-term memory capacity. *Cogn. Affect. Behav. Neurosci.* 5:144–55

Trick LM, Pylyshyn ZW. 1993. What enumeration studies can show us about spatial attention—evidence for limited capacity preattentive processing. *J. Exp. Psychol.: Hum. Percept. Perform.* 19(2):331–51

Ungerleider LG, Haxby JV. 1994. "What" and "where" in the human brain. *Curr. Opin. Neurobiol.* 4:157–65

Unsworth N, Engle RW. 2007. The nature of individual differences in working memory capacity: active maintenance in primary memory and controlled search from secondary memory. *Psychol. Rev.* 114:104–32

Vallar G, Baddeley AD. 1984. Fractionation of working memory: neuropsychological evidence for a phonological short-term store. *J. Verbal Learn. Verbal Behav.* 23:151–61

Vallar G, Papagno C. 2002. Neuropsychological impairments of verbal short-term memory. In *The Handbook of Memory Disorders*, ed. AD Baddeley, MD Kopelman, BA Wilson, pp. 249–70. Chichester, UK: Wiley. 2nd ed.

Verhaeghen P, Basak C. 2007. Aging and switching of the focus of attention in working memory: results from a modified N-Back task. *Q. J. Exp. Psychol. A*: In press

Verhaeghen P, Cerella J, Basak C. 2004. A working memory workout: how to expand the focus of serial attention from one to four items in 10 hours or less. *J. Exp. Psychol.: Learn. Mem. Cogn.* 30:1322–37

Vogel EK, Machizawa MG. 2004. Neural activity predicts individual differences in visual working memory capacity. *Nature* 426:748–51

Vogel EK, Woodman GF, Luck SJ. 2006. The time course of consolidation in visual working memory. *J. Exp. Psychol.: Hum. Percept. Perform.* 32:1436–51

Wager TD, Smith EE. 2003. Neuroimaging studies of working memory: a meta-analysis. *Neuroimage* 3:255–74

Warrington EK, Shallice T. 1969. The selective impairment of auditory verbal short-term memory. *Brain* 92:885–96

Waugh NC, Norman DA. 1965. Primary memory. *Psychol. Rev.* 72:89–104

Wheeler ME, Peterson SE, Buckner RL. 2000. Memory's echo: vivid remembering reactivates sensory-specific cortex. *Proc. Natl. Acad. Sci. USA* 97(20):11125–29

Wheeler ME, Shulman GL, Buckner RL, Miezin FM, Velanova K, Petersen SE. 2006. Evidence for separate perceptual reactivation and search processes during remembering. *Cereb. Cortex* 16(7):949–59

Wickens DD. 1970. Encoding categories of words—empirical approach to meaning. *Psychol. Rev.* 77:1–15

Wilken P, Ma WJ. 2004. A detection theory account of change detection. *J. Vis.* 4:1120–35

Wilson FAW, O'Scalaidhe SP, Goldman-Rakic PS. 1993. Dissociation of object and spatial processing domains in primate prefrontal cortex. *Science* 260:1955–58

Wixted JT. 2004. The psychology and neuroscience of forgetting. *Annu. Rev. Psychol.* 55:235–69

Woodman GF, Vogel EK, Luck SJ. 2001. Attention is not unitary. *Behav. Brain Sci.* 24(1):153

Xu YD, Chun MM. 2006. Dissociable neural mechanisms supporting visual short-term memory for objects. *Nature* 440:91–95

Yantis S, Serences JT. 2003. Cortical mechanisms of space-based and object-based attentional control. *Curr. Opin. Neurobiol.* 13:187–93

Zhang D, Zhang X, Sun X, Li Z, Wang Z, et al. 2004. Cross-modal temporal order memory for auditory digits and visual locations: an fMRI study. *Hum. Brain Mapp.* 22:280–89

Zucker RS, Regehr WG. 2002. Short-term synaptic plasticity. *Annu. Rev. Physiol.* 64:355–405

Relativity of Remembering: Why the Laws of Memory Vanished

Henry L. Roediger, III

Department of Psychology, Washington University in St. Louis, Missouri 63130;
email: roediger@wustl.edu

Annu. Rev. Psychol. 2008. 59:225–54

First published online as a Review in Advance on
September 12, 2007

The *Annual Review of Psychology* is online at
http://psych.annualreviews.org

This article's doi:
10.1146/annurev.psych.57.102904.190139

0066-4308/08/0203-0225$20.00

Key Words

learning, recall, recognition, retention, transfer

Abstract

For 120 years, cognitive psychologists have sought general laws of
learning and memory. In this review I conclude that none has stood
the test of time. No empirical law withstands manipulation across
the four sets of factors that Jenkins (1979) identified as critical to
memory experiments: types of subjects, kinds of events to be remembered, manipulation of encoding conditions, and variations in test
conditions. Another factor affecting many phenomena is whether a
manipulation of conditions occurs in randomized, within-subjects
designs rather than between-subjects (or within-subject, blocked)
designs. The fact that simple laws do not hold reveals the complex,
interactive nature of memory phenomena. Nonetheless, the science
of memory is robust, with most findings easily replicated under the
same conditions as originally used, but when other variables are manipulated, effects may disappear or reverse. These same points are
probably true of psychological research in most, if not all, domains.

Contents

INTRODUCTION

The *Annual Review of Psychology* is 58 years old. The intellectual heritage of this review on human memory began with Arthur W. Melton's article on *Learning* in the first volume in 1950. The topic of learning covered a wide band of research, and memory research was considered a subfield. Depending on the author of the learning chapters in the early volumes of the *Annual Review of Psychology*, human memory received either considerable attention (e.g., when B.J. Underwood was the author) or practically none (e.g., when H.F. Harlow was the author). The topic of learning continued to appear for the first nine years, with a review each year, but then became more specialized (e.g., perceptual learning). In 1968, the word "memory" appeared for the first time in a chapter title, when G. Keppel wrote a review on "Verbal Learning and Memory" (Keppel 1968). Two years later, E. Tulving & S.A. Madigan (1970) turned the title around for emphasis on memory, but they began their "Memory and Verbal Learning" review by commenting, "The domain of psychological research known today under the bifurcated title of verbal learning and memory has suffered through a long and dull history" (p. 437).

During the 1960s through much of the 1980s, authors took it upon themselves to cover the whole field, albeit selectively, in their reviews. Often they reported the exact period of months being covered. However, at some point along the way, that strategy became hopeless due to the explosion in research, and writers of these reviews (at least in the field of human memory) wisely concentrated on one or a few topics [e.g., Richardson-Klavehn & Bjork (1988) wrote on the study of implicit or indirect tests, in a heavily cited review, and ignored the rest of the field]. I have decided to follow in this tradition, and so my review does not pretend to cover the field or even to cover much recent research. Even making the bold assumption that it was once possible to knowledgeably survey the whole field of learning and memory, those days are long past. In some ways, my review would be more appropriate for a Centennial Review of Psychology.

The focus of this review is on relativity of remembering, using "remembering" in its generic sense of performance on a memory test rather than in its specialized sense developed by Tulving (1985a,b). The tradition of research considered here is that of the experimental/cognitive psychologist who, starting with Ebbinghaus (1885/1964), believes that incisive experimentation and judicious (but not expansive) theorizing is a powerful road to seeking truth about human memory. Of course, many other approaches to the topic of memory are perfectly valid in their own realm: cellular and molecular neurobiology studies with emphasis on synaptic change, long-term potentiation, and many other topics; approaches from animal learning and behavior that emphasize conditioning; ethological studies of foraging and homing, among other topics; neuropsychological studies of patients with various defects in learning and memory; behavioral neuroscience approaches studying animal models of memory; cognitive neuroscience approaches using various imaging techniques; social psychological approaches concerned with social remembering; and broad approaches from history and sociology on the study of collective memory and how it shapes personal identity (Wertsch 2002). All these fields have their own traditions for the study of learning and memory. We may someday hope for a unified science of memory, but that day is not yet at hand (see Roediger et al. 2007 for a start in this direction).

For purposes of this review, I follow in the tradition started by Ebbinghaus in assuming that scientists can wrest hard-won truths about memory from Mother Nature through careful, thorough (perhaps even compulsive) experimentation on adult human subjects. My review focuses further on long-term memory and not so much on short-term or working memory, a topic covered well in the review by Jonides et al. (2008).

LAWS OF MEMORY

The theme of this review—the relativity of remembering—contests a major assumption that shaped beliefs of the pioneers of our field, i.e., that there are general laws of learning and memory. Early researchers pronounced several laws of memory, and other generalizations and regularities have been proposed over the years. In *Animal Intelligence: Experimental Studies* (1911), E.L. Thorndike wrote, with breathtaking authority, "Two laws explain all learning." (They were the law of effect and the law of exercise.)

Dated from 1885, the experimental psychology tradition of the study of learning and memory is 123 years old. We have learned many fascinating facts about memory in this time, ones that would astonish Ebbinghaus. Yet the thesis of this review is that one central lesson to be gained from thousands of experimental studies is that no general laws of memory exist. All statements about memory must be qualified.

By a "law," I do not necessarily mean anything too grand, either, like Newton's three laws. Rather, I use the term "law" simply to mean an empirical regularity, an established functional relation, one that holds widely (ideally, universally) across manipulation of other variables. In an excellent article on "One Hundred Years of Laws in Psychology," Teigen (2002) proposed five criteria for laws in science: validity (the law should be a well-established regularity, with deterministic laws tolerating no exception and probabilistic laws having few); universality (the law should be independent of place and time); priority (laws take precedence over observations, such that when observations seem at odds with the law we tend to doubt the observations); explanatory power (the law is connected to other general principles); and autonomy (the law should be self-contained, able to be encapsulated in a brief description, preferably mathematical).

Many early researchers hoped that psychology would be like physics and produce general laws of behavior, to rival (say) Kepler's laws of planetary motion. Kepler was a devotee of numerology, and sought simple laws that would unite the whole solar system; he even sought a relation between musical harmonies and planetary motion. It took him 17 years of hard work to produce his famous third law. Commenting on Kepler's quest, Holton & Brush (1985) stated, "This conviction that a simple rule exists, so strong that it seems to us like an obsession, was partly a remnant of his earlier numerological preoccupations, and partly the good instinct of genius for the right thing to work on. But it also indicates a deep undercurrent running through the whole history of science: the belief in simplicity and uniformity of nature" (p. 44). The same tendency pervades any scientific field, but often the facts discomfort the belief, and calls for parsimony may be misguided if the parsimonious law is only about a circumscribed set of behaviors (Battig 1962).

Teigen (2002) examined 1.4 million abstracts in the PsychLit database from 1900 to 1999 for the occurrence of the word "law." His results reveal a striking regularity in that the term "law" has become much less frequent over this time, dropping from 266 mentions per 10,000 entries in 1900–1909 to a mere 10 from 1990 to 1999. "In other words, today one must read about 1000 journal articles before encountering a single law" (p. 108). Teigen's article was concerned with all of scientific psychology, but the same trends seem to be true in learning and memory research. The laws of memory have vanished from the scene.

Memory researchers have announced a number of laws of memory over the years. For example, some half dozen laws are provided in McGeoch's (1942) great textbook. Jost's (1897) two laws are still known today (and are considered below), but other "laws" of the day are not even recognizable 65 years later by those on the contemporary scene. Who today can even define the Kjerstad-Robinson law or the Müller-Schumann law of associative inhibition? (The first term refers to the form of the learning curve relating number of responses to its shape; the second essentially refers to the phenomenon of conditioned inhibition—see McGeoch 1942, p. 48 and p. 402, respectively.) As McGeoch (1942) reported in footnotes, the first law has rather immediate boundary conditions, so even as he wrote, the generality (and hence validity) of the law was called into question.

Besides a lack of generality of formal laws, even more commonsensical generalizations, ones that "everybody knows" (for example, that repetition improves memory), are either invalid or at least need to be qualified. No principles emerge that hold across various types of memory test, subject populations, retention intervals, instructional strategies, and so on. Although the relativity of remembering presents an uncomfortable fact for textbook writers and those of us wishing to communicate general principles to the lay public, the great truth of the first 120 years of the empirical study of human memory is captured in the phrase "it depends." Does repetition improve memory? Are spaced presentations better than massed presentations? Does deeper, more meaningful processing during encoding enhance retention relative to less meaningful, superficial analyses? Does generation (or active involvement) with learning materials improve retention relative to passive reading? Does the passage of time lead to forgetting? Do retrieval cues improve retention? If we cast our net of inquiry broadly across the field to consider these questions, the answer (as we shall see) is always, "it depends."

JENKINS' TETRAHEDRAL MODEL OF MEMORY EXPERIMENTS

In 1979, James J. Jenkins proposed a model of memory experiments, shown here (somewhat modified) in **Figure 1**. The ideas were presented in a book chapter, and the chapter by Jenkins was a commentary on other chapters and, indirectly, the whole volume. Furthermore, the chapter was tucked into the back of a very long edited book (Cermak & Craik 1979). The topic of the book was the levels-of-processing framework to learning and memory, which dominated the field in the 1970s (e.g., Craik & Lockhart 1972, Craik & Tulving 1975). Of course, many book chapters get lost in the shuffle, and the chapter by Jenkins was the twentieth of 21 chapters. Commentary types of chapters may get even shorter shrift than standard book chapters. It is perhaps for these reasons that the contribution from Jenkins has not (in my opinion) influenced the field as much as it should have. Although others have voiced somewhat similar ideas, Jenkins' contribution captures truths about memory simply, powerfully, and in just a few pages. His ideas were explicitly not intended as a theory of memory, but rather as a theory of memory experiments and how to

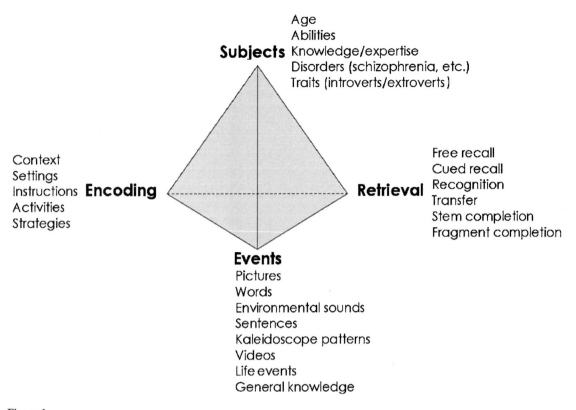

Age
Abilities
Subjects Knowledge/expertise
Disorders (schizophrenia, etc.)
Traits (introverts/extroverts)

Context
Settings
Instructions **Encoding**
Activities
Strategies

Retrieval Free recall
Cued recall
Recognition
Transfer
Stem completion
Fragment completion

Events
Pictures
Words
Environmental sounds
Sentences
Kaleidoscope patterns
Videos
Life events
General knowledge

Figure 1

Jenkins' tetrahedral model of memory experiments. Memory experiments can be considered a combination of four factors: subjects, encoding activities, events, and retrieval conditions. In a typical experiment, variations are made in one or two factors and others are randomized or held constant. Jenkins' point was that the effects obtained by manipulation of the independent variable on the dependent variable often depends on the levels of the control variables that are held constant. Adapted from Jenkins (1979).

interpret results from them. Yet his ideas can help lead to an appropriate theory. The general term for the theory might be contextualism, although that term has quite different meanings in various realms of social science and not all of them align with the view of Jenkins (see too his 1974 paper in which similar thoughts were expressed).

Jenkins' (1979) main point was that findings in any experiment about memory are *context sensitive* (italics are his, p. 431) and depend on the level of other variables that were not manipulated. That is, the control variables, those held constant, greatly influence the outcome of the experiment, but researchers usually remain blissfully ignorant

of their influence. Of course, it is natural at first to ignore variables that are not manipulated, but researchers should remain mindful of the fact that the particular outcomes in the research may be restricted in that they may only occur with particular settings of the control variables. Additional research in which these variables are manipulated is necessary to determine whether findings are robust (lawful) across a wide range of conditions, but often researchers repeatedly use a paradigm under the same conditions as in the original studies. Jenkins made his point with regard to memory experiments, but it actually holds across empirical research in all fields of psychology. In fact, Battig (1978) proposed broadening Jenkins' model of memory experiments to all psychological experiments.

Figure 1 reveals that experiments performed by cognitive psychologists are composed of a constellation of four basic factors. I have taken the liberty of updating the terminology used by Jenkins, or, less charitably, replacing a few terms with my own. One factor is the people involved in the research: college students (psychology's *Drosophila*), children, older adults, expert bridge players, depressed people, and so on. A second corner refers to events manipulated (or not) during encoding (context and setting, instructions given to subjects, activities or strategies used for learning, and more). For example, subjects can be told before receiving material that there will be a test (intentional learning instructions), or this fact may be omitted (incidental learning instructions) and the later test will be unexpected. A third corner refers to events to be remembered. These can be materials presented in a laboratory setting (word lists, stories, pictures, sentences, a crime scenario), general knowledge questions (What is the capital of Australia?), and events from one's life, among others. The fourth set of factors has to do with retrieval—the way retention is measured— and this factor has been much studied since the Jenkins (1979) chapter was published. A huge number of criterial task have been used to measure retention, from classic tasks like free recall, serial recall, paired associate learning, and various recognition procedures, to newer ones such as primed completion of word fragments or answering general knowledge questions. As with encoding, retrieval can be either intentional (when subjects are asked to remember events) or incidental (when the impact of prior experience is assessed through transfer or priming; see Jacoby 1984). This intentional/incidental contrast during retrieval corresponds to the distinction between explicit and implicit tests of memory (Schacter 1987).

Jenkins called **Figure 1** the "Problem Pyramid" or the "Theorist's Tetrahedron," and he noted, "The memory phenomena that we see depend on what kinds of subjects we study, what kinds of acquisition conditions we provide, what kinds of materials we choose to work with, and what kinds of criterial measures we obtain. Furthermore, the dependences themselves are complex; the variables interact vigorously with one another" (p. 431). Jenkins pointed to many interactions (second order and higher order) in his chapter, and the situation is surely more complex today than it was nearly 30 years ago. Even the separation of the factors above is not clear. For example, "instructions" is listed under encoding, but of course, the effect of the instructions will depend on the type of subjects receiving them and the knowledge the instructions activate.

Jenkins' model of memory experiments points up the possible complexity of the subject matter and the ways in which factors may interact. However, even it is incomplete. In later sections of this review, I consider cases in which all factors in Jenkins' pyramid are held constant and yet manipulation of another factor eliminates or even reverses experimental effects. This fact suggests that more faces might be added to the figure.

A CASE STUDY: THE LEVELS-OF-PROCESSING EFFECT

Following the spirit of the chapter by Jenkins and the volume in which it appeared, I apply Jenkins' scheme to the levels-of-processing effect (Craik & Lockhart 1972), the finding that semantic processing of materials (usually words in a list) leads to better retention on recall and recognition tests than do other types of processing, which channel attention to less meaningful aspects of the materials (e.g., phonemic or orthographic analyses). The levels-of-processing effect is enshrined in virtually all introductory, cognitive, and human memory textbooks, often without much qualification. Many in the field know of some limitations of the effect, but the power of semantic processing is often taken as first principle in the study of memory.

Let us take the famous experiments of Craik & Tulving (1975) as a reference point, because they were so powerful. Holding many classic variables of verbal learning constant (type of material, study time, general instructions to subjects, etc.), Craik and Tulving manipulated only the orienting task and the split-second judgment that subjects made about material during encoding. This orienting-task (or levels-of-processing) manipulation greatly affected the later recognition test, taking performance from nearly chance in one condition to close to perfect in another condition, as discussed below. In the basic procedure (similar in spirit to earlier experiments by Jenkins himself, e.g., Hyde & Jenkins 1969, 1973), students made judgments about 60 words (e.g., BEAR) on three different dimensions: Was the word printed in capital letters? Did it rhyme with chair? Did it refer to an animal? These tasks engender graphemic (case), phonemic (rhyme), and semantic (category) types (or levels) of processing, respectively. In the experiment, the answer to half of the 60 questions was yes, and for half the answer was no. In most of the experiments, the dependent measure was recognition memory.

Table 1 provides results from Experiment 9 (averaging across two replications) in the paper by Craik & Tulving (1975). Two basic effects are seen in **Table 1**, which were replicated several times in their experiments: Semantic processing of words provided better recognition than phonemic processing, which in turn led to better recognition than graphemic processing. In addition, items that

required a "yes" answer were generally better recognized than were those given a "no" answer (with two of the three orienting tasks). However, as is also apparent in **Table 1**, the two factors interacted such that the levels-of-processing effect was greater for "yes" than "no" answers.

Craik & Tulving (1975) reported ten or so experiments (some quite briefly), and their basic results have been replicated countless times when similar conditions have been used. As noted above, the typical levels-of-processing effects are huge, with recognition going from chance (33% under their test situation) in the case/graphemic conditions to 86% in the category/semantic condition when the task required subjects to provide a "yes" response. This experiment and ones like it using free recall measures (e.g., Tresselt & Mayzner 1960, Hyde & Jenkins 1969) are among the most powerful in the experimental study of memory. We still do not have a good theory of why the levels-of-processing effect (as it is called) occurs—Craik & Tulving's (1975) research showed that the original levels-of-processing ideas were wrong—but the fact that meaningful orienting tasks produce better retention than do ones that focus subjects' attention on phonemic or visual features is touted in practically all textbooks today. Roediger & Gallo (2002) discuss some of the mysteries left unexplained by the original levels-of-processing framework.

Surely the powerful effect of orienting tasks on later retention seems a good candidate for a general law of memory—meaningful encoding tasks produce better retention than phonemic or orthographic encoding tasks. In the 1970s, most researchers followed Craik and Tulving's procedures by using words, college student subjects, and recognition or recall tests. As noted, Craik & Tulving (1975) and others (Hyde & Jenkins 1969) did show generality over such variables as presentation rate and orienting instructions (intentional versus incidental learning). However, most variations were rather small ones, in retrospect.

Table 1 Proportion of words recognized after encoding words in relation to three types of questions (case, rhyme, and category) and their answers (yes or no). Adapted from Craik & Tulving (1975, Table 6)

	Yes	No
Case	0.33	0.33
Rhyme	0.62	0.42
Category	0.86	0.64

In applying Jenkins' ideas in **Figure 1**, we can also ask if the effect of orienting task (or the levels-of-processing effect) holds across subject groups, materials, and a variety of types of memory test. Considering subject groups first, in research to date, the effect seems quite secure when the standard procedure is used. Besides young adults, the effect has been shown to hold in preschool children (Murphy & Brown 1975), older adults (Craik 1977), and even patients with Korsakoff amnesia (Cermak & Reale 1978). Although exceptions may turn up in the future, so far all subject groups tested show the effect.

Turning to materials, the levels-of-processing effect holds widely across verbal materials (see Lockhart & Craik 1990 for a review). Relatively few studies have used nonverbal materials, but the effect has been obtained with faces (Smith & Winograd 1978) and chess positions (Lane & Robertson 1979). However, in a series of experiments, Intraub & Nicklos (1985) reported an exception: subjects studied pictures and answered questions about physical appearance (Is this horizontal or vertical?) or meaning (Is this edible or inedible?). Subjects were asked to recall the pictures using one- or two-sentence phrases, enough to indicate to the experimenter what picture was being recalled. Surprisingly, later recall was greater following physical encoding than following meaningful encoding. This advantage of physical encoding to meaningful encoding was replicated across six experiments but remains unexplained. In fairness, this is a rather isolated exception, and persistent experimental attention has not

been given to it. Still, it points to a possible lack of generality of the levels-of-processing effect across types of material.

Turning to type of criterial test, the evidence is quite mixed. On the positive side, for standard recall and recognition tests, the levels-of-processing effect holds quite well. On the other hand, when testing conditions are broadened, the effect disappears or even reverses. Type of criterial test is today widely acknowledged as a limiting condition of the effect. This is true of both implicit memory tests that are perceptual in nature (e.g., word identification, stem completion, fragment completion) and explicit memory tests that require subjects to access phonemic or orthographic information. Each case is considered in turn.

Jacoby & Dallas (1981) performed essentially the same type of experiment as Craik & Tulving (1975) except that they used two different measures of retention. That is, they manipulated question types to instantiate three levels of processing (case, rhyme, and category) and then gave subjects either a standard recognition test or what would today be called a perceptual implicit test. On the standard recognition test, they replicated Craik and Tulving's results, as can be seen on the left side of **Table 2**. Orienting task greatly affected level of recognition, as did whether the answer to the question was yes or no. However, on their second test, the outcome was quite different. The test they used is perceptual recognition (or word identification). In this test, subjects saw exactly the same sequence of items as on the standard recognition

Table 2 Proportion of words recognized (hit rates) in an explicit test (left side) and priming in identifying words on an implicit word identification test (right side). Priming is the difference in identifying studied relative to nonstudied words. Adapted from Jacoby & Dallas (1981, Experiment 1)

	Proportion recognized		Priming	
	Yes	**No**	**Yes**	**No**
Case	0.51	0.49	0.13	0.16
Rhyme	0.72	0.54	0.17	0.15
Category	0.95	0.78	0.15	0.18

test, but the words were presented very rapidly (about 35 msec per word, on average), and the subjects' task was to attempt to name the words as they whizzed by. The words were presented too fast to permit accurate recognition, so the measure of interest was how well subjects could name previously studied words relative to new words. Previous work had shown that prior study of words increased (or primed) the ability to name them on a word identification test, so the test can be used as an indirect (or implicit) measure of retention. The question of interest is whether orienting tasks would affect priming in word identification as they did in standard recognition and recall tests.

The answer was a resounding no. Shown on the right side of **Table 2** are priming scores derived from Jacoby and Dallas's results in their Experiment 1. The priming score is defined as the probability of correct identification of studied items minus identification of nonstudied items, which was relatively high in this experiment (0.65). Remarkably, the data on the right of **Table 1** show that neither the variable of orienting task nor the answer to the orienting task question (yes or no) systematically affected performance. Priming was about the same for all conditions in word identification under exactly the encoding conditions that had produced gigantic effects in episodic recognition (and, in other experiments, in recall). Yet priming definitely showed the effect of prior study (and hence measured retention), because the priming scores are positive— prior study increased identification. Jacoby & Dallas's (1981) results and many others since then argue that very different processes underlie certain types of explicit and implicit tests.

Graf & Mandler (1984) showed the same generally null results from the same type of encoding manipulation with word stem completion as the criterial test, and Roediger and colleagues (1992) replicated this result and showed the same null effects in primed word fragment completion. The conclusion from these (and many other) studies

is that manipulation of orienting tasks produces the levels-of-processing effects on some tests and not on others. In fact, Roediger et al. (1992) reported a situation in which the levels-of-processing effect was reversed, because priming was greater on verbal implicit tests following a graphemic encoding condition (subjects had to imagine the names of pictures and count the ascending and descending letters in the word) than following meaningful processing.

Perhaps this disparity in results between the left and right panels in **Table 2** arose because some researchers used explicit tests and others used implicit tests. This is not the case. Blaxton (1989) and Srinivas & Roediger (1990), among others, obtained the levels-of-processing effect using implicit memory tests (albeit ones conceptual rather than perceptual in nature). The explicit or implicit nature of the test does not determine whether the levels-of-processing effect occurs.

Even before Jacoby & Dallas's (1981) research, Morris et al. (1977) used a test that measured phonemic knowledge (Was a word that rhymed with care on the list?) and showed that prior phonemic encoding led to better performance on this type of criterial test than did prior meaningful encoding. That is, they showed that a reverse levels-of-processing effect can be obtained on explicit tests that ask subjects to consult the type of physical information encoded on "shallow" tasks. Morris et al. (1977) advanced the concept of transfer-appropriate processing, a contextualist idea in line with the arguments of Jenkins, and proposed that types of processing are not inherently deep or shallow (or good or bad) for later retention. Rather, whether types of encoding will enhance later retention depends on the properties of the test and whether information accessed during encoding will transfer to performance on the test. Processing must be appropriate for use on the test for positive transfer to occur. Other researchers reported either the same "reversed" levels-of-processing effect or no effect of orienting tasks on other explicit memory tests (Fisher

& Craik 1977, McDaniel et al. 1978), with the critical variable being the nature of retrieval cues and instructions given during the criterial task (see Jenkins 1979 for further examples).

In short, despite the powerful effects of orienting task judgments (semantic > phonemic > graphemic) observed by Craik & Tulving (1975) and many others, the effect does not constitute a general law because it depends on the nature of the test used (and perhaps other variables as well, such as type of material). If tests that draw on the perceptual record of experiences are used, no effect of orienting task generally occurs because perceptual characteristics of the stimuli are encoded in all the orienting tasks (Roediger et al. 1989b). If the test requires knowledge of the phonemic or graphemic characteristics that were encoded, a phonemic encoding task can produce greater performance than a semantic encoding task (Morris et al. 1977) and so can even a graphemic encoding task (McCabe & Jenkins 1978, as cited in Jenkins 1979, Stein 1978).

Challis et al. 1996 conducted the most systematic study illuminating the relativity of remembering in the levels-of-processing paradigm. In their ambitious experiment, five encoding conditions (manipulated within subjects) were crossed with six memory tests (examined between subjects), with performance in all conditions measured relative to a nonstudied baseline. The to-be-remembered items were words. Subjects simply learned them (intentional learning instructions), made judgments of whether the word could be related to the person (self-judgment), judged whether it referred to a living thing (living judgment), counted the number of syllables (count syllables), or counted the number of letters of a certain type (count letters). The tests were yes/no recognition, free recall, cued recall with semantic cues, cued recall with graphemic cues, or, finally, the two implicit memory tests of answering general knowledge questions and completing word fragments.

The results are presented in **Figure 2** in units of least significant differences relative to baseline performance (to put all tasks on

Figure 2

An experiment in which encoding conditions were manipulated within subjects and memory tests were administered between subjects. The results portray a complex interaction between encoding and retrieval conditions, showing that various measures of memory reflect different aspects of performance. Adapted from Challis et al. 1996.

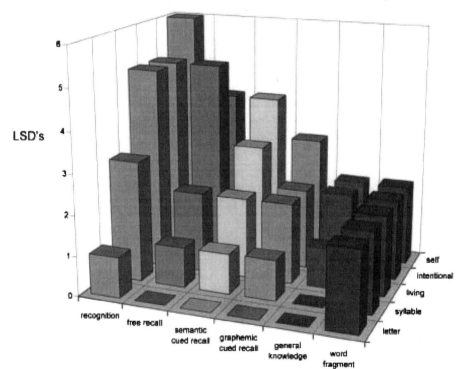

a common scale and so that any bars of different height are significantly different). Just a quick look at the figure shows that the results are complex—some encoding tasks produced better performance on some tests than others; tests differed markedly in revealing effects of past experience. All tests produced equivalent priming on the perceptual implicit memory test of word fragment completion, but the letter-encoding task produced significantly better performance than baseline only on this test and on recognition. The other tests picked up no effect of prior study in this encoding condition.

Consider just the nine bars in the upper left of **Figure 2**, comprising a 3 × 3 encoding/retrieval design. All the tests considered (recognition, free recall, and semantic cued recall) are based primarily on meaning (according to criteria spelled out by Roediger et al. 1989b), yet three different patterns of effect that occurred across encoding conditions (self-referential processing, intentional learning, and living/nonliving judgments) were observed. Recognition was best after self-encoding and equivalent after the other two manipulations. Free recall, on the other hand, was best after intentional learning, next best after self-encoding, and least good (among these three encoding conditions) after making living/nonliving judgments. Finally, for semantic cued recall, yet a different pattern emerged, with self > intentional > living. Thus, even though the three tests are similar in many ways (at least compared with, say, word-fragment completion), three different patterns of results emerged as a function of manipulation of encoding tasks (which themselves were rather similar, at least relative to rhyme or letter encoding tasks).

The point here (luckily) is not to explain the results in **Figure 2** (see Challis et al. 1996 for a valiant attempt), but rather to use the results to point to the relativity of remembering. In most experiments in which a variety of encoding manipulations are compared and contrasted across a variety of tests, the outcome is often just like that in **Figure 2**—a

complex interaction (see Kolers & Roediger 1984 and Roediger et al. 1989a for additional examples). When asking if Condition A provides better retention than Condition B, the answer is always "it depends" (on the type of test, or the materials, or the retention interval, and so on).

MEMORY TESTS

No comprehensive history of experimental studies of memory has ever been written (and we can pause briefly to wonder why, given how many researchers have devoted their lives to this field). However, if one were to be written, two dramatic changes that would be noted since 1970 would lie in the proliferation of different methods of testing memory (see Schacter 1987) and the explosion of different kinds of memory that have been postulated (e.g., Tulving 1972, 2007). The two changes are not unrelated, of course.

Here I focus on tests of memory. The field began with researchers measuring recall of presented items in order, as though serial recall were the natural starting place. Ebbinghaus (1885/1964) required himself to recall nonsense syllables in order, although the primary measure he used was trials to criterion (the number of study and test trials required to reach a single perfect recitation). He then measured the savings in the number or percentage of trials to repeat this feat at a later time. Ebbinghaus preferred the savings method because he regarded it as objective and much preferable to the "introspective methods" of recall or recognition. After all, in these latter measures, how could one know if the subject were performing optimally, or perhaps merely constructing plausible answers, or even blindly guessing? Savings methods overcame these problems to permit a more certain measure of retention.

Working at about the same time, Nipher (1876, 1878) presented digits and also measured serial recall, but he scored the number or percentage of correct responses in remembering digits in order, as in a telephone number (not that telephones were in use at that point; Nipher's materials were the mantissas of logarithms). He first reported the serial position effect, among other discoveries (Stigler 1978).

A bit later, Calkins (1894) developed the paired-associate learning technique, and other methods to measure retention quickly followed, primarily free recall (Kirkpatrick 1894) and recognition memory (e.g., Strong 1912). After these early developments, researchers generally stuck to these measures and used them and straightforward variations on them (such as measuring latencies) to ask many questions. Hall's (1971) *Verbal Learning and Retention*, a thorough text from the heyday of the verbal learning tradition, focused almost entirely on serial learning and paired-associate learning, although small sections were also devoted to free recall, recognition, and transfer procedures.

As far as I can tell, little was said in the early days about selection of dependent measures for analysis. The implicit assumption seems to have been that "memory" was a single entity and that most any measure would do, although some might be more convenient and more sensitive than others depending on the question being asked. For example, paired associate learning was appropriate if interest was in learning of single associations, whereas serial learning was more appropriate for learning a chain of associations. Recognition was often thought to be more sensitive than recall because it could detect memory traces of less strength (e.g., see Kausler 1974, p. 8). Free recall measures came to the fore later for intensive study. Deese (1957) introduced the technique of single-trial free recall and began the study of its serial position curve, which fueled much research in the 1960s and 1970s (and even today). Studies of multitrial free recall were introduced to study organizational processes, either subjects' tendencies to adopt organization inherent in materials (category clustering; Bousfield 1953) or organization imposed by the subject on materials selected to have no obvious orga-

nization (Mandler 1967, Tulving 1962). On the other hand, single-item (yes/no or free choice) recognition procedures were more appropriate for assessing item-specific knowledge. However, the overarching assumption seemed to be that all these methods were intended to study the same entity, memory. The procedures varied in their ability to elicit different aspects of retention, but of seemingly the same kind of memory.

Even as late as 1979, Jenkins noted that only "a few workers are interested in criterial tasks" (p. 432). He meant "few" in relation to the huge number of researchers interested in the other three prongs shown in **Figure 1** having to do with events (materials), encoding manipulations, and subject populations. However, since 1979, the number of memory measures that are in common use has exploded, fueled in large part by research on implicit or indirect measures of memory but also with a general broadening of scope of the field (e.g., autobiographical memory, prospective memory, among other topics).

The seeds for the cataclysmic changes in memory research had been sewn in the late 1960s, in papers by Warrington & Weiskrantz (1968, 1970), but no one knew it at the time. In their famous experiments, amnesic patients and control subjects studied lists of words and then were given tests of free recall, recognition and two novel tests. One of these tests involved completing words when given their initial letters, a task now called word stem completion. The other involved giving subjects fragmented words, words with parts missing. In both cases, the subjects' task was to complete the stem or fragment with a word. The finding from the experiment was that amnesic patients performed worse than control subjects on the recall and recognition tests, but the two groups performed about equally on the word stem and word fragment tests. Amnesic patients were not amnesic on all tests of memory. Warrington & Weiskrantz (1968) concluded, " . . . retention by partial information is a particularly favourable retrieval method for amnesics but not for controls" (pp. 629–630). In other words, they thought that the stem and fragment tests were simply powerful cues that were accessing the same type of memory as the other tests, the implicit assumption being there was only one form of memory to be accessed. Of course, from this standpoint, one could wonder why recognition performance was not also equivalent: How could a stem or fragment of a word serve as a more powerful cue than the whole word, when the target was the whole word? Warrington & Weiskrantz (1970) attempted to explain this paradox in terms of proactive interference being expressed differently on the different kinds of test (see p. 630).

Some controversy erupted about the replicability of these findings in the 1970s when other researchers did not find performance of amnesic patients equivalent to that of controls on stem and fragment tests (e.g., Squire et al. 1978). However, later research shows that the issue hinges on instructions subjects are given on these stem cued tests. If subjects are told to try to use each stem or fragment as a cue to retrieve a word from the list (in today's parlance, if they are given explicit memory instructions), amnesic patients perform worse than do normal subjects. On the other hand, if they are told to respond with the first word that comes to mind when they see the cue (implicit memory instructions), then equivalent priming is observed between groups (e.g., Graf et al. 1984). In general, on many tasks, when implicit memory instructions are used, researchers find equivalent priming between amnesic patients and control subjects (Shimamura 1986; see too Moscovitch et al. 1993). In their original paper, Warrington & Weiskrantz (1968, p. 974) pointed out, "...in addition to the rapidity and uniformity in learning this task [naming picture fragments], patients find it a much less exacting test than more conventional ones. They treat it more as a 'guessing game' than a formal test of memory."

Jenkins (1979) pointed out that the experimental set during encoding matters, but the literature shows that instructional set during testing greatly matters, too. In explicit memory tests, instructions to subjects require them to enter what Tulving (1983) called the retrieval mode, which is generally a necessary precursor for retrieval from episodic memory. By definition, instructions on implicit tests do not cause subjects to enter the retrieval mode, and often the instructions are designed to discourage such a mental set. Schacter et al. (1989) suggested that one strong form of evidence for distinguishing explicit and implicit forms of retention can be obtained by varying only instructions to subjects and holding all other aspects of the situation constant, a procedure they dubbed the retrieval intentionality criterion. If a researcher obtains different patterns of performance on explicit and implicit forms of a test holding everything else constant, then intentional and incidental (implicit) forms of retention are more secure. Of course, even on implicit tests subjects may sometimes produce an item that reminds them of the retrieval episode, leading to the phenomenon that has been labeled involuntary conscious memory and studied in its own right (e.g., Richardson-Klavehn et al. 1999).

Tulving (1972) proposed the distinction between episodic and semantic memory, and, for a time, the dissociations between performance on explicit memory tests and implicit memory tests were attributed to broad differences between episodic and semantic memory (Tulving 1983, 1985a) or between declarative and procedural memory in other classification schemes (e.g., Squire 1987). However, this broad heuristic did not survive empirical scrutiny, because it could be shown that tasks tapping the same putative system could be dissociated (e.g., Blaxton 1989, Srinivas & Roediger 1990; see Roediger et al. 1989a for a review). Researchers explained the different pattern of performance on certain implicit tests by proposing that performance on word stem or word fragment completion was caused by data-driven or perceptual processing (Roediger & Blaxton 1987), or reflected the perceptual record of experience (Kirsner

& Dunn 1985), or depended upon perceptual memory systems (Tulving & Schacter 1990).

Propelled by the flurry of research on implicit memory in the 1980s and 1990s, the number of tests used and the varieties of memory proposed has grown over the years. Toth (2000) listed 40 different tasks that have been (or in some cases, might be) used to study priming on implicit memory tests (see his Table 16.1 on p. 251). In a recent review, Tulving (2007) asked, semiseriously, "Are there 256 kinds of memory?" The large number of implicit and explicit memory tests tapping many varieties of memory point to a general problem for the field if one seeks general laws of learning and memory. Is it possible to find common laws across these many manifestations of learning and memory? The answer is clearly no.

Of course, one can wonder if the term "memory" has become too broad, encompassing all types of improvements with experience that might better be labeled with other terms (perceptual plasticity, priming, enhanced sensitivity, or whatever). Tulving (1983) has indeed argued that the term "memory" is too broad and is akin to similarly synoptic terms like locomotion. No one seeks general laws of locomotion and, similarly, perhaps no one should seek general laws of memory. Tulving (1985b) wrote, "[N]o profound generalizations can be made about memory as a whole, but general statements about particular kinds of memory may be perfectly possible" (p. 385). This statement is certainly true in principle, but even if a researcher looked for laws in only certain classes of test (e.g., explicit or implicit memory tests, or even free recall and recognition), the answer would be that there are none. No independent variable has even a monotonic effect on a variety of dependent measures of memory; exceptions to any broad generalizations exist. In the next section, I consider some of the most likely candidate variables for putative laws of memory and review why they do not survive close scrutiny.

CANDIDATE VARIABLES FOR LAWFUL RELATIONS

Many variables have been proposed as candidates for possible lawful relations. I consider here repetition, study time, spacing, generation, the mirror effect, imagery and the picture superiority effect, testing, and forgetting as the pre-eminent candidates. In all these cases attention is focused on exceptions to what has been proposed to be a general rule or a law.

Repetition

Perhaps the oldest generalization about learning is that it improves with repetition. Ebbinghaus (1885/1964) pointed to the gradual nature of learning and the effect of repetition in a passage in which he employed a metaphor for memory first used by Aristotle. In commenting on the relation between repetition and savings, he wrote:

> These relations can be described figuratively by speaking of the series as being more or less deeply engraved on some mental substratum. To carry out this figure: as the number of repetitions increases, the series are engraved more and more deeply and indelibly; if the number of repetitions is small, the inscription is but surface deep and only fleeting glimpses of the tracery can be caught; with a somewhat greater number the inscription can, for a time at least, be read at will; as the number of repetitions is still further increased, the deeply cut picture of the series fades out only after longer intervals. (Ebbinghaus 1885/1964, pp. 52–53)

Ebbinghaus provided a clear account, and one can find many confirmations of the general point that repetition on a task provides general improvement. However, many exceptions also exist in which repetitions do not improve performance at all, much less in accord with a particular function. We consider just a few exceptions here. Tulving (1966) exposed subjects to words under incidental learning conditions for six times before he placed the items in lists and required subjects to learn them. A control group performed the same initial task, but the words seen in the first list did not overlap with those later encountered in the to-be-learned list. The prior repetitions of the relevant words did not improve learning a whit, contrary to any account that strength accrues simply as a function of repetition.

Mandler & Pearlstone (1966) had one group of subjects sort 52 unrelated words into 2 to 7 idiosyncratic groups of their own choosing, with the requirement that subjects be able to make two consecutive sorts that were nearly identical. A yoked control group was required to do the same task, except that they had to discover the organization used by one of the subjects in the other group. Not surprisingly, the number of repetitions between the free choice and the yoked groups varied widely—an average of only 3.5 sorting trials in the free choice group compared to 7.5 trials in the yoked group. Nonetheless, when Mandler & Pearlstone (1966) later required both groups to recall the words, they did so equally well. Despite a doubling in the number of repetitions, the yoked group performed no better than the free choice group. However, for both groups the number of categories was strongly related to recall. As Crowder (1976) put it in summarizing these results, "the effect of repetition on recall was not direct; instead, repetition provided the occasion for organization to occur and organization was what supported good recall" (p. 340).

Many other examples could be provided showing that repetition does not always improve performance. Craik & Watkins (1973) reported two experiments that varied the amount of rehearsal (covert repetition) that subjects gave to words in lists. Despite huge variations in the amount of rehearsal across various experimental conditions, the number of rehearsals was unrelated to later recall. Glenberg et al. (1977) confirmed that rote repetition did not affect recall, but they showed that it did have an effect on recognition, an early indication that these measures

differ in important ways. Challis & Sidhu (1993) examined priming on implicit memory tests and manipulated the number of presentations before the test from 1 to 16. The amount of priming on a word fragment completion test was about as great from 16 presentations as from 1. In short, repetition does not always affect memory performance; there is no law of repetition.

Repetition also has to do with practice effects, and Newell & Rosenbloom (1981) argued for a "law of practice" that followed a power function. The law of practice is like Thorndike's law of exercise—as people repeatedly practice a task, they get better at it; they become more accurate and faster (Anderson 1982). The practice law is usually considered a law of learning, but of course, traditional concepts of learning and memory are hopelessly intermixed in traditional learning experiments with repeated practice. Unless previous practice sessions are retained, improvements on future trials will not occur. Although the power law of practice does hold over a wide variety of tasks, debate exists as to whether it is a general law. The research reviewed above shows that repetitions can have little impact on learning, contrary to the power law (albeit from different kinds of experiments than those usually considered). In addition, Heathcote et al. (2000) have argued that the power law is misnamed and that an exponential equation fits the data better than a power function. More importantly, Rickard (1997) reported an exception to the power law and argued that the type of function obtained depends on the types of tasks that are practiced.

Study Time

Bugelski (1962) and Cooper & Pantle (1967) offered the total time law of learning and memory. This law stated that, within limits, the probability of recall of an event is a direct result of the amount of study time afforded the event. The kind of evidence adduced for the law was from list learning experiments in which subjects studied items for two 10-second periods, four 5-second periods, or ten 2-second periods. Some results worked out well within this framework, showing equivalent recall with equal amounts of total study time. However many problems exist for the total time law. For one thing, all the results reviewed in the prior section indicating that amount of repetition is not always related to retention also show that the total time processing material is not always a relevant factor. Results reviewed in the next section about distribution and spacing of repetitions also undercut the total time law, because two study periods distributed in time produce better recall than the same amount of time spent in massed study. Thus, evidence accumulated since the 1960s shows that total time spent in study seems to play little role in retention except in circumscribed situations. Writing in 1970, Melton commented that "it seems clear that the Total-Time Law is in deep trouble as an empirical law . . . " (p. 601). Evidence since 1970 further undercuts the "law," which indicates that the claim of a total time law of memory represents another case where the term law was inappropriately applied.

Distribution and Spacing

Ebbinghaus (1885/1964, p. 89) discovered, more or less by accident, that presentations of material that were distributed in time were retained better than presentations presented close together in time. Crowder (1976, pp. 275–276) usefully distinguished among repetition, distribution, and lag (or spacing) effects. Repetition effects refer to any situation in which a repeated event is better retained than an event presented once; distribution effects refer to the case when events distributed in time are better recalled than ones presented back-to-back, or massed; and finally, spacing or lag effects refer to cases in which a systematic increase in retention occurs with the amount of lag or spacing between two events. We have seen that repetition effects do not qualify for laws of memory,

but might distribution of repetitions qualify? The answer seems to be no. Although spaced repetitions do lead to greater retention than massed repetitions under many circumstances, numerous experiments have failed to find such an effect.

Melton (1970) introduced one of the most widely used paradigms to study spacing effects, single-trial free recall, and many studies have shown that the more widely spaced two presentations of a word are in a list, the better is recall. However, exceptions to this rule are many in number. For example, in the earlier mentioned studies by Tulving (1966) and Mandler & Pearlstone (1966) that failed to find any evidence of repetition, the presentations of words were widely spaced. Even in Melton's (1970) paper, he spent considerable effort toward explaining why the spacing or lag effect did not always occur. For example, if testing occurs shortly after the second presentation, massed presentation produces greater recall than does spaced presentation in a paired associate paradigm (Balota et al. 1989, Peterson et al. 1963). Once again, although spacing of presentations may aid retention under some conditions, the spacing effect hardly qualifies as a general law of memory.

The experiments cited above generally used single items in long lists as the unit of repetition. In the 1950s, Underwood examined distributed practice effects using lists of material (generally paired associates) as the relevant unit of repetition, and he reviewed this work in "Ten Years of Massed Practice on Distributed Practice" (Underwood 1961). At the outset of the review, he commented, "The primary empirical goal at the time this series of studies was initiated was a straightforward one, namely, to determine the range of conditions and material within which distributed practice facilitated learning or retention. The fact that 10 years have passed since this goal was established indicates that it has proven to be an elusive objective to obtain. Indeed, no implication should be drawn from the present paper that the goal has now been reached; the pursuit continues" (Underwood 1961, p. 229).

Underwood's (1961) review showed that distributed practice effects occurred only under rather narrow conditions in his experiments and others like them, especially ones involving response interference. It is probably for this reason that most researchers have examined repetition, distribution, and spacing effects of single items in long lists rather than with larger units of material as the unit of repetition. Still, Underwood's (1961) research undercuts the idea of spacing effects generalizing across tasks.

Jost's (1897) two laws announced more than 100 years ago have to do with repetition and distribution effects. As stated by Alin (1997), the laws are, "1) Given two associations of the same strength, but of different ages, the older one will get a greater value on a new repetition; 2) Given two associations of the same strength, but of different ages, the older one will fall off less rapidly in a given length of time" (p. 2). The first law represents another statement of distribution and spacing effects, and Jost used Ebbinghaus's results to support the law (and he replicated those results). However, to the extent that distribution effects sometimes disappear (e.g., Underwood 1961) or even reverse at short retention intervals (Balota et al. 1989), exceptions to the law exist. Similarly, the second law depends on forgetting having a negatively accelerated function. To the extent that exceptions are obtained (in consolidation or hypermnesia experiments, as reviewed below), that law is limited, too.

The material cited in this section is not intended to discredit the generalization that distribution and spacing often obtain and have many general properties when they are observed. Rather, the point is that many experiments have failed to find such distribution and spacing effects and the precise boundary conditions for spacing effects have yet to be determined. Cepeda et al. (2006) provided a large-scale review that shows considerable consistency in certain types of experiments. However, they excluded studies in which the unit of analysis was greater than the single repeated item in a larger set of items to be recalled, which often do not show distribution effects (Underwood 1961).

Generation Effects

Active learning seems to be better than more passive learning in many situations. The generation effect refers to the fact that when people have to generate information they retain it better than if they read it. Jacoby (1978) showed this effect using simple materials such as "foot–sh_," where subjects in the generate condition had to name the related item (shoe, in this example), whereas subjects in the read condition were required to read it ("foot–shoe"). Recall of the target items such as "shoe" was generally greater following generation than reading. Slamecka & Graf (1978) showed this effect with other types of materials, such as telling subjects to generate opposites and then giving them items such as "hot – ????" Generating "cold" led to better retention than when subjects had previously read a pair such as "hot – cold."

Generation effects are often large and robust in within-subjects designs, but they can also be fragile. For example, when whole lists of items are read or generated in either between-subjects or within-subjects/between-lists designs, the generation effect is eliminated and often reversed; that is, under these conditions, read items are better retained than are generated items (Nairne et al. 1991, Schmidt & Cherry 1989). (I return to the issue of type of design in a section below.) Furthermore, even in conditions in which a robust generation effect is obtained on standard recall and recognition tests, the effect is reversed on perceptual implicit memory tests such as identification of words from brief flashes (perceptual identification; Jacoby 1983) or in word fragment completion (Blaxton 1989, Srinivas & Roediger 1990). Once again, although active learning and generation aid performance in some situations and on some types of memory tests, many exceptions exist.

The Mirror Effect

Glanzer & Adams (1985) noted a regularity in recognition memory they dubbed the mirror effect. When high- and low-frequency words are studied and tested on a yes/no recognition test, hit rates are higher for low- than high-frequency words, but false alarm rates show the opposite pattern (more false alarms occur for high- than low-frequency words). The effect is easily replicated under their conditions. The mirror pattern is puzzling, because it seems incompatible with signal detection theories attributing positive responses on recognition tests to familiarity or strength of representations. If low-frequency words have higher familiarity for studied items (hits), why should they have lower familiarity for non-studied items (false alarms)?

Theorists have taken the task of explaining the mirror effect seriously and created and modified models of recognition memory to do so (e.g., Murdock 2003). However, Greene (2007) has recently provided a review of the literature that shows the mirror effect is not very general. Many situations exist in which hits and false alarms are positively correlated for types of material. Perhaps most tellingly, when subjects study pseudowords (nonwords that can be easily pronounced, like "flirp") and words, the mirror effect disappears on a recognition test. That is, pseudowords show higher hit rates and higher false alarm rates than do words (e.g., Greene 2003, Hintzman & Curran 1997), rather than showing the mirror pattern. As Greene (2007) comments, "Ironically, the prototypical case of the mirror effect involved comparing high-frequency with low-frequency words. However, if extremely low frequency words are used instead, the mirror pattern is violated" (p. 61).

Imagery and the Picture Superiority Effect

The ancient Greeks discovered that imagery can aid memory, and the Romans taught imagery mnemonics to aid rhetoricians faced with making long speeches (Yates 1966).

Many studies have shown that pictures are recalled and recognized better than words, as well as showing that when the referents of concrete words are imagined, they are better remembered than when coded only in verbal form (e.g., Bower 1972, Paivio 1969). In addition, the advice to use bizarre images rather than common images to enable retrieval also has generated empirical support (Webber & Marshall 1978, among others). However, against this backdrop of positive findings, limitations and boundary conditions appear. For example, some imagery findings hinge on the type of experimental design used. When within-subjects (mixed-list) designs are used, for example, robust bizarre imagery effects are obtained (e.g., McDaniel & Einstein 1986). However, when between subjects or (within-subjects, between-list designs) are used, bizarre images often produce no better retention than common images (Collyer et al. 1972, Hauck et al. 1972). As noted in the section on generation effects, the same design issue occurs in that domain: When item types (generate or read) are mixed in within-subjects designs, strong effects are usually seen, but when the same variable is manipulated in blocks or between subjects, the effects disappear.

I noted in discussing the Jenkins tetrahedral model of memory experiments that one could hold constant all variables posited there and still eliminate or reverse experimental effects by manipulating another variable. The variable is type of design. Cognitive psychologists often prefer to study a variable by manipulating it within subjects, for reasons of economy. However, as we have seen with generation and imagery, manipulating the same variable between subjects (or within subjects, but with blocked lists of materials) can cause the effect to disappear or even reverse (see Schmidt 2007 for many examples). This fact suggests that the Jenkins (1979) model might need another face, although perhaps "type of design" might be considered under encoding factors. In terms of generality of effects to conditions outside the lab, people will probably believe that one particular strategy is better than another (say, forming images relative to not forming them) and so would use that technique exclusively rather than intermixing the techniques. However, under such blocked conditions, the technique may not be effective. Curiously, the fact that numerous manipulations at encoding change depending on the nature of the design has received little direct attention in the literature, at least in human memory (see Poulton 1982 for consideration of perceptual and attentional phenomena that vary with design changes). Nairne et al. (1991) proposed an account for the vicissitudes of the generation effect with design changes, and recently McDaniel & Bugg (2007) have broadened this approach to provide a general account to explain why design changes affect performance in many tasks. The main point here is that the effects of seemingly powerful variables such as generation and imagery do not generalize across design changes.

Pictures are better remembered than words (the picture superiority effect). This outcome occurs in between-subjects designs (e.g., Erdelyi & Becker 1974) as well as within-subjects designs. However, the positive effects of imagery are not found on all tests. In verbal implicit tests such as word fragment and word stem completion, words produce much more priming than do pictures (e.g., Rajaram & Roediger 1993, Weldon & Roediger 1987). Although effects of pictures and imagery are often powerful when they occur, they are hardly ubiquitous across types of test.

Testing

Generation effects refer to active processing during learning relative to more passive processing. Testing effects refer to the advantage often conferred on retention if subjects actively retrieve information (e.g., Carrier & Pashler 1992, Gates 1917; see Roediger & Karpicke 2006a for a review). The testing effect can be powerful; retrieving only some of the information and not receiving feedback usually produces better retention than does restudying the whole set of material, although obtaining this effect depends on the delays used in the first test. [If the first test is delayed so long that performance on it is quite poor, then the testing effect will not be obtained (Spitzer 1939).] Although the testing effect can be strong under the right conditions, it is not ubiquitous. For example, Roediger & Karpicke (2006b) had subjects study a prose passage twice or study it once and take a test on it. A final criterial test was given after five minutes, two days, or one week to independent groups. On the nearly immediate test, performance was better following massed studying rather than studying and testing, so in this limited context of immediate testing, cramming (repeated reading) produced better performance. However, after two days or a week, the study-plus-test condition outperformed the repeated-study condition, showing that taking a test (even without feedback) is better for long-term retention than an equivalent time spent in repeated study.

Testing for smaller units of information, such as in paired associates, can also lead to impressive testing effects (e.g., Carrier & Pashler 1992). However, testing of a pair is ineffective in promoting retention on a later test when the first test is given quite soon after studying the pair (Jacoby 1978, Karpicke & Roediger 2007). Testing probably does not help much when retrieval occurs from working memory but only when it occurs with some difficulty from secondary memory.

Testing can have a large influence on performance, as with the other variables considered in this section, but no general law exists in this case, either. As usual, if one were to ask if testing helps promote later retention, the answer is "under certain conditions."

Forgetting

Woodworth (1929) wrote, "The machinery developed in the process of learning is subject to the wasting effects of time" (p. 93). McGeoch (1932) argued that interference, not decay, is the cause of forgetting. The first forgetting curve was produced by Ebbinghaus (1885/1964), and Wixted & Carpenter (2007) argued that he even nailed the equation relating time since learning to performance, a particular logarithmic function that is for all practical purposes equivalent to a power function. Forgetting functions would seem to be universal in the study of learning and memory, so do they perhaps represent a law of memory? They can even be fit precisely by equations, as noted above, although some debate occurs over which function fits best (Rubin & Wenzel 1996, Wixted & Carpenter 2007). However, for our purposes we can note that the contending functions all account for around 98% or better of the variance.

The question then is, are exceptions found to this seemingly universal law of forgetting? The answer is yes. One perhaps trivial exception has to do with continued processing—if people are permitted to rehearse or otherwise continually process small amounts of information, the information can be retrieved nearly perfectly over time. Assuming we discount this situation, but look at short-term retention after distraction, forgetting over time still depends heavily on other variables. Using the Brown-Peterson paradigm, Keppel & Underwood (1962) showed that on the first trial there was hardly any forgetting even over fairly long periods of distraction, at least long in the context of short-term memory experiments (see too Reitman 1974). The amount of proactive interference heavily determines the amount of forgetting over time; the same generalization holds true in long-term retention (Underwood 1957).

One might object, quite rightly, that the forgetting function might still be the same, a power function, but that the intercept is raised and lowered by other variables. That is true, but the situation is worse than that: Sometimes performance actually improves with increasing amounts of time since learning. The phenomenon of hypermnesia (e.g., Erdelyi & Becker 1974) represents one such case. In hypermnesia experiments, subjects study a set of pictures and then take repeated tests

over time, usually using free or forced recall. The finding that is often obtained (see Payne 1987 for a review) is improved performance over time. Hypermnesia depends on repeated testing of the same information (Roediger & Payne 1982), whereas in standard forgetting experiments, different subjects (or different items) are tested at various intervals to avoid the "confound" of prior testing. Once again, the difference is in between- versus within-subject manipulations of tests. One might argue that using within-subjects testing to measure changes in performance over time is the wrong way to proceed, due to the influence of earlier tests on later tests (the testing effect). However, in normal life we often find ourselves attempting to recall the same events repeatedly, so ruling out hypermnesia experiments as not representing the proper design for studying forgetting seems rather arbitrary. A commonplace occurrence outside the lab is to fail to retrieve information (a name, a fact) at one point in time only to recover it a bit later. Such reminiscence or memory recoveries have been studied for nearly a century (Ballard 1913). Just as some encoding variables lead to different patterns of effect when manipulated within subjects or between subjects, so might some testing variables.

Roediger & Payne (1982) reported an experiment on hypermnesia that produced a puzzling result that did not depend on repeated testing. They had three separate groups of subjects study 60 pictures and required them to recall the names of the pictures later. After the study phase, subjects were kept busy with instructions and (in two cases, reading an article) for 2, 9, or 16 minutes before commencing with a series of three tests. Of course, performance on the very first test is uncontaminated by any prior testing and so might be expected to show the usual power function for forgetting, because the reading diverted subjects' attention. However, recall of the pictures was 43%, 42%, and 43%, respectively, across the three delays. No forgetting at all occurred. Of course, after studying pictorial material, a verbal task might not be expected to create much interference relative to other tasks, but keep in mind that subjects knew they would have to recall the names of the pictures and so doubtless used verbal encoding strategies during study. Luckily for Roediger & Payne (1982), the experiment was about repeated testing, and the editor did not ask the authors to explain why no forgetting occurred between 2 and 16 minutes on the first test given to the different groups.

Even if hypermnesia experiments are excluded, another huge class of experiments—those demonstrating consolidation—sometimes show improved recall over time with no intervening practice (Dudai 2004, McGaugh 2000). Wixted (2004) noted that researchers in the tradition of human experimental (i.e., cognitive) psychology have rarely incorporated (or even discussed) the issue of consolidation. The reason is that it does not fit with the notion, implicit in most accounts, that encoding happens quickly, immediately after perception. After that, the processes responsible for forgetting (usually assumed to be various types of interference) exert their inexorable influence. However, in consolidation experiments with animals and humans, performance can sometimes be shown to improve over time for relatively long periods (without repeated testing during that time). In the past ten years, much research has been directed at the issue of whether consolidation of certain types of memories occurs during sleep (see Payne et al. 2007 for a review). Several different types of task—visual and auditory discrimination, video games, various motor memory tasks, and even certain episodic memory paradigms—show actual improvements over time during sleep (relative to waking), an effect attributed to enhanced consolidation during sleep. In a typical study, subjects practice some relatively novel skill (e.g., the video game Tetris) either at night or in the morning. They are then tested 8–12 hours later after either a night of sleep or a day of waking activities. The typical pattern is that subjects will show improved perfor-

mance on the video game after a night of sleep (showing absolute increases in performance), whereas after the equivalent amount of time spent in waking activities, subjects will show no improvement or a drop in performance (Stickgold et al. 2001). Apparently, both REM sleep and slow-wave sleep contribute to these consolidation effects (Stickgold 2005).

Dudai (2004) argued for two types of consolidation, synaptic consolidation (which is relatively quick) and system consolidation (which occurs more gradually). Consolidation is usually measured by less interruption from application of some amnestic agent with time since a learning experience rather than with any absolute increase in performance over time, as in the sleep and learning experiments cited above. Still, the latter type of phenomenon argues that there is no general law that says forgetting always occurs in the time since presentation of information. Some consolidation experiments, as well as hypermnesia experiments, undercut the idea that a universal law of forgetting exists. Once again, whether retention declines or improves over time depends on other factors.

QUALIFICATIONS AND PROVISOS

The purview of this review is studies of long-term memory in the tradition of experimental/cognitive psychologists. However, as noted at the outset, this treatment does not consider many other valid studies of memory (and learning) from other traditions. I mention some possible laws here from other traditions, but am not knowledgeable enough to comment on their current status.

Other traditions within cognitive psychology, such as short-term/working memory and motor learning and memory, have received short shrift here. Some discoveries in these arenas suggest a general principle, at least. For example, is there a fixed capacity to short-term memory at about 3–4 items, as Cowan (2005) maintains? Although not a law, exactly,

Cowan's proposal at least suggests an interesting invariance. I must leave this discussion to others.

Teigen's (2002) review noted that nearly all putative laws of psychology date back many years. These include classic laws of learning, too, such as the laws of effect and exercise (Thorndike 1898, 1911). In my review, I rather casually lumped together studies traditionally considered those of learning and those of memory, because separating this boundary is difficult. However, from the tradition of animal learning and behavior studies, we can consider such entries as Premack's law (or principle) of the relativity of reinforcement (Premack 1962) and Herrnstein's (1961) matching law, as well as Thorndike's laws of effect and exercise (although the latter has been widely discredited by some of the results discussed above, among others). Further, in classical conditioning (and the learning of associations more generally), we may consider the principle arising from the Rescorla & Wagner (1972) model stating that a mismatch in the current state of knowledge and new information provided to the system drives learning (Rescorla 1988). (This idea is akin to discussions in cognitive psychology of distinctiveness and novelty in promoting memory.) As I say, I am not competent to judge whether the ideas cited above represent general laws and must leave the task for other people. Seligman (1970) reviewed "laws" then believed about classical conditioning and showed them invalid, but of course, we can all hope that researchers in all these areas will find general laws in the future. The fact that past laws have been undermined does not mean new ones will not be found.

This review raises the issue of whether there are laws of memory, but because psychology has seen a distinct decline in discussion of laws in general, we can ask if there are general laws of psychology. Teigen (2002) noted that most laws still described in psychology texts are those first proposed long ago (e.g., Weber's and Fechner's laws in psychophysics). Again, I leave this discussion to others, but finding general principles of behavior that hold widely across the variables in Jenkins' (1979) tetrahedron may be difficult. Also, Jenkins' (1979) approach does not explicitly take into account such factors as culture, species, or even type of experimental design.

In short, my claims are about a particular arena of study of learning and memory. Perhaps others can defend general laws of learning and memory (or of psychology) in other domains.

A COURSE FOR THE FUTURE

The message of this review should not, in my opinion, be taken as depressing. Although our search for general laws of memory has not succeeded, we have learned a huge amount about human memory and its complexities in the past 125 years. Some have argued that even seeking laws and general principles is misguided. Baddeley (1978, p. 150) argued that "the most fruitful way to extend our understanding of human memory is not to search for broader generalizations and 'principles', but is rather to develop ways of separating out and analyzing more deeply the complex underlying processes," a point made too by Battig (1978) at about the same time.

In the past 30 years, dozens of measures of retention deemed valid indicators of memory and knowledge have been studied. Although cognitive psychologists rely heavily on a certain restricted class of procedures to study recall and recognition, these are only two of many possible assessments of past learning. Despite the fact that researchers may spend their careers concentrating on one or another measure, consideration of many measures simultaneously can upset any general characterization of "how memory works." Claims from our research must therefore be specific rather than general, but this does not prevent our seeking more general principles at higher levels of analysis.

Research programs that examine the effects of several independent variables across many dependent variables almost always show complex interactions. Such studies reveal dissociations across variables and point to a multiplicity of forms of retention. One focus for the future is how various conditions of learning transfer across various measures of retention. Transfer as a topic of study per se has fallen a bit out of favor, but it remains a fundamental concept for the science of memory (McDaniel 2007). Ideas such as transfer appropriate processing (Morris et al. 1977) and the encoding specificity principle (Tulving & Thomson 1973), among others, help to focus on the complex interactions inherent in memory research (see too Jenkins 1979; Kolers & Roediger 1984; Roediger et al. 1989a,b). However, these broad classes of ideas are just the beginning step to understanding these puzzling facts, and clearly much theoretical work is needed to develop them.

The fact that our science does not provide straightforward laws is perhaps well known. McKeachie (1974) made similar points years ago. After all, hardly any researcher writes about general laws any longer (Teigen 2002). At the most, one sees a passing reference to, say, Jost's second law, in a particular context. The aim of this review has been to remind us of the quest for laws and the difficulty in achieving them. In a sense, this state of affairs is no surprise. E.O. Wilson, in *Consilience* (1998, p. 183), commented that the social sciences "are inherently far more difficult than physics and chemistry, and as a result they, not physics and chemistry, should be called the hard sciences." The reason is that in the social sciences, which deal with the huge number of variables that affect behavior of individuals and groups, pinpointing cause and effect relations for complex behaviors is a daunting challenge. The study of human memory may even seem tractable relative to many other issues. Therefore, confronting the complexity in the field of learning and memory is a strong challenge, but not an insurmountable one.

CONCLUSION

When one reads or hears the claim that "repetition improves retention" or that "generating information enhances recall" or that "forgetting follows a power function" or all other statements of the form that "variable X has a consistent effect on variable Y," one can be certain that the claim is both true and false. It is true in that conditions can be found under which the rule holds (otherwise the claim would not be made), but false in that a skeptic can always say: "Very nice work, but your finding depends on many other conditions. Change those and your effect will go away."

The proponent of a general rule that "X affects Y" is, on analysis, usually claiming, "Our study has shown that variable X has a positive effect on a particular measure of memory in a particular situation holding many other variables constant." If some other perfectly valid measure of retention were used in a slightly different situation, with other variables held constant at different levels, no effect, a different effect, or even the opposite effect can often be shown to obtain. The most fundamental principle of learning and memory, perhaps its only sort of general law, is that in making any generalization about memory one must add that "it depends." Of course, only future research can typically tell whether some finding is widely generalizable or holds under a narrow set of conditions.

Should we be discouraged that laws of memory do not seem to exist? I would argue that the answer is no, and that we should be all the more impressed by our science because of its inherent complexity. The cognitive psychology (and cognitive neuroscience) of memory have led to many wonderful discoveries with new ones occurring yearly (if not monthly). The great majority of the findings are highly replicable, at least under the same or similar conditions as in the original studies. The field has a strong scientific base. We have learned a tremendous amount in the years since Melton (1950) wrote the first *Annual Review of Psychology* article on this general topic. There may be no general laws of memory yet discovered, but there is an exciting, robust, and increasingly detailed scientific base in the study of memory. Further, many of the discoveries can make important applications outside the laboratory, in fields such as law and education. Future research can only profit from acknowledging the inherent complexity of the phenomena of memory.

ACKNOWLEDGMENTS

This review benefited from comments by Yadin Dudai, Gilles Einstein, John Jonides, Kathleen McDermott, James Nairne, Dan Schacter and, especially, Endel Tulving. I thank them all and apologize for some requests that remain unfulfilled. The writing of the review was supported by a Collaborative Activity Grant of the James S. McDonnell Foundation and through grant R305H060080 from the Cognition and Student Learning program of the Institute of Education Sciences, U.S. Department of Education. The opinions expressed are those of the author and do not represent views of the Institute or the U.S. Department of Education.

LITERATURE CITED

Alin LH. 1997. The memory laws of Jost. *Göteborg Psychol. Rep.* 27(1):1–21

Anderson JR. 1982. Acquisition of cognitive skill. *Psychol. Rev.* 89:369–406

Baddeley AD. The trouble with levels: a re-examination of Craik and Lockhart's framework for memory research. *Psychol. Rev.* 85:139–52

Ballard PB. 1913. Oblivescence and reminiscence. *Br. J. Psychol. Monogr. Suppl.* 1:1–82

Balota DA, Duchek JM, Paullin R. 1989. Age-related differences in the impact of spacing, lag, and retention interval. *Psychol. Aging* 4:3–9

Battig WF. 1962. Parsimony in psychology. *Psychol. Rep.* 11:555–72

Battig WF. 1978. *Parsimony or psychology.* Presidential Address, Rocky Mountain Psychol. Assoc., Denver, CO

Blaxton TA. 1989. Investigating dissociations among memory measures: support for a transfer-appropriate processing framework. *J. Exp. Psychol.: Learn. Mem. Cogn.* 15:657–68

Bousfield WA. 1953. The occurrence of clustering in the recall of randomly arranged associates. *J. Gen. Psychol.* 49:229–40

Bower GH. 1972. Mental imagery and associative learning. In *Cognition in Learning and Memory,* ed. LW Gregg, pp. 51–88. New York: Wiley

Bugelski BR. 1962. Presentation time, total time, and mediation in paired associate learning. *J. Exp. Psychol.* 63:409–12

Calkins MW. 1894. Association. Studies from the Harvard Psychology Laboratory. *Psychol. Rev.* 1:476–83

Carrier M, Pashler H. 1992. The influence of retrieval on retention. *Mem. Cogn.* 20:633–42

Cepeda NJ, Pashler H, Vul E, Wixted JT, Rohrer D. 2006. Distributed practice in verbal recall tasks: a review and quantitative synthesis. *Psychol. Bull.* 132:354–80

Cermak LS, Craik FIM, eds. 1979. *Levels of Processing in Human Memory.* Hillsdale, NJ: Erlbaum

Cermak LS, Reale L. 1978. Depth of processing and retention of words by alcoholic Korsakoff patients. *J. Exp. Psychol.: Hum. Learn. Mem.* 4:165–74

Challis BH, Sidhu R. 1993. Dissociative effect of massed repetition on implicit and explicit measures of memory. *J. Exp. Psychol.: Learn. Mem. Cogn.* 19:115–27

Challis BH, Velichkovsky BM, Craik FIM. 1996. Levels-of-processing effects on a variety of memory tasks: new findings and theoretical implications. *Conscious. Cogn.* 5:142–64

Collyer SC, Jonides J, Bevan W. 1972. Images as memory aids: Is bizarreness helpful? *Am. J. Psychol.* 85:31–38

Cooper EH, Pantle AJ. 1967. The total-time hypothesis in verbal learning. *Psychol. Bull.* 68:221–34

Cowan N. 2005. *Working Memory Capacity.* Hove, UK: Psychol. Press

Craik FIM. 1977. Age differences in human memory. In *Handbook of the Psychology of Aging*, ed. JE Birren, W Schaie, pp. 384–420. New York: Van Nostrand

Craik FIM, Lockhart RS. 1972. Levels of processing: a framework for memory research. *J. Verb. Learn. Verb. Behav.* 11:671–84

Craik FIM, Tulving E. 1975. Depth of processing and the retention of words in episodic memory. *J. Exp. Psychol. Gen.* 104:268–94

Craik FIM, Watkins MJ. 1973. The role of rehearsal in short-term memory. *J. Verb. Learn. Verb. Behav.* 12:599–607

Crowder RG. 1976. *Principles of Learning and Memory.* Hillsdale, NJ: Erlbaum

Deese J. 1957. Serial organization in the recall of disconnected items. *Psychol. Rep.* 3:577–82

Dudai Y. 2004. The neurobiology of consolidation, or, how stable is the engram? *Annu. Rev. Psychol.* 55:51–86

Ebbinghaus HE. 1885/1964. *Memory: A Contribution to Experimental Psychology.* Transl. HA Ruger, CE Bussenius, 1913. New York: Dover

Erdelyi MH, Becker J. 1974. Hypermnesia for pictures: incremental memory for pictures but not words in multiple recall trials. *Cogn. Psychol.* 6:159–71

Fisher RP, Craik FIM. 1977. Interaction between encoding and retrieval operations in cued recall. *J. Exp. Psychol.: Hum. Learn. Mem.* 3:701–11

Gates AI. 1917. Recitation as a factor in memorizing. *Arch. Psychol.* 40:104

Glanzer M, Adams JK. 1985. The mirror effect in recognition memory. *Mem. Cogn.* 13:8–20

Glenberg A, Smith SM, Green C. 1977. Type I rehearsal: maintenance and more. *J. Verb. Learn. Verb. Behav.* 16:339–52

Graf P, Mandler G. 1984. Activation makes words more accessible, but not necessarily more retrievable. *J. Verb. Learn. Verb. Behav.* 23:553–68

Graf P, Squire LR, Mandler G. 1984. The information that amnesic patients do not forget. *J. Exp. Psychol.: Learn. Mem. Cogn.* 10:164–78

Greene RL. 2003. Recognition memory for pseudowords. *J. Mem. Lang.* 50:259–67

Greene RL. 2007. Foxes, hedgehogs, and mirror effects: the role of general principles in memory research. In *The Foundations of Remembering: Essays in Honor of Henry L. Roediger, III*, ed. JS Nairne, pp. 53–66. New York: Psychol. Press

Hall JF. 1971. *Verbal Learning and Retention.* Philadelphia, PA: Lippincott

Hauck P, Walsh C, Kroll N. 1976. Visual imagery mnemonics: common vs bizarre mental images. *Bull. Psychon. Soc.* 7:160–62

Heathcote A, Brown S, Mewhort DJK. 2000. The power law repealed: the case for an exponential law of practice. *Psychon. Bull. Rev.* 7:185–207

Herrnstein RJ. 1961. Relative and absolute strength of response as a function of frequency of reinforcement. *J. Exp. Anal. Behav.* 4:267–72

Hintzman DL, Curran T. 1997. Comparing retrieval dynamics in recognition memory and lexical decision. *J. Exp. Psychol.: Gen.* 126:228–47

Holton GJ, Brush SG. 1985. *Introduction to Concepts and Theories in Physical Science.* Princeton, NJ: Princeton Univ. Press

Hyde TS, Jenkins JJ. 1969. Differential effects of incidental tasks on the organization of recall of a list of highly associated words. *J. Exp. Psychol.* 82:472–81

Hyde TS, Jenkins JJ. 1973. Recall for words as a function of semantic, graphic, and syntactic orienting tasks. *J. Verb. Learn. Verb. Behav.* 12:471–80

Intraub H, Nicklos S. 1985. Levels of processing and picture memory: the physical superiority effect. *J. Exp. Psychol.: Learn. Mem. Cogn.* 11:284–98

Jacoby LL. 1978. On interpreting the effects of repetition: solving a problem vs remembering a solution. *J. Verb. Learn. Verb. Behav.* 17:649–67

Jacoby LL. 1983. Remembering the data: analyzing interactive processes in reading. *J. Verb. Learn. Verb. Behav.* 22:485–508

Jacoby LL. 1984. Incidental vs intentional retrieval: remembering and awareness as separate issues. In *Neuropsychology of Memory*, ed. LR Squires, N Butters, pp. 145–56. New York: Guilford

Jacoby LL, Dallas M. 1981. On the relationship between autobiographical memory and perceptual learning. *J. Exp. Psychol.: Gen.* 110:306–40

Jenkins JJ. 1974. Remember that old theory of memory? Well forget it. *Am. Psychol.* 29:785–95

Jenkins JJ. 1979. Four points to remember: a tetrahedral model of memory experiments. In *Levels of Processing in Human Memory*, ed. LS Cermak, FIM Craik, pp. 429–46. Hillsdale, NJ: Erlbaum

Jonides J, Lewis RL, Nee DE, Lustig CA, Berman MG, Moore KS. 2008. The mind and brain of short-term memory. *Annu. Rev. Psychol.* 59:193–224

Jost A. 1897. Die Assoziationsfestigkeit in ihrer Abhängigkeit von der Verteilung der Wiederholungen. *Z. Psychol. Physiol. der Sinnesorg.* 14:436–72

Karpicke JD, Roediger HL. 2007. Expanding retrieval practice promotes short-term retention, but equally spaced retrieval enhances long-term retention. *J. Exp. Psychol.: Learn. Mem. Cogn.* 34:707–19

Kausler DH. 1974. *Psychology of Verbal Learning and Memory*. New York: Academic

Keppel G. 1968. Verbal learning and memory. *Annu. Rev. Psychol.* 19:169–202

Keppel G, Underwood BJ. 1962. Proactive inhibition in short-term retention of single items. *J. Verb. Learn. Verb. Behav.* 1:153–61

Kirkpatrick EA. 1894. An experimental study of memory. *Psychol. Rev.* 1:602–9

Kirsner K, Dunn JC. 1985. The perceptual record: a common factor in repetition priming and attribute retention. In *Mechanisms of Attention: Attention and Performance, XI*, ed. MI Posner, OWM Marrin, pp. 547–56. Hillsdale, NJ: Erlbaum

Kolers PA, Roediger HL III. 1984. Procedures of mind. *J. Verb. Learn. Verb. Behav.* 23:425–49

Lane DM, Robertson L. 1979. The generality of the levels of processing hypothesis: an application to memory for chess positions. *Mem. Cogn.* 7:253–56

Lockhart RS, Craik FIM. 1990. Levels of processing: a retrospective commentary on a framework for memory research. *Can. J. Psychol.* 44:87–112

Mandler G. 1967. Organization and memory. In *The Psychology of Learning and Motivation*, ed. KW Spence, JT Spence, 1:327–72. New York: Academic

Mandler G, Pearlstone Z. 1966. Free and constrained concept learning and subsequent recall. *J. Verb. Learn. Verb. Behav.* 5:126–31

McDaniel MA. 2007. Transfer: rediscovering a central concept. In *Science of Memory: Concepts*, ed. HL Roediger, Y Dudai, SM Fitzpatrick, pp. 267–70. Oxford: Oxford Univ. Press

McDaniel MA, Bugg JM. 2007. Instability in memory phenomena: a common puzzle and a unifying explanation. *Psychon. Bull. Rev.* In press

McDaniel MA, Einstein GO. 1986. Bizarre imagery as an effective memory aid: the importance of distinctiveness. *J. Exp. Psychol.: Learn. Mem. Cogn.* 12:54–65

McDaniel MA, Friedman A, Bourne LE. 1978. Remembering the levels of information in words. *Mem. Cogn.* 6:156–64

McGaugh JL. 2000. Memory: a century of consolidation. *Science* 287:248–51

McGeoch JA. 1932. Forgetting and the law of disuse. *Psychol. Rev.* 39:352–70

McGeoch JA. 1942. *The Psychology of Human Learning.* New York: Longmans, Green

McKeachie WJ. 1974. The decline and fall of the laws of learning. *Educ. Res.* 3:7–11

Melton AW. 1950. Learning. *Annu. Rev. Psychol.* 1:9–30

Melton AW. 1970. The situation with respect to the spacing of repetitions and memory. *J. Verb. Learn. Verb. Behav.* 9:596–606

Morris CD, Bransford JD, Franks JJ. 1977. Levels of processing vs transfer appropriate processing. *J. Verb. Learn. Verb. Behav.* 16:519–33

Moscovitch M, Vriezen E, Goshen-Gottstein Y. 1993. Implicit tests of memory in patients with focal lesions or degenerative brain disorders. In *Handbook of Neuropsychology*, ed. F Boller, J Grafman, pp. 133–73. Amsterdam: Elsevier

Murdock BB. 2003. The mirror effect and the spacing effect. *Psychon. Bull. Rev.* 20:570–88

Murphy MD, Brown AL. 1975. Incidental learning in preschool children as a function of level of cognitive analysis. *J. Exp. Child Psychol.* 19:509–23

Nairne JS, Riegler GL, Serra M. 1991. Dissociative effects of generation on item and order retention. *J. Exp. Psychol.: Learn. Mem. Cogn.* 17:702–9

Newell A, Rosenbloom PS. 1981. Cognitive skills and their acquisition. In *Mechanisms of Skill Acquisition and the Law of Practice*, ed. JR Anderson, pp. 1–51. Hillsdale, NJ: Erlbaum

Nipher FE. 1876. Probability of error in writing a series of numbers. *Am. J. Sci. Arts* 12:79–80

Nipher FE. 1878. On the distribution of errors in numbers written from memory. *Trans. Acad. Sci. St. Louis* 3:ccx–ccxi

Paivio A. 1969. Mental imagery in associative learning and memory. *Psychol. Rev.* 76:241–63

Payne DG. 1987. Hypermnesia and reminiscence in recall: a historical and empirical review. *Psychol. Bull.* 101:5–27

Payne JD, Ellenbogen JM, Walker MP, Stickgold R. 2007. The role of sleep in memory consolidation. In *Cognitive Psychology of Memory. Vol. 2 of Learning and Memory: A Comprehensive Reference*, ed. HL Roediger III, 4 vols. (J. Byrne, ed.). Oxford: Elsevier. In press

Peterson LR, Wampler R, Kirkpatrick M, Saltzman D. 1963. Effect of spacing presentations on retention of a paired-associate over short intervals. *J. Exp. Psychol.* 66:206–9

Poulton EC. 1982. Influential companions: effects of one strategy on another in the within-subjects designs of cognitive psychology. *Psychol. Bull.* 91:673–90

Premack D. 1962. Reversibility of the reinforcement relation. *Science* 136:255–57

Rajaram S, Roediger HL. 1993. Direct comparison of four implicit memory tests. *J. Exp. Psychol.: Learn. Mem. Cogn.* 19:765–76

Reitman JS. 1974. Without surreptitious rehearsal, information in short-term memory decays. *J. Verb. Learn. Verb. Behav.* 13:365–77

Rescorla RA. 1988. Pavlovian conditioning: It's not what you think it is. *Am. Psychol.* 43:151–60

Rescorla RA, Wagner AR. 1972. A theory of Pavlovian conditioning: variations in the effectiveness of reinforcement and nonreinforcement. In *Classical Conditioning II: Current Research and Theory*, ed. AH Black, WF Prokasy, pp. 64–99. New York: Appleton-Century-Crofts

Richardson-Klavehn A, Bjork RA. 1988. Measures of memory. *Annu. Rev. Psychol.* 39:475–543

Richardson-Klavehn A, Gardiner JM, Java RI. 1999. Involuntary conscious memory and the method of opposition. *Memory* 2:1–29

Rickard TC. 1997. Bending the power law: a CMPL theory of strategy shifts and the automatization of cognitive skills. *J. Exp. Psychol.: Gen.* 126:288–311

Roediger HL, Blaxton TA. 1987. Retrieval modes produce dissociations in memory for surface information. In *Memory and Learning: The Ebbinghaus Centennial Conference*, ed. DS Gorfein, RR Hoffman, pp. 349–79. Hillsdale, NJ: Erlbaum

Roediger HL, Dudai Y, Fitzpatrick SM, eds. 2007. *Science of Memory Concepts*. Oxford: Oxford Univ. Press

Roediger HL, Gallo DA. 2002. Levels of processing: some unanswered questions. In *Perspectives on Human Memory and Cognitive Aging: Essays in Honour of Fergus I.M. Craik*, ed. M Naveh-Benjamin, M Moscovitch, HL Roediger, pp. 28–47. Philadelphia, PA: Psychol. Press

Roediger HL, Karpicke JD. 2006a. The power of testing memory: basic research and implications for educational practice. *Perspect. Psychol. Sci.* 1:181–210

Roediger HL, Karpicke JD. 2006b. Test-enhanced learning: taking memory tests improves long-term retention. *Psychol. Sci.* 17:249–55

Roediger HL, Payne DG. 1982. Hypermnesia: the effects of repeated testing. *J. Exp. Psychol.: Learn. Mem. Cogn.* 8:66–72

Roediger HL, Srinivas K, Weldon MS. 1989a. Dissociations between implicit measures of retention. In *Implicit Memory: Theoretical Issues*, ed. S Lewandowsky, JC Dunn, K Kirsner, pp. 67–84. Hillsdale, NJ: Erlbaum

Roediger HL, Weldon MS, Challis BH. 1989b. Explaining dissociations between implicit and explicit measures of retention: a processing account. In *Varieties of Memory and Consciousness: Essays in Honour of Endel Tulving*, ed. HL Roediger, FIM Craik, pp. 3–39. Hillsdale, NJ: Erlbaum

Roediger HL, Weldon MS, Stadler ML, Riegler GL. 1992. Direct comparison of two implicit memory tests: word fragment and word stem completion. *J. Exp. Psychol.: Learn. Mem. Cogn.* 18:1251–69

Rubin DC, Wenzel AE. 1996. One hundred years of forgetting: a quantitative description of retention. *Psychol. Rev.* 103:734–60

Schacter DL. 1987. Implicit memory: history and current status. *J. Exp. Psychol.: Learn. Mem. Cogn.* 13:501–18

Schacter DL, Bowers J, Booker J. 1989. Intention, awareness, and implicit memory: the retrieval intentionality criterion. In *Implicit Memory: Theoretical Issues*, ed. S Lewandowsky, JC Dunn, K Kirsner, pp. 47–65. Hillsdale, NJ: Erlbaum

Schmidt SR. 2007. A theoretical and empirical review of the concept of distinctiveness in memory research. In *Cognitive Psychology of Memory. Vol. 2 of Learning and Memory: A Comprehensive Reference*, ed. HL Roediger III, 4 vols. (J. Byrne, ed.). Oxford: Elsevier. In press

Schmidt SR, Cherry K. 1989. The negative generation effect: delineation of a phenomenon. *Mem. Cogn.* 17:359–69

Seligman ME. 1970. On the generality of the laws of learning. *Psychol. Rev.* 77:406–18

Shimamura AP. 1986. Priming effects in amnesia: evidence for a dissociable memory function. *Q. J. Exp. Psychol.* 38A:619–44

Slamecka NJ, Graf P. 1978. The generation effect: delineation of a phenomenon. *J. Exp. Psychol.: Hum. Learn. Mem.* 4:592–604

Smith AD, Winograd E. 1978. Adult age differences in remembering faces. *Dev. Psychol.* 14:443–44

Spitzer HF. 1939. Studies in retention. *J. Educ. Psychol.* 30:641–56

Squire LR. 1987. *Memory and Brain*. New York: Oxford Univ. Press

Squire LR, Wetzel CD, Slater PC. 1978. Anterograde amnesia following ECT: an analysis of the beneficial effect of partial information. *Neuropsychologia* 16:339–47

Srinivas K, Roediger HL. 1990. Classifying implicit memory tests: category association and anagram solution. *J. Mem. Lang.* 29:389–412

Stein BS. 1978. Depth of processing reexamined: the effects of precision of encoding and test appropriateness. *J. Verb. Learn. Verb. Behav.* 17:165–74

Stickgold R. 2005. Sleep-dependent memory consolidation. *Nature* 437:1272–78

Stickgold R, Hobson JA, Fosse R, Fosse M. 2001. Sleep, learning, and dreams: off-line memory reprocessing. *Science* 294:1052–57

Stigler SM. 1978. Some forgotten work on memory. *J. Exp. Psychol.: Hum. Learn. Mem.* 4:1–4

Strong EK Jr. 1912. The effect of length of series upon recognition memory. *Psychol. Rev.* 19:447–62

Teigen KH. 2002. One hundred years of laws in psychology. *Am. J. Psychol.* 115:103–18

Thorndike EL. 1898. Animal intelligence: an experimental study of the association processes in animals. *Psychol. Rev. Monogr.* 2:Whole No. 8

Thorndike EL. 1911. *Animal Intelligence: Experimental Studies*. Lewiston, NY: MacMillan

Toth JP. 2000. Nonconscious forms of human memory. In *The Oxford Handbook of Memory*, ed. E Tulving, FIM Craik, pp. 245–61. New York: Oxford Univ. Press

Tresselt ME, Mayzner MS. 1960. A study of incidental learning. *J. Psychol.* 50:339–47

Tulving E. 1962. Subjective organization in free recall of "unrelated" words. *Psychol. Rev.* 69:344–54

Tulving E. 1966. Subjective organization and the effects of repetition in multi-trial free recall verbal learning. *J. Verb. Learn. Verb. Behav.* 5:193–97

Tulving E. 1972. Episodic and semantic memory. In *Organization and Memory*, ed. E Tulving, W Donaldson, pp. 381–403. New York: Academic

Tulving E. 1983. *Elements of Episodic Memory*. New York: Oxford Univ. Press

Tulving E. 1985a. How many memory systems are there? *Am. Psychol.* 40:385–98

Tulving E. 1985b. Memory and consciousness. *Can. Psychol.* 26:1–12

Tulving E. 2007. Are there 256 different kinds of memory? In *The Foundations of Remembering: Essays in Honor of Henry L. Roediger, III*, ed. JS Nairne, pp. 39–52. New York: Psychol. Press

Tulving E, Madigan SA. 1970. Memory and verbal learning. *Annu. Rev. Psychol.* 21:437–84

Tulving E, Schacter DL. 1990. Priming and human memory systems. *Science* 247:301–5

Tulving E, Thomson DM. 1973. Encoding specificity and retrieval processes in episodic memory. *Psychol. Rev.* 80:352–73

Underwood BJ. 1957. Interference and forgetting. *Psychol. Rev.* 53:49–60

Underwood BJ. 1961. Ten years of massed practice on distributed practice. *Psychol. Rev.* 68:229–47

Warrington EK, Weiskrantz L. 1968. New method of testing long-term retention with special reference to amnesic patients. *Nature* 217:972–74

Warrington EK, Weiskrantz L. 1970. Amnesic syndrome: consolidation or retrieval? *Nature* 228:629–30

Wertsch J. 2002. *Voices of Collective Memory*. New York: Cambridge Univ. Press

Webber SM, Marshall PH. 1978. Bizarreness effects in imagery as a function of processing level and delay. *J. Mental Imagery* 2:291–300

Weldon MS, Roediger HL. 1987. Altering retrieval demands reverses the picture superiority effect. *Mem. Cogn.* 15:269–80

Wilson EO. 1998. *Consilience*. New York: Knopf

Wixted JT. 2004. The psychology and neuroscience of forgetting. *Annu. Rev. Psychol.* 55:235–69

Wixted JT, Carpenter SK. 2007. The Wickelgren power law and the Ebbinghaus savings function. *Psychol. Sci.* 18:133–34

Woodworth RS. 1929. *Psychology*. New York: Holt & Co.

Yates FA. 1966. *The Art of Memory*. Middlesex, UK: Penguin

Dual-Processing Accounts of Reasoning, Judgment, and Social Cognition

Jonathan St. B. T. Evans

Center for Thinking and Language, School of Psychology, University of Plymouth, Plymouth PL4 8AA, United Kingdom; email: jevans@plymouth.ac.uk

Annu. Rev. Psychol. 2008. 59:255–78

First published online as a Review in Advance on May 31, 2007

The *Annual Review of Psychology* is online at http://psych.annualreviews.org

This article's doi: 10.1146/annurev.psych.59.103006.093629

Key Words

thinking, reasoning, decision-making, social cognition, dual-process theory

Abstract

This article reviews a diverse set of proposals for dual processing in higher cognition within largely disconnected literatures in cognitive and social psychology. All these theories have in common the distinction between cognitive processes that are fast, automatic, and unconscious and those that are slow, deliberative, and conscious. A number of authors have recently suggested that there may be two architecturally (and evolutionarily) distinct cognitive systems underlying these dual-process accounts. However, it emerges that (*a*) there are multiple kinds of implicit processes described by different theorists and (*b*) not all of the proposed attributes of the two kinds of processing can be sensibly mapped on to two systems as currently conceived. It is suggested that while some dual-process theories are concerned with parallel competing processes involving explicit and implicit knowledge systems, others are concerned with the influence of preconscious processes that contextualize and shape deliberative reasoning and decision-making.

Contents

INTRODUCTION

Dual-processing accounts of human behavior abound in cognitive and social psychology. So many authors have appealed to dual processes in so many different ways that it has proved a complex and challenging task to draw together any coherent overview of this topic. The review is restricted to "higher" cognitive processes typically described as thinking, reasoning, decision-making, and social judgment, although selected work from outside of these domains is also included where directly relevant. For example, there is some reference to work in the psychology of learning and memory, the philosophy of mind, and evolutionary psychology.

What dual-process theories have in common is the idea that there are two different modes of processing, for which I use the most neutral terms available in the literature, System 1 and System 2 processes (Kahneman & Frederick 2002, Stanovich 1999). Almost all authors agree on a distinction between processes that are unconscious, rapid, automatic, and high capacity, and those that are conscious, slow, and deliberative. Different authors have proposed a number of names for the two kinds of thinking they contrast, some of which are shown in **Table 1**. The labels are aligned in a manner consistent with generic dual-system theory (see below) under the headings System 1 and System 2. Despite the tidy way in which all these labels line up, readers should beware of inferring that there are necessarily just two systems or just two kinds of dual-processing theory for reasons that will become clear later. Some authors propose only dual-process distinctions without assumptions about underlying cognitive systems; some propose parallel and some sequential relationships between the two processes, and so on.

Attempts have been made to map various dual-process accounts into a generic dual-system theory (Evans 2003; Evans & Over 1996; Stanovich 1999, 2004). A major issue for this review is to consider whether such a grand theory is sustainable, or whether, in spite of first appearances, we need to classify dual-process theories as being of different and distinct kinds. I approach this question in part by considering the clusters of attributes supposedly belonging to System 1 and 2, which have been extracted from the numerous dual-process theories to be found in the literature. Of course, not all authors have made explicit statements about all of these attributes, but when they do so, they tend to make comments that are remarkably consistent from theory to theory. These putative features of Systems 1 and 2 are somewhat arbitrarily grouped here into four categories (see **Table 2**) and each is discussed in turn prior to the review of specific dual-process theories of higher cognition.

It should be noted that the attributes listed in **Table 2** do not include emotion, the discussion of which is generally beyond the scope of this review. Although many authors ignore emotion altogether in the fields reviewed here, it is clear that emotional processing would be placed in the System 1 rather than

Table 1 Labels attached to dual-processes in the literature, aligned on the assumption of a generic dual-system theory

References	System 1	System 2
Fodor (1983, 2001)	Input modules	Higher cognition
Schneider & Schiffrin (1977)	Automatic	Controlled
Epstein (1994), Epstein & Pacini (1999)	Experiential	Rational
Chaiken (1980), Chen & Chaiken (1999)	Heuristic	Systematic
Reber (1993), Evans & Over (1996)	Implicit/tacit	Explicit
Evans (1989, 2006)	Heuristic	Analytic
Sloman (1996), Smith & DeCoster (2000)	Associative	Rule based
Hammond (1996)	Intuitive	Analytic
Stanovich (1999, 2004)	System 1 (TASS)	System 2 (Analytic)
Nisbett et al. (2001)	Holistic	Analytic
Wilson (2002)	Adaptive unconscious	Conscious
Lieberman (2003)	Reflexive	Reflective
Toates (2006)	Stimulus bound	Higher order
Strack & Deustch (2004)	Impulsive	Reflective

Table 2 Clusters of attributes associated with dual systems of thinking

System 1	System 2
Cluster 1 (Consciousness)	
Unconscious (preconscious)	Conscious
Implicit	Explicit
Automatic	Controlled
Low effort	High effort
Rapid	Slow
High capacity	Low capacity
Default process	Inhibitory
Holistic, perceptual	Analytic, reflective
Cluster 2 (Evolution)	
Evolutionarily old	Evolutionarily recent
Evolutionary rationality	Individual rationality
Shared with animals	Uniquely human
Nonverbal	Linked to language
Modular cognition	Fluid intelligence
Cluster 3 (Functional characteristics)	
Associative	Rule based
Domain specific	Domain general
Contextualized	Abstract
Pragmatic	Logical
Parallel	Sequential
Stereotypical	Egalitarian
Cluster 4 (Individual differences)	
Universal	Heritable
Independent of general intelligence	Linked to general intelligence
Independent of working memory	Limited by working memory capacity

System 2 list. Emotion is explicitly linked to the first system in some dual-process accounts (Epstein 1994), implied by the neurological regions identified in others (Lieberman 2003), and specifically attributed to automatic processes in some recent accounts of social cognition (Hassin et al. 2005). Moreover, the idea that emotions play a key role in decision making is being developed in some contemporary work that contrasts a fast emotional basis for decision making with a slower and more deliberative cognitive basis (Haidt 2001, Hanoch & Vitouch 2004, Wang 2006).

FEATURES ATTRIBUTED TO DUAL PROCESSES AND SYSTEMS

Consciousness

A central concern for philosophers of mind, the problem of consciousness is one that has engendered a resurgence of interest in recent years in psychology and neuroscience (Velmans 2000). However, the concept of consciousness has had a somewhat checkered history in psychology. Mentalism and introspectionism dominated philosophy of mind and early laboratory studies of the nineteenth century when psychology first emerged as a distinct discipline. Thereafter, a series of movements led instead to an emphasis on what is automatic and unconscious in the control of human behavior. These are sometimes described as the psychoanalytic, behavioral, and cognitive unconscious (Uleman 2005). Each refers to a movement that undermined the concept of consciousness and the explanation (in scientific psychology) of behavior in terms of conscious beliefs and desires. Freud and other psychoanalysts introduced the world to the notion of an unconscious mind motivating our behavior with a combination of innate drives and repressed emotions as well as a conscious mind prone to rationalization and self-deception. Behaviorists such as Watson, Hull, and Skinner demonstrated associative and instrumental learning processes in both humans

and animals in theories that apparently allowed no place for consciousness and mentalistic accounts of behavior. However, the emergence of cognitive science and the widespread acceptance of a computational theory of mind led in the later part of the twentieth century to the idea of a cognitive unconscious (Kihlstrom 1987, Reber 1993) in the form of complex information processing in the brain that is conducted without conscious awareness. Some authors are now advocating a "new unconscious" that also incorporates motivation and emotion (Hassin et al. 2005).

While the problem of what consciousness *is* may seem intractable, the study of its function and evolution seems more promising. Dual-process theories of cognition effectively address the important question of the cognitive correlates of consciousness. The attributes listed for Systems 1 and 2 under Cluster 1 (**Table 2**) all reflect the proposed differences between the cognitive unconscious and the cognitive conscious. Authors talk of processes that are explicit and controlled (rather than implicit and automatic) reflecting two key concepts of consciousness: awareness and volition. Consciousness is also inherently slow, sequential, and capacity limited. This might be taken to mean that folk psychological accounts of mind are adequate at the System 2 level provided the System 1 level of mind is also recognized (Frankish 2004). In other words, System 2 is a form of thinking under intentional level control, supported by unconscious processes in System 1 that deliver percepts, memories, and so on. However, this happy state of affairs, which leaves "us" in control of our behavior, is contradicted by much psychological research. Many researchers have emphasized the fact that unconscious processes may control our behavior without us being aware of them doing so, and that conscious reasoning in System 2 is often used for the confabulation of explanations for these behaviors (Evans & Over 1996, Nisbett & Wilson 1977, Stanovich 2004, Wason & Evans 1975, Wilson 2002, Wilson &

Dunn 2004). It appears that we use the concepts of belief-desire psychology to theorize about our behavior as well as that of others. To muddy the waters further, some social psychologists are claiming evidence of intentionality in unconscious processing (Bargh et al. 2001, Bargh & Ferguson 2000).

The distinction between automatic and controlled cognition has been extensively researched in the study of lower-order cognition such as that involved in perception, attention, and the acquisition of motor skills, in a tradition dating from Schneider & Shiffrin (1977) and more recently linked with neuroscience (Monsell & Driver 2000). In this tradition, automatic processes are typically viewed as having been "automated" from those that were once controlled and conscious, an approach that seems to have had a strong influence on the development of dual-process accounts of social cognition (Chaiken & Trope 1999). However, as Sloman (2002) points out, this conception is too limited for the purposes of dual-process accounts of higher cognition, in which we may feel an experience of conflict between an intuition acquired from experience and a conscious piece of reasoning. Moreover, there is a contrasting literature on implicit learning (Berry & Dienes 1993, Reber 1993, Sun et al. 2005) that provides much evidence that people can acquire implicit knowledge, for example to predict or control a complex system, without ever knowing an explicit rule that they could state. Hence, the term "automatic" is used here simply as a contrastive with "controlled," implying no assumption about how such processes were acquired.

An operational definition of consciousness that seems to have appeared (often implicitly) in dual-process theories is that System 2 thinking requires access to a central working memory system of limited capacity, whereas System 1 does not. What we are aware of at a given time is represented in this working memory, through which conscious thinking flows in a sequential manner. This would seem to be a working memory of the kind originally described by Baddeley & Hitch (1974), which has not only short-term memory capacity but also executive and inhibitory functions, a theory that has engendered a huge research literature in its own right (see Gathercole 2003). (Consciousness is also closely associated with working memory in global workspace theory—see Baars & Franklin 2003.) The association of conscious thought with such a working memory explains the slow, sequential, and low-capacity nature of System 2 as well as its relation to individual differences in cognitive ability (see below). However, skeptics may see this as the only firm foundation on which the various dual-process theories stand: There is one conscious working memory system and everything else.

Age of Evolution

The idea that System 1 cognition evolved earlier than System 2 is a recurring theme in dual-process theories (Evans & Over 1996, Epstein & Pacini 1999, Reber 1993, Stanovich 1999). System 2 is thought to be associated with language, reflective consciousness, and higher-order control and with the capacity to think hypothetically about future and counterfactual possibilities. Authors have often asserted that such characteristics of thought are distinctively or uniquely human, while at the same time arguing that System 1 cognition, shared with other animals, continues to control much of our behavior. However, there is considerable evidence of a distinction between stimulus-bound and higher-order control process in many higher animals (Toates 2006), including rodents, which could be seen as the biological foundations for the System 1 and 2 cognition in humans. There is also evidence that primates, especially chimpanzees, have the capacity for higher-order mental representations, manifest as rudimentary theory of mind (Mithen 1996, Whiten 2000), albeit very limited in comparison with the ability of the human mind for meta-representation and higher-order intentionality.

The proposal that System 1 cognition is evolutionarily old and shared with other animals is also problematic because it is almost certainly not one system with a single evolutionary history. There are a number of distinct possible types of implicit cognitive processes, including forms of learning, automaticity, modular cognition, and the pragmatic processes that have been particularly studied in dual-process theories of deductive reasoning (see below). The concept of cognitive modules was introduced by Fodor (1983) in a dual-process theory that distinguished between input modules (such as those involved in vision and language) and general purpose, central cognition. Fodor proposed a number of strict criteria for modules including the requirements that they are innate, domain-specific, have specialized and isolated databases (knowledge encapsulation), are neurologically localized, and are associated with specific disorders. Some schools of evolutionary psychology later argued that the mind should consist mostly or entirely of domain-specific cognitive modules, even when engaged in higher order reasoning (Cosmides & Tooby 1992, 1996; Pinker 1997; Samuels 1998; Sperber 1994; Tooby & Cosmides 1992). This view included strong claims that domain-general processes would have little part to play in human cognition, such as that of Tooby & Cosmides (1992, p.112): "...there is a host of... reasons why content-free, general-purpose systems could not evolve, could not manage their own reproduction, and would be grossly inefficient and easily outcompeted if they did." Not surprisingly, this "massive modularity hypothesis" has been strongly attacked by dual-process theorists (Fodor 2001, Over 2003, Stanovich 2004, Stanovich & West 2003). More recent writings of evolutionary psychologists appear to have more compatibility with dual-processing frameworks, however, as they acknowledge the extraordinary and distinctive features of human higher cognition (Cosmides & Tooby 2000, Sperber 2000). There has also been a recent trend to weaken the criteria for modules to make massive modularity a more credible hypoth-

esis (Barrett & Kurzban 2006, Carruthers 2006).

It seems unsustainable to argue that there is just one form of implicit processing, in System 1, all of which is evolutionarily old and shared with other animals. For example, we may have forms of modular cognition that are relatively old (e.g., vision, attention) and others that are much more recent and distinctively human (e.g., language, theory of mind). Conditioning and other forms of associative learning appear to be ancient and shared with other animals, but forms of explicit memory, and in particular the human belief system, seem to be much more recent. However, although the notion that there are distinct implicit and explicit memory systems is central to a number of the dual-process theories that are considered in this review, it could well be an error to think of the latter as uniquely human in origin. There are powerful evolutionary arguments (as well as neurological evidence) for multiple systems of learning and memory in both humans and other animals (Carruthers 2006, Sherry & Schacter 1987). For example, Sherry & Schacter (1987), who interestingly referred to System 1 and 2 memory, noted that "... a strong case can be made for a distinction between a memory system that supports gradual or incremental learning and is involved in the acquisition of habits and skills and a system that supports rapid one-trial learning and is necessary for forming memories that represent specific situations and episodes" (p. 446). Taken in conjunction with the evidence of higher-order control systems in animals (Toates 2006), these arguments suggest that dual-system theorists would be better off claiming that System 2 cognition is uniquely developed, rather than uniquely present, in modern humans. Such an argument also has much greater evolutionary plausibility.

If Systems 1 and 2 incorporate different memory as well as reasoning systems, then it may be a mistake to assume that any influence of prior knowledge on reasoning necessarily arises in System 1. For example, Goel

(2005) has questioned the idea that the "belief bias" in reasoning that theorists have associated with System 1 processing (Evans & Over 1996, Stanovich 1999) could be ancient in origin or shared with animals that lack an explicit belief system. In support of this, he has evidence from neural imaging studies that belief bias arises in the prefrontal cortex, an area most strongly developed in the modern human brain (Goel et al. 2000, Goel & Dolan 2003). However, a dual-system theorist can reply that although System 1 has much in common with animal cognition, it looks very different in a brain that has System 2. Thus Stanovich (2004, Chapter 2), for example, suggests that goals that are acquired reflectively through System 2 can, through repeated activation, be installed into rigid implicit processing mechanisms—a kind of automation of thought. This may be why Stanovich (2004) now prefers to talk about TASS—the set of autonomous subsystems—rather than System 1. Certainly, there seems to be little foundation in arguments based on age of evolution for the claim that all implicit processes belong—in any useful sense—to a single system.

Functional Characteristics

Along with already discussed attributes of System 1 as rapid and automatic and System 2 as slow and controlled go a number of functional differences attributed to the two kinds of cognition, as shown in **Table 2** under Cluster 3. It appears that conscious thought is inherently sequential, whereas many theorists suppose the rapid processing and high capacity of System 1 reflects use of parallel processes. System 1 has been characterized as associative by Sloman (1996, 2002; see also Smith & DeCoster 2000), as contrasted with rule-based cognition in System 2. Those authors who are not focused on the idea of innate modules certainly emphasize the experiential nature of System 1 (for example, Epstein & Pacini 1999, Evans & Over 1996, Reber 1993), which could reflect implicit learning stored in functionally parallel neural networks (Dijksterhuis & Smith 2005; Smith & DeCoster 1999, 2000). However, although the notion that System 2 is in some sense rule-based is compatible with the proposals of most dual-process theorists, the characterization of System 1 as associative is not. The problem, as already identified, is that there are multiple systems of implicit processes and it is far from clear that the different theories can be mapped on to each at the System 1 end. In particular, theories that contrast heuristic with analytic or systematic processing (Chen & Chaiken 1999, Evans 2006) seem to be talking about something different from associative processing.

Other recurring themes in the writing of dual-process theorists are that System 1 processes are concrete, contextualized, or domain-specific, whereas System 2 processes are abstract, decontextualized, or domain-general. The notion that System 1 processes rapidly contextualize problems with prior knowledge and belief has been particularly emphasized in dual-process accounts of human reasoning (Evans 2006, Klaczynski & Lavallee 2005, Stanovich 1999). Such authors assume that belief-based reasoning is the default to which conscious effortful analytic reasoning in System 2 may be applied to overcome. However, it may be unwise to define System 2 as being abstract and decontextualized if we also want to retain its description as slow, sequential, explicit, and rule-based because none of these characteristics may be limited to abstract forms of reasoning (Sloman 2002, Verschueren et al. 2005). It would probably be more accurate to say that although abstract reasoning requires the use of System 2, concrete contexts do not preclude its application.

The consideration that System 2 thinking is not necessarily abstract and decontextualized is also one reason why it should not be equated with a mental logic. The idea that higher forms of thinking require a logic in the mind was popularized by Piaget (see Inhelder & Piaget 1958) and is particularly associated with the idea that people have natural logics composed of inference rules in their minds (Braine & O'Brien 1998a, Rips 1994). However, the popular mental models theory of deductive reasoning (Johnson-Laird 1983, Johnson-Laird & Byrne 1991) can also be regarded as a form of mental logic, accounting for deductive competence by semantic rather than syntactic principles (Evans & Over 1996, Oaksford & Chater 1995). Whichever account of deduction is preferred, it is clear that the System 2 concept is much broader than that of logical reasoning, including such ideas as an inhibitory role (suppressing pragmatic influences of System 1) and the ability to engage in hypothetical thought via supposition and mental simulations. This is probably why most dual-process theorists prefer broader terms such as "analytic" or "systematic" to describe the second system.

Individual Differences

Some dual-process theorists (Reber 1993, Stanovich 1999) have claimed a link between System 2 processing and general intelligence, with the corollary that System 1 processes are independent of general intelligence. This proposal has led to an increasing use of individual differences methodology in dual-process research, as revealed in the sections below. In addition to linking the effectiveness of analytic reasoning and decision making with general intelligence measures, researchers have also investigated two close correlates: working memory and age of development. It is now well established that individual differences in working memory capacity and general intelligence measures are very highly correlated (Colom et al. 2004). Working memory capacity is known to predict performance levels in a very wide range of cognitive tasks and has been directly linked with dual-process accounts of cognitive functions, albeit primarily at a lower level than those that form the focus of the current review (Barrett et al. 2004). Developmental studies are also relevant, as the analytic thinking skills that contribute to performance on general intelligence tests develop with age.

However, it has recently been claimed that it is ability and not age that is the important predictor of analytic reasoning, which may explain some inconsistencies in developmental research (Kokis et al. 2002). A further complication is that, as some researchers claim, System 1 may develop in parallel with System 2 (Klaczynski 2000, 2001).

Evolutionary psychologists such as Tooby & Cosmides (1992) have emphasized that their main interest lies in explaining intelligence that is universal and optimized across the human species. However, they have been strongly criticized (Stanovich 1999, Stanovich & West 2003) for downplaying the importance of heritable characteristics, particularly that of general intelligence, in their discussion of higher-order cognitive processes such as reasoning and decision making. In general, one of the stronger bases for dual-systems theory is the evidence that "controlled" cognitive processing correlates with individual differences in general intelligence and working memory capacity, whereas "automatic" processing does not. It seems at least to indicate that behavior may be controlled both with and without the use of executive working memory resources.

An important distinction in the individual differences approach is that between measures of cognitive capacity and dispositional thinking styles. The difference is between what people are able to do and what they are inclined to do. Stanovich (1999), for example, shows that residual variance in solution rates of reasoning and judgment task, when the effects of cognitive ability have been taken out, can be accounted for in terms of dispositions for critical thinking. Evidence for cross-cultural differences in thinking styles (Nisbett et al. 2001) are also dispositional as they can alter when people move to another culture. In the social cognition literature, there has been much attention to individual differences in thinking style as measured by such scales as "need for cognition" (Cacioppo & Petty 1982) or the rational-experiential inventory (Epstein et al. 1996). It is important to note that the observation of two thinking styles in itself does not constitute evidence for dual processes arising from two distinct cognitive systems.

APPLICATIONS OF DUAL-PROCESS THEORIES IN DIFFERENT DOMAINS

As the preceding discussion illustrates, System 2 appears to be a more coherent and consistent concept in the generic dual-system theory than does System 1 because multiple systems of implicit cognitive processes exist (Wilson 2002, Stanovich 2004). It is also likely that different dual-process theorists have different implicit systems in mind and that these systems do not have a single evolutionary history. I return to the issue of whether generic dual-system theory is sustainable at the end of the review. At this point, I look more closely at how dual-process theories are applied to the explanation of particular phenomena in higher cognition.

Dual-Process Theories of Reasoning

The psychology of deductive reasoning was largely established by the work of Peter Wason in the 1960s and 1970s (see Wason & Johnson-Laird 1972). Wason invented several famous tasks—including the four-card selection task—that are still used in current research. The field has expanded rapidly over the past 40 years and changed its character as authors have become progressively less attached to the normative standard of formal logic and more interested in the influence of contextual factors invoking prior belief and knowledge (Evans 2002). Dual-process ideas developed quite early on, with the first use of the term appearing in the title of a paper published by Wason & Evans (1975). This paper focused on the finding that card choices on the selection task were strongly influenced by a seemingly primitive matching bias (selecting cards explicitly mentioned in the conditional statement). Participants showed no

awareness of this in their verbal reports, instead justifying their choices with regard to the experimental instructions to prove the rule true or false. Wason & Evans concluded that participants were rationalizing with their conscious reasoning causes of behavior that were in fact unconscious. Their arguments were very much in accord with the famous critique of introspective reports presented by Nisbett & Wilson (1977).

The heuristic-analytic theory of reasoning (Evans 1989) shifted the emphasis of the heuristic processes responsible for biases to a pragmatic and preconscious level that preceded any attempt at analytic processing. This theory is narrower in scope than typical dual-process theories and is strongly focused on the explanation of biases in reasoning and judgment tasks. The idea was that heuristic processes selectively focused attention on task features that appeared relevant, introducing relevant prior knowledge in the process. Since analytic processing could only be applied to these selective representations, biases would be observed when either (*a*) logically relevant information was excluded or (*b*) logically irrelevant information was included by heuristic processing.

The sequential nature of the heuristic-analytic theory contrasts with parallel and interactive forms of dual-process theory, although many of the proposed features of the two processes correspond to those of the generic System 1 and 2: Heuristic processes are fast, automatic, and belief based, whereas analytic reasoning is slow, sequential, and can make an effort at deduction. In a recent reformulation of the theory, Evans (2006) has sought to reconcile it with conflict models by the proposal that heuristic responses can control behavior directly unless analytic reasoning intervenes. In other words, heuristics provide default responses that may or may not be inhibited and altered by analytic reasoning. Analytic system intervention may be cued by strong deductive reasoning instructions and may be more likely to occur when individuals have high cognitive ability or a disposition to think reflectively or critically (Stanovich 1999).

For much of its recent history, the psychology of deductive reasoning has been dominated by a debate between proponents of mental logic theorists, who attribute deductive competence to sets of abstract inference rules (Braine & O'Brien 1998a, Rips 1994), and mental model theorists (Johnson-Laird 1983, Johnson-Laird & Byrne 1991), who explain it in terms of a fundamental semantic principle: An argument is valid if there are no counterexamples to it. Although the writings of mental logic and mental model theorists include little explicit discussion of dual-process theory, the distinction is implicitly present in the theories. Mental logic theorists (for example, Braine & O'Brien 1998b) make great play of the distinction between direct rules of inference, which are applied effortlessly and accurately, and indirect rules, which require conscious effort and are much more error prone. They also explain errors in reasoning by reference to pragmatic implicatures and other contextual effects. Similarly, the mental model theory describes the formation of initial mental models as a relatively automatic and effortless process. The process of searching for counterexamples (Johnson-Laird & Bara 1984) or the fleshing-out of initially implicit mental models (Johnson-Laird & Byrne 2002) is, however, effortful and error prone and constrained by working memory capacity. Both theories include proposals that could account for pragmatic influences on reasoning and for the relation of reasoning accuracy to individual differences in cognitive capacity.

The paradigm case for dual processes in reasoning is belief bias. In the standard paradigm, people are given syllogisms and asked to evaluate their logical validity. Syllogisms vary in both their validity (whether the conclusion follows from premises) and their believability (whether the conclusion conforms or conflicts with prior belief). Thus, some syllogisms are belief-logic compatible, but some provide conflict—valid arguments with unbelievable conclusions and invalid arguments with believable conclusions. The basic phenomena of this paradigm were established by Evans et al. (1983), whose findings have been replicated many times since (see Klauer et al. 2000 for a recent extensive study). There is (a) a main effect of logic, in that valid conclusions are more often accepted than invalid conclusions, (b) a main effect of belief (belief bias) in that believable conclusions are much more often accepted, and (c) a belief by logic interaction, in that belief bias is much more marked on invalid syllogisms.

In the original study, Evans et al. (1983) argued, on the basis of protocol analyses and the examination of individual response patterns, that there was a within-person conflict between a logical and belief-based reasoning process. They offered two explanations of the belief by logic interaction, which were later augmented by one derived from mental model theory (Oakhill et al. 1989). More recently, accounts of the phenomena have been developed that are strongly compatible with dual-process theory (e.g., Klauer et al. 2000). These accounts are supported by evidence of a shift from logical to belief-based reasoning under severe time pressure (Evans & Curtis-Holmes 2005) and under concurrent working memory load (De Neys 2006).

There has been considerable interest in how people reason on belief-logic conflict problems; that is, the valid-unbelievable and invalid-believable syllogisms. Logical performance on such cases is known to decline with age (Gilinsky & Judd 1994) and to be related to individual differences in cognitive ability (Kokis et al. 2002, Newstead et al. 2004, Stanovich & West 1997). Stanovich (1999) argued on this basis that participants of higher cognitive ability are more able to inhibit belief-based reasoning. However, available data are more consistent with the view that although high-ability people reason more logically with belief-laden (as well as abstract) syllogisms, the belief bias effect is no less marked for them than for lower-ability people (Klaczynski 2000, Newstead et al. 2004,

Torrens et al. 1999). Thus, it may be that higher-ability people do not engage in more System 2 reasoning but rather are simply more successful when they do so.

A large literature exists on how people reason with the Wason four-card selection task (see Evans & Over 2004, Chapter 5, for a review). The task requires people to decide which of four cards to turn over to decide the truth of a conditional statement. For example, if the statement says, "If a card has an A on one side then it has a 3 on the other," and the visible sides display A, D, 3, and 7, then the logically correct choice is the A and the 7. This is because only a card that has an A and *not* a 3 could disprove the statement. Few people give this answer; most are more likely to choose A and 3, or just A. Although this abstract, indicative form of the task is very difficult, concrete and deontic forms (concerning rules and regulations) are much easier. For example, given the statement, "If a person is drinking beer in a bar, that person must be over 19 years of age," most participants readily see that they must check beer (rather than soda) drinkers and those who are under 19 years of age.

The heuristic-analytic theory explains the difficulty of the abstract task on the grounds of heuristics that focus attention on selected cards, a claim supported by the time that people spend observing individual cards (Evans 1996, but see Ball et al. 2003, Roberts 1998) and the accentuation of matching bias by a requirement to respond rapidly (Roberts & Newton 2001). Stanovich & West (1998) have produced strong evidence that analytic reasoning is involved in solving the abstract selection task, since solvers have much higher SAT scores than do nonsolvers. The relation to cognitive ability is, however, much weaker for concrete and deontic forms of the task, suggesting that it can be solved by pragmatic belief-based reasoning in System 1 (see also Newstead et al. 2004).

Recently, various authors have applied dual-process theory to the inferences people draw from conditional statements. Considerable evidence shows that reasoning with realistic conditionals is strongly influenced by pragmatic factors, including the availability of counterexamples to inferences from semantic memory (Cummins et al. 1991; Thompson 1994, 2000) and the strength of association of counterexamples as measured across both materials and individual participants (De Neys et al. 2005, Markovits et al. 1998, Markovits & Quinn 2002). Participants are also more likely to draw inferences from conditionals that they believe rather than disbelieve (George 1997; Liu et al. 1996; Newstead et al. 1997; Stevenson & Over 1995, 2001). However, evidence suggests that analytic System 2 reasoning processes, as well as heuristic System 1 processes, may be influenced by prior belief about the problem context (Verschueren et al. 2005).

In conclusion, dual-process theory has been widely applied to the study of syllogistic reasoning, the Wason selection task, and conditional inference. (For a critical review of the theory in the psychology of reasoning, see Osman 2005.) Experimental evidence has consistently shown that responses are partially consistent with logic but are also influenced by systematic biases such as matching bias and belief bias. Cognitive models have generally depicted these as competing influences in a within-participant conflict. Several different forms of evidence support dual-processing accounts, including (*a*) the observation of more logical and less belief-based reasoning under strong deductive reasoning instructions, (*b*) the association (in general) of better logical accuracy with higher-ability participants when problems cannot also be solved by a pragmatic route, and (*c*) the finding that working memory load or instructions to respond rapidly increase levels of typical biases as well as reduce logical accuracy.

Dual-Process Theories of Judgment and Decision Making

Three main research paradigms have dominated the psychology of judgment and decision making: (*a*) the "heuristics and biases" research program that is focused particularly on judgments of probability (Gilovich et al. 2002, Kahneman et al. 1982), (*b*) the study of decision making under risk (Wu et al. 2005), and (*c*) social judgment theory and the lens model (Doherty 1996). The last of these paradigms, which may be less familiar to readers, is focused on judgments made where multiple cues are available in the environment. An example might be medical diagnosis in light of a number of demographic factors, patient history, symptoms, diagnostic tests, and so on. It is possible to capture the implicit policy of judges by using multiple regression analysis to show which of the various cues predict their overall judgment.

Until recently, dual-process theory played a much smaller part in these fields than in the study of reasoning and social cognition. An exception is the cognitive continuum theory of Hammond (e.g., 1996), working in social judgment theory, which contrasts intuitive and analytic thinking. However, as the name suggests, this theory proposes two ends of a continuum rather than discrete processes or systems and hence is not the main type of theory with which this review is concerned.

Kahneman & Frederick (2002, 2005) recently developed a dual-process theory of probability judgment that they link to the generic dual-system theory. Heuristic judgments, which lead to biases, are associated with System 1, and analytic reasoning, which may intervene with these judgments and improve them, are linked to System 2. This helps explain general findings that although biases in probability judgment can be linked to heuristics such as representativeness (Kahneman & Tversky 1972, Teigen 2004) and availability (Reber 2004, Tversky & Kahneman 1973), these biases are not universally observed but do appear to compete with a tendency to give normatively correct answers. Such conflicts stand in parallel with the findings in the deductive reasoning literature, reviewed above, in which matching and beliefs biases compete with logically correct answers. In general, normatively correct solutions to problems from both literatures tend to be found more often by those of higher cognitive capacity (Stanovich 1999), who may be assumed to make more effective interventions with analytic or System 2 reasoning processes.

The processing assumptions of Kahneman & Frederick's theory are similar to those of the heuristic-analytic theory of reasoning (Evans 2006). It is assumed that fast System 1 (heuristic) processes cue default intuitive judgments that must nevertheless be endorsed by the (analytic) System 2, which often does so casually. This may involve attribute substitution, in which people actually answer a different (and easier) question than the one asked. However, high-effort deliberative reasoning may be applied, which can inhibit the biased response and replace it with one based on reflective reasoning. I call this kind of dual-process theory "default-interventionist" as compared with theories (e.g., that of Sloman, 1996) that are "parallel-competitive" in nature. Kahneman & Frederick suggest that even heuristics that are apparently conscious in application, such as the recognition heuristic (Gigerenzer et al. 1999), have an automatic component. In this case, feelings of familiarity are automatically recruited and then consciously interpreted as a basis for making a judgment, such as the relative size of foreign cities.

A major recent debate in the probability judgment literature has concerned the claim that probability problems are much easier if framed in terms of frequencies rather than in probabilities (Barbey & Sloman 2007, Cosmides & Tooby 1996, Gigerenzer & Hoffrage 1995), thus reducing biases such as base rate neglect in Bayesian reasoning (Kahneman & Tversky 1973, Koehler 1996). It was argued from an evolutionary perspective that we would have evolved a cognitive module for processing frequency information in the environment (Cosmides & Tooby 1996) that could not be applied to one-case probabilities. However, from a dual-process viewpoint, it appears that such a module would affect learning behavior in System 1 rather than in explicit System 2 reasoning about the quantitative word problems that are actually presented (Evans et al. 2000). Consistent with this, there is now much evidence that what facilitates Bayesian reasoning is a problem structure that cues explicit mental models of nested-set relationships (Evans et al. 2000, Girotto & Gonzalez 2001, Sloman et al. 2003) as originally proposed by Tversky & Kahnemant (1983). However, Hoffrage et al. (2002) have responded by arguing that such nested sets are intrinsic to natural sampling, a process that leads to the observation of natural frequencies that encode base rate information implicitly. Hence, they claim that Bayesian posterior probabilities can be derived from direct comparison of such frequencies with no difficult calculation involved. However, Barbey & Sloman (2007) have recently argued that this kind of evolutionary account, when examined in detail, is a good deal less parsimonious than an explanation in terms of dual processing.

Discussion of work on reasoning and judgment to this point may have suggested that System 2 processing is in some sense superior to that of System 1, in that the former is often associated with normatively correct responding and the latter with cognitive biases. However, those authors who have looked at expert judgment and decision-making provide a somewhat different perspective. For example, in Klein's (1999) naturalistic studies of decision making in groups such as fire officers and paramedics, the author argues that very little rational decision-making goes on, in the sense of deliberation between alternatives. What typically happens is that an expert recognizes a situation as of a kind encountered previously and rapidly retrieves a schema that provides a solution, a process Klein terms "recognition-primed" decision-making. The application will involve some explicit reasoning (sometimes mental simulations to check feasibility of solutions), but the key to intelligent action is the automatic retrieval process.

The value of System 1 processing has also been emphasized by other dual-process the-orists in applications to decision-making. For example, Reyna (2004) argues that experts acquire gist knowledge that allows them to make intuitive responses that are automatic, rapid, and effective, whereas novices need to rely on explicit analytic reasoning. However, Reyna notes also that the former kind of process can lead to bias and error when novel problems are presented, as is typically the case in laboratory studies of probability judgment. Perhaps more controversial is the recent claim of Dijksterhuis et al. (2006) that there are processes of conscious and unconscious reasoning, both of a deliberative nature, and that the unconscious reasoning leads to superior decision making. This is a very different kind of claim from those of the theories we have been considering that envisage fast heuristic processes delivering contextualized content for evaluation by a conscious, analytic process.

The evidence for superiority of unconscious decision-making is that people may make better decisions as measured by normative analysis or by correspondence with expert judgments (Wilson & Schooler 1991) when conscious deliberation is prevented by shortage of time or by competing tasks. This applies to fairly complex, multiattributed decision problems. However, it is unclear why any unconscious process of deliberative reasoning need be postulated. The evidence is consistent with the claim that where participants have a history of relevant experiential learning, fast recognition processes may provide accurate intuitive responses. What is interesting, however, is that conscious deliberative reasoning may then interfere with good decision-making. It may be that this reflects its sequential and low-capacity nature. An analogous finding in the learning literature is that complex rule learning may sometimes be inhibited by an instructional set for explicit learning (Reber 1993).

Dual processes would seem to be implicated when we contrast intuitive judgment with reflective decision-making. Many everyday decisions seem to involve rapid intuitive judgments in which courses of action spring to mind with little or no effort of conscious thinking. Much expert decision-making seems to have this character (Klein 1999). On the other hand, we can and do make some decisions in a manner much more akin to that prescribed by decision theory, exploring alternative actions and their consequences with extended mental simulations (Kahneman & Tversky 1982). Intuitive judgments seem to have the System 1 characteristics, whereas reflective decision-making seems much more like a System 2 process (see also Kahneman & Frederick 2002). Other examples familiar to us all concern phobias and compulsive behaviors like gambling, overeating, or smoking, where we may become aware of a System 1 and 2 conflict. We may judge our own behavior or that of others to be irrational because we compulsively behave in ways that are at odds with our explicitly stated (System 2) goals. Some authors have described these kinds of phenomena as implying two minds in one brain (Evans 2003) or a brain at war with itself (Stanovich 2004).

Dual-Process Theories of Social Cognition

Dual-process theories of social cognition emerged in the 1980s (Chaiken 1980, Petty & Cacioppo 1981) and developed in popularity to form the dominant paradigm for the past 20 years or more. Contemporary work particularly concerns the automatic and unconscious processing of social information in such domains as person perception, stereotyping, and attitude change (Bargh 2006, Chaiken & Trope 1999, Forgas et al. 2003, Hassin et al. 2005, Smith & DeCoster 2000, Wilson 2002) and its apparent dissociation from explicit beliefs and conscious processing. The proposal of new accounts or at least new labels for dual processes in social cognition has reached near epidemic proportions, causing some reaction in terms of a unimodel that instead emphasizes multiple parameters known to influence social judgments (Kruglanski et al. 2003).

Another interesting recent development is the quad model of Conrey et al. (2005), which proposes four kinds of process that should be distinguished in order to interpret research on automatic and controlled cognition.

Dual-processing accounts of social cognition have their roots in cognitive psychology, especially the study of automaticity and implicit memory, but have made curiously little connection with the dual-process theories of reasoning and decision-making discussed above. Although there is currently very little cross-referencing between these literatures, dual-process accounts in social psychology nevertheless share many common features with those in the cognitive psychology of reasoning and judgment. However, there are differences of emphasis. In general, the social cognition literature is less concerned with issues about cognitive architecture and evolution but more focused on issues concerning consciousness, free will, and the implications for moral and legal responsibilities of individuals.

A long-established dual-process theory is the heuristic-systematic model of Chaiken. According to Chen & Chaiken (1999, p. 74; Petty & Cacioppo 1981) "*Systematic processing* entails a relatively analytic and comprehensive treatment of judgment relevant information.... Given its nature, systematic processing requires both cognitive ability and capacity" whereas "*Heuristic processing* entails the activation and application of judgmental rules and 'heuristics' that are presumed to be learned and stored in memory.... Relative to systematic processing, heuristic processing make minimal cognitive demands on the perceiver." Systematic processing seems a similar concept here to that of analytic or System 2 reasoning in theories described above. However, heuristic processing in this theory sounds more like the recognition-primed decision making of Klein (1999) than the contextualization process postulated by reasoning theorists (Evans 2006, Stanovich 1999). In fact, heuristic processing so defined could be taken to be a form of System 2 or rule-based reasoning, albeit one less effortful than that which is called systematic processing (see Strack & Deutsch 2004).

The cognitive experimental self theory, or CEST (Epstein 1994, Epstein & Pacini 1999), proposes two cognitive systems—experiential and rational—that share many common features with the generic two-system theory of reasoning. Like System 1, the experiential system is described as having a long evolutionary history with clear links to animal cognition, whereas the rational system, like System 2, is recent and distinctively human. Many other features of the generic theory shown in **Table 1** are included: fast-slow, unconscious-conscious, associative-rule based, and so on, whereas emotion is explicitly linked to the experiential system. However, the theory has a parallel-competitive, rather than default-interventionist, structure, and it includes the proposal that each system has access to distinct forms of knowledge. Epstein's approach is distinctive in the linkage of the two systems to two competitive processing styles. In contrast with reasoning theorists like Stanovich, who keep a clear separation between cognitive systems and dispositional thinking styles, Epstein has developed a psychometric tool, the rational experiential inventory, or REI (Epstein et al. 1996), for measurement of the two styles based on self-report. Epstein & Pacini (1999) review a number of experimental studies that appear to support the existence of these two processing styles. However, neither people classified as rational thinkers nor those scoring highly on the related need-for-cognition scale appear to have any advantage on abstract tests of logical reasoning (Bors et al. 2006, Newstead et al. 2004).

Social psychologists have been particularly interested in links between unconscious processing and implicit forms of knowledge representation. For example, it has been proposed that people may have both implicit and explicit attitudes (Wilson et al. 2000), something that may help to explain the traditional dissociation between verbal and behavioral measure of attitude changes. It may be possible to change our explicit attitude while an implicit attitude continues to control our social behavior. Similarly, it has been argued that we may have both implicit and explicit stereotypes that are dissociated from one another (Bargh 1999, Bargh & Williams 2006, Devine 1989). Many studies have used the methodology of semantic priming, borrowed from the literature on implicit memory (Lucas 2000). For example, Macrae et al. (1997) showed that when people are asked to view photographs of males or females and required to process them in a semantic manner, their subsequent threshold for word recognition is primed for stereotype-consistent words. Although some authors have proposed an optimistic view that conscious processing can inhibit implicit stereotypes, the evidence suggests the contrary. Even people who have nonstereotypical explicitly stated beliefs and who are aware of the problem of stereotypical behavior can be shown experimentally to have much of their social behavior unconsciously controlled (Bargh 1999).

A recent attempt to link dual-process accounts in social cognition with those in cognitive psychology was made by Smith & DeCoster (2000), who build on the distinction of two kinds of memory, one based on slow acquisition through associative learning and one linked to explicit memory (McClelland et al. 1995). These led them to a parallel system account in which associative and rule-based processing (cf. Sloman 1996) are linked to the two forms of knowledge. This proposal is essentially similar to dual-process accounts that have been developed to distinguish implicit and explicit forms of learning (Berry & Dienes 1993, French & Cleeremans 2002, Reber 1993, Sun et al. 2005). Smith & DeCoster argue that the major dual-process theories in social psychology can be accommodated within this general framework. However, as noted earlier, this is doubtful in the case of the heuristic-systematic theory, which looks more like two forms of rule-based processing (Strack & Deutsch 2004).

An important development for dual-process and dual-system theory generally is the emergence of social cognitive neuroscience. Particularly interesting is the identification of reflexive (System 1) and reflective (System 2) cognitive processing, with two neurological systems described as the X-system and C-system, respectively (Lieberman 2003, Lieberman et al. 2004). The X-system is composed of the amygdala, basal ganglia, and lateral temporal cortex, brain areas known to be involved in conditioning and associative learning and now being linked by Lieberman and colleagues with social cognitive processes traditionally described as automatic or implicit. The C-system involves the anterior cingulate cortex, prefrontal cortex, and the medial-temporal lobe (including hippocampus), brain areas known to be involved with (among other things) explicit learning and inhibitory, executive control. This account is supported by recent findings concerning the neurological systems that underlie response to immediate and deferred rewards in decision-making (McClure et al. 2004), which correspond to X- and C-system regions of the brain. Although in its early stages, this research program provides perhaps the strongest basis in the literature for maintaining some form of dual-system distinction.

A final issue to note in this section is that of self-knowledge. Although the notion that System 2 reasoning may engage in rationalization or confabulation is mentioned in the cognitive literature (Evans & Over 1996, Stanovich 2004), this idea has been more thoroughly investigated in the social psychology literature, especially by Wilson and his colleagues (Nisbett & Wilson 1977, Wilson 2002, Wilson & Dunn 2004). The basic idea here is that although much of our behavior is unconsciously controlled, "we" (conscious beings) are not aware of this fact and may live with an illusion that we are much more in control of our behavior than we actually are. On this view, we observe and theorize about our own social behavior in much the same way

as we attempt to perceive and understand the behavior of others.

CONCLUSIONS

Although dual-process theories have been around in cognitive and social psychology for 30 years and more, it is only within the past 10 years or so that the terms System 1 and System 2 have come into common use. So popular are these terms now that it may be somewhat difficult to discourage their use and the implication of two underlying generic systems that they convey. However, close inspection of the evidence suggests that generic dual-system theory is currently oversimplified and misleading. In particular, (*a*) it is not possible coherently to link together all the attributes associated with Systems 1 and 2, respectively, in **Table 2**, certainly when moving between clusters, and (*b*) there are at least two quite distinct forms of dual-process theory to be found in these various literatures that cannot readily be mapped on to each other.

We might be better off talking about type 1 and type 2 processes since all theories seem to contrast fast, automatic, or unconscious processes with those that are slow, effortful, and conscious (Samuels 2006). Such terminology does not commit use to a two-system view. However, it would then be helpful to have some clear basis for this distinction. If we cannot associate all the System 1 (or type 1) features shown in **Table 2** together, for example, then which are the key ones that should distinguish them from System 2 (or type 2) processes? My suggestion is that type 2 processes are those that require access to a single, capacity-limited central working memory resource, while type 1 processes do not require such access. This implies that the core features of type 2 processes are that they are slow, sequential, and capacity limited. The last feature implies also that their functioning will correlate with individual differences in cognitive capacity and be disrupted by concurrent working memory load. Depending upon what else is assumed about working memory, there may be a rationale for describing such type 2 processes as registering in consciousness and having properties associated with executive processes and intentional, higher-order control. However, other proposed features of System 2 in the generic theory do not immediately follow from this definition of type 2 processes, for example, the proposal that such processes are uniquely human or associated with decontextualized thought or rule-based reasoning.

The problem with this distinction is that type 1 processes then simply refer to any processes in the mind that can operate automatically without occupying working memory space. As already indicated, there are a number of different kinds of such implicit processes. We may have innate cognitive modules with encapsulated processes for perception, attention, language processing, and so on. We appear to have an associative learning system that implicitly acquires knowledge of the world in a form similar to weights in neural networks; the knowledge cannot be called to mind as explicit knowledge, but it can directly affect our behavior. We have habitual and automated behavior patterns that once required conscious type 2 effort but seem to have become type 1 with practice and experience. We also have powerful pragmatic processes that rapidly identify and retrieve explicit knowledge for conscious processing. Type 2 processing requires supporting type 1 processes to supply a continuous stream of relevant content into working memory.

If there are indeed multiple kinds of type 1 processes, then it is to be expected that psychologists will have developed different kinds of dual-process theories, which seems to be the case. Parallel-competitive forms of dual-process theory seem to be rooted in the idea of two forms of learning, leading to two forms of knowledge (implicit and explicit) that can then lead to competing attempts to control behavior. Theories of this type include those of Sloman (1996), Reber (1993), and Smith & DeCoster (2000). As mentioned above,

there is promising evidence that these theories can be mapped onto neurologically distinct X- and C-systems (Lieberman 2003). However, the category of theories that I call "default-interventionist" assume, in contrast, that rapid preconscious processes supply content for conscious processing, cueing default behaviors that the analytic reasoning may approve or intervene upon with more effortful reasoning. This approach is reflected in dual-process theories of reasoning (Evans 2006, Stanovich 1999) as well as the theory of intuitive and reflective judgment proposed by Kahneman & Frederick (2002). If there are indeed two parallel cognitive and neurological systems, it is possible either that (a) the latter class of theories are mistaken in their architectural assumptions or (b) they are dealing with interactions between preconscious and conscious elements of the second system.

In short, my conclusion is that although dual-process theories enjoy good empirical support in a number of fields of psychology, the superficially attractive notion that they are all related to the same underlying two systems of cognition is probably mistaken, at least in the way that Systems 1 and 2 are being defined in the current literatures. For example, it is almost certainly wrong to think of System 1 as one system, all of which is old and shared with other animals. Equally, it is probably a mistake to think of System 2 as the conscious mind, all of whose processes are slow and sequential. If there is a second system, distinctively human, involving working memory and neurologically distinct structures, it does not follow that all of its workings are conscious and controlled. It is perfectly possible that one system operates entirely with type 1 processes and that the other includes a mixture of type 1 and type 2 processes, the latter being linked to the use of working memory, which this system uses—among other resources. Such a proposal could resolve the conflict between evidence for dual systems on the one hand with the proposals of different dual-process theorists on the other.

ACKNOWLEDGMENTS

The writing of this review was supported by a Research Fellowship award to the author by the Economic and Social Research Council of the United Kingdom (RES 000–27-0184). The author is grateful to Keith Stanovich, Tim Wilson, Phil Core, Eliot Smith, Shira Elqayam, and Yaniv Hanoch for their comments on an earlier draft of this review.

LITERATURE CITED

Baars BJ, Franklin S. 2003. How conscious experience and working memory interact. *Trends Cogn. Sci.* 7(4):166–72

Baddeley AD, Hitch GJ. 1974. Working memory. In *The Psychology of Learning and Motivation, Vol. 8*, ed. GA Bower, pp. 47–90. New York: Academic

Ball LJ, Lucas EJ, Gale AG, Miles JNV. 2003. Inspection times and the selection task: What do eye-movements reveal about relevance effects? *Q. J. Exp. Psychol.* 56A(6):1053–77

Barbey AK, Sloman SA. 2007. Base-rate respect: from ecological validity to dual processes. *Behav. Brain Sci.* In press

Bargh JA. 1999. The cognitive monster: the case against the controllability of automatic stereotype effects. See Chaiken & Trope 1999, pp. 361–82

Bargh JA, ed. 2006. *Social Psychology and the Unconscious*. New York: Psychol. Press

Bargh JA, Ferguson MJ. 2000. Beyond behaviorism: on the automaticity of higher mental processes. *Psychol. Bull.* 126(6):925–45

Bargh JA, Gollwitzer PM, Lee-Chai A, Barndollar K, Trötschel R. 2001. The automated will: nonconscious activation and pursuit of behavioral goals. *J. Personal. Soc. Psychol.* 81(6):1014–27

Bargh JA, Williams EL. 2006. The automaticity of social life. *Curr. Dir. Psychol. Sci.* 15(1):1–4

Barrett HC, Kurzban R. 2006. Modularity in cognition: framing the debate. *Psychol. Rev.* 113:628–47

Barrett LF, Tugade MM, Engle RW. 2004. Individual differences in working memory capacity and dual-process theories of the mind. *Psychol. Bull.* 130:553–73

Berry DC, Dienes Z. 1993. *Implicit Learning*. Hove, UK: Erlbaum

Bors DA, Vigneau F, Lalande F. 2006. Measuring the need for cognition: item polarity, dimensionality, and the relation with ability. *Personal. Individ. Differ.* 40(4):819–28

Braine MDS, O'Brien DP, eds. 1998a. *Mental Logic*. Mahwah, NJ: Erlbaum

Braine MDS, O'Brien DP. 1998b. The theory of mental-propositional logic: description and illustration. See Braine & O'Brien 1998a, pp. 79–89

Cacioppo JT, Petty RE. 1982. The need for cognition. *J. Personal. Soc. Psychol.* 42(1):116–31

Carruthers P. 2006. *The Architecture of the Mind*. Oxford, UK: Oxford Univ. Press

Chaiken S. 1980. Heuristic versus systematic information processing and the use of source versus message cues in persuasion. *J. Personal. Soc. Psychol.* 39:752–66

Chaiken S, Trope Y, eds. 1999. *Dual-Process Theories in Social Psychology*. New York: Guilford

Chen S, Chaiken S. 1999. The heuristic-systematic model in its broader context. See Chaiken & Trope 1999, pp. 73–96

Colom R, Rebollo I, Palacios A, Juan-Espinosa M, Kyllonen PC. 2004. Working memory is (almost) perfectly predicted by g. *Intelligence* 32(3):277–96

Conrey FR, Gawronski B, Sherman JW, Hugenberg K, Groom CJ. 2005. Separating multiple processes in implicit social cognition: the quad model of implicit task performance. *J. Personal. Soc. Psychol.* 89(4):469–87

Cosmides L, Tooby J. 1992. Cognitive adapations for social exchange. In *The Adapted Mind: Evolutionary Psychology and the Generation of Culture*, ed. JH Barkow, L Cosmides, J Tooby, pp. 163–228. Oxford, UK: Oxford Univ. Press

Cosmides L, Tooby J. 1996. Are humans good intuitive statisticians after all? Rethinking some conclusions from the literature on judgment under uncertainty. *Cognition* 58:1–73

Cosmides L, Tooby J. 2000. Consider the source: the evolution of adaptations for decoupling and metarepresentation. In *Metarepresentations*, ed. D Sperber, pp. 53–115. Oxford, UK: Oxford Univ. Press

Cummins DD, Lubart T, Alksnis O, Rist R. 1991. Conditional reasoning and causation. *Mem. Cogn.* 19:274–82

De Neys W. 2006. Dual processing in reasoning—two systems but one reasoner. *Psychol. Sci.* 17(5):428–33

De Neys W, Schaeken W, d'Ydewalle G. 2005. Working memory and everyday conditional reasoning: retrieval and inhibition of stored counterexamples. *Think. Reasoning* 11(4):349–81

Devine PG. 1989. Stereotypes and prejudice: their automatic and controlled components. *J. Personal. Soc. Psychol.* 56:680–90

Dijksterhuis A, Bos MW, Nordgren LF, von Baaren RB. 2006. On making the right choice: the deliberation-without-attention effect. *Science* 311:1005–7

Dijksterhuis A, Smith PK. 2005. What do we do unconsciously? And how? *J. Consum. Psychol.* 15(3):225–29

Doherty ME, ed. 1996. Social judgement theory. *Think. Reasoning* 2:2, 3

Epstein S. 1994. Integration of the cognitive and psychodynamic unconscious. *Am. Psychol.* 49:709–24

Epstein S, Pacini R. 1999. Some basic issues regarding dual-process theories from the perspective of cognitive-experiential theory. See Chaiken & Trope 1999, pp. 462–82

Epstein S, Pacini R, Denes-Raj V, Heier H. 1996. Individual differences in intuitive-experiential and analytic-rational thinking styles. *J. Personal. Soc. Psychol.* 71:390–405

Evans JStBT. 1989. *Bias in Human Reasoning: Causes and Consequences*. Brighton, UK: Erlbaum

Evans JStBT. 1996. Deciding before you think: relevance and reasoning in the selection task. *Br. J. Psychol.* 87:223–40

Evans JStBT. 2002. Logic and human reasoning: an assessment of the deduction paradigm. *Psychol. Bull.* 128:978–96

Evans JStBT. 2003. In two minds: dual process accounts of reasoning. *Trends Cogn. Sci.* 7:454–59

Evans JStBT. 2006. The heuristic-analytic theory of reasoning: extension and evaluation. *Psychon. Bull. Rev.* 13(3):378–95

Evans JStBT, Barston JL, Pollard P. 1983. On the conflict between logic and belief in syllogistic reasoning. *Mem. Cogn.* 11:295–306

Evans JStBT, Curtis-Holmes J. 2005. Rapid responding increases belief bias: evidence for the dual-process theory of reasoning. *Think. Reasoning* 11(4):382–89

Evans JStBT, Handley SJ, Perham N, Over DE, Thompson VA. 2000. Frequency versus probability formats in statistical word problems. *Cognition* 77:197–213

Evans JStBT, Over DE. 1996. *Rationality and Reasoning*. Hove, UK: Psychol. Press

Evans JStBT, Over DE. 2004. *If*. Oxford, UK: Oxford Univ. Press

Fodor J. 1983. *The Modularity of Mind*. Scranton, PA: Crowell

Fodor J. 2001. *The Mind Doesn't Work That Way*. Cambridge, MA: MIT Press

Forgas JP, Williams KR, von Hippel W, eds. 2003. *Social Judgments: Implicit and Explicit Processes*. New York: Cambridge Univ. Press

Frankish K. 2004. *Mind and Supermind*. Cambridge, UK: Cambridge Univ. Press

French RM, Cleeremans A, eds. 2002. *Implicit Learning and Consciousness*. Hove, UK: Psychol. Press

Gathercole S. 2003. *Short-Term and Working Memory*. London: Taylor & Francis

George C. 1997. Reasoning from uncertain premises. *Think. Reasoning* 3:161–90

Gigerenzer G, Hoffrage U. 1995. How to improve Bayesian reasoning without instruction: frequency formats. *Psychol. Rev.* 102:684–704

Gigerenzer G, Todd PM, ABC Research Group. 1999. *Simple Heuristics That Make Us Smart*. New York/Oxford: Oxford Univ. Press

Gilinsky AS, Judd BB. 1994. Working memory and bias in reasoning across the life-span. *Psychol. Aging* 9:356–71

Gilovich T, Griffin D, Kahneman D. 2002. *Heuristics and Biases: The Psychology of Intuitive Judgement*. Cambridge, UK: Cambridge Univ. Press

Girotto V, Gonzalez M. 2001. Solving probabilistic and statistical problems: a matter of information structure and question form. *Cognition* 78:247–76

Goel V. 2005. Cognitive neuroscience of deductive reasoning. In *The Cambridge Handbook of Thinking and Reasoning*, ed. K Holyoak, RG Morrison, pp. 475–92. Cambridge, UK: Cambridge Univ. Press

Goel V, Buchel C, Rith C, Olan J. 2000. Dissociation of mechanisms underlying syllogistic reasoning. *NeuroImage* 12:504–14

Goel V, Dolan RJ. 2003. Explaining modulation of reasoning by belief. *Cognition* 87:B11–22

Haidt J. 2001. The emotional dog and its rational tail: a social intuitionist approach to moral judgement. *Psychol. Rev.* 108(4):814–34

Hammond KR. 1996. *Human Judgment and Social Policy*. New York: Oxford Univ. Press

Hanoch Y, Vitouch O. 2004. Information, emotional arousal and the ecological reframing of the Yerkes-Dobson law. *Theor. Psychol.* 14:427–52

Hassin RR, Uleman JS, Bargh JA, eds. 2005. *The New Unconscious*. Oxford, UK: Oxford Univ. Press

Hoffrage U, Gigerenzer G, Krauss S, Martigon L. 2002. Representation facilitates reasoning: what natural frequencies are and what they are not. *Cognition* 84:343–52

Inhelder B, Piaget J. 1958. *The Growth of Logical Thinking*. New York: Basic Books

Johnson-Laird PN. 1983. *Mental Models*. Cambridge, UK: Cambridge Univ. Press

Johnson-Laird PN, Bara BG. 1984. Syllogistic inference. *Cognition* 16:1–61

Johnson-Laird PN, Byrne RMJ. 1991. *Deduction*. Hove & London: Erlbaum

Johnson-Laird PN, Byrne RMJ. 2002. Conditionals: a theory of meaning, pragmatics and inference. *Psychol. Rev.* 109:646–78

Kahneman D, Frederick S. 2002. Representativeness revisited: attribute substitution in intuitive judgement. In *Heuristics and Biases: The Psychology of Intuitive Judgment*, ed. T Gilovich, D Griffin, D Kahneman, pp. 49–81. Cambridge, UK: Cambridge Univ. Press

Kahneman D, Frederick S. 2005. A model of heuristic judgment. In *The Cambridge Handbook of Thinking and Reasoning*, ed. K Holyoak, RG Morrison, pp. 267–94. Cambridge, UK: Cambridge Univ. Press

Kahneman D, Slovic P, Tversky A. 1982. *Judgment Under Uncertainty: Heuristics and Biases*. Cambridge, UK: Cambridge Univ. Press

Kahneman D, Tversky A. 1972. Subjective probability: a judgment of representativeness. *Cogn. Psychol.* 3:430–54

Kahneman D, Tversky A. 1973. On the psychology of prediction. *Psychol. Rev.* 80:237–51

Kahneman D, Tversky A. 1982. The simulation heuristic. See Kahneman et al. 1982, pp. 201–10

Kihlstrom JF. 1987. The cognitive unconscious. *Science* 237:1445–52

Klaczynski PA. 2000. Motivated scientific reasoning biases, epistemological beliefs, and theory polarization: a two-process approach to adolescent cognition. *Child Dev.* 71(5):1347–66

Klaczynski PA. 2001. Framing effects on adolescent task representations, analytic and heuristic processing, and decision making: implications for the normative/descriptive gap. *Appl. Dev. Psychol.* 22:289–309

Klaczynski PA, Lavallee KL. 2005. Domain-specific identity, epistemic regulation, and intellectual ability as predictors of belief-biased reasoning: a dual-process perspective. *J. Exp. Child Psychol.* 92(1):1–24

Klauer KC, Musch J, Naumer B. 2000. On belief bias in syllogistic reasoning. *Psychol. Rev.* 107:852–84

Klein G. 1999. *Sources of Power*. Cambridge, MA: MIT Press

Koehler JJ. 1996. The base rate fallacy reconsidered: descriptive, normative and methodological challenges. *Behav. Brain Sci.* 19:1–53

Kokis JV, MacPherson R, Toplak ME, West RF, Stanovich KE. 2002. Heuristic and analytic processing: age trends and associations with cognitive ability and cognitive styles. *J. Exp. Child Psychol.* 83(1):26–52

Kruglanski AW, Chun WY, Erb HP, Pierro A, Mannett L, Spiegel S. 2003. A parametric unimodel of human judgment: integrating dual-process frameworks in social cognition from a single-mode perspective. See Forgas et al. 2003, pp. 137–61

Lieberman MD. 2003. Reflective and reflexive judgment processes: a social cognitive neuroscience approach. See Forgas et al. 2003, pp. 44–67

Lieberman MD, Jarcho JM, Satpute AB. 2004. Evidence-based and intuition-based self-knowledge: an fMRI study. *J. Personal. Soc. Psychol.* 87:421–35

Liu I-M, Lo K-C, Wu J-T. 1996. A probabilistic interpretation of "If-Then." *Q. J. Exp. Psychol.* 49A:828–44

Lucas M. 2000. Semantic priming without association: a meta-analytic review. *Psychon. Bull. Rev.* 7(4):618–30

Macrae CN, Bodenhausen GV, Milne AB, Thorn TMJ, Castelli L. 1997. Out of mind but back in sight: stereotypes on the rebound. *J. Exp. Soc. Psychol.* 33:471–89

Markovits H, Fleury M-L, Quinn S, Venet M. 1998. The development of conditional reasoning and the structure of semantic memory. *Child Dev.* 69:742–55

Markovits H, Quinn S. 2002. Efficiency of retrieval correlates with "logical" reasoning from causal conditional premises. *Mem. Cogn.* 30(5):696–706

McClelland JL, McNaughton BL, O'Reilly RC. 1995. Why there are complementary learning systems in the hippocampus and neocortex: insights from the successes and failures of connectionist models of learning and memory. *Psychol. Rev.* 102(3):419–57

McClure SM, Laibson DI, Loewenstein G, Cohen JD. 2004. Separate neural systems value immediate and delayed monetary rewards. *Science* 306(5695):503–7

Mithen S. 1996. *The Prehistory of the Mind*. London: Thames & Hudson

Monsell S, Driver J. 2000. *Control of Cognitive Processes*. Cambridge, MA: MIT Press

Newstead SE, Ellis C, Evans JStBT, Dennis I. 1997. Conditional reasoning with realistic material. *Think. Reasoning* 3:49–76

Newstead SE, Handley SJ, Harley C, Wright H, Farelly D. 2004. Individual differences in deductive reasoning. *Q. J. Exp. Psychol.* 57A:33–60

Nisbett R, Peng K, Choi I, Norenzayan A. 2001. Culture and systems of thought: holistic vs. analytic cognition. *Psychol. Rev.* 108:291–310

Nisbett RE, Wilson TD. 1977. Telling more than we can know: verbal reports on mental processes. *Psychol. Rev.* 84:231–95

Oakhill J, Johnson-Laird PN, Garnham A. 1989. Believability and syllogistic reasoning. *Cognition* 31:117–40

Oaksford M, Chater N. 1995. Theories of reasoning and the computational explanation of everyday inference. *Think. Reasoning* 1:121–52

Osman M. 2005. An evaluation of dual-process theories of reasoning. *Psychon. Bull. Rev.* 11:988–1010

Over DE. 2003. From massive modularity to metarepresentation: the evolution of higher cogntion. In *Evolution and the Psychology of Thinking: The Debate*, ed. DE Over, pp. 121–44. Hove, UK: Psychol. Press

Petty RE, Cacioppo JT. 1981. *Attitudes and Persuasions: Classical and Contemporary Approaches.* Dubuque, IA: Brown

Pinker S. 1997. *How the Mind Works.* New York: Norton

Reber AS. 1993. *Implicit Learning and Tacit Knowledge.* Oxford, UK: Oxford Univ. Press

Reber R. 2004. Availability. In *Cognitive Illusions*, ed. R Pohl, pp. 147–64. Hove, UK: Psychol. Press

Reyna VF. 2004. How people make decisions that involve risk: a dual-processes approach. *Curr. Dir. Psychol. Sci.* 13(2):60–66

Rips LJ. 1994. *The Psychology of Proof.* Cambridge, MA: MIT Press

Roberts MJ. 1998. Inspection times and the selection task: Are they relevant? *Q. J. Exp. Psychol.* 51A:781–810

Roberts MJ, Newton EJ. 2001. Inspection times, the change task, and the rapid-response selection task. *Q. J. Exp. Psychol.* 54(4):1031–48

Samuels R. 1998. Evolutionary psychology and the mass modularity hypothesis. *Br. J. Philos. Sci.* 49:575–602

Samuels R. 2006. The magical number two, plus or minus: some comments on dual-processing theories of cognition. *In Two Minds: Dual Process Theories of Reasoning and Rationality. 2006. Intl. Conf., Cambridge, UK*, July 5–7

Schneider W, Shiffrin RM. 1977. Controlled and automatic human information processing I: detection, search and attention. *Psychol. Rev.* 84:1–66

Sherry DF, Schacter DL. 1987. The evolution of multiple memory systems. *Psychol. Rev.* 94:439–54

Sloman SA. 1996. The empirical case for two systems of reasoning. *Psychol. Bull.* 119:3–22

Sloman SA. 2002. Two systems of reasoning. In *Heuristics and Biases: The Psychology of Intuitive Judgment*, ed. T Gilovich, D Griffin, D Kahneman, pp. 379–98. Cambridge, UK: Cambridge Univ. Press

Sloman SA, Over DE, Slovack L. 2003. Frequency illusions and other fallacies. *Organ. Behav. Hum. Decis. Process.* 91:296–309

Smith ER, DeCoster J. 1999. Associative and rule-based processing: a connectionist interpretation of dual-process models. See Chaiken & Trope 1999, pp. 323–60

Smith ER, DeCoster J. 2000. Dual-process models in social and cognitive psychology: conceptual integration and links to underlying memory systems. *Personal. Soc. Psychol. Rev.* 4(2):108–31

Sperber D. 1994. The modularity of thought and the epidemiology of representations. In *Mapping the Mind: Domain Specificity in Cognition and Culture*, ed. LA Hirschfield, SA Gelman, pp. 39–67. Cambridge, UK: Cambridge Univ. Press

Sperber D. 2000. Metarepresentations in an evolutionary perspective. In *Metarepresentations*, ed. D Sperber, pp. 117–38. Oxford, UK: Oxford Univ. Press

Stanovich KE. 1999. *Who is Rational? Studies of Individual Differences in Reasoning*. Mahwah, NJ: Elrbaum

Stanovich KE. 2004. *The Robot's Rebellion: Finding Meaning in the Age of Darwin*. Chicago: Chicago Univ. Press

Stanovich KE, West RF. 1997. Reasoning independently of prior belief and individual differences in actively open-minded thinking. *J. Educ. Psychol.* 89(2):342–57

Stanovich KE, West RF. 1998. Cognitive ability and variation in selection task performance. *Think. Reasoning* 4:193–230

Stanovich KE, West RF. 2003. Evolutionary versus instrumental goals: how evolutionary psychology misconceives human rationality. In *Evolution and the Psychology of Thinking*, ed. DE Over, pp. 171–230. Hove, UK: Psychol. Press

Stevenson RJ, Over DE. 1995. Deduction from uncertain premises. *Q. J. Exp. Psychol.* 48A:613–43

Stevenson RJ, Over DE. 2001. Reasoning from uncertain premises: effects of expertise and conversational context. *Think. Reasoning* 7(4):367–90

Strack F, Deutsch R. 2004. Reflective and impulsive determinants of social behavior. *Personal. Soc. Psychol. Rev.* 8(3):220–47

Sun R, Slusarz P, Terry C. 2005. The interaction of the explicit and the implicit in skill learning: a dual-process approach. *Psychol. Rev.* 112(1):159–92

Teigen KH. 2004. Judgments by representativeness. In *Cognitive Illusions*, ed. R Pohl, pp. 165–82. Hove, UK: Psychol. Press

Thompson VA. 1994. Interpretational factors in conditional reasoning. *Mem. Cogn.* 22:742–58

Thompson VA. 2000. The task-specific nature of domain-general reasoning. *Cognition* 76:209–68

Toates F. 2006. A model of the hierarchy of behaviour, cognition and consciousness. *Conscious. Cogn.* 15:75–118

Tooby J, Cosmides L. 1992. The psychological foundations of culture. In *The Adapted Mind: Evolutionary Psychology and the Generation of Culture*, ed. JH Barkow, L Cosmides, J Tooby, pp. 19–136. New York: Oxford Univ. Press

Torrens D, Thompson VA, Cramer KM. 1999. Individual differences and the belief bias effect: mental models, logical necessity, and abstract reasoning. *Think. Reasoning* 5:1–28

Tversky A, Kahneman D. 1973. Availability: a heuristic for judging frequency and probability. *Cogn. Psychol.* 5:207–32

Tversky A, Kahneman D. 1983. Extensional vs intuitive reasoning: the conjunction fallacy in probability judgment. *Psychol. Rev.* 90:293–315

Uleman JS. 2005. Introduction: becoming aware of the new unconscious. In *The New Unconscious*, ed. RR Hassin, JS Uleman, JA Bargh, pp. 9–15. Oxford, UK: Oxford Univ. Press

Velmans M. 2000. *Understanding Consciousness*. London: Routledge

Verschueren N, Schaeken W, d'Ydewalle G. 2005. A dual-process specification of causal conditional reasoning. *Think. Reasoning* 11(3):239–78

Wang XT. 2006. Emotions within reason: resolving conflicts in risk preference. *Cogn. Emot.* 20(8):1132–52

Wason PC, Evans JStBT. 1975. Dual processes in reasoning? *Cognition* 3:141–54

Wason PC, Johnson-Laird PN. 1972. *Psychology of Reasoning: Structure and Content*. London: Batsford

Whiten A. 2000. Chimpanzee cognition and the question of mental re-representation. In *Metarepresentations*, ed. D Sperber, pp. 139–67. Oxford, UK: Oxford Univ. Press

Wilson TD. 2002. *Strangers to Ourselves*. Cambridge, MA: Belknap

Wilson TD, Dunn EW. 2004. Self-knowledge: its limits, value, and potential for improvement. *Annu. Rev. Psychol.* 55:493–518

Wilson TD, Lindsey S, Schooler TY. 2000. A model of dual attitudes. *Psychol. Rev.* 107(1):101–26

Wilson TD, Schooler JW. 1991. Thinking too much: introspection can reduce the quality of preferences and decisions. *J. Personal. Soc. Psychol.* 60(2):181–92

Wu G, Zhang J, Gonzales R. 2005. Decision under risk. In *Blackwell Handbook of Judgment and Decision Making*, ed. DJ Koehler, N Harvey, pp. 299–423. Oxford, UK: Blackwell

Putting the Altruism Back into Altruism: The Evolution of Empathy

Frans B.M. de Waal

Living Links, Yerkes National Primate Research Center, and Psychology Department, Emory University, Atlanta, Georgia 30322; email: dewaal@emory.edu

Annu. Rev. Psychol. 2008. 59:279–300

First published online as a Review in Advance on June 5, 2007

The *Annual Review of Psychology* is online at http://psych.annualreviews.org

This article's doi: 10.1146/annurev.psych.59.103006.093625

Key Words

perception-action, perspective-taking, prosocial behavior, cooperation

Abstract

Evolutionary theory postulates that altruistic behavior evolved for the return-benefits it bears the performer. For return-benefits to play a motivational role, however, they need to be experienced by the organism. Motivational analyses should restrict themselves, therefore, to the altruistic impulse and its knowable consequences. Empathy is an ideal candidate mechanism to underlie so-called directed altruism, i.e., altruism in response to another's pain, need, or distress. Evidence is accumulating that this mechanism is phylogenetically ancient, probably as old as mammals and birds. Perception of the emotional state of another automatically activates shared representations causing a matching emotional state in the observer. With increasing cognition, state-matching evolved into more complex forms, including concern for the other and perspective-taking. Empathy-induced altruism derives its strength from the emotional stake it offers the self in the other's welfare. The dynamics of the empathy mechanism agree with predictions from kin selection and reciprocal altruism theory.

Contents

> Sympathy... cannot, in any sense, be regarded as a selfish principle.
> Smith (1759, p. 317)

> Empathy may be uniquely well suited for bridging the gap between egoism and altruism, since it has the property of transforming another person's misfortune into one's own feeling of distress.
> Hoffman (1981a, p. 133)

Altruism (biological definition): behavior that increases the recipient's fitness at a cost to the performers

Ultimate cause or goal: the benefits an organism or its close kin derive from a behavior, hence the probable reason why the behavior was favored by natural selection

Proximate cause: situation that triggers behavior and the mechanism (psychological, neural, physiological) that enables it

INTRODUCTION

Discussions of altruistic behavior tend to suffer from a lack of distinction between function and motivation. This is due to the contrasting emphasis of biologists and psychologists, with the former focusing on what a particular behavior is good for, and the latter on how it comes about.

Evolutionary explanations are built around the principle that all that natural selection can work with are the effects of behavior—not the motivation behind it. This means there is only one logical starting point for evolutionary accounts, as explained by Trivers (2002, p. 6):

"You begin with the effect of behavior on actors and recipients; you deal with the problem of internal motivation, which is a secondary problem, afterward.... [I]f you start with motivation, you have given up the evolutionary analysis at the outset."

This is a perfectly legitimate strategy that has yielded profound insights into the evolution of altruism (e.g., Dugatkin 2006). Unfortunately, however, these insights have not come with a new terminology: Evolutionary biology persists in using motivational terms. Thus, an action is called "selfish" regardless of whether or not the actor deliberately seeks benefits for itself. Similarly, an action is called "altruistic" if it benefits a recipient at a cost to the actor regardless of whether or not the actor intended to benefit the other. The prototypical altruist is a honeybee that stings an intruder—sacrificing her life to protect the hive—even though her motivation is more likely aggressive than benign. This usage of the terms "selfish" and "altruistic" oftentimes conflicts with their vernacular meaning (Sober & Wilson 1998).

The hijacking of motivational terminology by evolutionary biologists has been unhelpful for communication about motivation per se. The way to clear up the confusion is to do what Trivers did when he decided that evolutionary analyses require that effects be considered separate from motivation. Conversely, motivational analyses require us to keep motivation separate from evolutionary considerations. It is not for nothing that biologists hammer on the distinction between ultimate and proximate (Mayr 1961, Tinbergen 1963). The ultimate cause refers to why a behavior evolved over thousands of generations, which depends on its fitness consequences. The proximate cause, on the other hand, refers to the immediate situation that triggers behavior, and the role of learning, physiology, and neural processes—typically the domain of psychologists.

Proximate and ultimate viewpoints do inform each other, yet are not to be conflated. For example, primate cooperation is promoted by social tolerance. Through its effect on food-sharing, tolerance evens out payoff distributions (de Waal & Davis 2003, Melis et al. 2006). Tolerance likely is a proximate mechanism that evolved to serve the ultimate goal of cooperation, which is to yield benefits for all contributors.

Cooperation and altruistic behavior are thought to have evolved to help family members and those inclined to return the favor (Hamilton 1964, Trivers 1971). Regardless of whether this is the whole explanation or not (see Sober & DS Wilson 1998, EO Wilson 2005), the point is that ultimate accounts stress return-benefits, i.e., positive consequences for the performer and/or its kin. Inasmuch as these benefits may be quite delayed, however, it is unclear what motivational role, if any, they play. This becomes clear if we consider more closely what drives directed altruism, i.e., altruistic behavior aimed at others in need, pain, or distress. There are three ways in which directed altruism may come about:

1. Altruistic impulse. Spontaneous, disinterested helping and caring in reaction to begging or distress signals or the sight of another in pain or need.

2. Learned altruism. Helping as a conditioned response reinforced by positive outcomes for the actor.

3. Intentional altruism. Help based on the prediction of behavioral effects. One prediction could be that the help will be reciprocated, hence that the act will produce a net benefit. Since the actor seeks to benefit itself, we may call this intentionally selfish altruism. The second possibility is help based on an appreciation of how one's own behavior will help the other. Since the actor seeks to benefit the other, we may call this intentionally altruistic altruism.

Some directed altruistic behavior is promoted by built-in rewards, such as the oxytocin release during suckling that may underpin maternal care (Panksepp 1998). Empathy-based altruism may have similar intrinsically rewarding qualities in that it offers the actor an emotional stake in the recipient's well-being, i.e., if helping the other ameliorates the helper's internal state (see Empathy as Evolved Proximate Mechanism, below). Extrinsic rewards, on the other hand, are less likely to play a role. By definition, altruism carries an initial cost, and positive consequences occur only after a significant time interval (e.g., the recipient reciprocates) or not at all (e.g., care for dependent kin), making for rather poor learning conditions.

Intentionally selfish altruism would require the actor to explicitly expect others to return the favor. Despite the lack of evidence for such expectations in animals, they are often assumed. The common claim that humans are the only truly altruistic species, since all that animals care about are return-benefits (e.g., Dawkins 1976, Fehr & Fischbacher 2003, Kagan 2000, Silk et al. 2005), misconstrues reciprocity as a motivation. It assumes that animals engage in reciprocal exchange with a full appreciation of how it will ultimately benefit them. Helpful acts for immediate self-gain are indeed common (Dugatkin 1997), but the return-benefits of altruistic behavior typically remain beyond the animal's cognitive horizon, i.e., occur so distantly in time that the organism is unlikely to connect them with the original act. This applies to most reciprocal altruism in the animal kingdom.

Once evolved, behavior often assumes motivational autonomy, i.e., its motivation becomes disconnected from its ultimate goals. A good example is sexual behavior, which arose to serve reproduction. Since animals are, as far as we know, unaware of the link between sex and reproduction, they must be engaging in sex (as do humans much of the time) without progeny in mind. Just as sex cannot be motivated by unforeseen consequences, altruistic behavior cannot be motivated by unforeseen payoffs.

The altruistic impulse is to be taken very seriously, therefore, because even if altruistic behavior were partially learned based on

Directed altruism: helping or comforting behavior directed at an individual in need, pain, or distress

Intentional altruism: the altruist deliberately seeks to benefit either the other (intentionally altruistic altruism) or itself (intentionally selfish altruism)

Empathy-based altruism: help and care born from empathy with another

Empathy: the capacity to (a) be affected by and share the emotional state of another, (b) assess the reasons for the other's state, and (c) identify with the other, adopting his or her perspective. This definition extends beyond what exists in many animals, but the term "empathy" in the present review applies even if only criterion (a) is met

Motivational autonomy: independence of motivation from ultimate goals

Perception-action mechanism (PAM): automatically and unconsciously activated neural representations of states in the subject similar to those perceived in the object

Emotional contagion: emotional state-matching of a subject with an object

short-term intrinsic rewards or long-term extrinsic rewards, this by no means rules out the altruistic impulse. In fact, it presupposes this impulse given that a behavior's consequences cannot be learned without spontaneously engaging in it in the first place.

This review seeks to restore the altruism within altruism by exploring the role of empathy in the directed altruism of humans and other animals. Some definitions of empathy stress the sharing of emotions, whereas other definitions stress the capacity to put oneself into the other's "shoes." The latter definitions are so top-down, however, that they disconnect empathy from its possible antecedents. We follow a bottom-up approach instead, adopting the broadest possible definition, including mere emotional sensitivity to others. We first consider the various levels of empathy in animals and the underlying perception-action mechanism (PAM) proposed by Preston & de Waal (2002a). After this, we explore the relation between empathy and altruism.

A major question is whether evolution is likely to have selected empathy as proximate mechanism to generate directed altruism. Does empathy channel altruism in the direction that evolutionary theory would predict? So, even though motivation will be kept temporarily separate from evolutionary considerations, in the end the two will meet. Empathy may be motivationally autonomous, but it still needs to produce—on average and in the long run—evolutionarily advantageous outcomes. The central thesis to be argued here, then, is that empathy evolved in animals as the main proximate mechanism for directed altruism, and that it causes altruism to be dispensed in accordance with predictions from kin selection and reciprocal altruism theory.

ORIGIN OF EMPATHY

Empathy allows one to quickly and automatically relate to the emotional states of others, which is essential for the regulation of social interactions, coordinated activity, and cooperation toward shared goals. Even though cognition is often critical, it is a secondary development. As noted by Hoffman (1981b, p. 79), "[H]umans must be equipped biologically to function effectively in many social situations without undue reliance on cognitive processes."

The selection pressure to evolve rapid emotional connectedness likely started in the context of parental care long before our species evolved (Eibl-Eibesfeldt 1974 [1971], MacLean 1985). Signaling their state through smiling and crying, human infants urge their caregiver to come into action (Acebo & Thoman 1995, Bowlby 1958). Equivalent mechanisms operate in all animals in which reproduction relies on feeding, cleaning, and warming of the young. Avian or mammalian parents alert to and affected by their offspring's needs likely out-reproduced those who remained indifferent.

Once the empathic capacity existed, it could be applied outside the rearing context and play a role in the wider network of social relationships. The fact that mammals retain distress vocalizations into adulthood hints at the continued survival value of empathy-inducing signals. For example, primates often lick and clean the wounds of conspecifics (Boesch 1992), which is so critical for healing that adult male macaques injured during attempts to enter a new group often temporarily return to their native group, where they are more likely to receive this service (Dittus & Ratnayeke 1989).

LEVELS OF EMPATHY

Emotional Contagion

The lowest common denominator of all empathic processes is that one party is affected by another's emotional or arousal state. This broad perspective on empathy, which goes back as far as Lipps (1903), leads one to recognize continuity between humans and other animals as well as between human adults and young children. Emotional connectedness in humans is so common, starts so early in life (e.g., Hoffman 1975, Zahn-Waxler &

Radke-Yarrow 1990), and shows neural and physiological correlates (e.g., Adolphs et al. 1994, Decety & Chaminade 2003a, Rimm-Kaufman & Kagan 1996) as well as a genetic substrate (Plomin et al. 1993), that it would be strange indeed if no continuity with other species existed. Evolutionary continuity between humans and apes is reflected in the similarity of emotional communication (Parr & Waller 2007) as well as similar changes in brain and peripheral skin temperature in response to emotionally charged images (Parr 2001, Parr & Hopkins 2001).

A flock of birds taking off all at once because one among them is startled shows a reflex-like, highly adaptive spreading of fear that may not involve any understanding of what triggered the initial reaction. Similarly, when a room full of human newborns bursts out crying because one among them started to cry, there is an automatic spreading of distress (Hoffman 1975). At the core of these processes is adoption—in whole or in part—of another's emotional state, i.e., emotional contagion (Hatfield et al. 1993). Emotional contagion is not always a passive process, though: The object often aims to emotionally affect the subject, such as the extremely noisy temper tantrums of young apes when they are being rejected during weaning. Like human children (Potegal 2000), they exploit emotional contagion to induce maternal distress, which in turn may lead the mother to change her behavior to their advantage.

Emotional responses to displays of emotion in others are so commonplace in animals (de Waal 2003, Plutchik 1987, Preston & de Waal 2002b) that Darwin (1982 [1871, p. 77]) already noted that "many animals certainly sympathize with each other's distress or danger." For example, rats and pigeons display distress in response to perceived distress in a conspecific, and temporarily inhibit conditioned behavior if it causes pain responses in others (Church 1959, Watanabe & Ono 1986). A recent experiment demonstrated that mice perceiving other mice in pain intensify their own response to pain (Langford et al. 2006).

Miller et al. (1959) published the first of a series of pioneering studies on the transmission of affect in rhesus macaques. These monkeys tend to terminate projected pictures of conspecifics in a fearful pose even more rapidly than negatively conditioned stimuli. Perhaps the most compelling evidence for emotional contagion came from Wechkin et al. (1964) and Masserman et al. (1964), who found that monkeys refuse to pull a chain that delivers food to them if doing so delivers an electric shock to and triggers pain reactions in a companion. Whether their sacrifice reflects concern for the other (see below) remains unclear, however, as it might also be explained as avoidance of aversive vicarious arousal.

Sympathetic Concern

The next evolutionary step occurs when emotional contagion is combined with appraisal of the other's situation and attempts to understand the cause of the other's emotions. De Waal (1996) speaks of "cognitive empathy" when the empathic reaction includes such contextual appraisal.

The psychological literature distinguishes sympathy from personal distress, which in their social consequences are each other's opposites. Sympathy is defined as "an affective response that consists of feelings of sorrow or concern for a distressed or needy other (rather than sharing the emotion of the other). Sympathy is believed to involve an other-oriented, altruistic motivation" (Eisenberg 2000, p. 677). Personal distress, on the other hand, makes the affected party selfishly seek to alleviate its own distress, which mimics that of the object. Personal distress is not concerned, therefore, with the other (Batson 1991). A striking nonhuman primate example is how the continued screams of a punished infant rhesus monkey will cause other infants to embrace, mount, or even pile on top of the victim. Thus, one infant's distress spreads quickly to its peers, which then seek to reduce

Sympathetic concern: concern about another's state and attempts to ameliorate this state (e.g., consolation)

Cognitive empathy: empathy combined with contextual appraisal and an understanding of what caused the object's emotional state

Personal distress: self-centered distress born from empathy with another's distress

Consolation:
comforting behavior
directed at a
distressed party, such
as a recent victim of
aggression

their own negative arousal (de Waal 1996, p. 46).

Concern for others is different in that it relies on a separation between internally and externally generated emotions. This separation is observable in many mammals. In a study that sought to document children's responses to family members instructed to feign sadness (sobbing), pain (crying), or distress (choking), striking similarities emerged between the reactions of one-year-old children and pets, such as dogs and cats. The latter, too, showed comforting attempts, such as putting their head in the lap of the "distressed" person (Zahn-Waxler et al. 1984).

Yerkes (1925, p. 246) reported how his bonobo, Prince Chim, showed such concern for his sickly chimpanzee companion, Panzee, that the scientific establishment might reject his claims: "If I were to tell of his altruistic and obviously sympathetic behavior towards Panzee I should be suspected of idealizing an ape." Ladygina-Kohts (2001 [1935]) noticed similar tendencies in her young home-reared chimpanzee. She discovered that the only way to get him off the roof of her house (better than reward or threat of punishment) was by acting distressed, hence by inducing concern for herself in him.

Perhaps the best-documented example of sympathetic concern is consolation, defined as reassurance provided by an uninvolved bystander to one of the combatants in a previous aggressive incident (de Waal & van Roosmalen 1979). For example, a third party goes over to the loser of a fight and gently puts an arm around his or her shoulders (**Figure 1**). De Waal & van Roosmalen (1979) analyzed

Figure 1

Consolation is common in humans and apes, but virtually absent in monkeys. Here a juvenile chimpanzee puts an arm around a screaming adult male, who has just been defeated in a fight. Photograph by the author.

hundreds of consolations in chimpanzees, and de Waal & Aureli (1996) included an even larger sample. These studies show that bystanders contact victims of aggression more often than they contact aggressors, and bystanders contact victims of serious aggression more often than they contact those who had received mild aggression.

Subsequent studies have confirmed consolation in captive apes (Cordoni et al. 2004; Fuentes et al. 2002; Koski & Sterck 2006; Mallavarapu et al. 2006; Palagi et al. 2004, 2006), wild chimpanzees (Kutsukake & Castles 2004, Wittig & Boesch 2003), large-brained birds (Seed et al. 2007), and human children (Fujisawa et al. 2006). However, when de Waal & Aureli (1996) set out to apply the same observation protocol to detect consolation in monkeys, they failed to find any, as did others (Watts et al. 2000). The consolation gap between monkeys and the Hominoidea (i.e., humans and apes) extends even to the one situation where one would most expect consolation to occur: Macaque mothers fail to comfort their own offspring after a fight (Schino et al. 2004). O'Connell's (1995) content analysis of hundreds of reports confirms that reassurance of distressed others is typical of apes yet rare in monkeys. It still needs to be established, however, that this behavior actually does reduce the distressed party's arousal.

Empathic Perspective-Taking

Psychologists usually speak of empathy only when it involves perspective-taking. They emphasize understanding of the other, and adoption of the other's point of view. In this view, then, empathy is a cognitive affair dependent on imagination and mental state attribution, which may explain the skepticism about nonhuman empathy (Hauser 2000, Povinelli 1998). Perspective-taking by itself is, of course, hardly empathy: It is so only in combination with emotional engagement. The latter here is called "empathic perspective-taking," such as in one of the oldest

and best-known definitions by Smith (1759, p. 10) "changing places in fancy with the sufferer."

Menzel (1974) was the first to investigate whether chimpanzees understand what others know, setting the stage for studies of nonhuman theory-of-mind and perspective-taking. After several ups and downs in the evidence, current consensus seems to be that apes, but probably not monkeys, show some level of perspective-taking both in their spontaneous social behavior (de Waal 1996, 1998 [1982]) and under experimental conditions (Bräuer et al. 2005; Hare et al. 2001, 2006; Hirata 2006; Shillito et al. 2005).

A major manifestation of empathic perspective-taking is so-called targeted helping, which is help fine-tuned to another's specific situation and goals (de Waal 1996). The literature on primate behavior leaves little doubt about the existence of targeted helping, particularly in apes (see From Empathy to Altruism, below). A mother ape who returns to a whimpering youngster to help it from one tree to the next—by swaying her own tree toward the one the youngster is trapped in and then drape her body between both trees—goes beyond mere concern for the other. Her response likely involves emotional contagion (i.e., mother apes often briefly whimper themselves when they hear their offspring do so), but adds assessment of the specific reason for the other's distress and the other's goals. Tree bridging is a daily occurrence in orangutans, with mothers regularly anticipating their offspring's needs (van Schaik 2004, p. 104).

For an individual to move beyond being sensitive to others toward an explicit other-orientation requires a shift in perspective. The emotional state induced in oneself by the other now needs to be attributed to the other instead of the self. A heightened self-identity allows a subject to relate to the object's emotional state without losing sight of the actual source of this state (Hoffman 1982, Lewis 2002). The required self-representation is hard to establish independently, but one common avenue is to gauge reactions to a mirror.

Empathic perspective-taking: the capacity to take another's perspective—e.g., understanding another's specific situation and needs separate from one's own—combined with vicarious emotional arousal

Targeted helping: help and care based on a cognitive appreciation of the other's specific need or situation

The coemergence hypothesis predicts that mirror self-recognition (MSR) and advanced expressions of empathy appear together in both development and phylogeny.

Ontogenetically, the coemergence hypothesis is well-supported (Bischof-Köhler 1988, Johnson 1992, Zahn-Waxler et al. 1992). The relation between MSR and the development of empathic perspective-taking holds even after the data have been statistically controlled for age (Bischof-Köhler 1991). Gallup (1982) was the first to propose phylogenetic coemergence, a prediction empirically supported by the contrast between monkeys and apes, with compelling evidence for MSR, consolation, and targeted helping only in apes.

Apart from the great apes, the animals for which we have the most striking accounts of consolation and targeted helping are dolphins and elephants (see From Empathy to Altruism, below). Gallup (1983) had already predicted MSR in dolphins and elephants, and these predictions have now been confirmed by the mark test, in which an individual needs to locate a mark on itself that it cannot see without a mirror (Plotnik et al. 2006, Reiss & Marino 2001). MSR is believed to be absent in the rest of the animal kingdom (Anderson & Gallup 1999).

It should be added that self-representation is unlikely to have appeared de novo in a few large-brained animals. The framework of developmental psychologists, according to which self-representation emerges in small incremental steps (Lewis & Brooks-Gunn 1979, Rochat 2003), may apply also to phylogeny. Instead of adhering to an all-or-nothing division of self-representation, some animals may reach an intermediate stage similar to that of pre-MSR human infants (de Waal et al. 2005).

Possibly, the link between MSR and perspective-taking is relatively loose. Perspective-taking has recently been reported for species that appear to lack MSR, both mammals (Kuroshima et al. 2003, Virányi et al. 2005) and birds (Bugnyar & Heinrich 2005, Emery & Clayton 2001). These reports concern the finding or hiding of food, however, hence not empathic perspective-taking. In the future, we may be able to address the self-other distinction more directly through neural investigation (Decety & Chaminade 2003b). In humans, the right inferior parietal cortex, at the temporo-parietal junction, underpins empathy by helping distinguish between self- and other-produced actions (Decety & Grèzes 2006).

UNDERLYING MECHANISMS

Perception Action Mechanism

Preston & de Waal (2002a) propose that at the core of the empathic capacity lies a mechanism that provides an observer (the subject) with access to the subjective state of another (the object) through the subject's own neural and bodily representations. When the subject attends to the object's state, the subject's neural representations of similar states are automatically and unconsciously activated. The more similar and socially close two individuals are, the easier the subject's identification with the object, which enhances the subject's matching motor and autonomic responses. This lets the subject get "under the skin" of the object, bodily sharing its emotions and needs, which in turn may foster sympathy and helping. Preston & de Waal's (2002a) PAM fits Damasio's (1994) somatic marker hypothesis of emotions as well as evidence for a link at the cellular level between perception and action, such as the mirror neurons discovered in macaques by di Pellegrino et al. (1992).

Human data suggest that a similar physiological substrate underlies both observing and experiencing an emotion (Adolphs et al. 1997, 2000), and that affect communication creates matching physiological states in subject and object (Dimberg 1982, 1990; Levenson & Reuf 1992). Recent investigations of the neural basis of human empathy confirm the PAM in that they report neural similarity between self-generated and vicarious emotions

(Carr et al. 2003, Decety & Chaminade 2003a, Decety & Jackson 2006, de Gelder et al. 2004, Singer et al. 2004), such as activation of the anterior ventral insula both when we are disgusted and when we see another person expressing disgust (Wicker et al. 2003).

The idea that perception and action share representations is anything but new. Accordingly, empathy is a rapid routine, as confirmed by electromyographic studies of muscle contractions in the human face in response to pictures of facial expressions, even if presented so briefly that they cannot be consciously perceived (Dimberg et al. 2000). Accounts of empathy as a cognitive process often neglect such automatic reactions, which are far too rapid to be under voluntary control.

Russian Doll Model

Empathy covers all the ways in which one individual's emotional state affects another's, with simple mechanisms at its core and more complex mechanisms and perspective-taking abilities as its outer layers. Because of this layered nature of the capacities involved, we speak of the Russian doll model, in which higher cognitive levels of empathy build upon a firm, hard-wired basis, such as the PAM (de Waal 2003). The claim is not that PAM by itself explains sympathetic concern or perspective-taking, but that it underpins these cognitively more advanced forms of empathy, and serves to motivate behavioral outcomes. Without emotional engagement induced by state-matching, perspective-taking would be a cold phenomenon that could just as easily lead to torture as to helping (Deacon 1997, de Waal 2005).

Perception-action mechanisms are well known for motor perception (Prinz & Hommel 2002, Wolpert et al. 2001), so that we may assume PAM to underlie not only emotional state matching but also motor mimicry. This means that the Russian Doll also relates to doing as others do, including bodily synchronization, coordination, imitation, and emulation (**Figure 2**). If PAM is involved in both imitation and empathy, one expects correlations between both capacities. Highly empathic persons are indeed more inclined to unconscious mimicry (Chartrand & Bargh 1999) and humans with autism spectrum disorder are not only deficient in empathy but also imitation (Charman 2002, Charman et al. 1997). Functional magnetic resonance imaging studies neurally connect motor mimicry, such as contagious yawning, with empathic modeling (Platek et al. 2005).

Other primates, too, yawn when they see conspecifics yawn (Anderson et al. 2004, Paukner & Anderson 2006). In fact, behavioral copying ("aping") is pronounced in all of the primates. Social facilitation experiments show that satiated primates begin eating again when they see others eat (Addessi & Visalberghi 2001, Dindo & de Waal 2006), scratch themselves when others scratch themselves (Nakayama 2004), and show neonatal imitation similar to that of human infants (Bard 2006, Ferrari et al. 2006). Novel behavior is copied, too, at least by the apes. Examples are juveniles imitating the peculiar walk of others (de Waal 1998 [1982], Köhler 1925) as well as successful do-as-I-do experiments with human models (Custance et al. 1995, Myowa-Yamakoshi & Matsuzawa 1999).

Bodily similarity—such as with members of the same gender and species—likely enhances shared representation and identification, which has been proposed as the basis of true imitation (de Waal 1998, 2001), such as seen in the apes (Horner & Whiten 2005). The tendency of nonhuman primates to copy each other is as spontaneous as the empathic response. Thus, mirror neurons fire automatically to observed actions, even intentions (Fogassi et al. 2005), and monkeys require no extrinsic rewards to copy each other's behavior (Bonnie & de Waal 2006).

In accordance with the PAM (Preston & de Waal 2002a), the motivational structure of both imitation and empathy therefore includes (*a*) shared representations; (*b*) identification with others based on physical similarity, shared experience, and social closeness; and

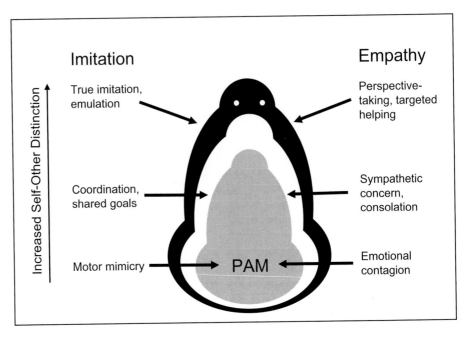

Figure 2

The Russian doll model of empathy and imitation. Empathy (*right*) induces a similar emotional state in the subject and the object, with at its core the perception-action mechanism (PAM). The doll's outer layers, such as sympathetic concern and perspective-taking, build upon this hard-wired socio-affective basis. Sharing the same mechanism, the doll's imitation side (*left*) correlates with the empathy side. Here, the PAM underlies motor mimicry, coordination, shared goals, and true imitation. Even though the doll's outer layers depend on prefrontal functioning and an increasing self-other distinction, these outer layers remain connected to its inner core.

(*c*) automaticity and spontaneity. All of this applies to the core mechanism, not necessarily to the more complex outer layers of the Russian doll model, which develop in interaction with the environment.

FROM EMPATHY TO ALTRUISM

Not all altruistic behavior requires empathy. When animals alert others to an outside threat, work together for immediate self-reward, or vocally attract others to discovered food, biologists may speak of altruism or cooperation, but this behavior is unlikely to be motivated by empathy with the beneficiary.

Emotional Contagion

Self-centered vicarious arousal, known as personal distress, represents the oldest kind of empathy. A good example seems the intensified pain response of mice seeing other mice in pain (Langford et al. 2006). Emotional contagion may lead individuals frightened by the alarm of others to hide or flee, a mother distressed by her offspring's distress to reassure both herself and her offspring by warming or nursing them, or inhibit an individual from inflicting pain upon another because of the vicarious negative arousal induced by the other's distress calls. Thus, simple empathic reactions may benefit both the actor and individuals close to them.

Behavioral copying, too, often produces adaptive outcomes. Imagine a group of animals in which every member was to eat, sleep, forage, or play independently: This would be impossible for nomadic animals, such as primates. Being in sync is often a matter of life or death (Boinski & Garber 2000).

Sympathetic Concern

Directed altruism requires the addition of other-orientation to emotional activation. In nonhuman primates, the most common empathy-based concern for others is defense against aggression. Exceptional urgency and extreme motivation are required because the reaction needs to be swift and actors may face bodily danger when assisting others against an attacker. For example, when a female reacts to the screams of her closest associate by defending her against a dominant male, she takes enormous risk on behalf of the other. She may very well be injured. What other than high emotional arousal can reasonably explain such bravery? Note the following description of two long-time chimpanzee friends in a zoo colony: "Not only do they often act together against attackers, but they also seek comfort and reassurance from each other. When one of them has been involved in a painful conflict, she goes to the other to be embraced. They then literally scream in each other's arms" (de Waal 1998 [1982], p. 67).

When Kagan (2000) argued against animal empathy by claiming that a chimpanzee would never jump into a lake to save another, Flack & de Waal (2000) replied with a quote from Goodall (1990, p. 213): "In some zoos, chimpanzees are kept on man-made islands, surrounded by water-filed moats... Chimpanzees cannot swim and, unless they are rescued, will drown if they fall into deep water. Despite this, individuals have sometimes made heroic efforts to save companions from drowning—and were sometimes successful. One adult male lost his life as he tried to rescue a small infant whose incompetent mother had allowed it to fall into the water."

To explain such behavior on the basis of expected return-benefits makes a huge cognitive leap by injecting ultimate goals into proximate decision-making (see Introduction, above). Admittedly, chimpanzees may deliberately engage in grooming as a way of gaining future return-favors (de Waal 1998 [1982], 1997b; Koyama et al. 2006), but grooming is

a low-cost service. It is hard to imagine that the chimpanzee's extreme hydrophobia could be overcome by a cognitive gamble on future returns. A male who jumps in the water must have an overwhelming immediate motivation, which probably only emotional engagement can produce.

Fortunately, with regard to primate altruism, we do not need to rely on qualitative accounts as there exists ample systematic data, such as a rich literature on support in aggressive contexts (Harcourt & de Waal 1992), cooperation (Kappeler & van Schaik 2006), and food-sharing (Feistner & Mcgrew 1989). Although some have argued that food-sharing may not be truly altruistic because it is subject to social pressure (Gilby 2006), the problem with this view is that top-ranking individuals (who have no trouble resisting pressure) are among the most generous (de Waal 1989), and sharing occurs even when individuals are separated by bars, hence insulated from pressure (de Waal 1997c, Nissen & Crawford 1932). Rather, the begging and distress signals typical of food beggars hint at a mediating role of empathy.

In short, empathy may motivate directed altruism in primates as often visible in the similarity of facial expressions and vocalizations of both altruists and beneficiaries. Empathy is the only mechanism capable of providing a unitary motivational explanation for a wide variety of situations in which assistance is dispensed according to need. Perhaps confusingly, the mechanism is relatively autonomous in both animals and humans. Thus, empathy often reaches beyond its original evolutionary context, such as when people send money to distant tsunami victims, when primates bestow care on unrelated juvenile orphans (Thierry & Anderson 1986), or when a bonobo tries to rescue an injured bird (de Waal 1997a).

Empathic Perspective-Taking

Evidence for altruism based on empathic perspective-taking mostly consists of striking anecdotes, which are admittedly open to multiple interpretations. However, anecdotes have traditionally provided productive starting points for research (debated between Kummer et al. 1990 and de Waal 1991).

Targeted helping has been described for cetaceans since the ancient Greeks. Dolphins are said to save companions by biting through harpoon lines or by hauling them out of nets in which they were entangled. Dolphins also support sick companions near the surface to keep them from drowning, and stay close to females in labor. Whales tend to interpose themselves between a hunter's boat and an injured conspecific, or capsize the boat (Caldwell & Caldwell 1966, Connor & Norris 1982).

Elephants are known to reassure distressed companions (Payne 1998, Poole 1996) and to support or lift up others too weak to stand (Hamilton-Douglas et al. 2006, Joubert 1991). Moss (1988, p. 73) offers a typical description of a young female, Tina, shot by a poacher: "Teresia and Trista became frantic and knelt down and tried to lift her up. They worked their tusks under her back and under her head. At one point they succeeded in lifting her into a sitting position but her body flopped back down. Her family tried everything to rouse her, kicking and tusking her, and Tallulah even went off and collected a trunkful of grass and tried to stuff it into her mouth."

For great apes, there exist literally hundreds of qualitative accounts of targeted helping, of which I cite just two striking examples:

Example 1:
During one winter at the Arnhem Zoo, before releasing the chimps, the keepers hosed out all rubber tires in the enclosure and hung them on a horizontal log. One day, Krom was interested in a tire in which water had stayed behind. Unfortunately, this particular tire was at the end of the row, with six or more heavy tires in front of it. Krom pulled and pulled at the one she wanted but couldn't remove it. She worked in vain for over ten minutes, ignored by everyone, except Jakie, a seven-year-old Krom had taken care of as a juvenile.
Immediately after Krom gave up and walked away, Jakie approached the scene. Without hesitation he pushed the tires one by one off the log, beginning with the front one, followed by the second, and so on, as any sensible chimp would. When he reached the last tire, he carefully removed it so that no water was lost, carrying it straight to his aunt, placing it upright in front of her. Krom accepted his present without any acknowledgment, and was already scooping up water with her hand when Jakie left (de Waal 1996, p. 83).

Example 2:
The two-meter-deep moat in front of the old bonobo enclosure at the San Diego Zoo had been drained for cleaning. After having scrubbed the moat and released the apes, the keepers went to turn on the valve to refill it with water when all of a sudden the old male, Kakowet, came to their window, screaming and frantically waving his arms so as to catch their attention. After so many years, he was familiar with the cleaning routine. As it turned out, several young bonobos had entered the dry moat but were unable to get out. The keepers provided a ladder. All bonobos got out except for the smallest one, who was pulled up by Kakowet himself (de Waal 1997a, p. 34).

Because it is almost impossible, and probably unethical, to create situations in the laboratory in which primates experience intense fear or distress, there is a scarcity of experiments on costly altruism of the kind described above. More often, experiments concern low-cost altruism, sometimes called "other-regarding preferences." A typical paradigm is to offer one member of a pair the option to either secure food for itself by manipulating part A of an apparatus or food for both itself and another by manipulating part B of the same apparatus. Colman et al. (1969) found 1 out of 4 tested macaques to be consistently other-regarding, yet two recent replications failed to find the same tendency in chimpanzees (Jensen et al. 2006, Silk et al. 2005). This has led authors to conclude that other-regarding preferences may be uniquely human. It is impossible to prove the null hypothesis, however. Given the overwhelming observational evidence for spontaneous helping and cooperation among primates, it seems only a matter of time until other-regarding preferences will be experimentally confirmed.

EMPATHY AS EVOLVED PROXIMATE MECHANISM OF DIRECTED ALTRUISM

A Russian doll is a satisfying plaything for the biologist since every outer layer encompasses an older, inner one. This is relevant to the origin of empathy: All prosocial behavior, even when dependent on prefrontal functioning, probably has PAM-based emotion sharing at its core (Preston & de Waal 2002a). Without this emotional component, it is hard to see why we or other animals would care.

Humans have so little control over empathic activation that they regularly shield themselves from it, e.g., by covering their eyes when in a movie something gruesome is about to happen. This is because they have already identified with the on-screen characters. One way to cognitively control empathy is to inhibit such identification. How self-imposed filters and contextual appraisal modulate the brain's empathic response remains a major unresolved issue (de Vignemont & Singer 2006). Sometimes, empathy appears wholly absent. For example, chimpanzees are capable of brutally killing each other (de Waal 1998 [1982], Wrangham & Peterson 1996),

hence must be capable of suppressing empathic activation in relation to conspecifics, which has led Goodall (1986, p. 532) to call their victims "dechimpized." (It is important to note, though, that a species' occasional violence by no means argues against it having empathic capacities—if so, human empathy would be the first to be denied.)

The PAM model predicts that the greater the similarity or familiarity of the subject and object, the more their representations will agree, hence the more accurate their state-matching. Generally, the empathic response is amplified by similarity, familiarity, social closeness, and positive experience with the other (Table 1 in Preston & de Waal 2002a). In human studies, subjects empathize with a confederate's pleasure or distress if they perceive the relationship as cooperative, yet show an antipathic response (i.e., distress at seeing the other's pleasure or pleasure at seeing the other's distress) if they perceive the relationship as competitive (Lanzetta & Englis 1989, Zillmann & Cantor 1977). These effects of previous experience have recently been confirmed by functional magnetic resonance imaging: Seeing the pain of a cooperative confederate activates pain-related brain areas, but seeing the pain of an unfair confederate activates reward-related brain areas, at least in men (Singer et al. 2006).

Relationship effects are also known for rodents, in which emotional contagion is measurable between cagemates but not between strangers (Langford et al. 2006). In monkeys, empathic responses to another's fear or pain are enhanced by familiarity between subject and object (Masserman et al. 1964, Miller at al. 1959). Thus, the empathy mechanism is biased the way evolutionary theory would predict. Empathy is (a) activated in relation to those with whom one has a close or positive relationship, and (b) suppressed, or even turned into Schadenfreude, in relation to strangers and defectors. The latter, retaliatory aspect corresponds with well-documented chimpanzee behavior: These apes not only reciprocate favors within positive relationships, but also take revenge upon those who have previously acted against them (de Waal & Luttrell 1988).

A common way in which mutually beneficial exchanges are achieved is through investment in long-term bonds to which both parties contribute. This reciprocity mechanism is commonplace in nonhuman primates (de Waal & Brosnan 2006) and has been suggested for human relations as well. Individual interests may be served by partnerships (e.g., marriages, friendships) that create a long-lasting communal "fitness interdependence" mediated by mutual empathy. Within these relationships, partners do not necessarily keep careful track of who did what for whom (Clark & Mills 1979), and derive psychological and health benefits not only from receiving but also from giving support (Brown & Brown 2006).

If altruism is produced by mechanisms, such as empathy and bonding, that produce emotional identification with the other, one may well ask if helping another does not boil down to helping oneself. It does, but as Smith (1759) argued, this is no reason to call empathy-based altruism selfish. A truly selfish individual would have no trouble walking away from another in need, whereas empathic engagement hooks one into the other's situation. Since the mechanism delivers intrinsic rewards exclusively via the other, it is genuinely other-oriented (Wispé 1991). At the same time, it is futile to try to extract the self from the process. There simply is no satisfactory answer to the question of how altruistic is altruism (debated among Batson et al. 1997, Cialdini et al. 1997, Hornstein 1991, Krebs 1991). This is, in fact, the beauty of the empathy-altruism connection: The mechanism works so well because it gives individuals an emotional stake in the welfare of others.

CONCLUSION

More than three decades ago, biologists deliberately removed the altruism from altruism. There is now increasing evidence that the brain is hardwired for social connection, and that the same empathy mechanism proposed to underlie human altruism (Batson 1991) may underlie the directed altruism of other animals. Empathy could well provide the main motivation making individuals who have exchanged benefits in the past to continue doing so in the future. Instead of assuming learned expectations or calculations about future benefits, this approach emphasizes a spontaneous altruistic impulse and a mediating role of the emotions. It is summarized in the five conclusions below:

1. An evolutionarily parsimonious account (cf. de Waal 1999) of directed altruism assumes similar motivational processes in humans and other animals.
2. Empathy, broadly defined, is a phylogenetically ancient capacity.
3. Without the emotional engagement brought about by empathy, it is unclear what could motivate the extremely costly helping behavior occasionally observed in social animals.
4. Consistent with kin selection and reciprocal altruism theory, empathy favors familiar individuals and previous cooperators, and is biased against previous defectors.
5. Combined with perspective-taking abilities, empathy's motivational autonomy opens the door to intentionally altruistic altruism in a few large-brained species.

ACKNOWLEDGMENTS

The author is grateful to Stephanie Preston for detailed comments on an earlier draft of the manuscript and to Jean Decety, Nancy Eisenberg, and Robert Trivers for constructive feedback. The author, however, remains responsible for the intellectual content.

LITERATURE CITED

Acebo C, Thoman EB. 1995. Role of infant crying in the early mother-infant dialogue. *Physiol. Behav.* 57:541–47

Addessi E, Visalberghi E. 2001. Social facilitation of eating novel food in tufted capuchin monkeys (*Cebus apella*): input provided by group members and responses affected in the observer. *Anim. Cogn.* 4:297–303

Adolphs R, Cahill L, Schul R, Babinsky R. 1997. Impaired declarative memory for emotional material following bilateral amygdala damage in humans. *Learn. Mem.* 4:291–300

Adolphs R, Damasio H, Tranel D, Cooper G, Damasio AR. 2000. A role for somatosensory cortices in the visual recognition of emotion as revealed by three-dimensional lesion mapping. *J. Neurosci.* 20:2683–90

Adolphs R, Tranel D, Damasio H, Damasio AR. 1994. Impaired recognition of emotion in facial expressions following bilateral damage to the human amygdala. *Nature* 372:669–72

Anderson JR, Gallup GG. 1999. Self-recognition in nonhuman primates: past and future challenges. In *Animal Models of Human Emotion and Cognition*, ed. M Haug, RE Whalen, pp. 175–94. Washington, DC: APA Books

Anderson JR, Myowa-Yamakoshi M, Matsuzawa T. 2004. Contagious yawning in chimpanzees. *Proc. R. Soc. Lond. B* (Suppl.)271:S468–70

Bard KA. 2007. Neonatal imitation in chimpanzees (*Pan troglodytes*) tested with two paradigms. *Anim. Cogn.* 10:233–42

Batson CD. 1991. *The Altruism Question: Toward a Social-Psychological Answer.* Hillsdale, NJ: Erlbaum

Batson CD, Sager K, Garst E, Kang M, Rubchinsky K, Dawson K. 1997. Is empathy-induced helping due to self-other merging? *J. Person. Soc. Psychol.* 73:495–509

Bischof-Köhler D. 1988. Über den Zusammenhang von Empathie und der Fähigkeit sich im Spiegel zu erkennen. *Schw. Z. Psychol.* 47:147–59

Bischof-Köhler D. 1991. The development of empathy in infants. In *Infant Development: Perspectives from German-Speaking Countries*, ed. M Lamb, M Keller, pp. 245–73. Hillsdale, NJ: Erlbaum

Boesch C. 1992. New elements of a theory of mind in wild chimpanzees. *Behav. Brain Sci.* 15:149–50

Boinski S, Garber PA. 2000. *On the Move: How and Why Animals Travel in Groups.* Chicago: Univ. Chicago Press

Bonnie KE, de Waal FBM. 2007. Copying without rewards: socially influenced foraging decisions among brown capuchin monkeys. *Anim. Cogn.* DOI: 10.1007/s10071-006-0069-9

Bowlby J. 1958. The nature of the child's tie to his mother. *Int. J. Psychoanal.* 39:350–73

Bräuer J, Call J, Tomasello M. 2005. All great ape species follow gaze to distant locations and around barriers. *J. Comp. Psychol.* 119:145–54

Brown SL, Brown RM. 2006. Selective investment theory: recasting the functional significance of close relationships. *Psychol. Inq.* 17:1–29

Bugnyar T, Heinrich B. 2005. Food-storing ravens differentiate between knowledgeable and ignorant competitors. *Proc. Roy. Soc. Lond. B* 272:1641–46

Caldwell MC, Caldwell DK. 1966. Epimeletic (care-giving) behavior in Cetacea. In *Whales, Dolphins, and Porpoises*, ed. KS Norris, pp. 755–89. Berkeley: Univ. Calif. Press

Carr L, Iacoboni M, Dubeau MC, Mazziotta JC, Lenzi GL. 2003. Neural mechanisms of empathy in humans: a relay from neural systems for imitation to limbic areas. *Proc. Natl. Acad. Sci. USA* 100:5497–502

Charman T. 2002. Understanding the imitation deficit in autism may lead to a more specific model of autism as an empathy disorder. *Behav. Brain Sci.* 25:29–30

Charman T, Swettenham J, Baron-Cohen S, Cox A, Baird G, Drew A. 1997. Infants with autism: an investigation of empathy, pretend play, joint attention, and imitation. *Dev. Psychol.* 33:781–89

Chartrand TL, Bargh JA. 1999. The chameleon effect: the perception-behavior link and social interaction. *J. Personal. Soc. Psychol.* 76:893–910

Church RM. 1959. Emotional reactions of rats to the pain of others. *J. Comp. Physiol. Psychol.* 52:132–34

Cialdini RB, Brown SL, Lewis BP, Luce CL, Neuberg SL. 1997. Reinterpreting the empathy-altruism relationship: when one into one equals oneness. *J. Personal. Soc. Psychol.* 73:481–94

Clark MS, Mills J. 1979. Interpersonal attraction in exchange and communal relationships. *J. Personal. Soc. Psychol.* 37:12–24

Colman AD, Liebold KE, Boren JJ. 1969. A method for studying altruism in monkeys. *Psychol. Record* 19:401–5

Connor RC, Norris KS. 1982. Are dolphins reciprocal altruists? *Am. Natural.* 119:358–72

Cordoni G, Palagi E, Borgognini TS. 2004. Reconciliation and consolation in captive Western gorillas. *Int. J. Primatol.* 27:1365–82

Custance DM, Whiten A, Bard KA. 1995. Can young chimpanzees imitate arbitrary actions? Hayes and Hayes 1952 revisited. *Behaviour* 132:835–59

Damasio AR. 1994. *Descartes' Error: Emotion, Reason, and the Human Brain.* New York: Putnam

Darwin C. 1982 [1871]. *The Descent of Man, and Selection in Relation to Sex.* Princeton, NJ: Princeton Univ. Press

Dawkins R. 1976. *The Selfish Gene.* Oxford, UK: Oxford Univ. Press

Deacon TW. 1997. *The Symbolic Species: The Co-Evolution of Language and the Brain.* New York: Norton

Decety J, Chaminade T. 2003a. Neural correlates of feeling sympathy. *Neuropsychology* 41:127–38

Decety J, Chaminade T. 2003b. When the self represents the other: a new cognitive neuroscience view on psychological identification. *Conscious Cogn.* 12:577–96

Decety J, Grèzes J. 2006. The power of simulation: imagining one's own and other's behavior. *Brain Res.* 1079:4–14

Decety J, Jackson PL. 2006. A social-neuroscience perspective on empathy. *Curr. Dir. Psychol. Sci.* 15:54–58

de Gelder B, Snyder J, Greve D, Gerard G, Hadjikhani N. 2004. Fear fosters flight: a mechanism for fear contagion when perceiving emotion expressed by a whole body. *Proc. Natl. Acad. Sci. USA* 101:16701–6

de Vignemont F, Singer T. 2006. The empathic brain: how, when and why? *Trends Cogn. Sci.* 10:435–41

de Waal FBM. 1989. Food sharing and reciprocal obligations among chimpanzees. *J. Hum. Evol.* 18:433–59

de Waal FBM. 1991. Complementary methods and convergent evidence in the study of primate social cognition. *Behaviour* 118:297–320

de Waal FBM. 1996. *Good Natured: The Origins of Right and Wrong in Humans and Other Animals.* Cambridge, MA: Harvard Univ. Press

de Waal FBM. 1997a. *Bonobo: The Forgotten Ape.* Berkeley: Univ. Calif. Press

de Waal FBM. 1997b. The chimpanzee's service economy: food for grooming. *Evol. Hum. Behav.* 18:375–86 de Waal FBM. 1997c. Food-transfers through mesh in brown capuchins. *J. Comp. Psychol.* 111:370–78

de Waal FBM. 1998 [1982]. *Chimpanzee Politics: Power and Sex Among Apes.* Baltimore, MD: Johns Hopkins Univ. Press

de Waal FBM. 1998. No imitation without identification. *Behav. Brain Sci.* 21:689

de Waal FBM. 1999. Anthropomorphism and anthropodenial: consistency in our thinking about humans and other animals. *Philos. Topics* 27:255–80

de Waal FBM. 2001. *The Ape and the Sushi Master.* New York: Basic Books

de Waal FBM. 2003. On the possibility of animal empathy. In *Feelings & Emotions: The Amsterdam Symposium*, ed. T Manstead, N Frijda, A Fischer, pp. 379–99. Cambridge, UK: Cambridge Univ. Press

de Waal FBM. 2005. *Our Inner Ape.* New York: Riverhead

de Waal FBM, Aureli F. 1996. Consolation, reconciliation, and a possible cognitive difference between macaque and chimpanzee. In *Reaching into Thought: The Minds of the Great Apes*, ed. AE Russon, KA Bard, ST Parker, pp. 80–110. Cambridge, UK: Cambridge Univ. Press

de Waal FBM, Brosnan SF. 2006. Simple and complex reciprocity in primates. In *Cooperation in Primates and Humans: Mechanisms and Evolution*, ed. PM Kappeler, CP van Schaik, pp. 85–105. Berlin: Springer

de Waal FBM, Davis JM. 2003. Capuchin cognitive ecology: cooperation based on projected returns. *Neuropsychology* 41:221–28

de Waal FBM, Dindo M, Freeman CA, Hall M. 2005. The monkey in the mirror: hardly a stranger. *Proc. Natl. Acad. Sci. USA* 102:11140–47

de Waal FBM, Luttrell LM. 1988. Mechanisms of social reciprocity in three primate species: symmetrical relationship characteristics or cognition? *Ethol. Sociobiol.* 9:101–18

de Waal FBM, van Roosmalen A. 1979. Reconciliation and consolation among chimpanzees. *Behav. Ecol. Sociobiol.* 5:55–66

di Pellegrino G, Fadiga L, Fogassi L, Gallese V, Rizzolatti G. 1992. Understanding motor events: a neurophysiological study. *Exp. Brain Res.* 91:176–80

Dimberg U. 1982. Facial reactions to facial expressions. *Psychophysiology* 19:643–47

Dimberg U. 1990. Facial electromyographic reactions and autonomic activity to auditory stimuli. *Biol. Psychol.* 31:137–47

Dimberg U, Thunberg M, Elmehed K. 2000. Unconscious facial reactions to emotional facial expressions. *Psychol. Sci.* 11:86–89

Dindo M, de Waal FBM. 2006. Partner effects on food consumption in brown capuchin monkeys. *Am. J. Primatol.* 69:1–9

Dittus WPJ, Ratnayeke SM. 1989. Individual and social behavioral responses to injury in wild toque macaques (*Macaca sinica*). *Int. J. Primatol.* 10:215–34

Dugatkin L. 1997. *Cooperation Among Animals: An Evolutionary Perspective.* New York: Oxford Univ. Press

Dugatkin L. 2006. *The Altruism Equation: Seven Scientists Search for the Origin of Goodness.* Princeton, NJ: Princeton Univ. Press

Eibl-Eibesfeldt I. 1974 [1971]. *Love and Hate.* New York: Schocken

Eisenberg N. 2000. Empathy and sympathy. In *Handbook of Emotion*, ed. M Lewis, JM Haviland-Jones, pp. 677–91. New York: Guilford. 2nd ed.

Emery NJ, Clayton NS. 2001. Effects of experience and social context on prospective caching strategies by scrub jays. *Nature* 414:443–46

Fehr E, Fischbacher U. 2003. The nature of human altruism. *Nature* 425:785–91

Feistner ATC, McGrew WC. 1989. Food-sharing in primates: a critical review. In *Perspectives in Primate Biology*, Vol. 3, ed. PK Seth, S Seth, pp. 21–36. New Delhi: Today Tomorrow's

Ferrari PF, Visalbergi E, Paukner A, Gogassi L, Ruggiero A, Suomi SJ. 2006. Neonatal imitation in rhesus macaques. *PLOS Biol.* 4:1501–8

Flack JC, de Waal FBM. 2000. Being nice is not a building block of morality: response to commentary discussion. *J. Consc. Stud.* 7:67–77

Fogassi L, Ferrari PF, Chersi F, Gesierich B, Rozzi S, et al. 2005. Parietal lobe: from action organization to intention understanding. *Science* 308:662–67

Fuentes A, Malone N, Sanz C, Matheson M, Vaughan L. 2002. Conflict and postconflict behavior in a small group of chimpanzees. *Primates* 43:223–35

Fujisawa KK, Kutsukake N, Hasegawa T. 2006. Peacemaking and consolation in Japanese preschoolers witnessing peer aggression. *J. Comp. Psychol.* 120:48–57

Gallup GG. 1982. Self-awareness and the emergence of mind in primates. *Am. J. Primatol.* 2:237–48

Gallup GG. 1983. Toward a comparative psychology of mind. In *Animal Cognition and Behavior*, ed. RL Mellgren, pp. 473–510. New York: North-Holland

Gilby IC. 2006. Meat sharing among the Gombe chimpanzees: harassment and reciprocal exchange. *Anim. Behav.* 71:953–63

Goodall J. 1986. *The Chimpanzees of Gombe: Patterns of Behavior.* Cambridge, MA: Belknap

Goodall J. 1990. *Through a Window: My Thirty Years with the Chimpanzees of Gombe.* Boston, MA: Houghton Mifflin

Hamilton WD. 1964. The genetical evolution of social behaviour I and II. *J. Theor. Biol.* 7:1–52

Hamilton-Douglas I, Bhalla S, Wittemyer G, Vollrath F. 2006. Behavioural reactions of elephants towards a dying and deceased matriarch. *Appl. Anim. Behav. Sci.* 100:87–102

Harcourt AH, de Waal FBM. 1992. *Coalitions and Alliances in Humans and Other Animals.* Oxford, UK: Oxford Univ. Press

Hare B, Call J, Tomasello M. 2001. Do chimpanzees know what conspecifics know? *Anim. Behav.* 61:139–51

Hare B, Call J, Tomasello M. 2006. Chimpanzees deceive a human competitor by hiding. *Cognition* 101:495–514

Hatfield E, Cacioppo JT, Rapson RL. 1993. Emotional contagion. *Curr. Dir. Psychol. Sci.* 2:96–99

Hauser MD. 2000. *Wild Minds: What Animals Really Think.* New York: Holt

Hirata S. 2006. Tactical deception and understanding of others in chimpanzees. In *Cognitive Development in Chimpanzees*, ed. T Matsuzawa, M Tomanaga, M Tanaka, pp. 265–76. Tokyo: Springer Verlag

Hoffman ML. 1975. Developmental synthesis of affect and cognition and its implications for altruistic motivation. *Dev. Psychol.* 11:607–22

Hoffman ML. 1981a. Is altruism part of human nature? *J. Personal. Soc. Psychol.* 40:121–37

Hoffman ML. 1981b. Perspectives on the difference between understanding people and understanding things: the role of affect. In *Social Cognitive Development*, ed. JH Flavell, L Ross, pp. 67–81. Cambridge, UK: Cambridge Univ. Press

Hoffman ML. 1982. Development of prosocial motivation: empathy and guilt. In *The Development of Prosocial Behavior*, ed. N Eisenberg, pp. 281–338. New York: Academic

Horner V, Whiten A. 2005. Causal knowledge and imitation/emulation switching in chimpanzees and children. *Anim. Cogn.* 8:164–81

Hornstein HA. 1991. Empathic distress and altruism: still inseparable. *Psychol. Inq.* 2:133–35

Jensen K, Hare B, Call J, Tomasello M. 2006. What's in it for me? Self-regard precludes altruism and spite in chimpanzees. *Proc. R. Soc. Lond. B Biol. Sci.* 273:1013–21

Johnson DB. 1992. Altruistic behavior and the development of the self in infants. *Merrill-Palmer Q. Behav. Dev.* 28:379–88

Joubert D. 1991. Elephant wake. *Natl. Geogr.* 179:39–42

Kagan J. 2000. Human morality is distinctive. *J. Consc. Stud.* 7:46–48

Kappeler PM, van Schaik CP. 2006. *Cooperation in Primates and Humans: Mechanisms and Evolution.* Berlin: Springer

Köhler W. 1925. *The Mentality of Apes.* New York: Vintage

Koski SE, Sterck EHM. 2007. Triadic post-conflict affiliation in captive chimpanzees: does consolation console? *Anim. Behav.* 73:133–42

Koyama NF, Caws C, Aureli F. 2006. Interchange of grooming and agonistic support in chimpanzees. *Int. J. Primatol.* 27:1293–309

Krebs DL. 1991. Altruism and egoism: a false dichotomy? *Psychol. Inq.* 2:137–9

Kummer H, Dasser V, Hoyningen-Huene P. 1990. Exploring primate social cognition: some critical remarks. *Behaviour* 112:84–98

Kuroshima H, Fujita K, Adachi I, Iwata K, Fuyuki A. 2003. A capuchin monkey (*Cebus apella*) recognizes when people do and do not know the location of food. *Anim. Cogn.* 6:283–91

Kutsukake N, Castles DL. 2004. Reconciliation and postconflict third-party affiliation among wild chimpanzees in the Mahale Mountains, Tanzania. *Primates* 45:157–65

Ladygina-Kohts NN. 2001 [1935]. *Infant Chimpanzee and Human Child: A Classic 1935 Comparative Study of Ape Emotions and Intelligence*, ed. FBM de Waal. New York: Oxford Univ. Press

Langford DJ, Crager SE, Shehzad Z, Smith SB, Sotocinal SG, et al. 2006. Social modulation of pain as evidence for empathy in mice. *Science* 312:1967–70

Lanzetta JT, Englis BG. 1989. Expectations of cooperation and competition and their effects on observers' vicarious emotional responses. *J. Personal. Soc. Psychol.* 56:543–54

Levenson RW, Reuf AM. 1992. Empathy: a physiological substrate. *J. Personal. Soc. Psychol.* 63:234–46

Lewis M. 2002. Empathy requires the development of the self. *Behav. Brain Sci.* 25:42

Lewis M, Brooks-Gunn J. 1979. *Social Cognition and the Acquisition of Self.* New York: Plenum

Lipps T. 1903. Einfühlung, innere Nachahmung und Organempfindung. *Arch. für die gesamte Psychol.* 1:465–519

MacLean PD. 1985. Brain evolution relating to family, play, and the separation call. *Arch. Gen. Psychiatry* 42:405–17

Mallavarapu S, Stoinski TS, Bloomsmith MA, Maple TL. 2006. Postconflict behavior in captive western lowland gorillas (*Gorilla gorilla gorilla*). *Am. J. Primatol.* 68:789–801

Masserman J, Wechkin MS, Terris W. 1964. Altruistic behavior in rhesus monkeys. *Am. J. Psychiatry* 121:584–85

Mayr E. 1961. Cause and effect in biology. *Science* 134:1501–6

Melis A, Hare B, Tomasello M. 2006. Engineering cooperation in chimpanzees: tolerance constraints on cooperation. *Anim. Behav.* 72:275–86

Menzel EW. 1974. A group of young chimpanzees in a one-acre field. In *Behavior of Non-human Primates*, Vol. 5, ed. AM Schrier, F Stollnitz, pp. 83–153. New York: Academic

Miller RE, Murphy JV, Mirsky IA. 1959. Relevance of facial expression and posture as cues in communication of affect between monkeys. *Arch. Gen. Psychiatry* 1:480–88

Moss C. 1988. *Elephant Memories: Thirteen Years in the Life of an Elephant Family.* New York: Fawcett Columbine

Myowa-Yamakoshi G, Matsuzawa T. 1999. Factors influencing imitation of manipulatory actions in chimpanzees. *J. Comp. Psychol.* 113:128–36

Nakayama K. 2004. Observing conspecifics scratching induces a contagion of scratching in Japanese monkeys (*Macaca fuscata*). *J. Comp. Psychol.* 118:20–24

Nissen H, Crawford M. 1932. A preliminary study of food-sharing behavior in young chimpanzees. *J. Comp. Psychol.* 22:383–419

O'Connell SM. 1995. Empathy in chimpanzees: evidence for theory of mind? *Primates* 36:397–410

Palagi E, Cordoni G, Borgognini Tarli S. 2006. Possible roles of consolation in captive chimpanzees (*Pan troglodytes*). *Am. J. Phys. Anthrop.* 129:105–11

Palagi E, Paoli T, Borgognini Tarli S. 2004. Reconciliation and consolation in captive bonobos (*Pan paniscus*). *Am. J. Primatol.* 62:15–30

Panksepp J. 1998. *Affective Neuroscience: The Foundations of Human and Animal Emotions.* New York: Oxford Univ. Press

Parr LA. 2001. Cognitive and physiological markers of emotional awareness in chimpanzees, *Pan troglodytes. Anim. Cogn.* 4:223–29

Parr LA, Hopkins WD. 2001. Brain temperature asymmetries and emotional perception in chimpanzees. *Pan troglodytes. Physiol. Behav.* 71:363–71

Parr LA, Waller BM. 2007. The evolution of human emotion. In *Evolution of Nervous Systems: A Comprehensive Reference*, Vol. 4, ed. JA Kaas, pp. 447–72. New York: Academic

Paukner A, Anderson JR. 2006. Video-induced yawning in stumptail macaques (*Macaca arctoides*). *Biol. Lett.* 2:36–38

Payne K. 1998. *Silent Thunder: In the Presence of Elephants.* New York: Penguin

Platek SM, Mohamed FB, Gallup GG. 2005. Contagious yawning and the brain. *Cogn. Brain Res.* 23:448–52

Plomin R, Emde RN, Braungart JM, Campos J, Corley R, et al. 1993. Genetic change and continuity from fourteen to twenty months: The MacArthur Longitudinal Twin Study. *Child Dev.* 64:1354–76

Plotnik J, de Waal FBM, Reiss D. 2006. Self-recognition in an Asian elephant. *Proc. Natl. Acad. Sci. USA* 103:17053–57

Plutchik R. 1987. Evolutionary bases of empathy. In *Empathy and Its Development*, ed. N Eisenberg, J Strayer, pp. 3–46. Cambridge, UK: Cambridge Univ. Press

Poole J. 1996. *Coming of Age with Elephants: A Memoir.* New York: Hyperion

Potegal M. 2000. Post-tantrum affiliation with parents: the ontogeny of reconciliation. In *Natural Conflict Resolution*, ed. F Aureli, FBM de Waal, pp. 253–55. Berkeley: Univ. Calif. Press

Povinelli DJ. 1998. Can animals empathize? Maybe not. *Sci. Am.* **http://geowords.com/lostlinks/b36/7.htm**

Preston SD, de Waal FBM. 2002a. Empathy: its ultimate and proximate bases. *Behav. Brain Sci.* 25:1–72

Preston SD, de Waal FBM. 2002b. The communication of emotions and the possibility of empathy in animals. In *Altruistic Love: Science, Philosophy, and Religion in Dialogue*, ed. SG Post, LG Underwood, JP Schloss, WB Hurlbut, pp. 284–308. Oxford, UK: Oxford Univ. Press

Prinz W, Hommel B. 2002. *Common Mechanisms in Perception and Action.* Oxford, UK: Oxford Univ. Press

Reiss D, Marino L. 2001. Mirror self-recognition in the bottlenose dolphin: a case of cognitive convergence. *Proc. Natl. Acad. Sci. USA* 98:5937–42

Rimm-Kaufman SE, Kagan J. 1996. The psychological significance of changes in skin temperature. *Motiv. Emot.* 20:63–78

Rochat P. 2003. Five levels of self-awareness as they unfold early in life. *Consc. Cogn.* 12:717–31

Schino G, Geminiani S, Rosati L, Aureli F. 2004. Behavioral and emotional response of Japanese macaque (*Macaca fuscata*) mothers after their offspring receive an aggression. *J. Comp. Psychol.* 118:340–46

Seed AM, Clayton NS, Emery NJ. 2007. Postconflict third-party affiliation in rooks, *Corvus frugilegus. Curr. Biol.* 17:152–58

Shillito DJ, Shumaker RW, Gallup GG, Beck BB. 2005. Understanding visual barriers: evidence for Level 1 perspective taking in an orangutan, *Pongo pygmaeus. Anim. Behav.* 69:679–87

Silk JB, Brosnan SF, Vonk J, Henrich J, Povinelli D, et al. 2005. Chimpanzees are indifferent to the welfare of unrelated group members. *Nature* 437:1357–59

Singer T, Seymour B, O'Doherty J, Kaube H, Dolan RJ, Frith CD. 2004. Empathy for pain involves the affective but not sensory components of pain. *Science* 303:1157–62

Singer T, Seymour B, O'Doherty JP, Stephan KE, Dolan RJ, Frith CD. 2006. Empathic neural responses are modulated by the perceived fairness of others. *Nature* 439:466–69

Smith A. 1976 [1759]. *A Theory of Moral Sentiments*, ed. DD Raphael, AL Macfie. Oxford, UK: Clarendon

Sober E, Wilson DS. 1998. *Unto Others: The Evolution and Psychology of Unselfish Behavior.* Cambridge, MA: Harvard Univ. Press

Thierry B, Anderson JR. 1986. Adoption in anthropoid primates. *Int. J. Primatol.* 7:191–216

Tinbergen N. 1963. On aims and methods of ethology. *Z. Tierpsychol.* 20:410–33

Trivers RL. 1971. The evolution of reciprocal altruism. *Q. Rev. Biol.* 46:35–57

Trivers RL. 2002. *Natural Selection and Social Theory.* Oxford, UK: Oxford Univ. Press

van Schaik CP. 2004. *Among Orangutans: Red Apes and the Rise of Human Culture.* Cambridge, MA: Belknap

Virányi Zs, Topál J, Miklósi Á, Csányi V. 2005. A nonverbal test of knowledge attribution: a comparative study on dogs and human infants. *Anim. Cogn.* 9:13–26

Watanabe S, Ono K. 1986. An experimental analysis of "empathic" response: effects of pain reactions of pigeon upon other pigeon's operant behavior. *Behav. Proc.* 13:269–77

Watts DP, Colmenares F, Arnold K. 2000. Redirection, consolation, and male policing: how targets of aggression interact with bystanders. In *Natural Conflict Resolution*, ed. F Aureli, FBM de Waal, pp. 281–301. Berkeley: Univ. Calif. Press

Wechkin S, Masserman JH, Terris W. 1964. Shock to a conspecific as an aversive stimulus. *Psychon. Sci.* 1:47–48

Wicker B, Keysers C, Plailly J, Royet JP, Gallese V, Rizzolatti G. 2003. Both of us disgusted in *my* insula: the common neural basis of seeing and feeling disgust. *Neuron* 40:655–64

Wilson EO. 2005. Kin selection as the key to altruism: its rise and fall. *Social. Res.* 72:159–66

Wispé L. 1991. *The Psychology of Sympathy.* New York: Plenum

Wittig R, Boesch C. 2003. The choice of postconflict interactions in wild chimpanzees (*Pan troglodytes*). *Behaviour* 140:1527–59

Wolpert DM, Ghahramani Z, Flanagan JR. 2001. Perspectives and problems in motor learning. *Trends Cogn. Sci.* 5:487–94

Wrangham RW, Peterson D. 1996. *Demonic Males: Apes and the Evolution of Human Aggression.* Boston, MA: Houghton Mifflin

Yerkes RM. 1925. *Almost Human.* New York: Century

Zahn-Waxler C, Hollenbeck B, Radke-Yarrow M. 1984. The origins of empathy and altruism. In *Advances in Animal Welfare Science*, ed. MW Fox, LD Mickley, pp. 21–39. Washington, DC: Humane Soc. U.S.

Zahn-Waxler C, Radke-Yarrow M. 1990. The origins of empathic concern. *Motiv. Emot.* 14:107–30

Zahn-Waxler C, Radke-Yarrow M, Wagner E, Chapman M. 1992. Development of concern for others. *Dev. Psychol.* 28:126–36

Zillmann D, Cantor JR. 1977. Affective responses to the emotions of a protagonist. *J. Exp. Soc. Psychol.* 13:155–65s

Social Bonds and Posttraumatic Stress Disorder

Anthony Charuvastra and Marylene Cloitre

Institute for Trauma and Resilience, New York University School of Medicine, New York, New York 10016; email: marylene.cloitre@nyumc.org

Annu. Rev. Psychol. 2008. 59:301–28

First published online as a Review in Advance on September 17, 2007

The *Annual Review of Psychology* is online at http://psych.annualreviews.org

This article's doi: 10.1146/annurev.psych.58.110405.085650

Key Words

PTSD, social support, social neuroscience, anxiety disorders, attachment

Abstract

Retrospective and prospective studies consistently show that individuals exposed to human-generated traumatic events carry a higher risk of developing Posttraumatic Stress Disorder (PTSD) than those exposed to other kinds of events. These studies also consistently identify perceptions of social support both before and after a traumatic event as an important factor in the determining vulnerability to the development of PTSD. We review the literature on interpersonal traumas, social support and risk for PTSD and integrate findings with recent advances in developmental psychopathology, attachment theory and social neuroscience. We propose and gather evidence for what we term the social ecology of PTSD, a conceptual framework for understanding how both PTSD risk and recovery are highly dependent on social phenomena. We explore clinical implications of this conceptual framework.

Contents

INTRODUCTION

There is accumulating evidence that phenomena such as social support, social cognition, and attachment organization contribute to emotion regulation under conditions of traumatic stress and, more particularly, contribute to risk for or protection against posttraumatic stress disorder (PTSD). In the past few years, several articles have been published summarizing the definition, risk factors, and treatment of PTSD (e.g., Ballenger et al. 2004, Davidson et al. 2004, Foa 2006, Nemeroff et al. 2006). Increasingly, researchers and clinicians emphasize the emotional components of PTSD. Specifically, an individual's inability to adequately modulate intensely emotional memories is increasingly seen as leading to symptoms of re-experiencing, hypervigilance, and ultimately avoidance and numbing (Cahill 1997, Cahill et al. 2003, Frewen & Lanius 2006, Kazui et al. 2000, Pitman & Delahanty 2005, Quirk et al. 2006, Rauch et al. 2006, Rothbaum & Davis 2003, Shin et al. 2006), and the resolution of fear and various other associated emotions is critical to recovery from the disorder. In this review, we propose and gather evidence for what we term the social ecology of PTSD, a conceptual framework for understanding how both PTSD risk and recovery are highly dependent on social phenomena.

We review and synthesize an understanding of PTSD in its social context, drawing from the fields of epidemiology and developmental psychology, the emerging sciences of attachment and social neuroscience, and the PTSD intervention literature. In Part 1, we review the evidence that interpersonal traumas are more pathogenic for PTSD, indicating the particular salience of human interactions in eliciting fear and other trauma-related responses. In Part 2, we describe research linking social support as it occurs both before and after a trauma, and we note the consistency with which this social phenomenon is among the most powerful influences in both risk for and recovery from PTSD. The data suggest that social support is an effective emotion regulator where the behaviors of others can soothe or exacerbate trauma-driven fears. In Part 3, we describe the first social bond, that between caregiver and child, within the context of attachment theory and review the literature on the ways in which the adult caregiver influences the child's responses to traumatic events, particularly in the modulation of feelings of fear versus those of safety. Childhood abuse and other early life adversities are significant risk factors for PTSD in adulthood. We suggest this risk factor exerts its influence in part through enduring diminished expectations of support from others and similarly chronic and possibly related compromised capacity for emotion regulation. We highlight studies in both humans and animals that identify the influences of parental stress and traumatic reactions on the biology of stress responsiveness in offspring, suggesting that social phenomena such as attachment behaviors and other parent-child interactions have immediate and enduring influences on stress-regulating biological systems. In Part 4, we report on studies investigating the neurobiological circuitry of fear, which identify ways in which social ties and social perceptions modulate fear reactivity in the brain, and discuss the implications for understanding the "social brain" of individuals with PTSD. In Part 5, we review the neurochemistry of social bonds to suggest that in addition to a fear system that has been well described, there may be a "safety" system based upon the brain circuits responsible for social affiliation. We focus on the neuropeptides oxytocin and arginovasopressin, which appear to be integral in mediating social affiliation. In Part 6, we conclude with the clinical implications of these findings.

In summary, we propose that human social experience has a particularly salient if not central role in the way an individual responds to trauma, beginning with the first social bond, the parent-child relationship, and extending to experiences in adulthood at both the dyadic and community or group level. Evidence from neurobiology and neurochemistry is beginning to identify ways in which social phenomena modulate fear circuitry in the brain and has suggested that social experience can shape and alter brain behavior and chemistry in the context of traumatic stress. PTSD may serve as a useful model in understanding the fundamental issues in the evolution of the role of social bonds in the assessment of threat and the management of fear responses.

PART 1: INTERPERSONAL TRAUMAS ARE WORSE

Humans experience traumatic events differently from all other animals because we ascribe meaning to events that befall us. The experience of fear associated with a trauma will reflect, in some way, the meaning ascribed to the event. Supporting this claim is the observation that not all traumas are equivalent in the risk of subsequent PTSD. Traumatic injuries caused by other people are the most likely to lead to PTSD. Indeed, this is so pervasive an observation that it is included in the characterization of PTSD in the *Diagnostic and Statistical Manual of Mental Disorders*, i.e., that PTSD may be especially severe or long lasting when the stressor is of "human design" (Am. Psychiatr. Assoc. 2000).

Three symptoms clusters comprise the diagnosis of PTSD: (*a*) re-experiencing symptoms (e.g., flashbacks, intrusive thoughts and images) (*b*) emotional numbing and avoidance of reminders of the trauma (e.g., places, people, thoughts), and (*c*) hyperarousal (e.g., increased startle response, irritability) (Am. Psychiatr. Assoc. 2000). However, for the diagnosis of PTSD to be considered, the individual must experience an event and have a response that entails certain characteristics. The event must involve an experience of threat to one's physical well-being or witnessing (seeing, hearing about) the death, injury, or threat to physical well-being of another person. In addition, the individual's subjective reaction must include but is not limited to the experience of fear, horror, and helplessness. If the event and the individual's reaction fulfill such criteria, the diagnosis of PTSD can be considered. The higher rate of PTSD related to events generated by "human intent" highlights the importance of subjective experience as a contributor to the development of PTSD. Although there is some room for argument, the cause of an event is often a subjective perception that varies from person to person and lends a specific meaning to the event and its long-term consequences. The appraisal of an event as human-caused appears to be particularly fear inducing. The following studies report on rates of PTSD by type of event. They support the observation of the salience of human-caused events in the generation of PTSD and allow some speculation about why this is so.

Epidemiological studies have consistently reported relatively higher rates of PTSD for events resulting from human intent. The most statistically and methodologically sound data on the incidence and prevalence of different types of mental illness in the United States comes from the National Comorbidity Survey (NCS) (Kessler et al. 1994, 2005; Kessler & Merikangas 2004). The NCS survey data indicate that among men and women who report rape as their most upsetting trauma, 65% of men and about 46% of women developed PTSD from this. For men, other traumas associated with a high rate of PTSD were combat exposure (conditional probability = 38.8%), childhood neglect (23.9%), and childhood physical abuse (22.3%), whereas among women, high rates of PTSD followed childhood physical abuse (48.5%), sexual molestation (26.5%), physical assault (21.3%), and being threatened with a weapon (32.6%). These findings are consistent with earlier studies (Kilpatrick & Resnick 1992, March 1992). Traumas of a nonpersonal nature (e.g., "accident" or "natural disaster with fire" or witnessing a trauma) had conditional probabilities for PTSD of less than 10% (Kessler et al. 1995), about half that associated with events related to human intent.

A Swedish national probability sample study of 3000 participants investigated trauma type as well as gender and ethnicity as factors influencing the development of PTSD following a trauma. Of the 1824 respondents reporting a traumatic event, type of trauma independently explained 16.7% of the variance in the rate of PTSD and was the strongest predictor of PTSD symptoms/severity. Of the specifically assessed traumas (robbery, physical assault, sexual assault, tragic death, war, and traffic accident), only traffic accidents did not independently contribute to predicting PTSD diagnosis, with sexual assault being the most likely to predict PTSD (Frans et al. 2005).

It should be noted that the study of interpersonal traumas (e.g., rape or childhood physical/sexual abuse), is often complicated by the problem of retrospective self-report, which is vulnerable to memory biases or distortions. Even events that have been corroborated by multiple observers, such as large-scale disasters, suffer from the absence of independent verification regarding the presence and exact type of exposure for any individual. For this reason, prospective studies or those from the military in which there is independent corroboration of trauma exposure (e.g., documentation of soldiers assigned to combat areas) are critical (e.g., Dorhenwend et al. 2006). The results of such studies have been consistent with retrospective studies, supporting the general finding of differential rates of PTSD by type of events. Accordingly, of particular importance is a prospective study by Shalev & Freedman (2005) that assessed rates of PTSD arising from terror attacks as compared to motor vehicle accidents within the same Israeli community, interviewing survivors at one-week and four-months post trauma (Shalev & Freedman 2005). Terror attack survivors developed PSTD at twice the rate of survivors of motor vehicle accidents (37.8% versus 18.7%). This study provided a rare opportunity to assess two different types of trauma (interpersonal and noninterpersonal) for which there is documentation and that result in differential rates of PTSD. Of interest, terror survivors who developed PTSD did not statistically differ from motor vehicle accident survivors with PTSD at one-week post trauma on scores of trauma symptoms, depression, anxiety, or dissociation. This would suggest that an as-yet unmeasured difference exists between the perceptions of victims of interpersonal and noninterpersonal traumas.

A few studies explore factors that provide some explanation for the apparent power of interpersonal violence as a risk factor for PTSD. First, appraisal of threat is higher when it is of an interpersonal nature. In a meta-analysis of PTSD risk factor studies, Ozer et al. (2003) found that in the civilian population, the predictive effect of perceived life threat on development of PTSD was greater when the traumatic event was interpersonal violence (effect size, or ES, = 0.36) than when the trauma was an accident (ES = 0.20), suggesting that fearing for one's life is more often associated with interpersonal violence. In addition, such traumas are associated with higher levels of subjective distress. Frans et al. (2005) found that perceived distress and trauma frequency explained 10 times more of the variance in the development of PTSD than did ethnicity or gender. In addition, for a given level of reported distress, women and men had similar odds of developing PTSD. This is of interest as it has been repeatedly demonstrated that, controlling for type of trauma, rates of PTSD are generally twice as high for women as for men. Thus, subjective distress seems to be a useful variable and potent mediator or moderator of risk for PTSD.

King et al. (1995) reported that in combat, the experience of seeing human beings severely maimed and killed, whether friend or foe, appears to be more subjectively disruptive than exposure to harm only. The authors reported a specific effect on PTSD risk from exposure to atrocities or episodes of extraordinarily abusive violence distinct from the effect of the perceived threat to one's own life. Thus, both the experience of threat to one's life as well as that to another share in common increased risk for PTSD. King and colleagues (1995) suggest that there is a special horror in violating basic norms of human conduct that is distinct from fearing for one's life. This may reflect the evolutionary significance of social bonding, whereby the species survival has depended on the ability to form cooperative social networks based on trust and norms of behavior. Exposure to cruelty, perversion, or betrayal may lead to a greater sense of threat or fear as this represents not just the risk of physical injury but also the breakdown of social norms as well as the sense of safety associated with being a member of a rule-guided community.

These data highlight the salience of perceptions of humans as actual or potential agents of harm, against oneself or others, in contributing to emotional distress and more

specifically to the development of PTSD. The relevance of the perception of others as helpful or hurtful before or after the event—as distinct from agents of the event—is discussed in the next section.

PART 2: SOCIAL NETWORKS AND SOCIAL SUPPORT

There is a large literature regarding the role of social support in influencing the mental health consequences of stressful life events (such as chronic illness and difficulties with employment), with the general and rather robust finding that support helps buffer against psychological distress (Cohen & Wills 1985). The salience of social support as it relates to PTSD has been demonstrated in two meta-analytic studies. Brewin et al. (2000) found that social support was the strongest correlate of PTSD (ES = 0.4). Ozer et al. (2003), who included 21 studies not analyzed by Brewin et al. (2000), also found that social support was a robust predictor of PTSD, with an effect size of 0.29, making social support the second strongest predictor of PTSD risk, after peritraumatic dissociation (ES = 0.35). Studies in these meta-analyses include both retrospective and prospective designs. Recognizing the potential limitations of retrospective studies, Brewin et al. (2000, p. 752) assessed the potential moderating effect of study design on predictors of PTSD and reported that the retrospective versus prospective nature of the study design did not influence the identified relationship between social support and PTSD.

Debate about the nature of the relationship between social support and PTSD persists, however, as some studies indicate that social support exerts its influence as a protective factor against the risk of PTSD, whereas other studies suggest that the relative absence of support is salient because it creates an increased risk for PTSD. Our review of the literature leads us to conclude that both types of experiences can occur, sometimes even simultaneously, and the relative impact of each is context sensitive relative to the nature of the trauma, the individual's needs, and the nature of the social or interpersonal relationships.

Measures of social support either ask people about functional support, which refers to the individual's perception or experience of social interactions as helpful or unhelpful, or assess structural support, which refers to external aspects of the individual's social network (e.g., size and complexity of the social network, actual support provided). Notably, both measures rely on self-report; investigators rarely, if ever, can independently verify the number of friends, the nature of the relationships, or the qualities of the interactions. Studies that have directly compared the contributions of functional support with those of structural support indicate that post-trauma distress is more greatly influenced by functional support than by structural support (Kaniasty & Norris 1992, Norris & Kaniasty 1996), and measures of quantitative aspects of social networks tend to be less predictive of mental health outcomes than do measures of the qualitative perception of social network interactions (Kessler et al. 1985, Sarason et al. 1987, Shinn et al. 1984). These findings indicate that the reported subjective experience of the helpfulness of others is more relevant than any quantitative measure of the social network reinforces the central role that subjective appraisal appears to have in determining the development and course of PTSD.

Studies in combat veterans provide a first picture of how social factors affect the development of PTSD. The National Vietnam Veterans Readjustment Study (NVVRS; Kulka et al. 1990) provides the most well characterized sample of combat veterans. Importantly, a recent reanalysis of the NVVRS sample confirmed the reports of traumatic exposures using multiple independent historical records, indicating that the retrospective reports of trauma in this sample were highly accurate (Dohrenwend et al. 2006). King et al. (1998) completed a series of studies on data from the NVVRS. Their initial findings indicated that for both

men and women, the most important postwar mediator of the risk for PTSD was perceived social support and that social support was negatively correlated with PTSD. The authors conclude that social support may serve to offset the deleterious consequences of traumas on PTSD risk (King et al. 1998). Several other studies show a consistent positive effect of social support on reducing risk of PTSD among prisoners of war (Engdahl et al. 1997), United Nations soldiers (Kaspersen et al. 2003), and among Albanian Kosovars after the Balkan civil war (Ahern et al. 2004).

At least one prospective study has identified social support as both a risk and protective factor (Koenen et al. 2003). In a 14-year prospective study of American Legionnaires whose combat exposure was in Vietnam, veterans with PTSD who showed more community involvement were more likely to show remission of their PTSD over the course of the study. On the other hand, veterans who reported more perceived negative community attitudes at homecoming were more likely to have a chronic course of PTSD. These two variables both indicate a degree of connectedness to a social network—greater community involvement suggests an ability to reintegrate into a social network and form social bonds, whereas experiencing negative community attitudes upon homecoming suggests a feeling of ostracism, isolation, and a weakening of social bonds. This study provides an example of the differing influences of social support: Positive social network interactions can facilitate resolution of PTSD while negative interactions contribute to its maintenance.

Retrospective studies of adults who have experienced childhood physical and sexual abuse provide another perspective on the interaction between traumatic events and social support. Positive social support appears to mitigate the negative effects of child abuse on measures of general psychological adjustment (Conte & Schuerman 1987, Everson et al. 1989, Gold et al. 1994, Runtz & Schallow 1997, Wyatt & Mickey 1987) and to attenuate PTSD symptom severity (Hyman et al.

2003). Schumm and colleagues (2006) studied a large community sample of low-income, predominantly minority women, and found that among women who were victims of both childhood abuse and adult sexual assault, social support had a large effect size in protecting against PTSD symptom severity (ES = 0.83). Similarly, in a prospective study, Bal et al. (2005) found that among adolescents, higher levels of crisis support immediately following disclosure of sexual abuse protected against the development of internalizing symptoms, which included posttraumatic stress symptoms, as measured by the Trauma Symptom Checklist for Children.

In contrast, several retrospective studies of adult rape victims have shown that the perception of blame and unsupportive social responses are strongly associated with psychological distress, whereas positive social interactions do not appear to bestow any benefit (Davis et al. 1991, Filipas & Ullman 2001, Ullman 1996a, Ullman & Filipas 2001). Similarly, a prospective study evaluating predictors of PTSD in adult survivors of sexual and nonsexual assault found that "interpersonal friction," defined as overt arguments and assessed at two-week post event in multiple social domains, predicted PTSD severity at three-month follow-up (Zoellner et al. 1999). In addition, after controlling for initial PTSD and depression symptoms, interpersonal friction was a stronger predictor of PTSD severity than was the type of assault. In contrast, initial positive social support was not predictive of later PTSD symptoms.

A second prospective study found that, controlling for baseline PTSD symptoms, negative reactions from the social network and dissatisfaction with support were predictive of both the onset and severity of PTSD symptoms at six months, whereas positive support had no effect on PTSD onset or course (Andrews et al. 2003). Compared with men, women had a higher frequency of self-reported negative responses from their social networks, but both sexes reported the same amount of positive support. These findings suggest that negative and positive reactions are distinct social processes, and that women victims have a higher risk for specifically negative social reactions.

In a study that addressed the notion that different kinds of social experiences may have different domains of influence, Borja et al. (2006) reported that among a nonclinical sample reporting histories of adult sexual assault, negatively experienced social interactions contributed specifically to the risk of developing PTSD symptoms. In contrast, positively experienced social interactions contributed to measures of posttraumatic growth (e.g., having a great appreciation for life, a greater sense of personal strength, or spiritual development). Importantly, positive social support was not correlated with PTSD symptoms, and conversely, negative support did not influence posttraumatic growth.

The study data in their totality suggest that negative and positive social support have different patterns of influence. The absence of support, or actual negative responses, appears rather consistently to exert a negative effect, while the benefit of positive social responses or interactions is less uniform. The psychological value of positive social support often depends on who gives the support (Pilisuk & Parks 1986) and whether the support offered matches a specific need (Kaniasty & Norris 1992, Punamaki et al. 2005). The buffering influence of positive social interactions on trauma response may be particularly limited by the vicissitudes of misunderstanding between the traumatized individual and his or her social network. Moreover, certain types of traumatic events are more likely than are others to elicit positive versus negative social reactions. As noted by Punamaki et al. (2005), traumas that typically mobilize positive social support are "visually distressing, unambiguous, collectively shared and ... often attribute heroic characteristics to the victims"; such as was the case with the 9/11 terrorist attack and its victims, particularly first responders. In contrast, traumatic events that elicit negative responses are often unseen and unshared, ambiguous in their acceptability, and associated with stigma and shame, as is often the case with sexual assault, sexual or physical abuse, or combat in an unpopular war. Several studies have reported the adverse impact of negative reactions from a social network on victims of marital violence and rape victims (Andrews & Brewin 1990, Campbell et al. 2001, Davis et al. 1991, Janoff-Bulman 1992). Similar effects have been described for returning Vietnam War veterans, who were harshly judged and in many ways socially rejected (Koenen et al. 2003, Summerfield & Hume 1993).

The most profound question, however, is why social support in either direction has such a potent influence on PTSD. A trauma is by definition an event that is threatening, unexpected, and uncontrollable, and from a cognitive perspective directly challenges beliefs that the world is safe, predictable, and controllable, contributing to the cardinal emotion of PTSD, namely fear (Am. Psychiatr. Assoc. 2000). In the case of interpersonal trauma, the event requires revision of the individual's fundamental "inner schemata of self in relation to the world," changing how safe the person feels in the world (Horowitz 1986) and ultimately, as Herman (1992) noted, revision of the systems of interpersonal bonds that connect the individual to his or her community.

During the course of natural recovery, fearful feelings decrease over time and the individual regains his or her emotional and cognitive equilibrium. At a cognitive level, positive social support may facilitate this process as it conveys the message that one is taken care of and is a member of a group whose task is in part the protection of its members. In contrast, negative support may reinforce beliefs that the world is hostile, contributing to feelings of fear and lack of safety. A prospective study assessing posttrauma beliefs among adult victims of sexual and physical assault found that posttrauma beliefs such as, "People who would stand by me have let me down" and "I feel like other people are ashamed of me now," were more predictive of PTSD than

were variables related to the traumatic event itself, including perceived threat to life and objective characteristics of the assault, such as presence of a weapon and severity of assault (Dunmore et al. 2001).

The finding that negative social support is consistently associated with the development of PTSD suggests that individuals who are vulnerable to PTSD are more likely to react with greater fear to negative interactions in comparison with those who do not develop PTSD following a traumatic exposure. Biases toward the perception of threat are consistent with emerging neurobiological models that suggest that variations in subcortical emotion processing may contribute to individual differences in vulnerability to various anxiety disorders (Phelps 2006), as discussed below. The findings of several psychosocial studies suggest that social support may be a significant mediator in emotional approach and avoidance of trauma-related reminders. Several retrospective studies have reported that following trauma, low social support is associated with avoidant coping in various forms, such as behavioral withdrawal and emotional disengagement (Irwin 1996, Runtz & Schallow 1997, Ullman 1996b). Furthermore, two prospective studies have shown that positive social support predicts lower subsequent PTSD avoidance symptoms (Dalgleish et al. 1996, Joseph et al. 1993). The influence of social support on avoidant symptomatology and behavior is significant because avoidant behaviors and symptoms are the most consistent predictors of poor outcome among trauma victims. For example, several studies have shown that avoidant coping (e.g., passive isolation) is associated with subsequent PTSD (North et al. 2001, Silver et al. 2002) and that trauma avoidance symptoms are the most predictive of developing full PTSD (North et al. 2002, Silva et al. 2000). In summary, there is evidence that low social support leads to avoidant coping, and that positive support decreases PTSD avoidant behaviors. These data, taken together, suggest that social support may modulate the trauma victim's capacity to approach and process trauma-related feelings, and this may account for some of its influence on the development of and recovery from PTSD.

Expanding on the concept that relationships within a social network affect how an individual processes thoughts and feelings, we suggest that a functional social network provides a sense of safety to an individual through the presence of stable, reliable interpersonal connections. Certain kinds of social interactions in this network may help trauma survivors regulate their emotions, particularly emotions of fear, anxiety, and mistrust. A consideration of the first social environment all individuals experience, the family, provides further evidence for this view of how social bonds affect PTSD.

PART 3: TRAUMATIC EVENTS IN CHILDHOOD AND THE FAMILY CONTEXT

The family is the first social network human beings experience. When children feel overwhelmed by fear or anxiety, they turn to salient attachment figures to restore their sense of safety. The theory of attachment as developed by Bowlby (1969, 1973) and Ainsworth et al. (1978) proposes that humans are born with an innate psychobiological system (the attachment behavioral system) that motivates them to seek proximity to significant others in times of danger, stress, or novelty. Proximity to the caretaker protects the child from threat, relieves distress through the receipt of comfort and soothing, and provides direction about how to negotiate the world at large so that the child can return to and be successful in exploration. Over time, such experiences result in the organization of an "internal working model" that specifies relational or interpersonal contingencies that guide expectations about when and from whom an individual can expect help during times of distress and difficulty. From an attachment theory perspective, effective adaptation over the course of development derives from evolving self-generated capacity for emotion regulation interacting with continuing reliance on the support of others when demand exceeds the individual's capacity (Ainsworth 1991, Bowlby 1988).

An emerging literature indicates that a child's proximity to its caretaker is a critical modulator of the child's sense of safety following a trauma. The first naturalistic observations concerning the impact of trauma on children were published during World War II, where it was noted that children exposed to trauma did not have a fear response proportional to the severity of the trauma. Rather, their response was proportional to the distance from their caretaker (Freud & Burlingham 1943). More recent work has indicated that the loss of parental presence, both threatened and actual, contributes to PTSD symptomatology. In a case series describing 41 traumatized preschool children, Scheeringa & Zeanah (1995) reported that of six proposed predictors, including age, gender, proximity to the event, duration, and injury to self, the only variable associated with significantly higher rates of PTSD was the child's observation of physical threat to the parent. Such traumas can signify to a child the loss of its "secure base" and the perception of a parent's lesser ability to respond to the child's needs, further contributing to a child's sense of separation and subsequent lack of safety (Scheeringa & Zeanah 1995).

More recently, a prospective study of children hospitalized for burns demonstrated the influence of loss of physical proximity to the parent as a contributor to PTSD symptomatology. Saxe et al. (2005) followed 72 children with acute burns and found that the degree of physical trauma sustained, as measured by total body area burned, and reported pain were linked to severity of PTSD symptoms through two factors: acute dissociation and, more strongly, through separation anxiety. Separation anxiety provides a measure of distress when the child is physically separated from its parent. This study gives some indication of the psychological processes involved in the disruption of the physical bond between child and caretaker and more particularly the presence of a significant relationship between separation anxiety and PTSD symptoms (Saxe et al. 2005).

When both parent and child are exposed simultaneously to the same stressor, the child and adult responses are highly related, suggesting that parental emotional and cognitive appraisal influences the child's response. Scheeringa & Zeanah (2001) reviewed 17 studies of children ranging from preschool to teen years who were exposed to clearly defined traumatic events. They reported that higher rates of diagnosed PTSD in parents were associated with higher rates in their children, although this relationship appears to be much more pronounced in infant and preschool-age children than in older children, consistent with the view that younger children are more dependent on parents to modulate emotional experience (Scheeringa & Zeanah 2001). At least four studies of a prospective nature have found that parental PTSD symptom status predicts children's PTSD symptoms at a later time (Koplewicz et al. 1994, Landolt et al. 1998, Laor et al. 1997, McFarlane 1987). These studies suggest a pattern of co-occurrence of posttraumatic symptoms between an adult caregiver and a young child and the risk of subsequent exacerbation of the child's symptoms related to the symptom status of the adult caregiver.

A child's PTSD appears to be influenced not only by parental PTSD symptoms but also by other parental behaviors, which suggests the role of parental behaviors as a modulator of emotional experience. These included avoidant behaviors in the parents with respect to the trauma as well as the child's perceived rejection by parents or feelings of guilt and anxiety caused by parents (Deblinger et al. 1999). Parental avoidant behavior can prevent the traumatic event from being discussed or processed within the relationship as may be needed by the child, or these behaviors can place constraints on exploratory activi-

ties that might allow the child to encounter and process traumatic reminders (Laor et al. 1997, 2001; Pynoos et al. 1995). In addition, parental behaviors of distancing or rejection, owing to a parent's own negative emotional reactions to the trauma or to the child's symptom expression, can disrupt the capacity of the child to regain equilibrium. In these situations, the social bond for the child will no longer be experienced as safe and durable, and this may be the most pernicious effect of a traumatic stress on a child and its family.

The final circumstance of trauma in the parent-child dyad is when the parent is the direct source of the child's trauma, as in the case of physical or sexual abuse and other forms of maltreatment. From the organization of care described by attachment theory, abuse describes a circumstance in which the child's source of safety is also a source of danger. Numerous studies in which the child's "safe harbor" or secure base is disturbed by maltreatment demonstrate the deleterious effects on emotional regulation and interpersonal ability when the relationship with a parent is unsafe.

Similar to findings in the adult literature, the rates of PTSD in children are higher for interpersonal traumas than for other kinds of trauma, such as accidents. Most of the PTSD data on the consequences of childhood trauma are retrospective because of the challenges of conducting research on victims of unpredictable events. Again, however, the findings from studies of children converge with findings in adults from prospectively and retrospectively obtained data. At least one study reported on the varying effects of diverse traumas among treatment-seeking children using the same measures and sampling methods across the traumas. Rates of PTSD for accidents were 11%; for war, 29%–33%; and for physical and sexual abuse, 65% (Saigh et al. 1999). When a child experiences physical or sexual abuse from a parent, the consequences are significant because the child not only experiences a traumatic event, with the parent as the agent of the trauma, but also loses an important source of soothing, comfort, emotional repair, and cognitive reorganization. At times, the parent is both agent of the trauma and an effective agent of comfort, creating a paradoxical or confusing state that further undermines a child's sense of safety.

Beyond the development of PTSD, the experiences of assault or abuse by a parent have a profound effect on developing capacities for modulation of affect and the use of others as support in times of need. A traumatizing parent clearly influences a child's ability to interact effectively with a social network. Children with histories of maltreatment show rigid and situationally inappropriate affective displays (Shields & Cicchetti 1998), diminished emotional self-awareness, difficulty modulating excitement in emotionally arousing situations, and difficulty recovering from episodes of upset or distress (Shields & Cicchetti 1997). Such children are more likely to isolate themselves or withdraw under conflictual circumstances (Sroufe et al. 1983) and are less likely to initiate social engagement with adults (Karrass & Walden 2005) and with their peers (Contreras et al. 2000). They expect little help under stressful circumstances and tend to interpret the ambiguous or even supportive efforts of others as hostile (Suess et al. 1992). Thus, the very ability to join and benefit from a social network is impaired by the effects of early childhood maltreatment, suggesting one of the ways in which early childhood traumas and their effects on attachment have such a profound influence on later risk of PTSD in adulthood.

Several retrospective studies and meta-analyses have identified childhood abuse as a strong predictor of PTSD following adult onset stressors of all kinds, including military/combat exposure (Andrews et al. 2000, Bremner et al. 1993, Breslau et al. 1999, Brewin et al. 2000). Data from the National Vietnam Veterans Readjustment Study reveal a link between childhood abuse and low negative social support in adulthood, which in turn is linked to risk for combat-related PTSD (King et al. 1999). Pretrauma risk factors from childhood appear to exert part of their influence on PTSD via their corrosive effects on social network formation over the course of an individual's lifetime.

It is assumed that the affective and social disturbances seen in maltreated children also occur in adults, negatively affecting function and in turn increasing risk for psychiatric disorders such as PTSD. However, scant data exist to support this assumption. In response to this gap, we investigated the status of emotion-regulation capacity and expectations of support and their relationship to current attachment status among treatment-seeking individuals with PTSD. We found that emotion regulation and social disturbances, so well documented among maltreated children, are also salient problems for adults with histories of childhood maltreatment. As in the developmental literature, we found that compromised attachment contributed directly to problems with emotion regulation and expectations of support, which in turn contributed separately and significantly to functional impairment (Cloitre et al. 2007). The study results identify parallel patterns of problems in emotion regulation and social relatedness in adults, suggesting some uniformity in the points of vulnerability in functioning as a result of abuse across the lifespan. The data, however, do not identify the degree to which such patterns are stable within any individual. Longitudinal prospective studies are needed to identify factors that contribute to developmental trajectories of impaired functioning and, more importantly, individual and environmental factors that support positive change and resilience.

Recent studies have suggested both the immediate and enduring biological effects of the parent-child dynamic with regard to safety and threat exposure. Infant stress-regulatory responses are substantially dependent on the infants' relationship to their primary caretaker. Experimental manipulation of caregiver responsiveness in the face of threat to the infant has been shown to be related to cortisol secretion. For example, experiences of separation during which the infants were left with substitute caretakers were associated with increased cortisol levels when the caretaker expressed negative affect (Schechter et al. 2004). Studies of holocaust survivors and their adult children provide biological data showing that parental trauma has a chronic and enduring influence on their offspring. The bonds between holocaust survivor-parents and their children were frequently disrupted by emotional distress, intense and terrifying memories, and other PTSD symptoms. Yehuda and colleagues (2001) found that adult offspring whose parents had PTSD were more likely to develop PTSD than those whose parents did not have PTSD (Yehuda et al. 2001). Additionally, having parents with PTSD contributed to a greater negative feedback inhibition of the hypothalamo-pituitary-adrenocortical (HPA) axis (i.e., greater dexamethasone suppression of cortisol), an effect that was independent of childhood traumatic stress or current PTSD symptoms (Yehuda et al. 2007). Yehuda has reported that PTSD-positive offspring reported more emotional abuse (Yehuda et al. 2001) and more over-protective parenting (personal communication, R. Yehuda), which suggests that disturbances in the parent-child relationship and parenting behaviors may mediate the observed PTSD relationship between parent and child. Moreover, the data suggest that parental PTSD symptoms can influence the parent-child relationship in ways that alter the child's HPA function in an enduring way. That is, it appears that disruptions to the safety of the parent-child bond may have lifelong effects on the response to traumatic stress and such disruptions imprint themselves into the biological organization of the stress response.

The fact that parental behavior can profoundly influence offspring emotional behavior and even organize the offspring biology has been demonstrated in several animal models. Early variations in maternal care produce lifelong alterations in the HPA axis and stress response, and such models demonstrate how sensitivity to stress may be transmitted across generations through behavioral interactions. These rodent and primate studies demonstrate some of the biological mechanisms by which emotional and social behavior become pervasively organized by early parent-child interactions and illustrate how variations in social experiences are essential to understanding gene-environment interactions that result in later behavioral phenotypes (Maestripieri 2005; Maestripieri et al. 2006a,b, 2007; Meaney & Szyf 2005a,b; Seckl & Meaney 2006; Shannon et al. 2005; Suomi 2005).

These recent discoveries in the developmental biology of stress response are consistent with Bowlby's view that the attachment system is active throughout the life cycle in times of stress. Attachment theory predicts that when an individual feels threatened, there will be an instinct to seek out safety in important relationships, whether these relationships are with the caregiver, as in the case of children, or within a selected social network, as in the case of adults. We have reviewed the data consistent with this proposal indicating that, following a trauma, parental response or the response of the social network influences the risk of developing PTSD in children and adults, respectively. We have also reviewed data suggesting that the impact of early traumatic experiences on the bonds between a child and its parents (in particular when the trauma comes from the parents) influences how an individual will later organize his social life, in the form of social bonds within a network, and his inner life, in terms of his ability to utilize social bonds to assist in coping with emotionally distressing events. The following sections describe how neurobiological insights into social bonding and social cognition provide the beginnings of a mechanistic account of the ways in which social bonds may contribute to a sense of safety and function to help an individual with emotion regulation.

PART 4: SOCIAL COGNITION—THE NEUROCIRCUITRY OF SOCIAL BONDS

With regard to PTSD, nearly all of the neurobiological research has focused on individual-level factors, such as neural circuits responsible for fear processing, modulation, and extinction (Phelps & LeDoux 2005, Rauch et al. 2006); alterations in the HPA axis (Marmar et al. 2006, Pitman et al. 2006, Yehuda 2006); or the nature of emotional memory (Cahill et al. 2003). Researchers have begun to identify the neural pathways underlying social affiliation, and emerging evidence shows the influence of social affiliations and evaluations on stress and fear systems in the brain. There have yet to be clinical studies examining the effect of stress or interpersonal trauma on brain regions implicated in social cognition and bonding. However, we believe that understanding at the neurobiological level how social information is processed and connected to states of fear, anxiety, safety, and reward will provide an important perspective on the social and psychological data reviewed above. In particular, considering the sizable impact that social factors have on the development of PTSD, it is important to connect the social and psychological paradigms to the rapidly advancing biological paradigms that have, so far, overlooked social interactions as they influence anxiety, fear, and stress responses. Conversely, a richer understanding of how social information affects the development of anxiety disorders, in this case PTSD, may suggest new ways to examine brain function in relation to stress and threat. For example, the feeling of safety may require not only an absence of fear but also an awareness of social connection and support, suggesting an interaction between subcortical fear-processing regions and higher cortical regions implicated in social knowledge.

Attachment theory posits the existence of an "internal working model" of attachment relationships that evolves with each significant attachment relationship and that guides an individual's use of attachment figures for emotional regulation and other interpersonal needs. Social neuroscience experiments have provided the first glimpses of the neural substrates of such an internal working model. Imaging research implicates certain regions or networks in the brain for representing the intentions of others within one's mind (so-called theory of mind), while other networks are responsible for comparing past experiences (memories) with present stimuli and context to make decisions about risk and reward seeking (Adolphs 2003, 2006; Adolphs et al. 1998). Similarly, other imaging data suggest that the feeling of trust involves an interaction between the amygdala and the prefrontal cortices (Adolphs 2002, Winston et al. 2002).

Coan et al. (2006) recently published the first functional magnetic resonance imaging (fMRI) study that demonstrates neural processes linking social support to emotion regulation. Sixteen highly satisfied married couples were selected, and the wife in each couple was exposed to a simple threat while the kind of social support she received was varied. When the wife was in the fMRI scanner, she was able to hold her husband's hand, the hand of a male experimenter (stranger), or no one's hand. The wife faced either the threat of receiving a mild but uncomfortable electric shock while in the scanner or a nonthreatening condition of knowing no shock would be delivered.

Both spouse and stranger handholding attenuated the neural response to threat in multiple brain areas implicated in the visceral and musculoskeletal responses to affect related arousal (e.g., ventral anterior cingulate, posterior cingulate). However, spousal handholding had a powerful and specific effect distinguishing it from stranger handholding. The women showed less activation in regions associated with emotion regulation (dorsolateral prefrontal cortex and caudate) and emotion-related homeostatic functions (superior colliculus) when holding their spouse's hands, compared with holding a stranger's hand, indicating that social knowledge influences emotion-regulation processes. The diminished activation in emotion-regulation areas correlated with subjective measures that under the threat condition, spouse handholding was less unpleasant than was stranger handholding. This suggests that there was less unpleasant affect to regulate in the spouse handholding condition, consistent with the observation of diminished neural activation. However, without more data, in particular pertaining to subcortical threat-processing activity (e.g., amygdala activity) and connectivity between the proposed emotion-regulation areas and the stress response areas, it is difficult to give a more precise interpretation of this specific finding.

Notably, the social support was nonverbal and of a sensory nature, namely touch, an elementary but perhaps universal form of comfort. Coan et al. (2006) also found that brain structures associated with more evaluative, attentional, and affective components of the threat response were attenuated more specifically by spousal handholding, suggesting that attachment figures influence both cognitive and emotion regulation processes in ways that strangers do not. Most interestingly, threat-related activations of the right anterior insula, superior frontal gyrus, and hypothalamus were sensitive to marital quality, with higher marital satisfaction predicting greater attenuation only during spousal handholding. Individuals with higher-quality relationships appear to benefit from a greater regulatory effect of attachment relationships on neural systems supporting the brain's stress response. Regulation of the hypothalamus suggests these benefits may be pervasive, as the hypothalamus regulates multiple systems within the brain and the body, including the HPA axis. The specific effect of marital quality on the spousal handholding condition is consistent with attachment theory's prediction that specific attachment experiences influence the quality of emotional regulation provided by contact with attachment figures. Furthermore, these effects are only apparent under conditions where the attachment system, or one of the members of the system, is under threat.

In addition to the above study, which suggests the role of intimate social bonds in attenuating fear reactions, data from other studies suggest that social distance can strengthen fear responses. Specifically, race bias has been shown to impede fear extinction. Olsson et al. (2005) assessed whether individuals of another race are more readily associated with an aversive stimulus than are individuals of one's own race, and whether these effects may be moderated by attitudes, beliefs, or contact with members of the racial outgroup. Using a standard fear-conditioning and fear-extinction paradigm with images of black and white faces as the conditioned stimuli, the investigators demonstrated that whereas all subjects acquired conditioned fear to faces of either race equally, subjects extinguished fearful associations only to faces from their own racial group. That is, white subjects could extinguish the fearful association with white faces but not black faces, and black subjects could extinguish the fearful association with black faces but not white faces. Of interest, the conditioning bias to racial outgroup faces was attenuated among those with more interracial dating experience, consistent with a large body of evidence that positive intergroup contact reduces negative reactions to outgroups. Social information appears to modulate very basic aspects of the fear system in humans, and positive social interactions can attenuate certain kinds of fear learning (Olsson et al. 2005). If fear extinction proves to be essential to the pathophysiology of PTSD, these findings suggest that social information and social experiences are essential modulators of fear extinction. Such findings also suggest new methods to investigate the effects of social support on PTSD. For example, certain types of social encounters may contribute to beliefs or attitudes that impair fear extinction.

Finally, emotional numbing has been identified as a symptom associated with significant impairment from PTSD (Breslau et al. 2005), and preliminary evidence links a diminished neural capacity to respond to social rewards to emotional numbing among PTSD sufferers. Elman et al. (2005) hypothesized that emotional numbing is related to deficits in the brain reward circuits, leading to altered responses to sources of pleasure. The investigators examined reactions to social and monetary reward using a validated reward paradigm for fMRI, and found that compared with controls, PTSD patients had smaller signal changes in the nucleus accumbens, cingulate gyrus, insula, and prefrontal cortex in response to reward stimuli. Thus, a decreased ability to respond to social reward may be either a risk factor for PTSD or a consequence of PTSD. These data suggest that failure of those with PTSD to seek out or use offers of social support (Norris & Kaniasty 1996) may reflect not only a desire to avoid fear reactions or hyperarousal, but also the absence of rewards associated with social contact. Such findings suggest that neural substrates for basic social responses may be implicated in the pathogenesis of PTSD and that these may be distinct from fear-related neural circuitry.

A separate line of inquiry shows that social events and information are processed by the brain at a subconscious level, before conscious cognitive activity comes online. Such stimuli can be conveyed by a variety of nonverbal cues in the social environment, including body language. In one study, normal subjects were presented with pictures of people (with the faces blurred) in nonfearful or fearful body postures. Although the test subjects were not making conscious appraisals, fMRI revealed increased amygdala and fusiform gyrus activity during viewing of the fearful body postures, consistent with the idea that the fear system processes such information early and automatically (Hadjikhani & de Gelder 2003). Furthermore, studies of social context processing show that cognitive appraisal can be influenced by emotional reactions to a social context. In a study of normal subjects discriminating fearful from surprised faces, the social context was varied prior to stimuli exposure. Facial expressions of surprise have been found to be somewhat ambiguous in regard to their affective "message" and were purposefully used to assess the potential influence of additional verbal information. When a surprised face was preceded by an emotionally congruent social context (e.g., conveyed verbally by being told "She just won 500 dollars"), there was less activation in the amygdala than when the social context preceding the surprised face suggested loss or threat (e.g., "He just lost 500 dollars") (Kim et al. 2004). These results suggest that information about social context regulates the fear system response to discrete stimuli and that social context may be particularly important in regulating the response to more ambiguous stimuli.

In summary, the fear system responds to and is modulated by a range of social information, including sensory information (touch), representations of bodily cues, stored social knowledge or assumptions (race), and contextual cues. Furthermore, such information has influence at both conscious and nonconscious levels of awareness (Phelps 2006). These findings suggest some of the mechanisms whereby discrete social experiences may influence fear processing, acquisition, and extinction. Consistent with the literature on social support and parent-child transmission of fear, these data suggest that positive information from socially relevant others can attenuate fear responses and that socially negative or even neutral information can heighten and maintain fear responses. It remains to be determined how such processes are different in people with PTSD and how such processes maintain or exacerbate PTSD symptoms, particularly with regard to victims of interpersonal traumas.

PART 5: SOCIAL COGNITION— THE NEUROCHEMISTRY OF SOCIAL BONDS

Investigation of the neuropeptides oxytocin (OT) and arginine vasopressin (AVP) suggests an intersection between the biology of social bonding and the biology of fear response that may parallel the intersection between social support and PTSD described above. Animal studies demonstrate that OT and AVP are involved in the neurocircuitry of fear. In rodents, OT acts on the amygdala to reduce fear (Amico et al. 2004, Gulpinar & Yegen 2004) and to modulate aggression (Bosch et al. 2005). Huber et al. (2005) recently demonstrated that receptors for OT and AVP are located within the central nucleus of the amygdala. The central nucleus appears to be a place where the expression of fear is modulated (Pare et al. 2004), suggesting that these neuropeptides may be related to distinct aspects of the fear response. Stimulation of OT receptors should lead to inhibition within the amygdala, suggesting a mechanism for the way in which OT downregulates fearful responses (Debiec 2005, Huber et al. 2005, LeDoux 2000).

More recently, OT and AVP have been identified as essential chemical mediators of social bonding in animals (Insel 2003, Keverne & Curley 2004, Young & Wang 2004). OT released at childbirth coordinates maternal response to the infant at both the physiologic and behavioral levels, whereas AVP regulates male social behaviors of territorial marking, social aggression, social recognition, anxiety, and male parenting behavior. In adult pair bonding, OT is integral for females, whereas AVP appears to be more central for males. Elegant experiments that transgenically alter the distribution of AVP1a receptors also alter male pair-bonding behavior, but have no effect on male parenting behavior, suggesting that there are separate AVP circuits for each kind of attachment in males. Partner bonds require the formation of social memory (e.g., that a particular individual is the mate) and reinforcement of that memory. Such memory and reinforcement depend upon an interaction between these neuropeptides and the dopamine reward system, with the release of dopamine during mating reinforcing the association between the familiar cues of the mate (e.g., odor) and reward. It appears that the neuropeptides are responsi-ble for linking the dopamine reward system to social bonding events. From an evolutionary viewpoint, such social memories of friendly others, particularly mates, are as essential to survival as the fear memories maintained by the amygdala.

It is notable that PTSD involves a disruption of social behavior, emotional reward (particularly from social experiences), and fear response. Only one study has examined the effects of these neuropeptides in PTSD. Pitman et al. (1993) explored whether OT and AVP would have inhibiting and enhancing effects, respectively, on fear-related memories in PTSD. The investigators used a combat imagery paradigm in subjects with combat-related PTSD and found that OT attenuated and AVP augmented autonomic responses. However, this initial study focused primarily on the stress-response effects of these neuropeptides on fear-related memories, but not in relation to social variables.

Heinrichs et al. (2003) explored the relationships between OT and stress response in social settings by administering OT and using the Trier Social Stress Test. The investigators found that OT interacts with received social support to suppress both the subjective and cortisol responses to psychosocial stress. Stress response was most affected by the combination of OT and social support, whereas the effect of receiving OT alone appeared to be about equivalent to the effect of receiving social support alone with regard to measures of physiologic and subjective measures of anxiety. OT also had an anxiolytic effect that social support alone did not have.

Kirsch et al. (2005) enrolled 15 normal human male subjects and administered either OT or placebo intranasally, followed by an fMRI paradigm, to assess amygdala activity and functional connectivity in response to a task involving visual stimuli that were either interpersonally threatening (angry or afraid faces), noninterpersonally threatening (fearful or threatening scenes devoid of social interaction of facial displays), or simple shapes. Compared with placebo, OT significantly suppressed amygdala activation, with the effect more pronounced for fearful faces than fearful scenes. Kirsch et al. (2005) demonstrated that the amygdala was functionally connected to the upper brainstem during the placebo condition and that this connectivity was significantly reduced with OT administration, consistent with the anatomic data from Huber et al. (2005) suggesting that OT inhibits outgoing signals from the central amygdala to the effector regions of the fear system (e.g., brainstem regions periaqueductal gray and reticular formation). Interestingly, OT administration had no effect on self-report scales of anger, dominance, or arousal, suggesting that the emotional effect is essentially subconscious.

It is unclear whether OT simply reduces fear-reactivity or promotes a sense of trust by involving brain areas distinct from fear circuitry. An interdisciplinary group of economists and psychologists recently showed that the administration of OT can increase trust in humans (Kosfeld et al. 2005). In this study, participants were asked to play an investing game that involved being either an investor or a trustee and participation in a series of investment exchanges with the same person (i.e., two subjects were paired as investor-trustee, and the social interaction of investment and return-on-investment took place several times within the same pair). The investors had real money, which they invested with the trustee. The trustee's job was to decide how much of a return, from zero to all, the investors would receive. Participants were given either placebo or OT intranasally, in a random, double-blind fashion, one hour before the game. Compared with placebo, recipients of OT behaved in a more trusting manner when they were investing.

This effect was specific to trusting behavior, because OT administration had no effect on the behavior of the trustees, whose job did not require trusting but did require a certain kind of strategic thinking to maximize their own share of the money. Furthermore, when the game was replayed, but a computer played

the trustee role and the investors knew that they were interacting with a computer rather than a person, OT had no effect on investor behavior. That is, the administration of OT only affected trusting behavior when the participants believed they were interacting with another human being, which suggests that OT does not simply lower an aversion to risk, but actually increases a certain kind of prosocial approach behavior that requires the mental representation of another human being with whom the subject is interacting. The authors postulate that this study reveals a specific system within the brain that maintains an aversion to betrayal or interpersonal rejection and that OT may be part of how this system is regulated.

Taken together, these studies suggest that OT does interact with the fear system to decrease fearful responses to stress, but that interaction with socially salient stimuli (e.g., other people) is necessary for OT to exert its modulating effect. Social bonds modulate the fear system, as demonstrated in the handholding study (Coan et al. 2006), and OT may be a neurochemical mediator of this effect. The fact that subjects in the investing game showed no response to OT when they believed they were interacting with a computer highlights the unique aspects of OT and social bonding in humans. The perception of human contact appears to be necessary for OT to influence behavior. Because PTSD often involves a disruption of interpersonal relationships, some of the social consequences of PTSD may be associated with disruptions of the neuropeptide circuitry responsible for linking social experiences with reward and fear systems in the brain.

Evidence of such disruption comes from a recent study of maltreated children. Fries et al. (2005) developed a novel method to measure the brain's output of OT and AVP using urine samples. They studied 18 adopted children who had experienced early neglect and had been in orphanages for an average of 16.6 months prior to adoption. Importantly, at the time of the study, these children had been living in stable, enriched, nurturing adoptive homes for an average of 34.6 months. Twenty-one children living in a typical home environment with their biological parents served as controls. The investigators probed the effect of a familiar social bond by having each child play an interactive computer game under two conditions: while sitting on either their mother's lap or on an unfamiliar female experimenter's lap. Through the 30-minute interaction, the mother or unfamiliar adult engaged in regularly timed physical contact (e.g., tickling, patting on the head, counting each other's fingers, whispering in ear), and a urine sample was collected about 15–20 minutes after the task. At baseline, compared with children without histories of neglect, those with a neglect history had lower levels of AVP and there was no difference in OT levels, suggesting that social deprivation may inhibit the full development of the AVP system. In response to the social interaction paradigm, children without histories of neglect showed an increase in OT secretion after interacting with their mothers, while those with histories of neglect did not. There were no group differences in OT levels after interaction with the stranger, and there were no group differences in AVP levels to either social interaction paradigm. This suggests that disruptions in early social bonding impair the OT response to active social bonding interactions with a caregiver later in life. Overall, early disruptions of attachment bonding may lead to long-term disruptions in the neural systems responsible for modulating social affiliation, including the ability to be calmed and comforted by social bonding interactions.

This experiment is the first example in humans of how early adversity programs the brain to respond in a fixed way to certain social stimuli, a phenomenon similar to that in which early maternal deprivation in rodents leads to lifelong programming of the glucocorticoid stress-response system (Seckl & Meaney 2006). This finding also suggests a possible biochemical mechanism for how early prior traumas function as risk factors for later PTSD. Early adversity may alter neural systems for social bonding, limiting an individual's ability to use social resources and build protective social networks later in life.

PART 6: CLINICAL IMPLICATIONS—THE THERAPEUTIC ALLIANCE AND THE CREATION OF SOCIAL NETWORKS IN THE TREATMENT OF POSTTRAUMATIC STRESS DISORDER

An individual with PTSD lives in a heightened and chronic fear state, which includes constant surveillance for and tendency toward perceiving threat in the environment, and this inevitably includes the therapist. The successful treatment of PTSD requires first and foremost providing a sense of safety to the client (Pearlman & Courtois 2005). It is a prerequisite to the treatment, and its most basic expression is realized in the ability of the client to stay in rather than flee from the treatment. The reduction of felt threat in the treatment context requires that the client experience the therapist as someone who is supportive, warm, and interested in the client, who appears to understand the meaning of the client's traumatic experiences and can identify resources (plans and interventions) to help the client. In this way, the therapeutic relationship shares some aspects in common with social support.

It may be useful to see the process of therapy as involving the creation of a social bond and to see the therapeutic alliance within therapy as a reflection of this bond. PTSD is almost inevitably associated with broken or distressed social bonds, either due to the nature of the trauma itself (e.g., sexual assault, combat), to the social repercussions of certain kinds of traumas (e.g., blaming, stigmatizing responses), or to weakened social networks (e.g., disaster victims). Consequently, the importance of the therapeutic alliance may be particularly salient in the treatment of PTSD. The client may be more sensitive to the interpersonal aspects of the therapy, particularly to lapses or imperfections in communication. This sensitivity can be attended to in the therapy, and the therapeutic relationship itself can be introduced either explicitly or implicitly as a model for the exploration of alternative and more positive relating.

A substantial empirical literature has identified that the therapeutic alliance is the most consistent predictor of psychotherapy outcome, although the relationship is often modest in size, with effect sizes ranging from 0.22 to 0.24 (Horvath & Symonds 1991, Martin et al. 2000). Alliance has proven to predict treatment outcome across different treatment modalities, including short-term cognitive-behavioral treatment (Raue & Goldfried 1994, Stiles et al. 1998), interpersonal therapy (Krupnick et al. 1996), psychodynamic therapy (Eaton et al. 1988, Stiles et al. 1998, Yeomans et al. 1994), gestalt therapy (Watson & Greenberg 1994), and cognitive therapy (Muran et al. 1994). In a recent study of PTSD examining the effect of therapeutic alliance, the influence of a positive relationship on PTSD symptom reduction was about twice the size typically reported in these other studies (ES = 0.46) (Cloitre et al. 2004). Thus, the strength of the patient-therapist relationship appears to be a critical common factor across treatment modalities and may be of particular importance in PTSD.

Formally, the therapeutic alliance has been defined as a collaboration that has three distinct dimensions: the presence of a feeling of mutual warmth and understanding, agreement on the goals of the treatment, and agreement on the means by which these goals will be attained (e.g., Raue & Goldfried 1994). Among individuals presenting for treatment of PTSD, the relative effectiveness of the treatment may vary according to the individual's sense of safety, essentially the antidote (or counterexperience) of the sense of fear that is the core emotional disturbance in PTSD. In a recent study, the strength of the therapeutic alliance established in the first three sessions of treatment was, among several early treatment indicators, the most powerful predictor of treatment outcome as measured by PTSD symptom reduction (Cloitre et al. 2002). Although all three components of the therapeutic alliance were predictive of this positive outcome, the strongest was the sense of a warm and understanding bond with the therapist, suggesting the importance of the positive emotional experience with the therapist.

The client's experience of felt safety is a prerequisite to the successful implementation of the various activities in the treatment. One of the essential components of treatment is the "emotional processing" of the memories of the trauma, with the goal of diminishing and resolving feelings of fear associated with memories. Psychological medicine has recognized the idea of therapeutic remembering since at least the early twentieth century (Freud 1914/1963). More recently, cognitive behavioral paradigms have framed PTSD treatment in terms of conditioning and habituation to feared internal or mental stimuli. Trauma memories are treated as the feared "objects," and if the client can bring forward the memory of the trauma with sufficient fidelity, intensity, and duration, the client's fearful reactions to the memory will diminish and PTSD will resolve (see Shalev 1997). The therapist must be sufficiently skilled in creating a safe enough context to allow a client to be persuaded to engage in such a process. A similar recovery process may occur for traumatized individuals who experience safety such that they engage in the processes of recollection and habituation on their own.

Increasingly, effective treatments address ways in which feelings of safety can be exported to a variety of aspects of the individual's life, and these include interventions to resolve fear responses in the individual's larger physical and social environment (e.g., Rothbaum & Foa 1999). Evidence relating social support to PTSD suggests the importance of incorporating interventions that take into account social support phenomena including the benefit to PTSD sufferers of positive social support, the risk to health and recovery when social support is low, and the need to effectively manage negative social support. More recently, interventions have considered that rather than simply reducing fear associated with traumatic interpersonal events by exposure to fear-eliciting people and places, treatment could additionally target improvement of interpersonal relationships.

In light of this evidence, we have added to traditional exposure-based treatments components that target the development of interpersonal skills and enhanced affect regulation abilities (Cloitre et al. 2002) through the use of role play and substantial practice both in and out of the treatment session. In addition to substantially reduced PTSD symptoms, the treatment led to the resolution of impairments in emotion regulation, significant increases in perceived social support, and improved positive relationships with significant others and individuals in the work, home, and social environments. The treatment was adapted to a real-world setting following the World Trade Center attack on September 11, 2001. The nature of this trauma was such that many survivors lost members of their social network through death or relocation. Moreover, many of those with PTSD associated with the World Trade Center attack suffered from diminished perceptions of social support despite its evident availability. The treatment was successful in resolving PTSD as well as improving interpersonal functioning and improving social support perceptions to normative levels (Levitt et al. 2007).

Finally, there has been exploration of treatment that focuses solely on interpersonal functioning without the use of any explicit fear-reduction intervention. In a pilot study of 14 individuals with PTSD, Bleiberg & Markowitz (2005) adapted interpersonal psychotherapy, an evidence-based standardized treatment, used initially for depression, that focuses on improving relationships. The treatment was successful in substantially reducing PTSD symptom severity in the majority of the study participants. Although the durability of these effects is unknown, the results suggest that specific efforts to improve the quality of social bonds can lead to improvement in individual PTSD symptoms, even in the absence of exposure-based work, potentially through self-initiated efforts to engage in emotional processing of the trauma.

Future studies are also needed to explore insights into the neurochemistry of feelings of trust and connectedness, how these relate to feelings of fear and anxiety, and their implications for improving treatments. Oxytocin has been widely used in humans already, albeit for nonpsychological purposes, and an efficient delivery system to the central nervous system already exists. Explorations of the therapeutic potential of this agent for PTSD and disorders of anxiety seem inevitable.

In conclusion, social bonds exert a powerful influence on the development and maintenance of PTSD as the location of important processes that influence how an individual responds to a traumatic event. Most crucially, it is within social bonds that individuals may receive or develop a sense of safety, which appears to be essential to the prevention of or recovery from PTSD. The process of therapy may by considered one type of social bonding, and measures of the therapeutic alliance begin to describe the social bond within therapy. Finally, insights into the neurobiology of social bonding may illuminate aspects of the neurobiology of PTSD and more generally may provide insights into the neurobiology of therapeutic change.

LITERATURE CITED

Adolphs R. 2002. Trust in the brain. *Nat. Neurosci.* 5(3):192–93

Adolphs R. 2003. Cognitive neuroscience of human social behaviour. *Nat. Rev. Neurosci.* 4(3):165–78

Adolphs R. 2006. How do we know the minds of others? Domain-specificity, simulation, and enactive social cognition. *Brain Res.* 1079(1):25–35

Adolphs R, Tranel D, Damasio AR. 1998. The human amygdala in social judgment. *Nature* 393(6684):470–74

Ahern J, Galea S, Fernandez WG, Koci B, Waldman R, Vlahov D. 2004. Gender, social support, and posttraumatic stress in postwar Kosovo. *J. Nerv. Ment. Dis.* 192(11):762–70

Ainsworth MDS. 1991. Attachments and other affectional bonds across the life cycle. In *Attachment Across the Life Cycle*, ed. CM Parkes, J Stevenson-Hinde, P Marris, pp. 33–51. London: Routledge

Ainsworth MDS, Blehar MC, Waters E, Wall S. 1978. *Patterns of Attachment: A Psychological Study of the Strange Situation*. Hillsdale, NJ: Erlbaum

Am. Psychiatr. Assoc. 2000. *Diagnostic and Statistical Manual of Mental Disorders (DSM-IV-TR)*. Washington, DC: Am. Psychiatr. Assoc. 4th ed., text rev.

Amico JA, Mantella RC, Vollmer RR, Li X. 2004. Anxiety and stress responses in female oxytocin deficient mice. *J. Neuroendocrinol.* 16(4):319–24

Andrews B, Brewin CR. 1990. Attributions of blame for marital violence: a study of antecedents and consequences. *J. Marriage Fam.* 52:757–67

Andrews B, Brewin CR, Rose S. 2003. Gender, social support, and PTSD in victims of violent crime. *J. Trauma Stress* 16(4):421–27

Andrews B, Brewin CR, Rose S, Kirk M. 2000. Predicting PTSD symptoms in victims of violent crime: the role of shame, anger, and childhood abuse. *J. Abnorm. Psychol.* 109(1):69–73

Bal S, De Bourdeaudhuij I, Crombez G, Van Oost P. 2005. Predictors of trauma symptomatology in sexually abused adolescents: a 6-month follow-up study. *J. Interpers. Violence* 20(11):1390–405

Ballenger JC, Davidson JR, Lecrubier Y, Nutt DJ, Marshall RD, et al. 2004. Consensus statement update on posttraumatic stress disorder from the international consensus group on depression and anxiety. *J. Clin. Psychiatry* 65(Suppl. 1):55–62

Bleiberg KL, Markowitz JC. 2005. A pilot study of interpersonal psychotherapy for posttraumatic stress disorder. *Am. J. Psychiatry* 162(1):181–83

Borja SE, Callahan JL, Long PJ. 2006. Positive and negative adjustment and social support of sexual assault survivors. *J. Trauma Stress* 19(6):905–14

Bosch OJ, Meddle SL, Beiderbeck DI, Douglas AJ, Neumann ID. 2005. Brain oxytocin correlates with maternal aggression: link to anxiety. *J. Neurosci.* 25(29):6807–15

Bowlby J. 1969. *Attachment and Loss: Vol. 1. Attachment*. New York: Basic Books

Bowlby J. 1973. *Attachment and Loss: Vol. 2. Separation: Anxiety and Anger*. New York: Basic Books

Bowlby J. 1988. *A Secure Base*. New York: Basic Books

Bremner JD, Southwick SM, Johnson DR, Yehuda R, Charney DS. 1993. Childhood physical abuse and combat-related posttraumatic stress disorder in Vietnam veterans. *Am. J. Psychiatry* 150(2):235–39

Breslau N, Chilcoat HD, Kessler RC, Davis GC. 1999. Previous exposure to trauma and PTSD effects of subsequent trauma: results from the Detroit Area Survey of Trauma. *Am. J. Psychiatry* 156(6):902–7

Breslau N, Reboussin BA, Anthony JC, Storr CL. 2005. The structure of posttraumatic stress disorder: latent class analysis in 2 community samples. *Arch. Gen. Psychiatry* 62(12):1343–51

Brewin CR, Andrews B, Valentine JD. 2000. Meta-analysis of risk factors for posttraumatic stress disorder in trauma-exposed adults. *J. Consult. Clin. Psychol.* 68(5):748–66

Cahill L. 1997. The neurobiology of emotionally influenced memory. implications for understanding traumatic memory. *Ann. NY Acad. Sci.* 821:238–46

Cahill L, Gorski L, Le K. 2003. Enhanced human memory consolidation with postlearning stress: interaction with the degree of arousal at encoding. *Learn. Mem.* 10(4):270–74

Campbell R, Ahrens CE, Sefl T, Wasco SM, Barnes HE. 2001. Social reactions to rape victims: healing and hurtful effects on psychological and physical health outcomes. *Violence Vict.* 16(3):287–302

Cloitre M, Koenen KC, Cohen LC, Han H. 2002. Skills training in affective and interpersonal regulation followed by exposure: a phase-based treatment for PTSD related to childhood abuse. *J. Consult. Clin. Psychol.* 70(5):1067–74

Cloitre M, Chase Stovall-McClough K, Miranda R, Chemtob CM. 2004. Therapeutic alliance, negative mood regulation, and treatment outcome in child abuse-related posttraumatic stress disorder. *J. Consult. Clin. Psychol.* 72(3):411–16

Cloitre M, Stovall-McClough KC, Zorbas P, Charuvastra A. 2007. *Attachment organization, emotion regulation and expectations of support among treatment-seeking adults with childhood maltreatment.* Work. Pap., Inst. Trauma Stress, N.Y. Univ. School Med., New York

Coan JA, Schaefer HS, Davidson RJ. 2006. Lending a hand: social regulation of the neural response to threat. *Psychol. Sci.* 17(12):1032–39

Cohen S, Wills TA. 1985. Stress, social support, and the buffering hypothesis. *Psychol. Bull.* 98(2):310–57

Conte JR, Schuerman JR. 1987. Factors associated with an increased impact of child sexual abuse. *Child Abuse Negl.* 11(2):201–11

Contreras JM, Kerns KA, Weimer BL, Gentzler AL, Tomich PL. 2000. Emotion regulation as a mediator of associations between mother-child attachment and peer relationships in middle childhood. *J. Fam. Psychol.* 14(1):111–24

Dalgleish T, Joseph S, Thrasher S, Tranah T, Yule W. 1996. Crisis support following the Herald of Free-Enterprise disaster: a longitudinal perspective. *J. Trauma Stress* 9(4):833–45

Davidson JR, Foa EB, eds. 1992. *Posttraumatic Stress Disorder: DSM-IV and Beyond.* Washington, DC: Am. Psychiatr. Press

Davidson JR, Stein DJ, Shalev AY, Yehuda R. 2004. Posttraumatic stress disorder: acquisition, recognition, course, and treatment. *J. Neuropsychiatry Clin. Neurosci.* 16(2):135–47

Davis RC, Brickman E, Baker T. 1991. Supportive and unsupportive responses of others to rape victims: effects on concurrent victim adjustment. *Am. J. Community Psychol.* 19(3):443–51

Debiec J. 2005. Peptides of love and fear: vasopressin and oxytocin modulate the integration of information in the amygdala. *BioEssays* 27(9):869–73

Deblinger E, Steer R, Lippmann J. 1999. Maternal factors associated with sexually abused children's psychosocial adjustment. *Child Maltreatment: J. Am. Prof. Soc. Abuse Child.* 4(1):13–20

Dohrenwend BP, Turner JB, Turse NA, Adams BG, Koenen KC, Marshall R. 2006. The psychological risks of Vietnam for U.S. veterans: a revisit with new data and methods. *Science* 313(5789):979–82

Dunmore E, Clark DM, Ehlers A. 2001. A prospective investigation of the role of cognitive factors in persistent posttraumatic stress disorder (PTSD) after physical or sexual assault. *Behav. Res. Ther.* 39(9):1063–84

Eaton TT, Abeles N, Gutfreund M. 1988. Therapeutic alliance and outcome: impact of treatment length and pretreatment symptomatology. *Psychotherapy* 25(4):536–42

Elman I, Frederick B, Ariely D, Dunlap S, Rodolico J, et al. 2005. Emotional numbing in PTSD: fMRI neuroimaging of reward circuitry. *Neuropsychopharmacology* 30(S1):s163 (Abstr.)

Engdahl B, Dikel TN, Eberly R, Blank A Jr. 1997. Posttraumatic stress disorder in a community group of former prisoners of war: a normative response to severe trauma. *Am. J. Psychiatry* 154(11):1576–81

Everson MD, Hunter WM, Runyon DK, Edelsohn GA, Coulter ML. 1989. Maternal support following disclosure of incest. *Am. J. Orthopsychiatry* 59(2):197–207

Filipas HH, Ullman SE. 2001. Social reactions to sexual assault victims from various support sources. *Violence Vict.* 16(6):673–92

Foa EB. 2006. Psychosocial therapy for posttraumatic stress disorder. *J. Clin. Psychiatry* 67(Suppl. 2):40–45

Frans O, Rimmo PA, Aberg L, Fredrikson M. 2005. Trauma exposure and post-traumatic stress disorder in the general population. *Acta Psychiatr. Scand.* 111(4):291–99

Freud A, Burlingham DT. 1943. *War and Children.* New York: Medical War Books

Freud S. 1914/1963. Further recommendations in the technique of psychoanalysis: recollection, repetition and working through. In *Therapy and Technique*, ed. P Reiff. New York: Macmillan

Frewen PA, Lanius RA. 2006. Toward a psychobiology of posttraumatic self-dysregulation: reexperiencing, hyperarousal, dissociation, and emotional numbing. *Ann. NY Acad. Sci.* 1071:110–24

Fries AB, Ziegler TE, Kurian JR, Jacoris S, Pollak SD. 2005. Early experience in humans is associated with changes in neuropeptides critical for regulating social behavior. *Proc. Natl. Acad. Sci. USA* 102(47):17237–40

Gold S, Milan L, Mayall A, Johnson A. 1994. A cross-validation study of the Trauma Symptom Checklist: the role of mediating variables. *J. Interpers. Violence* 9:12–26

Gulpinar MA, Yegen BC. 2004. The physiology of learning and memory: role of peptides and stress. *Curr. Protein Pept. Sci.* 5(6):457–73

Hadjikhani N, de Gelder B. 2003. Seeing fearful body expressions activates the fusiform cortex and amygdala. *Curr. Biol.* 13(24):2201–5

Heinrichs M, Baumgartner T, Kirschbaum C, Ehlert U. 2003. Social support and oxytocin interact to suppress cortisol and subjective responses to psychosocial stress. *Biol. Psychiatry* 54(12):1389–98

Herman J. 1992. *Trauma and Recovery.* New York: Basic Books

Horowitz M. 1986. *Stress Response Syndromes.* Northvale, NJ: Aronson

Horvath AO, Symonds, DB. 1991. Relation between working alliance and outcome in psychotherapy: a meta-analysis. *J. Counsel. Psychol.* 36(2):223–33

Huber D, Veinante P, Stoop R. 2005. Vasopressin and oxytocin excite distinct neuronal populations in the central amygdala. *Science* 308(5719):245–48

Hyman S, Gold S, Cott M. 2003. Forms of social support that moderate PTSD in childhood sexual abuse survivors. *J. Fam. Violence* 18(5):295–300

Insel TR. 2003. Is social attachment an addictive disorder? *Physiol. Behav.* 79(3):351–57

Irwin HJ. 1996. Traumatic childhood events, perceived availability of emotional support, and the development of dissociative tendencies. *Child Abuse Negl.* 20(8):701–7

Janoff-Bulman R. 1992. *Shattered Assumptions: Toward a New Psychology of Trauma.* New York: Free Press

Joseph S, Yule W, Williams R, Andrews B. 1993. Crisis support in the aftermath of disaster: a longitudinal perspective. *Br. J. Clin. Psychol.* 32(Part 2):177–85

Kaniasty K, Norris FH. 1992. Social support and victims of crime: matching event, support, and outcome. *Am. J. Community Psychol.* 20(2):211–41

Karrass J, Walden T. 2005. Effects of nurturing and non-nurturing caregiving on child social initiatives: an experimental investigation of emotion as a mediator of social behavior. *Soc. Dev.* 14:685–700

Kaspersen M, Matthiesen SB, Gotestam KG. 2003. Social network as a moderator in the relation between trauma exposure and trauma reaction: a survey among UN soldiers and relief workers. *Scand. J. Psychol.* 44(5):415–23

Kazui H, Mori E, Hashimoto M, Hirono N, Imamura T, et al. 2000. Impact of emotion on memory. Controlled study of the influence of emotionally charged material on declarative memory in Alzheimer's disease. *Br. J. Psychiatry* 177:343–47

Kessler RC, Berglund P, Demler O, Jin R, Merikangas KR, Walters EE. 2005. Lifetime prevalence and age-of-onset distributions of DSM-IV disorders in the National Comorbidity Survey Replication. *Arch. Gen. Psychiatry* 62(6):593–602

Kessler RC, McGonagle KA, Zhao S, Nelson CB, Hughes M, et al. 1994. Lifetime and 12-month prevalence of DSM-III-R psychiatric disorders in the United States. Results from the National Comorbidity Survey. *Arch. Gen. Psychiatry* 51(1):8–19

Kessler RC, Merikangas KR. 2004. The National Comorbidity Survey Replication (NCS-R): background and aims. *Int. J. Methods Psychiatr. Res.* 13(2):60–68

Kessler RC, Price RH, Wortman CB. 1985. Social factors in psychopathology: stress, social support, and coping processes. *Annu. Rev. Psychol.* 36:531–72

Kessler RC, Sonnega A, Bromet E, Hughes M, Nelson CB. 1995. Posttraumatic stress disorder in the National Comorbidity Survey. *Arch. Gen. Psychiatry* 52(12):1048–60

Keverne EB, Curley JP. 2004. Vasopressin, oxytocin and social behaviour. *Curr. Opin. Neurobiol.* 14(6):777–83

Kilpatrick D, Resnick H. 1992. Posttraumatic stress disorder associated with exposure to criminal victimization in clinical and community populations. See Davidson & Foa 1992, pp. 243–50

Kim H, Somerville LH, Johnstone T, Polis S, Alexander AL, et al. 2004. Contextual modulation of amygdala responsivity to surprised faces. *J. Cogn. Neurosci.* 16(10):1730–45

King DW, King LA, Foy DW, Keane TM, Fairbank JA. 1999. Posttraumatic stress disorder in a national sample of female and male Vietnam veterans: risk factors, war-zone stressors, and resilience-recovery variables. *J. Abnorm. Psychol.* 108(1):164–70

King DW, King LA, Gudanowski DM, Vreven DL. 1995. Alternative representations of war zone stressors: relationships to posttraumatic stress disorder in male and female Vietnam veterans. *J. Abnorm. Psychol.* 104(1):184–95

King LA, King DW, Fairbank JA, Keane TM, Adams GA. 1998. Resilience-recovery factors in post-traumatic stress disorder among female and male Vietnam veterans: hardiness, post-war social support, and additional stressful life events. *J. Personal. Soc. Psychol.* 74(2):420–34

Kirsch P, Esslinger C, Chen Q, Mier D, Lis S, et al. 2005. Oxytocin modulates neural circuitry for social cognition and fear in humans. *J. Neurosci.* 25(49):11489–93

Koenen KC, Stellman JM, Stellman SD, Sommer JF Jr. 2003. Risk factors for course of post-traumatic stress disorder among Vietnam veterans: a 14-year follow-up of American Legionnaires. *J. Consult. Clin. Psychol.* 71(6):980–86

Koplewicz HS, Vogel JM, Solanto MV, Morrissey RF, Alonso CM, et al. 2002. Child and parent response to the 1993 World Trade Center bombing. *J. Trauma Stress* 15(1):77–85

Kosfeld M, Heinrichs M, Zak PJ, Fischbacher U, Fehr E. 2005. Oxytocin increases trust in humans. *Nature* 435(7042):673–76

Krupnick JL, Sotsky SM, Simmens S, Moyer J, Elkin I, et al. 1996. The role of the therapeutic alliance in psychotherapy and pharmacotherapy outcome: findings in the National

Institute of Mental Health Treatment of Depression Collaborative Research Program. *J. Consult. Clin. Psychol.* 64(3):532–39

Kulka RA, Schlenger WE, Fairbank JA, Hough RL, Jordan BK, et al. 1990. *Trauma and the Vietnam War Generation: Report of Findings from the National Vietnam Veterans Readjustment Study.* New York: Brunner/Mazel

Landolt MA, Boehler U, Schwager C, Schallberger U, Nuessli R. 1998. Post-traumatic stress disorder in pediatric patients and their parents: an exploratory study. *J. Paediatr. Child Health* 34(6):539–43

Laor N, Wolmer L, Cohen DJ. 2001. Mothers' functioning and children's symptoms 5 years after a Scud missile attack. *Am. J. Psychiatry* 158(7):1020–26

Laor N, Wolmer L, Mayes LC, Gershon A, Weizman R, Cohen DJ. 1997. Israeli preschool children under Scuds: a 30-month follow-up. *J. Am. Acad. Child Adolesc. Psychiatry* 36(3):349–56

LeDoux JE. 2000. Emotion circuits in the brain. *Annu. Rev. Neurosci.* 23:155–84

Levitt JT, Malta LS, Martin A, Davis L, Cloitre M. 2007. The flexible application of a manualized treatment for PTSD in survivors of the 9/11 World Trade Center attack. *Behav. Res. Ther.* 45(7):1419–33

Maestripieri D. 2005. Early experience affects the intergenerational transmission of infant abuse in rhesus monkeys. *Proc. Natl. Acad. Sci. USA* 102(27):9726–29

Maestripieri D, Higley JD, Lindell SG, Newman TK, McCormack KM, Sanchez MM. 2006a. Early maternal rejection affects the development of monoaminergic systems and adult abusive parenting in rhesus macaques (*Macaca mulatta*). *Behav. Neurosci.* 120(5):1017–24

Maestripieri D, Lindell SG, Higley JD. 2007. Intergenerational transmission of maternal behavior in rhesus macaques and its underlying mechanisms. *Dev. Psychobiol.* 49(2):165–71

Maestripieri D, McCormack K, Lindell SG, Higley JD, Sanchez MM. 2006b. Influence of parenting style on the offspring's behaviour and CSF monoamine metabolite levels in crossfostered and noncrossfostered female rhesus macaques. *Behav. Brain Res.* 175(1):90–95

March J. 1992. What constitutes a stressor? The "criterion A" issue. See Davidson & Foa 1992, pp. 37–54

Marmar CR, McCaslin SE, Metzler TJ, Best S, Weiss DS, et al. 2006. Predictors of posttraumatic stress in police and other first responders. *Ann. NY Acad. Sci.* 1071:1–18

Martin DJ, Garske JP, Davis MK. 2000. Relation of the therapeutic alliance with outcome and other variables: a meta-analytic review. *J. Consult. Clin. Psychol.* 68(3):438–50

McFarlane AC. 1987. Family functioning and overprotection following a natural disaster: the longitudinal effects of posttraumatic morbidity. *Aust. N.Z. J. Psychiatry* 21(2):210–18

Meaney MJ, Szyf M. 2005a. Environmental programming of stress responses through DNA methylation: life at the interface between a dynamic environment and a fixed genome. *Dialogues Clin. Neurosci.* 7(2):103–23

Meaney MJ, Szyf M. 2005b. Maternal care as a model for experience-dependent chromatin plasticity? *Trends Neurosci.* 28(9):456–63

Muran JC, Segal ZV, Samstag LW, Crawford CE. 1994. Patient pretreatment interpersonal problems in therapeutic alliance in short-term cognitive therapy. *J. Consult. Clin. Psychol.* 62(1):185–90

Nemeroff CB, Bremner JD, Foa EB, Mayberg HS, North CS, Stein MB. 2006. Posttraumatic stress disorder: a state-of-the-science review. *J. Psychiatr. Res.* 40(1):1–21

Norris FH, Kaniasty K. 1996. Received and perceived social support in times of stress: a test of the social support deterioration deterrence model. *J. Personal. Soc. Psychol.* 71(3):498–511

North CS, Spitznagel EL, Smith EM. 2001. A prospective study of coping after exposure to a mass murder episode. *Ann. Clin. Psychiatry* 13(2):81–87

North CS, Tivis L, McMillen JC, Pfefferbaum B, Cox J, et al. 2002. Coping, functioning, and adjustment of rescue workers after the Oklahoma City bombing. *J. Trauma Stress* 15(3):171–75

Olsson A, Ebert JP, Banaji MR, Phelps EA. 2005. The role of social groups in the persistence of learned fear. *Science* 309(5735):785–87

Ozer EJ, Best SR, Lipsey TL, Weiss DS. 2003. Predictors of posttraumatic stress disorder and symptoms in adults: a meta-analysis. *Psychol. Bull.* 129(1):52–73

Pare D, Quirk GJ, LeDoux JE. 2004. New vistas on amygdala networks in conditioned fear. *J. Neurophysiol.* 92(1):1–9

Pearlman LA, Courtois CA. 2005. Clinical applications of the attachment framework: relational treatment of complex trauma. *J. Trauma Stress* 18(5):449–59

Phelps EA. 2006. Emotion and cognition: insights from studies of the human amygdala. *Annu. Rev. Psychol.* 57:27–53

Phelps EA, LeDoux JE. 2005. Contributions of the amygdala to emotion processing: from animal models to human behavior. *Neuron* 48(2):175–87

Pilisuk M, Parks SH. 1986. *The Healing Web: Social Networks and Human Survival.* Hanover, NH: Univ. Press N. Engl.

Pitman RK, Delahanty DL. 2005. Conceptually driven pharmacologic approaches to acute trauma. *CNS Spectr.* 10(2):99–106

Pitman RK, Gilbertson MW, Gurvits TV, May FS, Lasko NB, et al. 2006. Clarifying the origin of biological abnormalities in PTSD through the study of identical twins discordant for combat exposure. *Ann. NY Acad. Sci.* 1071:242–54

Pitman RK, Orr SP, Lasko NB. 1993. Effects of intranasal vasopressin and oxytocin on physiologic responding during personal combat imagery in Vietnam veterans with posttraumatic stress disorder. *Psychiatry Res.* 48(2):107–17

Punamaki RL, Komproe I, Qouta S, El-Masri M, de Jong JT. 2005. The deterioration and mobilization effects of trauma on social support: childhood maltreatment and adulthood military violence in a Palestinian community sample. *Child Abuse Negl.* 29(4):351–73

Pynoos RS, Steinberg AM, Wraith R. 1995. A developmental model of childhood traumatic stress. In *Developmental Psychopathology.* Volume 2: *Risk, Disorders, and Adaptation,* ed. D Cicchetti, DJ Cohen, pp. 72–95. New York: Wiley

Quirk GJ, Garcia R, Gonzalez-Lima F. 2006. Prefrontal mechanisms in extinction of conditioned fear. *Biol. Psychiatry* 60(4):337–43

Rauch SL, Shin LM, Phelps EA. 2006. Neurocircuitry models of posttraumatic stress disorder and extinction: human neuroimaging research—past, present, and future. *Biol. Psychiatry* 60(4):376–82

Raue PJ, Goldfried MR. 1994. The therapeutic alliance in cognitive-behavioral therapy. In *The Working Alliance: Theory, Research, and Practice,* ed. AO Horvath, LS Greenberg, pp. 131–52. Oxford, UK: Wiley

Rothbaum BO, Davis M. 2003. Applying learning principles to the treatment of post-trauma reactions. *Ann. NY Acad. Sci.* 1008:112–21

Rothbaum BO, Foa EB. 1999. *Reclaiming Your Life After Rape: Cognitive Behavioral Therapy for Posttraumatic Stress Disorder.* New York: Oxford Univ. Press

Runtz MG, Schallow JR. 1997. Social support and coping strategies as mediators of adult adjustment following childhood maltreatment. *Child Abuse Negl.* 21(2):211–26

Saigh P, Yasik A, Sack W, Koplewicz H. 1999. Child-adolescent posttraumatic stress disorder: prevalence, risk factors, and comorbidity. In *Posttraumatic Stress Disorder: A Comprehensive Text*, ed. P Saigh, JD Bremner, pp. 18–43. Boston: Allyn & Bacon

Sarason BR, Shearin EN, Pierce GR, Sarason IG. 1987. Interrelations of social support measures: theoretical and practical implications. *J. Personal. Soc. Psychol.* 52(4):813–32

Saxe GN, Stoddard F, Hall E, Chawla N, Lopez C, et al. 2005. Pathways to PTSD. Part I: Children with burns. *Am. J. Psychiatry* 162(7):1299–304

Schechter DS, Zeanah CH Jr, Myers MM, Brunelli SA, Liebowitz MR, et al. 2004. Psychobiological dysregulation in violence-exposed mothers: salivary cortisol of mothers with very young children pre- and postseparation stress. *Bull. Menninger Clin.* 68(4):319–36

Scheeringa MS, Zeanah CH. 1995. Symptom expression and trauma variables in children under 48 months of age. *Infant Ment. Health J.* 16:259–70

Scheeringa MS, Zeanah CH. 2001. A relational perspective on PTSD in early childhood. *J. Trauma Stress* 14(4):799–815

Schumm JA, Briggs-Phillips M, Hobfoll SE. 2006. Cumulative interpersonal traumas and social support as risk and resiliency factors in predicting PTSD and depression among inner-city women. *J. Trauma Stress* 19(6):825–36

Seckl JR, Meaney MJ. 2006. Glucocorticoid "programming" and PTSD risk. *Ann. NY Acad. Sci.* 1071:351–78

Shalev AY. 1997. Treatment of prolonged posttraumatic stress disorder learning from experience. *J. Trauma Stress* 10(3):415–23

Shalev AY, Freedman S. 2005. PTSD following terrorist attacks: a prospective evaluation. *Am. J. Psychiatry* 162(6):1188–91

Shannon C, Schwandt ML, Champoux M, Shoaf SE, Suomi SJ, et al. 2005. Maternal absence and stability of individual differences in CSF 5-HIAA concentrations in rhesus monkey infants. *Am. J. Psychiatry* 162(9):1658–64

Shields A, Cicchetti D. 1997. Emotion regulation among school-age children: the development and validation of a new criterion Q-sort scale. *Dev. Psychol.* 33(6):906–16

Shields A, Cicchetti D. 1998. Reactive aggression among maltreated children: the contributions of attention and emotion dysregulation. *J. Clin. Child Psychol.* 27(4):381–95

Shin LM, Rauch SL, Pitman RK. 2006. Amygdala, medial prefrontal cortex, and hippocampal function in PTSD. *Ann. NY Acad. Sci.* 1071:67–79

Shinn M, Lehmann S, Wong NW. 1984. Social interaction and social support. *J. Soc. Issues* 40(4):55–76

Silva RR, Alpert M, Munoz DM, Singh S, Matzner F, Dummit S. 2000. Stress and vulnerability to posttraumatic stress disorder in children and adolescents. *Am. J. Psychiatry* 157(8):1229–35

Silver RC, Holman EA, McIntosh DN, Poulin M, Gil-Rivas V. 2002. Nationwide longitudinal study of psychological responses to September 11. *JAMA* 288(10):1235–44

Sroufe LA, Fox NE, Pancake VR. 1983. Attachment and dependency in developmental perspective. *Child Dev.* 54(6):1615–27

Stiles WB, Agnew-Davies R, Hardy GE, Barkham M, Shapiro DA. 1998. Relations of the alliance with psychotherapy outcome: findings in the second Sheffield Psychotherapy Project. *J. Consult. Clin. Psychol.* 66(5):791–802

Suess GJ, Grossmann KE, Sroufe LA. 1992. Effects of infant attachment to mother and father on quality of adaptation in preschool: from dyadic to individual organisation of self. *Int. J. Behav. Dev.* 15(1):43–65

Summerfield D, Hume F. 1993. War and posttraumatic stress disorder: the question of social context. *J. Nerv. Ment. Dis.* 181(8):522

Suomi SJ. 2005. Aggression and social behaviour in rhesus monkeys. *Novartis Found. Symp.* 268:216–26

Ullman SE. 1996a. Do social reactions to sexual assault victims vary by support provider? *Violence Vict.* 11(2):143–57

Ullman SE. 1996b. Social reactions, coping strategies, and self-blame attributions in adjustment to sexual assault. *Psychol. Women Q.* 20(4):505–26

Ullman SE, Filipas HH. 2001. Predictors of PTSD symptom severity and social reactions in sexual assault victims. *J. Trauma Stress* 14(2):369–89

Watson JC, Greenberg LS. 1994. The alliance in experiential therapy: enacting the relationship conditions. In *The Working Alliance: Theory, Research and Practice*, ed. AO Horvath, LS Greenberg, pp. 153–72. Oxford, UK: Wiley

Winston JS, Strange BA, O'Doherty J, Dolan RJ. 2002. Automatic and intentional brain responses during evaluation of trustworthiness of faces. *Nat. Neurosci.* 5(3):277–83

Wyatt G, Mickey M. 1987. Ameliorating the effects of child sexual abuse: an exploratory study of support by parents and others. *J. Interpers. Violence* 2:403–14

Yehuda R. 2006. Advances in understanding neuroendocrine alterations in PTSD and their therapeutic implications. *Ann. NY Acad. Sci.* 1071:137–66

Yehuda R, Blair W, Labinsky E, Bierer LM. 2007. Effects of parental PTSD on the cortisol response to dexamethasone administration in their adult offspring. *Am. J. Psychiatry* 164(1):163–66

Yehuda R, Halligan SL, Grossman R. 2001. Childhood trauma and risk for PTSD: relationship to intergenerational effects of trauma, parental PTSD, and cortisol excretion. *Dev. Psychopathol.* 13(3):733–53

Yeomans FE, Gutfreund J, Selzer MA, Clarkin JF, Hull SW, Smith TE. 1994. Factors related to drop-outs by borderline patients: treatment contract and therapeutic alliance. *J. Psychother. Pract. Res.* 3(1):16–24

Young LJ, Wang Z. 2004. The neurobiology of pair bonding. *Nat. Neurosci.* 7(10):1048–54

Zoellner LA, Foa EB, Brigidi BD. 1999. Interpersonal friction and PTSD in female victims of sexual and nonsexual assault. *J. Trauma Stress* 12(4):689–700

Spontaneous Inferences, Implicit Impressions, and Implicit Theories

James S. Uleman, S. Adil Saribay,
and Celia M. Gonzalez

Department of Psychology, New York University, New York, New York 10003;
email: jim.uleman@nyu.edu, adil@nyu.edu, cmg250@nyu.edu

Annu. Rev. Psychol. 2008. 59:329–60

First published online as a Review in Advance on
September 12, 2007

The *Annual Review of Psychology* is online at
http://psych.annualreviews.org

This article's doi:
10.1146/annurev.psych.59.103006.093707

0066-4308/08/0203-0329$20.00

Key Words

automaticity, causality, folk psychology, traits, embodied
cognition, personhood

Abstract

People make social inferences without intentions, awareness, or effort, i.e., spontaneously. We review recent findings on spontaneous
social inferences (especially traits, goals, and causes) and closely related phenomena. We then describe current thinking on some of the
most relevant processes, implicit knowledge, and theories. These include automatic and controlled processes and their interplay; embodied cognition, including mimicry; and associative versus rule-based
processes. Implicit knowledge includes adult folk theories, conditions of personhood, self-knowledge to simulate others, and cultural
and social class differences. Implicit theories concern Bayesian networks, recent attribution research, and questions about the utility of
the disposition-situation dichotomy. Developmental research provides new insights. Spontaneous social inferences include a growing
array of phenomena, but they have been insufficiently linked to other
phenomena and theories. We hope the links suggested in this review
begin to remedy this.

Contents

INTRODUCTION

Over the past 20 years, evidence has grown that much, if not most, social behavior is governed by implicit, even automatic processes: implicit attitudes, inferences, goals and theories, and the affect and behaviors they produce (e.g., Bargh 2007, Hassin et al. 2005a). This has transformed our views of how people understand others. During the late 1960s and '70s, research on understanding others focused on self-reports of attributions of causality and responsibility. Then social cognition famously engulfed the field, using person memory paradigms and studies of errors and biases to understand how we process information about others. These approaches continue to yield rich rewards and have become part of normal science in social psychology. More recently, researchers in several other fields (developmental and cognitive psychology, neuroscience, and philosophy of mind) have made exciting theoretical and empirical advances that shed new light on social psychology's oldest questions; these researchers often call their work "social cognition," without reference to social psychology.

Within social psychology, spontaneous social inferences and implicit impressions of others have been widely documented. They occur and affect downstream events without our awareness or intentions. This review surveys the most recent work as well as some of the most important developments in related fields to suggest how they point to new directions for research on implicit impressions. It is beyond the scope of this brief review to consider other important related topics such as stereotyping (Major & O'Brien 2005), emotional intelligence (Mayer et al. 2008), accuracy in person perception (Kenny 2004), and social neuroscience (e.g., Lieberman 2007, Todorov et al. 2007).

IMPLICIT IMPRESSIONS

Implicit impressions of other people are not open to self-report. They include implicit attitudes toward others, implicit knowledge structures, implicit theories, and implicit behavioral tendencies. Uleman et al. (2005) described the wide range of evidence for the existence of implicit impressions, the ways in which they occur and have effects automatically, how they affect trait judgments of others, how the effects of simultaneous implicit and explicit impressions can be empirically distinguished, and how they may relate to errors in judging how well one knows someone, stereotypes, and ingroup/outgroup perceptions. We update that review in several areas.

Inferences Based on Faces

Faces play a special role in social perception, allowing us to easily distinguish individuals, establish mutual gaze, and infer "social category, identity, emotion, and psychological and physical traits, as well as the interdependence of attributes" (Zebrowitz 2006, p. 663, in Bodenhausen & Macrae 2006). Here we highlight recent findings most relevant to our main theme.

Social categories are extracted from faces very early in processing (Ito & Urland 2003), even when the faces are irrelevant to the task or presented suboptimally (e.g., inverted). But spontaneous categorization of faces may require a conceptual/semantic goal in the focal task (Macrae et al. 2005). Category-based construal of faces seems to be more efficient than identity-based construal (i.e., individuation), and this may underlie people's heavy reliance on categories in person perception (Cloutier et al. 2005). Personality traits can be inferred after 100 ms exposure to faces, though confidence increases and target impressions become more differentiated with more time (Willis & Todorov 2006). Perceivers' judgments of competence, after only one-second exposures to pairs of political candidates' faces, predict real-world election outcomes and margins of victory (Todorov et al. 2005).

Physiognomic information from faces affects interpreting other (verbal) information

about actors ("reading from faces"), and information about actors' personalities affects perception of their faces ("reading into faces") (Hassin & Trope 2000). Social categories are read into categorically ambiguous static faces (Eberhardt et al. 2003, Huart et al. 2005) and into dynamic facial expressions of emotions (Hugenberg & Bodenhausen 2003).

Impressions are also affected by subtle facial resemblances. When a connectionist network, trained to distinguish anomalous and baby faces from normal adult faces, was presented with novel normal adult faces, the extent to which anomalous and baby-face output units became activated (i.e., the extent to which the network "confused" normal faces with anomalous or baby faces) predicted human judges' trait impressions of these faces. The similarity of faces from particular categories (e.g., elderly) to anomalous and baby faces may partially explain stereotypes of those people (e.g., "unhealthy" and "weak," respectively) (Zebrowitz et al. 2003). Faces with more Afrocentric features attract more attention in the context of African American stereotype concepts (Eberhardt et al. 2004) and are seen to have more stereotypic African Americans attributes, even when they are European American (Blair et al. 2002, Maddox 2004). Since it is subtler, bias based on facial features might be harder to control than that based on categories (Blair et al. 2004).

Inferences Based on Behaviors

Spontaneous trait inferences. Spontaneous trait inferences (STIs) have usually been made from verbal descriptions of behavior, in the lab. For example, Todorov & Uleman (2003) used a false recognition paradigm to examine the automaticity of binding STIs to representations of actors. Participants under memory instructions viewed 60 pairs of actor photos and trait-implying behaviors (e.g., a woman's photo with "Alice solved the mystery halfway through the book," implying that she is clever). Then for a series of photo-trait pairs, they judged whether the trait had been explicit in the sentence with that photo. False recognition rates for implied traits paired with actual actors, relative to other actors, measured STIs. STIs occurred with very brief (two-second) initial exposures, when participants' goal was shallow processing (counting nouns) rather than memorization and when they were under a concurrent cognitive load. These findings suggest that STIs are automatically bound to actor representations.

Ham & Vonk (2003) obtained simultaneous trait and situational inferences from the same participants. Critical sentences (e.g., "John gets an A on the test") implied both traits ("smart") and properties of objects ("easy"). Probe recognition results showed both STIs and spontaneous situational inferences (SSIs). Ham & Vonk (2003, Study 2) used the savings-in-relearning paradigm and asked participants to form impressions of the actor, the situation, or the whole event. Later they learned associations between these implications and abstract cues associated with the sentences. Savings in this relearning task (evidence of prior spontaneous inferences) occurred for both traits and situations. And consistent with earlier findings for STIs, savings were unaffected by goal instructions.

Based on such findings, Ham & Vonk (2003) proposed an interesting integration of spontaneous and intentional inferences in person perception. Multiple (even inconsistent) inferences are made spontaneously in the first stage of the familiar three-stage models of person perception (Gilbert 1989, Trope & Alfieri 1997). In the second stage, goal-inconsistent inferences (if any) are automatically inhibited. Then remaining inferences are intentionally corrected or adjusted in the third stage. More direct tests of this proposal would be useful, especially if they included ambiguous behaviors.

These procedures might suggest that STI only occurs during text comprehension, and not during perception of raw behavior. However, Fiedler & Schenck (2001) showed that viewing static silhouettes of dyads that im-

ply traits (e.g., caring, mean) produces STI. They found shorter response times for identifying degraded trait words when preceded by silhouettes implying these traits. In Study 2, based on the Linguistic Category Model, identifying degraded trait words was preceded by a "verification task" designed to manipulate the level of linguistic abstraction about the silhouettes. Counterintuitively, the largest effect of silhouettes on trait word identification (STI) occurred when the intervening verification task was most concrete, involving direct action verbs rather than state verbs or adjectives. Thus, "focusing on the picture and refraining from abstract semantic interpretations…serves to enhance the STI" (Fiedler & Schenck 2001, p. 1543). Other evidence suggested that goals were also spontaneously inferred, even more quickly than traits.

Fiedler et al. (2005) replicated these findings with silhouettes and 15-second film clips. They also demonstrated simultaneous spontaneous inferences about both subjects (agents) and objects in dyadic interactions. The intervening verification task affected all these effects, suggesting that spontaneous encodings can be manipulated in several, sometimes counterintuitive, ways. Thus the verification task's verb type affected the target of spontaneous inferences, and verification "fit" with the dyadic behavior either closed off elaborative inferences (when fit was good) or left them "open" (when fit was poor). This interesting paradigm merits further research, particularly because of the many processes apparently invoked by the verification task that have opposing effects (semantic priming and inhibition, memory processes producing the picture superiority effect, open and closed mind-sets, etc.).

STI is also affected by individual differences such as perceivers' trait hostility and induced anger (Tiedens 2001). Others have used STI to characterize repressors (Caldwell & Newman 2005) and persons with chronic moral concerns (Narvaez et al. 2006). Tormala & Petty (2001) showed that perceivers high in the need to evaluate are more likely to spontaneously evaluate a target person online. They suggested this finding challenges the ubiquity of STI. However, we value these findings for indicating STI boundary conditions. STI refers to inferring the trait implication of a single (or very few related) behavior(s) and integrating that with the actor representation. As their results indicate, integrating meanings and/or evaluations of one target's many behaviors is less likely to occur spontaneously and requires high levels of relevant chronic goals.

STIs and stereotypes. Stereotypes of actors' social categories affect STIs. Wigboldus et al. (2003) examined how much reading about actors' stereotypic (or counterstereotypic or neutral) behaviors activates the trait concepts implied by the behavior. Stereotype-inconsistent (compared to stereotype-consistent or -neutral) STIs were inhibited. With ample cognitive resources, inhibition of stereotype-inconsistent inferences is attenuated (Wigboldus et al. 2004). Furthermore, processing goals dramatically influence the effect of stereotype-inconsistent information. Gonzalez et al. (2007) found that, as above, spontaneous processing inhibits STIs. But intentional processing (impression formation) produces stronger (more extreme) trait ratings for stereotype-inconsistent than stereotypic or neutral information. This latter effect is consistent with Biernat's (2005) shift-of-standards model, in which social categories shift the meaning of subjective scales, whereas the STI effect fits a simpler spreading activation/inhibition model. Thus, behavior-based trait inferences are influenced by stereotypes, and the direction of influence depends on perceivers' processing capacity and goals, including whether impression formation is spontaneous or intentional.

Spontaneous trait transference and evaluative conditioning. Considerable research has investigated when spontaneous trait transference (STT) does and does not occur, and many differences between STT and STI have

been identified. STT effect sizes are typically half those of STI. Carlston & Skowronski (2005), who discovered STT (Skowronski et al. 1998), proposed that STI entails attributional processing, whereas STT entails mere associations. They asked participants to familiarize themselves with a series of photo-behavior pairs in which those pictured described either themselves or someone else (of the other gender and not pictured). Participants then rated the people in the photos on several traits. Negative behaviors had more impact than did positive behaviors on STIs (from self-descriptions), consistent with attributional processing, but valence did not affect STTs (from describing others), which is more characteristic of associative processing. Study 2 ruled out encoding or retrieval errors as causes of STT, as did Study 3 (Carlston & Skowronski 2005). Study 3 also showed that asking whom the behaviors had described eliminated STT but increased STI. Participants were not affected by warnings to avoid STTs. All this suggests that "perceivers simply associate the informants with the trait implications of those descriptions . . . [which] then have an implicit effect on later impressions" (Carlston & Skowronski 2005, p. 895), and that STT is "unintentional and unconscious" (p. 896).

There are other dissociations. STIs are stronger for targets in low- rather than high-entitativity groups, as if they are more individuated. STT among such group members is weak. But the reverse (weaker STI and stronger within-group STT) occurs for members of high-entitativity groups (Crawford et al. 2002). Carlston & Mae's (2007) participants familiarized themselves with photos paired with trait-implying symbols (e.g., a flag) rather than sentences. STI but not STT effects were sensitive to the symbols' valence and memorability. Finally, Mae et al. (1999) showed that STT to popular celebrities is unaffected by prior knowledge of the celebrities. It seems likely (although it is untested) that STI is affected by prior knowledge of the actor.

Spontaneous trait transference (STT): a process wherein one person ("informant") describes another person's trait-implying behavior, and the trait implication of the behavior becomes associated with the informant

Crawford et al. (2007b) found that when participants' goal was to judge whether the trait-implying behaviors were reported truthfully, STT was unaffected, whereas STI was reduced entirely (Study 1) or almost (Study 2) to the level of STT. In their view, these and prior results suggest that in STT, behavior is categorized in trait terms; this category is associatively linked to informants at encoding, and this linked category is then used to respond to subsequent tasks. In contrast, STI involves inferring that the behavior category reflects the actor's trait at encoding. For some reason, truth detection interferes with such inferences but not with associations. These results also show that STI is surprisingly easy to disrupt, and STI is more goal dependent in this sense than was previously thought.

Does STT depend on the actor being absent at encoding? Todorov & Uleman (2004) showed that false recognition of implied traits is higher when they are paired with actors than when implied traits are paired with others who were also present at encoding. This was true even after a one-week delay as well as when there was equal attention to each photo at encoding and when targets had different physical orientations at test. However, these studies did not assess STT per se. Crawford et al. (2007a) did assess STT and found that when actors and either informants or bystanders were presented simultaneously with behaviors, STT did not occur, but STI did. One possible reason for this is that actors attracted more attention and processing. Unlike the studies of Todorov & Uleman (2004), these studies did not ensure equal attention to both photos at encoding. But Goren & Todorov (2007) ensured equal attention in four studies using false recognition and trait ratings. STT occurred only when actors were absent at encoding. Thus, STIs bind only to actors when they are there, but to other faces when they are not, producing STTs.

STT is a subtle way for informants to influence others' impressions of themselves. Even pairing people randomly with dogs associated with particular traits affects person impressions (Mae et al. 2004). Observers also attribute informant traits that differ from the direct implications of what informants say by inferring what kind of a person would say such things (Mae & Carlston 2005). Such meta-inferences may also be implicit.

Person evaluations are also subject to associative effects. In the "spreading attitude effect" based on evaluative conditioning, pairing a liked or disliked person (unconditioned stimulus, or US) with a formerly neutral person (conditioned stimulus, or CS) not only causes the CS person to acquire the valence of the US person, but also causes other persons associated only with the CS person to acquire the same valence (Walther 2002). This effect does not reflect cognitive balance, does not depend on awareness of contingencies, is resistant to extinction, and is enhanced under cognitive load. Cognitive balance processes can also affect evaluations of targets described by informants, when perceivers have prior attitudes toward the informants. So both implicit and explicit "attitudes toward targets were more positive when they were liked than when they were disliked by positive source [i.e., informant] individuals. In contrast, attitudes toward targets were less positive when they were liked than when they were disliked by negative source individuals" (Gawronski et al. 2005, p. 621).

Inferences Based on Relational Knowledge

Implicit impressions can be influenced by situationally triggered or chronically accessible relational knowledge. A clear example is the social-cognitive process of transference, in which the mental representation of a significant other is activated and applied to a novel person who bears minimal resemblance to this significant other (for a review, see Andersen & Saribay 2005). This happens unconsciously (Glassman & Andersen 1999). In transference, responses to a new person (e.g., how the new person is evaluated) are best predicted by the global qualities (e.g., positivity) of the significant-other representation.

Goals in important relationships can also influence perception of strangers. For instance, when people had a goal to understand a close friend and were subliminally primed with the name of this friend, they tried harder to understand a new person, as indicated by more situational attributions for that person's behavior (Fitzsimons & Bargh 2003). (See the review by Chen et al. 2007.)

OTHER SPONTANEOUS SOCIAL INFERENCES

Spontaneous Goal Inferences

Goals can be inferred spontaneously. In a study by Hassin et al. (2005b), participants read goal-implying sentences and then were given an unexpected cued-recall test, a probe recognition test, or lexical decision trials. Goals were spontaneously inferred, even from behaviors in which goal attainment was blocked (see also Fiedler & Schenck 2001).

Spontaneous goal inferences affect behavior. Aarts et al. (2004) showed that, given the opportunity, people will act on these goals even though they are unconscious and of unknown origin (goal contagion). However, if the inferred goal is unacceptable in some way (e.g., pursued by the actor through inappropriate means), then goal contagion does not occur and the goal is devalued. Goal contagion differs from mimicry (described below) in functioning like primed goals and having similar effects (e.g., Moskowitz et al. 2004). Furthermore, goal contagion can be deactivated through the co-occurrence of negative affect (Aarts et al. 2007).

Spontaneous Counterfactuals and Contradictions

Counterfactuals come to mind spontaneously, especially when events prompt negative affect (Roese et al. 2005) and provide a "but for" basis for inferring causality. Strong sit-

uational constraints prompt counterfactuals about what an actor would have done but for those constraints (Miller et al. 2005), and these influence trait attributions. Though counterfactuals may be triggered by situational cues, their content is also determined by perceivers' preexisting attitudes (e.g., Tetlock & Visser 2000) in ways that support initial attitudes and can serve to reaffirm and strengthen them (Crawford & McCrea 2004).

Actors' characteristics are represented differently when terms for the characteristics' negations come readily to mind (Sam is not warm → Sam is cold) than when they do not (Sam is not creative → Sam is?). This affects how person information is remembered, integrated with new information, and judged on truth-value (Mayo et al. 2004). Consistent with this, Hasson et al. (2005) showed that relations between comprehending statements and judging their truth-value depend on whether their negation is informative. As a consequence, when suspicion or distrust is aroused, words are only more likely to activate their opposites if a logical opposite comes to mind (Schul et al. 2004). Thus, semantic structures, preexisting attitudes and expectations, as well as episodes' logical possibilities constrain the spontaneous generation of counterfactuals and contradictions.

Spontaneous Belief Inferences

One counterfactual prominent in developmental research (discussed below) is false beliefs about the state of the world. Children younger than four years have difficulty representing others' false beliefs about reality while simultaneously maintaining a veridical representation of reality themselves. Apperly et al. (2006) devised an "incidental false-belief task" to see whether adults infer others' false beliefs automatically. Participants watched a visual display of a box and an observer, who was briefly absent while the location of the box was changed, and who then returned. When asked to track the location of the box, participants took longer to indicate where the observer believed the box was than where it actually was, whereas those who tracked the observer's belief answered both questions equally fast (2.2 s). Given this single test and the multifaceted nature of automaticity, their conclusion that "belief reasoning is not automatic" (Apperly et al. 2006, p. 844) is premature (see below). But this study raises important questions about which mental states are spontaneously inferred, and when.

Spontaneous Value Inferences

People spontaneously infer values relevant to social situations and even cultures. In a study by Ham & Van den Bos (2006), participants read vignettes about just and unjust situations, e.g., arbitrary grading procedures or unequal pay for equal work, and responded to recognition probes such as "just" or "unfair." Spontaneous justice inferences were stronger when the protagonists in the vignettes were personally relevant, i.e., described as "you" rather than "he/she," or "a friend" rather than "a stranger." Most interestingly, explicit justice judgments are not moderated by personal relevance (Ham & Van den Bos 2007). So personal relevance produces a dissociation between implicit and explicit justice inferences.

Fu et al. (2007) used the probe recognition paradigm to show that sentences with strong cultural referents (e.g., "A great emperor once produced an underground army of clay warriors") spontaneously activate that culture's values (e.g., obedience, modesty), even though they lack semantic or personal relevance to the sentence or actor. Bicultural participants not only showed such activations to Chinese and American cultural sentences (whereas Americans showed this only to American sentences), but they also showed rapid cultural frame switching between sentences within the same study session.

Broader Questions

To summarize, when we learn about or observe strangers performing trait-implying behaviors, we unintentionally and unconsciously (spontaneously) attribute traits (and goals) to them, creating implicit impressions. Though automatic in several senses, this inference process (STI) can be disrupted by some processing goals. It takes account of stereotypes about the actor. It is more complex than merely associating the activated trait category with someone, although this STT-linking process probably contributes to STI effects and has interesting consequences in its own right. Furthermore, relational knowledge activated during person perception affects implicit impressions. Spontaneous social inferences are not restricted to traits and goals.

Of course, we also form impressions of others intentionally. So one important question concerns how spontaneous (largely automatic) and intentional (controlled) processes interact. Other broad dichotomies seem particularly relevant to implicit impressions: abstract versus embodied cognition, and associative versus rule-based cognition (as in STT linking versus STI thinking, respectively). There is important progress on elaborating the (largely implicit) folk psychology that supports inferences about others. Another basic content domain (fundamental to traditional research on causal attribution) concerns causality: what it means, the role it plays in categories central to person perception, and how to model it. Finally, recent research on person perception in children, especially before language, supports symbolic reasoning and offers important insights.

BASIC PROCESSING DICHOTOMIES

Dual-process theories are widespread in social psychology (Chaiken & Trope 1999, Kruglanski & Orehek 2007). In this section, we describe the relevance of some of the most important ones to implicit impressions.

Automatic Versus Controlled Processes

This dichotomy has played a major role in the past 25 years of research in social psychology (see Andersen et al. 2007 for a review), even though control is only one of the four horsemen of automaticity singled out by Bargh (1994). As the impact of automatic processes extended to more and more phenomena previously considered intentional and controlled (Bargh 2007), some have been prompted to empirically examine the ways in which free will is illusory (Wegner 2005). Of course, this dichotomy is an oversimplification in at least three ways. First, automaticity refers to several features of cognitive processes, and these do not always covary. Second, control in the sense of self-regulation can be automatic and unconscious (Andersen et al. 2007, Hassin et al. 2005a). Third and most important, even when control is intended and conscious, controlled and automatic processes interact. As Jacoby (1991) has long noted, "no tasks are process pure." There are now techniques for separating effects of automatic and controlled processes on performance in several tasks relevant to person perception, and for modeling their interactions.

Uleman et al. (2005) used Jacoby's process dissociation procedure (PDP) to separately estimate effects of automatic and controlled processes in using STI-based implicit impressions. This work decomposes not the processes of forming STIs, but rather the processes involved in using STIs and explicit memory for intentional judgments. The PDP involves task performance under two conditions: an "inclusion" condition in which automatic and controlled processes both contribute to optimal performance, and an "exclusion" condition in which they are pitted against each other. The difference in performance in these two conditions provides an estimate of control. Thus, "automatic" means uncontrolled or uncontrollable. Participants rated actors who had previously been studied for a memory test, while paired with trait-implying behaviors that produced STIs. Then in an inclusion condition, they included any prior impression they could access in their trait ratings. In the exclusion condition, they tried to recall the behavior to exclude what-

ever bias it might create in forming impressions from the faces alone. Trait ratings were made immediately, after a 20-minute delay, or after a two-day delay. PDP estimates showed a significant effect of automatic processes on these ratings, regardless of delay. However (as expected), effects of controlled processes were significant immediately and after 20 minutes, but fell to nonsignificant after two days.

These studies demonstrate the feasibility of using the PDP to separate automatic from controlled effects of implicit impressions on trait ratings and show that both kinds of processes contribute to such ratings. It would be informative to include STT in such studies, to estimate and compare effects of automatic and controlled processes on trait ratings from STT and STI.

Payne et al. (2005; also Payne 2005) described a PDP approach to attitudes' (stereotypes') effects on behavior. Their results illustrate the utility of distinguishing automatic from controlled processes in responses to Black and White actors in Payne's weapon/tool task (Payne 2001). They showed that "participants were not 'blinded' by race so that they could only discriminate between weapons and tools when they inhibited the race bias. Instead, the actual objects and racial bias served as separate bases for responding, with decisions based on perceptual discrimination requiring cognitive control. When that control failed, the automatic race bias had its effect" (Payne et al. 2005, p. 415). The PDP also allowed Lambert et al. (2003) to show that a counterintuitive finding—more prejudiced behavior in an anticipated public (versus private) setting—occurred because the anticipation of behaving in public decreased cognitive control.

Conrey et al. (2005) generalized this approach to cases where two automatic and two controlled processes might operate; hence, their quad model. Using multinomial modeling to analyze responses to the Implicit Association Test (IAT) and Payne's task, they showed that the model "disentangles the influences of 4 distinct processes...: the

Four horsemen of automaticity: lack of awareness, lack of intention, cognitive efficiency, and lack of control

Process dissociation procedure (PDP): yields separate estimates of the effects of automatic and controlled processes on the same task

Payne's weapon/tool task: asks participants to rapidly judge whether an object is a weapon or tool. African American primes increase mistaking tools for weapons

Amodal: lacking or stripped of features that characterize particular sensory modalities

likelihood that automatic bias is activated by a stimulus; that a correct response can be determined; that automatic bias is overcome; and that, in the absence of other information, a guessing bias drives responses" (Conrey et al. 2005, p. 469). Thus, multiple simultaneous interacting automatic and controlled processes can be modeled and their separate effects estimated.

Burke & Uleman (2006) extended this work to effects of STI on trait ratings, as in Uleman et al. (2005). Participants viewed 80 face-behavior pairs for six seconds each, followed by a distracter task. Then they rated each of the 80 faces. Statistical procedures for separately estimating individual differences in trait scale use were added to the quad model. Parameter estimates were generally as predicted. Faces automatically activated the implied trait; participants were very poor at intentionally determining the correct response (i.e., recalling the paired behavior); participants overcame the automatic activation bias whenever they could determine the correct response; guessing was low; and including participants as a random effect accounted for significant variance.

All this demonstrates the advantages of using multinomial modeling (e.g., the quad model) to decompose component processes that underlie the use of implicit impressions (including STIs and stereotypes). These methods also put the focus back on control and enable us to test models that are more sophisticated and go beyond the false dichotomy of automatic versus controlled processes. (See also social neuroscience models of automatic and controlled processes, e.g., Amodio et al. 2004, Lieberman 2007.)

Abstract, Amodal, Disembodied Cognition Versus Situated, Modal, Embodied Cognition

Cognitive science has long harbored a "disembodied" view of cognition. The computer metaphor of the mind assumes an amodal architecture, despite little supporting evidence (Barsalou 1999). An alternative approach, usually called "embodied cognition," takes a modal view of knowledge representation (see Barsalou 2008) in which, "[w]hen a category is represented conceptually, the neural systems that processed it during perception and action become active" (Barsalou 2003, p. 523). This is not to say that perceptual and conceptual systems are isomorphic, but rather that they are nonmodular and employ common structures and processes.

Although social psychological conceptualizations of cognition are still primarily amodal, the field is replete with demonstrations of embodiment in both knowledge acquisition and knowledge use; see Niedenthal et al. 2005 for a review. Smith & Semin (2004), guided by their "situated social cognition" framework, integrate many of these demonstrations. For instance, the principle that "cognition is for action" implies that person "impressions are action-oriented representations"; that is, that "relational interdependence and its action implications are integral to the way we represent people" (Smith & Semin 2004, p. 64).

Mimicry as evidence of online embodied implicit impressions. Nonconscious behavioral mimicry provides evidence of implicit impressions that are clearly situated and embodied. A wide range of actions, such as facial expressions, body postures and gestures, speech patterns, and emotional states of others, are mimicked by perceivers without awareness (see Chartrand et al. 2005 for a review). This is a critical social skill whose impairment is related to difficulty in inferring others' mental states, such as emotions (McIntosh et al. 2006).

Nonconscious mimicry also suggests a direct yet flexible perception-behavior link (Dijksterhuis et al. 2007). Factors that facilitate (versus inhibit) how much a perceiver mimics a target person include induced positive (versus negative) mood (van Baaren et al. 2006), dispositional empathic ability (Sonnby-Borgström et al. 2003), and heightened affiliation needs (Lakin & Chartrand 2003). Thus, mimicry provides an unconscious means of accomplishing social goals (see also Chartrand & Dalton 2007).

Associative Versus Rule-Based Processes

Smith & DeCoster (2000) argued for the existence of two processing modes that function simultaneously. Associative processing depends on "associations that are structured by similarity and contiguity and are learned over many experiences. [It] occurs automatically and preconsciously, with awareness of the result of processing." Rule-based processing depends on "symbolically represented rules that are structured by language and logic and can be learned in just one or a few experiences. [It] occurs optionally when capacity and motivation are present and often with conscious awareness of steps of processing" (Smith & DeCoster 2000, p. 111). They used this dichotomy to integrate and extend many other domain-specific dual-process models in social psychology. Whereas earlier models of person perception and attribution tended to posit sequential steps or mutually exclusive modes of information processing, Smith & DeCoster (2000) suggest these modes function simultaneously (see also Lieberman et al. 2002). For example, reactions to stigmatized persons online demonstrate that each mode has its own time course and that they "interact dynamically over time to produce not only subjective states in the perceiver . . . but also overt behavior" (Pryor et al. 2004, p. 438). Smith & DeCoster (2000) note that "associative memory systems can perform attributional reasoning . . . and can combine multiple knowledge structures" (p. 128), contrary to the common assumption that such systems are unsophisticated and that attributions must rely on rule-based processes.

Useful as this distinction is, it does not capture all the differences between STI and STT described above. STT "associations" occur on a single trial, rather than being gradually established. Would multiple STT trials strengthen their effects, perhaps to the level of STI effects? Is STI best characterized as associative or rule-based? Neither STI nor STT results from the conscious deliberation that is often identified with rule-based learning.

According to Gawronski & Bodenhausen's (2006) dual-process model, attitudes result from two kinds of processes and their interplay. Implicit attitudes are grounded in associative processes, whereas explicit attitudes are grounded in syllogistic propositional reasoning. Automatic reactions are jointly determined by relatively stable associations available in memory and the differential pattern of such associations that particular input stimuli (and the general context and one's emotional-motivational states) trigger. Perceivers may view these automatic reactions as valid or invalid input for an evaluative judgment, depending on whether they are consistent with other propositions, e.g., beliefs about whether negatively evaluating a minority person is acceptable. Thus, propositional processes are concerned with consistency among and validity of evaluative reactions. Gawronski & Bodenhausen (2006) present a systematic analysis of factors responsible for changes in implicit and explicit attitudes, and cases that exemplify different patterns of implicit-explicit attitude change. The framework has broad applicability and can predict relations between implicit and explicit attitudes as well as the reason for and the direction of these relations (see also Fazio & Olson 2003).

In a clear demonstration that supports both conceptions of these two systems, Rydell and colleagues (2006) showed that perceivers' implicit impressions of a target person can be determined by subliminal primes paired with this person, whereas explicit impressions are determined by supraliminally presented behavioral descriptions of the person (see also DeCoster et al. 2006). When these two types of information are of opposite valence, so are the resulting implicit and explicit impressions. Furthermore, when perceivers are exposed to new information that contradicts the

Theory of mind:
the theory each of us
has about how the
mind (our own and
other people's)
works, particularly
regarding relations
among mental states
and behavior

Pragmatics: the
rules and situational
conditions that
enable
communication
through language,
but that are not
described by syntax
or semantics

valence of each type of earlier information, their implicit and explicit impressions change in opposite directions, reversing the direction of the initial dissociation. These impressions also affect behavior toward target persons differentially. For instance, one's preferred seating distance while interacting with another is related to implicit but not explicit impressions (Rydell & McConnell 2006).

ADULT FOLK THEORIES

Traditional attribution theory says little about the actual causes of others' behaviors (other than their locations in actors or situations) and the relationships of these causes to each other. But recent developments in philosophy and theory of mind are filling this gap and influencing empirical work in social psychology.

Malle's Model of the Folk Theory of Mind

Malle's (2004) model of the folk theory of mind is the most well developed in the literature, both conceptually and empirically. It identifies the significance of many basic concepts (intentionality, causes, and reasons) and their relationships; yields hypotheses about how and when they are used in explanations; and considers how language and the pragmatics of communication affect their expression. It is based on extensive evidence from experiments and content analyses of naturally occurring intentional explanations. The fundamental distinction is between intentional and unintentional behaviors rather than dispositional and situational causes. Only unintentional behaviors have causes. Intentional actions are explained in terms of reasons (mental states such as beliefs, desires, and valuings), or a causal history of reasons that provides the background but not the immediate reason(s), or enabling factors that make successful actions possible.

Traits, which occur in only 5% to 10% of all explanations, play multiple roles. They can

be explanations of unintentional behaviors (i.e., causes), what enables intended actions (e.g., abilities), or the history behind current reasons (e.g., chronic behaviors). It is beyond the scope of this review to summarize Malle's theory any further, but it generates many interesting hypotheses about the conditions that affect intentional explanations.

Adopting a theoretical framework that replaces the traditional situation-disposition dichotomy naturally prompts a reexamination of classic phenomena that were framed in these terms. In a meta-analysis of 173 studies, Malle (2006) reexamined the hypothesis that actors explain their own behaviors in situational terms and others' behaviors in personal or trait terms. He showed that the "actor-observer hypothesis appears to be a widely held yet false belief" (p. 907). The effect of perspective was virtually zero overall, but two interesting moderators were discovered. One was intimacy with the target, although the effect was the reverse of that classically predicted. The other was valence, with the classic asymmetry holding for negative events but reversing for positive ones. Calling the actor-observer asymmetry into question also challenges some explanations of the fundamental attribution error.

Degrees of Personhood

Adults do not always ascribe the full range of qualities of the human mind to other people, especially to outgroup members. Haslam (2006) proposed that there are two ways of dehumanizing others: "denying uniquely human attributes . . . represents them as animal-like, and denying human nature . . . represents them as objects or automata" (p. 253). His research suggests that the latter plays a large role in differentiating self from others at the interpersonal level.

Leyens et al. (2000) and Demoulin et al. (2004b) complement this work by showing that lay theories about essentialized social groups, and the degree of humanity ascribed to them, shape understandings of group members' emotions. Leyens et al. (2000) distinguish between primary emotions (simpler, physiological, and externally caused) and secondary emotions or sentiments (complex, cognitively oriented, and internally caused) that are more closely linked to human (versus animal) concepts and rated as more "uniquely human" (Demoulin et al. 2004a). Ingroups are accorded more uniquely human characteristics, i.e., sentiments, than are outgroups, and people are reluctant to attribute sentiments to outgroups (Cortes et al. 2005, Leyens et al. 2001). Sentiments are more strongly associated with ingroups on the IAT (Paladino et al. 2002) and suggest ingroup members' humanity more strongly than do sentiments in outgroup members (Vaes et al. 2006). More cognitive resources are required to process associations between sentiments and outgroups than ingroups (Gaunt et al. 2002), though primary emotions show no such bias (Gaunt et al. 2002, Paladino et al. 2002, Vaes et al. 2006).

Thus boundaries between social groups affect our understanding of social emotions and diminish the personhood ascribed to outgroup members. Recent functional magnetic resonance imaging research supports this. Harris & Fiske (2006) showed that viewing people from some social categories, while thinking about the emotions they evoke, does not activate brain regions typically activated by viewing others (the medial prefrontal cortex). Sampling from Fiske et al.'s (2002) two-dimensional stereotype content model, they found medial prefrontal cortex activation to people from each quadrant except those low in both competence and warmth, i.e., the homeless and drug addicts. Importantly, adopting a more individuating goal (judging their food preferences) eliminated this effect (Harris & Fiske 2007).

Continuous rather than categorical variables also moderate how much others are viewed as having complex mental lives. The longer a target is known, the more cognitive-affective units (e.g., feelings, thoughts, goals, beliefs, expectancies, plans, and needs) and the fewer traits used in describing him/her, as long as the target is positive or important (Idson & Mischel 2001). More IF-THEN observations, more explanations of these observations, and a higher proportion of cognitive-affective units are used to describe significant others (Chen 2003). When we evaluate others more positively, we make stronger mental state attributions to them and identify their actions at higher levels (e.g., as "expressing disappointment" versus "frowning"), especially when their actions are also positive (Kozak et al. 2006). When others are psychologically distant, perceivers give more weight to global dispositions (Nussbaum et al. 2003). Physical distance from actors even increases STIs (Rim et al. 2007).

Overall, when others are less positively valued, less important, less familiar, more distant, and/or outgroup members, they are accorded a simpler mental life and fewer conditional responses to life's exigencies.

Simulation or Social Projection

Much research on "the problem of other minds" (i.e., inferring other's mental states) emphasizes the self (see Alicke et al. 2005, Malle & Hodges 2005). Notwithstanding positive illusions about the self, researchers generally agree that people automatically use self-knowledge to make inferences about others, assuming self-other similarity by default (Epley et al. 2004b, Krueger 2003, Mussweiler 2003, Nickerson 1999), especially for ingroup members (Robbins & Krueger 2005). For instance, people spontaneously project their chronic and primed goals onto others (Kawada et al. 2004). People assimilate impressions of their partners to themselves, an adaptive process in high-functioning romantic relationships (Murray et al. 2002).

Children only start correcting these automatic egocentric inferences with sufficient practice (Epley et al. 2004a). Perspective taking seems to fit an "anchoring-and-adjustment" conceptualization. Egocentric biases increase under time pressure, decrease with accuracy motivation, and are adjusted serially and insufficiently, stopping at a satisfactory but not necessarily accurate point (Epley et al. 2004b). Although taking the self as a basis for social inference is a reasonable, even adaptive, strategy in the absence of other information (Krueger & Acevedo 2005), adults act egocentrically even when they have ready access to concrete knowledge of others' beliefs (Keysar et al. 2003).

According to Van Boven & Loewenstein's (2003) dual-judgment model, people first imagine being in the other's situation. Indeed, simply imagining another's feelings in another situation activates several self-related cognitions (Davis et al. 2004). Because people typically show an "empathy gap" in self-predictions (i.e., self-predictions are colored by current mental states), this gap also opens in predicting others. Thus, thirsty perceivers projected more thirst onto others in a different situation (mountain hikers led astray), and this was mediated by self-predictions for that situation (Van Boven & Loewenstein 2003).

Judging self versus others sometimes relies on different information (introspection versus lay theories, respectively), producing divergent inferences about self's and others' intrapersonal and interpersonal insight (Pronin et al. 2001). Self and others are also perceived as different in essential humanness (Haslam et al. 2005), being driven by ulterior motives or self-interest (Reeder et al. 2005), and being susceptible to influence and bias (Ehrlinger et al. 2005, Van Boven et al. 2003) (see Pronin et al. 2004 for a review). Perceivers project more when the targets are similar to themselves, even in unrelated domains, but they rely on stereotypes when others are dissimilar (Ames 2004).

Threatened self-esteem leads to "egocentric contrast" in perceiving others (Beauregard & Dunning 1998). More broadly, ego threat may lead people to defensively project threatening self-views, particularly when stereotypes are consistent with such derogation (Govorun et al. 2006). Traits

one abhors in oneself may be projected onto others (Mikulincer & Horesh 1999, Newman et al. 1997, Schimel et al. 2003). Hence, the influence of self on social judgment involves not only the actual self, but also possible selves (McElwee & Dunning 2006). Generally, perceivers are motivated to see others in ways that harmonize with current self-views, or better yet, enhance self-views (Dunning 2003).

By contrast, Karniol (2003) proposed that unique self information carries a "distinctiveness tag" in memory. When relevant information is not tagged, then "generic representations of prototypic situations and prototypic others serve as the default and are used to generate answers about the self" (Karniol 2003, p. 571). In this protocentric view, nonself exemplars play a larger role than does the self in judging unfamiliar others. Thus, judging unfamiliar others facilitates judging familiar others more than it facilitates judging the self, suggesting spontaneous recruitment of familiar others for the initial judgment (Karylowski et al. 2000). The self plays an even smaller role in judging others when task demands highlight its uniqueness or when judging observable (versus unobservable) manifestations of traits (Karylowski & Ranieri 2006). In response, Mussweiler (2003) noted that self-knowledge can still drive inferences about others who differ from the self and suggested that social prediction is still broadly egocentric.

In short, people are plagued by egocentric biases in perceiving others because of cognitive (e.g., high accessibility of the self) and motivational (e.g., self-enhancement) factors. Overall, mental state inferences have moved from a "haphazard enterprise" (Davis 2005, p. 53) to a systematic study of tools available to perceivers, when they are used, how they are used, and with what results. These issues are part of a heated debate between simulation theory versus theory-of-mind accounts of mind reading (Karniol 2003, Saxe 2005). Although these accounts assume universal cognitive skills, other researchers have focused on cultural differences.

Cultural, Subcultural, and Social Class Differences

Westerners (largely from the United States and Canada) emphasize personal causes of social behavior, whereas Asians emphasize situational or social structural factors (Fiske et al. 1998, Lehman et al. 2004, Nisbett 2003, Nisbett et al. 2001). Although Nisbett et al. (2001) emphasized differential weight given to situational information, cultural differences in STI occur when situational information is virtually absent. Zárate et al. (2001) used lexical decision response times to detect STI from single sentences. They found STI among Anglo but not among Latino students at the same U.S. university.

For Westerners, drawing trait inferences from behaviors is more likely than drawing behavior inferences from traits (Maass et al. 2001, 2006a). This "induction-deduction asymmetry" is reduced or even reversed among East Asians (Maass et al. 2006b). Knowles et al. (2001) suggested that situational correction varies cross-culturally. They found that Westerners made more extreme dispositional inferences from trait-diagnostic behaviors despite situational constraints, particularly under high cognitive load. Easterners may have more practice-induced facility with situational correction. Precisely where cultural differences have their effects within multistage conceptions of trait and situation inferences is unclear.

Differences in language use reflect, and likely contribute to, these cultural differences. Westerners use more trait adjectives than do Easterners, who use more behavioral verbs that incorporate contextual information to describe others and to remember and organize information about them (Maass et al. 2006b). Similarly, Westerners describe others in more abstract, decontextualized terms, whereas Easterners use more specific, contextual language (Kashima et al. 2006).

Lay beliefs may be influential in these findings. Easterners endorse situationist theories more than Westerners do, although there are no differences for dispositionist and interactionist theories (Norenzayan et al. 2002). Menon et al. (1999) argued that Easterners implicitly believe the social world (groups and collectives) is more invariant than Westerners do, whereas Westerners believe individuals are more invariant. Thus, Easterners make fewer trait attributions to individuals and more to groups. Church et al. (2003) examined lay theories of behavior across cultures. Ten components fell along two dimensions, implicit trait beliefs and implicit context beliefs. These were only modestly related and independently contributed to expectations of others' cross-situational consistency and the malleability of personality (see Church et al. 2005).

Intracultural and intranational variations also bear examination. Lillard (1998, Lillard & Skibbe 2005) notes that within both individualist and collectivist cultures, rural backgrounds foster contextual thinking whereas urban backgrounds foster more object-oriented dispositional thinking. Furthermore, in a nationally representative sample of U.S. ethnic and cultural groups, education level—more strongly than ethnic background—predicted rejection of dispositionist and situationist lay theories and acceptance of interactionist lay theories (Bauman & Skitka 2006).

Interestingly, beliefs about the trait- versus context-driven nature of human behavior (Church et al. 2003, 2005), or dispositionist, situationist, and interactionist thinking (e.g., Bauman & Skitka 2006, Norenzayan et al. 2002), are not negatively associated. Lay conceptions of causes of behaviors do not view dispositions and situations as mutually exclusive. Perhaps as Malle's (2004) model suggests, less global causal categories and more complex causal relations should be examined.

Other Implicit Theories

There is much promising research on other implicit theories, including Fiske et al.'s

(2002) stereotype content model that predicts affective responses to social groups. Ybarra (2002) presents considerable support for a lay theory of valenced behavior, in which positive behaviors are caused by situations and negative behaviors by dispositions. This "misanthropic bias" is only overridden under special conditions. Metaphor-based theories (e.g., light = good, Meier et al. 2004; up = good/down = bad, Meier & Robinson 2004; close = good/far = bad, Neumann & Strack 2000) may also spontaneously affect person perception.

Work by Dweck and her colleagues on implicit entity theories versus incremental theories continues to yield rich rewards. Molden et al. (2006) showed that under cognitive load, entity and incremental theorists selectively process information about others' behaviors that is consistent with their theories. Plaks et al. (2005) showed that theory-violating information is avoided under high load but scrutinized more under no load. It also produced more anxiety, which increased efforts to restore feelings of control on an unrelated task. McConnell (2001) showed that entity theorists' impressions are formed online, whereas incremental theorists' impressions are memory based.

Research on assimilation and contrast in person perception is another area where implicit theories (or mere mechanisms) are central. Space limitations preclude a review here, but two excellent sources are available: Biernat (2005) and Stapel & Suls (2007).

IMPLICIT CAUSAL THEORIES

Bayesian Networks

Attributions are traditionally understood in social psychology as being about causes, e.g., traits and attitudes. This is explicit when people answer questions about causality. But when inferences are spontaneous, what evidence is there that these concepts describe causes rather than semantic associates or summary characterizations? Sometimes their

causal status is clear from content and context (Hassin et al. 2002); more often, it is not (Carlston & Skowronski 2005). Recent developments in Bayesian networks (see Sloman 2005 for a nonmathematical introduction) provide new ways to approach these questions because they model probabilistic causal theories—including discounting, mental simulation, and counterfactual reasoning—more precisely than is possible with the verbal formulations traditionally used in social psychology. They essentially consist of directed graphs in which nodes (features or events) are linked by conditional probabilities, and a set of formalisms for calculating normative revisions in the network of beliefs following new information (Pearl 2000).

Bayesian nets underlie Gopnik et al.'s (2004) theory of how children acquire causal knowledge. Adults already have many causal theories and concepts based on them. Bayesian nets model how one should revise predictions following new observations versus interventions (Waldmann & Hagmayer 2005), use theory-based categories to predict unobserved features, and categorize exemplars from their observed features. They can also be used to discover what theories were used to perform such tasks.

For example, Rehder & Burnett (2005) used Bayesian nets to examine how people use newly learned categories in which category features are causally related. After participants learned the categories to criterion, they inferred unobserved features of new category members and categorized new exemplars described only by their features. Causal relations among features strongly affected performance on both of these tasks. More interestingly, participants' inferences violated the "causal Markov condition" of Bayesian nets, which holds that whenever causes are changed directly by interventions from outside the network, their consequences (descendents) are isolated from any effects of their antecedents (ancestors). Instead, participants seem to use these now causally irrelevant features to judge how much exemplars were well-functioning category members. And participants elaborated on the causal structure they were taught, inferring additional implicit causes and using these revised models to make judgments. Apparently, "people assume that categories possess a single underlying mechanism that varies in how well it functions, producing as a result either many or few characteristic features" (Rehder & Burnett 2005, p. 300). This "underlying mechanism" effect did not depend on domain specific knowledge, as it occurred for animate, economic, weather, and social systems. Would novel social categories (e.g., person types) exhibit this effect? Might this effect contribute to stereotype formation?

Perhaps traits are person categories based on causal theories that link mental states, situations, and behaviors. Could people use such categories rapidly (as suggested by STI research) in ways that reflect their causal structure? Luhmann et al. (2006) taught participants four novel categories based on causally related features and tested whether this knowledge was used in categorizing new exemplars under speeded conditions. It was, even when participants had as little as 500 ms to view the exemplar and 300 ms to respond.

The conceptual possibilities and computational tractability of Bayesian nets for modeling complex causal beliefs have not been exploited in social psychology. But they have great promise and power for extending our understanding of complex causal thinking, the use of theory-based categories in category and feature inferences, and the implicit inferences underlying causal mechanisms.

Causal Relations in Recent Attribution Research

The induction-deduction asymmetry (Maass et al. 2001) was shown when participants listened to descriptions of others in terms of traits and behaviors, matched for diagnosticity and memorability. Recognition errors and response times showed behavior-to-trait inferences were more likely and occurred online, whereas trait-to-behavior inferences were less

likely and were memory based. Because "traits serve more as potential prior causal aspects of behaviors" (Maass et al. 2001, p. 401) than vice versa, inferring trait causes is more likely than behavioral effects. Maass et al. (2006a) used free recall to show that the same asymmetry occurs under other processing goals. Adjectives (traits) were falsely recalled more often than verbs (behaviors), but tellingly, only when the agent was a person (versus the weather).

Discounting falls naturally out of Bayesian common effect networks. But as McClure's (1998) insightful review makes clear, discounting is neither as ubiquitous nor as simple as social psychology texts suggest, and several processes are implicated. Discounting is less likely when several causes are seen as joint contributors to the outcome (such as goals and preconditions). Sufficient causes discount others, whereas necessary causes are not discounted. Logical relations among causes and effects account for many discounting findings without resorting to cognitive bias or heuristics. But the anchor-and-adjust heuristic may underlie McClure's (1998) finding that, when causes are presented sequentially, the first cause is less likely to be discounted by subsequent causes than when they are presented simultaneously. Explanations (communicated causes) can differ from perceived causes. When rating causes, the "status of causal candidates can be clarified by distinguishing ... probability, necessity, sufficiency, and explanatory value" (McClure 1998, p. 16).

Extending this analysis, Roese & Morris (1999) showed that discounting versus conjunction effects, respectively, depend on causes (*a*) co-occurring or being mutually exclusive, (*b*) sharing a common causal mechanism or not, and (*c*) sharing the same valence or not. "People are more likely to discount an explanation ... that differs in valence from that implied by the initial explanation, and ... prefer conjunctions of two explanations if they imply the same impression valence" (Roese & Morris 1999, p. 446). Oppenheimer (2004) showed that

Common effect networks: causal networks with multiple causes that all contribute to the same effect. Differs from common cause networks, in which multiple effects are produced by the same cause

people "spontaneously discount ... availability in frequency judgments [of surnames or letters] when conspicuous alternative explanations [famous surnames or own initials] are available" (p. 104) but not made explicitly relevant. This suggests that people "make causal attribution to explain their own cognitive states, and do so spontaneously."

The Correspondence Bias and the Fundamental Attribution Error

Correspondence bias (CB) and the fundamental attribution error (FAE) are two phenomena that are often explained as failures to discount dispositional causes sufficiently in light of situational constraints and treated as synonymous. But Gawronski (2004, p. 209), as well as others, distinguishes between the CB ("to draw correspondent dispositional inferences from situationally constrained behavior") and the FAE ("the tendency to underestimate situational influences on human behavior"). Two recent reviews challenge the generality of each. As does McClure (1998), both reviewers reject the common hydraulic assumption that dispositional and situational causes always occur in a common effects causal model. Gawronski (2004) focuses on implicit theories of situational influences. He argues that people do have theories of situational causes and do believe that situations affect behavior. But they may fail to apply these theories (e.g., if the situation is not salient enough), or deliberately neglect situational causes (e.g., if they believe immoral behavior is highly diagnostic of immorality, regardless of the situation), or emphasize situational causes to interpret ambiguous behavior, thereby making stronger dispositional inferences. Even under concurrent cognitive load, people can characterize situational pressures if that is their goal (Krull 2001).

Sabini et al. (2001), like Malle (2004), believed the internal-external cause dichotomy is incoherent. They argued that research has "not shown that dispositions in general are significantly less important than laypeople believe them to be" (p. 1). Instead, "Americans (at least) think that they should ... treat as unimportant certain motives that are in fact not at all trivial ... to save face (for oneself and others) and to avoid embarrassment" (p. 2). Most of these studies entailed face-threatening (ego-dystonic) acts. But participants deny this and find other explanations, thereby saving face and exaggerating the importance of correspondent dispositions. Direct tests of this viewpoint would be welcome.

Reeder et al. (2004) also note the shortcomings of the internal-external dichotomy. Their multiple-inference model fits participants' ratings, open-ended explanations, and RT data better than either global situation/disposition inferences or Fein's (1996) work on suspecting ulterior motives. The multiple-inference model emphasizes that people make multiple inferences about motives in trying to understand voluntary behavior, integrate situational information into these motives, and base trait inferences on them. This theory is consistent with a substantial body of research, including Kammrath et al. (2005).

Nevertheless, leading researchers continue to frame findings in terms of the internal-external or disposition-situation dichotomy. Van Boven et al. (2003) showed that when making dispositional inferences, North Americans expect their peers to correct less for situational pressures than they themselves do. Yzerbyt et al. (2001) showed that correcting dispositional inferences for situational pressures involves suppressing the dispositions, which produces dispositional rebound when rating subsequent targets. But these results could be easily reframed in terms of specific mental states and situational causes. Such reframing may also be more accurate, as in Van Boven et al.'s (2003) Study 1, where the data violate a hydraulic relation between situational and dispositional causes. It is time to move beyond the CB and FAE as misleading overgeneralizations, and to focus instead on mapping people's specific theories (implicit and explicit) of the causal interrelations among mental states, situations, and behaviors.

DEVELOPMENTAL ANTECEDENTS

Developmental research is instructive because it draws on different theoretical and methodological traditions, yet deals with many of the same issues noted above.

Infants

Recent infant research shows that (*a*) to infants, other people are objects of special interest and attention from birth; (*b*) 1-year-old infants infer dispositions and future behaviors of others in relatively mature ways; (*c*) these inferences are necessarily implicit; (*d*) they usually occur in intensely reciprocal social interaction; and (*e*) language development adds new layers of complexity to these inferences (see also Saxe et al. 2004). Murphy (2002, chapters 9 and 10) reviews development of infants' basic conceptual processes, but without a focus on social concepts and interaction.

Cassia et al. (2001) showed that newborns preferentially track face-like high-contrast displays, relative to non-face-like displays matched on properties such as visual complexity. Within four days, infants are biased toward their mothers' faces (Bushnell 2001). Preferential attention to human speech occurs before birth (DeCasper et al. 1994), and newborns show many language discrimination skills (Ramus 2002).

Evidence for a fundamental person perception distinction—between animate and inanimate behavior—appears as early as six months. Much of this evidence shows that infants react differently to animate agents (those that demonstrate directed and internally caused movement, contingent behaviors, change after proximal contact, and goal-relevant and intentional acts) than to those without these attributes. Sensitivity to features of animacy emerges at different ages rather than all at once (see Rakison & Poulin-

Dubois 2001). Infants can also distinguish between intentional and accidental acts, a skill that requires mental state attributions that are more sophisticated. For instance, 16-month-olds are less likely to repeat an adult's action that is followed by "Whoops" (and hence accidental) than by "There!" (Carpenter et al. 1998). The distinction serves as an organizing principle for many theory-based categories (e.g., Gelman 2004) and is both fundamental and complex.

Person perception differs from object perception because, as people ourselves, we can use self-knowledge as a basis for knowing others (see Simulation Models, above). This requires distinguishing ourselves from others as well as mapping between others and ourselves. Newborns show immediate imitation of others (Meltzoff & Moore 1989), and by six weeks, they show delayed imitation, perhaps as a way of eliciting responses that identify others (Meltzoff & Moore 1994). Coordinated reciprocal interaction emerges by four to six months (Rochat et al. 1999). Moore (2006) notes that this gives infants a wide range of coordinated experiences from both a first- and a third-person perspective. Such social interactions teach how both self and others experience the world in similar and different ways (Barresi & Moore 1996).

In short, infants' "understanding" of others is based on distinguishing animate from inanimate motion, intentional acts from unintentional ones, and own actions from others' actions. This occurs largely without language production (although some language comprehension accompanies later developments). These complex achievements represent ways to understand others implicitly, i.e., without explicit reference to prior episodes.

However, most research on adults has focused on trait inferences. Can infants infer dispositions? Kuhlmeier et al. (2003) and Hamlin et al. (2007) addressed this question by having younger (5- to 6-month-old) and older (10- to 12-month-old) infants watch displays in which a ball was "helped" by a triangle and "hindered" by a square when climbing a hill, and then seemed to affiliate with one of the shapes. Older (but not younger) infants looked longer when the ball affiliated with the helper rather than the hinderer in a new context. The researchers interpreted this to mean that older infants attribute dispositional goals to an agent (the ball), as well as make the distinction between friend and foe. These carried over to the new context, producing expectations about the agent's behavior. Hamlin et al. (2007) also prompted infants to choose between the triangle and the square, and showed that infants of all ages preferred the helper. That is, choice preferences for "nice" rather than "mean" agents emerged at a younger age than attributions of goal dispositions to the ball.

Note that in these studies, dispositions are defined in several ways: in terms of goals, typical behaviors, and moral character; and that, as in Hamlin et al. (2007), different measures (looking times, preferences) show that different inferences are drawn from the same scenarios at different ages. Thus, evidence for dispositional inferences depends on the dependent variable employed and the response system(s) it engages. Second, the meanings of dispositions (e.g., merely valenced or related to behavioral intentions) change with age and experience, even among preverbal infants. This echoes Yuill's (1997) suggestion that understanding the development of trait inference and use may require classifying traits in terms of the mental states they involve. Attributions of different kinds of traits are likely to have different developmental histories, require different kinds of evidence (e.g., Rothbart & Park 1986), and refer to different mental states. There is recent evidence that infants measure up to the gold standard for inferring mental states, in that 15-month-olds can attribute false beliefs to others and hence "already possess (at least in a rudimentary and implicit form) a representational theory of mind" (Onishi & Baillargeon 2005, p. 257).

The development of language provides new layers of inferential, representational, and meta-representational possibilities. Baird &

Astington (2005) view language as causal in toddlers' growing ability to distinguish intentions from goals. Mastering standard theory-of-mind tasks is correlated with the child's use of relative clauses (Smith et al. 2003) and is caused by mothers' use of mental state language with their children during the preceding year (Ruffman et al. 2002).

Toddlers

Toddlers' understanding of personality traits is demonstrated most often by predicting others' behavior in new contexts. But many strategies can be used to predict future behavior. Alvarez et al. (2001) presented brief stories implying generosity or selfishness, neatness or messiness, bravery or fearfulness, etc. Kindergartners and fourth graders then predicted relevant behaviors in new situations, and finally gave trait and evaluative ratings. Even though both groups of children made the same explicit trait and evaluative inferences, mediational analyses showed that kindergartners relied on global evaluations, whereas fourth graders relied on traits. Thus, even when people make the same explicit trait attributions, they can use different aspects of the trait's meaning to predict future behavior.

Children also use other types of person information besides traits, valences, and mental states to make predictions. Kalish & Shiverick (2004) showed that 5-year-olds use deontic rules (e.g., prohibitions) to predict others' behaviors and affect, whereas 8-year-olds use others' preferences. Diesendruck & haLevi (2006) showed that 5-year-olds rely more heavily than adults do on social category memberships, and less on personality traits, when inferring mental states. Generally, younger children use traits less than older children or adults (Yuill 1997).

Trait labels can affect toddlers' inferences about mental states. Heyman & Gelman (1999) found that preschoolers' inferences about story characters' mental states were influenced by whether they were labeled "nice" or "mean" and "shy" or "not shy" (see also

Giles & Heyman 2005). Preschoolers even used novel trait labels more than physical appearance to predict novel (trait-unrelated) preferences (Heyman & Gelman 2000). Thus, "preschoolers appear to have some understanding that trait labels have implications for the mental lives of others" (p. 15). It remains to be seen whether toddlers understand such traits as simple person categories or in dimensional terms.

In sum, there is a growing array of methods for detecting children's implicit inferences that do not depend on verbal reports. These often depend on inferences having multiple consequences, and show that children of different ages use the "same" inference in different ways. There is ample evidence of implicit inferences about other people, including valence, animacy, agency, beliefs, goals, intentions, and traits. Note that the initial building blocks of person perception in infants are primarily perceptuomotor, multimodal, and procedural, and emerge largely from highly motivated social interaction.

SUMMARY POINTS

1. Implicit social inferences are ubiquitous, and spontaneous trait inferences are but one example.

2. Implicit social inferences are studied by varying processing goals, verbal information, visual (especially facial) information (static and dynamic), and social and cultural contexts. They affect online response times, memory, affect, judgments, and incidental and goal-directed behaviors.

3. Major theoretical processing dichotomies in social psychology capture many but not all of the phenomena they reveal. Multinomial models are useful for disentangling processes.

4. Recent models of adult folk theories and children's theory of mind are highly relevant but poorly integrated with work on implicit impressions.

5. Bayesian networks are similarly relevant but underutilized.

FUTURE DIRECTIONS

The suggestions below are only illustrative; others are in the text. The review itself should suggest more future directions to thoughtful readers.

1. How can STI, STT, evaluative conditioning, and spontaneous meta-inferences (based on the social contexts in which people provide information about themselves and others) be theoretically integrated?

2. How might major processing dichotomies be supplemented to encompass divergent phenomena such as STI and STT that are, for example, both automatic in some senses, and also apparently rule-based and associative (respectively)?

3. Which mental states, described in folk psychologies and theory of mind, are spontaneously inferred, and when do only more abstract inferences occur?

4. How might dehumanization affect these phenomena?

5. What roles do causal theories versus other processes (mere associations) play in phenomena such as STI or the induction-deduction asymmetry?

6. What might brain activity correlates of implicit versus explicit impressions reveal?

ACKNOWLEDGMENTS

Preparation of this article was supported in part by an NIH grant (MH-069842) to the first author and an NSF graduate research fellowship to the third author. We wish to thank Henk Aarts, Tanya Chartrand, Klaus Fiedler, Susan Fiske, Bertram Gawronski, Kiley Hamlin, Ying-yi Hong, Jacques-Phillippe Leyens, Anne Maass, Bertram Malle, John McClure, Bob Rehder, Diane Ruble, Yaacov Schul, Jeff Sherman, John Skowronski, Eliot Smith, Alex Todorov, and Dan Wigboldus for their useful comments. Any errors are our responsibility.

LITERATURE CITED

Aarts H, Custers R, Holland RW. 2007. The nonconscious cessation of goal pursuit: when goals and negative affect are coactivated. *J. Personal. Soc. Psychol.* 92:165–78

Aarts H, Gollwitzer PM, Hassin RR. 2004. Goal contagion: perceiving is for pursuing. *J. Personal. Soc. Psychol.* 87:23–37

Alicke MD, Dunning DA, Krueger JI, eds. 2005. *The Self in Social Judgment.* New York: Psychol. Press

Alvarez JM, Ruble DN, Bolger N. 2001. The role of evaluation in the development of person perception. *Child Dev.* 72:1409–25

Ames DR. 2004. Inside the mind reader's tool kit: projection and stereotyping in mental state inference. *J. Personal. Soc. Psychol.* 87:340–53

Amodio DM, Harmon-Jones E, Devine PG, Curtin JJ, Hartley SL, Covert AE. 2004. Neural signals for the detection of unintentional race bias. *Psychol. Sci.* 15:88–93

Andersen SM, Moskowitz GB, Blair IV, Nosek BA. 2007. Automatic thought. *Social Psychology: Handbook of Basic Principles*, ed. ET Higgins, AW Kruglanski, pp. 138–75. New York: Guilford. 2nd ed.

Andersen SM, Saribay SA. 2005. The relational self and transference: evoking motives, self-regulation, and emotions through activation of mental representations of significant others. In *Interpersonal Cognition*, ed. MW Baldwin, pp. 1–32. New York: Guilford

Apperly IA, Riggs KJ, Simpson A, Chiavarino C, Samson D. 2006. Is belief reasoning automatic? *Psychol. Sci.* 17:841–44

Baird JA, Astington JW. 2005. The development of the intention concept: from the observable world to the unobservable mind. See Hassin et al. 2005, pp. 256–76

Bargh JA, ed. 2007. *Social Psychology and the Unconscious: The Automaticity of Higher Mental Processes.* New York: Psychol. Press

Bargh JA. 1994. The four horsemen of automaticity: awareness, intention, efficiency, and control in social cognition. In *Handbook of Social Cognition: Vol. I, Basic Processes*, ed. RS Wyer, TK Srull, pp. 1–40. Hillsdale, NJ: Erlbaum. 2nd ed.

Barresi J, Moore C. 1996. Intentional relations and social understanding. *Behav. Brain Sci.* 19:107–22

Barsalou LW. 1999. Perceptual symbol systems. *Behav. Brain Sci.* 22:577–660

Barsalou LW. 2003. Situated simulation in the human conceptual system. *Lang. Cogn. Process.* 18:513–62

Barsalou LW. 2008. Grounded cognition. *Annu. Rev. Psychol.* 59: In press

Bauman CW, Skitka LJ. 2006. Ethnic group differences in lay philosophies of behavior in the United States. *J. Cross-Cult. Psychol.* 37:438–45

Beauregard KS, Dunning D. 1998. Turning up the contrast: self-enhancement motives prompt egocentric contrast effects in social judgments. *J. Personal. Soc. Psychol.* 74:606–21

Biernat M. 2005. *Standards and Expectancies: Contrast and Assimilation in Judgments of Self and Others*. New York: Psychol. Press

Blair IV, Judd CM, Fallman JL. 2004. The automaticity of race and Afrocentric facial features in social judgments. *J. Personal. Soc. Psychol.* 87:763–78

Blair IV, Judd CM, Sadler MS, Jenkins C. 2002. The role of Afrocentric features in person perception: judging by features and categories. *J. Personal. Soc. Psychol.* 83:5–25

Bodenhausen BW, Macrae CN, eds. 2006. Special issue: putting a face on person perception. *Soc. Cogn.* 24: Entire issue

Burke C, Uleman JS. 2006. *Mental control over effects of implicit impressions*. Presented at Annu. Meet. Soc. Personal. Soc. Psychol., Palm Springs, CA

Bushnell IWR. 2001. Mother's face recognition in newborn infants: learning and memory. *Infant Child Dev.* 10:67–74

Caldwell TL, Newman LS. 2005. The timeline of threat processing in repressors: more evidence for early vigilance and late avoidance. *Personal. Individ. Differ.* 38:1957–67

Carlston DE, Mae L. 2007. Posing with the flag: trait-specific effects of symbols on person perception. *J. Exp. Soc. Psychol.* 43:241–48

Carlston DE, Skowronski JJ. 2005. Linking vs thinking: evidence for the different associative and attributional bases of spontaneous trait transference and spontaneous trait inference. *J. Personal. Soc. Psychol.* 89:884–98

Carpenter M, Akhtar N, Tomasello M. 1998. Fourteen- through 18-month-old infants differentially imitate intentional and accidental actions. *Infant Behav. Dev.* 21:315–30

Cassia V, Simion F, Umiltá C. 2001. Face preference at birth: the role of an orienting mechanism. *Dev. Sci.* 4:101–8

Chaiken S, Trope Y, eds. 1999. *Dual-Process Theories in Social Psychology*. New York: Guilford

Chartrand TL, Dalton AN. 2007. Nonconscious mimicry: its ubiquity, importance, and functionality. In *The Psychology of Action, Vol. 2: Mechanisms of Human Action*, ed. E Morales, PM Gollwitzer, JA Bargh. New York: Oxford Univ. Press. In press

Chartrand TL, Maddux WW, Lakin JL. 2005. Beyond the perception-behavior link: the ubiquitous utility and motivational moderators of nonconscious mimicry. See Hassin et al. 2005, pp. 334–61

Chen S. 2003. Psychological-state theories about significant others: implications for the content and structure of significant-other representations. *Personal. Soc. Psychol. Bull.* 29:1285–302

Chen S, Fitzsimons GM, Andersen SM. 2007. Automaticity in close relationships. In *Automatic Processes in Social Thinking and Behavior*, ed. JA Bargh, pp. 133–72. New York: Psychol. Press

Church AT, Katigbak MS, Ortiz FA, del Prado AM, Vargas-Flores J, et al. 2005. Investigating implicit trait theories across cultures. *J. Cross-Cult. Psychol.* 36:476–96

Church AT, Ortiz FA, Katigbak MS, Avdeyeva TV, Emerson AM, et al. 2003. Measuring individual and cultural differences in implicit trait theories. *J. Personal. Soc. Psychol.* 85:332–47

Cloutier J, Mason MF, Macrae CN. 2005. The perceptual determinants of person construal: reopening the social-cognitive toolbox. *J. Personal. Soc. Psychol.* 88:885–94

Conrey FR, Sherman JW, Gawronski B, Hugenberg K, Groom CJ. 2005. Separating multiple processes in implicit social cognition: the quad model of implicit task performance. *J. Personal. Soc. Psychol.* 89:469–87

Cortes RP, Demoulin S, Rodriguez RT, Rodriguez AP, Leyens JP. 2005. Infrahumanization or familiarity? Attribution of uniquely human emotions to the self, the ingroup, and the outgroup. *Personal. Soc. Psychol. Bull.* 31:245–53

Crawford MT, McCrea SM. 2004. When mutations meet motivations: attitude biases in counterfactual thought. *J. Exp. Soc. Psychol.* 40:65–74

Crawford MT, Sherman SJ, Hamilton DL. 2002. Perceived entitativity, stereotype formation, and the interchangeability of group members. *J. Personal. Soc. Psychol.* 83:1076–94

Crawford MT, Skowronski JJ, Stiff C. 2007a. Limiting the spread of spontaneous trait transference. *J. Exp. Soc. Psychol.* 43:466–72

Crawford MT, Skowronski JJ, Stiff C, Scherer CR. 2007b. Interfering with inferential, but not associative, processes underlying spontaneous trait inference. *Personal. Soc. Psychol. Bull.* 33:677–90

Davis MH, Soderlund T, Cole J, Gadol E, Kute M, et al. 2004. Cognitions associated with attempts to empathize: How do we imagine the perspective of another? *Personal. Soc. Psychol. Bull.* 30:1625–35

Davis MH. 2005. A "constituent" approach to the study of perspective taking: what are its fundamental elements? In *Other Minds: How Humans Bridge the Divide Between Self and Others*, ed. BF Malle, SD Hodges, pp. 44–55. New York: Guilford

DeCasper AJ, Lecanuet J-P, Busnel M-C, Granier-Deferre C, Maugeais R. 1994. Fetal reactions to recurrent maternal speech. *Infant Behav. Dev.* 17:159–64

DeCoster J, Banner MJ, Smith ER, Semin GR. 2006. On the inexplicability of the implicit: differences in the information provided by implicit and explicit tests. *Soc. Cogn.* 24:5–21

Demoulin S, Leyens JP, Paladino MP, Rodriguez RT, Rodriguez AP, et al. 2004a. Dimensions of "uniquely" and "nonuniquely" human emotions. *Cogn. Emotion* 18:71–96

Demoulin S, Rodriguez RT, Rodriguez AR, Vaes J, Paladino PM, et al. 2004b. Emotional prejudice can lead to infrahumanization. *Eur. Rev. Soc. Psychol.* 15:259–96

Diesendruck G, haLevi H. 2006. The role of language, appearance, and culture in children's social category-based induction. *Child Dev.* 77:539–53

Dijksterhuis A, Chartrand TL, Aarts H. 2007. Effects of priming and perception on social behavior and goal pursuit. In *Social Psychology and the Unconscious: The Automaticity of Higher Mental Processes*, ed. JA Bargh, pp. 51–131. New York: Psychol. Press

Dunning D. 2003. The zealous self-affirmer: how and why the self lurks so pervasively behind social judgment. In *Motivated Social Perception: The Ontario Symposium, Vol. 9*, ed. SJ Spencer, S Fein, MP Zanna, JM Olson, pp. 45–72. Mahwah, NJ: Erlbaum

Eberhardt JL, Dasgupta N, Banaszynski TL. 2003. Believing is seeing: the effects of racial labels and implicit beliefs on face perception. *Personal. Soc. Psychol. Bull.* 29:360–70

Eberhardt JL, Goff PA, Purdie VJ, Davies PG. 2004. Seeing black: race, crime, and visual processing. *J. Personal. Soc. Psychol.* 87:876–93

Ehrlinger J, Gilovich T, Ross L. 2005. Peering into the bias blind spot: people's assessments of bias in themselves and others. *Personal. Soc. Psychol. Bull.* 31:680–92

Epley N, Keysar B, Van Boven L, Gilovich T. 2004b. Perspective taking as egocentric anchoring and adjustment. *J. Personal. Soc. Psychol.* 87:327–39

Epley N, Morewedge CK, Keysar B. 2004a. Perspective taking in children and adults: equivalent egocentrism but differential correction. *J. Exp. Soc. Psychol.* 40:760–68

Fazio RH, Olson MA. 2003. Implicit measures in social cognition research: their meaning and uses. *Annu. Rev. Psychol.* 54:297–327

Fein S. 1996. Effects of suspicion on attributional thinking and the correspondence bias. *J. Personal. Soc. Psychol.* 70:1164–84

Fiedler K, Schenck W. 2001. Spontaneous inferences from pictorially presented behaviors. *Personal. Soc. Psychol. Bull.* 27:1533–46

Fiedler K, Schenck W, Watling M, Menges JI. 2005. Priming trait inferences through pictures and moving pictures: the impact of open and closed mindsets. *J. Personal. Soc. Psychol.* 88:229–44

Fiske AP, Kitayama S, Markus HR, Nisbett RE. 1998. The cultural matrix of social psychology. In *Handbook of Social Psychology*, ed. DT Gilbert, ST Fiske, G Lindzey, pp. 915–81. New York: McGraw-Hill. 4th ed.

Fiske ST, Cuddy AJ, Glick P, Xu J. 2002. A model of (often mixed) stereotype content: competence and warmth respectively follow from perceived status and competition. *J. Personal. Soc. Psychol.* 82:878–902

Fitzsimons GM, Bargh JA. 2003. Thinking of you: nonconscious pursuit of interpersonal goals associated with relationship partners. *J. Personal. Soc. Psychol.* 84:148–64

Fu JH-y, Chiu C-y, Morris MW, Young MJ. 2007. Spontaneous inferences from cultural cues: varying responses of cultural insiders and outsiders. *J. Cross-Cult. Psychol.* 38:58–75

Gaunt R, Leyens JP, Demoulin S. 2002. Intergroup relations and the attribution of emotions. controllability of memory for secondary emotions associated with ingroup vs outgroup. *J. Exp. Psychol.* 38:508–14

Gawronski B. 2004. Theory-based bias correction in dispositional inference: the fundamental attribution error is dead, long live the correspondence bias. *Eur. Rev. Soc. Psychol.* 15:183–217

Gawronski B, Bodenhausen GV. 2006. Associative and propositional processes in evaluation: an integrative review of implicit and explicit attitude change. *Psychol. Bull.* 132:692–731

Gawronski B, Walther E, Blank H. 2005. Cognitive consistency and the formation of interpersonal attitudes: cognitive balance affects the encoding of social information. *J. Exp. Soc. Psychol.* 41:618–26

Gelman SA. 2004. Psychological essentialism in children. *Trends Cogn. Sci.* 8:404–9

Gilbert DT. 1989. Thinking lightly about others: automatic components of the social inference process. In *Unintended Thought*, ed. JS Uleman, JA Bargh, pp. 189–211. New York: Guilford

Giles JW, Heyman GD. 2005. Preschoolers use trait-relevant information to evaluate the appropriateness of an aggressive response. *Aggress. Behav.* 31:498–509

Glassman NS, Andersen SM. 1999. Activating transference without consciousness: using significant-other representations to go beyond what is subliminally given. *J. Personal. Soc. Psychol.* 77:1146–62

Gonzalez CM, Uleman JS, Todorov AT. 2007. A dissociation between spontaneous and intentional stereotyped trait inference. Unpubl. manuscr.

Gopnik A, Glymour C, Sobel DM, Schulz LE, Kushnir T, Danks D. 2004. A theory of causal learning in children: causal maps and Bayes nets. *Psychol. Rev.* 11:3–32

Goren A, Todorov A. 2007. *Stab in the front, praise in the back*. Poster presented at Annu. Meet. Soc. Personal. Social Psychol., Memphis, TN

Govorun O, Fuegen K, Payne KB. 2006. Stereotypes focus defensive projection. *Personal. Soc. Psychol. Bull.* 32:781–93

Ham J, Van den Bos K. 2006. Automatically inferring the justness of events: evidence from three implicit measurement paradigms. Manuscr. submitted

Ham J, Van den Bos K. 2007. Not fair for me! The influence of personal relevance on social justice inferences. *J. Exp. Soc. Psychol.* In press

Ham J, Vonk R. 2003. Smart and easy: co-occurring activation of spontaneous trait inferences and spontaneous situational inferences. *J. Exp. Soc. Psychol.* 39:434–47

Hamlin JK, Wynn K, Bloom P. 2007. *Social Evaluation in Preverbal Infants*. New Haven, CT: Yale Univ. Manuscr. under review

Harris LT, Fiske ST. 2006. Dehumanizing the lowest of the low: neuro-imaging responses to extreme outgroups. *Psychol. Sci.* 17:847–53

Harris LT, Fiske ST. 2007. Social groups that elicit disgust are differentially processed in mPFC. *Soc. Cogn. Affect. Neurosci.* 2:45–51

Haslam N. 2006. Dehumanization: an integrative review. *Personal. Soc. Psychol. Rev.* 10:252–64

Haslam N, Bain P, Douge L, Lee M, Bastian B. 2005. More human than you: attributing humanness to self and others. *J. Personal. Soc. Psychol.* 89:937–50

Hassin R, Trope Y. 2000. Facing faces: studies on the cognitive aspects of physiognomy. *J. Personal. Soc. Psychol.* 78:837–52

Hassin RR, Aarts H, Ferguson MJ. 2005b. Automatic goal inferences. *J. Exp. Soc. Psychol.* 41:129–40

Hassin RR, Bargh JA, Uleman JS. 2002. Spontaneous causal inferences. *J. Exp. Soc. Psychol.* 38:515–22

Hassin RR, Uleman JS, Bargh JA, eds. 2005a. *The New Unconscious.* New York: Oxford Univ. Press

Hasson U, Simmons JP, Todorov A. 2005. Believe it or not: on the possibility of suspending belief. *Psychol. Sci.* 16:566–71

Heyman GD, Gelman SA. 1999. The use of trait labels in making psychological inferences. *Child Dev.* 70:604–19

Heyman GD, Gelman SA. 2000. Preschool children's use of trait labels to make inductive inferences. *J. Exp. Child Psychol.* 77:1–19

Huart J, Corneille O, Becquart E. 2005. Face-based categorization, context-based categorization, and distortions in the recollection of gender ambiguous faces. *J. Exp. Soc. Psychol.* 41:598–608

Hugenberg K, Bodenhausen GV. 2003. Facing prejudice: implicit prejudice and the perception of facial threat. *Psychol. Sci.* 14:640–43

Idson LC, Mischel W. 2001. The personality of familiar and significant people: the lay perceiver as a social-cognitive theorist. *J. Personal. Soc. Psychol.* 80:585–96

Ito TA, Urland GR. 2003. Race and gender on the brain: electrocortical measures of attention to the race and gender of multiply categorizable individuals. *J. Personal. Soc. Psychol.* 85:616–26

Jacoby LL. 1991. A process dissociation framework: separating automatic from intentional uses of memory. *J. Mem. Lang.* 30:513–41

Kalish CW, Shiverick SM. 2004. Children's reasoning about norms and traits as motives for behavior. *Cogn. Dev.* 19:401–16

Kammrath LK, Mendoza-Denton R, Mischel W. 2005. Incorporating if . . . then . . . personality signatures in person perception: beyond the person-situation dichotomy. *J. Personal. Soc. Psychol.* 88:605–18

Karniol R. 2003. Egocentrism vs protocentrism: the status of self in social prediction. *Psychol. Rev.* 110:564–80

Karylowski JJ, Konarzewski K, Motes M. 2000. Recruitment of exemplars as reference points in social judgments. *J. Exp. Soc. Psychol.* 36:275–303

Karylowski JJ, Ranieri JF. 2006. Self as a default target in thinking about traits. *Self Identity* 5:365–79

Kashima Y, Kashima ES, Kim U, Gelfand M. 2006. Describing the social world: How is a person, a group, and a relationship described in the East and the West? *J. Exp. Soc. Psychol.* 42:388–96

Kawada CLK, Oettingen G, Gollwitzer PM, Bargh JA. 2004. The projection of implicit and explicit goals. *J. Personal. Soc. Psychol.* 86:545–59

Kenny DA. 2004. PERSON: a general model of interpersonal perception. *Personal. Soc. Psychol. Rev.* 8:265–80

Keysar B, Lin S, Barr DJ. 2003. Limits on theory of mind use in adults. *Cognition* 89:25–41

Knowles ED, Morris MW, Chiu Y, Hong Y. 2001. Culture and the process of person perception: evidence for automaticity among East Asians in correcting for situational influences on behavior. *Personal. Soc. Psychol. Bull.* 27:1344–56

Kozak MN, Marsh AA, Wegner DM. 2006. What do I think you're doing? Action identification and mind attribution. *J. Personal. Soc. Psychol.* 90:543–55

Krueger JI, Acevedo M. 2005. Social projection and the psychology of choice. See Alicke et al. 2005, pp. 17–41

Krueger JI. 2003. Return of the ego—self-referent information as a filter for social prediction: comment on Karniol 2003. *Psychol. Rev.* 110:585–90

Kruglanski AW, Orehek E. 2007. Partitioning the domain of social inference: dual mode and systems models and their alternatives. *Annu. Rev. Psychol.* 58:291–316

Krull DS. 2001. On partitioning the fundamental attribution error: dispositionalism and the correspondence bias. In *Cognitive Social Psychology*, ed. GB Moskowitz, pp. 211–27. Mahwah NJ: Erlbaum

Kuhlmeier V, Wynn K, Bloom P. 2003. Attribution of dispositional states by 12-month-olds. *Psychol. Sci.* 14:402–8

Lakin JL, Chartrand TL. 2003. Using nonconscious behavioral mimicry to create affiliation and rapport. *Psychol. Sci.* 14:334–39

Lambert AJ, Payne BK, Shaffer LM, Jacoby LL, Chasteen A, Khan S. 2003. Attitudes as dominant responses: on the "social facilitation" of prejudice in anticipated public contexts. *J. Personal. Soc. Psychol.* 84:277–95

Lehman DR, Chiu C, Schaller M. 2004. Psychology and culture. *Annu. Rev. Psychol.* 55:689–714

Leyens JP, Paladino PM, Rodriguez RT, Vaes J, Demoulin S, et al. 2000. The emotional side of prejudice: the attribution of secondary emotions to in-groups and out-groups. *Personal. Soc. Psychol. Rev.* 4:186–97

Leyens JP, Rodriguez AP, Rodriguez RT, Gaunt R, Paladino MP, et al. 2001. Psychological essentialism and the differential attribution of uniquely human emotions to in-groups and out-groups. *Eur. J. Soc. Psychol.* 31:395–411

Lieberman MD. 2007. Attention, control and automaticity: social cognitive neuroscience. *Annu. Rev. Psychol.* 58:259–89

Lieberman MD, Gaunt R, Gilbert DT, Trope Y. 2002. Reflection and reflexion: a social cognitive neuroscience approach to attributional inference. *Adv. Exp. Soc. Psychol.* 34:199–249

Lillard A. 1998. Ethnopsychologies: cultural variations in theories of mind. *Psychol. Bull.* 123:3–32

Lillard AS, Skibbe L. 2005. Theory of mind: conscious attribution and spontaneous trait inferences. See Hassin et al. 2005, pp. 277–305

Luhmann CC, Ahn W-K, Palmeri TJ. 2006. Theory-based categorization under speeded conditions. *Mem. Cogn.* 34:1102–11

Maass A, Cadinu M, Taroni M, Masserini M. 2006a. The induction-deduction asymmetry: fact or artifact? *Soc. Cogn.* 24:74–109

Maass A, Colombo A, Colombo A, Sherman SJ. 2001. Inferring traits from behaviors and behaviors from traits: the induction-deduction asymmetry. *J. Personal. Soc. Psychol.* 81:391–404

Maass A, Karasawa M, Politi F, Suga S. 2006b. Do verbs and adjectives play different roles in different cultures? A cross linguistic analysis of person representation. *J. Personal. Soc. Psychol.* 90:734–50

Macrae CN, Quinn KA, Mason MF, Quadflieg S. 2005. Understanding others: the face and person construal. *J. Personal. Soc. Psychol.* 89:686–95

Maddox KB. 2004. Perspectives on racial phenotypicality bias. *Personal. Soc. Psychol. Rev.* 8:383–401

Mae L, Carlston DE. 2005. Hoist on your own petard: when prejudiced remarks are recognized and backfire on speakers. *J. Exp. Soc. Psychol.* 41:240–55

Mae L, Carlston DE, Skowronski JJ. 1999. Spontaneous trait transference to familiar communicators: Is a little knowledge a dangerous thing? *J. Personal. Soc. Psychol.* 77:233–46

Mae L, McMorris LE, Hendry JL. 2004. Spontaneous trait transference from dogs to owners. *Anthrozoos* 17:225–43

Major B, O'Brien FT. 2005. Intergroup relations, stigma, stereotyping, prejudice, discrimination: the social psychology of stigma. *Annu. Rev. Psychol.* 56:393–421

Malle BF. 2004. *How the Mind Explains Behavior: Folk Explanations, Meaning, and Social Interaction.* Cambridge, MA: MIT Press

Malle BF. 2006. The actor-observer asymmetry in attribution: a (surprising) meta-analysis. *Psychol. Rev.* 132:895–913

Malle BF, Hodges SD, eds. 2005. *Other Minds: How Humans Bridge the Divide Between Self and Others.* New York: Guilford

Mayer JD, Roberts RD, Barsade SG. 2008. Emerging research in emotional intelligence. *Annu. Rev. Psychol.* 59: In press

Mayo R, Schul Y, Burnstein E. 2004. "I am not guilty" vs "I am innocent": successful negation may depend on the schema used for its encoding. *J. Exp. Soc. Psychol.* 40:433–49

McClure J. 1998. Discounting causes of behavior: Are two reasons better than one? *J. Personal. Soc. Psychol.* 74:7–20

McConnell A. 2001. Implicit theories: consequences for social judgments of individuals. *J. Exp. Soc. Psychol.* 37:215–27

McElwee RO, Dunning D. 2006. A broader view of "self" in egocentric social judgment: current and possible selves. *Self Identity* 4:113–30

McIntosh DN, Reichmann-Decker A, Winkielman P, Wilbarger JL. 2006. When the social mirror breaks: deficits in automatic, but not voluntary, mimicry of emotional facial expressions in autism. *Dev. Sci.* 9:295–302

Meier BP, Robinson MD. 2004. Why the sunny side is up: associations between affect and vertical position. *Psychol. Sci.* 15:243–47

Meier BP, Robinson MD, Clore GL. 2004. Why good guys wear white: automatic inferences about stimulus valence based on brightness. *Psychol. Sci.* 15:82–87

Meltzoff AN, Moore MK. 1989. Imitation in newborn infants: exploring the range of gestures imitated and the underlying mechanisms. *Dev. Psychol.* 25:954–62

Meltzoff AN, Moore MK. 1994. Imitation, memory, and the representation of persons. *Infant Behav. Dev.* 17:83–99

Menon T, Morris MW, Chiu C-Y, Hong Y-Y. 1999. Culture and the construal of agency: attribution to individual vs group dispositions. *J. Personal. Soc. Psychol.* 76:701–17

Mikulincer M, Horesh N. 1999. Adult attachment style and the perception of others: the role of projective mechanisms. *J. Personal. Soc. Psychol.* 76:1022–34

Miller DT, Visser PS, Staub BD. 2005. How surveillance begets perceptions of dishonesty: the case of the counterfactual sinner. *J. Personal. Soc. Psychol.* 89:117–28

Molden DC, Plaks JE, Dweck CS. 2006. "Meaningful" social inferences: effects of implicit theories on inferential processes. *J. Exp. Soc. Psychol.* 42:738–52

Moore C. 2006. *The Development of Commonsense Psychology.* Mahwah, NJ: Erlbaum

Moskowitz GB, Li P, Kirk ER. 2004. The implicit volition model: on the preconscious regulation of temporarily adopted goals. *Adv. Exp. Soc. Psychol.* 36:317–413

Murphy GL. 2002. *The Big Book of Concepts.* Cambridge, MA: MIT Press

Murray SL, Holmes JG, Bellavia G, Griffin DW, Dolderman D. 2002. Kindred spirits? The benefits of egocentrism in close relationships. *J. Personal. Soc. Psychol.* 82:563–81

Mussweiler T. 2003. When egocentrism breeds distinctness—comparison processes in social prediction: comment on Karniol 2003. *Psychol. Rev.* 110:581–84

Narvaez D, Lapsley DK, Hagele S, Lasky B. 2006. Moral chronicity and social information processing: tests of a social cognitive approach to the moral personality. *J. Res. Personal.* 40:966–85

Neumann R, Strack F. 2000. Approach and avoidance: the influence of proprioceptive and exteroceptive cues on encoding of affective information. *J. Personal. Soc. Psychol.* 79:39–48

Newman LS, Duff KJ, Baumeister RF. 1997. A new look at defensive projection: thought suppression, accessibility, and biased person perception. *J. Personal. Soc. Psychol.* 72:980–1001

Nickerson RS. 1999. How we know—and sometimes misjudge—what others know: imputing one's own knowledge to others. *Psychol. Bull.* 125:737–59

Niedenthal PM, Barsalou LW, Winkielman P, Krauth-Gruber S, Ric F. 2005. Embodiment in attitudes, social perception, and emotion. *Personal. Soc. Psychol. Rev.* 9:184–211

Nisbett RE. 2003. *The Geography of Thought: How Asians and Westerners Think Differently and Why.* New York: Free Press

Nisbett RE, Peng K, Choi I, Norenzayan A. 2001. Culture and systems of thought: holistic vs analytic cognition. *Psychol. Rev.* 108:291–310

Norenzayan A, Choi I, Nisbett RE. 2002. Cultural similarities and differences in social inference: evidence from behavioral predictions and lay theories of behavior. *Personal. Soc. Psychol. Bull.* 28:109–20

Nussbaum S, Trope Y, Liberman N. 2003. Creeping dispositionism: the temporal dynamics of behavior prediction. *J. Personal. Soc. Psychol.* 84:485–97

Onishi KH, Baillargeon R. 2005. Do 15-month-old infants understand false beliefs? *Science* 308:255–58

Oppenheimer DM. 2004. Spontaneous discounting of availability in frequency judgment tasks. *Psychol. Sci.* 15:100–5

Paladino PM, Leyens JP, Rodriguez RT, Rodriguez AP, Gaunt R, et al. 2002. Differential associations of uniquely and nonuniquely human emotions with the in-group and the out-group. *Group Proc. Intergroup Relat.* 5:105–17

Payne BK. 2001. Prejudice and perception: the role of automatic and controlled processes in misperceiving a weapon. *J. Personal. Soc. Psychol.* 81:181–92

Payne BK. 2005. Conceptualizing control in social cognition: how executive functioning modulates the expression of automatic stereotyping. *J. Personal. Soc. Psychol.* 89:488–503

Payne BK, Jacoby LL, Lambert AJ. 2005. Attitudes as accessibility bias: dissociating automatic and controlled processes. See Hassin et al. 2005, pp. 393–420

Pearl J. 2000. *Causality: Models, Reasoning, and Inference.* Cambridge, UK: Cambridge Univ. Press

Plaks JE, Grant H, Dweck CS. 2005. Violations of implicit theories and the sense of prediction and control: implications for motivated person perception. *J. Personal. Soc. Psychol.* 88:245–62

Pronin E, Gilovich T, Ross L. 2004. Objectivity in the eye of the beholder: divergent perceptions of bias in self vs others. *Psychol. Rev.* 111:781–99

Pronin E, Kruger J, Savitsky K, Ross L. 2001. You don't know me, but I know you: the illusion of asymmetric insight. *J. Personal. Soc. Psychol.* 81:639–56

Pryor JB, Reeder GD, Yeadon C, Hesson-McInnis M. 2004. A dual-process model of reactions to perceived stigma. *J. Personal. Soc. Psychol.* 87:436–52

Rakison DH, Poulin-Dubois D. 2001. Developmental origin of the animate-inanimate distinction. *Psychol. Bull.* 127:209–28

Ramus F. 2002. Language discrimination by newborns: teasing apart phonotactic, rhythmic, and intonational cues. *Annu. Rev. Lang. Acquis.* 2:85–115

Reeder GD, Pryor JB, Wohl MJA, Griswell ML. 2005. On attributing negative motives to others who disagree with our opinions. *Personal. Soc. Psychol. Bull.* 31:1498–510

Reeder GD, Vonk R, Ronk MJ, Ham J, Lawrence M. 2004. Dispositional attribution: multiple inferences about motive-related traits. *J. Personal. Soc. Psychol.* 86:530–44

Rehder B, Burnett RC. 2005. Feature inference and the causal structure of categories. *Cogn. Psychol.* 50:274–314

Rim S, Uleman JS, Trope Y. 2007. *Spatial distance affects implicit impressions of others.* Poster presented at 19th Annu. Meet. Assoc. Psychol. Sci., Washington, DC

Robbins JM, Krueger JI. 2005. Social projection to ingroups and outgroups: a review and meta-analysis. *Personal. Soc. Psychol. Rev.* 9:32–47

Rochat P, Querido J, Striano T. 1999. Emerging sensitivity to the timing and structure of protoconversation in early infancy. *Dev. Psychol.* 35:950–57

Roese NJ, Morris MW. 1999. Impression valence constrains social explanations: the case of discounting vs conjunction effects. *J. Personal. Soc. Psychol.* 77:437–48

Roese NJ, Sanna LJ, Galinsky AD. 2005. The mechanics of imagination: automaticity and control in counterfactual thinking. See Hassin et al. 2005, pp. 138–70

Rothbart M, Park B. 1986. On the confirmability and disconfirmability of trait concepts. *J. Personal. Soc. Psychol.* 50:131–42

Ruffman T, Slade L, Crowe E. 2002. The relation between children's and mothers' mental state language and theory-of-mind understanding. *Child Dev.* 73:734–51

Rydell RJ, McConnell AR. 2006. Understanding implicit and explicit attitude change: a systems of reasoning analysis. *J. Personal. Soc. Psychol.* 91:995–1008

Rydell RJ, McConnell AR, Mackie DM, Strain LM. 2006. Of two minds: forming and changing valence-inconsistent implicit and explicit attitudes. *Psychol. Sci.* 17:954–58

Sabini J, Siepmann M, Stein J. 2001. The really fundamental attribution error in social psychology research. *Psychol. Inq.* 12:1–15

Saxe R. 2005. Against simulation: the argument from error. *Trends Cogn. Sci.* 9:174–79

Saxe R, Carey S, Kanwisher N. 2004. Understanding other minds: linking developmental psychology and functional neuroimaging. *Annu. Rev. Psychol.* 55:87–124

Schimel J, Greenberg J, Martens A. 2003. Evidence that projection of a feared trait can serve a defensive function. *Personal. Soc. Psychol. Bull.* 29:969–79

Schul Y, Mayo R, Burnstein E. 2004. Encoding under trust and distrust: the spontaneous activation of incongruent cognitions. *J. Personal. Soc. Psychol.* 86:668–79

Skowronski JJ, Carlston DE, Mae L, Crawford MT. 1998. Spontaneous trait transference: communicators take on the qualities they describe in others. *J. Personal. Soc. Psychol.* 74:837–48

Sloman S. 2005. *Causal Models: How People Think About the World and Its Alternatives.* New York: Oxford Univ. Press

Smith ER, DeCoster J. 2000. Dual-process models in social and cognitive psychology: conceptual integration and links to underlying memory systems. *Personal. Soc. Psychol. Rev.* 4:108–31

Smith ER, Semin G. 2004. Socially situated cognition: cognition in its social context. *Adv. Exp. Soc. Psychol.* 36:53–117

Smith M, Apperly I, White V. 2003. False belief reasoning and the acquisition of relative clause sentences. *Child Dev.* 74:1709–19

Sonnby-Borgström M, Jönsson P, Svensson O. 2003. Emotional empathy as related to mimicry reactions at different levels of information processing. *J. Nonverbal Behav.* 27:3–23

Stapel DA, Suls J, eds. 2007. *Assimilation and Contrast in Social Psychology*. New York: Psychol. Press

Tetlock PE, Visser PS. 2000. Thinking about Russia: plausible past and probable futures. *Br. J. Soc. Psychol.* 39:173–96

Tiedens LZ. 2001. The effect of anger on the hostile inferences of aggressive and nonaggressive people: specific emotions, cognitive processing, and chronic accessibility. *Motiv. Emot.* 25:233–51

Todorov A, Fiske ST, Prentice D, eds. 2007. *Social Neuroscience: Toward Understanding the Underpinnings of the Social Mind*. New York: Oxford Univ. Press

Todorov A, Mandisodza AN, Goren A, Hall CC. 2005. Inferences of competence from faces predict election outcomes. *Science* 308:1623–26

Todorov A, Uleman JS. 2003. The efficiency of binding spontaneous trait inferences to actors' faces. *J. Exp. Soc. Psychol.* 39:549–62

Todorov A, Uleman JS. 2004. The person reference process in spontaneous trait inferences. *J. Personal. Soc. Psychol.* 87:482–93

Tormala ZL, Petty RE. 2001. On-line vs memory-based processing: the role of "need to evaluate" in person perception. *Personal. Soc. Psychol. Bull.* 27:1599–612

Trope Y, Alfieri T. 1997. Effortfulness and flexibility of dispositional judgment processes. *J. Personal. Soc. Psychol.* 73:662–74

Uleman JS, Blader SL, Todorov A. 2005. Implicit impressions. See Hassin et al. 2005, pp. 362–92

Vaes J, Paladino MP, Leyens JP. 2006. Priming uniquely human emotions and the ingroup (but not the outgroup) activates humanity concepts. *Eur. J. Soc. Psychol.* 36:169–81

van Baaren RB, Fockenberg DA, Holland RW, Janssen L, van Knippenberg A. 2006. The moody chameleon: the effect of mood on nonconscious mimicry. *Soc. Cogn.* 24:426–37

Van Boven L, Loewenstein G. 2003. Social projection of transient drive states. *Personal. Soc. Psychol. Bull.* 29:1159–68

Van Boven L, White K, Kamada A, Gilovich T. 2003. Intuitions about situational correction in self and others. *J. Personal. Soc. Psychol.* 85:249–58

Waldmann MR, Hagmayer Y. 2005. Seeing vs doing: two modes of accessing causal knowledge. *J. Exp. Psychol.: Learn. Mem. Cogn.* 31:216–27

Walther E. 2002. Guilty by mere association: evaluative conditioning and the spreading attitude effect. *J. Personal. Soc. Psychol.* 82:919–34

Wegner DM. 2005. Who is the controller of controlled processes? See Hassin et al. 2005, pp. 19–36

Wigboldus DH, Dijksterhuis A, van Knippenberg A. 2003. When stereotypes get in the way: Stereotypes obstruct stereotype-inconsistent trait inferences. *J. Personal. Soc. Psychol.* 84:470–84

Wigboldus DH, Sherman JW, Franzese HL, van Knippenberg A. 2004. Capacity and comprehension: spontaneous stereotyping under cognitive load. *Soc. Cogn.* 2:292–309

Willis J, Todorov A. 2006. First impressions: making up your mind after a 100-ms exposure to a face. *Psychol. Sci.* 17:592–98

Ybarra O. 2002. Naïve causal understanding of valenced behavior and its implications for social information processing. *Psychol. Bull.* 128:421–41

Yuill N. 1997. Children's understanding of traits. In *The Development of Social Cognition*, ed. S Hala, pp. 273–96. East Sussex, UK: Psychol. Press

Yzerbyt VY, Corneille O, Dumont M, Hahn K. 2001. The dispositional inference strikes back: situational focus and dispositional suppression in causal attribution. *J. Personal. Soc. Psychol.* 81:365–76

Zarate MA, Uleman JS, Voils CI. 2001. Effects of culture and processing goals on the activation and binding of trait concepts. *Soc. Cogn.* 19:295–323

Zebrowitz LA. 2006. Finally, faces find favor. *Soc. Cogn.* 24:657–701

Zebrowitz LA, Fellous J, Mignault A, Andreoletti C. 2003. Trait impressions as overgeneralized responses to adaptively significant facial qualities: evidence from connectionist modeling. *Personal. Soc. Psychol. Rev.* 7:194–215

Motives of the *Human* Animal: Comprehending, Managing, and Sharing Inner States

E. Tory Higgins[1] and Thane S. Pittman[2]

[1]Department of Psychology, Columbia University, New York, New York 10027;
[2]Department of Psychology, Colby College, Waterville, Maine 04901;
email: tory@psych.columbia.edu, tpittman@colby.edu

Annu. Rev. Psychol. 2008. 59:361–85

First published online as a Review in Advance on September 20, 2007

The *Annual Review of Psychology* is online at http://psych.annualreviews.org

This article's doi:
10.1146/annurev.psych.59.103006.093726

Key Words

motivation, self-regulation, social consciousness, understanding, attribution, affective forecasting, self-presentation, impression management, communication, shared reality

Abstract

We propose that four fundamental developments of the human animal together produce distinct human motives: (*a*) social consciousness or awareness that the outcomes or significance of a person's action (self or other) depend upon how another person (self or other) reacts to it; (*b*) recognizing that people's inner states can mediate their outward behaviors; (*c*) relating the present to both the past and the future (mental time travel); and (*d*) sharing reality with other people. We review a typology of four categories of concern for these motivational developments: thoughts, feelings/attitudes, competencies, and reference values (goals and standards). We then review the recent research on three specific areas related to these motivational concerns: imagining future-self inner states, managing how others comprehend us, and sharing knowledge about the world.

Contents

INTRODUCTION

What is it that humans want? What motives shape human behavior? The "rational man" perspective agrees with Descartes, and many other scholars since (e.g., Freud), who argued that humans' motivational inclinations are animal-like (e.g., the id and the pleasure principle). These animal-like motives need to be controlled by thought and reason (e.g., the ego and the reality principle), as well as by other basic hedonic contingencies (e.g., superego punishment). But what if one does not accept this assumption about the essence of human motivation? What if, motivationally, human "rationality" is not anchored in animal-like motivational inclinations and the hedonic principle? The objective of this review is to examine research on the human motives of comprehending, managing, and sharing inner states—inner states that include feelings but are not restricted to feelings (e.g., thoughts; goals), and not only inner states as they are but also as they might become. In our literature review, we emphasize publications since 2000, but we also attempt to provide an historical perspective on this issue given that previous *Annual Review of Psychology* chapters have not addressed it.

We are not suggesting that the human motives associated with comprehending, managing, and sharing inner states are the only ones that are distinct to humans. We have selected these human concerns because we believe that their motivational significance has received relatively little attention in the broader scientific community in comparison with other human motives (e.g., hedonic motivation). Most of our review focuses on research in the social-personality literature because of space limitations and the fact that these human motives have received the most attention in that literature (including the social-personality-abnormal literature and the social-personality-developmental literature). We recognize that there is work in other areas of psychology (e.g., cognitive and behavioral neuroscience), as well as in other disciplines (e.g., anthropology, sociology, and biology) that is clearly relevant to our general theme, but it was not possible to cover all such contributions.

Even within the social-personality literature, an exhaustive review of research examining people's concerns with comprehending, managing, and sharing the inner states of self and others is not feasible. Instead, we provide a structural framework for considering these concerns and direct the reader to those parts of the structure that have received considerable attention in the literature, such as the significance of reflective self-awareness (e.g., Leary 2007), managing others' attitudes (e.g., Crano & Prislin 2006), or sharing understandings with others (e.g., Keil 2006). We also point out those parts of the structure that have received little if any attention in the research literature.

MOTIVES OF THE HUMAN ANIMAL

Let us return to the questions with which we began: What is it that humans want? What motives shape human behavior? Perhaps more than anything else, Darwin's seminal work in the second half of the nineteenth century had a revolutionary effect on the approach that scientists took to answer these questions. The logic was that if humans evolved from other animals—if we were descended from them—then it would make sense to use the characteristics of nonhuman animals as reference points for discovering the characteristics of the human animal. Two very different general implications could be drawn from this logic, each associated with a different meaning of "evolve" (see *Webster's Ninth New Collegiate Dictionary* 1989). One meaning of evolve is "to develop," which has the meaning of growth, elaboration of possibilities, and improvement, suggesting that if humans evolved—developed—from other nonhuman animals in a direction of increasing complexity, then they must have some special or greater capacities that make them different from (better than?) other animals. Another meaning of evolve is "to derive," which in turn has the meaning of originate in, formed by, and made up of, suggesting that if humans evolved—derived—from other nonhuman animals, then they must share characteristics in common with these other animals.

Which of these two meanings of "evolve" directed psychology's research agenda? Interestingly, the answer is both, but not both

across all psychological domains. Psychologists primarily chose the "developed from" implication for the domain of cognition and the "derived from" implication for the domain of motivation. When it came to cognition, psychologists were inspired by how humans' creation and use of symbol systems and cultural artifacts (e.g., language, art, music, math, law, religion) were so special and advanced compared with the cognitive expressions of other animals. But when it came to motivation, psychologists were impressed by how humans' needs, drives, and self-regulatory mechanisms were so much like those of other animals. The "derived from" implication that was drawn for motivation suggested that a good way to learn what human motivation is really like is to study what motivates other animals. If sex, aggression, hunger, and thirst are the basic motives in other animals, then they are likely to be the basic motives in humans. If instincts or drives underlie the behaviors of animals, then they are likely to underlie human behavior as well. If the pleasure principle is the central motivational concept for explaining animal behavior, then it should be central when explaining human behavior as well. Thus, the predominant approach to studying human motivation was as follows: discover the motivational consequences of humans being animals. The historical asymmetry between emphasizing "developed from" for cognition and "derived from" for motivation produced, and continues to produce, an image of humans as having the mind of a god and the motives of a brute.

This image, we believe, is wrong and damaging. There are useful insights for both cognition and motivation from both of the general implications of the Darwinian logic. But what is most in need of correction is the failure to recognize what "developed from" implies for the domain of motivation.

We are not saying that there are only "improvements" in the evolution of human motivation. Without question, any development has trade-offs, and human motivation is no exception. We are also not suggesting that there is no overlap between the motives of humans and other animals. What we are saying is that there was development—a fundamental growth that resulted in human motives that are distinct from and advanced compared with other animals (producing both benefits and costs). The purpose of this review is to highlight and emphasize this development and the evidence for it in order to correct the balance of attention from the motives of the animal that happens to be human to the motives of the *human* animal.

We propose that four fundamental developments of the human animal together produce distinct human motives: (*a*) social consciousness or awareness that the outcomes or significance of a person's action (self or other) depend upon how another person (self or other) reacts to it; (*b*) recognizing that people's inner states can mediate their outward behaviors; (*c*) relating the present to both the past and the future (mental time travel); and (*d*) sharing reality with other people.

The literature has paid most attention to the differentiation of self from others that is involved in reflective self-consciousness (e.g., Leary 2004, 2007; Leary & Buttermore 2003; Terrace & Metcalfe 2005). But years ago, Cooley (1962/1909) argued against the traditional view (e.g., that of Descartes) that gave primacy and antecedence to self-consciousness as opposed to social consciousness or awareness of society. Social consciousness involves an awareness that the outcomes of a person (self or other) are determined by the reactions of others to what that person does.

Social consciousness could remain at the behavioral or action level—awareness of how the significance of one person's action depends on the reaction of another person. But another fundamental human development changes the game: the recognition that inner states, such as beliefs, feelings, expectancies, and goals, mediate the reactions of humans to one another. This startling discovery, which human children make between the ages of 3 and 6 (for recent reviews, see Higgins 2005, Nelson 2005),

involves an understanding that the social regulation of them by powerful others (e.g., parents) is determined by what these others want and believe. To control the reactions of others effectively and efficiently, you need to know about their inner states and not just their outward behaviors.

It could be that once you know what others want or expect you to be, then you are set going forward—what is true now about what is needed to satisfy what they want from you will always be true. But another fundamental human development complicates matters considerably—it is not only what you are now but also what you are becoming that matters (Higgins 2005). Parents, for example, respond to how their child is growing and developing. Positive responses from parents depend on a child improving and learning over time. Such responses by parents to what a child is becoming and the child's appreciation for the nature of such contingencies depends on another remarkable development—the ability to relate the present self to both the past self and the future self, or mental time travel (Tulving 2005). And not only the parent-child relationship involves a concern with "what is becoming" rather than just "what is." It is true of parent-teacher, boss-employee, and coach-player relationships, and beyond such cases, it is true of business executive–stockholder, politician-voter, and so on. Groups and nations are concerned with what they are becoming and not just what they currently are.

The fact that humans are aware that people have expectancies and desires about what is to become of them is a remarkable story with major implications for the nature of human motives. But there is one more remarkable development. Humans have a need to share their understanding of the world in general and the social world in particular (see Hardin & Higgins 1996). This includes sharing their beliefs about the inner experiences of self and others and sharing their inner motives for the becoming of self and others. Other animals will pay attention to what other animals are looking at (Call 2005), but only humans, including very young children, share their knowledge with one another, including creating joint attention and deliberate teaching (Nelson 2005, Terrace 2005). This need to share reality also has important implications for the nature of human motives.

Together, these four fundamental developments of the human animal have significant implications for human motivation. Social consciousness means that people are aware that others have power over their outcomes and that they can also have power over others' outcomes. Awareness of the significance of social power and influence produces central human motives when combined with recognizing that people's inner states can mediate their outward behaviors. First, it motivates people to comprehend others' inner thoughts, feelings, and desires, as well as the social rules and customs that influence others' inner states. It also motivates people to comprehend what are their own competencies, feelings, beliefs, and desires in order to learn about their relative strengths and weaknesses, and their own personal preferences and desires. Second, it motivates people to manage others' inner states to make others use their power and influence for them rather than against them. It also motivates people to manage their own feelings and beliefs in order to function effectively in the social world. Together, these central human motives can be characterized as the general human motivation to comprehend the inner states of self and others and to manage the comprehended inner states of self and others. We refer to this set of human motives as comprehending and managing concerns.

A final set of human motives evolved from humans wanting to share their comprehension of the past, present, and future with other people (see Hardin & Higgins 1996). Parents, for example, want their children to share their beliefs and attitudes about the world and, especially, to share the parents' goals and standards for them and self-regulate in relation to them (i.e., internalize them). Groups also want their members to share the group's goals and norms and commit to them (i.e., embrace the group identity). Once again, the shared reality is not restricted to performing certain behaviors in the present. At least as important is sharing future states, including future inner states, such as sharing what inner states a person or group should be striving to achieve in the future. These inner states include what future type of person or group, and which competencies, would make us happy, secure, proud, ready to meet challenges, or meet our potential in the future. Socialization processes, both by parents (see, for example, Higgins 1996) and by groups (Levine & Moreland 1994), work to create the desired shared reality. It should be emphasized that children and new group members (novices) also work to acquire a shared reality for the sake of effective and efficient regulation. We refer to this set of human motives as shared reality concerns.

HUMAN CONCERNS FOR COMPREHENDING, MANAGING, AND SHARING INNER STATES

This section provides an overview and a structural framework for considering human concerns for comprehending, managing, and sharing inner states. The framework is organized by the types of inner states with which people are concerned. We have selected broad categories for our typology. For each type of inner-state category, we consider the extent to which psychologists have studied humans' concerns regarding that type of inner state for self-as-target versus other-as-target and with respect to present states versus future states.

Thoughts

By thoughts, we are referring not only to people's thinking but also to the knowledge and beliefs underlying that thinking, and to people's reasoning and recollecting as well.

With respect to human motivation, people's concerns with thoughts as an inner state have been studied with respect to self and others' present and future thoughts. A substantial developmental literature on "theory of mind" reports that by approximately age 3 or 4, children begin to comprehend that another person's actions can be influenced by his or her thoughts, beliefs, and knowledge (e.g., Wellman et al. 2001). Evidence even suggests that distinct, domain-specific brain regions exist for such comprehension (e.g., Saxe et al. 2004). In addition to the developmental research, there is also renewed interest by social psychologists—following Heider's (1958) early work—in how people try to make sense of another person's actions by comprehending the thoughts that provided reasons for his or her actions (Kashima et al. 1998, Malle & Pearce 2001, O'Laughlin & Malle 2002), especially when the other person is familiar to them (Idson & Mischel 2001).

There is also a huge literature concerned with how people manage what others' thoughts will become. Indeed, a major characteristic of cultural socialization is people managing the development of another person's thoughts (especially a child's thoughts) and trying to ensure that the other person shares their thoughts—the process of "education." This educational motive of wanting to share with others some knowledge that you possess but that they do not (including gossip) is pervasive among humans but absent in other animals. It is not possible here to review this educational motive of managing and sharing thoughts as an inner state. It is ubiquitous among humans and fundamentally crucial for the development of human civilization. What is surprising, however, is that there is more scientific and popular literature prescribing how such education should be done than either studies of people's naïve theories of how it should be done (i.e., research on lay theories of how to educate others) or studies of how people actually do it motivationally. The motivational question has tended to be, "What motives underlie students' learning?"

rather than "What motives underlie teachers' instructing?"

It should be noted that there is one area regarding motives about thoughts that has received substantial attention by psychologists—managing one's own and others' unwanted thoughts. It is not possible here to review the vast literature on this issue that was inspired by Freud's psychoanalytic theory and continues to fascinate psychologists to this day (for a recent review, see Clark 2004). Suffice it to say that, historically, there has been greater interest in human motives to manage unwanted thoughts than on human motives to manage wanted thoughts. However, in the past decade there has been increasing interest in how people reflect on their cognitive processes (e.g., Metcalfe et al. 1998, Yzerbyt et al. 1998), such as the techniques people use to determine whether their memory experiences regarding their own past or their experiences of knowing something about the world are veridical (e.g., Johnson 2006, Koriat et al. 2000, Metcalfe 2000) or will be veridical in the future (Koriat et al. 2004).

Feelings and Attitudes

By feelings, we refer not only to affective and emotional experiences, experiencing pain or pleasure, but also to motivational experiences such as feeling that it is easy or difficult to do something and feeling the force of attraction to or repulsion from something. By attitudes, we refer to preferences as well, and we include them in this section because liking or disliking something, evaluating something as good or bad, are critical to attitudes and preferences and obviously have a close family resemblance to the emotional and motivational experiences that we are considering here. Regarding the inner state of attitudes alone, the bulk of psychological research has been concerned with managing the future attitudes of others; that is, how people persuade someone to change his or her present attitude to a new (future) attitude that they want him or her to have. We do not review this issue because it has been extensively and recently reviewed by others (e.g., Crano & Prislin 2006, Eagly & Chaiken 1993).

How people comprehend and manage their own present feelings is a major research question within the literature on self-control (e.g., Baumeister & Vohs 2004, Baumeister et al. 2007, Folkman & Moskowitz 2004; also see special issue on emotion regulation in *Psychological Inquiry*, Volume 11, 2000). As for others' thoughts, people try to make sense of another person's actions by comprehending the feelings or attitudes that provide reasons for or caused his or her actions. The causal schemata and inferential processes that people use in such comprehension have been examined quite extensively (e.g., Chun et al. 2002, Idson & Mischel 2001, Kashima et al. 1998, Malle & Pearce 2001, O'Laughlin & Malle 2002, Trope & Alfieri 1997). Interestingly, there is less research on the causal schemata and inferential processes that people use in comprehending their own actions. One possible reason for this is that people tend to comprehend their own action as being caused by the situation in which their action took place (including other people as the situation) and believe their action was the natural, objective response to seeing the world as it is (i.e., "naïve realism"; Pronin et al. 2004). Thus, there is little motive to consider how one's own inner states produced the action. There is some intriguing evidence that the motive to do so might be greater when considering one's past or future self than one's present self (Pronin & Ross 2006).

Competencies

By competencies, we refer not only to people's skills or abilities but also to other underlying personal characteristics that affect their performance and agency in the world, such as their self-confidence, energy, persistence, reliability, responsibility, and independence. Competencies also include social skills, such as knowing how to be helpful, polite, empathic, get along with others, and so on

(e.g., social intelligence). How people comprehend the competencies of self and others has received substantial attention in the social psychological literature. For example, people also use social category membership, such as their own or another person's gender, to infer underlying competencies, an inferential phenomenon extensively studied in the literature on stereotyping (e.g., Schneider 2004, Stangor 2000).

How their own and others' competencies are comprehended by themselves and by others matters to people. They want the competencies of people they like, and especially themselves, to be viewed positively by themselves and by others (e.g., Murray et al. 2000, Swann et al. 2002). This takes management. There is an extensive person perception literature in social psychology that reviews how people manage this. It includes research on how people manage their own comprehension of their own competencies, as found in self-enhancement strategies (e.g., Leary 2004, 2007), as well as how they manage their own comprehension of others' competencies.

People also attempt to manage how others perceive their own competencies, as when a person in power (e.g., parent, teacher, coach, manager, military officer) tries to influence the future performance-related motivation of subordinates (children, pupils, players, workers, soldiers) by shaping their comprehension of their current or future (potential) competencies. People also attempt to manage how others comprehend them (Schlenker & Weigold 1992), and they work toward a shared reality between themselves and their significant others regarding how their competencies are comprehended (McNulty & Swann 1994; Murray et al. 2000, 2006). There is evidence that to have a satisfying close relationship, people need to perceive that their partner, and even the family of their partner (MacDonald & Jessica 2006), shares their own comprehension of their competencies (Murray et al. 2000, 2006), even when those competencies are negative (Swan et al. 1992).

Reference Values: Goals and Standards

By goals and standards, we refer to reference values that function as desired end-states that both guide action and provide a comparison point for evaluating current states (Boldero & Francis 2002, Higgins 1991). These reference values include needs, purposes, objectives, aspirations, ideals, norms, demands, prescriptions, proscriptions, and oughts. In comparison with goals as ideal aspirations, hopes or future accomplishments, comprehending how others' actions are motivated by their ought goals or standards, by their sense of duty and responsibility, has received relatively little attention and deserves more study. In addition, with respect to human motivation, people's concerns with reference values as inner states have been studied mostly with respect to self and others' present reference values (Idson & Mischel 2001, Read et al. 1990, Trzebinski & Richards 1986) rather than with what self and others' reference values might become in the future (e.g., what will my child's standards be like when she becomes an adult?).

In close relationships (dating, marital), people want their partner to see them as becoming, if not having become already, the kind of person that they would ideally like to be (Murray et al. 2000, 2006; Swann et al. 2002). This requires managing their partner's comprehension of them, as well as their partner managing their own comprehension of them, to achieve a shared reality about their attaining their ideals. To accomplish this effectively, their partner needs to comprehend what it is they hope or wish to be or become. Although the literature has tended to focus on ideals, it would also be important for their partner to comprehend their oughts and believe that they are meeting them as well.

An especially significant concern is comprehending and managing whether self or other is or is not currently congruent with the reference values (goals and standards), and whether self or other is or is not in the process of becoming congruent with the reference values (e.g., Carver & Scheier 1998; Higgins 1987, 1991). This involves both self-regulation and social regulation, a fundamental aspect of human socialization, in the family, at school, and at work. Such socialization processes are not reviewed here because they are covered extensively in the developmental and clinical psychology areas, as well as in other disciplines such as sociology and anthropology. Regarding self-regulation, it is critical for people to comprehend their reference values for themselves and to manage the process of fulfilling the reference values by becoming the type of person so valued (e.g., acquiring the valued competencies).

Thus far, we have proposed a typology of four broad categories regarding people's concerns with comprehending, managing, and sharing inner state—thoughts, feelings/attitudes, competencies, and reference values (goals and standards). Within this general framework, we now select three specific areas to consider in more detail—imagining future-self inner states, managing how others comprehend you, and sharing knowledge about the world. We have selected these areas because of their general importance in self and social regulation, and because they provide especially strong examples of what is special about the motives of the *human* animal.

IMAGINING FUTURE-SELF INNER STATES

Self-regulation in humans and other animals involves making present decisions in relation to future goals and outcomes as desired and undesired end-states (Carver & Scheier 1998, Markus & Nurius 1986). Certainly humans differ from other animals in how far distant are the end-states they imagine, including even end-states in the afterlife (e.g., going to heaven or hell). However, there is another, perhaps even more critical, difference between humans and other animals in the nature of this self-regulation—the future states in relation to which the present decisions are made include imagined inner states of the self. For example, not only do humans imagine going to heaven or hell, they imagine the peace and joy they will feel in heaven or the anguish and suffering they will feel in hell. More commonly, people imagine how they will feel in the future if they were to make a particular decision now, how happy they will feel or how regretful they will feel. In addition to imagining what they will feel in the future, people imagine what type of person they might be or want to be in the future if they were to commit to a particular course of action now—what competencies they might possess, such as becoming an accomplished pianist or cook, a better student, or a more spiritual or patient person. These imagined future-self states can become reference values for self-regulation and self-evaluation. We review research on both imagining future-self thoughts and feelings as possible future outcomes and imagining future competencies that function as reference values in the present.

Imagining Future-Self Thoughts and Feelings

Imagining alternatives to the past is termed counterfactual thinking. Often the thoughts are conditional, such as, "If I had not done that, then . . ." or "If only I had done that instead, then . . ." (see Roese 1997). Counterfactuals can function not only to repair (negative) or maintain (positive) present feelings about past outcomes, but they can also be used to improve performance in the future, as by thinking about what one could have done better in the past and thus what should be done in the future (e.g., Sanna et al. 1999).

People can also imagine how they will think and feel in the future about a decision that they make now—prefactuals. For instance, they can imagine that if they were to make a particular choice now, it is likely that in the future they would think that another choice would have been better (i.e., self-criticism) and then feel regret over their past decision. Such anticipated counterfactual thinking and fear of future regret influence people's present decisions (Mandel et al. 2005, Tykocinski & Pittman 2004). Indeed, they may influence them too much because once an event has actually occurred, individuals are less susceptible to self-criticism and regret over a negative event than they imagined beforehand (Gilbert et al. 2004b). People can also think in the present about a past performance in a manner that will make them feel better were they to perform poorly in the future (i.e., self-protection; Sanna et al. 2001). For example, defensive pessimists benefit their future feelings and motivation by imagining negative outcomes in the future (e.g., a poor test grade) from something going wrong in the present (e.g., difficulty studying) that could be prevented next time. These self-protective thoughts are anticipated counterfactual thoughts of improvement that are prepared in the present to be used in the future if necessary (e.g., Sanna 1996, Showers 1992).

Affective forecasting, of which anticipated regret is one example, has attracted increasing attention in the decision-making literature. As Wilson & Gilbert (2003) point out, most earlier research on how people make predictions concerned imagining future external events in the world (e.g., "Will the stock market go up or down?") or in their own personal lives (e.g., "Will I still be living in New York City 15 years from now?"). In the past decade or so, however, there has been increasing interest in people's ability to forecast or imagine their own future feelings, such as "How happy will I be if I accept his proposal of marriage rather than staying single?" (e.g., Gilbert et al. 2004a, Hsee & Zhang 2004, Lowenstein & Schkade 1999, Mellers & McGraw 2001, Schkade & Kahneman 1998, Ubel et al. 2005, Wilson et al. 2000). Two general conclusions can be drawn from the literature. First, people care about predicting their future happiness and well-being. Second, for a variety of reasons, they frequently make mistakes when they do so. Not only do people overestimate the intensity of the pleasure or pain they will feel when an event occurs, they also overestimate how long the pleasure or pain will last after the event.

One major factor that can produce mistakes is focalism (see Schkade & Kahneman 1998, Wilson et al. 2000)—the tendency in the present to have in mind only the focal to-be-predicted event and not consider the surrounding circumstances that will co-occur with that event in the future. One technique that can reduce the focalism effect on misprediction is to have them imagine in the present not just the future event (e.g., a football game) but also all of the surrounding circumstances that could also produce feelings (studying, eating out with friends; Wilson et al. 2000). Another factor contributing to mispredictions is the failure in the present to take into account sufficiently how individuals (self or others) in the future will regulate their current thoughts or feelings. Once thoughts or feelings have actually occurred in the future, and especially when they are intense, mechanisms come into play that are designed to attenuate them, such as adaptation or sense-making processes (Gilbert et al. 2004a, Wilson & Gilbert 2003). It is difficult in the present to imagine the impact of those mechanisms because in many cases they only come into play when the thought or feeling is actually being experienced (cf. Ubel et al. 2005). Moreover, people have different lay theories about adaptation processes and their relation to affect progression or duration, and their use can depend on their current accessibility rather than their accuracy (Igou 2004). Individuals can also have incorrect implicit theories about the impact exposure to persuasive messages will have on their future attitudes (Wilson et al. 1998).

Imagined Future-Self Competencies Functioning as Present Reference Values

As discussed earlier, people want to comprehend both their present competencies and their personal reference values. A distinctive characteristic of humans is that they also imagine their future-self competencies—who they might become, hope to become, dream of becoming, fear becoming—and then use these future-self competencies as reference values for self-regulation in the present (e.g., Carver et al. 1994, Higgins 1987, Markus & Nurius 1986, Oettingen 1996, Oyserman & Markus 1990). Scholars have recognized for a long time that people imagine their future selves, but it was not until the late 1980s that the motivational and emotional significance of people's imagined future selves began to receive extensive empirical study as psychologists began to investigate two important functions of imagined future selves—as goals or incentives (to be approached or avoided) that influence current planning and decisions, and as standards or reference points for evaluating and interpreting the current self (Higgins 1987, Markus & Nurius 1986). We briefly review evidence for each of these functions.

Markus & Nurius (1986) found that about two-thirds of their sample of college students reported thinking about their possible selves in the future a great deal of the time or all the time, and the ratio of positive, "hoped-for" selves to negative, "feared" selves was almost 4 to 1. They imagine a very heterogeneous set of possible future selves that are relatively unconstrained by their current selves, even regarding their personality, and believe that change from their current selves is quite likely. Markus & Nurius (1986) describe how these possible selves, both positive and negative, provide direction and impetus for action and change. Often it is possessing a future self that is not only desirable but also possible that is critical. Imagining that one's desired future selves are possible is a form of optimism, and imagining that they are not possible is a form of pessimism; generally, optimistic thinking about the future yields higher motivation and better performance than pessimistic thinking does (e.g., Bandura 1997). Notably, simply imagining future desired selves and enjoying such fantasizing without considering the likelihood of these positive future selves can even impair motivation and performance (Oettingen & Mayer 2002).

Thus, imagining either desired future selves alone or possible selves alone is not sufficient for effective self-regulation. What is effective is imagining future selves that are both desirable and possible. But this is not the only combination of future selves that is motivationally effective. Indeed, imagining future difficulties and obstacles to attaining desired selves, as well as imagining feared selves that could occur instead in the future, have also been found to be effective. Oyserman & Markus (1990), for example, found that adolescents who varied in the degree of their delinquency were quite similar in their hoped-for selves, but differed markedly in their expected and feared selves (see also Carver et al. 1994). They found that the adolescents were less likely to be delinquents when they possessed a balance in their imagined future selves, where balance was defined as occurring when expected possible selves were offset by countervailing feared selves in the same domain (e.g., expecting a job, but fearing being unemployed). Similarly, combining desired future selves with feared future selves has been found to be an effective strategy employed by defensive pessimists who imagine what might happen if they were not careful enough in the future to do whatever would be necessary to avoid their feared future selves (Sanna 1996). Oettingen et al. (2001) have demonstrated in another way how effective it can be to combine imagining a desirable and possible future self and imagining obstacles to success. They found that contrasting enjoyment of fantasizing a desired future self that they believe is possible to attain and imagining how to change or overcome real current obstacles that could hinder success induces planning of and commitment to future goal-directed actions, as well as energizing and speeding up initiation of those actions.

People are more likely to experience an imagined desired self as being a truly possible self in the future to the extent that they can imagine themselves in the future carrying out a strategy to reach that desired self (e.g., "I can make it to high school by paying attention in class"). Oyserman et al. (2004), for example, found that low-income eighth graders who possessed possible selves with this strategic self-regulator quality, in contrast to purely self-enhancing possible selves, had superior academic outcomes. If the strategies used by strategic self-regulators are ways of overcoming current obstacles to attaining desired selves, i.e., strategies for change, then the work of Oyserman and her colleagues (2004) and the work of Oettingen and her colleagues (2001) can be seen as nicely complementing one another. Research by Gollwitzer and his colleagues on the self-regulatory effectiveness of implementation intentions ("If I encounter Situation X, then I'll perform Behavior Y") can be seen as complementing these other lines of work. Brandstatter et al. (2001), for example, have found that when people in the present imagine which particular future action they will perform when they encounter a specific future situation, they are more likely to actually initiate that action once that situation is encountered in the future, even when those future circumstances are demanding because of the actor's characteristics (e.g., the disruptive cognitive business associated with opiate addiction or schizophrenia) or situational characteristics (e.g., college students under high load conditions).

Thus far, we have discussed the impact on present self-regulation from imagining possible future selves that individuals want to approach or avoid (reference values). This involves future selves functioning as goals that guide present actions and decisions or commitments. As mentioned above, imagined future selves function not only as directive goals but also as standards to evaluate current actual selves. This self-evaluation process also has major motivational and emotional effects (e.g., Bandura 1986, Carver & Scheier 1998, Higgins 1987, Markus & Nurius 1986). For example, when people experience a discrepancy between their present state and the type of person they hope or aspire to become (their ideal self), they feel dejection-related emotions (e.g., sad, discouraged) and their engagement (e.g., eagerness) in what they are doing decreases. In contrast, when they experience a discrepancy between their present state and the type of person they believe they have a duty or obligation to become (their ought self), they feel agitation-related emotions (e.g., worried, nervous) and their engagement (e.g., vigilance) in what they are doing increases (Higgins 1987, Idson et al. 2000). Evidence also suggests that people's emotional appraisals of everyday objects (Shah & Higgins 2001) and the emotional tone of their autobiographical memories (Strauman 1996) are influenced by the nature of their future desired selves, with the emotional experiences being along the cheerfulness-dejection dimension for those possessing dominant ideal future selves and being along the quiescence-agitation dimension for those possessing dominant ought future selves. It should be noted as well that these different emotions, as pleasure and pain experiences that induce self-regulatory responses, have their own motivational effects.

People not only represent the future desired selves that they imagine for themselves but also the future desired selves that significant others imagine for them (Higgins 1987, 1996; Moretti & Higgins 1999). When a person's significant others are activated, those others' ideals and oughts for him or her are activated and function as standards for self-evaluation. In a study on transference by Andersen & Chen (2002), for example, one of the participants' parents was activated by learning about a new person who happened to resemble that parent. The participants' actual self was discrepant from either that parent's ideals for them or that parent's oughts for them. When the new person resembled a parent with ideal selves for them, the participants uniquely experienced more dejection-related feelings, whereas when the new person resembled a parent with ought selves for them, they

uniquely experienced more agitation-related feelings. In a different study by Shah (2003), half of the participants were primed with father-related words while they were working on an anagram task. After they had completed the task, the participants received either success or failure feedback. Earlier, the participants had been asked how much their father would ideally want them to do well on the anagram task, and how much their father would feel they ought to do well. Shah (2003) found that when "father" was primed, participants' father-ideal ratings uniquely predicted their cheerfulness-dejection reaction to the success or failure feedback, and their father-ought ratings uniquely predicted their quiescence-agitation reaction.

Humans' use of desired (and undesired) future selves to evaluate the current self is remarkable. Certainly, humans, like other animals, experience emotions from the actual or expected outcomes of their actions or decisions (with the outcomes typically occurring in a narrow time frame). In contrast, here we are describing human emotions being produced not by an outcome but rather by a comparison between the perceived present state of self and the imagined future state of self. Thus, the emotional significance of a present self state does not depend only on the current outcomes from that state but also on the extent to which that self state is becoming the imagined future self state. Notably, individuals with the same present selves can have different current emotional lives if they are imagining different future selves.

In this section, we have reviewed research on how people imagine their future thoughts, feelings, and competencies as inner self-states. These are future actual selves. Another type of inner self-state whose future people could imagine is their future desired end-state—in the future, who will they then want to become (e.g., "Now I want to become a tenured professor, but once I am a tenured professor, who will I want to become then?"). Just as actual selves can change and people can imagine them changing, so too can desired selves change and people can imagine them changing, too. This type of forecasting has not been examined in the literature. We expect that such forecasting would be especially difficult to do accurately because it is difficult to forecast how future events set new conditions that permit the creation of new desired end-states. For example, getting tenure at a university might create the new desired end-state of having an influence on university-wide affairs—an unlikely goal in the present when it is not clear that one will even be staying at the university for long. It should also be noted that this new desired end-state, in turn, could create a discrepancy to one's current state of having no such influence. Thus, in a short time, instead of being happy about getting tenure, one is discouraged about one's position in the university. Such unforeseen shifts in future desired end-states could be another contributing factor to poor forecasting of future affective duration and well-being.

MANAGING HOW OTHERS COMPREHEND YOU

The comprehensions that others develop about an actor (their thoughts, feelings and attitudes, competencies, and reference values and goals) will influence how those others react to and behave toward the actor, which in turn will have hedonic consequences for the actor. These potential hedonic consequences give actors a strong reason to want to influence how others comprehend them. In addition, because important aspects of the self (e.g., self-concept, self-esteem, or self-evaluation) are influenced by and dependent upon the ways in which one is comprehended by others, the wish to create and maintain desired comprehensions of self (i.e., desired self-concepts) will also produce motivation to influence the comprehensions of others. Human recognition of these two essential social realities, that both hedonic outcomes and the ability to acquire and sustain desired self-concepts are strongly affected by the comprehensions of others, provide the two basic human motiva-

tional reasons for wanting to manage how we are comprehended by others.

Successfully influencing the comprehensions of others in ways that are favorable to the actor is an extremely challenging task. One must accurately perceive how one is, has been, and/or will be comprehended by another— no easy feat. The difficulties, on both cognitive and motivational grounds, of coming to accurate rather than illusory understandings of self and others have been reviewed extensively elsewhere (see Macrae & Bodenhausen 2000, Pittman 1998, Pittman & Heller 1987, Pittman & Zeigler 2007). Even if one is successful at divining the comprehensions of others (or believing that one has successfully done so), one must also understand how effectively to alter or channel those comprehensions of self in desirable ways—also not a simple task but one that is mitigated significantly by the phenomena of self-fulfilling prophecies and behavioral confirmation (see Major & O'Brien 2005, Pittman & Heller 1987, Snyder & Stukas 1999).

In this section, we focus on the selection and use of self-presentational strategies to manage how we are comprehended by others. First, we review the motive to enhance social power over others by managing their comprehensions of self. Then we turn briefly to the motive to manage one's own desired self-concepts by managing others' comprehensions of self, specifically for the case of managing potentially negative comprehensions of self by others whom one has damaged.

Enhancing Social Power by Managing Others' Comprehensions of Self

Social power refers to the ability to influence the behavior of others (Jones & Pittman 1982; for another definition of social power, see Fiske & Berdahl 2007). Essential to the self-presentational process is the recognition that although social power may derive in large part from a person's formal role assignments and resources, the manner in which that power is exercised will be strongly affected by how that person is comprehended by others. Understanding these facts creates a powerful concern of an actor with influencing and managing the interpretations of the actor made by others in directions that will be favorable to the actor, and away from interpretations that will be unfavorable to the actor. Successful management of the comprehensions of others through strategic self-presentation is one of the primary ways that one's own social power can be enhanced and that of others can be controlled or blunted (Jones & Pittman 1982).

Early research on self-presentation (Jones & Pittman 1982) and impression management (Schlenker & Weigold 1992) focused on the types of impressions actors might wish to manage, and on tactics of management. The most extensively studied tactic is ingratiation (Jones 1964, Jones & Wortman 1973), a tactic designed to enhance thoughts and feelings of liking and attraction in the target person. One of its uniquely attractive properties for a self-presenter is that it works reasonably well even when its use is detected by the target (Jones 1964). This makes ingratiation a very safe strategy to employ, and it is routinely and effectively employed in a wide variety of settings (Blickle 2003, Strutton & Pelton 1998, Vonk 2002). Because managing the comprehensions of others is such a ubiquitous concern in daily social interaction, many tactics of strategic self-presentation (e.g., nodding in agreement and smiling to signal similarity, approval, and attraction in the service of ingratiation) are automatic habits rather than deliberate conscious choices.

More risky in the Jones & Pittman (1982) taxonomy are the strategies of intimidation (creating an attribution of dangerousness to force the target into desired behavior) and supplication (creating the impression of neediness designed to elicit help). Perhaps for this reason, in comparisons of the use of the five self-presentational strategies in the Jones & Pittman (1982) taxonomy, intimidation and supplication are least likely to be used in public settings (Schutz 1997). Intimidation is the most likely of the five strategies to involve the expression of negative emotion (Olson et al. 2001) and the use of aggressive target-oriented actions, such as focus of attention on the target and speed of entry into the influence situation (Bassett et al. 2002). Intimidation tends to produce reciprocal reactions of negativity, and its use by women in work settings is particularly problematic (Bolino & Turnley 2003). Although supplication can be very effective in eliciting help, it comes with the price of negative impressions that may undermine interactions (Bornstein 2006, Van Kleef et al. 2006).

The strategy of exemplification (attempting to create the attribution of moral worthiness), which in one study was shown to be more likely to be publicly employed by politicians than by entertainers or experts (Schutz 1997), is likely to be combined with ingratiation and not with intimidation (Bassett et al. 2002). This strategy carries with it the risk, if failed, of generating the judgment of hypocrisy by both others and self (Stone et al. 1997). Finally, the self-presentational strategy of self-promotion (attempting to create the attribution of competence and respect for one's capabilities) has been studied extensively. Developmentally, children begin to appreciate and use this strategy (and ingratiation as well) as their attributional knowledge increases (Aloise-Young 1993). Six-year-olds show little use of the strategy, but eight- and ten-year-old children show increasing use of self-promotion and ingratiation in social influence situations. More generally, whereas younger children (age ten or younger) will inhibit the expression of negative outgroup attitudes but only under situations of high public self-focus, older children generally inhibit such explicit attitudes, while still showing their existence on implicit measures (Rutland et al. 2005).

Using any of the strategies of self-presentation effectively means understanding the complexities and nuances of particular social situations. Capturing some of this complexity, Bornstein et al. (1996) demonstrated that individuals high in dependency modulate their use of self-promotion, minimizing it when dealing with a peer but using it when interacting with authority figures. Rudman (1998; see also Bolino & Turnley 2003) found that although self-promotion by women is an effective way to manage an image of competence, it comes at the cost of violating gender norms of modesty. The nature of the self-promotional tactics that are employed is also sensitive to the nature of the situation. Tyler & Feldman (2004) found that the number of untruthful statements in an interaction increased when participants were given the goal of self-promotion in an interaction of high importance. Interestingly, they also found that those participants were least able to recall the untruthful statements they had made, suggesting either that an effortful distraction under conditions of high importance led to poor recall or that a shared reality process (Higgins & Rholes 1978) led participants to believe in what they said (as we discuss in more detail below).

As the last cited study suggests, engaging in any of these strategies for managing the comprehensions of others can be motivationally effortful, particularly when the situation calls for self-presentations beyond those that are typical or well practiced. Consistent with this idea, Vohs et al. (2005) found that engaging in challenging or unusual self-presentation led to greater subsequent evidence of ego depletion than did engaging in familiar or well-practiced presentations. Conversely, prior ego depletion acted to disrupt subsequent attempts at self-presentation, leading to increased usage of ineffective strategies. This is consistent with the general finding that well-practiced, relatively automatic processes require less effort than those that require active self-control. However, even such disruptions can sometimes be beneficial. Pontari & Schlenker (2000) found that when extroverts were asked to self-present as introverts, the addition of a cognitive load interfered with their performance. However, when introverts were asked to self-present as extroverts, they actually performed better with a cognitive load, apparently because the load interfered with the self-defeating reactions that were normally present for those participants.

The motivational underpinnings of self-presentational efforts are likely both to stem from and to interact with other human motives. One of these complex interactions appears in the research on control motivation (see Pittman 1993, Weary et al. 1993) and managing the comprehensions of others. Acting to manage the comprehensions of others, in the service of increasing social power, is essentially an attempt to control one's social environment. Thus, we would expect that situations that enhance or activate a need for control would have consequences for the level and type of self-presentational activity. Self-verification theory is based in large part on this general premise. This research has been reviewed extensively elsewhere (Swann 1984, Swann et al. 2007), but generally it shows that individuals construct their social realities so that interaction partners are induced to comprehend and respond to them in self-consistent ways. But exceptions to this tendency do occur. For example, when a specific self-inconsistent conception on the part of an interaction partner will lead to increased social power, it is promoted (Swann et al. 2002). Consistent with this finding, Sechrist et al. (2004) first showed that targets of discrimination tend to inhibit attributions to discrimination under public (but not private) conditions as a self-presentational strategy. However, this tendency was eliminated when a need for personal control was induced.

More research can be expected on both the motivational underpinnings of managing the comprehensions of others and on how the activation of specific motives and motivational orientations affect management concerns and strategies.

Managing Damaged Identities

The research on self-verification processes blends the two motivational concerns mentioned at the beginning of this section: enhancing social power and creating, maintaining, and augmenting desired self-concepts. From a motivational perspective, things become very interesting when a person encounters a situation in which a damaged or threatened identity must be salvaged or protected, because this will certainly engage motivational concerns. Research on such circumstances has been reviewed recently (see Major & O'Brien 2005, Schneider 2004). We briefly reference here the research on the use of apologies, excuses, and expressions of remorse in managing potentially negative comprehensions of self by others.

In cases where harm has been done to another that could lead to negative comprehensions of self by that other, explanations in the form of excuses are an effective self-presentational response, both because they address (and diminish) responsibility for the negative outcome (Schlenker et al. 2001) and because they serve as an indirect signal of respect for the victim as they acknowledge the need for an explanation (Miller 2001). Apologies, on the other hand, can also be very effective reactions in cases in which an actor has harmed another, because harm is acknowledged, responsibility is accepted, and respect is shown for the victim's otherwise damaged status or standing (Miller 2001). Expressions of remorse, which may or may not include acceptance of responsibility, can also be effective in managing the reactions of others to an actual or perceived harm (Darley & Pittman 2003). In all of these cases, to be effective the actor has to understand the nature of the situation, including the norms governing it as seen by both the actor and the other, and to choose a response that balances the desire to repair social standing (social power) through mitigation of the other's feelings of injustice, indignation, and reduced status, as well as the effects of any such actions on the actor's own desired sense of self. In these cases of managing damaged identities, the aggrieved party will be particularly interested in the actor's state of mind, or intentions, at the

time of the transgression. Excuses, apologies, and expressions of remorse are all designed to create a particular shared comprehension of those circumstances in ways that benefit the actors' hedonic outcomes and sense of self.

SHARING KNOWLEDGE ABOUT THE WORLD

As discussed above, a special characteristic of people is their motivation to share their inner states with others. Recently, there has been increasing interest in how people share, and resist sharing, with others their thoughts or knowledge about the world. This section reviews that literature, paying particular attention to the role of social interaction in this process.

Knowledge Effects of Social Tuning to an Audience's Inner States

In an early study by Higgins & Rholes (1978), participants read behavioral descriptions of a male target person and then communicated about him, without using his name, to an audience whose task was to use the message to identify the target. The communicators believed that the target and the audience were members of the same group, and that the audience either liked or disliked the target. The study found that the communicators tuned or tailored their message to suit the audience's attitude; i.e., the message was more positive when the audience liked (versus disliked) the target. More significant, the communicators' own subsequent memory of the target's behaviors, even weeks later, was evaluatively consistent with their audience-tuned message rather than being based simply on the original behavioral information. Higgins (1992) proposed that this "saying-is-believing" effect, which has been replicated in many subsequent studies (for a review, see Echterhoff et al. 2005), involves communicators creating a shared reality with their audience. In the language of the present review, communicators first construct a message about the target that shares the inner attitude of the audience toward the target, and this action in turn creates communicator knowledge of the target that shares the evaluative viewpoint of the audience toward the target.

Recent studies have extended the earlier research on the saying-is-believing effect by examining both when it occurs and how it occurs. In one set of studies, Echterhoff et al. (2005) found that the audience-tuned message affected communicators' recall of the target person—creating shared knowledge with the audience—when communicators were told that their audience successfully identified the target from their message, but not when they were told that their audience failed to identify the target from their message. Thus, when communicators believed that they had failed to create a shared reality with their audience about the target, the shared knowledge reflected in recall was eliminated. There was also evidence that the communicators' epistemic trust in the audience was greater in the positive-feedback than in the negative-feedback condition.

In additional studies, Echterhoff et al. (2007) highlighted the importance of communicators' epistemic trust in the audience. Echterhoff et al. (2007) manipulated communication goals other than shared reality that also led communicators to tune their message to the audience's attitude, such as an entertainment goal of exaggerating the character of the target person or an instrumental goal of tuning to receive a possible reward from the audience. Although the magnitude of the message tuning toward the audience's attitude was at least as great in these non-shared reality goal conditions as in the standard shared reality goal condition, the message-related shared-knowledge effect was reduced or eliminated in these conditions (see also Todorov 2002). Moreover, the pattern of results regarding when the saying-is-believing effect did and did not occur was found to be mediated by the communicators' epistemic trust in the audience.

Additional studies by Hausmann et al. (2007) and by Higgins et al. (2007) investigated communicators' tuning toward the attitude of an audience composed of a group of persons rather than a single individual. These studies also found that epistemic trust in the audience is an important determinant of whether shared knowledge about a target is created in the communication process. Higgins et al. (2007) found that social tuning effects on knowledge do not require that a message actually be produced when the audience is a group of people sharing the same attitude about a target person; that is, a condition of high epistemic trust in the audience.

These studies suggest that the creation of epistemic trust from communicators' tuning their message to their audience's attitude is a possible mechanism for the social construction of knowledge about individuals and social category members (i.e., stereotypes). Studies by Hardin, Sinclair and their colleagues (Hardin & Conley 2001; Lowery et al. 2001; Sinclair et al. 2005a,b, 2006) highlight another possible mechanism underlying stereotype formation and maintenance—social relationship motives. The basic research paradigm of these studies involves participants interacting with someone who ostensibly has stereotypic views regarding some social category, i.e., stereotypic views of women or of African Americans. The participants' motivation to have a relationship with the audience varied as a function of personality or situational induction. These studies found that participants' stereotyping of themselves (self-stereotyping) and others (social stereotyping) was more likely to be tuned toward their audience's ostensible beliefs when social relationship motives were stronger.

The studies reviewed thus far concern tuning to the attitudes or beliefs of a particular audience. Social tuning can also involve tuning to a generalized other. Lyons & Kashima (2003), for example, examined communication chains where a story about a character who is a member of a stereotyped group is retold repeatedly through a four-person chain of storytellers. They found that stereotype-relevant information in the story became more consistent over the communication chain with the stereotypical views of the audience, and the shared nature of the stereotypes was an especially strong contributor to reconstructing the story in a more stereotypical form.

A classic case of creating a shared reality is groups' constructing a shared normative belief about some object or event. Levine et al. (2000) extended this research to the case of convergence in group members' risky or conservative strategic decision-making. They experimentally induced either a promotion or a prevention focus (see Higgins 1998) in three-person groups working on a multitrial recognition memory task. The group members' judgments converged over time, and this convergence was associated with a directional bias in strategic orientation (i.e., promotion groups became riskier than prevention groups).

Resistance to Creating a Shared Reality with Others

The literature has also found that there are conditions under which people resist creating a shared reality with others. Early studies on the saying-is-believing effect, for example, found that communicators vary in the extent to which they will tailor their message to suit their audience's attitude. Higgins & McCann (1984) found that when the audience was of higher status than was the communicator, message tuning was not just greater for high than for low authoritarians, but low authoritarians actively resisted tuning to the higher-status audience (antituning). Higgins & McCann (1984) also found that reduced audience tuning in the messages was associated with a reduced saying-is-believing effect, reflecting the fact that less shared knowledge about the target person was created.

More recent studies have found other forms of resistance to creating a shared reality with others. Echterhoff et al. (2005, 2007) compared the saying-is-believing effect when communicators tune their message for an in-group audience versus an out-group audience. Although there was significant message tuning toward the audience's attitude for both an in-group and out-group audience, the saying-is-believing effect was significantly reduced, and in some cases eliminated altogether, when the audience was an out-group. Thus, shared knowledge about a target person is not necessarily created by the social tuning of a message alone. As discussed above, Echterhoff et al. (2005, 2007) found that an experience of epistemic trust in the audience is also necessary for a shared reality to be created, and epistemic trust is reduced with an out-group audience. Within their self-stereotyping paradigm, Sinclair et al. (2005a) examined whether individuals might resist creating a shared reality with their audience's beliefs when affiliative motivation is low. In one condition, participants were primed with a social distance motive by giving them a scenario where they imagined feeling overwhelmed by social contact and needed some time to themselves. In this condition, the participants tended to contrast their self-evaluations away from the ostensible stereotypic views of their interaction partner.

In the above studies, resistance to creating a shared reality was successful in reducing shared beliefs or knowledge with the audience. Resistance is not always successful, however. Muller & Hirst (2007), for example, investigated what happens when participants discussing a story with others are warned that the information possessed by one member of the group is untrustworthy. They found that when this untrustworthy member was a dominant narrator of the story in the group, and the listener's own memory of the original story was poor, the listener paid careful attention to what the untrustworthy member had to say in order to resist it, paradoxically increasing the subsequent impact of the untrustworthy information on participants' recollections of the original story.

An especially interesting form of achieving versus resisting the creation of a new shared reality occurs when immigrants enter a new culture. Kosic et al. (2004) proposed that the motivation of immigrants to create a shared reality with the new cultural members depends on whether the new culture is personally a positive reference group for them, and whether they have a need for epistemic certainty about their beliefs (i.e., a high need for closure). Consistent with this shared reality perspective, they found that when the immigrants' initial reference group was (to a significant extent) the culture of the host country, their level of acculturation into the host society was higher as need for closure was higher, whereas when their initial reference group was their country of origin, acculturation was reduced as need for closure was higher.

CONCLUDING COMMENTS

It has been popular in recent decades to explain the wars and conflicts among nations, races, and religious and ethnic groups as deriving from the combination of human advancement in cognition, reflected in weapon-related advances, and human nonadvancement in our base animal-like motives. Indeed, at the same time as pundits trumpet the angel-like intellectual and artistic achievements of humans, they deplore our animal-like ferocity—one of the few animals who kills members of their own species. We beg to differ. Humans are not like other animals motivationally. Humans' motives to comprehend, manage, and share inner states are noncomparable to those of other animals. Indeed, these distinctive motives provide a better explanation for human conflict than our supposedly animal-like motives because it is precisely these motives that would produce the intensity of in-group versus out-group misunderstanding and mistrust that creates uniquely human conflicts.

We have argued for the importance to human motivation of the distinctive motives to comprehend, manage, and share inner states. A point that we have not made explicit is that, to the extent that we are correct, these motives would not have the same strength for everyone. It is a given that motivational states will differ as a function of many variables—situational, personality, developmental, cultural, and so on. In psychology, the variation in the motives to comprehend, manage, and share inner states has received the most attention for the dimension of developmental differences. We know, for example, that these motives are different for very young children than for adults. Although it is not a totally ignored issue, less attention has been given to the ways in which these motives vary as a personality difference, a historical difference, or a cross-cultural difference. This raises fascinating questions for future research. To what extent do different personalities reflect differences in strength of motivation to comprehend, manage, or share some inner states but not others? To what extent can cultures be understood in terms of their strength of motivation to comprehend, manage, or share some inner states but not others? What conflicts and misunderstandings arise between individuals and between cultures from differences in these motives?

ACKNOWLEDGMENTS

Work on this review was supported in part by National Institute of Mental Health Grant 39429 to E. Tory Higgins. The authors thank John Levine and Janet Metcalfe for their helpful comments on an earlier version of this review and Sheila Libby for her assistance with preparation of the manuscript.

LITERATURE CITED

Aloise-Young PA. 1993. The development of self-presentation: self-promotion in 6- to 10-year-old children. *Soc. Cogn.* 11:201–22

Andersen SM, Chen S. 2002. The relational self: an interpersonal social-cognitive theory. *Psychol. Rev.* 109:619–45

Bandura A. 1986. *Social Foundations of Thought and Action: A Social Cognitive Theory.* Englewood Cliffs, NJ: Prentice Hall

Bandura A. 1997. *Self-Efficacy: The Exercise of Control.* New York: Freeman

Bassett JF, Cate KL, Dabbs JM. 2002. Individual differences in self-presentation style: driving an automobile and meeting a stranger. *Self Identity* 13:281–88

Baumeister RF, Schmeichel BJ, Vohs KD. 2007. Self-regulation and the executive function: the self as controlling agent. See Kruglanski & Higgins 2007, pp. 516–39

Baumeister RF, Vohs KD, eds. 2004. *Handbook of Self-Regulation: Research, Theory, and Applications.* New York: Guilford

Blickle G. 2003. Some outcomes of pressure, ingratiation, and rational persuasion used with peers in the workplace. *J. Appl. Soc. Psychol.* 33:648–65

Boldero J, Francis J. 2002. Goals, standards, and the self: reference values serving different functions. *Personal. Soc. Psychol. Rev.* 6:232–41

Bolino MC, Turnley WH. 2003. More than one way to make an impression: exploring profiles of impression management. *J. Manag.* 29:141–60

Bornstein RF. 2006. The complex relationship between dependency and domestic violence. *Am. Psychol.* 61:595–606

Bornstein RF, Riggs JM, Hill EL, Calabrese C. 1996. Activity, passivity, self-denigration, and self-promotion: toward an interactionist model of interpersonal dependency. *J. Personal.* 64:637–74

Brandstatter V, Lengfelder A, Gollwitzer PM. 2001. Implementation intentions and efficient action initiation. *J. Personal. Soc. Psychol.* 81:946–60

Call J. 2005. The self and other: a missing link in comparative social cognition. See Terrace & Metcalfe 2005, pp. 321–41

Carver CS, Reynolds SL, Scheier MF. 1994. The possible selves of optimists and pessimists. *J. Res. Personal.* 28:133–41

Carver CS, Scheier MF. 1998. *On the Self-Regulation of Behavior.* New York: Cambridge Univ. Press

Chun WY, Spiegel S, Kruglanski AW. 2002. Assimilative behavior identification can also be resource dependent: a unimodel perspective on personal-attribution phases. *J. Personal. Soc. Psychol.* 83:542–55

Clark DA. 2004. *Intrusive Thoughts in Clinical Disorders: Theory, Research, and Treatment.* New York: Guilford

Cooley CH. 1962/1909. *Social Organization: A Study of the Larger Mind.* New York: Schocken

Crano WD, Prislin R. 2006. Attitudes and persuasion. *Annu. Rev. Psychol.* 57:345–74

Darley JM, Pittman TS. 2003. The psychology of compensatory and retributive justice. *Personal. Soc. Psychol. Rev.* 7:324–36

Eagly AH, Chaiken S. 1993. *The Psychology of Attitudes.* New York: Harcourt Brace Jovanovich

Echterhoff G, Higgins ET, Groll S. 2005. Audience-tuning effects on memory: the role of shared reality. *J. Personal. Soc. Psychol.* 89:257–76

Echterhoff G, Higgins ET, Kopietz R, Groll S. 2007. How communication goals determine when audience tuning biases memory. *J. Exp. Psychol.: Gen.* In press

Fiske ST, Berdahl J. 2007. Social power. See Kruglanski & Higgins 2007, pp. 678–92

Folkman S, Moskowitz JT. 2004. Coping: pitfalls and promise. *Annu. Rev. Psychol.* 55:745–74

Gilbert DT, Lieberman MD, Morewedge CK, Wilson TD. 2004a. The peculiar longevity of things not so bad. *Psychol. Sci.* 15:14–19

Gilbert DT, Morewedge CK, Risen JL, Wilson TD. 2004b. Looking forward to looking backward: the misprediction of regret. *Psychol. Sci.* 15:346–50

Hardin CD, Conley TD. 2001. A relational approach to cognition: shared experience and relationship affirmation in social cognition. In *Cognitive Social Psychology: The Princeton Symposium on the Legacy and Future of Social Cognition*, ed. GB Moskowitz, pp. 3–17. Mahwah, NJ: Erlbaum

Hardin CD, Higgins ET. 1996. Shared reality: how social verification makes the subjective objective. In *Handbook of Motivation and Cognition*. Vol. 3: *The Interpersonal Context*, ed. RM Sorrentino, ET Higgins, pp. 28–84. New York: Guilford

Hausmann LRM, Levine JM, Higgins ET. 2007. *Communication and group perception: extending the "saying is believing" effect.* Univ. Pittsburgh. Unpubl. manuscript.

Heider F. 1958. *The Psychology of Interpersonal Relations.* New York: Wiley

Higgins ET. 1987. Self-discrepancy: a theory relating self and affect. *Psychol. Rev.* 94:319–40

Higgins ET. 1991. Development of self-regulatory and self-evaluative processes: costs, benefits, and tradeoffs. In *Self Processes and Development: The Minnesota Symposia on Child Psychology*, ed. MR Gunnar, LA Sroufe, 23:125–65. Hillsdale, NJ: Erlbaum

Higgins ET. 1992. Achieving "shared reality" in the communication game: a social action that creates meaning. *J. Lang. Soc. Psychol.* 11:107–31

Higgins ET. 1996. Shared reality in the self-system: the social nature of self-regulation. *Eur. Rev. Soc. Psychol.* 7:1–29

Higgins ET. 1998. Promotion and prevention: regulatory focus as a motivational principle. In *Advances in Experimental Social Psychology*, ed. MP Zanna, 30:1–46. New York: Academic

Higgins ET. 2005. Humans as applied motivation scientists: self-consciousness from "shared reality" and "becoming." See Terrace & Metcalfe 2005, pp. 157–73

Higgins ET, Echterhoff G, Crespillo R, Kopietz R. 2007. Effects of communication on social knowledge: sharing reality with individual versus group audiences. *Jpn. Psychol. Res.* 49:89–99

Higgins ET, McCann CD. 1984. Social encoding and subsequent attitudes, impressions, and memory: "context-driven" and motivational aspects of processing. *J. Personal. Soc. Psychol.* 47:26–39

Higgins ET, Rholes WS. 1978. "Saying is believing": effects of message modification on memory and liking for the person described. *J. Exp. Soc. Psychol.* 14:363–78

Hsee CK, Zhang J. 2004. Distinction bias: misprediction and mischoice due to joint evaluation. *J. Personal. Soc. Psychol.* 86:680–95

Idson LC, Liberman N, Higgins ET. 2000. Distinguishing gains from nonlosses and losses from nongains: a regulatory focus perspective on hedonic intensity. *J. Exp. Soc. Psychol.* 36:252–74

Idson LC, Mischel W. 2001. The personality of familiar and significant people: the lay perceiver as a social-cognitive theorist. *J. Personal. Soc. Psychol.* 80:585–96

Igou ER. 2004. Lay theories in affective forecasting: the progression of affect. *J. Exp. Soc. Psychol.* 40:528–34

Johnson MK. 2006. Memory and reality. *Am. Psychol.* 61:760–71

Jones EE. 1964. *Ingratiation.* New York: Meredith

Jones EE, Pittman TS. 1982. Toward a general theory of strategic self-presentation. In *Psychological Perspectives on the Self*, ed. J Suls, 1:231–62. Hillsdale, NJ: Erlbaum

Jones EE, Wortman C. 1973. *Ingratiation: An Attributional Approach*. Morristown, NJ: Gen. Learn. Press

Kashima Y, McIntyre A, Clifford P. 1998. The category of the mind: folk psychology of belief, desire, and intention. *Asian J. Soc. Psychol.* 1:289–313

Keil FC. 2006. Explanation and understanding. *Annu. Rev. Psychol.* 57:227–54

Koriat A, Bjork RA, Sheffer L, Bar SK. 2004. Predicting one's own forgetting: the role of experience-based and theory-based processes. *J. Exp. Psychol.: Gen.* 133:643–56

Koriat A, Goldsmith M, Pansky A. 2000. Toward a psychology of memory accuracy. *Annu. Rev. Psychol.* 51:481–537

Kosic A, Kruglanski AW, Pierro A, Mannetti L. 2004. Social cognition of immigrants' acculturation: effects of the need for closure and the reference group at entry. *J. Personal. Soc. Psychol.* 86:796–813

Kruglanski AW, Higgins ET, eds. 2007. *Social Psychology: Handbook of Basic Principles*. New York: Guilford

Leary MR. 2004. *The Curse of the Self: Self-Awareness, Egotism, and the Quality of Human Life*. New York: Oxford Univ. Press

Leary MR. 2007. Motivational and emotional aspects of the self. *Annu. Rev. Psychol.* 58:317–44

Leary MR, Buttermore NE. 2003. The evolution of the human self: tracing the natural history of self-awareness. *J. Theory Soc. Behav.* 33:365–404

Levine JM, Higgins ET, Choi H-S. 2000. Development of strategic norms in groups. *Organ. Behav. Hum. Decis. Process.* 82:88–101

Levine JM, Moreland RL. 1994. Group socialization: theory and research. In *European Review of Social Psychology*, ed. W Stroebe, M Hewstone, 5:305–36. Chichester, UK: Wiley

Lowenstein G, Schkade D. 1999. Wouldn't it be nice? Predicting future feelings. In *Well-Being: The Foundations of Hedonic Psychology*, ed. D Kahneman, E Diener, N Schwarz, pp. 85–105. New York: Russell Sage Found.

Lowery BS, Hardin CD, Sinclair S. 2001. Social influence effects on automatic racial prejudice. *J. Personal. Soc. Psychol.* 81:842–55

Lyons A, Kashima Y. 2003. How are stereotypes maintained through communication? The influence of stereotype sharedness. *J. Personal. Soc. Psychol.* 85:989–1005

MacDonald G, Jessica M. 2006. Family approval as a constraint in dependency regulation: evidence from Australia and Indonesia. *Pers. Relat.* 13:183–94

Macrae N, Bodenhausen GV. 2000. Social cognition: thinking categorically about others. *Annu. Rev. Psychol.* 51:93–120

Major B, O'Brien LT. 2005. The social psychology of stigma. *Annu. Rev. Psychol.* 56:393–421

Malle BF, Pearce GE. 2001. Attention to behavioral events during interaction: two actor-observer gaps and three attempts to close them. *J. Personal. Soc. Psychol.* 81:278–94

Mandel DR, Hilton DJ, Catellani P. 2005. *The Psychology of Counterfactual Thinking*. London: Routledge

Markus H, Nurius P. 1986. Possible selves. *Am. Psychol.* 41:954–69

McNulty SE, Swann WB Jr. 1994. Identity negotiation in roommate relationships: the self as architect and consequence of social reality. *J. Personal. Soc. Psychol.* 67:1012–23

Mellers BA, McGraw AP. 2001. Anticipated emotions as guides to choice. *Curr. Dir. Psychol. Sci.* 10:210–14

Metcalfe J. 2000. Feelings and judgments of knowing: Is there a special noetic state? *Conscious. Cogn.* 9:178–86

Metcalfe J, Kerr NL, Brewer MB, Cantor N, eds. 1998. *Metacognition. Special Issue: Personality and Social Psychology Review*. Mahwah, NJ: Erlbaum

Miller DT. 2001. Disrespect and the experience of injustice. *Annu. Rev. Psychol.* 52:527–53

Moretti MM, Higgins ET. 1999. Own vs other standpoints in self-regulation: developmental antecedents and functional consequences. *Rev. Gen. Psychol.* 3:188–223

Muller F, Hirst W. 2007. Resistance to the influences of others: limits to the formation of a collective memory through conversational remembering. *Appl. Cogn. Psychol.* In press

Murray SL, Holmes JG, Collins NL. 2006. Optimizing assurance: the risk regulation system in relationships. *Psychol. Bull.* 132:641–66

Murray SL, Holmes JG, Griffin DW. 2000. Self-esteem and the quest for felt security: how perceived regard regulates attachment processes. *J. Personal. Soc. Psychol.* 78:478–98

Nelson K. 2005. Emerging levels of consciousness in early human development. See Terrace & Metcalfe 2005, pp. 116–41

Oettingen G. 1996. Positive fantasy and motivation. In *The Psychology of Action: Linking Cognition and Motivation to Behavior*, ed. PM Gollwitzer, JA Bargh, pp. 236–59. New York: Guilford

Oettingen G, Mayer D. 2002. The motivating function of thinking about the future: expectations vs fantasies. *J. Personal. Soc. Psychol.* 83:1198–212

Oettingen G, Pak H, Schnetter K. 2001. Self-regulation of goal setting: turning free fantasies about the future into binding goals. *J. Personal. Soc. Psychol.* 80:736–53

O' Laughlin MJ, Malle BF. 2002. How people explain actions performed by groups and individuals. *J. Personal. Soc. Psychol.* 82:33–48

Olson JM, Hafer CL, Taylor L. 2001. I'm mad as hell, and I'm not going to take it anymore: reports of negative emotions as a self-preservation tactic. *J. Appl. Soc. Psychol.* 31:981–99

Oyserman D, Bybee D, Terry K, Hart-Johnson T. 2004. Possible selves as roadmaps. *J. Res. Personal.* 38:130–49

Oyserman D, Markus HR. 1990. Possible selves and delinquency. *J. Personal. Soc. Psychol.* 59:112–25

Pittman TS. 1993. Control motivation and attitude change. In *Control Motivation and Social Cognition*, ed. G Weary, F Gleicher, K Marsh, pp. 157–75. New York: Springer-Verlag

Pittman TS. 1998. Motivation. In *Handbook of Social Psychology*, ed. D Gilbert, S Fiske, G Lindsay, pp. 549–90. Boston, MA: McGraw-Hill. 4th ed.

Pittman TS, Heller JF. 1987. Social motivation. *Annu. Rev. Psychol.* 38:461–89

Pittman TS, Zeigler K. 2007. Basic human needs. See Kruglanski & Higgins 2007, pp. 473–89

Pontari BA, Schlenker BR. 2000. The influence of cognitive load on self-presentation: Can cognitive busyness help as well as harm social performance? *J. Personal. Soc. Psychol.* 78:1092–108

Pronin E, Gilovich T, Ross L. 2004. Objectivity in the eye of the beholder: divergent perceptions of bias in self vs others. *Psychol. Rev.* 111:781–99

Pronin E, Ross L. 2006. Temporal differences in trait self-ascription: when the self is seen as an other. *J. Personal. Soc. Psychol.* 90:197–209

Read SJ, Jones DK, Miller LC. 1990. Traits as goal-based categories: the importance of goals in the coherence of dispositional categories. *J. Personal. Soc. Psychol.* 58:1048–61

Roese NJ. 1997. Counterfactual thinking. *Psychol. Bull.* 121:133–48

Rudman LA. 1998. Self-promotion as a risk factor for women: the costs and benefits of counterstereotypical impression management. *J. Personal. Soc. Psychol.* 74:629–45

Rutland A, Cameron L, Milne A, McGeorge P. 2005. Social norms and self-presentation: children's implicit and explicit intergroup attitudes. *Child Dev.* 76:451–66

Sanna LJ. 1996. Defensive pessimism, optimism, and simulating alternatives: some ups and downs of prefactual and counterfactual thinking. *J. Personal. Soc. Psychol.* 71:1020–36

Sanna LJ, Chang EC, Meier S. 2001. Counterfactual thinking and self-motives. *Personal. Soc. Psychol. Bull.* 27:1023–34

Sanna LJ, Turley-Ames KJ, Meier S. 1999. Mood, self-esteem, and simulated alternatives: thought-provoking affective influences on counterfactual direction. *J. Personal. Soc. Psychol.* 76:543–58

Saxe R, Carey S, Kanwisher N. 2004. Understanding other minds: linking developmental psychology and functional neuroimaging. *Annu. Rev. Psychol.* 55:87–124

Schkade DA, Kahneman D. 1998. Does living in California make people happy? A focusing illusion in judgments of life satisfaction. *Psychol. Sci.* 9:340–46

Schlenker BR, Pontari BA, Christopher AN. 2001. Excuses and character: personal and social implications of excuses. *Personal. Soc. Psychol. Rev.* 5:15–32

Schlenker BR, Weigold MF. 1992. Interpersonal processes involving impression regulation and management. *Annu. Rev. Psychol.* 43:133–68

Schneider DJ. 2004. *The Psychology of Stereotyping.* New York: Guilford

Schutz A. 1997. Self-presentational tactics of talk show guests: a comparison of politicians, experts, and entertainers. *J. Appl. Soc. Psychol.* 27:1941–52

Sechrist GB, Swim J, Stangor C. 2004. When do the stigmatized make attributions to discrimination occurring to the self and others? The roles of self-presentation and need for control. *J. Personal. Soc. Psychol.* 87:111–22

Shah J. 2003. The motivational looking glass: how significant others implicitly affect goal appraisals. *J. Personal. Soc. Psychol.* 85:424–39

Shah J, Higgins ET. 2001. Regulatory concerns and appraisal efficiency: the general impact of promotion and prevention. *J. Personal. Soc. Psychol.* 80:693–705

Showers C. 1992. The motivational and emotional consequences of considering positive or negative possibilities for an upcoming event. *J. Personal. Soc. Psychol.* 63:474–84

Sinclair S, Hardin CD, Lowery BS. 2006. Self-stereotyping in the context of multiple social identities. *J. Personal. Soc. Psychol.* 90:529–42

Sinclair S, Huntsinger J, Skorinko J, Hardin CD. 2005a. Social tuning of the self: consequences for the self-evaluations of stereotype targets. *J. Personal. Soc. Psychol.* 89:160–75

Sinclair S, Lowery BS, Hardin CD, Colangelo A. 2005b. Social tuning of automatic racial attitudes: the role of affiliative motivation. *J. Personal. Soc. Psychol.* 89:583–92

Snyder M, Stukas AA. 1999. Interpersonal processes: the interplay of cognitive, motivational, and behavioral activities in social interaction. *Annu. Rev. Psychol.* 50:273–303

Stangor C, ed. 2000. *Stereotypes and Prejudice: Key Readings in Social Psychology.* Philadelphia, PA: Psychol. Press

Stone J, Wiegand AW, Cooper J, Aronson E. 1997. When exemplification fails: hypocrisy and the motive for self-integrity. *J. Personal. Soc. Psychol.* 72:54–65

Strauman TJ. 1996. Stability within the self: a longitudinal study of the structural implications of self-discrepancy theory. *J. Personal. Soc. Psychol.* 71:1142–53

Strutton D, Pelton LE. 1998. Effects of ingratiation on lateral relationship quality within sales team settings. *J. Bus. Res.* 43:1–12

Swann WB Jr. 1984. Quest for accuracy in person perception: a matter of pragmatics. *Psychol. Rev.* 91:457–77

Swann WB Jr, Bosson JK, Pelham BW. 2002. Different partners, different selves: strategic verification of circumscribed identities. *Personal. Soc. Psychol. Bull.* 28:1215–28

Swann WB Jr, Chang-Schneider C, Angulo S. 2007. Self-verification in relationships as an adaptive process. In *Self and Relationships*, ed. J Wood, A Tesser, J Holmes. New York: Psychol. Press. In press

Swann WB Jr, Hixon JG, De La Ronde C. 1992. Embracing the bitter "truth": negative self-concepts and marital commitment. *Psychol. Sci.* 3:118–21

Terrace HS. 2005. Metacognition and the evolution of language. See Terrace & Metcalfe 2005, pp. 84–115

Terrace HS, Metcalfe J, eds. 2005. *The Missing Link in Cognition: Origins of Self-Reflective Consciousness*. Oxford: Oxford Univ. Press

Todorov A. 2002. Communication effects on memory and judgment. *Eur. J. Soc. Psychol.* 32:531–46

Trope Y, Alfieri T. 1997. Effortfulness and flexibility of dispositional judgment processes. *J. Personal. Soc. Psychol.* 73:662–74

Trzebinski J, Richards K. 1986. The role of goal categories in person impression. *J. Exp. Soc. Psychol.* 22:216–27

Tulving E. 2005. Episodic memory and autonoesis. Uniquely human? See Terrace & Metcalfe 2005, pp. 3–56

Tykocinski OE, Pittman TS. 2004. The dark side of opportunity: regret, disappointment, and the cost of prospects. In *The Psychology of Economic Decisions*, ed. I Brocas, J Carrillo, 2:179–96. New York: Oxford Univ. Press

Tyler JM, Feldman RS. 2004. Cognitive demand and self-presentation efforts: the influence of situational importance and interaction goal. *Self Identity* 3:364–77

Ubel PA, Loewenstein G, Jepson C. 2005. Disability and sunshine: Can hedonic predictions be improved by drawing attention to focusing illusions or emotional adaptation? *J. Exp. Psychol.: Appl.* 11:111–23

Van Kleef GA, De Dreu CKW, Manstead ASR. 2006. Supplication and appeasement in conflict and negotiation: interpersonal effects of disappointment, worry, guilt, and regret. *J. Personal. Soc. Psychol.* 91:124–42

Vohs KD, Baumeister RF, Ciarocco NJ. 2005. Self-regulation and self-presentation: regulatory resource depletion impairs impression management and effortful self-presentation depletes regulatory resources. *J. Personal. Soc. Psychol.* 88:632–57

Vonk R. 2002. Self-serving interpretations of flattery: why ingratiation works. *J. Personal. Soc. Psychol.* 82:515–26

Weary G, Gleicher F, Marsh K. 1993. *Control Motivation and Social Cognition*. New York: Springer-Verlag

Webster's Ninth New Collegiate Dictionary. 1989. Springfield, MA: Merriam-Webster

Wellman HM, Cross D, Watson J. 2001. Meta-analysis of theory-of-mind development: the truth about false belief. *Child Dev.* 72:655–84

Wilson TD, Gilbert DT. 2003. Affective forecasting. In *Advances in Experimental Social Psychology*, ed. MP Zanna, 35:345–411. New York: Elsevier

Wilson TD, Houston CE, Meyers JM. 1998. Choose your poison: effects of lay beliefs about mental processes on attitude change. *Soc. Cogn.* 16:114–32

Wilson TD, Wheatley TP, Meyers JM, Gilbert DT, Axsom D. 2000. Focalism: a source of durability bias in affective forecasting. *J. Personal. Soc. Psychol.* 78:821–36

Yzerbyt VY, Lories G, Dardenne B, eds. 1998. *Metacognition: Cognitive and Social Dimensions*. New York: Sage

Cognition in Organizations

Gerard P. Hodgkinson and Mark P. Healey

Leeds University Business School, University of Leeds, Leeds LS2 9JT,
United Kingdom; email: gph@lubs.leeds.ac.uk, busmph@leeds.ac.uk

Annu. Rev. Psychol. 2008. 59:387–417

First published online as a Review in Advance on
June 4, 2007

The *Annual Review of Psychology* is online at
http://psych.annualreviews.org

This article's doi:
10.1146/annurev.psych.59.103006.093612

Key Words

managerial and organizational cognition, organizational behavior,
information processing, decision making, cognitive engineering,
shared cognition

Abstract

This article reviews major developments from 2000 to early 2007
in the psychological analysis of cognition in organizations. Our review, the first in this series to survey cognitive theory and research
spanning the entire field of industrial and organizational psychology, considers theoretical, empirical, and methodological advances
across 10 substantive domains of application. Two major traditions,
the human factors and organizational traditions, have dominated
cognitively oriented research in this field. Our central message is
that the technological and human systems underpinning contemporary organizational forms are evolving in ways that demand greater
cooperation among researchers across both traditions. Such cooperation is necessary in order to gain theoretical insights of sufficient
depth and complexity to refine the explanation and prediction of behavior in organizations and derive psychologically sound solutions
to the unprecedented information-processing burdens confronting
the twenty-first century workforce.

Contents

INTRODUCTION

The study of cognition in organizations has been on the ascendancy for the past two decades. This should come as no surprise, for the vast scale of political, economic, social, and technological change confronting modern organizations is placing unprecedented information-processing burdens on the individuals and groups working within them. Ac-

I/O: industrial and organizational

cordingly, there has been a dramatic growth in psychological research directed toward advancing understanding of the cognitive capabilities and limitations of managers and employees, with a view to enhancing productivity and well-being in the workplace.

Our article is the first in the *Annual Review of Psychology* to cover advances in cognitive theory and research across the industrial and organizational (I/O) psychology field as a whole. Hence, we commence with a brief overview of historical developments, including the principal theoretical advances in cognitive psychology and social cognition that have informed the contemporary cognitive analysis of behavior in organizations. We then survey key developments across 10 major substantive domains of I/O psychology, namely, personnel selection and assessment, work groups and teams, training and development, stress and occupational health, work motivation, work design and cognitive ergonomics, leadership, organizational decision making, organizational change and development, and individual differences. Finally, we review recent methodological advances and highlight future directions for the field as a whole.

For the purposes of this review, it is useful to conceive of psychological research on cognition in organizations as falling into two major traditions: (*a*) the human factors tradition, and (*b*) the organizational tradition. Research in both traditions has important implications for the design of tasks, jobs, and new organizational forms, and for enriching the understanding of behavior both within and between organizations. As our review demonstrates, there are clear signs that in recent years human factors and organizational researchers have begun to cooperate across these traditions. Our overarching conclusion, however, is that such is the scale of the changes that have occurred in the world of work over recent decades that greater cooperation is now required in order to advance theoretical understanding of sufficient sophistication to inform the development of psychologically sound solutions to the increasingly complex challenges confronting the contemporary workforce.

HISTORICAL BACKGROUND AND THEORETICAL FOUNDATIONS

The purpose of this section is to outline, albeit briefly, the history of work on cognition in organizations, from its inception to the outset of the current review period, in order to provide the necessary background to inform a coherent and integrated review of contemporary developments across the 10 main domains of application.

The Human Factors Tradition

The human factors tradition subsumes the fields of engineering psychology and human performance, including psychological aspects of ergonomics, which blossomed as behaviorism gave way to cognitivism. The human information-processing approach to the analysis of skilled performance rose to prominence toward the end of the Second World War. Researchers attempted to refine understanding of the perceptual-motor tasks that predominated work in heavy industry at that time through the detailed analysis and modeling of the human-machine interface. Drawing on the computational metaphor that then predominated in cognitive experimental psychology, researchers in this tradition conceptualized the execution of skilled performance as a stage-based sequence of functions, including sensory and perceptual processes, memory, and decision making, culminating in the execution of skilled responses (see, e.g., Broadbent 1958).

As organizational technologies evolved, researchers turned to investigate more directly human operators' mental representations of complex industrial processes and systems in order to explore their nature and impact on system performance (see, e.g., Edwards & Lees 1974). Following Card et al.'s (1983) seminal volume, the so-called knobs

and dials era gave way to the era of human-computer interaction, informing the design of computer-based systems, from basic desktop machines to modern-day flight decks. Although the mental models concept, coined initially by Craik (1943), continues to play a central role in this more recent work, it has been the subject of increasingly critical scrutiny amid debates concerning its definition and usage, ranging from conceptions as temporary dynamic models in working memory, in similar vein to Johnson-Laird's (1983) notion of mental models, to enduring knowledge structures in long-term memory, akin to Bartlett's (1932) notion of schema (see Rouse & Morris 1986).

As observed by Wickens & Carswell (2006), in addition to the staged-based approach enumerated above, two other approaches to human information processing currently prevail within the human factors tradition. The first, known as the ecological approach, emphasizes human interaction with the environment and is characterized by the study of expertise in naturalistic settings. The second, the cognitive engineering approach, constitutes a hybrid approach bringing together key elements of the stage-based and ecological approaches, in an attempt to further understanding of the interactions between task and environmental constraints and operators' knowledge structures. Human factors researchers adopting the cognitive engineering approach (e.g., Zhang & Norman 1994) are beginning to examine the role of complex workplace technology as both a shaper and repository of knowledge (see also Hutchins 1995), a trend paralleled in the organizational tradition (cf. Walsh & Ungson 1991). Salvendy (2006) provides extensive coverage of work in the human factors tradition from its inception up to the current review period.

The Organizational Tradition

Theory and research within this tradition have gathered momentum over the past two decades. Its origins, however, can be traced to Simon's (1947) *Administrative Behavior*, in which he outlined the notion of bounded rationality, the idea that organizational decision makers strive for rationality within the limits of their cognitive capacities and information availability (see also March & Simon 1958). However, Weick (1979) subsequently called into question several of the core assumptions underpinning the bounded rationality notion through his work on enactment and the related concept of sensemaking. In particular, he challenged the idea that the environment is an objective entity that can only be partially comprehended due to limited processing capacity. On the contrary, he maintained that decision makers literally create their own constraints through an active constructive process, in which they rearrange, isolate, and demolish seemingly objective features of their surroundings, in turn giving rise to subjective differences in perception.

Hambrick & Mason's (1984) upper echelons perspective added further impetus to the organizational tradition. Drawing on Simon's notion of bounded rationality, this approach views strategic choice as a function of the demographic and psychological composition of the organization's top management team. Because of the difficulties of studying the mental representations and other psychological characteristics of the organization's executive team members in situ, Hambrick & Mason (1984) advocated indirect methods of cognitive assessment, whereby executives' background characteristics (e.g., education, functional specialization) are used as proxies for cognitive variables (i.e., values and beliefs) in the prediction of organizational outcomes (e.g., firm performance). From the early 1990s onward, the upper echelon approach has been the subject of growing theoretical and empirical scrutiny amid numerous contradictory and inconsistent findings. Responding to these challenges, more recent work has incorporated direct methods of cognitive assessment, thereby isolating the determinants and consequences of executive perceptions and beliefs

(e.g., Chattopadhyay et al. 1999, Markoczy 1997).

The development of direct methods to probe more deeply organizational decision makers' mental representations gathered pace throughout the 1990s, following the publication of Huff's (1990) influential volume and Walsh's (1995) landmark review, together with several special issues of key management and organization studies journals (e.g., *Journal of Management Studies, Organization Science*). Inter alia this body of work has enriched understanding of the nature and role of mental representations in both organizational inertia and strategic adaptation (e.g., Kiesler & Sproull 1982, Porac et al. 1995). However, as with the human factors tradition, construct validity issues and the proliferation and inconsistent use of terms and concepts relating to the mental representations notion have made conceptual integration and theoretical progression difficult.

Meanwhile, attribution theory (Kelley 1967) has enriched understanding in a range of substantive domains of application, from the analysis of personnel selection decisions to the investigation of managers' explanations of employee and organizational performance. Following Ashforth & Mael (1989), social identity theory (Tajfel & Turner 1979) and related conceptions of self- and social-categorization have similarly influenced research across a wide range of topics, from cooperation in the workplace to socio-cognitive processes in strategic management. Further work in social cognition emphasizing the tendency of individuals to seek consistency in their attitudes and beliefs (e.g., Heider 1958) has also been foundational in the development of several cognitive theories of work motivation, not least equity theory and related formulations (e.g., justice theory). Finally, various heuristics and biases elucidated by behavioral decision researchers (e.g., Tversky & Kahneman 1974) have been shown to influence judgment and choice in a range of personnel and organizational decision processes. The study of heuristic and intuitive processing has received added impetus over recent years (for a review, see Hodgkinson et al. 2008), following an explosion of interest in dual-process theories of cognition in cognitive psychology (e.g., Gilovich et al. 2002) and social cognition (e.g., Chaiken & Trope 1999). For further background and a detailed overview of the origins of the organizational tradition, see Walsh (1995) and Hodgkinson & Sparrow (2002).

Computation and Interpretation: Metaphors Bridging the Traditions

In sum, five major theoretical perspectives drawn from cognitive experimental psychology and social cognition pervade contemporary research on cognition in organizations, namely (*a*) schema theory and related conceptions of mental representations (especially the notion of mental models), (*b*) behavioral decision theory (especially work on heuristics and biases), (*c*) attribution theory, (*d*) social identity theory and related conceptions[1], and (*e*) enactment and the related notion of sensemaking.[2] To a greater or lesser extent, each perspective has shaped the direction of work within and across the human factors and organizational traditions.

It is helpful at this juncture to borrow Lant & Shapira's (2001) distinction between the computational and interpretive perspectives on cognition in organizations. The former, exemplified by the work on mental representations and behavioral decision research, draws attention to the fundamental information-processing limitations of orga-

nizational decision makers and the strategies they employ in an effort to overcome those limitations, thus emphasizing the downstream choice or calculation processes at the heart of decision making and problem solving. The latter, in contrast, exemplified by Weick's work, emphasizes the upstream processes of sensemaking used by individuals and groups to extract patterns of meaning from ambiguous environmental cues in the social construction of organizational realities. As demonstrated above and in the remaining sections of this article, these processes coexist in a dynamic interplay.

SUBSTANTIVE DOMAINS OF APPLICATION

In the following sections, we survey developments within the current review period across the 10 substantive domains. The terrain is vast. Accordingly, our review does not purport to be comprehensive. Rather, we focus on what we consider the pivotal advances informed by each of the five dominant theoretical perspectives and related formulations outlined above.

Personnel Selection and Assessment

Building on earlier work that adopted a social and political, as opposed to a psychometric, perspective on personnel selection and assessment (e.g., Cleveland & Murphy 1992, Herriot 1989), researchers have continued to explore the fundamental attributional processes influencing assessor judgments of candidates (Nemanick & Clark 2002, Silvester et al. 2002). However, there has been a shift of emphasis toward the analysis of candidates' reactions to the selection and assessment process, informed by justice-theoretic perspectives (Hausknecht et al. 2004, Ryan & Ployhart 2000), including the identification of antecedents of justice perceptions (Shaw et al. 2003, Truxillo et al. 2002) and an exploration of the effects of justice expectations on

---

[1]Many writers employ the term social identity theory, where strictly speaking the social identity approach is a more appropriate term. The latter comprises a combination of social identity theory and self/social categorization theory and thus constitutes an approach, rather than a theory as such (see Haslam 2001).

[2]The social cognitive theory of Bandura and colleagues is yet another highly influential approach that has contributed to the development of work on cognition in organizations, highlighting the interaction between personal goals, cognition, and environmental factors in the regulation of motivated behavior, encapsulated in the notion of self-efficacy (see, e.g., Bandura 1977, Wood & Bandura 1989).

applicants' reactions to the selection process (e.g., Bell et al. 2006).

Ployhart & Harold's (2004) Applicant Attribution-Reaction Theory views candidates' attributions of the causes of their experience of the selection process as the critical determinant of their affective, cognitive, and behavioral reactions, including their justice perceptions. Although potentially insightful, this theory has yet to be evaluated empirically and further work seeking to demonstrate the incremental gains in the prediction of candidate reactions through the integration of justice theory with attribution theory is now urgently required. In the meantime, however, Herriot (2004) has developed an alternative account of applicants' reactions, with a view to predicting their intention to exit the selection process, based on social identity theory. As with the Ployhart & Harold (2004) formulation, empirical work directed to the testing of this theory is now a priority. Meanwhile, social identity theory has also been used to explain the effects of demographic (dis)similarity between job candidates and assessors on selection decisions (Goldberg 2005).

A longstanding problem in the design of assessment and development centers concerns the lack of consistent behavioral ratings across exercises designed to tap common constructs. Interactionist models of behavior underpinned by social cognitive views of personality have been used in recent years to explain such inconsistencies, which are seen as a function of candidates responding differentially to the diversity of situational cues afforded by the various assessment tasks (e.g., Lievens et al. 2006). Work on the malleability of personal attributes has also been extended to the role of the performance appraiser. Heslin et al. (2005), for example, showed that appraisers who believe that personal attributes are relatively fixed are less likely to acknowledge changes in appraisees' behavior over time than those who believe these attributes are relatively changeable.

Although work continues on the cognitive mechanisms determining the accuracy of performance evaluations (e.g., Hennessey & Bernardin 2003, London et al. 2004, Martell & Evans 2005), it is clear that the appraisal process is being viewed increasingly in a wider socio-political context (Fletcher 2001). This has led some researchers to reconsider the implications of conventional work directed toward removing error and bias in rater judgments. Understanding divergence in performance assessments between parties requires an appreciation of their potentially disparate goals and motivations as well as the political processes operating within the wider organization.

It is important to emphasize that social constructionist perspectives do not negate the need for further work on rater cognitions. In the final analysis, rater judgments are central to the ongoing negotiated order that forms the basis of the psychological contract between employer and employee. Hence, the purpose of such work should be to develop insights that will assist all parties to the employment relationship to reach genuine agreement, a process foundational to the formation and maintenance of truly relational, as opposed to transactional, psychological contracts (cf. Rousseau 1995, Rynes et al. 2005). Recent applications of attribution theory and justice theory to the analysis of appraisers' and appraisees' perceptions of, and reactions to, the performance evaluation and reward allocation process (Johnson et al. 2002, Keeping & Levy 2000, Schroth & Shah 2000) stand to contribute to this richer agenda. Additional work that could also inform this agenda has examined the personal constructs underlying appraisers' and appraisees' perceptions of, and attitudes toward, performance evaluation systems (Wright 2004).

Work Groups and Teams

Interest in the cognitive basis of team functioning has increased dramatically. Fortunately, however, Ilgen et al. (2005) recently surveyed a number of the key developments arising from this work. Hence, we only consider major developments beyond the scope of their review.

Following Cannon-Bowers & Salas (2001), work on the conceptual refinement, measurement, and empirical analysis of shared cognition has gained momentum. For example, recent studies have differentiated task-specific knowledge from team process knowledge, finding that each form yields benefits in terms of team processes and task performance (e.g., Lim & Klein 2006, Mathieu et al. 2000). The notion of shared cognition has been defined variously (e.g., overlapping, complementary, distributed) amid growing recognition that the optimal form of sharing is contingent upon the nature of the task and situational variables (e.g., Ren et al. 2006), and varies as task demands evolve over time (Levesque et al. 2001). Cooke et al. (2000) and Langan-Fox et al. (2000) extensively reviewed developments in the measurement of shared cognition. Subsequently, researchers have advanced increasingly sophisticated metrics, distinguishing within-team sharing of mental models from the accuracy of such models relative to those of experts (e.g., Mathieu et al. 2005). In addition, Austin (2003) has developed a multidimensional instrument for assessing the transactive memory construct, i.e., knowing where to find particular expertise within the team. Doubtless, these advances will help inform emerging work exploring the antecedents (Brandon & Hollingshead 2004, Bunderson 2003) and consequences of transactive memory (Faraj & Sproull 2000), and shared cognition more generally (e.g., Rentsch & Klimoski 2001).

Increasingly, modern work practices involve the collaborative efforts of multiple teams, often drawn together temporarily from diverse organizations, as for example when teams drawn from multiple agencies come together in emergency and crisis situations. Mathieu et al. (2001) have proposed the concept of multiteam systems (MTSs) to address the information-processing problems arising in these "teams of teams." They extend work on the shared mental models posited to operate within conventional teams (e.g., task, team process), reviewed above, to encapsulate the varieties of knowledge structure required so that component teams within MTSs readily comprehend one another's purposes, resource capabilities, and limitations and requirements in order to respond effectively to shifting environmental contingencies. Elements of the MTSs notion have recently been tested in laboratory settings (DeChurch & Marks 2006, Marks et al. 2005), but its overall utility has yet to be scrutinized empirically in the field.

Given the concomitant increases in the pace of organizational change and allocation of work tasks to team units, researchers have continued to explore the cognitive bases of team adaptation, including team cognitive ability composition (LePine 2003). Burke et al. (2006) recently developed a multilevel conceptual model that brings together the individual cognitions (e.g., knowledge, cognitive ability, team orientation) and group cognitions (e.g., team situation awareness, shared mental models) that underpin team adaptation over time.

Notwithstanding the scale of criticisms leveled against the upper echelons approach and recent advances in the direct assessment of team cognition, a surprising number of studies within the current review period have merely sought to extend further this approach, using basic background variables as a proxy for cognitive and related psychological processes (e.g., Carpenter 2002, Herrmann & Datta 2006). Over the longer term, studies incorporating direct methods of cognitive assessment (e.g., Kilduff et al. 2000, Markoczy 2001) will surely lead to richer understanding of top management team processes and outcomes than those studies based on proxy measures. This is not to rule out the use of background characteristics in the analysis of cognitive processes in organizations. Indeed, a sizable volume of work informed by the social identity approach has postulated a central role for demographic variables in the processing of information by work groups and teams,

MTSs: multiteam system

as reviewed by van Knippenberg & Schippers (2007).

Training and Development

Ford & Kraiger (1995) revisited the foundational instructional systems framework (the origins of which lie in behaviorism) in order to map out a comprehensive agenda for organizational training and development from a cognitive perspective (see also Kraiger et al. 1993). Viewed from such a perspective, the central questions in respect of individual and team level training become how to impart, develop, and/or change trainees' knowledge structures (i.e., their mental models/schemata), not only to equip them to perform immediate day-to-day tasks, but also expand their repertoires for dealing with uncertainties in the wider transfer environment (see also Salas & Cannon-Bowers 2001).

At the individual level within the current review period, researchers have continued to investigate the potential of a range of interventions to enrich the content and/or structure of trainees' task-specific knowledge structures as an outcome of training, both in the laboratory (e.g., Bell & Kozlowski 2002, Kozlowski et al. 2001, Sauer et al. 2000, Schmidt & Ford 2003) and to a lesser extent in the field (e.g., Brown 2001, Ellis & Davidi 2005). The interventions investigated have included the provision of adaptive guidance (Bell & Kozlowski 2002) and the relative efficacy of rule- and system-based learning (Sauer et al. 2000). The conceptualization of knowledge-based training outcomes is becoming increasingly sophisticated; for example, researchers have begun to distinguish between procedural and declarative knowledge developed through training (e.g., Sitzmann et al. 2006). Unfortunately, however, based on differing conceptions, researchers have employed a diversity of methods to operationalize the notion of knowledge structures across studies spanning multiple knowledge domains. Content mea-

sures have included direct measures of declarative knowledge via questionnaires (e.g., Schmidt & Ford 2003) and the analysis of verbal protocols (Sauer et al. 2000). Structural measures have included the formal mapping of perceived relationships among task-related concepts using, for example, the Pathfinder algorithm (Kozlowski et al. 2001, Marks et al. 2002) and causal cognitive mapping techniques (Ellis & Davidi 2005). The domains investigated have been equally diverse, ranging from surgery (Arnold & Farrell 2002) to military navigation (Ellis & Davidi 2005). This basic confounding of research method with knowledge domain is impeding the development of cumulative insights. Hence, a program of work directed toward establishing the convergent and discriminant validity of the various measures in use for the assessment of the structure and content of trainees' knowledge structures, and the validation of a broader nomological network encompassing cognitive training outcomes, continues to be badly needed (cf. Kraiger et al. 1993).

At the team level within the current review period, substantial progress has been attained in the conceptualization and measurement of the team mental models construct as an outcome of training interventions such as cross-training (Marks et al. 2002) and computer-based training (Smith-Jentsch et al. 2001). These developments notwithstanding, the team mental models construct is still at an early stage of development and there are several outstanding issues concerning the application of this notion in the context of training and development. Specifically, it is unclear which variants of shared cognition (e.g., common, complementary, distributed knowledge) ultimately benefit the execution of various types of team task, or what training methods are best suited to the development of particular types of team mental model (e.g., task content related, team process related). Moreover, there is a pressing need for research to inform the design of interventions for imparting multiple variants of shared cognition and/or types of team mental model, with a view to maximizing positive transfer outcomes across the various component exercises.

Stress and Occupational Health

Work within this domain continues to be dominated by the measurement and modeling of social and physical factors as potential job stressors, accompanied by a recent proliferation of studies assessing the relative impact of individual difference variables and workplace characteristics on psychological and psychosomatic health (see Ferguson et al. 2006 for a meta-analysis of such studies). However, researchers have begun to open up the black box of stress appraisal and coping mechanisms (Lowe & Bennett 2003, Troup & Dewe 2002), thereby enriching earlier cognitive contributions to the understanding of workplace stress (Edwards 1992) and life stress more generally (e.g., Lazarus & Folkman 1984). Based on the assertion that current approaches to the analysis of stress in the workplace are cognitively underspecified (cf. Dewe & Cooper 2007), Daniels et al. (2004) proposed a model of stressor appraisal, coping choice, and affect predicated on several core cognitive principles (chiefly controlled and automatic processing, mental models, and inference by categorization). Several of the predictions of this relatively broad-based model have been supported empirically (e.g., Daniels et al. 2006). Related work of a more circumscribed nature has begun to explore in detail the nature and role of justice perceptions and related social comparison processes underpinning the experience of employee well-being, together with an analysis of the various situational and personal factors that trigger such judgments (Janssen 2004, Warr 2006). Another new line of inquiry, centered on the cognitive consequences of work-related stress, has begun examining the deleterious effects of stress on the formation and deployment of team mental models and transactive memory (Ellis 2006).

Research on job burnout within the current review period has also been informed by a variety of cognitively oriented perspectives. Maslach et al. (2001) have suggested that one prominent source of potential burnout arises from the "cognitive and emotional relationship" employees develop with their work and organizations. Specifically, violations of the psychological contract yield burnout because the erosion of a sense of reciprocity is inimical to the maintenance of employee well-being (Rousseau 1995). Drawing on the insights of attribution theory, Moore (2000) has offered an alternative conception in which the behavioral consequences of work-related emotional exhaustion (i.e., burnout) are mediated by employees' attributions of its causes.[3] Neither of these conceptions, however, has been subjected to the rigors of empirical scrutiny. In a third cognitively oriented conception, Haslam & Reicher (2006) demonstrated empirically that the social identity approach provides a potentially useful lens for analyzing the impact of intragroup processes as mediators of burnout and work-related stress more generally.

Work Motivation

Latham & Pinder (2005) extensively reviewed developments in the major cognitively based work motivation theories, arguing that three theories predominate, namely, goal-setting, social cognitive, and organizational justice theories. In a related forward-looking commentary, Locke & Latham (2004) called for greater integration of the dominant work motivation theories. There are encouraging signs that this is beginning to occur. Meyer et al. (2004), for example, outlined an integrative model of employee commitment and motivation, in which commitment is viewed as one of several forces that energize motivated behavior, building on the insights of goal

---

[3] Significantly, just outside of the current review period, Perrewe & Zellars (1999) argued for the incorporation of attributional processes in the modeling of work stress appraisal, whereas others (Frese & Zapf 1999, Schaubroeck 1999) maintained that studying the effects of "objective" environmental features is a more fruitful approach.

setting theory, self-determination theory,[4] and regulatory focus theory. In a second development, Steel & Konig (2006) combined the insights of cumulative prospect theory and the notion of hyperbolic discounting from behavioral decision theory with classic expectancy theory and need theory formulations. Their temporal theory of motivation purports to refine the understanding and prediction of a wide range of work-related phenomena, from goal setting to job design and the behavior of groups and stock markets.

Additional efforts to advance work motivation theory beyond Latham & Pinder's (2005) review include DeShon & Gillespie's (2005) motivated action theory, which seeks to unify differing accounts of the goal orientation construct, and the combined social identity and self-categorization theory perspective offered by Ellemers et al. (2004). The latter provides an account of how identification with workplace collectives shapes the motivation of individuals and groups. Behind these latest developments lies a major dilemma for the wider field of work motivation as a whole; the proliferation of constructs with the introduction of each new formulation is undermining the quest for greater conceptual unity.

Work Design and Cognitive Ergonomics

As noted at the outset, viewed from a cognitive standpoint the new organizational forms and work practices emerging in response to globalization and related economic and political developments pose significant design challenges to I/O psychologists. One particular design challenge that continues to attract much research attention concerns the system requirements for the effective cognitive functioning of geographically dispersed teams. As demonstrated by Cramton (2001), an inability to maintain "mutual knowledge" can compromise the effectiveness of these teams, thus placing a premium on human factors work directed toward the refinement of computer-mediated communication systems. These systems and related technologies have the potential to support the development of transactive memory and the various forms of team mental models reviewed above. Unfortunately, however, theory (Griffith & Neale 2001, Griffith et al. 2003) and empirical evidence (Baltes et al. 2002, Gibson & Gibbs 2006, Malhotra et al. 2001) concerning the effectiveness of these systems is somewhat mixed, thus implying a need to probe further, across a diversity of contexts, into the social psychological and technological dynamics that promote and inhibit the attainment of mutual knowledge in virtual teams.

Several empirical studies within the current review period have investigated the cognitive effects of job design. A field study reported by Leach et al. (2003), for example, demonstrated that an empowerment initiative significantly increased shop floor operatives' job knowledge, particularly among less-experienced employees. The initiative also significantly increased workers' self-efficacy and concomitantly decreased felt job strain. In related work, Elsbach & Hargadon (2006) examined ways of increasing organizational creativity by designing workdays to comprise an appropriate mix of cognitively challenging and "mindless" work.

Meanwhile, empirical work on operators' mental models of process control tasks and associated technological systems, both at the individual (e.g., Jones & Endsley 2000) and team (e.g., Sauer et al. 2006, Waller et al. 2004) levels of analysis, has also continued. The related construct of situation awareness also continues to enjoy widespread conceptual and empirical attention. Defined as knowledge of a more dynamic and fleeting form, as distinct from that which is more stable and long-term

---

[4]Building on cognitive evaluation theory, self-determination theory has only recently been applied to the systematic analysis of work motivation (Gagne & Deci 2005), although it has been widely applied in other domains. Self-determination theory models the interplay between extrinsic and intrinsic motivators and outlines the mechanisms by which they influence the controlled and autonomous regulation of behavior.

in nature, situation awareness has been postulated as a determinant of the successful operation of complex human-machine systems, both at the individual (Sohn & Doane 2004) and team (Gorman et al. 2006) levels of analysis. Research continues concerning the development and validation of psychometric tests for detecting the cognitive skills and abilities underpinning situation awareness (e.g., Sohn & Doane 2004), and the design of human-machine interfaces (e.g., Remington et al. 2000) and team processes (e.g., Roth et al. 2006), with a view to enhancing situation awareness. A further consideration concerns the allocation of function (i.e., individual versus team versus technology) to optimize system performance through the attainment and maintenance of situation awareness (see, e.g., Parasuraman 2000).

Recognizing that work design theory has not coevolved in line with modern work practices and organizational forms, there have been several recent attempted reconceptions to incorporate cognitive and emotional factors (Clegg & Spencer 2007, Daniels 2006, Parker et al. 2001). For example, Parker et al. (2001) have proposed an "elaborated model of work design," in which the traditional work characteristics of extant job and work design theories (e.g., skill variety, autonomy, feedback; Hackman & Oldham 1976) are augmented by the inclusion of cognitive demands (e.g., attentional and problem-solving demands). Within their model, cognitive outcomes relating to the use, creation, and transfer of knowledge can be facilitated or inhibited by work design factors. In a related methodological advance, Morgeson & Humphrey (2006) have reported the development and validation of a new work design questionnaire incorporating scales to assess cognitive demands (i.e., information processing and problem solving).[5] However, when this and the related recent reconceptions of work design are

considered in the light of the cognitive design challenges arising in the context of new work practices and organizational forms, some of which we have enumerated above, it is clear that there are many gaps in the current knowledge base that need addressing before designers of the contemporary workplace can derive psychologically sound solutions to meet these challenges.

Leadership

Lord & Emrich's (2000) review traced the origins and development of "the cognitive revolution in leadership research," covering major advances up to the commencement of the current review period. They identified two major streams of work, the first centering on individual and dyadic cognition, the second on collective cognition. A number of major advances have occurred in each stream within the current period.

Within the individual and dyadic stream, social information processing theories such as leadership categorization theory (e.g., Lord et al. 1984) and implicit leadership theory (e.g., Lord & Maher 1991) continue to inspire research on followers' perceptions and evaluations of leaders (e.g., Epitropaki & Martin 2005). More generally, work continues to explore the traits (e.g., intelligence; Judge et al. 2004a) and information processing capabilities and associated knowledge structures (i.e., expertise; Lord & Hall 2005) that underpin the emergence and development of leaders. The rich vein of work analyzing leader-member relations and trust in leaders has also taken a decidedly cognitive turn. For example, researchers have begun to explore followers' attributions of leader characteristics and associated behaviors and outcomes, including the attribution of charismatic influence attempts (e.g., Cha & Edmondson 2006, Dasborough & Ashkanasy 2002) and the attributional basis

---

[5]In a further methodological advance, Wallace & Chen (2005) have developed and validated a measure of cognitive failure. This instrument is potentially promising in a

variety of applications, not least for measuring the cognitive outcomes of work design interventions.

BDT: behavioral decision theory

of trust in leadership (e.g., Dirks 2000), including an examination of cross-cultural variations (Ensari & Murphy 2003).

Researchers have also investigated the nature and extent of variations in leadership prototypes across organizational (Dickson et al. 2006) and national (Brodbeck et al. 2000) cultures. These studies evidence a tension regarding the extent to which leadership prototypes and related mental representations should be viewed as relatively stable and enduring or as dynamic and fleeting. In a significant theoretical advance, Lord et al. (2001) developed a cognitive model of the way in which individuals mentally represent key leadership concepts (e.g., prototypes, schemas, implicit leadership theories) that allows for both the stability of leadership concepts and their changeability over time and across contexts, based on connectionist approaches to the modeling of cognitive architecture.

Arguably, the most significant developments during the current review period within the collective cognition research stream concern advances in understanding organizational sensemaking. A number of new concepts have been proposed to account more fully for the nature of leaders' attempts to influence and transform the attitudes and beliefs of their followers. For example, in an ethnographic study of a network marketing organization, Pratt (2000) demonstrated how successful leaders adopt "sense-breaking" tactics in an attempt to stimulate "seekership" among followers (i.e., the search for new meaning) with a view to increasing their identification with the organization. More generally, researchers are increasingly recognizing the importance of augmenting the analysis of such hierarchically driven, top-down sensemaking and sense-giving leadership processes with the study of the bottom-up influence processes adopted variously by a range of lower-level stakeholders, including middle managers, in the management of meaning (e.g., Balogun & Johnson 2004, Maitlis 2005).

The recent introduction of the social identity approach into the leadership domain holds considerable potential as a conceptual bridge across the individual/dyadic and collective cognition streams. Hogg's (2001) formulation, which brings together the voluminous literatures on prototypicality, social attraction, and attribution and information processing, provides a basis for understanding leadership processes in situations where group membership is particularly salient. Building on this approach, there has been an increasing volume of work demonstrating that individuals are recognized and evaluated as emergent leaders in accordance with their degree of fit with the prototype of the salient ingroup (e.g., Pierro et al. 2005, van Knippenberg & van Knippenberg 2005), as opposed to their fit with more generic leadership schemas or categories (cf. Lord et al. 1984). In two related developments, social identity theory has been applied to the analysis of leader-member exchange relationships (Hogg et al. 2005) and transformational leadership processes (Kark et al. 2003). For a more extensive review of social identity applications in leadership theory and research, see van Knippenberg et al. (2004).

Organizational Decision Making

In a previous section, we drew attention to the distinction between the computational and interpretive perspectives on cognition in organizations. Behavioral decision theory (BDT)—the epitome of the computational perspective—has historically dominated, and continues to dominate, much of the literature pertaining to the cognitive analysis of organizational decisions (for reviews, see Highhouse 2001, Neale et al. 2006). However, over recent years the adequacy of this approach has been called into question on philosophical, theoretical, and methodological grounds.

First, Gigerenzer and colleagues (e.g., Gigerenzer 1991, Gigerenzer & Goldstein 1996) maintain that many of the basic laboratory tasks employed in BDT experiments lack ecological validity (cf. Kahneman & Tversky 1996). Predicated upon a fundamentally different conception of Simon's bounded rationality notion from that construed by traditional BDT researchers, known as ecological rationality, they have identified a new class of heuristics, "fast and frugal," that they maintain are adaptively matched to the informational structure and demands of decision makers' environments. Within the current review period, there have been several extensions and applications of this research to organizationally relevant decisions. However, in the main this work has been conducted within the confines of the laboratory (e.g., Bryant 2007, Newell et al. 2003) or employed simulated data to test competitively the performance of fast and frugal heuristics against their conventional counterparts (e.g., Hogarth & Karelaia 2005), thus casting doubt on its generalizability to real-world contexts. Moreover, only a limited number of studies have investigated simple decision heuristics used by human participants in natural settings (e.g., Astebro & Elhedhli 2006). Overall, these studies have yielded mixed findings regarding the extent to which decision makers actually rely on fast and/or frugal heuristics and with what effect. Clearly, therefore, there is a need for further validation of this approach in both controlled and organizational field settings.

Second, researchers grouped under the umbrella of naturalistic decision making (NDM) reject the notion of equivalency between the sparse confines of the laboratory and the infinitely richer settings in which organizational decision makers conduct their everyday affairs, thus implying the need for NDM researchers to evolve their own context-specific concepts, theories, and methods. The origins of NDM lie in studies of domain experts making complex, high stakes, and ill-structured decisions under time pressure, often in dangerous situations (Lipshitz et al. 2001). In theoretical terms, Klein's (1993) recognition-primed decision making model, with its emphasis on the crucial role of pattern recognition in obviating the need for extensive deliberation of multiple alternatives, epitomizes the NDM approach. Within

the current review period, work on NDM has gathered momentum, both in organizational (Lipshitz et al. 2006) and human factors (e.g., Lipshitz & Cohen 2005, Perrin et al. 2001, Wiggins & Bollwerk 2006) applications. By way of illustration, Roth et al. (2006) employed cognitive task analysis to study the decision processes of dispersed employees in railroad operations, highlighting the potential of communication technologies for facilitating situation awareness. Several work design challenges identified in this study resonate with the problems outlined above concerning the attainment and maintenance of mutual knowledge and shared cognition in dispersed and collocated groups.[6]

The above developments notwithstanding, as noted above, conventional BDT research continues to play a central role in the analysis of organizationally relevant decisions. Within the current review period, there have been numerous applications and extensions of this work, ranging from the continued analysis of framing effects (Hodgkinson et al. 2002, Kuvaas & Selart 2004, Wright & Goodwin 2002), escalation behavior (Bragger et al. 2003), and confirmation bias (Russo et al. 2000), to the application of Janis & Mann's classic conflict theory of decision making (Hodgkinson & Wright 2002).

Organizational Change and Development

Organizational change and development was last reviewed in this series by Weick & Quinn (1999). During the interim period, there have been many advances. Accordingly, we review selectively developments centered on the cognitive analysis of the strategic management of organizations (for a more extensive survey of these developments, see Hodgkinson &

NDM: naturalistic decision making

---

[6]A third challenge to the conventional BDT orthodoxy comes from Sutcliffe & Weick's (2008) provocative essay in which they reconceptualize information overload in organizational decision making as a problem of interpretation rather than computation. However, it remains to be seen how far this perspective will inform new empirical work that goes beyond the insights of NDM research.

Sparrow 2002). The rationale for focusing on this work is its potential importance as a vehicle for leveraging up the strategic influence of the I/O psychology profession as a whole. For present purposes, it is analytically convenient to consider strategic management as encompassing three major sets of issues: analysis, choice, and implementation. In so doing, we do not seek to imply a linear or lockstep process. In practice, organizational strategies are as much the product of unplanned emergence as rational analysis, and a myriad of multilevel influences mediate and/or moderate the links between formal attempts to influence the strategic direction of the organization (i.e., its intended strategy) and its realized strategy (Mintzberg & Waters 1985).

Strategic analysis involves understanding the strategic position of the organization, its environment, resources, values, and objectives. Changes in cognitive representations can aid organizational adaptation by shifting attention, yet ingrained schemata can constitute barriers to organizational and industrial change (Bogner & Barr 2000). Accordingly, within the current review period, work has continued on the analysis of managers' mental representations of the structure and dynamics of competition in industries and markets, with a view to identifying patterns of belief convergence and divergence within and across organizations (e.g., Daniels et al. 2002, Hodgkinson 2005, Johnson & Hoopes 2003, McNamara et al. 2002, Osborne et al. 2001). The primary aim of this stream of work is to illuminate the socio-cognitive processes underpinning the development of competitive positioning strategies and associated adaptive mechanisms that afford collective protection to, and drive the performance advantages of, particular groups of competing firms, but also serve as potential sources of inertia and myopia. Recent studies have incorporated a range of methodological step changes, including prospective longitudinal research designs, mathematical simulation techniques, and the use of advanced multivariate analysis techniques, thereby overcoming the weaknesses of

the small scale, cross-sectional investigations that typified much of the earlier work in this stream. Complementing this stream of work centered on the external environment of the organization, there has been a growing interest in the cognitive microfoundations of the internal capabilities that promote sustainable competitive advantage, organizational learning and adaptation (e.g., Berson et al. 2006, Gavetti 2005, Lane et al. 2006).

Strategic choice involves the formulation, evaluation, and selection of possible courses of action. As discussed in the previous section, within the current review period researchers have applied and extended a range of BDT concepts and theories, with a view to explaining departures from rationality in strategic choice and related processes and the development of interventions to alleviate such effects. Although we have no wish to see this body of work discontinued, the fast and frugal and NDM approaches also surveyed above have much to offer in this domain of application, especially in the analysis of strategic choice processes in the high-velocity, uncertain business environments that characterize the operating conditions of many contemporary organizations (Brown & Eisenhardt 1997).

From a cognitive standpoint, arguably the most pressing research issue with regard to strategy implementation (the translation of strategy into action) is to develop insights into the processes and mechanisms that facilitate, or more frequently inhibit, attempts to equip employees to adapt to organizational change initiatives in ways that yield positive individual and collective outcomes, including personal well being and organizational citizenship behavior. Rousseau (2001) has advanced a schema theory of psychological contract formation and change that might account for employee resistance to such initiatives. Rousseau maintains that psychological contracts are encoded in mental models (i.e., schemas) that are relatively malleable during the early stages of the employment relationship. However, once established, like the mental models of competitive positioning strategies held by organizational decision makers, employees' mental models of the psychological contract become resistant to change, leading to inertia and inflexibility. Although Rousseau's theory closely accords with several other formulations concerning employee resistance to organizational change programs, including total quality (Reger et al. 1994) and empowerment (Labianca et al. 2000) initiatives, it has yet to be validated empirically. In addition to these schema-based theories, recently both attribution theory (Martinko et al. 2002, Repenning & Sterman 2002) and social identity theory (e.g., Fiol 2002, Haslam et al. 2003) have been posited as lenses through which to study the socio-cognitive mechanisms that might promote or inhibit adaptation to organizational change initiatives and the factors that give rise to counterproductive workplace behaviors.

Individual Differences

Many cognitively oriented studies within the nine domains surveyed above have routinely incorporated assessments of individual differences, including attributional style (Silvester et al. 2003), locus of control (Ng et al. 2006), and need for closure (Ellis & Davidi 2005, Pierro et al. 2005). However, two groups of variables are especially prominent in the overall body of work surveyed, namely, self-efficacy and related constructs (e.g., core-self evaluation) and cognitive style and associated constructs pertaining to the processing of information (e.g., decision style, cognitive strategy).[7]

Self-efficacy continues to be seen as a pervasive driver and outcome of cognitive functioning in organizations, influencing positively learning (Chen et al. 2000), cognitive, affective-motivational and behavioral training outcomes (Colquitt et al. 2000), and

responses to organizational change (Wanberg & Banas 2000). Despite this popularity, equivocality persists regarding the most appropriate way of conceptualizing task- and context-specific self-efficacy in relation to its putative antecedents and consequences and the higher-order generalized self-efficacy construct (e.g., Chen et al. 2000, Yeo & Neal 2006). In recent years, there has been marked interest in the emergence and effects of collective efficacy in organizational teams and groups (for a review, see Ilgen et al. 2005; see also Srivastava et al. 2006, Tasa et al. 2007). More generally, two challenges have recently been mounted to the primacy of self-efficacy. First, several replications and extensions of earlier findings have shown that high self-efficacy can impair performance by reducing effort once goals are within reach (Vancouver 2005, Vancouver et al. 2002, Yeo & Neal 2006), although these findings have been questioned on methodological grounds (Bandura & Locke 2003). Second, although meta-analytic findings from the beginning of the current review period support the idea that self-efficacy plays an important role in determining work-related performance (Judge & Bono 2001), a more recent meta-analysis conducted by Judge et al. (2007) showed that this effect is significantly reduced when controlling for more distal individual differences (e.g., mental ability, Big Five personality traits, and experience).

There have been recent attempts in several domains to group multiple specific traits pertaining to self-concept (e.g., self-esteem, self-efficacy, locus of control, and emotional stability) into a higher-order construct termed "core self-evaluation" (for a review, see Judge et al. 2004b). Hiller & Hambrick (2005), for example, have applied this construct to analyze the behavior of company executives, while Stajkovic (2006) has developed the related construct of core confidence. More generally, this approach reveals a wider tension in organizational research regarding the extent to which, and under what conditions, higher-order traits or more focused narrow-band traits are more appropriate

---

[7]In addition, numerous studies continue to demonstrate the power of general mental ability and specific cognitive abilities as predictors of work-related performance. However, a detailed consideration of this work would warrant a stand-alone review (for representative findings, see Salgado et al. 2003).

for capturing within- and between-individual variations in cognition and for predicting various work-related outcomes. Potentially, a myriad of individual differences could moderate or mediate the cognitive functioning of individuals and teams in organizational settings. One potentially fruitful approach to systematize the search for such links would be to map relevant narrow-band constructs onto higher-level organizing frameworks, such as the Five Factor Model, with a view to identifying the information processing characteristics and consequences of alternative configurations of personality.

Individual differences in information processing tendencies encompass a range of cognitively based variables that have been adopted widely in the analysis of organizational behavior, reflecting in general terms the distinction between analytic and intuitive processing (Chaiken & Trope 1999). For example, cognitive style has been shown to influence decision-making performance (Levin et al. 2000, Parker & Fischhoff 2005), perceptions of cognitive biases (Tetlock 2000), and the nature and quality of leader-member exchange (Allinson et al. 2001). However, debates have continued within the current review period regarding the psychometric status of measures of cognitive style, and views are now polarized. One view maintains that analysis and intuition are served by a common underlying cognitive system, that individuals have a stable overarching preference for one approach or the other, and that these tendencies are organized along a unidimensional, bipolar continuum (see, e.g., Allinson et al. 2001, Hayes et al. 2003). In contrast, a second perspective accords greater agency to individuals, arguing that analytic and intuitive processing capabilities are served by independent cognitive systems that permit individuals to switch back and forth from one approach to the other as required, albeit moderated to some extent by stylistic preferences (see, e.g., Dane & Pratt 2007; Hodgkinson et al. 2008; Hodgkinson & Sadler-Smith 2003a,b). These debates have

important implications for future work, following recent calls to examine the role individual differences in information processing might play in shaping cognitive functioning in various organizational domains, including the adoption of fast and frugal decision heuristics (e.g., Newell et al. 2003) and the selection, development, and leadership of strategy-making teams (Hodgkinson & Clarke 2007).

METHODOLOGICAL DEVELOPMENTS

Many important advances have occurred within the current review period in respect of cognitive task analysis methods and related cognitive mapping techniques for eliciting and representing individual (e.g., Fowlkes et al. 2000, Patrick & James 2004) and collective (e.g., Arthur et al. 2005) knowledge (for detailed overviews, see Cooke et al. 2000, Hodgkinson & Sparrow 2002, Langan-Fox et al. 2000, Schraagen et al. 2000). Four issues in respect of these methods continue to warrant scholarly attention.

The first issue concerns the question of what methods are best suited to what types of application. Researchers have established an impressive array of procedures for eliciting procedural and declarative knowledge, but the psychometric adequacy of many of these techniques across their various domains of application has yet to be determined.

The second issue concerns the relative merits of idiographic versus nomothetic approaches to knowledge elicitation. This debate has arisen in connection with repertory grid (Daniels & Johnson 2002; Hodgkinson 2002, 2005; Wright 2004) and causal cognitive mapping (Narayanan & Armstrong 2005) techniques. In recent years several hybrid approaches have been devised that combine the strengths of idiographic and nomothetic procedures. The main advantage of these approaches is that they yield data of a form amenable to systematic comparison, a vital prerequisite for developing cumulative insights across contexts and time periods, while ensuring that the elicitation task is meaningful to participants. In this connection, Clarkson & Hodgkinson (2005) have reported the development of new software to support hybrid approaches to causal cognitive mapping for use with large samples, while Hodgkinson (2005) has devised a hybrid approach to repertory grid elicitation and analysis for similar large-scale use.

The third issue concerns the nature of the cognitive processes triggered by the act of elicitation. For instance, different approaches to causal cognitive mapping have been shown to yield cause maps with significantly different structural characteristics (Hodgkinson et al. 2004), thus raising the question as to whether the products of various elicitation techniques should be viewed as mere artifacts of the production process or as isomorphic with the underlying cognitive processes and mental representations of substantive concern. The importance of this issue has been heightened following recent progress in cognitive science regarding the conceptualization of causal mental models and related constructs (Sloman & Hagmayer 2006), placing causal cognitive mapping techniques on firmer theoretical foundations.

Fourth, the vast majority of extant methods are designed to elicit conceptual knowledge of a form accessible through verbal report or other forms of conscious awareness. Although researchers have long recognized the importance of the less conscious aspects of cognition in organizational life (e.g., implicit knowledge, intuition), until recently there has been little advancement in methods for assessing these forms of knowledge in applied field settings. There are, however, encouraging signs of progress. Bing et al. (2007), for example, outline methods for assessing integratively the implicit and explicit knowledge underpinning personality prototypes. Developments in the assessment of implicit attitudes (e.g., Fazio & Olson 2003, Haines & Sumner 2006) and at the forefront of social cognitive neuroscience (Lieberman 2007) also hold considerable promise for exploring the various nonconscious processes that researchers are beginning to study in organizational contexts, including implicit affective processes (Kelly & Barsade 2001), subconscious motivation (Stajkovic et al. 2006), and nonconscious priming (Kay et al. 2004).

FUTURE CHALLENGES

Clearly, the period encompassed by this review has been most eventful. Looking ahead, researchers of cognition in organizations need to confront five major tensions if the field is to advance further.

Crossing the Traditions

We began this review with the observation that the complexities of the modern workplace are such that there is a need for increased cooperation across the organizational and human factors traditions. As we have seen, nowhere is this need more apparent than in the domain of work design and cognitive ergonomics. On the human factors side, concepts such as situation awareness and team mental models have provided useful insights into the cognitive functioning of complex human-machine systems and the system requirements for the attainment of shared cognition. On the organizational side, however, although work design theorists and researchers have called for the refinement of concepts and models to meet the design challenges implied by such systems, we are still a long way from a truly integrated approach capable of meeting these cognitive requirements while also ensuring that the positive benefits associated with interventions based on conventional job and work design principles are not lost in the process.

The work of Zhang and colleagues (e.g., Rinkus et al. 2005, Zhang et al. 2002) on the design of complex distributed information systems and the work of Agarwal & Karahanna (2000) on the intrinsic motivational properties of information technology provide convenient illustrations of the limitations of existing efforts to bring the two traditions together within a unified approach. Zhang and colleagues have drawn upon the distributed cognition, human-computer interaction, organizational learning, and organizational memory literatures in an attempt to derive a comprehensive framework for meeting the design challenges of distributed information systems, but they have failed to incorporate any of the insights of classic or contemporary theory and research on job and work design (e.g., Hackman & Oldham 1976, Parker et al. 2001). Agarwal & Karahanna (2000) have similarly drawn upon a diversity of literatures (e.g., work on the trait of absorption, the state of flow and cognitive engagement) to derive their notion of cognitive absorption, a multidimensional construct reflecting the extent to which individuals are immersed in information technology, yet neglected to consider the voluminous body of theory and research on work motivation. These oversights are understandable given the independent histories of the two traditions, but the time has surely come to develop appropriate bridging mechanisms to yield the required progress.

Crossing the Domains

Throughout our review, we have observed repeatedly that the five dominant theoretical perspectives identified at the outset pervade research across the 10 domains surveyed, albeit to varying extents. Schema theory and related notions of mental representations, for example, have emerged in a variety of guises as a basic mechanism for explaining cognitive bias and inertia at the individual, group, organizational, and interorganizational levels of analysis, from work groups and teams to leadership and organizational change and development. Social identity theory and related conceptions, attribution theory, and sensemaking notions have been no less ubiquitous.

Given this commonality, it is tempting to call for future research to focus on the development of theoretical accounts that cut across the various domains. Indeed, several noteworthy attempts have been made to develop such accounts. For instance, researchers have portrayed the social identity approach, combining self/social categorization and social identity theories, as an overarching conception capable of providing unified insights across multiple domains (see, e.g., Haslam 2001, Haslam et al. 2003, Hogg & Terry 2000). In general, however, it would be unwise to strive uniformly for broad theoretical accounts of cognitive mechanisms and processes that cut across domains to the exclusion of detailed theoretical specifications that offer intricate descriptions of domain-specific phenomena.

Integrative Understanding Within Domains

A third tension concerns the extent to which integrating the various theories that dominate particular domains might yield greater insights than if they continue to advance as independent formulations. As we saw in the domains of personnel selection and assessment (e.g., Ployhart & Harold 2004) and work motivation (e.g., DeShon & Gillespie 2005, Latham & Pinder 2005), there have been a number of such calls and attempts, with a view to developing more complete accounts of the focal phenomena. Over the longer term, however, it might prove more valuable for the advancement of science and practice within and between each domain to pit alternative formulations against one another, with a view to identifying the circumstances in which they provide greater or less understanding and predictive power. In the case of leadership, for example, future research could fruitfully investigate the relative contributions of social identity, attribution, and leader categorization formulations in the prediction and management of leader-member exchange relationships.

The Challenge of Emotion

In seeking to advance understanding of behavior in the workplace, a fourth tension concerns the extent to which it is possible and/or desirable to augment current cognitive conceptions by incorporating affective variables, as opposed to developing entirely new bodies of theory and research. Recent advances in social cognitive neuroscience (Phelps 2006) are providing vital signposts as to how the emerging work investigating the dynamic interplay between cognition and emotion in organizations might be elevated to a new level (cf. Brief & Weiss 2002, Fisher & Ashkanasy 2000). For example, the insights of this work could inform research that has begun to identify the mechanisms by which emotion impairs and aids learning (e.g., LePine 2004) and refine understanding of how emotional traits and states determine the extent to which organizational decision makers rely on controlled and automatic information processing (Daniels et al. 2004). Although it is acknowledged that both anticipated (e.g., fear, dread) and felt (e.g., anxiety, stress) emotions can constrain behavior relating to difficult decisions, current understanding of these mechanisms and their effects in organizational settings is limited (cf. Maitlis & Ozcelik 2004, Wong et al. 2006). In conceptual terms, researchers need to move beyond linear, single-step analyses of affective influences on cognition or conversely of the cognitive determinants of affect (cf. Brief & Weiss 2002). Suitably dynamic conceptions would encapsulate the recursive processes by which affectively informed appraisals produce discrete emotions, in turn shaping subsequent cognitions, both within discrete episodes and over time (for current progress in this regard, see Beal et al. 2005).

Laboratory Versus Field

The fifth tension constitutes a methodological challenge. Many of the articles across the substantive domains we have surveyed report studies of cognition in the laboratory rather than cognition in organizations, as such. However, the relative predominance of laboratory versus field studies varies considerably between domains. For example, research into cognition in work groups and teams continues to be heavily reliant on laboratory studies. In cases where the primary objective is merely to validate further well-established principles and concepts, researchers might usefully supplant such laboratory methods with methods of the sort pioneered by Hutchins (1995) and NDM researchers for studying cognition in situ (cf. Waller et al. 2004). However, in those cases where new concepts have begun to emerge (e.g., MTSs), a judicious combination of laboratory and field methods seems entirely appropriate. A blanket call for more field and fewer laboratory studies is, therefore, unwarranted. In the final analysis, researchers must select the mix of methods most appropriate to the research question(s) under investigation, taking into account the overall maturity of the theories and concepts underpinning their work.

CONCLUSIONS

Research on cognition in organizations is thriving. We have arrived at two general conclusions from the foregoing survey. First, reflecting the fact that this body of work now constitutes a multidisciplinary endeavor, there are clear signs of growing collaboration between researchers across the organizational and human factors traditions, but given the scale and complexity of the challenges confronting the modern workplace, we need even greater cooperation. Arguably, in going forward the greatest challenge is one of measurement—how best to capture, represent, and interpret conscious and nonconscious forms of cognition within and between organizations, as unobtrusively as possible in a time-sensitive manner. Second, although a number of common theoretical perspectives pervade each of the 10 substantive domains reviewed, it would be most unfortunate if the field were to degenerate into a series of internecine struggles for cross-domain theoretical supremacy. On the contrary, the plurality of perspectives augers well for the long-term health and vibrancy of research on managerial and organizational cognition and the I/O psychology field in general. As cognitive theories, concepts, and methods enter a new phase of maturity, we foresee a host of new insights emerging across the entire spectrum of organizational life.

ACKNOWLEDGMENTS

We thank Prithviraj Chattopadhyay, Chris Clegg, Susan T. Fiske, Kevin Ford, Alex Haslam, Peter Herriot, Denise Rousseau, Eduardo Salas, Mary Waller, and Karl Weick for their helpful and constructive comments on an earlier draft. We also gratefully acknowledge the financial support of the UK ESRC/EPSRC Advanced Institute of Management Research in the preparation of this article (under grant number RES-331-25-0028).

LITERATURE CITED

Agarwal R, Karahanna E. 2000. Time flies when you're having fun: cognitive absorption and beliefs about information technology usage. *MIS Q.* 24:665–94

Allinson CW, Armstrong SJ, Hayes J. 2001. The effects of cognitive style on leader-member exchange: a study of manager-subordinate dyads. *J. Occup. Organ. Psychol.* 74:201–20

Arnold P, Farrell MJ. 2002. Can virtual reality be used to measure and train surgical skills? *Ergonomics* 45:362–79

Arthur W, Edwards BD, Bell ST, Villado AJ, Bennett W. 2005. Team task analysis: identifying tasks and jobs that are team based. *Hum. Factors* 47:654–69

Ashforth BE, Mael F. 1989. Social identity theory and the organization. *Acad. Manage. Rev.* 14:20–39

Astebro T, Elhedhli S. 2006. The effectiveness of simple decision heuristics: forecasting commercial success for early-stage ventures. *Manage. Sci.* 52:395–409

Austin JR. 2003. Transactive memory in organizational groups: the effects of content, consensus, specialization, and accuracy on group performance. *J. Appl. Psychol.* 88:866–78

Balogun J, Johnson G. 2004. Organizational restructuring and middle manager sensemaking. *Acad. Manage. J.* 47:523–49

Baltes BB, Dickson MW, Sherman MP, Bauer CC, LaGanke JS. 2002. Computer-mediated communication and group decision making: a meta-analysis. *Organ. Behav. Hum. Decis. Process.* 87:156–79

Bandura A. 1977. Self-efficacy: toward a unifying theory of behavioral change. *Psychol. Rev.* 84:191–215

Bandura A, Locke EA. 2003. Negative self-efficacy and goal effects revisited. *J. Appl. Psychol.* 88:87–99

Bartlett FC. 1932. *Remembering: A Study in Experimental and Social Psychology.* Cambridge, UK: Cambridge Univ. Press

Beal DJ, Weiss HM, Barros E, MacDermid SM. 2005. An episodic process model of affective influences on performance. *J. Appl. Psychol.* 90:1054–68

Bell BS, Kozlowski SWJ. 2002. Adaptive guidance: enhancing self-regulation, knowledge, and performance in technology-based training. *Pers. Psychol.* 55:267–306

Bell BS, Wiechmann D, Ryan AM. 2006. Consequences of organizational justice expectations in a selection system. *J. Appl. Psychol.* 91:455–66

Berson Y, Nemanich LA, Waldman DA, Galvin BM, Keller RT. 2006. Leadership and organizational learning: a multiple levels perspective. *Leadersh. Q.* 17:577–94

Bing MN, LeBreton JM, Davison HK, Migetz DZ, James LR. 2007. Integrating implicit and explicit social cognitions for enhanced personality assessment: a general framework for choosing measurement and statistical methods. *Organ. Res. Methods* 10:136–79

Bogner WC, Barr PS. 2000. Making sense in hypercompetitive environments: a cognitive explanation for the persistence of high velocity competition. *Organ. Sci.* 11:212–26

Bragger JD, Hantula DA, Bragger D, Kirnan J, Kutcher E. 2003. When success breeds failure: history, hysteresis, and delayed exit decisions. *J. Appl. Psychol.* 88:6–14

Brandon DP, Hollingshead AB. 2004. Transactive memory systems in organizations: matching tasks, expertise, and people. *Organ. Sci.* 15:633–44

Brief AP, Weiss HM. 2002. Organizational behavior: affect in the workplace. *Annu. Rev. Psychol.* 53:279–307

Broadbent DE. 1958. *Perception and Communication*. London: Pergamon

Brodbeck FC, Frese M, Akerblom S, Audia G, Bakacsi G, et al. 2000. Cultural variation of leadership prototypes across 22 European countries. *J. Occup. Organ. Psychol.* 73:1–29

Brown KG. 2001. Using computers to deliver training: Which employees learn and why? *Pers. Psychol.* 54:271–96

Brown SL, Eisenhardt KM. 1997. The art of continuous change: linking complexity theory and time-paced evolution in relentlessly shifting organizations. *Admin. Sci. Q.* 42:1–34

Bryant DJ. 2007. Classifying simulated air threats with fast and frugal heuristics. *J. Behav. Decis. Mak.* 20:37–64

Bunderson JS. 2003. Recognizing and utilizing expertise in work groups: a status characteristics perspective. *Admin. Sci. Q.* 48:557–91

Burke CS, Stagl KC, Salas E, Pierce L, Kendall D. 2006. Understanding team adaptation: a conceptual analysis and model. *J. Appl. Psychol.* 91:1189–207

Cannon-Bowers JA, Salas E. 2001. Reflections on shared cognition. *J. Organ. Behav.* 22:195–202

Card S, Moran TP, Newel A. 1983. *The Psychology of Human-Computer Interaction*. Hillsdale, NJ: Erlbaum

Carpenter MA. 2002. The implications of strategy and social context for the relationship between top management team heterogeneity and firm performance. *Strateg. Manage. J.* 23:275–84

Cha SE, Edmondson AC. 2006. When values backfire: leadership, attribution, and disenchantment in a values-driven organization. *Leadersh. Q.* 17:57–78

Chaiken S, Trope Y, eds. 1999. *Dual Process Theories in Social Psychology*. New York: Guildford

Chattopadhyay P, Glick WH, Miller CC, Huber GP. 1999. Determinants of executive beliefs: comparing functional conditioning and social influence. *Strateg. Manage. J.* 20:763–89

Chen G, Gully SM, Whiteman JA, Kilcullen RN. 2000. Examination of relationships among trait-like individual differences, state-like individual differences, and learning performance. *J. Appl. Psychol.* 85:835–47

Clarkson GP, Hodgkinson GP. 2005. Introducing Cognizer™: a comprehensive computer package for the elicitation and analysis of cause maps. *Organ. Res. Methods* 8:317–41

Clegg CW, Spencer C. 2007. A circular and dynamic model of the process of job design. *J. Occup. Organ. Psychol.* 80:321–39

Cleveland JN, Murphy KR. 1992. Analyzing performance appraisal as a goal directed behavior. *Res. Pers. Hum. Resour. Manage.* 10:121–85

Colquitt JA, LePine JA, Noe RA. 2000. Toward an integrative theory of training motivation: a meta-analytic path analysis of 20 years of research. *J. Appl. Psychol.* 85:678–707

A field study exploring how group members attribute expertise using task and social category cues to develop transactive memory.

Cooke NJ, Salas E, Cannon-Bowers JA, Stout RJ. 2000. Measuring team knowledge. *Hum. Factors* 42:151–73

Craik K. 1943. *The Nature of Explanation*. Cambridge, UK: Cambridge Univ. Press

Cramton CD. 2001. The mutual knowledge problem and its consequences for dispersed collaboration. *Organ. Sci.* 12:346–71

Dane E, Pratt MG. 2007. Exploring intuition and its role in managerial decision making. *Acad. Manage. Rev.* 32:33–54

Daniels K. 2006. Rethinking job characteristics in work stress research. *Hum. Relat.* 59:267–90

Daniels K, Harris C, Briner RB. 2004. Linking work conditions to unpleasant affect: cognition, categorization and goals. *J. Occup. Organ. Psychol.* 77:343–63

Daniels K, Hartley R, Travers CJ. 2006. Beliefs about stressors alter stressors' impact: evidence from two experience-sampling studies. *Hum. Relat.* 59:1261–85

Daniels K, Johnson G. 2002. On trees and triviality traps: locating the debate on the contribution of cognitive mapping to organizational research. *Org. Stud.* 23:73–81

Daniels K, Johnson G, de Chernatony L. 2002. Task and institutional influences on managers' mental models of competition. *Org. Stud.* 23:31–62

Dasborough MT, Ashkanasy NM. 2002. Emotion and attribution of intentionality in leader-member relationships. *Leadersh. Q.* 13:615–34

DeChurch LA, Marks MA. 2006. Leadership in multiteam systems. *J. Appl. Psychol.* 91:311–29

DeShon RP, Gillespie JZ. 2005. A motivated action theory account of goal orientation. *J. Appl. Psychol.* 90:1096–127

Dewe P, Cooper CL. 2007. Coping research and the measurement of work related stress. In *International Review of Industrial and Organizational Psychology*, ed. GP Hodgkinson, JK Ford, pp. 141–91. Chichester, UK: Wiley

Dickson MW, Resick CJ, Hanges PJ. 2006. Systematic variation in organizationally-shared cognitive prototypes of effective leadership based on organizational form. *Leadersh. Q.* 17:487–505

Dirks KT. 2000. Trust in leadership and team performance: evidence from NCAA basketball. *J. Appl. Psychol.* 85:1004–12

Edwards E, Lees FP, eds. 1974. *The Human Operator in Process Control*. London: Taylor & Francis

Edwards JR. 1992. A cybernetic theory of stress, coping, and well-being in organizations. *Acad. Manage. Rev.* 17:238–74

Ellemers N, De Gilder D, Haslam SA. 2004. Motivating individuals and groups at work: a social identity perspective on leadership and group performance. *Acad. Manage. Rev.* 29:459–78

Ellis APJ. 2006. System breakdown: the role of mental models and transactive memory in the relationship between acute stress and team performance. *Acad. Manage. J.* 49:576–89

Ellis S, Davidi I. 2005. After-event reviews: drawing lessons from successful and failed experience. *J. Appl. Psychol.* 90:857–71

Elsbach KD, Hargadon AB. 2006. Enhancing creativity through "mindless" work: a framework of workday design. *Organ. Sci.* 17:470–83

Ensari N, Murphy SE. 2003. Cross-cultural variations in leadership perceptions and attribution of charisma to the leader. *Organ. Behav. Hum. Decis. Process.* 92:52–66

Epitropaki O, Martin R. 2005. From ideal to real: a longitudinal study of the role of implicit leadership theories on leader-member exchanges and employee outcomes. *J. Appl. Psychol.* 90:659–76

Faraj S, Sproull L. 2000. Coordinating expertise in software development teams. *Manage. Sci.* 46:1554–68

Fazio RH, Olson MA. 2003. Implicit measures in social cognition research: their meaning and use. *Annu. Rev. Psychol.* 54:297–327

Ferguson E, Daniels K, Jones D. 2006. Negatively oriented personality and perceived negative job characteristics as predictors of future psychological and physical symptoms: a meta-analytic structural modeling approach. *J. Psychosom. Res.* 60:45–52

Fiol CM. 2002. Capitalizing on paradox: the role of language in transforming organizational identities. *Organ. Sci.* 13:653–66

Fisher CD, Ashkanasy NM. 2000. The emerging role of emotions in work life: an introduction. *J. Organ. Behav.* 21:123–29

Fletcher C. 2001. Performance appraisal and management: the developing research agenda. *J. Occup. Organ. Psychol.* 74:473–87

Ford JK, Kraiger K. 1995. The application of cognitive constructs to the instructional systems model of training: implications for needs assessment, design and transfer. In *International Review of Industrial and Organizational Psychology, Volume 10*, ed. CL Cooper, IT Robertson, pp. 1–48. Chichester, UK: Wiley

Fowlkes JE, Salas E, Baker DP, Cannon-Bowers JA, Stout RJ. 2000. The utility of event-based knowledge elicitation. *Hum. Factors* 42:24–35

Frese M, Zapf D. 1999. On the importance of the objective environment in stress and attribution theory. Counterpoint to Perrewe & Zellars. *J. Organ. Behav.* 20:761–65

Gagne M, Deci EL. 2005. Self-determination theory and work motivation. *J. Organ. Behav.* 26:331–62

Gavetti G. 2005. Cognition and hierarchy: rethinking the microfoundations of capabilities development. *Organ. Sci.* 16:599–617

Gibson CB, Gibbs JL. 2006. Unpacking the concept of virtuality: the effects of geographic dispersion, electronic dependence, dynamic structure, and national diversity on team innovation. *Admin. Sci. Q.* 51:451–95

Gigerenzer G. 1991. How to make cognitive illusions disappear. Beyond heuristics and biases. In *European Review of Social Psychology*, ed. W Stroebe, M Hewstone, Vol 2, pp. 83–115. Chichester, UK: Wiley

Gigerenzer G, Goldstein DG. 1996. Reasoning the fast and frugal way: models of bounded rationality. *Psychol. Rev.* 103:650–69

Gilovich T, Griffith D, Kahneman D, eds. 2002. *Heuristics and Biases: The Psychology of Intuitive Judgment.* Cambridge, UK: Cambridge Univ. Press

Goldberg CB. 2005. Relational demography and similarity-attraction in interview assessments and subsequent offer decisions: Are we missing something? *Group Organ. Manage.* 30:597–624

Gorman JC, Cooke NJ, Winner JL. 2006. Measuring team situation awareness in decentralized command and control environments. *Ergonomics* 49:1312–25

Griffith TL, Neale MA. 2001. Information processing in traditional, hybrid, and virtual teams: from nascent knowledge to transactive memory. In *Research in Organizational Behavior, Volume 23*, pp. 379–421. Amsterdam: JAI Elsevier

Griffith TL, Sawyer JE, Neale MA. 2003. Virtualness and knowledge in teams: managing the love triangle of organizations, individuals, and information technology. *MIS Q.* 27:265–87

Hackman JR, Oldham GR. 1976. Motivation through design of work: test of a theory. *Organ. Behav. Hum. Perform.* 16:250–79

Haines EL, Sumner KE. 2006. Implicit measurement of attitudes, stereotypes, and self-concepts in organizations: teaching old dogmas new tricks. *Organ. Res. Methods* 9:536–53

Hambrick DC, Mason PA. 1984. Upper echelons: the organization as a reflection of its top managers. *Acad. Manage. Rev.* 9:193–206

Haslam SA. 2001. *Psychology in Organizations: The Social Identity Approach*. London: Sage

Haslam SA, Eggins RA, Reynolds KJ. 2003. The ASPIRe model: Actualizing Social and Personal Identity Resources to enhance organizational outcomes. *J. Occup. Organ. Psychol.* 76:83–113

Haslam SA, Reicher S. 2006. Stressing the group: social identity and the unfolding dynamics of responses to stress. *J. Appl. Psychol.* 91:1037–52

Hausknecht JP, Day DV, Thomas SC. 2004. Applicant reactions to selection procedures: an updated model and meta-analysis. *Pers. Psychol.* 57:639–83

Hayes J, Allinson CW, Hudson RS, Keasey K. 2003. Further reflections on the nature of intuition-analysis and the construct validity of the Cognitive Style Index. *J. Occup. Organ. Psychol.* 76:269–78

Heider F. 1958. *The Psychology of Interpersonal Relations*. New York: Wiley

Hennessey HW, Bernardin HJ. 2003. The relationship between performance appraisal criterion specificity and statistical evidence of discrimination. *Hum. Resour. Manage.* 42:143–58

Herriot P. 1989. Selection as a social process. In *Advances in Selection and Assessment*, ed. M Smith, IT Robertson, pp. 171–87. New York: Wiley

Herriot P. 2004. Social identities and applicant reactions. *Int. J. Sel. Assess.* 12:75–83

Herrmann P, Datta DK. 2006. CEO experiences: effects on the choice of FDI entry mode. *J. Manage. Stud.* 43:755–78

Heslin PA, Latham GP, VandeWalle D. 2005. The effect of implicit person theory on performance appraisals. *J. Appl. Psychol.* 90:842–56

Highhouse S. 2001. Judgment and decision-making research: relevance to industrial and organizational psychology. In *Handbook of Industrial, Work and Organizational Psychology: Volume 2—Organizational Psychology*, ed. N Anderson, DS Ones, HK Sinangil, C Viswesvaran, pp. 314–31. London: Sage

Hiller NJ, Hambrick DC. 2005. Conceptualizing executive hubris: the role of (hyper) core self-evaluations in strategic decision-making. *Strat. Manage. J.* 26:297–319

Hodgkinson GP. 2002. Comparing managers' mental models of competition: why self-report measures of belief similarity won't do. *Org. Stud.* 23:63–72

Hodgkinson GP. 2005. *Images of Competitive Space: A Study of Managerial and Organizational Strategic Cognition*. Basingstoke, UK: Palgrave Macmillan

Hodgkinson GP, Clarke I. 2007. Exploring the cognitive significance of organizational strategizing: a dual-process framework and research agenda. *Hum. Relat.* 60:243–55

Hodgkinson GP, Langan-Fox J, Sadler-Smith E. 2008. Intuition: a fundamental bridging construct in the behavioural sciences. *Br. J. Psychol.* 99:1–27

Hodgkinson GP, Maule AJ, Bown NJ. 2004. Causal cognitive mapping in the organizational strategy field: a comparison of alternative elicitation procedures. *Organ. Res. Methods* 7:3–26

Hodgkinson GP, Maule AJ, Bown NJ, Pearman AD, Glaister KW. 2002. Further reflections on the elimination of framing bias in strategic decision making. *Strat. Manage. J.* 23:1069–76

Hodgkinson GP, Sadler-Smith E. 2003a. Complex or unitary? A critique and empirical reassessment of the Allinson-Hayes Cognitive Style Index. *J. Occup. Organ. Psychol.* 76:243–68

Hodgkinson GP, Sadler-Smith E. 2003b. Reflections on reflections . . . on the nature of intuition, analysis and the construct validity of the Cognitive Style Index. *J. Occup. Organ. Psychol.* 76:279–81

Hodgkinson GP, Sparrow PR. 2002. *The Competent Organization: A Psychological Analysis of the Strategic Management Process*. Buckingham, UK: Open Univ. Press

Hodgkinson GP, Wright G. 2002. Confronting strategic inertia in a top management team: learning from failure. *Organ. Stud.* 23:949–77

Demonstrates how managers' beliefs regarding the malleability of personal attributes influence their ability to recognize employee performance variations.

Surveys theory, research, and methodological advances in the analysis of the strategic management process from a cognitive standpoint.

Hogarth RM, Karelaia N. 2005. Simple models for multiattribute choice with many alternatives: when it does and does not pay to face trade-offs with binary attributes. *Manage. Sci.* 51:1860–72

Hogg MA. 2001. A social identity theory of leadership. *Pers. Soc. Psychol. Rev.* 5:184–200

Hogg MA, Martin R, Epitropaki O, Mankad A, Svensson A, Weeden K. 2005. Effective leadership in salient groups: revisiting leader-member exchange theory from the perspective of the social identity theory of leadership. *Pers. Soc. Psychol. Bull.* 31:991–1004

Hogg MA, Terry DJ. 2000. Social identity and self-categorization processes in organizational contexts. *Acad. Manage. Rev.* **25:121–40**

Huff AS, ed. 1990. *Mapping Strategic Thought.* Chichester, UK: Wiley

Hutchins E. 1995. *Cognition in the Wild.* Cambridge, MA: MIT Press

Ilgen DR, Hollenbeck JR, Johnson M, Jundt D. 2005. Teams in organizations: from input-process-output models to IMOI models. *Annu. Rev. Psychol.* 56:517–43

Janssen O. 2004. How fairness perceptions make innovative behavior more or less stressful. *J. Organ. Behav.* 25:201–15

Johnson DE, Erez A, Kiker DS, Motowidlo SJ. 2002. Liking and attributions of motives as mediators of the relationships between individuals' reputations, helpful behaviors, and raters' reward decisions. *J. Appl. Psychol.* 87:808–15

Johnson DR, Hoopes DG. 2003. Managerial cognition, sunk costs and the evolution of industry structure. *Strat. Manage. J.* 24:1057–58

Johnson-Laird PN. 1983. *Mental Models: Towards a Cognitive Science of Language, Inference, and Consciousness.* Cambridge, MA: Cambridge Univ. Press

Jones DG, Endsley MR. 2000. Overcoming representational errors in complex environments. *Hum. Factors* 42:367–78

Judge TA, Bono JE. 2001. Relationship of core self-evaluations traits—self-esteem, generalized self-efficacy, locus of control, and emotional stability—with job satisfaction and job performance: a meta-analysis. *J. Appl. Psychol.* 86:80–92

Judge TA, Colbert AE, Ilies R. 2004a. Intelligence and leadership: a quantitative review and test of theoretical propositions. *J. Appl. Psychol.* 89:542–52

Judge TA, Jackson CL, Shaw JC, Scott BA, Rich BL. 2007. Self-efficacy and work-related performance: the integral role of individual differences. *J. Appl. Psychol.* 92:107–27

Judge TA, Van Vianen AEM, De Pater IE. 2004b. Emotional stability, core self-evaluations, and job outcomes: a review of the evidence and an agenda for future research. *Hum. Perform.* 17:325–46

Kahneman D, Tversky A. 1996. On the reality of cognitive illusions. *Psychol. Rev.* 103:582–91

Kark R, Shamir B, Chen G. 2003. The two faces of transformational leadership: empowerment and dependency. *J. Appl. Psychol.* 88:246–55

Kay AC, Wheeler SC, Bargh JA, Ross L. 2004. Material priming: the influence of mundane physical objects on situational construal and competitive behavioral choice. *Organ. Behav. Hum. Decis. Process.* **95:83–96**

Keeping LM, Levy PE. 2000. Performance appraisal reactions: measurement, modeling, and method bias. *J. Appl. Psychol.* 85:708–23

Kelley HH. 1967. Attribution theory in social psychology. In *Nebraska Symposium on Motivation*, ed. D Levine, pp. 192–240. Lincoln, NE: Univ. Nebraska Press

Kelly JR, Barsade SG. 2001. Mood and emotions in small groups and work teams. *Organ. Behav. Hum. Decis. Process.* 86:99–130

Kiesler S, Sproull L. 1982. Managerial response to changing environments: perspectives on problem sensing from social cognition. *Admin. Sci. Q.* 27:548–70

A highly cited article that draws on the social identity approach to analyze a wide range of organizational phenomena.

Reports five pioneering laboratory experiments that demonstrate exposure to business artifacts can influence judgments and behavior without conscious awareness.

Kilduff M, Angelmar R, Mehra A. 2000. Top management-team diversity and firm performance: examining the role of cognitions. *Organ. Sci.* 11:21–34

Klein GA. 1993. A recognition-primed decision (RPD) model of rapid decision making. In *Decision Making in Action: Models and Methods*, ed. G Klein, J Orasanu, R Calderwood, C Zsambok, pp. 138–47. Norwood, CT: Ablex

Kozlowski SWJ, Gully SM, Brown KG, Salas E, Smith EM, Nason ER. 2001. Effects of training goals and goal orientation traits on multidimensional training outcomes and performance adaptability. *Organ. Behav. Hum. Decis. Process.* 85:1–31

Kraiger K, Ford JK, Salas E. 1993. Application of cognitive, skill-based and affective theories of learning outcomes to new methods of training evaluation. *J. Appl. Psychol.* 78:311–28

Kuvaas B, Selart M. 2004. Effects of attribute framing on cognitive processing and evaluation. *Organ. Behav. Hum. Decis. Process.* 95:198–207

Labianca G, Gray B, Brass DJ. 2000. A grounded model of organizational schema change during empowerment. *Organ. Sci.* 11:235–57

Lane PJ, Koka BR, Pathak S. 2006. The reification of absorptive capacity: a critical review and rejuvenation of the construct. *Acad. Manage. Rev.* 31:833–63

Langan-Fox J, Code S, Langfield-Smith K. 2000. Team mental models: techniques, methods, and analytic approaches. *Hum. Factors* 42:242–71

Lant TK, Shapira Z. 2001. New research directions on organizational cognition. In *Managerial and Organizational Cognition: Computation and Interpretation*, ed. TK Lant, Z Shapira, pp. 367–76. Mahwah, NJ: Erlbaum

Latham GP, Pinder CC. 2005. Work motivation theory and research at the dawn of the twenty-first century. *Annu. Rev. Psychol.* 56:485–516

Lazarus RS, Folkman S. 1984. *Stress Appraisal and Coping*. New York: Springer

Leach DJ, Wall TD, Jackson PR. 2003. The effect of empowerment on job knowledge: an empirical test involving operators of complex technology. *J. Occup. Organ. Psychol.* 76:27–52

LePine JA. 2003. Team adaptation and postchange performance: effects of team composition in terms of members' cognitive ability and personality. *J. Appl. Psychol.* 88:27–39

LePine JA. 2004. Challenge and hindrance stress: relationships with exhaustion, motivation to learn, and learning performance. *J. Appl. Psychol.* 89:883–91

Levesque LL, Wilson JM, Wholey DR. 2001. Cognitive divergence and shared mental models in software development project teams. *J. Organ. Behav.* 22:135–44

Levin IP, Huneke ME, Jasper JD. 2000. Information processing at successive stages of decision making: need for cognition and inclusion-exclusion effects. *Organ. Behav. Hum. Decis. Process.* 82:171–93

Lieberman MD. 2007. Social cognitive neuroscience: a review of core processes. *Annu. Rev. Psychol.* 58:259–89

Lievens F, Chasteen CS, Day EA, Christiansen ND. 2006. Large-scale investigation of the role of trait activation theory for understanding assessment center convergent and discriminant validity. *J. Appl. Psychol.* 91:247–58

Lim BC, Klein KJ. 2006. Team mental models and team performance: a field study of the effects of team mental model similarity and accuracy. *J. Organ. Behav.* 27:403–18

Lipshitz R, Cohen MS. 2005. Warrants for prescription: analytically and empirically based approaches to improving decision making. *Hum. Factors* 47:102–20

Lipshitz R, Klein G, Carroll JS, eds. 2006. Special issue on "naturalistic decision making and organizational decision making: exploring the intersections." *Org. Stud.* 27:917–1057

Lipshitz R, Klein G, Orasanu J, Salas E. 2001. Focus article: taking stock of naturalistic decision making. *J. Behav. Decis. Mak.* 14:331–52

Large-scale investigation of the cognitive effects of stress on learning, integrating insights from personality, ability, stress, motivation, and learning theories.

Provides a state-of-the-art overview of the contributions and limitations of naturalistic decision making, accompanied by 16 peer commentaries.

Locke EA, Latham GP. 2004. What should we do about motivation theory? Six recommendations for the twenty-first century. *Acad. Manage. Rev.* 29:388–403

London M, Mone EM, Scott JC. 2004. Performance management and assessment: methods for improved rater accuracy and employee goal setting. *Hum. Resour. Manage.* 43:319–36

Lord RG, Brown DJ, Harvey JL, Hall RJ. 2001. Contextual constraints on prototype generation and their multilevel consequences for leadership perceptions. *Leadersh. Q.* 12:311–38

Lord RG, Emrich CG. 2000. Thinking outside the box by looking inside the box: extending the cognitive revolution in leadership research. *Leadersh. Q.* 11:551–79

Lord RG, Foti RJ, Devader CL. 1984. A test of leadership categorization theory: internal structure, information-processing, and leadership perceptions. *Organ. Behav. Hum. Perform.* 34:343–78

Lord RG, Hall RJ. 2005. Identity, deep structure and the development of leadership skill. *Leadersh. Q.* 16:591–615

Lord RG, Maher KJ. 1991. *Leadership and Information Processing: Linking Perception and Performance.* Boston, MA: Unwin Hyman

Lowe R, Bennett P. 2003. Exploring coping reactions to work-stress: application of an appraisal theory. *J. Occup. Organ. Psychol.* 76:393–400

Maitlis S. 2005. The social processes of organizational sensemaking. *Acad. Manage. J.* 48:21–49

Maitlis S, Ozcelik H. 2004. Toxic decision processes: a study of emotion and organizational decision making. *Organ. Sci.* 15:375–93

Malhotra A, Majchrzak A, Carman R, Lott V. 2001. Radical innovation without collocation: a case study at Boeing-Rocketdyne. *MIS Q.* 25:229–49

March JG, Simon HA. 1958. *Organizations.* New York: Wiley

Markoczy L. 1997. Measuring beliefs: accept no substitutes. *Acad. Manage. J.* 40:1228–42

Markoczy L. 2001. Consensus formation during strategic change. *Strat. Manage. J.* 22:1013–31

Marks MA, DeChurch LA, Mathieu JE, Panzer FJ, Alonso A. 2005. Teamwork in multiteam systems. *J. Appl. Psychol.* 90:964–71

Marks MA, Sabella MJ, Burke CS, Zaccaro SJ. 2002. The impact of cross-training on team effectiveness. *J. Appl. Psychol.* 87:3–13

Martell RF, Evans DP. 2005. Source-monitoring training: toward reducing rater expectancy effects in behavioral measurement. *J. Appl. Psychol.* 90:956–63

Martinko MJ, Gundlach MJ, Douglas SC. 2002. Toward an integrative theory of counterproductive workplace behavior: a causal reasoning perspective. *Int. J. Sel. Assess.* 10:36–50

Maslach C, Schaufeli WB, Leiter MP. 2001. Job burnout. *Annu. Rev. Psychol.* 52:397–422

Mathieu JE, Heffner TS, Goodwin GF, Cannon-Bowers JA, Salas E. 2005. Scaling the quality of teammates' mental models: equifinality and normative comparisons. *J. Organ. Behav.* 26:37–56

Mathieu JE, Heffner TS, Goodwin GF, Salas E, Cannon-Bowers JA. 2000. The influence of shared mental models on team process and performance. *J. Appl. Psychol.* 85:273–83

Mathieu JE, Marks MA, Zaccaro SJ. 2001. Multiteam systems. In *Handbook of Industrial, Work and Organizational Psychology: Volume 2—Organizational Psychology*, ed. N Anderson, DS Ones, HK Sinangil, C Viswesvaran, pp. 289–331. London: Sage

McNamara G, Luce RA, Tompson GH. 2002. Examining the effect of complexity in strategic group knowledge structures on firm performance. *Strat. Manage. J.* 23:153–70

Meyer JP, Becker TE, Vandenberghe C. 2004. Employee commitment and motivation: a conceptual analysis and integrative model. *J. Appl. Psychol.* 89:991–1007

Mintzberg H, Waters JA. 1985. Of strategies, deliberate and emergent. *Strat. Manage. J.* 6:257–72

Builds on advances in connectionist modeling to account for stability and flexibility in leadership prototypes.

Advances the multiteam systems concept, applying and extending principles of shared cognition from conventional teams to "teams of teams."

Moore JE. 2000. Why is this happening? A causal attribution approach to work exhaustion consequences. *Acad. Manage. Rev.* 25:335–49

Morgeson FP, Humphrey SE. 2006. The Work Design Questionnaire (WDQ): developing and validating a comprehensive measure for assessing job design and the nature of work. *J. Appl. Psychol.* 91:1321–39

Narayanan VK, Armstrong DJ, eds. 2005. *Causal Mapping for Research in Information Technology.* Hershey, PA: Idea Group Inc.

Neale MA, Tenbrunsel AE, Galvin T, Bazerman MH. 2006. A decision perspective on organizations: social cognition, behavioural decision theory and the psychological links to micro- and macro-organizational behaviour. In *The Sage Handbook of Organization Studies*, ed. SR Clegg, C Hardy, TB Lawrence, WR Nord, pp. 485–519. London: Sage

Nemanick RC, Clark EM. 2002. The differential effects of extracurricular activities on attributions in resume evaluation. *Int. J. Sel. Assess.* 10:206–17

Newell BR, Weston NJ, Shanks DR. 2003. Empirical tests of a fast-and-frugal heuristic: not everyone "takes-the-best." *Organ. Behav. Hum. Decis. Process.* 91:82–96

Ng TWH, Sorensen KL, Eby LT. 2006. Locus of control at work: a meta-analysis. *J. Organ. Behav.* 27:1057–87

Osborne JD, Stubbart CI, Ramaprasad A. 2001. Strategic groups and competitive enactment: a study of dynamic relationships between mental models and performance. *Strat. Manage. J.* 22:435–54

Parasuraman R. 2000. Designing automation for human use: empirical studies and quantitative models. *Ergonomics* 43:931–51

Parker AM, Fischhoff B. 2005. Decision-making competence: external validation through an individual-differences approach. *J. Behav. Decis. Mak.* 18:1–27

Parker SK, Wall TD, Cordery JL. 2001. Future work design research and practice: towards an elaborated model of work design. *J. Occup. Organ. Psychol.* 74:413–40

Patrick J, James N. 2004. Process tracing of complex cognitive work tasks. *J. Occup. Organ. Psychol.* 77:259–80

Perrewe PL, Zellars KL. 1999. An examination of attributions and emotions in the transactional approach to the organizational stress process. *J. Organ. Behav.* 20:739–52

Perrin BM, Barnett BJ, Walrath L, Grossman JD. 2001. Information order and outcome framing: an assessment of judgment bias in a naturalistic decision-making context. *Hum. Factors* 43:227–38

Phelps EA. 2006. Emotion and cognition: insights from studies of the human amygdala. *Annu. Rev. Psychol.* 57:27–53

Pierro A, Cicero L, Bonaiuto M, van Knippenberg D, Kruglanski AW. 2005. Leader group prototypicality and leadership effectiveness: the moderating role of need for cognitive closure. *Leadersh. Q.* 16:503–16

Ployhart RE, Harold CM. 2004. The applicant attribution-reaction theory (AART): an integrative theory of applicant attributional processing. *Int. J. Sel. Assess.* 12:84–98

Porac JF, Thomas H, Wilson F, Paton D, Kanfer A. 1995. Rivalry and the industry model of Scottish knitwear producers. *Admin. Sci. Q.* 40:203–27

Pratt MG. 2000. The good, the bad, and the ambivalent: managing identification among Amway distributors. *Admin. Sci. Q.* 45:456–93

Reger RK, Gustafson LT, Demarie SM, Mullane JV. 1994. Reframing the organization: why implementing total quality is easier said than done. *Acad. Manage. Rev.* 19:565–84

Remington RW, Johnston JC, Ruthruff E, Gold M, Romera M. 2000. Visual search in complex displays: factors affecting conflict detection by air traffic controllers. *Hum. Factors* 42:349–66

Ren YQ, Carley KM, Argote L. 2006. The contingent effects of transactive memory: When is it more beneficial to know what others know? *Manage. Sci.* 52:671–82

Rentsch JR, Klimoski RJ. 2001. Why do "great minds" think alike? Antecedents of team member schema agreement. *J. Organ. Behav.* 22:107–20

Repenning NP, Sterman JD. 2002. Capability traps and self-confirming attribution errors in the dynamics of process improvement. *Admin. Sci. Q.* 47:265–95

Rinkus S, Walji M, Johnson-Throop KA, Malin J, Turley JP, et al. 2005. Human-centered design of a distributed knowledge management system. *J. Biomed. Inform.* 38:4–17

Roth EM, Multer J, Raslear T. 2006. Shared situation awareness as a contributor to high reliability performance in railroad operations. *Org. Stud.* 27:967–87

Rouse WB, Morris NM. 1986. On looking into the black box: prospects and limits in the search for mental models. *Psychol. Bull.* 100:349–63

Rousseau DM. 1995. *Psychological Contracts in Organizations: Understanding Written and Unwritten Agreements.* Thousand Oaks, CA: Sage

Rousseau DM. 2001. Schema, promise and mutuality: the building blocks of the psychological contract. *J. Occup. Organ. Psychol.* 74:511–41

Russo JE, Meloy MG, Wilks TJ. 2000. Predecisional distortion of information by auditors and salespersons. *Manage. Sci.* 46:13–27

Ryan AM, Ployhart RE. 2000. Applicants' perceptions of selection procedures and decisions: a critical review and agenda for the future. *J. Manage.* 26:565–606

Rynes SL, Gerhart B, Parks L. 2005. Personnel psychology: performance evaluation and pay for performance. *Annu. Rev. Psychol.* 56:571–600

Salas E, Cannon-Bowers JA. 2001. The science of training: a decade of progress. *Annu. Rev. Psychol.* 52:471–99

Salgado JF, Anderson N, Moscoso S, Bertua C, De Fruyt F. 2003. International validity generalization of GMA and cognitive abilities: a European community meta-analysis. *Pers. Psychol.* 56:573–605

Salvendy G, ed. 2006. *Handbook of Human Factors and Ergonomics.* Hoboken, NJ: Wiley

Sauer J, Felsing T, Franke H, Ruttinger B. 2006. Cognitive diversity and team performance in a complex multiple task environment. *Ergonomics* 49:934–54

Sauer J, Hockey GRJ, Wastell DG. 2000. Effects of training on short- and long-term skill retention in a complex multiple-task environment. *Ergonomics* 43:2043–64

Schaubroeck J. 1999. Should the subjective be the objective? On studying mental processes, coping behavior, and actual exposures in organizational stress research. *J. Organ. Behav.* 20:753–60

Schmidt AM, Ford JK. 2003. Learning within a learner control training environment: the interactive effects of goal orientation and meta-cognitive instruction on learning outcomes. *Pers. Psychol.* 56:405–29

Schraagen JMC, Chipman SF, Shalin VL, eds. 2000. *Cognitive Task Analysis.* Mahwah, NJ: Erlbaum

Schroth HA, Shah PP. 2000. Procedures: Do we really want to know them? An examination of the effects of procedural justice on self-esteem. *J. Appl. Psychol.* 85:462–71

Shaw JC, Wild E, Colquitt JA. 2003. To justify or excuse? A meta-analytic review of the effects of explanations. *J. Appl. Psychol.* 88:444–58

Silvester J, Anderson-Gough FM, Anderson NR, Mohamed AR. 2002. Locus of control, attributions and impression management in the selection interview. *J. Occup. Organ. Psychol.* 75:59–76

Silvester J, Patterson F, Ferguson E. 2003. Comparing two attributional models of job performance in retail sales: a field study. *J. Occup. Organ. Psychol.* 76:115–32

Simon HA. 1947. *Administrative Behavior*. New York: Macmillan

Sitzmann T, Kraiger K, Stewart D, Wisher R. 2006. The comparative effectiveness of web-based and classroom instruction: a meta-analysis. *Pers. Psychol.* 59:623–64

Sloman SA, Hagmayer Y. 2006. The causal psycho-logic of choice. *Trends Cogn. Sci.* 10:407–12

Smith-Jentsch KA, Campbell GE, Milanovich DM, Reynolds AM. 2001. Measuring teamwork mental models to support training needs assessment, development, and evaluation: two empirical studies. *J. Organ. Behav.* 22:179–94

Sohn YW, Doane SM. 2004. Memory processes of flight situation awareness: interactive roles of working memory capacity, long-term working memory, and expertise. *Hum. Factors* 46:461–75

Srivastava A, Bartol KM, Locke EA. 2006. Empowering leadership in management teams: effects on knowledge sharing, efficacy, and performance. *Acad. Manage. J.* 49:1239–51

Stajkovic AD. 2006. Development of a core confidence-higher order construct. *J. Appl. Psychol.* 91:1208–24

Stajkovic AD, Locke EA, Blair ES. 2006. A first examination of the relationships between primed subconscious goals, assigned conscious goals, and task performance. *J. Appl. Psychol.* 91:1172–80

Steel P, Konig CJ. 2006. Integrating theories of motivation. *Acad. Manage. Rev.* 31:889–913

Sutcliffe KM, Weick K. 2008. Information overload revisited. In *The Oxford Handbook of Organizational Decision Making*, ed. GP Hodgkinson, WH Starbuck, pp. 56–75. Oxford, UK: Oxford Univ. Press

Tajfel H, Turner JC. 1979. An integrative theory of intergroup conflict. In *The Social Psychology of Intergroup Relations*, ed. WG Austin, S Worchel, pp. 33–47. Monterey, CA: Brooks-Cole

Tasa K, Taggar S, Seijts GH. 2007. The development of collective efficacy in teams: a multilevel and longitudinal perspective. *J. Appl. Psychol.* 92:17–27

Tetlock PE. 2000. Cognitive biases and organizational correctives: Do both disease and cure depend on the politics of the beholder? *Admin. Sci. Q.* 45:293–326

Troup C, Dewe P. 2002. Exploring the nature of control and its role in the appraisal of workplace stress. *Work Stress* 16:335–55

Truxillo DM, Bauer TN, Campion MA, Paronto ME. 2002. Selection fairness information and applicant reactions: a longitudinal field study. *J. Appl. Psychol.* 87:1020–31

Tversky A, Kahneman D. 1974. Judgment under uncertainty: heuristics and biases. *Science* 185:1124–31

van Knippenberg B, van Knippenberg D. 2005. Leader self-sacrifice and leadership effectiveness: the moderating role of leader prototypicality. *J. Appl. Psychol.* 90:25–37

van Knippenberg D, Schippers MC. 2007. Work group diversity. *Annu. Rev. Psychol.* 58:515–41

van Knippenberg D, van Knippenberg B, De Cremer D, Hogg MA. 2004. Leadership, self, and identity: a review and research agenda. *Leadersh. Q.* 15:825–56

Vancouver JB. 2005. The depth of history and explanation as benefit and bane for psychological control theories. *J. Appl. Psychol.* 90:38–52

Vancouver JB, Thompson CM, Tischner EC, Putka DJ. 2002. Two studies examining the negative effect of self-efficacy on performance. *J. Appl. Psychol.* 87:506–16

Wallace JC, Chen G. 2005. Development and validation of a work-specific measure of cognitive failure: implications for occupational safety. *J. Occup. Organ. Psychol.* 78:615–32

Waller MJ, Gupta N, Giambatista RC. 2004. Effects of adaptive behaviors and shared mental models on control crew performance. *Manage. Sci.* 50:1534–44

Walsh JP. 1995. Managerial and organizational cognition: notes from a trip down memory lane. *Organ. Sci.* 6:280–321

Demonstrates how shared cognition helps control room operatives adapt to crises in a nuclear power plant.

Walsh JP, Ungson GR. 1991. Organizational memory. *Acad. Manage. Rev.* 16:57–91

Wanberg CR, Banas JT. 2000. Predictors and outcomes of openness to changes in a reorganizing workplace. *J. Appl. Psychol.* 85:132–42

Warr P. 2006. Differential activation of judgments in employee well-being. *J. Occup. Organ. Psychol.* 79:225–44

Weick KE. 1979. *The Social Psychology of Organizing.* New York: McGraw-Hill. 2nd ed.

Weick KE, Quinn RE. 1999. Organizational change and development. *Annu. Rev. Psychol.* 50:361–86

Wickens CD, Carswell CM. 2006. Information processing. In *Handbook of Human Factors and Ergonomics*, ed. G Salvendy, pp. 111–49. Hoboken, NJ: Wiley

Wiggins MW, Bollwerk S. 2006. Heuristic-based information acquisition and decision making among pilots. *Hum. Factors* 48:734–46

Wong KF, Yik M, Kwong JYY. 2006. Understanding the emotional aspects of escalation of commitment: the role of negative affect. *J. Appl. Psychol.* 91:282–97

Wood RE, Bandura A. 1989. Social-cognitive theory of organizational management. *Acad. Manage. Rev.* 14:361–84

Wright G, Goodwin P. 2002. Eliminating a framing bias by using simple instructions to "think harder" and respondents with managerial experience: comment on "Breaking the Frame." *Strat. Manage. J.* 23:1059–67

Wright RP. 2004. Mapping cognitions to better understand attitudinal and behavioral responses in appraisal research. *J. Organ. Behav.* 25:339–74

Yeo GB, Neal A. 2006. An examination of the dynamic relationship between self-efficacy and performance across levels of analysis and levels of specificity. *J. Appl. Psychol.* 91:1088–101

Zhang JJ, Norman DA. 1994. Representations in distributed cognitive tasks. *Cogn. Sci.* 18:87–122

Zhang JJ, Patel VL, Johnson KA, Smith JW, Malin J. 2002. Designing human-centered distributed information systems. *IEEE Intell. Syst.* 17:42–47

Personnel Selection

Paul R. Sackett[1] and Filip Lievens[2]

[1]Department of Psychology, University of Minnesota, Minneapolis, Minnesota 55455; email: psackett@umn.edu [2]Department of Personnel Management and Work and Organizational Psychology, Ghent University, Henri Dunantlaan 2, 9000, Ghent, Belgium; email: filip.lievens@ugent.be

Annu. Rev. Psychol. 2008. 59:419–50

First published online as a Review in Advance on September 12, 2007

The *Annual Review of Psychology* is online at http://psych.annualreviews.org

This article's doi: 10.1146/annurev.psych.59.103006.093716

Key Words

job performance, testing, validity, adverse impact, ability, personality

Abstract

We review developments in personnel selection since the previous review by Hough & Oswald (2000) in the *Annual Review of Psychology*. We organize the review around a taxonomic structure of possible bases for improved selection, which includes (*a*) better understanding of the criterion domain and criterion measurement, (*b*) improved measurement of existing predictor methods or constructs, (*c*) identification and measurement of new predictor methods or constructs, (*d*) improved identification of features that moderate or mediate predictor-criterion relationships, (*e*) clearer understanding of the relationship between predictors or between predictors and criteria (e.g., via meta-analytic synthesis), (*f*) identification and prediction of new outcome variables, (*g*) improved ability to determine how well we predict the outcomes of interest, (*h*) improved understanding of subgroup differences, fairness, bias, and the legal defensibility, (*i*) improved administrative ease with which selection systems can be used, (*j*) improved insight into applicant reactions, and (*k*) improved decision-maker acceptance of selection systems.

Contents

INTRODUCTION

Personnel selection has a long history of coverage in the *Annual Review of Psychology*. This is the first treatment of the topic since 2000, and length constraints make this a selective review of work since the prior article by Hough & Oswald (2000). Our approach to this review is to focus more on learning (i.e., How has our understanding of selection and our ability to select effectively changed?) than on documenting activity (i.e., What has been done?). We envision a reader who vanished from the scene after the Hough & Oswald review and reappears now, asking, "Are we able to do a better job of selection now than we could in 2000?" Thus, we organize this review around a taxonomic structure of possible bases for improved selection, which we list below.

1. Better prediction of traditional outcome measures, as a result of:

    a. better understanding of the criterion domain and criterion measurement

    b. improved measurement of existing predictor methods or constructs

    c. identification and measurement of new predictor methods or constructs

    d. improved identification of features that moderate or mediate predictor-criterion relationships

    e. clearer understanding of the relationship between predictors or between predictors and criteria (e.g., via meta-analytic synthesis)

2. Identification and prediction of new outcome variables

3. Improved ability to determine how well we predict the outcomes of interest (i.e., improved techniques for estimating validity)

4. Improved understanding of subgroup differences, fairness, bias, and the legal defensibility of our selection systems

5. Improved administrative ease with which selection systems can be used

6. Improved methods obtaining more favorable applicant reactions and better insight into consequences of applicant reactions

7. Improved decision-maker acceptance of selection systems

Although our focus is on new research findings, we note that there are a number of professional developments important for anyone interested in the selection field. The Important Professional Developments sidebar briefly outlines these developments.

CAN WE PREDICT TRADITIONAL OUTCOME MEASURES BETTER BECAUSE OF BETTER UNDERSTANDING OF THE CRITERION DOMAIN AND CRITERION MEASUREMENT?

Conceptualization of the Criterion Domain

Research continues an ongoing trend of moving beyond a single unitary construct of job performance to a more differentiated model.

IMPORTANT PROFESSIONAL DEVELOPMENTS

Updated versions of the *Standards for Educational and Psychological Testing* (Am. Educ. Res. Assoc., Am. Psychol. Assoc., Natl. Counc. Meas. Educ. 1999) and the *Principles for the Validation and Use of Personnel Selection Procedures* (Soc. Ind. Organ. Psychol. 2003) have appeared. Jeanneret (2005) provides a useful summary and comparison of these documents.

Guidance on computer and Internet-based testing is provided in an American Psychological Association Task Force report (Naglieri et al. 2004) and in guidelines prepared by the International Test Commission (Int. Test Comm. 2006).

Edited volumes on a number of selection-related themes have appeared in the Society for Industrial and Organizational Psychology's two book series, including volumes on the management of selection systems (Kehoe 2000), personality in organizations (Barrick & Ryan 2003), discrimination at work (Dipboye & Colella 2004), employment discrimination litigation (Landy 2005a), and situational judgment tests (Weekley & Ployhart 2006). There are also edited volumes on validity generalization (Murphy 2003), test score banding (Aguinis 2004), emotional intelligence (Murphy 2006), and the Army's Project A (Campbell & Knapp 2001).

Two handbooks offering broad coverage of the industrial/organizational (I/O) field have been published; both containing multiple chapters examining various aspects of the personnel selection process (Anderson et al. 2001, Borman et al. 2003).

Campbell's influential perspective on the dimensionality of performance (e.g., Campbell et al. 1993) and the large-scale demonstrations in the military's Project A (Campbell & Knapp 2001) of differential relationships between predictor constructs (e.g., ability, personality) and criterion constructs (e.g., task proficiency, effort, maintaining personal discipline) contributed to making this a major focus of contemporary research on predictor-criterion relationships.

Two major developments in understanding criterion dimensions are the emergence of extensive literature on organizational citizenship behavior (Podsakoff et al. 2000; see also Borman & Motowidlo 1997, on the closely related topic of contextual performance) and on counterproductive work behavior (Sackett & Devore 2001, Spector & Fox 2005). Dalal (2005) presents a meta-analysis of relationships between these two domains; the modest correlations (mean $r = -0.32$ corrected for measurement error) support the differentiation of these two, rather than the view that they are merely opposite poles of a single continuum. Rotundo & Sackett (2002) review and integrate a number of perspectives on the dimensionality of job performance and offer task performance, citizenship performance, and counterproductive work behavior as the three major domains of job performance. With cognitively loaded predictors as generally the strongest correlates of task performance and noncognitive predictors as generally the best predictors in the citizenship and counterproductive behavior domains, careful attention to the criterion of interest to the organization is a critical determinant of the eventual makeup and success of a selection system.

Predictor-Criterion Matching

Related to the notion of criterion dimensionality, there is increased insight into predictor-criterion matching. This elaborates on the notion of specifying the criterion of interest and selecting predictors accordingly. We give several examples. First, Bartram (2005) offered an eight-dimensional taxonomy of performance dimensions for managerial jobs, paired with a set of hypotheses about specific ability and personality factors conceptually relevant to each dimension. He then showed higher validities for the hypothesized predictor-criterion combinations. Second, Hogan & Holland (2003) sorted criterion dimensions based on their conceptual relevance to various personality dimensions and then documented higher validity for personality dimensions when matched against these relevant criteria; see Hough & Oswald (2005) for additional examples in the personality domain. Third, Lievens et al. (2005a) classified

---

Predictor constructs: psychological characteristics underlying predictor measures

Counterproductive work behavior: behaviors that harm the organization or its members

Task performance: performance of core required job activities

medical schools as basic science–oriented versus patient care–oriented, and found an interpersonally oriented situational judgment test predictive of performance only in the patient care–oriented schools.

The Role of Time in Criterion Measurement

Apart from developments in better understanding the dimensionality of the criterion and in uncovering predictors for these different criterion dimensions, important progress has also been made in understanding the (in)stability of the criterion over time. Sturman et al. (2005) developed an approach to differentiating between temporal consistency, performance stability, and test-retest reliability. Removing the effects of temporal instability from indices of performance consistency is needed to understand the degree to which change in measured performance over time is a result of error in the measurement of performance versus real change in performance.

Predicting Performance Over Time

This renewed emphasis in the dynamic nature of the criterion has also generated studies that aim to predict change in the criterion construct. Studies have examined whether predictors of job performance differ across job stages. The transitional job stage, where there is a need to learn new things, is typically contrasted to the more routine maintenance job stage (Murphy 1989). Thoresen et al. (2004) found that the Big Five personality factor of Openness was related to performance and performance trends in the transition stage but not to performance at the maintenance stage. Stewart (1999) showed that the dependability aspects of the Conscientiousness factor (e.g., self-discipline) were related to job performance at the transitional stage, whereas the volitional facets of Conscientiousness (e.g., achievement motivation) were linked to job performance at the main-

tenance stage. Also worthy of note in understanding and predicting performance over time is Stewart & Nandleolyar's (2006) comparison of interindividual and intraindividual variation in performance over time. In a sales sample, they find greater intraindividual variation than interindividual variation in week-to-week performance. These intraindividual differences were further significantly determined by whether people benefited from situational opportunities (i.e., adaptability). There was also evidence that particular personality traits enabled people to increase their performance by effectively adapting to changes in the environment. Sales people high in Conscientiousness were better able to benefit from situational opportunities when they saw these opportunities as goals to achieve (task pursuit). The reverse was found for people high in Openness, who might be more effective in task revision situations.

Criterion Measurement

Turning from developments in the conceptualization of criteria to developments in criterion measurement, a common finding in ratings of job performance is a pattern of relatively high correlations among dimensions, even in the presence of careful scale development designed to maximize differentiation among scales. A common explanation offered for this is halo, as single raters commonly rate an employee on all dimensions. Viswesvaran et al. (2005) provided useful insights into this issue by meta-analytically comparing correlations between performance dimensions made by differing raters with those made by the same rater. Although ratings by the same rater were higher (mean interdimension $r = 0.72$) than those from different raters (mean $r = 0.54$), a strong general factor was found in both. Thus, the finding of a strong general factor is not an artifact of rater-specific halo.

With respect to innovations in rating format, Borman et al. (2001) introduced the computerized adaptive rating scale (CARS). Building on principles of adaptive testing,

Citizenship performance: behaviors contributing to organization's social and psychological environment

Temporal consistency: the correlation between performance measures over time

Performance stability: the degree of constancy of true performance over time

Test-retest reliability: the correlation between observed performance measures over time after removing the effects of performance instability. The term "test-retest reliability" is used uniquely in this formulation; the term more typically refers to the correlation between measures across time

Transitional job stage: stage of job tenure where there is a need to learn new things

Maintenance job stage: stage of job tenure where job tasks are constant

Criterion measurement: operational measures of the criterion domain

they scaled a set of performance behaviors and then used a computer to present raters with pairs of behaviors differing in effectiveness. The choice of which behavior best describes the ratee drives the selection of the next pair of behaviors, thus honing in on the ratee's level of effectiveness. Using ratings of videotaped performance episodes to compare CARS with graphic scales and behaviorally anchored scales, they reported higher reliability, validity, accuracy, and more favorable user reactions for CARS. Although this study is at the initial demonstration stage, it does suggest a potential route to higher-quality performance measures.

CAN WE PREDICT TRADITIONAL OUTCOME MEASURES BETTER BECAUSE OF IMPROVED MEASUREMENT OF EXISTING PREDICTOR METHODS OR CONSTRUCTS?

The prediction of traditional outcomes might be increased by improving the measurement of existing selection procedures. We outline five general strategies that have been pursued in attempting to improve existing selection procedures. Although there is research on attempts to improve measurement of a variety of constructs, much of the work focuses on the personality domain. Research in the period covered by this review continues the enormous surge of interest in personality that began in the past decade. Our sense is that a variety of factors contribute to this surge of interest, including (*a*) the clear relevance of the personality domain for the prediction of performance dimensions that go beyond task performance (e.g., citizenship and counterproductive behavior), (*b*) the potential for incremental validity in the prediction of task performance, (*c*) the common finding of minimal racial/ethnic group differences, thus offering the prospect of reduced adverse impact, and (*d*) some unease about the magnitude of validity coefficients obtained using personality measures. There seems to be a general

sense that personality "should" fare better than it does. Our sense is that what is emerging is that there are sizable relationships between variables in the personality domain and important work outcomes, but that the pattern of relationships is complex. We believe the field "got spoiled" by the relatively straightforward pattern of findings in the ability domain (e.g., relatively high correlations between different attempts to measure cognitive ability and consistent success in relating virtually any test with a substantial cognitive loading to job performance measures). In the personality domain, mean validity coefficients for single Big Five traits are indeed relatively small (e.g., the largest corrected validity, for Conscientiousness, is about 0.20), leading to some critical views of the use of personality measures (e.g., Murphy & Dzieweczynski 2005). However, overall performance is predicted much better by compound traits and by composites of Big Five measures. In addition, more specific performance dimensions (e.g., citizenship, counterproductive work behavior) are better predicted by carefully selected measures that may be subfacets of broad Big Five traits (Hough & Oswald 2005, Ones et al. 2005). As the work detailed below indicates, the field does not yet have a complete understanding of the role of personality constructs and personality measures.

Measure the Same Construct with Another Method

The first strategy is to measure the same construct with another method. This strategy recognizes that the constructs being measured (such as conscientiousness, cognitive ability, manual dexterity) should be distinguished from the method of measurement (such as self-report inventories, tests, interviews, work samples). In the personality domain, there have been several attempts at developing alternatives to traditional self-report measures. One has been to explicitly structure interviews around the Five-Factor Model (Barrick et al. 2000, Van Iddekinge et al.

2005) instead of using self-report personality inventories. Even in traditional interviews, personality factors (35%) and social skills (28%) are the most frequently measured constructs (Huffcutt et al. 2001a). Another is to develop implicit measures of personality. One example of this is Motowidlo et al.'s (2006) development of situational judgment tests designed to tap an individual's implicit trait theories. They theorize, and then offer evidence, that individual personality shapes individual judgments of the effectiveness of behaviors reflecting high to low levels of the trait in question. Thus, it may prove possible to make inferences about personality from an individual's judgments of the effectiveness of various behaviors. Another approach to implicit measurement of personality is conditional reasoning (James et al. 2005) based on the notion that people use various justification mechanisms to explain their behavior, and that people with varying dispositional tendencies will employ differing justification mechanisms. The basic paradigm is to present what appear to be logical reasoning problems, in which respondents are asked to select the response that follows most logically from an initial statement. In fact, the alternatives reflect various justification mechanisms. James et al. (2005) present considerable validity evidence for a conditional reasoning measure of aggression. Other research found that a conditional reasoning test of aggression could not be faked, provided that the real purpose of the test is not disclosed (LeBreton et al. 2007).

Improve Construct Measurement

A second strategy is to improve the measurement of the constructs underlying existing selection methods. For instance, in the personality domain, it has been argued that the validity of scales that were originally developed to measure the Five-Factor Model of personality will be higher than scales categorized in this framework post hoc. Evidence has been mixed: Salgado (2003) found such effects for Conscientiousness and Emotional Stability scales; however, Hurtz & Donovan (2000) did not. Another example is Schmit et al.'s (2000) development of a personality instrument based in broad international input, thus avoiding idiosyncrasies of a single nation or culture in instrument content. Apart from using better scales, one might also experiment with other response process models as a way of improving the quality of construct measurement in personality inventories. Existing personality inventories typically assume that candidates use a dominance response process. Whereas such a dominance response process is clearly appropriate for cognitive ability tests, ideal point process models seem to provide a better fit of candidates' responses to personality test items than do the dominance models (even though these personality inventories were developed on the basis of a dominance model; Stark et al. 2006).

These attempts to improve the quality of construct measurement are not limited to the personality domain. Advances have been made in unraveling the construct validity puzzle in assessment centers. Although there is now relative consensus that assessment center exercises are more important than assessment center constructs (Bowler & Woehr 2006, Lance et al. 2004), we have a better understanding of which factors affect the quality of construct measurement in assessment centers. First, well-designed assessment centers show more construct validity evidence (Arthur et al. 2000, Lievens & Conway 2001). For instance, there is better construct validity when fewer dimensions are used and when assessors are psychologists. High interassessor reliability is important; otherwise, variance due to assessors will be confounded with variance due to exercises because assessors typically rotate through the various exercises (Kolk et al. 2002). Third, various studies (Lance et al. 2000, Lievens 2002) identified the nature of candidate performance as another key factor. Construct validity evidence was established only for candidates whose performances varied across dimensions and were relatively consistent across exercises.

Implicit measures of personality: measures that permit inference about personality by means other than direct self-report

Situational judgment tests: method in which candidates are presented with a written or video depiction of a scenario and asked to evaluate a set of possible responses

Conditional reasoning: implicit approach making inferences about personality from responses to items that appear to measure reasoning ability

Dominance response process: response to personality items whereby a candidate endorses an item if he/she is located at a point on the trait continuum above that of the item

Ideal point process: response to personality items whereby a candidate endorses an item if he/she is located on the trait continuum near that of the item

Assessment center exercises: simulations in which candidates perform multiple tasks reflecting aspects of a complex job while being rated by trained assessors

Increase Contextualization

A third strategy is to increase the contextualization of existing selection procedures. We commonly view predictors on a continuum from sign to sample. General ability tests and personality inventories are then typically categorized as signs because they aim to measure decontextualized abilities and predispositions that signal or forecast subsequent workplace effectiveness. Conversely, assessment center exercises and work samples are considered to be samples because they are based on behavioral consistency between behavior during the selection procedure and job behavior. Increasing the contextualization of a personality inventory makes this distinction less clear. In particular, it has been argued that the common use of noncontextualized personality items (e.g., "I pay attention to details") is one reason for the relatively low criterion-related validities of personality scales. Because of the ambiguous nature of such items, a general frame of reference (how do I behave across a variety of situations) may be the basis for an individual's response for one item, whereas work behavior or some other frame of reference might serve as basis for completing another item. Contextualized personality inventories aim to circumvent these interpretation problems by using a specific frame of reference (e.g., "I pay attention to details at work"). Recent studies have generally found considerable support for the use of contextualized personality scales as a way of improving the criterion-related validity of personality scales (Bing et al. 2004, Hunthausen et al. 2003).

Reduce Response Distortion

A fourth strategy is to attempt to reduce the level of response distortion (i.e., faking). This approach seems especially useful for noncognitive selection procedures that are based on self-reports (e.g., personality inventories, biodata) rather than on actual behaviors. Recent research has compared different noncognitive selection procedures in terms of faking. A self-report personality measure was more prone to faking than a structured interview that was specifically designed to measure the same personality factors (Van Iddekinge et al. 2005). However, structured interviews themselves were more prone to impression management than were assessment center exercises that tapped interpersonal skills (McFarland et al. 2005). So, these results suggest that faking is most problematic for self-report personality inventories, followed by structured interviews and then by assessment centers.

Although social desirability corrections are still the single most used response-distortion reduction technique [used by 56% of human resource (HR) managers, according to a survey by Goffin & Christiansen (2003)], research has shown that this strategy is ineffective. For example, Ellingson et al. (1999) used a within-subjects design and determined that scores obtained under faking instructions could not be corrected to match scores obtained under instructions to respond honestly. Building on the conclusion that corrections are not effective, Schmitt & Oswald (2006) examined the more radical strategy of removing applicants with high faking scores from consideration for selection and found this had small effects on the mean performance of those selected.

One provocative finding that has emerged is that important differences appear to exist between instructed faking and naturally occurring faking. Ellingson et al. (1999) found that the multidimensional structure of a personality inventory collapsed to a single factor under instructed faking conditions; in contrast, Ellingson et al. (2001) found that the multidimensional structure was retained in operational testing settings, even among candidates with extremely high social desirability scores. This suggests the possibility that instructed faking results in a different response strategy (i.e., consistent choice of the socially desirable response across all items), whereas operational faking is more nuanced. Note also that instructed faking studies vary in terms of whether they focus on a specific job, on the workplace in general, or on a nonspecified context. This merits additional attention, given the extensive reliance on instructed faking as a research strategy.

We note that most research modeling the effects of faking have focused on top-down selection when using personality measures. However, in many operational settings, such measures are used with a relatively low fixed cutoff as part of initial screening. In such a setting, faking may result in an undeserving candidate succeeding in meeting the threshold for moving on to the next stage, but that candidate does not supplant a candidate who responds honestly on a rank order list, as in the case of top-down selection. The issue of unfairness to candidates responding honestly is less pressing here than in the case of top-down selection. In this vein, Mueller-Hanson et al. (2003) showed that faking reduced the validity of a measure of achievement motivation at the high end of the distribution but not at the low end, suggesting that faking may be less of an obstacle to screen-out uses of noncognitive measures than to screen-in uses.

Given these poor results for social desirability corrections, it seems important to redirect our attention to other interventions for reducing deliberate response distortion. So far, success has been mixed. A first preventive approach is to warn candidates that fakers can be identified and will be penalized. However, the empirical evidence shows only meager effects (around 0.25 standard deviation, or SD) for a combination of identification-only and consequences-only warnings on predictor scores and faking scale scores (Dwight & Donovan 2003). A second approach requires candidates to provide a written elaboration of their responses. This strategy seems useful only when the items are verifiable (e.g., biodata items). Elaboration lowered mean biodata scores but had no effect on criterion-related validity (Schmitt & Kunce 2002, Schmitt et al. 2003). Third, the use of forced response formats has received renewed attention. Although a multidimensional forced-choice response format was effective for reducing score inflation at the group level, it was affected by faking to the same degree as a traditional Likert scale at the individual-level analysis (Heggestad et al. 2006).

Impose Structure

A fifth strategy is to impose more structure on existing selection procedures. Creating a more structured format for evaluation should increase the level of standardization and therefore reliability and validity. Highly structured employment interviews constitute the best-known example of this principle successfully being put into action. For example, Schmidt & Zimmerman (2004) showed that a structured interview administered by one interviewer obtains the same level of validity as three to four independent unstructured interviews. The importance of question-and-response scoring standardization in employment interviews was further confirmed by the beneficial effects of interviewing with a telephone-based script (Schmidt & Rader 1999) and of carefully taking notes (Middendorf & Macan 2002).

Although increasing the level of structure has been especially applied to interviews, there is no reason why this principle would not be relevant for other selection procedures where standardization might be an issue. Indeed, in the context of reference checks, Taylor et al. (2004) found that reference checks significantly predicted supervisory ratings (0.36) when they were conducted in a structured and telephone-based format. Similarly, provision of frame-of-reference training to assessors affected the construct validity of their ratings, even though criterion-related validity was not affected (Lievens 2001, Schleicher et al. 2002).

Thus, multiple strategies have been suggested and examined with the goal of improving existing predictors. The result is several promising lines of inquiry.

Top-down selection: selection of candidates in rank order beginning with the highest-scoring candidate

Screen-out: selection system designed to exclude low-performing candidates

Screen-in: selection system designed to identify high-performing candidates

Elaboration: asking applicants to more fully justify their choice of a response to an item

Frame-of-reference training: providing raters with a common understanding of performance dimensions and scale levels

CAN WE PREDICT TRADITIONAL OUTCOME MEASURES BETTER BECAUSE OF IDENTIFICATION AND MEASUREMENT OF NEW PREDICTOR METHODS OR CONSTRUCTS?

Emotional intelligence: ability to accurately perceive, appraise, and express emotion

Emotional Intelligence

In recent years, emotional intelligence (EI) is probably the new psychological construct that has received the greatest attention in both practitioner and academic literature. It has received considerable critical scrutiny from selection researchers as a result of ambiguous definition, dimensions, and operationalization, and also as a result of questionable claims of validity and incremental validity (Landy 2005b, Matthews et al. 2004, Murphy 2006; see also Mayer et al. 2008). A breakthrough in the conceptual confusion around EI is the division of EI measures into either ability or mixed models (Côté & Miners 2006, Zeidner et al. 2004). The mixed (self-report) EI model views EI as akin to personality. A recent meta-analysis showed that EI measures based on this mixed model overlapped considerably with personality trait scores but not with cognitive ability (Van Rooy et al. 2005). Conversely, EI measures developed according to an EI ability model (e.g., EI as ability to accurately perceive, appraise, and express emotion) correlated more with cognitive ability and less with personality. Note too that measures based on the two models correlated only 0.14 with one another. Generally, EI measures (collapsing both models) produce a meta-analytic mean correlation of 0.23 with performance measures (Van Rooy & Viswesvaran 2004). However, this included measures of performance in many domains beyond job performance, included only a small number of studies using ability-based EI instruments, and included a sizable number of studies using self-report measures of performance. Thus, although clarification of the differing conceptualizations of EI sets the stage for further work, we are still far from being at the point of rendering a decision as to the incremental value of EI for selection purposes.

Situational Judgment Tests

Interest has recently surged in the class of predictors under the rubric of situational judgment tests (SJTs). Although not a new idea, they were independently reintroduced under differing labels and found a receptive audience. Motowidlo et al. (1990) framed them as "low fidelity simulations," and Sternberg and colleagues (e.g., Wagner & Sternberg 1985) framed them as measures of "tacit knowledge" and "practical intelligence." Sternberg presented these measures in the context of a generally critical evaluation of the use of general cognitive ability measures (see Gottfredson 2003 and McDaniel & Whetzel 2005 for responses to these claims), while current use in I/O generally views them as a potential supplement to ability and personality measures. An edited volume by Weekley & Ployhart (2006) is a comprehensive treatment of current developments with SJTs.

McDaniel et al. (2001) meta-analyzed 102 validity coefficients (albeit only 6 predictive validity coefficients) and found a mean corrected validity of 0.34. Similarly, SJTs had incremental validity over cognitive ability, experience, and personality (Chan & Schmitt 2002, Clevenger et al. 2001). With this regard, there is also substantial evidence that SJTs have value for broadening the type of skills measured in college admission (Lievens et al. 2005a, Oswald et al. 2004).

Now that SJTs have established themselves as valid predictors in the employment and education domains, attention has turned to better understanding their features. The type of response instructions seems to be a key factor, as it has been found to affect the cognitive loading and amount of response distortion in SJTs (McDaniel et al. 2007, Nguyen et al. 2005). Behavioral-tendency instructions (e.g., "What are you most likely to do?") exhibited lower correlations with cognitive ability and lower adverse impact but higher faking than knowledge-based instructions (e.g., "What is the best answer?"). The amount of fidelity appears to be another factor. For example, changing an existing video-based SJT to a written format (keeping content constant) substantially reduced the criterion-related validity of the test (Lievens & Sackett 2006). We also need to enhance our understanding of why SJTs predict work behavior. Recently, procedural knowledge and implicit trait policies have been advocated as two plausible explanations (Motowidlo et al. 2006). These might open a window of possibilities for more theory-based research on SJTs.

CAN WE PREDICT TRADITIONAL OUTCOME MEASURES BETTER BECAUSE OF IMPROVED IDENTIFICATION OF FEATURES THAT MODERATE OR MEDIATE RELATIONSHIPS?

In recent years, researchers have gradually moved away from examining main effects of selection procedures ("Is this selection procedure related to performance?") and toward investigating moderating and mediating effects that might explain when (moderators) and why (mediators) selection procedures factors are or are not related to performance. Again, most progress has been made in increasing our understanding of possible moderators and mediators of the validity of personality tests.

Situation-Based Moderators

With respect to situation-based moderators, Tett & Burnett's (2003) person-situation interactionist model of job performance provided a huge step forward because it explicitly focused on situations as moderators of trait

expression and trait evaluation. Hence, this model laid the foundation for specifying the conditions under which specific traits will predict job performance. This model goes much further than the earlier distinction between weak and strong situations. Its main hypothesis states that traits will be related to job performance in a given setting when (a) employees vary in their level on the trait, (b) trait expression is triggered by various situational (task, social, and organizational) cues, (c) trait-expressive behavior contributes to organizational effectiveness, and (d) the situation is not so strong as to override the expression of behavior. The model also outlines specific situational features (demands, distracters, constraints, and releasers) at three levels (task, social, and organizational); thus, it might serve as a welcome taxonomy to describe situations and interpret personality-performance relationships. Its value to understanding behavioral expression/evaluation as triggered by situations is not limited to personality but has also been fruitfully used in sample-based predictors such as assessment centers (Lievens et al. 2006).

Person-Based Moderators

The same conceptual reasoning runs through person-based moderators of personality-performance relationships. Similar to situational features, specific individual differences variables might constrain the behavior exhibited, in turn limiting the expression of underlying traits. For example, the relation between Big Five traits such as Extraversion, Emotional Stability, and Openness to Experience and interpersonal performance was lower when self-monitoring was high because people who are high in self-monitoring seem to be so motivated to adapt their behavior to environmental cues that it restricts their behavioral expressions (Barrick et al. 2005). Similar interactions between Conscientiousness and Agreeableness (Witt et al. 2002), Conscientiousness and Extraversion (Witt 2002), and Conscientiousness and social skills (Witt & Ferris 2003) have been discovered. In all of these cases, high levels of Conscientiousness coupled with either low levels of Agreeableness, low levels of Extraversion, or inadequate social skills were detrimental for performance. These results also have practical relevance. For example, they highlight that selecting people high in Conscientiousness but low in Agreeableness for jobs that require frequent collaboration reduces validities to zero.

A literature is emerging on retesting as a moderator of validity. Hausknecht et al. (2002, 2007) showed that retesters perform better and are less likely to turn over, holding cognitive ability constant, which they attribute to higher commitment to the organization. In contrast, Lievens et al. (2005) reported lower-criterion performance among individuals who obtained a given score upon retesting than among those obtaining the same score on the first attempt. They also reported within-person analyses showing higher validity for a retest than an initial test, suggesting that score improvement upon retesting reflects true score change rather than artifactual observed score improvement.

Mediators

Finally, in terms of mediators, there is some evidence that distal measures of personality traits relate to work behavior through more proximal motivational intentions (Barrick et al. 2002). Examples of such motivation intentions are status striving, communion striving, and accomplishment striving. A distal trait such as Agreeableness is then related to communion striving, Conscientiousness to accomplishment striving, and Extraversion to status striving. However, the most striking result was that Extraversion was linked to work performance through its effect on status striving. Thus, we are starting to dig deeper into personality-performance relationships in search of the reasons why and how these two are related.

CAN WE PREDICT TRADITIONAL OUTCOME MEASURES BETTER BECAUSE OF CLEARER UNDERSTANDING OF RELATIONSHIPS BETWEEN PREDICTORS AND CRITERIA?

In this section, we examine research that generally integrates and synthesizes findings from primary studies. Such work does not enable better prediction per se, but rather gives us better insight into the expected values of relationships between variables of interest. Such findings may affect the quality of eventual selection systems to the degree that they aid selection system designers in making a priori design choices that increase the likelihood that selected predictors will prove related to the criteria of interest. Much of the work summarized here is meta-analytic, but we note that other meta-analyses are referenced in various places in this review as appropriate.

Incremental Validity

A significant trend is a new focus in meta-analytic research on incremental validity. There are many meta-analytic summaries of the validity of individual predictors, and recent work focuses on combining meta-analytic results across predictors in order to estimate the incremental validity of one predictor over another. The new insight is that if one has meta-analytic estimates of the relationship between two or more predictors and a given criterion, one needs one additional piece of information, namely meta-analytic estimates of the correlation between the predictors. Given a complete predictor-criterion intercorrelation matrix, with each element in the matrix estimated by meta-analysis, one can estimate the validity of a composite of predictors as well as the incremental validity of one predictor over another. The prototypic study in this domain is Bobko et al.'s (1999) extension of previous work by Schmitt et al. (1997) examining cognitive ability, structured interviews, conscientiousness, and biodata as predictors of overall job performance. They reported considerable incremental validity when the additional predictors are used to supplement cognitive ability and relatively modest incremental validity of cognitive ability over the other three predictors. We note that this work focuses on observed validity coefficients, and if some predictors (e.g., cognitive ability) are more range restricted than others, the validity of the restricted predictor will be underestimated and the incremental validity of the other predictors will be overestimated. Thus, as we address in more detail elsewhere in this review, careful attention to range restriction is important for future progress in this area.

Given this interest in incremental validity, there are a growing number of meta-analyses of intercorrelations among specific predictors, including interview-cognitive ability and interview-personality relationships (Cortina et al. 2000; Huffcutt et al. 2001b), cognitive ability-situational judgment test relationships (McDaniel et al. 2001), and personality-situational judgment tests relationships (McDaniel & Nguyen 2001). A range of primary studies has also examined the incremental contribution to validity of one or more newer predictors over one or more established predictors (e.g., Clevenger et al. 2001, Lievens et al. 2003, Mount et al. 2000). All of these efforts are aimed at a better understanding of the nomological network of relationships among predictors and dimensions of job performance. However, a limitation of many of these incremental validity studies is that they investigated whether methods (i.e., biodata, assessment center exercises) added incremental validity over and beyond constructs (i.e., cognitive ability, personality). Thus, these studies failed to acknowledge the distinction between content (i.e., constructs measured) and methods (i.e., the techniques used to measure the specific content). When constructs and methods are confounded, incremental validity results are difficult to interpret.

Individual Predictors

There is also meta-analytic work on the validity of individual predictors. One particularly important finding is a revisiting of the validity of work sample tests by Roth et al. (2005). Two meta-analytic estimates appeared in 1984: an estimate of 0.54 by Hunter & Hunter (1984) and an estimate of 0.32 by Schmitt et al. (1984), both corrected for criterion unreliability. The 0.54 value has subsequently been offered as evidence that work samples are the most valid predictor of performance yet identified. Roth et al. (2005) documented that the Hunter & Hunter (1984) estimate is based on a reanalysis of a questionable data source, and they report an updated meta-analysis that produces a mean validity of 0.33, highly similar to Schmitt et al.'s (1984) prior value of 0.32. Thus, the validity evidence for work samples remains positive, but the estimate of their mean validity needs to be revised downward.

Another important finding comes from a meta-analytic examination of the validity of global measures of conscientiousness compared to measures of four conscientiousness facets (achievement, dependability, order, and cautiousness) in the prediction of broad versus narrow criteria (Dudley et al. 2006). Dudley and colleagues reported that although broad conscientiousness measures predict all criteria studied (e.g., overall performance, task performance, job dedication, and counterproductive work behavior), in all cases validity was driven largely by the achievement and/or dependability facets, with relatively little contribution from cautiousness and order. Achievement receives the dominant weight in predicting task performance, whereas dependability receives the dominant weight in predicting job dedication and counterproductive work behavior. For job dedication and counterproductive work behavior, the narrow facets provided a dramatic increase in variance accounted for over global conscientiousness measures. This work sheds light on the issue of settings in which broad versus narrow trait

Range restriction: estimating validity based on a sample narrower in range (e.g., incumbents) than the population of interest (e.g., applicants)

measures are preferred, and it makes clear that the criterion of interest leads to different decisions as to the predictor of choice.

In the assessment center domain, Arthur et al. (2003) reported a meta-analysis of the validity of final dimension ratings. They focused on final dimension ratings instead of on the overall assessment rating (OAR). Although the OAR is practically important, it is conceptually an amalgam of evaluations on a variety of dimensions in a diverse set of exercises. Several individual dimensions produced validities comparable to the OAR, and a composite of individual dimensions outperformed the OAR. Problem solving accounted for the most variance, followed by influencing others. In the cognitive ability domain, a cross-national team of researchers (Salgado et al. 2003a,b) reaffirmed U.S. findings of the generalizability of the validity of cognitive ability tests in data from seven European countries. Two meta-analyses addressed issues of "fit," with Arthur et al. (2006) focusing on person-organization fit and with Kristof-Brown et al. (2005) dealing more broadly with person-job, person-group, and person-organization fit. Both examined relationships with job performance and turnover, and both discussed the potential use of fit measures in a selection context. Correlations were modest, and there is virtually no information about the use of such measures in an actual selection context (with the exception of the interview; see Huffcutt et al. 2001a). Thus, this remains a topic for research rather than for operational use in selection.

IDENTIFICATION AND PREDICTION OF NEW OUTCOME VARIABLES

A core assumption in the selection paradigm is the relative stability of the job role against which the suitability of applicants is evaluated. However, rapidly changing organizational structures (e.g., due to mergers, downsizing, team-based work, or globaliza-tion) have added to job instability and have challenged personnel selection (Chan 2000, Kehoe 2000). As noted above, there has been a renewed interest in the notion of dynamic performance. In addition, a growing amount of studies have aimed to shed light on predictors (other than cognitive ability) related to the various dimensions of the higher-order construct of adaptability (Pulakos et al. 2000, 2002).

Creatively solving problems, dealing with uncertain work situations, cross-cultural adaptability, and interpersonal adaptability are adaptability dimensions that have been researched in recent years. With respect to the dimension of creatively solving problems, George & Zhou (2001) showed that creative behavior of employees was highest among those high on Openness to Experience and when the situation created enough opportunities for this trait to be manifested (e.g., unclear means, unclear ends, and positive feedback). Openness also played an important role in facilitating handling uncertain work situations. Judge et al. (1999) showed that Openness was related to coping with organizational change, which in turn was associated with job performance. Regarding cross-cultural adaptability, Lievens et al. (2003) found that cross-cultural training performance was predicted by Openness, cognitive ability, and assessment center ratings of adaptability, teamwork, and communication. Viewing desire to terminate an international assignment early as the converse of adaptability, Caligiuri (2000) found that Emotional Stability, Extraversion, and Agreeableness had significant negative relationships with desire to prematurely terminate the assignment in a concurrent validity study. Finally, interpersonal adaptability (measured by individual contextual performance of incumbents in team settings) was linked to structured interview ratings of social skills, Conscientiousness, Extraversion, and team knowledge (Morgeson et al. 2005).

Clearly, many of these results have practical ramifications for broadening and changing selection practices in new contexts. For instance, they suggest that a selection process for international personnel based on job knowledge and technical competence should be broadened. Yet, these studies also share some limitations, as they were typically concurrent studies with job incumbents. However, an even more important drawback is that they do not really examine predictors of change. They mostly examined different predictors in a new context. To be able to identify predictors of performance in a changing task and organization, it is necessary to include an assessment of people "unlearning" the old task and then "relearning" the new task. Along these lines, Le Pine et al. (2000) focused on adaptability in decision making and found evidence of different predictors before and after the change. Prechange task performance was related only to cognitive ability, whereas adaptive performance (postchange) was positively related to both cognitive ability and Openness to Experience and negatively to Conscientiousness.

IMPROVED ABILITY TO ESTIMATE PREDICTOR-CRITERION RELATIONSHIPS

The prototypic approach to estimating predictor-criterion relationships in the personnel selection field is to (a) estimate the strength of the linear relationship by correlating the predictor with the criterion, (b) correct the resulting correlation for measurement error in the criterion measure, and (c) further correct the resulting correlation for restriction of range. [The order of (b) and (c) is reversed if the reliability estimate is obtained on an unrestricted sample rather than from the selected sample used in step (a).] There have been useful developments in these areas.

Linearity

First, although relationships between cognitive ability and job performance have been found to be linear (Coward & Sackett 1990), there is no basis for inferring that this will generalize to noncognitive predictors. In fact, one can hypothesize curvilinear relationships in the personality domain (e.g., higher levels of conscientiousness are good up to a point, with extremely high levels involving a degree of rigidity and inflexibility resulting in lower performance). Investigations into nonlinear relationships are emerging, with mixed findings [e.g., no evidence for nonlinear conscientiousness-performance relationships in research by Robie & Ryan (1999), but evidence of such relationships in research by LaHuis et al. (2005)]. Future research needs to attend to a variety of issues, including power to detect nonlinearity, the possibility that faking masks nonlinear effects, and the conceptual basis for positing departures from linearity for a given job-attribute combination.

Meta-Analysis

Second, an edited volume by Murphy (2003) brings together multiple perspectives and a number of new developments in validity generalization. Important new developments include the development of new maximum likelihood estimation procedures (Raju & Drasgow 2003) and empirical Bayesian methods (Brannick & Hall 2003). These Bayesian methods integrate meta-analytic findings with findings from a local study to produce a revised estimate of local validity. This is an important reframing: In the past, the question was commonly framed as, "Should I rely on meta-analytic findings or on a local validity estimate?" These Bayesian methods formally consider the uncertainty in a local study and in meta-analytic findings and weight the two accordingly in estimating validity.

Range Restriction

Third, there have been important new insights into the correction of observed correlations for range restriction. One is the

Direct range restriction: reduction in the correlation between two variables due to selection on one of the two variables

Indirect range restriction: reduction in the correlation between two variables due to selection on a third variable correlated with one of the two

Synthetic validation: using prior evidence of relationships between selection procedures and various job components to estimate validity

Subgroup differences: differences in the mean predictor or criterion score between two groups of interest

Four-fifths rule: defining adverse impact as a selection rate for one group that is less than four-fifths of the selection rate for another group

presentation of a taxonomy of ways in which range restriction can occur and of methods of correction (Sackett & Yang 2000). Eleven different range restriction scenarios are treated, expanding the issue well beyond the common distinction between direct and indirect restriction. Another is an approach to making range restriction corrections in the context of meta-analysis. Sackett et al. (2007) note that common practice in meta-analysis is to apply a direct range restriction correction to the mean observed intercorrelations among predictors, which in effect applies the same correction to each study. They offer an approach in which studies are categorized based on the type of restriction present (e.g., no restriction versus direct versus indirect), with appropriate corrections made within each category.

The most significant development regarding range restriction is Hunter et al.'s (2006) development of a new approach to correcting for indirect range restriction. Prior approaches are based on the assumption that the third variable on which selection is actually done is measured and available to the researcher. However, the typical circumstance is that selection is done on the basis of a composite of measured and unmeasured variables (e.g., unquantified impressions in an interview), and that this overall selection composite is unmeasured. Hunter et al. (2006) developed a correction approach that does not require that the selection composite is measured. Schmidt et al. (2006) apply this approach to meta-analysis, which has implicitly assumed direct range restriction, and show that applying a direct restriction correction when restriction is actually indirect results in a 21% underestimate of validity in a reanalysis of four existing meta-analytic data sets.

We also note that two integrative reviews of the use of synthetic validation methods have appeared (Scherbaum 2005, Steel et al. 2006), which offer the potential for increased use of this family of methods for estimating criterion-related validity.

IMPROVED UNDERSTANDING OF SUBGROUP DIFFERENCES, FAIRNESS, BIAS, AND THE LEGAL DEFENSIBILITY OF OUR SELECTION SYSTEMS

Group differences by race and gender remain important issues in personnel selection. The heavier the weight given in a selection process to a predictor on which group mean differences exist, the lower the selection rate for members of the lower-scoring group. However, a number of predictors that fare well in terms of rated job relevance and criterion-related validity produce substantial subgroup differences (e.g., in the domain of cognitive ability for race/ethnicity and in the domain of physical ability for gender). This results in what has been termed the validity-adverse impact tradeoff, as attempts to maximize validity tend to involve giving heavy weight to predictors on which group differences are found, and attempts to minimize group differences tend to involve giving little or no weight to some potentially valid predictors (Sackett et al. 2001). This creates a dilemma for organizations that value both a highly productive and diverse workforce. This also has implications for the legal defensibility of selection systems, as adverse impact resulting from the use of predictors on which differences are found is the triggering mechanism for legal challenges to selection systems. Thus, there is interest in understanding the magnitude of group differences that can be expected using various predictors and in finding strategies for reducing group differences in ways that do not compromise validity. Work in this area has been very active since 2000, with quite a number of important developments. Alternatives to the U.S. federal government's four-fifths rule for establishing adverse impact have been proposed, including a test for the significance of the adverse impact ratios (Morris & Lobsenz 2000) and pairing the adverse impact ratio with a significance test (Roth et al. 2006). The issue of determining minimum qualifications (e.g., the lowest score a candidate can obtain and still be eligible for selection) has received greater attention because of court rulings (Kehoe & Olson 2005).

Subgroup Mean Differences

There have been important efforts at consolidating what is known about the magnitude of subgroup differences on various predictors. A major review by Hough et al. (2001) summarized the evidence for differences by race/ethnicity, gender, and age for a broad range of predictors, including cognitive abilities, personality, physical ability, assessment centers, biodata, interviews, and work samples. One theme emerging from that review is that there is considerable variation within subfacets of a given construct. For example, racial group differences on a number of specific abilities are smaller than differences on general cognitive ability, and race and gender differences vary within subfacets of the Big Five personality dimensions. A more focused review by Roth et al. (2001a) focused on differences by race/ethnicity on measures of cognitive ability. Roth and colleagues (2001a) add considerable nuance to the often-stated summary finding of white-black standardized mean differences of about 1.0 SD, noting (a) larger differences in applicant samples than incumbent samples, (b) larger differences in broad, pooled samples than in job-specific samples, and (c) larger differences in applicant samples for low-complexity jobs than for high-complexity jobs. The effects of range restriction mechanisms on subgroup differences were further explored by Roth et al. (2001b) in the context of multistage selection systems. Additional studies examined mean differences on other predictors, such as grade point average (Roth & Bobko 2000), educational attainment (Berry et al. 2006), and structured interviews (Roth et al. 2002). Two meta-analyses examined race differences in performance measures (McKay & McDaniel 2006, Roth et al. 2003); both reported overall uncorrected white-black mean differences of about 0.25 SD.

Mechanisms for Reducing Differences

There is new insight into several hypothesized mechanisms for reducing subgroup differences. Sackett et al. (2001) reviewed the cumulative evidence and concluded that several proposed mechanisms are not, in fact, effective in reducing differences. These include (a) using differential item functioning analysis to identify and remove items functioning differently by subgroup, (b) providing coaching programs (these may improve scores for all, but group differences remain), (c) providing more generous time limits (which appears to increase group differences), and (d) altering test taking motivation. The motivational approach receiving most attention is the phenomenon of stereotype threat (Steele et al. 2002). Although this research shows that the way a test is presented to students in laboratory settings can affect their performance, the limited research in employment settings does not produce findings indicative of systematic effects due to stereotype threat (Cullen et al. 2004, 2006). Finally, interventions designed to reduce the tendency of minority applicants to withdraw from the selection process are also not a viable approach for reducing subgroup differences because they were found to have small effects on the adverse impact of selection tests (Tam et al. 2004).

Sackett et al. (2001) did report some support for expanding the criterion as a means of reducing subgroup differences. The relative weight given to task, citizenship, and counterproductive behavior in forming a composite criterion affects the weight given to cognitive predictors. Sackett et al. cautioned against differential weighting of criteria solely as a means of influencing predictor subgroup differences; rather, they argued that criterion weights should reflect the relative emphasis the organization concludes is appropriate given its business strategy. They also reported some support for expanding the range of predictors used. The strategy of supplementing existing cognitive predictors with additional

Multistage selection: system in which candidates must pass each stage of a process before proceeding to the next

Differential item functioning: determining whether items function comparably across groups by comparing item responses of group members with the same overall scores

Stereotype threat: performance decrement resulting from the perception that one is a member of a group about which a negative stereotype is held

predictors outside the cognitive domain can reduce the overall subgroup differences in some circumstances. This strategy has received considerable attention because broadening the range of predictors has the potential to both reduce subgroup differences and increase validity.

There has been considerable activity regarding test score banding, including an integrative review featuring competing perspectives (Campion et al. 2001) and an edited volume (Aguinis 2004). Although banding is not advocated only as a device for reducing adverse impact, the potential for impact reduction is a key reason for the interest in banding. A clearer picture is emerging of the circumstances under which banding does or does not affect minority-hiring rates, with key features including the width of the band and the basis for selection within a band.

Forecasting Validity and Adverse Impact

New methods exist for forecasting the likely effects of various ways of combining multiple predictors on subsequent performance and on adverse impact. Although combining predictors via multiple regression is statistically optimal in terms of predicting performance, there may be alternative ways of combining that fare better in terms of adverse impact at what is judged to be an acceptably small reduction in validity. De Corte et al. (2007) applied the concept of Pareto optimality and provided a computer program that shows the set of predictor weights that give the lowest possible degree of subgroup difference at any given degree of reduction in validity. In other words, the procedure estimates the reduction in subgroup differences that would be attainable should the decision maker be willing to accept, say, a 1%, or a 5%, or a 10% reduction in validity. Thus, it makes the validity-diversity tradeoff very explicit. In another study, De Corte et al. (2006) offered a computer program for examining the effects

of different ways of sequencing predictors in a multistage selection system to achieve intended levels of workforce quality, workforce diversity, and selection cost. Also, Aguinis & Smith (2007) offered a program for examining the effect of the choice of selection ratio on mean criterion performance and adverse impact.

Differential Prediction

New methods have been developed for examining differential prediction (i.e., differences in slopes and intercepts between subgroups). Johnson et al. (2001) applied the logic of synthetic validity to pool data across jobs, thus making such analyses feasible in settings where samples within jobs are too small for adequate power. Sackett et al. (2003) showed that omitted variables that are correlated with both subgroup membership and the outcome of interest can bias attempts to estimate slope and intercept differences and offer strategies for addressing the omitted variables problem.

IMPROVED ADMINISTRATIVE EASE WITH WHICH SELECTION SYSTEMS CAN BE USED

To increase the efficiency and consistency of test delivery, many organizations have implemented Internet technology in their selection systems. Benefits of Internet-based selection include cost and time savings because neither the employer nor the applicants have to be present at the same location. Further, organizations' access to larger and more geographically diverse applicant pools is expanded. Finally, it might give organizations a "high-tech" image.

Lievens & Harris (2003) reviewed current research on Internet recruiting and testing. They concluded that most research has focused on either applicants' reactions or measurement equivalence with traditional paper-and-pencil testing. Two forms of the use of the

Internet in selection have especially been investigated, namely proctored Internet testing and videoconference interviewing.

With respect to videoconferencing interviews (and other technology-mediated interviews such as telephone interviews or interactive voice-response telephone interviews), there is evidence that their increased efficiency might also lead to potential drawbacks as compared with face-to-face interviews (Chapman et al. 2003). Technology-mediated interviews might result in less favorable reactions and loss of potential applicants. However, it should be emphasized that actual job pursuit behavior was not examined.

The picture for Internet-based testing is somewhat more positive. With regard to noncognitive measures, the Internet-based format generally leads to lower means, larger variances, more normal distributions, and larger internal consistencies. The only drawback seems to be the somewhat higher-scale intercorrelations (Ployhart et al. 2003). In within-subjects designs (Potosky & Bobko 2004), similar acceptable cross-mode correlations for noncognitive tests were found. However, this is not the case for timed tests. For instance, cross-mode equivalence of a timed spatial-reasoning test was as low as 0.44 (although there were only 30 minutes between the two administrations). On the one hand, the loading speed inherent in Internet-based testing might make the test different from its paper-and-pencil counterpart. In the Internet format, candidates also cannot start by browsing through the test to gauge the time constraints and type of items (Potosky & Bobko 2004, Richman et al. 1999). On the other hand, the task at hand (spatial reasoning) is also modified by the administration format change because it is not possible to make marks with a pen.

One limitation of existing Internet-based selection research is that explanations are seldom provided for why equivalence was or was not established. At a practical level, the identification of conditions that moderate measurement equivalence would also be insightful (see the aforementioned example of the spatial-reasoning test). More fundamentally, we believe that the current research on Internet testing is essentially conservative. Although an examination of equivalence is of key psychometric and legal importance, it does not advance our understanding of the new test administration format. That is, adapting traditional tests to the new technology is different from using the new technology to change existing tests/test administration and to enhance prediction. So, equivalence research per definition does not take the opportunity to improve the quality of assessment. Roznowski et al. (2000) offered an illustration of the use of cognitive processing measures that explicitly build on the possibilities of computerization to go beyond the type of measurement possible with paper-and-pencil testing and show incremental validity over a general cognitive measure in predicting training performance.

Unproctored Internet testing is a controversial example of the Internet radically changing the test administration process. Unproctored Internet testing might lead to candidate identification and test security concerns. Although test security problems might be partly circumvented by item banking and item-generation techniques (Irvine & Kyllonen 2002), user identification seems to be a deadlock (unless sophisticated techniques such as retinal scanning become widely available). To date, there seems to be relative consensus that unproctored testing is advisable only in low-stakes selection (Tippins et al. 2006). However, empirical evidence about the equivalence of proctored and unproctored testing in a variety of contexts is lacking.

Finally, it is striking that no evidence is available as to how Internet-based administration affects the utility of the selection system. So, we still do not know whether Internet selection affects the quantity and quality of the applicant pool and the performance of the people hired. However, utility studies of Internet-based selection seem necessary

Unproctored testing: testing in the absence of a test administrator

Utility: index of the usefulness of a selection system

as recent surveys show that technology-based solutions are not always a panacea for organizations (e.g., Chapman & Webster 2003). Frequently mentioned complaints included the decreasing quality of the applicant pool, the huge dependency on a costly and ever-changing technology, and a loss of personal touch.

IMPROVED MEASUREMENT OF AND INSIGHT INTO CONSEQUENCES OF APPLICANT REACTIONS

Consequences of Applicant Reactions

Since the early 1990s, a growing number of empirical and theoretical studies have focused on applicants' perceptions of selection procedures, the selection process, and the selection decision, and their effects on individual and organizational outcomes. Hausknecht et al.'s (2004) meta-analysis found that perceived procedural characteristics (e.g., face validity, perceived predictive validity) had moderate relationships with applicant perceptions. Person characteristics (e.g., age, gender, ethnic background, personality) showed near-zero correlations with applicant perceptions. In terms of selection procedures, work samples and interviews were perceived more favorably than were cognitive ability tests, which were perceived more positively than personality inventories.

This meta-analysis also yielded conclusions that raise some doubts about the added value of the field of applicant reactions. Although applicant perceptions clearly show some link with self-perceptions and applicants' intentions (e.g., job offer acceptance intentions), evidence for a relationship between applicant perceptions and actual behavioral outcomes was meager and disappointing. In fact, in the meta-analysis, there were simply too few studies to examine behavioral outcomes (e.g., applicant withdrawal, job performance, job satisfaction, and organizational citizenship behavior). Looking at

primary studies, research shows that applicant perceptions play a minimal role in actual applicant withdrawal (Ryan et al. 2000, Truxillo et al. 2002). This stands in contrast with introductions to articles about applicant reactions that typically claim that applicant reactions have important individual and organizational outcomes. So, in applicant perception studies it is critical to go beyond self-reported outcomes (see also Chan & Schmitt 2004).

Methodological Issues

The Hausknecht et al. (2004) meta-analysis also identified three methodological factors that moderated the results found. First, monomethod variance was prevalent, as the average correlations were higher when both variables were measured simultaneously than when they were separated in time. Indeed, studies that measured applicant reactions longitudinally at different points in time (e.g., Schleicher et al. 2006, Truxillo et al. 2002, Van Vianen et al. 2004) are scarce and demonstrate that reactions differ contingent upon the point in the selection process. For example, Schleicher et al. (2006) showed that opportunity to perform became an even more important predictor of overall procedural fairness after candidates received negative feedback. Similarly, Van Vianen et al. (2004) found that pre-feedback fairness perceptions were affected by different factors than were post-feedback fairness perceptions. Second, large differences between student samples and applicant samples were found. Third, correlations differed between hypothetical and authentic contexts. The meta-analysis showed that the majority of applicant reactions studies were not conducted with actual applicants (only 36.0%), in the field (only 48.8%), and in authentic contexts (only 38.4%); thus, these methodological factors suggest that some of the relationships found in the meta-analysis might be either under- or overestimated (depending on the issue at hand). Even among actual applicants, it is important that the issue examined is meaningful to applicants. This is nicely illustrated by Truxillo & Bauer (1999). They investigated applicants' reactions to test score banding in three separate actual applicant samples. Race differences in applicants' reactions to banding were found only in a sample wherein participants were really familiar with banding.

Influencing Applicant Reactions

Despite these critical remarks, the field of applicant reactions also made progress. New ways of obtaining more favorable applicant reactions were identified. In a longitudinal study, Truxillo et al. (2002) demonstrated that the provision of information to candidates prior to the selection process might be a practical and inexpensive vehicle to improve applicant reactions. Applicants who were given information about a video-based test perceived this test as fairer both at the time of testing and one month later, upon receiving their test results. However, more distal behavioral measures were not affected by the pretest information. The provision of an explanation for selection decisions was identified as another practical intervention for promoting selection procedure fairness (Gilliland et al. 2001, Ployhart et al. 1999). Although no one ideal explanation feature to reduce applicants' perceptions of unfairness was identified, explanations seemed to matter. It was noteworthy that Gilliland et al. (2001) even found evidence for a relationship between the type of explanation provided and actual reapplication behavior of applicants of a tenure-track faculty position.

Measurement of Applicant Reactions

Another important positive development in this field is improved measurement of applicants' perceptions and attitudes. Unidimensional and study-specific measures were replaced by newer multidimensional and theory-driven measures that have the potential to be used across many studies. Three

projects were most noteworthy. First, Bauer et al. (2001) developed the selection procedural justice scale. This scale was based on procedural justice theory and assessed 11 procedural justice rules. Second, Sanchez et al. (2000) used expectancy theory to develop a multifaceted measure of test motivation, called the Valence, Instrumentality, and Expectancy Motivation Scale. This measure proved to be a more theory-driven way of structuring and measuring the construct of test motivation as compared with the extant unidimensional motivation scale of the Test Attitude Scale (Arvey et al. 1990). Third, McCarthy & Goffin (2004) undertook a similar effort as they tried to improve on the unidimensional test-anxiety subscale of the Test Attitude Scale (Arvey et al. 1990). Specifically, they focused on anxiety in employment interviews and developed the Measure of Anxiety in Selection Interviews. To this end, McCarthy & Goffin (2004) borrowed on separate streams of anxiety research and conceptualized interview anxiety as consisting of five dimensions: communication anxiety, appearance anxiety, social anxiety, performance anxiety, and behavioral anxiety. Results confirmed that this context-specific multidimensional anxiety measure had a consistent negative relationship with interview performance and explained additional variance over and above noncontextualized anxiety scales.

In short, the field of applicant reactions has made strides forward in terms of better measuring applicant reactions as several multidimensional and theory-driven improvements over existing measures were developed. Some progress was also made in terms of devising ways of obtaining more favorable applicant reactions (i.e., through the use of pretest information and posttest explanations). Yet, we highlighted the meager evidence of a relationship between applicant perceptions and key individual and organizational consequences (e.g., actual withdrawal from the selection process, test performance, job satisfaction, and organizational citizenship behavior) as the Achilles heel of this field.

IMPROVED DECISION-MAKER ACCEPTANCE OF SELECTION SYSTEMS

Research findings outlined above have applied value only if they find inroads in organizations. However, this is not straightforward, as psychometric quality and legal defensibility are only some of the criteria that organizations use in selection practice decisions. Given that sound selection procedures are often either not used or are misused in organizations (perhaps the best known example being structured interviews), we need to better understand the factors that might impede organizations' use of selection procedures.

Apart from broader legal, economic, and political factors, some progress in uncovering additional factors was made in recent years. One factor identified was the lack of knowledge/awareness of specific selection procedures. For instance, the two most widely held misconceptions about research findings among HR professionals are that conscientiousness and values both are more valid than general mental ability in predicting job performance (Rynes et al. 2002). An interesting complement to Rynes et al's (2002) examination of beliefs of HR professionals was provided by Murphy et al.'s (2003) survey of I/O psychologists regarding their beliefs about a wide variety of issues regarding the use of cognitive ability measures in selection. I/O psychologists are in relative agreement that such measures have useful levels of validity, but in considerable disagreement about claims that cognitive ability is the most important individual-difference determinant of job and training performance.

In addition, use of structured interviews is related to participation in formal interviewer training (Chapman & Zweig 2005, Lievens & De Paepe 2004). Another factor associated with selection practice use was the type of work practices of organizations. Organizations use different types of selection methods contingent upon the nature of the work being done (skill requirements), training, and pay level (Wilk & Cappelli 2003). Finally, we also gained some understanding of potential operating factors in the international selection area. In that context, the issue of gaining acceptance for specific selection procedures is even more complicated due to tensions between corporate requirements of streamlined selection practices and local desires of customized ones. A 20-country study showed that national differences accounted for considerable variance in selection practice, whereas differences grounded in cultural values (uncertainty avoidance and power distance) explained only some of the variability (Ryan et al. 1999).

Taken together, this handful of studies produced a somewhat better understanding of potential factors (e.g., knowledge, work practices, and national differences) related to acceptance of selection procedures. Yet, there is still a long way to go. All of these studies were descriptive accounts. We need prescriptive studies that produce specific strategies for gaining acceptance of selection practices or successfully introducing new ones. Along these lines, Muchinsky (2004) presented an interesting case study wherein he used a balancing act (combining strategies of education, shared responsibility, negotiation, respect, and recognition of available knowledge of all stakeholders) to successfully implement psychometrically straightforward test development principles of a job knowledge test in an organizational context.

CONCLUSION

We opened with a big question: "Can we do a better job of selection today than in 2000?" Our sense is that we have made substantial progress in our understanding of selection systems. We have greatly improved our ability to predict and model the likely outcomes of a particular selection system, as a result of developments such as more and better meta-analyses, better insight into incremental validity, better range restriction corrections, and better understanding of validity-adverse impact tradeoffs. Thus, someone well informed about the research base is more likely to attend carefully to determining the criterion constructs of interest to the organization, more likely to select trial predictors with prior conceptual and empirical links to these criteria, more likely to select predictors with incremental validity over one another, and less likely to misestimate the validity of a selection system due to use of less-than-optimal methods of estimating the strength of predictor-criterion relationships.

We have identified quite a number of promising leads with the potential to improve the magnitude of predictor-criterion relationships should subsequent research support initial findings. These include contextualization of predictors and the use of implicit measures. We also have new insights into new outcomes and their predictability (e.g., adaptability), better understanding of the measurement and consequences of applicant reactions, and better understanding of impediments of selection system use (e.g., HR manager misperceptions about selection systems). Overall, relative to a decade ago, at best we are able to modestly improve validity at the margin, but we are getting much better at modeling and predicting the likely outcomes (validity, adverse impact) of a given selection system.

LITERATURE CITED

Aguinis H, ed. 2004. *Test-Score Banding in Human Resource Selection: Legal, Technical, and Societal Issues*. Westport, CT: Praeger

Aguinis H, Smith MA. 2007. Understanding the impact of test validity and bias on selection errors and adverse impact in human resource selection. *Pers. Psychol.* 60:165–99

Am. Educ. Res. Assoc., Am. Psychol. Assoc., Natl. Counc. Meas. Educ. 1999. *Standards for Educational and Psychological Testing*. Washington, DC: Am. Educ. Res. Assoc.

Anderson N, Ones DS, Sinangil HK, Viswesvaran C, eds. 2001. *Handbook of Industrial, Work and Organizational Psychology: Personality Psychology*. Thousand Oaks, CA: Sage

Arthur W, Bell ST, Villado AJ, Doverspike D. 2006. The use of person-organization fit in employment decision making: an assessment of its criterion-related validity. *J. Appl. Psychol.* 91:786–801

Arthur W, Day EA, McNelly TL, Edens PS. 2003. A meta-analysis of the criterion-related validity of assessment center dimensions. *Pers. Psychol.* 56:125–54

Arthur W, Woehr DJ, Maldegen R. 2000. Convergent and discriminant validity of assessment center dimensions: a conceptual and empirical reexamination of the assessment confer construct-related validity paradox. *J. Manag.* 26:813–35

Arvey RD, Strickland W, Drauden G, Martin C. 1990. Motivational components of test taking. *Pers. Psychol.* 43:695–716

Barrick MR, Parks L, Mount MK. 2005. Self-monitoring as a moderator of the relationships between personality traits and performance. *Pers. Psychol.* 58:745–67

Barrick MR, Patton GK, Haugland SN. 2000. Accuracy of interviewer judgments of job applicant personality traits. *Pers. Psychol.* 53:925–51

Barrick MR, Ryan AM, eds. 2003. *Personality and Work: Reconsidering the Role of Personality in Organizations*. San Francisco, CA: Jossey-Bass

Barrick MR, Stewart GL, Piotrowski M. 2002. Personality and job performance: test of the mediating effects of motivation among sales representatives. *J. Appl. Psychol.* 87:43–51

Bartram D. 2005. The great eight competencies: a criterion-centric approach to validation. *J. Appl. Psychol.* 90:1185–203

Bauer TN, Truxillo DM, Sanchez RJ, Craig JM, Ferrara P, Campion MA. 2001. Applicant reactions to selection: development of the Selection Procedural Justice Scale (SPJS). *Pers. Psychol.* 54:387–419

Berry CM, Gruys ML, Sackett PR. 2006. Educational attainment as a proxy for cognitive ability in selection: effects on levels of cognitive ability and adverse impact. *J. Appl. Psychol.* 91:696–705

Bing MN, Whanger JC, Davison HK, VanHook JB. 2004. Incremental validity of the frame-of-reference effect in personality scale scores: a replication and extension. *J. Appl. Psychol.* 89:150–57

Bobko P, Roth PL, Potosky D. 1999. Derivation and implications of a meta-analytic matrix incorporating cognitive ability, alternative predictors, and job performance. *Pers. Psychol.* 52:561–89

Borman WC, Buck DE, Hanson MA, Motowidlo SJ, Stark S, Drasgow F. 2001. An examination of the comparative reliability, validity, and accuracy of performance ratings made using computerized adaptive rating scales. *J. Appl. Psychol.* 86:965–73

Borman WC, Ilgen DR, Klimoski RJ, Weiner IB, eds. 2003. *Handbook of Psychology.* Vol. 12: *Industrial and Organizational Psychology.* Hoboken, NJ: Wiley

Borman WC, Motowidlo SJ. 1997. Organizational citizenship behavior and contextual performance. *Hum. Perform.* 10:67–69

Bowler MC, Woehr DJ. 2006. A meta-analytic evaluation of the impact of dimension and exercise factors on assessment center ratings. *J. Appl. Psychol.* 91:1114–24

Brannick MT, Hall SM. 2003. Validity generalization: a Bayesian perspective. See Murphy 2003, pp. 339–64

Caligiuri PM. 2000. The Big Five personality characteristics as predictors of expatriate's desire to terminate the assignment and supervisor-rated performance. *Pers. Psychol.* 53:67–88

Campbell JP, Knapp DJ, eds. 2001. *Exploring the Limits in Personnel Selection and Classification.* Mahwah, NJ: Erlbaum

Campbell JP, McCloy RA, Oppler SH, Sager CE. 1993. A theory of performance. In *Personnel Selection in Organizations*, ed. N Schmitt, WC Borman, pp. 35–70. San Francisco, CA: Jossey Bass

Campion MA, Outtz JL, Zedeck S, Schmidt FL, Kehoe JF, et al. 2001. The controversy over score banding in personnel selection: answers to 10 key questions. *Pers. Psychol.* 54:149–85

Chan D. 2000. Understanding adaptation to changes in the work environment: integrating individual difference and learning perspectives. *Res. Pers. Hum. Resour. Manag.* 18:1–42

Chan D, Schmitt N. 2002. Situational judgment and job performance. *Hum. Perform.* 15:233–54

Chan D, Schmitt N. 2004. An agenda for future research on applicant reactions to selection procedures: a construct-oriented approach. *Int. J. Select. Assess.* 12:9–23

Chapman DS, Uggerslev KL, Webster J. 2003. Applicant reactions to face-to-face and technology-mediated interviews: a field investigation. *J. Appl. Psychol.* 88:944–53

Chapman DS, Webster J. 2003. The use of technologies in the recruiting, screening, and selection processes for job candidates. *Int. J. Select. Assess.* 11:113–20

Chapman DS, Zweig DI. 2005. Developing a nomological network for interview structure: antecedents and consequences of the structured selection interview. *Pers. Psychol.* 58:673–702

Clevenger J, Pereira GM, Wiechmann D, Schmitt N, Harvey VS. 2001. Incremental validity of situational judgment tests. *J. Appl. Psychol.* 86:410–17

Cortina JM, Goldstein NB, Payne SC, Davison HK, Gilliland SW. 2000. The incremental validity of interview scores over and above cognitive ability and conscientiousness scores. *Pers. Psychol.* 53:325–51

Côté S, Miners CTH. 2006. Emotional intelligence, cognitive intelligence, and job performance. *Adm. Sci. Q.* 51:1–28

Coward WM, Sackett PR. 1990. Linearity of ability performance relationships—a reconfirmation. *J. Appl. Psychol.* 75:297–300

Cullen MJ, Hardison CM, Sackett PR. 2004. Using SAT-grade and ability-job performance relationships to test predictions derived from stereotype threat theory. *J. Appl. Psychol.* 89:220–30

Cullen MJ, Waters SD, Sackett PR. 2006. Testing stereotype threat theory predictions for math-identified and nonmath-identified students by gender. *Hum. Perform.* 19:421–40

Dalal RS. 2005. A meta-analysis of the relationship between organizational citizenship behavior and counterproductive work behavior. *J. Appl. Psychol.* 90:1241–55

De Corte W, Lievens F, Sackett PR. 2006. Predicting adverse impact and multistage mean criterion performance in selection. *J. Appl. Psychol.* 91:523–37

De Corte W, Lievens F, Sackett PR. 2007. Combining predictors to achieve optimal trade-offs between selection quality and adverse impact. *J. Appl. Psychol.* In press

Dipboye RL, Colella A, eds. 2004. *Discrimination at Work: The Psychological and Organizational Bases*. Mahwah, NJ: Erlbaum

Dudley NM, Orvis KA, Lebiecki JE, Cortina JM. 2006. A meta-analytic investigation of conscientiousness in the prediction of job performance: examining the intercorrelations and the incremental validity of narrow traits. *J. Appl. Psychol.* 91:40–57

Dwight SA, Donovan JJ. 2003. Do warnings not to fake reduce faking? *Hum. Perform.* 16:1–23

Ellingson JE, Sackett PR, Hough LM. 1999. Social desirability corrections in personality measurement: issues of applicant comparison and construct validity. *J. Appl. Psychol.* 84:55–166

Ellingson JE, Smith DB, Sackett PR. 2001. Investigating the influence of social desirability on personality factor structure. *J. Appl. Psychol.* 86:122–33

George JM, Zhou J. 2001. When openness to experience and conscientiousness are related to creative behavior: an interactional approach. *J. Appl. Psychol.* 86:513–24

Gilliland SW, Groth M, Baker RC, Dew AF, Polly LM, Langdon JC. 2001. Improving applicants' reactions to rejection letters: an application of fairness theory. *Pers. Psychol.* 54:669–703

Goffin RD, Christiansen ND. 2003. Correcting personality tests for faking: a review of popular personality tests and an initial survey of researchers. *Int. J. Select. Assess.* 11:340–44

Gottfredson LS. 2003. Dissecting practical intelligence theory: its claims and evidence. *Intelligence* 31:343–97

Hausknecht JP, Day DV, Thomas SC. 2004. Applicant reactions to selection procedures: an updated model and meta-analysis. *Pers. Psychol.* 57:639–83

Hausknecht JP, Halpert JA, Di Paolo NT, Moriarty MO. 2007. Retesting in selection: a meta-analysis of practice effects for tests of cognitive ability. *J. Appl. Psychol.* 92:373–85

Hausknecht JP, Trevor CO, Farr JL. 2002. Retaking ability tests in a selection setting: implications for practice effects, training performance, and turnover. *J. Appl. Psychol.* 87:243–54

Heggestad ED, Morrison M, Reeve CL, McCloy RA. 2006. Forced-choice assessments of personality for selection: evaluating issues of normative assessment and faking resistance. *J. Appl. Psychol.* 91:9–24

Hogan J, Holland B. 2003. Using theory to evaluate personality and job-performance relations: a socioanalytic perspective. *J. Appl. Psychol.* 88:100–12

Hough LM, Oswald FL. 2000. Personnel selection: looking toward the future—remembering the past. *Annu. Rev. Psychol.* 51:631–64

Hough LM, Oswald FL. 2005. They're right . . . well, mostly right: research evidence and an agenda to rescue personality testing from 1960's insights. *Hum. Perform.* 18:373–87

Hough LM, Oswald FL, Ployhart RE. 2001. Determinants, detection and amelioration of adverse impact in personnel selection procedures: issues, evidence and lessons learned. *Int. J. Select. Assess.* 9:152–94

Huffcutt AI, Conway JM, Roth PL, Stone NJ. 2001a. Identification and meta-analytic assessment of psychological constructs measured in employment interviews. *J. Appl. Psychol.* 86:897–913

Huffcutt AI, Weekley JA, Wiesner WH, Degroot TG, Jones C. 2001b. Comparison of situational and behavior description interview questions for higher-level positions. *Pers. Psychol.* 54:619–44

Hunter JE, Hunter RF. 1984. Validity and utility of alternative predictors of job performance. *Psychol. Bull.* 96:72–98

Hunter JE, Schmidt FL, Le H. 2006. Implications of direct and indirect range restriction for meta-analysis methods and findings. *J. Appl. Psychol.* 91:594–612

Hunthausen JM, Truxillo DM, Bauer TN, Hammer LB. 2003. A field study of frame-of-reference effects on personality test validity. *J. Appl. Psychol.* 88:545–51

Hurtz GM, Donovan JJ. 2000. Personality and job performance: the Big Five revisited. *J. Appl. Psychol.* 85:869–79

Int. Test Comm. (ITC). 2006. International guidelines on computer-based and Internet-delivered testing. **http://www.intestcom.org**. Accessed March 2, 2007

Irvine SH, Kyllonen PC, eds. 2002. *Item Generation for Test Development.* Mahwah, NJ: Erlbaum

James LR, McIntyre MD, Glisson CA, Green PD, Patton TW, et al. 2005. A conditional reasoning measure for aggression. *Organ. Res. Methods* 8:69–99

Jeanneret PR. 2005. Professional and technical authorities and guidelines. See Landy 2005, pp. 47–100

Johnson JW, Carter GW, Davison HK, Oliver DH. 2001. A synthetic validity approach to testing differential prediction hypotheses. *J. Appl. Psychol.* 86:774–80

Judge TA, Thoresen CJ, Pucik V, Welbourne TM. 1999. Managerial coping with organizational change: a dispositional perspective. *J. Appl. Psychol.* 84:107–22

Kehoe JF, ed. 2000. *Managing Selection in Changing Organizations: Human Resource Strategies.* San Francisco, CA: Jossey-Bass

Kehoe JF, Olson A. 2005. Cut scores and employment discrimination litigation. See Landy 2005, pp. 410–49

Kolk NJ, Born MP, van der Flier H. 2002. Impact of common rater variance on construct validity of assessment center dimension judgments. *Hum. Perform.* 15:325–37

Kristof-Brown AL, Zimmerman RD, Johnson EC. 2005. Consequences of individuals' fit at work: a meta-analysis of person-job, person-organization, person-group, and person-supervisor fit. *Pers. Psychol.* 58:281–342

LaHuis DM, Martin NR, Avis JM. 2005. Investigating nonlinear conscientiousness-job performance relations for clerical employees. *Hum. Perform.* 18:199–212

Lance CE, Lambert TA, Gewin AG, Lievens F, Conway JM. 2004. Revised estimates of dimension and exercise variance components in assessment center postexercise dimension ratings. *J. Appl. Psychol.* 89:377–85

Lance CE, Newbolt WH, Gatewood RD, Foster MR, French NR, Smith DE. 2000. Assessment center exercise factors represent cross-situational specificity, not method bias. *Hum. Perform.* 13:323–53

Landy FJ, ed. 2005a. *Employment Discrimination Litigation: Behavioral, Quantitative, and Legal Perspectives*. San Francisco, CA: Jossey Bass

Landy FJ. 2005b. Some historical and scientific issues related to research on emotional intelligence. *J. Organ. Behav.* 26:411–24

LeBreton JM, Barksdale CD, Robin JD, James LR. 2007. Measurement issues associated with conditional reasoning tests of personality: deception and faking. *J. Appl. Psychol.* 92:1–16

LePine JA, Colquitt JA, Erez A. 2000. Adaptability to changing task contexts: effects of general cognitive ability conscientiousness, and openness to experience. *Pers. Psychol.* 53:563–93

Lievens F. 2001. Assessor training strategies and their effects on accuracy, interrater reliability, and discriminant validity. *J. Appl. Psychol.* 86:255–64

Lievens F. 2002. Trying to understand the different pieces of the construct validity puzzle of assessment centers: an examination of assessor and assessee effects. *J. Appl. Psychol.* 87:675–86

Lievens F, Buyse T, Sackett PR. 2005a. The operational validity of a video-based situational judgment test for medical college admissions: illustrating the importance of matching predictor and criterion construct domains. *J. Appl. Psychol.* 90:442–52

Lievens F, Buyse T, Sackett PR. 2005b. The effects of retaking tests on test performance and validity: an examination of cognitive ability, knowledge, and situational judgment tests. *Pers. Psychol.* 58:981–1007

Lievens F, Chasteen CS, Day EA, Christiansen ND. 2006. Large-scale investigation of the role of trait activation theory for understanding assessment center convergent and discriminant validity. *J. Appl. Psychol.* 91:247–58

Lievens F, Conway JM. 2001. Dimension and exercise variance in assessment center scores: a large-scale evaluation of multitrait-multimethod studies. *J. Appl. Psychol.* 86:1202–22

Lievens F, De Paepe A. 2004. An empirical investigation of interviewer-related factors that discourage the use of high structure interviews. *J. Organ. Behav.* 25:29–46

Lievens F, Harris MM. 2003. Research on Internet recruiting and testing: current status and future directions. In *International Review of Industrial and Organizational Psychology*, ed. CL Cooper, IT Robertson, pp. 131–65. Chichester, UK: Wiley

Lievens F, Harris MM, Van Keer E, Bisqueret C. 2003. Predicting cross-cultural training performance: the validity of personality, cognitive ability, and dimensions measured by an assessment center and a behavior description interview. *J. Appl. Psychol.* 88:476–89

Lievens F, Sackett PR. 2006. Video-based vs. written situational judgment tests: a comparison in terms of predictive validity. *J. Appl. Psychol.* 91:1181–88

Matthews G, Roberts RD, Zeidner M. 2004. Seven myths about emotional intelligence. *Psychol. Inq.* 15:179–96

Mayer JD, Roberts RD, Barsade SG. 2008. Emerging research in emotional intelligence. *Annu. Rev. Psychol.* 59:501–36

McCarthy J, Goffin R. 2004. Measuring job interview anxiety: beyond weak knees and sweaty palms. *Pers. Psychol.* 57:607–37

McDaniel MA, Hartman NS, Whetzel DL, Grubb WL III. 2007. Situational judgment tests, response instructions and validity: a meta-analysis. *Pers. Psychol.* 60:63–91

McDaniel MA, Morgeson FP, Finnegan EB, Campion MA, Braverman EP. 2001. Use of situational judgment tests to predict job performance: a clarification of the literature. *J. Appl. Psychol.* 86:730–40

McDaniel MA, Nguyen NT. 2001. Situational judgment tests: a review of practice and constructs assessed. *Int. J. Select. Assess.* 9:103–13

McDaniel MA, Whetzel DL. 2005. Situational judgment test research: informing the debate on practical intelligence theory. *Intelligence* 33:515–25

McFarland LA, Yun GJ, Harold CM, Viera L, Moore LG. 2005. An examination of impression management use and effectiveness across assessment center exercises: the role of competency demands. *Pers. Psychol.* 58:949–80

McKay PF, McDaniel MA. 2006. A reexamination of black-white mean differences in work performance: more data, more moderators. *J. Appl. Psychol.* 91:538–54

Middendorf CH, Macan TH. 2002. Note-taking in the employment interview: effects on recall and judgments. *J. Appl. Psychol.* 87:293–303

Morgeson FP, Reider MH, Campion MA. 2005. Selecting individuals in team settings: the importance of social skills, personality characteristics, and teamwork knowledge. *Pers. Psychol.* 58:583–611

Morris SB, Lobsenz RE. 2000. Significance tests and confidence intervals for the adverse impact ratio. *Pers. Psychol.* 53:89–111

Motowidlo SJ, Dunnette MD, Carter GW. 1990. An alternative selection procedure: the low-fidelity simulation. *J. Appl. Psychol.* 75:640–47

Motowidlo SJ, Hooper AC, Jackson HL. 2006. Implicit policies about relations between personality traits and behavioral effectiveness in situational judgment items. *J. Appl. Psychol.* 91:749–61

Mount MK, Witt LA, Barrick MR. 2000. Incremental validity of empirically keyed biodata scales over GMA and the five factor personality constructs. *Pers. Psychol.* 53:299–323

Muchinsky PM. 2004. When the psychometrics of test development meets organizational realities: a conceptual framework for organizational change, examples, and recommendations. *Pers. Psychol.* 57:175–209

Mueller-Hanson R, Heggestad ED, Thornton GC. 2003. Faking and selection: considering the use of personality from select-in and select-out perspectives. *J. Appl. Psychol.* 88:348–55

Murphy KR. 1989. Is the relationship between cognitive ability and job performance stable over time? *Hum. Perform.* 2:183–200

Murphy KR, ed. 2003. *Validity Generalization: A Critical Review.* Mahwah, NJ: Erlbaum

Murphy KR, ed. 2006. *A Critique of Emotional Intelligence: What Are the Problems and How Can They Be Fixed?* Mahwah, NJ: Erlbaum

Murphy KR, Cronin BE, Tam AP. 2003. Controversy and consensus regarding the use of cognitive ability testing in organizations. *J. Appl. Psychol.* 88:660–71

Murphy KR, Dzieweczynski JL. 2005. Why don't measures of broad dimensions of personality perform better as predictors of job performance? *Hum. Perform.* 18:343–57

Naglieri JA, Drasgow F, Schmit M, Handler L, Prifitera A, et al. 2004. Psychological testing on the Internet: new problems, old issues. *Am. Psychol.* 59:150–62

Nguyen NT, Biderman MD, McDaniel MA. 2005. Effects of response instructions on faking a situational judgment test. *Int. J. Select. Assess.* 13:250–60

Ones DS, Viswesvaran C, Dilchert S. 2005. Personality at work: raising awareness and correcting misconceptions. *Hum. Perform.* 18:389–404

Oswald FL, Schmit N, Kim BH, Ramsay LJ, Gillespie MA. 2004. Developing a biodata measure and situational judgment inventory as predictors of college student performance. *J. Appl. Psychol.* 89:187–207

Ployhart RE, Ryan AM, Bennett M. 1999. Explanations for selection decisions: applicants' reactions to informational and sensitivity features of explanations. *J. Appl. Psychol.* 84:87–106

Ployhart RE, Weekley JA, Holtz BC, Kemp C. 2003. Web-based and paper-and-pencil testing of applicants in a proctored setting: Are personality, biodata, and situational judgment tests comparable? *Pers. Psychol.* 56:733–52

Podsakoff PM, MacKenzie SB, Paine JB, Bachrach DG. 2000. Organizational citizenship behaviors: a critical review of the theoretical and empirical literature and suggestions for future research. *J. Manag.* 26:513–63

Potosky D, Bobko P. 2004. Selection testing via the Internet: practical considerations and exploratory empirical findings. *Pers. Psychol.* 57:1003–34

Pulakos ED, Arad S, Donovan MA, Plamondon KE. 2000. Adaptability in the workplace: development of a taxonomy of adaptive performance. *J. Appl. Psychol.* 85:612–24

Pulakos ED, Schmitt N, Dorsey DW, Arad S, Hedge JW, Borman WC. 2002. Predicting adaptive performance: further tests of a model of adaptability. *Hum. Perform.* 15:299–323

Raju NS, Dragow F. 2003. Maximum likelihood estimation in validity generalization. See Murphy 2003, pp. 263–85

Richman WL, Kiesler S, Weisband S, Dragow F. 1999. A meta-analytic study of social desirability distortion in computer-administered questionnaires, traditional questionnaires, and interviews. *J. Appl. Psychol.* 84:754–75

Robie C, Ryan AM. 1999. Effects of nonlinearity and heteroscedasticity on the validity of conscientiousness in predicting overall job performance. *Int. J. Select. Assess.* 7:157–69

Roth PL, Bevier CA, Bobko P, Switzer FS, Tyler P. 2001a. Ethnic group differences in cognitive ability in employment and educational settings: a meta-analysis. *Pers. Psychol.* 54:297–330

Roth PL, Bobko P. 2000. College grade point average as a personnel selection device: ethnic group differences and potential adverse impact. *J. Appl. Psychol.* 85:399–406

Roth PL, Bobko P, McFarland LA. 2005. A meta-analysis of work sample test validity: updating and integrating some classic literature. *Pers. Psychol.* 58:1009–37

Roth PL, Bobko P, Switzer FS. 2006. Modeling the behavior of the 4/5ths rule for determining adverse impact: reasons for caution. *J. Appl. Psychol.* 91:507–22

Roth PL, Bobko P, Switzer FS, Dean MA. 2001b. Prior selection causes biased estimates of standardized ethnic group differences: simulation and analysis. *Pers. Psychol.* 54:591–617

Roth PL, Huffcutt AI, Bobko P. 2003. Ethnic group differences in measures of job performance: a new meta-analysis. *J. Appl. Psychol.* 88:694–706

Roth PL, Van Iddekinge CH, Huffcutt AI, Eidson CE, Bobko P. 2002. Corrections for range restriction in structured interview ethnic group differences: the values may be larger than researchers thought. *J. Appl. Psychol.* 87:369–76

Rotundo M, Sackett PR. 2002. The relative importance of task, citizenship, and counterproductive performance to global ratings of job performance: a policy-capturing approach. *J. Appl. Psychol.* 87:66–80

Roznowski M, Dickter DN, Hong S, Sawin LL, Shute VJ. 2000. Validity of measures of cognitive processes and general ability for learning and performance on highly complex computerized tutors: Is the g factor of intelligence even more general? *J. Appl. Psychol.* 85:940–55

Ryan AM, McFarland L, Baron H, Page R. 1999. An international look at selection practices: nation and culture as explanations for variability in practice. *Pers. Psychol.* 52:359–91

Ryan AM, Sacco JM, McFarland LA, Kriska SD. 2000. Applicant self-selection: correlates of withdrawal from a multiple hurdle process. *J. Appl. Psychol.* 85:163–79

Rynes SL, Colbert AE, Brown KG. 2002. HR professionals' beliefs about effective human resource practices: correspondence between research and practice. *Hum. Res. Manag.* 41:149–74

Sackett PR, Devore CJ. 2001. Counterproductive behaviors at work. See Anderson et al. 2001, pp. 145–64

Sackett PR, Laczo RM, Lippe ZP. 2003. Differential prediction and the use of multiple predictors: the omitted variables problem. *J. Appl. Psychol.* 88:1046–56

Sackett PR, Lievens F, Berry CM, Landers RN. 2007. A cautionary note on the effects of range restriction on predictor intercorrelations. *J. Appl. Psychol.* 92:538–44

Sackett PR, Schmitt N, Ellingson JE, Kabin MB. 2001. High-stakes testing in employment, credentialing, and higher education—prospects in a post-affirmative-action world. *Am. Psychol.* 56:302–18

Sackett PR, Yang H. 2000. Correction for range restriction: an expanded typology. *J. Appl. Psychol.* 85:112–18

Salgado JF. 2003. Predicting job performance using FFM and non-FFM personality measures. *J. Occup. Organ. Psychol.* 76:323–46

Salgado JF, Anderson N, Moscoso S, Bertua C, de Fruyt F. 2003a. International validity generalization of GMA and cognitive abilities: a European community meta-analysis. *Pers. Psychol.* 56:573–605

Salgado JF, Anderson N, Moscoso S, Bertua C, de Fruyt F, Rolland JP. 2003b. A meta-analytic study of general mental ability validity for different occupations in the European community. *J. Appl. Psychol.* 88:1068–81

Sanchez RJ, Truxillo DM, Bauer TN. 2000. Development and examination of an expectancy-based measure of test-taking motivation. *J. Appl. Psychol.* 85:739–50

Scherbaum CA. 2005. Synthetic validity: past, present, and future. *Pers. Psychol.* 58:481–515

Schleicher DJ, Day DV, Mayes BT, Riggio RE. 2002. A new frame for frame-of-reference training: enhancing the construct validity of assessment centers. *J. Appl. Psychol.* 87:735–46

Schleicher DJ, Venkataramani V, Morgeson FP, Campion MA. 2006. So you didn't get the job...now what do you think? Examining opportunity-to-perform fairness perceptions. *Pers. Psychol.* 59:559–90

Schmidt FL, Oh IS, Le H. 2006. Increasing the accuracy of corrections for range restriction: implications for selection procedure validities and other research results. *Pers. Psychol.* 59:281–305

Schmidt FL, Rader M. 1999. Exploring the boundary conditions for interview validity: meta-analytic validity findings for a new interview type. *Pers. Psychol.* 52:445–64

Schmidt FL, Zimmerman RD. 2004. A counterintuitive hypothesis about employment interview validity and some supporting evidence. *J. Appl. Psychol.* 89:553–61

Schmit MJ, Kihm JA, Robie C. 2000. Development of a global measure of personality. *Pers. Psychol.* 53:153–93

Schmitt N, Gooding RZ, Noe RA, Kirsch M. 1984. Meta-analysis of validity studies published between 1964 and 1982 and the investigation of study characteristics. *Pers. Psychol.* 37:407–22

Schmitt N, Kunce C. 2002. The effects of required elaboration of answers to biodata questions. *Pers. Psychol.* 55:569–87

Schmitt N, Oswald FL. 2006. The impact of corrections for faking on the validity of noncognitive measures in selection settings. *J. Appl. Psychol.* 91:613–21

Schmitt N, Oswald FL, Kim BH, Gillespie MA, Ramsay LJ, Yoo TY. 2003. Impact of elaboration on socially desirable responding and the validity of biodata measures. *J. Appl. Psychol.* 88:979–88

Schmitt N, Rogers W, Chan D, Sheppard L, Jennings D. 1997. Adverse impact and predictive efficiency of various predictor combinations. *J. Appl. Psychol.* 82:719–30

Soc. Ind. Organ. Psychol. 2003. *Principles for the Validation Use of Personnel Selection Procedures.* Bowling Green, OH: Soc. Ind. Organ. Psychol.

Spector PE, Fox S. 2005. A model of counterproductive work behavior. In *Counterproductive Workplace Behavior: Investigations of Actors and Targets*, ed. S Fox, PE Spector, pp. 151–74. Washington, DC: APA

Stark S, Chernyshenko OS, Drasgow F, Williams BA. 2006. Examining assumptions about item responding in personality assessment: Should ideal point methods be considered for scale development and scoring? *J. Appl. Psychol.* 91:25–39

Steel PDG, Huffcutt AI, Kammeyer-Mueller J. 2006. From the work one knows the worker: a systematic review of the challenges, solutions, and steps to creating synthetic validity. *Int. J. Select. Assess.* 14:16–36

Steele C, Spencer SJ, Aronson J. 2002. Contending with group image: the psychology of stereotype threat. In *Advances in Experimental Social Psychology*, ed. MP Zanna, pp. 379–440. San Diego, CA: Academic

Stewart GL. 1999. Trait bandwidth and stages of job performance: assessing differential effects for conscientiousness and its subtraits. *J. Appl. Psychol.* 84:959–68

Stewart GL, Nandkeolyar AK. 2006. Adaptation and intraindividual variation in sales outcomes: exploring the interactive effects of personality and environmental opportunity. *Pers. Psychol.* 59:307–32

Sturman MC, Cheramie RA, Cashen LH. 2005. The impact of job complexity and performance measurement on the temporal consistency, stability, and test-retest reliability of employee job performance ratings. *J. Appl. Psychol.* 90:269–83

Tam AP, Murphy KR, Lyall JT. 2004. Can changes in differential dropout rates reduce adverse impact? A computer simulation study of a multi-wave selection system. *Pers. Psychol.* 57:905–34

Taylor PJ, Pajo K, Cheung GW, Stringfield P. 2004. Dimensionality and validity of a structured telephone reference check procedure. *Pers. Psychol.* 57:745–72

Tett RP, Burnett DD. 2003. A personality trait-based interactionist model of job performance. *J. Appl. Psychol.* 88:500–17

Thoresen CJ, Bradley JC, Bliese PD, Thoresen JD. 2004. The Big Five personality traits and individual job performance growth trajectories in maintenance and transitional job stages. *J. Appl. Psychol.* 89:835–53

Tippins NT, Beaty J, Drasgow F, Gibson WM, Pearlman K, et al. 2006. Unproctored Internet testing in employment settings. *Pers. Psychol.* 59:189–225

Truxillo DM, Bauer TN. 1999. Applicant reactions to test score banding in entry-level and promotional contexts. *J. Appl. Psychol.* 84:322–39

Truxillo DM, Bauer TN, Campion MA, Paronto ME. 2002. Selection fairness information and applicant reactions: a longitudinal field study. *J. Appl. Psychol.* 87:1020–31

Van Iddekinge CH, Raymark PH, Roth PL. 2005. Assessing personality with a structured employment interview: construct-related validity and susceptibility to response inflation. *J. Appl. Psychol.* 90:536–52

Van Rooy DL, Viswesvaran C. 2004. Emotional intelligence: a meta-analytic investigation of predictive validity and nomological net. *J. Vocat. Behav.* 65:71–95

Van Rooy DL, Viswesvaran C, Pluta P. 2005. An evaluation of construct validity: What is this thing called Emotional Intelligence? *Hum. Perform.* 18:45–62

Van Vianen AEM, Taris R, Scholten E, Schinkel S. 2004. Perceived fairness in personnel selection: determinants and outcomes in different stages of the assessment procedure. *Int. J. Select. Assess.* 12:149–59

Viswesvaran C, Schmidt FL, Ones DS. 2005. Is there a general factor in ratings of job performance? A meta-analytic framework for disentangling substantive and error influences. *J. Appl. Psychol.* 90:108–31

Wagner RK, Sternberg RJ. 1985. Practical intelligence in real world pursuits: the role of tacit knowledge. *J. Personal. Soc. Psychol.* 49:436–58

Weekley JA, Ployhart RE, eds. 2006. *Situational Judgment Tests: Theory, Measurement and Application.* San Francisco, CA: Jossey Bass

Wilk SL, Cappelli P. 2003. Understanding the determinants of employer use of selection methods. *Pers. Psychol.* 56:103–24

Witt LA. 2002. The interactive effects of extraversion and conscientiousness on performance. *J. Manag.* 28:835–51

Witt LA, Burke LA, Barrick MR, Mount MK. 2002. The interactive effects of conscientiousness and agreeableness on job performance. *J. Appl. Psychol.* 87:164–69

Witt LA, Ferris GR. 2003. Social skill as moderator of the conscientiousness-performance relationship: convergent results across four studies. *J. Appl. Psychol.* 88:809–20

Zeidner M, Matthews G, Roberts RD. 2004. Emotional intelligence in the workplace: a critical review. *Appl. Psychol. Int. Rev.* 53:371–99

The Education of Dyslexic Children from Childhood to Young Adulthood

Sally E. Shaywitz,[1] Robin Morris,[2] and Bennett A. Shaywitz[3]

[1] Department of Pediatrics, Yale University School of Medicine, New Haven, Connecticut 06510; email: sally.shaywitz@yale.edu

[2] Department of Psychology, Georgia State University, Atlanta, Georgia 30302; email: robinmorris@gsu.edu

[3] Departments of Pediatrics and Neurology, Yale University School of Medicine, New Haven, Connecticut 06510; email: bennett.shaywitz@yale.edu

Annu. Rev. Psychol. 2008. 59:451–75

The *Annual Review of Psychology* is online at
http://psych.annualreviews.org

This article's doi:
10.1146/annurev.psych.59.103006.093633

0066-4308/08/0203-0451$20.00

Key Words

accommodations, classification, learning disabilities, neuroimaging, specific reading disability, reading remediation, reading intervention, dyslexia

Abstract

The past two decades have witnessed an explosion in our understanding of dyslexia (or specific reading disability), the most common and most carefully studied of the learning disabilities. We first review the core concepts of dyslexia: its definition, prevalence, and developmental course. Next we examine the cognitive model of dyslexia, especially the phonological theory, and review empiric data suggesting genetic and neurobiological influences on the development of dyslexia. With the scientific underpinnings of dyslexia serving as a foundation, we turn our attention to evidence-based approaches to diagnosis and treatment, including interventions and accommodations. Teaching reading represents a major focus. We first review those reading interventions effective in early grades, and then review interventions for older students. To date the preponderance of intervention studies have focused on word-level reading; newer studies are beginning to examine reading interventions that have gone beyond word reading to affect reading fluency and reading comprehension. The article concludes with a discussion of the critical role of accommodations for dyslexic students and the recent neurobiological evidence supporting the need for such accommodations.

Contents

BACKGROUND AND DEFINITION

For good readers, gaining meaning from print quickly and effortlessly, like breathing and speaking, is a natural part of life. For these men and women, it is almost unimaginable how something that seems to come so naturally could be difficult for others. Without doubt, since ancient times when man learned to use printed symbols to convey words and ideas, there have been those who struggled

Fluency: the ability to read words accurately, rapidly, and with good intonation

to decipher the code. Just how many are affected, the basis of the difficulty, and most importantly, the most effective, evidence-based approaches to educating dyslexic children and young adults were questions that had to wait until quite recently for resolution. We begin by reviewing the core concepts of dyslexia, including its definition, epidemiology, cognitive model, and etiology, especially neurobiological influences. We next consider specific evidence-based reading interventions for word-reading accuracy, fluency, and comprehension and then the exciting neurobiological findings that together have given rise to and must inform contemporary, evidence-based approaches to the education of dyslexic children. We conclude with a discussion of the critical role of accommodations for dyslexic students and the new neurobiological evidence supporting the need for such accommodations.

Historical Roots

Dyslexia has been described in virtually every ethnic group, language, and geographic region. The original report, published as *A Case of Congenital Wordblindness* on November 7, 1896, was prompted by the experience of a British physician, W. Pringle Morgan, with his patient Percy F., age 14, for whom he provided the following description:

> ...He has always been a bright and intelligent boy, quick at games, and in no way inferior to others his age. His great difficulty has been—and is now—his inability to read. He has been at school or under tutors since he was 7 years old, and the greatest efforts have been made to teach him to read, but, in spite of this laborious and persistent training, he can only with difficulty spell out words of one syllable ....

> ...I might add that the boy is bright and of average intelligence in conversation. His eyes are normal ... and his eyesight is good. The schoolmaster who has taught him for some years says that he would be the smartest

lad in the school if the instruction were entirely in oral... (Morgan 1896, p. 1378).

What is so striking is the similarity of Percy F. to the children we continue to see to this day. Such clinical descriptions from every corner of the globe attest to the invariance of dyslexia over both time and place. In his clinical vignette, Dr. Morgan captures the essence of dyslexia: an unexpected difficulty in reading.

Definition: Core Constancy Amid Refinements

Current definition. The basic notion of dyslexia as an unexpected difficulty in reading has remained constant across definitions of dyslexia (Critchley 1970, Lyon 1995) as evidenced by the most current definition provided by a working group meeting in Washington, D.C., in 2002:

> Dyslexia is a specific learning disability that is neurobiological in origin. It is characterized by difficulties with accurate and/or fluent word recognition and poor spelling and decoding abilities. These difficulties typically result from a deficit in the phonological component of language that is often unexpected in relation to other cognitive abilities and the provision of effective classroom instruction... (Lyon et al. 2003, p. 2).

Refinements from prior definitions. Dyslexia (also referred to as specific reading disability) is a member of the family of learning disabilities; in fact, reading disability is by far the most common learning disability, affecting over 80% of those identified as learning disabled (Lerner 1989). Although the recognition of dyslexia as a discrete entity dates back over a century, the concept of a learning disability is relatively new.

The term "learning disabilities," as initially proposed by Samuel Kirk (Kirk 1963) and later operationalized in the Federal Register (U.S. Office Educ. 1977), refers to a broad group of difficulties involving listening, speaking, reading, writing, and mathematics. In contrast to this undifferentiated construct, the current definition explicitly categorizes dyslexia as a "specific learning disability." New to the current definition over the previous one is reference to dyslexia's "neurobiological origin," reflecting the significant advances in neuroscience, particularly the brain imaging of reading and dyslexia that is discussed in detail below.

New, too, is the incorporation of, and emphasis on, the importance of fluent reading: the ability to read text not only accurately, but also rapidly and with proper expression (Rep. Natl. Reading Panel 2000). Thus, the previous reference to "single word decoding" is now supplanted by reference to "difficulties with accurate and/or fluent word recognition," acknowledging converging data pointing to the critical lack of the development of fluent reading as a hallmark of dyslexia that persists into adolescence and then adulthood, even when accuracy improves. The lack of fluent reading is observed clinically by reading that is effortful and slow; it is often considered the sine qua non of dyslexia, especially in young adult and adult readers (Bruck 1998, Lefly & Pennington 1991, Shaywitz 2003). This renewed appreciation of the importance of fluency should encourage its measurement; otherwise, many dyslexic children who can read accurately, but not fluently, will continue to go unnoticed (and untreated) within the classroom (Katzir et al. 2006).

As in the prior definition (Lyon 1995), emphasis is on the phonological weakness giving rise to the reading (and speaking) difficulties characterizing dyslexia. A range of studies has indicated phonological difficulties as the most robust (Fletcher et al. 1994, Shaywitz et al. 1999, Stanovich & Siegel 1994) and specific finding (Morris et al. 1998) in dyslexic children and adolescents, supporting the phonological-core variable differences model proposed earlier by Stanovich (1988). Critical to the notion of a phonological weakness as causal in the development of the concatenation of difficulties observed in

Accommodations: adaptations within the classroom, use of assistive technology, or provision of extra time allowing learning-disabled students to demonstrate their full knowledge

Decoding: determining the pronunciation of a word by analyzing the vowels and consonant combinations within the word

dyslexia has been the repeated demonstration that remediation of the phonological weakness leads to the amelioration of the decoding and word-reading weaknesses in dyslexia (Bradley & Bryant 1983; Byrne & Fielding-Barnsley 1995; Byrne et al. 2000; Foorman et al. 1998; Hatcher et al. 1994; Schneider et al. 1997; Torgesen et al. 1999, 2001).

Core definitional concept: an unexpected difficulty in reading. Perhaps the most consistent and enduring core of any definition of dyslexia is the concept of dyslexia as an unexpected difficulty in reading. "Unexpected" refers to the presence of a reading difficulty in a child (or adult) who appears to have all of the factors (intelligence, motivation, exposure to reasonable reading instruction) present to be a good reader but who continues to struggle (Shaywitz 1998). More challenging has been the question of how to operationalize the unexpected nature of dyslexia. Thus, using differing methods and criteria, definitions have attempted to capture the "unexpected" nature of dyslexia by requiring a discrepancy of a certain degree between a child's measured IQ and his reading achievement. For example, schools have typically relied on criteria based on an absolute discrepancy, most commonly one or one-and-one-half standard deviations between standard scores on IQ and reading tests; others, including many researchers, prefer regression-based methods adjusting for the correlation of IQ and reading achievement (Reynolds 1984, Stuebing et al. 2002).

We want to emphasize that the difficulty has been not with the notion of a discrepancy, but rather with the real-life practical effect of implementing this model in a primary school setting. For example, children who were clearly struggling as early as kindergarten or first grade had to wait, often until third grade or later, until their failure in reading was of such a magnitude that they met discrepancy requirements. And so it is understandable why this approach has often been referred to as a wait-to-fail model. Attempts to clarify the criteria by meta-analyses compar-

ing discrepant to simply low-achieving poor readers (defined on the basis of a reading score below a certain cut point, e.g., below a standard score of 90) find overlap between the two groups on reading-related constructs but not on IQ-related measures (Stuebing et al. 2002). In addition, both low-achieving and discrepant readers demonstrate comparable growth rates in word reading during the school years (Francis et al. 1996). Knowledge of long-term adult outcome may shed light on possible differences between the two groups not captured by studies during childhood; such efforts are now under way using data from the Connecticut Longitudinal Study (Ferrer et al. 2007, Shaywitz et al. 2003). Not only do poor readers identified by either discrepancy or low-achievement criteria resemble one another on measures of reading and growth rates of reading, but each group also differs along multiple dimensions from groups of typically achieving boys and girls (Fletcher et al. 1999, Lyon et al. 2001).

These findings have strong educational implications: It is not valid to assume that discrepant children require instructional strategies that differ from those for low-achieving readers. It also is not valid to deny the education services available for disabled or at-risk readers to low-achieving, nondiscrepant children. On the other hand, the observed similarity of the discrepant and low-achieving groups in reading-related constructs argues for identification approaches that include both low-achieving children and those struggling readers who are discrepant but who do not satisfy an arbitrary cut point for designation as low achieving. Seventy-five percent of children identified by discrepancy criteria also meet low-achievement criteria in reading; the remaining 25% who meet only discrepancy criteria may fail to be identified and yet still be struggling to read (Shaywitz et al. 1992a).

A recognition of these difficulties combined with accumulating data indicating the importance of early intervention (Lyon et al. 2001; Torgesen et al. 1999, 2001) has prompted researchers and educators to search for alternative approaches that would promote earlier intervention or prevention for at-risk readers. One such approach focuses on a more dynamic assessment, particularly applicable to early grades, where the ongoing development of fluency in component reading skills (e.g., letter recognition, word reading) is measured frequently and is compared with expected norms (Kame'enui et al. 2000). Another approach, termed "response to intervention" (RTI; Fuchs & Fuchs 2006), has generated considerable interest. Here, all children are first provided with evidence-based reading instruction and their progress is frequently monitored; those who are not making progress are selected to receive additional support (see below for fuller discussion of RTI).

Definitional framework of dyslexia: categorical or dimensional. How best to more broadly conceptualize dyslexia has long been of theoretical interest to investigators and of more practical import to educators who must set policies to identify struggling readers in need of support. Earlier views, mainly stemming from the influential Isle of Wight study (Rutter & Yule 1975, Yule & Rutter 1985), posited a categorical view of dyslexia envisioning reading ability as bimodally distributed, with children with specific reading retardation (dyslexia) forming a so-called hump at the lower tail of the distribution (Rutter & Yule 1975, Yule & Rutter 1985). In contrast, more recent data from an epidemiologic sample, the Connecticut Longitudinal Study, suggests that reading difficulties, including dyslexia, occur as part of a continuum that includes nonimpaired as well as disabled readers (Shaywitz et al. 1992b). Other investigators, too, have pointed out methodological flaws in the British study (van der Wissel & Zegers 1985) or failed to replicate its findings (Jorm et al. 1986, Rodgers 1983, Silva et al. 1985, Stevenson 1988). The importance of the Connecticut data is that these findings place dyslexia within the same dimensional framework as other important disorders that affect the health and welfare of children and adults.

Thus, like hypertension and obesity, dyslexia occurs in degrees of severity. A dimensional model also argues that although cut points are placed to help define groups, these are arbitrary and may have no biological validity; those on one or the other side of such a cut point will differ from one another by degree, but not kind. Clinically, for school identification of children for special services, this means that "children who do not meet these arbitrarily imposed criteria may still require and profit from special help" in reading (Shaywitz et al. 1992b, p. 149).

EPIDEMIOLOGY OF DYSLEXIA

Prevalence

Reading difficulties are highly prevalent; the specific prevalence rate will reflect the particular definition and cut points established as criteria for identification. For example, results of the 2005 National Assessment of Educational Progress indicate 27% of high school seniors are reading below the most basic levels (minimum level at which a student can demonstrate an understanding of what she or he has read) (Grigg et al. 2007). Even more primary grade students—36% of fourth grade children—are reading below basic levels (Perie et al. 2005). In our epidemiological Connecticut Longitudinal Study sample in which each participant was individually assessed, we found that 17.5% of students were reading below age or ability levels (Shaywitz et al. 1994).

Developmental Course

Converging data indicate that reading difficulties are persistent and do not remit with age or time (Francis et al. 1994, Shaywitz et al. 1995) (**Figure 1**, see color insert).

This should put an end to the unsupported, but unfortunately, too widely held notion that reading problems are outgrown or somehow represent a developmental lag. The implication is that reading problems expressed early

RTI: response to intervention

Evidence-based reading instruction: programs and methods for which there is reliable and valid evidence published in a peer-reviewed journal of effectiveness in teaching children to read

Phonemes: elemental particles of speech; the smallest unit of speech distinguishing one spoken word from another

must be addressed or they will persist with time. Here, also, it is important to keep in mind that the expression of the difficulty may change, so that difficulties with reading accuracy, especially in very bright children, often evolve into relatively accurate, but not fluent, reading. Given the knowledge of the unremitting course of dyslexia, early intervention takes on a new urgency; particularly since the data strongly indicate a much more positive response to interventions that are provided in the very first few years of school compared with those delivered in the later years of primary school (Torgesen et al. 2006).

Sex Differences in Dyslexia

The belief that reading difficulties affect predominantly or exclusively males reflects the overwhelmingly larger number of boys compared with girls identified by schools as having a reading problem. However, a series of epidemiological studies, including ones that compare school-identified disabled readers with objective, individually assessed, criterion-identified disabled readers, indicate that a referral bias favors boys in school-identification procedures reflecting boys' disruptive classroom behavior (Shaywitz et al. 1990). Since boys are generally more active and impulsive, they are more likely to be identified through traditional school-identification procedures, whereas girls—who are generally quiet and who may struggle to read—often go unnoticed. A range of data now indicate that although there are somewhat more boys, significant numbers of girls struggle to read (Flynn & Rahbar 1994, Shaywitz et al. 1990). Awareness of a student's reading difficulties should not be dependent on overt signs of a behavioral difficulty; the increased reliance on ongoing monitoring of reading fluency (for example, use of dynamic indicators of basic early literacy skills, or DIBELS; Kame'enui et al. 2000) should help to ensure that all children who are failing to make progress will be identified and receive appropriate interventions.

COGNITIVE MODEL OF DYSLEXIA AND ITS IMPLICATIONS

Phonological Theory

Print emerged from the language system, and the relationship between print and spoken language is perhaps best captured by the statement, "Writing is not language, but merely a way of recording [spoken] language by visible marks" (Bloomfield 1933, p. 21). Of the several theories suggested, an explanation reflecting what is known about the relationship between spoken and written language, the phonological model, has received the most support (Hulme et al. 2005, Ramus et al. 2003, Rayner et al. 2001, Shaywitz 2003, Snowling 2000).

Most contemporary approaches to diagnosis and to teaching dyslexic children to read derive from a phonological model of how children gain access to print. In particular, knowledge of this model enables the reader to understand the basis and logic of current evidence-based reading instruction. Here we discuss the nature and educational implications of this model; in a later section, specific evidence-based approaches to reading intervention are presented. To understand why print has meaning and why reading presents a challenge, we first consider the language system and then discuss why reading is more difficult than speaking.

The language system. The language system is conceptualized as a hierarchy of component modules (Fodor 1983); at the lowest level is the phonological module, dedicated to processing the elemental units of language, phonemes. Language is generative; different combinations of just 44 phonemes in the English language produce tens of thousands of words (Abler 1989). The phonological module assembles the phonemes into words for the speaker and disassembles the words back into phonemes for the listener. Reflecting a process referred to as coarticulation, spoken language appears seamless to the listener, with

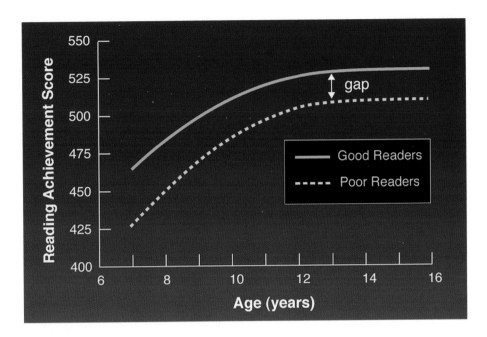

Figure 1

Trajectory of reading skills over time in nonimpaired and dyslexic readers. Ordinate is Rasch scores
(W scores) from the Woodcock-Johnson reading test (Woodcock & Johnson 1989) and abscissa is age
in years. Both dyslexic and nonimpaired readers improve their reading scores as they get older, but the
gap between the dyslexic and nonimpaired readers remains. Thus, dyslexia is a deficit and not a developmental lag. (Figure derived from data in Francis et al. 1996 and reprinted from Shaywitz 2003 with
permission.)

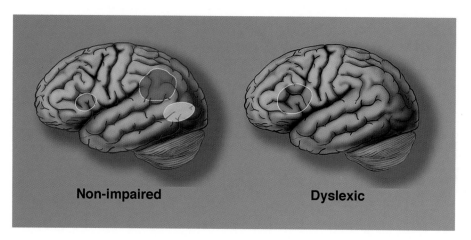

Figure 2

Neural signature for dyslexia. Schematic view of left hemisphere brain systems for reading observed during fMRI in nonimpaired (*left*) and dyslexic (*right*) readers. In nonimpaired readers, three systems are evident: one anterior in the area of the inferior frontal gyrus and two posterior, the top system around the parieto-temporal region and the bottom system around the occipito-temporal region. In dyslexic readers, the anterior system is slightly overactivated compared with systems of nonimpaired readers; in contrast, the two posterior systems are underactivated. This pattern of underactivation in left posterior reading systems is referred to as the neural signature for dyslexia. Figure reprinted from (Shaywitz 2003) with permission.

no clues to its segmental nature (Liberman et al. 1967). Thus, the word "bat" is composed of three phonemes, "b," "aaaa," and "t," but the listener hears this as the holistic word "bat" and not as three separate sounds. It is the seamless nature of spoken language, giving no clue to its underlying segmental nature, that presents a challenge to the would-be reader.

Spoken language is innate, observed in all societies on earth, and has been with us for tens of thousands of years. Exposing a baby to a natural speaking environment results in the development of spoken language; spoken language is spontaneous and does not need to be taught. In contrast, print is artificial; many societies still rely primarily on spoken language. From an evolutionary perspective, print is rather new, only several thousand years old (Lawler 2001). Consequently, as opposed to spoken language, written language is acquired and must be taught. Converging data suggest that the prime challenge for beginning readers is to map the orthography (letters) onto the elemental sounds of spoken language (phonemes), and this serves as the major focus of early reading instruction. However, reflecting the seamless nature of spoken language, perhaps as many as 30% of the population has difficulty noticing the phonemes within words, resulting in difficulty learning to associate the letters with specific sounds within each word (Liberman et al. 1974).

Phonological awareness. Phonological awareness (PA), referring to the ability to recognize, identify, and manipulate syllables and phonemes within spoken language, is at the core of reading and reading difficulties (Snow et al. 1998, Torgesen & Mathes 2000, Wagner & Torgesen 1987). PA predicts reading acquisition (Bradley & Bryant 1983, Hatcher et al. 1994, Hoien et al. 1995) and differentiates good and poor readers (Goswami & Bryant 1990, Wagner & Torgesen 1987), and instruction aimed at improving PA improves reading (Bradley & Bryant 1983; Byrne & Fielding-Barnsley 1995; Byrne et al. 2000; Foorman et al. 1998;

Hatcher et al. 1994; Torgesen et al. 1999, 2001). Acquisition of phonological awareness follows a systematic, hierarchical model of word structure, progressing from larger to smaller phonological units (Anthony et al. 2003). Accordingly, children first develop a sensitivity to, or awareness of, spoken whole words, then syllables, then phoneme-level units of language. The latter is referred to as phonemic awareness. Good evidence supports the belief that reading itself is critical for the development of PA. Thus, PA is primarily developed following introduction to reading instruction, independent of age (Goswami & Bryant 1990), and not surprisingly, (illiterate) adults who have never received reading instruction lack phonemic awareness (Morais et al. 1979). The importance of reading instruction to the development of the critical skill of phonemic awareness was demonstrated in a study of four-, five-, and six-year-old children (Liberman et al. 1974) in which none of the four-year-olds, 17% of the five-year-olds, and 70% of the six-year-olds (following a year of schooling and presumed reading instruction) performed well on a test of phonemic awareness. A major advance has been the availability of standardized tests of phonological abilities (e.g., the Comprehensive Test of Phonological Processing; Wagner et al. 1999) that can be administered as early as age five.

Dyslexia in Different Orthographies

Dyslexia has been described in all writing systems, including alphabetic and logographic orthographies (Stevenson et al. 1982). Alphabetic orthographies use letters and letter clusters to represent phonemes, whereas logographic ones (Chinese, Korean, and Japanese Kanji) use characters to represent monosyllabic morphemes of spoken language. Within alphabetic writing systems, dyslexia occurs in languages with highly predictable relations between letters and sounds (e.g., Finnish, German, and Italian) and those described as dense orthographies with a more erratic

Orthography: the specific writing system of a language

Morphemes: the smallest meaningful linguistic units, for example, prefixes, suffixes

Functional magnetic resonance imaging (fMRI): using the magnetic properties of blood to measure blood flow and localize brain processes while subjects perform a cognitive task

relationship between letters and sounds (e.g., especially English, but also Danish, Portuguese, and French) (Caravolas 2005, Goulandris 2003, Ziegler & Goswami 2005). Although dyslexia occurs in all languages, variations in the consistency of the mapping of the orthography to the phonology will influence reading acquisition and strategies, resulting in differences in reading development among languages (Ziegler & Goswami 2005). Of importance from an educational perspective is that the more consistent the letter-sound mappings are, the easier it is for children to learn to read words accurately. Thus, the initial steps of literacy acquisition occur earlier and with more ease in languages such as Finnish and Italian, where there is greater predictability of sound-symbol linkages. Variations in consistency, in turn, will influence the expression of dyslexia across different languages. For example, in orthographies that are more consistent, learning to read words accurately generally occurs readily in dyslexic as well as in good readers. As a result, in these readers, dyslexia may not present itself until later on in school, perhaps after fourth grade or so, and may be expressed only as a problem in reading fluency, with reading accuracy relatively intact (Ziegler & Goswami 2005). The inconsistencies between the sounds and their spellings, not surprisingly, also affect dyslexic children and cause difficulties in spelling. Ziegler & Goswami (2005) posit that these variations will affect how well dyslexic children develop phonemic awareness once literacy instruction begins. They argue that consistent phonemic-letter linkages tend to be held and kept in memory more easily so that they are better instantiated in response to reading instruction; as a result, dyslexic children demonstrate phonological deficits only very early on in these languages. In contrast, in languages such as English, with more unpredictable letter-sounds mappings, deficits in phonemic awareness are noted early on in school and persist through adolescence (Shaywitz et al. 1999) and into adulthood (Bruck & Treiman 1992).

ETIOLOGY

Genetic Influences

Dyslexia is both familial and heritable: The disorder is found in 23% to 65% of the children of parents who are dyslexic, and 40% of the siblings of a dyslexic child are also affected (Pennington & Gilger 1996). Interestingly, a higher heritability for dyslexia has been reported in children with higher IQs (Olson et al. 1999, Wadsworth et al. 2000). Genetic transmission is complex, with both recessive and dominant transmission observed in different cases, with at least 50% or more of the variance explained by genetic factors and the remainder attributed to environmental influences (Olson & Byrne 2005). Linkage studies have implicated genes on four chromosomes—2, 6, 15, and 18—in dyslexia (Fisher & DeFries 2002). At least nine loci have been reported to be associated with the disorder. Much attention has recently centered on DCDC2, located on the short arm (p) of chromosome 6 in band 22 (6p22), and its association with dyslexia has been independently reported by two different investigative groups (Meng et al. 2005, Schumacher et al. 2006). These findings of a strong genetic influence have educational implications: If a child has a parent or sibling who is dyslexic, that child should be considered at risk and observed carefully for signs of a reading difficulty. It is also important to emphasize that a genetic etiology does not constrain a positive response to reading intervention (Torgesen & Mathes 2000; Wise et al. 1999, 2000); once identified, dyslexic children deserve and will benefit from evidence-based interventions.

Neurobiological Influences

Within the past two decades, the development of neuroimaging, particularly functional magnetic resonance imaging (fMRI), has provided investigators and clinicians with the opportunity to examine and treat learning disabilities at a previously dreamed of, but unattainable, level of understanding (Anderson &

Gore 1997, Frackowiak et al. 2004, Jezzard et al. 2001). Using this technology, neuroscientists have been able to identify and localize several interrelated left hemisphere neural networks in reading: an anterior network in the inferior frontal gyrus (Broca's area), long associated with articulation that also serves an important function in silent reading and naming (Fiez & Peterson 1998, Frackowiak et al. 2004), and two in left hemisphere posterior brain regions, one around the parieto-temporal region serving word analysis, the other in the left occipito-temporal region, the word form area, critical for skilled, fluent reading. A number of functional brain imaging studies in disabled readers converge to indicate a failure of left hemisphere posterior brain systems to function properly during reading (Brunswick et al. 1999; Helenius et al. 1999; Horwitz et al. 1998; Paulesu et al. 2001; Rumsey et al. 1992, 1997; Salmelin et al. 1996; Shaywitz et al. 1998) (**Figure 2**, see color insert). This neurobiological evidence of dysfunction in left hemisphere posterior reading circuits is already present in reading-disabled children and cannot be ascribed simply to a lifetime of poor reading (Seki et al. 2001, Shaywitz et al. 2002, Simos et al. 2000, Temple et al. 2000). Anterior systems, especially involving regions around the inferior frontal gyrus, have also been implicated in disabled readers in reports of individuals with brain lesions (Benson 1994) as well as in functional brain imaging studies (Brunswick et al. 1999, Corina et al. 2001, Georgiewa et al. 2002, Paulesu et al. 1996, Rumsey et al. 1997, Shaywitz et al. 1998). Although dyslexic readers exhibit a dysfunction in posterior reading systems, they appear to develop compensatory systems involving areas around the inferior frontal gyrus in both hemispheres as well as the right hemisphere homologue of the left occipito-temporal word form area (Shaywitz et al. 2002).

Malleability of neural systems for reading. A number of investigators have focused on whether the neural systems for reading are malleable and whether the disruption in these systems in struggling readers can be influenced by a reading intervention. Specific interventions are discussed below; here, we focus on brain imaging as a tool to interrogate the plasticity of these systems and to examine the influence of reading instruction on the development or reorganization (repair) of these neural systems. For example, in a study of second- and third-grade dyslexic and nonimpaired readers, compared with dyslexic readers who received other types of intervention, children who received an experimental evidence-based phonological intervention not only improved their reading but also demonstrated increased activation both in left anterior (inferior frontal gyrus) and left posterior (middle temporal gyrus) brain regions (Shaywitz et al. 2004). These findings indicate that teaching matters and that how children are taught can foster the development of those automatic neural systems that serve skilled reading. Other investigators, too, have found that reading interventions influence neural systems in brain. For example, one study in adults demonstrated greater activation in the left prefrontal cortex after training compared with before training (Temple et al. 2000). Other studies in children have reported intervention-associated changes including fMRI changes in left inferior frontal and posterior areas as well as in right hemisphere and cingulate cortex (Temple et al. 2003); changes in lactate concentration during magnetic resonance spectroscopy in the left frontal regions (Richards et al. 2000); fMRI changes in left frontal and left posterior regions (Aylward et al. 2003); changes in magnetoencephalography in the left superior temporal gyrus (Simos et al. 2002); and changes in fMRI in dyslexic adults in posterior reading systems (Eden et al. 2004). Still to be determined is the precise relationship among the type of intervention, changes in brain activation, and clinical improvement in reading.

fMRI and mechanisms of reading. fMRI has also been very useful in understanding

LPMOT: left posterior and medial occipito-temporal region

LALOT: left anterior and lateral occipito-temporal region

the mechanisms of reading, knowledge that offers the possibility of providing more individualized interventions to dyslexic children and adults. Neurobiological evidence is beginning to emerge to support behavioral data indicating that many dyslexics are not able to make good use of sound-symbol linkages as they mature, and instead, they come to rely on memorized words. Behavioral studies indicate phonologic deficits continue to characterize struggling readers, even as they enter adolescence and adult life (Bruck & Treiman 1992, Shaywitz et al. 1999). In addition, persistently poor adult readers appear to read words by memorization so that they are able to read familiar words but have difficulty reading unfamiliar words. Brain imaging now reveals that such readers demonstrate an aberrant neural connectivity pattern. Thus, in nonimpaired readers, functional connections were observed between the left occipito-temporal word form area and other components of the left hemisphere reading system. In contrast, in persistently poor readers, functional connections were observed between the left occipito-temporal word form area and right frontal neural systems regions associated with memory (Shaywitz et al. 2003).

A more recent fMRI study (Shaywitz et al. 2007) also demonstrates the importance of memory systems in dyslexic readers. This study found that brain regions developing with age in dyslexic readers differ from those in nonimpaired readers, primarily in being localized to a more left posterior and medial (LPMOT), rather than a more left anterior and lateral (LALOT) occipito-temporal region. This difference in activation patterns between dyslexic and nonimpaired readers has parallels to reported brain activation differences observed during reading of two Japanese writing systems, Kana and Kanji. Kana script employs symbols that are linked to the sound or phoneme (comparable to English and other alphabetic scripts); Kanji script uses ideographs where each character must be memorized. In the imaging study of these writing systems, LALOT activation, similar

to that seen in nonimpaired readers, occurred during reading Kana. In contrast, LPMOT activation, comparable to that observed in dyslexic readers, was noted during reading of Kanji script (Nakamura et al. 2005), suggesting that the LPMOT region functions as part of a memory-based system. Together, these behavioral and recent neurobiological findings lead us to suppose that as dyslexic children mature, this posterior medial system supports memorization rather than the progressive sound-symbol linkages observed in nonimpaired readers.

Implications of brain imaging studies. The brain imaging studies reviewed above provide neurobiological evidence that illuminates and clarifies current understanding of the nature of dyslexia and its treatment. For example, brain imaging has taken dyslexia from what had previously been considered a hidden disability to one that is visible—the findings of a disruption in posterior reading systems are often referred to as a neural signature for dyslexia.

Important, too, is the demonstration of a disruption in the occipito-temporal or word form system, a system that converging brain imaging studies now show is linked to fluent (automatic, rapid) reading. Disruption in this system for skilled reading has very important practical implications for the dyslexic reader—it provides the neurobiological evidence for the biologic necessity for additional time on high stakes tests (see Accommodations section below).

Studies demonstrating the effects of a reading intervention on neural systems for reading have important implications for public policy regarding teaching children to read: The provision of an evidence-based reading intervention at an early age improves reading fluency and facilitates the development of those neural systems that underlie skilled reading (see section on interventions). fMRI studies focusing on the mechanisms of reading indicate that poor readers rely on memory rather than understanding how letters link to sounds. Furthermore, these studies underscore the importance of fluency; many bright but struggling readers memorize words and can read them relatively accurately but not automatically, and so they read slowly and with great effort.

Thus, evidence is beginning to emerge to indicate that many dyslexics compensate for their poor reading by memorizing words. The problem, of course, for poor readers, is that memory has a limited capacity. For example, by third or fourth grade, a reader comes across perhaps 3000 or more new words a year. Many of these words are difficult to memorize because they are long, complicated, new, or rare words. Those typical readers who have learned about the sound-symbol organization of written language are able to analyze words based on the letter-sound linkages and have a distinct advantage over the dyslexic reader. The reliance on memory systems in these populations of older disabled readers may have implications for treatment of dyslexia. For example, it suggests that more pragmatic interventions focusing on sight words (such as those occurring in assigned reading materials) and provision of accommodations such as aural presentation of literature (e.g., books on tape; see Accommodations section below) might take on a more significant role in these older dyslexic individuals than would an approach used in younger students that is based primarily on teaching sound-symbol associations.

DIAGNOSIS AND TREATMENT

Diagnosis of Dyslexia

Dyslexia is more than simply a score on a reading test. Reflecting the core phonological deficit, a range of downstream effects is observed in spoken as well as in written language. Phonological processing is critical to both spoken and written language. Although most attention has centered on the print difficulties (and they are the most severe), the ability to notice, manipulate, and retrieve phonological elements has an important function in speaking—for example, in retrieving phonemes from the internal lexicon and serially ordering them to utter the spoken word. Thus, it should not be surprising that problems with spoken language, albeit more subtle than those in reading, are often observed. These include late speaking, mispronunciations, difficulties with word retrieval, needing time to summon an oral response, and confusing words that sound alike, for example, saying "recession" when the individual meant to say "reception." A range of problems are noted in reading (especially small function words and unfamiliar words, slow reading); difficulties in spelling; ability to master a foreign language; handwriting; and attention (Shaywitz 2003). The lack of reading fluency brings with it a need to read "manually" (a process consuming great effort) rather than automatically; the cost of such reading is a tremendous drain on attentional resources. This is often observed in the classroom when struggling readers, asked to read quietly, deplete their attentional resources as they struggle with the print, and consequently appear to be daydreaming or not attending to the assigned reading. Some have posited that the need to call upon exceptional attentional resources during reading leads to the clinical appearance of attentional difficulties, in this instance, secondary to the reading difficulty and not primary (Pennington et al. 1993). That is, it is to be viewed as distinct from a primary attentional problem. In addition, it has long been known that there is also a high comorbidity between dyslexia and attention deficit/hyperactivity disorder, ranging from 15% to 50% (Biederman et al. 1996, Shaywitz et al. 1994). Therefore, both primary and secondary attentional difficulties are often noted in individuals who are dyslexic.

In contrast to these difficulties, other cognitive abilities, including thinking, reasoning, vocabulary, and listening comprehension, are usually intact. Intact higher-level abilities offer an explanation of why reading comprehension is often appreciably above single-word

Phonological processing: a category of oral language processing involved with accessing the specific sounds making up spoken words

National Reading Panel: Congressionally mandated in 1998 to review research literature on teaching reading, and in 2000 reported on the most effective methods and approaches

Phonics: an approach to early reading instruction emphasizing letter-sound linkages

reading accuracy and fluency in dyslexia (reviewed in Shaywitz 2003).

Dyslexia is a clinical diagnosis, best made by an experienced clinician who has taken a careful history, observed the child or young adult reading, and administered a battery of tests that assess the child's cognitive ability, academic skills including reading accuracy, fluency, and comprehension, spelling, and mathematics (an area in which skills are often high), and language skills, particularly phonological processing (Marzola & Shepherd 2005, Shaywitz 2003). The uneven peaks and valleys of both cognitive and academic functioning contribute to the clinical picture of dyslexia: a weakness in phonologically based skills in the context of often-stronger cognitive and academic skills in nonreading-related areas.

As children mature, compensation often occurs that results in relatively accurate, but not fluent, reading. Awareness of this developmental pattern is critically important for the diagnosis in older children, young adults, and beyond. The consequence is that such dyslexic older children may appear to perform reasonably well on a test of word reading or decoding; on these tests, credit is given irrespective of how long it takes the individual to respond or if initial errors in reading are later corrected. Accordingly, tests of reading fluency—how quickly and accurately individual words and passages are read—and tests assessing reading rate are keystones of an assessment for, and an accurate diagnosis of, dyslexia.

Teaching Reading to Dyslexic Students

Within the past decade, an evidence-based approach to teaching children (including dyslexic children) to read has emerged. Much of the evidence base was synthesized by the National Reading Panel established by the U.S. Congress in 1998 with a mandate to review existing research on teaching children to read and then to present the data

in a Report to Congress. The panel worked for two years reviewing the extant data on teaching children to read published in peer-reviewed journals, performing meta-analyses where the data allowed, and reporting to Congress on its findings in April 2000. As a result of its exhaustive review, the panel found that five essential elements should be incorporated into effective reading instruction—phonemic awareness, phonics, fluency, vocabulary, and comprehension (Rep. Natl. Reading Panel 2000)—and that these are optimally taught systemically and explicitly. These empirically rooted findings converge with what we know about why print has meaning. As noted above, a core deficit in phonological processing is observed in a majority of children and adults with developmental dyslexia (Liberman & Shankweiler 1991). Thus, it is not surprising that a majority of the many recent well-controlled research studies have focused on preventing or remediating these core phonological deficits.

Early Intervention

Probably the most hopeful research has been early intervention studies of children at-risk for dyslexia based on their problems with phonological processing or initial word-identification skills (Lonigan 2003) in kindergarten or the first grade. Both classroom-level interventions (Adams & Carnine 2003, Foorman et al. 1998, Fuchs & Fuchs 2005) and pullout remedial approaches (Blachman 1997, D'Agostino & Murphy 2004, Torgesen et al. 1999, Vellutino et al. 2006) and combinations of classroom and pullout approaches (O'Connor 2000, Simmons et al. 2003, Vaughn et al. 2003) have reported positive results. Although definitions of reading-disabled or dyslexic subjects in these studies varied, on average, large effects sizes (>0.70) were reported. Together, these studies suggest that prevention programs that explicitly focus on phonemic awareness, phonics, and meaning of text in the earliest grades of reading instruction reduce the base rates of at-risk students to below 5%. Although one cannot explicitly define such children as having dyslexia because they are typically just learning to read, and it is difficult to define a word-reading deficit at this level of reading development, it appears that these systematic programs can significantly improve core reading skills in the weakest readers at these ages.

Interventions for Older Students

For older students the remedial research literature includes a range of intervention programs, including those described as direct instruction and those that are more strategy based (Swanson et al. 1999). Here, the evidence is less encouraging than for younger children. Investigations using remedial interventions that begin after the second grade indicate it is more challenging to bring children or adults up to expected grade levels once they fall behind, although significant improvements in reading can still occur (effect sizes >0.60). As an example, Lovett et al. (2000) combined a program referred to as an explicit, scripted direct-instruction approach (based on Reading Mastery; Engelmann & Bruner 1988) that focused on phonological analysis and blending of phonemes with a strategy-based program (an expanded and adapted version of the Benchmark program; Gaskins et al. 1986) that focused on teaching children metacognitive strategies to assist in word identification. This combined program, and adaptations of it for different grade levels, have been evaluated with severe dyslexic students in both elementary and middle school in randomized experimental designs with control groups. Results of implementation of such combination programs indicated that this approach resulted in significantly better standardized reading measure outcomes than the individual components alone or other contrast programs (Lovett et al. 2003).

In an intensive eight-week evaluation of two different phonologically based programs, Torgesen et al. (2001) focused on older elementary students with word-reading abilities below the fifth percentile. The investigators showed that these explicit programs resulted in significant improvements in reading on standardized reading measures following the interventions, and many of the students tested in the average range on word identification measures (but not fluency measures). More importantly, the gains made in word identification lasted for more than two years post intervention.

These and many other studies (for more comprehensive reviews, see Fletcher et al. 2007; Shaywitz 2003; Swanson et al. 1999, 2003) have provided the evidence that phonologically based decoding and word recognition skills are "teachable aspects of reading for most children" (Moats & Foorman 1997, p. 188). This corpus of evidence indicates that focused, intense, systematic, and explicit interventions can positively impact word-reading development, with some expected transfer impacting comprehension, in even the most severely disabled dyslexic readers and that many different types of remediation programs can be effective. This is an important finding, for there is often a tendency to search for the one (magical) program that will address all struggling readers' difficulties. Current knowledge supports several types of intervention programs as effective. Evidence is not yet available that would allow the selection of one specific program over others or to support the choice of an individual program that would be specifically more beneficial to particular groups of dyslexic readers.

Beyond Word Accuracy

Fluency. The consistent improvement in phonologically based word attack and decoding skills has not always generalized to accurate, fluent text reading or adequate reading comprehension, the ultimate goal of all reading interventions (Lovett et al. 1989, Torgesen et al. 1997). Moats & Foorman (1997) review this problem and state, "generalization and transfer of decoding proficiency to fluent word recognition and better reading

Scaffolding: a teaching strategy where the teacher provides scaffolds (supports) that facilitate the child's ability. For example, the teacher reads a passage slightly more difficult than the child is able to read by him/herself. The child then reads the same passage repeatedly and gradually learns to read this previously difficult section with facility

comprehension was not automatic..." (p. 188), a conclusion that has continued to be echoed by other studies and reviews (Lyon & Moats 1997, Rayner et al. 2001, Rep. Natl. Reading Panel 2000, Snow 2002, Torgesen et al. 1997).

These results and questions have more recently raised significant interest in whether fluency deficits can be treated in reading-disabled and dyslexic subjects and whether such interventions (see Kuhn & Stahl 2003, Rep. Natl. Reading Panel 2000 for more comprehensive reviews) should be focused on connected-text or word-level strategies. Meyer & Felton (1999) found that most fluency programs use repeated reading of connected text, although some newer programs focus on broader developmental models of fluency encompassing both building semantic knowledge and orthographic pattern awareness (Wolf et al. 2000).

As examples of the repeated reading approaches, Stahl & Heuback (2005) and Young and associates (1996) reported significant gains in their poor readers' text reading fluency using connected text methods, whereas Levy and associates (1997) and Tan & Nicholson (1997) focused their interventions at the word level and showed similar but less robust gains in connected text fluency. A key aspect of most fluency-focused intervention programs with dyslexic students is that they require significant reading of connected text with scaffolding support by either peers or teachers. The conceptual framework behind these approaches is that as word identification becomes more automatic, due to increasing orthographic awareness via practice, an improving reader requires less strategic attention on the act of reading as it becomes automatic and can direct more cognitive energy and focus on comprehension of meaning. Kuhn & Stahl's (2003) review of fluency-oriented instructional approaches found that repeated reading of text with scaffolding typically produces gains in fluency and reading-related skills similar to reading the equivalent amounts of nonrepetitive text (average

effect sizes 0.35–0.50). This finding suggests that it's the amount of reading that is critical in supporting the development of fluent and automatic reading. Chard and associates' (2002) review of studies specific to students with dyslexia found slightly higher average effect sizes (0.50–0.70) for a range of intervention approaches focused on fluency.

Reading comprehension. Although children and adults with dyslexia are defined by their word identification and decoding problems, some may also have reading comprehension difficulties that are not due to an underlying oral language disorder. Because of this, some researchers have focused on intervention programs aimed at reading comprehension abilities. Most remedial approaches have developed comprehension-related strategy instruction or specific comprehension-related skill instructional types of programs. Strategy-related programs have focused on developing critical thinking skills related to understanding of text and constructing its meaning based on the reader's prior knowledge, prediction of text, monitoring of text structure, and question asking, as examples. Skill-related programs focus more on finding ideas and facts, developing multiple meaning of words and increasing vocabulary, and summarizing text.

Several reviews (Jenkins & O'Connor 2003, Swanson et al. 1999, Vaughn & Klingner 2004) suggest that various types of comprehension-focused intervention studies in reading-disabled children and adults, particularly those using explicit, strategy-focused approaches, were effective. Unfortunately, because of the wide range of methodologies used in these studies and the variety of programmatic approaches, the resulting range of effect sizes seen in comprehension-focused intervention studies of dyslexic students is typically broad (0.20–0.70). It appears that many of these studies support the efficacy of the comprehension-focused remediation programs' ability to teach their specific strategies, but the ability of students to apply those strategies in new text reading and comprehension situations is less consistent.

Treatment Resisters

In their focus on treatment resisters, Torgesen & Mathes (2000) highlighted a key set of findings across all intervention studies: A number of children and adults do not respond to programs that are shown to be effective in their peers. Such results highlight the heterogeneity of the dyslexia population, but also suggest that no one explicit remedial instructional program, whether focused at the level of word identification, fluency, or comprehension, or any combination of these processes, will be able to successfully address the needs of all such readers. The kinds of issues raised by such consistent findings of treatment-resisters across different interventions focus on contextual or procedural factors rather than content itself. Questions include how best to understand the role of (*a*) instructional intensity (length of intervention, hours of instruction, optimal ratios of teachers to students, reading time, etc.); (*b*) program integrity/fidelity; (*c*) teacher ability/experience; (*d*) program focus/explicitness/multidimensionality; and (*e*) individual student prior instructional experiences/exposure and reading abilities. The ways in which these factors, individually and together, affect treatment outcomes is just beginning to be addressed, particularly for treatment resisters. The answers to these unresolved questions will provide critical information to better understand the ways in which effective instructional programs may affect any specific student with dyslexia.

Response to Intervention

It has become increasingly apparent that several causes exist for students' deficiencies in reading. Such students may be instructional casualties resulting from poor, inappropriate, or noneffective reading instruction. On the other hand, some reading-deficient students have received quality reading instruction but still have not mastered reading due to their underlying individual core phonological and linguistic deficits. In addition, some students have experienced both factors. Such problems are not easily addressed via one-time evaluations or interventions without some developmental perspective and sequential evaluations over time.

The thrust of RTI frameworks (Fuchs & Fuchs 2006) is to address these traditional limitations in the treatment of persons with dyslexia by focusing on change over time. A typical model would screen all students on core academic abilities—in this case reading—and identify those at risk using somewhat liberal criteria (resulting in more false positives). These students are then followed using frequently repeated reading-focused evaluation probes during an academic year (or years) while they are receiving systematic reading instruction. Those students who do not make adequate progress compared with their typically developing peers (comparing the amount of change over a given time period) are then provided with increasingly intense and, as needed, alternative approaches to reading interventions and continue to be monitored over time. Students who receive the best available quality instruction and who do not respond to these increasingly explicit, intense, and alternative approaches over time would then be classified as dyslexic or learning disabled (Presid. Commiss. Excell. Spec. Educ. 2002). Clearly, such multitiered models still depend on measures sensitive to change, definitions of adequate change, validated interventions of increasing intensity, instructional integrity, and a systematic approach at the school/teacher level to ensure that all students are monitored. McMaster and colleagues (2005) have provided one of the better examples of this approach to children across 33 classrooms. Less than 5% of those children who, via the ongoing weekly monitoring of reading, received increasingly intense and ultimately one-on-one instruction were still considered not to have made adequate progress in reading, compared with nearly 15% of the control classrooms using standard reading instruction and practices. The use of RTI models is expected to be a rapidly growing trend in the school identification of reading difficulties.

Summary of Interventions

Explicit, intense, systematic, and developmentally appropriate interventions are effective and provide an evidence-based approach in treating dyslexia. Interventions focused at word decoding and single-word identification levels have had the most consistent evidence and have been shown to be the most effective, particularly in prevention and early childhood studies. Fluency- and comprehension-focused interventions have had less investigation but have still shown significant, albeit more variable, effects on reading outcomes in these students. Programs that systematically integrate multiple-focused interventions are considered the most effective, although their specific sequencing, degree of overlap, and level of focus on each component during each phase are still open to critical investigation. At this point, determining which instructional program works best is not necessarily important, but rather determining what program works best for what kind of dyslexic student with what kind of characteristics in what kind of implementation.

Overall, significant progress has been made in understanding the cognitive basis of dyslexia and in using this knowledge to inform instructional practices. At the same time, it must be kept in mind that we are only in the early stages of discovering and developing specific reading interventions that will consistently improve all components of reading, including accuracy, fluency, and comprehension. Broad-stroke gains have been made in developing an overall template for providing reading interventions to dyslexic students; however, we await evidence to guide the more fine-grained selection of specific interventions for individual struggling readers at all ages and at all levels of reading ability.

Accommodations

A complete education for a dyslexic student includes evidence-based reading interventions and accommodations. As noted above, intervention data, although promising, have yet to indicate that the gap has been closed in the ability of dyslexic students to read words fluently beyond the first few grades. Accordingly, although dyslexic children will improve their accuracy, deficient fluency continues to be a concern at all grade levels, and increasingly so as children move up into middle and high school and then into postsecondary education.

Accommodations are of three general types: (*a*) those that by-pass the reading difficulty by providing information through an auditory mode, (*b*) those that provide compensatory assistive technologies, and (*c*) those that provide additional time so that the dysfluent reader can demonstrate his/her knowledge.

First, beginning quite early in their schooling, dyslexic readers require alternative modes of acquiring information so that their vocabulary and fund of knowledge better reflect their intellectual level than does their impaired reading ability. Access to recorded materials, whether they are based on the school curriculum or reflect what peers are reading for pleasure, are a necessity for such children if they are to keep up with their classmates and with their own intellectual curiosity and interests. Next, assistive technology, computers, and both print-to-speech as well as speech-to-print software provide further compensation for oft-noted difficulties with handwriting, spelling, and lack of fluency. A major advance has been the convergence of behavioral and neuroimaging data providing evidence for the critical need for extra time on examinations for dyslexic students, particularly as they progress toward high school graduation and beyond. Behavioral data indicating the persistence of dysfluent reading are now supported by neurobiological data demonstrating that the left anterior lateral occipito-temporal (word-form) region responsible for fluent, rapid reading is disrupted in dyslexic children and adults (Dehaene et al. 2005; Shaywitz et al. 1998, 2003). As the neurobiological data indicate, dyslexic readers develop compensatory neural pathways, and these systems support increased accuracy over time. However, the word-form region does not develop (Shaywitz et al. 2007), and compensatory pathways do not provide fluent or automatic reading. Accordingly, if such students are to demonstrate the full range of their knowledge, provision of additional time on examinations is a necessity to compensate for the lack of availability of the efficient word-form area. Currently, no quantitative data are available to serve as a reliable metric for gauging the specific amount of extra time needed by a student, and this determination is best guided by the student's own experience over the years. Because the persistence of the reading difficulty is indicated by both behavioral and imaging longitudinal data, requiring that students in postsecondary settings be tested every three or five years is not consistent with scientific knowledge. Furthermore, it is extremely expensive and even problematic. As students progress through school to higher grades and compensate in reading accuracy, simple reading measures of word identification fail to capture difficulties in fluent reading and so are often misleading. In addition, since such nonautomatic readers must call upon attentional resources during reading, these students are highly susceptible to noise and other distractions. Study and test taking in quiet, separate rooms allow these dysfluent readers to concentrate and make maximum use of their often strained attentional resources.

In summary, given that dyslexia represents a disparity between an individual's reading and intellectual abilities; accommodations are critical to assure fairness and equity. Contemporary management of dyslexia provides evidence-based accommodations; these include access to recorded materials; computers and print-to-speech software; and additional time on examinations, with the amount of time determined by the student's experience (Shaywitz 2003). Such accommodations are provided based on a student's history, observations of his/her reading aloud, and test results. With the provision of such accommodations, dyslexic students are entering and succeeding in a range of professions, including journalism, literary writing, science, medicine, law, and education (Shaywitz 2003).

SUMMARY POINTS

1. The core concept of dyslexia as an unexpected difficulty in reading has remained invariant over the century since its first description; dyslexia is found in all languages including both alphabetic and logographic scripts.

2. A deficit in phonological processing, accessing the individual sounds of spoken words, represents the core weakness in dyslexia, and its remediation is the focus of early intervention programs for at-risk and struggling readers.

3. Dyslexia is a chronic, persistent difficulty and is neither a developmental lag nor outgrown; the implication is that reading problems must be recognized and addressed early.

4. Evidence-based interventions are now available and have positive effects on reading. The most consistent and largest effect sizes are associated with provision of prevention programs explicitly focused on phonological awareness, phonics, and meaning of text.

5. Intervention programs for children beyond second grade, though effective, are challenging and have produced less-consistent results. Such evidence-based programs focus on systematic, phonologically based instruction and teaching metacognitive

strategies to assist in word identification. No single program is the most effective; many types of remediation programs can be effective.

6. Fluency deficits have proven much more difficult to remediate than word accuracy problems. Many children who respond to programs aimed at improving word identification skills remain dysfluent, slow readers. Approaches that focus on repeated oral reading with feedback and guidance have shown the most consistent positive results. For readers who are not fluent and cannot read individual words automatically, reading remains effortful and slow.

7. Neurobiological studies have revealed differences in the neural circuitry for reading between nonimpaired and dyslexic readers and identified a neural signature for dyslexia. Brain imaging has also indicated a target (the left occipito-temporal word form area) for intervention for skilled or fluent reading and that these systems are malleable and respond to effective reading interventions. Such findings demonstrate the importance and powerful impact of effective reading instruction.

8. Interventions, while promising, have yet to close the gap in the ability of dyslexic children to read fluently; dyslexic children often remain accurate but slow readers. Neurobiological evidence indicates that the failure of the word form area to function properly in dyslexic children and young adults is responsible for their characteristic inefficient, slow reading. Accommodations, particularly the provision of extra time, are essential for dyslexic students to fully demonstrate their knowledge.

FUTURE ISSUES

1. To identify which specific instructional components/programs work best for which specific types of dyslexic students and under what kinds of implementation practices.

2. To identify which specific instructional elements in which specific combination improve fluency and reading comprehension, particularly in older students.

3. To identify the role of attentional difficulties in dyslexic readers.

4. To determine effective methods of identifying at-risk children earlier and more accurately.

5. To determine mechanisms by which the phonology and orthography are integrated in the word form region and how this process could be facilitated.

ACKNOWLEDGMENTS

The work described in this article was supported by grants from the National Institute of Child Health and Human Development (P50 HD25802, RO1 HD046171, and R01 HD057655) to Sally Shaywitz and Bennett Shaywitz.

LITERATURE CITED

Abler W. 1989. On the particulate principle of self-diversifying systems. *J. Soc. Biol. Struct.* 12:1–13

Adams G, Carnine D. 2003. Direct instruction. In *Handbook of Learning Disabilities*, ed. H Swanson, K Harris, S Graham, pp. 403–16. New York: Guilford

Anderson A, Gore J. 1997. The physical basis of neuroimaging techniques. In *Child and Adolescent Psychiatric Clinics of North America*, ed. M Lewis, B Peterson, pp. 213–64. Philadelphia, PA: Saunders

Anthony J, Lonigan C, Driscoll K, Phillips B, Burgess S. 2003. Phonological sensitivity: a quasi-parallel progression of word structure units and cognitive operations. *Read. Res. Q.* 38:470–87

Aylward E, Richards T, Berninger V, Nagy W, Field K, et al. 2003. Instructional treatment associated with changes in brain activation in children with dyslexia. *Neurology* 61:212–19

Benson DF. 1994. *The Neurology of Thinking*. New York: Oxford Univ. Press

Biederman J, Faraone S, Milberger S, Curtis S, Chen L, et al. 1996. Predictors of persistence and remission of ADHD into adolescence: results from a four-year prospective follow-up study. *J. Am. Acad. Child Adolesc. Psychiatry* 35:343–51

Blachman B. 1997. *Early Intervention and Phonological Awareness: A Cautionary Tale*. Mahwah, NJ: Erlbaum

Bloomfield L. 1933. *Language*. New York: Spansuls, Rinehart, & Winston

Bradley L, Bryant PE. 1983. Categorizing sounds and learning to read—a causal connection. *Nature* 301:419–21

Bruck M. 1998. Outcomes of adults with childhood histories of dyslexia. In *Cognitive and Linguistic Bases of Reading, Writing, and Spelling*, ed. C Hulme, R Joshi, pp. 179–200. Mahwah, NJ: Erlbaum

Bruck M, Treiman R. 1992. Learning to pronounce words: the limitations of analogies. *Read. Res. Q.* 27:375–88

Brunswick N, McCrory E, Price CJ, Frith CD, Frith U. 1999. Explicit and implicit processing of words and pseudowords by adult developmental dyslexics: a search for Wernicke's Wortschatz. *Brain* 122:1901–17

Byrne B, Fielding-Barnsley R. 1995. Evaluation of a program to teach phonemic awareness to young children: a 2- and 3-year follow-up, and a new preschool trial. *J. Educ. Psychol.* 87:488–503

Byrne B, Fielding-Barnsley R, Ashley L. 2000. Effects of preschool phoneme identity training after six years: outcome level distinguished from rate of response. *J. Educ. Psychol.* 92:659–67

Caravolas M. 2005. *The Nature and Causes of Dyslexia in Different Languages*. Cambridge, MA: Blackwell

Chard D, Vaughn S, Tyler B. 2002. A synthesis of research on effective interventions for building reading fluency with elementary students with learning disabilities. *J. Learn. Disabil.* 35:386–406

Corina D, Richards T, Serafini S, Richards A, Steury K, et al. 2001. fMRI auditory language differences between dyslexic and able reading children. *NeuroReport* 12:1195–201

Critchley M. 1970. *The Dyslexic Child*. Springfield, IL: Thomas

D'Agostino J, Murphy J. 2004. A meta-analysis of reading recovery in United States schools. *Educ. Eval. Policy Anal.* 26:23–28

Dehaene S, Cohen L, Sigman M, Vinckier F. 2005. The neural code for written words: a proposal. *Trends Cogn. Sci.* 9:335–41

Eden G, Jones K, Cappell K, Gareau L, Wood F, et al. 2004. Neural changes following remediation in adult developmental dyslexia. *Neuron* 44:411–22

Engelmann S, Bruner E. 1988. *Reading Mastery I/II Fast Cycle: Teacher's Guide*. Chicago: Sci. Res. Assoc.

Ferrer E, McArdle J, Shaywitz B, Holahan J, Marchione K, Shaywitz S. 2007. Longitudinal models of developmental dynamics between reading and cognition from childhood to adolescence. *Dev. Psychol.* In press

Fiez JA, Peterson SE. 1998. Neuroimaging studies of word reading. *Proc. Natl. Acad. Sci. USA* 95:914–21

Fisher S, DeFries J. 2002. Developmental dyslexia: genetic dissection of a complex cognitive trait. *Nat. Rev. Neurosci.* 3:767–80

Fletcher J, Foorman B, Shaywitz S, Shaywitz B. 1999. *Conceptual and Methodological Issues in Dyslexia Research: A Lesson for Developmental Disorders.* Cambridge, MA: MIT Press

Fletcher J, Lyon G, Fuchs L, Barnes M. 2007. *Learning Disabilities: From Identification to Intervention.* New York: Guilford

Fletcher J, Shaywitz S, Shankweiler D, Katz L, Liberman I, et al. 1994. Cognitive profiles of reading disability: comparisons of discrepancy and low achievement definitions. *J. Educ. Psychol.* 86:6–23

Flynn J, Rahbar M. 1994. Prevalence of reading failure in boys compared with girls. *Psychol. Sch.* 31:66–71

Fodor JA. 1983. *The Modularity of Mind.* Cambridge, MA: MIT Press

Foorman B, Francis D, Fletcher J, Schatschneider C, Mehta P. 1998. The role of instruction in learning to read: preventing reading failure in at-risk children. *J. Educ. Psychol.* 90:37–55

Frackowiak R, Friston K, Frith C, Dolan R, Price C, et al. 2004. *Human Brain Function.* San Diego, CA: Academic/Elsevier Sci.

Francis D, Shaywitz S, Stuebing K, Shaywitz B, Fletcher J. 1994. *The Measurement of Change: Assessing Behavior Over Time and Within a Developmental Context.* Baltimore, MD: Brookes

Francis D, Shaywitz S, Steubing K, Shaywitz B, Fletcher J. 1996. Developmental lag vs. deficit models of reading disability: a longitudinal, individual growth curves analysis. *J. Educ. Psychol.* 88:3–17

Fuchs D, Fuchs L. 2005. Peer-assisted learning strategies: promoting word recognition, fluency and reading comprehension in young children. *J. Spec. Educ.* 39:34–44

Fuchs D, Fuchs L. 2006. Introduction to response to intervention: What, why and how valid is it? *Read. Res. Q.* 41:93–99

Gaskins I, Downer M, Gaskins R. 1986. *Introduction to the Benchmark School Word Identification/Vocabulary Development Program.* Media, PA: Benchmark Sch.

Georgiewa P, Rzanny R, Gaser C, Gerhard UJ, Vieweg U, et al. 2002. Phonological processing in dyslexic children: a study combining functional imaging and event related potentials. *Neurosci. Lett.* 318:5–8

Goswami U, Bryant P. 1990. *Phonological Skills and Learning to Read.* Hillsdale, NJ: Erlbaum

Goulandris N, ed. 2003. *Dyslexia in Different Languages: Cross-Linguistic Comparisons.* London: Whurr

Grigg W, Donahue P, Dion G. 2007. *The Nation's Report Card: 12th-Grade Reading and Mathematics 2005.* Natl. Cent. Educ. Stat., U.S. Dept. Educ. Washington, DC: U.S. Govt. Print. Off.

Hatcher P, Hulme C, Ellis A. 1994. Ameliorating early reading failure by integrating the teaching of reading and phonological skills: the phonological linkage hypothesis. *Child Dev.* 65:41–57

Helenius P, Tarkiainen A, Cornelissen P, Hansen PC, Salmelin R. 1999. Dissociation of normal feature analysis and deficient processing of letter-strings in dyslexic adults. *Cereb. Cortex* 4:476–83

Hoien T, Lundberg I, Stanovich K, Bjaalid I. 1995. Components of phonological awareness. *Read. Writing* 7:171–88

Horwitz B, Rumsey JM, Donohue BC. 1998. Functional connectivity of the angular gyrus in normal reading and dyslexia. *Proc. Natl. Acad. Sci. USA* 95:8939–44

Hulme C, Snowling M, Caravolas M, Carroll J. 2005. Phonological skills are (probably) one cause of success in learning to read: a comment on Castles and Coltheart. *Sci. Stud. Read.* 9:351–65

Jenkins J, O'Connor R. 2003. Cooperative learning for students with learning disabilities: evidence from experiments, observations, and interviews. In *Handbook of Learning Disabilities*, ed. H Swanson, K Harris, S Graham, pp. 417–30. New York: Guilford

Jezzard P, Matthews P, Smith S. 2001. *Functional MRI: An Introduction to Methods*. Oxford, UK: Oxford Univ. Press

Jorm A, Share D, Matthews M, Matthews R. 1986. Cognitive factors at school entry predictive of specific reading retardation and general reading backwardness: a research note. *J. Child Psychol.* 27:45–54

Kame'enui E, Simmons D, Good R, Harn B. 2000. *The Use of Fluency-Based Measures in Early Identification and Evaluation of Intervention Efficacy in Schools*. Parkton, MD: York

Katzir T, Youngsuk K, Wolf M, O'Brien B, Kennedy B, et al. 2006. Reading fluency: The whole is more than the parts. *Ann. Dyslexia* 56:51–82

Kirk S. 1963. *Behavioral Diagnosis and Remediation of Learning Disabilities*. Evanston, IL: Fund Percept. Handicapped Child

Kuhn M, Stahl S. 2003. Fluency: a review of developmental and remedial practices. *J. Educ. Psychol.* 95:3–21

Lawler A. 2001. Archaeology. Writing gets a rewrite. *Science* 292:2418–20

Lefly DL, Pennington BF. 1991. Spelling errors and reading fluency in compensated adult dyslexics. *Ann. Dyslexia* 41:143–62

Lerner J. 1989. Educational interventions in learning disabilities. *J. Am. Acad. Child Adolesc. Psychiatry* 28:326–31

Levy B, Abello B, Lysynchuk L. 1997. Transfer from word training to reading in context: gains in reading fluency and comprehension. *Learn. Disabil. Q.* 20:173–88

Liberman A, Cooper F, Shankweiler D, Studdert-Kennedy M. 1967. Perception of the speech code. *Psychol. Rev.* 74:431–61

Liberman I, Shankweiler D. 1991. *Phonology and Beginning Reading: A Tutorial*. Hillsdale, NJ: Erlbaum

Liberman IY, Shankweiler D, Fischer F, Carter B. 1974. Explicit syllable and phoneme segmentation in the young child. *Exp. Child Psychol.* 18:201–12

Lonigan C. 2003. *Development and Promotion of Emergent Literacy Skills in Children at Risk of Reading Difficulties*. Baltimore, MD: York

Lovett M, Barron, Benson N. 2003. *Effective Remediation of Word Identification and Decoding Difficulties in School-Age Children with Reading Disabilities*. New York: Guilford

Lovett M, Lacerenza L, Borden S, Frijters J, Steinback K, Palma M. 2000. Components of effective remediation for developmental reading disabilities: combining phonological and strategy-based instruction to improve outcomes. *J. Educ. Psychol.* 92:263–83

Lovett M, Ransby M, Hardwick N, Johns M, Donaldson S. 1989. Can dyslexia be treated? Treatment-specific and generalized treatment effects in dyslexic children's response to remediation. *Brain Lang.* 37:90–121

Lyon G. 1995. Toward a definition of dyslexia. *Ann. Dyslexia* 45:3–27

Lyon G, Fletcher J, Shaywitz S, Shaywitz B, Torgesen J, et al. 2001. *Rethinking learning disabilities*. Washington, DC: Fordham Found. Progress. Policy Inst.

Lyon G, Moats L. 1997. Critical conceptual and methodological considerations in reading intervention research. *J. Learn. Disabil.* 30:578–88

Lyon G, Shaywitz S, Shaywitz B. 2003. A definition of dyslexia. *Ann. Dyslexia* 53:1–14

Marzola E, Shepherd M. 2005. Assessment of reading difficulties. In *Multisensory Teaching of Basic Language Skills*, ed. JR Birsh, pp. 171–85. Baltimore, MD: Brookes

McMaster K, Fuchs D, Fuchs L, Compton D. 2005. Responding to nonresponders: an experimental field trial of identification and intervention methods. *Except. Child.* 71:445–63

Meng H, Smith S, Hager K, Held M, Liu J, et al. 2005. DCDC2 is associated with reading disability and modulates neuronal development in the brain. *Proc. Natl. Acad. Sci. USA* 102:17053–58

Meyer M, Felton R. 1999. Repeated reading to enhance fluency: old approaches and new direction. *Ann. Dyslexia* 49:283–306

Moats L, Foorman B. 1997. Introduction to special issue of *SSR*: components of effective reading instruction. *Sci. Stud. Read.* 1:187–89

Morais J, Cary L, Alegria J, Bertelson P. 1979. Does awareness of speech as a sequence of phones arise spontaneously? *Cognition* 7:323–31

Morgan WP. 1896. A case of congenital word blindness. *Br. Med. J.*, p. 1378

Morris R, Stuebing K, Fletcher J, Shaywitz S, Lyon G, et al. 1998. Subtypes of reading disability: coherent variability around a phonological core. *J. Educ. Psychol.* 90:347–73

Nakamura K, Dehaene S, Jobert A, Le Bihan D, Kouider S. 2005. Subliminal convergence of kanji and kana words: further evidence for functional parcellation of the posterior temporal cortex in visual word perception. *J. Cogn. Neurosci.* 17:954–68

O'Connor R. 2000. Increasing the intensity of intervention in kindergarten and first grade. *Learn. Disabil. Res. Pract.* 15:43–54

Olson R, Byrne B. 2005. Genetic and environmental influences on reading and language ability and disability. In *The Connections Between Language and Reading Disability*, ed. H Catts, A Kamhi, pp. 173–200. Hillsdale, NJ: Erlbaum

Olson R, Datta H, Gayan J, DeFries J. 1999. *A Behavioral-Genetic Analysis of Reading Disabilities and Component Processes*. Cambridge, MA: MIT Press

Paulesu E, Demonet J-F, Fazio F, McCrory E, Chanoine V, et al. 2001. Dyslexia-cultural diversity and biological unity. *Science* 291:2165–67

Paulesu E, Frith U, Snowling M, Gallagher A, Morton J, et al. 1996. Is developmental dyslexia a disconnection syndrome? Evidence from PET scanning. *Brain* 119:143–57

Pennington B, Gilger J. 1996. *How Is Dyslexia Transmitted?* Baltimore, MD: York

Pennington B, Grossier D, Welsh M. 1993. Contrasting cognitive deficits in attention deficit hyperactivity disorder vs. reading disability. *Dev. Psychol.* 29:511–23

Perie M, Grigg W, Donahue P. 2005. *National Assessment of Educational Progress: The Nation's Report Card, Reading 2005*. U.S. Dept. Educ. Inst. Educ. Sci., Washington, DC: U.S. Gov. Print. Off.

Presid. Commiss. Excell. Spec. Educ. 2002. *A New Era: Revitalizing Special Education for Children and Their Families*. U.S. Dept. Educ. Inst. Educ. Sci., Washington, DC: U.S. Gov. Print. Off.

Ramus F, Rosen S, Dakin S, Day B, Castellote J, et al. 2003. Theories of developmental dyslexia: Insights from a multiple case study of dyslexic adults. *Brain* 126:841–65

Rayner K, Foorman B, Perfetti C, Pesetsky D, Seidenberg M. 2001. How psychological science informs the teaching of reading. *Psychol. Sci. Public Int.* 2:31–74

Rep. Natl. Reading Panel. 2000. *Teaching Children to Read: An Evidence-Based Assessment of the Scientific Research Literature on Reading and Its Implications for Reading Instruction*: U.S. Dept. Health Human Serv., Public Health Serv., Natl. Inst. Health, Natl. Inst. Child Health Human Dev., Washington, DC

Reynolds C. 1984. Critical measurement issues in learning disabilities. *J. Spec. Educ.* 18:451–76

Richards T, Corina D, Serafini S, Steury K, Echeland D, et al. 2000. Effects of a phonologically driven treatment for dyslexia on lactate levels measured by proton MRI spectroscopic imaging. *Am. J. Neuroradiol.* 21:916–22

Rodgers B. 1983. The identification and prevalence of specific reading retardation. *Br. J. Educ. Psychol.* 53:369–73

Rumsey JM, Andreason P, Zametkin AJ, Aquino T, King C, et al. 1992. Failure to activate the left temporoparietal cortex in dyslexia. *Arch. Neurol.* 49:527–34

Rumsey JM, Nace K, Donohue B, Wise D, Maisog JM, Andreason P. 1997. A positron emission tomographic study of impaired word recognition and phonological processing in dyslexic men. *Arch. Neurol.* 54:562–73

Rutter M, Yule W. 1975. The concept of specific reading retardation. *J. Child Psychol. Psychiatry* 16:181–97

Salmelin R, Service E, Kiesila P, Uutela K, Salonen O. 1996. Impaired visual word processing in dyslexia revealed with magnetoencephalography. *Ann. Neurol.* 40:157–62

Schneider W, Kispert P, Roth E, Vise M, Marx H. 1997. Short- and long-term effects of training phonological awareness in kindergarten: evidence from two German studies. *J. Educ. Psychol.* 92:284–95

Schumacher J, Anthoni H, Dahdou F, Konig I, Hillmer A, et al. 2006. Strong genetic evidence of DCDC2 as a susceptibility gene for dyslexia. *Am. J. Hum. Genet.* 78:52–62

Seki A, Koeda T, Sugihara S, Kamba M, Hirata Y, et al. 2001. A functional magnetic resonance imaging study during reading in Japanese dyslexic children. *Brain Dev.* 23:312–16

Shaywitz B, Fletcher J, Holahan J, Shaywitz S. 1992a. Discrepancy compared to low achievement definitions of reading disability: results from the Connecticut Longitudinal Study. *J. Learn. Disabil.* 25:639–48

Shaywitz B, Holford T, Holahan J, Fletcher J, Stuebing K, et al. 1995. A Matthew effect for IQ but not for reading: results from a longitudinal study. *Read. Res. Q.* 30:894–906

Shaywitz B, Shaywitz S, Blachman B, Pugh K, Fulbright R, et al. 2004. Development of left occipito-temporal systems for skilled reading in children after a phonologically-based intervention. *Biol. Psychiatry* 55:926–33

Shaywitz B, Shaywitz S, Pugh K, Mencl W, Fulbright R, et al. 2002. Disruption of posterior brain systems for reading in children with developmental dyslexia. *Biol. Psychiatry* 52:101–10

Shaywitz B, Skudlarski P, Holahan J, Marchione K, Constable R, et al. 2007. Age-related changes in reading systems of dyslexic children. *Ann. Neurol.* 61:363–70

Shaywitz S. 1998. Current concepts: dyslexia. *N. Eng. J. Med.* 338:307–12

Shaywitz S. 2003. *Overcoming Dyslexia: A New and Complete Science-Based Program for Reading Problems at Any Level.* New York: Knopf

Shaywitz S, Escobar M, Shaywitz B, Fletcher J, Makuch R. 1992b. Evidence that dyslexia may represent the lower tail of a normal distribution of reading ability. *N. Engl. J. Med.* 326:145–50

Shaywitz S, Fletcher J, Holahan J, Shneider A, Marchione K, et al. 1999. Persistence of dyslexia: the Connecticut Longitudinal Study at adolescence. *Pediatrics.* 104:1351–59

Shaywitz S, Fletcher J, Shaywitz B. 1994. Issues in the definition and classification of attention deficit disorder. *Topics Lang. Disord.* 14:1–25

Shaywitz S, Shaywitz B, Fletcher J, Escobar M. 1990. Prevalence of reading disability in boys and girls: results of the Connecticut Longitudinal Study. *J. Am. Med. Assoc.* 264:998–1002

Shaywitz S, Shaywitz B, Fulbright R, Skudlarski P, Mencl W, et al. 2003. Neural systems for compensation and persistence: young adult outcome of childhood reading disability. *Biol. Psychiatry* 54:25–33

Shaywitz S, Shaywitz B, Pugh K, Fulbright R, Constable R, et al. 1998. Functional disruption in the organization of the brain for reading in dyslexia. *Proc. Natl. Acad. Sci. USA* 95:2636–41

Silva P, McGee R, Williams S. 1985. Some characteristics of 9-year-old boys with general reading backwardness or specific reading retardation. *J. Child Psychol. Psychiatry* 53:407–21

Simmons D, Kame'enui E, Stoolmiller M, Coyne M, Harn B. 2003. *Accelerating Growth and Maintaining Proficiency: A Two-Year Intervention Study of Kindergarten and First Grade Children At Risk for Reading Difficulties.* Baltimore, MD: York

Simos PG, Breier JI, Fletcher JM, Foorman BR, Bergman E, et al. 2000. Brain activation profiles in dyslexic children during nonword reading: a magnetic source imaging study. *Neurosci. Lett.* 290:61–65

Simos PG, Fletcher JM, Bergman E, Breier JI, Foorman BR, et al. 2002. Dyslexia-specific brain activation profile becomes normal following successful remedial training. *Neurology* 58:1203–13

Snow C. 2002. Reading for understanding: toward an R&D program in reading comprehension. In *Prepared for the Office of Education Research and Improvement Science and Technology Policy Institute.* Santa Monica, CA: RAND Read. Study Group, RAND Corp.

Snow C, Burns S, Griffin P, eds. 1998. *Preventing Reading Difficulties in Young Children.* Washington, DC: Natl. Acad. Press

Snowling M. 2000. *Dyslexia.* Oxford, UK: Blackwell

Stahl S, Heuback K. 2005. Fluency-oriented reading instruction. *J. Literacy Res.* 37:25–60

Stanovich K. 1988. Explaining the differences between the dyslexic and the garden-variety poor reader: the phonological core variable difference model. *J. Learn. Disabil.* 21:590–604

Stanovich K, Siegel L. 1994. Phenotypic performance profile of children with reading disabilities: a regression-based test of the phonological-core variable-difference model. *J. Educ. Psychol.* 86:24–53

Stevenson H, Stigler J, Lucker G, Lee S, Hsu C, Kitamura S. 1982. Reading disabilities: the case of Chinese, Japanese, and English. *Child Dev.* 53:1164–81

Stevenson J. 1988. Which aspects of reading disability show a "hump" in their distribution? *Appl. Cogn. Psychol.* 2:77–85

Stuebing K, Fletcher J, LeDoux J, Lyon GR, Shaywitz S, Shaywitz B. 2002. Validity of IQ-discrepancy classifications of reading disabilities: a meta-analysis. *Am. Educ. Res. J.* 39:469–518

Swanson H, Harris K, Graham S. 2003. *Handbook of Learning Disabilities.* New York: Guilford

Swanson H, Hoskyn M, Lee C. 1999. *Interventions for Students with Learning Disabilities: A Meta-Analysis of Treatment Outcomes.* New York: Guilford

Tan A, Nicholson T. 1997. Flashcards revisited: training poor readers to read words faster improves their comprehension of text. *J. Educ. Psychol.* 89:276–88

Temple E, Deutsch G, Poldrack R, Miller S, Tallal P, et al. 2003. Neural deficits in children with dyslexia ameliorated by behavioral remediation: evidence from fMRI. *Proc. Natl. Acad. Sci. USA* 100:2860–65

Temple E, Poldrack R, Protopapas A, Nagarajan S, Salz T, et al. 2000. Disruption of the neural response to rapid acoustic stimuli in dyslexia: evidence from functional MRI. *Proc. Natl. Acad. Sci. USA* 97:13907–12

Torgesen J, Alexander A, Wagner R, Rashotte C, Voeller K, Conway T. 2001. Intensive remedial instruction for children with severe reading disabilities: immediate and long-term outcomes from two instructional approaches. *J. Learn. Disabil.* 34:33–58

Torgesen J, Mathes P. 2000. *A Basic Guide to Understanding, Assessing and Teaching Phonological Awareness.* Austin, TX: Pro-Ed

Torgesen J, Myers D, Schirm A, Stuart E, Vartivarian S, et al. 2006. *National Assessment of Title I Interim Report to Congress: Volume II: Closing the Reading Gap, First Year Findings from a Randomized Trial of Four Reading Interventions for Striving Readers.* Washington, DC: U.S. Dept. Educ., Inst. Educ. Sci.

Torgesen J, Wagner R, Rashotte C. 1997. *Approaches to the Prevention and Remediation of Phonologically-Based Reading Disabilities.* Mahwah, NJ: Erlbaum

Torgesen J, Wagner R, Rashotte C, Rose E, Lindamood P, et al. 1999. Preventing reading failure in children with phonological processing difficulties: group and individual responses to instruction. *J. Educ. Psychol.* 81:579–93

U.S. Office Educ. 1977. Definition and criteria for defining students as learning disabled. In *Federal Register*, U.S. Office Educ., pp. 65–83. Washington, DC: U.S. GPO

van der Wissel A, Zegers F. 1985. Reading retardation revisited. *Br. J. Dev. Psychol.* 3:3–9

Vaughn S, Klingner J. 2004. Teaching reading comprehension to students with learning disabilities. In *Handbook of Language and Literacy: Development and Disorders*, ed. C Stone, E Silliman, B Ehren, KK Apel, pp. 541–55. New York: Guilford

Vaughn S, Linar-Thompson S, Hickman P. 2003. Response to treatment as a way of identifying students with learning disabilities. *Except. Child.* 69:391–409

Vellutino FR, Scanlon DM, Small S, Fanuele DP. 2006. Response to intervention as a vehicle for distinguishing between children with and without reading disabilities: evidence for the role of kindergarten and first-grade interventions. *J. Learn. Disabil.* 39:157–69

Wadsworth S, Olson R, Pennington B, DeFries J. 2000. Differential genetic etiology of reading disability as a function of IQ. *J. Learn. Disabil.* 33:192–99

Wagner R, Torgesen J. 1987. The nature of phonological processes and its causal role in the acquisition of reading skills. *Psychol. Bull.* 101:192–212

Wagner R, Torgesen J, Rashotte C. 1999. *CTOPP: Comprehensive Test of Phonological Processing.* Austin, TX: PRO-ED

Wise B, Ring J, Olson R. 1999. Training phonological awareness with and without attention to articulation. *J. Exp. Child Psychol.* 72:271–304

Wise B, Ring J, Olson R. 2000. Individual differences in gains from computer-assisted remedial reading. *J. Exp. Child Psychol.* 77:197–235

Wolf M, Miller L, Donnelly K. 2000. Retrieval, automaticity, vocabulary elaboration, orthography (RAVE-O): a comprehensive, fluency-based reading intervention program. *J. Learn. Disabil.* 33:375–86

Woodcock R, Johnson M. 1989. *Woodcock-Johnson Psycho-Educational Battery-Revised (WJ-R).* Allen, TX: Dev. Learn. Mater.

Young A, Bowers P, MacKinnon G. 1996. Effects of prosodic modeling and repeated reading on poor readers' fluency and comprehension. *Appl. Psycholing.* 17:59–84

Yule W, Rutter M. 1985. *Reading and Other Learning Difficulties.* Oxford, UK: Blackwell Sci.

Ziegler J, Goswami U. 2005. Reading acquisition, developmental dyslexia, and skilled reading across languages: a psycholinguistic grain size theory. *Psychol. Bull.* 131:3–29

Health Psychology: The Search for Pathways between Behavior and Health

Howard Leventhal,[1] John Weinman,[2]
Elaine A. Leventhal,[1] and L. Alison Phillips[1]

[1]Institute for Health, Health Care Policy and Aging Research, Rutgers, The State University of New Jersey, New Brunswick, New Jersey 08901-1293; [2]Health Psychology Section, Psychology Department, Institute of Psychiatry, King's College London, London SE1 9RT, United Kingdom; email: hleventhal@ifh.rutgers.edu

Annu. Rev. Psychol. 2008. 59:477–505

The *Annual Review of Psychology* is online at
http://psych.annualreviews.org

This article's doi:
10.1146/annurev.psych.59.103006.093643

Copyright © 2008 by Annual Reviews.
All rights reserved

0066-4308/08/0203-0477$20.00

Key Words

behavioral interventions, self-management, chronic illness

Abstract

This review of the current status of theoretically based behavioral research for chronic illness management makes the following points: (*a*) Behavioral interventions have demonstrated effectiveness for improving health outcomes using biomedical indicators, (*b*) current interventions are too costly and time consuming to be used in clinical and community settings, (*c*) translation of the conceptual models generated from studies of the problem-solving processes underlying self-management and the relationship of these processes to the self system and cultural and institutional contexts suggest new avenues for developing effective and efficient cognitive-behavioral interventions, and (*d*) it is proposed that integration of the conceptual developments in self-management with new approaches to the design of clinical trials can generate tailored, behavioral interventions that will improve quality of care.

Contents

INTRODUCTION

Health psychology research needs to satisfy two goals: the development of theoretical models describing the processes underlying risky and healthy behaviors, and the creation of effective procedures for behavioral change that are usable in clinical and community settings. The primary steps required for a practice-oriented theory are to increase the specificity and predictive power of theory by adding concepts generated from observations in clinical and community settings and to develop increasingly complex models to better understand how behavioral factors contribute to health outcomes. The steps required for practice are to develop interventions that are theory-based and are usable in clinical and community settings as well as effective for helping individuals initiate and sustain behaviors that will improve their personal health. These goals are reflected in the three major lines of research examined in previous contributions to the *Annual Review of Psychology*: biobehavioral studies of direct pathways from behavior to illness (e.g., stress illness research; Ader & Cohen 1993, Baum & Posluszny 1999), behavioral interventions to control these direct pathways (Kiecolt-Glaser et al. 2002, Schneiderman et al. 2001), and behavioral studies focused on the prevention and control of chronic conditions (Rodin & Salovey 1989). This review focuses on a subset of this third area of behavioral studies: the processes involved in initiating and maintaining behaviors for reducing risk and controlling existent chronic disease. These behaviors include lifestyle changes such as diet, exercise, and adherence to medication for reducing risk and control of diabetes, hypertension, and congestive heart failure. A narrow focus is necessary because it is impossible to cover in the space allotted the enormous number of behavioral studies that have appeared since a previous and able review by Rodin & Salovey (1989).

Our chapter is organized as follows: First, we provide a brief justification for focusing on prevention and control of chronic illnesses. We argue that the movement for evidence-based practice in the medical field has created pressure on health psychologists for effective and efficient (usable) theory-based behavioral interventions for the control of chronic illness. Second, we review models and evidence respecting the self-management process, i.e., how people manage (control and prevent) chronic conditions in their home settings. This section is organized around the proposition that the social-cognitive-behavioral model, with an emphasis on cognitive processes, is the most comprehensive model for understanding behavioral processes relevant to health. Third, we briefly review new approaches to clinical trials for increasing the effectiveness of behavioral interventions and whether integrating these innovative approaches with self-regulation models could create interventions that are usable in clinical settings.

WHY FOCUS ON PREVENTION AND CONTROL OF CHRONIC ILLNESS?

Advances in public health and the economic well-being of populations in the early twentieth century in Western nations resulted in chronic conditions, such as cardiovascular diseases and cancers, replacing infectious diseases as one of the top ten killers in Western nations (Fries 2005, McKinlay & McKinlay 1977). The recent surge in HIV AIDS, an infectious condition, is not an exception to this trend, because existing HIV treatments are lifelong, i.e., chronic, and require chronic, intensive self-management (Siegel & Lekas 2002). Treatment of chronic illnesses also absorbs well over half of the health care budget of developed nations (McKinlay & McKinlay 1977), and because chronic conditions are more common with advancing age, the financial burden will increase as the population ages. The focus of this chapter on chronic illness management is congruent, therefore, with a major problem for society and the health care system. As human behaviors, including food intake, physical activity, and cigarette smoking, are causally related to both vulnerability and management of chronic conditions, it is fully justified to focus on their prevention and control (Baum & Posluszny 1999).

Narrowing the focus to behaviors for the prevention and management of chronic diseases sets constraints on how we cover the pathways to chronic illness that have been identified by social, behavioral, and biomedical investigators. For example, although statistical models have shown direct effects to health through economic, ecological, and cultural pathways (House et al. 1992, Kaplan 1992), we argue that many of these effects are produced by behavior. Failure to detect behavioral mediators at the individual level may be due to deficits in assessment of relevant behaviors and to narrow definitions of behavior that include only overt risky (smoking) or healthy (exercise) behaviors and ignore generalized behaviors or sets such as chronic vigilance. We also propose that direct pathways from psychological traits such as trait negative affect (trait NA) and cognitive competency to health are often mediated by behavioral factors, though many relationships between traits and health indicators reflect interactions of behaviors with third factors such as genetic make-up and/or gene expression. All of the pathways impact the individual and the individual's behaviors—healthy, risky, treatment adherence, and lifestyle behaviors. It is reasonable to expect, therefore, that the best way to affect health outcomes will be through the pathways influencing these behaviors.

EVIDENCE-BASED PRACTICE AND BEHAVIORAL INTERVENTIONS FOR CONTROLLING CHRONIC ILLNESSES

Translational Research and Evidence-Based Medicine

Translational research is critical for both theory and practice, and "the recasting of clinical science along the principles of evidence-based medicine provide[s] a better environment where translational research may now materialize its goals" (Ioannidis 2004, p. 5). The growth of evidence-based practice in medicine has created pressure on health psychologists for effective and efficient theory-based behavioral interventions for the control of chronic illness. Even though clinical outcome trials provide information on the efficacy of treatments, the mechanisms for change are not delineated in clinical outcome studies, a fact that limits their use for practice and theoretical development, and so we must move beyond clinical outcome studies to translational research that investigates the effects of individual, theoretical components (Lerman 2003). In this way, our research can be translated for and used by those in clinical practice. A broad literature search was conducted using two Ovid information sources, PsycINFO and Medline, for randomized, controlled trials of behavioral interventions conducted in the past decade whose purpose was to study the prevention and management of chronic conditions. General subject terms were used in both search engines, including all terms that were related to "behavioral intervention" or "lifestyle intervention," "chronic illness," and "randomized trials." A total of 137 studies were collected using the specified search terms; the studies were then cut down to only those that met criteria of being behavioral interventions, using randomized and controlled trials, and having to do with chronic conditions in the past decade. The search results were further eliminated if they were related to drug addictions or smoking rather than chronic illnesses such as diabetes and heart failure. After all inclusion and exclusion criteria were implemented, 26 studies remained. Of these 26 trials, 21 reported significant and substantial benefits from a behavioral intervention. Although these trials are few in number, 80% of them produced some or all of their predicted benefits in health outcomes. Thus, the best trials clearly satisfied the key criterion for effectiveness—the behavioral changes reduced the onset and/or progression of chronic disease—but fell short of a second criterion: They were not efficient and usable in the vast majority of clinical settings, as has been the case for most effective interventions (McDonald et al. 2002). In the following section, we focus on two diabetes prevention trials that are excellent examples of effective behavioral interventions, and then we address behavioral models that point to possible directions for achieving efficiency and/or the clinical usability of such behavioral interventions. To be clinically usable, behavioral interventions must be efficient, not only effective, so that physicians, nurses, and health institutions have the time and resources for implementation.

The Diabetes Prevention Trials

The Finnish Diabetes Prevention Study Group (Lindström et al. 2003, Tuomilehto et al. 2001), which conducted a randomized trial comparing lifestyle with standard-care treatment conditions, reported that 58% fewer lifestyle participants became diabetic relative to those in standard care over the average four years of its intervention. Most importantly, the benefit of lifestyle change was sustained for three years following termination of the intervention, though the effect shrank somewhat at final follow-up (58% to 46%). The trial of individuals at high risk for diabetes that was conducted in the United States (Diabetes Prev. Prog. Res. Group 2002) confirmed the Finnish findings; 58% fewer of the 1079 participants in the lifestyle intervention became diabetic in the 2.8-year post-intervention period (average per-participant observation) in comparison with the 1082 standard-care participants. The 1073 participants taking medication also fared better than control participants, 31% fewer became diabetic, though they fared significantly less well than the participants in the lifestyle intervention. The quality of these trials appears to be very high; adherence to the interventions was excellent (80% or more), and mediating factors, weight loss, and hours engaged in physical activity increased more in the lifestyle than in the control conditions. Although it is difficult to compare the time demands and extent of coverage for specific topics in these complex interventions, the Finnish study appears to have been significantly less time demanding than that used by the U.S. working group (for reviews, see Heneghan et al. 2006, Tuomilehto et al. 2005).

Do the Trials Meet Criteria for Evidence-Based Practice?

Although the incidence of diabetes is clearly lower, and impressively so, for participants in lifestyle interventions than for those in control or medication treatment conditions (see Gillies et al. 2007, Yamaoka & Tango 2005), support for lifestyle interventions as an evidence-based practice requires that the interventions meet additional benchmarks. First, diabetes is a lifetime condition, and although the seven-year follow-up in the Finnish trial is encouraging, it remains to be seen if the behavioral changes and their benefits will be sustained over a lifetime and can be replicated in other trials. Second, there are issues of cost effectiveness and usability in clinical settings. The U.S. program involved 16 one-on-one, hour-long sessions with a cognitive-behavioral therapist as well as meetings with nutritionists and nurses and phone calls to reinforce and sustain behavior change. Economic analyses of the U.S. and a similar lifestyle program conducted in the United Kingdom suggest they are cost effective for the health care system and for society as a whole; the costs include direct medical and nonmedical expenses and various indirect costs (Diabetes Prev. Prog. Res. Group 2003, Teutsch 2003). Cost effectiveness on a national scale does not, however, translate into usability in clinical settings, where personnel skilled in the conduct of such interventions are lacking and the savings may go to units (e.g., hospitals) other than those in which interventions are conducted (e.g., specialty clinics). Furthermore, cost effectiveness on a national scale does not necessarily translate into cost effectiveness for the individual patient, the people for whom the intervention is aimed, because patient time is rarely considered in cost analyses (Russell et al. 2005).

We propose that understanding the processes underlying how patients act to detect and manage chronic conditions will provide ideas for effective and efficient interventions. This proposal is consistent with, although different from, efforts to tune interventions to stages that define participants' readiness for change (Prochaska et al. 2005), to target the intervention to groups of participants, or to tailor the interventions to individuals' needs (De Bourdeaudhuij & Brug 2000). A review of tailored informational interventions (Ryan & Lauver 2002) concluded that they were significantly more effective than were standard interventions for some but not all types of behavior (e.g., effective for dietary behaviors but not for smoking behaviors), and these interventions were more likely to be effective when they used ipsative feedback, which compares a participant's present and past behaviors. All of the reviewed tailored informational interventions that were significant had only very small effect sizes. Therefore, although these interventions may be more efficient than the lifestyle interventions to date, they are not as effective. The challenge for interventions is to be effective and efficient, and therefore usable.

THE PROCESS OF SELF-MANAGEMENT OF CHRONIC ILLNESS

The creation of effective and efficient evidence-based practices requires something in addition to the translation of theory-based interventions to practice settings: These additions can be identified by the systematic investigation and conceptualization of the processes underlying how patients use treatments in their homes, workplaces, and communities—their lived environments. We propose that the incorporation of models and concepts developed in field settings into the conceptual structure of behavioral theory developed in laboratory settings, i.e., translation from the field to the laboratory, will facilitate the development and testing of efficient and effective interventions for enhancing healthy behaviors. Translation from the field is critical given that medical treatments and lifestyle behaviors are performed in lived environments.

Factors Affecting Chronic Illness Management: Emotion and Cognitive Traits

Studies of health care usage, disease risk screening, and behavior for the prevention and management of chronic conditions provide insights into mechanisms underlying effective self-management behaviors. The social-cognitive-behavioral framework that is the basis for behavioral health research encompasses factors ranging from the cultural and social environment through individual or person factors, and most importantly, the behavioral processes that initiate and sustain healthy and risky behaviors. The framework encompasses a multilevel set of control systems (Carver et al. 1989, Cooper & Shallice 2006, Powers 1973), with each level generating goals and strategies that influence adjacent levels in the hierarchy. Understanding how variables interact either within or across levels is not captured by structural or hierarchical statistical models that depict the architecture of a system but do not describe its software, i.e., how factors communicate with one another. How factors communicate with one another is critical information for the design of interventions. For example, there is little evidence on how typical individual difference measures relate to within-individual variation in behavior over time because individual difference measures may not identify and assess the self-perceptions and strategies that control the temporal variation in intraperson problem solving (Cervone 2004). We illustrate these points below in our description of what is known about the processes involved in the regulation of treatment adherence behaviors.

Emotion traits. For more than 30 years, studies have reported on the relationship between individual differences in emotion characteristics and healthy and risky behaviors and health outcomes, e.g., mortality and morbidity. Although measures of negative affect such as trait anxiety are more or less consistent predictors of morbidity and mortality (Friedman & Booth-Kewley 1987), they are somewhat less effective in predicting healthy and/or risky behaviors (Mora et al. 2002, 2007). Individual differences in depressive affect and angry/hostile behavioral styles are somewhat an exception, as they have been consistent predictors of morbidity and mortality from cardiovascular disease (Barefoot et al. 1983). Questions about these relationships include the extent to which these constructs overlap with one another and with variables such as burnout and vital exhaustion, and whether they affect health through the same or through different physiological pathways (Suls & Bunde 2005).

Although studies have generally failed to detect robust direct effects of factors such as neuroticism or trait anxiety on care seeking, theory has suggested and data have identified indirect pathways that merit further examination. One such path shows, as predicted, that individuals with high scores on trait NA are more likely to report asthma-specific health worries that mediate the connection between trait NA and the reporting of symptoms specific to asthma. Asthma-specific worries, however, do not affect the relationship of the trait NA to reporting of generic, emotional symptoms (Moral et al. 2007). Thus, being high on trait NA increases susceptibility to feeling fearful in response to illness threats and focuses attention on the physical indicators of threat, allowing the individual to distinguish clearly between symptoms of illness and symptoms of emotional distress. Because illness-specific worry enhances attention to and accurate identification of illness symptoms, and because symptoms are powerful initiators of health behaviors, it is clear that illness-specific worry should predict seeking health care; a specific worry, cancer worry, has been shown to predict cancer screening (Diefenbach et al. 1999, Hay et al. 2006). Imaging studies have identified neural centers that are likely the loci for memories that integrate symptoms, subjective worry, and action tendencies (Critchley 2005).

Depression appears to have direct effects on a range of health behaviors. For example, depression has been shown to reduce adherence to treatment in patients who have had a myocardial infarction (MI) (Ziegelstein et al. 2000), to reduce attendance at programs for lowering blood lipids post-MI and post-bypass surgery (Sebregts et al. 2003), and to delay care seeking following an MI (see review by Dracup et al. 1995) and bowel obstruction (Bickell et al. 2005). The data suggest, however, that these effects often reflect only one of the components of depression, i.e., its affective, cognitive, or somatic feature, and not the entire construct. For example, a cognitive component of depression, the belief that other people disrespect and dislike you, predicted reductions in perceived social support over a two-year period in a sample of 851 elderly individuals, whereas depressed mood and somatic symptoms had no relationship to reductions in perceived support (Maher et al. 2006). Social support is associated with better health outcomes (Cohen 2004), and thus its erosion would increase risk of illness, thereby defining an indirect pathway from depression to physical illness. Consistent with prior data (Dracup et al. 1995), interviews with 433 post-MI patients found that patients reporting depressive symptoms two weeks prior to hospitalization delayed longer (40+ hours) before seeking care in comparison with patients who did not report depressive symptoms (22+ hours; Bunde & Martin 2006). This direct effect however, was due entirely to two items in the Patient Health Questionnaire-9 depression measure: fatigue and sleep disturbance. Delay was not related to the other components of depression, mood, anhedonia, or feeling bad about the self, or to the neuroticism scale from the Big Five In-

ventory (Costa & McCrae 1992). The findings for white coat hypertension reported by Spruill and colleagues (2007) resonate with the Bunde & Martin (2006) data: situational fear levels and not trait anxiety were associated with (white coat) hypertension in the clinical setting; white coat hypertension was detected for individuals who had labeled themselves as hypertensive regardless of their actual ambulatory blood pressure status. Kemeny's (2003) summary of multiple studies also shows that situation-specific measures, and not general measure of stress, predict HIV progression. Thus, the results of these studies converge in showing that situation-specific rather than general conceptualizations and measurements of emotion concepts are needed to predict health outcomes (Leventhal et al. 2007a).

Cognitive/behavioral traits. The Big Five factor of conscientiousness and its subfactor of conventionality appear to have consistent, modest relationships with lower levels of risky and higher levels of healthy behaviors and better health outcomes (Bogg & Roberts 2004). A recent analysis of existent data found that teacher ratings of conscientiousness were positively related to better health in their former pupils 40 years later; some of the effect was clearly indirect, i.e., from conscientiousness through educational attainment and higher levels of healthy and lower levels of risky behaviors, although some of the relationship was direct and unaccounted for by mediators in the best-fitting model (Hampson et al. 2007). Conscientiousness may affect self-management at many points in the behavioral process: It may affect risk aversion, nondiscounting of remote rewards, skills in generating action plans, and/or adherence to well-organized, nonrisky, and not overly complex lifestyles (Park et al. 1999). Behavioral processes related to conscientiousness may play a role in the "healthy adherer effect" (Simpson et al. 2006); participants adherent to protocol in placebo conditions have been found to have outcomes as favorable as those of treated patients.

Summary comment. It is clear that person traits are related to health. What is not well understood is how person factors relate to specific behaviors or biological vulnerabilities that mediate these effects. The identification of the processes underlying how traits influence problem solving (i.e., how health threats are viewed, the strategies skills and specific responses for threat management) and how the outcomes of problem solving are evaluated and translated into intermediate beliefs (worries; strategies) requires analyses that focus on intraindividual assessment rather than individual-difference assessment. As Cervone (2004) argues, stable factors (traits) may have little or no relationship to the process-level variables that affect the day-by-day fluctuation in health-relevant behaviors. The identification of relationships to health behaviors and health outcomes of specific health worries, components of depression, or representations of specific self vulnerabilities, and behavioral styles specific to particular types of settings are consistent with the proposition that domain-specific person factors will better predict behavioral episodes over time. This is true because they are tuned to the specific cues, internal and external, that activate behavioral processes in that domain (Cervone et al. 2006). As we argue in the final section, understanding how moderators such as traits affect process-level variables will be critical for the development of effective and efficient interventions.

Factors Affecting Chronic Illness Management: Process Analyses

Studies have identified a broad array of cultural, community, and personal values and beliefs and associated triggering factors that initiate and sustain behaviors affecting the development of chronic illnesses. For example, obesity, a multiplier of risk factors for many chronic conditions (Pi-Sunyer 1993), is affected by factors ranging from availability and cost of healthy foods to cultural values associated with portliness and thinness, to individual pathology affecting food intake (Wadden et al. 2002). The picture for addictions, smoking, and alcohol use is equally complex; cultural, peer, and family environments as well as individual propensity to risk taking and emotional reactivity affect likelihood of initiation, rapidity of addiction, and difficulty of cessation (Galea et al. 2004, Turner et al. 2004). Models depicting the processes involved in healthy and risky behaviors typically place environmental factors (availability; cost; socioeconomic status) on the far left, belief variables such as personal vulnerability next, then triggers that activate these beliefs and motivate action, followed by response alternatives and their associated expectations (e.g., response efficacy and self-efficacy for execution), a plan for action (Bandura 1989, Leventhal 1970, MacGregor et al. 2006), and post-action satisfaction (Baldwin et al. 2006, Finch et al. 2005). Consistent with earlier data (Leventhal 1970), a combination of motivating variables (attitudes, intentions) and action variables, i.e., plans and efficacy (Leventhal et al. 1965, Sheeran & Orbell 2000), appears to be essential for healthy or risk-reducing behaviors; neither set alone appears to be sufficient to generate behavior (Leventhal 1970, Rothman 2000, Witte & Morrison 2000). For example, a recent study of volunteer parent participants in a smoking-cessation intervention found that predictors of participation in the program included recently receiving medical care, a motivating factor, and planning to make changes in smoking behavior (Mak et al. 2006). Action plans play a key role in converting attitudes to action; the associations are especially large with respect to performing single, time-limited behaviors such as screening for and inoculation against disease threats (e.g., Orbell et al. 1997). Suggestions as to how cultural-, social-, and person-level factors affect the processes involved in self-management of chronic illness are a central concern of this review because interactions among these factors are crucial for research aiming to develop effective and efficient interventions. Since lifetime management of diseases such as asthma, diabetes, and hypertension is highly dependent upon contact with the medical care system, we concentrate on empirical studies examining the processes underlying the use of health care and adherence to lifestyle behaviors and medication for the control of chronic conditions.

Triggers. When we distinguish visits to health care providers that are patient driven from those that are routine annual exams—practitioner or employer scheduled visits—it is no surprise that patient-driven visits are the visits triggered by somatic changes. For example, new symptoms triggered use of care for 100% of 121 elderly individuals whose use of care was tracked over a year; only 30% of their matched controls reported new symptoms (Cameron et al. 1995). The new symptoms reported by the 30% of noncare users were seen as not severe or of sufficient duration to merit attention. Care-seeking delay can be similarly predicted by a lack of perceived relevance of a symptom to illness. Burgess and colleagues (1998) found, for example, that women who delayed care seeking for breast cancer symptoms were more likely to have nonlump symptoms than were those who did not delay care seeking; that is, because there was no lump in the breast, the women who delayed seeking care did not realize the severity of the initial, nonlump symptom.

Heuristics. The numerous empirical studies describing differences in how young and elderly individuals evaluate and respond to their symptoms (see Brody & Kleban 1983, Stoller 1998) make up a vast repository of information with rich theoretical implications for the appraisals that underlie seeking health care. Investigators have begun to identify the specific heuristics, or mental rules, that people use to interpret somatic events and to identify the illness schemata underlying their use (Brownlee et al. 2000). Four classes of heuristics have been identified (Leventhal et al. 2007b): first, heuristics involving innate, spatial-temporal maps of symptoms into

cerebral architecture (e.g., location, duration, severity); second, heuristics involving patterns of symptoms based on prior experience (e.g., schema related—chest pain means a heart problem), novelty (ambiguous or incongruous with underlying schema), trajectory (worsening, fluctuating), and control (e.g., did it or did it not improve with self-care); third, heuristics based upon cultural beliefs and social experience (e.g., age-illness, gender stereotypes, stress/illness, good feeling = good health); and last, heuristics involving active social comparisons (e.g., prevalence and severity in one's community, and similarity rules such as similarity in exposure, temperament, physical characteristics). Heuristics give meaning to somatic changes. For example, changes of long duration and high severity imply that an experienced somatic change may be a serious threat to function and/or life; both are associated with high levels of care seeking among elderly individuals (Mora et al. 2002). Mild, chronic symptoms with unchanging trajectories that lack a specific pattern and are systemic rather than localized are readily attributed to age rather than illness (Brody & Kleban 1983, Prohaska et al. 1987). Since multiple heuristics are involved in the interpretation of a somatic event, it is possible to predict interactions among them. For example, in comparison to symptoms that are distinctive (e.g., patterned or in a specific location, such as sore throats, stuffed nose, or swelling), symptoms that are vague (e.g., in a nonspecific location and/or lacking pattern, such as fatigue or aching body) are readily attributed to life stress and are unlikely to trigger motivation for seeking medical care (Cameron et al. 1995). However, when vague symptoms were experienced in association with life events a month or more in duration, care seeking was just as likely as it was for distinctive symptoms. The perception that vague symptoms may be indicators of illness when associated with stressors of long duration is consistent with empirical data that prolonged stress increases the likelihood of developing a cold after exposure to rhinoviruses

(Cohen et al. 1998, Cohen & Williamson 1991). There are instances, therefore, in which people's mental tool boxes, that is, their heuristics, provide rules in accord with empirical data.

The studies of heuristics suggest at least three directions for future research. First, in their study of delay in care seeking following a myocardial infarction, Bunde & Martin (2006) found opposite effects on delay for mental rules and depression: location (chest pain), pattern (left chest and arm), and novelty (sweating) reduced delay, whereas depression increased delay. Consistent with the parallel-processing assumption that underlies illness cognition models (Leventhal 1970), the effects of heuristics and depression were independent of one another; i.e., the bivariable relationships of depression and/or heuristics to delay were unchanged in multivariable models. The effect of context on the independence or interdependence of heuristics and affect needs to be studied. Second, an individual will act differently when heuristics join potentially unique experiences into a common conceptual framework versus when they do not; e.g., an individual will seek health care if chest pain, sweating, and arm pain are framed within the concept of "heart attack" and not as discrete events. Concepts allow the individual to see similarities over occasions (prior history was related to swift care seeking; Bunde & Martin 2006, Dracup et al. 1995), to see current symptoms as signals for later ones, and to regulate behavior in line with the expectations associated with the more abstract, conceptual framework of "heart attack." By contrast, cardiac diseases such as congestive heart failure lack the features necessary to be coded as coronary events; the chronic symptoms are often mild (breathlessness, fatigue, swollen legs), attributed to age, and are not conceptualized as heart related (Horowitz et al. 2004). Although patients are told they have heart disease, failure to connect their symptoms to a cardiac concept (absence of depth) results in failure to see worsening of chronic symptoms as an indicator that more severe symptoms are on the horizon. Patients who say they do not understand their conditions do not act to counter, change, and avoid hospitalization. The conditions necessary for linkage to occur, i.e., the time needed to see relationships among embedded experiences, require research.

The third direction for future research in relevant health heuristics concerns the relationship of these illness-oriented heuristics to cognitive-search rules, such as representativeness and availability, which are factors related to limitations in processing capacity (Tversky & Kahneman 1974). Within the illness cognition framework, availability and representativeness are conceptualized as attributes of the domain-specific rules. Thus, the availability and representativeness of a somatic/health heuristic is a function of the schemata or database underlying the search process. Investigations in this domain will be important for understanding the conditions involved in the biases affecting self-appraisals and sustained self-management of chronic conditions.

Schemata and illness representations. The initial question likely addressed by heuristic processing is, "Am I sick or am I well?" Crossing the threshold from perceiving no illness to perceiving illness involves consideration of alternative schemata on the "sickness" side of the equation. Early multidimensional scaling and cluster analysis of illness labels found four clusters of illness representations in a two-dimensional space: contagious illnesses that are a threat to life and those that are not, and noncontagious illnesses that are a threat to life and those that are not (Bishop 1991). Although scaling did not assess the availability or salience of these categories, Bishop (1991) identified a clear indicator of salience by showing that memory for illness information was better retained if consistent with an underlying prototype. Evidence that prototypes affect behavioral management of chronic conditions was clear in the early studies of hypertension showing that diagnostic labeling was associated with symptom reporting both for patients (Meyer et al. 1985) and for subjects in laboratory studies (Baumann et al. 1989); the linkage of symptoms to a label reflects the fundamental symmetry between the prototype and experience: "to be sick means being symptomatic." Patients hospitalized for severe attacks of asthma agreed that they "will have asthma all of their lives" and then agreed that they "have asthma only when they have symptoms" (Halm et al. 2006); behavior was consistent with these beliefs as they took both prevention medication (which is to be used daily when asymptomatic) and controller medication (which is to be used for attacks) only when they were symptomatic. Symptom management is also a pattern for HIV, a contagious, chronic condition; when symptoms clear up, patients with HIV are likely to stop medication (Horne et al. 2004).

The schema most consistent with symptom management is the acute illness model, a schema with five domains identified by the Illness Perception Questionnaire (Weinman et al. 1996): (a) identity—symptoms and label, (b) time line (time limited), (c) cause (external cause), (d) consequences (not life threatening), and (e) control via self-care or with medical treatment (Diefenbach & Leventhal 1996). The acute representation is linked to procedures for management that alleviate (control) both symptoms and condition (identity), are time limited (time line), nonthreatening (consequences), and work through routes that are plausible given the underlying condition (cause; Horne 2003). The acute or time-limited nature of symptom-focused models is consistent with clinical observations and data showing that patients stop treatment both when symptoms resolve and when objective indicators return to "normal values" (Horne et al. 2004). An excellent study by Henderson et al. (2007) showed that priming an illness schema for the common cold (e.g., by writing about a recent experience with a cold) increases color-naming response time to words related to the common cold in the Stroop color-naming test: Response times to neutral words and words related to cardiovascular disease were unaffected. When a schema for car-

diovascular disease was primed, color-naming response time was affected for words related to cardiovascular disease but not to neutral words or words related to the common cold. Schemata are implicit, organized, and affect behavior when activated.

Representations of treatment and health behaviors. When a health threat is perceived as imminent or as probable, procedures will be entertained and elaborated for threat avoidance and control (Wakslak et al. 2006). Thus, stimulus events or inputs, such as symptoms, physical dysfunctions, illnesses in others, and a variety of social and media messages, initiate the development of mental representations of the output, or the behavioral side of the control system for the regulation of a chronic illness threat. Treatment behaviors, whether prescribed or self-initiated, carry an implicit set of expectations respecting their consequences, time lines, efficacy (control), and route of action (causal), and these expectations are appraised against both experiential and abstract criteria. For example, patients in the Meyer et al. (1985) study were adherent to medication and in better blood pressure control if they perceived that medication was controlling symptoms they attributed to hypertension; symptoms however, were not related to blood pressure. Jamison (1995) gives numerous examples of the conflict between abstract, verbalized expectations and implicit concrete expectations in the treatment of depression. Although depressed patients have the abstract knowledge, i.e., they "know" it will take several weeks for medication to work, they experience medication symptoms at the onset of treatment without an improvement in mood. Experience overwrites knowledge: They feel the medication is working (creating symptoms) but they also feel it is not working (not improving mood) these feelings often lead to nonadherence. Treatments are embedded in implicit schemata or representations, and a treatment schema is linked to the representation of the illness that is the target for control.

Examinations of treatment beliefs held by chronically ill patients have identified general and specific concerns about medication use (general: doctors overprescribe medication; specific: medication can be addictive) and about specific beliefs respecting its necessity (efficacy for maintaining health) and harmfulness (Horne & Weinman 1999). Endorsement of these beliefs differs across chronic conditions: Necessity of medication is more strongly endorsed by patients with diabetes than by patients with coronary and psychiatric conditions, and concerns about medication are somewhat higher among patients with asthma (Horne & Weinman 1999). Since these beliefs are focused on the response part of the regulatory system, the data show, as would be expected, that these beliefs about treatments are more strongly associated with treatment adherence than are related beliefs about the illness. For example, adherence is better among patients holding strong beliefs about the necessity of their prescribed medication than among patients who are highly concerned about the illness but do not see the medication as necessary (Horne & Weinman 1999, 2002). Medication beliefs were also related to participation in antiretroviral treatment in the Highly Active Antiretroviral Therapy study (Horne 2003, Horne et al. 2004) and to treatment adherence (Horne et al. 2004).

The Theory of Planned Behavior (TPB; Ajzen 1991) has been used to examine the relationships of behavioral and/or treatment beliefs to adherence for issues such as use of condoms (Albarracin et al. 2001), mammography (Tolma et al. 2006), screening for colon-cancer (McCaffery et al. 2003), and dietary and exercise behaviors (see Hagger et al. 2002 and Smith 2004). In the majority of TPB studies, as in several of the studies from the perspective of self-regulation theory, treatment/behavioral beliefs were found to be more strongly related to behavioral intentions and action than to illness beliefs. For example, attendance at a colposcopy clinic for detection of possible cervical dysplasia was predicted by (*a*) the belief that one could readily attend, (*b*) a belief of behavioral control, and (*c*) intentions to attend. Measures of illness representations did not predict behavior (Orbell et al. 2006). Illness representations did predict attendance as did perceptions of behavioral control and intentions to act when attendance at a colposcopy clinic was differentiated into three categories of patients: did not attend, attended when prompted, and attended without prompting (Orbell et al. 2006, p. 611). Representations of cancer, perceptions of behavioral control, and intentions predicted attendance for patients in need of prompting. Prompting likely primed implicit illness models for these patients.

In their fine study, Orbell and colleagues stated their major goal to be the comparison of "two theories of health behavior": self-regulation and TPB (Orbell et al. 2006). This goal merits comment because the study and others similar to it compare the predictive power of measures, not theories. Moreover, the selection of measures was inappropriate for a comparison of theories. Comparing illness representations as the measure of self-regulation theory to behavioral beliefs and intentions as the measure of TPB is inadvisable because it compares only the first component of the self-regulatory control loop and ignores both treatment representations and outcome expectations, components that are essential for the completion of a self-regulatory loop. A comparison of theories would assess the action stage of the self-regulatory model with the action components of TPB. And if treatment beliefs (TPB) are conceptually the same as treatment representations, then the comparison would be between the two implementations of these components and not the entire theories. In addition, it is arbitrary to include intention in TPB and to exclude it from social-learning or self-regulation theory; intentions are conscious verbalizations of readiness to act; they are at home in any theory that conceptualizes action readiness at implicit and explicit levels. In summary, comparisons among measures are not equivalent to comparisons among models (Leventhal et al. 2007c).

Coherence between illness and treatment representations; converting schemas into scripts. The concept of coherence, i.e., whether an individual can make sense of her or his illness experience, was introduced by Antonovsky (1993). The concept influenced other investigators (Moss-Morris et al. 2002) and provided a link between health research and basic research in experimental psychology (Broadbent et al. 2006). Whether a representation of illness and a representation of its possible treatments form a cohesive pattern is a core issue for self-regulation theory. Self-regulation theory would hypothesize that coherence between illness and treatment representations arises when the actions taken to manage an illness are seen as congruent with the treatment representation, that is, that they are perceived to be effective treatments. Perceived effectiveness emerges when the experienced outcome of treatment matches the individual's expectations for both subjective and objective indicators; these indicators or targets are generated from the representation of the illness. The importance of coherence, or "goodness of fit," between illness and treatment representations can be seen in studies of patients with hypertension. For example, patients who believed treatment was necessary (assessed using the Horne necessity scale) were more adherent, and they perceived their hypertension to have a longer time line, more negative consequences, and to be more amenable to control by treatment (Ross et al. 2004); their illness belief that treatment could control their hypertension was coherent with their treatment belief that their hypertension medication was effective. Patients with coherent asthma illness and treatment representations who saw treatment as necessary and who were more adherent represented asthma as a chronic condition. In contrast, patients with noncoherent representations had concerns about treatment, were less adherent, believed asthma to be less controllable, and perceived their symptoms as side effects of treatment (Horne & Weinman 2002). Patients resist treatments that are inconsistent with their illness representations; for example, patients resisted the recommendation to exercise for joint and back pain following myocardial infarction if they perceived excessive activity as the cause of their heart attack (Weinman et al. 2000). Rothman and colleagues (Baldwin et al. 2006) found that maintenance of smoking cessation was related to satisfaction with the change is an alternative way of assessing coherence.

Motivating behavioral change for disease prevention may prove problematic for individuals identified as at genetic risk; behavioral change may seem inappropriate for a disease that is programmed in one's genes. For example, it was expected that testing people at increased risk for familial hypercholesterolemia would increase motivation for medication and diet change among participants with positive test findings, but this was not the case (Marteau et al. 2004). Although the evidence to date is not entirely consistent, there are several indications that people are likely to choose medical treatment over lifestyle change (diet and exercise) for risk reduction when an illnesses is perceived as genetically caused (Marteau et al. 2004, Wright et al. 2006). It is sometimes the case that simple communications can reverse the lack of coherence between representations of illness and treatment; women given a coherent explanation as to how smoking could affect cervical cancer were more likely to undergo cervical screening and express motivation for smoking cessation (Hall et al. 2004). Unpacking the coherence concept suggests that it might be better reframed as converting discrete representations, that of illness and treatment, into behavioral scripts that are generated when behavioral management produces an expected and satisfying outcome, i.e., when behaviors affect objective and subjective criteria as anticipated (Baldwin et al. 2006, Finch et al. 2005, Meyer et al. 1985, Rothman 2000).

Factors Affecting Chronic Illness Management: Contextual Factors of Self, Social Networks, and Culture

Illness and treatment representations are constructed within the perceived self and may lead to revised perceptions of the durability and competence of the physical self and its ability to function in a variety of cognitive tasks and social roles (Epstein 1973). Investigators have focused on two aspects of the self concept that are directly related to the problem-solving process described in the prior section: self-efficacy and beliefs respecting control—both oriented toward the behavioral component of the regulatory system, and optimism and disengagement—two factors affecting the appraisal of movement toward goals. To this point, however, relatively few studies have explicitly examined how feedback from the problem-solving level, that is, feedback from illness management, affects these factors or other aspects of the self system. There also is little empirical data showing how aspects of the self, e.g., self-assessments of health and feelings of vulnerability to specific diseases, affect the construction and content of illnesses and treatment representations.

Self as context. Self-efficacy, or the perception that one is able to perform a specific action in an efficacious manner (Bandura 1989, 2004), and internal control, or the perception of personal control over and responsibility for daily events (Rodin & Langer 1996), are two self system concepts commonly used in health behavior research. Although some studies have treated these variables as traits, they are basically dynamic concepts—beliefs that are shaped by behavior and that in turn affect behavior. It is easier, however, to identify studies that demonstrate how efficacy affects behavior than to identify studies that examine how behavior affects efficacy; for example, studies have looked at the effect of level of self-efficacy on taking medication (e.g., Barclay et al. 2007), for healthy eating (e.g., Shields & Brawley 2006), and for exercising (e.g., Renner & Schwarzer 2005). To be complete, studies of efficacy should also include how and the conditions under which the behavior affects or mediates changes in self-efficacy (Maibach & Murphy 1995). For example, exercise builds self-efficacy for exercise behaviors if the exerciser experiences positive affect and social support during the activity (e.g., Dechamps et al. 2007). Experiencing positive affect and engaging in social comparison as a result of the behavior elaborates the meaning of the action in cognitive and experiential memory; experience-based positive feedback conveys the value of the behavior to the cognitive system.

Treating self-efficacy as a static trait in research ignores two additional findings in health research in addition to the data showing how efficacy is modified by action. First, self-efficacy may be more important for the initiation than the maintenance of a behavioral change. For example, self-efficacy was important for initiating smoking cessation, but satisfaction with cessation, not efficacy, was related to maintaining cessation (Rothman 2000) (see Coherence Between Illness and Treatment Representation, above), and neither self-efficacy nor satisfaction was related to long-term maintenance once nonsmoking became habitual (Baldwin et al. 2006). Second, efficacy is domain specific; thus, an individual's self-efficacy for regulating diet is ineffective for regulating exercise (Baldwin et al. 2006). Domain-specific differentiations of self-efficacy have also proven essential to understand the findings and processes involved in rehabilitation following myocardial infarction (Schwarzer & Fuchs 1995), initiation and maintenance of exercise (Sallis et al. 1992), and in regulation of healthy diets (Schwarzer & Fuchs 1995). The differentiation of efficacy across domains and its change over time is consistent with its conceptualization as a dynamic factor rather than as a trait, and it is consistent with the importance of specificity respecting the assessment of affective and cognitive traits.

Investigators have questioned whether efficacy is merely a correlate or is an actual causal mediator of performance—i.e., whether efficacy has a functional relationship to subsequent performance. Heggestad & Kanfer's (2005) studies show that prior behaviors can build efficacy but that the individual's prior behavior and not efficacy has a causal relationship to subsequent behavior. It has yet to be determined whether their findings will hold for maintenance of a health behavior versus only initiation of the health behavior and whether efficacy can affect success for some health behavior changes and not others (Vancouver & Kendall 2006). When efficacy is assessed as an ability to achieve an outcome rather than an ability to perform a specific act or sequence of actions, it might be an indicator of coherence; i.e., as mentioned in the prior section, it might be an indicator that control has been scripted and is on the way to becoming automatic.

In addition to factors such as efficacy that are related to performance skills, other aspects of the self affect motivation for the initiation, cessation, and/or maintenance of healthy and risky behaviors. Three self-appraisals that affect motivation for health behaviors are optimism (Carver et al. 1989), a self-regulation strategy to conserve resources (e.g., not exercising in order to conserve physical energy) (Leventhal & Crouch 1997), and a strategy for goal disengagement (e.g., giving up on an unattainable goal by focusing on a new goal) (Wrosch et al. 2003). For example, Duke et al. (2002) found that community-dwelling older adults who appraised themselves as optimistic were more likely to initiate less vigorous activities (walking) to replace more vigorous activities (jogging) they had given up due to illness a year earlier. These elderly adults were less likely to make replacements, however, if they believed it important to conserve resources. In their examination of strategies for disengagement, Wrosch and colleagues (2003) argue that failing to give up unattainable goals can be a source of emotional distress that will reduce quality of life and have adverse effects on health. Wrosch et al. theorize that elderly people high on internal control are more likely to experience this syndrome of distress, as well as reduced quality of life and negative effects on their health, because they are more likely to be motivated to reach for goals that are unattainable within their limited remaining life spans. In contrast, elderly people low on control will more readily yield and identify more attainable goals. Interestingly, Wrosch and colleagues (2003) propose that internal control beliefs will be beneficial for giving up and replacing goals among younger persons. Finally, rather than focusing on specific strategies, Heidrich and colleagues (1994) showed that the discrepancy between ideal and perceived self accounted for the effects of cancer and social adjustment; the discrepancy between how the individuals wanted to be and how they saw themselves accounted for, i.e., mediated, their social adjustment and most of the effects of their illness on depression. Although these studies have clear implications for behaviors to prevent and control chronic illness, such as medication adherence, dietary control, and exercise, few provide evidence directly related to these behaviors.

Comment on self studies. It is clear that the perceived and conceptual self (Kihlstrom 1993) and its overall and specific properties (Swann et al. 2007) are intimately related to risk perception and behaviors for the prevention and control of chronic illness. Few studies, however, examine direct connections between factors of the self and the problem-solving processes involved in chronic illness management. For example, heuristics such as novelty (e.g., if a symptom is novel it is more likely to be perceived as serious; Leventhal & Scherer 1987), location (e.g., chest pain is often assumed to indicate heart problems rather than a lung problem, since the chest is most salient as the location of the heart), severity, and timeline are rules for appraising deviation from an underlying, stable image of the bodily self, but little attention has been given to this aspect of self by health investigators (see Petrie & Weinman 1997 for examples). Self-appraisals such as optimism, conservation of resources, and willingness to yield life goals are coping strategies that lead to the formation of coherent cognitive, emotional, and expressive behavioral scripts by encouraging similar and repeated approaches to life and health problems. The behavioral scripts and expressive behaviors associated with these self-ascribed orientations could affect physical health outcomes through the chronic activation of central autonomic pathways. These issues need to be explored in longitudinal studies that examine behavioral processes at both psychological and physiological levels. A possible approach to conceptualizing one aspect of the process involved in communication between the self and ongoing problem-solving processes would be to set the social comparison process, i.e., whether patients select upward or downward comparisons (Taylor & Lobel 1989), within the context of patient models of disease and treatment: upward when the representations and current evidence suggest the need for acquiring skills and hopeful outcomes, downward when they point to a need to bolster self-esteem. Finally, it is unclear whether person factors, such as optimism or disengagement, are traits and are less usable for predicting intraindividual outcomes or if they are products of domain-specific behavioral episodes that capture both inter- and intraperson effects (Cervone 2004). Person factors generated within specific domains, such as conservation of resources for physical survival, may generalize to other areas at a conceptual level, although instruments for assessment would need to be worded to reflect the content of each domain.

Cultural and social influences on health outcomes. Historians and social scientists alike have been quick to recognize the effects of environmental, cultural, and societal resources on disease and longevity. Braudel's (1979, p. 39) sobering review of the expansion and contraction in European and world populations illustrates how cycles of expansion and contraction are related to changes in climate, agricultural practices, and expanding trade. Recent data show substantial associations between mortality, aging, and disease and risk indicators with measures of social stratification, e.g., county of residence, income, education, religious involvement, etc. (House et al. 1992, Kaplan 1992). The data highlight the need for further investigation in three areas. First, information is needed as to how specific cultural and socioeconomic factors affect factors at the individual/psychological level. Studies of religion and health provide a more detailed view about how religious participation, spirituality, and a sense of self reduce risky behaviors and encourage healthy behaviors that affect health outcomes (See Schaie et al. 2004). It is not always clear, however, whether or how a particular feature of the ecological context and/or culture, e.g., religious attendance, social engagement, prayer, spirituality, or the body as a temple of God (Hill et al. 2006), affect the specific beliefs and behaviors that affect health outcomes. The association of cultural factors with healthy and risky behaviors could be mediated by common, culturally generated personal traits, social relationships, lifestyles, representations of illness and treatments, and/or approaches to planning for prevention and management of illness and illness risks. Second, when social and cultural analyses identify the specific behavioral factors correlated with disease, there are often ambiguities as to how these behaviors "get under the skin," that is, how they influence the physiological pathways leading to disease and mortality (Taylor et al. 1997). Thus, although associations between disease risk and factors such as ecology, socioeconomic status, and religious involvement identify important areas for research, the data often fail to indicate whether one or some combination of environmental or social factors might be responsible for the increase in disease. The importance of identifying mediators between superordinate factors such as socioeconomic status and disease indicators can be seen by the changing relationship between a superordinate factor, in this case gender, and lung cancer. Lung cancer rates declined among physician cigarette smokers approximately 20 years after Doll & Hill's (1950) report relating lung cancer to smoking. A similar decline occurred for men in the United States after the 1964 Surgeon General's report (U.S. Dept. Health Human Serv. 1964). Lung cancer rates and prevalence of smoking gradually increased, however, among women during this same period, when marketing campaigns focused on women and the "light cigarette" (Kozlowski et al. 1998). Identifying mediators for these changes, particularly for the failure to observe a decline in smoking among women, is not a simple issue. Depression was thought to be responsible for greater difficulties in smoking cessation among women than among men, but meta-analyses cast doubt on this hypothesis as at least one type of depression, major depressive disorder, neither moderates short- or long-term cessation nor affects gender differences in ease of quitting (Hitsman et al. 2003). Variation across studies in identifying mediators may reflect inadequacies in sample size and the conceptualization and time of assessment of mediating variables. Diary data are beginning to describe the details of social interactions responsible for behavioral and affective factors that may lead to adverse health outcomes (Rook 2003). The task remains, however, to identify the factors that mediated the relationship of social marketing to the social context and role definitions that are involved in the gender differences in initiation and cessation of smoking. As many of the physiological pathways relating smoking to lung cancer have been described, the data succeed in identifying specific factors bridging the social environment and individual behavior to "get under the skin."

Cognitive-behavioral anthropologists (see, e.g., Garro 2000) have described some of the processes involved in the link of culture to health behaviors by assessing whether beliefs about specific illnesses are shared by multiple individuals within a specific ethnic community. Garro (2000) identified a culturally shared schema or prototype for hypertension and two prototypes for diabetes—one Western in nature, the other specific to ethnic beliefs and practices. Each of the diabetes prototypes identified specific causes and routes for treatment that made sense to individuals and guided their management of diabetes. Narratives of personal history with diabetes meld personal experience with cultural prototypes and reflect the storyteller's degree of belonging to ethnic or Western cultures. Cultural beliefs and their associated use of Western, traditional, and alternative care have been examined in mental health (Cabassa et al. 2007, Karasz et al. 2003), cancer genetic counseling (Eichmeyer et al. 2005), and other conditions (Buchwald et al. 2000). This research was stimulated in part by Pachter's (1994) paper, which alerted medical practitioners to the effects of ethnic disparities in representations of diseases among patients and practitioners that lead to conflict between doctors and patients and ineffective use of medical treatments by patients.

Comments on social factors. The emphasis on the cognitive and affective components of beliefs and the individual acculturation to Western practices is directly relevant to the cognitive processes examined in the construction of illness and treatment representations discussed in the section above on problem solving processes in health and illness, The Process of Self-Management of Chronic Illness. It is important, however, not to overlook the role played by institutions in the formation of patient representations of illness and treatment: Culturally established institutions train practitioners in the management of illness, determine the mixture of folk and Western biomedical models involved in the training of practitioners, establish the appearance of the health care system, and establish how care is delivered (Chrisman & Kleinman 1983). Three points related to social factors are worthy of mention for the present review.

First, practitioners have been sensitized to the role of acculturation as a factor in rates of life-threatening chronic illnesses—the causal factors of illnesses such as prostate cancer and obesity ranging from diet and stress in new environments to issues in migration (Jasso et al. 2004). Second, an extensive literature has emerged on the role of linguistic competency (e.g., Ngo-Metzger et al. 2003) and ethnic match of patient and practitioner (e.g., Tarn et al. 2005) in communication and trust in primary care settings. Third, practitioners' questions and procedures in the medical examination reinforce the heuristics patients use in self-appraisal. Asking, "Where does it hurt," "How long has it been going on," and "How does it feel" reinforces heuristics of location, duration, and pattern for self-diagnosis and management. For example, by examining the lungs, legs, and feet (location heuristic) of patients with congestive heart failure, doctors reinforce to the patients that their illness is not related to the heart but instead to respiratory function and circulation in the legs and feet. The detailed analysis of the processes involved in the contacts between patients and practitioners should be helpful for the development of interventions that are both effective and efficient for enhancing patients' understanding and management of chronic conditions.

COGNITIVE-BEHAVIORAL INTERVENTIONS TO IMPROVE SELF-MANAGEMENT

Our review of processes from problem solving through self and social contexts was designed to raise questions and suggest directions for innovative approaches for interventions that will meet criteria for effectiveness and efficiency—i.e., for the development of interventions that are as effective as those in the diabetes prevention trials reviewed above but simpler and less demanding of time and skill by practitioners and patients. Current findings provide both support and doubt as to the feasibility of reaching this dual goal of efficiency and effectiveness. For example, meta-

analyses show that forming intentions and/or plans for action (Leventhal 1970) are effective for crossing the gap between intention to action for simple, one-time behaviors, though generally are ineffective for complex, time-demanding behaviors that prevent and control chronic illnesses (exercise, dietary change; Webb & Sheeran 2006). Moderate levels of success have also been reported for behavioral interventions for the control of chronic illness that are implemented from a social-learning framework (a process approach that is identical in many respects to the problem-solving approach described in the present review) for the control of some chronic conditions. For example, hemoglobin A1c and blood sugar levels for diabetes and blood pressure for hypertension have been successfully controlled through such interventions but symptoms of osteoarthritis or rheumatoid arthritis have not (Chodosh et al. 2005, Lorig et al. 2005). The success of diabetes and hypertension interventions is also balanced by mixed outcomes for congestive heart failure—negative outcomes have been obtained, including failure to prevent recurrent episodes and hospitalization in some sites (DeBusk et al. 2004), but positive outcomes have been obtained in other sites (Sisk et al. 2006).

The successes of social learning interventions indicate that they have captured essential elements needed for improvement of hard outcomes of chronic illnesses (Lorig et al. 1999). Although the interventions are less complex and time demanding than the diabetes trials, their success rates are also less impressive, due perhaps to the generality of the interventions; they are not focused on specific aspects of particular chronic conditions (Wagner 2004). A central theme underlying our review is that increasing the specificity of behavioral management for particular diseases requires the addition of concepts to self-regulation theory generated from observations in the clinic and community, i.e., bidirectional translation. This may entail changes as simple as identifying the invalid subjective cues that patients use to guide self-management (medication use) and developing behavioral procedures that teach them to ignore subjective targets and use objective indicators (blood pressure and/or blood sugar readings) to guide self-management (Dunbar 2007). Other simple procedures may involve reframing how a behavioral intervention is implemented to insure, for example, that patients see their depressive symptoms as part of their chronic physical illness and not as a separate and unmanageable mental illness. In short, current social learning interventions may not have adequately considered how patients and their medical practitioners represent illnesses and how the treatment experience fits with the patients' representations of their chronic conditions. Once such issues are considered, the effectiveness of the interventions may improve substantially.

Process Theories and Design of Clinical Trials

Investigators have recognized the need to increase the effectiveness and efficiency of behavioral interventions and are proposing new approaches to the analysis and design of clinical trials. For example, Kraemer et al. (2002) have discussed the need for assessments to define subgroups of participants (moderators) prior to the implementation of behavioral interventions and to identify and measure mediators, i.e., factors recorded post intervention that affect treatment adherence. They indicate the need for such analyses in completed multicenter trials and the need for a theoretically based approach to implementation of such measures in ongoing and proposed large-scale trials (Kraemer et al. 2002). These recommendations assume that interventions targeting specific subgroups are potentially more effective and more efficient than interventions using common methods for all participants. Cervone's (2004) analysis suggests the need for extreme caution, however, in expecting measures of traits or *Diagnostic and Statistical Manual of Mental Disorders* (DSM) categories to isolate the within-person fac-

tors that are responsible for the initiation and maintenance of healthy and risky behaviors in specific domains. Assessing factors such as health worry that interact with specific situational triggers (Bem & Funder 1978) would move individual-difference assessment closer to the intraperson or process level by capturing how participants experience and understand health threats and preventive and treatment behaviors. Most clinical trials, however, have selected traits and/or DSM categories as moderators and therefore have not assessed patients' perceptions of their chronic health problems, the psychological accompaniments of these problems, or the procedures they have used or prefer to use for their management. The deficits associated with using interindividual differences as moderators are seen in clinical trials testing whether reducing depressive symptoms would increase treatment adherence in comorbid conditions. The expectation that addressing depression would improve patient care of comorbid conditions seems reasonable because medication adherence has been observed to be poorer in those who are depressed [e.g., aspirin was not taken daily, as prescribed, by patients hospitalized with acute coronary syndrome who scored higher on the Beck Depression Inventory (Gehi et al. 2005)]. The expectation is also reasonable given that decline in depression was associated prospectively with increased adherence (Rieckmann et al. 2006). Interventions to reduce depression have been unsuccessful, however, in improving adherence (Haynes et al. 2005). It is unclear precisely which aspects of patients' physical illness or social and personal contexts elicit and sustain these depressive states or which aspects of patients' affective reactions are responsible for nonadherence. Inconsistent and negative findings of depression interventions may be the result of using measures of interindividual difference rather than intraindividual, self-management processes for matching patients to treatments (Sobell & Sobell 2000). Identification of intraindividual moderators at the level of process rather than trait calls for sophisticated, content-specific theory and instruments (Cervone et al. 2006, Evans 2006) with sufficient validity to identify and assess these factors at the outset of a clinical trial.

Two alternatives for the development of effective and efficient behavioral interventions that are now being tested are stepwise treatment and self-assignment to treatment. In stepwise treatments, all patients are assigned to the least costly (with regard to time, effort, and negative side effects), highly effective first-step treatment; the second-step treatment is reserved for patients for whom the first step of treatment fails. Second-step treatments are often more tailored to the individual's behavioral or biological system and are often more intensive in terms of time and effort than are first-step treatments. Stepwise approaches to behavioral interventions may have problems less frequently encountered in medication trials. For example, patients in a medical trial may be more likely to attribute failure of a first-step treatment to deficiencies in the medication, whereas patients in behavioral interventions may be likely to attribute failure of a first-step treatment to deficiencies in themselves, a self-attribution that can increase feelings of hopelessness and reduce self-efficacy and motivation for the second-step treatment (Wilson et al. 2000). Improvements in stepwise behavioral treatments will require conditions that prime patients to attribute initial failure to treatment rather than to themselves; this is similar to the goals of treatments for addictions, in which patients demonstrate the "abstinence violation effect" by blaming themselves for losing control over the negative, addictive behavior (Curry et al. 1987).

A direct approach to patient perceptions of illness and treatment is involved in clinical trials in which patients select their preferred treatments; discussion of the conduct and analysis of these trials is under way (see TenHave et al. 2003, Thornett 2001). Assignment to pharmacological- or psychological-behavioral treatments that is inconsistent with patients' preferences has been shown to have negative effects on the treatment alliance. For example, the perceived treatment alliance improves over time for patients assigned to their preferred psychological treatment but declines if these patients are assigned to a nonpreferred pharmacological treatment (Iacoviello et al. 2007). Consistency with preferences does not seem to affect the alliance for patients who prefer a pharmacological treatment. Because positive alliances are associated with treatment benefits (Martin et al. 2000), treating patients based on their preferences may prove to be important for behavioral interventions for chronic illnesses. It is unknown whether the benefits of consistency in assignment are mediated by the patient's perception of congruity between the representations of the illness and the treatment or from improved communication allowing practitioners and patients to develop shared goals respecting benefits in both subjective experience and objective function. In addition to the above approaches to clinical trial design, Dunn & Bentall (2007) have proposed the use of the instrumental variable method to identify process variables in treatment interventions. These methods are able to assess not only whether an intervention is effective but also are able to examine how it achieves effectiveness. Thus, the method will allow researchers to examine causal processes involved in effective and efficient interventions.

PAST, PRESENT, FUTURE: CONCLUDING COMMENTS

Our view of the status of behavioral research for chronic illness can be summarized as follows. First, changes in behavior can improve health outcomes. The reductions in lung cancer (Ebbert et al. 2003) and breast cancer and the intervention trials for individuals at high risk for diabetes are examples of the effectiveness of behavioral change. Second, to this point in time, interventions focused on changing the behavior of individual patients that have proven effective for long-term behavioral change are complex and time consuming; they meet the effectiveness criteria for evidence-based practice but are not cost effective or usable in most practice settings. Third, the development of theoretical concepts supported by substantial data show that patients represent specific chronic illnesses and treatments based upon their experience and perception of somatic changes in themselves and observations and exposure to information about illness in others. These exposures affect the behavioral strategies they perceive to be effective and within their competence to perform for the prevention and control of chronic illness. Fourth, the translation of what has been learned about how patients self-regulate health into effective and usable interventions is at beginning stages; interventions work for some diseases, though it is unclear which components are necessary and/or sufficient for success. Finally, investigators are considering approaches to clinical trial design that may make behavioral interventions more usable, i.e., efficient and accessible to the clinical environment, and these innovative approaches appear to address models of the processes underlying self-management. The integration of self-regulatory models with new approaches to clinical trials is, however, a nontrivial problem because the models suggest that interventions must focus on practitioners and not just on patients. How patients' and practitioners' models affect communication with one another, with family members, and in response to messages from the surrounding culture will determine whether interventions for broad lifestyle changes or for use of specific medications are successful in meeting expectations for changes in objective as well as subjective criteria of benefit. Behavioral interventions of the future may parallel the features of individualized medicine; the former involves treatments matched to specific cognitive-affective patterns of the individual patient, and the latter involves treatments matched to the specific expression of genes underlying the patient's disease. Treatment effectiveness would be evaluated by the accumulation of case-by-case outcomes and, hopefully, the posterior probabilities of success will exceed the prior.

ACKNOWLEDGMENTS

This review was written with support from a National Institute of Aging grant, R24AG023958, the Center for the Study of Health Beliefs and Behaviors. The authors thank Tamara Musumeci for her help with the references.

LITERATURE CITED

Ader R, Cohen N. 1993. Psychoneuroimmunology: conditioning and stress. *Annu. Rev. Psychol.* 44:53–85

Ajzen I. 1991. The theory of planned behavior. *Organ. Behav. Hum. Dec. Process.* 50:179–211

Albarracin D, Johnson BT, Fishbein M, Muellerleile PA. 2001. Theories of reasoned action and planned behavior as models of condom use: a meta-analysis. *Psychol. Bull.* 127:142–61

Am. Pyschol. Assoc. 2000. *Diagnostic and Statistical Manual of Mental Disorders*. Arlington, VA: Am. Psychiatr. Publ. 4th ed., text rev.

Antonovsky A. 1993. The structure and properties of the Sense of Coherence Scale. *Soc. Sci. Med.* 36:725–33

Baldwin AS, Rothman AJ, Hertel AW, Linde JA, Jeffery RW, et al. 2006. Specifying the determinants of the initiation and maintenance of behavior change: an examination of self-efficacy, satisfaction, and smoking cessation. *Health Psychol.* 25(5):626–34

Bandura A. 1989. Self-regulation of motivation and action through internal standards and goal systems. In *Goal Concepts in Personality and Social Psychology*, ed. LA Pervin, pp. 19–85. Hillsdale, NJ: Erlbaum

Bandura A. 2004. Health promotion by social cognitive means. *Health Educ. Behav.* 31(2):143–64

Barclay TR, Hinkin CH, Castellon SA, Mason KI, Reinhard MJ, et al. 2007. Age-associated predictors of medication adherence in HIV-positive adults: health beliefs, self-efficacy, and neurocognitive status. *Health Psychol.* 26(1):40–49

Barefoot JC, Dahlstrom WG, Williams RB Jr. 1983. Hostility, CHD incidence, and total mortality: a 25-year follow-up study of 255 physicians. *Psychosom. Med.* 45(1):59–63

Baum A, Posluszny DM. 1999. Health psychology: mapping biobehavioral contributions to health and illness. *Annu. Rev. Psychol.* 50:137–63

Baumann L, Cameron LD, Zimmerman R, Leventhal H. 1989. Illness representations and matching labels with symptoms. *Health Psychol.* 8:449–69

Bem DJ, Funder DC. 1978. Predicting more of the people more of the time: assessing the personality of situations. *Psychol. Rev.* 85(6):485–500

Bickell BA, Federman AD, Aufses AH Jr. 2005. Influence of time on risk of bowel resection in complete small bowel obstruction. *J. Am. Coll. Surg.* 201:847–54

Bishop GD. 1991. Understanding the understanding of illness: lay disease representations. In *Mental Representation in Health and Illness*, ed. JA Skelton, RT Croyle, pp. 32–59. New York: Springer-Verlag

Bogg T, Roberts BW. 2004. Conscientiousness and health-related behaviors: a meta-analysis of the leading behavioral contributors to mortality. *Psychol. Bull.* 130(6):887–919

Braudel F. 1979. *Civilization and Capitalism, 15th–18th Century*, Vols. I, II, & III. New York: Harper & Row

Broadbent E, Petrie KJ, Main J, Weinman J. 2006. The Brief Illness Perception Questionnaire. *J. Psychosom. Res.* 60(6):631–37

Brody EM, Kleban MH. 1983. Day-to-day mental and physical health symptoms of older people: a report on health logs. *Gerontologist* 23(1):75–85

Brownlee S, Leventhal EA, Leventhal H. 2000. Regulation, self-regulation and construction of the self in maintaining physical health. In *Handbook of Self-Regulation*, ed. M Boekartz, PR Pintrich, M Zeidner, pp. 369–416. San Diego, CA: Academic

Buchwald D, Beals J, Manson SM. 2000. Use of traditional health practices among native Americans in a primary care setting. *Med. Care* 38(12):1191–99

Bunde J, Martin R. 2006. Depression and prehospital delay in the context of myocardial infarction. *Psychosom. Med.* 68:51–57

Burgess CC, Ramirez A, Richards M, Love S. 1998. Who and what influences delayed presentation in breast cancer? *Br. J. Cancer* 77(8):1343–48

Cabassa LJ, Lester R, Zayas LH. 2007. "It's like being in a labyrinth": Hispanic immigrants' perceptions of depression and attitudes toward treatments. *J. Immigrant Health* 9:1–16

Cameron L, Leventhal EA, Leventhal H. 1995. Seeking medical care in response to symptoms and life stress. *Psychosom. Med.* 57(1):37–47

Carver CS, Scheier MF, Weintraub JK. 1989. Assessing coping strategies: a theoretically based approach. *J. Personal. Soc. Psychol.* 56:267–83

Cervone D. 2004. Personality architecture: within-person structures and processes. *Annu. Rev. Psychol.* 56:423–52

Cervone D, Shadel WG, Smith RE, Fiori M. 2006. Self-regulation: reminders and suggestions from personality science. *Appl. Psychol. Int. Rev.* 55(3):333–85

Chodosh J, Morton SC, Mojica W, Maglione M, Suttorp MJ, et al. 2005. Meta-analysis: chronic disease self-management programs for older adults. *Ann. Intern. Med.* 143:427–38

Chrisman NJ, Kleinman A. 1983. Popular health care, social networks, and cultural meanings: the orientation of medical anthropology. In *Handbook of Health, Healthcare, and the Health Professions*, ed. D Mechanic, pp. 569–90. New York: Free Press

Cohen S. 2004. Social relationships and health. *Am. Psychol.* 59(8):676–84

Cohen S, Frank E, Doyle WJ, Skoner DP, Rabin BS, Gwaltney JM Jr. 1998. Types of stressors that increase susceptibility to the common cold in healthy adults. *Health Psychol.* 17(3):211–13

Cohen S, Williamson GM. 1991. Stress and infectious disease in humans. *Psychol. Bull.* 109(1):5–24

Cooper RP, Shallice T. 2006. Hierarchical schemas and goals in the control of sequential behavior. *Psychol. Rev.* 113(4):887–916

Costa PT Jr, McCrae RR. 1992. Normal personality assessment in clinical practice: the NEO Personality Inventory. *Psychol. Assess.* 4:5–13

Critchley HD. 2005. Neural mechanisms of autonomic, affective, and cognitive integration. *J. Comp. Neurol.* 493:154–66

Curry S, Marlatt GA, Gordon JR. 1987. Abstinence violation effect: validation of an attributional construct with smoking cessation. *J. Consult. Clin. Psychol.* 55(2):145–49

De Bourdeaudhuij I, Brug J. 2000. Tailoring dietary feedback to reduce fat intake: an intervention at the family level. *Health Educ. Res.* 15(4):449–62

DeBusk RF, Miller NH, Parker KM, Bandura A, Kraemer HC, et al. 2004. Care management for low-risk patients with heart failure. *Ann. Intern. Med.* 141:606–13

Dechamps A, Lafont L, Bourdel-Marchasson I. 2007. Effects of Tai Chi exercises on self-efficacy and psychological health. *Eur. Rev. Aging Physical Activity* 4(1):25–32

Diabetes Prev. Prog. Res. Group. 2002. Reduction in the incidence of type 2 diabetes with lifestyle intervention or metformin. *New Engl. J. Med.* 346(6):393–403

Diabetes Prev. Prog. Res. Group. 2003. Within-trial cost-effectiveness of lifestyle intervention or metformin for the primary prevention of type 2 diabetes. *Diabetes Care* 26:2518–23

Diefenbach MA, Leventhal H. 1996. The common-sense model of illness representation: theoretical and practical considerations. *J. Soc. Distress Homeless.* 5(1):11–38

Diefenbach MA, Miller SM, Daly MB. 1999. Specific worry about breast cancer predicts mammography use in women at risk for breast and ovarian cancer. *Health Psychol.* 18(5):532–36

Doll R, Hill AB. 1950. Smoking and carcinoma of the lung; preliminary report. *Br. Med. J.* 2(4682):739–48

Dracup K, Moser DK, Eisenberg M, Meischke H, Alonzo AA, Braslow A. 1995. Causes of delay in seeking treatment for heart attack symptoms. *Soc. Sci. Med.* 40(3):379–92

Duke J, Brownlee S, Leventhal EA, Leventhal H. 2002. Giving up and replacing activities in response to illness. *J. Gerontol. Psychol. Sci.* 57B(4):367–76

Dunbar L, Schneider SH, Burns E, Leventhal H. 2007. Does patient blood glucose monitoring improve diabetes control: Always, sometimes, never? A systematic review from the framework of the common-sense model. *Diabetes Educ.* In press

Dunn G, Bentall R. 2007. Modelling treatment effect heterogeneity in randomized controlled trials of complex interventions (psychological treatments). *Stat. Med.* DOI: 10.1002/sim.2891

Ebbert JO, Yang P, Vachon CM, Vierkant RA, Cerhan JR, et al. 2003. Lung cancer risk reduction after smoking cessation: observations from a prospective cohort of women. *J. Clin. Oncol.* 21(5):921–26

Eichmeyer JN, Northrup H, Assel MA, Goka TJ, Johnston DA, Williams AT. 2005. An assessment of risk understanding in Hispanic genetic counseling patients. *J. Genet. Couns.* 14(4):319–28

Epstein S. 1973. The self-concept revisited: or a theory of a theory. *Am. Psychol.* 28(5):404–16

Evans J St BT. 2006. The heuristic-analytic theory of reasoning: extension and evaluation. *Psychon. Bull. Rev.* 13(3):378–95

Finch EA, Linde JA, Jeffery RW, Rothman AJ, King CM, Levy RL. 2005. The effects of outcome expectations and satisfaction on weight loss and maintenance: correlational and experimental analyses—a randomized trial. *Health Psychol.* 24(6):608–16

Friedman HS, Booth-Kewley S. 1987. The "disease-prone personality": a meta-analytic view of the construct. *Am. Psychol.* 42:539–55

Fries JF. 2005. The compression of morbidity. *Milbank Q.* 83(4):897–907

Galea S, Nandi A, Vlahov D. 2004. The social epidemiology of substance use. *Epidemiol. Rev.* 26(1):36–52

Garro LC. 2000. Remembering what one knows and the construction of the past: a comparison of cultural consensus theory and cultural schema theory. *Ethos* 28(3):275–319

Gehi A, Haas D, Pipkin S, Whooley MA. 2005. Depression and medication adherence in outpatients with coronary heart disease. *Arch. Intern. Med.* 165:2508–13

Gillies CL, Abrams KR, Lambert PC, Cooper NJ, Sutton AJ, et al. 2007. Pharmacological and lifestyle interventions to prevent or delay type 2 diabetes in people with impaired glucose tolerance: systematic review and meta-analysis. *Br. Med. J.* 334:299

Hagger MS, Chatzisarantis NLD, Biddle SJH. 2002. A meta-analytic review of the theories of reasoned action and planned behavior in physical activity: predictive validity and the contribution of additional variables. *J. Sport Exerc. Psychol.* 24:3–32

Hall S, Weinman J, Marteau TM. 2004. The motivating impact of informing women smokers of a link between smoking and cervical cancer: the role of coherence. *Health Psychol.* 23(4):419–24

Halm EA, Mora P, Leventhal H. 2006. No symptoms, no asthma: the acute episodic disease belief is associated with poor self-management among inner city adults with persistent asthma. *Chest* 129:573–80

Hampson SE, Goldberg LR, Vogt TM, Dubanoski JP. 2007. Mechanisms by which childhood personality traits influence adult health status: educational attainment and health behaviors. *Health Psychol.* 26(1):121–25

Hay JL, McCaul KD, Magnan RE. 2006. Does worry about breast cancer predict screening behaviors? A meta-analysis of the prospective evidence. *Prev. Med.* 42(6):401–8

Haynes RB, Yao X, Degani A, Kripalani S, Garg A, McDonald HP. 2005. Interventions to enhance medication adherence. *Cochrane Database Syst. Rev.* DOI: 10.1002/14651858.CD000011.pub2

Heggestad ED, Kanfer R. 2005. The predictive validity of self-efficacy in training performance: little more than past performance. *J. Exp. Psychol. Appl.* 11:84–97

Heidrich SM, Forsthoff CA, Ward SE. 1994. Psychological adjustment in adults with cancer: the self as mediator. *Health Psychol.* 13:346–53

Henderson C, Hagger M, Orbell S. 2007. Does priming a specific illness schema result in an attentional information-processing bias for specific illnesses? *Health Psychol.* 26:165–73

Heneghan C, Thompson M, Perera R. 2006. Prevention of diabetes: drug trials show promising results, but have limitations. *Br. Med. J.* 333:764–65

Hill TD, Burdette AM, Ellison CG, Musick MA. 2006. Religious attendance and health behaviors of Texas adults. *Prev. Med.* 42:309–12

Hitsman B, Borrelli B, McChargue DE, Spring B, Niaura R. 2003. History of depression and smoking cessation outcome: a meta-analysis. *J. Consult. Clin. Psychol.* 71(4):657–63

Horne R. 2003. Treatment perceptions and self-regulation. In *The Self-Regulation of Health and Illness Behavior*, ed. LD Cameron, H Leventhal, pp. 138–53. London: Routledge

Horne R, Buick D, Fisher M, Leake H, Cooper V, Weinman J. 2004. Doubts about necessity and concerns about adverse effects: identifying the types of beliefs that are associated with nonadherence to HAART. *Int. J. STD AIDS* 15(1):38–44

Horne R, Weinman J. 1999. Patients' beliefs about prescribed medicines and their role in adherence to treatment in chronic physical illness. *J. Psychosom. Res.* 47(6):555–67

Horne R, Weinman J. 2002. Self-regulation and self-management in asthma: exploring the role of illness perceptions and treatment beliefs in explaining nonadherence to preventer medication. *Psychol. Health* 17(1):17–33

Horowitz CR, Rein SB, Leventhal H. 2004. A story of maladies, misconceptions and mishaps: effective management of heart failure. *Soc. Sci. Med.* 58:631–43

House JS, Kessler RC, Herzog AR, Mero RP, Kinney AM, Breslow MJ. 1992. Social stratification, age, and health. In *Aging, Health Behaviors, and Health Outcomes*, ed. KW Schaie, D Blazer, JS House, pp. 1–32. Hillsdale, NJ: Erlbaum

Iacoviello BM, McCarthy KS, Barrett MS, Rynn M, Gallop R, Barber JP. 2007. Treatment preferences affect the therapeutic alliance: implications for randomized controlled trials. *J. Consult. Clin. Psychol.* 75(1):194–98

Ioannidis J. 2004. Materializing research promises: opportunities, priorities and conflicts in translational medicine. *J. Transl. Med.* 2:5–10

Jamison KR. 1995. *An Unquiet Mind*. New York: Knopf

Jasso G, Massey DS, Rosenzweig MR, Smith JP. 2004. *Immigrant health: selectivity and acculturation*. Work. Pap. 04/23, Inst. Fiscal Stud., London

Kaplan GA. 1992. Health and aging in the Alameda county study. In *Aging, Health Behaviors, and Health Outcomes*, ed. KW Schaie, D Blazer, JS House, pp. 69–88. Hillsdale, NJ: Erlbaum

Karasz A, Sacajiu G, Garcia N. 2003. Conceptual models of psychological distress among low-income patients in an inner-city primary care clinic. *J. Gen. Intern. Med.* 18:475–77

Kemeny MA. 2003. The psychobiology of stress. *Curr. Direct. Psychol. Sci.* 12:124–29

Kiecolt-Glaser JK, McGuire L, Robles TF, Glaser R. 2002. Emotions, morbidity, and mortality: new perspectives from psychoneuroimmunology. *Annu. Rev. Psychol.* 53(1):83–107

Kihlstrom JF. 1993. What does the self look like? In *The Mental Representation of Trait and Autobiographical Knowledge About the Self*, ed. TK Srull, pp. 79–90. Hillsdale, NJ: Erlbaum

Kozlowski LT, Goldberg ME, Yost BA, White EL, Sweeney CT, Pillitteri JL. 1998. Smokers' misperceptions of light and ultralight cigarettes may keep them smoking. *Am. J. Prev. Med.* 15(1):78–79

Kraemer HC, Wilson T, Fairburn CG, Agras S. 2002. Mediators and moderators of treatment effects in randomized clinical trials. *Arch. Gen. Psychiatry* 59(10):877–83

Lerman DC. 2003. From the laboratory to community application: translational research in behavior analysis. *J. Appl. Behav. Anal.* 36:415–19

Leventhal EA, Crouch M. 1997. Are there differences in perceptions of illness across the lifespan? In *Perceptions of Health and Illness: Current Research and Applications*, ed. KJ Petrie, JA Weinman, pp. 77–102. Amsterdam, Netherlands: Harwood Acad.

Leventhal H. 1970. Findings and theory in the study of fear communication. *Adv. Exp. Soc. Psychol.* 5:119–86

Leventhal H, Contrada R, Leventhal EA. 2007a. Lessons from white coat hypertension: Comment on Spruill et al., "The Impact of Perceived Hypertension Status on Anxiety and the White Coat Hypertension Effect." *Ann. Behav. Med.* In press

Leventhal H, Forster R, Leventhal EA. 2007b. Self-regulation of health threats, affect, and the self: lessons from older adults. In *Handbook of Health Psychology and Aging*, ed. CM Aldwin, CL Park, A Spiro III, pp. 341–66. New York: Guilford

Leventhal H, Musumeci T, Contrada R. 2007c. Current issues and new directions in psychology and health: theory, translation, and evidence-based practice. *Psychol. Health* 22(4):381–86

Leventhal H, Scherer K. 1987. The relationship of emotion to cognition: a functional approach to a semantic controversy. *Cogn. Emot.* 1(1):3–28

Leventhal H, Singer R, Jones S. 1965. Effects of fear and specificity of recommendation upon attitudes and behavior. *J. Personal. Soc. Psychol.* 2(1):20–29

Lindstrom J, Louheranta A, Mannelin M. 2003. The Finnish Diabetes Prevention Study (DPS): lifestyle intervention and 3-year results on diet and physical activity. *Diabetes Care* 26:3230–36

Lorig KR, Hurwicz ML, Sobel D, Hobbs M, Ritter PL. 2005. A national dissemination of an evidence-based self-management program: a process evaluation study. *Patient Educ. Couns.* 59:69–79

Lorig KR, Sobel DS, Stewart AL, Brown BW Jr, Bandura A, et al. 1999. Evidence suggesting that a chronic disease self-management program can improve health status while reducing hospitalization: a randomized trial. *Med. Care* 37(1):5–14

MacGregor K, Handley M, Wong S, Sharifi C, Gjeltema K, et al. 2006. Behavior-change action plans in primary care: a feasibility study of clinicians. *J. Am. Board Fam. Med.* 19:215–23

Maher MJ, Mora PA, Leventhal H. 2006. Depression as a predictor of perceived social support and demand: a componential approach using a prospective sample of older adults. *Emotion* 6(3):450–58

Maibach E, Murphy DA. 1995. Self-efficacy in health promotion research and practice: conceptualization and measurement. *Health Educ. Res.* 10(1):37–50

Mak YW, Loke AY, Lam TH, Abdullah AS. 2006. Predictors of the participation of smoking parents in a proactive telephone-based smoking cessation program. *Addict. Behav.* 31(10):1731–43

Marteau T, Senior V, Humphries SE, Bobrow M, Cranston T, et al. 2004. Psychological impact of genetic testing for familial hypercholesterolaemia in a previously aware population: a randomised controlled trial. *Am. J. Med. Genet.* 128A:285–93

Martin DJ, Garske JP, Davis MK. 2000. Relation of the therapeutic alliance with outcome and other variables: a meta-analytic review. *J. Consult. Clin. Psychol.* 68(3):438–50

McCaffery K, Wardle J, Waller J. 2003. Knowledge, attitudes, and behavioral intentions in relation to the early detection of colorectal cancer in the United Kingdom. *Prev. Med.* 36(5):525–35

McKinlay JB, McKinlay SM. 1977. The questionable contribution of medical measures to the decline of mortality in the United States in the twentieth century. *Milbank Q.* 55(3):405–28

McDonald HP, Garg AX, Haynes RB. 2002. Interventions to enhance patient adherence to medication prescriptions: scientific review. *JAMA* 288(22):2868–79

Meyer D, Leventhal H, Gutmann M. 1985. Common-sense models of illness: the example of hypertension. *Health Psychol.* 4:115–35

Mora PA, Halm EA, Leventhal H, Ceric F. 2007. Elucidating the relationship between negative affectivity and symptoms: the role of illness-specific affective responses. *Ann. Behav. Med.* In press

Mora PA, Robitaille C, Leventhal H, Swigar M, Leventhal EA. 2002. Trait negative affect relates to prior week symptoms, but not to reports of illness episodes, illness symptoms and care seeking among older people. *Psychosom. Med.* 64(3):436–49

Moss-Morris R, Weinman J, Petrie KJ, Horne R, Cameron LD, Buick D. 2002. The Revised Illness Perception Questionnaire (IPQ-R). *Psychol. Health* 17(1):1–16

Ngo-Metzger Q, Massagli MP, Clarridge BR, Manocchia M, Davis RB, et al. 2003. Linguistic and cultural barriers to care. *J. Gen. Intern. Med.* 18:44–52

Orbell S, Hagger M, Brown V, Tidy J. 2006. Comparing two theories of health behavior: a prospective study of noncompletion of treatment following cervical cancer screening. *Health Psychol.* 25(5):604–15

Orbell S, Hodgkins S, Sheeran P. 1997. Implementation intentions and the theory of planned behavior. *Personal. Soc. Psychol. Bull.* 23(9):945–54

Pachter LM. 1994. Culture and clinical care: folk illness beliefs and behaviors and their implications for health care delivery. *JAMA* 271:690–94

Park DC, Hertzog C, Leventhal H, Morrell R, Leventhal E, et al. 1999. Medication adherence in rheumatoid arthritis patients: older is wiser. *J. Am. Geriatr. Soc.* 47:172–83

Petrie KJ, Weinman JA. 1997. *Perceptions of Health and Illness: Current Research and Applications.* Amsterdam: Harwood Acad.

Pi-Sunyer FX. 1993. Medical hazards of obesity. *Ann. Intern. Med.* 119(7):655–60

Powers WT. 1973. Feedback: beyond behaviorism. *Science* 179:351–56

Prochaska JO, Velicer WF, Redding C, Rossi JS, Goldstein M, et al. 2005. Stage-based expert systems to guide a population of primary care patients to quit smoking, eat healthier, prevent skin cancer, and receive regular mammograms. *Prev. Med.* 41:406–16

Prohaska TR, Keller ML, Leventhal EA, Leventhal H. 1987. Impact of symptoms and aging attribution on emotions and coping. *Health Psychol.* 6:495–514

Renner B, Schwarzer R. 2005. The motivation to eat a healthy diet: how intenders and nonintenders differ in terms of risk perception, outcome expectancies, self-efficacy, and nutrition behavior. *Polish Psychol. Bull.* 36(1):7–15

Rieckmann N, Gerin W, Kronish IM, Burg MM, Chaplin WF, et al. 2006. Course of depressive symptoms and medication adherence after acute coronary syndromes. *J. Am. Coll. Cardiol.* 48(11):2218–22

Rodin J, Langer EJ. 1996. Long-term effects of a control-relevant intervention with the institutionalized aged. In *Readings in Social Psychology: The Art and Science of Research*, ed. S Fein, S Spencer, pp. 175–80. Boston, MA: Houghton Mifflin

Rodin J, Salovey P. 1989. Health psychology. *Annu. Rev. Psychol.* 40:533–79

Rook KS. 2003. Exposure and reactivity to negative social exchanges: a preliminary investigation using daily diary data. *J Gerontol. B Psychol. Sci. Soc. Sci.* 58B(2):100–11

Ross S, Walker A, MacLeod MJ. 2004. Patient compliance in hypertension: role of illness perceptions and treatment beliefs. *J. Human Hypertens.* 18:607–13

Rothman AJ. 2000. Toward a theory-based analysis of behavioral maintenance. *Health Psychol.* 19(Suppl.):64–69

Russell LB, Suh D, Safford MM. 2005. Time requirements for diabetes self-management: too much for many? *J. Fam. Pract.* 54(1):52–56

Ryan P, Lauver DR. 2002. The efficacy of tailored interventions. *J. Nurs. Scholarsh.* 34(4):331–37

Sallis JF, Hovell MF, Hofstetter CR. 1992. Predictors of adoption and maintenance of vigorous physical activity in men and women. *Prev. Med.* 21(2):237–51

Schaie KW, Krause N, Booth A, eds. 2004. *Religious Influences on Health and Well-Being in the Elderly.* New York: Springer

Schneiderman N, Antoni MH, Saab PG, Ironson G. 2001. Health psychology: psychosocial and biobehavioral aspects of chronic disease management. *Annu. Rev. Psychol.* 52:555–80

Schwarzer R, Fuchs R. 1995. Self-efficacy and health behaviors. In *Predicting Health Behaviour*, ed. M Connor, P Norman, pp. 163–96. Buckingham, UK: Open Univ. Press

Sebregts EH, Falger PR, Bar FW, Kester AD, Appels A. 2003. Cholesterol changes in coronary patients after a short behavior modification program. *Int. J. Behav. Med.* 10(4):315–30

Sheeran P, Orbell S. 2000. Using implementation intentions to increase attendance for cervical cancer screening. *Health Psychol.* 19(3):283–89

Shields CA, Brawley LR. 2006. Preferring proxy-agency: impact on self-efficacy for exercise. *J. Health Psychol.* 11(6):904–14

Siegel K, Lekas HM. 2002. AIDS as a chronic illness: psychosocial implications. *AIDS* 16(Suppl. 4):S69–76

Simpson SH, Eurich DT, Majumdar SR, Padwal RS, Tsuyuki RT, et al. 2006. A meta-analysis of the association between adherence to drug therapy and mortality. *Br. Med. J.* 333:15–21

Sisk JE, Hebert PL, Horowitz CR, McLaughlin MA, Wang JJ, Chassin MR. 2006. Effects of nurse management on the quality of heart failure care in minority communities. *Ann. Intern. Med.* 145:273–83

Smith JL. 2004. Food, health and psychology: Competing recipes for research and understanding. *J. Health Psychol.* 9:483–96

Sobell MB, Sobell LC. 2000. Stepped care as a heuristic approach to the treatment of alcohol problems. *J. Consult. Clin. Psychol.* 68(4):573–79

Spruill TM, Pickering TG, Schwartz JE, Mostofsky, Ogedegbe G, et al. 2007. The impact of perceived hypertension status on anxiety and the White Coat Hypertension Effect. *Ann. Behav. Med.* In press

Stoller EP. 1998. Dynamics and processes of self-care in old age. In *Self-Care in Later Life*, ed. MG Ory, GH DeFriese, pp. 24–61. New York: Springer

Suls J, Bunde J. 2005. Anger, anxiety, and depression as risk factors for cardiovascular disease: the problems and implications of overlapping affective dispositions. *Psychol. Bull.* 131(2):260–300

Swann WB, Chang-Schneider C, McClarty KL. 2007. Do people's self-views matter? *Am. Psychol.* 62(2):84–94

Tarn DM, Meredith LS, Kagawa-Singer M, Matsumura S, Bito S, et al. 2005. Trust in one's physician: the role of ethnic match, autonomy, acculturation, and religiosity among Japanese and Japanese Americans. *Ann. Fam. Med.* 3:339–47

Taylor SE, Lobel M. 1989. Social comparison activity under threat: downward evaluation and upward contacts. *Psychol. Rev.* 96(4):569–75

Taylor SE, Repetti RL, Seeman T. 1997. Health psychology: What is an unhealthy environment and how does it get under the skin? *Annu. Rev. Psychol.* 48:411–47

TenHave TR, Coyne J, Salzer M, Katz I. 2003. Research to improve the quality of care for depression: alternatives to the simple randomized clinical trial. *Gen. Hosp. Psychiatry* 25(2):115–23

Teutsch S. 2003. The cost-effectiveness of preventing diabetes. *Diabetes Care* 26:2693–94

Thornett A. 2001. Assessing the effect of patient and prescriber preference in trials of treatment of depression in general practice. *Med. Sci. Monit.* 7(5):1086–91

Tolma EL, Reininger BM, Evans A, Ureda J. 2006. Examining the theory of planned behavior and the construct of self-efficacy to predict mammography intention. *Health Educ. Behav.* 33:233–51

Tuomilehto J, Lindstrom J, Eriksson JG, Valle TT, Hamalainen H, et al. 2001. Prevention of type 2 diabetes mellitus by changes in lifestyle among subjects with impaired glucose tolerance. *New Engl. J. Med.* 344(18):1343–50

Tuomilehto J, Lindstom J, Qiao Q. 2005. Strategies for the prevention of type 2 diabetes and cardiovascular disease. *Eur. Heart J. Suppl.* 7(Suppl. D):18–22

Turner L, Mermelstein R, Flay B. 2004. Individual and contextual influences on adolescent smoking. *Ann. NY Acad. Sci.* 1021:175–97

Tversky A, Kahneman D. 1974. Judgement under uncertainty: heuristics and biases. *Science* 185(4157):1124–31

U.S. Dept. Health Human Serv. 1964. *Smoking and Health: Report of the Advisory Committee to the Surgeon General of the Public Health Service.* Public Health Serv. Publ. No. 1103. Rockville, MD: US GPO

Vancouver JB, Kendall LN. 2006. When self-efficacy negatively relates to motivation and performance in a learning context. *J. Appl. Psychol.* 91(5):1146–53

Wadden TA, Brownell KD, Foster GD. 2002. Obesity: responding to the global epidemic. *J. Consult. Clin. Psychol.* 70(3):510–25

Wagner EH. 2004. Deconstructing heart failure disease management. *Ann. Intern. Med.* 141(8):644–46

Wakslak CJ, Trope Y, Liberman N, Alony R. 2006. Seeing the forest when entry is unlikely: probability and the mental representation of events. *J. Exp. Psychol.* 4:641–53

Webb TL, Sheeran P. 2006. Does changing behavioral intentions engender behavior change? A meta-analysis of the experimental evidence. *Psychol. Bull.* 132(2):249–68

Weinman J, Petrie KJ, Moss-Morris R, Horne R. 1996. The Illness Perception Questionnaire: a new method for assessing the cognitive representation of illness. *Psychol. Health* 11(3):431–45

Weinman J, Petrie KJ, Sharpe N, Walker S. 2000. Causal attributions in patients and spouses following first-time myocardial infarction and subsequent lifestyle changes. *Br. J. Health Psychol.* 5(3):263–73

Wilson GT, Vitousek KM, Loeb KL. 2000. Stepped care treatment for eating disorders. *J. Consult. Clin. Psychol.* 68(4):564–72

Witte K, Morrison K. 2000. Examining the influence of trait anxiety/repression sensitization on individuals' reactions to fear appeals. *West. J. Commun.* 64:1–27

Wright A, French D, Weinman J, Marteau T. 2006. Can genetic risk information enhance motivation for smoking cessation? *Health Psychol.* 25:740–52

Wrosch C, Scheier MF, Carver CS, Schulz R. 2003. The importance of goal disengagement in adaptive self-regulation: when giving up is beneficial. *Self Identity* 2:1–20

Yamaoka K, Tango T. 2005. Efficacy of lifestyle education to prevent type 2 diabetes. *Diabetes Care* 28(11):2780–86

Ziegelstein RC, Fauerbach JA, Stevens SS, Romanelli J, Richter DP, Bush DE. 2000. Patients with depression are less likely to follow recommendations to reduce cardiac risk during recovery from a myocardial infarction. *Arch. Intern. Med.* 160:1818–23

Human Abilities: Emotional Intelligence

John D. Mayer,[1] Richard D. Roberts,[2]
and Sigal G. Barsade[3]

[1]Department of Psychology, University of New Hampshire, Durham,
New Hampshire 03824; email: jack.mayer@unh.edu

[2]Center for New Constructs, R&D, Educational Testing Service, Princeton,
New Jersey 08541; email: RRoberts@ets.org

[3]Wharton School, University of Pennsylvania, Philadelphia, Pennsylvania 19104;
email: sigal.barsade@wharton.upenn.edu

Annu. Rev. Psychol. 2008. 59:507–36

The *Annual Review of Psychology* is online at
http://psych.annualreviews.org

This article's doi:
10.1146/annurev.psych.59.103006.093646

Key Words

emotional intelligence, cognitive abilities, emotional knowledge,
emotional perception, psychological assessment

Abstract

Emotional intelligence (EI) involves the ability to carry out accurate reasoning about emotions and the ability to use emotions and emotional knowledge to enhance thought. We discuss the origins of the EI concept, define EI, and describe the scope of the field today. We review three approaches taken to date from both a theoretical and methodological perspective. We find that Specific-Ability and Integrative-Model approaches adequately conceptualize and measure EI. Pivotal in this review are those studies that address the relation between EI measures and meaningful criteria including social outcomes, performance, and psychological and physical well-being. The Discussion section is followed by a list of summary points and recommended issues for future research.

Contents

EMERGING RESEARCH IN EMOTIONAL INTELLIGENCE

Emotion: an integrated feeling state involving physiological changes, motor-preparedness, cognitions about action, and inner experiences that emerges from an appraisal of the self or situation

EI: emotional intelligence

In Ancient Greece, the development of logical thought—syllogisms, arguments, inquiry—was the burgeoning information technology of the day. The Stoics of Ancient Greece believed that logic was superior to feelings because people could agree as to rational arguments but often disagreed as to feelings. Although Stoic philosophy was influential, the idea that rationality was superior to emotionality was not accepted by all. For example, the sentimentalists of eighteenth-century Europe espoused a "follow your heart" credo, arguing that truth might be a property of one's feelings

and intuition, and that such feelings were truer than reason (Reddy 2001). The recently introduced concept of emotional intelligence (EI) offers a new way of looking at the debate—that people can reason about emotions and use emotions to assist reasoning.

If EI were to exist, some argued, it could strengthen our current understanding of both emotions and intelligence (e.g., Sternberg 2001). It might enrich our sense of the functionality of human emotion and the breadth of human intelligence. EI also directs attention to the role of emotion at home, in schools, and at the workplace and how the effects of emotion may ripple through groups and society (Barsade 2002, Barsade et al. 2003, Ciarrochi et al. 2006, Elias et al. 1997, Izard 2002, Matthews et al. 2007).

In this review, we describe research on EI covering a roughly 18-year span from 1990 to early 2007. During that time, work on the topic expanded from a few articles and book chapters to an active research area. Over the same period, research continued in emotion, intelligence, and their interaction, as reflected in *Annual Review of Psychology* coverage (a partial list includes Cacioppo & Gardner 1999, Eisenberg 2000, Lubinski 2000, Oatley & Jenkins 1992, Phelps 2006, Rosenbaum et al. 2001, Sternberg & Kaufman 1998, Voss & Wiley 1995). EI is related to both emotion and intelligence, but it also is distinct from them.

Our aim has been to collect what represents, to us, some of the best and most promising research in the EI field. A review of such research can help define EI, indicate its relation to other concepts, and illustrate its influence on practical outcomes. In the opening of our review, we provide a context for the present-day field, examine uses of the term "emotional intelligence," and describe the scope of research in the area. Our challenge in covering the field is considerable because the term "emotional intelligence" is used in many different ways. One of our goals is to identify the core elements of EI and its study.

THE SCOPE OF EMOTIONAL INTELLIGENCE

What Is Emotional Intelligence?

The term "emotional intelligence" has been employed on an occasional basis at least since the mid-twentieth century. Literary accounts of Jane Austen's *Pride and Prejudice* refer to various characters possessing this quality (Van Ghent 1953, p. 106–107). Scientific references date to the 1960s. For example, emotional intelligence had been mentioned in relation to psychotherapy treatments (Leuner

1966) and to promoting personal and social improvement more generally (Beasley 1987, Payne 1986).

During the 1980s, psychologists expressed a renewed openness to the idea of multiple intelligences (Gardner 1983, Sternberg 1985). Simultaneously, research on emotion and on how emotions and cognition interacted were on the ascendancy (for historical background, see Matthews et al. 2002, Mayer 2000, Mayer et al. 2000a, Oatley 2004). It was amid such lively inquiry that scientific articles on EI first began to appear (Mayer et al. 1990, Salovey & Mayer 1990).

Interest in studying EI grew dramatically throughout the late 1990s, propelled by a popularization of the topic (Goleman 1995). With the term's newly found cachet, and with the excitement surrounding the identification of a potential new intelligence, many used the term—but often in markedly different ways (Bar-On 1997, Elias et al. 1997, Goleman 1995, Mayer & Salovey 1993, Picard 1997). So, what does the term "emotional intelligence" really mean?

Can Emotional Intelligence Be Conceptualized Validly?

By 2007, the wide diversity of those interested in EI was matched by the wide diversity in the conceptions of EI they employed. Some researchers defined EI as an ability to reason about emotion; others equated the concept with a list of traits such as achievement motivation, flexibility, happiness, and self-regard. Still others found the addition of such traits, which seemed to be ad hoc, to be troubling, and wondered whether a theoretically sound conceptualization of EI could be identified (Locke 2005).

The conceptual network of psychological concepts. A scientific concept such as EI arises in the context of associated scientific terms and their meanings. Cronbach & Meehl (1955) referred to this context as a nomological network—a system of meanings

Intelligence: a mental ability (or set of mental abilities) that permit the recognition, learning, memory for, and capacity to reason about a particular form of information, such as verbal information

Nomological network: the interconnected terms and ideas that scientists use to understand their field of study. Scientists' ideas are characterized as connected with one another in logical fashion, and as tied to real-world phenomena, in an integrated, meaningful way

with which most scientists are familiar and that have been established because of their utility. For the term "emotional intelligence" to be valid, it must fit with such a network of concepts (or provide a rationale for why it does not). We begin by examining some concepts that are closely related to EI and then consider how EI might fit within this nomological network.

Our view and definition of human mental abilities and intelligence. Intelligence is a type of mental ability that concerns the handling of—and reasoning about—information of various sorts (Carroll 1993, Spearman 1927, Sternberg & Detterman 1986). The information involved can be very specific (relations among auditory frequencies) or very general (strategic planning). Often, these abilities are described as falling along a hierarchy from simple perceptual processes and information processing to higher and more general forms of problem solving (Carroll 1993).

We view intelligence as a general descriptive term referring to a hierarchy of mental abilities. At the lowest level of this hierarchy are basic, discrete, mental abilities. These include, for example, the ability to recognize words and their meanings in the verbal realm, or, as another instance, to see how puzzle pieces fit together in the perceptual realm, or to understand how objects are rotated in space. At a middle level of the hierarchy are broader, cohesive groups of abilities. These abilities include verbal-comprehension intelligence—a group of abilities focused on understanding and reasoning about verbal information, and, as a second example, perceptual-organizational intelligence—a group of abilities focused on recognizing, comparing, and understanding perceptual patterns. At the highest level of the hierarchy, general intelligence, or *g*, involves abstract reasoning across all such domains. Our working definition of intelligence appears in the margin.

Our view and definition of emotion. As an emotion emerges, it entails coordinated changes in physiology, motor readiness, behavior, cognition, and subjective experience (Izard 1993; Parrott 2002, p. 342; Simon 1982). For example, as a person becomes happy, she may experience lower blood pressure and greater motor readiness to approach others; she also may smile, think happy thoughts, and feel good inside. These emotional reactions emerge in response to perceived or actual alterations in the person's environment. Our working definition of emotion appears in the margin.

Our definitions of both intelligence and emotion are consistent with longstanding—we would say, consensual—approaches in their respective disciplines, but there are alternative views of both concepts (Averill & Nunley 1993, Kleinginna & Kleinginna 1981, Sternberg 1985, Sternberg & Detterman 1986). For example, some views of intelligences divide the concept into a crystallized, learned portion, including especially verbal aspects, and into a fluid portion that involves on-the-spot reasoning and emphasizes perceptual-organizational and spatial skill (e.g., Carroll 1993, Vernon 1971). Alternative views of emotion exist as well (Averill 1992, Averill & Nunley 1993). Acknowledging such complexities, we continue to examine how intelligence and emotion might connect with EI in a conceptual network.

The General Scope and Boundaries of Emotional Intelligence

Emotional intelligence is a term parallel to such others as verbal-comprehension intelligence, perceptual-organizational intelligence, or broad-visualization intelligence (Carroll 1993). In each such term, the descriptor—verbal-comprehension, perceptual-organizational, broad-visualization—modifies the noun: intelligence. For example, verbal comprehension concerns an individual's understanding and reasoning with verbal information.

Many forms of intelligence concern learning and reasoning about a particular type of material and then are enhanced further by the learning they have fostered. For example, verbal-comprehension intelligence describes the capacity to learn and reason about words and their meanings. The more words one understands, however, the more the verbal knowledge one already has gained promotes the intelligence. Thus, verbal intelligence is the ability to reason about words and the use of acquired verbal knowledge to promote such reasoning. Perceptual-organizational intelligence concerns the ability to reason about visual patterns and the use of acquired knowledge about patterns to enhance the intelligence. Following such precedents, an initial working description of EI is as follows:

> Emotional intelligence concerns the ability to carry out accurate reasoning about emotions and the ability to use emotions and emotional knowledge to enhance thought.

To study EI means to focus on the ability itself. Some have made the case that characteristics such as assertiveness and self-regard should be considered part of EI because both involve emotion and intelligence to some degree. Virtually all mental activities, however, from color perception to self-insight, potentially involve emotion and intelligence, simply because emotion and intelligence are active throughout most of one's mental processes; that is, mental functions are highly interconnected (Hilgard 1980, LeDoux 2000). EI is distinct from other mental processes in involving a primary focus on a specific area of problem solving.

As an analogy, consider again verbal-comprehension intelligence. The primary focus on the meaning conveyed by language is crucial. Someone could argue, for example, that assertiveness (or self-regard, etc.) is a part of verbal intelligence because asserting oneself often requires words. The argument fails, however, in regard to the criterion of the primary focus. Assertiveness is not part of the ability to reason verbally, although it may be influenced by such reasoning; equating characteristics such as assertiveness with the ability diverts attention from the intelligence itself. Returning to EI, its primary focus has to do with reasoning about emotions and the use of emotions to enhance thought.

APPROACHES TO EMOTIONAL INTELLIGENCE IN THE SCIENTIFIC LITERATURE

Theoretical Approaches to Emotional Intelligence

EI represents abilities that join intelligence and emotion to enhance thought. Some of the abilities that make up EI can be found in the top of **Figure 1** (see color insert), in the box labeled "emotional intelligence." The box contains specific skills, such as the ability to accurately identify emotion, and indicates that these individual skills may also be viewed as forming an integrated, global EI. Theoretical approaches to EI, in fact, can be divided according to whether they focus on specific abilities or on more global integrations of those capacities.

The specific-ability approaches concern individual mental capacities important to EI. The integrative-model approaches regard EI as a cohesive, global ability. There exists a third approach to EI as well, called a mixed-model approach to the field (Matthews et al. 2004, Mayer et al. 2000b, McCrae 2000, Neubauer & Freudenthaler 2005). This approach mixes in a variety of non-EI qualities, and, consequently, appears to fall partway or largely outside the boundaries of the concept (**Figure 1**, *bottom*). These three approaches to EI are described in detail below.

Specific-Ability Approaches to Emotional Intelligence

Emotional perception and identification. Specific-ability approaches to EI focus on a particular skill or skills that can be considered fundamental to EI. In this section, we outline some of these abilities, beginning with accuracy in emotional perception. The study of perceptual accuracy grew out of an extensive body of research in nonverbal perception. Nonverbal perception includes deciphering social information, such as power and intimacy relationships, along with the accurate recognition of emotional expression. From the nonverbal research, specialized models of emotional accuracy emerged. For example, one model aimed to study a person's accuracy at perceiving emotion in child and adult faces, voices, and postures (Nowicki & Duke 1994). A number of reviews and key papers provide excellent descriptions of research in nonverbal sensitivity more generally (e.g., Buck 1984, Hall & Bernieri 2001, Rosenthal et al. 1979).

Two frequently used measures of perceptual accuracy in emotion are the Diagnostic Analysis of Nonverbal Accuracy Scales (DANVA and DANVA-2; Nowicki & Duke 1994) and the Japanese and Caucasian Brief Affect Recognition Test (JACBART; Matsumoto et al. 2000), though there are others (e.g., Elfenbein et al. 2006). Generally speaking, these scales present pictures of faces and of postures, gestures, or recordings of voice tones; the participant's task is to correctly identify the emotion expressed. For example, the DANVA-2 employs stimuli that express one of the four emotions of happiness, sadness, anger, and fear.

Use of emotional information in thinking. Some specific-ability models address the ways in which emotions facilitate thinking. For example, emotions may prioritize thinking (Mandler 1975) or allow people to be better decision makers (Lyubomirsky et al. 2005). A person who responds emotionally to important issues will attend to the more crucial aspects of his or her life. By contrast, if the person is constantly frustrated, say, by her subordinate's minor clerical errors, then broader concerns that are more important may not be addressed (Parrott 2002). In addition, certain specific emotions can foster given types

of thinking. For example, positive emotions promote greater creativity in some contexts (Amabile et al. 2005, Averill & Nunley 1992, Isen 2001, Lyubomirsky et al. 2005).

Part of emotional facilitation is to know how to include emotions in, and exclude emotions from, thought. On the Emotional Stroop test (Richards et al. 1992), people first see neutral words printed in varying colors and must say the colors without being distracted by the words. In a second condition, negative/anxiety emotion words are employed; in a third condition, positive emotion words might be employed. It is common for people to be distracted and read the emotion word rather than say the color. Those with higher EI might exhibit less interference from the emotion words (e.g., Masia et al. 1999, Richards et al. 1992).

Reasoning about emotions: emotional appraisal, labeling, and language. Another set of specific-ability models concerns emotional reasoning and understanding. For example, emotion-appraisal researchers have developed decision rules for matching a given emotion to the class of situation that has elicited it. If a person experiences fear, for example, it is likely that he is facing a situation that is threatening, raises thoughts of bad things happening, and elicits a need to escape (Roseman 1984, p. 210; Scherer et al. 2001). Related to such appraisals also are the accurate labeling and categorization of feelings (Clore et al. 1987, Innes-Ker & Niedenthal 2002). Theorists have argued that accurate appraisal may be a hallmark of emotionally intelligent responding (MacCann et al. 2004, p. 41; Parrott 2002, pp. 354–355). If a person's appraisal process is awry, then he or she may misunderstand an event or its consequences and react inappropriately.

As another example, emotional understanding may involve being able to describe one's own and others' feelings. For instance, the Levels of Emotional Awareness Scale (LEAS; Lane et al. 1990) presents 20 emotionally evocative situations involving the test taker and a fictional person. Participants write both about how they and the other person would feel in the situation. Responses are scored according to whether the test taker appropriately includes emotional responses and the degree of sophistication (complexity) of those responses, including, for example, the individual's capacity to differentiate between his or her own and others' responses.

Emotion management. Another relevant ability area concerns emotional self-management. This area grew out of clinical findings that, for example, one's emotionality could become more positive by reframing perceptions of situations (Beck et al. 1979), as well as from the idea that when at work, individuals often exert considerable emotional self-control (Hochschild 1983). A sizeable amount of research on emotional self-management and regulation has emerged in parallel with that on EI (Gross 1998, Lazarus 1994), including in the child development domain (Eisenberg 2000). Denham and colleagues (2003), for instance, have used behavioral observations of children in order to assess their frustration tolerance, asking observers to rate the children's degree of distress, crying, and tantrums, among other indices.

Integrative-Model Approaches to Emotional Intelligence

Izard's Emotional Knowledge Approach. The key element in integrative models of EI is the joining of several specific abilities to obtain an overall sense of EI. For example, Izard's Emotional Knowledge Test (EKT; Izard et al. 2001) asks test takers to match an emotion such as sadness with a situation such as "your best friend moves away," as well as to identify emotions in faces. It provides an integrative measure of EI, focusing in particular on emotional perception and understanding. Izard's test also is important because it is designed for use with younger age groups (e.g., as early as 3–4 years old) relative to other measures of EI.

Izard (2001) sometimes prefer to speak of emotional knowledge as opposed to emotional intelligence. Psychologists often speak about an aptitude-knowledge continuum (e.g., Lichten & Wainer 2000). At one end of this continuum, aptitude refers to the capacity to reason and learn; at the other end, knowledge refers to what a person actually has learned. Both intelligence and knowledge tests operate according to similar principles and rely on assessing a person's knowledge. Generally speaking, intelligence tests emphasize general breadth and rate of learning as well as the ability to reason with unfamiliar problems. Knowledge tests, by contrast, measure attained knowledge. Both concepts fit within the scope of EI studies, as defined here.

The Four-Branch Model of Emotional Intelligence. The Four-Branch Model of EI is another integrative approach (Mayer & Salovey 1997, Salovey & Mayer 1990). The model views overall EI as joining abilities from four areas: (*a*) accurately perceiving emotion, (*b*) using emotions to facilitate thought, (*c*) understanding emotion, and (*d*) managing emotion (Mayer & Salovey 1997, Mayer et al. 2003). Each of these areas is viewed as developing from early childhood onward. For example, in perceiving emotion, a person's ability to recognize basic emotions in faces is likely to precede the ability to detect the faking of emotional expressions (Mayer & Salovey 1997, p. 10). As skills grow in one area (e.g., perceiving emotions), so will skills in other areas, such as understanding emotions and being able to regulate them.

The Four-Branch Model has been measured by a series of instruments, the most recent of which is the Mayer-Salovey-Caruso Emotional Intelligence Test, or MSCEIT (Mayer et al. 2002b). This test is composed of eight individual tasks similar to those described in individual areas above. Two tasks are used to measure each branch of the model. For example, emotional perception is measured by asking participants to identify

EKT: Emotional Knowledge Test

MSCEIT: Mayer-Salovey-Caruso Emotional Intelligence Test

MEIS: Multifactor Emotional Intelligence Scale

Mixed Model: a theoretical approach that equates diverse psychological traits, abilities, styles, and other characteristics to EI

emotions in faces and landscapes. Emotional facilitation is assessed, in one subscale, by asking participants to identify which emotions promote which kinds of thoughts and activities. Emotional understanding is measured via understanding how emotions blend [e.g., "Which two emotions together are closest to contempt: (*a*) sadness and fear or (*b*) anger and disgust?"]. Emotional management of oneself and others is measured by presenting test takers with vignettes describing a social situation and asking them how emotions might be managed in the situation (Mayer et al. 2002a). The MSCEIT replaced the earlier, lengthier, Multifactor Emotional Intelligence Scale (MEIS; Mayer et al. 1999).

Mixed-Model Approaches to Emotional Intelligence

The third approach to EI is often referred to as a Mixed Model approach because of the mixed qualities that such models target. These approaches use very broad definitions of EI that include "noncognitive capability, competency, or skill" (Bar-On 1997) and/or "emotionally and socially intelligent behavior" (Bar-On 2004, p. 122), and "dispositions from the personality domain" (Petrides & Furnham 2003, pp. 278–280). Tett et al. (2005) drew on Salovey & Mayer's (1990) original EI model, which they interpreted in a broader, more mixed-model fashion than the authors had intended (see Mayer et al. 2000b, p. 401).

More concretely, most measures in this category assess one or more EI attributes, such as accurate emotional perception, but then to varying degrees mix in other scales of happiness, stress tolerance, and self-regard (Bar-On 1997); adaptability, (low) impulsiveness and social competence (Boyatzis & Sala 2004, Petrides & Furnham 2001); and creative thinking, flexibility, and intuition versus reason (Tett et al. 2005). Relative to the conceptual development we described above, these mixed-in attributes lack a primary focus on EI, as described in this review.

Relating Emotional Intelligence to Other Psychological Variables

Variables included in mixed models such as assertiveness and need for achievement surely are important to study—but are not part of EI, as that concept is developed here. A clearer approach is to consider EI a discrete variable and then study it in relation to such other characteristics. Several theorists have examined EI in the context of positive and negative affect and stress tolerance (Izard 2001; Parrott 2002, pp. 351–355; Zeidner et al. 2003); others have positioned EI, the need for achievement, and other diverse traits in the context of personality (Mayer 2005, 2006). These latter models connect EI to related variables in a way that is consistent with the great majority of psychologists' nomological networks.

MEASURES OF EMOTIONAL INTELLIGENCE

An Evaluation of Emotional Intelligence Measures

In this section, we examine more closely the measures proposed to assess emotionally intelligent skills and abilities. Our focus is on several of the scales introduced above, including scales of emotional perception (e.g., the DANVA and JACBART) and emotional understanding (e.g., the LEAS), as well as measures that integrate across such areas (e.g., the MSCEIT and EKT). We categorize and summarize these and other scales in **Table 1**.

The key purpose of this section is to ask, "Do these tests measure what they claim to?" In particular, do they measure EI? Standards of test validity have changed and developed over the past century, and still are developing. We have distilled from the current *Standards for Educational and Psychological Testing* (Joint Comm. Standards 1999) a group of desirable criteria that seem particularly relevant to EI research at this time. These criteria are grouped into three broad categories: (*a*) adequate test design relative to theories of EI, (*b*) the structure of EI measurement (which tells

Table 1 A guide to emotional intelligence measures frequently mentioned in the review

Key test name, related tests, and source(s)	Acronym(s)	Description of the test
Specific Ability measures		
Diagnostic Analysis of Nonverbal Accuracy 2 The test has three versions: 1. Adult Facial Expressions (Nowicki & Carton 1993) 2. Adult Paralanguage (e.g., auditory) (Baum & Nowicki 1998) 3. Posture Test (Pitterman & Nowicki 2004)	1. DANVA 2-AF 2. DANVA 2-AP 3. DANVA 2-POS	The Adult Facial version consists of 24 photographs of an equal number of happy, sad, angry, and fearful facial expressions of high and low intensities, balanced also by gender. For this and the related tests described below, the participants' task is to indicate which of the four emotions is present in the stimuli. A youth form is also available. The Paralanguage version includes two professional actors (one male, the other female) who say a neutral sentence, "I am going out of the room now but I'll be back later" in one of four emotional states. The Posture test includes 32 stimuli of two men and two women in standing and sitting postures representing high- and low-intensity happiness, sadness, anger, and fear.
Japanese and Caucasian Brief Affect Recognition Test (Matsumoto et al. 2000)	JACBART	Fifty-six Japanese and Caucasian faces are presented in a video format. Each target face portrays one of seven emotions: happiness, contempt, disgust, sadness, anger, surprise, and fear. Each such facial expression is presented for 0.2 seconds between identical initial and trailing neutral facial expressions posed by the same individual—that is, between backward and forward masks. The test-taker's task is to identify correctly the emotion present.
Levels of Emotional Awareness Scale (Lane et al. 1990)	LEAS	Twenty social scenes involving two characters, "you" and an additional individual, elicit four types of emotion: anger, fear, happiness, and sadness. After a test taker reads a scene, he or she is asked, "How would you feel?" and "How would the other person feel?" Participants are required to describe their anticipated feelings (and those of a second person) for each scene. Scoring is according to a continuum of low emotional awareness (no emotional response) to high emotional awareness (appropriate emotions for "you" and the character).
Integrative Model measures		
Emotion Knowledge Test (umbrella label for an evolving set of tests, including the Assessment of Children's Emotional Skills, Perceiving and Labeling Emotion, and Emotion Matching Test) (Izard et al. 2001, Mostow et al. 2002, Trentacosta & Izard 2007)	EKT (or ACES, PLE, or EMT)	The most recent ACES contains three subscales. Facial Expressions contains 26 faces; children are asked if they are happy, sad, mad, scared, or express no feeling. The Social Situations subscale includes 15 two- to three-sentence vignettes describing a social situation; the Social Behavior scale similarly contains 15 two- to three-sentence descriptions of behavior; children respond to each scale by estimating the emotion of the main character. An overall emotion-knowledge score is calculated.
Mayer-Salovey-Caruso Emotional Intelligence Scale (Mayer et al. 2002a, Mayer et al. 2003) Multibranch Emotional Intelligence Scale (Mayer et al. 1999)	MSCEIT; MEIS	Eight tasks (141 items) measure various aspects of EI including emotional perception in (*a*) faces and (*b*) landscapes, using emotions in (*c*) synesthesia and in (*d*) facilitating thought, understanding emotional (*e*) changes across time and (*f*) blends, and managing emotions in (*g*) oneself and (*h*) relationships. Responses are scored for correctness (e.g., against answers from an expert or consensus-based scoring). Each task uses a different item type; different response scales are used by different tasks. Scores for overall EI as well as Perceiving, Facilitating, Understanding, and Managing emotions, and other composites, can be calculated. The longer MEIS test (402 items) consists of 12 scales, also arranged into four branches; there is considerable conceptual overlap, but no item overlap, between the two tests.
Mixed Model measures		
Emotional Quotient Inventory (Bar-On 1997)	EQ-i	A 133-item self-judgment inventory. Items are divided over 15 subscales such as adaptability, assertiveness, and self-regard that also can be formed into five higher-order factors: intrapersonal, interpersonal, adaptation, stress management, and general mood.

(Continued)

Table 1 *(Continued)*

Key test name, related tests, and source(s)	Acronym(s)	Description of the test
Self-Report Emotional Intelligence Test (Schutte et al. 1998)	SREIT	A 33-item self-report inventory that has most often been used to assess an over all level of EI.
Multidimensional Emotional Intelligence Assessment (Tett et al. 2005, 2006)	MEIA	A 118-item self-report inventory employing 10 scales, many of which are based on the original Salovey & Mayer (1990) model of EI and some of which are added.

Measures are organized according to the categories presented in the main body of the text.

DANVA scores are usually reported in articles as "Coding Errors"—we have reversed this to "Coding Skill" in the main body of the text.

us whether EI is one thing or many things), and (*c*) test relationships with key benchmarks.

Adequate Test Design

We use the term "adequate test design" to refer to evidence of appropriate test content, evidence that test takers employ proper response processes to answer a question, and evidence of acceptable test reliability.

Content evidence of validity. Evidence for a test's validity includes the extent to which a test's content addresses what should be measured. For example, evidence that the DANVA-2 measures EI comes from the fact that the scale presents pictures of emotionally laden faces and body postures to participants who must then identify whether the content they see is mostly happy, angry, sad, or fearful. As another example, evidence that the MSCEIT measures EI stems from its content, which is divided into four areas corresponding to the Four-Branch model of EI: the capacities to (*a*) perceive emotions, (*b*) use emotions to facilitate thought, (*c*) understand emotions, and (*d*) manage emotions. For example, item content reflecting understanding emotion provides a participant with an emotion definition and then asks him or her to select the emotion that was defined (see **Figure 2**, see color insert).

Response-process evidence of validity. The standard practice in measuring mental abilities is to ask people to solve problems and then compare their answers to a criterion of correctness. Such ability testing elicits a response process in which a person demonstrates an ability by actively solving the problem and then recording a correct answer. Significant reviews of intelligence—including those covering dozens of diverse abilities—rely exclusively on such ability testing (Carroll 1993). In other words, response-process evidence for the validity of an EI measure includes that the test poses questions of a test taker and then matches the individual's answers to a criterion of correctness.

The Specific Ability and Integrative Model scales discussed here meet such standards. For example, the JACBART asks participants to look at an emotional facial expression and then match the expression to an emotion. The correct answer is decided by reference to the Facial Affect Coding system, a well-regarded system for determining emotional facial expressions (Ekman & Friesen 1975). The MSCEIT has employed two scoring systems. The expert-consensus scoring method involves matching a participant's response to the correct answers nominated by emotion experts. The general-consensus scoring method matches participant answers to the preferred responses of the standardization sample. The rationale for the latter method is that, because human beings have evolved to understand emotional information, unselected groups of people can identify correct scores almost as well as can experts. A study of test scores, assessed across roughly 2000 individuals, indicated that these two scoring methods are

Response-process evidence: a form of validity evidence that concerns whether the questions posed by a test elicit the actual to-be-measured mental activities targeted for study

Specific ability approach: a theoretical approach to EI focused on a specific skill area within the domain (e.g., effective emotional management)

correlated, $r = 0.96$ to 0.98 (Mayer et al. 2003); that is, the two methods converge well on correct answers (for a discussion, see Mayer et al. 2001, Roberts et al. 2001).

Reliability of emotional intelligence measures. Reliability refers to the consistency with which a test measures; without consistency, measurement is compromised. One way to assess reliability is through a scale's internal consistency—that is, whether a participant's responses are consistent across items. The measures listed in **Table 1** generally possess moderate to high internal-consistency reliability. For example, the coefficient alpha (α) reliability of the LEAS ranges from 0.81 to 0.89 (Ciarrochi et al. 2003, Lane et al. 1990). Reported αs for the JACBART range from 0.73 to 0.92 (see Matsumoto et al. 2004, Roberts et al. 2006). Reports of the MSCEIT indicate total scale split halves of $r = 0.91$ and 0.93; split half estimates of reliability are employed because of the test's item heterogeneity (Mayer et al. 2003). However, the reliability of several other tests of emotion perception, especially those involving auditory modalities, are closer to $r = 0.45$ (MacCann 2006, Roberts et al. 2006). A second sort of reliability—test-retest reliability—concerns consistency across time. The MSCEIT's test-retest reliability is $r = 0.86$, with an $N = 60$ (Brackett & Mayer 2003). The test-retest reliability of the JACBART is $r = 0.78$ with an $N = 56$ (Matsumoto et al. 2000).

In sum, reliability ranges from $r = 0.80$ to 0.92 for most full-scales measures, which is adequate for research and, in the higher instances, for reliable assessment of an individual.

Validity Evidence from Factor Structure

Few topics concerning EI are as central as whether the abilities it consists of can be modeled as a unified intelligence. If so, then it is possible to speak of EI as a coherent area of information processing. Moreover, it would become possible to develop a taxonomic model that placed component abilities in relation to one another in a relatively invariant manner across subpopulations, time, and test administrators (e.g., Carroll 1993).

A number of studies suggest that measures of EI do form coherent, recognizable factors, despite the often low correlations among them (see below). Most centrally, a single, global EI factor can be used to describe both MEIS and MSCEIT test data (Ciarrochi et al. 2000; Mayer et al. 2003, 2005; Palmer et al. 2005; Roberts et al. 2001). The same studies also extract intercorrelated, more specific factors within the general factors. For example, two factors, Experiential and Strategic EI, are often obtained (Ciarrochi et al. 2000, Mayer et al. 2003, Roberts et al. 2006), as well as a three- or four-factor model emphasizing Emotional Perception, Understanding, and Management (Mayer et al. 1999, 2003; Palmer et al. 2005, Roberts et al. 2001). These findings are consistent with a hierarchical view of intelligence, in which a general EI divides into more specific factors and then into subfactors.

Test Relations to Key Benchmarks

Convergent validity evidence among emotional intelligence measures. We have identified a number of measures as related to EI. If they are all measures of EI, then they should correlate with one another—that is, converge toward a common criterion. Here, however, there is some concern. It has long been observed that correlations among various measures of the ability to perceive nonverbal expressions are low (Boone & Buck 2004, Buck 1984, Hall 2001). For example, most correlations among measures of perceiving interpersonal affect (and other nonverbal behavior) are in the range $r = -0.10$ to 0.20 s (Hall 2001, p. 135). One exception is a reported $r = 0.80$ between two newer scales, the DANVA-2 and the

JACBART (Nowicki 2007, p. 6). Comparisons between such scales and the perception scales of the MSCEIT seem consistent with the less strong, earlier findings: The JACBART and emotional perception scales of the MSCEIT correlated essentially zero, although the JACBART correlated $r = 0.20$ to 0.26 with other scales of the MSCEIT and MSCEIT Total EI (Roberts et al. 2006). Turning to other measures, the MSCEIT and the LEAS intercorrelate at about the $r = 0.15$ to 0.20 level (Ciarrochi et al. 2003). Yet, in principle, it seems possible to develop scales that intercorrelate more highly. For example, the four branches of the MSCEIT (which share no items in common and use different response scales) intercorrelate $r = 0.27$ to 0.51 (Mayer et al. 2003).

These measures appear, on a theoretical level, to be assessing abilities within the EI domain, yet reports to date indicate that the scales tap different sources of variance. Although the correlations within a test such as the MSCEIT are reassuring, the lack of correlation across tests is both perplexing and troubling. More studies relating these scales are needed, as is a better understanding of the basis of their divergence.

Relation to biopsychological processes. Another key question concerns how EI relates to biopsychological processes. One argument for EI is that distinctly emotional regions of the brain might carry out information processing differently from more purely cognitive centers. A recent fMRI study indicated that the brain areas most activated when solving MSCEIT problems are the left frontal polar and left anterior temporal regions, which are closely linked with social cooperation (Reis et al. 2007). Similarly, people with higher LEAS scores exhibit greater responsiveness to stimuli in area 24 of the anterior cingulate cortex, which is involved in emotional processing (Lane et al. 1998). Intelligence researchers have long found that higher-IQ participants are able to solve problems with less brain activity (i.e., more efficiently) than those

with a lower IQ. Employing this paradigm, researchers have found that those higher in EI exert less brain activity to solve emotional problems, as indicated by brain wave activity (Jausovec & Jausovec 2005, Jausovec et al. 2001).

Relation to intelligences and related mental abilities. Based on the conceptualizations of EI as a form of intelligence, moderate relations should exist between EI and other measures of cognitive abilities. Studies with the MEIS, MSCEIT, LEAS, and various developmental measures do exhibit positive correlations with verbal, knowledge-based intelligence tests. The overall relationships between the MSCEIT and MEIS scales with verbal intelligence and verbal SAT are about $r = 0.36$; the correlations are lower ($r = 0.10$ to 0.20) for other cognitive intelligences such as perceptual-organizational intelligence. MSCEIT Emotional Understanding scores show the strongest individual relations with verbal/crystallized intelligence measures, with an average $r = 0.38$ across seven studies (Roberts et al. 2007).

The vast majority of EI measures of emotional perception are related $r = 0.20$ or less to tests of reasoning ability (often equated to fluid intelligence; Barchard 2003, Ciarrochi et al. 2000, Mayer et al. 1999, Roberts et al. 2001). One exception to this general finding is the JACBART, which, perhaps because of its speeded component, relates $r = 0.27$ to fluid intelligence (Roberts et al. 2006, Roberts & Stankov 1999).

Some aspects of EI also may intersect with social intelligence. In a factor analysis bearing both on the structure of EI and its relation to other intelligences, the MSCEIT subscales divided into two factors, the first related to Experiential EI (MSCEIT Perception and Facilitation) and the second, Strategic EI, related to socio-emotional reasoning that loaded MSCEIT Understanding as well as scales from the O'Sullivan-Guilford Social Intelligence measure (Barchard & Hakstian 2004).

Intelligence tests (including EI) assess the ability of participants to converge on a correct answer. This contrasts with creativity tests, which emphasize divergent forms of thinking—that is, the capacity to think in novel ways (Averill & Thompson-Knowles 1991). In fact, emotional creativity measured as an ability and MSCEIT Total EI appear entirely independent of one another (Ivcevic et al. 2007).

Overall, the evidence above suggests that ability-based EI measures index emotional knowledge, which is related to verbal-comprehension and/or crystallized intelligence. The magnitude of this correlation is typically $r = 0.30$ to 0.40, which indicates that EI is different from, say, verbal-comprehension intelligence. EI also may exhibit relations with social intelligence, but apparently not with creativity.

Relation to ongoing emotion and emotional empathy. EI theories, although specifying accurate reasoning about emotions, generally are agnostic as to the emotions a person might feel at a given time. Research evidence indicates that few relations exist: MEIS Total EI was unrelated to emotional state in a large sample (Mayer et al. 1999). Nevertheless, the definition of EI includes key aspects of empathy—especially that part of empathy having to do with recognizing others' feelings. Higher EI on the LEAS, MEIS, and MSCEIT does correlate, $r = 0.20$ to 0.43, with self-judgments of empathic feeling (Brackett et al. 2006; Caruso et al. 2002; Ciarrochi et al. 2000, 2003; Mayer et al. 1999; Mayer & Geher 1996).

Relation to benchmark personality traits. EI measures also have been examined in relation to benchmark personality traits such as the Big Five. The frequently studied Big Five traits are Extraversion-Introversion, Neuroticism-Emotional Stability, Openness-Closedness, Conscientiousness-Careless-ness, and Agreeableness-Disagreeableness (Goldberg 1993). Mayer & Salovey (1993) predicted EI would have a low but significant relation to the trait Openness (with which many intelligences correlate; Ackerman & Heggestad 1997). Two reviews of studies indicate that Total MEIS/MSCEIT EI does correlate with Openness, $r = 0.17$ to 0.18, but has its highest relation among the Big Five with Agreeableness, $r = 0.21$ to 0.28, a scale sometimes viewed as reflecting compassion and cooperation.

Measurement Issues Regarding Mixed-Model Scales

Conceptual issues. Mixed Model scales—those that mix in attributes from outside EI—have their own specific measurement characteristics and concerns. The theories behind these instruments mix many attributes with EI, and their measures reflect this (Bar-On 2000, Schutte et al. 1998, Tett et al. 2005). Mixed Model tests include items such as "I can express my needs much of the time" (e.g., assertiveness) or "I am a fairly easygoing person" (e.g., flexibility). Consequently, the instruments lack content evidence for their validity in assessing EI because they fail to focus either on intelligent reasoning about emotion or on using emotions and emotional knowledge to enhance intelligence.

As a matter of practice, Mixed Models all are operationalized with self-judgment scales rather than ability items (Bar-On 2000, Schutte et al. 1998, Tett et al. 2005). (Some scales also use observer reports as a secondary operationalization.) Self-judgment assessments ask questions that measure a person's self-estimated ability, such as "Do you usually clearly perceive the emotional state you are in?" Conceptually, such a response process is not valid for the direct assessment of a mental ability. Moreover, empirical evidence indicates that, generally, self-estimates of intelligence are related only minimally to measured ability (Paulhus et al. 1998); self-estimates of EI appear even less related to such abilities (Brackett et al. 2006). In the case of EI, appropriate feedback may be hard to come

The Big Five: a set of five personality traits: Extraversion, Neuroticism, Openness, Conscientiousness, and Agreeableness, each of which is a composite of more specific intercorrelated traits

by, and low ability can impede accurate self-understanding. Self-judgments, therefore, introduce a substantial proportion of variance unrelated to EI.

Indicative findings. The mixed-model scales' use of self-judgment questions, combined with their diverse content, leads to measures that are difficult to assess empirically, and often appear to assess a global pleasant versus unpleasant emotional style. Empirically, for example, many of the individual subscales or test totals of the Bar-On EQ-i, the Self-Report Emotional Intelligence Test, and the Multidimensional Emotional Intelligence Assessment correlate in the range of $r = 0.60$ to 0.70 with single scales of established personality dimensions such as (lower) Neuroticism from the Big Five (Brackett & Mayer 2003, Study 2; Dawda & Hart 2000; Petrides & Furnham 2001; Tett et al. 2005). Two studies indicate that the Big Five scales together predict EQ-i scores in a range of multiple r's $= 0.75$ to 0.79 (Brackett & Mayer 2003, Grubb & McDaniel 2007). Similarly, a scale of psychological well-being predicts the Schutte Self-Report Emotional Intelligence Scale at $r = 0.70$ (Brackett & Mayer 2003); EI ability scales have far lower relations in comparison (see Relation to Benchmark Personality Traits, above).

Empirical research confirms that self-reported EI does not predict ability assessments of EI well. Brackett and colleagues (2006) developed a self-judgment scale based on the Four-Branch Model, correlated it with the MSCEIT's measure of the same four branches, and found a correlation of only $r = 0.19$ between 275 participants' estimates and their actual abilities. More commonly used self-judgment scales of EI, such as the Bar-On EQ-i and Schutte scales, predict the MSCEIT at about the same level (Brackett & Mayer 2003, Zeidner et al. 2005).

Moreover, participants can readily portray more positive self-judgments under conditions of high-stakes selection. For example, under "fake good" conditions, participants raised their average score on the (self-judgment) Bar-On EQ-i by 0.80 of a standard deviation—before any coaching or training (Grubb & McDaniel 2007).

Mixed Model scales do not define EI in a manner consistent with reasonable scientific terminology. They further employ measurement approaches that are invalid for assessing EI, as the concept is developed here. That said, some of the scales do possess specific merits, such as good standardization, reliability, or factorial validity, as measures of other constructs (e.g., Barchard & Christensen 2007, Grubb & McDaniel 2007).

A growing number of researchers have questioned whether there is a good rationale to label Mixed Models as measuring EI at all (Davies et al. 1998, Matthews et al. 2007, Mayer & Ciarrochi 2006, Murphy 2006). Our review leads us to the same question. The remainder of the review focuses on measures from the specific ability and integrative model approaches that we judge as possessing validity for assessing EI.

WHAT DOES EMOTIONAL INTELLIGENCE PREDICT (OR NOT) IN LIFE OUTCOMES?

A more complete understanding of EI requires an appreciation of how its measures relate to life outcomes. In this section, we attempt to create a condensed version of what one might take away from reading, one by one, a series of articles relevant to this literature. The summary conveys some of the major topics of study, some of the methods, and some of the many findings—both consistent and inconsistent. We present the material without much commentary, allowing readers to obtain a sense of the relationships on their own. In the Discussion section below, we offer some observations on the work, which are further developed in our Summary Points section. Our overview is divided into EI in social relationships, in school, at work, and in relation to well-being.

The Scope of Emotional Intelligence

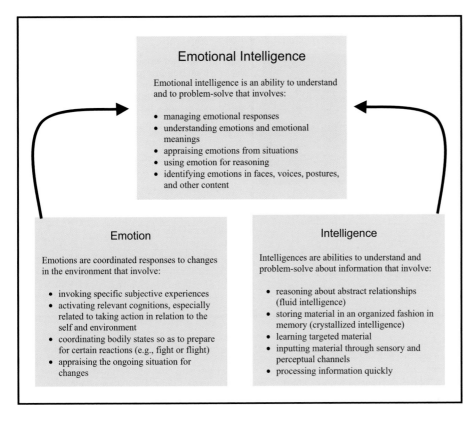

Emotional Intelligence

Emotional intelligence is an ability to understand and to problem-solve that involves:

- managing emotional responses
- understanding emotions and emotional meanings
- appraising emotions from situations
- using emotion for reasoning
- identifying emotions in faces, voices, postures, and other content

Emotion

Emotions are coordinated responses to changes in the environment that involve:

- invoking specific subjective experiences
- activating relevant cognitions, especially related to taking action in relation to the self and environment
- coordinating bodily states so as to prepare for certain reactions (e.g., fight or flight)
- appraising the ongoing situation for changes

Intelligence

Intelligences are abilities to understand and problem-solve about information that involve:

- reasoning about abstract relationships (fluid intelligence)
- storing material in an organized fashion in memory (crystallized intelligence)
- learning targeted material
- inputting material through sensory and perceptual channels
- processing information quickly

Mixed Models of Emotional Intelligence

Mixed models of emotional intelligence begin with emotional intelligence-related qualities such as the ability to perceive emotions accurately, and mix in with them:

- motives such as *need for achievement*
- social styles such as *gregariousness* and *assertiveness*
- self-related qualities such as *self-esteem*
- control-related qualities such as *flexibility* and *impulse control*

Figure 1

Emotional Intelligence (EI; *upper box*) is closely related to two other scientific concepts: intelligence and emotion. Intelligence and emotion have consensual meanings for most psychologists. For example, intelligences (*box to right*) involve abilities to understand information; emotions (*box to left*) are coordinated responses to the environment. EI is the ability to reason about emotions as well as the capacity to use emotions and emotional information to assist reasoning. Specific-Ability approaches to EI (*upper box, bulleted items*) study such matters as how well a person identifies emotions in faces or how well a person understands emotional meanings. Integrative-Model approaches to EI (*upper box, overall*) concern the study of specific abilities together. Mixed-Model approaches (*bottom*) are less related to EI and to the other two approaches. Although they typically study some relevant emotion-specific abilities, they also add in motives, social styles, self-related qualities, and other traits that do not concern a primary focus on emotion or emotional reasoning.

Two Items of the Sort Found on Emotional Intelligence Scales

1.	2.
	**Tom felt worried when he thought about all the work he needed to do. He believed he could handle it – if only he had the time. When his supervisor brought him an additional project, he felt _____. (Select the best choice.)**

Emotion	Select one:
a. Happy	O
b. Angry	O
c. Fearful	O
d. Sad	O

Emotion	Select one:
a. Frustrated and anxious	O
b. Content and calm	O
c. Ashamed and accepting	O
d. Sad and guilty	O

Figure 2

The two test items, *1* and *2*, are typical of those that measure emotional intelligence. Item *1* measures emotional accuracy with a face of the sort found on the Diagnostic Analysis of Nonverbal Accuracy Scales-2. The participant's job is to identify the emotion expressed in the face (alternative *b*, angry, is the correct choice in this case). Item *2* represents an emotion understanding item of the sort that appears on the Mayer-Salovey-Caruso Emotional Intelligence Test. The participant's job is to identify the correct feeling that the individual might experience (alternative *a* is most likely, given the information supplied).

Social Relations in Childhood and Adolescence

EI consistently predicts positive social and academic outcomes in children (Eisenberg et al. 2000, Schultz et al. 2004). For example, Izard et al. (2001a) found that EKT Emotional Knowledge scores assessed among 5-year-old preschoolers positively predicted the students' third-grade social skills, such as assertion, cooperation, and self-control, as rated by teachers. The same assessment also negatively predicted a composite of problem behaviors such as internalizing and hyperactivity. These findings from economically disadvantaged families held after verbal ability, sex, and selected personality traits all were controlled. Similar findings have been reported by Fine et al. (2003).

Children's skill at emotional regulation appears to influence their social well-being as well (for reviews, see Cole et al. 2004, Eisenberg 2000). In a longitudinal study of children ages 3–4, Denham et al. (2003), collected multimethod ratings of children's emotional regulation and emotion knowledge. In a structural equation model, children's higher emotional regulation and emotional knowledge predicted social competence at ages 3–4 and later on in kindergarten (Denham et al. 2003).

In a study of adolescents, Mestre et al. (2006) found that 15-year-old Spanish students with higher MSCEIT Strategic (Understanding and Management) scores were more frequently nominated as friends by their peers. This finding still held for young women after controlling for IQ and the Big Five personality factors.

Social Relations in Adulthood

Diary studies and self-perceptions of social competence. Lopes and colleagues (2004) conducted a two-week daily diary study of German undergraduates' social interactions, for which participants reported every face-to-face social interaction they participated in lasting 10 minutes or longer. In these

UNCOVERING NEW INTELLIGENCES

The 1980s and 1990s saw a resurgence in theoretical attention to specific intelligences (e.g., Gardner 1983, Sternberg 1985). For many years, some scientists argued that general intelligence (or *g*) could suffice empirically to represent an individual's many cognitive abilities in predicting occupational, educational, and life success generally (Jensen 1998). Although *g* is a plainly powerful and efficient index of mental ability, the idea that one construct might have such universal importance was hotly debated.

From the 1990s to present, researchers have explored the possibility that intelligences are a more diverse and looser confederation of abilities than once was thought. A particular focus among researchers has been the exploration of "hot intelligences"—intelligences that pertain to personally relevant information—such as practical, social, and emotional intelligence. Social intelligence for example, includes capacities to appraise and understand human relationships (Lee et al. 2000, Weis & Süß 2007). Practical intelligence involves the ability to understand often unstated rules (technically, tacit information) that surround us (Sternberg et al. 2006, Wagner 2000). A specific but often overlooked cognitive intelligence—spatial intelligence—is coming into its own as well (Lubinski 2000, Lubinski et al. 2001). Empirical investigations of many of these intelligences are advancing in a promising fashion. It appears likely that other intelligences beyond EI will add to the prediction of critical life outcomes such as academic and work performance, social relationships, and how well one attains psychological well-being.

interactions, one or more of participants' scores on MSCEIT Perceiving, Facilitating, and Managing (but not Understanding) significantly predicted participants' perceptions of how enjoyable and/or interested, wanted, and respected they felt in the interactions.

Brackett and colleagues (2006, Study 2) found that higher EI among close friends led to higher self-perceived competence in reacting to their friends' life events. Among friendship pairs, higher EI participants reported making fewer critical remarks, $r = -0.33$, in response to others' successes (perhaps better managing their envy) as well as fewer passive-destructive responses such as "I don't pay much attention" to the other's positive event. In the same study, higher EI also predicted fewer destructive responses to conflict in close relationships, $r = -0.22$ to -0.27, including fewer active responses, such as "I scream at him," and fewer passive responses, such as "I avoid her." This latter pattern held only for males in the sample.

Others' perceptions of the emotionally intelligent person. A number of findings indicate that having high EI leads others to perceive an individual more positively. For example, Brackett et al. (2006, Study 3) videotaped U.S. undergraduate students engaged in a "get to know you" conversation with a confederate. Four judges later rated the videotape of the target interaction for various attributes. For men, MSCEIT Total EI correlated in the $r = 0.50$ range with judges' ratings of the participants' overall social competence, including how much of a team player they were, how socially engaged they were, and their expressed level of interest in the confederate. There was, however, no significant relationship between EI and any of these variables for the women in the study.

Similar findings come from Lopes et al. (2005). In this study, undergraduates first completed self-report measures that asked about the general quality of their social interactions. The participants then nominated up to eight peers in their same college class who exhibited several aspects of EI. Similar to the findings above, MSCEIT Managing scores correlated $r = 0.28$ to 0.29 with the participants self-reports—and with peer nominations—for such attributes as "sensitive to the feelings and concerns of others" and "willing to help others." These relationships were significant above and beyond variance accounted for by other personality traits and verbal intelligence. In this same study, people high in EI, compared with those who scored lower, more often nominated as friends those people who also had nominated them. Additional support for this phenomenon was found by Lopes et al. (2004).

Conversely, MSCEIT Total EI correlated $r = -0.20$ with social deviance, as indexed by getting into fights or vandalizing property (Brackett & Mayer 2003). In a partial replication, the relationship was also found, but for men only, $r = -0.40$ (Brackett et al. 2004).

Emotional intelligence, family, and intimate relationships. EI also relates to one's family and other intimate relationships. In two studies of parental relations, MEIS EI skills in Perception, Understanding, and Management correlated $r = 0.15$ to 0.23 with self-judgments of perceived parental warmth (Ciarrochi et al. 2000, Mayer et al. 1999). However, perceived social support from parents (as opposed to warmth) shows a more mixed relationship: Only the MSCEIT Managing scale correlated with perceived support from parents, after controlling for the Big Five traits and verbal intelligence ($r = 0.22$; Lopes et al. 2003). No relationship was identified between MSCEIT EI and a report of interacting with one's mother and father (Brackett et al. 2004).

Although a few studies show weak or no influence of EI on intimate relationships (Brackett et al. 2005, Hampel 2003), several studies demonstrate significant correlations between the two. For example, higher DANVA-2 Face and Voice Perception accuracy scores correlated, $r = 0.57$ and 0.63, respectively, to relationship well-being (Carton et al. 1999). MEIS General EI also predicted relationship quality, $r = 0.22$, remaining significant after controlling for the Big Five personality traits and general intelligence (Ciarrochi et al. 2000). MSCEIT Managing Emotion also was positively correlated to the perceived quality of romantic partners (Lopes et al. 2004).

Brackett and colleagues (2005) examined the MSCEIT EI match between partners within a couple. If both members of the couple were low on EI, they experienced more conflict and poorer relationship quality overall, as predicted. Unexpectedly, couples in which one partner was higher in EI than the other had equivalent (or often better) relationship quality than the high-high EI couples.

Scholastic Outcomes from Grade School to College

A number of studies have examined the impact of EI on academic performance. The previously discussed developmental study by Izard et al. (2001a) found that five-year-old preschoolers' emotional knowledge predicted third-grade teachers' ratings of academic competencies (e.g., arithmetic skills, reading skills, the motivation to succeed), $r = 0.43$. The correlation remained significant after controlling for verbal ability, sex, and socio-emotional traits.

Moving upward from elementary- through college-age students, Halberstadt & Hall (1980) reviewed 22 studies (5 of which included adult populations) of nonverbal sensitivity (including emotional perception) and found a small but significant positive relationship between the ability to identify nonverbal expressions, on the one hand, and cognitive ability assessed by standard tests and school performance, on the other.

Mestre et al. (2006) found that MSCEIT Strategic (Understanding and Managing) EI correlated, $r = 0.47$, with teacher ratings of academic achievement among 15-year-old Spanish boys—above and beyond IQ and the Big Five personality traits. A similar relation for teacher ratings for girls dropped below significance after controlling for IQ and personality. Scores on the MSCEIT Total EI also were higher for gifted compared to nongifted seventh- through tenth-grade Israeli students (Zeidner et al. 2005).

The MSCEIT Total, Strategic, and Understanding scales can predict school grades, between $r = 0.14$ and 0.23 (Brackett et al. 2004, O'Connor & Little 2003). This relationship (as well as others discussed above), however, may be accounted for in part by the overlap between these scales and cognitive intelligence. Predictions from the MSCEIT and LEAS regarding academic achievement often

decrease or become nonsignificant when controlling for cognitive intelligence and other personality measures (Amelang & Steinmayr 2006, Barchard 2003, Bastian et al. 2005, Brackett & Mayer 2003).

Emotional Intelligence at Work

Decision making and negotiation. People's work performance—and EI's relation to it—can be studied by simulating work environments in a laboratory setting. For example, Day & Carroll (2004) studied research participants in a group decision-making task. The participants' task was to determine the order in which employees should be laid off during an organizational downsizing. The ranking of which employees to layoff was first completed individually and then together in a meeting to achieve group consensus. Participants with high MSCEIT Total scores received higher organizational-citizenship ratings from other group members. MSCEIT Perception exhibited an $r = 0.17$ relation with individual (but not group) performance on the layoff task.

Managerial in-basket exercises allow researchers to study participants' performance at fact-finding, analyzing problems, and decision making more generally. In an organizational simulation with undergraduates, JACBART Emotional Perception correlated $r = 0.28$ with successful problem analyses, although not with related criteria (Matsumoto et al. 2004, Study 3).

In a negotiation study, Elfenbein et al. (2007) studied undergraduate buyers and sellers. Their Emotion Perception accuracy was measured on the Singapore Picture Scale, a test similar to the JACBART. Higher Emotion Perception on the part of sellers increased the amount of money gained overall by the negotiating pair and was marginally related to the proportion of money the seller individually received. Buyers' Emotional Perception showed no effect.

Mueller & Curhan (2007) examined a group of U.S. negotiators, all students in a Master of Business Administration program.

They found that high MSCEIT Understanding predicted that one's negotiation partner would feel more positively about his/her outcome, $r = 0.23$, even after controlling for the partner's positive affect and how much the negotiation partner received. The creation of positive affect by people with higher EI may be especially important because it can spread among groups via emotional contagion (Barsade 2002, Hatfield et al. 1994).

Field studies of emotional intelligence and performance. In a meta-analysis, Elfenbein et al. (2007) found that Emotion Recognition Accuracy predicted a modest but significant and consistent rise in workplace effectiveness in professionals as diverse as physicians, human service workers, school teachers and principals, and business managers. Also, Elfenbein & Ambady (2002) found that DANVA Facial (but not Vocal) Emotional Perception scores correlated $r = 0.25$ to 0.45 with employee performance, measured via senior staff members' ratings, in a yearlong U.S. not-for-profit public service program.

Lopes et al. (2006) examined the work performance of a sample of 44 analysts and clerical/administrative employees from the financial staff of a U.S.-based insurance company. After controlling for relevant personality and demographic variables, MSCEIT Total EI correlated $r = 0.28$ to 0.45 with company rank, higher merit increases, peer and supervisor rated sociability, and rated contribution to a positive work environment. A similar study by Rosete & Ciarrochi (2005) examined 41 executives from a large Australian public service organization. Executives' MSCEIT Total, Perception, and Understanding scores correlated in the $r =$ mid 0.30s range with rated "cultivates productive working relationships" and rated personal drive and integrity—but not with "achieves results." In this case, their EI scores, in other words, correlated with how they achieved rather than with what they achieved. Correlations remained significant after controlling for IQ and other personality traits.

A recent study builds on research that extraverts, relative to introverts, may be better able to employ emotional information since they are stimulated rather than overwhelmed by the emotion information. In a study of 177 managers in a U.S.-based global corporation, DANVA Facial Recognition correlated with transformational leadership styles as rated by 480 subordinates, and this relationship was strongest for managers higher in extraversion (Rubin et al. 2005). Turning to the moderating influence of cognitive intelligence, Côté & Miners (2006) found that MSCEIT EI predicted supervisor-assessed task performance and organizational citizenship (in some instances) in a sample of 175 full-time university employees, and it did so more strongly for people with lower cognitive intelligence. This suggests that higher EI may compensate for lower skill levels in other areas.

Psychological and Physical Well-Being

Psychological well-being. A person's inner well-being and external performance often mutually influence one another. Given that high EI appears to influence positive relationships and other outcomes, does it enhance a person's overall psychological well-being? The MSCEIT Total EI correlates $r = 0.16$ to 0.28 with psychological well-being (Brackett & Mayer 2003, Brackett et al. 2006), whereas MEIS Total EI relates to life satisfaction between $r = 0.11$ and 0.28 after controlling for other personality variables, including cognitive intelligence and socio-emotional variables (Ciarrochi et al. 2000, Mayer et al. 1999). The MEIS and MSCEIT Total EI, as well as the DANVA 2 Standing scales, correlate with self-esteem from $r = 0.19$ to 0.33 (Brackett et al. 2006, Ciarrochi et al. 2000, Pitterman & Nowicki 2004), though the relationship for the DANVA held for men only. Moving from well-being to distress, DANVA-2 Emotional Accuracy scores relate inversely overall with depression, $r = -0.42$ (Carton et al. 1999). MSCEIT EI relates $r = -0.24$ with anxiety (Bastian et al.

2005), and controlling for relevant personality variables, $r = -0.23$ and -0.16 with feeling worried and distressed before beginning a challenging task (Bastian et al. 2005, Matthews et al. 2006).

Physical health behaviors. EI also has been studied in relation to some health behaviors. For example, higher MEIS Total EI scores correlated $r = -0.16$ and -0.19, respectively, with lower tobacco and alcohol use among adolescents (Trinidad & Johnson 2002). The MSCEIT Total EI did not predict tobacco use among college students in two other studies; however, it again predicted alcohol use in one study (for men only, $r = -0.28$) (Brackett & Mayer 2003, Brackett et al.

2004). The MSCEIT Total EI either did not predict (Brackett & Mayer 2003) or moderately predicted illegal drug use, $r = -0.32$, for men only (Brackett et al. 2004). Finally, high emotional perception skills reduced the risk of (self-reported) Internet addiction, as measured among a sample of 41 undergraduates from the Stockholm School of Economics (Engelberg & Sjöberg 2000).

Overall Trends and Intriguing Findings

As we examined these and other findings, we identified trends that appeared to extend across several studies or more; these are summarized in **Table 2**. The trends include, for

Table 2 Summary of selected trends in emotional intelligence outcome studies

General effect	EI measures	Representative studies[*]
1. Better social relations for children. Among children and adolescents, EI positively correlates with good social relations and negatively correlates with social deviance, measured both in and out of school as reported by children themselves, their family members, and their teachers.	DANVA ER Q-Sort EKT ESK MSCEIT	• Denham et al. (2003) • Eisenberg et al. (2000) • Fine et al. (2003) • Izard et al. (2001)
2. Better social relations for adults. Among adults, higher EI leads to greater self-perception of social competence and less use of destructive interpersonal strategies.	EARS MEIS MSCEIT	• Brackett et al. (2006) • Lopes et al. (2004)
3. High-EI individuals are perceived more positively by others. Others perceive high-EI individuals as more pleasant to be around, more empathic, and more socially adroit than those low in EI.	MSCEIT	• Brackett et al. (2006) • Lopes et al. (2004) • Lopes et al. (2005)
4. Better family and intimate relationships. EI is correlated with some aspects of family and intimate relationships as reported by self and others.	DANVA-2 MEIS MSCEIT	• Brackett et al. (2005) • Carton et al. (1999)
5. Better academic achievement. EI is correlated with higher academic achievement as reported by teachers, but generally not with higher grades once IQ is taken into account.	LEAS MSCEIT	• Barchard (2003) • Izard et al. (2001) • O'Connor & Little (2003)
6. Better social relations during work performance and in negotiations. EI is correlated with more positive performance outcomes and negotiation outcomes in the laboratory and with more success at work, according to some preliminary research.	DANVA JACBART MEIS MSCEIT	• Côté & Miners (2006) • Elfenbein et al. (2007) • Rubin et al. 2005
7. Better psychological well-being. EI is correlated with greater life satisfaction and self-esteem and lower ratings of depression; EI also is correlated inversely with some negative physical health behaviors, but this has not yet been found as a strong set of relationships.	MSCEIT LEAS	• Bastian et al. (2005) • Gohm et al. (2005) • Matthews et al. (2006)

[*]More studies are indicated in the corresponding portion of the Outcomes section of the review.
Acronyms: DANVA, Diagnostic Analysis of Nonverbal Accuracy Scales; EARS, Emotional Accuracy Research Scale; EI, emotional intelligence; EKT, Emotional Knowledge Test; ER Q-Sort, emotional regulation Q-Sort; ESK, emotion situation knowledge; JACBART, Japanese and Caucasian Brief Affect Recognition Test MEIS, Multifactor Emotional Intelligence Scale; MSCEIT, Mayer-Salovey-Caruso Emotional Intelligence Test.

example, that EI correlates with better social relationships for both children and adults, including in family relationships. Higher EI also predicts academic achievement (although this may be due to its overlap with cognitive intelligence), better social relationships at work, and better psychological well-being (see **Table 2**).

A few other individual findings caught our eye as well, including correlations between EI and (*a*) career interests (Caruso et al. 2002), (*b*) attitudes toward money (Engelberg & Sjöberg 2004), (*c*) money gained in a negotiation (Elfenbein et al. 2007), (*d*) emotional eavesdropping (Elfenbein & Ambady 2002), and (*e*) knowing how one would feel after an event—emotional forecasting (Dunn et al. 2007). Another set of studies concerned whether people who are more emotionally overwhelmed may be unable to use their EI (Gohm et al. 2005) and how EI related to adult attachment (Kafetsios 2004). Finally, we note the beginnings of research on EI training and its outcomes (e.g., Brackett & Katulak 2006, Izard et al. 2004).

DISCUSSION

The Scope and Measure of Emotional Intelligence

Over the past 18 years, research on EI has emerged and a remarkable amount has been learned. At the same time, EI is still a new field of research, and much remains to be done. In the preceding sections of this review, we examined mainstream conceptions of intelligence and emotion, defined EI, and described the scope of research in the field. We also described Specific-Ability, Integrative-Model, and Mixed-Model approaches to studying the field. We noted that there have been some real inroads into providing construct validity evidence for a range of EI measures since the field's inception. Specific Ability and Integrative Models, in particular, have generated promising measures of a unique psychological construct.

Outcomes of Emotional Intelligence

In the Outcomes section, we surveyed key findings regarding EI. Accumulating findings indicate that EI may predict important criteria in several areas, which are summarized in **Table 2**. Those findings include, for example, that EI correlates with better social relationships and with fewer problem social behaviors, and that this relationship begins in childhood continuing through adulthood.

As with much research of this sort, the overall consistencies in research findings that we have identified are accompanied by many inconsistencies as well. For example, measures of EI such as the MSCEIT sometimes predicted an outcome with one subscale, and in another study, predicted the same outcome but with a different subscale. Another inconsistency is that higher EI predicted some but not other specific indices of a general outcome such as good work performance.

Such issues reflect the realities of empirical research, in which research designs may be less than perfect, chance effects may lead to spurious significant or nonsignificant outcomes, samples may not be large enough, the range of target behavior may be restricted in a sample, and many other less-than-desirable factors may impinge. As research continues, these ambiguities likely will be clarified.

Concluding Comments

In the Summary Points below, we have distilled what we regard as the key ideas of this review. In the Future Issues section, we have highlighted some of the more important unresolved issues of today. Whatever the future holds for the science of EI, we believe that the concept has proven a valuable addition to contemporary science and practice. Consideration of EI theory and assessment has proven beneficial to the study of emotions and the study of intelligence, and raised awareness of the importance of emotional components in diverse domains of human abilities and their application in people's lives.

SUMMARY POINTS

1. Emotional intelligence (EI) is the ability to carry out accurate reasoning focused on emotions and the ability to use emotions and emotional knowledge to enhance thought.

2. Theoretical approaches to EI divide into two categories. Specific-Ability approaches examine relatively discrete mental abilities that process emotional information. Integrative-Model approaches describe overarching frameworks of mental abilities that combine skills from multiple EI areas.

3. Aside from the central Specific Ability and Integrative Model approaches to EI, some psychologists have suggested a third approach to the field: Mixed Model approaches. Such models mix diverse attributes, such as assertiveness, flexibility, and the need for achievement, that are not primarily focused on emotional reasoning or emotional knowledge. These models do not fall within the scope of EI as it is developed here.

4. EI measures based on Specific Ability and Integrative Models exhibit test validity as a group. This conclusion is based on an analysis of (*a*) the tests' design, including the tests' contents, response processes, and reliabilities, (*b*) the tests' structures, including their factorial validity, and (*c*) the tests' convergent and divergent validity, including their relations with criterion variables. One serious concern is that different scales of accurate emotional perception often do not correlate highly with each other. This lack of convergence among measures in the emotion perception domain is not yet understood.

5. Measures of EI based on Mixed Model approaches do not provide valid assessments in the area. This conclusion is based on an analysis that concludes such measures (*a*) employ response processes that assess self-concept rather than actual ability, (*b*) draw on attributes, such as flexibility and assertiveness, that are not part of the EI concept as understood here, and (*c*) empirically exhibit substantial overlap with other commonly studied personality traits.

6. EI is a predictor of significant outcomes across diverse samples in a number of real-world domains. It predicts social relations, workplace performance, and mental and physical well-being.

7. EI often shows incremental validity in predicting social outcomes over other measures of intelligence and socio-emotional traits.

8. The relation between EI and life outcomes suggests that EI may valuably inform practitioners' understandings of, and interventions in, human behavior.

FUTURE ISSUES

1. *Does EI fit into a comprehensive taxonomy of mental abilities?* Empirically supported taxonomies of cognitive mental abilities already exist (Carroll 1993). Could such taxonomies be enlarged to include emotional and social intelligences? Such taxonomies promote an understanding of mental abilities, define their interrelations, and ensure that the most important among those abilities are assessed. For example, recent

iterations of the Wechsler and Standford-Binet tests, drawing in part on such taxonomies, added scales to assess previously underemphasized abilities.

2. *What else does EI predict beyond the findings summarized here?* Researchers already have examined the relationships between EI and valued criteria. Are there more possibilities? For example, EI might predict a wider range of outcomes at school and work than studied thus far, such as attrition, attendance, and satisfaction. Research on EI in the home, as well as across different psychiatric groups, and patients' success in psychotherapy is of interest as well. Such research can help psychologists better understand the meaning and utility of the EI concept.

3. *What can meta-analyses clarify about EI?* Reviews of EI outcomes already exist. Future reviews could rely more on more formal techniques such as meta-analyses of effects in the area, focusing in particular on the correlates of measures based on Specific-Ability and Integrative-Model approaches. For example, a number of studies seem to indicate that EI's predictive effects may be stronger for men than women, but is this impression correct? Conducting such analyses will place such findings and claims concerning EI on a firmer footing.

4. *What is the effect of teaching emotional knowledge?* Studies of teaching emotional knowledge and reasoning in the home, school, and workforce already have begun. Are such applications effective and, if so, in what ways? Laboratory analogues, such as the experimental manipulation of emotional management, can help researchers understand EI's effect on outcomes. Field research also has the potential to indicate EI's impact if the effects of emotional teachings are clearly distinguished from other ameliorative practices. The results from experimental and applied research often are valuable guides to theory.

ACKNOWLEDGMENTS

The authors come from several independent laboratories and have endeavored to create a consensus review of the field. They thank the collaborators with whom they more usually work, who were generous and supportive of this project. These include Marc Brackett, Art Brief, David Caruso, Glenn Geher, Patrick Kyllonen, Gerald Matthews, Carolyn MacCann, Peter Salovey, Ralf Schulze, Barry Staw, and Moshe Zeidner. Many of these individuals, as well as additional colleagues, read and commented on the manuscript. These additional colleagues included Kim Barchard, Joseph Ciarrochi, Arla Day, Vanessa Druskat, Daniel Eignor, Judith Hall, Cal Izard, David Matsumoto, Steve Nowicki, Maureen O'Sullivan, and Lennart Sjoberg. We are grateful to them all, and extend special thanks to Kim Barchard and Vanessa Druskat for their detailed, multiple sets of comments on particularly challenging sections of the review. The authors also thank Marina Milonova and Chia-Jung Tsay who helped identify and organize much of the psychometric and outcome literature that makes up this review, and in addition assisted in recording the results of many individual articles.

The views expressed here are those of the authors and do not necessarily reflect the views of their respective institutions, or the views of the researchers with whom they have collaborated at other times, or the views of those who have read and commented on the manuscript.

DISCLOSURES

John D. Mayer is an author of the Mayer-Salovey-Caruso Emotional Intelligence Test and receives royalties from that test. Richard D. Roberts works at the Center for New Constructs of Educational Testing Service and is developing for that organization, and also for other organizations through contract work, a range of assessments, some of which could be considered alternatives to or competitors with contemporary measures of EI.

LITERATURE CITED

Ackerman PL, Heggestad ED. 1997. Intelligence, personality, and interests: evidence for overlapping traits. *Psychol. Bull.* 121:219–45

Amabile TM, Barsade SG, Mueller JS, Staw BM. 2005. Affect and creativity at work. *Adm. Sci. Q.* 50:367–403

Amelang M, Steinmayr R. 2006. Is there a validity increment for tests of emotional intelligence in explaining the variance of performance criteria? *Intelligence* 34:459–68

Averill JR. 1992. The structural bases of emotional behavior: a metatheoretical analysis. *Rev. Personal. Soc. Psychol.* 13:1–24

Averill JR, Nunley EP. 1992. *Voyages of the Heart: Living an Emotionally Creative Life.* New York: Free Press

Averill JR, Nunley EP. 1993. Grief as an emotion and as a disease: a social-constructionist perspective. In *Handbook of Bereavement: Theory, Research, and Intervention*, ed. MS Stroebe, W Stroebe, RO Hansson, pp. 77–90. New York: Cambridge Univ. Press

Averill JR, Thompson-Knowles. 1991. Emotional creativity. In *International Review of Studies on Emotion*, ed. KT Strongman, pp. 269–99. London: Wiley

Bar-On R. 1997. *BarOn Emotional Quotient Inventory: Technical Manual.* Toronto: Multi-Health Systems

Bar-On R. 2000. Emotional and social intelligence: insights from the Emotional Quotient Inventory. In *The Handbook of Emotional Intelligence: Theory, Development, Assessment, and Application at Home, School, and in the Workplace*, ed. R Bar-On, JDA Parker, pp. 363–88. San Francisco: Jossey-Bass

Bar-On R. 2004. The BarOn Emotional Quotient Inventory (EQ-i): rationale, description and summary of psychometric properties. See Geher 2004, pp. 115–45

Barchard KA. 2003. Does emotional intelligence assist in the prediction of academic success? *Educ. Psychol. Meas.* 63:840–58

Barchard KA, Christensen MM. 2007. Dimensionality and higher-order factor structure of self-reported emotional intelligence. *Personal. Individ. Differ.* 42:971–85

Barchard KA, Hakstian RA. 2004. The nature and measurement of emotional intelligence abilities: basic dimensions and their relationships with other cognitive ability and personality variables. *Educ. Psychol. Meas.* 64:437–62

Barsade SG. 2002. The ripple effect: emotional contagion and its influence on group behavior. *Adm. Sci. Q.* 47:644–75

Barsade SG, Brief AP, Spataro SE. 2003. The affective revolution in organizational behavior: the emergence of a paradigm. In *Organizational Behavior: The State of the Science*, ed. J Greenberg, pp. 3–52. Mahwah, NJ: Erlbaum

Bastian VA, Burns NR, Nettelbeck T. 2005. Emotional intelligence predicts life skills, but not as well as personality and cognitive abilities. *Personal. Individ. Differ.* 39:1135–45

Baum KM, Nowicki S. 1998. Perception of emotion: measuring decoding accuracy of adult prosodic cues varying in intensity. *J. Nonverbal Behav.* 22:89–107

Beasley K. 1987. The emotional quotient. *Br. Mensa Mag.*, May, p. 25

Beck AT, Rush AJ, Shaw BF, Emery G. 1979. *Cognitive Therapy of Depression.* New York: Guilford

Boone RT, Buck R. 2004. Emotion receiving ability: a new view of measuring individual differences in the ability to accurately judge others' emotions. See Geher 2004, pp. 73–89

Boyatzis RE, Sala F. 2004. The Emotional Competence Inventory (ECI). See Geher 2004, pp. 147–80

Brackett M, Mayer JD. 2003. Convergent, discriminant, and incremental validity of competing measures of emotional intelligence. *Personal. Soc. Psychol. Bull.* 29:1147–58

Brackett M, Mayer JD, Warner RM. 2004. Emotional intelligence and the prediction of behavior. *Personal. Individ. Differ.* 36:1387–402

Brackett MA, Katulak NA. 2006. Emotional intelligence in the classroom: skill-based training for teachers and students. In *Applying Emotional Intelligence: A Practitioner's Guide*, ed. J Ciarrochi, JD Mayer, pp. 1–27. New York: Psychol. Press/Taylor & Francis

Brackett MA, Rivers SE, Shiffman S, Lerner N, Salovey P. 2006. Relating emotional abilities to social functioning: a comparison of self-report and performance measures of emotional intelligence. *J. Personal. Soc. Psychol.* 91:780–95

Brackett MA, Warner RM, Bosco J. 2005. Emotional intelligence and relationship quality among couples. *Pers. Relat.* 12:197–212

Buck R. 1984. *The Communication of Emotion.* New York: Guilford

Cacioppo JT, Gardner WL. 1999. Emotions. *Annu. Rev. Psychol.* 50:191–214

Carroll JB. 1993. *Human Cognitive Abilities: A Survey of Factor Analytic Studies.* New York: Cambridge Univ. Press

Carton JS, Kessler EA, Pape CL. 1999. Nonverbal decoding skills and relationship well-being in adults. *J. Nonverbal Behav.* 23:91–100

Caruso DR, Mayer JD, Salovey P. 2002. Relation of an ability measure of emotional intelligence to personality. *J. Personal. Assess.* 79:306–20

Ciarrochi JV, Caputi P, Mayer JD. 2003. The distinctiveness and utility of a measure of trait emotional awareness. *Personal. Individ. Differ.* 34:1477–90

Ciarrochi JV, Chan AY, Caputi P. 2000. A critical evaluation of the emotional intelligence concept. *Personal. Individ. Differ.* 28:539–61

Ciarrochi JV, Forgas JP, Mayer JD, eds. 2006. *Emotional Intelligence in Everyday Life: A Scientific Inquiry.* Philadelphia, PA: Psychol. Press 2nd ed.

Clore GL, Ortony A, Foss MA. 1987. The psychological foundations of the affective lexicon. *J. Personal. Soc. Psychol.* 53:751–66

Cole PM, Martin SE, Dennis TA. 2004. Emotion regulation as a scientific construct: methodological challenges and directions for child development research. *Child Dev.* 75:317–33

Côté S, Miners CTH. 2006. Emotional intelligence, cognitive intelligence and job performance. *Adm. Sci. Q.* 51:1–28

Cronbach LJ, Meehl PE. 1955. Construct validity in psychological tests. *Psychol. Bull.* 52:281–302

Davies M, Stankov L, Roberts RD. 1998. Emotional intelligence: in search of an elusive construct. *J. Personal. Soc. Psychol.* 75:989–1015

Dawda D, Hart SD. 2000. Assessing emotional intelligence: reliability and validity of the Bar-On Emotional Quotient Inventory (EQ-i) in university students. *Personal. Individ. Differ.* 28:797–812

Day AL, Carroll SA. 2004. Using an ability-based measure of emotional intelligence to predict individual performance, group performance, and group citizenship behaviours. *Personal. Individ. Differ.* 36:1443–58

Presents a taxonomy of mental abilities based on the most extensive analysis of perceptual and cognitive test data up to that time.

Denham SA, Blair KA, DeMulder E, Levitas J, Sawyer K, Auerbach-Major S. 2003. Preschool emotional competence: pathway to social competence. *Child Dev.* 74:238–56

Dunn EW, Brackett MA, Ashton-James C, Schneiderman E, Salovey P. 2007. On emotionally intelligent time travel: individual differences in affective forecasting ability. *Personal. Soc. Psychol. Bull.* 33:85–93

Eisenberg N. 2000. Emotion, regulation, and moral development. *Annu. Rev. Psychol.* 51:665–97

Eisenberg N, Fabes RA, Guthrie IK, Reiser M. 2000. Dispositional emotionality and regulation: their role in predicting quality of social functioning. *J. Personal. Soc. Psychol.* 78:136–57

Ekman P, Friesen WV. 1975. *Unmasking the Face: A Guide to Recognizing the Emotions from Facial Cues.* Englewood Cliffs, NJ: Prentice Hall

Elfenbein HA, Ambady N. 2002. Predicting workplace outcomes from the ability to eavesdrop on feelings. *J. Appl. Psychol.* 87:963–71

Elfenbein HA, Der Foo M, Boldry JG. 2006. Dyadic effects in nonverbal communication: a variance partitioning analysis. *Cogn. Emot.* 20:149–59

Elfenbein HA, Der Foo MD, White J, Tan HH. 2007. Reading your counterpart: the benefit of emotion recognition accuracy for effectiveness in negotiation. *J. Nonverbal Behav.* In press

Elias MJ, Zins JE, Weissberg RP, Frey KS, Greenberg MT, et al. 1997. *Promoting Social and Emotional Learning: Guidelines for Educators.* Alexandria, VA: Assoc. Supervision Curric. Dev.

Engelberg E, Sjöberg L. 2000. Internet use, social skills, and adjustment. *CyberPsychol. Behav.* 7:41–47

Engelberg E, Sjöberg L. 2004. Money attitudes and emotional intelligence. *J. Appl. Soc. Psychol.* 36:2027–47

Fine SE, Izard CE, Mostow AJ, Trentacosta CJ, Ackerman BP. 2003. First grade emotion knowledge as a predictor of fifth grade self-reported internalizing behaviors in children from economically disadvantaged families. *Dev. Psychopathol.* 15:331–42

Gardner H. 1983. *Frames of Mind: The Theory of Multiple Intelligences.* New York: Basic Books

Geher G, ed. 2004. *Measuring Emotional Intelligence: Common Ground and Controversy.* New York: Nova Sci.

Gohm CL, Corser GC, Dalsky DJ. 2005. Emotional intelligence under stress: useful, unnecessary, or irrelevant? *Personal. Individ. Differ.* 39:1017–28

Goldberg LR. 1993. The structure of phenotypic personality traits. *Am. Psychol.* 48:26–34

Goleman D. 1995. *Emotional Intelligence.* New York: Bantam

Gross JJ. 1998. The emerging field of emotional regulation: an integrative review. *Rev. Gen. Psychol.* 2:271–99

Grubb WL, McDaniel MA. 2007. The fakability of Bar-On's emotional quotient inventory short form: Catch me if you can. *Hum. Perform.* 20:43–59

Halberstadt AG, Hall JA. 1980. Who's getting the message? Children's nonverbal skill and their evaluation by teachers. *Dev. Psychol.* 16:564–73

Hall JA. 2001. The PONS Test and the psychometric approach to measuring interpersonal sensitivity. In *Interpersonal Sensitivity: Theory and Measurement,* ed. JA Hall, FJ Bernieri, pp. 143–60. Mahwah, NJ: Erlbaum

Hall JA, Bernieri FJ. 2001. *Interpersonal Sensitivity: Theory and Measurement.* Mahwah, NJ: Erlbaum

Hampel V. 2003. Exploring associations between emotional intelligence and relationship quality utilizing the Mayer, Salovey, and Caruso Emotional Intelligence Test (MSCEIT). *Dissert. Abstr. Intl. B: Sci. Eng.* 63(8-B):3915

Best-selling trade book that popularized EI; its scientific coverage is a matter of dispute.

Hatfield E, Cacioppo J, Rapson RL. 1994. *Emotional Contagion*. New York: Cambridge Univ. Press

Hilgard ER. 1980. The trilogy of mind: cognition, affection, and conation. *J. Hist. Behav. Sci.* 16:107–17

Hochschild AR. 1983. *The Managed Heart: Commercialization of Human Feeling*. Berkeley: Univ. Calif. Press

Innes-Ker Å, Niedenthal PM. 2002. Emotion concepts and emotional states in social judgment and categorization. *J. Personal. Soc. Psychol.* 83:804–16

Isen AM. 2001. An influence of positive affect on decision making in complex situations: theoretical issues with practical implications. *J. Consum. Psychol.* 11:75–86

Ivcevic Z, Mayer JD, Brackett M. 2007. Exploring personality the natural way: an inquiry into open-ended self descriptions. *Imagination Cogn. Personal.* 26:65–86

Izard CE. 1993. Four systems for emotion activation: cognitive and noncognitive processes. *Psychol. Rev.* 100:68–90

Izard CE. 2001. Emotional intelligence or adaptive emotions? *Emotion* 1:249–57

Izard CE. 2002. Translating emotion theory and research into preventive interventions. *Psychol. Bull.* 128:796–824

Izard CE, Fine S, Schultz D, Mostow AJ, Ackerman B, Youngstrom E. 2001. Emotion knowledge as a predictor of social behavior and academic competence in children at risk. *Psychol. Sci.* 12:18–23

Izard CE, Trentacosta CJ, King KA. 2004. An emotion-based prevention program for Head Start children. *Early Educ. Dev.* 15:407–22

Jausovec N, Jausovec K. 2005. Differences in induced gamma and upper alpha oscillations in the human brain related to verbal/performance and emotional intelligence. *Int. J. Psychophysiol.* 56:223–35

Jausovec N, Jausovec K, Gerlic I. 2001. Differences in event-related and induced electroencephalography patterns in the theta and alpha frequency bands related to human emotional intelligence. *Neurosci. Lett.* 311:93–96

Jensen AR. 1998. *The g Factor: The Science of Mental Ability*. Westport, CT: Praeger/Greenwood

Joint Comm. Standards. 1999. *Standards for Educational and Psychological Testing*. Washington, DC: Am. Educ. Res. Assoc

Kafetsios K. 2004. Attachment and emotional intelligence abilities across the life course. *Personal. Individ. Differ.* 37:129–45

Kleinginna PR, Kleinginna AM. 1981. A categorized list of emotion definitions, with suggestions for a consensual definition. *Motiv. Emot.* 5:345–79

Lane RD, Quinlan DM, Schwartz GE, Walker PA, Zeitlin SB. 1990. The Levels of Emotional Awareness Scale: a cognitive-developmental measure of emotion. *J. Personal. Assess.* 55:124–34

Lane RD, Reiman EM, Axelrod B, Lang-Sheng Y, Holmes A, Schwartz GE. 1998. Neural correlates of levels of emotional awareness: evidence of an interaction between emotion and attention in the anterior cingulate cortex. *J. Cogn. Neurosci.* 10:525–35

Law KS, Wong C-S, Song LJ. 2004. The construct and criterion validity of emotional intelligence and its potential utility for management studies. *J. Appl. Psychol.* 89:483–96

Lazarus RS. 1994. *Emotion and Adaptation*. Oxford, UK: Oxford Univ. Press

LeDoux JE. 2000. Emotion circuits in the brain. *Annu. Rev. Neurosci.* 23:155–84

Lee J-E, Wong C-MT, Day JD, Maxwell SE, Thorpe P. 2000. Social and academic intelligence: a multitrait-multimethod study of their crystallized and fluid characteristics. *Personal. Individ. Differ.* 29:539–53

Reviews key scientific research relevant to enhancing emotional development and emotional knowledge among youth to promote their social competence.

Provides a key reference guide for understanding psychological tests and their validity; endorsed by major stakeholder associations such as American Psychological Association.

Leuner B. 1966. Emotional intelligence and emancipation. *Praxis Kinderpsychol. Kinderpsychiatrie* 15:193–203

Lichten W, Wainer H. 2000. The aptitude-achievement function: an aid for allocating educational resources, with an advanced placement example. *Educ. Psychol. Rev.* 12:201–28

Locke EA. 2005. Why emotional intelligence is an invalid concept. *J. Organ. Behav.* 26:425–31

Lopes PN, Brackett MA, Nezlek JB, Schütz A, Sellin I, Salovey P. 2004. Emotional intelligence and social interaction. *Personal. Soc. Psychol. Bull.* 30:1018–34

Lopes PN, Côté S, Grewal D, Kadis J, Gall M, Salovey P. 2006. Emotional intelligence and positive work outcomes. *Psichothema* 18(Suppl.):132–38

Lopes PN, Salovey P, Côté S, Beers M. 2005. Emotion regulation abilities and the quality of social interaction. *Emotion* 5:113–18

Lopes PN, Salovey P, Straus R. 2003. Emotional intelligence, personality, and the perceived quality of social relationships. *Personal. Individ. Differ.* 35:641–58

Lubinski D. 2000. Scientific and social significance of assessing individual differences: "sinking shafts at a few critical points." *Annu. Rev. Psychol.* 51:405–44

Lubinski DW, Mary R, Morelock MJ. 2001. Top 1 in 10,000: a 10-year follow-up of the profoundly gifted. *J. Appl. Psychol.* 86:718–29

Lyubomirsky S, King L, Diener E. 2005. The benefits of frequent positive affect: Does happiness lead to success? *Psychol. Bull.* 131:803–55

MacCann C. 2006. *New Approaches to Measuring Emotional Intelligence: Exploring Methodological Issues with Two New Assessment Tools*. Sydney, Australia: Univ. Sydney

MacCann C, Matthews G, Zeidner M, Roberts RD. 2004. The assessment of emotional intelligence: on frameworks, fissues, and the future. In *Measuring Emotional Intelligence: Common Ground and Controversy*, ed. G Geher, pp. 21–52. Hauppauge, NY: Nova Sci.

Mandler G. 1975. *Mind and Emotion*. New York: Wiley

Masia CL, McNeil DW, Cohn LG, Hope DA. 1999. Exposure to social anxiety words: treatment for social phobia based on the Stroop paradigm. *Cogn. Behav. Pract.* 6:248–58

Matsumoto D, LeRoux JA, Wilson-Cohn C, Raroque J, Kooken K, et al. 2000. A new test to measure emotion recognition ability: Matsumoto and Ekman's Japanese and Caucasian Brief Affect Recognition Test (JACBART). *J. Nonverbal Behav.* 24:179–209

Matsumoto D, LeRoux JA, Bernhard R, Gray H. 2004. Unraveling the psychological correlates of intercultural adjustment potential. *Int. J. Intercult. Relat.* 28:281–309

Matthews G, Emo AK, Funke G, Zeidner M, Roberts RD, et al. 2006. Emotional intelligence, personality, and task-induced stress. *J. Exp. Psychol. Appl.* 12:96–107

Matthews G, Roberts RD, Zeidner M. 2004. Seven myths about emotional intelligence. *Psychol. Inq.* 15:179–96

Matthews G, Zeidner M, Roberts RD. 2002. *Emotional Intelligence: Science and Myth*. Cambridge, MA: MIT Press

Matthews G, Zeidner M, Roberts RD, eds. 2007. *Emotional Intelligence: Knowns and Unknowns*. Cambridge, MA: Oxford Univ. Press

Mayer JD. 2000. Emotion, intelligence, emotional intelligence. In *The Handbook of Affect and Social Cognition*, ed. JP Forgas, pp. 410–31. Mahwah, NJ: Erlbaum

Mayer JD. 2005. A tale of two visions: Can a new view of personality help integrate psychology? *Am. Psychol.* 60:294–307

Mayer JD. 2006. A new field guide to emotional intelligence. See Ciarrochi et al. 2006, pp. 3–26

Mayer JD, Caruso DR, Salovey P. 1999. Emotional intelligence meets traditional standards for an intelligence. *Intelligence* 27:267–98

Empirical study that assesses how EI may impact social interactions; extensive and particularly well done.

Addresses EI theory, its measurement, and future research directions in a collection of writings by diverse experts.

Mayer JD, Ciarrochi J. 2006. Clarifying concepts related to emotional intelligence: a proposed glossary. See Ciarrochi et al. 2006, pp. 261–67

Mayer JD, DiPaolo MT, Salovey P. 1990. Perceiving affective content in ambiguous visual stimuli: a component of emotional intelligence. *J. Personal. Assess.* 54:772–81

Mayer JD, Geher G. 1996. Emotional intelligence and the identification of emotion. *Intelligence* 17:89–113

Mayer JD, Panter AT, Salovey P, Sitaraneos G. 2005. A discrepancy in analyses of the MSCEIT—resolving the mystery and understanding its implications: a reply to Gignac 2005. *Emotion* 5:236–37

Mayer JD, Salovey P. 1993. The intelligence of emotional intelligence. *Intelligence* 17:433–42

Mayer JD, Salovey P. 1997. What is emotional intelligence? In *Emotional Development and Emotional Intelligence: Educational Implications*, ed. P Salovey, D Sluyter, pp. 3–31. New York: Basic Books

Mayer JD, Salovey P, Caruso DR. 2000a. Emotional intelligence as zeitgeist, as personality, and as a standard intelligence. In *Handbook of Emotional Intelligence*, ed. R Bar-On, JDA Parker, pp. 92–117. New York: Jossey-Bass

Mayer JD, Salovey P, Caruso DR. 2000b. Models of emotional intelligence. In *Handbook of Intelligence*, ed. RJ Sternberg, pp. 396–420. Cambridge, UK: Cambridge Univ. Press

Mayer JD, Salovey P, Caruso DR. 2002a. *Mayer-Salovey-Caruso Emotional Intelligence Test (MSCEIT) Item Booklet*. Toronto: MHS Publ.

Mayer JD, Salovey P, Caruso DR. 2002b. *Mayer-Salovey-Caruso Emotional Intelligence Test (MSCEIT) User's Manual*. Toronto: MHS Publ.

Mayer JD, Salovey P, Caruso DR, Sitarenios G. 2001. Emotional intelligence as a standard intelligence. *Emotion* 1:232–42

Mayer JD, Salovey P, Caruso DR, Sitarenios G. 2003. Measuring emotional intelligence with the MSCEIT V2.0. *Emotion* 3:97–105

McCrae RR. 2000. Emotional intelligence from the perspective of the five-factor model of personality. In *The Handbook of Emotional Intelligence: Theory, Development, Assessment, and Application at Home, School, and in the Workplace*, ed. R Bar-On, JDA Parker, pp. 263–76. San Francisco, CA: Jossey-Bass

Mestre JM, Guil R, Lopes PN, Salovey P, Gil-Olarte P. 2006. Emotional intelligence and social and academic adaptation to school. *Psicothema* 18:112–17

Mostow AJ, Izard CE, Fine S, Trentacosta CJ. 2002. Modeling emotional, cognitive, and behavioral predictors of peer acceptance. *Child Dev.* 73:1775–87

Mueller J, Curhan J. 2006. Emotional intelligence and counterpart mood induction in a negotiation. *Int. J. Conflict Manag.* 17:110–28

Murphy KR, ed. 2006. *A Critique of Emotional Intelligence: What Are the Problems and How Can They Be Fixed?* Mahwah, NJ: Erlbaum

Neubauer AC, Freudenthaler HH. 2005. Models of emotional intelligence. In *Emotional Intelligence: An International Handbook*, ed. R Schulze, RD Roberts, pp. 31–50. Ashland, OH: Hogrefe & Huber

Nowicki SJ. 2007. *A Manual for the DANVA Tests*. Atlanta, GA: Dept. Psychol., Emory Univ.

Nowicki SJ, Carton J. 1993. The measurement of emotional intensity from facial expressions. *J. Soc. Psychol.* 133:749–50

Nowicki SJ, Duke MP. 1994. Individual differences in the nonverbal communication of affect: the Diagnostic Analysis of Nonverbal Accuracy Scale. *J. Nonverbal Behav.* 19:9–35

Oatley K. 2004. *Emotions: A Brief History*. Malden, MA: Blackwell Sci.

Introduces the MSCEIT, an integrative ability-based measure of EI.

Introduces the DANVA, a measure of accurate emotion perception.

Oatley K, Jenkins JM. 1992. Human emotions: function and dysfunction. *Annu. Rev. Psychol.* 43:55–85

O'Connor RMJ, Little IS. 2003. Revisiting the predictive validity of emotional intelligence: self-report vs ability-based measures. *Personal. Individ. Differ.* 35:1893–902

Palmer BR, Gignac G, Manocha R, Stough C. 2005. A psychometric evaluation of the Mayer-Salovey-Caruso Emotional Intelligence Test Version 2.0. *Intelligence* 33:285–305

Parrott WG. 2002. The functional utility of negative emotions. In *The Wisdom in Feeling: Psychological Processes in Emotional Intelligence*, ed. L Feldman Barrett, P Salovey, pp. 341–59. New York: Guilford

Paulhus DL, Lysy DC, Yik MSM. 1998. Self-report measures of intelligence: Are they useful as proxy IQ tests? *J. Personal.* 66:525–54

Payne WL. 1986. A study of emotion: developing emotional intelligence; self-integration; relating to fear, pain and desire. *Dissert. Abstr. Int. A: Human. Social Sci.* 47:203A

Petrides KV, Furnham A. 2001. Trait emotional intelligence: psychometric investigation with reference to established trait taxonomies. *Eur. J. Personal.* 15:425–48

Petrides KV, Furnham A. 2003. Trait emotional intelligence: behavioural validation in two studies of emotion recognition and reactivity to mood induction. *Eur. J. Personal.* 17:39–57

Phelps EA. 2006. Emotion and cognition: insights from studies of the human amygdala. *Annu. Rev. Psychol.* 57:27–53

Picard R. 1997. *Affective Computing*. Cambridge, MA: MIT Press

Pitterman H, Nowicki SJ. 2004. A test of the ability to identify emotion in human standing and sitting postures: the diagnostic analysis of nonverbal accuracy-2 posture test (DANVA2-POS). *Genet. Soc. Gen. Psychol. Monogr.* 130:146–62

Reddy WM. 2001. *The Navigation of Feeling: A Framework for the History of Emotions*. Cambridge, UK: Cambridge Univ. Press

Reis DL, Brackett MA, Shamosh NA, Kent AK, Salovey P, Gray JR. 2007. Emotional intelligence predicts individual differences in social exchange reasoning. *NeuroImage.* 35:1385–91

Richards A, French CC, Johnson W. 1992. Effects of mood manipulation and anxiety on performance of an emotional Stroop task. *Br. J. Psychol.* 83:479–91

Roberts RD, Schulze R, MacCann C. 2007. The measurement of emotional intelligence: a decade of progress? In *Sage Personality Handbook Series*, ed. G Boyle, G Matthews, D Saklofske. In press

Roberts RD, Schulze R, O'Brien K, MacCann C, Reid J, Maul A. 2006. Exploring the validity of the Mayer-Salovey-Caruso Emotional Intelligence Test (MSCEIT) with established emotions measures. *Emotion* 6:663–69

Roberts RD, Stankov L. 1999. Individual differences in speed of mental processing and human cognitive abilities: towards a taxonomic model. *Learn. Individ. Differ.* 11:1–120

Roberts RD, Zeidner M, Matthews G. 2001. Does emotional intelligence meet traditional standards for an intelligence? Some new data and conclusions. *Emotion* 1:196–231

Roseman IJ. 1984. Cognitive determinants of emotion: a structural theory. *Rev. Personal. Soc. Psychol.* 5:11–36

Rosenbaum DA, Carlson RA, Gilmore RO. 2001. Acquisition of intellectual and perceptual-motor skills. *Annu. Rev. Psychol.* 52:453–70

Rosenthal R, Hall JA, DiMatteo MR, Rogers PL, Archer D. 1979. *The PONS Test*. Baltimore, MD: Johns Hopkins Univ. Press

Rosete D, Ciarrochi J. 2005. Emotional intelligence and its relationship to workplace performance of leadership effectiveness. *Leadersh. Organ. Dev. J.* 26:388–99

Rubin RS, Munz DC, Bommer WH. 2005. Leading from within: the effects of emotion recognition and personality on transformational leadership behavior. *Acad. Manage. J.* 48:845–58

Seminal article that introduces a theory of EI and argues for its study by the scientific community.

Salovey P, Mayer JD. 1990. Emotional intelligence. *Imagination Cogn. Personal.* 9:185–211

Scherer KR, Schorr A, Johnstone T, eds. 2001. *Appraisal Processes in Emotion: Theory, Methods, Research*. New York: Oxford Univ. Press

Schultz D, Izard CE, Bear G. 2004. Children's emotion processing: relations to emotionality and aggression. *Dev. Psychopathol.* 16:371–87

Schutte NS, Malouff JM, Hall LE, Haggerty DJ, Cooper JT, et al. 1998. Development and validation of a measure of emotional intelligence. *Personal. Individ. Differ.* 25:167–77

Simon HA. 1982. Affect and cognition: comments. In *Affect and Cognition: The Seventeenth Annual Carnegie Symposium on Cognition*, ed. MS Clark, ST Fiske, pp. 333–42. Hillsdale, NJ: Erlbaum

Spearman C. 1927. *The Abilities of Man*. New York: Macmillan

Sternberg RJ. 1985. Human intelligence: the model is the message. *Science* 230:1111–18

Sternberg RJ. 2001. Measuring the idea of an idea: How intelligent is the idea of emotional intelligence? In *Emotional Intelligence in Everyday Life*, ed. J Ciarrochi, JP Forgas, JD Mayer, pp. 187–94. Philadelphia: Psychol. Press

Sternberg RJ, Detterman DR. 1986. *What is Intelligence?* Norwood, NJ: Ablex

Sternberg RJ, Kaufman JC. 1998. Human abilities. *Annu. Rev. Psychol.* 49:479–502

Sternberg RJ, Rainbow Proj. Collab. 2006. The Rainbow Project: enhancing the SAT through assessments of analytical, practical, and creative skills. *Intelligence* 34:321–50

Tett RP, Fox KE, Wang A. 2005. Development and validation of a self-report measure of emotional intelligence as a multidimensional trait domain. *Personal. Soc. Psychol. Bull.* 31:859–88

Tett RP, Wang A, Fox KE. 2006. *MEIA: Multidimensional Emotional Intelligence Assessment Manual*. Port Huron, MI: Sigma Assess. Syst.

Trentacosta CJ, Izard CE. 2007. Kindergarten children's emotion competence as a predictor of their academic competence in first grade. *Emotion* 7:77–88

Trinidad DR, Johnson CA. 2002. The association between emotional intelligence and early adolescent tobacco and alcohol use. *Personal. Individ. Differ.* 32:95–105

Van Ghent D. 1953. *The English Novel: Form and Function*. New York: Harper & Row

Vernon PE. 1971. *The Structure of Human Abilities*. New York: Methuen

Voss JF, Wiley J. 1995. Acquiring intellectual skills. *Annu. Rev. Psychol.* 46:155–81

Wagner RK. 2000. Practical intelligence. In *Handbook of Intelligence*, ed. RJ Sternberg, pp. 380–95. Cambridge, UK: Cambridge Univ. Press

Weis S, Süß H-M. 2007. Reviving the search for social intelligence—a multitrait-multimethod study of its structure and construct validity. *Personal. Individ. Differ.* 42:3–14

Zeidner M, Matthews G, Roberts RD. 2003. Development of emotional intelligence: towards a multi-level investment model. *Hum. Dev.* 46:69–96

Zeidner M, Shani-Zinovich I, Matthews G, Roberts RD. 2005. Assessing emotional intelligence in gifted and nongifted high school students: outcomes depend on the measure. *Intelligence* 33:369–91

Sample Size Planning for Statistical Power and Accuracy in Parameter Estimation

Scott E. Maxwell,[1] Ken Kelley,[2] and Joseph R. Rausch[3]

[1] Department of Psychology, University of Notre Dame, Notre Dame, Indiana 46556; email: smaxwell@nd.edu

[2] Inquiry Methodology Program, Indiana University, Bloomington, Indiana 47405; email: kkiii@indiana.edu

[3] Department of Psychology, University of Minnesota, Minneapolis, Minnesota 55455; email: rausch@umn.edu

Annu. Rev. Psychol. 2008. 59:537–63

The *Annual Review of Psychology* is online at http://psych.annualreviews.org

This article's doi: 10.1146/annurev.psych.59.103006.093735

Key Words

effect size, confidence intervals, cumulative science

Abstract

This review examines recent advances in sample size planning, not only from the perspective of an individual researcher, but also with regard to the goal of developing cumulative knowledge. Psychologists have traditionally thought of sample size planning in terms of power analysis. Although we review recent advances in power analysis, our main focus is the desirability of achieving accurate parameter estimates, either instead of or in addition to obtaining sufficient power. Accuracy in parameter estimation (AIPE) has taken on increasing importance in light of recent emphasis on effect size estimation and formation of confidence intervals. The review provides an overview of the logic behind sample size planning for AIPE and summarizes recent advances in implementing this approach in designs commonly used in psychological research.

Contents

INTRODUCTION AND OVERVIEW

One of the most frequently asked questions of a statistical consultant is how large a sample is needed for a specific research project. This question is usually couched in terms of designing a study with sufficient statistical power to achieve a statistically significant result. Given recent arguments in favor of reducing the role of null hypothesis significance testing (NHST), such sample size planning might seem less important. In fact, we believe that sample size planning remains a vital aspect of research, regardless of one's position on the NHST controversy. In particular, we argue that sample size planning is important not only for an individual investigator who aspires to publish, but also for a discipline that aspires to create a cumulative science.

From the standpoint of an individual investigator, statistical power is clearly important because most publication outlets in psychology implicitly require statistically significant results as a prerequisite for publication. Thus, investigators who want to publish need to have adequate power. Despite the obvious nature of this statement, literature reviews continue to show that underpowered studies persist, not just in psychology but also in other disciplines (Bezeau & Graves 2001, Cashen & Geiger 2004, Chan & Altman 2005, Maggard et al. 2003). Maxwell (2004) suggests that one reason for their persistence is the simple fact that most studies involve multiple hypothesis tests. Even though the power of any single test may be low by any reasonable standard, the opportunity to conduct multiple tests makes it highly likely that something of interest will emerge as statistically significant. Unfortunately, Maxwell (2004) goes on to show that the consequence for the discipline is an abundance of apparent contradictions in the published literature. Other authors such as Greenwald (1975) and Ioannidis (2005) have similarly shown the importance of power for the development of a cumulative science.

O'Brien & Castelloe (2007) extend this idea through what they define to be "crucial Type I" and "crucial Type II" error rates. The crucial Type I error rate is the probability that the null hypothesis is true when the null hypothesis is rejected. Similarly, the crucial Type II error rate is the probability that the null hypothesis is false when the null hypothesis is not rejected. All too many researchers may be under the false impression that these crucial error rates are simply α and β. In reality, however, as O'Brien & Castelloe (2007) show, these crucial error rates in fact are given by

$$\alpha^* = Prob(H_0 \, true | p \leq \alpha)$$
$$= \frac{\alpha(1 - \gamma)}{\alpha(1 - \gamma) + (1 - \beta)\gamma} \quad (1)$$
$$\beta^* = Prob(H_0 \, false | p > \alpha)$$
$$= \frac{\beta\gamma}{\beta\gamma + (1 - \alpha)(1 - \gamma)}, \quad (2)$$

where α^* is the crucial Type I error rate, β^* is the crucial Type II error rate, α is the usual Type I error rate, β is the usual Type II error rate, and γ is the prior probability that the null hypothesis is false (or, from a frequentist perspective, the proportion of all relevant studies for which the null hypothesis is false). A key point emphasized by O'Brien & Castelloe (2007) is that all other things being equal, greater power reduces both types of crucial error. As a result, statistical results are more trustworthy when power is high.

Thus, adequate power is an issue not only for an individual investigator who aspires to publish, but also for a discipline that aspires to develop a cumulative literature. The effect on the field may in fact be one reason why old theories in psychology never seem to die, but rather only fade away due to what is claimed to be the slow progress in psychology (Meehl 1978). O'Brien & Castelloe (2007) provide a related perspective by discussing the relation between crucial error rates and the "March of Science."

The concept of power is relevant only in the context of hypothesis testing, because the very definition of power is the probability of rejecting the null hypothesis in favor of an alternative hypothesis when the alternative hypothesis is true. While acknowledging the controversial nature of significance testing (Harlow et al. 1997, Nickerson 2000), we believe that power analysis should play an important role in psychological research. A full treatment of this issue is beyond the scope of this review, so instead we borrow from Jones & Tukey (2000), who among others have pointed out that in many situations a two-tailed hypothesis test provides information about a potentially important question, namely the direction of an effect. In particular, single-degree-of-freedom two-tailed hypothesis tests generally lead to one of three conclusions about a parameter or about a difference between parameters: (*a*) it is negative, (*b*) it is positive, or (*c*) the sign cannot be determined, so it plausibly could be negative, zero, or positive.

How relevant to psychological research is the information provided by hypothesis tests? We submit that sometimes it is of crucial importance, whereas other times it may be a foregone conclusion. For example, consider Festinger's & Carlsmith's (1959) classic study of cognitive dissonance. Would participants rate a boring study more highly if they received a payment of $1 or a payment of $20 (roughly $7 and $140, respectively, in 2006 dollars)? As predicted by cognitive dissonance theory, participants who received $1 rated the study more highly than participants who received $20. How does this relate to sample size planning? We would maintain that the primary goal of this study was to determine the sign of the difference in mean rating between the two participant groups. In particular, which group would produce the higher mean rating could not be predicted with certainty prior to conducting the study. Thus, the hypothesis test allowed the investigators to answer their primary research question. Notice that this question was not literally whether the groups would produce identical ratings, but rather which group would produce the larger rating. This study continues to be a classic at least in part because competing theories predicted different directions for the difference. Whether the mean difference was small, medium, or large was basically irrelevant. Thus, sample size planning for power should play a critical role here because the goal is to establish the direction of the mean difference.

Now consider a different example. Sternberg & Williams (1997) examined the ability of Graduate Record Examinations (GRE) scores to predict various measures of graduate school success. Here it is difficult to imagine that the direction of the correlation would not be positive. Instead, the question of interest is the magnitude of the correlation. As a result, power takes on reduced importance. However, this hardly makes sample size planning irrelevant, because the size of the sample will directly affect the precision and thus the accuracy with which the population correlation is estimated. For example, a correlation of 0.40 obtained in a sample of 100 yields a 95% confidence interval for the correlation that stretches from 0.22 to 0.55. The fact that the interval excludes zero allows a conclusion that the population correlation is positive, but the magnitude could be anywhere from halfway between small and medium to larger than large according to Cohen's (1988) conventions. If this interval is deemed too wide, the simplest solution (other than decreasing the level of confidence below 95%) is to obtain a larger sample.

Notice the different emphases in the cognitive dissonance and GRE examples. In the first example, sample size should be driven primarily by considerations of power. In the second example, the main goal is to estimate the magnitude of a parameter, which leads to a different approach to sample size planning. In particular, this review describes a variety of procedures for choosing sample size to obtain accurate parameter estimates, in the sense that there is a sufficiently narrow range of plausible values for the parameter of interest, as judged by the width of the corresponding confidence interval. However, we need to be clear that methods of sample size planning for accuracy have only recently begun to be widely developed for many statistical methods. Thus, certain sections of this review focus exclusively on sample size planning for power. We should also add that sample size planning for power is not at all incompatible with sample size planning for accuracy; instead, both perspectives will often be important and need to be considered together because often the goal should be to obtain an accurate estimate of a parameter and also to ascertain whether the parameter is negative, zero, or positive.

Confidence intervals provide a useful organizational framework for simultaneously considering the direction, the magnitude, and the accuracy of an effect. Direction is unambiguous (within the usual limits of probabilistic certainty) when a confidence interval fails to include zero as a plausible value. Thus, from this perspective, power can often be construed in terms of desiring a sufficiently high probability that a confidence interval based on one's observed data will not contain a value of zero. Magnitude requires consideration of precision and accuracy. If estimating the magnitude of a parameter is important, it follows immediately that the width of a confidence interval for this parameter should be considered, along with the center of the interval. A narrow interval results when the standard error of the parameter estimate is small, which is equivalent to saying that the parameter is estimated precisely. Accuracy entails not only precision but also an interval that tends to contain the true population value. In many situations, accuracy and precision go hand in hand, because many estimators are unbiased or at least consistent. Readers interested in additional discussion of the relationship between accuracy and precision can consult Kelley & Maxwell (2003, 2008), Kelley et al. (2003), and Kelley & Rausch (2006).

A CLOSER EXAMINATION OF POWER AND ACCURACY

Consider a researcher who is planning a two-group study where the goal is to compare mean scores in the treatment and control groups. For simplicity, assume that participants are randomly assigned to groups, with responses independently determined. Further suppose that normality and homogeneity of variance are plausible assumptions, so the researcher plans to analyze these data with an independent groups t-test with a two-tailed alpha level of 0.05.

Suppose this researcher desires a power of 0.80. One immediate dilemma is the necessity of specifying an effect size. Suppose the researcher decides to follow Cohen's (1988) guidelines and on this basis specifies a medium effect size (i.e., a population Cohen's d of 0.50). The researcher discovers that he or she will need to have 64 participants per group, or a total sample size of 128, assuming no attrition. Now suppose the researcher conducts the study, and it so happens that the standardized sample mean difference between groups turns out to be exactly 0.50, and thus is exactly medium according to Cohen's (1988) conventions. The corresponding t value equals 2.83, which is statistically significant at the 0.05 level. This might seem to be a happy ending to the story—the apparent conclusion is that there is a true mean difference between the groups, and the difference corresponds to a medium effect size. However, this effect size value of 0.50 is only an estimate and is itself subject to variability. Recent authoritative sources have recommended that confidence intervals accompany effect size estimates. For example, the *Publication Manual of the American Psychological Association* (Am. Psychol. Assoc. 2001) follows earlier advice offered by Wilkinson et al. (1999) in stating that "The reporting of confidence intervals (for estimates of parameters, for functions of parameters such as differences in means, and for effect sizes) can be an extremely effective way of reporting results . . . . The use of confidence intervals is therefore strongly recommended" (2001, p. 22). Similarly, the American Educational Research Association reporting standards state that "an indication of the uncertainty" of effect size indices "should

be included" (Am. Educ. Res. Assoc. 2006, p. 10).

Heeding the advice of the *Publication Manual of the American Psychological Association* (Am. Psychol. Assoc. 2001) and the *Standards for Reporting on Empirical Social Science Research in AERA Publications* (Am. Educ. Res. Assoc. 2006), our hypothetical researcher proceeds to form a confidence interval. Specifically, a 95% confidence interval for the population value of Cohen's d turns out to range from 0.15 to 0.85. Suddenly, it is not at all clear that the true effect here is medium even though the sample value of Cohen's d was exactly 0.50. In fact, the confidence interval reveals that the effect could plausibly be smaller than small (i.e., less than 0.20) or larger than large (i.e., greater than 0.80).

Goodman & Berlin (1994) provide a link between power and precision. In particular, they derive the following simple rule-of-thumb approximate relations between confidence intervals and detectable differences:

Predicted 95% CI

$$= \text{observed difference} \pm 0.7\Delta_{0.80} \quad (3)$$

$$= \text{observed difference} \pm 0.6\Delta_{0.90}, \quad (4)$$

where $\Delta_{0.80}$ = true difference for which there is 80% power and $\Delta_{0.90}$ = true difference for which there is 90% power.

Equation 3 shows why our conscientious hypothetical investigator obtained such a wide confidence interval for Cohen's d even while planning a study with adequate power. Recall that the researcher chose a sample size that would provide power of 0.80 for a medium effect size of 0.50. Substituting a value of 0.50 into Equation 3 produces an interval stretching 0.35 below and 0.35 above the observed difference. Because the observed Cohen's d was 0.50, the accompanying confidence interval ranges from 0.15 to 0.85. Notice by implication that regardless of the observed effect size, a total sample size of 128 (assuming equal sample sizes of 64 per group) will result in a 95% confidence interval for Cohen's d whose total width will be approximately 0.70.

The clear message here is that although a total sample size of 128 may be adequate for power, this sample size does not provide a highly accurate estimate of the population Cohen's *d*. We revisit procedures for designing studies to obtain a sufficiently accurate estimate of Cohen's *d* below.

It is important to emphasize that Equations 3 and 4 provide a useful rule of thumb for sample size planning for any parameter estimate or effect size; the accuracy of the approximation will depend on the extent to which the relevant standard error is independent of the effect size, an issue to which we return below. For example, consider the goal of ascertaining the relation between GRE scores and graduate school success. Suppose the sample size is chosen to be 84 to have power of 0.80 to detect a medium correlation of 0.30 according to Cohen's (1988) conventions. It immediately follows from Equation 3 that the total width of a 95% confidence interval for the population correlation coefficient will be approximately 0.42. For example, if the observed correlation in the sample happens to equal 0.30, the corresponding 95% confidence interval will stretch from 0.09 to 0.48, close to but not literally identical to the width implied by Equation 3 because the standard error of the sample correlation coefficient depends partly on the value of the correlation itself. The confidence interval once again reveals all too clearly, just as it did in the previous example of Cohen's *d*, that considerable uncertainty remains about the true value of the population correlation coefficient.

These examples illustrate that even if sample sizes are sufficiently large to guarantee adequate power, they may not be large enough to guarantee accurate parameter estimates. In reality, these examples probably underestimate the severity of the problem in the current psychological literature because, as mentioned above, literature reviews continue to show that studies tend to be underpowered to detect a medium effect. If studies are adequately powered to detect only a large effect, Equations 3 and 4 show that the ensuing con-

fidence intervals will be wider yet. This underscores Cohen's hypothesis about why confidence intervals tend not to be reported in the literature. In his classic 1994 *American Psychologist* article, he stated, "I suspect that the main reason they are not reported is that they are so embarrassingly large!" (Cohen 1994, p. 1002). However, failing to report confidence intervals simply provides a false sense of certainty, and sets readers up to interpret seemingly discrepant values reported in different studies as being contradictory of one another. Such embarrassment may also reflect an unrealistic expectation about the extent to which a single study can provide a definitive answer, a topic that we discuss below.

The most general point here is that sample size planning should sometimes focus on obtaining a sample large enough to have an adequate probability to reject the null hypothesis, whereas other times the focus should be on an adequate probability of obtaining a sufficiently narrow confidence interval. The sample size necessary to obtain an accurate estimate can be larger than the sample size necessary for adequate power, but the reverse can also be true, depending primarily on the size of effect to be detected. In fact, in many situations it should be important to achieve two goals: (*a*) reject the null hypothesis and establish the direction of an effect, and (*b*) estimate the effect accurately. The first of these implies the need to plan sample size in terms of power, whereas the second implies the need to plan sample size in terms of accuracy. Work that is described below has begun to develop sample size planning methods that accomplish both of these goals simultaneously.

CONCEPTUAL FOUNDATION FOR SAMPLE SIZE PLANNING FOR ACCURACY

Most behavioral researchers realize the importance of sample size planning and power analysis in order to have an appropriate probability of rejecting the null hypothesis when it is false. However, fewer researchers are as familiar with the role of sample size planning in order to avoid having to present "embarrassingly large" confidence intervals. The current section will provide a general conceptual framework for the specific examples that follow in later sections.

The basic idea of sample size planning for accuracy (i.e., accuracy in parameter estimation, or AIPE) is based on controlling the width of the confidence interval of interest. For example, consider the case of a confidence interval for a difference between two independent means. Assuming normality, homogeneity of variance, and equal group sizes, a 95% confidence interval for a difference between independent means can be written as

$$(\bar{Y}_1 - \bar{Y}_2) \pm t_{.975, 2n-2} \, s_P \sqrt{2/n}, \qquad (5)$$

where $\bar{Y}_1$ and $\bar{Y}_2$ are the sample means for each group, $t_{.975, 2n-2}$ is a critical t value corresponding to an alpha level of 0.05 two-tailed with $2n-2$ degrees of freedom, s_P is the pooled sample standard deviation, and n is the sample size per group. Suppose a researcher wants his or her confidence interval to have a "half width" of ω. In other words, the desired ensuing 95% confidence interval will be

$$(\bar{Y}_1 - \bar{Y}_2) \pm \omega. \qquad (6)$$

Notice that the effect of interest here, namely the population mean difference, has a desired precision equal to ω, in the sense that the true population difference should (with probability of 0.95) be within ω units of the sample difference (notice the full confidence interval width is 2ω).

Equations 5 and 6 show that the confidence interval will have the desired width if

$$\omega = t_{.975, 2n-2} s_P \sqrt{2/n}. \qquad (7)$$

It might seem that we could easily obtain the necessary sample size simply by solving Equation 7 for n:

$$n = \frac{2t_{.975, 2n-2}^2 s_P^2}{\omega^2}. \qquad (8)$$

However, three factors prevent Equation 8 from providing the actual desired sample size

per group. First, the t value in the numerator depends on n, and thus n is necessarily on both sides of the equation. However, except for very small sample sizes, the z is very close to the t, so introducing a z value of 1.96 for a two-sided 95% confidence interval only very slightly underestimates the actual desired sample size. Second, the variance term in the numerator is a sample statistic. This dilemma can be solved by replacing s^2 with a population variance σ^2. Of course, this leads to other issues, because σ^2 is itself unknown. Nevertheless, the sample size obtained from using σ^2 can be thought of as a conditional sample size, based on a working value of the population variance. Ongoing research addresses the possibility of updating this variance quantity based on early looks at one's data (Coffey & Muller 2003, Proschan 2005). Yet another alternative is to express the desired half-width ω in standard deviation units, in which case σ^2 appears in both the numerator and denominator and thus cancels itself out of the equation.

A third complication is less obvious and pertains specifically to sample size planning for accuracy. Even if a researcher were fortunate enough to use the correct value of σ^2 in the equation for sample size, the actual confidence interval will be based on the sample variance s_P^2, not on σ^2. As a result, even if the correct value of σ^2 is substituted into the expression for sample size, the result will be an interval whose expected width approximately equals the desired width. However, whenever the sample variance happens by chance to be larger than the population variance, Equation 5 shows that the interval obtained from the sample data will be wider than desired. As a result, AIPE requires the specification of "tolerance," which is the probability that the interval will be wider than desired. For example, a researcher might specify that he or she wants to be 80% certain of obtaining an interval no wider than the desired width, in which case tolerance would equal 0.20. Such a goal clearly requires a larger sample size than if the researcher were willing to tolerate only the expected interval width being sufficiently narrow. Sections of the review below provide references for incorporating this tolerance value into sample size planning for various effects.

SPECIFICATION OF EFFECT SIZE

One of the most troublesome aspects of sample size planning is the necessity to specify an effect size. In fact, as Lipsey (1990, p. 47) puts it in his chapter entitled "Effect Size: The Problematic Parameter," "The problem that is perhaps most responsible for inhibiting statistical power analysis in the design of treatment effectiveness research, however, is the fact that the effect size is generally both unknown and difficult to guess." Senn (2002, p. 1304) addresses this criticism of power analysis by pointing out, "The difference you are seeking is not the same as the difference you expect to find, and again you do not have to know what the treatment will do to find a figure. This is common to all science. An astronomer does not know the magnitude of new stars until he has found them, but the magnitude of star he is looking for determines how much he has to spend on a telescope." Also important is the point that power is not literally a single number but instead is a function defined over parameter values consistent with the alternative hypothesis. As such, power curves and response surfaces show how power changes as a function of such factors as effect size and sample size and thereby provide much more information than a single number.

Adding to the confusion is considerable disagreement about what magnitude of effect is truly important. McCartney & Rosenthal (2000) and Prentice & Miller (1992), among others, have argued that psychologists tend not to realize that effects conventionally thought of as small or even less than small may in fact be very important, either scientifically or practically. Unfortunately, in practice, sample size planning often is based on exactly the opposite perspective, whereby power be-

comes adequate to detect only large effects. As Goodman & Berlin (1994, p. 203) state, "A typical sample size consultation often resembles a ritualistic dance. The investigator usually knows how many participants can be recruited and wants the statistician to justify this sample size by calculating the difference that is 'detectable' for a given number of participants rather than the reverse . . . . The 'detectable difference' that is calculated is typically larger than most investigators would consider important or even likely." This description makes it abundantly clear why some researchers may view the sample size planning process as anything but scientific.

In principle, it would seem that researchers who design studies with sufficient power to detect only large effects would end up only hurting themselves, because unless they obtain statistically significant results, they may be unlikely to publish their results. However, any such self-correcting mechanism is likely to operate very gently if at all because almost all studies involve multiple hypothesis tests. As Kelley et al. (2003) and Maxwell (2004) point out, even if the power of any single test is low, the power to detect some effect among multiple tests can easily be quite high. In this sense, the system provides little direct incentive for researchers to adopt a procedure whereby they choose sample size based on a serious consideration of an effect size.

The discipline pays a price for underpowered studies even if individual researchers may not. First, as we have already mentioned, underpowered studies tend to produce a literature with apparent contradictions. Second, as Goodman & Berlin (1994), Hunter & Schmidt (2004), and Maxwell (2004) have pointed out, such apparent contradictions may in fact reflect nothing more than inherent sampling variability. Third, reporting results only as either significant or nonsignificant exacerbates the problem. Much better would be to report results in terms of confidence intervals because they display the uncertainty in effects, thus preventing readers from overinterpreting the presence of multiple asterisks next to small p-values.

A major advantage of sample size planning for accuracy is that sample size formulas for narrow confidence intervals can be much less dependent on the actual value of the population parameter in question than are sample size formulas for power. For example, the mean difference between groups does not appear in Equation 8, so sample size planning here is independent of effect size. In some situations (described below), the desired sample size is not independent of the underlying effect size. However, in such situations sample size for accuracy is often less dependent on the parameter value than is sample size for power. As a result, sample size planning from the AIPE perspective frequently overcomes Lipsey's (1990) major stumbling block for sample size planning because the unknown effect size may be relatively unimportant.

SAMPLE SIZE PLANNING FOR SPECIFIC DESIGNS AND ANALYSES

Comparing Two Independent Groups

The comparison of means via the two-group t-test is common in psychological research. As with most sample size planning procedures, obtaining sufficient power has dominated sample size planning for comparing two independent groups. Since Cohen's (1962) cataloging of typical standardized effect sizes in abnormal-social psychological research, researchers have often used Cohen's rules of thumb regarding small, medium, and large effects sizes for the standardized mean difference when planning sample size and interpreting study results.

Of course, rejecting a null hypothesis concerning mean differences may not be as informative as forming a confidence interval for the mean difference or Cohen's d. Thus, the AIPE approach to sample size planning is more appropriate than the power analytic approach in some situations. Due to the distributional differences between the unstandardized and standardized mean difference, AIPE sample size planning is not equivalent for these two effect sizes. Kelley et al. (2003) discuss sample size planning from an AIPE perspective in the context of two groups for the unstandardized mean difference (see also Beal 1989). Kelley & Rausch (2006) develop sample size planning procedures from the AIPE perspective for the population standardized mean difference. Both Kelley et al. (2003) and Kelley & Rausch (2006) also compare the power analytic and AIPE approaches to one another. In the context of AIPE for the unstandardized mean difference, the width of the confidence interval is independent of the size of the mean difference (recall Equation 5), which implies that the only parameter specification required is the common variance (Kelley et al. 2003). Necessary sample size for the standardized mean difference is not independent of the population standardized mean difference, but in practice, it depends relatively little on the size of the effect (Kelley & Rausch 2006).

Figure 1 shows necessary sample size per group as a function of the size of the population standardized mean difference (between 0.10 and 0.50) for power of 0.50, 0.80, and 0.95 (where $\alpha = 0.05$, two-tailed) and for desired 95% confidence interval widths of 0.35, 0.25, and 0.15. The smaller the value of the population standardized mean difference, the larger the sample size for a specified level of power. However, the larger the standardized mean difference, the larger the sample size for a specified confidence interval width, albeit the increase in sample size for larger standardized mean differences is minimal. Thus, necessary AIPE sample size for Cohen's d depends almost entirely on the desired confidence interval width. Such a realization should help to ease qualms about Lipsey's (1990) "problematic" unknowable effect size parameter in this situation.

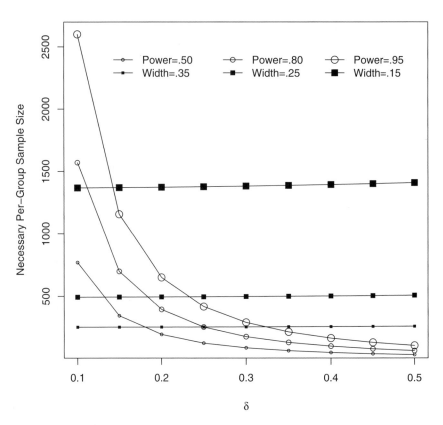

Figure 1

Necessary per-group sample size as a function of effect size for desired power and desired confidence interval width. Adapted from Kelley & Rausch (2006), with permission.

Adjustment for Multiple Comparison Procedures

In the analysis of variance (ANOVA) framework, multiple comparisons are commonly performed to address targeted questions about mean differences. Such contrasts are generally evaluated with a modified critical value due to the effect of multiplicity on the Type I error rate. Miller (1981) and Hsu (1996) provide comprehensive reviews on issues surrounding multiple comparisons. When a multiple comparison procedure will be used in data analysis, sample size planning should take this into account. Without such consideration, sample size will likely be too small.

Pan & Kupper (1999) develop methods for planning sample size from the AIPE perspective (both for the expected width and desired tolerance) for multiple comparisons, and Hsu (1989, 1996) provides an analogous discussion from the power analytic perspec-

tive. Both Pan & Kupper (1999) and Hsu (1989, 1996) develop methods for the most commonly used multiple comparison procedures (e.g., Bonferroni, Tukey, Scheffé, and Dunnett). Williams et al. (1999) discuss alternative multiple comparison procedures, including a sequential procedure for controlling the false discovery rate (FDR; Benjamini & Hochberg 1995). Although controlling the FDR tends to yield more power than controlling the familywise error rate, as of yet no formal sample size planning procedures currently exist for the FDR.

Multiple Regression

Kelley & Maxwell (2008) discuss sample size planning for multiple regression in a two-by-two framework, where one dimension represents the goal of the study, power or accuracy, and the other represents the effect size of interest, omnibus or targeted. Operationally, in multiple regression the omnibus effect is the squared multiple correlation coefficient, and the targeted effect is a specific regression coefficient. Thus, the way in which sample size is planned, and indeed the sample size itself, should depend on the question of interest.

Cohen (1988) details sample size planning for desired power for the omnibus effect (i.e., the squared multiple correlation coefficient) and a targeted effect (i.e., a particular regression coefficient). Commonly cited rules of thumb that pervade the literature on sample size for multiple regression are rarely appropriate (Green 1991, Maxwell 2000). Maxwell (2000) develops a set of procedures to plan sample size for targeted effects (see also Cohen 1988). Something not obvious is the fact that it is entirely possible for each regression coefficient to require a different sample size in order for there to be the same degree of power. More importantly, and not previously well documented in the literature, is that an appropriate sample size for the test of the squared multiple correlation coefficient in no way implies an appropriate sample size for the test of a particular regression coefficient.

Kelley & Maxwell (2003), later updated and generalized in Kelley & Maxwell (2008), develop methods for planning sample size for a targeted regression coefficient from the AIPE perspective. Much like the discussion regarding unstandardized and standardized mean differences, the value of an unstandardized regression coefficient is independent of confidence interval width, yet for standardized regression coefficients, a relatively small relation exists between the size of the standardized regression coefficient and the width of the confidence interval (Kelley & Maxwell 2008). This demonstrates that the AIPE approach to sample size planning for a targeted regression coefficient is easier to implement than the corresponding power analysis in the sense that the appropriate sample size is much less sensitive to the unknown effect size.

Kelley & Maxwell (2008) and Kelley (2007) develop AIPE sample size planning methods for the squared multiple correlation

coefficient for fixed and random regressors, respectively. The necessary AIPE sample size for the squared multiple correlation coefficient, contrary to a targeted regression coefficient, depends heavily on the value of the effect size. Algina & Olejnik (2000) develop a related method of planning sample size so that the observed squared multiple correlation coefficient is within a specified distance from the population value with some desired probability. Algina and colleagues have also developed sample size procedures for other important effects not often considered when planning sample size for multiple regression. In a cross-validation context, Algina & Keselman (2000) present methods to ensure that the squared cross-validity coefficient is sufficiently close to its upper limit, the squared population multiple correlation coefficient. Along the same lines as Algina & Olejnik (2000), Algina & Olejnik (2003) develop sample size planning procedures for the zero-order, the zero-order squared, and the partial correlation coefficient. Algina et al. (2002) also apply the sample size approach of Algina & Olejnik (2000) to the difference between squared multiple correlation coefficients (i.e., the squared semipartial correlation coefficient) in nested models.

The General Linear Multivariate Model

Reviews of sample size planning for the multivariate general linear model have been provided by Muller et al. (1992) and O'Brien & Muller (1993). A notable development in sample size planning for the general linear multivariate model is the work of Jiroutek et al. (2003). Their work combines the power analytic approach with an approach similar to AIPE, where the goal is to obtain a narrow confidence interval, conditional on the population value being contained within the observed interval. Thus, the approach of Jiroutek et al. (2003) accomplishes three things simultaneously with a single method: (*a*) an estimate that leads to a rejection of the null hypothesis, (*b*) a corresponding confidence interval that is sufficiently narrow, and (*c*) a confidence interval that correctly brackets the population parameter, all with some specified probability. The fundamental idea of this approach is to formalize sample size planning to ensure a specified probability for obtaining an estimate that is simultaneously accurate and statistically significant. Thus, the work of Jiroutek et al. (2003) is especially valuable for researchers whose goals include establishing both the direction and magnitude of an effect.

Most methods of sample size planning for the general linear model assume fixed predictors. Many psychological predictor variables are continuous, and most continuous variables in psychology are random instead of fixed. Glueck & Muller (2003) review the limited availability of sample size planning methods with random predictors. They also discuss the ramifications of incorporating a random baseline covariate for the calculation of sample size and power. Their methods extend directly to the context of generalized estimation equations (e.g., Liang & Zeger 1986), where not only are discrete and continuous outcomes possible, so too is a flexible correlational structure.

Exploratory Factor Analysis

Various suggestions and rules of thumb for sample size planning permeate the literature on exploratory factor analysis. Many rules of thumb stipulate a desired ratio of sample size to the number of factors, variables, or free parameters. MacCallum et al. (1999, 2001), Hogarty et al. (2005), Nasser & Wisenbaker (2001), and Velicer & Fava (1998) each review the existing literature and show that, in general, such rules of thumb regarding necessary sample size are oversimplified and should not be trusted.

Monte Carlo simulations have clearly shown that necessary sample size depends to a large extent on the goals of the researcher, and planning sample size cannot generally be reduced to rules of thumb. Basing sample size

on a ratio relative to the number of variables or an absolute sample size ignores communalities, which greatly affect necessary sample size. MacCallum et al. (1999) develop an approach that explicitly considers communalities as a necessary part of the procedure, with the goal of obtaining more valid factor analysis solutions. MacCallum et al. (2001) extend this work by allowing the factor model to be misspecified.

Confirmatory Factor Analysis and Structural Equation Modeling

Confirmatory factor analysis (CFA) and structural equation modeling (SEM) have become indispensable in much psychological research. SEM and CFA generally evaluate the overall model with chi-square likelihood ratio tests and/or with fit indices. The chi-square likelihood ratio test evaluates exact fit, whereas fit indices quantify how well a model fits the data. One can also consider sample size for specific path coefficients (i.e., targeted effects). Also, instead of considering only power, the AIPE approach could also be used for model fit and targeted effects. Currently, however, AIPE has not been developed in this context. Such a limitation is one that can certainly benefit from future research. As in multiple regression, the way in which sample size is planned should depend on the particular research goals (power and/or AIPE for omnibus and/or targeted effects).

Satorra & Saris (1985) provide an early approach to sample size planning based on the chi-square likelihood ratio test, where a specific but incorrect null model is hypothesized and the noncentrality parameter is determined based on the correct alternative model in order to calculate the probability of rejecting the specified null model.

Muthén & Muthén (2002), Mooijaart (2003), and Yuan & Hayashi (2003) all extend Satorra & Saris (1985) by developing computational approaches to sample size planning, such that data are generated given a specific set of parameters from a specified model in order to determine power empirically. As Kim (2005) points out, such approaches are based on an alternative model being correctly specified, where all of the model parameters are explicitly stated. Due to the sheer number of parameters of many models, specification of the set of parameters generally proves to be quite difficult.

Rather than approaching sample size from an exact fit perspective, MacCallum et al. (1996) develop sample size planning methods by defining the null hypothesis to be a particular value (generally not zero and thus not a perfect fit) of the root mean square error of approximation (RMSEA; Browne & Cudeck 1993, Steiger 1990, Steiger & Lind 1980). The idea is not necessarily to test an exact model, but rather to determine sample size so that not-good-fitting models could be rejected. This approach is implemented by determining sample size so that the upper limit of a confidence interval for the population RMSEA, given the hypothesized RMSEA value, is less than what is operationally defined as a not-good-fitting model. Such an approach overcomes the problem with the likelihood ratio test that very large samples will essentially always reject the null hypothesis, even for models that are useful (Browne & Cudeck 1993). In this framework, unlike the approach of Satorra & Saris (1985) where a specific null model is specified, the relationship between fit indices and the noncentrality parameter from a noncentral chi-square distribution is exploited so that the fit index itself is specified instead of a large number of individual parameters. For example, given the model-specified degrees of freedom and a hypothesized value of the population RMSEA equal to 0.05, sample size can be planned so that 0.08 is excluded from the confidence interval for the population RMSEA with some specified probability.

MacCallum & Hong (1997) and Kim (2005) extend the methods of MacCallum et al. (1996) to commonly used fit indices other than the RMSEA. MacCallum et al. (2006) further extend the methods of MacCallum et al. (1996) so that differences between the fit of competing models can be tested. Because different fit indices can be used, necessary sample size depends in part on the particular fit index chosen. Hancock & Freeman (2001) provide a tutorial for applied researchers on using the MacCallum et al. (1996) approach, and Hancock (2006) provides a tutorial chapter on general sample size issues in SEM with CFA as a special case. The effect of missing data (e.g., Dolan et al. 2005, Muthén & Muthén 2002) and type of manifest variable (continuous versus discrete; Lei & Dunbar 2004) on power has also been considered.

Longitudinal Data Analysis

Latent growth curve (LGC) models (Bollen & Curran 2006; McArdle 1988; McArdle & Epstein 1987; Meredith & Tisak 1984, 1990) and multilevel models for longitudinal data (Raudenbush & Bryk 2002, Singer & Willett 2003) have become increasingly popular methods for analyzing change. A number of recent approaches have been developed to calculate power and sample size for these models, with continuous or discrete outcomes.

For continuous outcomes, Muthén & Curran (1997) provide an extensive treatment of using LGC models for the analysis of randomized trials and illustrate an approach to power analysis in this context. Hedeker et al. (1999) provide a general framework for sample size planning from a power perspective when designing longitudinal studies to detect group differences, focusing on a mixed/multilevel model approach. Hedeker et al. (1999) also allow for differing degrees and patterns of attrition to be specified for the purpose of examining the effect of missing data on power in longitudinal studies. Similar to the work of Hedeker et al. (1999), Jung & Ahn (2003) provide sample size expressions for sufficient power for group comparisons in longitudinal data analysis that also allow for varying degrees and patterns of attrition. An important difference in these two approaches, however, lies in Jung & Ahn's (2003) choice of generalized estimating equations (GEE) for the derivation of their results. Winkens et al. (2006) provide expressions and an illustration of the effects of increasing the number of participants per group and the number of measurement occasions on necessary sample size and power for group comparisons in longitudinal data analysis. Winkens et al. (2006) differ from other researchers in this area, however, in that these authors also explicitly incorporate a cost function into their expressions to directly weigh the cost of adding participants versus time points.

Raudenbush & Xiao-Feng (2001) provide expressions for calculating power on group differences in orthogonal polynomial growth model parameters as a function of group sample size, study duration, and the number of measurement occasions. Also in the context of polynomial growth models, Biesanz et al. (2004) note that recoding time generally leads to "a change in the question asked" (p. 43) with respect to the lower-order polynomial growth parameters. Thus, changes in the corresponding power functions due to recoding time are generally due to changes in the meanings of these lower-order growth model parameters. Yan & Su (2006) provide methods for sample size calculation for sufficient power for group differences in longitudinal studies, but also allow nonlinear models (e.g., Bates & Watts 1988) for the growth functions of the two groups.

Other studies have contributed to sample size and power analysis for longitudinal studies of discrete outcome variables. For example, Rochon (1998) proposes a general approach to calculating minimum sample size for power analysis in repeated measures designs based on GEE, where the outcome variable can be discrete or continuous. Rochon (1998) also provides illustrative examples based on binary and Poisson outcome variables. Leon (2004) uses previous work of Diggle et al. (2002) to provide sample size tables for power to detect a treatment effect between two groups as a function of Type I error, the number of repeated binary observations, the group response rates, and the intraclass correlation. Jung & Ahn (2005) derive sample size expressions for sufficient power when comparing group differences in rates of change on a binary variable. Their approach is based on GEE, and it allows researchers to specify the degree and certain patterns of attrition.

Generalized Linear Models

The generalized linear model represents a well-known class of statistical methods that are useful for modeling categorical variables and contingency tables, and more generally, variables that are not normally distributed. A number of sample size planning methods have recently been proposed for this modeling approach, all from a power analysis perspective. Shieh (2005) presents an approach to power and sample size calculation for generalized linear models, which allows researchers to test multiple parameters simultaneously using a Wald test, among other extensions. Lyles et al. (2007) and Newson (2004) provide general, practical approaches for power calculations in the context of the generalized linear model.

The logistic regression model, which can be conceptualized as a special case of the generalized linear model, is used to model categorical or ordinal outcome variables. Recent articles on sample size and power for logistic regression have provided a variety of perspectives on power issues. Tsonaka et al. (2006) describe sample size and power calculations for discrete bounded outcome variables in a randomized trial. Taylor et al. (2006) illustrate the loss of power and necessary increase in sample size to achieve the same level of power when a continuous variable is categorized, either for the purpose of simplifying the analysis or via the process of measuring a continuous variable with ordinal categories. These authors also illustrate the potential utility in utilizing logistic or probit ordinal regression models to minimize the loss of efficiency in such situations.

Vergouwe et al. (2005) illustrate sample size planning for externally validating various logistic regression models using data from patients with metastatic testicular cancer. They argue that this approach is especially useful for model/variable selection. Furthermore, Vaeth & Skovlund (2004) and Hsieh et al. (1998) provide simple approaches to sample size calculations for power in logistic regression. In particular, Hsieh et al.'s (1998) simplified calculations are based on comparisons of means or proportions with a modification based on a variance inflation factor. Also, Strickland & Lu (2003) provide sample size calculations for comparing two groups in pre-post designs when the outcome variable is categorical or ordinal.

Whereas some authors have focused directly on the role of sample size in increasing power in the context of logistic regression, others have focused upon the utility of collecting pretreatment covariates in randomized studies for attaining increases in power. For example, Hernandez et al. (2004) illustrate the potential gain in efficiency either through smaller required sample sizes or through increased power in randomized studies of dichotomous outcomes by incorporating a baseline covariate into the logistic regression model. In fact, Hernandez et al. (2004) report up to a 46% reduction in required sample size for a prespecified level of power for the treatment effect through incorporating a baseline covariate into the analysis.

Cluster Randomized Trials

Cluster randomized trials are often used when it is more practical or feasible to randomly assign groups (i.e., clusters of individuals), as opposed to individual participants, to various treatment conditions (e.g., randomly assigning classrooms instead of students). Sample size planning may be especially important in such situations because even if there are a large number of participants per cluster, power and accuracy will suffer if the number of clusters is small. Thus, researchers should consider a number of alternatives in designing cluster randomized trials. Raudenbush (1997) uses a multilevel modeling framework to evaluate a number of key variables, including the study cost, the number of participants within cluster, the number of clusters, and the increase in statistical efficiency that can be attained by incorporating a pretreatment covariate into the statistical analysis.

Campbell et al. (2004) present a sample size–calculating tool that can be used to determine the necessary number of clusters and participants within cluster to detect a minimally meaningful treatment effect. Moerbeek (2006) evaluates the cost of two approaches for increasing power in a cluster randomized trial: increasing the number of clusters and incorporating pretreatment covariates into the statistical model. In particular, Moerbeek derives expressions that researchers can use to weigh these two alternatives against one another in terms of their relative costs. While also focusing one aspect of their study on the utility of a pretreatment covariate in cluster randomized trials, Murray et al. (2006) compare mixed ANOVA/ANCOVA models to multilevel models with respect to the power to detect an effect and conclude that the mixed model ANCOVA with a pretreatment covariate is preferable.

Federov & Jones (2005) provide a general exposition of a variety of issues in the analysis of cluster randomized trials. In particular, they express a preference for a random-effects model for the analysis of cluster randomized trials and also emphasize the importance of accounting for a number of important variables when designing a cluster randomized trial. Finally, Kraemer & Robinson (2005) clearly describe a number of important methodological issues that need to be carefully considered when designing, conducting, and analyzing cluster randomized trials.

Survival Analysis

Survival analysis is often the method of choice when the outcome variable of interest is the duration of time until a particular event occurs (e.g., Singer & Willett 2003). Recent work on study design for sufficient power in survival analysis includes Maki (2006), who presents expressions for power and sample size when using a form of the Weibull model to represent hazard functions. In contrast, Vaeth & Skovlund (2004) provide an approach to sample size and power calculations based on the Cox regression model. Furthermore, Schulgen et al. (2005) and Bernardo & Harrington (2001) introduce formulations necessary for sufficient power when comparing two groups in survival analysis, whereas Barthel et al. (2006) present a general approach to power in survival analysis.

Mixture Modeling

The general goal of mixture modeling is to decompose an observed distribution into multiple unobserved distributions. The observed distribution is often termed a composite, as the model implies it is the sum of component distributions. One goal is simply to model an observed, generally nonnormal, distribution. Another goal is to decompose a nonnormal distribution into multiple component distributions, where it is believed the components represent unobserved (i.e., latent) classes/groups. In so doing, the grouping variable can be regarded as missing with the goal of the mixture model then being the recovery of the parameters from each class and/or classification of individuals into the class to which they belong. McLachlan & Peel (2000) provide a survey of mixture models.

Mixture models have been extended to many models, such as regression, confirmatory factor analysis, structural equation modeling, and longitudinal models, among others. Sample size planning for mixture models is thus specific to the particular type of mixture analysis of interest. Furthermore, sample size planning can be based on several different goals: distinguishing between different competing models, assigning each individual to the appropriate class, AIPE for parameter estimates, etc. Thus, crossing the different types of mixture models with the different goals leads to a large set of possible ways to plan an appropriate sample size. Due to the rich questions that mixture models can address, sample size planning in mixture modeling certainly deserves increased attention.

Muñoz & Acuña (1999) and Zheng & Frey (2004) evaluate different combinations of parameters and sample size on the effectiveness of parameter recovery from mixed distributions. Not surprisingly, the consensus is that results are better when sample size is larger. Lubke & Neale (2006) evaluate the role sample size plays in factor mixture models when comparing two-class single-factor mixture models with single-class two-factor models. Again, the general conclusion is that the correct model tends to be selected with higher probability for larger sample sizes and larger class separations. Not obvious, however, is the fact that larger sample sizes are also associated with overestimation of the number of classes. Such a finding supports a common recommendation in the mixture modeling literature that theory should play a role in determining the number of latent classes.

EQUIVALENCE, NONINFERIORITY, AND THE GOOD ENOUGH PRINCIPLE

Equivalence is commonly studied in the medical sciences where two treatments, often drugs, are evaluated to investigate if there is no meaningful clinical difference between them. Evaluation of noninferiority is related to equivalence, except instead of implying there is no meaningful difference, noninferiority implies that one treatment is no worse than the other(s). Tryon (2001) provides a review of equivalence with connection to the psychological literature and the controversy that sometimes surrounds null hypothesis testing. Basic sample size issues for equivalence and noninferiority are discussed in Julious (2004). Liu et al. (2002),

Tang et al. (2002), and Chan (2002) discuss methods for equivalence/noninferiority for binary data, the ratio of proportions in matched-pair designs, and the difference between two proportions, respectively.

Such issues are related to the "good enough" principle and the "good enough belt," where the limits of the belt define what is considered a nontrivial effect (Serlin & Lapsley 1985, 1993). The AIPE approach to sample size planning can be helpful in this context, because if the upper and lower confidence limits are contained within the good enough belt, then evidence exists that meaningful differences are implausible at the specified confidence level. Because AIPE has not yet been developed for all important statistical methods, there is a corresponding deficiency in the sample size planning literature with regard to the good enough principle.

SIMULATION-BASED APPROACHES TO SAMPLE SIZE PLANNING

As has been detailed, sample size planning procedures have been developed for a wide variety of statistical tests. However, these procedures are typically based on standard techniques when all assumptions have been met. Sample size planning procedures for nonstandard analyses (e.g., classification and regression trees) and/or computationally based techniques (e.g., the bootstrap approach to statistical inference) have not generally been developed. Even when sample size planning for power has been developed, at this time there are often no corresponding methods for AIPE. However, a general principle of sample size planning appears to hold: Sample size can be planned for any research goal, on any statistical technique, in any situation with an a priori Monte Carlo simulation study.

An a priori Monte Carlo simulation study for planning an appropriate sample size involves generating random data from the population of interest (e.g., the appropriate parameters, distributional form), implementing the particular statistical technique, and repeating a large number of times (e.g., 10,000) with different sample sizes until the minimum sample size is found where the particular goal is accomplished (e.g., 90% power, expected confidence interval width of 0.15, 85% power and a 1% percent tolerance that the confidence interval is sufficiently narrow). Conducting such an a priori Monte Carlo simulation to plan sample size requires knowledge of the distributional form and population parameters, but this is also true with traditional analytic methods of sample size planning (where normality of the errors is almost always assumed). Muthén and Muthén (2002) discuss sample size planning for CFA and SEM via an a priori Monte Carlo simulation study. In the context of Bayesian inference, M'Lan et al. (2006) and Wang & Gelfand (2002) discuss similar a priori Monte Carlo simulation approaches for AIPE and power.

PLANNED AND POST HOC POWER ANALYSES

Although the fifth edition of the *Publication Manual of the American Psychological Association* (Am. Psychol. Assoc. 2001) encourages researchers to take power considerations seriously, it does not distinguish between planned and post hoc power analysis (also called "observed power" or "retrospective power" in some sources). Hoenig & Heisey (2001) cite 19 journals across a variety of disciplines advocating post hoc power analysis to interpret the results of a nonsignificant hypothesis test. It is important to clarify that post hoc power relies on using the sample effect size observed in the study to calculate power, instead of using an a priori effect size.

Hoenig & Heisey (2001) argue convincingly that many researchers have misunderstood post hoc power. Specifically, a low value of post hoc power does not necessarily imply that the study was underpowered, because it may simply reflect a small observed sample effect size. Yet another limitation of post hoc power is that Yuan & Maxwell (2005) have shown that post hoc power does not necessarily provide a good estimate of the actual population power even in large samples. Taken together, these perspectives show that confidence intervals and equivalence tests are superior to post hoc power as methods for interpreting the magnitude of statistically nonsignificant effect sizes, whether the goal is to assess support for a trivially small effect size, such as for assessing equivalence or noninferiority, or the goal is to argue that a study was underpowered.

METHODS TO INCREASE POWER AND ACCURACY

The emphasis placed on sample size in most discussions of power and accuracy may lead researchers to conclude that the only factor under their control that can influence power and accuracy is in fact sample size. In reality, although sample size clearly plays a vital role, there are often many other factors under an investigator's control that can increase power and accuracy. In the specific case of a linear model with m predictors, McClelland (2000) notes that the confidence interval for a regression coefficient can be expressed as

$$b \pm t_{N-m-1;\alpha} \sqrt{\frac{MSE}{NV_X(1 - R_X^2)}}, \qquad (9)$$

where b is the estimated coefficient, $t_{N-m-1;\alpha}$ is a critical value, N is sample size, MSE is the model mean square error, V_X is the variance of the predictor variable, and R_X^2 is the proportion of variance in the predictor shared with other predictor variables in the model. McClelland describes a variety of possible methods for decreasing the width of the confidence interval, and thereby increasing power, in addition to simply increasing sample size. More generally, Shadish et al. (2002) and West et al. (2000) provide explanations of a number of factors that researchers should consider in their efforts to increase power and accuracy.

META-ANALYSIS AND STUDY REGISTRIES

Researchers who engage in appropriate methods of sample size planning may quickly discover that the sample size needed to obtain adequate power or accuracy exceeds their resources. Investigators who need only determine that effect sizes expected to be large are in fact nonzero in the expected direction may be perfectly able to continue designing studies with relatively modest sample sizes. However, investigators who need to detect small effects or who need to obtain accurate parameter estimates will typically need quite large samples. If psychology is to take seriously the mission to estimate magnitude of effects accurately, researchers may be shocked at how large their samples will need to be.

For example, the standard error of the sample correlation depends on the value of the population correlation coefficient, but for small values of the population correlation, the standard error is approximately $\sqrt{1/n}$. Suppose a researcher wants to pinpoint the true population value of the correlation coefficient to within ± 0.05. A 95% confidence interval for the correlation needs to be based on roughly 1500 cases in order for the interval to have an expected half-width of 0.05 unless the correlation itself is sizable [a large correlation of 0.50 according to Cohen's (1988) conventions would still require more than 850 cases]. Experimentalists do not get the last laugh, because the sample size necessary to obtain a 95% confidence interval with a half-width of 0.05 for a standardized mean difference between two independent means is more than 3000 per group. Sample sizes of such magnitudes presumably explain Hunter & Schmidt's (2004, p. 14) statements that "for correlational studies, 'small sample size' includes all studies with less than a thousand persons and often extends above that" and "for experimental studies, 'small sample size' begins with 3000 and often extends well beyond that."

One way out of this conundrum is to decide that intervals do not need to have half-widths as narrow as 0.05 to be regarded as sufficiently precise. Other considerations include the same factors besides sample size that can increase precision, such as using a within-subjects design or incorporating covariates in the analysis. Even so, the fact remains that for many types of research programs, very large samples will be required to estimate effects with any reasonable degree of precision, and it will thus generally be difficult to obtain sufficient resources to obtain accurate parameter estimates in a single study.

Meta-analysis provides one potential solution to the lack of precision often observed in individual studies. Cohn & Becker (2003) point out that meta-analysis typically reduces the standard error of the estimated effect size, and thus leads to narrower confidence intervals and therefore more precision. In addition, power is often increased.

Hedges & Pigott (2001, 2004) argue for the importance of conducting power analyses before investing resources in a meta-analysis. They show that standard tests performed as part of meta-analyses do not necessarily have high statistical power, especially tests of heterogeneity of effect sizes, reinforcing the need to conduct a power analysis prior to undertaking a meta-analysis. These two articles together demonstrate how to conduct a power analysis for a variety of tests that might be of interest in a meta-analysis.

Although a major goal of meta-analysis is often to increase power and accuracy, resultant power and accuracy in meta-analysis "can be highly dependent on the statistical model used to meta-analyze the data" (Sutton et al. 2007). In fact, Hedges & Pigott (2001, p. 216) state that "The inclusion in meta-analysis of studies with very small sample sizes may have a paradoxical effect of decreasing the power of random-effects tests of the mean effect size." Along related lines, Lau et al. (1992) suggest that meta-analysis can be used to summarize the state of knowledge at each stage of research. Sutton et al. (2007) implicitly adopt this perspective and thereby argue that sample size planning should often be done not from a perspective of designing a single study with sufficient power, but instead should be done in the context of designing a new study to contribute to a larger body of literature in such a way that an ensuing meta-analysis adding the new study to the extant literature will have sufficient power. They then proceed to present a simulation approach to sample size planning based on this idea. One important result they demonstrate is that in a random effects meta-analytic model, multiple smaller studies can sometimes provide much more power than a single larger study with the same total sample size. This result converges with cautions offered by Schmidt (1996) and Wilson & Lipsey (2001) regarding the hazards of overinterpreting any single study, regardless of how large its sample size might be.

An important limitation of meta-analysis is its susceptibility to biased effect size estimates as a result of such factors as publication bias (such as the "file drawer" effect due to unpublished studies). Although methodologists continue to develop new methods to identify and adjust for publication bias, concerns remain about how well current methods work. For example, Kromrey & Rendina-Gobioff (2006) conclude that current methods to identify publication bias often either fail to control Type I error rates or else lack power. Furthermore, Kraemer et al. (1998) have shown that including underpowered studies in a meta-analysis can create bias, underscoring the importance of designing individual studies with sufficient power. Beyond problems caused by entire studies not being reported, a related problem is selective reporting of results, even in published studies. Chan et al. (2004) find clear evidence of selective reporting within studies in a large literature review they conducted. Chan et al. (2004) recommend that studies should be registered and protocols published online prior to the actual execution of a study. Toward this goal, the member journals of the International Committee of Medical Journal Editors adopted a policy in 2004 requiring registration of all clinical trials in a public trials registry as a condition of consideration for publication.

Multisite studies offer an alternative to meta-analysis and at least in principle are less prone to the "file drawer" effect. Kelley & Rausch (2006, p. 375) point out that "The idea of such multisite studies is to spread the burden but reap the benefits of estimates that are accurate and/or statistically significant." However, Kraemer & Robinson (2005, p. 528) point out that it is important to "prevent premature multicenter RCTs [randomized clinical trials] that may waste limited funding, investigator time and resources, and burden participants for little yield." They discuss various aspects of sample size planning in multicenter studies and provide a model of the respective roles of multicenter studies and individual studies in creating a cumulative science.

SUMMARY AND CONCLUSIONS

Advances continue to be made in methods for sample size planning. Some of these advances reflect analytic contributions for specific statistical methods, whereas others reflect new perspectives on fundamental goals of empirical research. In addition to the developments we have described, other important advances are taking place in the role of pilot studies in sample size planning (e.g., Kraemer et al. 2006), methods for dealing with the fact that the effect size is unknowable prior to conducting a study (e.g., O'Hagan et al. 2005), accounting for uncertainty in sample size due to estimating variance (e.g., Muller & Pasour 1997), adaptive sample size adjustments based on interim analyses (e.g., Jennison & Turnbull 2006, Mehta & Patel 2006), complications in planning subgroup analyses (e.g., Brookes et al. 2004, Lagakos 2006), the impact of noncompliance on power in randomized studies (e.g., Jo 2002), and Bayesian approaches to sample size planning (e.g., Berry 2004, 2006; Inoue et al. 2005; Lee & Zelen 2000). As psychologists consider the importance of effect size measures, it becomes incumbent to recognize the inherent uncertainty in effect size measures observed in small samples. Thus, the AIPE approach to sample size planning should assume an increasing role in psychological research. At the same time, it is important for researchers to appreciate the role of statistical power and AIPE not only for their own individual research but also for the discipline's effort to build a cumulative science.

SUMMARY POINTS

1. Sample size planning is important to enhance cumulative knowledge in the discipline as well as for the individual researcher.

2. Sample size planning can be based on a goal of achieving adequate statistical power, or accurate parameter estimates, or both.

3. Researchers are actively involved in developing methods for sample size planning, especially for complex designs and analyses.

4. Sample sizes necessary to achieve accurate parameter estimates will often be larger than sample sizes necessary to detect even a small effect.

5. Sample sizes necessary to obtain accurate parameter estimates or power to detect small effects may often require resources prohibitive to the individual researcher, thus suggesting the desirability of study registries accompanied by meta-analytic methods.

ACKNOWLEDGMENTS

We thank Chrystyna Kouros for help in the preparation of this review, and Lyle Jones, Helena Kraemer, Russell Lenth, Gitta Lubke, Robert MacCallum, Keith Muller, and Ralph O'Brien for their helpful comments on an earlier version of this review.

LITERATURE CITED

Algina J, Keselman HJ. 2000. Cross-validation sample sizes. *Appl. Psychol. Meas.* 24(2):173–79

Algina J, Moulder BC, Moser BK. 2002. Sample size requirements for accurate estimation of squared semipartial correlation coefficients. *Multivariate Behav. Res.* 37(1):37–57

Algina J, Olejnik S. 2000. Conducting power analyses for ANOVA and ANCOVA in between-subjects designs. *Eval. Health Prof.* 26(3):288–314

Algina J, Olejnik S. 2003. Sample size tables for correlation analysis with applications in partial correlation and multiple regression analysis. *Multivariate Behav. Res.* 38(3):309–23

Am. Educ. Res. Assoc. 2006. *Standards for Reporting on Empirical Social Science Research in AERA Publications.* Washington, DC: Am. Educ. Res. Assoc. **http://www.aera.net/opportunities/?id=1850**

Am. Psychol. Assoc. 2001. *Publication Manual of the American Psychological Association.* Washington, DC: Am. Psychol. Assoc. 5th ed.

Barthel FMS, Babiker A, Royston P, Parmar MKB. 2006. Evaluation of sample size and power for multi-arm survival trials allowing for nonuniform accrual, nonproportional hazards, loss to follow-up and cross-over. *Stat. Med.* 25:2521–42

Bates DM, Watts DG. 1988. *Nonlinear Regression Analysis and Its Applications.* New York: Wiley

Beal SL. 1989. Sample size determination for confidence intervals on the population mean and on the difference between two population means. *Biometrics* 45(3):969–77

Benjamini Y, Hochberg Y. 1995. Controlling the false discovery rate: a practical and powerful approach to multiple testing. *J. R. Stat. Soc. B* 57(1):289–300

Bernardo MVP, Harrington DP. 2001. Sample size calculations for the two-sample problem using the multiplicative intensity model. *Stat. Med.* 20:557–79

Berry DA. 2004. Bayesian statistics and the efficiency and ethics of clinical trials. *Stat. Sci.* 19(1):175–87

Berry DA. 2006. Bayesian clinical trials. *Nature* 5:27–36

Bezeau S, Graves R. 2001. Statistical power and effect sizes of clinical neuropsychology research. *J. Clin. Exp. Neuropsychol.* 23:399–406

Biesanz JC, Deeb-Sossa N, Papadakis AA, Bollen KA, Curran PJ. 2004. The role of coding time in estimating and interpreting growth curve models. *Psychol. Methods* 9(1):30–52

Bollen KA, Curran PJ. 2006. *Latent Curve Models: A Structural Equation Perspective.* Hoboken, NJ: Wiley

Brookes ST, Whitely E, Egger M, Smith GD, Mulheran PA, Peters TJ. 2004. Subgroup analyses in randomized trials: risks of subgroup-specific analyses; power and sample size for the interaction test. *J. Clin. Epidemiol.* 57:229–36

Browne MW, Cudeck R. 1993. Alternative ways of assessing model fit. In *Testing Structural Equation Models*, ed. K Bollen, S Long, pp. 136–62. Newbury Park, NJ: Sage

Campbell MK, Thomson S, Ramsay CR, MacLennan GS, Grimshaw JM. 2004. Sample size calculator for cluster randomized trials. *Comput. Biol. Med.* 34:113–25

Cashen LH, Geiger SW. 2004. Statistical power and the testing of null hypotheses: a review of contemporary management research and recommendations for future studies. *Organ. Res. Methods* 7(2):151–67

Chan A. 2002. Power and sample size determination for noninferiority trials using an exact method. *J. Biopharm. Stat.* 12(4):457–69

Chan A, Altman DG. 2005. Epidemiology and reporting of randomized trials published in PubMed journals. *Lancet* 365:1159–62

Chan A, Hróbjartsson A, Haahr MT, Gotzsche PC, Altman DG. 2004. Empirical evidence for selective reporting of outcomes in randomized trials: comparison of protocols for published articles. *JAMA* 2291(20):2457–65

Coffey CS, Muller KE. 2003. Properties of internal pilots with the univariate approach to repeated measures. *Statist. Med.* 22:2469–85

Cohen J. 1962. The statistical power of abnormal-social psychological research: a review. *J. Abnorm. Soc. Psychol.* 65(3):145–53

Cohen J. 1988. *Statistical Power Analysis for the Behavioral Sciences.* Hillsdale, NJ: Erlbaum. 2nd ed.

Cohen J. 1994. The earth is round (p < .05). *Am. Psychol.* 49(12):997–1003

Cohn LD, Becker BJ. 2003. How meta-analysis increases statistical power. *Psychol. Methods* 8(3):243–53

Diggle PJ, Heagerty P, Liang KY, Zeger SL. 2002. *Analysis of Longitudinal Data.* Oxford: Oxford Univ. Press. 2nd ed.

Dolan C, Van Der Sluis S, Grasman R. 2005. A note on normal theory power calculation in SEM with data missing completely at random. *Struct. Equ. Model.* 12(2):245–62

Federov V, Jones B. 2005. The design of multicentre trials. *Stat. Methods Med. Res.* 14:205–48

Festinger L, Carlsmith JM. 1959. Cognitive consequences of forced compliance. *J. Abnorm. Soc. Psychol.* 58(2):203–10

Glueck DH, Muller KE. 2003. Adjusting power for a baseline covariate in linear models. *Stat. Med.* 22:2535–51

Goodman SN, Berlin JA. 1994. The use of predicted confidence intervals when planning experiments and the misuse of power when interpreting results. *Ann. Intern. Med.* 121:200–6

Green SB. 1991. How many subjects does it take to do a regression analysis? *Multivariate Behav. Res.* 26:499–510

Greenwald AG. 1975. Consequences of prejudice against the null hypothesis. *Psychol. Bull.* 82:1–20

Hancock GR. 2006. Power analysis in covariance structure modeling. In *Structural Equation Modeling: A Second Course*, ed. GR Hancock, RO Mueller, pp. 69–115. Greenwich, CT: Inf. Age Publ.

Hancock GR, Freeman MJ. 2001. Power and sample size for the root mean square error of approximation test of not close fit in structural equation modeling. *Educ. Psychol. Meas.* 61(5):741–58

Harlow LL, Mulaik SA, Steiger JH. 1997. *What If There Were No Significance Tests?* Mahwah, NJ: Erlbaum

Hedeker D, Gibbons RD, Waternaux C. 1999. Sample size estimation for longitudinal designs with attrition: comparing time-related contrasts between two groups. *J. Educ. Behav. Stat.* 24(1):70–93

Hedges LV, Pigott TD. 2001. The power of statistical tests in meta-analysis. *Psychol. Methods* 6(3):203–17

Hedges LV, Pigott TD. 2004. The power of statistical tests for moderators in meta-analysis. *Psychol. Methods* 9(4):426–45

Hernandez AV, Steyerberg EW, Habbema DF. 2004. Covariate adjustment in randomized controlled trials with dichotomous outcomes increases statistical power and reduces sample size requirements. *J. Clin. Epidemiol.* 57:454–60

Hoenig JM, Heisey DM. 2001. The abuse of power: the pervasive fallacy of power calculations for data analysis. *Am. Stat.* 55(1):19–24

Hogarty KY, Hines CV, Kromrey JD, Ferron JM, Mumford KR. 2005. The quality of factor solutions in explanatory factor analysis: the influence of sample size, communality, and overdetermination. *Educ. Psychol. Meas.* 65(2):202–26

Hsieh FY, Bloch DA, Larsen MD. 1998. A simple method of sample size calculation for linear and logistic regression. *Stat. Med.* 17:1623–34

Hsu JC. 1989. Sample size computation for designing multiple comparison experiments. *Comput. Stat. Data Anal.* 7:79–91

Hsu JC. 1996. *Multiple Comparisons: Theory and Methods.* London: Chapman & Hall

Hunter JE, Schmidt FL. 2004. *Methods of Meta-Analysis: Correcting Error and Bias in Research Findings.* Thousand Oaks, CA: Sage. 2nd ed.

Ioannidis JPA. 2005. Why most published research findings are false. *PLoS Med.* 2(8):696–701

Inoue LY, Berry DA, Parmigiani G. 2005. Relationship between Bayesian and frequentist sample size determination. *Am. Stat.* 59(1):79–87

Jennison C, Turnbull BW. 2006. Adaptive and nonadaptive group sequential tests. *Biometrika* 93(1):1–21

Jiroutek MR, Muller KE, Kupper LL, Stewart PW. 2003. A new method for choosing sample size for confidence interval-based inferences. *Biometrics* 59:580–90

Jo B. 2002. Statistical power in randomized intervention studies with noncompliance. *Psychol. Methods* 7(2):178–93

Jones LV, Tukey JW. 2000. A sensible formulation of the significance test. *Psychol. Methods* 5(4):411–14

Julious SA. 2004. Sample sizes for clinical trials with normal data. *Stat. Med.* 23:1921–86

Jung S, Ahn C. 2003. Sample size estimation for GEE method for comparing slopes in repeated measurements data. *Stat. Med.* 22:1305–15

Jung S, Ahn C. 2005. Sample size for a two-group comparison of repeated binary measurements using GEE. *Stat. Med.* 24:2583–96

Kelley K. 2007. Sample size planning for the squared multiple correlation coefficient: accuracy in parameter estimation via narrow confidence intervals. *Behav. Res. Methods.* In press

Kelley K, Maxwell SE. 2003. Sample size for multiple regression: obtaining regression coefficients that are accurate, not simply significant. *Psychol. Methods* 8(3):305–21

Kelley K, Maxwell SE. 2008. Sample size planning with applications to multiple regression: power and accuracy for omnibus and targeted effects. In *The Sage Handbook of Social Research Methods*, ed. P Alasuutari, L Bickman, J Brannen, pp. 166–92. London: Sage

Kelley K, Maxwell SE, Rausch JR. 2003. Obtaining power or obtaining precision: delineating methods of sample-size planning. *Eval. Health Prof.* 26(3):258–87

Kelley K, Rausch JR. 2006. Sample size planning for the standardized mean difference: accuracy in parameter estimation via narrow confidence intervals. *Psychol. Methods* 11(4):363–85

Kim KH. 2005. The relation among fit indexes, power, and sample size in structural equation modeling. *Struct. Equ. Model.* 12(3):368–90

Kraemer HC, Gardner C, Brooks JO, Yesavage JA. 1998. The advantages of excluding underpowered studies in meta-analysis: inclusionist vs exclusionist viewpoints. *Psychol. Methods* 3:23–31

Kraemer HC, Mints J, Noda A, Tinklenberg J, Yesavage JA. 2006. Caution regarding the use of pilot studies to guide power calculations for study proposals. *Arch. Gen. Psychiatry* 63:484–89

Kraemer HC, Robinson TN. 2005. Are certain multicenter randomized clinical trial structures misleading clinical and policy decisions? *Contemp. Clin. Trials* 26:518–29

Kromrey JD, Rendina-Gobioff G. 2006. On knowing what we do not know. *Educ. Psychol. Meas.* 66(3):357–73

Lagakos SW. 2006. The challenge of subgroup analyses—reporting without distorting. *N. Engl. J. Med.* 354:1667–70

Lau J, Antman EM, Jimenez-Silva J, Kupelnick B, Mosteller F, Chalmers TC. 1992. Cumulative meta-analysis of therapeutic trials for myocardial infarction. *N. Engl. J. Med.* 327:248–54

Lee SJ, Zelen M. 2000. Clinical trials and sample size considerations: another perspective. Rejoinder. *Stat. Sci.* 15(2):108–10

Lei PW, Dunbar SB. 2004. Effects of score discreteness and estimating alternative model parameters on power estimation methods in structural equation modeling. *Struct. Equ. Model.* 11(1):20–44

Leon AC. 2004. Sample size requirements for comparisons of two groups on repeated observations of a binary outcome. *Eval. Health Prof.* 27(1):34–44

Liang KY, Zeger SL. 1986. Longitudinal data analysis using generalized linear models. *Biometrika* 73:13–22

Lipsey MW. 1990. *Design Sensitivity: Statistical Power for Experimental Research*. Thousand Oaks, CA: Sage

Liu J, Hsueh H, Hsieh E, Chen JJ. 2002. Tests for equivalence or noninferiority for paired binary data. *Stat. Med.* 21:231–45

Lubke G, Neale MC. 2006. Distinguishing between latent classes and continuous factors: resolution by maximum likelihood? *Multivariate Behav. Res.* 41:499–532

Lyles RH, Lin H, Williamson JM. 2007. A practical approach to computing power for generalized linear models with nominal, count, or ordinal responses. *Stat. Med.* 26:1632–48

MacCallum RC, Browne MW, Cai L. 2006. Testing differences between nested covariance structure models: power analysis and null hypotheses. *Psychol. Methods* 11(1):19–35

MacCallum RC, Browne MW, Sugawara HM. 1996. Power analysis and determination of sample size for covariance structure modeling. *Psychol. Methods* 1(2):130–49

MacCallum RC, Hong S. 1997. Power analysis in covariance structure modeling using GFI and AGFI. *Multivariate Behav. Res.* 32(2):193–210

MacCallum RC, Widaman KF, Preacher KJ, Hong S. 2001. Sample size in factor analysis: the role of model error. *Multivariate Behav. Res.* 36(4):611–37

MacCallum RC, Widaman KF, Zhang S, Hong S. 1999. Sample size in factor analysis. *Psychol. Methods* 4(1):84–99

Maggard MA, O'Connell JB, Liu JH, Etzioni DA, Ko CK. 2003. Sample size calculations in surgery: Are they done correctly? *Surgery* 134(2):275–79

Maki E. 2006. Power and sample size considerations in clinical trials with competing risk endpoints. *Pharm. Stat.* 5:159–71

Maxwell SE. 2000. Sample size and multiple regression analysis. *Psychol. Methods* 5(4):434–58

Maxwell SE. 2004. The persistence of underpowered studies in psychological research: causes, consequences, and remedies. *Psychol. Methods* 9(2):147–63

McArdle JJ. 1988. Dynamic but structural equation modeling of repeated measures data. In *The Handbook of Multivariate Experimental Psychology*, Vol. 2, ed. JR Nesselroade, RB Cattell, pp. 561–614. New York: Plenum

McArdle JJ, Epstein D. 1987. Latent growth curves within developmental structural equation models. *Child. Dev.* 58:110–33

McCartney K, Rosenthal R. 2000. Effect size, practical importance, and social policy for children. *Child. Dev.* 71(1):173–80

McClelland GH. 2000. Increasing statistical power without increasing sample size. *Am. Psychol.* 55(8):963–64

McLachlan GJ, Peel D. 2000. *Finite Mixture Models*. New York: Wiley

Meehl PE. 1978. Theoretical risks and tabular asterisks: Sir Karl, Sir Ronald, and the slow progress of soft psychology. *J. Consult. Clin. Psychol.* 46(4):806–34

Mehta CR, Patel NR. 2006. Adaptive, group sequential and decision theoretic approaches to sample size determination. *Stat. Med.* 25:3250–69

Meredith W, Tisak J. 1984. *"Tuckerizing" curves*. Presented at Annu. Meet. Psychometric Soc., Santa Barbara, Calif.

Meredith W, Tisak J. 1990. Latent curve analysis. *Psychometrika* 55:107–22

Miller RG. 1981. *Simultaneous Statistical Inference*. New York: Springer-Verlag. 2nd ed.

M' Lan CE, Joseph L, Wolfson DB. 2006. Bayesian sample size determination for case-control studies. *J. Am. Stat. Assoc.* 101(474):760–72

Moerbeek M. 2006. Power and money in cluster randomized trials: When is it worth measuring a covariate? *Stat. Med.* 25:2607–17

Mooijaart A. 2003. Estimating the statistical power in small samples by empirical distributions. In *New Development in Psychometrics*, ed. H Yanai, A Okada, K Shigemasu, Y Kano, JJ Meulman, pp. 149–56. Tokyo: Springer-Verlag

Muller KE, LaVange LM, Ramey SL, Ramey CT. 1992. Power calculations for general linear multivariate models including repeated measures applications. *J. Am. Stat. Assoc.* 87:1209–26

Muller KE, Pasour VB. 1997. Bias in linear model power and sample size due to estimating variance. *Commun. Stat.: Theory Methods* 26:839–51

Muñoz MA, Acuña JD. 1999. Sample size requirements of a mixture analysis method with applications in systematic biology. *J. Theor. Biol.* 196:263–165

Murray DM, van Horn ML, Hawkins JD, Arthur MW. 2006. Analysis strategies for a community trial to reduce adolescent ATOD use: a comparison of random coefficient and ANOVA/ANCOVA models. *Contemp. Clin. Trials* 27:188–206

Muthén BO, Curran PJ. 1997. General longitudinal modeling of individual differences in experimental designs: a latent variable framework for analysis and power estimation. *Psychol. Methods* 24(4):371–402

Muthén LK, Muthén BO. 2002. How to use a Monte Carlo study to decide on sample size and determine power. *Struct. Equ. Model.* 9(4):599–620

Nasser F, Wisenbaker J. 2001. Modeling the observation-to-variable ratio necessary for determining the number of factors by the standard error scree procedure using logistic regression. *Educ. Psychol. Meas.* 61(3):387–403

Newson R. 2004. Generalized power calculations for generalized linear models and more. *Stata J.* 4(4):379–401

Nickerson RS. 2000. Null hypothesis significance testing: a review of an old and continuing controversy. *Psychol. Methods* 5(2):241–301

O'Brien RG, Castelloe JM. 2007. Sample size analysis for traditional hypothesis testing: concepts and issues. In *Pharmaceutical Statistics Using SAS: A Practical Guide*, ed. A Dmitrienko, C Chuang-Stein, R D'Agostino, pp. 237–71. Cary, NC: SAS

O'Brien RG, Muller KE. 1993. Unified power analysis for t-tests through multivariate hypotheses. In *Applied Analysis of Variance in Behavioral Science*, ed. LK Edwards, pp. 297–344. New York: Marcel Dekker

O'Hagan A, Steves JW, Campbell MJ. 2005. Assurance in clinical trial design. *Pharm. Stat.* 4:187–201

Pan Z, Kupper LL. 1999. Sample size determination for multiple comparison studies treating confidence interval width as random. *Stat. Med.* 18:1475–88

Prentice DA, Miller DT. 1992. When small effects are impressive. *Psychol. Bull.* 112(1):160–64

Proschan MA. 2005. Two-stage sample size re-estimation based on a nuisance parameter: a review. *J. Biopharm. Stat.* 15(4):559–74

Raudenbush SW. 1997. Statistical analysis and optimal design for cluster randomized trials. *Psychol. Methods* 2:173–85

Raudenbush SW, Bryk AS. 2002. *Hierarchical Linear Models: Applications and Data Analysis Methods.* Thousand Oaks, CA: Sage. 2nd ed.

Raudenbush SW, Xiao-Feng L. 2001. Effects of study duration, frequency of observation, and sample size on power in studies of group differences in polynomial change. *Psychol. Methods* 6(4):387–401

Rochon J. 1998. Application of GEE procedures for sample size calculations in repeated measures experiments. *Stat. Med.* 17:1643–58

Satorra A, Saris WE. 1985. Power of the likelihood ratio test in covariance structure analysis. *Psychometrika* 50(1):83–90

Schmidt FL. 1996. Statistical significance testing and cumulative knowledge in psychology: implications for training of researchers. *Psychol. Methods* 1:115–29

Schulgen G, Olschewski M, Krane V, Wanner C, Ruff G, Schumacher M. 2005. Sample size for clinical trials with time-to-event endpoints and competing risks. *Contemp. Clin. Trials* 26:386–96

Senn SJ. 2002. Power is indeed irrelevant in interpreting completed studies. *BMJ* 325:1304

Serlin RC, Lapsley DK. 1985. Rationality in psychological research: the good-enough principle. *Am. Psychol.* 40(1):73–83

Serlin RC, Lapsley DK. 1993. Rational appraisal of psychological research and the good-enough principle. In *A Handbook for Data Analysis in the Behavioral Sciences: Methodological Issues*, ed. G Keren, C Lewis, pp. 199–228. Hillsdale, NJ: Erlbaum

Shadish WR, Cook TD, Campbell DT. 2002. *Experimental and Quasi-Experimental Designs for Generalized Causal Inference.* Boston, MA: Houghton Mifflin

Shieh G. 2005. Power and sample size calculations for multivariate linear models with randomized explanatory variables. *Psychometrika* 70(2):347–58

Singer JD, Willett JB. 2003. *Applied Longitudinal Data Analysis: Modeling Change and Event Occurrence.* New York: Oxford Univ. Press

Steiger JH. 1990. Structural model evaluation and modification: an interval estimation approach. *Multivariate Behav. Res.* 25:173–80

Steiger JH, Lind JM. 1980. *Statistically Based Tests for the Number of Common Factors.* Presented at Annu. Meet. Psychometric Soc., Iowa City, IA

Sternberg RJ, Williams WW. 1997. Does the Graduate Record Examination predict meaningful success in the graduate training of psychology? A case study. *Am. Psychol.* 52(6):630–41

Strickland PA, Lu S. 2003. Estimates, power and sample size calculations for two-sample ordinal outcomes under before-after study designs. *Stat. Med.* 22:1807–18

Sutton AJ, Cooper NJ, Jones DR, Lambert PC, Thompson JR, Abrams KR. 2007. Evidence-based sample size calculations based upon updated meta-analysis. *Stat. Med.* 26:2479–500

Tang M, Tang N, Chan IS, Chan BP. 2002. Sample size determination for establishing equivalence/noninferiority via ratio of two proportions in matched-pair design. *Biometrics* 58:957–63

Taylor AB, West SG, Aiken LS. 2006. Loss of power in logistic, ordinal logistic, and probit regression when an outcome variable is coarsely categorized. *Educ. Psychol. Meas.* 66(2):228–39

Tsonaka R, Rizopoulos D, Lesaffre E. 2006. Power and sample size calculations for discrete bounded outcome scores. *Stat. Med.* 25:4241–52

Tryon WW. 2001. Evaluating statistical difference, equivalence, and indeterminacy using inferential confidence intervals: an integrated alternative method of conducting null hypothesis statistical tests. *Psychol. Methods* 6(4):371–86

Vaeth M, Skovlund E. 2004. A simple approach to power and sample size calculations in logistic regression and Cox regression models. *Stat. Med.* 23:1781–92

Velicer WF, Fava JL. 1998. Effects of variable and subject sampling on factor pattern recovery. *Psychol. Methods* 3(2):231–51

Vergouwe Y, Steyerberg EW, Eijkemans MJC, Habbema JDF. 2005. Substantial effective sample sizes were required for external validation studies of predictive logistic regression models. *J. Clin. Epidemiol.* 58:475–83

Wang F, Gelfand AE. 2002. A simulation-based approach to Bayesian sample size determination for performance under a given model and for separating models. *Stat. Sci.* 17:193–208

West SG, Biesanz JC, Pitts SC. 2000. Causal inference and generalization in field settings: experimental and quasi-experimental designs. In *Handbook of Research Methods in Social and Personality Psychology*, ed. HT Reis, CM Judd, pp. 40–84. New York: Cambridge Univ. Press

Wilkinson L, Task Force Statistical Inference. 1999. Statistical methods in psychology journals: guidelines and explanations. *Am. Psychol.* 54(8):594–604

Williams VSL, Jones LV, Tukey JW. 1999. Controlling error in multiple comparisons, with examples from state-to-state differences in educational achievement. *J. Educ. Behav. Stat.* 24:42–69

Wilson DB, Lipsey MW. 2001. The role of method in treatment effectiveness research: evidence from meta-analysis. *Psychol. Methods* 6:413–29

Winkens B, Schouten HJA, van Breukelen GJP, Berger MPF. 2006. Optimal number of repeated measures and group sizes in clinical trials with linearly divergent treatment effects. *Contemp. Clin. Trials* 27:57–69

Yan X, Su X. 2006. Sample size determination for clinical trials in patients with nonlinear disease progression. *J. Biopharm. Stat.* 16:91–105

Yuan K, Hayashi K. 2003. Bootstrap approach to inference and power analysis based on three test statistics for covariance structure models. *Br. J. Math. Stat. Psychol.* 56(1):93–110

Yuan K, Maxwell SE. 2005. On the post hoc power in testing mean differences. *J. Educ. Behav. Stat.* 30(2):141–67

Zheng J, Frey HC. 2004. Quantification of variability and uncertainty using mixture distributions: evaluation of sample size, mixing weights, and separation between components. *Risk Anal.* 24(3):553–71

A Comprehensive Review of the Placebo Effect: Recent Advances and Current Thought

Donald D. Price,[1] Damien G. Finniss,[2] and Fabrizio Benedetti[3]

[1]Division of Neuroscience, Oral and Maxillofacial Surgery, University of Florida, Gainesville, Florida 32610-0416, [2]University of Sydney Pain Management and Research Center, Royal North Shore Hospital, Sydney, Australia, [3]Department of Neuroscience, University of Turin Medical School, and National Institute of Neuroscience, Turin 10125 Italy; email: dprice@dental.ufl.edu, placebo@bigpond.net.au, fabrizio.benedetti@unito.it

Annu. Rev. Psychol. 2008. 59:565–90

First published online as a Review in Advance on June 5, 2007

The *Annual Review of Psychology* is online at http://psych.annualreviews.org

This article's doi: 10.1146/annurev.psych.59.113006.095941

Key Words

natural history, emotions, analgesia, biological models

Abstract

Our understanding and conceptualization of the placebo effect has shifted in emphasis from a focus on the inert content of a physical placebo agent to the overall simulation of a therapeutic intervention. Research has identified many types of placebo responses driven by different mechanisms depending on the particular context wherein the placebo is given. Some placebo responses, such as analgesia, are initiated and maintained by expectations of symptom change and changes in motivation/emotions. Placebo factors have neurobiological underpinnings and actual effects on the brain and body. They are not just response biases. Other placebo responses result from less conscious processes, such as classical conditioning in the case of immune, hormonal, and respiratory functions. The demonstration of the involvement of placebo mechanisms in clinical trials and routine clinical practice has highlighted interesting considerations for clinical trial design and opened up opportunities for ethical enhancement of these mechanisms in clinical practice.

Contents

INTRODUCTION

The placebo effect has been a topic of interest in scientific and clinical communities for many years, and our knowledge of the mechanisms of the placebo effect has advanced considerably within the past decade. A significant proportion of the research has occurred in the fields of pain and analgesia, and the placebo analgesic response appears to be the best-understood model of placebo mechanisms. Placebo mechanisms in other clinical conditions and populations have only recently begun to be identified. This article reviews and synthesizes current knowledge on placebo mechanisms and identifies potential implications for clinical practice. Although emphasis is placed on placebo analgesia, the commonality of factors and mechanisms of other placebo phenomena are also discussed along with possible differences.

HISTORICAL AND CONCEPTUAL BACKGROUND

The placebo effect has been a phenomenon of significant interest and debate in medicine. Although the use of the word "placebo" dates back several centuries in the medical literature, the placebo effect has only recently

---

Placebo effect: the average placebo response in a group of individuals

Analgesia: a reduction in the magnitude of pain on the sensory or affective dimension or on both dimensions, depending on what is measured

gained the attention and interest of many researchers and clinicians. The author of what is believed to be the first placebo controlled trial (conducted in 1799) stated, "[A]n important lesson in physic is here to be learnt, the wonderful and powerful influence of the passions of the mind upon the state and disorder of the body" (de Craen et al. 1999). Some 200 years later, advances in research design and technology have allowed scientists to identify some of the neurobiological and psychological mechanisms of the placebo effect and to further explore the complexities of the mind-brain-body interaction.

Placebos have typically been identified as inert agents or procedures aimed at pleasing the patient rather than exerting a specific effect. However, this conceptualization presents us with a paradox: If a placebo is inert, it can't cause an effect, as something that is inert has no inherent properties that allow it to cause an effect. This paradox is highlighted in the many attempts to define placebos and the placebo effect, resulting in a degree of confusion and debate. More recently, our conceptualization of placebos and the placebo effect has changed, clarifying some of the issues relating to definitions and the paradox of how an inert substance or procedure can be believed to cause an effect.

Researchers who study the placebo effect are examining the psychosocial context surrounding the patient and the effect that this context has on the patient's experience, brain, and body (Colloca & Benedetti 2005). The focus has shifted from the "inert" content of the placebo agent (e.g., starch capsules) to the concept of a simulation of an active therapy within a psychosocial context. This capacity of simulation empowers the influence of placebo. The placebo response may be driven by many different environmental factors involved in the context of a patient, factors that influence patients' expectations, desires, and emotions. To the extent that it differs from the untreated natural history condition, the response seen in a given individual following administration of a placebo is the placebo response. The responses of a population to placebo administration, such as in a clinical trial, represent the group effect or placebo effect.

Historically, one of the problems of analyzing placebo effects has been the misinterpretation of other phenomena as placebo effects. This results in confusion and misunderstanding about placebo phenomena and mechanisms. Therefore, it is important to note that the true placebo effect (a real psychobiological response) is seen in carefully designed experiments and in clinical populations where the responses to administration of a placebo are compared with a natural history group or untreated baseline condition. This is particularly important in studies of pain, where many painful conditions exhibit varied temporal patterns of intensity, and a reduction in pain following administration of a placebo may be either a placebo effect or something that would have happened regardless of the intervention. Another example is regression to the mean, a statistical phenomenon that assumes that in a given population, extremes in reported pain intensity will change over time toward the average of that population. In the case of pain, this phenomenon asserts that individuals tend to experience a higher level of pain intensity on initial assessment and lower pain intensity at subsequent assessments. If in this case a group of patients were given placebos, one could not be sure that the changes in reported pain scores were a placebo effect or a statistical phenomenon. Both these cases highlight the possible misinterpretation of other phenomena as placebo effects and the importance of a natural history group or baseline condition when assessing true placebo effects. In the case of clinical trials, it is particularly important to be able to differentiate the effect of a placebo from the changes due to the natural history of a particular condition.

Placebo response: the change in a symptom or condition of an individual that occurs as a result of placebo (natural history minus placebo condition)

Expectation (in relation to placebo literature): expected magnitude of symptom or condition or perceived likelihood of an outcome

Desire: the experience of wanting to avoid something (avoidance goal) or wanting to obtain a pleasant or happy outcome (approach goal)

Natural history: the magnitude of a symptom or condition that occurs over a specified amount of time in the absence of treatment

Regression to the mean: individuals with extreme scores on any measure at one point probably will have less extreme scores, for purely statistical reasons, the next time they are tested

ENVIRONMENTAL AND PSYCHOSOCIAL DETERMINANTS OF THE PLACEBO EFFECT

Contextual Factors that Influence Placebo Effects

Environmental and psychosocial determinants of placebo responses/effects include conditioning, verbal suggestions, and behaviors manifested by healthcare providers. These factors are likely to vary greatly across clinical and research contexts and consequently generate considerable variability in the placebo effect itself. This variability is evident among placebo effect sizes for studies of pain treatments. Three meta-analyses have shown that although placebo effect sizes are small on average in studies that use placebo treatments only as a control condition (Cohen's d or pooled standardized mean difference = 0.15–0.27), there is considerable variability in placebo effect sizes (Hrobjartsson & Goetsche 2001, 2004; Vase et al. 2002). Thus, in the meta-analysis by Vase et al. (2002), the mean Cohen's d was only 0.15, but placebo effect sizes ranged from −0.95 to +0.57. Placebo analgesic effect sizes, although controversial, are larger in studies that use placebo treatments to analyze the mechanism of placebo analgesia (0.51 and 0.95 according to Hrobjartsson & Goetsche 2006 and Vase et al. 2002, respectively), but again considerable variability exists across studies (Vase et al. 2002). As a working hypothesis, it is reasonable to propose that factors that promote placebo effects are more likely to be limited in clinical trials and to be enhanced in studies that are about placebo mechanisms.

Meta-analyses are limited in providing understanding of the factors that contribute to placebo analgesia because they do not systematically vary factors that affect its magnitude. Mechanism studies have the potential to provide greater insight into sources of variability of placebo effects because they can provide experimental control of some of the relevant factors. Most importantly, such studies can even be designed using human pain patients in the contexts of actual clinical treatments. Thus, the contribution of placebo analgesia to the effectiveness of analgesic drugs has been tested in clinical postoperative settings using hidden and open injections of traditional painkillers such as buprenorphine (Amanzio et al. 2001, Benedetti et al. 2003, Levine & Gordon 1984). The open-hidden paradigm represents a novel way of studying placebo mechanisms and the specific effects of a treatment, such as a drug. In this paradigm, the patient can receive a treatment in the standard clinical "open" manner, where the treatment is given by the clinician and in full view of the patient. Alternatively, the treatment can be received in a "hidden" manner, by means of a computer-programmed drug infusion pump, where the clinician is not present and the patient is unaware that the treatment is being administered (Levine & Gordon 1984). Several analgesia studies have used the open-hidden paradigm, demonstrating that open administration of a drug is significantly more effective than hidden administration (Amanzio et al. 2001, Benedetti 2003, Colloca et al. 2004, Levine & Gordon 1984). In one study wherein medication was administrated openly by a doctor who gave verbal suggestions for pain relief, pain reduction was greater than when the medication was administered by a hidden machine (Amanzio et al. 2001), as shown in **Figure 1**. In another open-hidden paradigm study, patients needed less medication to reach postoperative analgesia in comparison to hidden administration (Amanzio et al. 2001, Colloca et al. 2004). The difference in medication needed for analgesia between open and hidden injections directly reflects the placebo analgesic effect.

An important goal of placebo analgesia research is to identify factors that contribute to perceived efficacy of the therapeutic intervention. Factors associated with open injections and with suggestions that the agent is an effective analgesic may be especially useful in

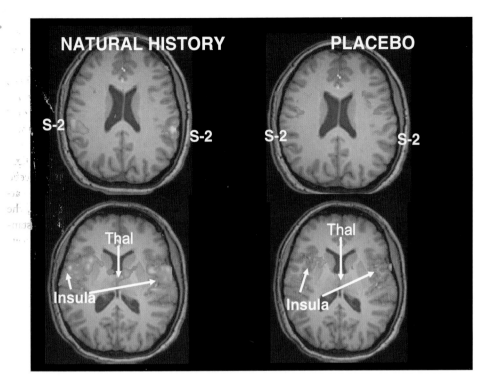

Figure 4

Brain regions showing large reductions in pain-related brain activity, as represented by red-yellow regions, during the placebo condition (*right horizontal brain slices*) compared with untreated natural history or baseline condition (*left horizontal brain slices*). The thalamus (Thal), second somatosensory area (S-2), and insular cortical regions (Insula) showed reduced activity. These functional magnetic resonance images are based on data from Price et al. 2007.

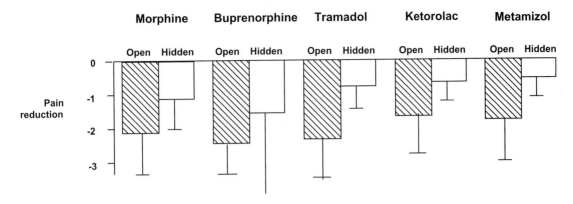

Figure 1

Comparison of analgesic effects of opioid (morphine, tramadol, buprenorphine) and nonopioid (ketorolac, metamizol) medications across hidden versus open intravenous injections in patients with postoperative pain. (Data are from Amanzio et al. 2001.)

clarifying how these factors either mediate or moderate placebo analgesia effects. A number of studies have now analyzed these factors.

Factors that Influence the Magnitude of Placebo Analgesia

The magnitude of placebo analgesia may range from no responses to large responses. It has long been known that there are placebo responders and nonresponders, although why this occurs is less clear. In placebo studies, differences between group averages are usually recorded rather than observations of individual responses to a placebo intervention. This point is very important because an identical mean change between a placebo group and a no-treatment group might be seen if all individuals in the placebo group exhibit a moderate response or, otherwise, a relatively small subset of individuals exhibit a large magnitude response and others show no response at all.

Beecher's widely cited study of clinical analgesic trials (Beecher 1955), from which he concluded that an average of 30% of patients respond to placebo treatments for pain, means little, if anything, because none of the studies he mentioned included no-treatment groups. However, more recent studies have tried to answer the same question. For example, Levine et al. (1979) found that 39% of

patients had an analgesic response to placebo treatment, and in a study of normal volunteers using ischemic arm pain, Benedetti (1996) found that 26.9% of the subjects responded to a placebo analgesic, as compared with a no-treatment control group. Another study involving cutaneous heating of the left hand found that 56% of subjects responded to the placebo treatment, as compared with the no-treatment controls (Petrovic et al. 2002).

Assessing the magnitude of the placebo analgesic effect is not an easy task, as the experimental conditions change across different studies. By measuring the average change in pain experienced by all the individuals who receive placebo and comparing this to the average change in the no-treatment group, several studies have found that the magnitude of the placebo analgesic effect is about 2 out of 10 units on a visual analogue scale (VAS) or numerical rating scale (NRS) (Amanzio et al. 2001; Benedetti et al. 1995, 1998; Gracely et al. 1983; Levine & Gordon 1984; Price 2001).

In studies where the known placebo responders in a group are separated for analysis, the average magnitude of analgesia found has been, not surprisingly, significantly greater. For example, Benedetti (1996), looking only at responders, found an average placebo analgesia magnitude of 5 units on the 10-unit

NRS. This is similar to results from a postoperative dental study that found a 3.3 cm (out of 10) lower mean post-treatment VAS score for placebo responders as compared with nonresponders (Levine et al. 1978).

Today it appears clear that the experimental manipulation used to induce placebo analgesia plays a fundamental role in the magnitude of the response. Among different manipulations that have been performed, both the type of verbal suggestions and the individual's previous experience have been found to be important.

Verbal suggestions that induce certain expectations of analgesia induce larger placebo responses than those inducing uncertain expectations. This point is illustrated by a study carried out in the clinical setting to investigate the differences between the double-blind and the deceptive paradigm (Pollo et al. 2001). Postoperative patients were treated with buprenorphine, on request, for three consecutive days, and with a basal infusion of saline solution. However, the symbolic meaning of this saline basal infusion varied in three different groups of patients. The first group was told nothing (natural history or no-treatment group), the second was told that the infusion could be either a potent analgesic or a placebo (classic double-blind administration), and the third group was told that the infusion was a potent painkiller (deceptive administration). The placebo effect of the saline basal infusion was measured by recording the doses of buprenorphine requested over the three-day treatment. It is important to stress once again that the double-blind group received uncertain verbal instructions ("It can be either a placebo or a painkiller. Thus we are not certain that the pain will subside"), whereas the deceptive administration group received certain instructions ("It is a painkiller. Thus pain will subside soon"). Compared with the natural history group, a 20.8% decrease in buprenorphine intake was found with the double-blind administration and an even greater 33.8% decrease was found in the group given deceptive administration

of the saline basal infusion. It is important to point out that the time-course of pain was the same in the three groups over the three-day period of treatment. Thus the same analgesic effect was obtained with different doses of buprenorphine. The above studies teach us that subtle differences in the verbal context of the patient may have a significant impact on the magnitude of the response.

Previous experience can also influence the magnitude of placebo analgesia. In one study, the intensity of painful stimulation was reduced surreptitiously after placebo administration to make the subjects believe that an analgesic treatment was effective (Colloca & Benedetti 2006). This procedure induced strong placebo responses after minutes, and these responses, albeit reduced, lasted from four to seven days. In a second group of subjects of the same study, the same procedure was repeated four to seven days after a totally ineffective analgesic treatment. The placebo responses were remarkably reduced compared with the first group. Thus, small and large placebo responses were obtained, depending on several factors, such as the previous positive or negative experience of an analgesic treatment and the time lag between the treatment and the placebo responses. These findings indicate that placebo analgesia is finely tuned by prior experience and these effects may last, albeit reduced, several days. These results emphasize that the placebo effect may represent a learning phenomenon involving several factors and may explain the large variability of the magnitude of placebo responses among studies.

PLACEBO EFFECTS CAUSED BY COGNITIVE AND EMOTIONAL CHANGES

Patients are likely to perceive environmental factors in different ways, and these differences are likely to contribute to the magnitude, duration, and qualities of placebo responses. Cognitive and emotional factors that have been proposed to contribute to placebo effects include expected symptom intensity, desire for symptom change, changes in emotion, and distortions in memory.

Expectancy

Expectancy is the experienced likelihood of an outcome or an expected effect. For example, within the context of pain studies it can be measured by asking people about the level of pain they expect to experience. Montgomery and Kirsch conducted one of the first studies in which expected pain levels were manipulated and directly measured (Montgomery & Kirsch 1997). They used a design in which subjects were given cutaneous pain via iontopheretic stimuli. Once baseline stimuli were applied, subjects were secretly given stimuli with reduced intensities in the presence of an inert cream (i.e., conditioning trials). Then the stimulus strength was restored to its original baseline level and several stimuli were then used in placebo trials to test the effect of conditioning. Subjects rated expected pain levels just before placebo test trials and were divided into two groups. The first did not know about the stimulus manipulation, and prior conditioning markedly diminished their pain ratings during placebo trials. However, regression analyses showed that this effect was mediated by expected pain levels. Expectancy accounted for 49% of the variance in postmanipulation pain ratings. The second group was informed about the experimental design and learned that the cream was inert. There was no placebo analgesic effect in this second group. The regression analysis and difference in results across groups show that conscious expectation is necessary for placebo analgesia.

Price and colleagues further tested the extent to which expectations of pain relief can be graded and related to specific areas of the body (Price et al. 1999). Using a similar paradigm, they applied placebo creams and graded levels of heat stimulation on three adjacent areas of the subjects' forearm to give subjects expectations that cream A was a strong analgesic, cream B a weak analgesic, and cream C a control agent. Immediately after these conditioning trials, subjects rated their expected pain levels for the placebo test trials wherein the stimulus intensity was the same for all three areas. The conditioning trials led to graded levels of expected pain (C > B > A) for the three creams as well as graded magnitudes of actual pain (C > B > A) when tested during placebo test trials. Thus, magnitudes of placebo analgesia could be graded across three adjacent skin areas, demonstrating a high degree of somatotopic specificity for placebo analgesia. Expected pain levels accounted for 25% to 36% of the variance in postmanipulation pain ratings.

Expectancy and Memory

The memory of previous experiences is also likely to influence the experience of pain. Price et al. (1999) assessed the placebo effect based on both concurrent ratings of pain during the placebo condition and on retrospective ratings of pain that were obtained approximately two minutes after the stimuli were applied. The magnitude of placebo analgesic effects based on retrospective ratings was three to four times greater than the magnitude based on concurrent ratings. The main reason for this difference was that subjects remembered their baseline pain intensity as being much larger than it actually was. Similar to placebo analgesia effects assessed concurrently, the remembered placebo effects were strongly correlated with expected pain intensities ($R = 0.5$–0.6). Thus, placebo analgesia effects may be enhanced by distorted memories of pretreatment levels of pain. Furthermore, as remembered pain and expected pain are closely related, these psychological factors seem to interact. These findings were replicated by De Pascalis et al. (2002).

Are Placebo Effects Related to a Desire-Expectation Emotion Model?

Although expectancy seems to be an important psychological mediator of placebo effects, it is unlikely to operate alone. Desire, which is the experiential dimension of wanting something to happen or wanting to avoid something happening, is also likely to be involved in placebo phenomena. Desire and expectation also interact and underlie common human emotions, such as sadness, anxiety, and relief (Price & Barrell 2000; Price et al. 1985, 2001). In the context of analgesic studies, it is quite plausible that patients and subjects have some degree of desire to avoid, terminate, or reduce evoked or ongoing pain. On the other hand, some placebo effects involve appetitive or approach goals, such as positive moods or increased arousal. In the following discussion, we provide an account of how decreased desire may contribute to placebo analgesia and increased desire may contribute to placebo effects during appetitive goals. We then propose that the roles of goals, expectation, desire, and emotional feelings all can be accommodated within the same explanatory model.

To further understand how desire and expectation influence placebo analgesia, Verne et al. (2003) and Vase et al. (2003) conducted two similar studies. Patients with irritable bowel syndrome (IBS) were exposed to rectal distention by means of a balloon barostat, a type of visceral stimulation that simulates their clinical pain, and tested under the conditions of untreated natural history (baseline), rectal placebo, and rectal lidocaine. Pain was rated immediately after each stimulus within each condition. The first study was conducted as a double-blind crossover clinical trial in which patients were given an informed consent form that stated they "may receive an active pain reducing medication or an inert placebo agent" (Verne et al. 2003). In this study, there was a significant pain-relieving effect of rectal lidocaine as compared with rectal placebo ($p < 0.001$), and there was a significant pain-relieving effect of rectal placebo (pain in placebo < natural history). In a second similarly designed study, patients were told, "The agent you have just been given is known to significantly reduce pain in some patients" at the onset of each treatment condition (rectal placebo, rectal lidocaine) (Vase et al. 2003). A much larger placebo analgesic effect (Cohen's $d = 2.0$) was found in the second study, and it did not significantly differ from that of rectal lidocaine. These two studies show that adding an overt suggestion for pain relief can increase placebo analgesia to a magnitude that matches that of an active agent. Comparison of the placebo effect sizes of the two studies is shown in **Figure 2**.

In both studies, patients were asked to rate their expected pain level and desire for pain relief right after the agent was administered. Data from the two studies were pooled in order to determine whether changes in desire/expectancy ratings predicted changes in pain ratings across natural history and placebo conditions (i.e., placebo responses) (Vase et al. 2004). The placebo effect (natural history pain intensity–rectal placebo pain intensity), change in expected pain (natural history pain expectation–rectal placebo pain expectation), and change in desire for pain relief (natural history desire–rectal placebo desire) were all calculated for each of 23 subjects. The changes in expectation and desire were entered into a hierarchical regression equation along with their interaction, and the placebo response served as the predicted variable (**Table 1**). First, desire change scores and expected pain change scores were entered into the model. This component accounted for 16% of the variance in placebo effects but this factor alone was not statistically significant (**Table 1**). Second, after statistically controlling for this component, a second component, change in desire × change in expectation, was entered into the regression equation, and it accounted for an additional 22% of the variance in the placebo effect. This second component was statistically significant (**Table 1**). The entire model accounted for 38% of the variance in the placebo effect (**Table 1**). This analysis suggests that both desire for pain relief and expected pain relief contribute to placebo analgesia, and a main factor is a multiplicative interaction between desire for pain reduction and expected pain intensity.

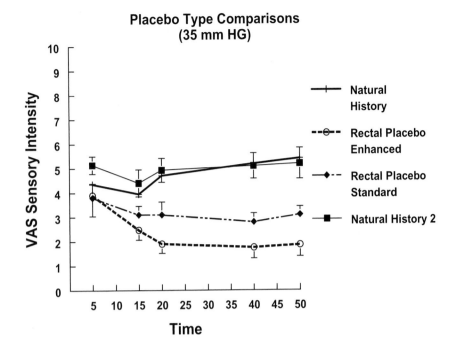

Placebo Type Comparisons (35 mm HG)

Y-axis: VAS Sensory Intensity

X-axis: Time

Legend:
- Natural History
- Rectal Placebo Enhanced
- Rectal Placebo Standard
- Natural History 2

Figure 2

Comparisons of natural history, rectal placebo, and rectal lidocaine scores on a visual analogue scale (VAS) during a 50-minute session within a clinical trial design, where no suggestions for pain relief are given (*left*) and within a placebo design with verbal suggestions for pain relief (*right*). The X-axis refers to time in minutes. (Data are from Vase et al. 2003 and Verne et al. 2003.)

Table 1 The contribution of changes in expectancy and desire to rectal placebo analgesia

Model	R^2 change	P
Δ Expectancy + Δ desire	0.16	0.17
Δ Expectancy × Δ desire	0.22	0.02
Total model	0.38	0.02

This interaction is consistent with Price and Barrell's desire-expectation model of emotions, which shows that ratings of negative and positive emotional feelings are predicted by multiplicative interactions between ratings of desire and expectation (Price et al. 1984, 1985, 2001; **Figure 3**). Desire to reduce pain would be considered an avoidance goal, according to the desire-expectation model, and these results suggest that analgesia would be related to a reduction in negative emotions, as illustrated in the top panel of **Figure 3**. This prediction was supported by significant reductions in anxiety ratings in the two experiments (Vase et al. 2003, Verne et al. 2003). It is further supported by a subsequent study showing that ratings of desire for pain reduc-

tion, expected pain, and anxiety all decreased over time as the placebo effect increased over time (Vase et al. 2005). All of these studies support the desire-expectation model.

Interestingly, the desire-expectation model predicts that placebo responses in approach or appetitive goals would relate to increased levels of desire in the placebo condition, unlike avoidance goals (compare top and lower panels of **Figure 3**). The reason that this is so is that increased desire for a pleasant outcome is associated with increased positive emotional feelings throughout most of the range of expectation (**Figure 3**, lower panel). Support for this prediction was obtained in an experiment wherein participants were given placebo pills that were said to have a sedating effect (Jensen & Karoly 1991). The desire to feel such effects were manipulated by telling participants that individuals who react to the pills have either positive or more negative personality characteristics. The authors found greater placebo responses in subjects who were told that sedative effects were related to positive traits, and they had larger ratings of desire to experience sedation than did the other participants who associated sedation with negative consequences.

Based on several interrelated experiments, Geers et al. (2005) argue that the placebo effect is most likely to occur when individuals have a goal that can be fulfilled by confirmation of the placebo expectation, consistent with the model just described. Their results demonstrated a role for desire for an effect across a variety of symptom domains, including those related to positive (approach or appetitive) and negative (avoidance) goals. For

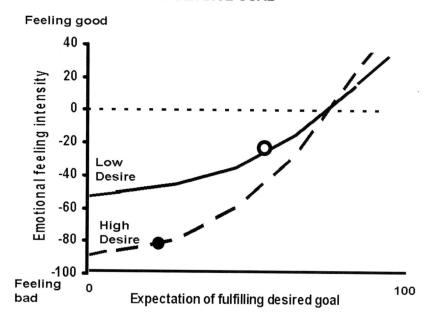

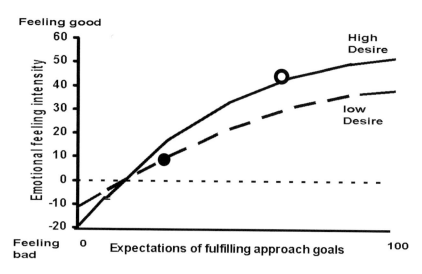

example, participants listened to a piece of music in one of their experiments. One group was given a suggestion that the music would improve mood, and another was not given any suggestion. Two additional groups also were either given this suggestion or no suggestion; in addition, they were either primed with a goal of independence or cooperation. Only the latter was compatible with the goal of improving mood. Placebo responses were calculated as differences in mood ratings across baseline and postplacebo conditions. The placebo effect was largest in the subjects given placebo suggestion coupled with the cooperation priming that was compatible with mood improvement. The remaining groups had low to negligible placebo effects. Taken together, these results show the importance of motivation (desire) across different types of placebo responses involving approach and avoidance goals.

Somatic Focus Moderates Effects of Goals and Expectancy

In addition to the roles of goals, desires, and expectations in placebo responding, there is evidence that the degree of somatic focus has a moderating influence on these psychological factors (Geers et al. 2006, Lundh 1987). In an experiment that induced expectations of unpleasant symptoms, individuals who expected they were taking a drug but given placebo tablets reported more placebo symptoms when they closely focused on their symptoms (Geers et al. 2006). This type of interaction also has been proposed for approach goals. Thus, Lundh (1987) proposes a cognitive-emotional model of the placebo effect in which positive placebo suggestions for improvements in physical health lead individuals to attend selectively to signs of improvement. When they closely notice these signs, they are said to take them as evidence that the placebo treatment has been effective.

If somatic focus operates as a kind of feedback that supports factors underlying placebo responding, increasing the degree or frequency of somatic focusing could increase the magnitudes of placebo responses over time. This possibility is supported by observations showing that the growth of the placebo effect at least partly depends on the frequency of test stimuli. As discussed above, ratings of desire, expectation, and anxiety decrease over time along with the increase in placebo effect (Vase et al. 2005). As shown in **Figure 2**, it took about 20 minutes for the placebo effect to increase to its maximum level in conditions wherein stimuli were applied at seven times per 50 minutes (**Figure 2**) (Vase et al.

Figure 3

The desire-expectation model of emotions (Price & Barrell 1984; Price et al. 1985, 2001), showing hypothetical improvements in emotional states associated with a placebo response during an avoidance goal, such as wanting to be relieved of pain (*top panel*) and during an approach goal, such as wanting to feel energetic (*bottom panel*). These curves are similar to those empirically derived from ratings of desire, expectation, and positive/negative feelings (Price et al. 1985, 2001) and show a multiplicative interaction between desire intensity and expectation with respect to their effects on positive and negative emotional feeling intensity (the curves intersect between 0 and 100). The closed circle in the top panel reflects a baseline negative feeling state. It is associated with a high desire for pain relief in combination with a low expectation of pain relief (or high levels of pain). After placebo administration, the postplacebo feeling state becomes less negative as a consequence of a lowering of desire (high desire to low desire) and an increased expectation of pain relief (or lower levels of pain). This change is represented by the upper open circle in the top panel. Likewise, the closed and open circles in the bottom panel reflect changes from the pre- to the postplacebo condition. In this case, the placebo response (e.g., feeling more energetic) is accompanied by an increased desire for an effect, an increased expectation of an effect, and an increased positive feeling state. According to the model, placebo responses are driven by decreased negative or increased positive emotional feeling states for avoidance and approach goals, respectively.

fMRI: functional
magnetic resonance
imaging

2003, Verne et al. 2003). This same pattern of increase was found in a subsequent experiment that applied seven stimuli in 10 minutes (Price et al. 2007). The placebo effect increased to its maximum level during the first three stimuli and over 3–4 minutes with this more rapid stimulus frequency. Taken together, the results of Geers et al. (2006) and Vase et al. (2005) support a model of placebo mechanism wherein goals, desire, expectation, and consequent emotional feelings codetermine the placebo response. Somatic focus provides a self-confirming feedback that facilitates these factors over time, leading to more positive (or less negative) emotional feelings about prospects of avoiding aversive experiences or obtaining appetitive experiences (**Figure 2**).

If the desire-expectation model is accurate, then placebo phenomena occur within the context of emotional regulation and symptoms should be influenced by desire, expectation, and emotional feeling intensity regardless of whether these factors are evoked by placebo manipulations. A separate line of evidence for the role of expectancy in placebo analgesia includes studies that manipulate expectancy in nonplacebo contexts. Three studies found large reductions in pain from expectancy manipulations, and two of these studies found corresponding reductions in pain-related brain activity (Keltner et al. 2006, Koyama et al. 2005, Rainville et al. 2005). Desire and emotions also influence pain in nonplacebo contexts. Rainville et al. (2005) recently have shown that hypnotic inductions of changes in desire for relief as well as inductions of positive and negative emotional states modulate pain in directions they claim are consistent with the desire-expectation model.

Thus, to put it simply, placebo responses seem to relate to feeling good (or less bad) about prospects of relief (avoidance goal) or pleasure (approach goal) that are associated with treatments or medications. These feelings can be separately influenced by desire and expectation or by the combination of both factors. An explanation at a more mechanistic level is needed. For example, do placebo-induced changes in expectations, desires, and emotions simply lead to subjective biases about symptoms/effects, or do they affect their biological causes?

NEUROBIOLOGY OF THE DESIRE-EXPECTATION MODEL

The Functional Role of Placebo-Related Increases and Decreases in Brain Activity

Several neurobiologists have found that placebo effects are accompanied by reductions in neural activity within brain areas known to process symptoms such as anxiety and pain. They also have found that these reductions are accompanied by increases in neural activity within brain areas known to be involved in emotional regulation (Fields 2004, Petrovic et al. 2005, Zubieta et al. 2001). They propose that placebo responses are generated as a function of reward and/or aversion and associated neural circuitry.

In two functional magnetic resonance imaging (fMRI) experiments published in a single study, Wager et al. (2004) found that placebo analgesia was related to decreased neural activity in pain processing areas of the brain. Pain-related neural activity was reduced within the thalamus, anterior insular cortex, and anterior cingulate cortex during the placebo condition as compared with the baseline condition. In addition, the magnitudes of these decreases were correlated with reductions in pain ratings.

Another important aspect of Wager et al.'s (2004) study was that they imaged not only the period of pain but also the period of anticipation of pain. They hypothesized increases in neural activity within brain areas involved in expectation. In support of their hypothesis, they found significant positive correlations ($r = 0.4$–0.7) between increases in brain activity in the anticipatory period and decreases in pain and pain-related neural activity during stimulation within the placebo condition. The brain areas showing positive correlations during the anticipatory phase included the orbitofrontal cortex (OFC), dorsolateral prefrontal cortex (DLPFC), rostral anterior cingulate cortex (rACC), and midbrain periaqueductal gray (PAG). The DLPFC has been consistently associated with the representation of and maintenance of information needed for cognitive control, consistent with a role in expectation (Miller & Cohen 2001). On the other hand, the OFC is associated with functioning in the evaluative and reward information relevant to allocation of control, consistent with a role in affective or motivational responses to anticipation of pain (Dias et al. 1996). Such a role is consistent with results showing that desire for relief is a factor in placebo analgesia.

A limitation of Wager et al.'s (2004) study is that most of the decreases in neural activity within pain-related areas occurred during the period that subjects rated pain, leaving open the possibility that placebo effects mainly reflected report biases. In a subsequent fMRI study, brain activity of IBS patients was measured in response to rectal distension by a balloon barostat (Price et al. 2007). As shown in **Figure 4** (see color insert), a large placebo effect was produced by suggestions and accompanied by large reductions in neural activity in known pain-related areas, such as thalamus, S-1, S-2, insula, and ACC, during the period of stimulation, thereby reflecting effects unlikely to result from report biases. It was also accompanied by increases in neural activity in the rostral ACC, bilateral amygdale, and PAG (unpublished observations), areas known to be involved in reward/aversion, emotions, and the classical descending pain modulatory pathway (Basbaum & Fields 1978). The latter includes a core rACC-amygdala-PAG-rostroventral medulla-spinal cord connection, wherein pain-related signals are inhibited in the dorsal horn of the spinal cord (Basbaum & Fields 1978, Mayer & Price 1976). This network contains endogenous opioids.

However, the involvement of brain areas involved in emotional regulation and hence in placebo responses is not restricted only to pain modulation. Petrovic et al. (2005) demonstrated a placebo effect related to the reduction of anxiety associated with viewing unpleasant pictures. Reductions in experienced unpleasantness were accompanied by increases in brain areas involved in reward/aversion and previously shown to be involved in placebo analgesia. These areas included those previously implicated in emotional modulation, such as the OFC, rACC, and amygdala. They also included areas involved in treatment expectation, such as ventrolateral prefrontal cortex and rACC.

Future Directions in Relating Brain Activity to Psychological Variables Associated with Placebo

Large placebo effects that accompany corresponding decreases in activity within symptom-related areas of the brain underscore both the psychological and biological reality of the placebo response and support current models of mind-brain interactions (Schwartz et al. 2005).

However, elucidating the relationships between cognitive and emotional factors to placebo responses is an enormous challenge, as is determining their neurobiological underpinnings. Psychological studies of placebo responses have included progressively more variables, such as expectancy, desire, somatic focus, and type of goal. Measures of these variables potentially can be incorporated into brain imaging and other types of neurobiological studies so that explicit mechanistic hypotheses about these factors can be tested at both a more refined psychological and neurobiological level. Such improvements should provide increasing potential for utilizing knowledge of these mechanisms in clinical research and practice.

CCK:
cholecystokinin

EVIDENCE FOR OPIOID AND NONOPIOID MECHANISMS IN PLACEBO ANALGESIA

Opioid Mechanisms

An important step in understanding the mechanisms of placebo-induced analgesia was made in the clinical setting when Levine et al. (1978) provided evidence that placebo analgesia is antagonized by naloxone, an opioid antagonist, which indicates mediation by endogenous opioid systems. Other studies subsequently further confirmed this hypothesis (Benedetti 1996, Grevert et al. 1983, Levine & Gordon 1984). These include studies described above that use verbal suggestion, conditioning, and open-hidden injections. For example, enhanced analgesia with open as compared to hidden injections was eliminated by naloxone (Amanzio et al. 2001). In addition, cholecystokinin (CCK) was found to inhibit placebo-induced analgesia, as CCK antagonists are capable of potentiating the placebo analgesic effect (Benedetti 1996, Benedetti et al. 1995). In fact, CCK is an antiopioid peptide that antagonizes endogenous opioid neuropeptides, so that its blockade results in the potentiation of opioid effects (Benedetti 1997).

Fields & Levine (1984) hypothesized that the placebo response may be subdivided into opioid and nonopioid components. In fact, they suggested that different physical, psychological, and environmental situations could affect the endogenous opioid systems differently. This problem was addressed by Amanzio & Benedetti (1999), who showed that both expectation and a conditioning procedure could result in placebo analgesia. The former is capable of activating opioid systems, whereas the latter activates specific subsystems. In fact, if the placebo response is induced by means of strong expectation cues, it can be blocked by the naloxone. Conversely, as described below, if the placebo response is induced by means of prior conditioning with a nonopioid drug, it is naloxone-insensitive.

Regional placebo analgesic responses can be obtained in different parts of the body (Montgomery & Kirsch 1996, Price et al. 1999), and these responses are naloxone-reversible (Benedetti et al. 1999b). If four noxious stimuli are applied to the hands and feet and a placebo cream is applied to one hand only, pain is reduced only on the hand where the placebo cream had been applied. This effect is blocked by naloxone, which suggests that the placebo-activated endogenous opioids have a somatotopic organization (Benedetti et al. 1999b). An additional study supporting the involvement of endogenous opioids in placebo analgesia was performed by Lipman et al. (1990) in chronic pain patients. It was found that those patients who responded to placebo showed higher concentrations of endorphins in the cerebrospinal fluid compared with those patients who did not respond.

A likely candidate for the mediation of placebo-induced analgesia is the opioid neuronal network described above (Fields & Basbaum 1999, Fields & Price 1997), and this hypothesis is supported by a brain imaging study that found similar regions in the cerebral cortex and in the brainstem affected by both a placebo and the rapidly acting opioid agonist remifentanil. This suggests a related mechanism in placebo-induced and opioid-induced analgesia (Petrovic et al. 2002).

The direct demonstration of placebo-induced release of endogenous opioids has been obtained by using in vivo receptor binding with positron emission tomography by Zubieta et al. (2005). By using an experimental model of pain in healthy volunteers, these authors found an increase of μ-opioid receptor neurotransmission in different brain regions, such as the anterior cingulate cortex, the orbitofrontal cortex, the insula, and the nucleus accumbens.

As is described in detail below, placebo-activated endogenous opioids have also been shown to affect the respiratory centers (Benedetti et al. 1998, 1999a) and the cardiovascular system (Pollo et al. 2003), thus indicating that they act not only on pain transmission but on other systems as well.

Nonopioid Agents and Mechanisms in Placebo Analgesia

Placebo analgesic responses have been found to be mediated by mechanisms other than opioids in other circumstances. For example, they have been found to be naloxone insensitive, thus nonopioid mediated, if the subjects were previously exposed to a nonopioid drug, such as ketorolac (Amanzio & Benedetti 1999). When ketorolac was administered for two days in a row and then replaced with a placebo on the third day, the placebo analgesic response was not reversed with naloxone. This suggests that specific pharmacological mechanisms are involved in a learned placebo response, depending on the previous exposure to opioid or nonopioid substances. Another example of placebo analgesia that is nonopioid-mediated has been studied in IBS patients who exhibit strong placebo responses. Placebo effects in these patients were found to be naloxone-insensitive, suggesting mediation by nonopioid mechanisms (Vase et al. 2005).

Although other neurochemical mechanisms have not yet been identified, it is worth noting that the possible involvement of some neurotransmitters has been found in some conditions. For instance, by using the analgesic drug sumatriptan, a serotonin agonist of the $5-HT_{1B/1D}$ receptors that stimulates growth hormone (GH) and inhibits cortisol secretion, it was shown that a conditioning procedure is capable of producing hormonal placebo responses. In fact, if a placebo is given after repeated administrations of sumatriptan, a placebo GH increase and a placebo cortisol decrease can be found (Benedetti et al. 2003b). Interestingly, verbally induced expectations of increase/decrease of GH and cortisol did not have any effect on the secretion of these hormones. Therefore, whereas hormone secretion is not affected by expectations, it is affected by a conditioning procedure. Although we do not know whether these placebo responses are really mediated by serotonin, a pharmacological preconditioning appears to affect serotonin-dependent hormone secretion. These new findings may help in the investigation of nonopioid mechanisms in placebo analgesia.

The verbal instructions that induce expectations may have either a hopeful and trust-inducing meaning, eliciting a placebo effect, or a fearful and stressful meaning, inducing a nocebo effect (Benedetti & Amanzio 1997; Hahn 1985, 1997; Moerman 2002). In a study performed using postoperative patients (Benedetti et al. 1997) and healthy volunteers (Benedetti et al. 2006), negative expectations were induced by administering an inert substance along with the suggestion that pain was going to increase. In fact, pain increased and this increase was prevented by the CCK antagonist proglumide. This indicates that expectation-induced hyperalgesia of these patients was mediated, at least in part, by CCK. The effects of proglumide were not antagonized by naloxone (Benedetti et al. 1997), which suggests that endogenous opioids were not involved. Since CCK plays a role in anxiety and negative expectations themselves are anxiogenic, these results suggest that proglumide acts on a CCK-dependent link between anxiety and pain (Benedetti et al. 2006). Although this study analyzed nocebo hyperalgesia and not placebo analgesia, it shows that CCK-ergic systems may be activated by negative verbal suggestions that induce negative expectations.

MECHANISMS OTHER THAN EXPECTATION AND CONDITIONS OTHER THAN PAIN

Evidence for Classical Conditioning Mechanisms

Some of the placebo analgesia studies discussed so far suggest that conditioning can have a role in at least some placebo responses, although in most cases the proximate psychological mediators seem to be expectations, motivations, and emotions. These findings do not negate conditioning as a factor, only a classical Pavlovian model that doesn't require conscious expectations. Classical conditioning seems to play a key role for phenomena other than pain.

In classical conditioning, repeated associations between a neutral stimulus (conditioned stimulus, or CS), for example a syringe or a pill, and an unconditioned stimulus (US), for instance the active drug inside the syringe or pill, lead to a conditioned response (CR), whereby the CS alone induces a physiological response that is similar in all respects to that of the US. This mechanism emphasizes once again that there is not just a single placebo effect; rather, there are many, with different mechanisms taking place in different conditions on the one hand and in different systems and apparatuses on the other. Two of the best examples of placebo responses as conditioned responses come from the immune and endocrine system.

Placebo Responses in the Immune and Endocrine System

McKenzie (1896) reported an interesting observation relevant to the understanding of the placebo effect in the immune system. In this study, it was shown that some people who are allergic to flowers show an allergic reaction when presented with something that superficially looks like a flower, but contains no pollen (i.e., an artificial flower). Ader & Cohen (1982) provided experimental evidence that immunological placebo responses can be obtained by pairing a solution of sodium saccharin (CS) with the immunosuppressive drug cyclophosphamide (US). In fact, mice treated in this way show conditioned immunosuppression, that is, immune responses to sodium saccharin alone. Ader et al. (1993) also showed that a conditioned enhancement of antibody production is possible using an antigen as un-

conditioned stimulus of the immune system. In this case, mice were given repeated immunizations with keyhole limpet hemocyanin (KLH) paired with a gustatory conditioned stimulus. A classically conditioned enhancement of anti-KLH antibodies was observed when the mice were re-exposed to the gustatory stimulation alone.

These studies in animals have been repeated in humans. Olness & Ader (1992) presented a clinical case study of a child with lupus erithematosus. The child received cyclophosphamide paired with taste and smell stimuli, according to the conditioning procedure used in animals. During the course of twelve months, a clinically successful outcome was obtained by using taste and smell stimuli alone on half the monthly chemotherapy sessions. In another study, multiple sclerosis patients received four intravenous treatments with cyclophosphamide (US) paired with anise-flavored syrup (CS) (Giang et al. 1996). Eight out of ten patients displayed decreased peripheral leukocyte counts following the syrup alone, an effect that mimics that of cyclophosphamide. Recently, these findings have been confirmed in humans (Goebel et al. 2002). In fact, repeated associations between cyclosporin A (US) and a flavored drink (CS) induced conditioned immunosuppression, in which the flavored drink alone produced a suppression of the immune functions, as assessed by means of interleukin-2 and interferon-gamma messenger ribonucleic acid expression, in vitro release of interleukin-2 and interferon-gamma, as well as lymphocyte proliferation.

Some hormonal placebo responses, similar to the conditioning-induced immunological responses, have been described. As noted in the previous section on nonopioid mechanisms, by using an analgesic drug—the serotonin agonist sumatriptan, which stimulates GH and inhibits cortisol secretion—it was shown that a conditioning procedure is capable of producing placebo secretive responses of hormones (Benedetti et al. 2003). In fact, if a placebo is given after repeated administrations of sumatriptan, a placebo GH increase and a placebo cortisol decrease can be found. Interestingly, verbally induced expectations of increase/decrease of GH and cortisol did not have any effect on the secretion of these hormones, indicating that hormone secretion is not affected by verbal suggestions and expectations, but rather by a form of conditioning that does not require conscious expectations.

All these findings in the immune and endocrine system suggest that a CS may acquire all the properties and characteristics of a placebo. These findings also have important clinical implications, as the pharmacotherapeutic doses in different diseases can be reduced by pairing chemotherapies with a number of conditioned stimuli.

Other Biological Models of Placebo

Besides these conditioning studies in the immune and endocrine systems, which clearly show the involvement of systems and mechanisms other than pain transmission in the placebo effect, a number of studies exist in which some biological responses to placebo administration have been described in detail. These studies are now emerging as interesting models to better understand the placebo effect across different diseases. These models, which are described below, are the respiratory and cardiovascular system, Parkinson's disease, and depression.

Respiratory and cardiovascular placebo responses. Placebo-activated endogenous opioids have been shown to produce a typical side effect of opioids, that is, respiratory depression (Benedetti et al. 1998, 1999a). After postoperative patients receive repeated administrations of analgesic doses of buprenorphine, which induces a mild reduction of ventilation, a placebo is capable of mimicking the same respiratory depressant response. Remarkably, this respiratory placebo response is totally blocked by naloxone, indicating that it is mediated by en-

dogenous opioids. The involvement of other systems in the action of placebo-activated endogenous opioids is further supported by a study in which the sympathetic control of the heart was analyzed during placebo analgesia (Pollo et al. 2003). In a pharmacological study in healthy volunteers, it was found that placebo analgesia in experimental ischemic arm pain was accompanied by a reduction of heart rate. Both the placebo analgesic effect and the concomitant heart rate decrease were reversed by the opioid antagonist naloxone, whereas the β-blocker propranolol antagonized the placebo heart rate reduction but not placebo analgesia. There are at least two possible mechanisms through which the heart is affected during placebo analgesia. It might be a consequence of pain reduction itself or, otherwise, the placebo-activated endogenous opioids might inhibit the cardiovascular system directly. Further research is necessary to differentiate between these two mechanisms.

Parkinson's disease. Recently, Parkinson's disease has emerged as an interesting model to understand the neurobiological mechanisms of the placebo response. In this model, patients are given an inert substance (placebo) and are told that it is an anti-Parkinsonian drug that produces an improvement in motor performance. It has been shown that Parkinsonian patients respond to placebos quite well (Goetz et al. 2000, Shetty et al. 1999), and a study that used positron emission tomography to assess endogenous dopamine release shows that placebo-induced expectation of motor improvement activates dopamine in the striatum of Parkinsonian patients (de la Fuente-Fernandez et al. 2001). In addition, Pollo et al. (2002) showed that different and opposite expectations of bad and good motor performance modulate the therapeutic effect of subthalamic nucleus stimulation in Parkinsonian patients who had undergone chronic implantation of electrodes for deep brain stimulation. For example, in an analysis of the effect of subthalamic stimulation on the velocity of movement of the right hand, the hand movement was found to be faster when the patients expected a good motor performance (Pollo et al. 2002). The expectation of good performance was induced through a placebo-like procedure, thus indicating that placebo-induced expectations have an influence on the outcome of the treatment. All these effects occurred within minutes, which suggests that expectations induce neural changes very quickly.

The ability to study Parkinsonian patients who are implanted with electrodes for deep brain stimulation has been exploited recently to record from single neurons after placebo administration (Benedetti et al. 2004). In this study, the activity from single neurons in the subthalamic nucleus was recorded before and after placebo administration to see whether neuronal changes were linked to the clinical placebo response. The placebo consisted of a saline solution that was given to patients along with the suggestion that it was an anti-Parkinsonian drug. It was found that the placebo responders showed a significant decrease of neuronal discharge and the disappearance of bursting activity of subthalamic neurons, whereas the placebo nonresponders did not exhibit these changes. These findings in Parkinson's disease patients offer opportunities to administer an exciting and innovative approach with the possibility of recording from single neurons in awake patients during the placebo response.

Depression. The neural mechanisms of placebo treatments have also been studied in depression. However, these studies need further research and confirmation since, due to ethical constraints, they did not include appropriate control groups. Depressed patients who received a placebo treatment showed both electrical and metabolic changes in the brain. In one study, placebos induced electroencephalographic changes in the pre-frontal cortex of patients with major depression, particularly in the right hemisphere (Leuchter et al. 2002). It has been suggested

that this finding of brain functional changes during placebo treatment can be used to identify the subjects who are likely to be placebo responders. In particular, Leuchter et al. (2004) found that placebo responders had lower pretreatment frontocentral cordance (a measure of electroencephalogram activity) in comparison with all other subjects. Placebo responders also had faster cognitive processing time, as assessed by neuropsychological testing, and lower reporting of late insomnia. Based on these data, the authors suggest a combination of clinical, neurophysiological, and cognitive assessments for identifying depressed subjects who are likely to be placebo responders.

In another study, changes in brain glucose metabolism were measured by using positron emission tomography in subjects with unipolar depression (Mayberg et al. 2002). Placebo treatments were associated with metabolic increases in the prefrontal, anterior cingulate, premotor, parietal, posterior insula, and posterior cingulate cortex, and metabolic decreases in the subgenual cingulate cortex, para-hippocampus, and thalamus. Interestingly, these regions also were affected by the selective serotonin reuptake inhibitor fluoxetine, a result that suggests a possible role for serotonin in placebo-induced antidepressant effects (see Benedetti et al. 2005 for a review).

IMPLICATIONS FOR CLINICAL TRIALS AND CLINICAL PRACTICE

Recent advances in our understanding of placebo responses have raised some implications for clinical trials and clinical practice. Some of these implications center on the ethical enhancement of factors that drive placebo mechanisms during administration of an active therapy. It is important to note that the clinical implications for placebo use involve exploitation of placebo factors and mechanisms when there is an active treatment being administered, not the deliberate use of a placebo when there is an active treatment available, which is unethical. The research on the placebo effect has highlighted the involvement of several factors in placebo responses, and studies of placebo mechanisms have started to identify the ways in which these factors drive responses. Despite increases in the number of studies of placebo mechanisms, there has been limited investigation of the harnessing of these mechanisms to improve clinical trials and clinical practice.

A recent study illustrates the long-term clinical benefits of placebo factors when patients believe they have been given active treatments. In a double-blind study of human fetal mesencephalic transplantation (an experimental treatment for Parkinson's disease), investigators studied the effect of this treatment compared with a placebo treatment for twelve months, using a standard randomized controlled trial design (McRae et al. 2004). They also assessed the patient's perceived assignment to either the active (fetal tissue implant) or placebo treatment (sham surgery). There were no differences between the transplant and sham surgery groups on several physical and quality-of-life measures made by both medical staff and patients. Instead, the perceived assignment of treatment group had a beneficial impact on the overall outcome, and this difference was present at least twelve months after surgery. Patients who believed they received transplanted tissue had significant improvements in both psychological (quality of life) and physiological (motor function) outcomes, regardless of whether they received sham surgery or fetal tissue implantations. This study is unusual in providing evidence that the placebo effect can last a long time, quite possibly due to the elaborate and invasive nature of the placebo treatment.

In two similar studies (Bausell et al. 2005, Linde et al. 2007), real acupuncture was compared with sham acupuncture for different painful conditions, such as migraine, tension-type headache, chronic low back pain, and osteoarthritis. These studies examined the effects of patients' expectations on the therapeutic outcome, regardless of the group to which the patient belonged. To do this, patients were asked either which group they believed they belonged to (either placebo or real treatment) (Bausell et al. 2005) or whether they considered acupuncture to be an effective therapy in general and what they personally expected from the treatment (Linde et al. 2007). These studies found that patients who believed they belonged to the real treatment group experienced larger clinical improvement than those patients who believed they belonged to the placebo group (Bausell et al. 2005). Likewise, patients with higher expectations about acupuncture treatment experienced larger clinical benefits than did patients with lower expectations, regardless of their allocation to real or sham acupuncture (Linde et al. 2007). Thus, it did not really matter whether the patients actually received the real or the sham procedure. What mattered was whether they believed in acupuncture and expected a benefit from it.

We think that these studies represent a good example of how clinical trials should be viewed from a theoretical perspective and how they should be conducted from a practical viewpoint. They underscore the necessity to consider clinical trials from a different perspective, in order to make their interpretation more reliable. Some confusing outcomes of clinical trials could be clarified by the simple questions, "What do you expect from this treatment?", or "Which group do you believe you are assigned to?"

These studies also illustrate how incorporation of placebo-related measures can improve clinical trials. Assessing variables that contribute to the placebo effect, such as perceived group assignment, expected changes, and desire for clinical benefits, could provide a means of assessing the contribution of placebo even when there is no natural history condition. Recall that factors such as these account for large amounts of variance in placebo responses. A secondary benefit would be a means of assessing the extent to which double-blind conditions are maintained. Enhancing and maintaining the placebo component of a proven therapy could occur because of several psychosocial factors and suggestions that are ethically permissible (e.g., "The agent you have just been given is known to significantly reduce pain in some patients").

Further implications of the role of placebo mechanisms on the outcome of an active therapy are seen with the differences between a standard administration of a treatment and a hidden administration, a paradigm described earlier. This difference in effect has been demonstrated not only for pain (**Figure 1**) but also for other conditions such as Parkinson's disease. In the case of Parkinson's disease, deep brain stimulation of the subthalamic nucleus has been shown to be less effective (by means of autonomic and motor responses) when administered covertly rather than in a standard clinical (open) manner (Colloca et al. 2004). Similar to analgesia studies, this study shows that the overall effect of a treatment such as administration of an active agent is a combination of the pharmacological properties of the drug and the placebo mechanisms that are driven by the psychosocial context surrounding the drug administration. The larger the difference between the two administrations, the more significant the placebo mechanisms are in the overall effect. On the other hand, a smaller difference between the administrations indicates that the pharmacological properties of the drug are playing a more significant role rather than placebo mechanisms. The factors involved in this difference are those that mediate placebo effects, as the difference in the administrations represents the psychosocial context of the treatment.

The open-hidden paradigm underscores the importance of placebo mechanisms, particularly expectations, on the outcome of a given treatment. In doing so, it demonstrates that the therapeutic interaction between a clinician and a patient can play a significant role in the outcome of a therapy. It also presents researchers with a different paradigm to study the overall effect of a drug, where one can establish the pharmacological and placebo components of a drug without actually administering a placebo. The paradigm also highlights the potentially negative impact of a loss of placebo mechanisms on the outcome of a therapy and highlights the clinical importance of assessment of these factors prior to therapy in some instances. One such instance is analgesic therapy for patients with Alzheimer's disease. In this condition, there is a disruption of expectation mechanisms due to cognitive impairment.

In a recent study, one of us assessed overt and covert administration of a local anesthetic following venipuncture in Alzheimer's disease sufferers (Benedetti et al. 2006). In this experiment, the placebo component, represented by the differences in response to open and hidden local anesthetic administration, was correlated with both cognitive status and functional connectivity between different brain regions. Interestingly, patients with reduced frontal assessment battery scores showed a decreased placebo component to the therapy. Similar disruption of the placebo component was seen with reduced connectivity between the prefrontal lobes and the rest of the brain. Of clinical importance is the fact that the reductions in the placebo component had an effect on treatment efficacy, with those patients with greater losses of placebo mechanisms requiring larger doses of the drug to produce adequate analgesia. This study further highlights the importance of expectancy-related (placebo) mechanisms in the overall therapeutic outcome and the need for consideration of these mechanisms when prescribing an analgesic regime to patients with cognitive impairment (Benedetti et al. 2006).

CONCLUSIONS

Our understanding and conceptualization of the placebo effect has changed in recent times, shifting from a focus on the inert content of a physical placebo agent to the overall simulation of a therapeutic intervention. Research has allowed for the identification of not one but many placebo responses, each of which may be driven by different psychological and neurobiological mechanisms depending on the particular context in which the placebo is given. We are still some way from understanding the relationships between the identified psychological variables and their neurobiological underpinnings, although a body of literature is emerging that identifies the roles of certain cognitive and emotional factors and various biochemical and neuroanatomical mechanisms in driving placebo responses. This literature also shows that placebos have actual biological effects on the brain and body and are more than response biases. The demonstration of the involvement of placebo mechanisms in routine clinical practice and clinical trials has opened up opportunities to look at the ethical enhancement of these mechanisms in clinical practice. Further experimental and clinical research will hopefully provide for improved understanding of placebo mechanisms and the ability to harness them for the advancement of clinical practice.

SUMMARY POINTS

1. The concept of placebo response has shifted in emphasis from viewing it as caused by an inert physical agent to viewing it as the result of simulation of an active therapy.

2. Placebo effects can be produced by suggestions, past effects of active treatments, and cues that signal that an active medication or treatment has been given.

3. Proximate psychological mediators of placebo responses include expectations, desires, and emotions that target prospective symptom changes.

4. Psychological mediators are related to brain structures involved in reward/aversion and regulation of emotions.

5. Placebo analgesic effects require endogenous opioids in some circumstances (e.g., prior conditioning with opioids) and not in others (e.g., prior conditioning with non-opioid drugs).

6. Although desire, expectations, and emotions may be required for some placebo phenomena, such as pain, Parkinson's disease, depression, and mood changes, other placebo responses (immune, hormonal, and respiratory responses) result from less conscious processes such as classical conditioning.

7. Assessment of mediators of placebo responses, such as expected benefits and perceived group assignment, could improve clinical trials by providing a means of separately assessing the contributions of placebo factors and factors related to active treatment, as well as monitoring the extent of blinding within the trial.

8. Knowledge concerning mediators and mechanisms of placebo effects within active therapies could serve to enhance this component through ethical use of suggestions and optimum caregiver-patient interactions.

FUTURE ISSUES

1. There is a need to further characterize relationships between psychological mediators of placebo responses and their associated neural mechanisms.

2. Healthcare professionals need to be educated about the characteristics and underlying mechanisms of placebo so that they can optimize placebo components of therapy.

3. Powerful placebo effects reflect mind-brain-body relationships, and there is a need to philosophically resolve explanations of these relationships without resorting to eliminative materialism or forms of dualism that completely divide the mind from the body.

ACKNOWLEDGMENTS

Support for this research was provided by grant RO1 (AT001424) from the National Center for Complementary and Alternative Medicine to Dr. Michael Robinson. This work was also supported by grants from Istituto San Paolo di Torino and Regione Piemonte to Fabrizio Benedetti. We thank our many colleagues who participated in some of the research reviewed here. We thank Drs. Michael Robinson, Nicholas Verne, and Lene Vase for data and data analysis associated with **Table 1**.

LITERATURE CITED

Ader R, Cohen N. 1982. Behaviorally conditioned immunosuppression and murine systemic lupus erythematosus. *Science* 215:1534–36

Ader R, Kelly K, Moynihan JA, Grota LJ, Cohen N. 1993. Conditioned enhancement of antibody production using an antigen as the unconditioned stimulus. *Brain Behav. Immun.* 7:334–43

Amanzio M, Benedetti F. 1999. Neuropharmacological dissection of placebo analgesia: expectation-activated opioid systems versus conditioning-activated specific subsystems. *J. Neurosci.* 19:484–94

Amanzio M, Pollo A, Maggi G, Benedetti F. 2001. Response variability to analgesics: a role for non-specific activation of endogenous opioids. *Pain* 90:205–15

Basbaum AI, Fields HL. 1978. Endogenous pain control mechanisms: review and hypothesis. *Ann. Neurol.* 4(5):451–62

Bausell RB, Lao L, Bergman S, Lee WL, Berman BM. 2005. Is acupuncture analgesia an expectancy effect? Preliminary evidence based on participants' perceived assignments in two placebo-controlled trials. *Eval. Health Prof.* 28:9–26

Beecher HK. 1955. The powerful placebo. *JAMA* 159:1602–6

Benedetti F. 1996. The opposite effects of the opiate antagonist naloxone and the cholecystokinin antagonist proglumide on placebo analgesia. *Pain* 64:535–43

Benedetti F. 1997. Cholecystokinin type-A and type-B receptors and their modulation of opioid analgesia. *News Physiol. Sci.* 12:263–68

Benedetti F, Amanzio M. 1997. The neurobiology of placebo analgesia: from endogenous opioids to cholecystokinin. *Prog. Neurobiol.* 52:109–25

Benedetti F, Amanzio M, Baldi S, Casadio C, Cavallo A, et al. 1998. The specific effects of prior opioid exposure on placebo analgesia and placebo respiratory depression. *Pain* 75:313–19

Benedetti F, Amanzio M, Baldi S, Casadio C, Maggi G. 1999a. Inducing placebo respiratory depressant responses in humans via opioid receptors. *Eur. J. Neurosci.* 11:625–31

Benedetti F, Amanzio M, Casadio C, Oliaro A, Maggi G. 1997. Blockade of nocebo hyperalgesia by the cholecystokinin antagonist proglumide. *Pain* 70:431–36

Benedetti F, Amanzio M, Maggi G. 1995. Potentiation of placebo analgesia by proglumide. *Lancet* 346:1231

Benedetti F, Arduino C, Amanzio M. 1999b. Somatotopic activation of opioid systems by target-expectations of analgesia. *J. Neurosci.* 9:3639–48

Benedetti F, Arduino C, Costa S, Vighetti S, Tarenzi L, et al. 2006. Loss of expectation-related mechanisms in Alzheimer's disease makes analgesic therapies less effective. *Pain* 121:133–44

Benedetti F, Colloca L, Torre E, Lanotte M, Melcarne A, et al. 2004. Placebo-responsive Parkinson patients show decreased activity in single neurons of subthalamic nucleus. *Nat. Neurosci.* 7:587–88

Benedetti F, Mayberg HS, Wager TD, Stohler CS, Zubieta JK. 2005. Neurobiological mechanisms of the placebo effect. *J. Neurosci.* 25:10390–402

Benedetti F, Pollo A, Lopiano L, Lanotte M, Vighetti S, et al. 2003. Conscious expectation and unconscious conditioning in analgesic; motor and hormonal placebo/nocebo responses. *J. Neurosci.* 23:4315–23

Colloca L, Benedetti F. 2005. Placebos and painkillers: Is mind as real as matter? *Nat. Rev. Neurosci.* 6(7):545–52

Colloca L, Benedetti F. 2006. How prior experience shapes placebo analgesia. *Pain* 124:126–33

Colloca L, Lopiano L, Lanotte M, Benedetti F. 2004. Overt versus covert treatment for pain, anxiety, and Parkinson's disease. *Lancet Neurol.* 3:679–84

de Craen AJ, Kaptchuk TJ, Tijssen JG, Kleijnen J. 1999. Placebos and placebo effects in medicine: historical overview. *J.R. Soc. Med.* 92(10):511–15

de la Fuente-Fernandez R, Ruth TJ, Sossi V, Schulzer M, Calne DB, et al. 2001. Expectation and dopamine release: mechanism of the placebo effect in Parkinson's disease. *Science* 293:1164–66

De Pascalis V, Chiaradia C, Carotenuto E. 2002. The contribution of suggestibility and expectation to placebo analgesia phenomenon in an experimental setting. *Pain* 96:393–402

Dias R, Robbins TW, Roberts AC. 1996. Dissociation in prefrontal cortex of affective and attentional shifts. *Nature* 380(6569):69–72

Fields HL. 2004. State-dependent opioid control of pain. *Nat. Rev Neurosci.* 5:565–75

Fields HL, Basbaum AI. 1999. Central nervous system mechanisms of pain modulation. In *Textbook of Pain*, ed. PD Wall, R Melzack, pp. 309–29. Edinburgh, UK: Churchill Livingstone

Fields HL, Levine JD. 1984. Placebo analgesia—a role for endorphins? *Trends Neurosci.* 7:271–73

Fields HL, Price DD. 1997. Toward a neurobiology of placebo analgesia. In *The Placebo Effect: An Interdisciplinary Exploration*, ed. A Harrington, pp. 93–116. Cambridge, MA: Harvard Univ. Press

Geers AL, Helfer SG, Weiland PE, Kosbab K. 2006. Expectations and placebo response: a laboratory investigation into the role of somatic focus. *J. Behav. Med.* 29(2):171–78

Geers AL, Weiland PE, Kosbab K, Landry SJ, Helfer SG. 2005. Goal activation, expectations, and the placebo effect. *J. Personal. Soc. Psychol.* 89(2):143–59

Giang DW, Goodman AD, Schiffer RB, Mattson DH, Petrie M, et al. 1996. Conditioning of cyclophosphamide-induced leukopenia in humans. *J. Neuropsychiatry Clin. Neurosci.* 8:194–201

Goebel MU, Trebst AE, Steiner J, Xie YF, Exton MS, et al. 2002. Behavioral conditioning of immunosuppression is possible in humans. *FASEB J.* 16:1869–73

Goetz CG, Leurgans S, Raman R, Stebbins GT. 2000. Objective changes in motor function during placebo treatment in PD. *Neurology* 54:710–14

Gracely RH, Dubner R, Wolskee PJ, Deeter WR. 1983. Placebo and naloxone can alter post-surgical pain by separate mechanisms. *Nature* 306:264–65

Grevert P, Albert LH, Goldstein A. 1983. Partial antagonism of placebo analgesia by naloxone. *Pain* 16:129–43

Hahn RA. 1985. A sociocultural model of illness and healing. In *Placebo: Theory, Research, and Mechanisms*, ed. L White, B Tursky, GE Schwartz, pp. 167–95. New York: Guilford

Hahn RA. 1997. The nocebo phenomenon: scope and foundations. In *The Placebo Effect: An Interdisciplinary Exploration*, ed. A Harrington, pp. 56–76. Cambridge, MA: Harvard Univ. Press

Hrobjartsson A, Gøtzsche PC. 2001. Is the placebo effect powerless? An analysis of clinical trials comparing placebo with no-treatment. *N. Engl. J. Med.* 344:1594–602

Hrobjartsson A, Gøtzsche PC. 2004. Is the placebo effect powerless? Update of a systematic review with 52 new randomized trials comparing placebo with no treatment. *J. Int. Med.* 256:91–100

Hrobjartsson A, Gøtzsche PC. 2006. Unsubstantiated claims of large effects of placebo on pain: serious errors in meta-analysis of placebo analgesia mechanism studies. *J. Clin. Epidemiol.* 59:336–38

Jensen MP, Karoly P. 1991. Motivation and expectancy factors in symptom perception: a laboratory study of the placebo effect. *Psychosomatic Med.* 53(2):144–52

Keltner JR, Furst A, Fan C, Redfern R, Inglis R, et al. 2006. Isolating the modulatory effect of expectation on pain transmission: a functional magnetic resonance imaging study. *J. Neurosci.* 26(16):4437–43

Koyama T, McHaffie JG, Laurienti PJ, Coghill RC. 2005. The subjective experience of pain: where expectations become reality. *Proc. Natl. Acad. Sci. USA* 102(36):12950–55

Leuchter AF, Cook IA, Witte EA, Morgan M, Abrams M. 2002. Changes in brain function of depressed subjects during treatment with placebo. *Am. J. Psychiatry* 159:122–29

Leuchter AF, Morgan M, Cook IA, Dunkin J, Abrams M, et al. 2004. Pretreatment neurophysiological and clinical characteristics of placebo responders in treatment trials for major depression. *Psychopharmacology* 177:15–22

Levine JD, Gordon NC. 1984. Influence of the method of drug administration on analgesic response. *Nature* 312:755–56

Levine JD, Gordon NC, Bornstein JC, Fields HL. 1979. Role of pain in placebo analgesia. *Proc. Natl. Acad. Sci. USA* 76:3528–31

Levine JD, Gordon NC, Fields HL. 1978. The mechanisms of placebo analgesia. *Lancet* 2:654–57

Linde K, Witt CM, Streng A, Weidenhammer W, Wagenpfeil S, et al. 2007. The impact of patient expectations on outcomes in four randomized controlled trials of acupuncture in patients with chronic pain. *Pain* 128(3):264–71

Lipman JJ, Miller BE, Mays KS, Miller MN, North WC, et al. 1990. Peak B endorphin concentration in cerebrospinal fluid: reduced in chronic pain patients and increased during the placebo response. *Psychopharmacology* 102:112–16

Lundh LG. 1987. Placebo, belief, and health. A cognitive-emotional model. *Scand. J. Psychol.* 28(2):128–43

Mayberg HS, Silva AJ, Brannan SK, Tekell JL, Mahurin RK, et al. 2002. The functional neuroanatomy of the placebo effect. *Am. J. Psychiatry* 159:728–37

Mayer DJ, Price DD. 1976. Central nervous mechanisms of analgesia. *Pain* 2:379–404

McKenzie JN. 1896. The production of the so-called "rose-cold" by means of an artificial rose. *Am. J. Med. Sci.* 91:45

McRae C, Cherin E, Yamazaki G, Diem G, Vo AH, et al. 2004. Effects of perceived treatment on quality of life and medical outcomes in a double-blind placebo surgery trial. *Arch. Gen. Psychiatry* 61:412–20

Miller EK, Cohen JD. 2001. An integrative theory of prefrontal cortex function. *Annu. Rev. Neurosci.* 24:167–202

Moerman DE. 2002. Meaningful dimensions of medical care. In *The Science of the Placebo: Toward an Interdisciplinary Research Agenda*, ed. HA Guess, A Kleinman, JW Kusek, LW Engel, pp. 77–107. London: BMJ Books

Montgomery GH, Kirsch I. 1996. Mechanisms of placebo pain reduction: an empirical investigation. *Psychol. Sci.* 7:174–76

Montgomery GH, Kirsch I. 1997. Classical conditioning and the placebo effect. *Pain* 72:107–13

Olness K, Ader R. 1992. Conditioning as an adjunct in the pharmacotherapy of lupus erythematosus. *J. Dev. Behav. Pediatr.* 13:124–25

Petrovic P, Dietrich T, Fransson P, Andersson J, Carlsson K. 2005. Placebo in emotional processing—induced expectations of anxiety relief activate a generalized modulatory network. *Neuron* 46(6):957–69

Petrovic P, Kalso E, Petersson KM, Ingvar M. 2002. Placebo and opioid analgesia—imaging a shared neuronal network. *Science* 295:1737–40

Pollo A, Amanzio M, Arslanian A, Casadio C, Maggi G, et al. 2001. Response expectancies in placebo analgesia and their clinical relevance. *Pain* 93:77–84

Pollo A, Torre E, Lopiano L, Rizzone M, Lanotte M, et al. 2002. Expectation modulates the response to subthalamic nucleus stimulation in Parkinsonian patients. *NeuroReport* 13:1383–86

Pollo A, Vighetti S, Rainero I, Benedetti F. 2003. Placebo analgesia and the heart. *Pain* 102:125–33

Price DD. 2001. Assessing placebo effects without placebo groups: an untapped possibility? *Pain* 90:201–3

Price DD, Barrell JE, Barrell JJ. 1985. A quantitative-experiential analysis of human emotions. *Motiv. Emot.* 9:19–38

Price DD, Barrell JJ. 1984. Some general laws of human emotion: interrelationships between intensities of desire, expectation and emotional feeling. *J. Personal.* 52(4):389–409

Price DD, Barrell JJ. 2000. Mechanisms of analgesia produced by hypnosis and placebo suggestions. *Prog. Brain Res.* 122:255–71

Price DD, Craggs J, Verne GN, Perlstein WM, Robinson ME. 2007. Placebo analgesia is accompanied by large reductions in pain-related brain activity in irritable bowel syndrome patients. *Pain* 127:63–72

Price DD, Milling LS, Kirsch I, Duff A, Montgomery GH, et al. 1999. An analysis of factors that contribute to the magnitude of placebo analgesia in an experimental paradigm. *Pain* 83:147–56

Price DD, Riley J, Barrell JJ. 2001. Are lived choices based on emotional processes? *Cogn. Emot.* 15(3):365–79

Rainville P, Bao QV, Chetrien P. 2005. Pain-related emotions modulate experimental pain perception and autonomic responses. *Pain* 118(3):306–18

Schwartz JM, Stapp HP, Beauregard M. 2005. Quantum physics in neuroscience and psychology: a neurophysical model of mind-brain interaction. *Philos. Trans. R. Soc. London B Biol. Sci.* 360:1309–27

Shetty N, Friedman JH, Kieburtz K, Marshall FJ, Oakes D. 1999. The placebo response in Parkinson's disease. Parkinson study group. *Clin. Neuropharmacol.* 22:207–12

Vase L, Price DD, Verne GN, Robinson ME. 2004. The contribution of changes in expected pain levels and desire for pain relief to placebo analgesia. In *Psychological Modulation of Pain*, ed. DD Price, M Catherine Bushnell, pp 207–34. Seattle, WA: IASP Press

Vase L, Riley JL III, Price DD. 2002. A comparison of placebo effects in clinical analgesic trials versus studies of placebo analgesia. *Pain* 99:443–52

Vase L, Robinson ME, Verne GN, Price DD. 2003. The contributions of suggestion, expectancy and desire to placebo effect in irritable bowl syndrome patients. *Pain* 105:17–25

Vase L, Robinson ME, Verne GN, Price DD. 2005. Increased placebo analgesia over time in irritable bowel syndrome (IBS) patients is associated with desire and expectation but not endogenous opioid mechanisms. *Pain* 115(3):338–47

Verne GN, Robinson ME, Vase L, Price DD. 2003. Reversal of visceral and cutaneous hyperalgesia by local rectal anesthesia in irritable bowl syndrome (IBS) patients. *Pain* 105:223–30

Wager T, Rilling JK, Smith EE, Sokolik A, Casey KL, et al. 2004. Placebo-induced changes in fMRI in the anticipation and experience of pain. *Science* 303(5661):1162–67

Zubieta J, Smith YR, Bueller JA, Ketter B, Kilbourn MR, et al. 2001. Regional μ-opioid receptor regulation of sensory and affective dimensions of pain. *Science* 293:311–15

Zubieta JK, Bueller JA, Jackson LR, Scott DJ, Xu Y, et al. 2005. Placebo effects mediated by endogenous opioid activity on μ-opioid receptors. *J. Neurosci.* 25:7754–62

Children's Social Competence in Cultural Context

Xinyin Chen[1] and Doran C. French[2]

[1]Department of Psychology, University of Western Ontario, London, Ontario N6A 5C2 Canada; email: xchen@uwo.ca

[2]Department of Psychology, Illinois Wesleyan University, Bloomington, Illinois 61702; email: dfrench@titan.iwu.edu

Annu. Rev. Psychol. 2008. 59:591–616

First published online as a Review in Advance on May 31, 2007

The *Annual Review of Psychology* is online at http://psych.annualreviews.org

This article's doi: 10.1146/annurev.psych.59.103006.093606

Key Words

social functioning, peer relationship, culture

Abstract

Social initiative and behavioral control represent two major dimensions of children's social competence. Cultural norms and values with respect to these dimensions may affect the exhibition, meaning, and development of specific social behaviors such as sociability, shyness-inhibition, cooperation-compliance, and aggression-defiance, as well as the quality and function of social relationships. The culturally guided social interaction processes including evaluations and responses likely serve as an important mediator of cultural influence on children's social behaviors, relationships, and developmental patterns. In this article, we review research on children's social functioning and peer relationships in different cultures from an integrative contextual-developmental perspective. We also review research on the implications of the macro-level social and cultural changes that are happening in many societies for socialization and development of social competence.

Contents

INTRODUCTION

More than 25 years ago, Ogbu (1981) wrote a classic article in which he argued that children's competence should be judged within the framework of their culture, and in particular, the socioecological demands that children were being socialized to address. In the past decades, cross-cultural and developmental researchers have been increasingly interested in how cultural factors may be involved in the development of social competence (e.g., Edwards et al. 2006). In this article, we review and discuss the work in this area with a particular focus on the role of cultural norms and values in the exhibition and developmental processes of social competence.

SOCIAL FUNCTIONING, INTERACTION, AND CULTURAL CONTEXT: A CONCEPTUAL FRAMEWORK

Social competence is generally defined as the ability to attain personal or group success in social situations (Waters & Sroufe 1983, Zigler 1973). Although there are some differences in specific definitions of social competence, most conceptualizations emphasize active participation or initiative in social interactions and the appropriateness of the behaviors in social settings (Rubin & Rose-Krasnor 1992). Social initiative refers to the tendency to initiate and maintain social activities, especially in challenging settings. High social initiative is driven by the child's approach motive in social situations and is reflected in high interest in social activities. In contrast, internal anxiety or feelings of insecurity may impede spontaneous engagement in social participation, leading to a low level of social initiative (Asendorpf 1990). Behavioral control, representing self-regulatory ability to modulate behavioral and emotional reactivity, is closely related to the maintenance of social appropriateness (Eisenberg & Fabes 1992, Kochanska & Aksan 1995, Rothbart & Bates 2006). The dimension of control, which is indicated mostly by the exhibition of cooperative, compliant, and aggressive-defiant behaviors, is concerned with "fit in with others" and thus is particularly important for the achievement of interpersonal harmony and group well-being. The broad construct of control also incorporates the components of social responsibility and concerns for others (Kochanska & Aksan 1995).

Social competence:
the ability to attain personal or group success in social situations

Culture and Social Initiative and Behavioral Control

Different societies have been found to place different values on the dimensions of social initiative and norm-based behavioral control in children and adolescents (e.g., Chen et al. 2006b,c; Greenfield et al. 2006). In Western self-oriented or individualistic cultures, acquiring autonomy and assertive social skills is an important socialization goal (Triandis 1995). Social initiative is viewed as a major index of social maturity and accomplishment, and the lack of active social participation and initiative is considered maladaptive (Rubin et al. 2002). In contrast, although self-regulation and control are encouraged, the cultural emphasis on individual decision-making and freedom requires socialization agents to help children learn to balance the needs of the self with those of others (Maccoby & Martin 1983). Consequently, behavioral control is often regarded as less important, especially when it is in conflict with the attainment of individual social and psychological goals (Oyserman et al. 2002, Triandis 1995).

Social initiative may not be highly appreciated or valued in group-oriented or collectivistic societies, such as many East Asian and Latin American societies, because it may not facilitate harmony and cohesiveness in the group. To maintain interpersonal and group harmony, individuals need to restrain personal desires in an effort to address the needs and interests of others (Tamis-LeMonda 2007, Triandis 1995). Thus, self-control may be emphasized in a more consistent and absolute manner; the lack of control is often regarded as a serious problem during childhood and adolescence (Ho 1986, Zhou et al. 2004). In cultures such as China, not only are children encouraged to comply with external demands, but also to understand general social expectations and requirements concerning their conduct. These understandings are believed to help children demonstrate committed and internalized control (Chen et al. 2003a).

In short, as manifestations of the two fundamental socioemotional dimensions (Rothbart & Bates 2006) in social domains, social initiative and behavioral control may be valued differently in self-oriented and group-oriented cultures. This framework provides an approach toward understanding how cultural context may be involved in social interpretations and evaluations of specific behaviors including aggression-disruption (based on high social initiative and low control), shyness-inhibition (low initiative and adequate control to constrain behavioral and emotional reactivity toward self, rather than others), and different aspects of adaptive social functioning such as sociability and prosocial-cooperative behavior.

The Mediating Role of Social Interaction

Hinde (1987) argues that social interaction helps form the links between culture and individual behavior. Similarly, the sociocultural theory (Cole 1996, Rogoff 2003, Vygotsky 1978) highlights the importance of interpersonal collaborative experiences, particularly with adults and skilled peer tutors, in the transmission or internalization of cultural values. Based on these arguments, we have recently proposed a contextual-developmental perspective in which social interaction processes serve to mediate cultural influence on human development (Chen et al. 2006b). This perspective focuses on how social evaluations and responses and the active participation of the child in interactions are guided by cultural norms and values and, at the same time, regulate individual behavior and development.

According to the contextual-developmental perspective, there may exist individual and group biases in early disposition that constitute a major developmental origin of socioemotional functioning. Peers and adults may perceive and evaluate specific socioemotional characteristics such as

Social initiative: a dimension of social competence representing the tendency to initiate and maintain social activities, especially in challenging settings

Behavioral control: self-regulatory ability to modulate behavioral and emotional reactivity in order to maintain social appropriateness

Contextual-developmental perspective: a perspective emphasizing the role of social interaction processes including mutual evaluations and responses in mediating cultural influence on human development

shyness-inhibition and defiance in ways consistent with cultural belief and value systems in the society. Moreover, peers and adults in different cultures may respond differently to these socioemotional characteristics and express different attitudes (e.g., acceptance, rejection) toward children who display the characteristics in social interactions. Social evaluations and responses, in turn, may affect children's behaviors and ultimately the developmental patterns and outcomes of socioemotional functioning. Cultural norms and values, which are changing themselves, provide a basis for the social processes (Chen et al. 2006b, French et al. 2006a). At the same time, children actively engage in social interactions through displaying their reactions to social influence and through participating in constructing peer cultures (Corsaro & Nelson 2003). Whereas some children are sensitive to social evaluations and attempt to adjust their socioemotional functioning according to social expectations, others are more resistant to social influence. Moreover, children play an active role in selecting and adopting existing culture and creating cultural norms and values for social evaluations and other peer group activities. Thus, the social processes are bidirectional and transactional in nature. Through these processes, personal characteristics, socialization, and cultural factors collectively shape children's social behaviors and social relationships.

In the following sections, we review children's social functioning, focusing on social initiative (sociability and shyness-social inhibition) and behavioral control (cooperation and aggression-defiance), in cultural context. We discuss cultural meanings of social behaviors, the role of socialization in their development, and their developmental patterns in different cultures. A major index of social competence in children is how they establish and sustain positive peer relationships (Ladd 2005). Thus, we review cultural influences on peer relationships. We focus on how cultural values of initiative and control affect the quality and functional roles of peer relationships

such as friendship and how cultural norms guide children to engage in negotiation and resolve conflict in peer interactions. In addition, we review and discuss studies concerning the implications of macro-level social and cultural changes for the development of social competence.

The overriding theme of this article is how social functioning and peer relationships reflect social competence in specific cultural contexts. Our review and discussion of social functioning and relationships are guided by (a) the conceptual framework concerning cultural values of social initiative and behavioral control, and (b) the contextual-developmental perspective focusing on the mediating role of the social interaction processes in development.

CHILDREN'S SOCIAL FUNCTIONING ACROSS CULTURES: PREVALENCE, MEANINGS, AND DEVELOPMENTAL PATTERNS

Culture and Social Initiative: Sociability and Shyness-Inhibition

According to Asendorpf (1990, 1991), sociability is derived from motives of high approach and low avoidance in social situations and is often indicated by active engagement in interaction with peers. In contrast, shyness-inhibition results from an internal approach-avoidance conflict that is manifested in wary and restrained behaviors in challenging settings. Cultural norms and values may affect the display and the functional meanings of sociability and shyness in childhood (e.g., Chen et al. 2006c).

Sociability and peer interaction. Interaction with peers is a fundamental part of human development in most societies. Even in cultures where children are required to spend much of their time helping with family duties such as caring for their younger siblings, children often do this in the company of peers (Tietjen 2006). In many contemporary societies, schools provide children with the primary context for interaction because they congregate large numbers of nonkin same-age children, thus allowing gender- and age-segregated peer groups to exist. Traditionally, girls tend to assume more household responsibilities such as childcare and engage in fewer interactions with peers than do boys in some cultures (Whiting & Edwards 1988). With the introduction of the Western style of schooling, however, the gender difference in overall peer interactions has been diminishing, although the forms of peer interactions may differ somewhat for boys and girls (Maccoby 1998).

Developmental researchers have investigated children's sociability and peer interactions in different societies by observing children's play. The findings indicate that cultural and social conditions are related to levels of social participation; cultures that value social initiative tend to facilitate children's social interactions. Edwards (2000), for example, reanalyzed the data from the Six Culture Study and found that children in relatively open communities (e.g., Okinawa and the United States), where peer interactions were encouraged, had significantly higher scores on overall social engagement than did children in more "close" and agricultural communities (e.g., Kenya and India). In a more recent study, Chen et al. (2006d) found that Canadian preschool-age children more actively participated in peer interactions than did their Chinese counterparts; in contrast, Chinese children displayed more nonsocial behaviors, including passive solitary and parallel play behaviors, than did Canadian children. Relatively low social interaction was also found in Indonesian children, who were less likely to respond positively to play initiations than were American children (Farver & Howes 1988). The differences in the overall engagement of peer interactions are likely reflective of the different cultural expectations concerning the development of sociability, as it is less valued in some cultures than in others (Parmar

et al. 2004, Rothbaum & Trommsdorff 2006).

Self-expression in social interaction. Cultural norms and values may influence both the level and characteristics of peer interaction. Researchers have found consistent cultural variations in the extent to which children engage in socio-dramatic activities. According to Howes (1992), the ability to engage in socio-dramatic behavior and pretense represents the mastery of skills that promote the coordination of decontextualized and substitutive activities. As indicated by Farver et al. (1995) and Edwards (2000), however, this form of social behavior requires children to control their social-evaluative anxiety, to express their inner interests and personal styles, and to engage in self-explanation and negotiation. Cultural values of assertiveness and self-expression may impact the display of socio-dramatic behavior in social interactions.

In North American societies, children are socialized to behave in a self-directive and autonomous manner and are encouraged to exhibit personal styles (e.g., Smetana 2002, Triandis 1995). As a result, North American children tend to engage in more socio-dramatic play behaviors than do children in many other, particularly group-oriented, cultures. For example, children in Maya (Gaskins 2000), Bedouin Arab (Ariel & Sever 1980), Kenya, Mexico, and India (Edwards 2000) have been found to engage in little socio-dramatic activity. In a study of play behavior in Korean preschools in the United States, Farver et al. (1995) found that Korean American children displayed less social and pretend play than did Anglo American children. Moreover, Korean children's pretend play included more everyday and family role activities and fewer fantastic themes (i.e., extraordinary actions performed by fantasy characters), and Korean children used less self-assertive communicative strategies (Farver & Shin 1997). These results were consistent with the findings from an earlier study conducted with preschool children in Korea

(Tieszen 1979). Farver et al. (1995) argued that the cross-cultural differences might be related to the cultural practices in structuring the environment in which children's social interactions occur.

Sociability and social and psychological adjustment. Children who are active in social settings are regarded as socially competent by peers and adults in North America (e.g., Rubin et al. 2002). Assertiveness and self-expression involved in sociable behavior make it desirable in social interactions in individualistic cultures. Indeed, North American sociable children are likely to obtain social status in the peer group and achieve success in social and emotional areas (Buhrmester et al. 1988, Rubin et al. 2006a).

Sociability is often less emphasized in group-oriented cultures than in more individualistic cultures because such behavior may not clearly contribute to effective group functioning. In a longitudinal study, Chen et al. (2000) found that sociability in Chinese children positively predicted social impact or salience in the peer group, but did not predict social acceptance or preference. Moreover, after its overlap with prosocial behavior was controlled, sociability did not predict social or academic outcomes, and it positively predicted later externalizing problems.

Nevertheless, the active participation of sociable children in social interactions may be conducive to psychoemotional adjustment. In Chen et al.'s (2000) study, sociability was found to be associated positively with self-regard and negatively with loneliness in Chinese children. A follow-up study (Chen et al. 2002) showed that sociability in childhood was associated positively with perceived self-worth and negatively with internalizing symptoms in late adolescence. Active social participation of sociable children may facilitate their formation of interpersonal support systems that in turn help these children cope with psychoemotional difficulties, particularly under adverse circumstances.

Shyness-inhibition. Shyness-inhibition, as it is manifested in wary, vigilant, and sensitive behavior, is generally assumed to reflect internal anxiety and lack of self-confidence in stressful and social-evaluative situations (Asendorpf 1990). Western researchers have typically viewed children who display shy-inhibited behaviors as socially incompetent and immature (e.g., Fox et al. 2005). Shy-inhibited children, especially during the school years, are likely to experience low peer acceptance and poor social adjustment (Rubin et al. 2002). Over time, these children tend to develop negative self-perceptions and self-feelings such as depression, in part because they receive negative social feedback and become aware of their social difficulties (e.g., Rubin et al. 2006a). Nevertheless, the prevalence and functional significance of children's shy-inhibited behavior are likely to vary across cultures because this behavior is not necessarily perceived as incompetent or associated with adjustment problems in societies where social initiative and assertiveness are not valued.

Cross-cultural differences in the display of shyness-inhibition have been reported in childhood and adolescence (e.g., Farver & Howes 1988, Freedman & Freedman 1969, Kagan et al. 1978, Lee et al. 2006). Farver et al. (1995), for example, found that Korean American children displayed more shy and unoccupied behaviors than did European American children in a naturalistic peer interaction setting. The results were consistent with Rubin et al.'s (2006b) recent findings that Korean and Chinese toddlers exhibited higher inhibition than did Italian and Australian toddlers in laboratory free-play sessions.

Chen et al. (1998) conducted a comprehensive analysis of children's shy-inhibited behavior in various free-play and stressful situations and found that Chinese toddlers were more shy, vigilant, and inhibited than their Canadian counterparts. Chinese toddlers stayed closer to their mothers and were less likely to explore in free-play sessions. Moreover, Chinese toddlers displayed more anxious and fearful behaviors when interacting with a stranger, as indicated by their higher scores on the latency to approach the stranger and to touch a toy truck and a "robot" when they were invited to do so. Similar cross-cultural differences in self-reported shyness have been found between Chinese and Western adolescents (Gong 1984, Yang 1986).

Parent and peer attitudes and responses. Researchers have examined how adults and children in different cultures perceive and react to shy-inhibited behavior. North American parents typically react to shy-inhibited behavior with concern, disappointment, and punishment (Rubin et al. 2002). Chen et al. (1998) found, however, that shy-inhibited behavior in Chinese children was associated with parents' acceptance and approval. Peers in China and North America also respond differently to shy-inhibited behaviors. Chen et al. (2006d) found that, compared with others, shy-inhibited Canadian children who made passive and low-power social initiations received fewer positive responses and more rejection from peers, whereas shy-inhibited Chinese children who displayed the same behavior more often received positive responses. These different adult and peer attitudes and responses reflect cultural values and socialization goals (Chen et al. 2006c). In traditional Chinese culture, shy and wary behavior is thought to be associated with virtuous qualities such as modesty, cautiousness, and self-control. Socially sensitive and restrained behavior is often regarded as indicating accomplishment and maturity, and shy-sensitive children are perceived to be well behaved and understanding (e.g., Liang 1987).

Shyness and social and psychological adjustment. The distinct social attitudes and responses in China and North America may constitute different social environments in which shy-inhibited children develop. In North America, shy children, particularly boys, are likely to experience difficulties in so-cial and life adjustment in the later years (e.g., Caspi et al. 1988, Coplan et al. 2004, Rubin et al. 2002). Unlike their counterparts in the West, shy children in China are accepted by peers and perform well socially and academically in childhood and adolescence (e.g., Chen et al. 1992, 1999). Shy children are more likely than are others to obtain leadership status and the award of distinguished studentship in the school. Given the social and cultural endorsement, it is not surprising that shy Chinese children perceive themselves positively and do not feel lonely or depressed (Chen et al. 1995, 2004a). It should be noted that as China is undergoing dramatic reforms toward a market economy, the adaptive value of shyness has been declining in urban children (Chen et al. 2005). Recent findings indicate that shyness is still associated with social and psychological adjustment among children in rural areas of China (Chen & Wang 2006), but the association will likely change rapidly as the massive transformation expands to these areas.

Shyness may be unassociated with adjustment problems in countries in addition to China. Although the results may not be highly consistent, there is evidence that shyness is viewed as less deviant and problematic in some Asian cultures, such as Indonesia (Eisenberg et al. 2001) and Korea (Farver et al. 1995), than in North America. Shyness has also been found to lead to less negative outcomes in Swedish youth than in U.S. youth. Kerr et al. (1996) followed a sample of children born in Sweden in the mid 1950s to adulthood. Although shyness predicted later marriage and parenthood, it did not affect adulthood education and careers, which differed from the findings of Caspi et al. (1988) for U.S. youth. According to Kerr et al. (1996), the social welfare and support systems that evolved from the egalitarian values in Sweden assured that people did not need to be assertive or competitive to achieve career success. Perhaps because similar social support systems were not yet available for girls during the period in which the study was conducted, Swedish shy girls appeared to attain lower levels of education than did non-shy girls. Kerr et al. (1996) expected that shy and non-shy girls would not differ in Sweden today.

Summary. The cultural values that different societies (e.g., North American versus East Asian) place on social initiative may affect the prevalence of children's sociable and shy-inhibited behaviors, as well as the nature of social interactions such as self-expressivity in interactions. Social interpretations and evaluations and the responses of the child may reflect the values and, at the same time, shape the experiences (e.g., peer acceptance, psychoemotional adjustment) and development (e.g., career establishment) of sociable and shy children.

Culture and Behavioral Control: Cooperation-Compliance and Aggression-Defiance

Cross-cultural differences in children's cooperative-compliant and aggressive-defiant behaviors have been observed in many studies (e.g., Whiting & Edwards 1988), differences believed to be associated with the extent to which the culture emphasizes the control or regulation of coercive behavior (Bond 2004). From a developmental perspective, socialization practices may play an important role in children's learning of the social norms and the exhibition of cooperative and aggressive behaviors. A variety of other social and cultural factors, such as religion, SES, and organizational and structural characteristics of the society (e.g., political and economic systems, childcare practices), may also be involved in the development of these behaviors through the socialization processes (Super & Harkness 1986).

Cooperative and compliant behavior. Cultures that emphasize social obligation, group harmony, and family interdependence appear to promote the development of cooperative and compliant behavior (Eisenberg et al. 2006a). Whiting & Edwards (1988),

for example, found that children in societies where extended families lived together in traditional styles and where children were required to assume family responsibilities (e.g., Nyansongo in Kenya, Juxtlahuaca in Mexio, and Tarong in Philippines) displayed more prosocial-cooperative and compliant behaviors than did children in economically complex societies with class structures and occupational division of labor (Taira in Okinawa, Khalapur in India, and Orchard Town in the United States). In Kenyan communities where families lived on large, isolated farms, children displayed the most frequent cooperation in household and agricultural work (Edwards 2000). Graves & Graves (1983) found that Aituaki (Cook Islands) children from rural and extended families displayed similar patterns of cooperative and compliant behavior.

In a series of studies of cooperation, competition, and allocation behavior, Kagan and his colleagues (Kagan & Knight 1981, Kagan & Madson 1972) found that Mexican American children were more cooperative than were children from urban and westernized cultures. The tendency to be cooperative in distribution of objects declined from second to third generation of Mexican American children, which suggests that cooperation was affected by the acculturation process (Knight & Kagan 1977).

Recent studies have shown that children in China, India, and Korea and some other Asian countries display more cooperative and compliant behaviors than do children in North America and Western Europe (e.g., Farver et al. 1995, Orlick et al. 1990). Orlick et al. (1990), for example, found that kindergarten children in China displayed more cooperative peer interaction behavior than did children in Canada. Whereas approximately 85% of the social behavior of Chinese children was coded as cooperative, the comparable percentage of Canadian children was only 22%. Similar results have been reported by Navon & Ramsay (1989). Stevenson (1991) argues that the cooperative and prosocial tendency of children toward others in some Asian countries such as China and Japan is related to the greater emphasis that the society puts on socializing children to strive for group, rather than individual, accomplishment.

Autonomy versus obligation in prosocial-cooperative behavior. Cultural variations in prosocial-cooperative behaviors may be due, in part, to the influence of cultural norms on children's understanding of the behaviors. Miller (1994) argues that individuals in sociocentric societies view responsiveness to the needs of others to be a fundamental commitment, whereas individuals in Western societies attempt to maintain a balance between prosocial concerns and individual freedom of choice. Consistent with this argument, Miller et al. (1990) found that Indian adults and children held a broader and higher standard of social responsibility than Americans.

The autonomy versus obligation orientation may partially characterize cultural differences in children's prosocial-cooperative behaviors across various situations. Prosocial behavior and interpersonal cooperation are often seen in Western cultures as a personal decision based on such factors as how much one likes the target person(s) (Eisenberg et al. 2006a, Greenfield et al. 2006). In societies that emphasize group harmony and social relationships, there is considerable pressure on children to view prosocial-cooperative behavior as obligatory (e.g., Miller 1994). In these societies, socialization of responsibility often emerges in the early years with an emphasis on children's self-control and regulation.

Early self-regulation, socialization, and the development of prosocial-cooperative behavior. Children's self-regulatory ability and parental effort to socialize control and responsibility in the early years are major factors that contribute to prosocial-cooperative behavior. Eisenberg and her colleagues (Eisenberg et al. 2004, 2006b; Zhou et al. 2004) have found that children's regulation in China, Indonesia,

France, and other cultures is associated with, and predictive of, adaptive social functioning, particularly prosocial-cooperative behavior. It has been argued that early self-regulatory ability may serve as a basis for the internalization of social norms and rules (Kochanska & Aksan 1995). Moreover, well-regulated children can modulate their emotions and behaviors and thus focus their attention on others' needs and interests (Eisenberg et al. 2006a).

Although the emergence of self-regulation in early childhood may be considered a significant early achievement in most societies, parents in different cultures may socialize children's regulation at different paces and in different ways. Keller et al. (2004) assessed the relations between parenting and self-regulation in Cameroonian Nso, Costa Rican, and Greek children. As expected, rural Cameroonian Nso mothers had higher scores than did Costa Rican mothers, who in turn had higher scores than did middle-class Greek mothers, on proximal parenting style (body contact, body stimulation), which was believed to facilitate child obedience and regulation. Accordingly, Cameroonian Nso toddlers displayed more regulated behaviors, as indicated by their compliance with maternal requests and prohibitions, than did their counterparts in the other two groups. Costa Rican toddlers also had higher regulation scores than Greek toddlers. Keller et al. (2004) argue that whereas behavioral training and control may be viewed as interference into the child's behavior and an infringement of the child's freedom in individualistic cultures, self-regulation and compliance are viewed as a duty, expressing social maturity and competence, in group-oriented cultural contexts.

Chinese parents also socialize children to be compliant and self-regulated at an early age. According to traditional Confucian views, it is important to learn and follow the dictates of "*li*" (propriety)—a set of rules for actions—to cultivate and strengthen innate virtues (Ho 1986). Chen et al. (2003a) found that Chinese mothers expected their toddlers to exert a higher level of behavioral regulation than did Canadian mothers. When children failed to do so, Chinese mothers were more likely than Canadian mothers to express concern and dissatisfaction. Indeed, Chinese children displayed a more committed and mature form of compliance than their Canadian counterparts on various tasks.

Cultural differences in the socialization of child cooperative and responsible behaviors appear more consistent and evident from middle childhood to adolescence. Larson & Verma (1999) reviewed evidence suggesting that children ages four to six years, particularly girls, in preindustrialized societies start to be assigned household responsibilities and that these responsibilities increase rapidly with age (six to seven hours/day for 10- to 12-year-olds). In contrast, children in postindustrialized societies spend considerably less time doing household work. The context of performing household duties and childcare appears to be particularly relevant to eliciting and facilitating prosocial-cooperative behaviors in children (De Guzman et al. 2005).

Finally, general parenting styles may be related to children's cooperative and compliant behaviors. It has been demonstrated that the fundamental parenting dimensions of warmth and inductive reasoning are positively associated with child prosocial-cooperative behaviors across cultures (Chen et al. 1997, Nelson et al. 2006, Rohner 1986). Nevertheless, it remains to be examined how parental warmth and control are reflected in specific parenting behaviors and contribute to the development of social competence in culturally distinct manners (Chao 1994, Steinberg et al. 1992).

Aggression and defiance. It has been argued that cultural context may facilitate or inhibit the expression of aggressive and defiant behaviors (Weisz et al. 1988). Munroe et al. (2000), for example, found that boys displayed more aggressive behaviors such as assaulting and verbal attack in patrilineal cultures with a system of kinship linkage through the male

(e.g., Kenya and Nepal) than in nonpatrilineal cultures. In general, cultures that value competitiveness and the pursuit of personal goals seem to allow for more coercive and aggressive behavior, whereas cultures that emphasize group harmony and personal control tend to inhibit aggressive behavior (Bergeron & Schneider 2005, Weisz et al. 1988). This argument has been supported by findings that children in some Asian countries, such as China, Korea, and Thailand, Australia, and some European nations, such as Sweden and the Netherlands, tend to display relatively fewer aggressive and externalizing behaviors than do North American children (e.g., Bergeron & Schneider 2005, Farver et al. 1995, Kessen 1975, Russell et al. 2003, Weisz et al. 1988).

Cultural norms, socialization, and individual beliefs and attitudes about aggression and anger. Developmental researchers have long been interested in the role of socialization in the development of aggression and anger (e.g., Cummings et al. 1981). Cultural influences may take place during the socialization process through shaping individual beliefs and attitudes about aggressive behaviors (Huesmann & Guerra 1997), as these beliefs and attitudes constitute a basis for attributions and the activation of scripts about aggressive acts (Dodge et al. 2006). This is illustrated by studies of Brahman and Tamang children's anger and aggression in rural Nepal (Cole et al. 2002, 2006). Brahmans are high-caste Hindus who value hierarchy and dominance in the caste, whereas Tamangs, with a background of Tibetan Buddhism, value social equality, compassion, modesty, and nonviolence. When the child displays anger and aggression, Tamang caregivers disapprove and rebuke the child, whereas Brahman caregivers respond with yielding and attempting to coax the child to feel better (Cole et al. 2006). The socialization effect is reflected in children's attitudes; Brahman children are more likely to endorse anger and aggressive behaviors than are Tamang children. Moreover, Brahman children react to difficult social situations such as peer conflict with anger and other negative emotions more often than Tamang children (Cole et al. 2002). In a study using hypothetical interpersonal dilemmas, Zahn-Waxler et al. (1996) found that Japanese children showed less anger and less aggressive behavior and language than did U.S. children in their responses to conflict and distress. The cultural differences may be attributable to the greater emphasis of Japanese mothers on control of negative emotions and impulses and on upholding standards for appropriate behaviors.

Social evaluations and adjustment of aggressive children. Although aggression is generally discouraged in Western individualistic cultures, aggressive children and adolescents may receive social support from peers and sometimes be perceived as popular and treated as "stars" in their groups (e.g., Cairns et al. 1988, Rodkin et al. 2000). As a result, despite their social and behavioral problems, aggressive children often have biased self-perceptions, overestimate their social competence, and do not report internalizing psychoemotional problems (Asher et al. 1990, Hoza et al. 1995).

Aggressive, disruptive, and defiant behaviors are strictly prohibited in Chinese society because of their potential threat to group harmony. Chinese schools regularly engage in collective and public evaluations in which children are required to evaluate themselves in the group in terms of whether their behaviors reach the school standards and whether they have made improvement over the time. Peers and teachers provide feedback on the child's self-evaluations. This social interactive process makes it difficult for aggressive children to develop inflated or "biased" self-perceptions of their competence and social status. Consequently, aggressive children in China display pervasive social and psychological difficulties including low social status, poor quality of peer relationships, negative self-perceptions, and feelings of loneliness and depression (Chen et al. 1995, 2004a)

Summary. Cultural beliefs and values with respect to behavioral control in the society may be associated with the exhibition of cooperative-compliant and aggressive-defiant behaviors as well as the meanings of these behaviors (e.g., autonomy versus obligation in prosocial-cooperative behavior) in children. Socialization experiences such as children's participation in household work and parenting practices likely contribute to the development of self-regulatory and responsible behaviors. Culturally directed adult and peer-group attitudes and specific social-evaluative processes in the society may determine, to a large extent, the developmental patterns of cooperative and aggressive behaviors.

CHILDREN'S PEER RELATIONSHIPS IN CULTURAL CONTEXT

A major developmental outcome of social behaviors is children's success in developing and maintaining relationships with peers (Rubin et al. 2006a). One aspect of success with peer relationships is to become accepted by peers and integrated into social networks. As we discussed in the previous sections, peer acceptance is associated with culturally valued behaviors, and, as such, the characteristics of those accepted by peers tend to reflect these values. A second important aspect of peer relationships is the ability to establish specific friendship bonds with others. The ability to develop friendships has been found to be associated with indexes of social and psychological adjustment in Western as well as some non-Western cultures (French et al. 2003). In the sections below, we focus on peer group integration and friendship as well as conflict management, a feature of peer interaction essential to both aspects of relationships.

Peer group involvement and friendship are associated but not necessarily identical (Gest et al. 2001). Some children who are well integrated within a peer group do not have close friends, whereas the opposite is true for others. At the cultural level, there appear to be differences in the extent to which broad social integration or development of specific friendships is encouraged. Sharabany & Wiseman (1993) found that children in kibbutz communities focused on group involvement and had limited dyadic friendships. In other cultures, such as South Korea, individuals develop extremely strong dyadic friendships, many of these lasting throughout the life span (French et al. 2006a). A third variation appears in some societies, such as the Yucatan Mayan, in which involvement with age mates typically occurs within extended family networks of siblings and cousins, leaving little space for relationships with non-kin (Gaskins 2006). In most societies, such as the United States, there is a mixed emphasis on network integration and development of specific friendships.

Peer Group Involvement

Peer involvement increases in North American children from childhood to early adolescence, which may derive from the desire of youths to become autonomous from the family (Furman & Buhrmester 1985). Once they enter the peer world, children are encouraged to learn independence and self-direction while maintaining positive relationships with others, and eventually they are expected to acquire a sense of self-identity within the peer context (Brown 1990, Mead 1934). Thus, peer group involvement provides a social context for children to understand themselves in relation to others and experience self-validation (Rubin et al. 2006a, Sullivan 1953). In studies of North American youth, it has been found that intensive interaction within the small clique appears to be the major form of peer activity in childhood, but this tends to decline from middle childhood to adolescence, when affiliation with multiple groups and larger crowds becomes more salient (e.g., Brown 1990). During development, there is a general loosening of clique ties, and children's sense of belongingness and the intensity of group boundaries decline steadily with age (see Rubin et al. 2006a).

Children and adolescents' peer experiences likely vary across cultures in part because of different expectations regarding individual independence in the group (Rothbaum et al. 2000). In collectivistic societies, the tension between the pursuit of independence and personal identity and the commitment to group undertaking may be less evident than in Western cultures. This argument appears to be consistent with the findings that adolescents in Arabic, Chinese, Indonesian, Israeli kibbutz, and Latino societies and the former Soviet Union maintain high group affiliations (Azmitia et al. 2006, French et al. 2005a, Kiesner et al. 2003, Sharabany 2006). More important, in these cultures, there are often a strong requirement of loyalty and commitment to the group and great pressure on group members to conform to group norms. Children are expected and encouraged to identify with the group (Sharabany 2006). It is likely that collectivistic cultural values may reinforce and facilitate the regulatory effect of the peer group on children's behavior and development (e.g., Azmitia & Cooper 2004; Chen et al. 2003b, 2006b).

Dyadic Relationships

Much of the literature on dyadic relationships with friends has focused on the qualities of these relationships and the functional roles that they serve. Most relevant to the present discussion is the provision of enhancement of self-worth, instrumental assistance, and intimacy.

Enhancement of self-worth. A major socialization goal, particularly for children in Western cultures (Tietjen 1989), is to develop confidence and positive views about themselves, and the support of friends may be an important mechanism to accomplish this goal (Rubin et al. 2006a, Sullivan 1953). The role of friendship in promoting self-worth may be less salient in many non-Western cultures, where the development of the self is not considered a major developmental task. This has been supported by findings from qualitative and quantitative studies that Chinese (e.g., Chen et al. 2004b, Cho 2005) and Indonesian (French et al. 2005a) children and children with an Arab and Caribbean background (Dayan et al. 2001) often do not report the enhancement of self-worth as an important function of friendship.

Instrumental assistance. Mutual assistance is likely an important aspect of most friendships (Hartup 1992, Hays 1988), although such assistance among European American children may focus more on advice giving and cognitive support than on providing tangible resources (French et al. 2005a). Instrumental aid appears to be particularly important for friendships of children in many group-oriented cultures (Smart 1999, Tietjen 1989). Way (2006) found that sharing of money and protecting friends from harm were salient aspects of the friendships of low-income black and Hispanic adolescents in the United States, which appears consistent with suggestions that social relationships serve a more utilitarian function in societies or communities where relying on others for basic needs is essential (Guthrie 2006, Kagitcibasi 2005). Instrumental assistance has been documented to be a highly salient feature of friendships in some Asian nations, such as China (Chen et al. 2004b), Indonesia (French et al. 2005a), South Korea (French et al. 2006a), and the Philippines (Hollnsteiner 1979), and in Latino societies, such as Cuba (Gonzalez et al. 2004) and Costa Rica (DeRosier & Kupersmidt 1991). In these societies, instrumental assistance may also be reflected in broad nonmaterial areas such as helping others solve problems, learn skills, and develop socially acceptable behaviors (Sun 1995). For example, a theme that has emerged from the interviews with Chinese adolescents in mainland China, Taiwan, and the United States is the high appreciation of mutual assistance of friends in learning and school achievement (Chen et al. 2004b, Sun 1995, Way 2006).

Intimacy. Conceptualizing and measuring friendship intimacy across cultures is complex. Although most researchers focus on self-disclosure, such as sharing secrets, intimacy is closely associated with some other constructs, such as sensitivity, mutual understanding, exclusivity, attachment, emotional closeness, and trust (Sharabany 2006). The extent to which these different aspects of intimacy are emphasized likely differs across cultures. As a result, intimacy may result from different underlying processes (e.g., spontaneous self-disclosure versus mutual understanding), making it difficult to interpret the results of cross-cultural studies.

There are two conflicting arguments about culture and friendship intimacy. On the one hand, Triandis et al. (1988) argue that the friendships of persons in collectivistic cultures tend to be more intimate and more exclusive than the friendships of those in individualistic cultures. Sharabany (2006), on the other hand, suggests that in at least certain collectivistic societies, friendships are characterized as low in intimacy because of the availability of other sources of emotional support, reduced privacy inherent in collectivistic lifestyles, and the potential threat that exclusive friend dyad may pose to the cohesiveness of the larger group. There is empirical evidence supporting each of these positions.

Consistent with the Triandis et al. (1988) study, friendships in South Korean children and adolescents are often described as highly intimate (French et al. 2006a, Shwalb et al. 2007). The degree of intimacy, mutual receptiveness, and harmonious communication within these relationships is expressed by an ideal in which personal autonomy becomes secondary to the importance of maintaining a shared sense of identity (Shwalb et al. 2007). In a series of studies with Korean children, adolescents, and college students, French et al. (2006a,b) found that high exclusivity and strong boundaries existed such that interactions typically occurred in small groups of close friends that did not include non-friends. Friendships among Japanese youth also appear to be very close; friendships are established early in life and remain close throughout adulthood (Gudukunst & Nishida 1994). Within the United States, it has been found that Latino and black adolescents perceive their friendships as more intimate and close than do adolescents in European American and other cultural groups (Gonzalez & Schneider 2004, Way et al. 2006). These results appear to be consistent with the argument of Triandis et al. (1988).

Support for Sharabany's (2006) argument comes mainly from studies in Indonesian, rural Arab, and Israeli kibbutz cultures. Youths in these cultures have reported lower intimacy than their North America counterparts reported (e.g., French 2005a, 2006a; Sharabany 2006). Anthropological findings suggest that compared with American students, Indonesian students are less likely to develop close friendships because they are encouraged to focus on integration into general peer networks and the larger community (Jay 1969). Similarly, in a study concerning parental values of friendship, Beit-Hallahmi et al. (1982) found that kibbutz adults preferred a large number of friends with superficial or "shallow" connections to a few close, in-depth friends.

French and his colleagues (French et al. 2005a, 2006a) argue that there may be multiple prototypes of peer experience, each of which provides for interaction with age-mates that facilitates the development of competence. The nature of this peer experience may depend on complex social, historical, and ecological factors. For example, the Confucian value on trust and obligation between friends may be associated with the salience of loyalty and exclusivity in friendships in Korea and other countries that have been influenced by this tradition (French et al. 2006a). It is also possible that relatively intimate social relationships in Latino youths are related to the cultural encouragement of emotional expressivity, especially in conveying warmth and affection in social interactions (Argyle et al. 1986, Valdivia et al. 2005).

Peer Conflict

Effective management of conflict is essential for the development and maintenance of social relationships, particularly friendships (de Waal 1996). It is also important to manage interpersonal conflicts within communities because conflicts, if uncontrolled, can disrupt community organizations (Lambert 1971). In numerous studies in the United States, it has been shown that success in managing potential or overt conflict episodes is related to other indexes of competence, including sociometric status, aggression, emotional control, and social adjustment (e.g., Murphy & Eisenberg 2002, Putallaz & Sheppard 1990).

Considerable research, much of which has been conducted with adults, has documented cultural differences in the manner in which conflicts are addressed (e.g., Markus & Linn 1999). Researchers have found that individuals across cultures differ in their tolerance of overt conflict, methods of resolution, and mechanisms by which relationships are restored following conflict episodes (Bond 2004, Fry 2000). Markus & Linn (1999) suggest that persons with an independent worldview tend to see conflicts as impingements on individual freedom or action and regard assertive engagement and attempts to find correct solutions as the appropriate response. In contrast, persons with an interdependent worldview typically view conflicts as relationship issues and see it as more important to minimize the disturbance and maintain valued relationships than to find solutions to resolve it. Similarly, Rothbaum et al. (2000) and Shantz & Hobart (1989) have discussed conflicts as struggles between personal interests, assertiveness, and expressiveness, on the one hand, and group well-being and conformity to the expectations of others, on the other.

The study of culture and conflict in children has yielded evidence consistent with the argument that persons in individualistic cultures are more likely than are those in more group-oriented cultures to emphasize individual goals and to use direct and assertive strategies to solve conflicts. For example, Medina et al. (2001) found that preschool children in the Netherlands more often than children in Andalusia, a more collectivistic society, focused on maintaining individual perspectives and displayed assertiveness and imposition of personal views during conflicts. Differences also emerged in the causes and resolutions of conflicts. Dutch children's conflicts often focused on object possession or control of personal space, whereas those of Andalusian children focused on the organization of social activities. Moreover, whereas conflicts in Dutch children tended to result in rupture of activities or interactions, Andalusian children tended to resolve conflicts and reach agreement by compromise or submission. Schneider et al. (2000) also found that children in Central Italy were more efficient than Canadian children were in avoiding and resolving conflicts between friends, mainly by maintaining respect for rules. Benjamin et al. (2001) found that children in Taiwan reported significantly less conflict and greater agreement in their friendships than did children in Canada. Similar findings, obtained by French et al. (2005b), indicated that Indonesian children more frequently reported exhibiting disengagement and submission during conflict than did U.S. children. Finally, Gabrielidis et al. (1997) found that Mexican youths reported using concessions and shared principles to resolve interpersonal conflicts to a greater extent than did U.S. youths.

Much of the research on culture and conflict has been descriptive, focusing on the incidence, processes, and resolutions of conflict (e.g., Butovskaya et al. 2000). As a rare exception, French et al. (2005b) assessed relations between disengagement in conflict and indexes of social adjustment in Indonesian and U.S. children. Whereas disengagement was positively associated with teacher ratings of peer preference and negatively asso-

ciated with social problems for Indonesian children, the opposite pattern emerged for U.S. children. The results suggest that disengagement may have different meanings in these two cultures—in the U.S. reflecting unassertiveness, and in Indonesia reflecting a culturally valued approach based on self-control to addressing conflict by avoiding direct confrontation.

In summary, cultural values of individual assertiveness/initiative and conformity to social expectations are reflected in major aspects of children's peer relationships, including peer group involvement, functions of friendships, and conflict management strategies. Culture serves to guide children to enter the peer world and to pursue personal or group goals, to construct friendships that fulfill various functional roles in development (e.g., enhancing self-worth, assistance in social and school performance), and to develop appropriate strategies (e.g., assertive engagement, submission, or withdrawal) to resolve conflicts in peer interactions. Further research is needed on how cultural context affects the developmental significance of children's experiences in peer relationships.

THE IMPACT OF SOCIAL AND CULTURAL CHANGES ON CHILDREN'S SOCIAL COMPETENCE

According to social ecological theory (Bronfenbrenner & Morris 1998, Elder & Shanahan 2006), human lives carry the imprint of their social worlds, which are themselves subject to continuous historical change. The impact of macro-level societal changes on human development has been demonstrated by the considerable implications of the Great Depression in the 1930s and by more recent employment policy reform in the United States for family organization, parenting, and child behavior (Elder 1974, Yoshikawa & Hsueh 2001).

Social and cultural changes may have a significant influence on parental socialization goals. Kagitcibasi & Ataca (2005) found that the developmental goals of Turkish parents changed over the past three decades as a function of the transformation of the society. With urbanization and socioeconomic development, material dependence within the family decreased, which has been associated with more-positive parental perceptions of the child's autonomy. Turkish parents in 2003, particularly those in urban families with a high socioeconomic status, valued autonomy more than did those in 1975, and parents in 2003 were more likely than parents in 1975 to appreciate the "psychological value of the child" (e.g., pleasure watching children grow, fun to have young children around, to have someone to love and care for).

Societal changes may affect the development of various aspects of social competence, including self-control and social initiative. For example, the urbanization of traditional rural societies (e.g., Graves & Graves 1983, Madsen & Lancy 1981, Nadler et al. 1979) seems to have resulted in children having fewer interactions with their extended kin group and participating to a lesser extent in family labor and household work, and a decrease in children's cooperative and obedient behaviors. The reduced opportunities to learn and practice nurturant and responsible skills by performing subsistence tasks, such as caring for younger siblings, may be a main contributing factor in children's behavioral changes. Kagitcibasi (2005) argued, however, that social and economic changes toward urbanization may not necessarily weaken interpersonal socioemotional support and psychological interdependence in group-oriented societies. Although urban lifestyles and increased affluence with modernization may allow for greater individual autonomy, they may have limited impact on the enduring influence of the culture of relatedness.

The impact of social and cultural changes on child and adolescent social initiative is documented in recent studies in Eastern European nations (Flanagan 2000, Silbereisen 2000). Silbereisen (2000), for example, found that the dramatic societal change after the fall of the Berlin Wall transformed the life course of adolescents, including their patterns of individual planning and decision-making. The transition to adulthood and becoming financially self-supportive among Eastern German young people occurred significantly later after the German unification than it did in the preunification era.

The dramatic change in China since the 1980s from a command economy to a market economy has affected children's shy-inhibited behavior and its functional meanings in social interactions and adjustment. Chen et al. (2005) examined relations between shyness-inhibition and adjustment in Chinese children in three urban cohorts (1990, 1998, and 2002), which represented different phases of the massive social and economic reform in China. The results indicated that the relations differed significantly across the cohorts. Specifically, shyness was perceived positively by peers and adults and was associated with peer acceptance, leadership, and school adjustment in the 1990 cohort. In contrast, shyness was associated with peer rejection, school problems, and depression in the 2002 cohort. The relations between shyness and peer relationships and adjustment variables were either nonsignificant or mixed in the 1998 cohort. Chen et al. (2005) argued that the extensive change toward the market economy and the introduction of some individualistic values might have led to the decline in the adaptive value of shy-inhibited behavior. In the new competitive environment, shy-inhibited behavior that may impede self-expression and active exploration is no longer regarded as adaptive and competent (Chang 2003, Chang et al. 2005, Hart et al. 2000). Interestingly, Chen et al. (2005) found that shyness was positively associated with both peer acceptance and peer rejection in the 1998 cohort, indicating mixed attitudes of peers toward shy-inhibited children, which may reflect the cultural conflict between imported Western values of social initiative and autonomy and traditional Chinese values of self-control.

Finally, the increased value on social initiative in China may also be reflected in the function of social relationships. Tamis-LeMonda et al. (2007) have noticed that the traditional utilitarian and instrumental type of relationship, *Guan Xi*, is losing significance in the society as China moves to a market economy and stronger legal infrastructure. Parents and children increasingly appreciate the function of friendship and other relationships in fulfilling individual psychoemotional needs.

In short, the global shift toward urbanization and modernization may have produced rapid changes in the values on the basic dimensions of social competence, such as social initiative and self-control, and specific social behaviors, such as shyness. These changes have considerable implications for children's social and psychological adjustment.

CONCLUSIONS AND FUTURE DIRECTIONS

The findings from a variety of studies indicate the importance of cultural context for the development of social competence. According to the contextual-developmental perspective (Chen et al. 2006b), cultural influence on children's social competence is a dynamic process, which is reflected at three levels: the changing cultural context, the developing child, and the mediating role of social interaction between the child and peers, parents, and others. To understand the nature of children's social competence, it is important to examine how the child's characteristics and socialization practices contribute to the social interaction processes, which in turn shape developmental outcomes in cultural context.

In this review, we focus on different values that self- and group-oriented cultures place on two main dimensions of social competence—social initiative and behavioral control. Whereas cross-cultural research indicates that these cultural values may be associated with children's social behaviors and relationships, it is important to note that the political, economic, and cultural exchanges and interactions may lead to the merging and coexistence of diverse value systems (Kagitcibasi 2005, Tamis-LeMonda et al. 2007). Moreover, within-culture variations are likely to be remarkably increased during this process. Many of the studies we reviewed have indicated that subcultures related to social class, religion, and ethnicity within a society may influence the development of social competence (e.g., Cole et al. 2006, Graves & Graves 1983, Nucci et al. 1996). The influences associated with social class are likely to be substantial across cultures (Kohn & Schooler 1983) and may be stronger in societies in which the gaps between different social classes are large and there are relatively minimal opportunities for social mobility. Researchers should pay great attention to these within-culture factors in the future.

With globalization, Western values may have a significant impact on the views of children and adults on social competence in other societies. However, Western values are unlikely to be adopted completely in their original forms, but instead may be integrated with the cultural traditions in the society. It will be interesting to investigate how social competence developed on the basis of integrated and sophisticated value systems helps children adapt and succeed in the changing global community.

The cultural influence on children needs to be understood from a developmental perspective. Parents may adjust their socialization goals and practices as children develop (Rothbaum & Trommsdorff 2006, Tamis-LeMonda et al. 2007). Parents may also attempt to maintain a balance according to the child's developmental level in providing opportunities and constraints when helping children learn different cultural values. At the same time, children's personal characteristics, such as compliance and defiance, become more noticeable with age in affecting parental socialization efforts and the developmental processes.

The increasingly active role of the child is also reflected in peer interactions, including the choices of playmates, settings, and activities, and the reactions to peer influence (Edwards et al. 2006). From middle childhood, peer relationships provide a major social milieu in which children negotiate with each other to adopt existing cultural standards and values and create their own peer cultures.

How peer interaction processes, particularly mutual evaluations and responses in group activities, are involved in transmitting and constructing cultures and in regulating children's social functioning and development need to be examined thoroughly in future research.

SUMMARY POINTS

1. Different societies place different values on social initiative and norm-based behavioral control in children and adolescents, which affect the interpretation and evaluation of specific aspects of social functioning including sociability, shyness-inhibition, cooperation-compliance, and aggression-defiance.

2. The prevalence, meanings, and developmental patterns of children's social functioning and peer relationships are determined to a large extent by culturally guided peers and adults' attitudes and social-evaluative processes in the society.

3. Cultural norms and values are reflected in major aspects of peer relationships including peer group involvement, functions of friendships, and peer conflict management strategies.

4. Macro-level social, economic, and cultural changes may have a significant impact on socialization goals and practices and the development of social competence.

5. Future research on children's social competence should further explore the dynamic processes among the changing cultural context, the developing child, and the mediating role of social interaction.

LITERATURE CITED

Argyle M, Henderson M, Bond M, Iizuka Y, Contarello A. 1986. Cross-cultural variations in relationship rules. *Int. J. Psychol.* 21:287–315

Ariel S, Sever I. 1980. Play in the desert and play in the town: on play activities of Bedouin Arab children. In *Play and Culture*, ed. HB Schwartzman, pp. 164–75. West Point, NY: Leisure Press

Asendorpf J. 1990. Beyond social withdrawal: shyness, unsociability and peer avoidance. *Hum. Dev.* 33:250–59

Asendorpf J. 1991. Development of inhibited children's coping with unfamiliarity. *Child Dev.* 62:1460–74

Asher S, Parkhurst JT, Hymel S, Williams GA. 1990. Peer rejection and loneliness in childhood. In *Peer Rejection in Childhood*, ed. SR Asher, JD Coie, pp. 253–73. New York: Cambridge Univ. Press

Azmitia M, Ittel A, Brenk C. 2006. Latino-heritage adolescents' friendship. See Chen et al. 2006a, pp. 426–51

Azmitia M, Cooper CR. 2004. Good or bad? Peer influences on Latino and European American adolescents' pathways through school. *J. Educ. Students Placed Risk* 6:45–71

Beit-Hallahmi B, Sharabany R, Dana-Engelstein H, Rabin AI, Regev E. 1982. Patterns of interpersonal attachment: sociability, friendship and marriage. In *Twenty Years Later: Kibbutz Children Grow Up*, ed. AI Rabin, B Beit-Hallahmi, pp. 119–44. New York: Springer

Benjamin WJ, Schneider BH, Greenman PS, Hum M. 2001. Conflict and childhood friendship in Taiwan and Canada. *Can. J. Behav. Sci.* 33:203–11

Bergeron N, Schneider BH. 2005. Explaining cross-national differences in peer-directed aggression: a quantitative synthesis. *Aggress. Behav.* 31:116–37

Bond MH. 2004. Culture and aggression—from context to coercion. *Personal. Soc. Psychol. Rev.* 8:62–78

Bronfenbrenner U, Morris PA. 1998. The ecology of developmental processes. In *Handbook of Child Psychology: Vol 1. Theoretical Models of Human Development*, ed. RM Lerner, pp. 993–1028. New York: Wiley

Brown BB. 1990. Peer groups and peer cultures. In *At the Threshold: The Developing Adolescent*, ed. SS Feldman, GR Elliott, pp. 171–96. Cambridge, MA: Harvard Univ. Press

Buhrmester D, Furman W, Wittenberg MT, Reis HT. 1988. Five domains of interpersonal competence in peer relationships. *J. Personal. Soc. Psychol.* 55:991–1008

Butovskaya M, Verbeek P, Ljungberg T, Lunardini A. 2000. A multicultural view of peacemaking among young children. In *Natural Conflict Resolution*, ed. F Aureli, FBM de Waal, pp. 243–58. Berkeley, CA: Univ. Calif. Press

Cairns RB, Cairns BD, Neckerman HJ, Gest S, Gariepy JL. 1988. Social networks and aggressive behavior: peer support or peer rejection? *Dev. Psychol.* 24:815–23

Caspi A, Elder GH Jr, Bem DJ. 1988. Moving away from the world: life-course patterns of shy children. *Dev. Psychol.* 24:824–31

Chang L. 2003. Variable effects of children's aggression, social withdrawal, and prosocial leadership as functions of teacher beliefs and behaviors. *Child Dev.* 74:538–48

Chang L, Lei L, Li KK, Liu H, Guo B, et al. 2005. Peer acceptance and self-perceptions of verbal and behavioural aggression and withdrawal. *Int. J. Behav. Dev.* 29:49–57

Chao RK. 1994. Beyond parental control and authoritarian parenting style: understanding Chinese parenting through the cultural notion of training. *Child Dev.* 65:1111–19

Chen X, Cen G, Li D, He Y. 2005. Social functioning and adjustment in Chinese children: the imprint of historical time. *Child Dev.* 76:182–95

Chen X, Chang L, He Y. 2003b. The peer group as a context: mediating and moderating effects on the relations between academic achievement and social functioning in Chinese children. *Child Dev.* 74:710–27

Chen X, DeSouza A, Chen H, Wang L. 2006d. Reticent behavior and experiences in peer interactions in Canadian and Chinese children. *Dev. Psychol.* 42:656–65

Chen X, French D, Schneider B, eds. 2006a. *Peer Relationships in Cultural Context*. New York: Cambridge Univ. Press

Chen X, French D, Schneider B. 2006b. Culture and peer relationships. See Chen et al. 2006a, pp. 3–20

Chen X, Hastings P, Rubin KH, Chen H, Cen G, Stewart SL. 1998. Childrearing attitudes and behavioral inhibition in Chinese and Canadian toddlers: a cross-cultural study. *Dev. Psychol.* 34:677–86

Chen X, He Y, De Oliveira AM, Lo Coco A, Zappulla C, et al. 2004a. Loneliness and social adaptation in Brazilian, Canadian, Chinese and Italian children. *J. Child Psychol. Psychiatry* 45:1373–84

Chen X, Kaspar V, Zhang Y, Wang L, Zheng S. 2004b. Peer relationships among Chinese and North American boys: a cross-cultural perspective. In *Adolescent Boys in Context*, ed. N Way, J Chu, pp. 197–218. New York: N.Y. Univ. Press

Chen X, Li D, Li Z, Li B, Liu M. 2000. Sociable and prosocial dimensions of social competence in Chinese children: common and unique contributions to social, academic and psychological adjustment. *Dev. Psychol.* 36:302–14

Identifies cross-cultural differences in childhood behavioral inhibition and its associations with parental childrearing attitudes.

Chen X, Dong Q, Zhou H. 1997. Authoritative and authoritarian parenting practices and social and school adjustment in Chinese children. *Int. J. Behav. Dev.* 20:855–73

Chen X, Liu M, Rubin KH, Cen G, Gao X, Li D. 2002. Sociability and prosocial orientation as predictors of youth adjustment: a seven-year longitudinal study in a Chinese sample. *Int. J. Behav. Dev.* 26:128–36

Chen X, Rubin KH, Li B. 1995. Depressed mood in Chinese children: relations with school performance and family environment. *J. Consult. Clin. Psychol.* 63:938–47

Chen X, Rubin KH, Li B, Li Z. 1999. Adolescent outcomes of social functioning in Chinese children. *Int. J. Behav. Dev.* 23:199–223

Chen X, Rubin KH, Liu M, Chen H, Wang L, et al. 2003a. Compliance in Chinese and Canadian toddlers. *Int. J. Behav. Dev.* 27:428–36

Chen X, Rubin KH, Sun Y. 1992. Social reputation and peer relationships in Chinese and Canadian children: a cross-cultural study. *Child Dev.* 63:1336–43

Chen X, Wang Z. 2006. *Social and cultural changes and the development of social functioning.* Presented at Bienn. Meet. Int. Soc. Study Behav. Dev., 19th, Melbourne, Australia

Chen X, Wang L, DeSouza A. 2006c. Temperament and socio-emotional functioning in Chinese and North American children. See Chen et al. 2006a, pp. 123–47

Cho GE, Sandel TL, Miller PJ, Wang S. 2005. What do grandmothers think about self-esteem? American and Taiwanese folk theories revisited. *Soc. Dev.* 14:701–21

Cole M. 1996. *Cultural Psychology.* Cambridge, MA: Harvard Univ. Press

Cole PM, Bruschi C, Tamang BL. 2002. Cultural differences in children's emotional reactions to difficult situations. *Child Dev.* 73:983–96

Examines how Brahman and Tamang adults differed in socializing children's anger, conflict, and aggressive behaviors in social situations.

Cole PM, Tamang BL, Shrestha S. 2006. Cultural variations in the socialization of young children's anger and shame. *Child Dev.* 77:1237–51

Coplan RJ, Prakash K, O'Neil K, Armer M. 2004. Do you "want" to play? Distinguishing between conflicted-shyness and social disinterest in early childhood. *Dev. Psychol.* 40:244–58

Corsaro WA, Nelson E. 2003. Children's collective activities and peer culture in early literacy in American and Italian preschools. *Sociol. Educ.* 76:209–27

Cummings EM, Zahn-Waxler C, Radke-Yarrow M. 1981. Young children's responses to expressions of anger and affection by others in the family. *Child Dev.* 52:1274–82

Dayan J, Doyle AB, Markiewicz D. 2001. Social support networks and self-esteem of idiocentric and allocentric children and adolescents. *J. Soc. Pers. Relat.* 18:767–84

de Guzman MRT, Edwards CP, Carlo G. 2005. Prosocial behaviors in context: a study of the Gikuyu children of Ngecha, Kenya. *Appl. Dev. Psychol.* 26:542–58

de Waal FBM. 1996. Conflict as negotiation. In *Great Ape Societies*, ed. WC McGrew, LF Marchant, T Nishida, pp. 159–72. New York: Cambridge Univ. Press

DeRosier ME, Kupersmidt JB. 1991. Costa Rican children's perceptions of their social networks. *Dev. Psychol.* 27:656–62

Dodge KA, Coie JD, Lynam D. 2006. Aggression and antisocial behavior in youth. In *Handbook of Child Psychology: Vol. 3. Social, Emotional, and Personality Development*, ed. N Eisenberg, pp. 719–88. New York: Wiley

Comprehensively discusses the active role of the child in social development and peer interaction through self-socialization.

Edwards CP. 2000. Children's play in cross-cultural perspective: a new look at the Six Culture Study. *Cross-Cult. Res.* 34:318–38

Edwards CP, Guzman MRT, Brown J, Kumru A. 2006. Children's social behaviors and peer interactions in diverse cultures. See Chen et al. 2006a, pp. 23–51

Eisenberg N, Fabes RA. 1992. Emotion, regulation, and the development of social competence. In *Review of Personality and Social Psychology: Vol. 14. Emotion and Social Behavior*, ed. MS Clark, pp. 119–50. Newbury Park, CA: Sage

Eisenberg N, Fabes RA, Spinrad TL. 2006a. Prosocial development. In *Handbook of Child Psychology: Vol. 3. Social, Emotional, and Personality Development*, ed. N Eisenberg, pp. 646–718. New York: Wiley

Eisenberg N, Liew J, Pidada S. 2004. The longitudinal relations of regulation and emotionality to quality of Indonesian children's socioemotional functioning. *Dev. Psychol.* 40:805–12

Eisenberg N, Pidada S, Liew J. 2001. The relations of regulation and negative emotionality to Indonesian children's social functioning. *Child Dev.* 72:1747–63

Eisenberg N, Zhou Q, Liew J, Champion C, Pidada S. 2006b. Emotion, emotion-related regulation, and social functioning. See Chen et al. 2006a, pp. 170–97

Elder GH Jr. 1974. *Children of the Great Depression*. Chicago, IL: Univ. Chicago Press

Elder GH Jr, Shanahan MJ. 2006. The life course and human development. In *Handbook of Child Psychology: Vol 1. Theoretical Models of Human Development*, ed. RM Lerner, pp. 665–715. New York: Wiley

Farver JM, Howes C. 1988. Cross-cultural differences in social interaction: a comparison of American and Indonesian children. *J. Cross-Cult. Psychol.* 19:203–15

Farver JM, Kim YK, Lee Y. 1995. Cultural differences in Korean- and Anglo-American preschoolers' social interaction and play behaviors. *Child Dev.* 66:1088–99

Farver JM, Shin YL. 1997. Social pretend play in Korea- and Anglo-American preschoolers. *Child Dev.* 68:544–56

Flanagan CA. 2000. Social change and the "social contract" in adolescent development. In *Negotiating Adolescence in Times of Social Change*, ed. LJ Crockett, RK Silbereisen, pp. 191–98. New York: Cambridge Univ. Press

Fox HA, Henderson HA, Marshall PJ, Nichols KE, Ghera MM. 2005. Behavioral inhibition: linking biology and behavior within a developmental framework. *Annu. Rev. Psychol.* 56:235–62

Freedman DG, Freedman M. 1969. Behavioral differences between Chinese-American and American newborns. *Nature* 224:1227

French DC, Bae A, Pidada S, Lee O. 2006b. Friendships of Indonesian, S. Korean and U.S. college students. *Pers. Relat.* 13:69–81

French DC, Jansen EA, Riansari M, Setiono K. 2003. Friendships of Indonesian children: adjustment of children who differ in friendship presence and similarity between mutual friends. *Soc. Dev.* 12:605–21

French DC, Pidada S, Denoma J, McDonald K, Lawton A. 2005b. Reported peer conflicts of children in the United Status and Indonesia. *Soc. Dev.* 14:458–72

French DC, Lee O, Pidada S. 2006a. Friendships of Indonesian, S. Korean and United States youth: exclusivity, intimacy, enhancement of worth, and conflict. See Chen et al. 2006a, pp. 379–402

French DC, Pidada S, Victor A. 2005a. Friendships of Indonesian and United States youth. *Int. J. Behav. Dev.* 29:304–13

Fry DP. 2000. Conflict management in cross-cultural perspective. In *Natural Conflict Resolution*, ed. F Aureli, FBM de Waal, pp. 334–51. Berkeley, CA: Univ. Calif. Press

Furman W, Buhrmester D. 1985. Age and sex differences in perceptions of networks of social relationships. *Child Dev.* 63:103–15

Gabrielidis C, Ybarra O, Villareal L. 1997. Preferred styles of conflict resolution: Mexico and the United States. *J. Cross-Cult. Psychol.* 28:661–77

Gaskins S. 2000. Children's daily activities in a Mayan village: a culturally grounded description. *J. Cross-Cult. Res.* 34:375–89

Gaskin S. 2006. The cultural organization of Yucatec Mayan children's social interactions. See Chen et al. 2006a, pp. 283–309

Demonstrates that cultural practices may affect children's social behaviors and peer interaction styles.

Reveals cultural variations in the quality and function of children's and adolescents' friendship, such as exclusivity and intimacy.

Gest SD, Graham-Bermann SA, Hartup WW. 2001. Peer experience: common and unique features of number of friendships, social network centrality, and sociometric status. *Soc. Dev.* 10:23–40

Gong Y. 1984. Use of the Eysenck Personality Questionnaire in China. *Personal. Individ. Differ.* 5:431–38

Gonzalez Y, Moreno DS, Schneider BH. 2004. Friendship expectations of early adolescents in Cuba and Canada. *J. Cross-Cult. Psychol.* 35:436–45

Graves NB, Graves TD. 1983. The cultural context of prosocial development: an ecological model. In *The Nature of Prosocial Development*, ed. DL Bridgeman, pp. 795–824. San Diego, CA: Academic

Greenfield PM, Suzuki LK, Rothstein-Fisch C. 2006. Cultural pathways through human development. In *Handbook of Child Psychology: Vol. 4. Child Psychology in Practice*, ed. KA Renninger, IE Sigel, pp. 655–99. New York: Wiley

Gudukunst W, Nishida T. 1994. *Bridging Japanese/North American Differences*. Thousand Oaks, CA: Sage

Guthrie D. 2006. *China and Globalization: The Social, Economic, and Political Transformation of Chinese Society*. New York: Routledge

Hart CH, Yang C, Nelson LJ, Robinson CC, Olson JA, et al. 2000. Peer acceptance in early childhood and subtypes of socially withdrawn behaviour in China, Russia and the United States. *Int. J. Behav. Dev.* 24:73–81

Hartup WW. 1992. Friendships and their developmental significance. In *Childhood Social Development*, ed. H McGurk, pp. 175–205. Grove, UK: Erlbaum

Hays RB. 1988. Friendship. In *Handbook of Personal Relationships*, ed. SW Duck, pp. 391–408. New York: Wiley

Hinde RA. 1987. *Individuals, Relationships and Culture*. Cambridge, UK: Cambridge Univ. Press

Ho DYF. 1986. Chinese pattern of socialization: a critical review. In *The Psychology of the Chinese People*, ed. MH Bond, pp. 1–37. New York: Oxford Univ. Press

Hollnsteiner MR. 1979. Reciprocity as a Filipino in value. In *Culture and the Filipino*, ed. MR Hollnsteiner, pp. 38–43. Quezon City, Phillippines: Atteneo de Manila Univ.

Howes C. 1992. *The Collaborative Construction of Pretend*. Albany, NY: SUNY Press

Hoza B, Molina BG, Bukowski WM, Sippola LK. 1995. Peer variables as predictors of later childhood adjustment. *Dev. Psychopathol.* 7:787–802

Huesmann LR, Guerra NG. 1997. Children's normative beliefs about aggression and aggressive behavior. *J. Personal. Soc. Psychol.* 72:408–19

Jay RR. 1969. *Javanese Villagers: Social Relations in Rural Modjokuto*. Cambridge, MA: MIT Press

Kagan J, Kearsley RB, Zelazo PR. 1978. *Infancy: Its Place in Human Development*. Cambridge, MA: Harvard Univ. Press

Kagan S, Knight GP. 1981. Social motives among Anglo-American and Mexican-American children: experimental and projective measures. *J. Res. Personal.* 15:93–106

Kagan S, Madsen MC. 1972. Experimental analyses of cooperation and competition of Anglo-American and Mexican-American children. *Dev. Psychol.* 6:49–59

Keller H, Yovsi R, Borke J, Kartner J, Jensen H, Papaligoura Z. 2004. Developmental consequences of early parenting experiences: self-recognition and self-regulation in three cultural communities. *Child Dev.* 75:1745–60

Kerr M, Lambert WW, Bem DJ. 1996. Life course sequelae of childhood shyness in Sweden: comparison with the United States. *Dev. Psychol.* 32:1100–5

Argues that social interactions and relationships play an important role in cultural influence on individual behaviors and development.

Kessen W. 1975. *Childhood in China.* New Haven, CT: Yale Univ. Press

Kagitcibasi C. 2005. Autonomy and relatedness in cultural context: implications for self and family. *J. Cross-Cult. Psychol.* 36:403–22

Kagitcibasi C, Ataca B. 2005. Value of children and family change: a three-decade portrait from Turkey. *Appl. Psychol.: An. Int. Rev.* 54:317–37

Kiesner J, Poulin F, Nicotra E. 2003. Peer relations across contexts: individual-network homophily and network inclusion in and after school. *Child Dev.* 74:1328–43

Knight GP, Kagan S. 1977. Acculturation of prosocial and competitive behaviors among second- and third-generation Mexican-American children. *J. Cross-Cult. Psychol.* 8:273–84

Kochanska G, Aksan N. 1995. Mother-child mutually positive affect, the quality of child compliance to requests and prohibitions, and maternal control as correlates of early internalization. *Child Dev.* 66:236–54

Kohn ML, Schooler C. 1983. *Work and Personality: An Inquiry into the Impact of Social Stratification.* Norwood, NJ: Ablex

Ladd G. 2005. *Children's Peer Relations and Social Competence: A Century of Progress. Current Perspectives in Psychology.* New Haven, CT: Yale Univ. Press

Lambert WW. 1971. Cross-cultural backgrounds to personality development and the socialization of aggression: findings from the Six Cultures Study. In *Comparative Perspectives on Social Psychology,* ed. WW Lambert, R Weisbrod, pp. 49–61. Boston, MA: Little, Brown

Larson RW, Verma S. 1999. How children and adolescents spend time across the world: work, play, and developmental opportunities. *Psychol. Bull.* 125:701–36

Lee MR, Okazaki S, Yoo HC. 2006. Frequency and intensity of social anxiety in Asian Americans and European Americans. *Cult. Divers. Ethnic Minority Psychol.* 12:291–305

Liang S. 1987. *The Outline of Chinese Culture.* Shanghai, China: Xue Lin

Maccoby EE. 1998. *The Two Sexes: Growing Up Apart, Coming Together.* Cambridge, MA: Harvard Univ. Press

Maccoby EE, Martin CN. 1983. Socialization in the context of the family: parent-child interaction. In *Handbook of Child Psychology. Vol. 4. Socialization, Personality and Social Development,* ed. EM Hetherington, pp. 1–102. New York: Wiley

Madsen MC, Lancy DF. 1981. Cooperative and competitive behavior: experiments related to ethnic identity and urbanization in Papua New Guinea. *J. Cross-Cult. Psychol.* 12:389–408

Markus HR, Lin LR. 1999. Conflictways: cultural diversity in the meanings and practices of conflict. In *Cultural Divides: Understanding and Overcoming Group Conflict,* ed. DA Prentice, DT Miller, pp. 302–33. New York: Russell Sage Found.

Mead GH. 1934. *Mind, Self, and Society.* Chicago: Univ. Chicago Press

Medina JAM, Lozano VM, Goudena PP. 2001. Conflict management in preschoolers: a cross-cultural perspective. *Int. J. Early Years Educ.* 9:153–60

Miller JG. 1994. Cultural diversity in the morality of caring: individually oriented versus duty-based interpersonal moral codes. *Cross-Cult. Res.* 28:3–39

Miller JG, Bersoff DM, Harwood RL. 1990. Perceptions of social responsibilities in India and in the United States: Moral imperatives or personal decisions? *J. Personal. Soc. Psychol.* 58:33–47

Munroe RL, Hulefeld R, Rodgers JM, Tomeo DL, Yamazaki SK. 2000. Aggression among children in found cultures. *Cross-Cult. Res.* 34:3–25

Murphy BC, Eisenberg N. 2002. An integrative examination of peer conflict: children's reported goals, emotions, and behaviors. *Soc. Dev.* 11:534–57

Nadler A, Romek E, Shapira-Friedman A. 1979. Giving in the kibbutz: pro-social behavior of city and kibbutz children as affected by social responsibility and social pressure. *J. Cross-Cult. Psychol.* 10:57–72

Navon R, Ramsey PG. 1989. Possession and exchange of materials in Chinese and American preschools. *J. Res. Childhood Educ.* 4:18–29

Nelson DA, Nelson LJ, Hart CH, Yang C, Jin S. 2006. Parenting and peer-group behavior in cultural context. See Chen et al. 2006a, pp. 213–46

Nucci L, Camino C, Sapiro CM. 1996. Social class effects on Northeastern Brazilian children's conceptions of areas of personal choice and social regulation. *Child Dev.* 67:1223–42

Ogbu JU. 1981. Origins of human competence: a cultural-ecological perspective? *Child Dev.* 52:413–29

Orlick T, Zhou QY, Partington J. 1990. Co-operation and conflict within Chinese and Canadian kindergarten settings. *Can. J. Behav. Sci.* 22:20–25

Oyserman D, Coon HM, Kemmelmeier M. 2002. Rethinking individualism and collectivism: evaluation of theoretical assumptions and meta-analyses. *Psychol. Bull.* 128:3–72

Parmar P, Harkness S, Super CM. 2004. Asian and Euro-American parents' ethnotheories of play and learning: effects on preschool children's home routine and school behaviour. *Int. J. Behav. Dev.* 28:97–104

Putallaz M, Sheppard BH. 1990. Children's social status and orientations to limited resources. *Child Dev.* 61:2022–27

Rodkin PC, Farmer TW, Pearl R, van Acker R. 2000. Heterogeneity of popular boys: antisocial and prosocial configurations. *Dev. Psychol.* 36:14–24

Rogoff B. 2003. *The Cultural Nature of Human Development.* New York: Oxford Univ. Press

Rohner RP. 1986. *The Warmth Dimension: Foundation of Parental Acceptance-Rejection Theory.* Newbury Park, CA: Sage

Rothbart MK, Bates JE. 2006. Temperament. In *Handbook of Child Psychology: Vol. 3. Social, Emotional, and Personality Development*, ed. N Eisenberg, pp. 99–166. New York: Wiley

Rothbaum F, Pott M, Azuma H, Miyake K, Weisz J. 2000. The development of close relationships in Japan and the United States: paths of symbiotic harmony and generative tension. *Child Dev.* 71:1121–42

Rothbaum F, Trommsdorff G. 2006. Do roots and wings complement or oppose one another? The socialization of relatedness and autonomy in cultural context. In *Handbook of Socialization: Theory and Research*, ed. J Grusec, P Hastings, pp. 461–89. New York: Guilford

Rubin KH, Bukowski W, Parker JG. 2006a. Peer interactions, relationships, and groups. In *Handbook of Child Psychology: Vol 3. Social, Emotional, and Personality Development*, ed. N Eisenberg, pp. 571–645. New York: Wiley

Rubin KH, Burgess KB, Coplan RJ. 2002. Social withdrawal and shyness. In *Blackwell Handbook of Childhood Social Development*, ed. PK Smith, CH Hart, pp. 330–52. Malden, MA: Blackwell Sci.

Rubin KH, Hemphill SA, Chen X, Hastings P, Sanson A, et al. 2006b. A cross-cultural study of behavioral inhibition in toddlers: east-west-north-south. *Int. J. Behav. Dev.* 30:219–26

Rubin KH, Rose-Krasnor L. 1992. Interpersonal problem-solving and social competence in children. In *Handbook of Social Development: A Lifespan Perspective*, ed. VB van Hasselt, M Hersen, pp. 283–323. New York: Plenum

Russell A, Hart CH, Robinson CC, Olsen SF. 2003. Children's sociable and aggressive behavior with peers: a comparison of the US and Australia, and contributions of temperament and parenting styles. *Int. J. Behav. Dev.* 27:74–86

Schneider BH, Fonzi A, Tomada G, Tani F. 2000. A cross-national comparison of children's behavior with their friends in situations of potential conflict. *J. Cross-Cult. Psychol.* 31:256–66

Shantz CU, Hobart CJ. 1989. Social conflict and development: peers and siblings. In *Peer Relationships and Child Development*, ed. TJ Berndt, GW Ladd, pp 71–94. New York: Wiley

Argues that children's competence needs to be judged in cultural context.

Sharabany R. 2006. The cultural context of children and adolescents: peer relationships and intimate friendships among Arab and Jewish children in Israel. See Chen et al. 2006a, pp. 452–78

Sharabany R, Wiseman H. 1993. Close relationships in adolescence: the case of the kibbutz. *J. Youth Adolesc.* 22:671–95

Shwalb DW, Shwalb BJ, Nakazawa J, Hyun JH, Hao LV, Satiadarma M. 2007. Child and adolescent development in Japan, South Korea, Vietnam, and Indonesia. In *Handbook of Cross-Cultural Developmental Psychology*, ed. M Bornstein, Hillsdale, NJ: Erlbaum. In press

Silbereisen RK. 2000. German unification and adolescents' developmental timetables: continuities and discontinuities. In *Negotiating Adolescence in Times of Social Change*, ed. LA Crockett, RK Silbereisen, pp. 104–22. New York: Cambridge Univ. Press

Smart A. 1999. Expressions of interest: friendship and *guanxi* in Chinese societies. In *The Anthropology of Friendship*, ed. S Bell, S Coleman, pp. 119–36. Oxford, UK: Berg

Smetana J. 2002. Culture, autonomy, and personal jurisdiction. In *Advances in Child Development and Behavior*, ed. R Kail, H Reese, 29:52–87. New York: Academic

Steinberg L, Dornbusch S, Brown BB. 1992. Ethnic differences in adolescent achievement: an ecological perspective. *Am. Psychol.* 47:723–29

Stevenson HW. 1991. The development of prosocial behavior in large-scale collective societies: China and Japan. In *Cooperation and Prosocial Behaviour*, ed. RA Hinde, J Groebel, pp. 89–105. Cambridge, UK: Cambridge Univ. Press

Sullivan HS. 1953. *The Interpersonal Theory of Psychiatry*. New York: Norton

Sun SL. 1995. *The development of social networks among Chinese children in Taiwan*. Ph.D dissert. Univ. N. Carolina, Chapel Hill

Super CM, Harkness S. 1986. The developmental niche: a conceptualization at the interface of child and culture. *Int. J. Behav. Dev.* 9:545–69

Tamis-LeMonda CS, Way N, Hughes D, Yoshikawa H, Kalman RK, Niwa E. 2007. Parents' goals for children: the dynamic coexistence of collectivism and individualism in cultures and individuals. *Soc. Dev.* In press

Tieszen HR. 1979. Children's social behavior in a Korean preschool. *J. Korean Home Econ. Assoc.* 17:71–84

Tietjen A. 1989. The ecology of children's social support networks. In *Children's Social Networks and Social Support*, ed. D Belle, pp. 37–69. New York: Wiley

Tietjen A. 2006. Cultural influences on peer relations: an ecological perspective. See Chen et al. 2006a, pp. 52–74

Triandis HC. 1995. *Individualism and Collectivism*. Boulder, CO: Westview

Triandis HC, Bontempo R, Villareal MJ, Asai M, Lucca N. 1988. Individualism and collectivism: cross-cultural perspectives on self-ingroup relationships. *J. Personal. Soc. Psychol.* 54:323–33

Valdivia IA, Schneider BH, Chavez KL, Chen X. 2005. Social withdrawal and maladjustment in a very group-oriented society. *Int. J. Behav. Dev.* 29:219–28

Vygotsky LS. 1978. *Mind in Society: The Development of Higher Psychological Processes*. Cambridge, MA: Harvard Univ. Press

Waters E, Sroufe LA. 1983. Social competence as a developmental construct. *Dev. Rev.* 3:79–97

Way N. 2006. The cultural practice of close friendships among urban adolescents in the United States. See Chen et al. 2006a, pp. 403–25

Way N, Becker BE, Greene ML. 2006. Friendships among black, Latino, and Asian American adolescents in an urban context. In *Child Psychology: A Handbook of Contemporary Issues*, ed. L Balter, C Tamis-Lemonda, pp. 415–43. New York: Psychol. Press

Weisz JR, Suwanlert S, Chaiyasit W, Weiss B, Walter BR, Anderson WW. 1988. Thai and American perspectives on over- and undercontrolled child behavior problems: exploring the threshold model among parents, teachers, and psychologists. *J. Consult. Clin. Psychol.* 56:601–9

Whiting BB, Edwards CP. 1988. *Children of Different Worlds.* Cambridge, MA: Harvard Univ. Press

Yang KS. 1986. Chinese personality and its change. In *The Psychology of the Chinese People*, ed. MH Bond, pp. 106–70. New York: Oxford Univ. Press

Yoshikawa H, Hsueh H. 2001. Child development and public policy: toward a dynamic systems perspective. *Child Dev.* 72:1887–903

Zahn-Waxler C, Friedman RJ, Cole PM, Mizuta I, Hiruma N. 1996. Japanese and United States preschool children's responses to conflict and distress. *Child Dev.* 67:2462–77

Zigler E. 1973. Project Head Start: success or failure? *Learning* 1:43–47

Zhou Q, Eisenberg N, Wang Y, Reiser M. 2004. Chinese children's effortful control and dispositional anger/frustration: relations to parenting styles and children's social functioning. *Dev. Psychol.* 40:352–66

Grounded Cognition

Lawrence W. Barsalou

Department of Psychology, Emory University, Atlanta, Georgia 30322;
email: barsalou@emory.edu

Annu. Rev. Psychol. 2008. 59:617–45

First published online as a Review in Advance on
August 15, 2007

The *Annual Review of Psychology* is online at
http://psych.annualreviews.org

This article's doi:
10.1146/annurev.psych.59.103006.093639

Key Words

cognitive architecture, imagery, representation, simulation,
situated action

Abstract

Grounded cognition rejects traditional views that cognition is computation on amodal symbols in a modular system, independent of
the brain's modal systems for perception, action, and introspection. Instead, grounded cognition proposes that modal simulations,
bodily states, and situated action underlie cognition. Accumulating
behavioral and neural evidence supporting this view is reviewed from
research on perception, memory, knowledge, language, thought, social cognition, and development. Theories of grounded cognition are
also reviewed, as are origins of the area and common misperceptions
of it. Theoretical, empirical, and methodological issues are raised
whose future treatment is likely to affect the growth and impact of
grounded cognition.

Contents

WHAT IS GROUNDED COGNITION?

Standard theories of cognition assume that knowledge resides in a semantic memory system separate from the brain's modal systems for perception (e.g., vision, audition), action (e.g., movement, proprioception), and introspection (e.g., mental states, affect). According to standard theories, representations in modal systems are transduced into amodal symbols that represent knowledge about experience in semantic memory. Once this knowledge exists, it supports the spectrum of cognitive processes from perception to thought.

Conceptions of grounded cognition take many different forms (Gibbs 2006, Wilson 2002). In general, however, they reject the standard view that amodal symbols represent knowledge in semantic memory. From the perspective of grounded cognition, it is unlikely that the brain contains amodal symbols; if it does, they work together with modal representations to create cognition.

Some accounts of grounded cognition focus on roles of the body in cognition, based on widespread findings that bodily states can cause cognitive states and be effects of them (e.g., Barsalou et al. 2003, Lakoff & Johnson 1980, Smith 2005b). Most accounts of grounded cognition, however, focus on the roles of simulation in cognition (e.g., Barsalou 1999, Decety & Grèzes 2006, Goldman 2006). Simulation is the reenactment of perceptual, motor, and introspective states acquired during experience with the world, body, and mind. As an experience occurs (e.g., easing into a chair), the brain captures states across the modalities and integrates them with a multimodal representation stored in memory (e.g., how a chair looks and feels, the action of sitting, introspections of comfort and relaxation). Later, when knowledge is needed to represent a category (e.g., chair), multimodal representations captured during experiences with its instances are reactivated to simulate how the brain represented perception, action, and introspection associated with it.

According to this account, a diverse collection of simulation mechanisms, sharing a common representational system, supports the spectrum of cognitive activities. The presence of simulation mechanisms across diverse cognitive processes suggests that simulation provides a core form of computation in the brain. Mental imagery constitutes the best known case of these simulation mechanisms (e.g., Kosslyn 1980, 1994). Whereas mental imagery typically results from deliberate attempts to construct conscious representations in working memory, other forms of simulation often appear to become active automatically and unconsciously outside working memory.

Still other accounts of grounded cognition focus on situated action, social interaction, and the environment (e.g., Barsalou 2003, Barsalou et al. 2007a, Glenberg 1997, W. Prinz 1997, Rizzolatti & Craighero 2004, Robbins & Aydede 2007, E. Smith & Semin 2004, Yeh & Barsalou 2006). From this perspective, the cognitive system evolved to support action in specific situations, including social interaction. These accounts stress interactions between perception, action, the body, the environment, and other agents, typically during goal achievement.

It is important to note that the phrase "embodied cognition" is often used when referring to this collection of literatures. Problematically, however, "embodied cognition" produces the mistaken assumption that all researchers in this community believe that bodily states are necessary for cognition and that these researchers focus exclusively on bodily states in their investigations. Clearly, however, cognition often proceeds independently of the body, and many researchers address other forms of grounding. "Grounded cognition" reflects the assumption that cognition is typically grounded in multiple ways, including simulations, situated action, and, on occasion, bodily states. Perhaps grounding will one day become such a widely accepted assumption that "grounded" falls away, leaving "cognition" and thereby solving this problem.

Origins of Grounded Cognition

Perhaps surprisingly, grounded cognition has been the dominant view of cognition for most of recorded history. Nearly all prescientific views of the human mind going to back to ancient philosophers (e.g., Epicurus 341–270 B.C.E./1987) assumed that modal representations and imagery represent knowledge (Barsalou 1999, J. Prinz 2002), analogous to current simulation views. Even nativists, such as Kant (1787/1965) and Reid (1785/1969), frequently discussed modal images in knowledge (among other constructs).

In the early twentieth century, behaviorists attacked late nineteenth-century studies of introspection, banishing imagery from much of psychology for not being sufficiently scientific, along with other cognitive constructs (Watson 1913). When cognitive constructs reemerged during the Cognitive Revolution of the mid-twentieth century, imagery was not among them, probably for two reasons. First, the new cognitivists remembered Watson's attacks on imagery and wanted to avoid the same criticisms. Second, they were enthralled with new forms of representation inspired by major developments in logic, linguistics, statistics, and computer science. As a result, theories of knowledge adopted a wide variety of amodal representations, including feature lists, semantic networks, and frames (Barsalou & Hale 1993).

When early findings for mental imagery were reported in the 1960s (for reviews, see Paivio 1971, Shepard & Cooper 1982), the new cognitivists dismissed and discredited them (e.g., Pylyshyn 1973). Nevertheless, the behavioral and neural evidence for imagery eventually became so overwhelming that imagery is now accepted as a basic cognitive mechanism (Kosslyn et al. 2006).

Most recently, research in grounded cognition has challenged theories that originated during the Cognitive Revolution on numerous grounds (e.g., Barsalou 1999, Glenberg 1997, Harnad 1990, Lakoff 1987, Searle 1980). First, little empirical evidence supports the presence of amodal symbols in cognition. Instead, amodal symbols were adopted largely because they provided elegant and powerful formalisms for representing knowledge, because they captured important intuitions about the symbolic character of cognition, and because they could be implemented in artificial intelligence. Second, traditional theories have been challenged on the grounds that they fail to explain how cognition interfaces with perception and action (the grounding problem). Third, traditional theories increasingly face a lack of understanding about where the brain stores amodal symbols and about how amodal symbols could be consistent with neural principles of computation.

In place of traditional theories, researchers in grounded cognition have turned away from amodal symbols, focusing instead on simulation, situated action, and bodily states. In many respects, these researchers have rediscovered the classic philosophical assumption that modal representations are central to knowledge, reinventing this assumption in the modern contexts of psychology, cognitive science, and neuroscience. As a result, grounded theories focus increasingly on neural representations in the modalities, and less on conscious imagery.

Common Misperceptions of Grounded Cognition

Because modern grounded approaches are so new, we are far from having a unified view. Furthermore, the diverse approaches that exist are not specified computationally or formally. For these reasons, vagueness exists and misperceptions follow.

Grounded theories are often viewed as completely empiricist and therefore inconsistent with nativism. As noted above, however, classic nativists assumed that imagery played central roles in knowledge. Indeed, there are no a priori reasons why simulation cannot

have a strong genetic basis. Genetic contributions almost certainly shape the modal systems and memory systems that capture and implement simulations. Some simulations could have a genetic basis.

Grounded theories are often viewed as recording systems that only capture images (e.g., cameras) and are unable to interpret these images conceptually (e.g., Haugland 1991, Pylyshyn 1973). As described below, however, grounded theories are capable of implementing the classic symbolic functions that underlie conceptual interpretation (e.g., Barsalou 1999, 2005a).

Grounded theories are often viewed as only using sensory-motor representations of the external world to represent knowledge. As a result, it is argued that grounded theories cannot represent abstract concepts not grounded externally. Importantly, however, embodiment researchers since the classic empiricists have argued that internal states such as meta-cognition and affect constitute sources of knowledge no less important than external experience. Recent embodiment theorists propose that knowledge acquired from introspection is central to the representation of abstract concepts (e.g., Barsalou 1999, Barsalou & Wiemer-Hastings 2005).

Finally, grounded theories are often viewed as necessarily depending on bodily states or full-blown simulations that recreate experience. Researchers in grounded cognition make neither assumption. Bodily states are not necessary for cognitive activity, although they can be closely related to it. Although simulation is a central construct, these researchers agree that simulations rarely, if ever, recreate full experiences. Instead, simulations are typically partial recreations of experience that can contain bias and error (e.g., Barsalou 1999).

THEORIES OF GROUNDED COGNITION

All grounded theories represent negative reactions to standard theories of cognition based on amodal symbols. Additionally, grounded theories contain insights about mechanisms central to cognition that standard theories have largely ignored, such as simulation, situated action, and bodily states. Although most theories have been descriptive, they have nevertheless generated testable hypotheses addressed in empirical research. Clearly an important goal for future theory is to implement and formalize these theories.

Cognitive Linguistics Theories

Some of the first theories to champion grounded cognition in modern times arose in cognitive linguistics. These theories were negative reactions to amodal theories of syntax originating in the Cognitive Revolution (e.g., Chomsky 1957), and positive champions for the roles of bodies, situations, and simulations in language.

Lakoff & Johnson (1980, 1999) proposed that abstract concepts are grounded metaphorically in embodied and situated knowledge (also see Gibbs 1994). Specifically, these researchers argued that people possess extensive knowledge about their bodies (e.g., eating) and situations (e.g., verticality), and that abstract concepts draw on this knowledge metaphorically. For example, love can be understood as eating ("being consumed by a lover"), and affective experience can be understood as verticality ("happy is up, sad is down"). Extensive linguistic evidence across languages shows that people talk ubiquitously about abstract concepts using concrete metaphors. Such metaphors also arise extensively in literature (e.g., Turner 1996). A key issue is whether these metaphors simply reflect linguistic convention or whether they actually represent how people think (e.g., Murphy 1997). Increasing evidence suggests that these metaphors play central roles in thought (e.g., Boroditsky & Ramscar 2002, Gibbs 2006).

Other theories in cognitive linguistics have grounded the syntax and semantics of natural language in components of experience, such as paths, spatial relations, processes, and forces (e.g., Lakoff 1987; Langacker 1987, 1991; Talmy 1983, 1988). Cognitive linguists have also grounded reasoning in experience (e.g., Fauconnier 1985). Other cognitive linguists have developed grammars that use frames and constructions to capture the structure of situations (e.g., Fillmore 1985, A. Goldberg 1995). All these theories provide rich sources of hypotheses for scientific research (e.g., Coulson 2001, Kaschak & Glenberg 2000, Kemmerer 2006, Mandler 1992, Tomasello 2003).

Theories of Situated Action

These theories reflect another reaction to standard theories of cognition, again rejecting the idea that cognition revolves around computation on amodal symbols. Positively, many of these theories focus on the central roles of perception and action in cognition.

Following Gibson (1979), theories of situated action propose that the environment plays central roles in shaping cognitive mechanisms. Additionally, these theories focus on the close coupling of perception and action during goal achievement (e.g., Clark 1997, W. Prinz 1997, Thelen & L. Smith 1994, Steels & Brooks 1995), and increasingly on social interaction (e.g., Breazeal 2002). Many of these theories have originated in robotics. As a result, they are implemented computationally in robots operating in the physical world with other agents. Robotics provides a powerful test bed for developing and evaluating grounded theories of cognition that attempt to explain unified agents, not just component processes (Barsalou et al. 2007a).

Rather than adopting computational architectures that manipulate amodal symbols, theories of situated action often adopt dynamic systems as their architecture. From this perspective, fixed representations do not exist in the brain. Instead, multiple systems implement perception, action, and cognition, where each system is capable of residing in one of infinitely many continuous states. Over learning, states of these systems become coupled to reflect patterns of interaction with each other and with the environment effective in achieving goals (attractors). Such theories have been applied to perception and action (e.g., Van Orden et al. 2005), development (e.g., Thelen et al. 2001), and cognition (e.g., Spivey 2007).

Cognitive Simulation Theories

Perceptual symbol systems. The attacks on standard theories from cognitive linguistics, situated action, dynamic systems, and elsewhere might suggest that standard theories have nothing to offer. To the contrary, Barsalou's (1999) theory of Perceptual Symbol Systems (PSS) argued that traditional approaches are correct in postulating the importance of symbolic operations for interpreting experience (Fodor & Pylyshyn 1988, Pylyshyn 1973). Although grounded theories are viewed widely as recording systems (Haugeland 1991), PSS demonstrated that grounded theories can implement symbolic functions naturally (also see Barsalou 2005a, 2007). Through the construct of simulators—corresponding roughly to concepts and types in standard theories—PSS implements the standard symbolic functions of type-token binding, inference, productivity, recursion, and propositions. This approach retains the symbolic functionality of traditional theories but implements it differently, using simulation and dynamic systems. Thus, PSS is a synthetic approach that integrates traditional theories with grounded theories.

PSS further assumes that a single, multimodal representation system in the brain supports diverse forms of simulation across different cognitive processes, including high-level perception, implicit memory, working memory, long-term memory, and conceptual knowledge. According to PSS, differences between these cognitive processes reflect differences in the mechanisms that capture multimodal states and simulate them later. In high-level perception and implicit memory, association areas in a modality capture representations (e.g., in vision) and later trigger simulations that produce perceptual completion, repetition priming, etc. Working memory utilizes the same representation system but controls it differently during simulation, using frontal mechanisms to keep a modal representation active temporarily. Long-term memory again utilizes the same representation system to simulate episodic events but controls it via medial temporal systems and different frontal areas. Finally, conceptual knowledge uses the same representational system to simulate knowledge but controls it via association areas in the temporal, parietal, and frontal lobes. According to PSS, simulation is a unifying computational principle across diverse processes in the brain, taking different forms for each. The convergence zone architecture proposed by Damasio (1989) and extended by Simmons & Barsalou (2003) offers one way to implement a single representation system controlled by multiple simulation mechanisms.

Barsalou (2003) integrated PSS with situated cognition, proposing that simulations typically contextualize the categories that they represent in background situations, which include objects, agents, actions, events, and mental states (also see Yeh & Barsalou 2006). Barsalou et al. (2003) similarly proposed that situated simulations explain embodiment effects in social psychology through a pattern-completion inference mechanism.

In humans, the simulation system central to PSS is closely integrated with the linguistic system. Paivio (1971, 1986) developed an account of how language and simulation interact—Dual Code Theory—and amassed considerable evidence for it. Glaser (1992) and Barsalou and colleagues (2007b) offered revisions of this theory that place deep conceptual processing in the simulation system, not in the linguistic system. Barsalou (2005b) further proposed that nonhumans have roughly the same simulation system as humans but lack a linguistic system to control it. Barsalou (2007) proposed that humans' powerful symbolic capabilities emerge from interactions between language and simulation.

Memory theories. Glenberg (1997) argued that traditional accounts of memory focus too much on the passive storage of information and too little on the importance of situated action. Glenberg proposed that memory primarily serves to control situated action, and that the patterns stored in memory reflect the nature of bodily actions and their ability to mesh with situations during goal pursuit. Drawing on Gibson (1979), Glenberg suggested that the perception of relevant objects triggers affordances for action stored in memory. Conversely, reasoning about future actions relies on remembering affordances while suppressing perception of the environment (Glenberg et al. 1998).

Rubin (2006) argued that traditional accounts of memory are limited by only attempting to explain simple laboratory paradigms. When richer forms of memory are considered, such as autobiographical memory and oral history, more complex theories are required. Rubin proposed Basic Systems Theory as an account of complex memory phenomena. Similar to PSS and its situated extensions, Basic Systems Theory proposes that a complex memory contains many multimodal components from vision, audition, action, space, affect, language, etc., and that retrieving a memory involves simulating its multimodal components together. Conway (1990, 2002) similarly stressed the centrality of multimodal representations in autobiographical memory.

Social Simulation Theories

Simulation plays increasingly important roles in theories of social cognition (Goldman 2006). Of particular interest is explaining how we represent the mental states of other people. Simulation theories propose that we represent other people's minds using simulations of our own minds. To feel someone else's pain, we simulate our own pain.

Mirror neuron circuits typically underlie social simulation theories. In primates, a subset of the neural circuit used to manipulate objects becomes active when perceiving another agent perform an action to achieve a goal (Rizzolatti & Craighero 2004). To recognize and understand another agent's action, primates simulate the perceived action in their own motor system. Notably, mirror neurons within these circuits respond strongest to the goal of the action, not to the action itself. Thus, mirror circuits help perceivers infer an actor's intention, not simply recognize the action performed.

More generally, social neuroscientists propose that mirror circuits provide a general mechanism for understanding diverse mental states in others (e.g., Decety & Grèzes 2006, Gallese et al. 2004, 2007). To understand how someone else feels when disgusted, we simulate how we feel when disgusted. From this perspective, simulation provides a general mechanism for establishing empathy. Simulation theorists further propose that simulation supports other important social processes, such as imitation and social coordination. Some simulation theorists propose that mirror circuits contributed to the evolution of human language (Arbib 2005, Rizzolatti & Arbib 1998).

EMPIRICAL EVIDENCE

Surprisingly little research has attempted to test the widely accepted assumption that amodal symbols represent knowledge. Indeed, hardly any research before the past ten years attempted to assess directly the format in which knowledge is represented (e.g., amodal symbols, simulation). Furthermore, relatively little research assessed other aspects of the grounded view, such as the roles of situations and bodily states in cognition. During the past ten years, however, many researchers have designed experiments to assess grounded theories explicitly. The results of these experiments increasingly suggest that simulations, situations, and bodily states play central roles in cognition. Because of space limitations, many important findings are not cited.

Perception and Action

Perceptual inference. The simulation process central to accounts of grounded cognition plays ubiquitous roles in perception. During perception, states of perceptual systems become stored in memory (e.g., for vision and audition). Similar stimuli perceived later trigger these memories, simulating the perceptual states they contain. As these simulations become active, they produce perceptual inferences that go beyond perceived stimuli in useful ways.

Goldstone (1995) taught people simple associations between a shape (e.g., square) and a color (e.g., dark red). Later, when a colored shape was flashed (e.g., a red square), and participants had to reproduce its color, they distorted the color towards the prototypical color associated with the shape seen earlier. Perceiving the object's shape activated a simulation of its prototypical color, which then distorted perception of the current color. Hansen et al. (2006) similarly showed that simulations of an object's natural color (e.g., yellow for banana) distort achromatic perception of the object (e.g., a gray banana) toward the opponent color (e.g., a bluish banana).

During the perception of motion, visual simulations similarly arise that go beyond the physical motion present. In motion continuation, viewers simulate the visual trajectory of an object beyond its actual trajectory, falsely remembering anticipated motion (e.g., Freyd 1987). Knowledge about whether an object moves quickly or slowly affects the perceived speed of these simulated trajectories (e.g., Reed & Vinson 1996). During apparent motion, simulations of possible human action similarly shape perception of interpolated motion (e.g., Shiffrar & Freyd 1990, 1993). Stevens et al. (2000) showed that simulations in the motor system underlie these inferences. Analogous simulations produce somatosensory anticipations of an object tracing a trajectory over the body (Blankenburg et al. 2006).

Lexical knowledge produces simulations that contribute to speech perception. In the phoneme restoration effect, listeners use auditory knowledge about a word to simulate a missing phoneme (e.g., Warren 1970). Samuel (1997) showed that these simulations utilize early auditory systems.

Perception-action coordination. As people perceive visual objects, simulations of potential actions become active in preparation for situated action. Tucker & Ellis (1998) showed that the perceived handle of a cup activates a grasping simulation that inadvertently affects motor responses on an unrelated task. Tucker & Ellis (2001) showed that viewing an object grasped with a precision or power grip (e.g., a grape versus a hammer) produces a simulation of the appropriate action. Symes et al. (2007) showed that these simulations are sensitive to whether an object's orientation makes it easily graspable. Glover et al. (2004) showed that the size of an object affects these simulations. Bub et al. (2007) showed that a perceived object (or object name) automatically triggers simulations of both grasping and functional actions. Tucker & Ellis (2004) also showed that these simulations occur when the name of an object is read (e.g., "grape"). Helbig et al. (2006) showed that action simulations speed visual recognition of objects on which these actions are performed. Using fMRI, Chao & Martin (2000) showed that perceived objects activate the brain's grasping circuit (see Lewis 2006 for a review).

Researchers increasingly extend these original findings in creative ways. In Bosbach et al. (2005), accurately judging the weight of an object lifted by another agent requires simulating the lifting action in one's own motor and somatosensory systems. In Repp & Knoblich (2004), a pianist's ability to identify auditory recordings of his or her own playing depends on simulating the motor actions underlying it. In Pulvermüller et al. (2006), hearing a word activates the articulatory actions associated with producing it. In Proffitt (2006), simulations of perceived effort affect visual perception (but not action-guided movement). Being tired from a run makes a hill look steeper. Carrying a heavy pack makes a path look longer.

Motor simulations are also central to basic motor control. As a simple action is performed, the motor system constructs a feed-forward simulation of the action to guide and correct it (e.g., Grush 2004, Wolpert et al. 1999). These motor simulations also play roles in generating visual inferences about the anticipated actions of perceived agents (Wilson & Knoblich 2005).

Perception of space. Rather than being isotropic, the perception of space is shaped by the body, the body's relation to the environment, and the body's potential for action (Franklin & Tversky 1990). Locating objects along the vertical axis of the body is easiest because of the body's perceived asymmetry with respect to the ground. Locating objects along the front-back axis is next easiest because of the potential for action to the front. Locating objects along the left-right axis is most difficult because environmental and bodily cues are lacking. Longo & Laurenco (2007) found that people's perception of near space extends further outward as their arm length increases, suggesting that individual differences in bodies produce individual differences in space perception.

Memory

Implicit memory. Implicit memory appears closely related to perceptual inference. In both, perceptual memories become active and affect perception. As described above, simulations during perceptual inference create perceptions that go beyond stimulus information. In implicit memory, simulations increase perceptual fluency and the likelihood that perceptions are categorized correctly (i.e., repetition priming). If, for example, a perceived face activates an implicit memory, the face may be perceived more quickly and accurately.

Several general findings support the conclusion that implicit memory results from the simulation of perceptual memories (Roediger & McDermott 1993, Schacter et al. 2004). First, perceptual processing is typically important for establishing robust implicit learning, suggesting that perceptual memories are responsible (e.g., Jacoby 1983). Second, repetition priming is strongest when the modalities of the memory and the perceived stimulus match, for example, when an auditory memory exists to help process an auditory stimulus (e.g., Kirsner et al. 1989). Third, repetition priming is strongest when perceptual details of the memory and perceived stimulus match, such as orientation, size, font, etc. (e.g., Jacoby & Hayman 1987, Jolicoeur 1985). Fourth, imagining a stimulus produces repetition priming similar to actually perceiving it, suggesting that shared perceptual representations underlie both (e.g., Roediger & Blaxton 1987, Schacter & Graf 1989). For all these reasons, the simulation of perceptual states appears central to implicit memory.

Explicit memory. Similar to implicit memory, conscious memory of previous episodes relies heavily on modal representations. Extensive reviews of supporting findings can be found in Paivio (1971, 1986), Conway (1990, 2002), and Rubin (2006), who build theories of explicit memory from this evidence. In general, these theories assume that multimodal simulations of previous episodes are central to episodic recollection. Simulation also appears central to constructing future events based on memories of past events (Schacter & Addis 2007).

Although particularly strong evidence for multimodal simulation comes from research on autobiographical memory, even simple laboratory experiments demonstrate simulation. Consider experiments that manipulate whether words are studied visually or auditorally (e.g., Wheeler et al. 2000). When retrieval of these words is tested later in a scanner, visual areas become active following visual study, whereas auditory areas become active following auditory study. Thus, the retrieval of a word simulates the modal operations performed at encoding. Buckner & Wheeler (2001) review many such findings.

Within a single modality, the distributed brain states associated with studying different kinds of stimuli are simulated later at retrieval. Polyn et al. (2005) found that the distributed neural pattern associated with studying faces later reappeared when remembering them, as did the patterns for studying locations or objects. Kent & Lamberts (2006) similarly found that the speed of processing different perceptual dimensions at encoding was linearly related to the speed of processing them at retrieval.

Simulation also provides a natural explanation of various memory effects. Because a stimulus leaves memories in the modal areas that encoded it, greater activation in modal areas occurs when remembering something that actually occurred than when falsely remembering something that did not (Slotnick & Schacter 2004). Remembering a stimulus specifically produces greater activation in modal areas than remembering it generally (Garoff et al. 2005). Simulating a scene at encoding that extends the boundary of a studied picture produces reconstructive error later at retrieval (e.g., Intraub et al. 1998). Reinstating actions at retrieval performed earlier during encoding facilitates memory (Ross et al. 2007).

Working memory. Neuroscience research with nonhumans established the distributed neural circuits that store an absent stimulus in working memory (e.g., Levy & Goldman-Rakic 2000). To maintain a working memory, neurons in the frontal lobes maintain a simulation of the absent stimulus in the modal system that processed it originally. More specifically, different regions of frontal cortex maintain working memories for different types of modal content. For example, some regions maintain working memories of objects, whereas others maintain working memories of spatial locations. Even more specifically, different populations of frontal neurons are highly selective for the specific features they

maintain (Pasternak & Greenlee 2005). For example, different frontal populations maintain working memories for motion in different directions, for textures of different spatial frequency, etc.

Research on imagery has further established the central role of modal simulation in working memory. Considerable behavioral evidence indicates that visual imagery in working memory simulates visual processing (e.g., Finke 1989, Kosslyn 1980, Shepard & Cooper 1982). Neural evidence strongly corroborates this conclusion (e.g., Kosslyn et al. 2000). Analogously, motor imagery simulates motor processing (e.g., Grèzes & Decety 2001, Jeannerod 1995), and auditory imagery simulates auditory processing (e.g., Halpern et al. 2004).

When action is relevant to visual imagery, the motor system becomes engaged, consistent with theories of situated action. For example, when visual rotation of a body part is imagined, bodily constraints shape the rotational trajectory (e.g., Parsons 1987a,b). Similarly, mental rotation of visual objects is accompanied by motor simulations of making them turn (e.g., Richter et al. 2000).

Knowledge and Conceptual Processing

Although simulation in working memory has been accepted for many years, simulation as the basis of knowledge representation is still considered a radical proposal. Nevertheless, considerable evidence now demonstrates the presence of simulation during conceptual processing.

Behavioral evidence. Researchers have used the property verification task to assess whether conceptual processing utilizes simulation. On each trial, the word for a category is presented (e.g., HORSE) followed by a word for a property that is either true or false of the category (e.g., mane versus horns). According to standard theories, participants assess relations between amodal symbols for concepts and properties to verify properties. According to grounded views, participants simulate the concept and the property and then assess whether the simulated property can be found in the simulated concept.

Consistent with the simulation view, Solomon & Barsalou (2004) found that perceptual variables such as size best predicted verification times and errors. As properties became larger, verifying them became more difficult, consistent with the finding that verifying properties perceptually becomes more difficult as properties become larger (cf. Morrison & Tversky 1997). Solomon & Barsalou (2001) similarly found that property representations contain detailed perceptual information, difficult to verbalize, suggesting that participants simulated properties to verify them. Borghi et al. (2004) found that the positions of properties in space are simulated during their verification.

If participants simulate properties to verify them, then having to switch from one modality to another while simulating properties should incur a switching cost, analogous to the cost of switching attention from one modality to another in perception (e.g., Spence et al. 2000). Pecher at al. (2003, 2004) found support for this hypothesis, as did Marques (2006) and Vermeulen et al. (2007).

Lesion evidence. Neuropsychologists have reported that lesions in a particular modality increase the likelihood of losing categories that rely on it for processing a category (e.g., Cree & McRae 2003, Damasio & Damasio 1994, Gainotti 2006, Gainotti et al. 1995, Humphreys & Forde 2001, Simmons & Barsalou 2003, Warrington & McCarthy 1987, Warrington & Shallice 1984). For example, damage to visual areas increases the likelihood of losing animals because visual processing is often the dominant modality for interacting with this category. Conversely, damage to motor areas increases the likelihood of losing the tools category, because motor processing is often the dominant modality. Similarly, damage to color process-

ing areas can produce deficits in color knowledge (e.g., Miceli et al. 2001), and damage to spatial processing areas can produce deficits in location knowledge (e.g., Levine et al. 1985). Additional research demonstrates that other mechanisms beside modal representations contribute to category-specific deficits (e.g., Caramazza & Shelton 1998, Cree & McRae 2003, Simmons & Barsalou 2003, Tyler et al. 2000).

Neuroimaging evidence. Neuroimaging research further confirms that simulation plays a central role in conceptual processing (Martin 2001, 2007). When conceptual knowledge about objects is represented, brain areas that represent their properties during perception and action become active. In particular, brain areas that represent the shape and color of objects (fusiform gyrus), the motion they exhibit (middle and superior temporal lobe), and the actions that agents perform on them (premotor and parietal areas) become active to represent these properties conceptually. When people perform the property verification task described above, modal areas for the properties tested become active, including brain areas for shape, color, size, sound, taste, action, and touch (e.g., R. Goldberg et al. 2006, Kan et al. 2003, Kellenbach et al. 2001, Simmons et al. 2007).

Further evidence comes from different profiles of multimodal activation for different categories. When people process animals conceptually, visual areas are especially active; when people process artifacts, motor areas become active (e.g., Kiefer 2005; Martin 2001, 2007; Thompson-Schill 2003). Similarly, when people process foods conceptually, gustatory areas become active (e.g., Simmons et al. 2005). When people process things that smell, olfactory areas become active (e.g., Gonzalez et al. 2006). Additionally, the property areas just noted are often segregated by category (Martin 2007). Within the motion processing system, for example, distinct areas represent motion conceptually for animals versus artifacts.

Language Comprehension

Situation models. Although the presence of modal representations in such a high-level cognitive task as comprehension might seem implausible, supporting evidence has existed for decades. Early work on comprehension inferences strongly suggested the presence of spatial representations (e.g., Bransford & Johnson 1973). Bower & Morrow (1990) found that people represent text meaning with situation models that have spatial properties (also see Glenberg et al. 1987, Rinck & Bower 2004). Other research has shown that readers take spatial perspectives on scenes described in texts (e.g., Black et al. 1979, Spivey et al. 2000). Intraub & Hoffman (1992) found that readers confused pictures with texts, suggesting that readers simulated text meaning. Gernsbacher et al. (1990) found that individual abilities for comprehending events visually versus verbally were highly correlated, suggesting that modal representations underlie both. Potter et al. (1986) showed that replacing words with pictures did not disrupt sentence processing, suggesting that the pictures were integrated effortlessly into modal representations of sentence meaning (also see Glaser 1992).

Perceptual simulation. More recently, researchers have addressed the role of perceptual simulation in representing texts. In much research reviewed by Zwaan & Madden (2005), participants read a sentence and then processed a picture that either matched or mismatched something implied but not stated literally. For example, participants read "The ranger saw the eagle in the sky" and then named a subsequent picture of an eagle either with its wings outstretched or folded. If readers constructed simulations to represent sentences, these simulations should have contained implicit perceptual information such as object shape. Consistent with this prediction, participants were faster to name the eagle with outstretched wings. Many experiments have demonstrated these matching effects, consistent with the simulation view.

In another line of research, participants maintained irrelevant information in working memory while processing sentences about scenes (Fincher-Kiefer 2001, Fincher-Kiefer & D'Agostino 2004). Drawing predictive spatial inferences about the described scenes was worse when working memory contained interfering visual information than when it contained noninterfering verbal information, suggesting that readers represented the texts with simulations.

Motor simulation. Many researchers have demonstrated the presence of motor simulations in comprehension. Across several lines of research, Pulvermüller (2005) found that when participants simply read the word for an action, the motor system becomes active to represent its meaning. More specifically, verbs for head, arm, and leg actions produce head, arm, and leg simulations in the respective areas of the motor system. These simulations become active quickly, within a few hundred milliseconds, as illustrated by magnetoencephalography (MEG). These simulations also play causal roles in lexical processing, given that transcranial magnetic stimulation (TMS) over the relevant motor areas affects behavioral performance (e.g., Buccino et al. 2005, Pulvermüller et al. 2005). Myung et al. (2006) similarly showed that motor simulations triggered by words produce priming across lexical decision trials.

Many other researchers have assessed whether physical actions affect comprehension. Klatzky et al. (1989) showed that priming a motor action affected the time to judge the sensibility of a simple phrase describing an action. Similarly, comprehension is facilitated when the action to make a response is consistent with text meaning (Glenberg & Kaschak 2003) and also when the action to control text presentation is consistent (Zwaan & Taylor 2006). When reading about a sport, such as hockey, experts produce motor simulations absent in novices (Holt & Beilock 2006).

Other research shows that participants simulate motion through space as they read texts. Richardson et al. (2003) found that readers simulate horizontal and vertical paths implied by both concrete and abstract verbs (e.g., push versus lift, argue versus respect). Matlock (2004) found that implied fictive motion (e.g., the road runs through the valley) produces corresponding simulations of motion through space. Richardson & Matlock (2007) found that these simulations produce related eye movements. Meier & Robinson (2004) found that reading positively valenced words orients attention up, whereas reading negatively valenced words orients attention down. Schubert (2005) similarly found that reading words associated with high versus low power orients attention up versus down, respectively. Meier & Robinson (2006) found that depression increases downward orientation.

Affective simulation. Researchers have also shown that people simulate affective states during comprehension. When people read taboo words and reprimands, affective reactions, as measured by skin conductance, are stronger when read in a first language than in a second language acquired at a later age (Harris et al. 2003). Because greater affect is associated with these expressions at younger ages, native language speakers continue to simulate these affective responses when reading them as adults.

A reader's affective state interacts with the affective content of a text. In Havas et al. (2007), participants' faces were configured discretely into states associated with particular emotions prior to judging the sensibility of sentences that contained emotional content. When facial emotion matched sentence emotion, comprehension was better than when they mismatched. Embodied states of the face triggered emotional states, which in turn interacted with sentence comprehension. Barrett (2006) suggests that affective simulation underlies the conceptualization of emotion that occurs in comprehension and other processes.

Gesture. Another important form of embodiment in language is the gesture that spontaneously accompanies speech (McNeill 2005). Producing gestures helps speakers retrieve words whose meanings are related to the gestures (e.g., Krauss 1998). Speakers also produce gestures to help listeners comprehend what they say (e.g., Alibali et al. 2001, Kelly 2001, Valenzeno et al. 2003). In child development, gesture can convey an emerging conceptualization that cannot yet be articulated in speech (e.g., Goldin-Meadow 2003). Kelly et al. (2002) integrate gesture with grounded theories of language.

Thought

Physical reasoning. Much work shows that simulations play central roles in reasoning about physical situations (Hegarty 2004). When people view a static configuration of gears, for example, they use simulation to infer the direction in which a particular gear will turn. People similarly use simulation to draw inferences about how a configuration of pulleys will work or when water will spill from a tipped glass.

Numerous sources of evidence support the use of simulation in these tasks. The time to draw an inference is often correlated with the duration of a physical event, such as how long a gear takes to turn (e.g., Schwartz & Black 1996). Drawing inferences often produces associated gestures (e.g., Hegarty et al. 2005). Carrying out associated actions can improve inference (e.g., Schwartz 1999). When working memory is filled with visuospatial information, inferences suffer compared with when working memory is filled with verbal information (e.g., Sims & Hegarty 1997). Individual differences in spatial ability correlate with the ability to draw inferences (e.g., Hegarty & Steinhoff 1997). Hegarty (2004) concludes that spatial simulation, not visual imagery, plays the central role in reasoning about physical situations. Furthermore, the simulations that underlie this reasoning appear piecemeal and sketchy, not holistic and detailed.

Abstract reasoning. Abstract forms of reasoning have not received as much attention as physical reasoning. Although Johnson-Laird's (1983) mental model theory could be made compatible with grounded views, the mental models in his theory typically contain amodal symbols, not simulations. Much circumstantial evidence, however, suggests that simulation plays central roles in abstract reasoning. For example, philosophers of science observe frequently that scientific and mathematical discoveries typically arise from simulation (e.g., Barwise & Etchemendy 1991, Hadamard 1949, Nersessian 1999). Widespread content effects in reasoning similarly implicate simulations and situations in abstract reasoning (e.g., Cheng & Holyoak 1985).

Further evidence that abstract reasoning is grounded comes from research inspired by metaphor theory. When people reason about the abstract concept of time, they use space metaphorically to draw inferences (e.g., Boroditsky 2000, Boroditsky & Ramscar 2002). For example, when people hear, "Next Wednesday's meeting has been moved forward two days," their inference about whether the new meeting day is Monday or Friday depends on their current spatial trajectory. Similarly, how people conceptualize time reflects whether their language describes space horizontally or vertically (Boroditsky 2001).

Social Cognition

Embodiment effects. Social psychologists have reported embodiment effects for decades (Barsalou et al. 2003, Niedenthal et al. 2005). Bodily states can be effects of social cognition. For example, activating the elderly stereotype causes people to walk slowly and to perform lexical decision slowly (e.g., Dijksterhuis & Bargh 2001). Similarly, seeing an in-group member engages the smiling musculature (e.g., Vanman et al. 1997).

Bodily states are not simply effects of social cognition; they also cause it. When a facial expression or posture is adopted, it elicits associated mental states. For example, engaging the smiling musculature produces positive affect (e.g., Strack et al. 1988), whereas slumping produces negative affect (e.g., Stepper & Strack 1993). Actions produce similar outcomes. Nodding one's head produces positive affect (e.g., Wells & Petty 1980), whereas pushing away with the arms produces negative affect (e.g., Cacioppo et al. 1993).

Barsalou et al. (2003) proposed that these embodiment effects reflect a pattern-completion inference mechanism that supports situated action. According to this view, representations of familiar situations that contain embodiments become established in memory (e.g., receiving a gift, feeling positive affect, and smiling). When part of this situation occurs (e.g., receiving a gift), it activates the remainder of the situational pattern, producing associated embodiments (e.g., smiling). Similarly, if smiling is engaged, it activates representations of situations that contain it, producing associated pattern components (e.g., positive affect, generosity). E. Smith & Semin (2004) review much further evidence that situated action organizes social cognition. Barsalou et al. (2005) examine embodiment in religious cognition.

Social mirroring. Accumulating evidence implicates simulation in many social processes (Decety & Grèzes 2006, Gallese et al. 2004, Goldman 2006, Iacoboni 2007, Rizzolatti & Craighero 2004). In general, mirror circuits appear to underlie these simulations, establishing empathy between perceivers and perceived actors. Using mirror circuits, perceivers infer the goals of others (e.g., Kohler et al. 2002) and infer their affective states, such as pain and disgust (e.g., Jackson et al. 2005, Wicker et al. 2003). Mirror circuits underlie a variety of other social activities, including imitation (e.g., Iacoboni et al. 1999) and social coordination (e.g., Sebanz et al. 2006).

In general, a mirror circuit does not provide a complete account of a social activity but contributes to a larger system. For example, additional brain areas beyond mirror circuits prevent perceivers from confusing someone else's mental state with their own (Decety & Grèzes 2006). In imitation, simulating how the imitation of an action will look and feel is also important (Iacoboni et al. 1999). Joint attention and timing are also central in social coordination (Sebanz et al. 2006).

Individual differences in simulation ability produce individual differences in social cognition. For example, individual differences in the ability to simulate other people's mental states, such as pain, correlate with rated empathy (e.g., Jackson et al. 2005). Individual differences in expertise, such as ballet, correlate with the ability to mirror relevant action (Calvo-Merino et al. 2005).

Development

Newborn infants imitate the facial expressions and bodily movements of adults, simulating the actions that they see physically (Meltzoff & Moore 1983). As infants grow older, they understand the perceived actions of others in terms of what they have come to understand about their own actions and intentions (Meltzoff 2007). Once infants experience the occluding effects of a blindfold, for example, they understand that an adult wearing a blindfold cannot see. Thus, mirroring plays a central role in development, as infants use simulations of their own experience to understand the goals and actions of others.

Researchers increasingly demonstrate that development depends critically on bodily states (e.g., L. Smith 2005b) and situated action (e.g., L. Smith & Gasser 2005). For example, L. Smith et al. (1999) showed that the development of object permanence is not simply a cognitive achievement (as long believed) but also a grounded one. Specifically, motor perseveration plays a major role in tasks that measure object permanence. Longo & Bertenthal (2006) similarly showed that motor simulations contribute to perseveration.

Other developmental tasks also exhibit strong dependence on action. For example, the motor actions performed while learning a category influence the visual features abstracted into its representation (L. Smith 2005a). Similarly, the actions performed on objects during play later cause children to place the objects in spatial clusters that reflect shared categories (Namy et al. 1997). In general, extensive amounts of learning occur between perception, action, and cognition as development progresses (e.g., Greco et al. 1990, Rochat & Striano 1999).

THEORETICAL AND EMPIRICAL ISSUES

Grounded cognition in its modern form is sufficiently new and controversial that many issues surround it. A sample of these issues follows.

Does the Brain Contain Amodal Symbols?

Researchers who once denied that the modalities had anything to do with cognition now acknowledge their potential relevance. The empirical evidence that the modalities have something to do with cognition has become compelling. Nevertheless, most researchers in cognitive psychology and cognitive science are not ready to completely abandon traditional theories. One widely held view is that simulations in the modalities play peripheral roles in cognition, while classic operations on amodal symbols still play the central roles.

It will be important for future research to assess this mixed view. Can empirical evidence be found for the amodal symbols still believed by many to lie at the heart of cognition? As mentioned above, surprisingly few attempts have been made to establish empirical support for amodal symbols. If amodal symbols are to remain central in cognitive theories, empirical support is necessary. It will not be enough to rely on the fact that theories built from amodal symbols can mimic cognitive abilities. It will also be important to demonstrate that computation on amodal symbols constitutes the underlying mechanism.

Furthermore, modal symbols must be localized in the brain, and neural principles for processing them explained.

Does Simulation Implement Classic Symbolic Operations?

Conversely, can simulation mechanisms be shown to be more than merely peripheral to cognition? Can simulation implement the core cognitive functions that many researchers still believe require amodal symbols? As described above, grounded theories, such as PSS and cognitive linguistics grammars, have illustrated how simulation mechanisms can implement, in principle, core cognitive functions, including type-token binding, inference, productivity, recursion, and propositions. The existence of these operations in the cognitive system is not in question. How the brain actually implements them is. Amodal formalisms for symbolic operations may provide a theoretical shorthand for expressing what the brain computes, but simulation, or something else, may be the mechanism that actually implements these operations.

Clearly, computational implementations are required to demonstrate convincingly that simulation can implement symbolic operations. Empirical evidence will be required to support these accounts. If future research succeeds in these projects, the viability of amodal symbols as plausible cognitive constructs may increasingly come into question.

Are Simulations and Embodiments Causal or Epiphenomenal?

Proponents of amodal views often suggest that amodal symbols play the central causal roles in cognitive computation, with simulations and embodiments simply being epiphenomenal. Establishing whether simulations and embodiments play causal roles is indeed an important issue. Considerable evidence exists already, however, that they do. For example, TMS over motor areas affects linguistic processing (e.g., Buccino et al. 2005, Pulvermüller et al. 2005). If simulations in motor areas are epiphenomenal, then modulating brain activity in these areas should have no effect on the causal sequence of processes underlying language, but it does. Similarly, experimentally manipulated bodily states, assigned randomly to participants, produce extensive effects throughout social cognition (Barsalou et al. 2003), situated action (e.g., Tucker & Ellis 1998, 2001, 2004), and linguistic processing (e.g., Glenberg & Kaschak 2003). If these bodily states are epiphenomenal, they should have no effect on the causal sequence of processes underlying behavioral performance, but again they do.

Conversely, it is essential for proponents of amodal views to demonstrate that amodal symbols play causal roles in cognition (assuming that evidence for their existence in the brain can be found). Consider neuroimaging studies that find activations in modal areas during conceptual processing (e.g., Martin 2007). If these activations are epiphenomenal, then it is essential to identify alternative amodal brain areas that play the causal role in producing conceptual performance. Interestingly, many of these studies fail to find significant activations outside modal areas, suggesting that amodal processes do not contribute to conceptual processing, and that the active modal areas observed play the causal roles, given that they are the only areas active.

Assessing the causal roles of simulations and embodiments clearly requires much further research. Nevertheless, significant evidence exists already that they are not epiphenomenal.

What Roles Do Statistical Representations Play?

Research inspired by neural networks and Bayesian statistics has clearly shown that the brain is exquisitely sensitive to the statistical structure of experience. Interestingly, these two approaches often (but not always) assume that statistical processing occurs in a modular system separate from the brain's modal systems, much like traditional symbolic theories. In other words, these approaches have remained relatively ungrounded.

By no means is this necessary. To the contrary, statistical processing is central to grounded cognition, as illustrated by dynamic systems approaches. Similarly, theories such as PSS assume that neural networks underlie the convergence zone architecture that implements simulation. Furthermore, Bayesian statistics can be viewed as statistical accounts of the multimodal information stored in the dynamic systems that generate simulations and guide situated action. Depending on the particular distribution of multimodal content captured for a category, the Bayesian statistics describing it will vary, as will the simulations and situated actions generated from it. Bayesian theories provide a powerful tool for describing the content and behavior of these systems.

How Is Language Grounded?

Language provides an excellent domain in which to combine symbolic operations, statistical processing, and grounding. Symbolic operations are clearly central to linguistic processing. Thematic roles of verbs are bound to values (e.g., binding the instrument role for "eat" to spoon). Open-class words for nouns, modifiers, and verbs, and adverbs combine productively to form novel phrasal and sentential structures (e.g., combining different color modifiers with different object head nouns to form noun phrases such as red hair, blond hair, and red wine). Phrasal structures embed recursively (e.g., "The dog the cat chased howled"). Propositions extracted from linguistic utterances represent meaning beyond surface structure [e.g., extracting chase (cat, dog) from either "The cat chased the dog" or the "The dog was chased by the cat"].

Statistical processing is also central to language use. Much research shows that statistical distributions of word senses contribute to

ambiguity resolution during syntactic analysis (e.g., Trueswell 1996). Similarly, statistical distributions of argument structures and their instantiations contribute to sentence processing (e.g., McRae et al. 2005).

Finally, grounding is also central to comprehension, as we saw earlier. As people comprehend a text, they construct simulations to represent its perceptual, motor, and affective content. Simulations appear central to the representation of meaning.

Thus, language use is a domain where the study of symbolic operations, statistical processing, and grounding can be integrated. Numerous issues challenge the integration of these perspectives. Do amodal symbols or simulation mechanisms implement the symbolic operations that underlie linguistic processing? As sentences are processed incrementally, are simulations constructed incrementally to reflect the semantic contribution of each incoming word? Does the compositional structure of syntax correspond to the compositional structure of simulations? Do language statistics affect the specific simulations constructed during comprehension? Do cognitive linguistics grammars offer useful frameworks for integrating symbolic operations, statistical processing, and grounding?

Does the Brain Contain a Single Representational System?

As described above, some simulation theories propose that a single multimodal representation system underlies diverse cognitive processes, including top-down perception, implicit memory, working memory, explicit memory, and conceptual knowledge. According to this view, simulation is a unifying computational principle throughout the brain, with different control systems operating on a shared representational system to produce different forms of simulation in different processes.

Is this proposal correct? If so, what is the nature of the shared representational system? Within a given modality, is the representational system organized hierarchically, as appears to be the case in the visual and motor systems? If so, do some processes access these hierarchical representations at higher or lower levels than others? For example, explicit memory, conceptual processing, and language might tend to access high-level representations, whereas top-down perception, implicit memory, and working memory might tend to access lower-level representations. Another central issue concerns the different control mechanisms for different processes. Where are they located in the brain, and why do they reside in these particular locations? How do differences between them implement different processes?

How Does the Brain Represent Abstract Concepts?

Abstract concepts pose a classic challenge for grounded cognition. How can theories that focus on modal simulations explain concepts that do not appear modal? This concern often reflects the misperception described above that conceptual content in grounded theories can only come from perception of the external world. Because people perceive internal states, however, conceptual content can come from internal sources as well. Preliminary evidence suggests that introspective information is indeed central to the representation of abstract concepts (e.g., Barsalou & Wiemer-Hastings 2005, Wiemer-Hastings et al. 2001). Such findings suggest that we need to learn much more about how people perceive and conceptualize internal states. Notably, people simulate internal states similar to how they simulate external states (e.g., Havas et al. 2007, Niedenthal et al. 2005). Thus, simulations of internal states could provide much of the conceptual content central to abstract concepts (Barsalou 1999).

Abstract concepts also appear to depend heavily on situations and situated action (Schwanenflugel 1991). Processing an abstract concept by itself is difficult but becomes much easier when a background situation contextualizes it. Barsalou & Wiemer-Hastings (2005) report evidence for extensive situational content in abstract concepts.

Because the scientific study of concepts has primarily focused so far on concrete concepts, we actually know remarkably little about abstract concepts, even from the perspective of traditional cognitive theories. Nevertheless, abstract concepts appear to play central roles throughout human cognition, especially in meta-cognition, social interaction, education, industry, and social institutions. Regardless of whether simulations of introspections and situations underlie the representation of abstract concepts, much more effort should be devoted to understanding them.

Do Mirror Neuron Systems Pervade Social Cognition?

Much excitement surrounds the discovery of mirror neuron systems. As described above, social simulation theories propose that these systems underlie many important social phenomena. One central issue is assessing whether mirror systems do indeed play all these roles, and perhaps others. If so, then why do humans exhibit such different social abilities than nonhuman primates who also have mirror systems? What other systems contribute to these differences? Also, to what extent do compromised mirror systems underlie psychopathologies associated with a lack of intersubjectivity, such as autism and schizophrenia (e.g., Gallese 2003)?

METHODOLOGICAL ISSUES

Besides addressing theoretical and empirical issues, grounded cognition must address various methodological issues. Future growth and impact of this area is likely to depend on addressing these issues successfully.

Computational and Formal Theories

Grounded cognition suffers from an obvious lack of well-specified theories. Often experiments simply attempt to demonstrate the presence of modal processing in higher cognition. Given the widespread skepticism about grounded cognition ten years ago, demonstration experiments made sense. Now that modal processing in higher cognition is becoming well documented, it is time to develop computational accounts of grounded theories, along with experiments that test them. Transitioning from demonstration experiments to analytic experiments is a natural trajectory in science, and it will undoubtedly occur in grounded cognition. This trajectory is also likely to include increasing attempts to build computational implementations, followed by formal accounts of the principles underlying them. For examples of initial attempts to implement grounded theories, see Cangelosi et al. (2000), Cangelosi & Riga (2006), Garagnani et al. (2007), Wennekers et al. (2006), and Goldreich (2007).

Integrating Disciplines and Levels of Explanation

One strength of grounded cognition is its natural fit with the brain. Because grounded cognition rests on the modalities, knowledge of how the brain implements the modalities informs grounded cognition. Furthermore, assessing neural activity in the modalities provides a natural way to test predictions of grounded theories. Clearly, however, much greater integration of cognitive and neural mechanisms must occur than the relatively simple mappings established so far. Nevertheless, the grounded approach appears to have unusual potential for integrating cognition with the brain.

Grounded cognition has significant potential to integrate other research areas as well. For example, a core principle of grounded cognition is that cognition shares mechanisms with perception, action, and introspection. Increasingly specified accounts of how cognition, perception, action, and introspection interact during situated action are likely to follow from future research. Similarly, grounded cognition has also shown potential to integrate cognitive, social, and developmental processes. Research in all three fields has increasingly incorporated simulation, situations, and bodily states as important constructs. Thus, further integration of these areas seems like another natural outcome of research in grounded cognition. As described above, robotics offers considerable potential for accomplishing this integration (Barsalou et al. 2007a).

Grounding Classic Research Paradigms

It is unlikely that grounded cognition will be fully accepted until classic research paradigms can be understood within its framework. In cognitive psychology, for example, how would a classic paradigm such as recognition memory be understood as grounded? Similarly, how might the construct of a production in a production system be understood?

One possibility is that many empirical results and their interpretations would remain roughly the same within the framework of ground cognition. Analogous to how symbolic operations can be retained in grounded views but be realized differently, well-established empirical results and explanations may often retain much of their original form. One focus of change is likely to be at the representational level. In recognition memory, for example, rather than assuming that a vector of amodal symbols represents a learning episode, its representational elements could instead be mapped into a multimodal state. At higher theoretical levels, much of the original theory might remain. Similarly, in production systems, rather than viewing the condition and action sides of a production as amodal symbols, the condition could be represented as the state of a perceptual modality, and the action could be represented as a state of the motor system. From the grounded perspective, a production is simply an association between a perception and an action. Above the representational level, the remaining structure of a production system might again remain largely intact.

Clearly, the reinvention of classic paradigms requires careful theoretical and empirical assessment. Until grounding is integrated with classic paradigms, however, it is unlikely that it will be accepted fully. Thus, another major goal for the grounded cognition community is to illustrate how classic paradigms can be made compatible with grounding, and perhaps how grounding can take understandings of these paradigms to new levels.

ACKNOWLEDGMENT

This work was supported by National Science Foundation Grant BCS-0212134 and by DARPA contract BICA FA8650-05-C-7256 to Lawrence Barsalou.

LITERATURE CITED

Alibali MW, Heath DC, Myers HJ. 2001. Effects of visibility between speaker and listener on gesture production: Some gestures are meant to be seen. *J. Mem. Lang.* 44:169–88

Arbib MA. 2005. From monkey-like action recognition to human language: an evolutionary framework for neurolinguistics. *Behav. Brain Sci.* 28:105–67

Barrett LF. 2006. Solving the emotion paradox: categorization and the experience of emotion. *Pers. Soc. Psychol. Rev.* 10:20–46

Barsalou LW. 1999. Perceptual symbol systems. *Behav. Brain Sci.* 22:577–660

Barsalou LW. 2003. Situated simulation in the human conceptual system. *Lang. Cogn. Process.* 18:513–62

Barsalou LW. 2005a. Abstraction as dynamic interpretation in perceptual symbol systems. In *Building Object Categories*, Carnegie Sympos. Ser., ed. L Gershkoff-Stowe, D Rakison, pp. 389–431. Mahwah, NJ: Erlbaum

Barsalou LW. 2005b. Continuity of the conceptual system across species. *Trends Cogn. Sci.* 9:309–11

Barsalou LW. 2007. Grounding symbolic operations in the brain's modal systems. In *Embodied Grounding: Social, Cognitive, Affective, and Neuroscientific approaches*, ed. GR Semin, ER Smith. New York: Cambridge Univ. Press. In press

Barsalou LW, Barbey AK, Simmons WK, Santos A. 2005. Embodiment in religious knowledge. *J. Cogn. Cult.* 5:14–57

Barsalou LW, Breazeal C, Smith LB. 2007a. Cognition as coordinated noncognition. *Cogn. Process.* 8:79–91

Barsalou LW, Hale CR. 1993. Components of conceptual representation: from feature lists to recursive frames. In *Categories and Concepts: Theoretical Views and Inductive Data Analysis*, ed. I Van Mechelen, J Hampton, R Michalski, P Theuns, pp. 97–144. San Diego, CA: Academic

Barsalou LW, Niedenthal PM, Barbey A, Ruppert J. 2003. Social embodiment. In *The Psychology of Learning and Motivation*, Vol. 43, ed. B Ross, pp. 43–92. San Diego, CA: Academic

Barsalou LW, Santos A, Simmon WK, Wilson CD. 2007b. Language and simulation in conceptual processing. In *Symbols, Embodiment, and Meaning*, ed. M De Vega AM, Glenberg AC, Graesser A. Oxford: Oxford Univ. Press. In press

Barsalou LW, Wiemer-Hastings K. 2005. Situating abstract concepts. In *Grounding Cognition: The Role of Perception and Action in Memory, Language, and Thought*, ed. D Pecher, R Zwaan, pp. 129–63. New York: Cambridge Univ. Press

Barwise J, Etchemendy J. 1991. Visual information and valid reasoning. In *Visualization in Mathematics*, ed. W Zimmerman, S Cunningham, pp. 9–24. Washington, DC: Math. Assoc. Am.

Black JB, Turner TJ, Bower GH. 1979. Point of view in narrative comprehension, memory, and production. *J. Verbal Learn. Verbal Behav.* 18:187–98

Blankenburg F, Ruff CC, Deichmann R, Rees G, Driver J. 2006. The cutaneous rabbit illusion affects human primary sensory cortex somatotopically. *PLoS Biol.* 4:459–66

Borghi AM, Glenberg A, Kaschak M. 2004. Putting words in perspective. *Mem. Cogn.* 32:863–73

Boroditsky L. 2000. Metaphoric structuring: understanding time through spatial metaphors. *Cognition* 75:1–28

Boroditsky L. 2001. Does language shape thought? English and Mandarin speakers' conceptions of time. *Cogn. Psychol.* 43:1–22

Boroditsky L, Ramscar M. 2002. The roles of body and mind in abstract thought. *Psychol. Sci.* 13:185–88

Bosbach S, Cole J, Prinz W, Knoblich G. 2005. Inferring another's expectation from action: the role of peripheral sensation. *Nat. Neurosci.* 8:1295–97

Bower GH, Morrow DG. 1990. Mental models in narrative comprehension. *Science* 247:44–48

Bransford JD, Johnson MK. 1973. Considerations of some problems of comprehension. In *Visual Information Processing*, ed. WG Chase, pp. 383–438. New York: Academic

Breazeal C. 2002. *Designing Sociable Robots*. Cambridge, MA: MIT Press

Bub DN, Masson MEJ, Cree GS. 2007. Evocation of functional and volumetric gestural knowledge by objects and words. *Cognition*. In press

Buccino G, Riggio L, Melli G, Binkofski F, Gallese V, Rizzolatti G. 2005. Listening to action-related sentences modulates the activity of the motor system: a combined TMS and behavioral study. *Cogn. Brain Res.* 24:355–63

Buckner RL, Wheeler ME. 2001. The cognitive neuroscience of remembering. *Nat. Rev. Neurosci.* 2:624–34

Cacioppo JT, Priester JR, Bernston GG. 1993. Rudimentary determination of attitudes: II. Arm flexion and extension have differential effects on attitudes. *J. Personal. Soc. Psychol.* 65:5–17

Calvo-Merino B, Glaser DE, Grèzes J, Passingham RE, Haggard P. 2005. Action observation and acquired motor skills: an fMRI study with expert dancers. *Cereb. Cortex* 8:1243–49

Cangelosi A, Greco A, Harnad S. 2000. From robotic toil to symbolic theft: grounding transfer from entry-level to higher-level categories. *Connect. Sci.* 12:143–62

Cangelosi A, Riga T. 2006. An embodied model for sensorimotor grounding and grounding transfer: experiments with epigenetic robots. *Cogn. Sci.* 30:673–89

Caramazza A, Shelton JR. 1998. Domain-specific knowledge systems in the brain: the animate-inanimate distinction. *J. Cogn. Neurosci.* 10:1–34

Chao LL, Martin A. 2000. Representation of manipulable man-made objects in the dorsal stream. *Neuroimage* 12:478–84

Cheng PW, Holyoak KJ. 1985. Pragmatic reasoning schemas. *Cogn. Psychol.* 17:391–416

Chomsky N. 1957. *Syntactic Structures*. The Hague: Mouton

Clark A. 1997. *Being There: Putting Brain, Body, and World Together Again*. Cambridge, MA: MIT Press

Conway MA. 1990. *Autobiographical Memory: An Introduction*. Buckingham, UK: Buckingham Univ. Press

Conway MA. 2002. Sensory-perceptual episodic memory and its context: autobiographical memory. In *Episodic Memory: New Directions in Research*, ed. A Baddeley, JP Aggleton, MA Conway, pp. 53–70. Oxford: Oxford Univ. Press

Coulson S. 2001. *Semantic Leaps: Frame Shifting and Conceptual Blending in Meaning Construction*. New York: Cambridge Univ. Press

Cree GS, McRae K. 2003. Analyzing the factors underlying the structure and computation of the meaning of chipmunk, cherry, chisel, cheese, and cello (and many other such concrete nouns). *J. Exp. Psychol.: Gen.* 132:163–201

Damasio AR. 1989. Time-locked multiregional retroactivation: a systems-level proposal for the neural substrates of recall and recognition. *Cognition* 33:25–62

Damasio AR, Damasio H. 1994. Cortical systems for retrieval of concrete knowledge: the convergence zone framework. In *Large-Scale Neuronal Theories of the Brain*, ed. C Koch, JL Davis, pp. 61–74. Cambridge, MA: MIT Press

Decety J, Grèzes J. 2006. The power of simulation: imagining one's own and other's behavior. *Brain Res.* 1079:4–14

Dijksterhuis A, Bargh JA. 2001. The perception-behavior expressway: automatic effects of social perception on social behavior. In *Advances in Experimental Social Psychology*, Vol. 23, ed. MP Zanna, pp. 1–40. San Diego, CA: Academic

Epicurus (341–270 B.C.E.). 1987. Sensation, imagination, and memory. In *The Hellenistic Philosophers*, Vol. 1, ed. AA Long, DN Sedley, pp. 72–78. New York: Cambridge Univ. Press

Fauconnier G. 1985. *Mental Spaces*. Cambridge, MA: MIT Press

Fillmore CJ. 1985. Frames and the semantics of understanding. *Quad. di Semantica* 6:222–55

Fincher-Kiefer R. 2001. Perceptual components of situation models. *Mem. Cogn.* 29:336–43

Fincher-Kiefer R, D'Agostino PR. 2004. The role of visuospatial resources in generating predictive and bridging inferences. *Discourse Process.* 37:205–24

Finke RA. 1989. *Principles of Mental Imagery*. Cambridge, MA: MIT Press

Fodor JA, Pylyshyn ZW. 1988. Connectionism and cognitive architecture: a critical analysis. *Cognition* 28:3–71

Franklin N, Tversky B. 1990. Searching imagined environments. *J. Exp. Psychol.: Gen.* 119:63–76

Freyd JJ. 1987. Dynamic mental representations. *Psychol. Rev.* 94:427–38

Gainotti G. 2006. Anatomical functional and cognitive determinants of semantic memory disorders. *Neurosci. Biobehav. Rev.* 30:577–94

Gainotti G, Silveri MC, Daniele A, Giustolisi L. 1995. Neuroanatomical correlates of category-specific semantic disorders: a critical survey. *Memory* 3:247–64

Gallese V. 2003. The roots of empathy: the shared manifold hypothesis and the neural basis of intersubjectivity. *Psychopathology* 36:171–80

Gallese V, Keysers C, Rizzolatti G. 2004. A unifying view of the basis of social cognition. *Trends Cogn. Sci.* 8:396–403

Garagnani M, Wennekers T, Pulvermüller F. 2007. A neural model of the language cortex. *Neurocomputing* 70:1914–19

Garoff RJ, Slotnick SD, Schacter DL. 2005. The neural origins of specific and general memory: the role of the fusiform cortex. *Neuropsychologia* 43:847–59

Gernsbacher MA, Varner KR, Faust ME. 1990. Investigating differences in general comprehension skill. *J. Exp. Psychol.: Learn. Mem. Cogn.* 16:430–45

Gibbs RW Jr. 1994. *The Poetics of Mind: Figurative Thought, Language, and Understanding*. New York: Cambridge Univ. Press

Gibbs RW Jr. 2006. *Embodiment and Cognitive Science*. New York: Cambridge Univ. Press

Gibson JJ. 1979. *The Ecological Approach to Visual Perception*. New York: Houghton Mifflin

Glaser WR. 1992. Picture naming. *Cognition* 42:61–105

Glenberg AM. 1997. What memory is for. *Behav. Brain Sci.* 20:1–55

Glenberg AM, Kaschak MP. 2003. The body's contribution to language. In *The Psychology of Learning and Motivation*, Vol. 43, ed. B Ross, pp. 93–126. New York: Academic

Glenberg AM, Meyer M, Lindem K. 1987. Mental models contribute to foregrounding during text comprehension. *J. Mem. Lang.* 26:69–83

Glenberg AM, Schroeder JL, Robertson DA. 1998. Averting the gaze disengages the environment and facilitates remembering. *Mem. Cogn.* 26:651–58

Glover S, Rosenbaum DA, Graham J, Dixon P. 2004. Grasping the meaning of words. *Exp. Brain Res.* 154:103–8

Goldberg A. 1995. *Constructions. A Construction Grammar Approach to Argument Structure*. Chicago: Univ. Chicago Press

Goldberg RF, Perfetti CF, Schneider W. 2006. Perceptual knowledge retrieval activates sensory brain regions. *J. Neurosci.* 26:4917–21

Goldin-Meadow S. 2003. *Hearing Gesture: How Our Hands Help Us Think*. Cambridge, MA: Harvard Univ. Press

Goldman A. 2006. *Simulating Minds: The Philosophy, Psychology, and Neuroscience of Mindreading*. Oxford: Oxford Univ. Press

Goldreich D. 2007. A Bayesian perceptual model replicates the cutaneous rabbit and other tactile spatiotemporal illusions. *PLoS ONE* 2:e333

Goldstone RL. 1995. Effects of categorization on color perception. *Psychol. Sci.* 5:298–304

Gonzalez J, Barros-Loscertales A, Pulvermüller F, Meseguer V, Sanjuán A, et al. 2006. Reading cinnamon activates olfactory brain regions. *Neuroimage* 32:906–12

Greco C, Hayne H, Rovee-Collier C. 1990. Roles of function, reminding, and variability in categorization by 3-month-old infants. *J. Exp. Psychol.: Learn. Mem. Cogn.* 16:617–33

Grèzes J, Decety J. 2001. Functional anatomy of execution, mental simulation, observation, and verb generation of actions: a meta-analysis. *Hum. Brain Mapp.* 12:1–19

Grush R. 2004. The emulation theory of representation: motor control, imagery, and perception. *Behav. Brain Sci.* 27:377–442

Hadamard J. 1949. *The Psychology of Invention in the Mathematical Field*. New York: Dover

Halpern AR, Zatorre RJ, Bouffard M, Johnson JA. 2004. Behavioral and neural correlates of perceived and imagined timbre. *Neuropsychologia* 42:1281–92

Hansen T, Olkkonen M, Walter S, Gegenfurtner KR. 2006. Memory modulates color appearance. *Nat. Neurosci.* 9:1367–68

Harnad S. 1990. The symbol grounding problem. *Physica D* 42:335–46

Harris CL, Aycicegi A, Berko Gleason J. 2003. Taboo words and reprimands elicit greater autonomic reactivity in a first than in a second language. *Appl. Linguistics* 24:561–79

Haugeland J. 1991. Representational genera. In *Philosophy and Connectionist Theory*, ed. W Ramsey, SP Stitch, DE Rumelhart, pp. 61–89. Hillsdale, NJ: Erlbaum

Havas DA, Glenberg AM, Rinck M. 2007. Emotion simulation during language comprehension. *Psychon. Bull. Rev.* In press

Hegarty M. 2004. Mechanical reasoning as mental simulation. *Trends Cogn. Sci.* 8:280–85

Hegarty M, Mayer S, Kriz S, Keehner M. 2005. The role of gestures in mental animation. *Spat. Cogn. Comput.* 5:333–56

Hegarty M, Steinhoff K. 1997. Use of diagrams as external memory in a mechanical reasoning task. *Learn. Individ. Differ.* 9:19–42

Helbig HB, Graf M, Kiefer M. 2006. The role of action representations in visual object recognition. *Exp. Brain Res.* 174:221–28

Holt LE, Beilock SL. 2006. Expertise and its embodiment: examining the impact of sensorimotor skill expertise on the representation of action-related text. *Psychon. Bull. Rev.* 13:694–701

Humphreys GW, Forde EME. 2001. Hierarchies, similarity, and interactivity in object recognition: "category-specific" neuropsychological deficits. *Behav. Brain Sci.* 24:453–509

Iacoboni M. 2007. Understanding others: imitation, language, empathy. In *Perspectives on Imitation: From Cognitive Neuroscience to Social Science*, ed. S Hurley, N Chater. Cambridge, MA: MIT Press. In press

Iacoboni M, Woods RP, Brass M, Bekkering H, Mazziotta JC, Rizzolatti G. 1999. Cortical mechanisms of human imitation. *Science* 286:2526–28

Intraub H, Gottesman CV, Bills AJ. 1998. Effects of perceiving and imagining scenes on memory for pictures. *J. Exp. Psychol.: Learn. Mem. Cogn.* 24:186–201

Intraub H, Hoffman JE. 1992. Reading and visual memory: remembering scenes that were never seen. *Am. J. Psychol.* 105:101–14

Jackson PL, Meltzoff AN, Decety J. 2005. How do we perceive the pain of others: a window into the neural processes involved in empathy. *NeuroImage* 24:771–79

Jacoby L. 1983. Remembering the data: analyzing interactive processes in reading. *J. Verbal Learn. Verbal Behav.* 22:485–508

Jacoby LL, Hayman CAG. 1987. Specific visual transfer in word identification. *J. Exp. Psychol.: Learn. Mem. Cogn.* 13:456–63

Jeannerod M. 1995. Mental imagery in the motor context. *Neuropsychologia* 33:1419–32

Johnson-Laird PN. 1983. *Mental Models.* Cambridge, MA: Harvard Univ. Press

Jolicoeur P. 1985. The time to name disoriented natural objects. *Mem. Cogn.* 13:289–303

Kan IP, Barsalou LW, Solomon KO, Minor JK, Thompson-Schill SL. 2003. Role of mental imagery in a property verification task: fMRI evidence for perceptual representations of conceptual knowledge. *Cogn. Neuropsychol.* 20:525–40

Kant E. 1787/1965. *The Critique of Pure Reason.* Transl. NK Smith. New York: St. Martin's Press

Kaschak MP. Glenberg AM. 2000. Constructing meaning: the role of affordances and grammatical constructions in sentence comprehension. *J. Mem. Lang.* 43:508–29

Kellenbach ML, Brett M, Patterson K. 2001. Large, colorful, or noisy? Attribute- and modal activations during retrieval of perceptual attribute knowledge. *Cogn. Affect. Behav. Neurosci.* 1:207–21

Kelly SD. 2001. Broadening the units of analysis in communication: speech and nonverbal behaviours in pragmatic comprehension. *J. Child Lang.* 28:325–49

Kelly SD, Iverson J, Terranova J, Niego J, Hopkins M, Goldsmith L. 2002. Putting language back in the body: speech and gesture on three timeframes. *Dev. Neuropsychol.* 22:323–49

Kemmerer D. 2006. The semantics of space: integrating linguistic typology and cognitive neuroscience. *Neuropsychologia* 44:1607–21

Kent C, Lamberts K. 2006. Modeling the time course of feature perception and feature information retrieval. *J. Mem. Lang.* 55:553–71

Kiefer M. 2005. Repetition priming modulates category-related effects on event-related potentials: further evidence for multiple cortical semantic systems. *J. Cogn. Neurosci.* 17:199–211

Kirsner K, Dunn JC, Standen P. 1989. Domain-specific resources in word recognition. In *Implicit Memory: Theoretical Views*, ed. S Lewandowsky, JC Dunn, K Kirsner, pp. 99–122. Hillsdale, NJ: Erlbaum

Klatzky RL, Pelligrino JW, McCloskey BP, Doherty S. 1989. The role of motor representations in semantic sensibility judgments. *J. Mem. Lang.* 28:56–77

Kohler E, Keysers Cl, Umiltá MA, Fogassi L, Gallese V, Rizzolatti G. 2002. Hearing sounds, understanding actions: action representation in mirror neurons. *Science* 297:846–48

Kosslyn SM. 1980. *Image and Mind*. Cambridge, MA: Harvard Univ. Press

Kosslyn SM. 1994. *Image and Brain*. Cambridge, MA: MIT Press

Kosslyn SM, Ganis G, Thompson WL. 2000. Neural foundations of imagery. *Nat. Rev. Neurosci.* 2:635–42

Kosslyn SM, Thompson WL, Ganis G. 2006. *The Case for Mental Imagery*. Oxford: Oxford Univ. Press

Krauss RM. 1998. Why do we gesture when we speak? *Curr. Dir. Psychol. Sci.* 7:54–59

Lakoff G. 1987. *Women, Fire, and Dangerous Things: What Categories Reveal About the Mind*. Chicago: Univ. Chicago Press

Lakoff G, Johnson M. 1980. *Metaphors We Live By*. Chicago: Univ. Chicago Press

Lakoff G, Johnson M. 1999. *Philosophy in the Flesh: The Embodied Mind and Its Challenge to Western Thought*. New York: Basic Books

Langacker RW. 1987. *Foundations of Cognitive Grammar: Vol. 1. Theoretical Prerequisites*. Stanford, CA: Stanford Univ. Press

Langacker RW. 1991. *Foundations of Cognitive Grammar, Vol. II: Descriptive Application*. Stanford, CA: Stanford Univ. Press

Lewis JW. 2006. Cortical networks related to human use of tools. *Neuroscientist* 12:211–31

Levine DN, Warach J, Farah MJ. 1985. Two visual systems in mental imagery: dissociation of "what" and "where" in imagery disorders due to bilateral posterior cerebral lesions. *Neurology* 35:1010–18

Levy R, Goldman-Rakic PS. 2000. Segregation of working memory functions within the dorsolateral prefrontal cortex. *Exp. Brain Res.* 133:23–32

Longo MR, Bertenthal BI. 2006. Common coding of observation and execution of action in 9-month-old infants. *Infancy* 10:43–59

Longo MR, Laurenco SF. 2007. Space perception and body morphology: extent of near space scales with arm length. *Exp. Brain Res.* 177:285–90

Mandler M. 1992. How to build a baby: II. Conceptual primitives. *Psychol. Rev.* 99:587–604

Marques JF. 2006. Specialization and semantic organization: evidence for multiple semantics linked to sensory modalities. *Mem. Cogn.* 34:60–67

Martin A. 2001. Functional neuroimaging of semantic memory. In *Handbook of Functional Neuroimaging of Cognition*, ed. R Cabeza, A Kingstone, pp. 153–86. Cambridge, MA: MIT Press

Martin A. 2007. The representation of object concepts in the brain. *Annu. Rev. Psychol.* 58:25–45

Matlock T. 2004. Fictive motion as cognitive simulation. *Mem. Cogn.* 32:1389–400

McNeill D. 2005. *Gesture and Thought*. Chicago: Univ. Chicago Press

McRae K, Hare M, Elman JL, Ferretti TR. 2005. A basis for generating expectancies for verbs from nouns. *Mem. Cogn.* 33:1174–84

Meier BP, Robinson MD. 2004. Why the sunny side is up: associations between affect and vertical position. *Psychol. Sci.* 15:243–47

Meier BP, Robinson MD. 2006. Does "feeling down" mean seeing down? Depressive symptoms and vertical selective attention. *J. Res. Personal.* 40:451–61

Meltzoff AN. 2007. "Like me": a foundation for social cognition. *Dev. Sci.* 10:126–34

Meltzoff AN, Moore MK. 1983. Newborn infants imitate adult facial gestures. *Child Dev.* 54:702–9

Miceli G, Fouch E, Capasso R, Shelton JR, Tomaiuolo F, Caramazza A. 2001. The dissociation of color from form and function knowledge. *Nat. Neurosci.* 4:662–67

Morrison JB, Tversky B. 1997. Body schemas. In *Proceedings of the Cognitive Science Society*, ed. MG Shafto, P Langley, pp. 525–29. Mahwah, NJ: Erlbaum

Murphy GL. 1997. Reasons to doubt the present evidence for metaphoric representation. *Cognition* 62:99–108

Myung J, Blumstein SE, Sedivy JC. 2006. Playing on the typewriter, typing on the piano: manipulation knowledge of objects. *Cognition* 98:223–43

Namy LL, Smith LB, Gershkoff-Stowe L. 1997. Young children discovery of spatial classification. *Cogn. Dev.* 12:163–84

Nersessian NJ. 1999. Model-based reasoning in conceptual change. In *Model-Based Reasoning in Scientific Discovery*, ed. L Magnani, NJ Nersessian, P Thagard, pp. 5–22. New York: Kluwer Acad./Plenum

Niedenthal PM, Barsalou LW, Winkielman P, Krauth-Gruber S, Ric F. 2005. Embodiment in attitudes, social perception, and emotion. *Pers. Soc. Psychol. Rev.* 9:184–211

Paivio A. 1971. *Imagery and Verbal Processes*. New York: Holt, Rinehart & Winston

Paivio A. 1986. *Mental Representations: A Dual Coding Approach*. New York: Oxford Univ. Press

Parsons LM. 1987a. Imagined spatial transformations of one's body. *J. Exp. Psychol.: Gen.* 116:172–91

Parsons LM. 1987b. Imagined spatial transformations of one's hands and feet. *Cogn. Psychol.* 19:178–241

Pasternak T, Greenlee MW. 2005. Working memory in primate sensory systems. *Nat. Rev. Neurosci.* 6:97–107

Pecher D, Zeelenberg R, Barsalou LW. 2003. Verifying properties from different modalities for concepts produces switching costs. *Psychol. Sci.* 14:119–24

Pecher D, Zeelenberg R, Barsalou LW. 2004. Sensorimotor simulations underlie conceptual representations: modality-specific effects of prior activation. *Psychon. Bull. Rev.* 11:164–67

Polyn SM, Natu VS, Cohen JD, Norman KA. 2005. Category-specific cortical activity precedes retrieval memory search. *Science* 310:1963–66

Potter MC, Kroll JF, Yachzel B, Carpenter E, Sherman J. 1986. Pictures in sentences: understanding without words. *J. Exp. Psychol.: Gen.* 115:281–94

Prinz J. 2002. *Furnishing the Mind: Concepts and Their Perceptual Basis*. Cambridge, MA: MIT

Prinz W. 1997. Perception and action planning. *Eur. J. Cogn. Psychol.* 9:129–54

Proffitt DR. 2006. Embodied perception and the economy of action. *Perspect. Psychol. Sci.* 1:110–22

Pulvermüller F. 2005. Brain mechanisms linking language and action. *Nat. Rev. Neurosci.* 6:576–82

Pulvermüller F, Hauk O, Nikulin VV, Ilmoniemi RJ. 2005. Functional links between motor and language systems. *Eur. J. Neurosci.* 21:793–97

Pulvermüller F, Huss H, Kherif F, Martin FMP, Hauk O, Shtyrov Y. 2006. Motor cortex maps articulatory features of speech sounds. *Proc. Natl. Acad. Sci. USA* 103:7865–70

Pylyshyn ZW. 1973. What the mind's eye tells the mind's brain: a critique of mental imagery. *Psychol. Bull.* 80:1–24

Reed CL, Vinson NG. 1996. Conceptual effects on representational momentum. *J. Exp. Psychol.: Hum. Percept. Perform.* 22:839–50

Reid T. 1785/1969. *Essays on the Intellectual Powers of Man*. Cambridge, MA: MIT Press

Repp BH, Knoblich G. 2004. Perceiving action identity: how pianists recognize their own performances. *Psychol. Sci.* 15:604–9

Richardson DC, Matlock T. 2007. The integration of figurative language and static depictions: an eye movement study of fictive motion. *Cognition* 102:129–38

Richardson DC, Spivey MJ, Barsalou LW, McRae K. 2003. Spatial representations activated during real-time comprehension of verbs. *Cogn. Sci.* 27:767–80

Richter W, Somorjai R, Summers R, Jarmasz M, Menon RS, et al. 2000. Motor area activity during mental rotation studied by time-resolved single-trial fMRI. *J. Cogn. Neurosci.* 12:310–20

Rinck M, Bower GH. 2004. Goal-based accessibility of entities within situation models. In *The Psychology of Learning and Motivation: Advances in Research and Theory*, Vol. 44, ed. BH Ross, pp. 1–33. New York: Elsevier Sci.

Rizzolatti G, Arbib MA. 1998. Language within our grasp. *Trends Neurosci.* 21:188–94

Rizzolatti G, Craighero L. 2004. The mirror-neuron system. *Annu. Rev. Neurosci.* 27:169–92

Robbins P, Aydede M, eds. 2007. *Cambridge Handbook of Situated Cognition*. New York: Cambridge Univ. Press

Rochat P, Striano T. 1999. Emerging self-exploration by 2-month-old infants. *Dev. Sci.* 2:206–18

Roediger HL, Blaxton TA. 1987. Effects of varying modality, surface features, and retention interval on priming in word fragment completion. *Mem. Cogn.* 15:379–88

Roediger HL, McDermott KB. 1993. Implicit memory in normal human subjects. In *Handbook of Neuropsychology*, Vol. 8, ed. F Boller, J Grafman, pp. 63–131. Amsterdam: Elsevier

Ross BH, Wang RF, Kramer AF, Simons DJ, Crowell JA. 2007. Action information from classification learning. *Psychon. Bull. Rev.* In press

Rubin DC. 2006. The basic-systems model of episodic memory. *Perspect. Psychol. Sci.* 1:277–311

Samuel AG. 1997. Lexical activation produces potent phonemic percepts. *Cogn. Psychol.* 32:97–127

Schacter DL, Addis DR. 2007. The cognitive neuroscience of constructive memory: remembering the past and imagining the future. *Philos. Trans. R. Soc. Lond. B Biol. Sci.* 362:773–86

Schacter DL, Dobbins IG, Schnyer DM. 2004. Specificity of priming: a cognitive neuroscience perspective. *Nat. Rev. Neurosci.* 5:853–62

Schacter DL, Graf P. 1989. Modality specificity of implicit memory for new associations. *J. Exp. Psychol.: Learn. Mem. Cogn.* 15:3–12

Schubert T. 2005. Your Highness: vertical positions as perceptual symbols of power. *J. Personal. Soc. Psychol.* 89:1–21

Schwanenflugel PJ. 1991. Why are abstract concepts hard to understand? In *The Psychology of Word Meaning*, ed. PJ Schwanenflugel, pp. 223–50. Mahwah, NJ: Erlbaum

Schwartz DL. 1999. Physical imagery: kinematic vs dynamic models. *Cogn. Psychol.* 38:433–64

Schwartz DL, Black JB. 1996. Analog imagery in mental model reasoning: depictive models. *Cogn. Psychol.* 30:154–219

Searle JR. 1980. Minds, brains, and programs. *Behav. Brain Sci.* 3:417–24

Sebanz N, Bekkering H, Knoblich G. 2006. Joint action: bodies and minds moving together. *Trends Cogn. Sci.* 10:70–76

Shepard RN, Cooper LA. 1982. *Mental Images and Their Transformations*. New York: Cambridge Univ. Press

Shiffrar M, Freyd JJ. 1990. Apparent motion of the human body. *Psychol. Sci.* 4:257–64

Shiffrar M, Freyd JJ. 1993. Timing and apparent motion path choice with human body photographs. *Psychol. Sci.* 6:379–84

Simmons WK, Barsalou LW. 2003. The similarity-in-topography principle: reconciling theories of conceptual deficits. *Cogn. Neuropsychol.* 20:451–86

Simmons WK, Martin A, Barsalou LW. 2005. Pictures of appetizing foods activate gustatory cortices for taste and reward. *Cereb. Cortex* 15:1602–8

Simmons WK, Ramjee V, Beauchamp MS, McRae K, Martin A, Barsalou LW. 2007. Common neural substrates for perceiving and knowing about color and action. *Neuropsychologia* 45:2802–10

Sims VK, Hegarty M. 1997. Mental animation in the visual-spatial sketchpad: evidence from dual-task studies. *Mem. Cogn.* 25:321–32

Slotnick SD, Schacter DL. 2004. A sensory signature that distinguishes true from false memories. *Nat. Neurosci.* 7:664–72

Smith ER, Semin GR. 2004. Socially situated cognition: cognition in its social context. *Adv. Exp. Soc. Psychol.* 36:53–117

Smith LB. 2005a. Action alters shape categories. *Cogn. Sci.* 29:665–79

Smith LB. 2005b. Cognition as a dynamic system: principles from embodiment. *Dev. Rev.* 25:278–98

Smith LB, Gasser M. 2005. The development of embodied cognition: six lessons from babies. *Artif. Life* 11:13–30

Smith LB, Thelen E, Titzer R, McLin D. 1999. Knowing in the context of acting: the task dynamics of the A-not-B Error. *Psychol. Rev.* 106:235–60

Solomon KO, Barsalou LW. 2001. Representing properties locally. *Cogn. Psychol.* 43:129–69

Solomon KO, Barsalou LW. 2004. Perceptual simulation in property verification. *Mem. Cogn.* 32:244–59

Spence C, Nicholls MER, Driver J. 2000. The cost of expecting events in the wrong sensory modality. *Percept. Psychophys.* 63:330–36

Spivey M. 2007. *The Continuity of Mind.* New York: Oxford Univ. Press

Spivey M, Tyler M, Richardson D, Young E. 2000. Eye movements during comprehension of spoken scene descriptions. *Proc. 22nd Annu. Conf. Cogn. Sci. Soc.*, pp. 487–92. Mahwah, NJ: Erlbaum

Steels L, Brooks R. 1995. *The Artificial Life Route to Artificial Intelligence: Building Embodied Situated Agents.* Mahwah, NJ: Erlbaum

Stepper S, Strack F. 1993. Proprioceptive determinants of emotional and nonemotional feelings. *J. Personal. Soc. Psychol.* 64:211–20

Stevens JA, Fonlupt P, Shiffrar M, Decety J. 2000. New aspects of motion perception: selective neural encoding of apparent human movements. *NeuroReport* 11:109–15

Strack F, Martin LL, Stepper S. 1988. Inhibiting and facilitating conditions of the human smile: a nonobtrusive test of the facial feedback hypothesis. *J. Personal. Soc. Psychol.* 54:768–77

Symes E, Ellis R, Tucker M. 2007. Visual object affordances: object orientation. *Acta Psychol.* 124:238–55

Talmy L. 1983. How language structures space. In *Spatial Orientation: Theory, Research, and Application*, ed. H Pick, L Acredelo, pp. 225–82. New York: Plenum

Talmy L. 1988. Force dynamics in language and cognition. *Cogn. Sci.* 12:49–100

Thelen E, Schoner G, Scheier C, Smith LB. 2001. The dynamics of embodiment: a field theory of infant perseverative reaching. *Behav. Brain Sci.* 24:1–86

Thelen E, Smith LB. 1994. *A Dynamic Systems Approach to the Development of Cognition and Action.* Cambridge, MA: MIT Press

Thompson-Schill SL. 2003. Neuroimaging studies of semantic memory: inferring "how" from "where." *Neuropsychologia* 41:280–92

Tomasello M. 2003. *Constructing a Language: A Usage-Based Theory of Language Acquisition.* Cambridge, MA: Harvard Univ. Press

Trueswell JC. 1996. The role of lexical frequency in syntactic ambiguity resolution. *J. Mem. Lang.* 35:566–85

Tucker M, Ellis R. 1998. On the relations between seen objects and components of potential actions. *J. Exp. Psychol.: Hum. Percept. Perform.* 24:830–46

Tucker M, Ellis R. 2001. The potentiation of grasp types during visual object categorization. *Visual Cogn.* 8:769–800

Tucker M, Ellis R. 2004. Action priming by briefly presented objects. *Acta Psychol.* 116:185–203

Turner M. 1996. *The Literary Mind.* New York: Oxford Univ. Press

Tyler LK, Moss HE, Durrant-Peatfield MR, Levy JP. 2000. Conceptual structure and the structure of concepts: a distributed account of category-specific deficits. *Brain Lang.* 75:195–231

Valenzeno L, Alibali MW, Klatzky RL. 2003. Teachers' gestures facilitate students' learning: a lesson in symmetry. *Contemp. Educ. Psychol.* 28:187–204

Van Orden GC, Holden JG, Turvey MT. 2005. Human cognition and 1/f scaling. *J. Exp. Psychol.: Gen.* 134:117–23

Vanman EJ, Paul BY, Ito TA, Miller N. 1997. The modern face of prejudice and structural features that moderate the effect of cooperation on affect. *J. Personal. Soc. Psychol.* 73:941–59

Vermeulen N, Niedenthal PM, Luminet O. 2007. Switching between sensory and affective systems incurs processing costs. *Cogn. Sci.* In press

Warren RM. 1970. Perceptual restoration of missing speech sounds. *Science* 167:392–93

Warrington EK, McCarthy RA. 1987. Categories of knowledge: further fractionations and an attempted integration. *Brain* 110:1273–96

Warrington EK, Shallice T. 1984. Category specific semantic impairments. *Brain* 107:829–54

Watson JB. 1913. Psychology as the behaviorist sees it. *Psychol. Rev.* 20:158–77

Wells GL, Petty RE. 1980. The effects of overt head movements on persuasion: compatibility and incompatibility of responses. *Basic Appl. Soc. Psychol.* 1:219–30

Wennekers T, Garagnani M, Pulvermüller F. 2006. Language models based on Hebbian cell assemblies. *J. Physiol. Paris* 100:16–30

Wheeler ME, Petersen SE, Buckner RL. 2000. Memory's echo: vivid remembering reactivates sensory-specific cortex. *Proc. Natl. Acad. Sci. USA* 97:11125–29

Wicker B, et al. 2003. Both of us disgusted in my insula: the common neural basis of seeing and feeling disgust. *Neuron* 40:655–64

Wiemer-Hastings K, Krug J, Xu X. 2001. Imagery, context availability, contextual constraint, and abstractness. *Proc. 23rd Annu. Conf. Cogn. Sci. Soc.*, pp. 1134–39. Mahwah, NJ: Erlbaum

Wilson M. 2002. Six views of embodied cognition. *Psychon. Bull. Rev.* 9:625–36

Wilson M, Knoblich G. 2005. The case for motor involvement in perceiving conspecifics. *Psychol. Bull.* 131:460–73

Wolpert DM, Ghahramani Z, Jordan MI. 1999. An internal model for sensorimotor integration. *Science* 269:1880–82

Yeh W, Barsalou LW. 2006. The situated nature of concepts. *Am. J. Psychol.* 119:349–84

Zwaan RA, Madden CJ. 2005. Embodied sentence comprehension. In *Grounding Cognition: The Role of Perception and Action in Memory, Language, and Thought*, ed. D Pecher, R Zwaan, pp. 224–45. New York: Cambridge Univ. Press

Zwaan RA, Taylor LJ. 2006. Seeing, acting, understanding: motor resonance in language comprehension. *J. Exp. Psychol.: Gen.* 135:1–11

Neuroeconomics

George Loewenstein,[1] Scott Rick,[2]
and Jonathan D. Cohen[3]

[1] Department of Social and Decision Sciences, Carnegie Mellon University,
Pittsburgh, Pennsylvania 15213, [2] Department of Operations and Information
Management, The Wharton School, University of Pennsylvania, Philadelphia,
Pennsylvania 19104, [3] Department of Psychology, Center for the Study of Brain, Mind
and Behavior, Princeton University, Princeton, New Jersey 08540, and Department of
Psychiatry, Western Psychiatric Institute and Clinic, University of Pittsburgh,
Pittsburgh, Pennsylvania 15260; email: gl20@andrew.cmu.edu,
srick@wharton.upenn.edu, jdc@princeton.edu

Annu. Rev. Psychol. 2008. 59:647–72

First published online as a Review in Advance on
September 17, 2007

The *Annual Review of Psychology* is online at
http://psych.annualreviews.org

This article's doi:
10.1146/annurev.psych.59.103006.093710

Key Words

decision making, emotions, dual-process theories, neuroscience,
behavioral economics

Abstract

Neuroeconomics has further bridged the once disparate fields of
economics and psychology. Such convergence is almost exclusively
attributable to changes within economics. Neuroeconomics has inspired more change within economics than within psychology because the most important findings in neuroeconomics have posed
more of a challenge to the standard economic perspective. Neuroeconomics has primarily challenged the standard economic assumption that decision making is a unitary process—a simple matter of
integrated and coherent utility maximization—suggesting instead
that it is driven by the interaction between automatic and controlled
processes. This article reviews neuroeconomic research in three domains of interest to both economists and psychologists: decision
making under risk and uncertainty, intertemporal choice, and social
decision making. In addition to reviewing new economic models inspired by this research, we also discuss how neuroeconomics may
influence future work in psychology.

Contents

Man is equipped with the psychical and physical make-up of his first human ancestors; he is the sort of being who functions best in the exhilarations and the fatigues of the hunt, of primitive warfare, and in the precarious life of nomadism. He rose superbly to the crises of these existences. Strangely and suddenly he now finds himself transported into a different milieu, keeping, however, as he must, the equipment for the old life. Fortunately his power of reflecting (there seems to be an innate tendency to reflect and learn which is a distinguishing characteristic of our species) has enabled him to persist under the new conditions by modifying his responses to stimuli.

Rexford G. Tugwell,
Journal of Political Economy, 1922

INTRODUCTION

Rexford Tugwell's brilliant analysis of human behavior represents one of the last gasps of a sophisticated psychological account of economic behavior that was once integral to economics (cf. Ashraf et al. 2005), but was lost to the field for almost a century. This psychological perspective took account of the different cognitive and motivational processes driving human behavior—the "equipment for the old life" and the human "power of reflecting"—and of the problems caused by using equipment adapted to the old life to solve problems in "a different milieu"—a human civilization that is dramatically different from that which prevailed when the equipment for the old life evolved.

Even by the time the passage reproduced above was published, the field of economics had rejected the theoretical perspective that can be gleaned from it in favor of a far simpler "rational choice" perspective that treated the power of reflecting, which Tugwell viewed as "the distinguishing characteristic of our species," as the lone force driving human behavior.[1] Indeed, the *Journal of Political Economy*, where Tugwell's paper appeared, was to become the standard-bearer of this perspective. Coupled with a belief in the efficiency of markets, economists' embracing of the rational choice perspective gave them a worldview very different from that of psychologists. Whereas psychologists tend to view humans as fallible and sometimes even self-destructive, economists tend to view people as efficient maximizers of self-interest who make mistakes only when imperfectly informed about the consequences of their actions.

Despite the divergent worldviews of contemporary psychologists and economists, the two disciplines are essentially siblings separated at birth. Both have a fundamental interest in understanding human behavior. Psychology chose early on to focus on empirical questions, largely deferring attempts to formalize the resulting insights until there were sufficient data to constrain theory. By contrast, economics chose to build a foundation of formal theory, at the expense of adopting highly simplified and, ultimately, unrealistic

---

[1] The rational choice perspective may therefore be a manifestation of the "isolation effect," a general tendency to "disregard components that the alternatives share, and focus on the components that distinguish them" (Kahneman & Tversky 1979).

assumptions about the processes governing human behavior.[2] Thus, while psychology became a predominantly empirical discipline, economics became a predominantly theoretical one. This may be one reason why the first journal devoted exclusively to experimental research in psychology, known then as the *Journal of Experimental Psychology*, predates the first analogous journal in economics, *Experimental Economics*, by 82 years (1916 versus 1998).

This is unfortunate, as success in science relies on the interconnection of theory and data. However, there have been attempts to bridge the disciplines. Beginning with the publication of Richard Thaler's (1980) remarkable article, "Toward a Positive Theory of Consumer Choice," a number of economists drew on the nascent field of behavioral decision research for clues about the limitations of the rational choice perspective and insights into alternative assumptions that could better explain real-world human economic behavior. Behavioral decision research arrived, in a sense, custom-made for application to economics, because much of its focus was already on the limitations of the rational choice perspective. Behavioral economics, so named in part because it drew on behavioral decision research, has been a great success story due in part to the strength of the psychological research upon which it drew [for details of these developments, see Angner & Loewenstein (2007)].

Inevitably and fortunately, however, behavioral economics has now moved beyond an exclusive reliance on behavioral decision research; indeed, part of its dynamism has been its willingness to draw upon other lines of research in psychology, including social psychology and cognitive psychology. And, given the increasing prominence of neuroscience within the field of psychology and the openness of behavioral economics to new methods and ideas, it was only a matter of time before behavioral economics would embrace neuroscience. When that happened, in the late 1990s, the new field of neuroeconomics was born.

Neuroeconomics, we argue, has further bridged the once disparate fields of economics and psychology. However, this convergence is almost exclusively attributable to changes within economics. Neuroeconomics has inspired more change within economics than within psychology because the most important findings in neuroeconomics have posed more of a challenge to the standard economic perspective than to dominant perspectives within psychology. For example, much of the research in neuroscience and more recently in neuroeconomics challenges the bedrock assumption within economics that decision making is a unitary process—a simple matter of integrated and coherent utility maximization. One of the most important insights of neuroscience is that the brain is not a homogeneous processor, but rather involves a melding of diverse specialized processes that are integrated in different ways when the brain faces different types of problems. More specifically, some economists have come to appreciate a distinction between automatic processes, which roughly correspond to what Tugwell called the "equipment for the old life," and controlled processes, which correspond to what Tugwell referred to as the "power of reflecting."

Indeed, neuroeconomics has already inspired a spate of economic models that attempt to formalize the idea that judgment and behavior are the result of the interaction between multiple, often conflicting, processes. For example, Bernheim & Rangel (2004) model the brain as operating in either a "cold" mode or a "hot" mode. Which mode is triggered depends (stochastically) on

Behavioral economics: a subdiscipline of economics that incorporates more psychologically realistic assumptions to increase the explanatory and predictive power of economic theory

---

[2] Kenneth Binmore (1988, p. 421), an economist, once described the contrast between psychology and economics more bluntly: "Psychologists accuse economists of having 'no respect for the data', and they are right to do so. It is a disgrace that so little experimental work has been done on the basic tenets on which economic theory is founded... But if economists 'have no respect for the data', it is at least as true that psychologists 'have no respect for theory'."

situational factors, which are partly a function of previous behavior (e.g., whether or not one chooses to enter into a situation that is likely to trigger craving). Loewenstein & O'Donoghue (2004) similarly assume that behavior is the result of the interaction between "deliberative" and "affective" systems. However, rather than assuming that the determination of which system is in control is a stochastic process, they assume that the affective system is normally in control of behavior, and that the deliberative system can influence the affective system's preference by exerting costly cognitive effort or "willpower." Fudenberg & Levine (2006) model choice as the outcome of a struggle between a long-run player and a short-run player (cf. Thaler & Shefrin's 1981 planner-doer model). Benhabib & Bisin (2005) propose that controlled, executive processes "constrain" automatic processes; they monitor the decisions of automatic processes, intervening only when those decisions become excessively suboptimal. Brocas & Carrillo (2006) propose that controlled processes constrain emotional processes that display limited rationality because they are imperfectly informed.

These models represent a shift within economics toward a view that, according to one review of dual processes (Evans 2008), is widely accepted by both cognitive (Posner & Snyder 1975, Shiffrin & Schneider 1977) and social psychologists (Chaiken 1980, Petty & Cacioppo 1981). As the assumptions underlying economic models become increasingly consistent with psychological intuition and empirical reality, psychologists will likely find the techniques and insights offered by these models more readily importable, leading to disciplinary cross-fertilization in the opposite direction of what has mainly occurred until now.

The resulting fresh predictions need not be limited to domains typically studied by psychologists. Economics is centrally focused on tracing out the aggregate implications of individual behavior. Indeed, as Edward Glaeser (2003, p. 10), an economist, notes, "[T]he great achievement of economics is understanding aggregation." Economic models informed by neuroeconomics may offer new insight to psychologists interested in large-scale phenomena.

Another possible avenue for importation of ideas from economics to psychology and neuroscience involves the coordination and orchestration of neural systems. Most neuroscientists tend to be, at least by economic standards, rather microscopic in their focus—typically focusing on a single information-processing task and a very limited range of neural regions. Economics, in contrast, has developed both analytical and simulation methods for modeling the coordination of diverse resources in pursuit of specific goals. The brain is, in fact, much like a modern economy. Like an economy, which consists of diverse specialized units, such as firms, the brain consists of diverse subsystems adapted for various functions (Cohen 2005). And, much as the economy changes when there is a new development such as a war (the famous problem of a transition from "butter" to "guns") or a new technology such as the Internet, the brain is constantly adapting itself to new types of tasks (e.g., using computers, playing video games, functioning in a new job). Neuroscience research has begun to identify some of the mechanisms that are involved in such learning of new tasks (see Hill & Schneider 2006 for a review), but has only recently begun to address how the brain solves the complex problem of allocating scarce processing resources to competing tasks (e.g., Botvinick et al. 2001, Braver & Cohen 2000, Cohen et al. 2007). Given its central focus on the allocation of scarce resources, economics may ultimately provide an analytic framework for addressing this issue.

As suggested above, neuroeconomics has great potential to contribute to psychology, both directly and through its influence on economics. However, these contributions mainly lie in the future. This review focuses on neuroeconomics research that has primarily influenced economics. Specifically, we focus our review on three domains of behavior of interest to both economists and psychologists: decision making under risk and uncertainty, intertemporal choice, and social decision making.

DECISION MAKING UNDER RISK AND UNCERTAINTY

When choosing between alternative courses of action, people rarely know with certainty what consequences those actions will produce; most decisions are made under conditions of risk. The still dominant theory of how they do so is the expected utility (EU) model, which was first proposed by Daniel Bernoulli in 1738. According to EU, people choose between alternative courses of action by assessing the desirability or "utility" of each action's possible outcomes, weighing those utilities by their probability of occurring, and selecting the course of action that yields the greatest sum—i.e., "expected utility."

Although the model seems superficially plausible and can be derived from a set of seemingly sensible axioms (von Neumann & Morgenstern 1944), researchers have uncovered a wide range of expected utility anomalies—common patterns of behavior that are inconsistent with EU (see Starmer 2000 for a review). Initial attempts by behavioral economists to explain these anomalies adhered to the unitary decision-making perspective, but modified it in the direction of greater psychological realism. For example, EU assumes that the utility of a particular outcome is not simply based on that outcome, but rather on the integration of that outcome with all assets accumulated to that point. Consider, for example, a gamble that offers a 50% chance of winning $20 and a 50% chance of losing $10. If your current wealth totals $1 million, then EU assumes that you view the gamble as offering a 50% chance of experiencing the utility of $1,000,020 and a 50% chance of experiencing the utility of $999,990. However, as originally noted by Markowitz (1952) and developed more fully by Kahneman & Tversky (1979), people typically make decisions with a more local focus; they "bracket" their decisions more narrowly (Read et al. 1999). Most people would, for example, not view the gamble just discussed in terms of different final levels of wealth, but would instead process it as presented— as a 50% chance of winning $20 and a 50% chance of losing $10. Moreover, people tend to dislike losses more than they like gains, a phenomenon known as loss aversion (Tversky & Kahneman 1991). Combined with narrow bracketing, loss aversion can help to explain a wide range of phenomena, from the almost universal tendency to reject symmetric bets— e.g., a 50-50 chance to gain or lose $100— to the preference for investing in bonds over stocks (Benartzi & Thaler 1995, Gneezy & Potters 1997), to the tendency to hold on to stocks and houses that fall in value (Genesove & Mayer 2001).

EU: expected utility

Other behavioral research has focused not only on the utility or "value" function, but also on probability weighting. Whereas EU assumes that people weigh outcomes according to their raw probability of occurring, behavioral modifications to EU have assumed instead that people overweight small probabilities and underweight large ones (Kahneman & Tversky 1979) or that they tend to place disproportionate attention on the worst and best outcomes that could occur (e.g., Quiggin 1982), either of which can help to make sense of why people often play the lottery *and* buy insurance. In combination, these modifications to EU's standard assumptions can explain a wide range of risky decision-making phenomena while adhering to a unitary decision-making framework.

There is, however, a range of decision-making phenomena that do not appear to be well explained by any existing unitary models of risky decision making. For example, at an experiential level, people often seem to be of two minds when it comes to risks: they fear outcomes that they know are not objectively serious but experience little trepidation toward outcomes that they know to be seriously threatening. The former is well illustrated by the behavior of phobics who are typically aware that the object of their fear is objectively nonthreatening, but are prevented by their emotional reactions from acting on this judgment (Barlow 1988, Epstein 1994). Such conflicts are not limited to phobics; many people greatly fear outcomes they cognitively recognize as highly unlikely (e.g., airplane crashes).

To account for regularities of this type, Loewenstein et al. (2001) proposed the "risk as feelings" (RAF) hypothesis, which postulated that people react to risks at two levels—by evaluating them in the dispassionate fashion posited by unitary models, but also at an emotional level; that is, different evaluative mechanisms using different cost functions may each respond differently to the same circumstances. For example, emotional responses to risks tend to be strongly related to newness; we overreact emotionally to new risks (often low-probability events) and underreact to those that are familiar (though they may be much more likely to occur). This can explain why, for instance, people seemed to initially overreact to the risk of terrorism in the years immediately following 9/11 but tend to underreact to the much more familiar risk of driving—eating, drinking, and talking on the cell phone while driving and failing to take full advantage of seatbelts and child seats.

Neuroeconomic research on decision making under risk and uncertainty has thus far focused on examining the extent to which EU anomalies can be attributed to emotions experienced at the moment of choice. Although many studies have found a relationship between immediate emotions and risky decision making, the evidence for multiple systems is mixed. Below, we review some of the major findings.

LITERATURE REVIEW

Risk Aversion and Loss Aversion

Several early studies in neuroeconomics focused on understanding why people are sen-

sitive to differences between outcomes and reference points, rather than to absolute end-states. Knutson et al. (2003), for example, found that activation in medial prefrontal cortex (MPFC; a target of dopaminergic projections) was lower after failing to receive an anticipated reward than after anticipating, and then receiving, no reward (cf. Abler et al. 2005). Similarly, several studies have found that activation in another dopaminergic target, nucleus accumbens (NAcc), was greater following the unanticipated delivery of juice and water than after the anticipated delivery of juice and water (Berns et al. 2001, McClure et al. 2003). This is consistent with earlier animal research, which has found that dopamine neurons within the ventral striatum of monkeys are sensitive to new information about anticipated rewards, which can be viewed as changes relative to the reference point of expectations (e.g., Montague et al. 1996). This research suggests that the tendency to encode gambles as gains and losses rather than as final levels of wealth may not simply be due to the greater simplicity of the former, but rather to a hardwired tendency for specific neural circuits to respond to deviations from expectations.

Other neuroeconomic research has examined whether the prospect of risky outcomes elicits anticipatory emotions. For instance, Kahn et al. (2002) conducted an experiment in which participants played a game that required occasional bluffing, which exposed them to the risk of being caught and suffering a loss. When a choice had been made but the outcome remained unknown, activation in amygdala was greater following bluffs than following honest play. The amygdala is closely associated with the processing of fear (LeDoux 1996), though it is often more generally associated with maintaining vigilance (e.g., Phelps et al. 2000). Knutson et al. (2001) found that self-reported happiness and NAcc activation increased as anticipated (probabilistic) gains increased (cf. Breiter et al. 2001). These studies support the RAF hypothesis that salient risky outcomes elicit emotional reactions, but note that they did not focus on the key RAF prediction, namely whether emotion actually influenced decision making.

Damasio (1994) and Bechara et al. (1997) have proposed, consistent with RAF, that decision makers encode the consequences of alternative courses of action affectively and that such "somatic markers" serve as an important input to decision making. As a consequence, individuals with damage to regions that affectively encode information should be disadvantaged relative to individuals without such damage in situations in which emotions lead to better decision making. Damasio (1994) originally argued that the ventromedial prefrontal cortex (VMPFC) plays a critical role in this affective encoding process, and Bechara et al. (1997) therefore compared the behavior of individuals with and without VMPFC damage in a gambling task. On any given turn, players could draw cards from one of four decks, two of which included $100 gains and two of which contained $50 gains. The high-paying decks also included a small number of substantial losses, resulting in a net negative expected value for these decks. Bechara et al. (1997) found that both nonpatients and those with VMPFC damage avoided the high-paying decks immediately after incurring substantial losses. However, individuals with VMPFC damage resumed sampling from the high-paying decks more quickly than nonpatients did after encountering a substantial loss. Bechara et al. (1997) argued that nonpatients' ability to generate somatic markers allowed them to play advantageously before consciously understanding the advantageous strategy.

The Bechara et al. (1997) study stimulated much interest and subsequent research (901 citations according to Google Scholar when this review went to press), but it has not been immune to criticism (see Dunn et al. 2005 for a review). Maia & McClelland (2004), for example, propose that the questionnaires Bechara et al. (1997) used were insufficiently powerful to uncover all the knowledge consciously held by participants. Maia & McClelland (2004) created a more sensitive measure and found that verbal reports (among nonpatients only) indicated knowledge of the advantageous strategy more reliably than did actual behavior and that participants were rarely able to play advantageously without being able to report the advantageous strategy.

VMPFC:
ventromedial
prefrontal cortex

Although subsequent critiques have further challenged the findings of Bechara et al. (1997), the somatic marker hypothesis has remained intuitively appealing and has received renewed support. Recently, Bechara and colleagues (Shiv et al. 2005) compared the behavior of individuals with and without damage to the amygdala, the orbitofrontal cortex, the right insular cortex, or the somatosensory cortex (regions critical for the processing of emotions; e.g., Davidson et al. 2000, Dolan 2002) in a new gambling task. Participants were given a chance to bet on a series of coin flips that would each result in winning $2.50 or losing $1. Because each gamble has a positive expected value, participants who are fearful of risk are at a disadvantage. Consistent with the hypothesis that the regions of interest in this study are critical for the processing of emotions, participants with damage to those regions earned more money than did participants without such damage. The results are consistent with the somatic marker hypothesis, but they also suggest that the extent to which emotional deficits lead to poor decision making depends critically on the specific decision context.

Negative affect has also been proposed as an explanation for loss aversion in other contexts. One phenomenon that is typically attributed to loss aversion is the "endowment effect" (Thaler 1980), which refers to the tendency for people to value an object more highly if they possess it than they would value the same object if they did not. Kahneman et al. (1990), for example, demonstrated the effect by endowing one group of participants (sellers) with an object and giving them the option of selling it for various amounts of cash. They did not endow another group of participants (choosers) and then gave them a series of choices between receiving the object and receiving various amounts of cash. Although sellers and choosers are in identical wealth positions, and face identical choices (leave with money or object), sellers hold out for significantly more money than choosers are willing to forgo to obtain the object.

Weber et al. (2007) attempted to examine the neural underpinnings of the endowment effect in an experiment in which participants had the opportunity to buy and sell digital copies of songs. Specifically, participants were endowed with 32 songs and asked to state how much money they would require to sell the songs. They were also asked to state how much money they would be willing to pay to buy another 32 songs. Weber et al. (2007) found that amygdala activation was greater in the selling condition than in the buying condition. Caution is required when interpreting the results of this study, however. Note that the endowment effect is not the difference between how much people demand to sell a good and how much they are willing to pay to acquire it. Both selling and buying involve one loss and one gain (selling involves losing the good and getting money; buying involves losing money and getting the good). A more natural comparison is between selling and choosing (getting the good or getting money), which holds the money side constant but varies whether one is obtaining or giving up the good. This limitation of the study makes it difficult to interpret the significance of the difference in amygdala activation across the selling and buying conditions, and in particular to identify it as the source of loss aversion.

Indeed, conflicting with the conclusion of Weber et al. (2007) that losses bring qualitatively different processes into play is a study by Tom et al. (2007) that more directly investigated the neural underpinnings of loss aversion. Participants in the experiment were given a series of options to accept or reject a series of gambles that offered a 50% chance of winning money and a 50% chance of losing money. The authors found that no brain regions, including those associated with experiencing fear, showed significantly increasing activation as the size of the potential loss increased. Rather, activation in dorsal and ventral striatum and VMPFC, dopaminergic targets previously shown to be associated with the anticipation and receipt of monetary rewards (e.g., Knutson et al. 2001), showed increasing activation as gains increased and decreasing activation as losses increased (with the latter effect about twice the magnitude of the former). Their conclusion is that loss aversion appears to be driven by an asymmetric response to gains and losses within regions targeted by dopamine projections.

Loss aversion can explain the great dislike of playing "mixed" gambles, which offer a chance of gaining or losing money. However, in and of itself, loss aversion makes no prediction about whether and how risk-taking will change when it comes to gambles that involve all gains (e.g., $10 versus a 10% chance of $100) or all losses. In fact, there is good evidence that people generally tend to be risk-averse when it comes to gambles involving gains (as long as probabilities are in the mid-range) and to be risk-seeking for gambles involving all losses. In a canonical demonstration of this phenomenon, Tversky & Kahneman (1981) asked participants to imagine that the United States is preparing for the outbreak of an unusual Asian disease that is expected to kill 600 people. Participants are then asked to choose between two pairs of programs to combat the problem. In the gain condition, participants are told, "If program A is adopted, 200 people will be saved. If program B is adopted, there is a 1/3 probability that 600 people will be saved and a 2/3 probability that no one will be saved." In the loss condition, participants are told, "If program C is adopted, 400 people will die. If program D is adopted, there is a 1/3 probability that nobody will die and a 2/3 probability that 600 people will die." Most people presented with these decisions prefer A to B *and* D to C, which is surprising because program A is identical to program C, and B to D.

Naturally, such a pattern of choices is anomalous from the rational choice perspective, which assumes that decisions are based on the likelihood and desirability of final outcomes. Kahneman & Tversky (1979) account for this "reflection effect" by proposing that the marginal value of both gains and losses generally decreases with their magnitude. Such diminishing sensitivity produces risk-aversion in the domain of gains (i.e., a preference for a certain gain of x over a gamble with an expected value of x), and risk-seeking in the domain of losses (i.e., a preference for a gamble with an expected value of $-x$ over a certain $-x$), which explains why people like a program that will save 200 lives with certainty but not an (equivalent) program that will lose 400 lives with certainty.

Recent neuroeconomic research suggests, however, that fear may also play a role in producing the reflection effect. De Martino et al. (2006) asked participants to choose between certain and risky gains and losses while having their brains scanned with fMRI. The authors found that amygdala activation was greater when participants chose certain gains over risky gains as well as when participants chose risky losses over certain losses. Moreover, De Martino et al. (2006) found that activity in anterior cingulate cortex (ACC) was greater when participants made choices that ran counter to the reflection effect (i.e., risky gains over certain gains, certain losses over risky losses). The ACC has been hypothesized to detect and signal the occurrence of conflicts in information processing (Botvinick et al. 2001, Carter et al. 1998). Accordingly, the results suggest that greater conflict must be resolved before expressing preferences inconsistent with the reflection effect than before expressing preferences consistent with the effect. Contrary to Tom et al. (2007), the results of De Martino et al. (2006) are consistent with the operation of qualitatively different systems within the brain (Kahneman & Frederick 2006).

Ambiguity Aversion

Thus far we have focused on situations in which probabilities are known and presented in numerical form to subjects. However, in the real world, people often make decisions without explicit knowledge of probabilities—under conditions of "ambiguity." Some decision-researchers have argued that there is no meaningful difference between uncertain (probabilistic) and ambiguous events. Savage (1954), among others, argued that, even when people cannot articulate the probability of a particular event, they still behave as if the event has a specific "subjective probability." However, Daniel Ellsberg (1961), in a famous paper, argued that people treat ambiguous probabilities differently from unambiguous ones. In one illustration of this point, Ellsberg presents the reader with two hypothetical urns, each containing red and/or black balls. Urn I contains 100 red and black balls, but in an unknown ratio. Urn II contains exactly 50 red and 50 black balls. Drawing a ball of a designated color from an urn wins $100.

People tend to be indifferent between betting on red or black from Urn I, which in subjective probability terms can be taken to imply that they believe that each has a 50% chance of occurring. Similarly, people are indifferent to betting on red or black from Urn II, which has the equivalent interpretation. However, most people prefer betting on red from Urn II to betting on red from Urn I *and* betting on black from Urn II to betting on black from Urn I, which is impossible to make sense of if one believes that people are behaving as if they hold coherent probabilities for the different events.

Although ambiguity aversion has received much attention since Ellsberg's seminal work in 1961, the explanation for the anomaly has itself remained ambiguous. Many explanations have been proposed (Curley et al. 1986), and they can be divided into three major classes. One type of explanation assumes that people react pessimistically to ambiguous

fMRI: functional magnetic resonance imaging

ACC: anterior cingulate cortex

probabilities, as if they assume that when the odds are unknown they will be stacked against the decision maker. Ellsberg himself offered such an account. A second class of explanation assumes that people treat probabilities as if they were outcomes and, much as they tend to be risk-averse with respect to outcomes (e.g., they prefer a sure $500 over a 50-50 chance to gain zero or $1000), they are also risk-averse with respect to probabilities (e.g., they prefer a "sure" 50% chance of winning over a 50-50 chance of having either a 0% or 100% chance of winning). Finally, a third explanation assumes that ambiguity aversion involves the overapplication of a heuristic that often makes sense: Avoid betting when other people possess information that you lack, or when you lack information that would be helpful in making a decision.

Curley et al. (1986) tested several proposed explanations behaviorally. They found that participants who said the ambiguous urn could not be biased against them were still ambiguity-averse, suggesting ambiguity aversion is not driven by pessimism about a "hostile" generation of outcomes. The authors also found that ambiguity aversion was uncorrelated with risk aversion, casting doubt on the second class of explanations discussed above. Finally, Curley et al. (1986) found that participants were significantly more ambiguity-averse when they were told that the chosen gamble would be played and the urn's contents revealed in front of other participants than when the gamble was resolved privately. The authors thus surmised that ambiguity aversion is due to social presentation concerns. However, their findings essentially reveal a situational moderator rather than an explanation for why people are generally ambiguity-averse. Subsequent studies have revealed other interesting moderators (e.g., Fox & Tversky 1995, Heath & Tversky 1991, Kühberger & Perner 2003), but a general explanation for ambiguity aversion has remained somewhat elusive.

Hsu et al. (2005) investigated the neural underpinnings of ambiguity aversion by asking participants to make choices between certain outcomes and risky gambles and between certain outcomes and ambiguous gambles. In a Card-Deck condition, gambles offer either clear probabilities (e.g., a 50% chance of winning $10) or ambiguous probabilities (e.g., an unknown chance of winning $10). In a Knowledge condition, gambles are based on either events participants have some knowledge about (e.g., win $10 by correctly guessing whether the high temperature in New York City on November 7, 2003 was above 50°F) or events participants likely have far less knowledge about (e.g., win $10 by correctly guessing whether the high temperature in Dushanbe, Tajikistan on November 7, 2003 was above 50°F). Finally, in an Informed Opponent condition, participants are presented with a deck that contains 20 red and blue cards, but in an unknown ratio. In the ambiguous condition, the opponent is allowed to sample three cards from the deck; in the risk condition, the opponent is not allowed to sample from the deck. Both participants then choose a color. Finally, a card is drawn from the deck, and participants win if they chose the realized color and their opponent chose the opposite color.

Across all conditions, Hsu et al. (2005) found that activation in amygdala as well as orbitofrontal cortex (OFC; a region thought to integrate cognitive and emotional inputs, e.g., Critchley et al. 2001) was significantly greater in the ambiguity condition than in the risk condition.[3] The findings appear most consistent with the first and last accounts of ambiguity aversion discussed above. Interestingly, an analysis of the time course of activity within the amygdala and OFC revealed no strong differences between the Informed Opponent condition and the Card-Deck or Knowledge conditions, suggesting that ambiguity-induced negative affect was no greater when others had information the

---

[3]The same paper reported that a sample of people with OFC lesions were both risk- and ambiguity-neutral, whereas people without OFC lesions were both risk- and ambiguity-averse.

participant lacked. Though the results do not explicitly favor any one particular explanation for ambiguity aversion, what is clear is that people appear to have an immediate negative emotional reaction to ambiguity.

SUMMARY

The neuroeconomic research on decision making under risk and uncertainty has yielded some provocative findings, but remains largely unintegrated. Consistent with the somatic marker hypothesis, Shiv et al. (2005) find evidence suggesting that mild emotions play an advisory role in the decision-making process. Weber et al. (2007) claim that amygdala activation underlies the endowment effect, but unfortunately, their experimental design (comparing selling prices to buying prices) does not permit such an inference. And while De Martino et al.'s (2006) work on the reflection effect is readily interpreted as evidence for multiple systems (Kahneman & Frederick 2006), Tom et al. (2007) explicitly interpret their results regarding loss aversion as evidence against dual-systems accounts. Finally, the results of Hsu et al. (2005) suggest that negative affect plays a role in ambiguity aversion. Thus, while some of the reviewed research has provided fairly compelling support for the proposed role of emotion in risky decision making, the extent to which such results generally support a dual-system account of behavior is still unclear. Stronger evidence for the multiple systems perspective comes from neuroeconomic research on intertemporal choice. We turn to that work below.

INTERTEMPORAL CHOICE

Another central topic in economics is intertemporal choice—decisions involving alternatives whose costs and benefits are distributed over time. The discounted utility (DU) model is the dominant model of intertemporal choice in economics (Samuelson 1937). Although the DU model, like the EU model, can be derived from a set of primitive, intuitively compelling axioms (Koopmans 1960), several anomalies have been identified that call the model's descriptive validity into question (see Frederick et al. 2002 for a review).

One of the most important, and frequently criticized, assumptions of DU is the assumption of exponential discounting, which implies that a given time delay leads to the same amount of discounting regardless of when it occurs. Delaying the delivery of a good by one day, for example, presumably leads to the same degree of time discounting whether that delay makes the difference between consuming the good tomorrow rather than today or in a year and a day rather than in a year. However, there is strong evidence that people (as well as animals) do not discount the future exponentially (Kirby & Herrnstein 1995, Rachlin & Raineri 1992). Rather, people care more about the same time delay if it is proximal rather than distal, a general pattern that has been referred to as "hyperbolic time discounting" (Ainslie 1975). For instance, delaying consumption of a pleasurable good from today to tomorrow is more distressing than delaying consumption from a year from now to a year and a day from now.

Several hypotheses have been advanced to explain why people discount the future hyperbolically. The most common has been to simply assume that hyperbolic time discounting is, in effect, hardwired into our evolutionary apparatus. Advocates of this approach often draw attention to the observation that all animals in whom discounting has been measured also discount the future hyperbolically. However, despite the superficial similarity, there is an enormous discontinuity between humans and other animals. Even after long periods of training, our nearest evolutionary relatives have measured discount functions that fall in value nearly to zero after a delay of about one minute. For example, Stevens et al. (2005) report that cotton-top tamarin monkeys are unable to wait more than eight seconds to triple the value of an immediately available

DU: discounted utility

food reward. Although it is possible that the same mechanism could produce functions that differ so dramatically in magnitude of discounting, it seems unlikely. Moreover, much as people often feel of two minds when it comes to decision making under risk, such intrapersonal conflicts are even more prevalent and dramatic when it comes to intertemporal choice (e.g., the choice between a piece of chocolate cake on the dessert cart and adhering to one's diet).

Neuroeconomic research on intertemporal choice has largely focused on whether behavior can be better explained by the interaction of multiple systems. The central debate in this domain of research has focused on the role of the limbic system in intertemporal choice. The limbic system, which commonly refers to the medial and orbital regions of frontal cortex (along the inner surfaces and base of the frontal lobes, respectively), the amygdala (along the inner surface of the temporal lobes), the insular cortex (at the junction of the frontal and temporal lobes), and their subcortical counterparts, is thought to be critical to emotional processing (Dalgleish 2004). Some evidence suggests that these structures preferentially respond to immediately available rewards (McClure et al. 2004b, 2007), but recent research argues that these structures respond to rewards at all delays (Glimcher et al. 2007). Below we examine the competing claims as well as related neuroeconomic research on intertemporal choice.

LITERATURE REVIEW

Instead of assuming that hyperbolic discounting is hardwired into our evolutionary apparatus, some researchers have proposed that hyperbolic discounting reflects the operation of two fundamentally different systems, one that heavily values the present and cares little about the future, and the other deliberative, which discounts outcomes more consistently across time (e.g., Loewenstein 1996, Shefrin & Thaler 1988).

McClure et al. (2004b) tested the hypothesis by measuring the brain activity of participants while they made a series of intertemporal choices between small proximal rewards ($R available at delay d) and larger delayed rewards ($R' available at delay d'), where $R < R' and $d < d'$. Rewards ranged from \$5 to \$40 Amazon.com gift certificates, and the delay ranged from the day of the experiment to six weeks later. The purpose of the study was to examine whether there were brain regions that show elevated activation (relative to a resting-state benchmark) only when immediacy is an option (i.e., activation when $d = 0$, but no activation when $d > 0$) and whether there were regions that show elevated activation when making any intertemporal decision. McClure et al. (2004b) found that time discounting results from the combined influence of two neural systems. Limbic and paralimbic cortical structures, which are known to be rich in dopaminergic innervation, are preferentially recruited for choices involving immediately available rewards. In contrast, fronto-parietal regions, which support higher cognitive functions, are recruited for all intertemporal choices (as contrasted with rest periods). Moreover, the authors find that when choices involved an opportunity for immediate reward, thus engaging both systems, greater activity in fronto-parietal regions than in limbic regions is associated with choosing larger delayed rewards, whereas greater activity in limbic regions than in fronto-parietal regions is associated with choosing smaller immediate rewards. Other research arriving at the same conclusion with different methods found that people with greater activation in these limbic reward regions in response to gaining or losing money also place greater weight on immediate rewards relative to delayed rewards (Hariri et al. 2006).

Note, however, that since the rewards were gift certificates, the consumption they afforded was not immediate in any conventional sense. To address this limitation,

McClure et al. (2007) ran an experiment in which the brains of thirsty participants were scanned with fMRI while they made a series of choices between receiving a small amount of juice or water immediately (by having it squirted into their mouth) and receiving a larger amount of juice or water up to 20 minutes later. Like McClure et al. (2004b), McClure et al. (2007) found that limbic regions were preferentially recruited for choices involving immediately available juice or water, whereas fronto-parietal regions were recruited for all choices.

The extent to which such findings actually support a two-system account of intertemporal choice is not uncontroversial, however (see, e.g., Ainslie & Monterosso's 2004 commentary on McClure et al. 2004b). Glimcher et al. (2007; Experiment 2) recently conducted a study in which participants made two types of choices. In the Immediate-Option condition, participants chose between small proximal rewards and larger delayed rewards. In the Delayed-Option condition, participants chose between small rewards available at a delay of 60 days and larger rewards available at a delay of more than 60 days. Glimcher et al. (2007) found that limbic and paralimbic structures such as MPFC, ventral striatum, and posterior cingulate were not preferentially recruited for choices involving immediately available rewards. However, this may due to a counterintuitive finding in the Delayed-Option condition. Inconsistent with previous behavioral research on intertemporal "preference reversals" (Green et al. 1994, Kirby & Herrnstein 1995, Millar & Navarick 1984, Solnick et al. 1980), Glimcher et al. (2007) found that participants adopted an "as soon as possible" strategy in the Delayed-Option condition. Specifically, participants tended to prefer the small reward in both the Immediate-Option and Delayed-Option conditions. Evidence against multiple systems would be more compelling if it were obtained in an experiment that replicated the behavioral regularity under investigation.

While the above studies examined how people choose between well-defined immediate and delayed rewards, note that consumers rarely face such explicit choices. Although the standard economic perspective assumes that the price of a good represents how much future pleasure must be forgone to finance immediate consumption, it is not at all clear that people spontaneously consider such "opportunity costs" in their purchasing decisions. Consider, for instance, a study by Frederick et al. (2006) in which participants were asked if they would (hypothetically) be willing to purchase a desirable video for $14.99. The researchers simply varied whether the decision not to buy it was framed as "not buy this entertaining video" or "keep the $14.99 for other purchases." Although the two phrases represent equivalent actions, the latter highlights the pleasure that is forgone by purchasing the video. Frederick et al. (2006) found that drawing attention to opportunity costs significantly reduced the proportion of participants willing to purchase the video, suggesting that some participants are not spontaneously considering opportunity costs.

If prices do not always deter spending through a deliberative consideration of opportunity costs, then what role do prices play in spending decisions? Knutson et al. (2007) investigated this question in an experiment in which participants chose whether or not to purchase a series of discounted consumer goods while having their brains scanned with fMRI. Participants were given $20 to spend and were told that one of their decisions would ultimately be randomly selected to count for real. At the conclusion of the experiment, participants indicated how much they liked each product and how much they would be willing to pay for it.

Knutson et al. (2007) found that the extent to which participants reported liking the products correlated positively with NAcc activation, which itself positively correlated with actual purchasing decisions. However, Knutson et al. (2007) also found that activation in insula during the period when subjects first saw the price correlated negatively with purchasing decisions. Insula activation has previously been observed in connection with aversive stimuli such as disgusting odors (Wicker et al. 2003), unfairness (Sanfey et al. 2003), and social exclusion (Eisenberger et al. 2003). Thus, when delayed rewards are not explicitly represented (as in, e.g., McClure et al. 2004b), but rather implicitly captured by prices, participants appear to rely on an anticipatory "pain of paying" (Prelec & Loewenstein 1998) to deter their spending, rather than an exclusively deliberative consideration of pleasures forgone by consuming immediately.

Subsequent research by Rick et al. (2007) suggests that the pain of paying produces a divergence between desired and typical spending behavior. The authors developed a Spendthrift-Tightwad scale to measure individual differences in the pain of paying. Tightwads report experiencing the pain of paying intensely and also report that they typically spend less than they would ideally like to spend. Spendthrifts report experiencing minimal pain of paying and also report that they typically spend more than they would ideally like to spend. In both cases, emotional reactions to the prospect of spending appear to prevent the implementation of more deliberative goals.

Other evidence suggestive of dual systems in the domain of consumer choice comes from a study of soft drink preferences. McClure et al. (2004a) first asked participants whether they preferred Coke or Pepsi. Participants were then asked to drink unlabeled cups of Coke and Pepsi and indicate which they preferred. Finally, participants had their brains scanned with fMRI while receiving squirts of Coke and Pepsi, and they were again not told which soda they were receiving. The correlation between stated and behavioral (i.e., taste-test) preferences failed to reach signif-

icance. Unlabeled cups of Coke were about as well liked by self-proclaimed Coke-lovers as they were by self-proclaimed Pepsi-lovers. However, while participants were drinking Coke and Pepsi, the difference in activation in VMPFC (a region often associated with the experience of reward; Bechara et al. 1994, Knutson et al. 2001, McClure et al. 2007, O'Doherty et al. 2003) strongly correlated with behavioral preferences. Why did experienced pleasure correlate with behavioral preferences, but not stated preferences?[4] To begin to answer this question, McClure et al. (2004a) ran another study in which participants were either told that they were about to receive Coke or that they were about to receive either Coke or Pepsi; after both signals, participants received Coke. Activation in several regions (e.g., hippocampus, dorsolateral prefrontal cortex) was significantly greater when participants knew they were about to receive Coke than when they did not know what was coming. However, activation in VMPFC, and other regions commonly implicated in the experience of pleasure, did not vary across conditions.[5] The authors concluded that structures associated with the experience of pleasure and structures that retain cultural information (e.g., about brands) may function separately to influence stated preferences.

SUMMARY

The extent to which intertemporal choice is generated by multiple systems with conflicting priorities is a hotly debated issue within neuroeconomics. McClure et al. (2004b, 2007) found that limbic and paralimbic cortical structures, which are known

---

[4]Note that in the real world, "stated preferences" would manifest themselves behaviorally, as supermarkets typically do not allow customers to choose between Coke and Pepsi by taking blind taste-tests.

[5]Analogous results were not found in another study in which participants were told that they were about to receive Pepsi or that they were about to receive either Coke or Pepsi. Activation in no brain regions varied significantly across conditions.

to be rich in dopaminergic innervation, are preferentially recruited for choices involving immediately available rewards, whereas fronto-parietal regions, which support higher cognitive functions, are recruited for all intertemporal choices. Knutson et al. (2007) found evidence consistent with the hypothesis that pain, rather than attention to opportunity costs, acts to deter the desire to consume immediately. Subsequent behavioral research by Rick et al. (2007) suggests that the pain of paying can produce a divergence between desired and typical spending behavior. McClure et al. (2004a) suggested that separable systems are involved in generating brand preferences. Glimcher and colleagues (2007), however, have argued against a dual-system interpretation of intertemporal choice. However, as noted above, their study failed to observe many intertemporal "preference reversals," a regularity commonly found in purely behavioral studies and other neuroimaging experiments. Although the majority of the evidence therefore supports a multiple systems account of intertemporal choice, the debate will undoubtedly continue.

SOCIAL DECISION MAKING

Although there are widely accepted normative benchmarks for risky decision making and intertemporal choice, no such benchmarks exist for how people should behave toward others. Some hard-line economists have assumed that pure self-interest is, or should be, the norm, but this is almost surely a minority position. To adhere to the belief that people are purely selfish would not only require that one ignores wide-ranging experimental results showing the contrary, but would also clash with commonplace observations of behavior. The experimental research on "other-regarding" behavior not only demonstrates that people care about the welfare of others, but also challenges the validity of some of the more primitive models of social preferences—e.g., those that assume that social preferences can be captured by a function that puts a fixed

weight on the welfare of other persons. Although in some cases (e.g., parents toward children) there may be an element of altruism that could potentially be modeled in this fashion, more generally people tend to care about their own payoff and either the difference between their own payoff and others' payoffs or the difference between their own payoff and what they view as a fair payoff (Andreoni & Miller 2002, Bolton 1991, Bolton & Ockenfels 2000, Charness & Rabin 2002, Fehr & Schmidt 1999, Loewenstein et al. 1989, Rabin 1993).[6]

Although models of this type take major strides in the direction of providing a more realistic account of other-regarding preferences, once again they leave out important dimensions of the phenomenon. Specifically, as is true for risky decision making and intertemporal choice, people often react to other people at both an emotional and a more intellectual/deliberative level. In some cases, such as crying in a movie, we can be deeply moved by people who do not warrant sympathy—even fictional movie characters who do not actually exist. Other cases, such as mass calamities, if they occur in distant parts of the world to people with whom we are not familiar, can barely touch our heartstrings, even if we realize at an intellectual level that those victims are highly deserving of our sympathy and aid. To capture these phenomena, as well as a variety of experimental findings, Loewenstein & Small (2007) have proposed a dual-process model of helping behavior in which a sympathetic but highly immature emotional system interacts with a more mature but uncaring deliberative system.

The neuroeconomics literature is, in this case, highly supportive of such a perspective overall, although, as discussed below,

Welfare:
well-being; neuroeconomists and standard economists debate whether welfare is synonymous with objective happiness or (behaviorally) revealed preferences

---

[6]Distaste for inequality is not an exclusively human property. Brosnan & de Waal (2003) find that capuchin monkeys will forgo consuming cucumbers when similar monkeys are given grapes, a more desirable reward. Rather than exchanging their tokens for the inferior reward, the deprived monkeys sometimes threw their token out of the test chamber or at the experimenter.

some of the major findings seem somewhat contradictory. For example, some research has suggested that self-interest sometimes relies on deliberate (and possibly even deliberative) suppression of a more emotional desire for fairness (Sanfey et al. 2003), whereas other work has suggested that self-interest is the more evolutionarily primitive desire that is sometimes suppressed by fairness concerns (Knoch et al. 2006). Below we examine the relevant evidence as well as other neuroeconomic research on social preferences.

LITERATURE REVIEW

Some recent research has suggested that conflicts between affect and deliberation are particularly likely when people face certain moral dilemmas. Consider, for example, one of the classic "trolley" dilemmas (Thomson 1986), in which a runaway trolley is headed for five people who will be killed if it continues its present course. The only way to save them is to hit a switch that will turn the trolley onto an alternate set of tracks where it will kill one person instead of five. Most people say it is morally acceptable to hit the switch (Greene et al. 2001). In an objectively equivalent "footbridge" dilemma (Thomson 1986), a trolley again threatens to kill five people. This time there is a large stranger on a footbridge spanning the tracks, between the oncoming trolley and the would-be victims. The only way to save them is to push the stranger off the bridge and onto the tracks below, which would kill him but save the others. Most people say it is morally unacceptable to push the stranger (Greene et al. 2001).

Why is it only sometimes morally acceptable to kill one to save five? To test this hypothesis, Greene et al. (2001) proposed that the thought of pushing someone to his death is more emotionally distressing than the thought of flipping a switch that would cause a trolley to inflict identical damage. To investigate whether "personal" moral dilemmas that require the direct infliction of harm to achieve a greater utilitarian good elicit more intense emotional responses than "impersonal" moral dilemmas that require a less direct infliction of harm, they confronted participants with several versions of each dilemma while scanning their brains with fMRI. Participants also faced several nonmoral dilemmas that required a similar degree of mental effort, as judged by reaction times (e.g., deciding between traveling by bus or train given certain time constraints).

As predicted, brain regions consistently associated with emotional processing, such as medial frontal and posterior paracingulate cortex, were more active when participants considered personal moral dilemmas than when participants considered impersonal moral or nonmoral dilemmas. Supporting the notion that emotions play a causal role in personal moral dilemmas, Greene et al. (2001; see also Greene et al. 2004) found that participants took significantly longer to make utilitarian judgments that went against the emotional response in the personal moral dilemmas (e.g., judging that it is appropriate to push the stranger to his death) than to make emotionally congruent judgments, but that reaction times did not differ by judgment in the other two conditions. The results suggest that the personal moral dilemmas elicit a strong prepotent emotional response that must be cognitively overcome in order to respond in a manner inconsistent with the emotion.

Koenigs et al. (2007) also found that emotions play a causal role in personal moral judgments. Participants either had lesions to VMPFC, lesions to brain regions not directly associated with emotional processing, or no brain lesions, and were confronted with a series of moral and nonmoral dilemmas. Given that patients with VMPFC lesions typically show diminished emotional responsivity in general and severely reduced social emotions (e.g., shame) in particular (e.g., Anderson et al. 1999), these participants were predicted to find utilitarian judgments more palatable in the personal moral dilemmas as compared with normal and lesion control participants. Indeed, Koenigs et al. (2007) found that the frequency of utilitarian judgments did not differ by participant type in the nonmoral and impersonal moral conditions, but that participants with VMPFC lesions were most likely to make utilitarian judgments in the personal moral condition.

In combination, the results of Greene et al. (2001, 2004) and Koenigs et al. (2007) lend strong support to a dual-process perspective. People seem to evaluate these types of moral dilemmas deliberatively (e.g., which choice will lead to fewer people dying) and affectively (which choice would feel worse). Since the deliberative element is intentionally kept constant across the dilemmas, whereas the affective element differs, people with emotion deficiencies (who evaluate all of the dilemmas deliberatively) make decisions that are more consistent.

Another context in which affect and deliberation appear to conflict is that of the "ultimatum game" (Guth et al. 1982). In the typical ultimatum game, a "proposer" offers some portion of an endowment to a "responder" who can either accept the offer or reject it. If the responder accepts the offer, the money is divided according to the proposed split. If the responder rejects the offer, both players leave with nothing. Since purely self-interested responders should accept any positive offer, self-interested proposers should offer no more than the smallest positive amount possible. However, average offers typically exceed 30% of the pie, and offers of less than 20% are frequently rejected (see Camerer 2003). These results are typically obtained in one-shot games, meaning responders' unwillingness to accept small offers cannot be interpreted as an attempt to elicit larger offers in the future. Also, participants typically play the game anonymously, so the results cannot be attributed to immediate reputational or self-presentation concerns.

Several behavioral economic models have emerged to account for such findings.

Reciprocity-based theories of fairness (e.g., Dufwenberg & Kirchsteiger 2004, Rabin 1993), for example, propose that people enjoy reciprocating intentional kindness with kindness, and intentional unkindness with unkindness. Inequality-aversion models (Bolton & Ockenfels 2000, Fehr & Schmidt 1999) propose that people are averse to outcomes that deviate from equality, whether that inequality is advantageous or disadvantageous. Thus, according to the former account, responders reject low offers because they enjoy reciprocating unkindness with unkindness, whereas the latter account proposes that responders reject low offers because they find the proposed inequality painful.

Sanfey et al. (2003) studied ultimatum game behavior using fMRI to better understand why responders reject positive offers. Participants in their study, all responders, were told they would play the ultimatum game with 10 different human proposers (though offers were actually predetermined by the experimenters). Responders received five "fair" offers ($5 for proposer, $5 for respondent), and five unfair offers. In ten other trials, responders received the same offer, but this time from a computer (although what it means to receive an offer from a computer is somewhat ambiguous, given that the computer cannot literally keep the residual money). Consistent with intention-based theories of reciprocity and behavioral work by Blount (1995), participants were more willing to accept low offers from computer proposers than from human proposers. Moreover, activation in the anterior insula, an emotional region of the cortical pain matrix, was greater in response to unfair offers from human proposers than in response to unfair offers from computer proposers. In fact, whether players reject unfair offers from human proposers can be predicted reliably by the level of their insula activity. The insula findings thus appear to support the inequality-aversion models: Responders appear to be rejecting offers not because they enjoy reciprocating unkindness with unkindness, but rather because the prospect of inequality pains them (cf. Pillutla & Murnighan 1996).

A second finding from Sanfey et al. (2003), and follow-up work inspired by it, raises the question of whether self-interest or a desire for fairness is more evolutionarily ancient. Specifically, Sanfey et al. (2003) found that activation in the right dorsolateral prefrontal cortex (DLPFC), a region involved in executive control, goal maintenance, and overriding prepotent responses (e.g., Miller & Cohen 2001), was greater than activation in the insula when responders accepted unfair offers. By contrast, insula activation was greater than right DLPFC activation when responders rejected unfair offers. Sanfey et al. (2003) interpreted this pattern as evidence that the prepotent, emotional response was to reject unfair offers, and that regions associated with higher-level cognition had to override that impulse in order to accept such offers.

Knoch et al. (2006) devised a way to test this hypothesis experimentally. Participants in this experiment played ultimatum games, and proposers could offer anywhere between none and half of their endowment. In the period before making their decisions, some responders received repetitive transcranial magnetic stimulation (rTMS), a method that uses pulsed magnetic fields to temporarily disrupt brain function in specific regions. Some responders received rTMS to the right DLPFC, some received rTMS to the left DLPFC, and others received "sham" (placebo) rTMS to the right or left DLPFC.[7] By experimentally

manipulating activation in the DLPFC, the authors were equipped to make causal conclusions about its role in responder behavior. Knoch et al. (2006) found that responders who had rTMS to the right DLPFC were significantly more likely to accept unfair offers than were responders who had rTMS to the left DLFPC or responders who had sham rTMS. Note that the effect was not mediated by perceptions of fairness: Participants who had rTMS to the right DLPFC were no less likely than other participants to rate low offers as very unfair. Thus, the right DLPFC appears to influence what one is willing to accept, rather than what one considers fair. Contrary to Sanfey et al. (2003), these results suggest that the right DLPFC plays a key role in overriding or weakening self-interested impulses, allowing people to implement their taste for fairness.[8]

Of course, the results need to be interpreted with caution, as we still have a relatively limited understanding of the effects of rTMS, with respect to both where it has its effects (at the targeted site or on distal components of connected circuits) and its influence on neural function. For example, although it is believed that rTMS disrupts activation in regions thought to be involved in a particular task, it may actually stimulate activation in other regions that would not have normally been involved in a targeted task (E. Fehr, personal communication). Some researchers are

---

[7] van't Wout et al. (2005) were actually the first to conduct such an experiment. Specifically, van't Wout et al. (2005) varied, *within-subject*, whether seven ultimatum game responders received rTMS to right DLPFC or sham rTMS to right DLPFC. Given that participants who experience both real rTMS and sham rTMS are likely to detect a difference between the procedures, demand effects are clearly a concern in this study. Moreover, van't Wout et al. (2005) did not include an active rTMS control, unlike Knoch et al. (2006), who include a condition in which responders receive rTMS to left DLPFC. Taken together, the design of van't Wout et al. (2005) makes it difficult to attribute any observed treatment difference in behavior to the disruption

of right DLPFC. Further complicating matters, little treatment difference was actually observed (48% of unfair offers were accepted under rTMS; 42% under sham rTMS).

[8] The Knoch et al. (2006) results are consistent with behavioral work by Skitka et al. (2002), who showed participants a number of case studies of people who had contracted AIDS in different ways. Different cases made the victim appear more or less responsible (e.g., sexual contact versus a blood transfusion). Participants were asked for each case study to indicate whether the individual should be given subsidized access to drug treatment. Half of the participants made their decisions under cognitive load, while half made their decisions under no load. Participants were less likely to advocate subsidized treatment under cognitive load, suggesting that deliberation played a role in overcoming self-interest.

already combining rTMS with fMRI, and we will undoubtedly continue to learn about this promising procedure.

SUMMARY

In the domain of social preferences, the growing neuroscientific literature is highly supportive of a dual-system account of behavior. For example, Greene et al. (2001) and Koenigs et al. (2007) present evidence suggesting that personal moral dilemmas elicit prepotent emotional responses that must be cognitively overriden in order to make judgments incongruent with the prepotent response. The findings of Sanfey et al. (2003) and Knoch et al. (2006) both suggest that fairness preferences and self-interest operate via different systems, though they come to conflicting conclusions regarding which desire is the prepotent response in ultimatum games. While the Sanfey et al. (2003) results are correlational, Knoch et al. (2006) experimentally manipulated activation in right DLPFC and can thus draw causal conclusions about its role in ultimatum game behavior. However, given the uncertainty that still surrounds the rTMS procedure, future research should continue to examine how self-interest and fairness preferences interact at the neural level.

CONCLUSION

Neuroeconomics has bridged economics and psychology, largely because of movement within economics. Recent models in economics (Benhabib & Bisin 2005, Bernheim & Rangel 2004, Brocas & Carrillo 2006, Fudenberg & Levine 2006, Loewenstein & O'Donoghue 2004) have come to embrace a multiple systems perspective, which has long been popular among psychologists (Chaiken & Trope 1999, Posner & Snyder 1975, Schiffrin & Schneider 1977). Although neuroeconomics has not yet produced many findings that directly challenge assumptions held within psychology (only one of the neuroeconomics papers discussed above, Shiv et al.

2005, was published in a psychology journal), the field will undoubtedly eventually focus on issues of importance to both fields. For example, psychologists have often questioned how multiple systems interact to influence behavior. They may compete, or one system may provide a default response that can subsequently be overridden by another system, hypotheses that Evans (2008) respectively refers to as "parallel-competitive" and "default-interventionist." Economists who attempt to formally model the interaction of multiple systems are certainly interested in this question, and it is only a matter of time before neuroeconomists attempt to address it empirically.

Although neuroeconomics has encouraged positive changes within economics, reactions to neuroeconomics within economics too often seem to take one of two extreme forms. On the one hand, neuroeconomics has inspired some economists to adopt more psychologically realistic views of the world. This is undoubtedly beneficial to those economists and to the field. However, such views probably should have been adopted much earlier based on behavioral research. The overweighting of neural relative to behavioral evidence is illustrated in the bibliographies of the five new economic models mentioned above. For example, only one cites Chaiken & Trope's (1999) well-known review of dual-process research, whereas citations of neuroscientific studies abound. On the other hand, some economists, still reeling from the incorporation of psychology into economics and the rise of behavioral economics, are even more aghast at the infiltration of economics by neuroscience. They reject the "new phrenology" (Harrison 2005, p. 794) based on the argument that neural data cannot refute economic models, which make predictions about behavior rather than underlying processes (Gul & Pesendorfer 2005). According to this view, the failure to find neural correlates of "as-if" processes in economic models is not a failure of the models, but rather a failure to test them properly. Economists generally evaluate assumptions about underlying processes based on the accuracy of their implications, and psychologically implausible assumptions are often tolerated if they lead to satisfactory behavioral predictions.

However, to the extent that correct assumptions about underlying processes make better (and fresh) predictions, researchers should strive to refine those assumptions. Neuroeconomic research aims to facilitate this refinement and suggest new models. Indeed, as discussed above, neuroeconomics has already inspired a spate of individual choice models within economics.

Beyond its potential for refining economic theories, a better understanding of the neural processes underlying behavior could have other far-reaching consequences. For example, economists have typically assumed an equivalence between preference and welfare—i.e., that satisfying people's preferences will make them better off. However, dual-process models of behavior challenge this assumption by postulating the existence of different systems with competing motivational propensities.

Neuroscience methods also hold out the promise of making it possible to measure happiness more directly, or at least mechanisms more proximal to the experience of happiness, which could have profound implications for public policy. Currently, it is widely believed that it is impossible to make interpersonal comparisons of desire or well-being. Deprived of such data, economists have been very reluctant to take a strong position on issues of resource distribution. Person A may have 10 times as much wealth as person B, which might lead one to assume that person B would benefit more than person A would be hurt by a transfer of wealth from A to B. However, lacking any ability to compare the two individuals' utilities, such an inference would be logically unsound; perhaps person A has a much greater appreciation of luxury than B, so that overall happiness would actually be enhanced by a further transfer of wealth from B to A. Neuroscientific measurement of hedo-

nic states might help to disarm such logical defenses of inequality.

Looking ahead, neuroeconomics will continue to capitalize on the latest technologies developed by neuroscientists. Ideally, the technology will become increasingly portable (e.g., wearable sensors). Critics of laboratory research often lament the alien-like, context-free nature of experiments. Studies in which participants must remain almost perfectly still inside multi-ton magnets are even more vulnerable to such critiques. Another important technological advance is known as hyperscanning, which refers to the simultaneous scanning of several interacting brains (Montague et al. 2002).[9] Finally, the combination of multiple methods (e.g., rTMS and fMRI) will undoubtedly lead to new insights.

Armed with rapidly improving technology and new insights emerging from neuroscience and psychology, we believe that the future of neuroeconomics is bright. Its promise is great, in part, because 50 years of dominance by the rational choice model has left so many important questions unanswered. What, for example, is the enormous appeal of gambling? Why are disputes, whether between individuals or countries, so often jointly destructive? What causes the boom and bust cycles that are so clearly present in financial and other markets? How does advertising work? Why do credit cards promote spending? Why do people fail to save for retirement? A refined understanding of human behavior has the potential to shed light on these and many other important phenomena, and a better understanding of neural processing, in turn, cannot help but inform our understanding of human behavior.

---

[9]King-Casas et al. (2005) used hyperscanning to examine behavior in a repeated trust game. They found that activation in the trustee's head of caudate originally responded to the revelation of the investor's decisions, but this activation eventually came to precede such revelation, indicating that the trustee had developed a model to predict the investor's likely next move. Tomlin et al. (2006) similarly studied a repeated trust game and found that activation along the cingulate cortex distinguishes between the revelation of one's own decision and the revelation of the decision of one's opponent.

SUMMARY POINTS

1. Neuroeconomics has further bridged the once disparate fields of economics and psychology, largely due to movement within economics. Change has occurred within economics because the most important findings in neuroeconomics have posed a challenge to the standard economic perspective.

2. Neuroeconomics has primarily challenged the standard economic assumption that decision making is a unitary process—a simple matter of integrated and coherent utility maximization—suggesting instead that it is driven by the interaction between automatic and controlled processes.

3. Neuroeconomic research has focused most intensely on decision making under risk and uncertainty, but this line of research provides only mixed support for a dual-systems perspective.

4. The extent to which intertemporal choice is generated by multiple systems with conflicting priorities is perhaps the most hotly debated issue within neuroeconomics. However, a majority of the evidence favors a multiple systems perspective.

5. Neuroeconomic research on social preferences is highly supportive of a dual-systems account, although the most prominent studies come to conflicting conclusions regarding how self-interest and fairness concerns interact to influence behavior.

6. Neuroeconomics may ultimately influence psychology indirectly, via its influence on economics (e.g., by inspiring economic models increasingly grounded in psychological reality), and directly, by addressing debates of interest within psychology (e.g., whether multiple systems operate sequentially or in parallel to influence behavior).

LITERATURE CITED

Abler B, Walter H, Erk S. 2005. Neural correlates of frustration. *NeuroReport* 16:669–72

Ainslie G. 1975. Specious reward: a behavioral theory of impulsiveness and impulse control. *Psychol. Bull.* 82:463–96

Ainslie G, Monterosso J. 2004. A marketplace in the brain? *Science* 306:421–23

Anderson SW, Bechara A, Damasio H, Tranel D, Damasio AR. 1999. Impairment of social and moral behavior related to early damage in human prefrontal cortex. *Nat. Neurosci.* 2:1032–37

Andreoni J, Miller J. 2002. Giving according to GARP: an experimental test of the consistency of preferences for altruism. *Econometrica* 70:737–53

Angner E, Loewenstein G. 2007. Behavioral economics. In *Philosophy of Economics*, ed. D Gabbay, P Thagard, J Woods, Vol. 13. Amsterdam: Elsevier. In press

Ashraf N, Camerer CF, Loewenstein G. 2005. Adam Smith, behavioral economist. *J. Econ. Perspect.* 19:131–45

Barlow DH. 1988. *Anxiety and Its Disorders: The Nature and Treatment of Anxiety and Panic.* New York: Guilford

Bechara A, Damasio AR, Damasio H, Anderson SW. 1994. Insensitivity to future consequences following damage to human prefrontal cortex. *Cognition* 50:7–15

Bechara A, Damasio H, Tranel D, Damasio AR. 1997. Deciding advantageously before knowing the advantageous strategy. *Science* 275:1293–95

Benartzi S, Thaler RH. 1995. Myopic loss aversion and the equity premium puzzle. *Q. J. Econ.* 110:73–92

Benhabib J, Bisin A. 2005. Modeling internal commitment mechanisms and self-control: a neuroeconomics approach to consumption-saving decisions. *Games Econ. Behav.* 52:460–92

Bernheim BD, Rangel A. 2004. Addiction and cue-triggered decision processes. *Am. Econ. Rev.* 94:1558–90

Bernoulli D. 1738. Exposition of a new theory on the measurement of risk. Transl. L Sommer, 1954, in *Econometrica* 22:23–36 (from Latin)

Berns GS, McClure SM, Pagnoni G, Montague PR. 2001. Predictability modulates human brain response to reward. *J. Neurosci.* 21:2793–98

Binmore K. 1988. The individual in the economy: a textbook of economic psychology. *Economica* 55:421–22

Blount S. 1995. When social outcomes aren't fair: the effect of causal attributions on preferences. *Organ. Behav. Hum. Decis. Processes* 63:131–44

Bolton GE. 1991. A comparative model of bargaining: theory and evidence. *Am. Econ. Rev.* 81:1096–136

Bolton GE, Ockenfels A. 2000. ERC: a theory of equity, reciprocity, and competition. *Am. Econ. Rev.* 90:166–93

Botvinick MM, Braver TS, Carter CS, Barch DM, Cohen JD. 2001. Conflict monitoring and cognitive control. *Psychol. Rev.* 108:624–52

Braver TS, Cohen JD. 2000. On the control of control: the role of dopamine in regulating prefrontal function and working memory. In *Attention and Performance XVIII: Control of Cognitive Processes*, ed. S Monsell, J Driver, pp. 713–37. Cambridge, MA: MIT Press

Breiter HC, Aharon I, Kahneman D, Dale A, Shizgal P. 2001. Functional imaging of neural responses to expectancy and experience of monetary gains and losses. *Neuron* 21:619–39

Brocas I, Carrillo JD. 2006. *The brain as a hierarchical organization.* Work. Pap., Dept. Econ., Univ. South. Calif., Los Angeles

Brosnan SF, de Waal FBM. 2003. Monkeys reject unequal pay. *Nature* 425:297–99

Camerer CF. 2003. *Behavioral Game Theory: Experiments in Strategic Interaction.* New York: Russell Sage Found.

Carter CS, Braver TS, Barch DM, Botvinick MM, Noll DC, Cohen JD. 1998. Anterior cingulate cortex, error detection and the on-line monitoring of performance. *Science* 280:747–49

Chaiken S. 1980. Heuristic vs systematic information processing and the use of source vs message cues in persuasion. *J. Personal. Soc. Psychol.* 39:752–66

Chaiken S, Trope Y, eds. 1999. *Dual-Process Theories in Social Psychology.* New York: Guilford

Charness G, Rabin M. 2002. Understanding social preferences with simple tests. *Q. J. Econ.* 117:775–816

Cohen JD. 2005. The vulcanization of the human brain: a neural perspective on interactions between cognition and emotion. *J. Econ. Perspect.* 19:3–24

Cohen JD, McClure SM, Yu AJ. 2007. Should I stay or should I go? How the human brain manages the tradeoff between exploitation and exploration. *Philos. Trans. R. Soc. London Ser. B* 362:933–42

Critchley HD, Mathias CJ, Dolan RJ. 2001. Neural activity in the human brain relating to uncertainty and arousal during anticipation. *Neuron* 29:537–45

Curley SP, Yates JF, Abrams RA. 1986. Psychological sources of ambiguity avoidance. *Organ. Behav. Hum. Decis. Processes* 38:230–56

Dalgleish T. 2004. The emotional brain. *Nat. Rev. Neurosci.* 5:583–89

Damasio AR. 1994. *Descartes' Error: Emotion, Reason, and the Human Brain*. New York: Putnam

Davidson RJ, Jackson DC, Kalin NH. 2000. Emotion, plasticity, context, and regulation: perspectives from affective neuroscience. *Psychol. Bull.* 126:890–909

De Martino B, Kumaran D, Seymour B, Dolan RJ. 2006. Frames, biases, and rational decision-making in the human brain. *Science* 313:684–87

Dolan RJ. 2002. Emotion, cognition, and behavior. *Science* 298:1191–94

Dufwenberg M, Kirchsteiger G. 2004. A theory of sequential reciprocity. *Games Econ. Behav.* 47:268–98

Dunn BD, Dalgleish T, Lawrence AD. 2005. The somatic marker hypothesis: a critical evaluation. *Neurosci. Biobehav. Rev.* 30:239–71

Eisenberger NI, Lieberman MD, Williams KD. 2003. Does rejection hurt: an fMRI study of social exclusion. *Science* 302:290–92

Ellsberg D. 1961. Risk, ambiguity and the Savage axioms. *Q. J. Econ.* 75:643–69

Epstein S. 1994. Integration of the cognitive and the psychodynamic unconscious. *Am. Psychol.* 49:709–24

Evans JStBT. 2008. Dual-processing accounts of reasoning, judgment, and social cognition. *Annu. Rev. Psychol.* 59:In press

Fehr E, Schmidt K. 1999. A theory of fairness, competition and cooperation. *Q. J. Econ.* 114:817–68

Fox CR, Tversky A. 1995. Ambiguity avoidance and comparative ignorance. *Q. J. Econ.* 110:585–603

Frederick S, Loewenstein G, O'Donoghue T. 2002. Time discounting and time preference: A critical review. *J. Econ. Lit.* 40:351–401

Frederick S, Novemsky N, Wang J, Dhar R, Nowlis S. 2006. *Opportunity costs and consumer decisions*. Work. Pap., Sloan School Manag., MIT, Cambridge, MA

Fudenberg D, Levine DK. 2006. A dual-self model of impulse control. *Am. Econ. Rev.* 96:1449–76

Genesove D, Mayer C. 2001. Loss aversion and seller behavior: evidence from the housing market. *Q. J. Econ.* 116:1233–60

Glaeser EL. 2003. *Psychology and the market*. Harvard Inst. Econ. Res. Discuss. Pap. 2023

Glimcher PW, Kable J, Louie K. 2007. Neuroeconomic studies of impulsivity: now or just as soon as possible? *Am. Econ. Rev.* 97:142–47

Gneezy U, Potters J. 1997. An experiment on risk taking and evaluation periods. *Q. J. Econ.* 112:631–45

Green L, Fristoe N, Myerson J. 1994. Temporal discounting and preference reversals in choice between delayed outcomes. *Psychon. Bull. Rev.* 1:383–89

Greene JD, Nystrom LE, Engell AD, Darley JM, Cohen JD. 2004. The neural bases of cognitive conflict and control in moral judgment. *Neuron* 44:389–400

Greene JD, Sommerville RB, Nystrom LE, Darley JM, Cohen JD. 2001. An fMRI investigation of emotional engagement in moral judgment. *Science* 293:2105–8

Gul F, Pesendorfer W. 2005. *The case for mindless economics*. Work. Pap., Dept. Econ., Princeton Univ.

Guth W, Schmittberger R, Schwarze B. 1982. An experimental analysis of ultimatum bargaining. *J. Econ. Behav. Organ.* 3:367–88

Hariri AR, Brown SM, Williamson DE, Flory JD, de Wit H, et al. 2006. Preference for immediate over delayed rewards is associated with magnitude of ventral striatal activity. *J. Neurosci.* 26:13213–17

Harrison GW. 2005. Book review: advances in behavioral economics. *J. Econ. Psychol.* 26:793–95

Argues that neural data cannot refute economic theories, which are silent regarding underlying processes. The most prominent critique of neuroeconomics.

Heath C, Tversky A. 1991. Preference and belief: ambiguity and competence in choice under uncertainty. *J. Risk Uncertain.* 4:5–28

Hill NM, Schneider W. 2006. Brain changes in the development of expertise: neurological evidence on skill-based adaptations. In *Cambridge Handbook of Expertise and Expert Performance*, ed. KA Ericsson, N Charness, P Feltovich, R Hoffman, pp. 653–82. New York: Cambridge Univ. Press

Hsu M, Bhatt M, Adolphs R, Tranel D, Camerer CF. 2005. Neural systems responding to degrees of uncertainty in human decision-making. ***Science*** **310:1680–83**

Kahn I, Yeshurun Y, Rotshtein P, Fried I, Ben-Bashat D, et al. 2002. The role of the amygdala in signaling prospective outcome of choice. *Neuron* 33:983–94

Kahneman D, Frederick S. 2006. Frames and brains: elicitation and control of response tendencies. *Trends Cogn. Sci.* 11:45–46

Kahneman D, Knetsch JL, Thaler RH. 1990. Experimental tests of the endowment effect and the Coase theorem. *J. Polit. Econ.* 98:1325–48

Kahneman D, Tversky A. 1979. Prospect theory: an analysis of decision under risk. *Econometrica* 47:263–91

King-Casas B, Tomlin D, Anen C, Camerer CF, Quartz SR, et al. 2005. Getting to know you: reputation and trust in a two-person economic exchange. *Science* 308:78–83

Kirby KN, Herrnstein RJ. 1995. Preference reversals due to myopic discounting of delayed reward. *Psychol. Sci.* 6:83–89

Knoch D, Pascual-Leone A, Meyer K, Treyer V, Fehr E. 2006. Diminishing reciprocal fairness by disrupting the right prefrontal cortex. ***Science*** **314:829–32**

Knutson B, Fong GW, Adams CM, Varner JL, Hommer D. 2001. Dissociation of reward anticipation and outcome with event-related fMRI. *NeuroReport* 12:3683–87

Knutson B, Fong GW, Bennett SM, Adams CM, Hommer D. 2003. A region of mesial prefrontal cortex tracks monetarily rewarding outcomes: characterization with rapid event-related fMRI. *NeuroImage* 18:263–72

Knutson B, Rick S, Wimmer GE, Prelec D, Loewenstein G. 2007. Neural predictors of purchases. ***Neuron*** **53:147–56**

Koenigs M, Young L, Adolphs R, Tranel D, Cushman F, et al. 2007. Damage to the prefrontal cortex increases utilitarian moral judgments. *Nature* 446:908–11

Koopmans TC. 1960. Stationary ordinal utility and impatience. *Econometrica* 28:287–309

Kühberger A, Perner J. 2003. The role of competition and knowledge in the Ellsberg task. *J. Behav. Decis. Mak.* 16:181–91

LeDoux JE. 1996. *The Emotional Brain.* New York: Simon & Schuster

Loewenstein G. 1996. Out of control: visceral influences on behavior. *Organ. Behav. Hum. Decis. Processes* 65:272–92

Loewenstein G, O'Donoghue T. 2004. *Animal spirits: affective and deliberative processes in economic behavior.* Work. Pap., Carnegie Mellon

Loewenstein G, Small DA. 2007. The scarecrow and the tin man: the vicissitudes of human sympathy and caring. *Rev. Gen. Psychol.* 11:112–26

Loewenstein G, Thompson L, Bazerman MH. 1989. Social utility and decision making in interpersonal contexts. *J. Personal. Soc. Psychol.* 57:426–41

Loewenstein G, Weber EU, Hsee CK, Welch N. 2001. Risk as feelings. *Psychol. Bull.* 127:267–86

Maia TV, McClelland JL. 2004. A reexamination of the evidence for the somatic marker hypothesis: what participants really know in the Iowa gambling task. *Proc. Natl. Acad. Sci. USA* 101:16075–80

Ambitiously combined fMRI and lesion patient data to test various explanations for ambiguity aversion. Results implicated immediate negative emotions.

Unlike most neuroeconomic studies that rely on correlational evidence, Knoch et al. use rTMS to experimentally manipulate activation in DLPFC.

Found that insula activation correlated negatively with spending, suggesting people do not control their spending strictly by considering opportunity costs.

Markowitz H. 1952. The utility of wealth. *J. Polit. Econ.* 60:151–58

McClure SM, Berns GS, Montague PR. 2003. Temporal prediction errors in a passive learning task activate human striatum. *Neuron* 38:339–46

McClure SM, Ericson KM, Laibson DI, Loewenstein G, Cohen JD. 2007. Time discounting for primary rewards. *J. Neurosci.* 27:5796–804

McClure SM, Laibson DI, Loewenstein G, Cohen JD. 2004a. Separate neural systems value immediate and delayed monetary rewards. *Science* 306:503–7

McClure SM, Li J, Tomlin D, Cypert KS, Montague LM, et al. 2004b. Neural correlates of behavioral preference for culturally familiar drinks. *Neuron* 44:379–87

Millar A, Navarick DJ. 1984. Self-control and choice in humans: effects of video game playing as a positive reinforcer. *Learn. Motiv.* 15:203–18

Miller EK, Cohen JD. 2001. An integrative theory of prefrontal cortex function. *Annu. Rev. Neurosci.* 24:167–202

Montague PR, Berns GS, Cohen JD, McClure SM, Giuseppe P, et al. 2002. Hyperscanning: simultaneous fMRI during linked social interactions. *NeuroImage* 16:1159–64

Montague PR, Dayan P, Sejnowski TJ. 1996. A framework for mesencephalic dopamine systems based on predictive Hebbian learning. *J. Neurosci.* 16:1936–47

O'Doherty JP, Critchley H, Deichmann R, Dolan RJ. 2003. Dissociating valence of outcome from behavioral control in human orbital and ventral prefrontal cortices. *J. Neurosci.* 23:7931–39

Petty RE, Cacioppo JT. 1981. *Attitudes and Persuasion: Classical and Contemporary Approaches.* Dubuque, IA: Brown

Phelps EA, O'Connor KJ, Cunningham WA, Funayama ES, Gatenby JC, et al. 2000. Performance on indirect measures of race evaluation predicts amygdala activation. *J. Cogn. Neurosci.* 12:729–38

Pillutla MM, Murnighan JK. 1996. Unfairness, anger, and spite: emotional rejections of ultimatum offers. *Organ. Behav. Hum. Decis. Processes* 68:208–24

Posner MI, Snyder CRR. 1975. Attention and cognitive control. In *Information Processing and Cognition: The Loyola Symposium*, ed. R Solso, pp. 55–85. Hillsdale, NJ: Erlbaum

Prelec D, Loewenstein G. 1998. The red and the black: mental accounting of savings and debt. *Mark. Sci.* 17:4–28

Quiggin J. 1982. A theory of anticipated utility. *J. Econ. Behav. Organ.* 3:323–43

Rabin M. 1993. Incorporating fairness into game theory and economics. *Am. Econ. Rev.* 83:1281–302

Rachlin H, Raineri A. 1992. Irrationality, impulsiveness, and selfishness as discount reversal effects. In *Choice Over Time*, ed. G Loewenstein, J Elster, pp. 93–118. New York: Russell Sage Found.

Read D, Loewenstein G, Rabin M. 1999. Choice bracketing. *J. Risk Uncertain.* 19:171–97

Rick S, Cryder C, Loewenstein G. 2007. Tightwads and spendthrifts. *J. Consum. Res.* In press

Samuelson P. 1937. A note on measurement of utility. *Rev. Econ. Stud.* 4:155–61

Sanfey AG, Rilling JK, Aronson JA, Nystrom LE, Cohen JD. 2003. The neural basis of economic decision-making in the ultimatum game. *Science* 300:1755–58

Savage LJ. 1954. *The Foundations of Statistics*. New York: Wiley

Shefrin HM, Thaler RH. 1988. The behavioral life-cycle hypothesis. *Econ. Inq.* 26:609–43

Shiffrin RM, Schneider W. 1977. Controlled and automatic human information processing: II. Perceptual learning, automatic attending, and a general theory. *Psychol. Rev.* 84:127–90

Shiv B, Loewenstein G, Bechara A, Damasio H, Damasio AR. 2005. Investment behavior and the negative side of emotion. *Psychol. Sci.* 16:435–39

Concluded that limbic/paralimbic structures are preferentially recruited for intertemporal choices involving immediately available rewards, as opposed to fronto-parietal regions.

Results suggested unfair ultimatum game offers elicit a negative emotional response favoring rejection. Knoch et al. (2006) questioned this interpretation.

Skitka LJ, Mullen E, Griffin T, Hutchinson S, Chamberlin B. 2002. Dispositions, ideological scripts, or motivated correction? Understanding ideological differences in attributions for social problems. *J. Personal. Soc. Psychol.* 83:470–87

Solnick J, Kannenberg C, Eckerman D, Waller M. 1980. An experimental analysis of impulsivity and impulse control in humans. *Learn. Motiv.* 11:61–77

Starmer C. 2000. Developments in nonexpected utility theory: the hunt for a descriptive theory of choice under risk. *J. Econ. Lit.* 38:332–82

Stevens JR, Hallinan EV, Hauser MD. 2005. The ecology and evolution of patience in two New World monkeys. *Biol. Lett.* 1:223–26

Thaler RH. 1980. Toward a positive theory of consumer choice. *J. Econ. Behav. Organ.* 1:39–60

Thaler RH, Shefrin HM. 1981. An economic theory of self-control. *J. Polit. Econ.* 89:392–406

Thomson JJ. 1986. *Rights, Restitution and Risk.* Cambridge. MA: Harvard Univ. Press

Tom SM, Fox CR, Trepel C, Poldrack RA. 2007. The neural basis of loss aversion in decision-making under risk. *Science* 315:515–18

Tomlin D, Kayali MA, King-Casas B, Anen C, Camerer CF, et al. 2006. Agent-specific responses in the cingulate cortex during economic exchanges. *Science* 312:1047–50

Tugwell RG. 1922. Human nature in economic theory. *J. Polit. Econ.* 30:317–45

Tversky A, Kahneman D. 1981. The framing of decisions and the psychology of choice. *Science* 211:453–58

Tversky A, Kahneman D. 1991. Loss aversion in riskless choice: a reference-dependent model. *Q. J. Econ.* 106:1039–61

van't Wout M, Kahn RS, Sanfey AG, Aleman A. 2005. Repetitive transcranial magnetic stimulation over the right dorsolateral prefrontal cortex affects strategic decision-making. *NeuroReport* 16:1849–52

von Neumann J, Morgenstern O. 1944. *Theory of Games and Economic Behavior.* New York: Wiley

Weber B, Aholt A, Neuhaus C, Trautner P, Elger CE, Teichert T. 2007. Neural evidence for reference-dependence in real-market-transactions. *NeuroImage* 35:441–47

Wicker B, Keysers C, Plailly J, Royet J-P, Gallese V, Rizzolatti G. 2003. Both of us disgusted in *my* insula: the common neural basis of seeing and feeling disgust. *Neuron* 40:655–64

Attributed loss aversion to an asymmetric response to gains and losses within dopaminergic targets rather than to multiple systems.

Cumulative Indexes

Contributing Authors, Volumes 49–59

Kazdin AE, 54:253–76
Keefe FJ, 56:601–30
Keil FC, 57:227–54
Keller H, 54:461–90
Kelley K, 59:537–63
Kelman HC, 57:1–26
Kerr NL, 55:623–55
Kersten D, 55:271–304
Kestler L, 55:401–30
Kiecolt-Glaser JK, 53:83–107
Kingdom FAA, 59:143–66
Klin A, 56:315–36
Kolb B, 49:43–64
Koob GF, 59:29–53
Kopta SM, 50:441–69
Koriat A, 51:481–537
Koutstaal W, 49:289–318
Kramer RM, 50:569–98
Krantz DS, 53:341–69
Krosnick JA, 50:537–67
Kruglanski AW, 58:291–316

L

Lachman ME, 55:305–31
Lackner JR, 56:115–47
Ladd GW, 50:333–59
Langenbucher JW, 50:79–107
Latham GP, 56:485–516
Lavie P, 52:277–303
Leary MR, 58:317–44
LeBoeuf RA, 53:491–517
Lehman DR, 55:689–714
Leiter MP, 52:397–422
Le Moal M, 59:29–53
Leonardo ED, 57:117–37
Lerner RM, 49:413–46
Leventhal EA, 59:477–505
Leventhal H, 59:477–505
Levine B, 53:401–33
Lewis RL, 59:193–224
Lieberman MD, 58:259–89
Lievens F, 59:419–50
Lilienfeld SO, 53:519–43
Lindenberger U, 50:471–507
Lipsey MW, 51:345–75
Logan GD, 55:207–34
Loken B, 57:453–85
López SR, 51:571–98
Lotto AJ, 55:149–79
Lubinski D, 51:405–44

Lucas RE, 54:403–25
Lueger RJ, 50:441–69
Lussier JP, 55:431–61
Lustig CA, 59:193–224
Lynch EB, 51:121–47

M

MacCallum RC, 51:201–26
Maccoby EE, 51:1–27
MacCoun RJ, 49:259–87
MacKinnon DP, 58:593–614
Macrae CN, 51:93–120
MacWhinney B, 49:199–227
Maddox WT, 56:149–78
Maier SF, 51:29–57
Major BN, 56:393–421
Mamassian P, 55:271–304
Margolin G, 51:445–79
Markman AB, 52:223–47
Marshall PJ, 56:235–62
Martin A, 58:25–45
Martin RC, 54:55–89
Mashek DJ, 58:345–72
Maslach C, 52:397–422
Maxwell SE, 59:537–63
Mayer JD, 59:507–36
Mayer RE, 55:715–44
Maynard A, 54:461–90
Mays VM, 58:201–25
McCeney MK, 53:341–69
McDermott C, 55:519–44
McFall RM, 50:215–41
McGuffin P, 54:205–28
McGuire L, 53:83–107
McKenna KYA, 55:572–90
McKoon G, 49:25–42
McNally RJ, 54:229–52
Medin DL, 51:121–47
Meece JL, 57:487–503
Mehl MR, 54:547–77
Mellers BA, 49:447–77
Mesquita B, 58:373–403
Metzger A, 57:255–84
Miller DT, 52:527–54
Miller GA, 50:1–19
Mineka S, 49:377–412
Mischel W, 49:229–58; 55:1–22
Monahan J, 56:631–59
Moore DA, 51:279–314
Moore KS, 59:193–224
Morrin M, 49:319–44

Morris AS, 52:83–110
Morris R, 59:451–75
Morrison C, 59:55–92
Moskowitz JT, 55:745–74
Murphy KR, 49:141–68

N

Nairne JS, 53:53–81
Nathan PE, 50:79–107
Nee DE, 59:193–224
Nezworski MT, 53:519–43
Nichols KE, 56:235–62
Niederhoffer KG, 54:547–77
Nitschke JB, 53:545–74
Norman KA, 49:289–318
Nowlis SM, 52:249–75

O

O'Brien LT, 56:393–421
Ochsner KN, 58:373–403
Oishi S, 54:403–25
Ollendick TH, 52:685–716
Olson EA, 54:277–95
Olson GM, 54:491–516
Olson JS, 54:491–516
Olson MA, 54:297–327
Orehek E, 58:291–316
Oswald FL, 51:631–64
Ozer DJ, 57:401–21

P

Palincsar AS, 49:345–75
Paloutzian RF, 54:377–402
Pansky A, 51:481–537
Paradise R, 54:175–203
Parke RD, 55:365–99
Parks L, 56:571–600
Pashler H, 52:629–51
Pearce JM, 52:111–39
Peissig JJ, 58:75–96
Penn DC, 58:97–118
Pennebaker JW, 54:547–77
Penner LA, 56:365–92
Peplau LA, 58:405–24
Peretz I, 56:89–114
Pettigrew TF, 49:65–85
Phelps EA, 57:27–53
Phillips LA, 59:477–505

Piliavin JA, 56:365–92
Pinder CC, 56:485–516
Pittman TS, 59:361–85
Pizzagalli D, 53:545–74
Plomin R, 54:205–28
Polivy J, 53:187–213
Posluszny DM, 50:137–63
Posner MI, 58:1–23
Poulos AM, 56:207–34
Povinelli DJ, 58:97–118
Price DD, 59:565–90
Prislin R, 57:345–74
Putnam K, 53:545–74

Q

Quevedo K, 58:145–73
Quinn RE, 50:361–86

R

Rafaeli E, 54:579–616
Ratcliff R, 49:25–42
Ratnam R, 51:699–725
Raudenbush SW, 52:501–25
Rausch JR, 59:537–63
Recanzone GH, 59:119–42
Rensink RA, 53:245–77
Reppucci ND, 50:387–418
Revenson TA, 58:565–92
Rhodes G, 57:199–226
Rick S, 59:647–72
Roberts BW, 56:453–84
Roberts RD, 59:507–36
Robinson A, 49:117–39
Robinson GE, 50:651–82
Robinson TE, 54:25–53
Robles TF, 53:83–107
Roediger HL III, 59:225–54
Rogoff B, 54:175–203
Rollman GB, 50:305–31
Rolls ET, 51:599–630
Rosenbaum DA, 52:453–70
Rosenthal R, 52:59–82
Rothbart MK, 58:1–23
Rourke BP, 53:309–39
Rubin M, 53:575–604
Runco MA, 55:657–87
Rusbult CE, 54:351–75
Russell JA, 54:329–49
Ruthruff E, 52:629–51
Rutter M, 53:463–90

Ryan RM, 52:141–66
Rynes SL, 56:571–600

S

Saab PG, 52:555–80
Sackett PR, 59:419–50
Salas E, 52:471–99
Sankis LM, 51:377–404
Sargis EG, 57:529–55
Saribay SA, 59:329–60
Saunders SM, 50:441–69
Saxe R, 55:87–124
Schacter DL, 49:289–318
Schall JD, 55:23–50
Schaller M, 55:689–714
Schaufeli WB, 52:397–422
Schippers MC, 58:515–41
Schneiderman N, 52:555–80
Schroeder DA, 56:365–92
Schultz W, 57:87–115
Schwartz A, 49:447–77
Schwartz MW, 51:255–77
Seeley RJ, 51:255–77
Serbin LA, 55:333–63
Seyfarth RM, 54:145–73
Shafir E, 53:491–517
Shaywitz BA, 59:451–75
Shaywitz SE, 59:451–75
Sherry DF, 57:167–97
Shevell SK, 59:143–66
Shiffrar M, 58:47–73
Shiner RL, 56:453–84
Shinn M, 54:427–59
Shoda Y, 49:229–58
Shors TJ, 57:55–85
Siegel JM, 55:125–48
Silberg J, 53:463–90
Simon AF, 51:149–69
Simonson I, 52:249–75
Simonton DK, 54:617–40
Sincharoen S, 57:585–611
Skinner EA, 58:119–44
Skitka LJ, 57:529–55
Smetana JG, 57:255–84
Snyder DK, 57:317–44
Snyder M, 50:273–303
Solomon KO, 51:121–47
Spears R, 53:161–86
Staddon JER, 54:115–44
Stanton AL, 58:565–92
Staudinger UM, 50:471–507

Steel GD, 51:227–53
Steinberg L, 52:83–110
Sternberg RJ, 49:479–502
Stewart AJ, 55:519–44
Stewart MO, 57:285–315
Stickgold R, 57:139–66
Strunk D, 57:285–315
Stuewig J, 58:345–72
Stukas AA Jr, 50:273–303
Stuss DT, 53:401–33
Suedfeld P, 51:227–53
Suh EM, 53:133–60
Sullivan JL, 50:625–50
Sutter ML, 59:119–42

T

Tangney JP, 58:345–72
Tarr MJ, 58:75–96
Tees RC, 50:509–35
Tennen H, 58:565–92
Thompson RF, 56:1–23
Tindale RS, 55:623–55
Tolan P, 57:557–83
Toohey SM, 54:427–59
Tourangeau R, 55:775–801
Transue JE, 50:625–50
Treat TA, 50:215–41
Triandis HC, 53:133–60
Tulving E, 53:1–25
Tyler TR, 57:375–400

U

Uleman JS, 59:329–60

V

Valley KL, 51:279–314
van Knippenberg D, 58:515–41
Van Lange PAM, 54:351–75
Velleman PF, 52:305–35
Volkmar F, 56:315–36

W

Wahlsten D, 50:599–624
Wainer H, 52:305–35
Walker BM, 58:453–77
Walker E, 55:401–30

Walker MP, 57:139–66
Warriner EM, 53:309–39
Watkins LR, 51:29–57
Watson D, 49:377–412
Wegner DM, 51:59–91
Weick KE, 50:361–86
Weinman J, 59:477–505
Weiss H, 53:279–307
Weisz JR, 56:337–63
Wells GL, 54:277–95
Wenzlaff RM, 51:59–91
Werker JF, 50:509–35
Whishaw IQ, 49:43–64

Whisman MA, 57:317–44
Wickens TD, 49:537–57
Widiger TA, 51:377–404
Wigfield A, 53:109–32
Williams KD, 58:425–52
Willis H, 53:575–604
Wilson TD, 55:493–518
Wingate LR, 56:287–314
Winter DA, 58:453–77
Wixted JT, 55:235–69
Wood JM, 53:519–43
Wood W, 51:539–70
Woods SC, 51:255–77

Woolard JL, 50:387–418
Wulfeck B, 52:369–96

Y

Yuille A, 55:271–304

Z

Zatorre RJ, 56:89–114
Zimmer-Gembeck MJ,
    58:119–44

Chapter Titles, Volumes 49–59

Career Development and Counseling

Chemical Senses

See Sensory Processes

Clinical and Counseling Psychology (See also Psychopathology)

Adult Clinical Neuropsychology

Child/Family Therapy

Clinical Assessment

Industrial Psychology

See Personnel-Organizational Psychology

Learning and Memory

Marketing and Consumer Behavior

Motivation

Organizational Psychology or Organizational Behavior

Cognition in Organizations

Groups and Teams

Leadership

Work Motivation

Perception

Psychology in Other Countries

ANNUAL REVIEWS

Intelligent Synthesis of the Scientific Literature

Annual Reviews – Your Starting Point for Research Online
http://arjournals.annualreviews.org

- Over 1150 Annual Reviews volumes—more than 26,000 critical, authoritative review articles in 35 disciplines spanning the Biomedical, Physical, and Social sciences—available online, including all Annual Reviews back volumes, dating to 1932
- Current individual subscriptions include seamless online access to full-text articles, PDFs, Reviews in Advance (as much as 6 months ahead of print publication), bibliographies, and other supplementary material in the current volume and the prior 4 years' volumes
- All articles are fully supplemented, searchable, and downloadable — see http://psych.annualreviews.org
- Access links to the reviewed references (when available online)
- Site features include customized alerting services, citation tracking, and saved searches

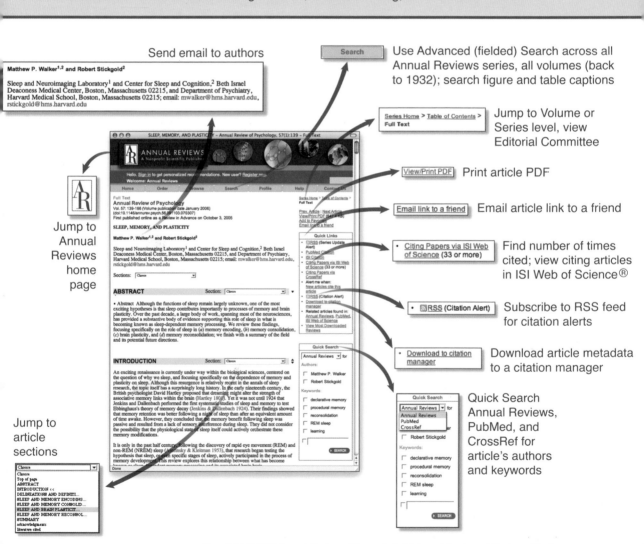

Send email to authors

Search — Use Advanced (fielded) Search across all Annual Reviews series, all volumes (back to 1932); search figure and table captions

Series Home > Table of Contents > Full Text — Jump to Volume or Series level, view Editorial Committee

View/Print PDF — Print article PDF

Email link to a friend — Email article link to a friend

Jump to Annual Reviews home page

Citing Papers via ISI Web of Science (33 or more) — Find number of times cited; view citing articles in ISI Web of Science®

RSS (Citation Alert) — Subscribe to RSS feed for citation alerts

Download to citation manager — Download article metadata to a citation manager

Quick Search Annual Reviews, PubMed, and CrossRef for article's authors and keywords

Jump to article sections